WOLVERINE
OFFICIAL INDEX to the MARVEL UNIVERSE

HEAD WRITER
Jeph York
with Al Sjoerdsma (Spider-Man vs. Wolverine)
& Daron Jensen (Scorpio Connection, Scorpio Rising)

COORDINATORS
Daron Jensen & Stuart Vandal

CHRONOLOGY CONSULTANT
Paul Bourcier

OFFICIAL INDEX STAFF
Chris Buchner, Russ Chappell, Chris McCarver,
Sean McQuaid, Jacob Rougemont, Robert J. Sodaro
& Kevin Wasser

EDITOR
Jeff Youngquist

EDITORS, SPECIAL PROJECTS
Jennifer Grünwald & Mark D. Beazley

ASSISTANT EDITORS
Alex Starbuck & Nelson Ribeiro

SVP OF PRINT & DIGITAL PUBLISHING SALES
David Gabriel

BOOK DESIGN
Spring Hoteling

PRODUCTION
Joe Frontirre

EDITOR IN CHIEF
Axel Alonso

CHIEF CREATIVE OFFICER
Joe Quesada

PUBLISHER
Dan Buckley

EXECUTIVE PRODUCER
Alan Fine

Special thanks to George Olshevsky for starting it all and setting
the standard so high, the folks at the Marvel Chronology Project for
appreciating what we get right and pointing out what we get wrong,
the Marvel Appendix, the Marvel Masterworks Message Board,
spiderfan.org, Sol Comics' Variant Mafia, Jason Aaron, Larry Hama,
Todd Klein, Erik Larsen, Tom Orzechowski, Mark Powers, Jeanine
Schaefer, Chris Sotomayor, Mike Baygerstock, Kendra Brown, Heroes
Haven's Peter Carbonaro, Empire Comics' Jim & Tony Fraffieri,
Andrew Hallett, Mike Hansen, Alex Lea, Jed Raven, John Rhett
Thomas, Kirsten Weinrich, Greg York, Carolyn Ziering, Ronald Byrd,
Jeff Christiansen, Mike O'Sullivan, and the rest of the Handbook team.

Welcome to the new *Official Index to the Marvel Universe*'s ninth and final collected edition, featuring the Wolverine!

Entry format: Credits include all the known creators. Where the cover artists are different from those handling the interior, we credit them separately. Pencilers and inkers are separate credits, unless the same person did both, whereby they are credited for "art." Feature Characters are the lead, often title, characters in the comic. Supporting Cast are the regular cast. Villains should be obvious. Guest Stars cover other heroes and major characters who turn up in the story, while Other Characters covers everyone else. When multiple characters have used a given codename, we identify which version the character is the first time they appear in a given title; thereafter, unless otherwise stated, all subsequent appearances can be assumed to be the same version. Locations/Items serves to list places plus unusual, unique, or significant equipment. The Synopsis covers the events depicted in the story. Flashbacks are placed in their own section for ease of reference and divided into four types (fb, dfb, pfb, & rfb) described in the Abbreviation Key. The Note section covers interesting information and anomalies that don't fit the other headings.

Chronologies: Along with telling you which characters turn up in which issues, we also try to let you know where they were beforehand, and where they go afterwards. After so many years of flashbacks and retroactive continuity (retcons), this can become a tricky process. For Feature Characters, we list, in order, all appearances between the issue being covered and the character's next appearance in the series. For all other reoccuring characters, we list their last and next appearances. However, so that readers can enjoy tracking a character's appearances both in the genuine historical order, and in the revised order created by the insertions of flashbacks over the years, we distinguish between real world and flashback-revised "chronologically" last and next appearances. We omit "next in" if the subsequent issue is that character's next appearance (or if the issue in question is their final appearance to date), and, for Supporting Cast, we omit "last in" if the previous appearance is within the last five issues of the same series. We also include characters' next and last "behind-the-scenes" appearances, if applicable. As confusion has arisen in the past over volume numbers, we distinguish between different volumes sharing the same cover title by including the publication year. Issue numbers with a slash and extra digit indicate later stories in the same issue; for example, 50/3 is the third story in issue 50.

D1393129

A CENTURY OF SNIKT: THE HISTORY OF THE WOLVERINE

Wolverine has one of the most complicated backstories in the Marvel Universe. Over a century old, he has been a soldier, spy, adventure samurai, mercenary, assassin, hero and more. He has crisscrossed the globe, fought in two World Wars, and romanced many beautif women. He has wielded mutant claws of bone and metal, and been brainwashed and manipulated time and again. And with every passin year, more of his labyrinthine past is revealed.

James Howlett was born in Alberta, Canada in the last decades of the 19th century to John and Elizabeth Howlett. A sickly child, he grew u with companions Rose O'Hara and Dog Logan, son of alcoholic groundskeeper Thomas Logan (Origin #1, '01, W:O #33, '09 fb, X:Prelud #4, '11 fb, W&X #26, '13 fb). However, James was unaware that Thomas was his biological father. One night Thomas tried to convinc Elizabeth to leave with him, but a fight broke out and Thomas shot John dead. Enraged, James popped bone claws from his hands for th first time, and killed Thomas (Origin #2, '01). James and Rose fled, eventually finding employment at a quarry, where James took the alia Logan (Origin #3, '02). His newfound healing factor dealt with his recent trauma by "healing over" much of his memory. Young Logan grew t manhood at the quarry (Origin #4, '02, X:Prelude #4, '11 fb, W:BC, '91 fb), learning to hunt and earning the nickname "Wolverine" (Origin #5 '02). Dog eventually located and attacked Logan; in the confusion of the brawl, Logan accidentally stabbed Rose with his claws, killing he Horrified, he fled into the woods (Origin #6, '02, X:Prelude #4, '11 fb), where he lived with wolves. Dog tracked the feral "Wolverine" (AstSMV #3-4, '10-11) until he encountered a mine full of mysterious diamonds that hurled him into the timestream. Wolverine eventually returned t civilization (W:WX #10, '10 fb); working as a fur trapper, he battled the monstrous Uncegila (MCP #93 fb, 94-97 & 98 fb, '91-92). He soo became a mercenary; in Tokyo, he first encountered the savage Victor Creed, the Hand ninja clan, and — though he was unaware at the time — the long-lived manipulator Romulus, who had plans for Wolverine (W #52-53, '07 fbs). Returning to Canada, Wolverine fell in love wit a Blackfoot named Silver Fox (W:O #49, '10 fb); they lived together near the frontier town Mount Logan (W #49, '91 fb, W #65, '93 fb). Cree arrived in town; Wolverine befriended him (XO:Sabre, '09, W #47, '91 fb), but on Wolverine's next birthday, Creed raped and seemingly kille Silver Fox (W #50, '07 fb, W:O #5, '06 fb). Wolverine attacked Creed but was eventually defeated (W #41, '91 fb, W #50, '07 fb, W #10, '89 f XO:Sabre, '09, W:O #5, '06 fb, UXM #213, '87 fb). Romulus arrived and convinced Wolverine that the townspeople had allowed Silver Fox t die. Grief-stricken, Wolverine massacred them — the first step down a long road of being unknowingly conditioned to act as Romulus' pawn (W:O #5, '06 fb).

Wolverine worked for the Hudson Bay Company for a time (W:O #33, '09 fb, W:O #15, '07 fb), and was soon molded into a soldier at thei training facility by Silas Burr, later known as Cyber (W:O #15, '07 fb, W:O #33, '09 fb, W:O #12, '07 fb). Unbeknownst to Wolverine, Romulu ran the training facility using Wolverine's uncle Elias Hudson as his figurehead. During WWI, Wolverine joined Burr's elite squad, the Devil' Brigade. In 1915, Wolverine dueled and defeated Azrael, the Angel of Death, on a Belgium battlefield (W #57-60, '07-08 fbs). At the Hudso Bay facility, Wolverine fell for an employee named Janet, but Burr murdered her on Romulus' orders — to teach Wolverine the folly of trying t live like a normal man (W:O #12, 15 & 17, '07 fbs). After WWI, Wolverine wandered the world. In Japan, he encountered the samurai Ogun, bu declined an offer to train with him (W #113, '97 fb). In 1921, Wolverine joined Mystique's band of Kansas City grifters for a time, but ultimate betrayed them to the police (W #62-65, '08 fbs). In the 1930s, working as a strikebreaker-fighting union "negotiator," Wolverine killed a corrup coal mine owner, whose son swore revenge (W #10, '11 fb). Wolverine later spent time in a circus as the "Immortal Man" (W:Amaz, '08 and traveled to the island nation Madripoor, where he romanced the diminutive Seraph. Unbeknownst to Wolverine, Seraph also worked fo Romulus; she taught Wolverine how to kill with finesse (W:O Ann, '07). When a Hand ninja nearly killed Wolverine, he found himself duelin Azrael in the afterlife for the right to return to life — an unexpected benefit of having defeated Azrael in WWI (W #58, '07 fb, W:O Ann, '07 In late 1934, the mysterious Covenant hired Wolverine to kill the Dreaming Maiden, but he instead took pity on her and hid her away (W #314-317, '12-13 fbs). By 1936, Wolverine had become a partner in Mystique and her lover Destiny's detective agency; they allied with a time-traveling Shadowcat and saved the future Queen Elizabeth II from the Shadow King (X:TF #2-3, '99). Promising Seraph that he woul learn control, Wolverine returned to Japan and trained with Ogun (W #126, '98 fb, W #103, '96 fb bts, W #89, '95 fb, W #169, '01 fb). In 1937 Wolverine fought in the Spanish Civil War with Eugene Judd, later Puck; the two were briefly displaced by their time-traveling future selves (W #35-37, '91). Later that year, Seraph assigned Wolverine to study under spymaster Taras Romanov (W:O #9, '07 fb). Wolverine trained Taras ward Natasha Romanov, later the Black Widow, to fight (BW:DO #1, '10 fb) — but his true mission was to kill Taras if he suspected their mutua master Romulus' identity. Wolverine shot Taras but spared Natasha (W:O #9, '07 fb, W:O #24, '08 fb).

When WWII began, Wolverine returned to the Devil's Brigade (W:O #17, '07 fb), his memories of Janet suppressed either thanks to Romulus manipulations or his healing factor. In early 1940, Wolverine nearly crossed paths with Hercules in Paris (W/Herc #1, '11 fb). His main stagin ground became Madripoor, where Seraph and Cyber assigned him espionage tasks (W:O #17, '07 fb). In mid-1941, Wolverine allied wit Captain America to rescue Natasha from the Hand (UXM #268, '90 fb, W:O #16, '07 fb), an elaborate ploy to assassinate the Hand leader. Tha November, Wolverine and Captain America battled Baron Strucker and his nascent Hydra organization in Tunisia; there Wolverine met Nic Fury and suspected, correctly, that Captain America's sidekick Bucky was also an espionage agent. Mid-battle, Seraph gave Wolverine ne orders to kill Captain America, but Wolverine admired him too much, and let himself be defeated (W:O #17-20, '07-08 fbs). In 1942, Wolverin was imprisoned in the Sobibor death camp, where he tormented the Commandants (W #32, '05). In 1943, he romanced fellow spy Catharin (I M:MMH, '06 fb) and, on Romulus' orders, oversaw horrific experiments performed on Japanese-Americans (W:O #26, '08 fb). Later re enlisting as a soldier (W #50, '92 fb), Wolverine fought by Captain America and Bucky's sides once again (WWHs:C/W #1-2, '10 fbs), taugh fighting techniques to Greek resistance soldiers (W #106, '96 fb), and fought at Normandy (W #34, '90 fb), where he encountered the vampiri Bloodscream (W #78, '94 fb). In December 1944, Wolverine fought in the Battle of the Bulge (W #1000/5, '11); in April 1945, he battled a Naz werewolf and was dismayed to learn of Captain America's apparent death (W #1000, '11). In summer 1945, Wolverine romanced the beautifu Atsuko in Hiroshima, and survived the atomic bombing that ended WWII (Logan #1-3, '08 fbs). Turning mercenary again, Wolverine worke with Landau, Luckman & Lake's Chang (W #97, '96 fb), saved the life of Eric Brooks, later Blade (Blade #5, '07 fb), and befriended Korea fishermen near Madripoor (RamW, '09 fb). In the late 1940s, the other-dimensional Kimora defeated Wolverine soundly (L:PW, '96). Decidin to retire, Wolverine settled in Jasmine Falls (W #40, '06 fb), but years later, Chang convinced him to face Kimora again; this time Wolverin triumphed (L:PW, '96). Back in Jasmine Falls, Wolverine married Itsu (W:O #27, '08 fb). She soon became pregnant, but one night in 195 Wolverine found her murdered (W #40, '06 fb). Unbeknownst to Wolverine, Romulus had ripped his unborn son from Itsu's womb. Wolverin sought out the swordsmith Muramasa, who distilled his murderous rage into a mystical sword that could kill nearly anything (W:O #35, '09 f W #40, '06 fb), but Bucky, now the brainwashed Russian agent the Winter Soldier, intervened and "liberated" Wolverine (W #38, '06 fb); it woul be decades before Wolverine claimed the sword — or learned that Bucky had killed Itsu, on Romulus' orders.

eturning to his old life, Wolverine continued running missions for Romulus' shadow organization, including recruiting young Frank Simpson (W:O #3, '06 fb). The coal miner's son tried to kill Wolverine many times, but failed (W #10, '11 fb). Wolverine later assassinated a conspiracy theorist, traumatizing his daughter (W #11, '11 fb). In 1958, Wolverine encountered Jimmy Woo's G-Men while investigating mind-controlling insects in Cuba (W:AoAtlas #1-3, '08-09). In San Francisco he killed Chinatown's tyrannical crimelord the Black Dragon, but refused to accept the position himself; his girlfriend Lin Fong took up the role (W:MD #2-4, '09 fbs). Circa 1961, Wolverine and Creed, now called Sabretooth, were hired by the Weapon X Program, which was putting together a mutant black ops group, Team X. At first the two fought bitterly (XO:Sabre, '09), but Weapon X altered their memories, along with those of their new teammates — including Silver Fox, who had survived Sabretooth's assault decades earlier and had seemingly not aged since, likely due to Romulus' machinations. Weapon X initially altered the team's memories using elaborate stage sets (W #50, '92 fb), but soon hired telepath Aldo Ferro, later Psi-Borg (W #63, '92 fb), who added gruesome details to pre-existing traumas (W #10, '89 fb, W #41, '91 fb), enhanced the stage-created memories (W #48-49, '91 fbs) and added entirely new ones (W #62 & 60, '92 fbs), muddying the team members' true relationships to one another. In 1963, Silver Fox betrayed Team X in Cuba (W #49, '91 fb, W #61, '92 fb) and fled, joining Hydra. Sabretooth, subconsciously recalling his birthday assault of Silver Fox, began a tradition of celebrating Wolverine's birthday by fighting him (XO:Sabre, '09). Team X continued their undercover missions (W #87, '94 fb, Mvk #2, '97 fb), but Sabretooth grew more savage: when Wolverine was sent to kill Russian super-soldier prototype Epsilon Red, Sabretooth arrived with orders canceling the mission, but murdered Red's pregnant wife (W #68, '93 fb). Itsu's son Daken, who had been secretly raised by Romulus and taught to hate Wolverine, allied with the coal miner's son (D:DW #1, '10 fb), giving him ideas for a long-term revenge plan. Soon after, Team X killed a conspiracy theorist, coincidentally the husband of the traumatized young woman whose father Wolverine had killed years before (W #11, '11 fb).

the early 1970s, the Weapon X Program decided to experiment on Wolverine, discovering that the radioactive Carbonadium dulled his healing factor (W:O #6, '06 fb, W:O #25, '08 fb). They intended to erase his memories of the experiment, but Wolverine awakened early, recovering many of his original memories (W:O #7, '06 fb) and now dimly aware that his team was manipulated by Romulus. On a mission to Berlin to assassinate Russian super-agent Omega Red and obtain a Carbonadium synthesizer (X #5 & 7, '92 fbs), the team extracted their mole, Janice Hollenbeck — but Sabretooth, well aware of Romulus, realized that Wolverine had suspicions. He killed Janice, reinforcing Romulus' lifelong lesson that people die when Wolverine tries to think for himself (W:O #8, '07 fb, X #5-6, '92 fbs). Omega Red attacked; the Team escaped (Mvk Dec, '97 fb, X #6, '92 fb, W #60-61, '92 fbs), but Wolverine, now extremely distrustful, hid the synthesizer inside Janice's corpse (X #7, '92 fb). Wolverine quit Team X (X #6, '92 fb, XO:Sabre, '09) but couldn't escape Romulus' reach. His memories soon suppressed again, Wolverine was sent to "condition" Frank Simpson, now a POW in Vietnam (W:O #2, '06 fb). Weapon X's parent program, Weapon Plus, would soon make Frank into the super-soldier Nuke. Wolverine eventually joined Canada's Department K, becoming a spy and once again traveling the world. In China, he battled Chen Yu with the immortal Adam Destine (W Ann #1, 12 fb). On Coney Island, he romanced mobster Phil DeBlasio's girlfriend (W:Bwalk, '10 fb). In Canada, he encountered Interpol agent Sean Cassidy, later Banshee (CX #26/2, '88 fb), and was handed a crippling defeat by sorcerer Abdul Alhazred (MCP #154, '94 fb). Meanwhile, Sabretooth continued his tradition of attacking Wolverine every year on his birthday (XO:Sabre, '09). Wolverine helped Viktoria Suhkarov defect from Russia, but the lycanthropic assassin Volk killed her father Dimitri (W Ann '97 fb). On a joint mission with the CIA, Wolverine was captured by Baron Strucker and freed by agents Richard and Mary Parker (UToS #-1, '97), later the parents of Peter Parker, who became Spider-Man. Between assignments, Wolverine spent time as a bouncer for his friend Antonio Vargas' bar (W:BR, '98 fb). Partnered with Squee, Wolverine was tasked with locating mobster Monte. He seduced Abeline, Monte's girlfriend, but Abeline and the Winter Soldier kidnapped and tortured him (WWHs:C/W #1-2, '10 fbs).

earing rumors that the world's governments were seeking to control or eliminate the world's growing mutant population, Wolverine convinced Sabretooth to help him locate and protect mutants. A young Charles Xavier, an embittered Max Eisenhardt (later Magneto) and the amnesiac Sub-Mariner declined their invitation, but the two recruited several young mutants. Unfortunately, when the US government sent Bolivar Trask's prototype Sentinels against them, most of the recruits were killed (FX #1-5, '12-13). Weapon X agents approached a dejected Wolverine, offering to make him the "perfect soldier"; Wolverine agreed, re-enlisting in the military to train, where he served in Southeast Asia with Xavier and Carmen Pryde (Ex #14, '05 fb). After his tour of duty, he visited his friend Saburo Bando (W #26, '90 fb) and returned to espionage work; when his partner Neil Langram was killed, he and CIA agent Carol Danvers investigated, learning that groups including the Hellfire Club and Canada's nascent Dept. H were starting to recruit mutants. Wolverine again battled Sabretooth, who had killed Neil; he came away disillusioned (:SS, '96). Turning to alcohol, Wolverine accidentally shot a fellow agent and was fired from Dept. K. The Weapon X Program then kidnapped Wolverine (MCP #72, '91, WX #23, '04 fb, MCP #73, '91 fb, W #48, '91 fb). Romulus, hoping to create a weapon to combat the emerging new generation of super heroes, ordered Wolverine's memory wiped (W #54, '97 fb). The Weapon X staff were surprised to learn of Wolverine's claws, now Adamantium-coated as well, but they incorporated the discovery into their plan to create a brainwashed killer (MCP #74-76, '91, X:Prelude #4, '11 fb, MCP #77-78, '91, NX #130, '02 fb, W #58, '07 fb, MCP #78, '91). After pitting him against animals (W #49, '91 fb, MCP #79, '91), Weapon X unleashed Wolverine on a "field test"; he slaughtered the entire town of Roanoke (WX #24-25, '04 fbs). With Psi-Borg's telepathic help, Weapon X then made Wolverine think he had broken free and escaped (MCP #79-80, W #49 fb, MCP #80, W #48 fb, MCP #80-84, all '91); however, following the scenario Wolverine actually did escape (MCP #84, '91, W #14, '04 fb bts, X23 #1, '05), mauling new recruit Malcolm Colcord (W #166, '01 fb, W #175, '02 fb). Fleeing into the wilderness, Wolverine saved a family from a wolf attack (W:Hunger, '09). Reduced to an animalistic state, he lived ferally in Wood Buffalo National Park (W #118, '97 fb) for a time, where he encountered the near-mythical Hunter in Darkness (W #34, '90 fb).

olverine spotted honeymooners James and Heather Hudson (W #92, '95 fb). Assuming them to be poachers, he attacked, but they shot and captured him (AFlt #33, '86 fb, AFlt #-1, '97 fb). Eventually bringing the feral Wolverine back to lucidity, James and Heather befriended him. James invited Wolverine to join Dept. H, which he now ran; Wolverine agreed, having lost all memory of their more sinister agendas (AFlt #3/2, '83) and unaware that James was descended from his uncle Frederick Hudson. James arranged a meeting between Wolverine and Adamantium inventor Dr. Myron MacLain, hoping to find answers about Wolverine's forgotten past, but Sabretooth, Hydra and the Black Widow attacked and Carol Danvers and Nick Fury rescued Wolverine; he remembered none of them (W #-1, '97). After months of psychotherapy to try to control his primal rage and regain his memories (UXM #147, '81 fb, X #140, '80 fb), Wolverine helped James battle unbalanced Canadian hero Chinook, and attended James and Heather's second wedding ceremony (AFlt #-1, '97). Dressing Wolverine in a heroic costume, James pitched him to Dept. H as a super-agent, coincidentally codenamed Weapon X. On an early mission, Wolverine recruited mutant Madison Jeffries (W:FCBD, '09); he then helped free Iraq's American embassy from insurgents, promising a dying hostage that he would avenge her (W #9, '89 fb bts). Wolverine began working mainly in Siberia and Asia. He teamed with pilot Ben Grimm, later the Thing, on a Russian mission that pitted them against the Black Widow (BFF:Ben #1-3, '00). In Japan, he battled the Hand (W #13, '11 fb); in Hong Kong, he romanced Ai-Chia and befriended killer Roddy McLeish — but when McLeish murdered Ai-Chia's father, Wolverine attacked him, leaving him for dead (W #119-121, 119 & 12 '97-98 fbs). Shortly after the Fantastic Four made their public debut, Wolverine adventured with Seraph and Viper in Madripoor until Sabretoo seemingly killed Seraph (W #126, '98 fb). Wolverine romanced druglord Takeshi Kishimoto's daughter (SM/W #2, '03 fb) and allied with th time-traveling Nathan Dayspring to capture D'von Kray, a menace from the 39th century. Dept. H tried to transform Kray into a Canadian ager but he ran amok and Wolverine killed him (W/Cable, '99). Wolverine teamed with CIA agent Rick Stoner to retrieve James' stolen body arm prototype from Hydra (Fury, '94), while James tried to mutate a murderer into another super-agent over Wolverine's objections (AFlt #52, '87 ft Magneto contacted the world's mutants, asking them to band together under him, but Wolverine did not respond (X #14, '11 fb).

James recruited several superhumans into a team called the Flight, which he hoped Wolverine would lead. After a disastrous battle agains Egghead and several other villains (AFlt Spec, '92), James broke the Flight into skill-based tiers: Alpha, Beta and Gamma. Wolverine traine Gamma Flight's Wild Child, but was disgusted by his savagery (MCP #51, '90 fb); when Wild Child injured teammate Stitch during trainin Wolverine nearly killed him (AFlt #127/2, '93 fb). Finally locating the Iraqi insurgents, Wolverine fulfilled his years-old promise of revenge (\ #9, '89 fb). When assassins gunned Wolverine down in the desert, David Nanjiwarra helped him survive (W/NF:SC, '89 fb). Later, Wolverin battled Russian super-agent Vladimir Zaitsev (UXM #228, '88 fb) and recruited Aurora for Alpha Flight (AFlt #9/2, '84). The Leader kidnappe Wolverine, along with Hercules and the Deviant Karkas, but the three soon escaped (W #144, '99 fb). When the Hulk arrived in Canada, Dep H ordered Wolverine to neutralize him (W:FCBD, '09) — but Wolverine received secondary orders from Romulus: to get noticed by an unknow entity who was planning to recruit mutants. Once noticed and recruited, Wolverine was to kill this unknown party (W:O #28, '08 fb). Wolverin found the Hulk battling a Wendigo (IHulk #180, '74); he helped Hulk defeat his foe, then turned on him, but was unable to defeat the jade gia (IHulk #181, '74, W:O #28 & 30, '08-09 fbs, IHulk #181-182, '74). Later, Wolverine saved his old friend Charlemagne from Russian agent (SMvW, '87 fb) and helped James defeat Bedlam, the murderer James had begun mutating years before (AFlt #53, '87 fb). Soon after, during training exercise, Wolverine's berserker rage overcame him and he stabbed James in the chest (AFlt #1, '97 fb); James barely survived. Xavie now X-Men leader Professor X, traveled to Dept. H to recruit Wolverine (XO:W, '09). After secretly killing some Dept. H "loose ends" (W:O #28 '08 fb), Wolverine agreed to join Xavier (GSX #1, '75, W:O #28, '08 fb). James and Major Chasin objected (XO:W, '09, GSX #1, '75, AFlt #52 '87 fb) and Dept. H tried to capture Xavier, but Wolverine fought free and left for the USA (XO:W, '09). Meeting Professor X's other "new X-Men Wolverine sized them up in the Danger Room (GSX #3, '05). Cyclops briefed the recruits about the original X-Men's capture by Krakoa (XO:C '08, GSX #1, '75, CX #1, '86, GSX #1, '75, X:Lib #2, '98 fb), but Professor X, aware that Wolverine was meant to assassinate him, met with him privately and telepathically removed Romulus' brainwashing (X:OS fb, X:L #217 fb, W:O #29 fb, X:L #216 fb, all '08, XO:W, '09). For the first tim in decades, Wolverine's mind was unclouded, though his memories were more shattered than ever.

From this point onward, Wolverine's history is chronicled in much more detail in the *Uncanny X-Men: Official Index to the Marvel Universe* GN The new X-Men freed the originals (GSX #1, '75, X:WA, '94 fb, X:DG #6, '06 fb, GSX #1, '75); Wolverine was immediately attracted to Jean Gre (CX #1, '86), but she and most of the original X-Men quit (X #94, '75). Cyclops and Professor X trained the new team (CX #2, '86, W:WX #16, '1 fb, X #94, '75, X:L #218, '09 fb, W #118, '97 fb, X #94, '75, GSX #4, '05), but Sabretooth still attacked Wolverine on every birthday (CX #10/2, '87 a throat wound from his old foe caused Wolverine to once again duel Azrael in the afterlife (W #58, '07 fb, CX #10/2, '87, CX #2, '86, X #94-95 '75, CX #3, '86, X #95, '75, CX #3/2, '86, X #96, '75, UO #9, '97, X #106, '77 fb). Wolverine and Nightcrawler soon became close friends (CX #4/2, '86, X #97, '76, ASM #161, '76, XMU #25, '99 fb, MHol #1, '91). Sentinels abducted Jean Grey and several X-Men, including Wolverine to an orbiting space station (X #98, '76, CX #6, '87, X #98-99, '76, CX #7, '87, X #99, '76). The X-Men freed themselves and Jean piloted a shuttle back to Earth, but she was caught in a lethal radiation storm. Dying, she was secretly saved and replaced by the cosmic Phoenix Force (X #100, '76, CX #8 & 8/2, '87, X #101, '76, CX #9, '87, X #101, '76, MTU Ann #1, '76, MTU #53, '77, MT #262/2, '92). "Jean" was hospitalize soon after, and Wolverine realized the depth of his feelings for her (CX #9/2, '87, X #101-104, '76-77, CX #12, '87, X #104, '77, CX #13, '87, X #105 & 108 fb, '77, CX #14, '87 fb, X #107-108, '77, CX #15, '87, X #109, '78 fb, X #108, '77, IF #15, '77). James Hudson, now called Weapor Alpha, tried unsuccessfully to force Wolverine to return to Canada (X #109, '78, AFlt #17, '84 fb, X #109, '78, W #176, '10 fb, CX #28/2, '88, X #110, '78). After encountering Hercules again (MTE #26/5, '80), Wolverine made his affections for Phoenix clear, but despite a small spark o attraction, the feelings were not mutual (CX 18/2 & 27/2, '88, Girl #1/6, '10). When Magneto attacked, Phoenix and Beast were separated from the team in Antarctica, each group believing the other killed in the battle (CX #17/2, '88, X #111-112, '78, CX #18, '88, X #112-113, '78, CX #19 '88, X #113, '78, X #125, '79 fb, CX #20, '88 fb). Wolverine grieved for Phoenix, but as the X-Men made their way home via Japan (X #114, '78 CX #21/2, '88, X #114-116, '78, CX #22 & 22/2, '88, X #116-117, '78-79, CX #23, '88), he met a young woman named Mariko Yashida (X #118 '79, W:O #46, '10 fb, X #118-119, '79, CX #25, '88, X #119-120, '79, W:O #46, '10 fb).

James Hudson and Alpha Flight attempted again to force Wolverine back to Canada, but failed (X #120-121, '79, CX #27, '88, X #121, '79). The X-Men finally returned home and learned that Phoenix and Beast were alive (CX #26/2 & 25/2, '88; X #122-124, X Ann #3, all '79, BA #27/3, '81 X #125-126, '79, CX #32/2, '89, X #126-127, '79, CX #33/2, '89, X #127-129, '79-80, CX #39/2, '89, SSol #7, '93 fb, X #130, '80 fb, CX #35/2, '89, X #129-131, '80), but although Wolverine was overjoyed, he was falling in love with Mariko (W:O #46, '10 fb). Phoenix was soon corrupted by her own cosmic power; rather than continue menacing the galaxy, she killed herself (X #132-137, '80, FF Ann #18, '84, X #137, '80, X Ann #199, '85 fb, BICMW #1/2, '10, X #138, '80, W:WX #16, '10 fb). Carmen Pryde's daughter Kitty soon joined the X-Men; Wolverine mentored her (X Ann #4, '80, W #126, '98 fb) and teamed with Alpha Flight to battle the Wendigo (X #139-140, '80). Returning Wolverine's affection, Mariko visited for Christmas (W:O #46, '10 fb, X:Lib #1, '98 fb; X #141, UXM #142, Daz #1-2, all '81, Ex #85, '95 fb, UXM #143, '81, W Ann #95 fb, UXM #144, '81, MTU #100, '80; Rom #17-18, SW #37, UXM #145-147, all '81, UXM #187, '84 fb, UXM #148, '81); she was kidnapped shortly thereafter by a Japanese criminal and Wolverine rescued her (W:WX #16, '10 fb, BMC HC/13, '87; UXM #149, Av Ann #10, UXM #150, X Ann #5, all '81, MFan #3-4, '82, UXM #151-152, '81; Micro #37, UXM #153, MGN #1, all '82, SS Ann #6, '93 fb bts, XMU #29/2, '00, MFan #4, '82, UXM #154-159, '82). After a number of adventures, Wolverine noticed that Mariko had stopped writing to him (UXM #160, '82, Magik #1, '83 fb; UXM #160-161, MTU #117-118, CoC #1, 2 bts & 3, all '82, IHulk #277 bts & 278-279, '82-83, W:O #46, '10 fb). The alien Brood abducted the X-Men into space and implanted them with their eggs. Wolverine's healing factor destroyed his; the other X-Men were soon able to cure themselves (UXM #162, '82 fb, UXM #161-166, '82-83, Ex #116, '98 fb) and returned home (NM #3, '83 bts, UXM #167, '83, X Ann #6, '82, MTIO Ann #7, '82, MTIO #96, '83, SpEdX/2, '83). Wolverine, perturbed by Mariko's recent lack of contact, decided to take a short vacation from the team (UXM #168, '83) — which is where the Wolverine Index begins…

WOLVERINE #1 (September 1982)

"I'm Wolverine" (22 pages)

CREDITS: Chris Claremont (writer), Frank Miller (pencils), Josef Rubinstein (finishes), Tom Orzechowski (letters, logo), Glynis Wein (colors), Louise Jones (editor)
FEATURE CHARACTER: Wolverine (James "Logan" Howlett, fast-healing mutant X-Man with retractable claws & Adamantium-coated skeleton, last in UXM #160, '82, chr last in UXM #168, '83, also in MGN #5, '83, X/AFlt #1-2, '98, XvHulk, '09, MTU #135, '83, W:Carni, '10 & W:O #46, '10 fb)
SUPPORTING CAST: Mariko Yashida (Wolverine's beloved, also in photo, last in UXM #143, '81, chr last in BMC HC, '87, chr last bts in XMU #29/2, '00)
VILLAINS: Noburu-Hideki (Mariko's husband, 1st, unnamed), Yukio (Yukiko, ronin, 1st, unnamed, chr last in W/Gam #3, '95 fb), Lord Shingen Harada (Mariko's father, Oyabun (leader) of Clan Yashida, see NOTE; 1st on-panel app, last in SecWs #26, '11 fb, last bts in DD #111, '74), street gang (dies)
OTHER CHARACTERS: Asano Kimura (Japanese Secret Service agent, 1st, next in W #3, '82) & his superiors (bts assigning Asano to Wolverine, next bts in W #3, '82), Josie's Bar 'N' Grill bartender & patrons inc hunter, Shingen's sumo, Alberta Mounties (bts arresting hunter), Japanese Embassy employee, Yashida servant (prev 2 bts on phone), Japan Air Lines pilot (bts piloting plane); grizzly bear (dies), Shingen's guard dogs; Masamune (master swordsmith, mentioned, forged Honor Sword), bear's victims: 2 Mounties, 5 men, 3 women & 5 children (prev mentioned, dead); Buddha (as statue)
LOCATIONS/ITEMS: Canada inc bear's Rocky Mountain den & Josie's Bar 'N' Grill (Coalspur, Alberta); Honshu, Japan inc Yashidas' ancestral manor (Ou Sanmyaku mountains, outside Agarashima, Miyagi Prefecture) w/garden & Tokyo w/Ginza alley & Wolverine's hotel room; skies over Pacific Ocean; X-Mansion (X-Men's Westchester, New York headquarters), New York City's Japanese Embassy (prev 2 bts) / Wolverine's Adamantium skeleton (hereinafter considered part of his standard equipment and not listed separately), photo & returned letters, hunter's poisoned arrow (bts) & beer mug, Japan Air Lines plane, Clan Yashida swords inc Honor Sword (unnamed), Shingen's bokken, gang's weapons, Yukio's poisoned shuriken & throwing blades
SYNOPSIS: In the Rockies, Wolverine hunts and kills a murderous grizzly bear. Realizing that the bear was driven mad by a poisoned arrow, Wolverine tracks down the hunter responsible and brings him to justice. Returning to the X-Mansion, Wolverine learns that his love Mariko Yashida has returned to Japan and refuses to acknowledge him. Wolverine travels to Japan, where his friend Asano Kimura reveals that Mariko's father, Shingen Harada, has made her marry an associate, Noburu-Hideki, to repay a debt he owes. Sneaking into the Yashida estate, Wolverine finds that Noburu has beaten Mariko. He nearly kills Noburu, but Mariko begs him to stop, as she is honor-bound to remain married. Wolverine is suddenly incapacitated by poisoned shuriken; when he awakens, Shingen challenges him to mock combat — however, Shingen's wood strikes are for real, causing Wolverine to pop his claws and attack savagely, shaming him in Mariko's eyes. Shingen defeats Wolverine and has him dumped in an alley, where a street gang confronts him — but they are suddenly killed by a mysterious woman…
NOTE: Wolverine's real name is revealed in Origin #1, '01 though it is not linked to him until Origin #2, '01. Only Shingen's title and given name are revealed here. His surname is given as Yashida in UXM #172, '83 and Harada in OHMU #10, '83. Subsequent appearances and mentions have used both names seemingly interchangeably, but all Handbooks have consistently named him Harada, and this Index will do so as well. Noburu and Yukio are named next issue, which also reveals that Yukio works for Shingen, hence her listing as a Villain here. W:Soul #1, '05 reveals that Yukio shortened her name from Yukiko to sound more masculine. To keep consistent with the comics, Japanese characters are named here in "Western" style, with given names first and surnames last. Clan Yashida's Honor Sword is named in W #4, '82. Clan Yashida's manor, located only "in the hills" here, is revealed to be in the Ou Sanmyaku (Ou Mountains) in KP&W #4, '85. Miyagi Prefecture is misspelled "Miyago" here, and bokken, wooden practice swords, are spelled "bokan." Inker Josef Rubinstein's last name is misspelled "Rubinstien" here. Wolverine mentions here that he knows his father, but later issues clarify that he has very few memories of his past, and reveal that his memories have been altered many times. Also, Origin #1, '01 implies that his biological father was Thomas Logan, the Howlett family gardener, not John Howlett, his mother's husband. Therefore, it is uncertain who Wolverine believes his father to be here, and very unlikely that he is correct.

WOLVERINE #2 (October 1982)

"Debts and Obligations" (22 pages)

CREDITS: Chris Claremont (writer), Frank Miller (pencils), Josef Rubinstein (finishes), Tom Orzechowski (letters), Glynis Wein (colors), Louise Jones (editor)
FEATURE CHARACTER: Wolverine
SUPPORTING CAST: Mariko Yashida (also in Wolverine's thoughts, next in W #4, '82)
VILLAINS: Hand (Ninja assassin clan, many die, others last in DD #190, '83), Katsuyori (Japanese crimelord, dies) & his assassins (also as Kabuki troupe), Noburu-Hideki (next in W #4, '82), Yukio (prev 2 named), Shingen Harada
OTHER CHARACTERS: Tokyo police (1 in silhouette, others bts in cars), Katsuyori's wife (dies) & bodyguards (some die), Shingen's receptionist
LOCATIONS/ITEMS: Tokyo inc Yukio's apartment, Wolverine's hotel room, Shingen's Meguro District office & Katsuyori's Kabuki theatre (remodeled castle) w/moat / Hand's swords, bows & arrows, police cars, Yukio's knife, throwing blades, explosives & remote detonator, guards' guns, Katsuyori's security systems (bts) & car (destroyed), assassins' katanas (1 destroyed) & Kabuki costumes
SYNOPSIS: Yukio frantically awakens Wolverine, who sees Hand ninjas surrounding them. Wolverine battles and kills the ninjas, and Yukio explains that they work for a local crimelord. She comes on to Wolverine but, thinking of Mariko, he turns her down. Later, Yukio angrily storms into the office of her employer — Shingen — who explains that the attack had to be real to fool Wolverine. Shingen then orders Yukio to kill a rival crimelord, Katsuyori, during a meeting with Noburu and Mariko — and then to kill Wolverine, to which Yukio reluctantly agrees. Yukio tells Wolverine that Katsuyori sent the Hand, and the two infiltrate his castle and spy on the meeting. Katsuyori, aware of Shingen's intent, disguises assassins as Kabuki actors. They attack Noburu and Mariko during a performance, and Wolverine leaps to defend Mariko. He brutally battles the troupe onstage, horrifying Mariko, who has never seen his berserker rage. Outside, Yukio blows up the fleeing Katsuyori's car — and as Mariko turns away from Wolverine, Yukio grins.

NOTE: Although Wolverine does not seem to recognize the Hand here, he has fought them several times in the past, including W #52, '07 fb, W:O Ann, '07 fb & UXM #268, '90 fb; his memory alterations have likely suppressed his recollection of these events.

WOLVERINE #3 (November 1982)

"Loss" (22 pages)

CREDITS: Chris Claremont (writer), Frank Miller (pencils), Josef Rubinstein (finishes), Tom Orzechowski (letters), Glynis Wein (colors), Louise Jones (editor)
FEATURE CHARACTER: Wolverine (also as feudal warrior in his own dream)
VILLAINS: Shingen Harada (bts sending Hand after Yukio, also as feudal lord in Wolverine's dream), Hand ninjas (die), Yukio
OTHER CHARACTERS: Takahashi (blacklisted Sumo), Asano Kimura (last in W #1, '82, dies) & his superiors (bts assigning Asano to Shingen, last bts in W #1, '82), Japanese underworld (bts, newly united under Shingen), Shinkansen driver (bts operating train), bar patrons, bellhop; Mariko Yashida (as feudal princess), horse (dies), feudal warriors (prev 3 in Wolverine's dream); models (on billboards)
LOCATIONS/ITEMS: Tokyo inc bar, train tracks, rooftops, private Zen garden & Wolverine's hotel w/room, feudal Japanese castle (in dream) / Wolverine's sword & armor, feudal warriors' armor, bows & arrows, Mariko's bow & arrow, Shingen's swords (all in dream), Asano's car & gun, Hand's swords, ropes, bows & arrows, Wolverine's bottle (destroyed), Shinkansen bullet train, Yukio's throwing blades
SYNOPSIS: Wolverine drowns his sorrow over losing Mariko in beer, bar brawls and Yukio, with whom he has become involved. Asano asks him to help investigate a new crimelord who has taken over the Japanese underworld, but the embittered Wolverine refuses. Yukio lives dangerously by dodging a bullet train, while Wolverine falls asleep and dreams of Mariko's rejection. Hand ninjas arrive and insist that Yukio kill Wolverine, but Yukio kills the ninjas instead. Wolverine awakens and mutters Mariko's name, upsetting Yukio. At Wolverine's hotel room, she mistakes Asano for a ninja and kills him — and when Wolverine arrives, he smells the poison on her blades, recognizes it from the shuriken that struck him at Shingen's manor, and realizes that Shingen is the new crimelord and that Yukio works for him. Wolverine chases Yukio to a Zen garden, but as he is about to kill her the Hand attack. Wolverine and Yukio defeat the ninjas and Yukio flees — while Wolverine takes time to rebuild the tranquil Zen garden, coming to terms with his recent losses and betrayals, and deciding to rise above them.

WOLVERINE #4 (December 1982)

"Honor" (22 pages)

CREDITS: Chris Claremont (writer), Frank Miller (pencils), Josef Rubinstein (finishes), Tom Orzechowski (letters), Lynn Varley (colors), Louise Jones (editor)
FEATURE CHARACTER: Wolverine (next in UXM #172-173, '83, W #96, '95 fb; UXM #174-175, X Ann #7, all '83, MFan #24/2, '86, Cap #289, '84 bts, UXM #175, '83, UXM #223, '87 fb, UXM #176, '83, DD #196, '83; MK #35, UXM #178-179, all '84, X:Lib #3, '99 fb; X&M #1-4, NM #14, UXM #180, all '84; W #150, '00 fb, UXM #180, '84; SecWars #1-7, 8 bts & 9-12, all '84-85, FF #265, '84 bts, UXM #181, '84, 1985 #6, '08, UXM #183, '84, MGN #12, '84, Fs #2, '86, DC #4, '89 fb, KP&W #1, '84)
GUEST STARS: X-Men (Wolverine's mutant teammates): Colossus (Piotr "Peter" Rasputin, organic steel strength), Nightcrawler (Kurt Wagner, blue-furred teleporter), Storm (Ororo Munroe, controls weather) (all chr last in NM #7, '83), Ariel (Katherine "Kitty" Pryde, phaser, chr last in MTU #135, '83); Cyclops (Scott Summers, retired X-Man, fires optic force blasts, chr last in UXM #171, '83) (all last in UXM #164, '82, chr next in UXM #172, '83)
SUPPORTING CAST: Mariko Yashida, Yukio (both next in UXM #172, '83)
VILLAINS: Shingen Harada (dies, possibly next as spirit in W #176, '02, see NOTE, next in W #60, '08), Noburu-Hideki (last in W #2, '82, dies), Japanese criminals inc Morita & Goro, Hand ninjas (some bts, defeated by Wolverine, rest die, some or others next in UXM #255, '89)
OTHER CHARACTERS: Shingen's servant & advisors inc Agami, hotel cleaning staff (bts cleaning Wolverine's carpet); Shingen's guard dogs (dead); Hirohito (Emperor of Japan, mentioned on invitation)
LOCATIONS/ITEMS: X-Mansion, Japan inc police station, mountains (prev 2 bts), several underworld bases, Wolverine's Tokyo hotel room & Yashida ancestral manor w/family history room / Wolverine's package & note, criminal's gun (bts) & suitcases of money & heroin, Hand's radio (bts), hoods, net & weapons inc shuriken, knives, swords, bows, crossbow & arrows, Yashida ancestral armor & Honor Sword (named), Yukio's throwing blades, Shingen's ropes & radio, Noburu's helicopter (bts) & gun, Mariko's kimono, Mariko & Wolverine's wedding invitation
SYNOPSIS: Wolverine assaults underworld operations one by one, dismantling Shingen's newly formed organization. Shingen sends the Hand after him, but Wolverine returns the defeated ninjas' hoods in a box, with a note challenging Shingen to combat. Wolverine arms himself with the ninjas' stolen weapons, while Mariko, now knowing that her father is evil and responsible for stopping him, but honor-bound to obey him, agonizes over her dilemma. Yukio sneaks into Shingen's manor, hoping to kill him to make up for killing Asano, but is captured. Wolverine battles his way into the manor and Noburu tries to flee with Mariko as a hostage, but Yukio kills Noburu. Wolverine and Shingen fight an intense duel, and Wolverine eventually triumphs, killing Shingen. He worries that Mariko may swear vengeance on him for killing her father, but instead she explains that she would have killed Shingen herself for dishonoring her family, and awards Wolverine Clan Yashida's Honor Sword. Months later, in America, the X-Men receive an invitation to Wolverine and Mariko's wedding.
NOTE: Yukio's reversal here moves her from Villain status to Supporting Cast. Mariko, mentally influenced by the villain Mastermind (Jason Wyngarde), calls off the wedding in UXM #173, '83. In W #176, '02, Shingen's spirit appears when Wolverine visits the afterlife, along with many other deceased characters' spirits — but Colossus' spirit also appears, and AX #5-6, '04 imply that Colossus is not actually dead during that time. Therefore it is uncertain if any other spirits Wolverine see in that issue are real, including Shingen. They could be illusions, as demons like Mephisto often manipulate living people who visit the afterlife — or Wolverine may have simply hallucinated the entire experience while healing from grave wounds. Because of the general uncertainty of afterlife experiences, this Index will qualify all appearances of any character's dead spirit as "possible" appearances, and where applicable will give additional chronologies to indicate the character's subsequent appearance in the event that their spirit later proves to be a hallucination or illusion.

KITTY PRYDE AND WOLVERINE #1 (November 1984)

"Lies" (23 pages)

CREDITS: Chris Claremont (writer), Al Milgrom (art), Tom Orzechowski (letters, logo), Glynis Wein (colors), Louise Jones & Ann Nocenti (editors)
FEATURE CHARACTERS: Ariel (last in UXM #183, '84, chr last in DC #4, '89 fb), Wolverine
SUPPORTING CAST: Carmen Pryde (Ariel's father, bank president, last in UXM #143, '81, last bts in X Ann #6, '82)
VILLAINS: Ogun (Wolverine's former sensei, 1st but chr last in W #169, '01 fb), Heiji Shigematsu (Yakuza Oyabun & corporation owner, 1st), Shumai (Shigematsu's bodyguard, 1st), Mr. Delano, Mr. Walsh (prev 2 Shigematsu's US branch managers)
OTHER CHARACTERS: Theresa "Terri" Pryde (Ariel's mother, bts sending letters, last in UXM #143, '81, last bts in X Ann #6, '82, next in Ex #78, '94), Mr. Casey (Deerfield Bank guard), Mrs. Lysinski (Prydes' housekeeper, bts in their home), bank employees (bts, sent home early), Chicago cabbie & baggage handlers, Japan Air Lines pilot (bts flying plane), stewardess & passengers, Shigematsu's staff: "command" (bts, alerted about Ariel), janitor & security guard, Tokyo police inc Saburo, airport security & ground crew inc chief, bus driver (bts driving bus), operators (bts on phone), reporter (voice only, on TV) & bystanders; Professor X (mentioned, taught Ariel Japanese)
LOCATIONS/ITEMS: Deerfield, Illinois (Ariel's hometown) inc skating rink (bts) & Deerfield Bank and Trust w/Carmen's office; Chicago's O'Hare Airport w/International Concourse & runway; skies above Pacific Ocean; Tokyo inc Narita International Airport w/runway & bus terminal, Matsushino Bank, sewer, TV studio (bts) & Shigematsu Industries building (unnamed, Seigikahara Plaza, Otemachi District) w/Shigematsu's executive suite; X-Mansion / Ariel's ice skates, hat, blanket, money & stolen yen, Ogun's limousine, Shigematsu's private jet, Carmen's note (bts) & money, taxi, luggage trucks & modules w/luggage, Japan Air Lines 747, chief's radio, security's radio (bts), Tokyo bus, public telephones, car & televisions, janitor's bucket & mop, guard's handgun, office windows (destroyed), bank camera (bts), ATM & alarm, police truncheons
SYNOPSIS: Taking a break from the X-Men after her breakup with Colossus, Ariel visits her father Carmen's bank. She overhears two men pressuring Carmen, and interrupts. Carmen reveals that Shigematsu's corporation bought the bank and is flying him to Tokyo for a meeting. Ogun takes notice of Ariel, who suspects that the men are Yakuza. Ariel follows Carmen to the airport and stows away on a flight to Japan. A stewardess finds her, but Ariel slips away when the plane lands. Locating Shigematsu's office building, she phases inside but, exhausted, falls asleep. A cleaning woman discovers her and a guard opens fire, and Ariel flees into a rainstorm. Desperate, she phases money out of an ATM, but police arrive and Ariel phases through the street, landing in the sewer; she spends the rest of the night huddled in a doorway. The next morning Ariel calls the X-Mansion, but hangs up when Wolverine answers. Returning to Shigematsu's office, Ariel overhears her father agreeing to launder money through his bank…
NOTE: Despite being a title character, Wolverine appears in only two panels of this issue. Mrs. Lysinski's last name is also spelled Lysinsky. This issue establishes that Professor X telepathically taught Ariel Japanese prior to UXM #172, '83. Shigematsu's given name is revealed in KP&W #5, '85. Ariel's suspicion that he is Yakuza is confirmed in KP&W #3, '85, which also reveals his company's name and plaza address. The criminal acts that got Carmen involved with Shigematsu are revealed in KP&W #5, '85. Ogun is revealed as Wolverine's former sensei next issue.

KITTY PRYDE AND WOLVERINE #2 (December 1984)

"Terror" (23 pages)

CREDITS: Chris Claremont (writer), Al Milgrom (art), Tom Orzechowski (letters), Glynis Wein (colors), Ann Nocenti (editor)
FEATURE CHARACTERS: Ariel (also as a child in her own hallucination), Wolverine (also in photo)
SUPPORTING CAST: Carmen Pryde
VILLAINS: Ogun (also in photo), Heiji Shigematsu (both next in KP&W #5, '85), Mr. Delano, Mr. Walsh, Shigematsu's bodyguards inc Shumai & Hideo, Ogun's ninjas inc Matsuo
OTHER CHARACTERS: Shigematsu's employees & guards, airport security guard & travelers, Ogun's servants (in photo); Buddha (as statue)
LOCATIONS/ITEMS: Shigematsu Industries building w/lobby, basement & Shigematsu's executive suite, JFK Airport, Ogun's Japan home (also in photo) / Ogun's demon mask, sleep powder, spotlight & photo, hurled chair, airport metal detector w/handheld wand, Wolverine's passport & ticket, Ogun & Ariel's shuriken, practice targets, bo staffs, sais, tiger claws (prev in hallucination) & katanas (also in hallucination), bodyguards' handguns & hair pins, ninjas' sais, katanas, daggers, tiger claws, nunchuks & chained scythe
SYNOPSIS: Ariel cries out to her father and is discovered. Shigematsu orders her captured, but she evades his goons and flees. Ogun requests Ariel as payment for his services to Shigematsu; when Carmen objects, Ogun forcefully coerces him. In the basement, a demon-masked Ogun surprises and captures Ariel; in New York, Wolverine boards a plane for Japan. Ariel awakens paralyzed under a spotlight; Ogun cuts her hair off, mystically strips her of her senses and begins brainwashing her. Ariel imagines that she has reverted to infancy, and Ogun trains her in the martial arts as she grows, molding her in his image. When she reaches her proper age again, they are completely in sync. Awakening, Ariel dons Ogun's demon mask. Arriving in Japan, Wolverine confronts Shigematsu, overpowering his bodyguards and demanding Ariel's whereabouts. Shigematsu calls Ogun, who supervises Ariel as he ruthlessly defeats several ninjas simultaneously. Ogun tells Shigematsu to set up a meeting, and instructs Ariel to kill Wolverine when he arrives. Ariel eagerly agrees.
NOTE: The "services" that Ogun rendered to Shigematsu remain unrevealed. Ogun is revealed as Wolverine's former sensei here.

"Death" (23 pages)

CREDITS: Chris Claremont (writer), Al Milgrom (art), Tom Orzechowski (letters), Glynis Wein (colors), Ann Nocenti (editor)
FEATURE CHARACTERS: Ariel, Wolverine
SUPPORTING CAST: Yukio (last in UXM #173, '83), Carmen Pryde
VILLAIN: Shumai (next in KP&W #6, '85)
OTHER CHARACTERS: Yukio's sources (bts informing Yukio), Tokyo train drivers (bts operating trains), police, commuters & bystanders; model (on billboard)
LOCATIONS/ITEMS: Tokyo inc temple w/rooftop, Zen garden & nearby alley, Shigematsu Industries building (named) w/Shigematsu's executive suite & Tokyo Station w/tunnels & railyard / Yukio's throwing blades & car w/ police band radio (bts), Ariel's tiger claws (1 destroyed), nunchuks (destroyed), bow (bts), arrows, poison, stink bomb, shuriken, katanas, sai, flash bomb & demon mask, dumpster w/garbage, Shigematsu's brandy, Carmen's briefcase, office windows (destroyed) & alarm, window-washing scaffold & tools, police radio (bts) & truncheon, trains inc Shinkansen bullet train
SYNOPSIS: As Wolverine waits on a temple rooftop, Yukio attacks him. When Wolverine defeats her she kisses him, welcoming him back to Japan. He explains that he arranged Ariel's release, but Yukio suspects treachery and leaves to investigate Shigematsu. A ninja attacks Wolverine, blinding his enhanced senses with a stink bomb and attacking him with poisoned weapons. Wolverine slashes at the ninja, but somehow seems to miss each time. Wolverine retreats as the poison takes effect, hiding in a dumpster to heal. At Shigematsu's office, Yukio battles Shumai. She dangles him out a window and interrogates him, learning that Wolverine was to be ambushed. When a drunken Carmen distracts Yukio, Shumai throws both her and Carmen off the balcony; Yukio saves them by grabbing a scaffolding. The ninja finds Wolverine, but he has healed and pursues her through a train station, as Yukio and Carmen arrive following police reports. Wolverine unmasks the ninja, revealing her as Ariel — who takes advantage of Wolverine's hesitation and stabs him through the chest.
NOTE: Shigematsu is confirmed as a Yakuza crimelord here.

"Rebirth" (23 pages)

CREDITS: Chris Claremont (writer), Al Milgrom (art), Joe Rosen (letters), Glynis Wein (colors), Ann Nocenti (editor)
FEATURE CHARACTERS: Wolverine (also bts on phone in UXM #188, '84), Ariel (both also in Ariel's dream, rfb & pfb)
GUEST STAR: Professor X (Charles Francis Xavier, X-Men's telepathic founder, last in UXM #186, '84, last bts & next in UXM #188, '84)
SUPPORTING CAST: Yukio, Carmen Pryde (both also in pfb)
OTHER CHARACTERS: Tokyo airline announcer (voice only) & travelers; birds; Ogun (in legend & Ariel's dream), Miyamoto Musashi (Japan's greatest swordsman, in legend); Storm (mentioned as having lost her powers), Guardian (James MacDonald Hudson, mentioned as having died)
LOCATIONS/ITEMS: Ou Sanmyaku (Ou Mountains, Honshu, Japan) inc highway & Yashidas' ancestral manor w/Zen garden & waterfall, X-Mansion, Agarashima Airport, Tokyo Station railyard (in dream, rfb & pfb), 17th-century Japanese river w/bridge (in legend) / Yukio's drugged throwing blades (in pfb) & car, Wolverine's bandages & walking stick, Ariel's katanas (bts, also in dream, rfb & pfb), demon mask (in rfb), bonds, rake, luggage & ticket, Ogun's katana (in dream & legend) & demon mask (in dream), Musashi's katana (in legend), Clan Yashida's Sno-Cat (bts) & Honor Sword, Carmen's broom, Casket of Ancient Winters (Asgardian artifact, bts, see NOTE), airplanes
FLASHBACKS: Ariel stabs Wolverine (last issue). Yukio incapacitates Ariel with drugged throwing blades (p).
SYNOPSIS: Yukio drives frantically to the Yashidas' manor with Carmen, a bound Ariel and a grievously injured Wolverine. Ariel phases out of the car, and Yukio chases her and knocks her out again. Back in her right mind, Ariel awakens to a weakened Wolverine and is horrified to realize what she did. Wolverine tells her a legend about Ogun and Miyamoto Musashi "dueling" solely through eye contact. He has Ariel rake a Zen garden, but the results are perfection, frightening Ariel. Wolverine explains that Ogun imprinted his psyche over hers, and that her mind will eventually be subsumed unless she fights back. Wolverine trains Ariel, but she remains unable to complete a Zen test of holding a sword at arm's length indefinitely. Ariel twists her ankle jogging, and Wolverine leaves her behind. She finds the strength of will to get up and continue; coming to an epiphany, she holds the sword for a full day without pause. Ariel then heads to the airport, frightened but determined to face her destiny.
NOTE: Clan Yashida's ancestral manor is specified to be in the Ou Sanmyaku mountains here. Professor X's middle name is revealed in UXM #304, '93. Storm lost her powers in UXM #185, '84 and regains them in UXM #226, '88. Guardian, Wolverine's old friend and the founder of Canadian superteam Alpha Flight, was thought to have died in AFlt #12, '84, but is revealed to have survived in AFlt #88-90, '90. This issue's snow is the Fimbulwinter, caused by the Casket of Ancient Winters being opened in Thor #348-349, '84.

"Courage" (23 pages)

CREDITS: Chris Claremont (writer), Al Milgrom (art), Tom Orzechowski (letters), Glynis Wein (colors), Ann Nocenti (editor)
FEATURE CHARACTERS: Ariel (also as Mariko & in her own thoughts; becomes Shadowcat), Wolverine (also as Shadowcat's drawing)
GUEST STAR: Professor X (bts confirming that Ariel didn't return home, last in UXM #188, '84, next in NM #22, '84)
SUPPORTING CAST: Amiko Kobayashi (Wolverine's foster daughter), Mariko Yashida (both last in UXM #181, '84), Yukio, Carmen Pryde
VILLAINS: Ogun (also as Mariko & in Shadowcat's hallucination), Heiji Shigematsu (both last in KP&W #2, '84)
OTHER CHARACTERS: Tokyo police: Tetsuro, Goro (prev 2 "Thunderblue" helicopter unit) & their commander (voice only, on radio), Yashidas' servant (bts plowing airstrip) & pilot (voice only, piloting plane), bystanders; Tamsin

(Amiko's friend), Amiko's crush (prev 2 mentioned)

LOCATIONS/ITEMS: Tokyo (also in Ariel's thoughts) inc police helicopter base, Haneda Airport (prev 2 bts), Shigematsu's executive suite, subway w/station bathroom & Yashidas' Meguro District penthouse apartment w/rooftop & Mariko's bedroom; Yashidas' ancestral manor w/ airstrip (bts), skies above Japan / Shigematsu's pen & papers, Ariel's ninja costume, katanas (prev 2 also in Ariel's thoughts, destroyed), makeup & new costume, police helicopter w/spotlight & radio headsets, base's radio (bts), subway train, Yashidas' snowplow (bts) & private jet, Mariko's high heels, robe & wig, Ogun's demon mask (also in hallucination), body armor (bts), katanas (1 destroyed), bo staff, drugged shuriken & flash bomb, penthouse's electronic surveillance equipment (bts) & windows (destroyed), painting tools & scaffold w/winch

SYNOPSIS: Ariel confronts Shigematsu in full ninja garb, demanding that he release Carmen from his "employ" or suffer the consequences. Phasing through the wall, she drops into a nearby subway station, where she changes into a new costume. Thinking about her recent life-changing experiences, she decides on a new identity: Shadowcat. Mariko Yashida returns to her apartment, where she relaxes with her ward Amiko, but becomes uneasy when she hears noises. On a plane to Tokyo, Carmen explains how he illicitly used his bank to help debt-ridden local families, and Wolverine chides him for letting Shigematsu blackmail him. Ogun invades Mariko's apartment, hoping to kill her to punish Wolverine — but finds Shadowcat waiting for him instead. The two duel, but Shadowcat is frightened of her new ruthlessness. Ogun hits Shadowcat with a drugged shuriken, inhibiting her phasing power. Their battle spills onto the rooftop, where Ogun tries to hypnotize Shadowcat again. This time she proves resistant, and he prepares to kill her … when Wolverine arrives.

NOTE: Shigematsu's given name is revealed here. Wolverine adopted Amiko after her mother was killed in UXM #181, '84. She is incorrectly called "Akiko" here and next issue; her surname is revealed in SecWar:FNF, '05. Kitty Pryde adopts a new codename and costume this issue. She references having worn a short wig in UXM #183, '84, an attempt to cover an art error depicting her with short hair in that issue.

KITTY PRYDE AND WOLVERINE #6 (April 1985)

"Honor" (24 pages)

CREDITS: Chris Claremont (writer), Al Milgrom (art), Tom Orzechowski (letters), Glynis Wein (colors), Ann Nocenti (editor)

FEATURE CHARACTERS: Shadowcat (next in UXM #192, '85), Wolverine (next in UXM #192, '85; AFlt #16-17, X Ann #8, all '84; Rom #65-66, Daz #38, all '85, W/NF:SC, '89, X/AFlt #1-2, '85-86, UXM #193-194, '85, SH #29, '91; UXM #194-195, SecWars2 #1, NM #31 bts, UXM #196, SecWars2 #5, UXM #199, X Ann #9, all '85, UXM #200-201, '85-86, MFan #33, '87; PP #19, AFlt #33-34, HFHX, all '86, W:WX #16, '10 fb; SecWars2 #7, UXM #202, SecWars2 #8, UXM #203, SecWars2 #9, Cap Ann #8, UXM #205 & 207-210, X Ann #10, UXM #211, PP #27, NM #46, all '86, UXM #212-214, '86-87; MVs #3-4, UXM #215-216, all '87, UXM #228, '88 fb, UXM #219, '87 fb, SMvW, '87)

SUPPORTING CAST: Amiko Kobayashi (next in W #82, '94), Mariko Yashida (chr next in W:Doom, '97, next in XFac #63, '91), Yukio (next in W #55, '92), Carmen Pryde (next in Ex #76, '94)

VILLAINS: Ogun (also in legend, dies, next in W #89, '95), Shumai (last in KP&W #3, '85), Heiji Shigematsu (bts ordering Mariko's death)

OTHER CHARACTERS: Mr. Shapiro (ice cream parlor owner) & his patrons, pachinko parlor players & proprietor, US Embassy Federal agents (bts hearing Carmen's confession) & guard, bystanders, Amiko's relatives (mentioned as having died in a tsunami); Miyamoto Musashi (in legend)

LOCATIONS/ITEMS: Tokyo inc Yashidas' penthouse rooftop, pachinko parlor, US Embassy, Shapiro's ice cream parlor & construction site w/elevator shaft; 17th-century Japanese river (in legend) / Ogun's katanas (1 also in legend, 1 destroyed), demon mask (destroyed), shuriken & daggers, Yukio's car (destroyed), Shumai's rocket launcher (bts), pachinko parlor window (destroyed) & machines, proprietor's handgun w/ armor-piercing bullets, elevator (destroyed) w/brake system (bts), guard's rifle, Wolverine's walking stick, Shadowcat's ice cream sundae

SYNOPSIS: Wolverine stares down Ogun, hoping to duplicate his legendary eye-contact battle with Miyamoto Musashi, but Ogun attacks. They duel, but Ogun gains the upper hand; Wolverine flees, goading Ogun away from Shadowcat. Yukio and Carmen check on Mariko and Amiko, but Shumai blows up Yukio's car. Shadowcat phases through Shumai, breaking his concentration; Yukio quickly defeats him. Ogun steals a handgun and shoots Wolverine, who limps to an elevator. Ogun cuts the cables and the elevator plummets; Wolverine applies the emergency brakes and escapes. Inspired by Wolverine and Shadowcat's examples, Carmen goes to the US Embassy and reveals Shigematsu's money-laundering scheme, while Shadowcat catches up to Wolverine and Ogun. Badly injured, Wolverine gives in to a berserker rage, savagely attacking and defeating Ogun. He tells Shadowcat to kill the helpless Ogun, but she cannot — passing Wolverine's test of her character. Ogun reclaims his sword and charges; Shadowcat phases and Wolverine stabs through her body, killing Ogun. Later, Wolverine reassures Mariko and Carmen that Shadowcat will eventually be fine.

NOTE: This issue's story has the same title as W #4, '82, the conclusion of Wolverine's first miniseries. Amiko is again incorrectly called "Akiko." It is unclear which of her relatives died in the tsunami, but her mother did not; she was crushed by falling debris in UXM #181, '84. Ex #21, '90 reveals that Shadowcat's parents entered the Witness Protection Program after this issue. Their plotline is then dropped, but they must have left the program by Ex #78, '94, where Shadowcat calls her mother without any difficulty.

SPIDER-MAN VERSUS WOLVERINE (February 1987)

"High Tide" (64 pages)

CREDITS: Jim Owsley (writer), Mark Bright (pencils), Al Williamson (inks), Bill Oakley (letters), Petra Scotese (colors), Ann Nocenti (editor), Evan Skolnick (2nd print editor), Keith Williams (2nd print c inks)

FEATURE CHARACTERS: Spider-Man (Peter Parker, spider-powered hero, also as "Mr. Simmons," last in WoSM #28, '87, chr last in Web:TS #18, '00, next in ASM #289, '87), Wolverine (also as "Peter Richards," also in pfb, also in fb between XO:W, '09 & AFlt #53, '87 fb; next in WoSM #29, FFvX #1-4, XvA #1-4, all '87, X&SM #2, '09; X Ann #11, UXM #220, DD #248-249, AFlt #52-53, UXM #221-222, all '87, UXM #228, '88 photo; UXM #223-224, IHulk #340, all '87, W #12, '11 fb,

IHulk #340, '87; UXM #225-226, NM #61, UXM #226-227 & 229-231, all '88, Whead #1, '92; AFlt #61, MCP #1-5, all '88, W #58, '07 fb; MCP #5-6, 7 fb, 6 bts & 7-10, '88-89, W #1, '88)

GUEST STARS: X-Men: Havok (Alex Summers, fires plasma blasts), Storm (both in pfb, last in UXM #219, '87, next in FFvX #1, '87) (1 or more also bts answering phone, exact members unspecified, team last in UXM #219, '87, next in FFvX #1, '87; see NOTE)

SUPPORTING CAST: Kate Cushing (Daily Bugle city editor, last in DD #242, '87, next in ASM #296, '88), J. Jonah Jameson (Daily Bugle editor-in-chief, last in WoSM #26, '87, next in ASM #289, '87), Ned Leeds (Daily Bugle reporter, dies, last in ASM #288, also in ASM #289 fb, next bts in ASM #289, all '87), Nathan Lubensky (May's love interest, last in WoSM #24, '87, next in ASM #300, '88), May Parker (Spider-Man's aunt, last in ASM #288, last bts in PPSSM #126, next in ASM #290, all '87), Mary Jane Watson (Spider-Man's love interest, last in WoSM #28, next bts in ASM #289, next in PPSSM #129, all '87)

VILLAINS: Charlemagne ("Charlie," freelance espionage agent, dies; also in fb prior to issue), 1400 Club (Foreigner's assassins) inc Hans (unnamed) (1st bts, arranging Ned's body, chr last in ASM #289, '87 fb, some or others next in WoSM #92, '92); KGB agents ("core group" that hired Charlemagne, all die): "Sophie," "Burt" (prev 2 as shopowners), Heinreicht, some bts (found dead, some also in photos; some as teachers, gas station attendants, etc), others (group also bts in fb prior to issue, sending operatives after Charlemagne); KGB field operatives (some bts, some die; others dead in fb, most bts) & East German undercover operatives (many die; others in fb, die) inc Ganymed staff & patrons; German muggers (some die), international espionage agents

OTHER CHARACTERS: Victor & Rose Palermo (May's boarders, see NOTE, both last in ASM #288, '87, next in WoSM #47, '89), Daily Bugle staff inc Gloria Grant (Jameson's secretary, bts phoning May, last in PPSSM #120, '86, next in WoSM #38, '88), "Molly-Fulla-Tears" (teenage girl, finds Sophie & Burt's bodies), derelict, Manhattan police & SWAT team, Wolverine's contact (bts informing him), West Berlin police inc Fritz (bus station attendant & customers, costume shopkeeper & his son (bts, shopkeeper made Die Spinne costume for him), East German border patrol, hotel guests & customs agents, Charlemagne's servants, airplane pilot (bts piloting plane), stewardess & passengers, New York & West Berlin bystanders; Fritz's mother & wife (prev 2 mentioned); Liz Allan, Harry Osborn, Gwen Stacy, Flash Thompson (prev 4 Peter & MJ's friends, bts in photos); Silvester Rambone (actor, named on marquee); Frankenstein, Chewbacca, Stormtrooper, gorilla, clown, devil, others (prev 7 as masks & costumes), bird (as statue)

LOCATIONS/ITEMS: New York City inc Sophie & Burt's Hell's Kitchen store, Daily Bugle, May's Forest Hills home, Mary Jane & Spider-Man's apartments, LaGuardia airport (bts) & Times Square w/movie theater; X-Mansion (in pfb); East Berlin, East Germany (also in fb) inc hotel, Charlemagne's house, Ganymed (Friedrich Strasse restaurant), Treptow Soviet cemetery, customs checkpoint & Berlin Wall (also in fb) w/minefield; West Berlin, West Germany inc Pottsdämmer Platz Tiergarten, Kurfürstendamm, bus station, costume shop, airport & Wolverine, Spider-Man & Ned's hotel rooms / Spider-Man's web shooters (hereinafter considered his standard equipment and not listed separately), spider-tracer, belt w/mini-camera & spotlight, photos, gift for May, luggage, German/English translation book & tossed rock, Wolverine's luggage (in pfb), note & fake passports, Charlemagne's heart-shaped charms (1 in fb, others bts), semi-automatic 9mm pistol & car, KGB weapons (others in fb, some destroyed), F Train (bts), Nathan's wheelchair, New York police guns, SWAT helicopter, van & rifles, Mary Jane's photo album, Ned's missions list, photos, ropes & gag, mugger's knife, shop's masks & costumes inc "Die Spinne," West Berlin police lighter & cigar, East Berlin border patrol rifles, mines, razor-wire & truck, poisoned fruit, agents' helicopter, floodlights & guns, airplane

FLASHBACKS: When Charlemagne begins her killing spree, Wolverine informs Storm and Havok that he must find her (p). KGB agents try to kill Charlemagne after she performs a job for them, but Wolverine saves her. Charlemagne escapes, leaving her heart charm as a memento of Ned's investigation in West Berlin.

SYNOPSIS: Spider-Man discovers shopowners Burt and Sophie killed; a sniper attacks Times Square. Ned Leeds tells Jonah that all the victims were KGB agents; heart charms at the scenes imply that Charlemagne wants revenge on her former clients. Jonah assigns Peter to Ned's investigation in West Berlin. There, Wolverine searches for Charlemagne; he recognizes Peter's scent as Spider-Man, and insists that Peter leave. Peter soon finds Ned murdered in his hotel room. Armed agents confront Peter, but Wolverine kills them. Peter gets a "Die Spinne" Spider-Man suit from a costume shop and follows Wolverine to East Berlin. There, Wolverine finds Charlemagne amidst more KGB bodies. They patronize a restaurant full of undercover KGB agents; when Spider-Man blunders in, sparking a fight, Charlemagne flees. Wolverine and Spider-Man attack several KGB fronts but find that Charlemagne has been there first, killing the remaining agents. Wolverine berates Spider-Man for interfering, claiming that he could have stopped Charlemagne. Later, Charlemagne contacts Wolverine, wanting him to kill her before the KGB does, but Spider-Man intervenes. As Spider-Man and Wolverine battle, Charlemagne intentionally steps into one of Spider-Man's punches, committing suicide. Haunted by Ned and Charlemagne's deaths, Peter returns home and takes solace in Mary Jane's arms.

NOTE: Rose is incorrectly called "Maude" here; Ned is incorrectly called "Jake" once. ASM #289, '87 reveals that Jack O'Lantern (Jason Macendale), believing Ned to be the Hobgoblin, hired the Foreigner to have Ned killed; that issue's flashback names Hans. SM:HL #3, '97 reveals that Ned's informant was the Kingpin, and that Ned believed himself to be the Hobgoblin, brainwashed by the true Hobgoblin (Roderick Kingsley). This issue was reprinted in 1990 as a squarebound prestige-format edition with a new cover.

THE BEST OF MARVEL COMICS (1987)

"The Black Panther!" (20 pages)

NOTE: This hardcover special edition, sold via the 1987 Sears holiday catalog, has an embossed faux-leather cover. It contains 3 origin features, 12 reprints and an all-new Wolverine story. The cover is labeled "Volume One," but future volumes were not published. The first story, reprinted from FF #52, '66, is preceded by a 1-page feature "The Origin of the Fantastic Four!", recapping the FF's origin from FF #1, '61 (but incorrectly showing the Thing mutating into his standard rocky form, not his original lumpy form) and featuring Human Torch, Invisible Girl, Mr Fantastic and Thing.

2ND STORY: "The Way It Began…!" (20 pages)

NOTE: Reprinted from FF #53, '66. Story is followed by a 1-page feature, "The Origin of the Incredible Hulk!" (Sal Buscema, pencils), recapping the Hulk's origin from IHulk #1, '62 and clashes with the US Army from IHulk #3 & 6, '62-63, and featuring Hulk, Rick Jones, Air Force pilots (bts in planes), soldiers and a doctor.

3RD STORY: "Sasquatch!" (34 pages)
NOTE: Reprinted from IHulk Ann #8, '79.

4TH STORY: "The Kid Who Collects Spider-Man!" (11 pages)
NOTE: Reprinted from ASM #248, '84.

5TH STORY: "If This Be My Destiny…!" (20 pages)
NOTE: Reprinted from ASM #31, '65.

6TH STORY: "Man On a Rampage!" (20 pages)
NOTE: Reprinted from ASM #32, '66.

7TH STORY: "The Final Chapter!" (20 pages)
NOTE: Reprinted from ASM #33, '66.

8TH STORY: "The Living Legend" (22 pages)
NOTE: Reprinted from Cap #255, '81. Pages 20-21, a double-page splash image, are printed on the front and back of the same page, disrupting the image.

9TH STORY: "The Answer At Last!" (18 pages)
NOTE: Reprinted from Thor #159, '68. Pages 3 & 14 of the original story are omitted.

10TH STORY: "The Wrath of the Wrecker!" (20 pages)
NOTE: Reprinted from Thor #171, '68.

11TH STORY: "A Mystic Reborn!" (22 pages)
NOTE: Reprinted from DrS #56, '82. Story is followed by a 1-page feature, "The Origin of the Uncanny X-Men," reprinting and reformatting GSX #1, '75 p.31 panels 4 & 3, p.8 panel 1, p.3 panel 2, p.10 panel 4, p.6 panel 5, p.5 panel 5, p.15 panel 3 & p.13 panel 8 with added dialogue, recapping that issue's formation of the new X-Men team (but incorrectly showing Professor X contacting everyone telepathically, not in person) and featuring Colossus, Cyclops, Nightcrawler, Professor X, Storm and Wolverine.

12TH STORY: "He'll Never Make Me Cry" (18 pages)
NOTE: Reprinted from UXM #183, '84. Pages 6-7, 11 & 22 of the original story are omitted, and p.21's footnote is replaced with "Fin." This story is not listed on the contents page.

13TH STORY: "The Hunter" (6 pages)
CREDITS: Chris Claremont (writer), Marshall Rogers (pencils), Randy Emberlin (inks, uncredited), Tom Orzechowski (letters), Bob Sharen (colors, uncredited), Michael Higgins (editor), John Romita (c pencils)
FEATURE CHARACTER: Wolverine (chr last in W:WX #16, '10 fb, chr next in UXM #149, '81)
SUPPORTING CAST: Mariko Yashida (chr last in UXM #143, '81, chr next bts in XMU #29/2, '00, chr next in W #1, '82)
VILLAINS: Sabuko (would-be Yakuza gangster) & his henchmen (some in Mandroid armor, some die)
OTHER CHARACTERS: Tokyo bystanders; Sabuko's guard dogs; Spider-Man (cover only)
LOCATIONS/ITEMS: Tokyo inc Sabuko's replica fortress / Sabuko's ransom note, remote control unit (both bts) & laser security system, guards' omnium-steel Mandroid armor (destroyed), Samurai armor & rifles
SYNOPSIS: Sabuko has kidnapped Mariko, hoping to capture and kill Wolverine to gain Yakuza prestige. Wolverine sneaks into Sabuko's fortress and allows himself to be captured. He is brought before Sabuko, but breaks free, massacres the Mandroid-armored guards and corners Sabuko — who reveals that Mariko was inside one of the Mandroids. However, Wolverine had smelled her, and only damaged her suit enough to free her. Wolverine orders Sabuko to abandon crime, and leaves with Mariko.
NOTE: This story occurs prior to Wolverine and Mariko's breakup in UXM #173, '83. Emberlin and Sharen's credits are given in the '91 book, *Marvel: Five Fabulous Decades of the World's Greatest Comics.*

WOLVERINE #1 (November 1988)

"Sword Quest" (22 pages)

CREDITS: Chris Claremont (writer), John Buscema (pencils), Al Williamson (inks), Tom Orzechowski (letters), Glynis Oliver (colors), Daryl Edelman (asst editor, uncredited), Bob Harras (editor)
FEATURE CHARACTER: Wolverine (also unnamed as "Patch," see NOTE)
SUPPORTING CAST: Lindsay McCabe (Jessica's private detective partner, former actress), Jessica Drew (bts meeting Kojima imposter) (both last in UXM #206, '86)
VILLAINS: Banapur Khan ("prince of pirates," dies) & his crew (all die) inc Cheong, Hanrahan, Krause, Lal, Roger, Rohmer & Amram Singh; Black Blade ("Muramasa Sword," 1st bts, carried by Jessica, see NOTE); Cult of the Black Blade (Muramasa cult, 1st): Mei Yin, Tsuboro (prev 2 unnamed), bellhop (prev 3 next in W #3, '89), others (bts hiring pirates, inc 1 as Kojima); Cult's hired Madripoor goons
OTHER CHARACTERS: Captain Kwan Pen Lee (airline pilot, dies), Noboru Kojima (Mariko's secretary, dies), Flight 49 survivors inc stewardess, pirates' victims (bts in mass grave, dead), Madripoor airline announcer (voice only), customs agent, travelers & cabbie; Muramasa (sword's creator, mentioned only as part of sword's name)
LOCATIONS/ITEMS: Principality of Madripoor (cutthroat East Asian island nation): "Hightown" (upscale half of Madripoor's capital city, also named Madripoor) inc airport & Imperial Hotel w/Lindsay's room; Telambang (Indonesian island) inc Banapur's village, abandoned airstrip & dock / Banapur's sword, knife & speedboat, crew's booby traps (all but 1 bts), ropes, netting & weapons inc swords (1 destroyed), guns & Uzi, Flight 49 (Sovereign Airways jet), stewardess' gun, Madripoor newspaper, Concorde jet, Lindsay's lamp (destroyed), passport, luggage & taxi, Wolverine's eyepatch (hereinafter considered his standard equipment whenever he operates as "Patch" and not listed separately), goons' car, bellhop's knife, Tsuboro's handgun & ID

SYNOPSIS: Pirate leader Banapur Khan beheads the captain of an airplane that his crew has hijacked. Wolverine infiltrates the pirates' camp and saves the plane's stewardess from being assaulted. He then locates Noburo Kojima, a passenger on the plane, who has been tortured for information. The pirates attack, but Wolverine kills them all; Banapur flees, but is shot by the stewardess. Dying, Noburo warns Wolverine that the pirates were hired by a Muramasa-worshipping cult who want the fabled Black Blade — which is being delivered by courier to Madripoor. Staking out the airport, Wolverine spots courier Lindsay McCabe arrive, and realizes that he will have to keep his identity secret, as she knew the X-Men, who the world believe dead. At her hotel, cultists ambush Lindsay, but Wolverine arrives as "Patch" and helps her defeat them. Lindsay realizes that a cultist posed as Noburo to contact her — and that her partner, Jessica Drew, is on her way to deliver the sword to him!

NOTE: This issue also has a back cover pin-up by John Byrne. The X-Men died in UXM #227, '88, their deaths broadcast on worldwide TV. Although the goddess Roma resurrected them, they decided to let the world continue thinking they were dead. As such, Wolverine began using the name "Patch" when in Madripoor, wearing an eyepatch and avoiding overt use of his claws to hide his identity — although W #14-15, '89 reveal that much of the supporting cast knew he was Wolverine, and were just humoring him. Wolverine also debuts a new black costume here, only used when adventuring in Madripoor. The name "Patch" is first used next month, both next issue and in MCP #9, '88. The Black Blade is revealed as sentient next issue, hence its bts inclusion as a Villain here. MyA:Book, '07 clarifies that it is a different sword than the Muramasa Sword forged from Wolverine's rage, first seen in W #40, '06. Muramasa first appears in W #38, '06 fb. Mei Yin and Tsuboro are named in W #3, '89.

WOLVERINE #2 (December 1988)

"Possession Is the Law" (22 pages)

CREDITS: Chris Claremont (writer), John Buscema (pencils), Klaus Janson (inks), Tom Orzechowski (letters), Glynis Oliver (colors), Daryl Edelman (asst editor, uncredited), Bob Harras (editor)
FEATURE CHARACTER: Wolverine (as "Patch," also possessed by Black Blade, also in rfb)
SUPPORTING CAST: Jessica Drew (private investigator, formerly Spider-Woman, also possessed by Black Blade), Lindsay McCabe (also in rfb)
VILLAINS: Silver Samurai (Kenuichio Harada, Mariko's criminal half-brother, last in NM #53, '87), Black Blade (sentient evil sword, 1st on-panel app), Cult of the Black Blade (some bts offering reward for sword, others dead, inc Noburo imposter)
OTHER CHARACTERS: Belle (Lowtown bartender), Lowtown saloon patrons inc Roscoe (dies) & Rufe, police, bystanders; Noburo Kojima, Mei Yin, Tsuboro, pirates, airport patrons, bellhop (prev 6 in rfb)
LOCATIONS/ITEMS: "Lowtown" (seedy, impoverished half of Madripoor's capital city) inc saloon (destroyed) & docklands warehouse, Hightown: airport & Imperial Hotel, Telambang (prev 3 in rfb) / Lindsay's luggage, Tsuboro's handgun, pirate's sword (all in rfb), Belle's Long Island Iced Teas, Silver Samurai's armor & katana, hurled chair, Lindsay's dress, patron's club, Rufe's gun, Roscoe's knife, rubble, police cars & ambulance, flammable warehouse goods (destroyed)
FLASHBACK: Wolverine finds Noburo, kills pirates, locates Lindsay and battles cultists (last issue).
SYNOPSIS: Wolverine and Lindsay visit the saloon where Jessica was to deliver the Black Blade. Determined to match Wolverine shot for shot, Lindsay quickly becomes drunk and befriends the bartender. Wolverine investigates upstairs and discovers Jessica's would-be ambush, several cultists, dead. The Silver Samurai bursts in, seeking the sword; Wolverine fights without his claws to maintain his cover, and is soon defeated. Suddenly Jessica, possessed by the sword, attacks the Samurai. As they battle, several saloon patrons join the fight, hoping for the reward for the sword. Jessica kills one and lunges for Lindsay, and Wolverine intervenes. Finding that the sword has heightened her strength and stamina, Wolverine collapses the saloon wall, burying the combatants. Jessica flees and Wolverine pursues her; Lindsay digs out the Samurai and allies with him. Wolverine battles Jessica, briefly slipping into a berserker rage to overcome her. He grabs the sword — but the malevolent spirit of the blade releases Jessica and possesses Wolverine…
NOTE: This issue also has a "Wolverine Gallery" back cover pin-up by Bill Sienkiewicz. Wolverine's alias "Patch" is first used this month, both here and in MCP #9, '88. The Black Blade is revealed as sentient here. The Silver Samurai's given name is misspelled "Keniuchio" here.

WOLVERINE #3 (January 1989)

"The Black Blade" (22 pages)

CREDITS: Chris Claremont (writer), John Buscema (pencils), Al Williamson (inks), Tom Orzechowski (letters), Glynis Oliver (colors), Daryl Edelman (asst editor, uncredited), Bob Harras (editor)
FEATURE CHARACTER: Wolverine (as "Patch," also possessed by Black Blade, next in W:Doom, '97; MA Ann #4, UXM #232-234, X Ann #12, UXM #235-238, all '88, MCP #16/3, '89, UXM #239-241, '88-89; XFac #37, UXM #242, XFac #38, UXM #243, XFac #39, X Ann #13/2, PWJ #6-7, all '89)
SUPPORTING CAST: Jessica Drew, Lindsay McCabe (both next in MA Ann #4, '88), O'Donnell (Princess Bar owner, last in MCP #10, '89, next in W #8, '89), Madripoor's Police Chief Tai (1st, unnamed)
VILLAINS: Silver Samurai (chr next in W:Doom, '97), Black Blade (both next in W #56, '92), Cult of the Black Blade inc Mei Yin, Tsuboro (prev 2 named) & bellhop (prev 3 last in W #1, '88)
OTHER CHARACTERS: Princess Bar staff; rats; Vietnam veterans (mentioned, taught Lindsay about weapons), demon (as statue)
LOCATIONS/ITEMS: Madripoor: Lowtown inc dockside warehouse (destroyed) & Princess Bar (O'Donnell's bar) w/cellar, cultists' highland temple / Silver Samurai's armor & katana, Lindsay's dress, knife & binoculars, rubble, cultists' ropes & swords, O'Donnell's stage blood & modified sniper rifle w/scope, Wolverine's dragon mask (destroyed)
SYNOPSIS: Possessed, Wolverine escapes with the unconscious Jessica, the Black Blade intending to have him sacrifice her to complete its bond with Wolverine. Lindsay and the Samurai head for the Princess Bar, where Tai questions O'Donnell about the night's events. After Tai leaves, the three hatch a plan to interrogate the cultists that Wolverine captured at Lindsay's hotel. Dragging one into the darkness, Lindsay play-acts a gruesome killing, scaring another into revealing the cult's plans. The Samurai wonders aloud if the Black Blade is looking for a warrior worthy of wielding it. Lindsay and the Samurai infiltrate the cult's temple, and Lindsay shoots Wolverine as he is about to sacrifice Jessica. The Samurai battles the cultists and the possessed Wolverine, who eventually rejects the sword's influence, flinging it away. The Samurai claims the sword, and the others are shocked when it does not possess him — he is the warrior worthy of taming its will. The Samurai departs peacefully, and Wolverine, Jessica and Lindsay celebrate a happy ending.

NOTE: This issue also has a "Wolverine Gallery" back cover pin-up by Kevin Nowlan. Tai's surname is revealed next issue; his given name is unreveled to date. O'Donnell reveals that his name is actually an alias in W #15, '89. Tai mentions here that O'Donnell has taken on a "silent partner"; next issue reveals that Wolverine bought a half-interest in the Princess Bar.

WOLVERINE/NICK FURY: THE SCORPIO CONNECTION (1989)

"The Scorpio Connection" (62 pages)

CREDITS: Archie Goodwin (writer), Howard Chaykin (art), Ken Bruzenak (letters), Richard Ory & Barb Rausch (colors & special effects), Sara Tuchinsky & Evan Skolnick (asst editors), Gregory Wright & Mark Gruenwald (editors)

FEATURE CHARACTERS: Nick Fury (Executive Director of SHIELD (Supreme Headquarters International Espionage Law-Enforcement Division, covert intelligence agency), also as boy in photo & bts as guard & Swift Sword member, also in fb2 between M:LG #10, '00 & W #-1, '97; chr last in Cap #304, '85, chr next in Cap #309, '85), Wolverine (also in fb1 between W #9, '89 fb & UXM #228, '88 fb; chr last in Daz #38, '85, chr next in X/AFlt #1, '85)

GUEST STARS: X-Men: Rogue (Anna Marie, absorbs powers & memories via touch), Colossus (both chr next in X/AFlt #1, '85) & Dazzler (Alison Blaire, converts sound to light, chr next in NM #29, '85) (all chr last in Daz #38, '85)

SUPPORTING CAST: SHIELD Special Directors: Timothy "Dum Dum" Dugan (Nick's confidante, chr last in Rom #53, '84, chr next in MGN #18, '85), la Contessa Valentina de Fontaine (Nick's romantic interest, chr last in UXM #182, '84, chr next in MHol '93/2); Jake Fury (Nick's brother, Dimension Research scientist, in fb2 between SgtF #69, '69 & SecWs #25, '11 fb; also as boy in photo)

VILLAINS: Scorpio (Mikel Fury, Nick's brainwashed son, 1st, next in W/NF:SR, '94), Amber D'Alexis (Mikel's mother, Amber Palace proprietor & Swift Sword ally, dies; also in dfb, also in fb2 prior to issue), Arcade (funhouse-themed assassin, voice only), Miss Locke (Arcade's assistant) (prev 2 chr last in UXM #177, '84, chr next in DDs #4, '83), Swift Sword (terrorist support network): David Nanjiwarra (Aborigine SHIELD agent & traitor, also in photo, dies; also in fb1 prior to issue), Skorzeny (Rio Cobre mining corporation director, also in photo, dies) & his employees, others (some as Amber Palace employees, others bts aiding Amber); terrorist assassin (bts in fb1, tracked by Wolverine, dies); terrorists (in fb1, most bts in base, die; others bts in helicopter)

OTHER CHARACTERS: SHIELD agents (some or others chr last in Cap #304, '85, chr next in MGN #18, '85) inc Bellini, Cross, Giulietta, Hazeltine, Palo, guards, medical team (all but 1 bts on helicopter, 1 chr next in W #14, '11 fb, next in W #20, '04) & anti-terrorist unit (as archeological team, also in photos, die) inc Lars, Arcade's androids (destroyed) inc guards & duplicates of Arcade, Mario (Kelly's bartender), Kelly's patrons & band, Blair & Tracy (vacationing dental hygienists), Venice gondolier, Istanbul restaurant patrons & waiter, Atlanta SWAT team inc snipers, David's ASIO (Australian Security Intelligence Organisation) superiors (bts informing David about Wolverine), bigoted bush outpost employee (prev 2 in fb1), espionage ring (bts, investigated by Fury), Amber Palace patrons, Dimension Research secretary, Macao band, police & bystanders (prev 6 in fb2), Manhattan bystanders inc Scott, Kevin & their parents; birds, cats; Scorpio (Jake Fury LMD, in Nick's thoughts, see NOTE); Richard Ory (colorist), others (prev 2 in photos in fb2); cartoon women (on Arcade's monitors), Giulietta's boyfriend's mother, David's prejudiced SHIELD supervisor (prev 2 mentioned), rodent, camel (prev 2 as statues)

LOCATIONS/ITEMS: Machu Picchu, Peru inc SHIELD outpost & Rio Cobre copper mine (Swift Sword front) w/airstrip; Manhattan inc Nick's penthouse, SHIELD headquarters, Kelly's bar & Hotel Adirondak w/SHIELD gym; Murderworld (Arcade's funhouse-themed deathtrap base, Queens); Aegean Islands, Greece inc Andros & Amber's villa w/media room (also in dfb) & nearby deserted house (destroyed); Venice, Italy inc SHIELD outpost; Istanbul, Turkey inc Amber Palace (Amber's casino) & restaurant; Atlanta, Georgia inc SHIELD's underground Information Central complex & nearby hotel w/roof & atrium mall; Australia's Tanami desert (in fb1) inc terrorist training camp (bts, destroyed) & bush outpost; Macao, China (in fb2) inc original Amber Palace & Dimension Research office; SHIELD outposts in Taiwan & Balkans (prev 2 mentioned, attacked) / SHIELD security net (bts) w/generator, survey equipment (prev 3 destroyed), gas antidote, master computer (prev 2 bts), HAWK (High Altitude Wing Kite) glide suits, helicopters, workout equipment, files, body bags, electromagnetic & infrared sensors, audio monitors, guns, blast armor, truncheons & stretcher, David's gun & grenade, Scorpio's Scorpio Key replica & calling card, Nick's homing tracer, circuit disruptor (prev 2 bts), photo, olive, blacklight bomb, infrared goggles, tracking unit, gun & jetpack, Arcade's spy monitors (some destroyed), Hazeltine's pipe, girls' cruise ship, Amber's VTOL plane (destroyed), tracking unit (bts), yacht, chandelier, iron shutters, computer & paralyzing gas, Swift Sword agents' plane (destroyed), guns, fire extinguisher & files, canal sludge (bts), hotel skylight (destroyed) & elevator, SWAT helicopters & guns, Wolverine's cigar, band's instruments (others in fb2), terrorists' helicopter, David's water can, Wolverine & David's beers (prev 3 in fb1), Amber's gambling chips, Nick's disguise, newspaper & badge (prev 4 in fb2), Scorpio Key (in Nick's thoughts)

FLASHBACKS: Assassins gun down Wolverine in the Australian desert. ASIO agent David Nanjiwarra helps him survive, and Wolverine encourages David to join SHIELD (1). Undercover in Macao, CIA agent Nick Fury investigates casino owner Amber D'Alexis for espionage, but discovers that she is his brother Jake's lover. Fury seduces her, then when enough evidence is gathered, has her arrested (2). Amber records a vindictive message for Fury (d).

SYNOPSIS: In Peru, Scorpio slaughters a SHIELD unit including David Nanjiwarra. In New York, Nick Fury regrets never having children. The X-Men battle Arcade, who tells Wolverine of David's death. Fury worries that Scorpio, his brother Jake, may have returned. Wolverine demands to be part of the investigation. In Greece, Amber plots to use the Swift Sword organization and her son Mikel, the new Scorpio, against Fury. In Peru, Wolverine follows Scorpio's scent to a Swift Sword operation. Later, Scorpio attacks a Venice SHIELD installation, but Fury is waiting for him. They fight, but Scorpio escapes, claiming to be Jake's son. Later, Wolverine tracks a Swift Sword operative to Istanbul, where Amber and Scorpio ambush him. Fury rescues Wolverine and they track Amber to her Aegean villa. A prerecorded message greets Fury before he and Wolverine are gassed. Scorpio attacks SHIELD's Atlanta computer complex, but finds Fury and Wolverine already there, recovered from the gas. Amber reveals that Scorpio is Fury's son, and Nick is forced to shoot Scorpio to save Wolverine. Wolverine kills Amber, but spares Scorpio when Fury reveals that David was a double agent working for Swift Sword. Later, Logan congratulates Nick on being a father.

NOTE: This issue was published as a MGN hardcover with a dust jacket; the interior flap has a Wolverine & Nick Fury image by Chaykin. That image was used as the cover of the 1990 softcover reprint, which strangely omits Wolverine's name from the indicia. The story is preceded by a title/credits page and a Scorpio frontispiece taken from p.19 panel 1. This issue occurs well before SHIELD'S dissolution in NFVS #6, '88; Dazzler is not an X-Man here, but is adventuring with them following their appearance in her own series. Rogue's first name is revealed in Rogue #2, '04; her last name is unrevealed to date. SecWs #26, '11 reveals that the Jake Fury who becomes Scorpio is a schizophrenic LMD (Life Model Decoy). Colorist Richard Ory inserted his name into the background of several panels, as well as a short note to co-colorist Barb Rausch: "Barb – go for it."

WOLVERINE #4 (February 1989)

"Bloodsport" (22 pages)

CREDITS: Chris Claremont (writer), John Buscema (pencils), Al Williamson (inks), Tom Orzechowski (letters) Glynis Oliver (colors), Daryl Edelman (asst editor, uncredited), Bob Harras (editor)
FEATURE CHARACTER: Wolverine (also as "Patch")
GUEST STAR: Karma (Xi'an Coy Manh, former New Mutant, possesses minds, last in NM #54, '87)
SUPPORTING CAST: Jessica Drew, Lindsay McCabe (both last in MA Ann #4, '88), Col. Archibald "Archie" Corrigan (South Seas Skyways owner, 1st but chr last in W:Doom, '97), Tyger Tiger (Jessan Hoan, Madripoor new crimelord, last in MCP #10, '89), Police Chief Tai (named, next in W #8, '89)
VILLAINS: Bloodsport (vampiric mercenary, 1st but chr last as Bloodscream in W:Carni, '10, see NOTE) Roughouse (Asgardian mercenary, 1st), General Nguyen Ngoc Coy (Karma's crimelord uncle, last in MA Ann #4, '88), Prince Baran (bts summoning Tyger, unnamed, last bts in MCP #10, '89, next in W #6, '89), Madripoor drug & slave-peddling crimelords (bts supporting Coy)
OTHER CHARACTERS: Lord Chancellor Ranjamaryan (Baran's chancellor, dies) & his guard, Madripoor police & detective, Lowtown bystanders, Tyger's "protection" (bts, attacked) & "bank managers" (1 dies, others dead), Coy's servant; worms; Buddha (as statue)
LOCATIONS/ITEMS: Lowtown inc South Seas Skyways hangar, Princess Bar, Tyger's "bank," canal & central bazaar, Hightown: Ranjamaryan palace & Sovereign Hotel's Imperial penthouse / Archie's airplanes & 12-gauge shotgun, police radio (bts), car, ambulance, hook & bodybag guard's rifle, Karma's glass (destroyed) & handkerchief, "bank's" chained door & safe (prev 2 destroyed), Tyger's Rolls-Royce (destroyed) finger-claws, Coy's champagne
SYNOPSIS: Roughouse and Bloodsport pursue and catch Chancellor Ranjamaryan; later, the police fish his bloodless corpse out of a canal and Wolverine decides to investigate. Elsewhere, the two enforcers threaten Archie Corrigan. They insist that he stop working for Tyger Tiger and begin working for General Coy, and Bloodsport brands Archie's chest with his palm. Wolverine detects Karma's scent at Ranjamaryan palace and tracks her to Hightown, learning that Coy plans to take over Madripoor's underworld, and she is aiding him for an unknown reason. Jessica and Lindsay discover another of Tyger's operations wiped out by Roughouse and Bloodsport. The Prince summons Tyger to discuss the gang war — but en route, Roughouse and Bloodsport attack Tyger and Wolverine. Karma intervenes, briefly possessing the two enforcers and allowing Wolverine to flee with a badly wounded Tyger. Later, Jessica and Lindsay minister to Tyger while Wolverine approaches Archie for a favor, as Coy, the enforcers and a reluctant Karma plan their next move...
NOTE: This issue also has a "Wolverine Gallery" back cover pin-up by Barry Windsor-Smith. Ranjamaryan's name is also spelled "Ranjamaryam." Baran's name is revealed in W #7, '89. W #6, '89 reveals Archie's rank and Baran's covert support of Coy; W #10, '89 confirms that Ranjamaryan was killed because he supported Tyger. This issue establishes that Tyger is a crimelord with a conscience, refusing to deal in drugs or slaves. W #6, '89 explains that Karma works for Coy reluctantly because he promised to help locate her siblings Leong and Nga, kidnapped by unknown parties in NM #46, '86. Hence, neither will be listed as Villains. Roughouse references trolls here, the first hint that he is Asgardian. He is confirmed as Asgardian in IM:DoS Ann, '08. Wolverine reveals here that he purchased a half-interest in the Princess Bar UXM #268, '90 reveals that the bar used to be owned by his diminutive lover Seraph. Bloodsport's codename changes without explanation to Bloodscream in W #17, '89. W:Carni, '10 reveals that his codename was also Bloodscream prior to this issue, so it seems that his "Bloodsport" identity was merely a brief name change.

WOLVERINE #5 (March 1989)

"Hunter's Moon!" (22 pages)

CREDITS: Chris Claremont (writer), John Buscema (pencils), Al Williamson (inks), Janice Chiang (letters) Glynis Oliver (colors), Daryl Edelman (asst editor), Bob Harras (editor)
FEATURE CHARACTER: Wolverine (also as "Patch," also in photo & symbolic image)
GUEST STAR: Karma
SUPPORTING CAST: Lindsay McCabe (chr next in W #6, '89 fb), Archie Corrigan, Jessica Drew, Tyger Tiger
VILLAINS: Hardcase (Sgt.-Major Harry Malone, chr last in UXM #262, '90 fb) & his Harriers (mercenary team): Battleaxe (Jerome Hamilton, also as "'Axe") & Shotgun (Zeke Sallinger) (all 1st, next in UXM #261, '90) Bloodsport, Roughouse (prev 2 chr next in W #6, '89 fb), General Coy (bts hiring Harriers), Coy's hired soldiers inc Chief, pilot (prev 2 die) & Chollo
OTHER CHARACTERS: Chang (LL&L's local expediter, 1st, dies, also in photo, chr last in L:PW, '96, also in W #6, '89 fb), US Drug Enforcement Administration officials (bts hiring Harriers, see NOTE)
LOCATIONS/ITEMS: Sovereign Hotel's Imperial Penthouse; Lowtown's Landau, Luckman & Lake (interdimensional firm, 1st mention) branch office (23 Hotei Way, destroyed); "Golden Triangle" (border of Thailand, Burma & Laos) inc soldiers' headquarters / Karma's shattered glass, Archie's gun & Douglas DC-3 w/radio (bts) & M61 Vulcan cannons, soldiers' P-51 Mustang, opium, vans (prev 3 destroyed), jeeps (destroyed, w/spare gas cans), radio, machetes & rifles, Shotgun's rifle w/infrared scope, Battleaxe's axes, grenades & radio, Harriers' uniforms & emergency signal, Hardcase & Chief's pistols, Chang's photo & armor (see NOTE) w/facemask, Wolverine's short-wave radio (bts) & ropes
SYNOPSIS: Bloodsport notices that an upset Karma has shattered a glass, cutting herself, and tastes her blood. Wolverine has Archie fly him to the "Golden Triangle" to destroy Coy's opium crop, hoping to cripple his growing power base. Archie, remembering Bloodsport's threat, debates shooting Wolverine, but decides against it. A Mustang strafes their plane, and Wolverine bails out, slicing the Mustang's wing off before plummeting to Earth. In Lowtown, Jessica and Lindsay bring the injured Tyger to Landau, Luckman & Lake's office. In the Golden Triangle, the Harriers and Coy's local soldiers grudgingly work together to find Wolverine, but he ambushes the Harriers. Chang gives Lindsay a set of impenetrable armor for Tyger, just as Roughouse and Bloodsport burst in. As the soldiers retrieve the Harriers, Wolverine infiltrates their camp, causing chaos and starting fires. The soldiers retreat with Coy's opium, but Wolverine calls in an airstrike from Archie, who destroys their vans once they are in the open. In Lowtown, the LL&L office lies in ruins...
NOTE: This issue also has a "Wolverine Gallery" back cover pin-up by John Bolton, featuring Wolverine and two brawlers. UXM #261, '90 reveals Hardcase and the Harriers' real names, and also that they were secretly working for the DEA here to ensure Coy's opium was destroyed Coy is also incorrectly called a Colonel here. Landau, Luckman & Lake is revealed as interdimensional in W #97, '96; their Lowtown office

address is revealed in W #98, '96. The armor Chang loans Lindsay is identical to Wolverine's teammate Psylocke's armor, first seen in UXM #232, '88. Chang says Wolverine ordered it for "a friend"; presumably it is a replacement for Psylocke's original armor, warped during "Inferno" and damaged by Sabretooth in UXM #243, '89. The series' letters page, "Cutting Edge," debuts here.

WOLVERINE #6 (April 1989)

"Roughouse!" (22 pages)

CREDITS: Chris Claremont (writer), John Buscema (pencils), Al Williamson (inks), Janice Chiang (letters), Glynis Oliver (colors), Daryl Edelman (asst editor, uncredited), Bob Harras (editor)
FEATURE CHARACTER: Wolverine (also as "Patch")
GUEST STAR: Karma
SUPPORTING CAST: Lindsay McCabe (also in fb between W #5-6, '89), Archie Corrigan, Jessica Drew, Tyger Tiger
VILLAINS: Bloodsport, Roughouse (both also in fb between W #5-6, '89), Prince Baran (Prince of Madripoor, 1st on-panel app, last bts in W #4, '89), General Coy
OTHER CHARACTERS: Chang (in fb during W #5, '89, dies), Baran's servant & household guard (1st) inc Lieutenant, Coy's servants; Baran's sea creature (dies, see NOTE); Buddha, demons (prev 2 as statues); Napoleon, soldiers, horse (prev 3 in painting)
LOCATIONS/ITEMS: Baran's Madripoor palace, Lowtown's LL&L office (in fb, destroyed) / Karma's umbrella & car, Baran's riches & pool, Archie's gun (see NOTE), Lindsay & Jessica's slave collars, rubble (in fb), Tyger's armor w/facemask, Jessica's protective drapery, guards' rifles
FLASHBACK: Roughouse levels the LL&L office, and Bloodsport kills Chang.
SYNOPSIS: Karma possesses a guard and infiltrates Baran's palace, having decided to oppose her uncle and free Tyger. She encounters Wolverine and Archie, who have the same intention. Elsewhere in the palace, Coy gloats to the captured Jessica and Lindsay, but Roughouse is unable to break the armor that encases Tyger. Wolverine suddenly attacks, slicing Bloodsport's throat and stabbing Roughouse, but both recover, revealing that mortal weapons cannot kill them. Karma possesses Bloodsport briefly, distracting him. Archie bluffs Coy, threatening to shoot Karma, but Bloodsport disarms him. Roughouse knocks Jessica into Baran's pool, where a tentacled sea creature grabs her. Wolverine knocks Roughouse in as well and dives in, freeing Jessica, but Roughouse kills the creature. Tyger attacks Bloodsport and Lindsay points out that her armor may not have been forged by mortals, rattling Bloodsport enough for Tyger to knock him out. Wolverine and Jessica defeat Roughouse and corner Coy — but the battle is interrupted by Baran and his armed guard…
NOTE: This issue also has a "Wolverine Gallery" back cover pin-up by Todd McFarlane. Baran's covert support of Coy and Archie's rank are revealed here, as is Karma's motivation for serving Coy, an exchange for his help finding her kidnapped siblings. Roughouse swears by "Ymir's icy breath" here, the second hint that he is Asgardian. Although Lindsay was wearing the armor when Roughouse and Bloodsport attacked last issue, Tyger wears it now; presumably Lindsay quickly dressed Tyger while Jessica delayed the villains. Archie's gun, a 9mm pistol last issue, changes from a revolver to a pistol between panels of this issue. The Prince's sea creature's death is confirmed next issue.

WOLVERINE #7 (May 1989)

"Mr. Fixit Comes to Town" (22 pages)

CREDITS: Chris Claremont (writer), John Buscema (art), Ken Bruzenak (letters), Mike Rockwitz (colors), Daryl Edelman (asst editor), Bob Harras (editor)
FEATURE CHARACTER: Wolverine (also as "Patch")
GUEST STARS: Hulk (Dr. Robert Bruce Banner, gamma-powered goliath, as Las Vegas enforcer "Mr. Fixit" & Bruce Banner, last in IHulk #354, '89, chr last in MA Ann #4/3, '88), Karma
SUPPORTING CAST: Lindsay McCabe (also as statues & on posters), Archie Corrigan (next in W #11, '89), Jessica Drew, Tyger Tiger
VILLAINS: Prince Baran (named, next bts in W #11, '89, next in W #15, '89), Bloodsport, Roughouse, General Coy, preppy biker gang inc Chaz, Dex, Laurence & Muffy, Las Vegas Don (Coy's mobster supporter, unnamed), hired goons (1 as skycap)
OTHER CHARACTERS: Michael Berengetti (Coliseum casino owner, Fixit's employer, bts offering Fixit's help, last in IHulk #354, chr next in MCP #38/3, next in IHulk #357, all '89), Connie (Fixit's driver), baggage handlers inc Arnie & Lou, Baran's Royal Couturier (bts providing Lindsay clothes) & household guard (some or others next in W #14, '89) inc Captain, LAX airline announcer (voice only), gangster's men & butler, Coy's servants, Fixit's Madripoor driver, Madripoor travelers; Lindsay's co-stars, horse (prev 2 on posters)
LOCATIONS/ITEMS: Hightown inc airport & Sovereign Hotel w/Imperial Penthouse & Fixit's room, Baran's palace; Don's Tahoe, Nevada estate; California gas station (Rte. 395, near Naval Air Weapons Station China Lake), Los Angeles International Airport / Fixit's money, sedatives (both bts), limousines & luggage, Tyger's armor w/facemask, guards' rifles, bikers' motorcycles (all but 1 destroyed), Chaz's pocketknife, Connie's makeup kit, Flight 007 (Sovereign Airways jet), baggage carts, Jessica & Lindsay's new clothes, Prince's film prints, videos (prev 2 bts), solid gold pen, posters & statues w/prop weapons, hurled furniture, Roughouse's alcohol, Madripoor driver's carphone (bts), goons' motorcycles (bts, destroyed), grenade & weapons inc pipes & guns, alley lights (bts, destroyed)
SYNOPSIS: A mobster asks Mr. Fixit, aka the gray-skinned Hulk, to look into his ally Coy's recent setbacks. In Madripoor, Baran reveals himself as Lindsay's biggest fan. He invites everyone to be his guests, rattling Coy, who had counted on Baran's support. En route to LAX, Fixit's driver is attacked by teenage bikers; Fixit demolishes their motorcycles and scares them straight. In Madripoor, Wolverine informs Tyger of Baran's offer: that she and Coy share the position of crimelord. With them checking and balancing one another, no rivals will have room to gain footholds. Tyger and Coy reluctantly agree and are escorted out; Baran then shows Lindsay and Jessica his room of Lindsay-related memorabilia. Later, Karma tells Wolverine that a Las Vegas enforcer is on his way. Wolverine spots Fixit at the airport, and lends a hand when a gang of goons tries to kill him. Wolverine later spies on Fixit at his hotel, and, realizing that he turns back to Banner during the day, starts planning some fun…
NOTE: An accident in IHulk #324, '86 let Banner's "gray Hulk" persona become dominant. The gray-skinned Hulk is smarter than the green Hulk, but transforms back to Bruce Banner during daylight hours. Hulk became the Las Vegas bodyguard "Mr. Fixit" just prior to IHulk #347, '88. The Don's title is revealed next issue. Baran's sea creature's implied death last issue is made explicit here. Lindsay McCabe has acted in *Demon Debs, Demon Blues, Last Train From Moscow, Cyber Witch, Lethal Latex Lovelies* and *Ms. Merc*.

WOLVERINE #8 (June 1989)

"If It Ain't Broke—!" (22 pages)

CREDITS: Chris Claremont (writer), John Buscema (art), Ken Bruzenak (letters), Glynis Oliver (colors), Dary▮ Edelman (asst editor, uncredited), Bob Harras (editor)
FEATURE CHARACTER: Wolverine (as "Patch")
GUEST STARS: Hulk (as "Joe Fixit," also in dfb as Bruce Banner, chr next in MCP #38/3, '89, next in IHulk #355 '89), Karma (next in W #27, '90)
SUPPORTING CAST: Jessica Drew, Lindsay McCabe, Police Chief Tai (all next in W #10, '89), O'Donnell (next in W #13, '89), Tyger Tiger (next in W #17, '89)
VILLAINS: General Coy, Roughouse (both next in W #17, '89), Bloodsport (next as Bloodscream in W #17 '89), Shen (slave trader) & his thugs, Mr. Liu (Coy's inspector), Kobe (drug manufacturer) & his Manbot androids (destroyed) & employees
OTHER CHARACTERS: Heng (tailor, bts providing Fixit's suit), Jasmine (madam, bts arranging entertainment) & her prostitutes (also in dfb), Sovereign employee (bts providing wake-up call), Princess Bar piano player, staff & patrons, Madripet driver (bts driving truck), kidnapped women, Madripoor travelers, stewardesses & bystanders; John "Hannibal" Smith (A-Team member, quoted, see NOTE)
LOCATIONS/ITEMS: Hightown airport, Fixit's Sovereign Hotel room, Lowtown inc Mr. Max's Spa (brothel & slave-trading front) w/cellblock Coy's cocaine processing facility (prev 2 destroyed), Princess Bar & cliffside house w/balcony / Fixit's new suits (2 destroyed), pajamas (destroyed), luggage & money, Wolverine's purple pants & note, Lindsay's microphone, Madripoor tanker truck, girls' cages, Kobe's drug refining equipment (prev 3 destroyed), prostitutes' wine & food (also in dfb), Manbots' weapons, Sovereign Airways jet
FLASHBACK: Jasmine's "ladies" pamper Bruce Banner all day long (d).
SYNOPSIS: Fixit angrily discovers that someone replaced all his suits with purple pants. After buying a new suit, Fixit asks "Patch" to help find Coy, but a passing truck splashes him. He smashes the truck but is covered in its cargo, industrial sludge, and Wolverine finds him replacement clothes — purple pants. Wolverine takes Fixit to a brothel that hides a slave ring, and tricks him into destroying the operation. Fixit awakens the next night, angered by vague memories of Bruce Banner enjoying "his" reward. Wolverine then lures the increasingly annoyed Fixit to a cliffside balcony, collapsing it; Fixit plummets onto Coy's cocaine refining facility below. Its android guards attack and Fixit smashes the operation, but an enraged Coy confronts him, revealing that Fixit was sent to help him against Tyger. Realizing that both the Don and Wolverine had manipulated him, Fixit punches Wolverine and angrily leaves town. Wolverine arranges Fixit a pampered first-class flight home — into the sunrise, where Bruce Banner will enjoy the ride.
NOTE: This issue also has a "Wolverine Gallery" back cover pin-up by Rob Liefeld, featuring Wolverine and ninjas. The Don's title is revealed here Wolverine paraphrases the line "I love it when a plan comes together" as that of his "old army buddy" — a reference to the A-Team's Hannibal.

WOLVERINE #9 (July 1989)

"Promises to Keep" (23 pages)

CREDITS: Peter David (writer), Gene Colan (art), Bill Oakley (letters), Mark Chiarello (colors), Daryl Edelman (asst editor, uncredited), Bob Harras (editor)
FEATURE CHARACTER: Wolverine (as "Patch," also bts in fb3 as Weapon X between W:FCBD, '09 & BFF:Ben #1, '00; also in fb2 & fb1 between AFlt #127/2, '93 fb & W/NF:SC, '89 fb)
VILLAINS: Mercenary crew: Bruno, Needle, Rollins, Van Slyke (all in fb3 (some or all possibly bts), fb2 & fb1 die), Malone (in fb3, fb2 & fb1, dies), Schmidt (dies), Shelly (dies off-panel) (prev 2 in fb3 (both possibly bts) & fb2), 2 others (in fb2 (possibly die); also possibly in fb3 (1 or both possibly bts) prior to fb2, see NOTE), others (in fb3, die); Iraqi militants (in fb3, all but 1 bts, 1 dies)
OTHER CHARACTERS: American Embassy hostages inc Canadian nun (dies off-panel), Delta Force (US Special Forces, 1 dies), US Government officials (bts sending Delta Force), Weapon X's handlers (bts sending Weapon X) (all in fb3), motel receptionist, vacationers (prev 2 in fb1), Madripoor waitress & bar patrons; deer (in fb2, dies); Playboy models (in fb1 in magazine photos)
LOCATIONS/ITEMS: Woodland inc river, waterfall & motel w/cabin (all in fb1), crew's campsite (in fb2), Iraq's American Embassy (in fb3) Madripoor bar / Rollins' knife, receptionist's Playboy & key, Malone's money, crew's handguns, Wolverine's sheet, vacationers' canoe (destroyed w/oars (all in fb1), crew's rifles (some in fb1 & fb2, Schmidt's in fb1, others in fb3), Bruno's drugs (bts), Malone's pistol, Delta Force's rifles, dead soldier's uniform & gear, Iraqi's rifle (prev 6 in fb3), Wolverine's cross
FLASHBACKS: Wolverine hunts a crew of mercenaries, killing Van Slyke and promising to kill them one by one. Rollins takes watch, but the others awaken to find Wolverine instead, who mentions their Iraq mission five years prior. The remaining mercenaries find Rollins dead, steal a canoe and flee downriver, but Wolverine destroys it and kills Needle. Bruno turns on Malone, offering to kill him if Wolverine spares him but Malone shoots Bruno. Wolverine confronts Malone, revealing that the woman Malone tormented in Iraq was a Canadian nun who asked Wolverine to avenge her. Rather than let Wolverine kill him, Malone shoots himself — which Wolverine considers good enough (1). The night before, Wolverine ambushes the crew, killing Schmidt and Shelly (2). Five years prior, Iraqi insurgents hire the crew to help capture the American Embassy. They take hostages, including a woman Malone whom repeatedly rapes. Special forces including Weapon X kill the insurgents and some mercenaries, but several escape, including Malone (3).
SYNOPSIS: On the anniversary of the nun's death, Wolverine remembers his vengeance on her tormentors.
NOTE: This issue also has a "Wolverine Gallery" back cover pin-up. "Weapon X" was Wolverine's designation during his time as a Canadian Dep H operative; it is also the name of the program that implanted his Adamantium, as revealed in X #7, '92. Malone's five-man crew references two men that Wolverine killed in fb2, but the crew is shown as a group of nine; either Wolverine killed four men, or two weren't on the original Iraqi mission and he let them escape.

WOLVERINE #10 (August 1989)

"24 Hours" (23 pages)

CREDITS: Chris Claremont (writer), John Buscema (pencils), Bill Sienkiewicz (inks, c art), Ken Bruzenak (letters), Mike Rockwitz (colors), Daryl Edelman (asst editor, uncredited), Bob Harras (editor)
FEATURE CHARACTER: Wolverine (also as "Patch," also in fb1 between W #50, '07 fb & W:O #5, '06 fb, also in XO:Sabre, '09 & W #50, '07 fb during fb; also in fb2/implant between W #63, '92 fb & W #41, '91 fb, see NOTE)
SUPPORTING CAST: Silver Fox (Wolverine's Native American lover, 1st, seemingly dead, see NOTE; in fb1 between W #50, '07 fb & XO:Sabre, '09), Lindsay McCabe, Police Chief Tai (prev 2 next in W #14, '89), Jessica Drew
VILLAINS: Sabretooth (Victor Creed, animalistic mutant with healing factor, in shadow, also in fb1 between W #55, '07 fb & W:O #5, '06 fb, also in XO:Sabre, '09 & W #50, '07 fb during fb; also in fb2/implant between W #63, '92 fb & W #41, '91 fb; last in XFac #39, next bts in ASM #321, next in ASM #322, all '89), Vole (unnamed, 1st bts in fb2/implant between W #63, '92 fb & W #41, '91 fb), 2 bruisers (both named Daryl, die), street gang
OTHER CHARACTERS: Madame Joy (brothel owner, last in MCP #7, '88) & her prostitutes (some or others last in MCP #7, '88) inc Mavis (bts), Inga & Inza, saloon bartender (in fb) & patrons (in fb1, some or others chr last & also in XO:Sabre, '09, also bts in W #50, '07 fb, chr next in W:O #5, '06 fb; others bts in fb2/implant prior to W #41, '91 fb, possibly disguised Weapon X agents, see NOTE), Tai's contacts (bts researching Sabretooth), bartender, bar patrons inc brawlers; US Navy soldiers; Dr. Fong (Lowtown doctor, mentioned)
LOCATIONS/ITEMS: Lowtown inc dockside warehouse (destroyed), bar, rooftops, Princess Bar & Madame Joy's (brothel) w/dispensary (bts) & "Drew & McCabe Resolutions" (Jessica & Lindsay's upstairs detective agency/apartment), Tai's police headquarters office; Mount Logan (Yukon, Canada frontier town, unnamed) saloon w/nearby woods & cliff (prev 3 in fb1), Weapon X Program's warehouse (Windsor, Ontario; in fb2) / Wolverine's makeshift club, woodpile (both in fb1), saloon stage set, props inc cake slice (prev 3 in fb2), bar's clock, gang's gun & knives, US Navy submarine (bts), Tai's files, Daryls' Cadillac, submachine gun, grenade launcher & flamethrower, Sabretooth's ribbons & note
FLASHBACKS: An enraged Wolverine, having found his lover Silver Fox dead, attacks Sabretooth in a saloon. The two brawl furiously until Sabretooth collapses a woodpile on Wolverine, who flees. Wolverine climbs a cliff, but finds Sabretooth at the top. Desperate, Wolverine throws them both over the cliff. Sabretooth recovers first and leaves, impressed (1). In an implanted memory, Sabretooth taunts Wolverine, licking icing off a birthday cake and saying that Silver Fox told him "no" (2).
SYNOPSIS: Wolverine avoids his usual haunts, suspecting that Sabretooth will attack him that day. He breaks up a bar fight and rescues two Navy soldiers from a street gang, taking them to Madame Joy's for first aid, where Jessica and Lindsay reveal that they have opened a detective agency upstairs. Wolverine checks in with Tai, who explains that as far as his sources know, Sabretooth is dead. Jessica follows Wolverine, but bruisers from the bar briefly attack. In the confusion, Wolverine and Jessica each think the other defeated the bruisers, but Wolverine later finds them dead at the Princess Bar, with a note from Sabretooth warning that only he gets to kill Wolverine — especially on his birthday.
NOTE: This issue also has a "Wolverine Gallery" back cover pin-up by Kent Williams. Sabretooth's last name is revealed in X #5, '92, though it is not linked to him until X #6, '92; his first name is revealed in Sabre #3, '93. The frontier town is named as Mount Logan in W #125, '98. This issue confirms that Chancellor Ranjamaryan was killed for supporting Tyger Tiger in W #4, '89. Wolverine calls the Daryls brothers, meaning that "Daryl" might be their last name. Their names may be a reference to the TV show *Newhart*, which featured brothers named Larry, Darryl and Darryl. Part of this issue's flashback is a memory implant inserted by the Weapon X Program. W #50, '92 reveals that Silver Fox did not die, and implies that the entire fight was a staged event; Weapon X agents may have acted out the roles of bystanders. Vole's Team X codename is revealed in W #50, '92, although it is not linked to him until W #62, '92, his first on-panel appearance. His standard codename, Psi-Borg, is revealed in W #63, '92; W #64, '92 implies that he helped implant the memory telepathically. However, W #125, '98 implies and W:O #5, '06 reveals that the fight actually occurred. It seems that Weapon X simply added details to make the memory more traumatic and convince Wolverine that Silver Fox had died. This issue was reprinted in 2006 as part of the Marvel Legends toy line, featuring a slightly modified cover with most of the lettering removed, and released with the Wolverine vs. Sabretooth "Face-Off" two-pack.

WOLVERINE #11 (Early September 1989)

"Brother's Keeper" (22 pages)

CREDITS: Peter David (writer), John Buscema (pencils), Bill Sienkiewicz (inks), Ken Bruzenak (letters), Mark Chiarello (colors), Daryl Edelman (asst editor), Bob Harras (editor), Kevin Nowlan (c art)
FEATURE CHARACTER: Wolverine (as "Patch")
SUPPORTING CAST: Archie Corrigan, Jessica Drew
VILLAINS: Prince Baran (bts directing Jessica, see NOTE, last in W #7, next bts in W #14, next in W #15, all '89), Ba'al (1st bts, spirit within Gehenna Stone fragment, chr last in W #13, '89 fb), Sà-Bal-Bal (unnamed, 1st bts, directing Followers), Followers of Ba'al (would-be vampires, 1st, unnamed) inc Jarocha & Ernst
OTHER CHARACTERS: Burt Corrigan (Archie's unstable brother, 1st, also as Indiana Jones, see NOTE), Trish (Princess Bar waitress), Jakes (Burt's butler), Mr. Tuttle (Museum of Antiquities curator), Judge Fenster (San Francisco judge, unnamed), Mr. Schoenfeld (Burt's lawyer), Ruth (Archie's aunt), Jessica's landlord (bts demanding rent), Museum of Antiquities security guard, Princess Bar patrons, bar brawlers, cabbie, Ruth's lawyer, bailiff, Madripoor & San Francisco bystanders; Burt's horse; Morris (Ruth's husband), Archie & Burt's father (prev 2 mentioned); Rudyard Kipling (poet, quoted), Dorothy Gale, Sherlock Holmes, Sam Spade, Tarzan (prev 4 mentioned as Burt's prior personas), Harrison Ford (Indiana Jones actor, mentioned as Burt's persona, see NOTE); Roman warrior, knight, horse, others (prev 4 as statues)
LOCATIONS/ITEMS: San Francisco, California inc Archie's hotel (bts), Museum of Antiquities, courthouse; Jake's townhouse & Jessica's detective agency; Lowtown inc Princess Bar, skies over Pacific Ocean / Followers' suction cups, glass cutter & fake fangs, guard's flashlight & gun, glass case & fake Gehenna Stone fragment (prev 2 destroyed), museum's alarm system (bts), Wolverine's fake passport (bts) & darts, bystander's wallet, Archie's Douglas DC-3, Burt's whip (bts), letter, art, dissertation on ancient cultures, Gehenna Stone fragment & gun, bar & courtroom windows (destroyed), cabbie's taxi & comic book, Jessica's mail, judge's gavel

SYNOPSIS: Thieves try to steal a Gehenna Stone fragment from a San Francisco museum, but discover that it is a fake. A security guard confronts them and they attack, revealing themselves as vampires. In Madripoor, Archie explains that his aunt is trying to declare his mentally unstable brother Burt incompetent, because he obsesses about films and believes he is the title character. Believing that she wants his inherited fortune, Archie convinces Wolverine and Jessica to see Burt with him — but although Burt acts normal during their visit, he returns to admiring the real Gehenna Stone fragment when they leave. Jessica checks in on her San Francisco detective agency, where the museum curator promptly hires her to investigate the break-in and find the real fragment. The next day, Burt crashes through the window of his competency hearing on a horse, believing he is Indiana Jones and warning of evil forces. As Archie tells him there's no such thing, vampires leap through the window in hot pursuit…

NOTE: Cover-labeled "The Gehenna Stone Affair! Part One of Six." The series was published biweekly for the duration of the storyline. Judge Fenster and the Followers of Ba'al are named next issue; Sà-Bal-Bal is named in OHMU #1, '06. The "vampires" are revealed as frauds next issue; Ba'al's presence in the Gehenna Stone is revealed in W #13, '89. W #14, '89 reveals that Baran had secretly hired Jessica to keep tabs on persons of interest; as this is her first on-panel mission for him, she is listed as bts here. Although Burt is clearly living as Indiana Jones, this arc identifies him only as Harrison Ford, the actor who played Indy. This issue's letters page has a Comic Buyers' Guide 1988 Fan Awards ballot, and an unofficial Marvel Assistant Editors 1988 Fan Awards ballot, created by assistants who jokingly note that their category is not on the CBG ballot.

WOLVERINE #12 (Late September 1989)

"Straits of San Francisco" (22 pages)

CREDITS: Peter David (writer), John Buscema (pencils), Bill Sienkiewicz (inks), Ken Bruzenak (letters), Glynis Oliver (colors), Daryl Edelman (asst editor), Bob Harras (editor), Kevin Nowlan (c art)
FEATURE CHARACTER: Wolverine (as "Patch")
SUPPORTING CAST: Archie Corrigan, Jessica Drew
VILLAINS: Sà-Bal-Bal (Ba'al's descendant, 1st on-panel app), Ba'al (bts, spirit within Gehenna Stone), Followers of Ba'al (group named) inc Maroney
OTHER CHARACTERS: Burt Corrigan (also as Indiana Jones), Judge Fenster (named), Lyn Pederson ("Page After Page" owner, unnamed), airfield employee (dead), San Francisco police, trolley passengers, bystanders, Burt's horse; Bill Liebowitz (Lyn's friend, mentioned), Marion Ravenwood, Wilhelmina "Willie" Scott (prev 2 Indiana Jones characters, mentioned by Burt); Spider-Man (in window display)

LOCATIONS/ITEMS: San Francisco inc police station, Fisherman's Wharf, "Page After Page" comic book store & courthouse w/judge's chambers; nearby airfield w/office / Burt's Gehenna Stone fragment (in bag), whip & gun, judge's telephone, Followers' fake fangs (1 set destroyed), car (destroyed), handgun & rifle, police cars (1 destroyed) & guns, airplanes, Gehenna Stone (mostly assembled), Pederson's window display (destroyed), sign & ladder, San Francisco Cable Cars trolley (destroyed), stolen car w/lockbar (destroyed)

SYNOPSIS: As Wolverine and the Corrigans battle a horde of bloodthirsty attackers, Wolverine breaks one's fangs, revealing that they are not true vampires. Jessica arrives, and leaps on the back of Burt's horse as he flees from more "vampires," who pursue him in a car. The police arrive, but Wolverine and Archie steal a patrol car and chase after Burt, and other "vampires" steal another and pursue them. Elsewhere, Ba'al's descendant gloats over the nearly rebuilt Gehenna Stone. Burt reveals to Jessica that he stole the fragment from the museum to keep it from the Followers of Ba'al. Wolverine leans out the window and slashes the pursuing car's tires, and it crashes into a comic book storefront. However, the Followers in the other patrol car slam their car into him. Wolverine hooks the Followers' car with his claws, forcing it to crash into a trolley. Wolverine and Archie catch up with Jessica and Burt, steal another car, and decide to return to Madripoor…

NOTE: Cover-labeled "The Gehenna Stone Affair! Part Two of Six." Sà-Bal-Bal is revealed as Ba'al's descendant next issue. Burt's Gehenna Stone segment changes size and shape, from a blocky fist-sized object last issue to a small fragment here. Lyn Pederson and his parents ran the Las Vegas comic book store "Page After Page" from 1982-1995.

WOLVERINE #13 (Early October 1989)

"Blood Ties" (22 pages)

CREDITS: Peter David (writer), John Buscema (pencils), Bill Sienkiewicz (inks), Ken Bruzenak (letters), Glynis Oliver (colors), Daryl Edelman (asst editor, uncredited), Bob Harras (editor), Kevin Nowlan (c art)
FEATURE CHARACTER: Wolverine (as "Patch")
SUPPORTING CAST: Archie Corrigan, Jessica Drew, O'Donnell
VILLAINS: Ba'al (Ba'al-Hadad, corrupt Annunaki storm god, bts, spirit within Gehenna Stone fragments; also in fb, his 1st on-panel & chr 1st app, prior to W #11, '89, dies), Sà-Bal-Bal, ancient Followers of Ba'al (original cult, in fb, most or all die), modern Followers of Ba'al
OTHER CHARACTERS: Burt Corrigan (also as Indiana Jones), Larry & "Gar" (prev 2 twins, see NOTE, die), Hand of God (righteous warrior, 1st, next bts in W #16, '89), archaeologists (prev 2 in fb), Princess Bar staff & patrons, San Francisco police, airfield employee (dead), twins' buyer (bts in Singapore)

LOCATIONS/ITEMS: Princess Bar w/upstairs room, San Francisco highway, nearby airfield w/office & hangar, Gehenna (unholy town outside ancient Jerusalem), tomb (prev 2 in fb) / Ba'al's axe & bowl of human blood, Hand of God's sword & shield, Gehenna Stone (destroyed), ancient Followers' axes, archeologists' tools & lantern (all in fb), twins' Gehenna Stone fragment (also in fb), money & knives, Patch's stolen car, police car, bullhorn & gun, Burt's Gehenna Stone fragment (in bag, also in fb) & gun, vampires' fake fangs & weapons inc knives, gun & clubs, Sà-Bal-Bal's airplane

FLASHBACK: Ba'al and his original Followers practice unspeakable acts in Gehenna until the Hand of God wipes them out. The dying Ba'al transfers his soul into the Gehenna Stone, but the Hand of God shatters it. Centuries later, archeologists begin finding fragments of the Stone.

SYNOPSIS: Twins arrive at the Princess Bar, showing off a fragment of the Gehenna Stone. In San Francisco, police pursue Wolverine and his friends in their stolen car, but Wolverine leaps onto the police cruiser and disables it. In the Princess Bar, the twins briefly have an uncharacteristic squabble, then purchase a room for the night. In San Francisco, Burt explains the Gehenna Stone's history, and explains that recovered fragments have been disappearing from museums over the past two years. When Wolverine asks to see Burt's fragment, he becomes oddly possessive. In the twins' room, they become suspicious, each believing the other wants the fragment for himself. Enraged, they attack one another with knives. Wolverine and his friends arrive at the airfield where Archie landed, but are ambushed by the Followers of Ba'al, who steal Burt's fragment. Sà-Bal-Bal easily defeats Wolverine, frying him with energy, then escapes on a plane with the Followers. In the

Princess Bar, O'Donnell discovers the twins' corpses.

NOTE: Cover-labeled "The Gehenna Stone Affair! Part Three of Six." Sà-Bal-Bal is revealed as Ba'al's descendant here. Ba'al's full name is revealed and he is clarified as one of the Annunaki, the Mesopotamian pantheon, in OHMU #1, '06; he is further clarified as the god of rain and thunderstorms in OHMU #3, '07. Gar's full first name is likely Gary (he also calls Larry "Lar"), making the twins Larry and Gary. Their Gehenna Stone fragment changes shape between panels, from a small cube to a larger, crystalline form.

WOLVERINE #14 (Late October 1989)

"Flying Wolves" (23 pages)

CREDITS: Peter David (writer), John Buscema (pencils), Bill Sienkiewicz (inks), Ken Bruzenak (letters), Gregory Wright (colors), Daryl Edelman (asst editor, uncredited), Bob Harras (editor), Kevin Nowlan (c art)
FEATURE CHARACTER: Wolverine (also as "Patch," also in rfb)
SUPPORTING CAST: Archie Corrigan (also bts in rfb), Jessica Drew, Lindsay McCabe, O'Donnell, Police Chief Tai
VILLAINS: Prince Baran (bts sending Johann, also in Jessica's thoughts, last in W #7, '89, last bts in W #11, '89), Sà-Bal-Bal (as "Ba'al," see NOTE; also as image in flames & in rfb), Ba'al (bts, spirit within Gehenna Stone), Followers of Ba'al (die, some or others also bts in rfb inc Maroney)
OTHER CHARACTERS: Burt Corrigan (also as Indiana Jones, also in rfb), Johann (Baran's aide, 1st), Baran's household guard (some or others last in W #7, '89), Larry & "Gar" (prev 2 dead, under sheets), Madripoor police, paramedics & bystanders; shark (bts eating Follower); Ruth & her lawyer, Burt's horse (prev 3 in rfb)
LOCATIONS/ITEMS: Princess Bar w/O'Donnell's chambers, skies over Pacific Ocean; San Francisco (in rfb) inc courthouse & nearby airfield / Sà-Bal-Bal's airplane (destroyed) w/electrical panel, Archie's Douglas DC-3, 2 stolen police cars (in rfb), Wolverine's brown costume & briefcase, paramedics' ambulance, stretchers & sheets, O'Donnell's Gehenna Stone fragment, Followers' fake fangs, strap (destroyed) & weapons inc machine guns (1 destroyed), pistol, machetes, swords & truncheon, Archie's rope ladder & fire extinguisher, O'Donnell's handgun, Lindsay's lingerie, Gehenna Stone inc Burt's fragment, guards' rifles
FLASHBACK: Burt bursts into court on a horse, Wolverine and Archie chase the Followers' police car, and Sà-Bal-Bal fries Wolverine (W #11-13, '89).
SYNOPSIS: Over the Pacific, Archie's plane gains on Sà-Bal-Bal's. At the Princess Bar, Tai questions O'Donnell, but when he asks for the Gehenna Stone fragment, O'Donnell is suddenly possessive. On Archie's plane, Jessica notices Burt's agitation over his lost fragment, and decides that she should obtain the Stone for her secret employer, Baran. The Followers open fire on Archie, and Jessica leaps onto their plane, followed by Wolverine, openly wearing his costume. The two battle the Followers while Burt deploys a rope ladder; unfortunately, Followers seize it and begin climbing. At the Princess Bar, Lindsay seduces O'Donnell, hoping to save the fragment. Sà-Bal-Bal adds Burt's fragment to the nearly complete Gehenna Stone, and uses it to mutate a Follower into a monster, who attacks Wolverine. Burt kicks the Followers off the ladder while Wolverine electrocutes the monster. Sà-Bal-Bal's plane catches fire and explodes; Wolverine leaps clear with Jessica, catching Archie's ladder. At the Princess Bar, Baran's men burst into O'Donnell's chambers, demanding the fragment.
NOTE: Cover-labeled "The Gehenna Stone Affair! Part Four of Six." Sà-Bal-Bal goes by the name Ba'al here; W #16, '89 implies that he believes he is Ba'al reincarnated. Jessica reveals here that Baran hired her to keep tabs on people of interest, including "Patch," and that she has known that "Patch" was Wolverine all along. Deciding to end his subterfuge this issue, Wolverine dons his standard brown and tan costume for the first time in this series. To mark the occasion, the cover corner box changes to an image of Wolverine in this costume (taken from next issue's cover art).

WOLVERINE #15 (Early November 1989)

"Homecoming" (22 pages)

CREDITS: Peter David (writer), John Buscema (pencils), Bill Sienkiewicz (inks), Ken Bruzenak (letters), Glynis Oliver (colors), Daryl Edelman (asst editor), Bob Harras (editor), Kevin Nowlan (c art)
FEATURE CHARACTER: Wolverine (also as "Patch," also in rfb1 & pfb1)
SUPPORTING CAST: Lindsay McCabe, O'Donnell (both also in rfb2 & pfb2), Jessica Drew (also in rfb1 & pfb1), Archie Corrigan, Police Chief Tai
VILLAINS: Sà-Bal-Bal (as "Ba'al"), Ba'al (bts in pfb2, spirit within Gehenna Stone fragment), Followers of Ba'al (2 die)
OTHER CHARACTERS: Burt Corrigan (also as Indiana Jones), Johann (also in rfb2 & pfb2), Baran's household guard (in rfb2 & pfb2) & servants inc Saloman, Princess Bar patrons & bartender, Madripoor police inc Kwan, hobo, prostitute, bystanders; cat, dog; tiger (as statue)
LOCATIONS/ITEMS: Lowtown inc Princess Bar w/O'Donnell's chambers (in rfb2 & pfb2), skies over Pacific Ocean (in rfb1 & pfb1), Baran's palace / Archie's Douglas DC-3 (in rfb1 & pfb1), guards' rifles (in rfb2 & pfb2), O'Donnell's Gehenna Stone fragment & gun (prev 2 in pfb2), Tai's gun, police billy clubs (1 destroyed), Followers' fake fangs, Burt's whip, Jessica's pistol, hurled chair (destroyed), Wolverine's pad & paper
FLASHBACKS: Jessica reveals that she knew "Patch" was Wolverine (last issue). Johann demands the fragment from O'Donnell (last issue). Jessica explains that she was humoring Wolverine the whole time (p1). Despite Lindsay's desperate pleas, O'Donnell gives Johann the fragment (p2).
SYNOPSIS: Back in Madripoor, Wolverine spots Tai and his policemen roughly questioning Lindsay about O'Donnell's fragment. Wolverine interferes, fighting the officers and vainly trying to calm Tai down while Lindsay flees. Returning to the Princess Bar, Wolverine finds Lindsay screaming at O'Donnell for giving the fragment away. She and O'Donnell reveal that they know Wolverine's identity as Archie arrives, concerned about Burt, still upset over his stolen fragment. In Lowtown, Burt stumbles across three Followers kidnapping a prostitute for a sacrifice, and tries to stop them Indiana Jones-style. The Followers overpower Burt, but Jessica arrives and shoots two, then tails the third as he flees. At the Princess Bar, Tai and his officers burst in demanding the fragment, and a brawl erupts. Wolverine soon realizes that the Gehenna Stone fragments make people possessive and violent, and learns that Baran has the final fragment. He, Archie, O'Donnell and Tai head for the palace, but Jessica has already arrived — to see Baran meeting with Sà-Bal-Bal!
NOTE: Cover-labeled "The Gehenna Stone Affair! Part Five of Six." O'Donnell reveals here that his name is an alias. Lindsay and O'Donnell reveal that they knew "Patch" was Wolverine. Tai appears not to know, but W:O Ann, '07 reveals that he is an operative of shadowy mastermind Romulus, who has been manipulating Wolverine for decades, so Tai likely does know "Patch's" identity. Archie doesn't appear overly shocked by Wolverine's claws, so presumably he knew as well. Sà-Bal-Bal continues to use the name Ba'al here.

WOLVERINE #16 (Mid November 1989)

"Electric Warriors" (24 pages)

CREDITS: Peter David (writer), John Buscema (pencils), Bill Sienkiewicz (inks), Ken Bruzenak (letters), Glynis Oliver (colors), Daryl Edelman (asst editor, uncredited), Bob Harras (editor), Kevin Nowlan (c art)
FEATURE CHARACTER: Wolverine (also as "Patch," next in UXM #245, Pun #18, X Ann #13, all '89, MSM #6-8, '91-92; MCP #29-31, HW:Melt #1-2, all '89, HW:Melt TPB, '90, HW:Melt #3-4, '89, MCP #40, '90 fb, MCP #38-47 & 51-53, '89-90, W:Jun, '90 fb)
SUPPORTING CAST: Jessica Drew, Lindsay McCabe (both next in W #27, '90), Archie Corrigan, O'Donnell, Police Chief Tai
VILLAINS: Sà-Bal-Bal (as "Ba'al" & possessed by Ba'al, dies), Ba'al (bts possessing Sà-Bal-Bal, also in symbolic image, next bts in GR #50, '94, next in Blaze #3, '94), Prince Baran, Followers of Ba'al
OTHER CHARACTERS: Burt Corrigan (as Indiana Jones & James Bond), Hand of God (bts possessing Wolverine, also in symbolic image, last in W #13, '89 fb), Johann (dies), Baran's household guard (some or others next in W #27, '90, all but bts), Princess Bar waiter, Monte Carlo Grande Casino dealer, owner & patrons, Madripoor bystanders
LOCATIONS/ITEMS: Baran's palace w/throne room & nearby road, ocean & beach, Lowtown inc Princess Bar; Monte Carlo Grande Casino, Monaco / Tai's gun, Followers' fake fangs & weapons inc knives, pipes, machete & sword, guards' rifles, Jessica's pistol, Burt's jeep, whip & chips, Gehenna Stone (reassembled & destroyed) inc O'Donnell's fragment, Baran's knife & swords, Ba'al's axe, Hand of God's sword & shield (prev 3 in symbolic image), dealer's cards
SYNOPSIS: Followers of Ba'al attack Wolverine and his allies. Wolverine allows the fight to separate him from the others, and heads for the palace. Baran negotiates with Sà-Bal-Bal for the final Gehenna Stone fragment, but Sà-Bal-Bal loses his temper and guts Johann, who had swallowed it. Baran calls his guards as the Followers burst in and Wolverine arrives, and a savage battle erupts. Sà-Bal-Bal reassembles the Gehenna Stone and is filled with Ba'al's power and essence. He mutates his Followers into actual vampires, but suddenly fears Wolverine. The two battle, but Burt arrives and knocks the Stone from Ba'al's grasp with his whip. Ba'al blasts Wolverine, who utters a prayer and blindly lashes out. Briefly possessed by the Hand of God, Wolverine shatters the Gehenna Stone and impales Ba'al. The Followers revert to human and are quickly subdued. Later, Jessica speculates that Wolverine may be descended from the Hand of God — while in Monaco, Burt turns up at a casino, now believing that he is James Bond.
NOTE: Cover-labeled "The Gehenna Stone Affair! Part Six of Six." Although Sà-Bal-Bal believes he is Ba'al reincarnated, he is not; Ba'al's spirit was in the Gehenna Stone until Sà-Bal-Bal reassembled it and Ba'al possessed him. Marvel at this time was shifting their comics' cover dates from four months ahead of the publication date to two months ahead; every title transitioned over by carrying an apparent biweekly cover date for two months. In Wolverine's case, this shift overlapped the end of his actual biweekly schedule, producing the illusion that the title shipped three issues in November '89.

WOLVERINE: THE JUNGLE ADVENTURE (1990)

(Untitled, 48 pages)

CREDITS: Walter Simonson (writer), Mike Mignola (pencils, c art, back c art), Bob Wiacek (inks), Ken Bruzenak (letters), Mark Chiarello (colors), Daryl Edelman (asst editor), Bob Harras (editor)
FEATURE CHARACTER: Wolverine (in fb2 & fb1 between MCP #53, '90 & W #17, '89)
VILLAINS: Apocalypse (En Sabah Nur, immortal Darwinist conqueror, in fb2 as theatre employee & fb1 as hologram between XFac Ann #3, '88 & FF #335, '89), Apocalypse's rogue robot double (bts in fb2 sending cyborg after Wolverine, bts in dfb guiding Tyrannosaurus, also in fb1, destroyed) & his cyborg assassin (former Tribe of Fire member, in fb2, dies) & cyborg Tyrannosaurus rex ("honker of doom," also in Tribe's thoughts, in dfb & fb1, dies)
OTHER CHARACTERS: Tribe of Fire (Savage Land tribe, also briefly as Tribe of the Wolverine in fb1): Gahck (chieftain), shaman (both also in fb1 prior to issue), Erista (Wolverine & Gahck's newborn son, unnamed), Falk (Chakel's father), Glumph (prev 2 in fb1), Chakel (young hunter), Kaffkal (prev 2 also in dfb & fb1 prior to issue) & his hunting party (in dfb & fb1), Apocalypse robot's victims (in fb1, die), others (some or others also in fb1 prior to issue), 1 other (mentioned, escaped Apocalypse robot but went mad & died); supply ship crew (bts, gave Wolverine passage), actors (bts performing play) & theatre patrons (prev 3 in fb2); Savage Land creatures inc Dimetrodon ("spiny honker"), cobra (prev 2 in fb1, die), Tyrannosaurus' scavenger birds (bts in dfb, heard by Wolverine, also in fb1), tiger (dead, shaman's headdress, also in fb1 prior to issue) & dinosaurs ("honkers," 1 dead in fb1, skull inc Pteranodons (in fb2, some or others also in fb1) & Apatosauri (in fb1); Nick Fury (mentioned, gave Wolverine lighter), Cyclops (mentioned briefed X-Men on Apocalypse), Marvel Girl (named in Apocalypse's note)
LOCATIONS/ITEMS: Savage Land (prehistoric jungle under Antarctic icecap): Tribe of Fire's lands (also in fb1) w/Gahck's cave (in fb1) & "Great Green Wood" (in fb1 & dfb), "Mountain of Thunder" (Apocalypse robot's volcano laboratory, in fb1, destroyed) & skies above Savage Land (in fb2); Apocalypse's base (bts in fb1), Broadway theatre w/back alley, Antarctica's McMurdo Sound (prev 3 in fb2) / Gahck's war mask, furs & hurled pipe, Stone of Silence, Wolverine's spear & ropes, Tribe's spears (some also in dfb), blankets (bts), stone axes & sacred ochres, fire-hardened sticks, cut saplings, Tyrannosaurus' cyborg implants, Apocalypse robot's machinery, cage, cyborg creation tubes & Adamantium skull, Cyclops' visor (in hologram), Apocalypse's hologram projector (all in fb1), Apocalypse's theatre tickets (bts) & note, cyborg's flamethrower, fire hydrant, Wolverine's brick shield (prev 3 destroyed) & hurled pavement chunk, supply ship (prev 7 in fb2), Chakel's cyborg implants (also in fb1), Wolverine's explosive SHIELD lighter (bts in fb2, also in fb1) & Ultralite aircraft (in fb2 & fb1)
FLASHBACKS: Arriving in the Savage Land, Wolverine finds the Tribe of Fire worshipping his lighter. They hail him as a god, but Gahck challenges him; Wolverine defeats her and becomes chieftain. Wolverine, seeking answers about a cyborg that attacked him, begins living with the tribe; soon, hunters report that a Tyrannosaurus who often attacks their village has eaten Chakel. They set a trap, but the dinosaur avoids it and consumes Wolverine. He cuts his way free, learning that it too is a cyborg. The Tribe shows Wolverine an "evil" volcano; he investigates and is captured by Apocalypse, who is transforming captured Tribesmen into cyborgs. Gahck follows and is captured; Wolverine attacks "Apocalypse," discovering that he is a robot and destroying him. The real Apocalypse appears, explaining that the robot had malfunctioned, that he manipulated Wolverine into confronting its cyborg and gave the Tribe Wolverine's lighter. While Gahck frees Chakel, Wolverine uses the lighter, which doubles as a SHIELD explosive, to destroy the laboratory. He heads home, blowing Gahck a kiss (1). Apocalypse lures Wolverine

o a public confrontation with a cyborg. Wolverine dispatches it, but it smells of the Savage Land, so he travels there (2). The Tyrannosaurus
ats" Chakel (d).

YNOPSIS: As the shaman retells the story of the Wolverine, Gahck holds her infant son in her arms.

OTE: This is the first of several squarebound prestige-format Wolverine one-shots, originally intended as Annuals. This issue's framing
quence occurs nearly a year in the future; the flashbacks occur concurrently with other comics published at this time. Erista is named in
HMU:X, '04, which also confirms that he is Wolverine's son. Apocalypse's real name is revealed in Cable #2, '93, though it is not linked to
m until Cable #5, '93. Wolverine thinks the cyborgs smell familiar, and finds an Adamantium skull in Apocalypse's lab, seeming to hint that
pocalypse was involved with Wolverine's Adamantium implantation. These hints were never touched on again; however, Apocalypse re-
planted Wolverine's Adamantium in W #145, '99 fb. Dimetrodons are not dinosaurs; they are pelycosaurs, distantly related to mammals and
edating dinosaurs by roughly 35-50 million years.

WOLVERINE #17 (Late November 1989)

"Basics!" (22 pages)

CREDITS: Archie Goodwin (writer), John Byrne (breakdowns, c art), Klaus Janson (finishes), Jim Novak (letters),
Glynis Oliver (colors), Daryl Edelman (asst editor), Bob Harras (editor)
FEATURE CHARACTER: Wolverine (also as "Patch," also in rfb & pfb)
GUEST STARS: Daredevil (Matt Murdock, blind hero, in fb between MCP #19/4, '89 & DD #253, '88), Gateway
(Aborigine mutant teleporter, in pfb, last in X Ann #13, '89, chr last in MSH #8, '92, next bts in W #19, '89, next in
UXM #247, '89), Storm (in pfb, last in FF Ann #22, '89, chr last in MCP #48/4, '90, next in UXM #246, '89)
SUPPORTING CAST: Tyger Tiger (last in W #8, '89), Police Chief Tai (next in PWZ #22, '93), Archie Corrigan, O'Donnell
VILLAINS: General Coy, Roughouse (both last in W #8, '89), Bloodscream (last as Bloodsport in W #8, '89, next
in W #77, '94), Geist (Nikolaus Geist, cybernetic former Nazi, 1st but chr last in W #18, '89 fb) & his hired goons,
President Caridad (1st bts, selling Coy cocaine, chr last in W #18, '89 fb) & his soldiers (bts on ship), Spore (1st
s, unnamed, inside Cody in fb between W #21, '90 fb & this issue; also bts in cocaine), Prince Baran, Cody's cocaine dealers (bts in fb, dead)
THER CHARACTERS: Hammer Cody (drug-using ex-boxer, in fb, dies), Princess Bar patrons inc a US senator & his entourage, Madripoor
lice (bts seizing cocaine), Baran's servant, NYC & Federal law enforcement agencies (bts in fb, disputing case's jurisdiction), warship captain
comm officer (prev 2 bts on ship), NYC police & bystanders (prev 2 in fb), Madripoor bystanders; wild boar (in pfb, dies), birds (some in fb &
b), dog; Shingen Harada, Mariko Yashida, Noburu-Hideki (prev 3 in rfb); Buddha (as statue)
OCATIONS/ITEMS: Lowtown inc docks & Princess Bar w/upstairs room, Baran's palace, South China Sea, Australian outback (Northern
rritory, in pfb), Yashidas' ancestral manor (in rfb); Hell's Kitchen, Manhattan (in fb) inc crackhouse / Daredevil's billy club, crack house door,
ore window (prev 2 destroyed), hurled trash can, police car & guns (all in fb), Wolverine & Shingen's bokken (in rfb), Gateway's bull-roarer (in
b), Princess Bar window (destroyed), O'Donnell's lease, Archie's winnings, Geist's money, motorboat & exoskeleton w/bionic hand & razor
achment, goons' truck, Roughouse's bonds, Caridad's tainted cocaine (more also bts in fb) & US Navy warship
LASHBACKS: Shingen defeats and degrades Wolverine (W #1, '82). Wolverine, feeling feral, kills a wild boar and decides to take some time
ay from the X-Men (p). Hammer Cody, high on cocaine, battles Daredevil with heightened strength until he suddenly dies.
YNOPSIS: Wolverine brawls with Roughouse in Madripoor, enjoying fighting one of few opponents he can go all-out with. Wolverine wins and
lebrates with the Princess Bar regulars, but Coy sells Roughouse's unconscious form to Geist. At the palace, Baran discusses Tai's recent
izure of Coy's imported cocaine. Displeased at hard drugs entering his island, Baran sells the product back to Geist, the intermediary for Coy's
pplier. Wolverine smells the cocaine on a passing truck and follows, witnessing Geist load it — and the captive Roughouse — onto a US Navy
arship. On board, Geist explains that Coy's cocaine was tainted with an unknown substance that grants heightened strength to its users, but
on kills them. Geist wants to field-test the effects on Roughouse, a much hardier man. He attaches a razor to his bionic arm — and Wolverine,
eaking aboard, hears Roughouse screaming…
OTE: The series returns to monthly publication here, although Marvel's cover-date shifting at this time makes it appear otherwise. Bloodsport's
ame changes to Bloodscream here without explanation; as discussed in W #4, '89's NOTE, Bloodscream seems to be his primary codename.
ore is named in W #21, '90; Geist's first name is revealed in MAtlas #1, '08. W #23, '90 reveals that Geist is a CIA mole; nonetheless as a
mer Nazi he will still be listed as a Villain. Archie's company, South Seas Skyways, is referred to as "South Sea Airways" here and next issue.

WOLVERINE #18 (December 1989)

"All at Sea" (22 pages)

CREDITS: Archie Goodwin (writer), John Byrne (breakdowns, c art), Klaus Janson (finishes), Jim Novak
(letters), Glynis Oliver (colors), Daryl Edelman (asst editor, uncredited), Bob Harras (editor)
FEATURE CHARACTER: Wolverine (also as "Patch," see NOTE, next in Cap #363, '89, UXM #246, '89)
SUPPORTING CAST: Archie Corrigan (next in W #31, '90), O'Donnell (next in W #87, '94), Tyger Tiger (next
in W #27, '90)
VILLAINS: Geist (also in fb between Av1959 #5, '12 & W #17, '89), President Felix Guillermo Caridad (president
of Tierra Verde, 1st on-panel app, also in fb prior to W #17, '89) & his soldiers (some die), Nuke (Frank Simpson,
unbalanced super-soldier, in fb between W:O #2, '06 fb & DD #230, '86 bts), Spore (bts in Roughouse & cocaine),
General Coy, Prince Baran (prev 2 next in W #23, '90), Roughouse
OTHER CHARACTERS: Sister Salvation (Caridad's estranged wife, healing touch, 1st) & her parishioners
ie, most bts in mission), Tierra Verde rebels (die), US Colonel, Caridad's pilots (prev 3 in fb), warship comm officer (bts sending messages) &
ptain, Coy's pilot (bts on helicopter), Baran's pilots; birds; Captain America, Thor, Iron Man (prev 3 monitor images in fb)
OCATIONS/ITEMS: Republic of Tierra Verde (Central American nation, 1st, also in fb) inc Caridad's Puerto Verde palace (unnamed), rebel
ronghold (prev 2 in fb) & Sister Salvation's mission (prev 2 destroyed), South China Sea, Pacific Ocean / Caridad's binoculars, helicopter &
per hero videotapes, pilots' rifles, Nuke's submachine gun ("Betsy"), red pills (see NOTE) & grenades (all in fb), Caridad's US Navy warship,
nted cocaine & yacht w/helicopter, soldiers' explosives (bts), handguns & rifles w/laser sights, Geist's exoskeleton (also in fb) w/bionic hand,
mputer & dart gun attachment w/tranquilizer darts, Roughouse's bonds (destroyed), hurled machine gun, wreckage & ammo belt, Coy's
licopter & money, Baran's airplane & money, captain's binoculars, Archie's Douglas DC-3 w/radio, Tyger's motorboat w/radio

FLASHBACK: The US military demonstrates Nuke, who wipes out a Tierra Verde rebel village. Envious, President Caridad tells his advis
Geist that he wants to create a super hero of his own.

SYNOPSIS: Wolverine battles the ship's guards until Geist arrives, wondering why his foe is dressed like a dead hero. Demanding to s
Roughouse, Wolverine learns that Geist shaved his head and beard, revealing old scars, and drugged him with the tainted cocaine. When Ge
explains that he is trying to create a super hero for Caridad, a disgusted Wolverine cuts Roughouse free. Madness overtakes Roughouse and
battles Wolverine savagely, but Geist tranquilizes both men. Coy and Baran arrive on the ship; Geist sells Coy some of the tainted cocaine, a
sells Baran Wolverine's unconscious body. Baran, wishing to be rid of the nuisance of "Patch," throws him into the ocean. In Tierra Verde, Carid
forces his estranged wife, a nun with healing powers nicknamed Sister Salvation, to rejoin him by destroying her mission house. O'Donnell a
Tyger, who had been shadowing Wolverine, fish him out of the ocean, and he resolves to invade Tierra Verde.

NOTE: Although Geist, Coy and Baran see "Patch" in full Wolverine costume, they all believe the X-Men to be dead, and therefore assume th
he is merely imitating Wolverine for effect. Puerto Verde is named next issue. Nuke says "gimme a red" here, but takes a blue pill. W:O #2, '
reveals Nuke's first name, and that the "reds" were placebos; Nuke's heightened adrenaline came from within himself. NX #145, '03, reveals th
Weapon Plus, the parent program behind the Weapon X project that gave Wolverine his Adamantium, also sponsored the project that creat
Nuke. W:O #2-3, '06 reveal that Wolverine, under orders from Romulus, helped recruit Frank Simpson into the project as a youth, and tortur
him years later to condition his mind and direct his rage.

WOLVERINE #19 (Mid December 1989)

"Heroes & Villains" (22 pages)

CREDITS: Archie Goodwin (writer), John Byrne (layouts, c art), Klaus Janson (finishes), Jim Novak (letter
Mike Rockwitz (colors), Daryl Edelman (asst editor), Bob Harras (editor)
FEATURE CHARACTER: Wolverine
GUEST STAR: Gateway (bts teleporting Wolverine, last in W #17, '89, next in UXM #247, '89)
VILLAINS: Dr. Doom (Victor von Doom, monarch of Latveria, last in DD #275, '89), Kingpin (Wilson Fisk, oversiz
crimelord, last in Pun #28, '89) (prev 2 next in WoSM #60, '90), Magneto (Max "Erik Magnus Lehnsherr" Eisenhar
magnetic mutant, next in UXM #253, '89), Red Skull (Johann Shmidt, Nazi super villain, next bts in ASM #328, '9
next in WoSM #61, '90) (prev 2 last in Cap #366, '90), Tiger Shark (Todd Arliss, aquatic villain, last in WCA #16, '8
chr last in MCP #56/3, '90), Geist (also in fb between X:TF #3, '99 & Av1959 #5, '12), Adolf Hitler (in fb betwe
Cap:ME, '94 fb & DF:Av #4.8, '00 fb), Spore (bts in Roughouse), President Caridad & his soldiers, Roughouse
OTHER CHARACTERS: La Bandera (1st, transforms inspiration into mutant energy) & her revolutionaries, Jack Bascomb (CIA agent, 1
next in W #23, '90), Sister Salvation, Caridad's political prisoners (bts, unnamed, location leaked to Bandera) inc Enríque Rosales, Chubas
& Luis, guards & researchers, OSS (Office of Strategic Services) officials (bts), German rocket scientist, CIA official (prev 3 in fb), New Yc
police, others (prev 2 on Kingpin's monitors), Puerto Verde cabbie (bts in taxi), tourists, press, waiter & bystanders inc newlyweds; Palo Carid
(Caridad & Salvation's son, 1st mention, unnamed), Bandera's father (mentioned, died from drugs); Aztec gods (in Caridad's thoughts, all bu
bts); historical figures (prev 2 as paintings & busts)
LOCATIONS/ITEMS: Puerto Verde (Tierra Verde's capital city, named) inc news office (destroyed), beach, docks, café, Tierra Verde Medi
Center w/filtration sublevel & Caridad's palace w/tunnels, el Jardín del Rey (Tierra Verde cocaine field, bts, also in Caridad's thought
Washington DC's Capitol & White House, Queens' Unisphere (prev 3 on monitors), Kingpin's New York office, Loki's meeting chamber, Hitle
headquarters, OSS & CIA offices (prev 3 in fb), Pacific Ocean / Tiger Shark's water circulation suit, Bandera's staff, soldiers' gun, club
firebomb, revolutionaries' weapons inc hook, club, bricks, guns, axe & cleaver, Caridad's US Navy warship, comm unit & monitor, taxi, Kingpi
monitors & comm equipment, Geist's shaving tools, machine pistol & exoskeleton w/bionic hand (destroyed) & razor attachment, guards' rifl
meteors, god's sword & shield (prev 3 in thoughts), Roughouse's bonds, palace's water filtration system w/grating (destroyed) & ocean pipeli
FLASHBACK: Geist serves Hitler during WWII, and delivers a German scientist to the OSS and aids the CIA in the following decades.
SYNOPSIS: Gateway teleports Wolverine to Puerto Verde, where he finds Tiger Shark attacking heroine la Bandera. The two drive Tiger Sha
off, and Wolverine realizes that Bandera can rally and channel inspiration. Jack Bascomb, an old friend, warns Wolverine that more is happeni
in Tierra Verde than he knows. Kingpin tells Caridad that he sent Tiger Shark to kill Bandera for her anti-drug actions in Florida. Carida
researchers reveal that the tainted cocaine grew in a single crop from el Jardín del Rey, where legends say gods once battled. Wolveri
sneaks into the palace and attacks Geist, demanding to be taken to Roughouse — even as Caridad tries to convince Sister Salvation to he
Roughouse, who is developing sores. Bandera inspires revolutionaries to attack the palace, responding to Geist's leaked rumor of politi
prisoners. Geist leads Wolverine through the water filtration complex, where Tiger Shark leaps from a tank and attacks. Wolverine swims throu
a pipeline to the sea, but Tiger Shark follows…
NOTE: Cover-labeled "Acts of Vengeance!", part of a line-wide event where Loki, Norse god of mischief, convinces villains to attack unfami
heroes. Magneto's longtime alias is revealed in XMU #2, '93, and his real name in X:MT #1, '08. Palo is named in W #22, '90. Enríque's f
name is revealed next issue, and his last name in MAtlas #2, '08. Chubasco and Luis are named in W #22, '90.

WOLVERINE #20 (January 1990)

"Miracles" (22 pages)

CREDITS: Archie Goodwin (writer), John Byrne (breakdowns, c art), Klaus Janson (finishes), Jim Nov
(letters), Mike Rockwitz (colors), Daryl Edelman (asst editor, uncredited), Bob Harras (editor)
FEATURE CHARACTER: Wolverine (also in dfb)
VILLAINS: Tiger Shark (next in MCP #77/4, '91), Spore (bts in Roughouse), Geist, Roughouse, President Carid
OTHER CHARACTERS: Sister Salvation, la Bandera & her revolutionaries (die), Caridad's doctors, scientists, pi
soldiers inc Colonel & political prisoners inc Enríque Rosales, Chubasco & Luis; sharks; Palo Caridad (mentioned)
LOCATIONS/ITEMS: Pacific Ocean (also in dfb), Tierra Verde Medical Center w/prison ward, roof, laborato
& filtration sublevel / Tiger Shark's water circulation suit, coral shelf (also in dfb, destroyed), Bandera's sta
revolutionaries' guns, soldiers' handguns & rifles, prisoners' shackles, Geist's exoskeleton w/bionic hand &
dart gun attachment w/cocaine-filled darts, Caridad's tainted cocaine (bts) & helicopter, Roughouse's bon
(destroyed), scientist's tranquilizer, hospital security cameras (bts) & monitors

FLASHBACK: Wolverine breaks free of the coral shelf (d).

SYNOPSIS: Wolverine and Tiger Shark battle underwater. Tiger Shark embeds Wolverine's claws in a coral shelf and leaves him to drown. La Bandera and her allies assault the hospital, but find that the political prisoners have been moved. Geist reveals that he leaked their location to lure Bandera there. Tiger Shark kills the revolutionaries and Bandera flees. Sister Salvation uses her healing touch on Roughouse, now covered in sores. Tiger Shark tracks Bandera but encounters an enraged Wolverine, who savagely defeats him. Wolverine and Bandera free Roughouse and corner Caridad; Geist threatens to kill the prisoners, but they revolt, giving Wolverine time to steal Caridad's helicopter, taking Sister Salvation along with Roughouse and Bandera. As Sister Salvation finishes healing Roughouse, Tiger Shark leaps from the ocean and tries to drag Wolverine down — but blood from his injuries attracts sharks, which swarm him. The heroes celebrate a clean getaway, but Wolverine is unaware that Geist shot him with several cocaine-filled darts…

NOTE: Cover-labeled "Acts of Vengeance!" This issue also has a "Wolverine Gallery" pin-up.

WOLVERINE #21 (February 1990)

"Battleground" (22 pages)

CREDITS: Archie Goodwin (writer), John Byrne (breakdowns, c art), Klaus Janson (finishes), Jim Novak (letters), Glynis Oliver (colors), Daryl Edelman (asst editor), Bob Harras (editor)
FEATURE CHARACTER: Wolverine (also in his own hallucination)
GUEST STARS: X-Men: Psylocke (Elizabeth "Betsy" Braddock, telepath), Colossus, Havok (all during UXM #249, '89), Dazzler (last in UXM #248, chr last in UXM #249 fb, next in UXM #249, all '89)
VILLAINS: Spore (bts in Wolverine, named, also in Wolverine's hallucination & bts in rfb; also in fb, its 1st on-panel & chr 1st app, prior to W #17, '89 fb, also in W #22, '90 fb during fb), Deviants (mutated offshoot of humanity, in fb, some or others chr last in WI? #23/2, '80, chr next in Et #2, '76 fb), Geist (also in Wolverine's hallucination), President Caridad & his soldiers
OTHER CHARACTERS: Sister Salvation (also in Wolverine's hallucination), Roughouse, la Bandera & her revolutionaries (former political prisoners) inc Enrique Rosales, Chubasco & Luis, Tierra Verde natives, Eternals (immortal offshoot of humanity, some or all die, others chr last in WI? #24/2, '80, chr next in WI? #25/2, '80), Celestials (evolution-altering "space gods," all but 1 bts destroying Spore, some or others chr last in WI? #23/2, '80, chr next in Et #1, '06 fb), cocaine farmers (prev 3 in fb), jungle creatures (bts, die); Palo Caridad (mentioned); Daredevil, Hammer Cody (prev 2 in rfb); Nazis (die), Adolf Hitler (prev 2 in Wolverine's hallucination); historical figure (as painting)
LOCATIONS/ITEMS: X-Men's outback HQ (Cooterman's Creek, Northern Territory, Australia; unnamed), Tierra Verde: el Jardín del Rey (in fb), jungle, swamp & Caridad's Puerto Verde palace, Deviant & Eternal cities (prev 2 in fb), Hell's Kitchen (in rfb), German city (in hallucination) inc Hitler's chambers / Psylocke's armor, Caridad's comm unit & helicopters (1 destroyed) w/radio, Geist's cocaine-filled darts (all but 1 bts), radio & exoskeleton (also in hallucination) w/razor attachment (in hallucination), bionic hand & computer, soldiers' rifles & floodlights, vines (destroyed), Bandera's staff, natives' spears, bow & arrow, Sister Salvation's habit, Nazis' tank (destroyed), machine guns & grenades, Wolverine's bag (prev 2 in hallucination), Deviants' genetic equipment, farmers' bales (prev 2 in fb)
FLASHBACKS: Hammer Cody dies (W #17, '89 fb). Millennia ago, the Deviants create Spore to battle the Eternals. Spore goes rogue, attacking both sides, until the Celestials destroy him. His substance sinks into the earth, and eventually inhabits the field's cocaine crop.
SYNOPSIS: In Australia, Psylocke detects something wrong with Wolverine's mind. In the jungle, Caridad's soldiers hunt the escapees as the tainted cocaine sends Wolverine into a feral rage. Roughouse restrains him while Sister Salvation tries to heal him as, nearby, la Bandera and the freed prisoners encounter a tribe of natives. Wolverine hallucinates a battle against Nazis, Adolf Hitler and Geist. Sister Salvation appears and gives him strength, but Geist transforms into Spore, revealing that it is a living virus present in the tainted cocaine, and that it wants to claim Wolverine's body for itself. Sister Salvation, leaving her habit behind, tries to heal Wolverine again. He hallucinates his healing factor manifesting and destroying Spore, and awakens cured — but Caridad and his troops surround and capture Wolverine and Roughouse. Sister Salvation's habit had been a clue; she betrayed them in hopes that Caridad would let her see her son.
NOTE: Cooterman's Creek is named in OHMU:ME #29, '93. Next issue reveals that when Sister Salvation healed Roughouse, she cleansed his violent rage; hence he is no longer listed as a Villain. The Celestials split off the Eternals and Deviants from baseline humanity during the First Host, their initial visit to Earth millennia ago; Spore was destroyed by the Celestials' Second Host, who visited Earth 20,000 years ago to see the progress their creations had made.

WOLVERINE #22 (March 1990)

"Outburst!" (22 pages)

CREDITS: Archie Goodwin (writer), John Byrne (breakdowns, c art), Klaus Janson (finishes), Jim Novak (letters), Glynis Oliver (colors), Daryl Edelman (asst editor, uncredited), Bob Harras (editor)
FEATURE CHARACTER: Wolverine (also as himself & a wolverine in his own hallucination)
VILLAINS: Spore (manifests in Caridad, also in fb during W #21, '90 fb), President Caridad (dies) & his soldiers (some die) inc Sergeant & Lieutenant, Geist
OTHER CHARACTERS: Sister Salvation (also in Wolverine's hallucination), Palo Caridad (Tierra Verde army private, 1st on-panel app), Roughouse, la Bandera & her revolutionaries inc Chubasco, Luis (prev 2 named, die) & Enrique Rosales, Tierra Verde natives, Spore's victims (in fb, die); Roughouse's father (mentioned; beat him with sticks); Mariko Yashida (in Wolverine's hallucination)
LOCATIONS/ITEMS: Caridad's Tierra Verde training camp w/mud pit, cellblock & lab, Central America (in fb), snowscape (in hallucination) / Mariko & Salvation's katana (in hallucination), Wolverine's bonds (some destroyed), Caridad's flamethrowers (all but 1 bts), electrical torture device, tainted cocaine & lab equipment, Geist's exoskeleton w/bionic hand, razor attachment & dart gun attachment w/cocaine-filled darts, soldiers' sticks, mortars, rockets (prev 3 bts), rifles & machine gun, Palo & Sergeant's padding & pugil sticks, Roughouse's chains (destroyed), natives' bows (bts), arrows & spears, hurled tubing, Bandera's staff, revolutionaries' guns
FLASHBACK: Spore absorbs several cavemen.
SYNOPSIS: Wolverine hallucinates as Caridad tortures him, not believing Wolverine's story about Spore living in the cocaine. Outside, Caridad reunites Sister Salvation with their son Palo, now a private in Tierra Verde's army. In the cells, Roughouse explains to Wolverine that his father

beat him as a child, giving him scars, but that Sister Salvation washed away his lifelong anger. Caridad debates burning the tainted cocain but instead decides to use it on Palo, hoping to transform him into a national hero. Sister Salvation panics at this news, and Roughouse hea her screams and snaps his chains. He frees Wolverine, who bursts in and deflects most of Geist's darts. One hits Palo, but the rest hit Carida Sister Salvation decides to cure her son instead of her husband — just as la Bandera's revolutionaries attack, aided by the natives. Carida injects himself with the rest of the cocaine and is swiftly subsumed by Spore, who absorbs several revolutionaries. Wolverine attacks with flamethrower, but Spore engulfs him…

WOLVERINE #23 (April 1990)

"Endings" (22 pages)

CREDITS: Archie Goodwin (writer), John Byrne (art), Jim Novak (letters), Glynis Oliver (colors), Daryl Edelma (asst editor), Bob Harras (editor)
FEATURE CHARACTER: Wolverine (next in UXM #251-253 & 257-258, '89-90; AFlt #87-90, UXM #261, Ann #14/2, UXM #268, all '90, W:RT, '91, NM #93, '90, Cable&NM TPB, '92; NM #93-94, MCP #48-50 & 54-6 all '90, Whead #1, '92 fb)
VILLAINS: Reavers: Bonebreaker, Wade Cole, Lady Deathstrike, Angelo Macon, Donald Pierce, Murray Rees (all last in UXM #249, '89), Pretty Boy, Skullbuster (prev 2 last in UXM #248, '89) (all bts in outback HQ, next UXM #251, '89); Prince Baran (chr next in W #29, '90 fb, next in W #27, '90), General Coy (next in NM #93, '9 (both last in W #18, '89), Magneto (last in AWC #60, '90, next in UXM #269, '90), Geist (possibly next as spirit W #176, '02, see NOTE), Spore (dies), President Caridad's soldiers

OTHER CHARACTERS: Roughouse (next in W #123, '98), Jack Bascomb (last in W #19, '89), Sister Salvation, Palo Caridad, la Bande & her revolutionaries (some die, some become new cabinet) inc Enríque Rosales, Tierra Verde natives & citizens inc looters (bts, ransacke palace), CIA officials (bts arranging Geist's extradition), Coy's bodyguards (bts, incapacitated, some or others next in W #27, '90), Madripo bystanders, Baran's servants & horse; historical figure (as bust)

LOCATIONS/ITEMS: Caridad's training camp, Puerto Verde w/café, Tierra Verde Medical Center prison ward (bts) & Caridad's form palace, Sovereign Hotel's Imperial penthouse, Baran's palace w/grounds, Lowtown inc sewers, Reavers' Australian outback HQ (see NOTE Geist's Washington DC safehouse / Bandera's staff, revolutionaries' guns & armed caravan, natives' spears, bows & arrows, soldiers' rifles floodlights, Sister Salvation's bandages, Palo's stretcher & straps, Wolverine's helicopter (bts), leaflets, eyepatch & jeep, Geist's stolen true (bts), getaway stash (bts, destroyed), shotgun & exoskeletons (1 destroyed) w/bionic hand & shaving attachment, Caridad's tainted cocai samples (destroyed, all but 1 bts), citizens' signs & fireworks, Coy & Baran's bonds & blindfolds, Magneto's robot (destroyed)

SYNOPSIS: Wolverine cuts his way free of Spore and la Bandera rallies the revolutionaries, but Spore easily withstands their attack. The retreat and Sister Salvation suggests a plan; Bandera distracts Spore, Wolverine knocks him down, and Sister Salvation touches him. Spo ignites with searing flame and burns to ashes. Bandera and her revolutionaries head to the capital, while Roughouse stays behind with Sist Salvation. Wolverine tracks down Geist and destroys his exoskeleton. Later, as the citizens celebrate the revolution, Wolverine angrily confron the new cabinet, having learned that they released Geist to the USA. He warns Bandera that running a country is more difficult than she think and Jack Bascomb reveals that Geist was a CIA mole. Wolverine returns to Madripoor, destroys Coy's tainted cocaine sample, and kidnaps C and Baran. He chases them through the sewers, payback for their betrayals, and returns home to the X-Men. Later, Magneto confronts Geist his safehouse. A Holocaust survivor, Magneto looks forward to "talking" with the former Nazi…

NOTE: John Byrne signs the front cover "John 'n' Mac," referring to the Macintosh computer that he used to digitally stretch Geist's reflectio on Wolverine's claws. The cyborg Reavers, former owners of the X-Men's outback HQ, reclaimed it in UXM #251, '89; they are waiting there ambush Wolverine. MAtlas #2, '08 reveals that Enríque was later elected President of Tierra Verde. Magneto incorrectly tells Geist that his w died in a concentration camp. He and Magda escaped from Auschwitz and were together for many years afterwards; Magneto may have bee lying for effect here. In W #176, '02, Geist's spirit appears when Wolverine visits the afterlife, implying that he died sometime between here ar that issue. However, as discussed in W #4, '82's NOTE, it is uncertain if anything Wolverine witnesses there is real. Cap #442, '95 reveals th the hero-killing Zeitgeist later murders la Bandera.

WOLVERINE #24 (May 1990)

"Snow Blind" (22 pages)

CREDITS: Peter David (writer), Gene Colan (art), Jim Novak (letters), Mark Chiarello (colors), Daryl Edelma (asst editor), Bob Harras (editor), Jim Lee (c art)
FEATURE CHARACTER: Wolverine (as "Patch")
VILLAINS: Snow Queen (Brigitte "Gitte" Lahti, sense-scrambling assassin, dies) & her employer (bts hiring he
OTHER CHARACTERS: Ganif (thieves' mentor) & his beggar children inc Aldo, Rashi & Rose, Madripo bartender (also in photo), bar patrons & bystanders inc Henry
LOCATIONS/ITEMS: Madripoor inc bar, rooftops, Snow Queen's rented room, Aldo's basement hideaway & Ganif thieves' quarter base / Snow Queen's knife, photo, plastic explosive earrings, detonation wire necklace, ropes, gu (destroyed) w/silencer & briefcase (destroyed) w/money & bomb w/timer, Rose's cup & sunglasses, Ganif's mone beggar's knife, Aldo's headband (bts), bolted iron door (destroyed), Wolverine's improvised tourniquet

SYNOPSIS: Snow Queen readies a briefcase bomb, preparing for an assassination. However, on the street, beggar child Aldo grabs the briefcase and flees. Snow Queen chases him, shooting; Wolverine hears fellow beggar Rose's cries for help. He confronts Snow Queen, wh scrambles his senses and escapes. Hiding, Aldo unknowingly triggers the bomb's countdown timer, and finds a photo of Snow Queen's targ — a bartender, who coincidentally is serving Wolverine. The bartender tells Wolverine to talk to Ganif, the beggars' mentor, as Snow Quee forces Rose to help find Aldo. Ganif gives Aldo's headband to Wolverine, who tracks his scent. Snow Queen finds Aldo, but Wolverine arrive and attacks. She scrambles his senses again and cuts him with a knife, but Wolverine slowly gets his bearings and slashes her arm. Sno Queen shoots at Aldo but hits Rose. As Wolverine and Aldo help Rose, Snow Queen flees with the briefcase. She opens it, but finds that th timer has counted down to zero; Wolverine and the beggars witness the explosion.

WOLVERINE #25 (June 1990)

"Heir Aid" (22 pages)

CREDITS: Jo Duffy (writer), John Buscema (art), Ken Bruzenak (letters), Glynis Oliver (colors), Daryl Edelman (asst editor), Bob Harras (editor), Jim Lee (c art)
FEATURE CHARACTER: Wolverine (also as a boy in his own story, see NOTE)
VILLAINS: Piggot (would-be Wharfside ganglord) & his men (some die)
OTHER CHARACTERS: Mr. Morrow (would-be Wharfside ganglord) & his men (some die) inc Loo; Gabriel (Morrow's son), Polly & Rebecca (prev 2 Gabriel's attendants), Madripoor police; boy's father & his people (bts casting boy out, see NOTE), fur trappers (die) & their catches (dead, all but 1 bts, ruined by wolverines & boy); wolverines (some die, 1 also in symbolic image), rabbits (1 dies), reindeer (dies), deer, mountain lion (prev 9 in Wolverine's story); clown (as Gabriel's doll), historical figure (as painting)
LOCATIONS/ITEMS: Wharfside (Lowtown dockland district) inc Morrow's house w/Gabriel's bedroom, Canadian wilderness (in story) / Wolverine's eyepatch (see NOTE), Morrow's men's guns, Gabriel's teddy bear & serving cart, Piggot's men's guns, knives, machetes, pipe & chain, Piggot's sword cane; boy's cloak (destroyed) & stick, hunters' cage, ropes (prev 2 destroyed), traps, shotguns & net (prev 7 in story)
SYNOPSIS: Morrow calls in a favor from Wolverine. He and his men plan to attack their Wharfside turf war rival, Piggot. Fearing that Piggot will harm his son Gabriel, Morrow asks Wolverine to safeguard him for the night. Gabriel asks for a bedtime story; Wolverine tells him of a small boy, cast out by his family for being weak and cowardly. In the Canadian wilderness, a pack of wolverines adopt the boy, who soon grows strong and feral. Fur trappers capture and cage him, but the wolverines attack the trappers. When some are shot, the enraged boy breaks free and kills the trappers. Wolverine hears some of Piggot's men sneaking in; they grab Gabriel, but he kills them. Morrow's men retreat into the house, and Piggot's men follow. Wolverine joins the fray, but Morrow is pinned down. Piggot gloatingly prepares to kill Morrow — but Gabriel, having learned courage from Wolverine's story, rams Piggot with a serving cart. Police arrive to stop the battle, and Morrow embraces his son.
NOTE: "Morrow" is heavily implied to be an alias, therefore it cannot be assumed to be Gabriel's last name. The debt Wolverine owes him is unrevealed to date. Although Wolverine wears his eyepatch here, he is deliberately appearing as himself, not as "Patch." Wolverine's bedtime story may have been based on actual events from his past: although Wolverine was not cast out for being small and weak, Origin #1 established that he was indeed a frail, sickly boy. Origin #6, '02 & XO:W, '09 reveal that he lived ferally in the Canadian wilderness with wolves for a time; the wolverines in his story could have been stand-ins for those wolves, and hunters might have briefly captured him during that time. If similar events happened in Wolverine's youth, they would have occurred somewhere between Origin #6, '02 & W:WX #10, '10 fb. In W #30, '90, Wolverine comments that the man who runs Wharfside owes him, implying that Morrow may have won the turf war by that point.

WOLVERINE #26 (Early July 1990)

"Memory of Peace" (22 pages)

CREDITS: Jo Duffy (writer), Klaus Janson (pencils), Tom Palmer (inks), Jim Novak (letters), Glynis Oliver (colors), Bob Harras (editor)
FEATURE CHARACTER: Wolverine (also as "Patch," also in pfb, also in fb between Ex #14, '05 fb & L:SS, '96)
VILLAINS: Gene Claymore (criminal gambler, dies), Masaki Weston (Bando's nephew; prev 2 also bts in pfb, smelled by Wolverine; also in fb prior to pfb) & hired thugs (in pfb, die)
OTHER CHARACTERS: Saburo Bando (Wolverine's old friend), his wife (both also in fb prior to pfb) & their family & servants (all dead in pfb), Claymore's bodyguards & fish; Weston's parents (mentioned)
LOCATIONS/ITEMS: Bando's Japan home (in fb & pfb) & gravesite, Madripoor inc Claymore's Hightown skyscraper suite & Weston's home / Claymore's window (destroyed), art collection, cards & chips, thugs' knives (2 destroyed) & gun (prev 2 in pfb), Bando's glazed bowl (also in fb), teamaking tools (in fb), letter & gravestone, bodyguards' guns, Wolverine's car & cigar, Weston's knife, servant's sword
FLASHBACKS: At Bando's home, Wolverine finds the servants dead. He confronts and kills the thugs who murdered them, then finds Bando and his wife also dead, and vows revenge (p). Years ago, Wolverine visits Bando, and comments on the beauty of a glazed bowl. Bando explains that it is his family's most treasured heirloom, and mentions that he made his nephew Masaki, troubled because his father was poor, his heir.
SYNOPSIS: Wolverine plays cards with Claymore, who now owns Bando's bowl. Reading Claymore's body language with his senses, Wolverine continues raising the stakes until he wins everything Claymore owns, then demands the bowl and the name of its seller. Claymore reveals that Masaki sold it to him, and charges at Wolverine — who trips him, sending Claymore plummeting out a window. Wolverine travels to Masaki's home and finds him preparing to commit suicide. Wolverine reveals that Masaki didn't need to kill his family for the bowl; Bando had cancer and would have died shortly anyway. Masaki attacks Wolverine, who kills him. Later, Wolverine leaves the bowl on Bando's grave.
NOTE: This issue also has a "Wolverine Gallery" pin-up by Todd McFarlane. The series begins biweekly publication again here; although the cover date is "Early July," the indicia date is "Mid-July." This issue consistently names Bando as Bando Saburo. This issue mentions his lineage as "the house of Bando," it should be assumed that the issue is presenting his name in Eastern style, with surname first and given name last. Saburo's name is extremely similar to that of Wolverine's post-WWII friend Suboro Bando, seen in W #40, '06 fb; Saburo may be Suboro's grandson or another relative. This issue's assistant editor is unknown; it is either Daryl Edelman or Suzanne Gaffney.

WOLVERINE #27 (Late July 1990)

"The Lazarus Project, Part One: Predators and Prey!" (22 pages)

CREDITS: Jo Duffy (writer), John Buscema (pencils), Dan Green (inks), Ken Bruzenak (letters), Glynis Oliv (colors), Suzanne Gaffney (asst editor), Bob Harras (editor), Jim Lee (c art)
FEATURE CHARACTER: Wolverine (also as "Patch," also in Karma's thoughts, also in W #29, '90 fb)
GUEST STAR: Karma (last in W #8, '89, chr next in W #29, '90 fb)
SUPPORTING CAST: Jessica Drew, Lindsay McCabe (both last in W #16, '90, next in SenSM Ann '96/2), Tyg Tiger (last in W #18, '89, next in W #31, '90)
VILLAINS: Captain Merrick (Lazarus Project officer, see NOTE), Dr. Page (Lazarus Project scientist) (both 1st but c last in W #30, '90 fb), Broker (Andover, Lazarus Project liaison, 1st), Pinocchio (Rick, self-repairing cyborg, 1st but c last as Rick in W #30, '90 fb) (prev 3 next in W #30, '90), Prince Baran (last in W #23, chr last in W #29 fb, next bts in W #30, next in W #31, all '90), General Coy (last in NM #93, '90, chr last & next in W #29, '90 fb), Madripoor thugs inc L

OTHER CHARACTERS: Target (Ted, marksman, unnamed, 1st but chr last in W #29, '90 fb), Coy's bodyguards (some or others last in W #23, '90), Baran's household guards (all but 1 bts, some or others last in W #16, '89, next in W #30, '90), Rumikan villagers inc elders, Madripo pilot, crew & bystanders; New Mutants: Wolfsbane, Cannonball, Sunspot, Psyche (prev 4 Karma's former teammates, in Karma's thought Leong Coy Manh, Nga Coy Manh (prev 2 Karma's siblings, mentioned by Coy, also in Karma's thoughts); lion (as statue)
LOCATIONS/ITEMS: Lowtown inc alley, airfield & Princess Bar, Sovereign Hotel's Imperial penthouse, Baran's palace w/Page's lab, Rumi (village on small island, also called Rumika, off Madripoor's coast) inc elder's home / Lim's knife, thugs' chain, machete, knives, gun & crowb Nga's doll (in Karma's thoughts), bystander's wallet (bts), Master Form (Lazarus Project item, also in photo), Target's bow, guns & kniv Merrick & guard's rifles, Broker's photo & paperwork, Pinocchio's self-healing cyborg armor, Wolverine's hired airplane, Jessica's stretcher straps, Page's window (destroyed), map & chemical beaker
SYNOPSIS: In Lowtown, Wolverine and Tyger make short work of a street gang. Noticing the fight, Karma helps by surreptitiously possessi one of the thugs. Wolverine and Tyger arrive at the Princess Bar, where Jessica reveals that Baran has hired her as a bodyguard. On Rumi Merrick leaves an object called the Master Form with the villagers, who promise to protect it. Meanwhile, the Broker discusses the Form, and t Lazarus Project that relies upon it, with his new business partners Coy and Baran. Jessica patrols the palace, but discovers a lab and overhea a scientist, Dr. Page, talking with a shadowed figure about attacking Rumika. Page notices her, and orders a giant robot called Pinocchio attack. Later, Wolverine finds a badly beaten Jessica in the streets, and sends her and Lindsay back to the US for their own safety. Investigatin Wolverine finds and battles Pinocchio, who proves resistant to his claws. Page throws chemicals in Wolverine's face, and he staggers out t window and falls into the ocean…
NOTE: Cover-labeled "The Lazarus Project, Part One." Target's codename is revealed next issue. W #29, '90 reveals his first name along w that of his cousin Rick; W #30, '90 clarifies that Rick is Pinocchio. Their last names are unrevealed to date, as is the Broker's first name. Merri is named here only as the shadowed figure talking to Dr. Page; next issue reveals him to also be the Lazarus Project officer, and reveals b rank. Although Merrick is black, the figure's hand is incorrectly colored white. Next issue's fb reveals that Merrick was present off-panel wh Wolverine fought Pinocchio, whose armor is revealed as self-healing in W #30, '90.

WOLVERINE #28 (Early August 1990)

"The Lazarus Project: the Stranger" (23 pages)

CREDITS: Jo Duffy (writer), Barry Kitson (pencils), Keith Williams (inks), Jim Novak (letters), Nel Yomtov (color Suzanne Gaffney (asst editor, uncredited), Bob Harras (editor), Mark Chiarello (c pencils), Mike Mignola (c ink
FEATURE CHARACTER: Wolverine (also bts in rfb1 & rfb3, also in rfb2)
GUEST STAR: Karma (also in fb during MTU #100, '80 fb; chr last in W #29, '90 fb)
VILLAINS: Captain Merrick (also in shadow in rfb3, also bts in W #29, '90 fb, dies) & his mercenaries (chr last b in W #29, '90 fb, die), Karma's mother's killer (bts in fb during MTU #100, '80 fb bts, see NOTE)
OTHER CHARACTERS: Tranh Coy Manh, Leong Coy Manh, Nga Coy Manh (all Karma's siblings), Karma mother (dies) & father (see NOTE) (all in fb during MTU #100, '80 fb), Target (named), Rumikan villagers (d inc Jian & his brother, Lum (Jian's son) & elders inc Jian's father; fish (dead), boar (dies), birds, shark, pig, rabb Pinocchio (in rfb1), Dr. Page (in rfb3)
LOCATIONS/ITEMS: Sovereign Hotel's Imperial penthouse, island of Rumika inc beach & village of Rumika w/Wolverine's hut (also in rfb. Vietnamese jungle, Pacific Ocean (prev 2 in fb1), Page's lab (in rfb3) / Merrick's rifle & helicopter w/radio, Target's guns & knives, Karma's ph & stolen boat, villagers' knives, spears, scythe & fishing equipment inc nets (1 destroyed), mercenaries' guns, Master Form (also in photo Karma's mother's killer's gun (bts), Karma's father's rifle (prev 2 in fb), Pinocchio's armor (in rfb1), Page's chemical beaker (in rfb3)
FLASHBACKS: Pinocchio menaces Wolverine (last issue). Wolverine recovers by a fire (this issue). Dr. Page and Merrick gloat (last issue). young Karma walks through the jungle with her siblings, her father prepares to leave for war, and her mother is shot (see NOTE).
SYNOPSIS: An amnesiac Wolverine washes up on Rumika, startling a group of fishing villagers. When a shark snags a net, dragging a m underwater, Wolverine saves him. The elders decide that Wolverine is not after the Master Form, and the villagers welcome him. As days pas Wolverine bonds with the Rumikans, but regains only flashes of memory. Elsewhere, Merrick reassures Target that his enemies will not fin the Form, even as Karma learns that Rumika is in danger. The next day, mercenaries attack, shooting Wolverine and all the villagers; Jian fle with the Form but is killed. Arriving, Karma tries to save two children by possessing a mercenary, but others knock her host out and shoot th children. Enraged, Wolverine slaughters the attackers. Merrick arrives, lamenting the tragedy, but Wolverine smells his scent on the mercenari and reveals his duplicity. A horrified Target shoots Merrick; the sight of the dead children brings back Wolverine's memory.
NOTE: Cover-labeled "The Lazarus Project, Part Two." Merrick's name is clarified here, and his rank is revealed. Karma's account of her paren deaths here differs from her origin in MTU #100, '80 fb; there, Thai pirates killed her father on a boat, and her mother died after they repeate assaulted her. Here, Karma claims that her mother was shot by "those who claimed they would liberate us," and that her father died in jung warfare. It is possible that the US soldiers who defeated the pirates accidentally shot Karma's mother, or that the pirates initially claimed to liberators before assaulting and shooting Karma's mother, thus making both versions true — but the two versions of her father's death cann be reconciled. The art for rfb2 is taken directly from this issue's p.7 panel 1.

WOLVERINE #29 (Late August 1990)

"The Lazarus Project: the Road Back" (23 pages)

CREDITS: Jo Duffy (writer), Barry Kitson (pencils), Al Milgrom (inks), Jim Novak (letters), Gregory Wright (colors), Suzanne Gaffney (asst editor, uncredited), Bob Harras (editor), Mark Chiarello (c pencils), Klaus Janson (c inks)
FEATURE CHARACTER: Wolverine (also in rfb1, also in fb2 during W #27, '90)
GUEST STAR: Karma (also in Wolverine's thoughts, rfb1 & rfb2, also in fb3 between W #27-28, '90)
VILLAINS: Prince Baran (in fb1 between W #23 & 27, '90), General Coy (in fb1 between NM #93 & W #27, also in fb3 between W #27 & 30, all '90) (both also in Wolverine's thoughts & rfb2), Captain Merrick (dead, also in shadow in rfb1; also in fb4, his chr 1st app, prior to W #30, '90 fb; also bts in fb3 during W #28, '90, contacted by Coy) & his soldiers (in fb4) & mercenaries: 1st unit (dead, also bts in fb3 prior to W #28, '90, detected) & 2nd unit (die)
OTHER CHARACTERS: Target (also as Ted in fb4 between W #30, '90 fb & W #27, '90), Rick (in fb4 between W #30, '90 fbs, also as Pinocchio in rfb) (both also in W #30, '90 fb during fb), Senator Delman, Ted's town's mayor
ev 2 bts contacting Ted's father), Lazarus Project drill sergeant (prior to W #30, '90 fb) & officials, Ted's parents (die) & neighbors (some die),
ice (die, 1 bts in car, 1 voice only), a Teenage Mutant Ninja Turtle (on TV) (prev 8 in fb4), tracking station operator (in fb3), Rumikan villagers
ad, 1 also in rfb1) inc Jian & his brother, Lum & elders inc Jian's father; Tyger Tiger, Dr. Page, thug, airplane captain & crew, birds (prev 6 in
), Broker (in rfb2); Jessica Drew, Lindsay McCabe, Baran's household guard (prev 3 in Wolverine's thoughts & rfb1); Leong Coy Manh, Nga
Manh (prev 2 in Wolverine's thoughts)
CATIONS/ITEMS: Village of Rumika w/nearby beach (in rfb1), Lowtown (in rfb1) inc Princess Bar & airfield, Baran's palace (in Wolverine's
ughts, rfb1, rfb2, fb1 & fb3) w/Page's lab (in rfb1) & nearby road (in fb2), Sovereign Hotel's Imperial penthouse (in Wolverine's thoughts), Ted's
dhood home (destroyed), Lazarus Project training grounds (prev 2 in fb4) / Wolverine's torch, funeral pyre & loincloth, villager's spear, elder's
e, Master Form (also in Karma's thoughts & fb4), Target's guns (1 also in fb4) & knives, follow-up unit's machine guns, Karma's flowers,
a's doll (in Wolverine's thoughts), guards' rifles (in Wolverine's thoughts, 1 also in rfb1), thug's crowbar, Wolverine's hired airplane, Jessica's
etcher w/straps, Pinocchio's armor, Page's map & chemical beaker (prev 7 in rfb1), mercenaries' boat (bts), tracking station sensors (bts)
printout (prev 3 in fb3), Ted & Rick's baseball & gloves, Ted's father's safe, soldiers' tank, bazooka & machine gun, police car (destroyed) w/
dspeaker (prev 8 in fb4)
ASHBACKS: Wolverine and Tyger walk in Lowtown; Karma possesses a thug; Jessica leaves for the palace; Wolverine finds a beaten Jessica
d sends her and Lindsay home; Wolverine fights Pinocchio and Page and ends up amnesiac on Rumika (W #27-28, '90). The Broker meets
h Coy and Baran (W #27, '90). Coy kisses Baran's hand (1). Coy detects mercenaries headed for Rumika (3).
ars ago, Merrick entrusts the Master Form to Ted's father. However, soldiers come for it, killing many civilians including Ted's parents. He and his
usin Rick survive and hide the Form, returning it to Merrick, who recruits them. Years later, Ted has become a marksman (4).
NOPSIS: Guilt-ridden, Wolverine builds a funeral pyre for the dead Rumikans. He, Karma and Target compare stories, trying to deduce
rrick and the Lazarus Project's true motives. A second unit of mercenaries arrives; Karma distracts them and Wolverine kills them. Adding
ir bodies to the pyre, Wolverine leaves the Master Form behind to commemorate what the Rumikans died for, and heads for Madripoor.
TE: Cover-labeled "The Lazarus Project, Part Three." Target and his cousin Rick's first names are revealed here. Target's father paraphrases
losopher Edmund Burke's famously attributed quote, saying "all that's needed for evil to flourish is for men of conscience to do nothing."
ntrary to fb3, Coy reveals next issue that he knew about the mercenaries' attack all along; he must have been play-acting here to fool Karma.

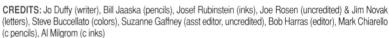

WOLVERINE #30 (Early September 1990)

"The Lazarus Project, Conclusion: Family Matters" (23 pages)

CREDITS: Jo Duffy (writer), Bill Jaaska (pencils), Josef Rubinstein (inks), Joe Rosen (uncredited) & Jim Novak (letters), Steve Buccellato (colors), Suzanne Gaffney (asst editor, uncredited), Bob Harras (editor), Mark Chiarello (c pencils), Al Milgrom (c inks)
FEATURE CHARACTER: Wolverine (also in Broker's thoughts)
GUEST STAR: Karma (next in NW #45, '94)
VILLAINS: Dr. Page (also in fb1, her chr 1st app, prior to W #27, '90), Broker (both last in W #27, '90), Captain Merrick (in fb1 between W #29, '90 fb & W #27, '90), Pinocchio (also as Rick in fb2, his chr 1st app, prior to W #29 fb; also as Rick in fb1 between W #29 fb & W #27, also in W #29 fb, all '90, during fb1), Prince Baran (bts at summer home, last in W #27, '90), General Coy (last in W #29, '90 fb)
OTHER CHARACTERS: Target (also as Ted in fb2, his chr 1st app, prior to W #29, '90 fb; also as Ted in fb1
ing & also in W #29, '90 fb), Genji, Hikaru (prev 2 Broker's employees, die), Broker's follow-up force (bts reporting deaths on Rumika),
zarus Project drill sergeant (in fb1 following W #29, '90 fb), Baran's household guards (some or others last in W #27, '90, some die) & aide
CATIONS/ITEMS: Baran's palace w/Page's lab, Wharfside dock, South China Sea, Rumika (bts), Lazarus Project training grounds (in fb1),
's childhood home (in fb1 & fb2) / Page's tools & remote control, Master Form (bts, also in Wolverine's thoughts & fb1), Broker's files (bts),
rma's stolen boat, Ted & Rick's pugil sticks (in fb1) & baseball gloves (in fb2, 1 bts), Target's rifle, guards' guns, Pinocchio's self-healing cyborg
nor w/forearm blades, Genji & Hikaru's sword
ASHBACKS: Young Ted and Rick volunteer for the Lazarus Project. As they train, Ted discovers a talent for marksmanship (see NOTE), and
k volunteers for a project (1). Ted and Rick play catch as children (2).
NOPSIS: The Broker's employees inform him that the mercenaries are dead, and the Master Form was found abandoned on Rumika.
lverine, Karma and Target sail back to Madripoor, thinking about their lost loved ones. Karma possesses a palace guard and has him lead
m in as prisoners, but other guards expose their ruse and the trio fight past them. Coy discovers that Baran has left, leaving him to deal with
situation. Page sends Pinocchio against Wolverine, and Karma discovers that Coy knew about the planned Rumikan massacre. Pinocchio
ognizes Target, who realizes that the cyborg is his cousin Rick. Wolverine deactivates Page's remote control and Target talks Rick back to
senses; Karma angrily rejects Coy and leaves his employ. The Broker's employees, fearing Wolverine, commit suicide; Broker hides under
ir bodies when Wolverine arrives and flees after he leaves. As Target and Pinocchio reunite, Wolverine is glad that the Lazarus Project has
en terminated.

NOTE: Cover-labeled "The Lazarus Project, Part Four." Wolverine implies here that Morrow, seen in W #25, '90, may have won his Wharfside ti war against Piggot. Although the art and coloring on p.11 implies that Target shoots a guard, the dialogue implies that he's just threatening h with a gun. This issue's flashbacks have some confusion over which boy is which; fb1 incorrectly states that Rick is the one with marksmans skills, and Ted and Rick's dialogue is swapped in fb2. The Master Form's importance and function are never revealed. It may have neith Merrick's plan seems to be simply placing the Form with various communities, then sending "enemies" to slaughter them, and recruiting anyc strong and loyal enough to survive and protect the Form.

WOLVERINE #31 (Late September 1990)

"Killing Zone" (22 pages)

CREDITS: Larry Hama (writer), Marc Silvestri (pencils), Dan Green (inks), Pat Brosseau (letters), Glynis Oli (colors), Suzanne Gaffney (asst editor), Bob Harras (editor)
FEATURE CHARACTER: Wolverine (also as "Patch")
SUPPORTING CAST: Archie Corrigan (last in W #18, '89), Tyger Tiger
VILLAINS: Dai-Kumo (Osaka Yakuza boss), Goro (Dai-Kumo's enforcer), Dr. Malheur (Dai-Kumo's chem (all 1st), Dragonhead (Goro's lieutenant), Seven, Eleven (prev 2 Dragonhead's bodyguards) (prev 3 die), Yaku gangsters (die) inc Kenzo & Makoto, Prince Baran (next in W #98, '96), General Coy
OTHER CHARACTERS: Reiko (Goro's aide, 1st), Princess Bar patrons & bartender, Tyger's maid, Bara motor pool employees, Madripoor police & bystanders; Madripoorian spider-monkey, sharks (prev 2 die); Cc opium harvesters, Tyger's smugglers (prev 2 mentioned); Ryu (mythical dragon), spider (prev 2 as tattoos)
LOCATIONS/ITEMS: Lowtown inc Princess Bar (partly destroyed) w/crawlspace & back alley, South Seas Skyways hangar (bts) & doc Baran's palace w/carport, Tyger's Hightown penthouse / Yakuza guns, Goro's katana & car, Reiko's umbrella sword, Wolverine's new s (destroyed), Malheur's syringe & vial, monkey's cage & hypothalamic fluid, hurled chair (destroyed), police jeep & gold Rolex watches, pho booth, Kenzo's sword, Princess Bar window & support pillar (prev 3 destroyed), Dragonhead's limousine, sword & grenades, Thunderl (Raiden, drug made from super-refined hypothalamic fluid), motor pool umbrella & polishing cloth, Tyger's Ferrari, Baran's solid gold Merced Benzes (all but 1 bts), Archie's shotgun
SYNOPSIS: As Wolverine and Archie drink, a gang of Yakuza enter the Princess Bar and challenge Wolverine. Archie leaves quickly encounters Goro, who nearly beheads him until Reiko intercedes. At the palace, Dai-Kumo and Dr. Malheur explain that they can cure can using Madripoorian spider-monkeys' hypothalamic fluid, and seek Baran, Coy and Tyger's aid to harvest and process the endangered creatur Wolverine and the Yakuza fight a brutal battle that wrecks half the bar and pushes Wolverine's healing factor to its limit. Archie discovers that police have been bribed; at the palace, Dai-Kumo explains that he is having Patch killed in case he opposes him. Tyger declines Dai-Kum offer, not believing his cancer-cure story. When Dragonhead sees that his Yakuza soldiers are losing, he and his bodyguards ingest Thunderb the powerful amphetamine that Malheur truly creates from the monkeys' brains, and attack Wolverine savagely. Dragonhead tackles Wolver into the harbor holding grenades, but Wolverine feeds him to sharks and climbs to shore, exhausted.
NOTE: O'Donnell, jokingly noted here as owning the Princess Bar's destroyed half, is incorrectly spelled "O'Donnel" in this issue and next. N issue reveals that Dai-Kumo and his Yakuza outfit are from Osaka, Japan; it also reveals that Reiko serves Goro grudgingly to fulfill her fathe gambling debts, hence she is not listed as a Villain here. W #55, '92 reveals that Dai-Kumo secretly worked for the Hand. Seven and Elev each have a pair of dice tattooed on their forehead, showing a roll of 7 and 11 respectively. "Malheur" is French for "misfortune." Thunderbolt's name (Raiden the Thunderbolt) is a play on words; its users are said to be "riding the thunderbolt."

WOLVERINE #32 (October 1990)

"Terminal Trauma" (22 pages)

CREDITS: Larry Hama (writer), Marc Silvestri (pencils), Dan Green (inks), Pat Brosseau (letters), Glynis Oli (colors), Suzanne Gaffney (asst editor, uncredited), Bob Harras (editor)
FEATURE CHARACTER: Wolverine (also in photo & his own dreams)
SUPPORTING CAST: Archie Corrigan, Tyger Tiger
VILLAINS: General Coy (chr next bts in NThr #3, '93 fb, next bts in MCP #85, '91, next in MCP #86, '91), Malheur (also in photo), Goro, Dai-Kumo & his bodyguard, Coy's opium harvesters
OTHER CHARACTERS: Reiko, Tyger's enforcers (die) & underworld contacts (bts informing Tyger), Madrip native mountain tribesman & bystanders; Madripoorian spider-monkeys (die); Mongaku (blind seer, mention prophesied Goro's death); Marvel Girl, dragons inc Ryu (also as Dragonhead, Seven & Eleven) (prev 3 Wolverine's dreams); Kwannon ("Kwan-Yin," Buddhist goddess of mercy), spider (prev 2 as tattoos)
LOCATIONS/ITEMS: Tyger's Hightown penthouse, Madripoor's Central Highlands, Lowtown inc docks & Dai-Kumo's warehouse Dragonhead, Seven & Eleven's swords (in dream), Tyger's furniture (destroyed) & first aid supplies, Wolverine's bandages, harvesters' g nets, truck & gas grenade launcher, Malheur's caliper, Dai-Kumo's limousine, cellphone & seaplane, Goro's binoculars, camera, car w/pho & bouquet w/hidden sword, enforcers' knife & gun, Reiko's umbrella sword, monkeys' hypothalamic fluid, Tyger's Ferrari & Interpol paperwo
SYNOPSIS: Wolverine dreams of fighting Dragonhead, and awakens in Tyger's penthouse, still not fully healed. Coy's harvesters force native to find Madripoor's spider-monkeys, and use gas grenades to capture them. Goro calls Dai-Kumo to report that Wolverine still lives, a Dai-Kumo orders him to finish the job. Tyger and Archie leave the bedridden Wolverine to learn more about Dai-Kumo's operation. Goro a Reiko arrive, killing Tyger's enforcers; Goro stabs Wolverine through the chest and photographs his prone body. Near death, Wolverine drea of Marvel Girl exhorting him to pull the sword out; he does so just as Tyger and Archie return with Dai-Kumo's operation's location. Malh and Dai-Kumo discuss creating two drugs: Zap, a progressively-addictive drug that they will sell cheaply, and Thunderbolt, which is lethal produces an ultimate high, for which they will charge thousands per dose. Goro confirms Wolverine's death to Dai-Kumo, and they leave Japan. Wolverine arrives at their warehouse, finds thousands of dead monkeys, and prepares to follow Dai-Kumo.
NOTE: The series returns to monthly publication here. Wolverine has had feelings for former X-Men teammate Marvel Girl almost since joined the team. This issue establishes that Dai-Kumo's crew are based out of Osaka, Japan, and that Reiko is only serving Goro to help rep her father's gambling debt to him. O'Donnell's name is misspelled "O'Donnel" again. "Zap" stands for Zootoxic Acid Psychogalvanide, a d made from monkeys' hypothalamic fluid, cane sugar, vinegar and peanut shell fiber. Refining Zap creates Thunderbolt.

WOLVERINE #33 (November 1990)

"Grave Undertakings" (22 pages)

CREDITS: Larry Hama (writer), Marc Silvestri (pencils), Dan Green (inks), Pat Brosseau (letters), Glynis Oliver (colors), Suzanne Gaffney (asst editor), Bob Harras (editor)

FEATURE CHARACTER: Wolverine (also as "Logan W. Patch," also in his own dream, next in MCP #62-63, '90)

SUPPORTING CAST: Archie Corrigan, Tyger Tiger (both next in MCP #62, '90)

VILLAINS: Goro (also in Wolverine's dream, presumably dies, see NOTE), Dr. Malheur (dies), Dai-Kumo (dies, next in W #107, '96 fb) & his customs agents & party guests inc Yakuza gangsters (die, some next in W #107, '96 fb)

OTHER CHARACTERS: Reiko (next in W #55, '92), Tyger's smugglers (bts aiding Tyger), Dai-Kumo's gravediggers & servant; tigers (die), bats, wolf; Dragonhead, Seven, Eleven (prev 3 also as dragon), Marvel Girl (prev 4 in Wolverine's dream); spider (as wall scroll & tattoo)

LOCATIONS/ITEMS: Honshu, Japan: Kobe (bts), Osaka inc airport & Dai-Kumo's cemetery & mansion w/refining plant & animal pit / Wolverine's fin (destroyed) & bandages, agents' crowbar & gun, Tyger's car, forged landing permits (prev 2 bts), cargo manifest, curare drug & gun, Archie's otgun & Douglas DC-3 w/radio (bts), Dai-Kumo's van, Reiko's flower, car & umbrella sword, gravediggers' shovel, Thunderbolt (also in dream) w/ othalamic catalyst, Malheur's gun & refining equipment (some destroyed) inc catwalk w/control device, Dragonhead's sword (in dream), wolf's ge, Yakuza guns & swords, Goro's sword (also in dream)

NOPSIS: Osaka customs agents open a coffin containing Wolverine. Tyger gave him a death-simulating drug to smuggle him into Japan, Dai-Kumo arrives and claims the body, deciding to honor his foe by burying him in his private cemetery. Goro buries Wolverine and taunts iko, aware that she wanted Wolverine to kill him and release her from his service. At his mansion, Dai-Kumo and Dr. Malheur mix a large vat of underbolt. Wolverine awakens and claws out of the grave, startling the mourning Reiko. Dai-Kumo throws a party, demonstrating Thunderbolt drugging a wolf, which savagely kills tigers. Wolverine barges in; Dai-Kumo's gangsters attack but he plows through them and stares down wolf, which flees. Malheur tricks Wolverine into falling into the Thunderbolt vat, but Wolverine pulls Malheur with him, who overdoses and s while Wolverine is unaffected. Goro takes Thunderbolt and challenges Wolverine to battle, but Wolverine slashes Goro's legs and leaves to die. As Archie and Tyger arrive, Wolverine finds Dai-Kumo impaled by Reiko's sword.

OTE: Archie's company, South Seas Skyways, is called "South East Asia Airways" here. W #31-32, '90 establish that Goro believed in a phecy that only "a blade wielded by a dead man" could kill him, but although Wolverine spared him, Goro consumed the lethal Thunderbolt d presumably died shortly after the issue's end.

WOLVERINE #34 (December 1990)

"The Hunter in Darkness" (22 pages)

CREDITS: Larry Hama (writer), Marc Silvestri (pencils), Dan Green (inks), Pat Brosseau (letters), Glynis Oliver (colors), Suzanne Gaffney (asst editor), Bob Harras (editor)

FEATURE CHARACTER: Wolverine (also in rfb, also as Cpl. Logan in fb2 & fb4 between W #106, '96 fb & W #78, '94 fb; also in fb3 & fb1 between W #118, '97 fb & W #92, '95 fb; next in UXM #271, NM #96, XFac #61, UXM #272, NM #97, XFac #62, W:BI, all '90)

VILLAINS: Athabasca Ike (escaped murderer, also in photo, also in pfb, dies), 21st Panzergrenadier patrol (Nazi soldiers, in fb2 & fb4, some or all die, 1 possibly next in W #78, '94 fb) inc Oberleutnant

OTHER CHARACTERS: Hunter in Darkness ("He Who Stalks on Moonless Nights," predatory woodland creature, also in fb3 prior to issue, next bts in W #43, '91, next in W #45, '91), Sgt. Doolin (also in rfb, also in fb2 & fb4 prior to W #46, '91 fb; also in fb1 during W #46, '91 fb; next bts in W #46, '91 fb), Constable Morris (prev lberta Mounties, die), courtroom guard (dies), judge, Mr. & Mrs. Golightly (prev 2 dead) (prev 4 in pfb) & their daughter (also in pfb), 1st nadian Parachute Battalion (in fb2); fish (1 dies)

LOCATIONS/ITEMS: Alberta, Canada inc Wood Buffalo National Park (also in fb1 & fb3, see NOTE), Edmonton courthouse & Golightlys' Fort ipewyan home (prev 2 in pfb); Ranville, Normandy, France (in fb2 & fb4) / Wolverine's Fairbairn knife (in fb2 & fb4) & pack, Doolin's jeep (destroyed), e (also in fb1 & rfb), parachute (in fb2 & fb4), knife, lighter (prev 2 in fb2), ammo belt & flashlight, Morris' handgun (destroyed) & wanted poster, ard's handgun (in pfb), bear trap (in fb3) w/chain (destroyed, in fb1 & fb3), Ike's stolen jeep (bts, also bts in pfb), rope, knife, lighter & rifle w/scope, uglas C-47, battalion's rifles (all but 1 bts) & parachutes (prev 3 in fb2), Nazi knife (in fb4), flare & rifles w/bayonets (prev 3 in fb2 & fb4)

ASHBACKS: Doolin shoots Wolverine (this issue's fb1). Doolin shoots a feral Wolverine, thinking him to be the Hunter in Darkness (1). Cpl. gan's battalion, including Doolin, parachute into Normandy but get tangled in tree branches; Doolin lights his lighter and Nazis spot them (2). eral Wolverine frees the Hunter in Darkness from a bear trap, and leaves a false trail to confuse hunters (3). Cpl. Logan savagely kills Nazis h a knife (4). Athabasca Ike escapes from court, kills the Golightlys and kidnaps their daughter (p).

NOPSIS: As Wolverine hunts in Wood Buffalo park, Mounties Doolin and Morris warn him of Athabasca Ike's escape; Wolverine smells Ike the mountains and offers to help track him. Doolin and Morris discuss the mythical Hunter in Darkness who supposedly lives in the woods. , dragging his hostage, notices his pursuers and shoots Morris. Night falls and Wolverine begins sneaking up on Ike, but the Hunter attacks n. Doolin shines his flashlight on the battle, but Ike sees the light and shoots Doolin; fatally injured, he begins recalling his WWII experiences. then shoots the Hunter, but his hostage escapes. The wounded Hunter kills Ike, Wolverine recovers the hostage, and Doolin recalls his rporal's name as he dies: Logan.

OTE: The world learns that the X-Men are still alive in the "X-Tinction Agenda" crossover, occurring between this issue and next. Wolverine is found living ferally in Wood Buffalo National Park years before by James and Heather Hudson (later Alpha Flight's Guardian and Vindicator); CP #84, '91 reveals that he lived there after escaping the Weapon X Program. Wolverine looks at a scar on his chest when Doolin mentions ooting a creature years ago, but given his prodigious healing factor, it cannot be from that injury. The Battle of Normandy was fought from June September 1944; Logan's Canadian battalion was an element of the 6th British Airborne Division and parachuted into Normandy on "D-Day," ne 6, 1944. The Oberleutnant uses several German slang terms here: an Alte Hase ("old hare") is a seasoned trooper; Gruenschnabel reen beaks," new troops) and Landsers ("grunts," troopers) are both misspelled. Marc Silvestri's name is misspelled "Sivestri," Edmonton is sspelled "Edmunton," and Wood Buffalo National Park is incorrectly called Buffalo Woods State Park.

WOLVERINE: BLOODLUST (December 1990)

"Bloodlust" (48 pages)

CREDITS: Alan Davis (writer, pencils), Paul Neary (inks), Michael Heisler (letters), Bernie Jaye (colors), Suzan Gaffney (asst editor), Bob Harras (editor)
FEATURE CHARACTER: Wolverine (next in MFan #54/2-55/2, '90-91, FF #347-349, '90-91, SM&FF #3, ' MCP #64-71, '90-91, W #35, '91)
VILLAINS: Neuri renegades (cannibal mystics, die, 1 also as Saskia; all also in fb (some bts) prior to issue)
OTHER CHARACTERS: Neuri (peaceful Gaea-attuned race): survivors (also in fb prior to issue) inc Wolverin guide (dies), others (in fb, some die, 1 prior to Ex #46, '92 fb, see NOTE), their ancestors (in fb; see NOTE); Ga (Elder Goddess of Earth, bts granting Neuri power as "the great Earth-mother" in fb between Thor Ann #11, & Thor #300, '80 fb), renegades' victims: Axel DuBois, Nelson, Jeanette (prev 2 young couple) & their childr Siberians (in fb), brawlers inc Moose (prev 7 die), others (some bts, dead; others dead as bones); bank offici in fb); policemen (bts finding Axel's body), sheriff, bar patrons & bartender, Mongols, their victims (some die) (prev in fb); bear (bts, previously lived in cave); baby animals (as teddy bears & mobile)
LOCATIONS/ITEMS: Dawson City, Yukon, Canada inc Yukon Mudslide Bar, Nelson & Jeanette's cabin & nearby woods w/Saskia's ca (destroyed); Alshra (spiritual plane); Russia's Ural Mountains inc Neuri's valley home, Siberia inc factories, research outpost & Neu underground home (prev 2 destroyed), outer space (prev 7 in fb) / Mongols' swords, shields, axes & spear, victims' swords & shield, Ne ancestors' packs & walking sticks, research station Sno-Cat (all in fb), Wolverine's beer glass (destroyed) & pack, bar table, whiskey bottle (pr 2 destroyed), sheriff's cruiser, brawlers' rifles, bear spoor (bts)
FLASHBACK: A millennium ago, the peaceful Neuri achieve harmony with Gaea and become empowered. Encroaching barbarians force the to migrate north, transforming themselves into Yeti-like creatures and making a home in the Siberian ice. Over time, they evolve a group mind a psychically explore space, but human development damages their home. Angry, some Neuri begin murdering humans and learning dark mag
SYNOPSIS: In the Yukon, Wolverine telepathically experiences a renegade Neuri killing a man. Unsettled, he starts a bar brawl but finds bloodlust artificially heightened. He befriends a young woman named Saskia, but renegade Neuri attack, and although Wolverine kills son the others vanish with Saskia. Wolverine struggles for control of his heightened murderous urges as the bar brawlers pursue him, believ him a killer. The renegades murder a family, which Wolverine again experiences telepathically. Several peaceful Neuri approach, transport Wolverine to the calming Alshra spirit plane. Wolverine agrees to help stop the renegades and a guide accompanies him. The renegades atta the brawlers but Wolverine intercedes. He fights a brutal battle, killing all but one, but is badly injured; the guide heals him. The final renega slaughters the brawlers and harnesses the Alshra's energies, mystically attacking Wolverine and killing the guide. Wolverine pursues renegade to a cave, where he finds a frightened Saskia. Straining to sense the renegade, Wolverine realizes Saskia has no scent and atta her. She reveals herself as the renegade and battles Wolverine, who kills her. The Neuri thank Wolverine and return to their damaged home
NOTE: This issue's indicia reads "Wolverine Annual #2 — Bloodlust." Marvel considered W:Jun, '90 to be "Annual #1," though it was not labe as such. Ex #46, '92 fb reveals that a Neuri from this issue's fb was captured by gypsies 70 years ago; he appears next bts in Ex #44, '91 a next in Ex #46, '92. MCP #108, '92 reveals that some of the Neuri's ancestors split from the group over a millennium ago and settled n Winzeldorf, Germany. They did not adapt their bodies to the Siberian cold; their descendants resembled pale, veiny vampires. This offshoot ra appears chr last in UO #8, '97 and next in MCP #101, '92.

WOLVERINE #35 (January 1991)

"Blood, Sand and Claws!" (22 pages)

CREDITS: Larry Hama (writer), Marc Silvestri (pencils), Dan Green (inks), Pat Brosseau (letters), Glynis Oli (colors), Suzanne Gaffney (asst editor), Bob Harras (editor)
FEATURE CHARACTER: Wolverine (also as "Logan W. Patch" on monitor)
GUEST STAR: Puck (Eugene Judd, diminutive Alpha Flight acrobat, also in photo, last in AFlt #91, '90; a inhabiting his past self, last in chr 1st app)
SUPPORTING CAST: Tyger Tiger (also on monitor, last in MCP #63, '90, next in MCP #85, '91)
VILLAINS: Reavers (anti-mutant cyborgs): Donald Pierce (Hellfire Club's former White Bishop, also on monite Lady Deathstrike (Yuriko Oyama, Adamantium-taloned samurai), Pretty Boy (mind-manipulating eye filamer chr next voice only in W/Pun #1, '93, next in UXM #281, '91), Bonebreaker (tank-like lower body) (all last in U) #269, '90); Legion Kondor (Nazi unit assigned to Spain) inc Hauptmann Horst Schlachter (1st), recon pa (dead) & Stuka pilots (1 dies, others bts in planes)
OTHER CHARACTERS: Gateway (last in FF Ann #24, '91), Ernest Hemingway (war correspondent, as "Ernesto"), Inez (partisan revolution 1st) (prev 2 also in photo), Bambi Bolinsky (bouncer), Akira, Tetsuo (prev 2 Japanese police, die), Jade-Faced Lum, Three-Finger Fat (prev Tyger's bodyguards), Maera (bullfighter, dies), Freight-Train (roughneck) & his friends, Alpha Flight employee (bts giving Puck's location), patrons & bartender, casino patrons & employees inc waitress & maitre d', bullfighting audience (some die) inc Loyalist soldiers (some or oth also in photo); flies, bull (prev 2 die), birds; Bambi's attackers, Inez's partisan rebels (prev 2 mentioned), Pablo Picasso, Gertrude Stein, Alice Toklas (prev 3 mentioned as being in Paris)
LOCATIONS/ITEMS: Canada: Alpha Flight's temporary Ottawa, Ontario base (bts), Vancouver, British Columbia inc harbor (also in photo Gastown Bar; Guernica, Spain inc bullfighting ring (also in photo); Dai-Kumo's Osaka mansion w/refining plant, Reavers' Australian outback H Hightown casino / Bambi's cast, knife & sugar, police car w/computer & radio, Akira's handgun & flashlight, refining tank (destroyed), Reave cybernetic implants (hereinafter considered their standard equipment and not listed separately) inc Deathstrike's Adamantium finger-talo roughnecks' chainsaw, axe & crowbar, Gateway's bull-roarer, Pretty Boy's rifle, Tyger's dice & postcard, bodyguards' guns, Puck's rowbo fishing pole, novel, photo, cape & sword, Hemingway's car, Legion Kondor's recon car (destroyed), binoculars, half-track, rifles & Stuka di bombers (1 destroyed) w/bombs (1 dies) & machine guns
SYNOPSIS: Wolverine visits his old Alpha Flight friend Puck, who is temporarily working as a Vancouver bouncer. In Osaka, Lady Deathstr follows Wolverine's trail, learning from a police computer that he was recently in Madripoor. Forcing Gateway to teleport her there, she mak Tyger Tiger reveal Wolverine's current location. Puck and Wolverine reminisce; as Puck shows Wolverine a photo of himself with Ern Hemingway in 1937 Guernica, Deathstrike orders Gateway to transport her to the location Wolverine is looking at. Gateway generates a cyclo

e vortex, throwing Deathstrike, Wolverine and Puck back to the Spanish Civil War, reuniting them with Hemingway and partisan fighter Inez. Puck discovers that he is back to his full height, Nazi planes bomb Guernica. Wolverine downs a Stuka with a bullfighters' sword, and he, ck, Inez and Hemingway drive off to rendezvous with Inez's rebels. Deathstrike, having killed a Nazi recon unit, watches them go — but uptmann Schlachter arrives, sees her handiwork and orders her killed.

TE: Cover-labeled "Blood and Claws!" Puck's body hosted the demonic Black Raazer for decades, slowing his aging but transforming him o a dwarf. Lady Deathstrike hates Wolverine, believing that his Adamantium bones resulted from a process her father invented, which was len years before. Working unwillingly for the Reavers, Gateway is not considered a Villain; UXM #269, '90 revealed that he is compelled to ve the town's residents. W #36-37, '91 imply that while Wolverine and Deathstrike physically went back in time, Puck's spirit inhabited his past f's body. Wolverine knows Inez, but does not recall how; his memory alterations may be to blame. Apparently he had already met Hemingway d Inez by 1937; they are on first-name terms with him here. In the real world, Legion Kondor bombed Guernica on April 26, 1937, although lfram Freiherr von Richthofen led its ground troops. Schlachter gives his rank as "Kaptain" here, a bastardized translation of Hauptmann. icemen Akira and Tetsuo are named after characters from the anime "Akira." Archie Corrigan's company, South Seas Skyways, is again led "South East Asia Airways" here.

WOLVERINE #36 (February 1991)

"…It Tolls For Thee!" (22 pages)

CREDITS: Larry Hama (writer), Marc Silvestri (pencils), Dan Green (inks), Pat Brosseau (letters), Mark Chiarello (colors), Suzanne Gaffney (asst editor), Bob Harras (editor), Josef Rubinstein (c inks)
FEATURE CHARACTER: Wolverine
GUEST STAR: Puck (inhabiting his past self)
VILLAINS: Reavers: Murray Reese (former Hellfire Club soldier, last in UXM #269, '90, next in W #38, '91), Bonebreaker, Lady Deathstrike, Donald Pierce; Legion Kondor (some die) inc Hauptmann Horst Schlachter, Oberfeldwebel, recon pilot (dies) & Stuka pilots (bts in planes), Falangist soldiers (Spanish fascists, some die) inc their Nazi Hauptmann (dies) & Guardia Civil: Jaime, others (bts battling rebels, die)
OTHER CHARACTERS: Gateway (next in UXM #281, '91), Ernest Hemingway (as "Ernesto"), Inez & her partisan rebels: Eric "Ricky" Blair (American writer, also as "Enrico," see NOTE), Vicente, others (bts, dead in ves); Guernica victims (dead); Kenji Oyama (Deathstrike's father), US navy soldiers (bts on aircraft carrier) (prev 2 in rfb); birds (1 dies), rses (die); Jaime's sisters, Spanish Republican Army (prev 2 mentioned)
CATIONS/ITEMS: Guernica, Spain inc cantina (destroyed), railroad bridge (bts) & nearby mountains inc partisans' camp & Eroica mountain ss; Reavers' Australian outback HQ, Pacific Ocean (in rfb) / Hemingway's car (destroyed) inc toolkit w/wrench & ball-peen hammer, Inez's guns, angists' roadblock (destroyed), guns (some bts) & machine gun (destroyed) w/firing pin (bts), ammo belt & tripod, Legion Kondor's Stuka dive-mbers, fencing wire, rifles, grenades, half-track w/radio & Messerschmitt (destroyed) w/radio & bomb, Pierce's money, partisans' blasting caps s), guns & shovels, horses' hobbles (bts), Puck's bandages & makeshift litter; Kenji's Zero aircraft (destroyed), US aircraft carrier (prev 2 in rfb)
ASHBACK: WWII kamikaze pilot Kenji Oyama flies toward a US aircraft carrier (AFlt #34, '86 fb), and crashes on its deck (DD #197, '83 fb).
NOPSIS: Wolverine, Puck, Inez and Hemingway battle Falangist fascists as they escape Guernica; Wolverine captures a large machine n. Elsewhere, Lady Deathstrike resists Legion Kondor's efforts to hang her, and allies herself with Schlachter. A time vortex manifests in the sent, and Pierce realizes that Deathstrike is tampering with the past. Wolverine and the others reach Inez's partisan rebel base, but find that arly everyone has been killed in battle; the two survivors have taken a teenage boy prisoner. Deathstrike convinces Schlachter to help her kill lverine; a Legion Kondor recon aircraft locates and bombs the partisans' base, grievously injuring Puck. Wolverine shoots the plane down, d they decide to take Puck through a mountain pass to a partisan hospital. Their prisoner swears not to reveal their route and they let him go, Deathstrike captures the boy and forces the information from him. As Legion Kondor attacks the pass, Wolverine stays behind to cover the ers' escape, donning his costume and attacking the Nazis.
TE: Cover-labeled "Blood and Claws! Part II." This issue's title, part of a John Donne quote, refers to the Hemingway novel *For Whom the ll Tolls*, which took its name from the same quote. The novel, about a young American in the Spanish Civil War, is based on Hemingway's n experiences. As in Hemingway's novel, some characters here use the archaic pronouns "thou" and "thee." Rebel Eric Blair is better known George Orwell; Wolverine calls him "George" once here. Murray Reese is one of three Hellfire Club soldiers badly injured by Wolverine in #133, '80. The soldiers' first and last names were revealed piecemeal over the years; OMIX #3, '94 clarified which names belong to whom.

WOLVERINE #37 (March 1991)

"Fall Back & Spring Forward" (22 pages)

CREDITS: Larry Hama (writer), Marc Silvestri (pencils), Dan Green (inks), Pat Brosseau (letters), Glynis Oliver (colors), Suzanne Gaffney (asst editor), Bob Harras (editor)
FEATURE CHARACTER: Wolverine (also in photo, next in X Ann #15/4, UXM #273-277, all '91, MTU #19, '06, W/Pun #1-3, '93; UXM #278-279, XFac #69, UXM #280, XFac #70, all '91, W:Saud, '06 fb; DC #4, NF:AoS #25-29, Av #332-333, W #44 fb, all '91)
GUEST STARS: Puck (also in photo, next in AFlt #94, '91; also inhabiting his past self, chr next in AFlt #32, '86 fb), Energizer (Katie Power, pre-teen Power Pack member, during UXM #205, '86)
VILLAINS: Reavers: Lady Deathstrike (also her past self, chr last in AFlt #34, '86, chr next in UXM #205, '86), Bonebreaker, Donald Pierce; Murray Reese (chr last in MGN #4, '83), Spiral ("Ricochet" Rita Wayword, Mojo's six-armed sorceress, chr last in Ls #6, '86) (prev 2 chr next in UXM #205, '86), Elsie-Dee (android little girl, 1st), rce's Wolverine android (1st), Legion Kondor (some die) inc Hauptmann Horst Schlachter (dies) & Hegel (see NOTE), Falangists (die), Kenji ama (bts in plane in scene from AFlt #34, '86 fb & DD #197, '83 fb)
HER CHARACTERS: Ernest Hemingway (as "Ernesto"), Inez (prev 2 also in photo), Eric Blair (as "Enrico"), Vicente, US Navy soldiers (in ene from AFlt #34, '86 fb & DD #197, '83 fb), bystanders (in scene from UXM #205, '86); birds (others in past); Loyalist soldiers (in photo); enage Mutant Ninja Turtles (mentioned, see NOTE)
CATIONS/ITEMS: Guernica, Spain inc bullfighting ring (in photo) & nearby Eroica mountain pass; Reavers' Australian outback HQ, Pacific ean, Body Shoppe (Spiral's workshop), Vancouver Harbor, Manhattan inc South Street Seaport, construction site & East River / Falangists'

guns, Legion Kondor's half-track (destroyed) w/radio (bts) & rifles (some destroyed) w/bayonets, Schlachter's binoculars, map & hat, Puc
rowboat, book, photo, bandages & makeshift litter, Pierce's android creation equipment & computer w/printout, Kenji's Zero aircraft (destroye
US aircraft carrier w/planes, Spiral's nutrient-bath tank (destroyed & restored)

SYNOPSIS: Wolverine defeats Legion Kondor's men, and Lady Deathstrike attacks him as another time vortex appears. Unable to see throu
the fog, Schlachter drives closer, accidentally running over Deathstrike's bionic arm. Enraged, she stabs Schlachter and the vortex becom
a whirlwind. In the present, Schlachter's hat blows out of the vortex; Pierce runs a computer search, learning that Schlachter was suppose
have lived six more years. Distracted, Bonebreaker fails to halt a logic program installation in Pierce's android project. In the past, Puck recov
and leaps into the vortex with Wolverine and Deathstrike. The three tumble through time, seeing Deathstrike's father's failed kamikaze attem
her cyborg transformation and her previous battle with Wolverine. Puck and Wolverine arrive back in the present; Puck recalls nothing of
adventure, and is confused to see that his 1937 photo now includes Wolverine. Deathstrike arrives back at the Reavers' base, where Pie
debuts two androids: one resembling a little girl, the other a duplicate of Wolverine.

NOTE: Cover-labeled "Blood and Claws: the Conclusion!" Inez notes feeling the earth move during a tremor, a reference to *For Whom the E
Tolls'* well-known line "did they feel the earth move?" Although some soldiers survive Wolverine and Deathstrike's attacks, Pierce learns t
they all died in an avalanche at Eroica; presumably it occurred shortly after Wolverine and Deathstrike depart. Pierce notes that Deathstrik
temporal meddling erased the fifth Teenage Mutant Ninja Turtle from history. It is unclear when the altered photo was taken, as Wolverine a
Puck had no opportunity to pose for it in 1937. The fact that Spiral is a future version of Ricochet Rita, a supporting character from the Ls, '85
series, is revealed in XFac Ann #7, '92; Rita's last name is revealed in OHMU #10, '06.

WOLVERINE #38 (April 1991)

"See Venice & Die!" (22 pages)

CREDITS: Larry Hama (writer), Marc Silvestri (pencils), Dan Green (inks), Pat Brosseau (letters), Glynis Oli
(colors), Suzanne Gaffney (asst editor), Bob Harras (editor)
FEATURE CHARACTER: Wolverine
GUEST STAR: Storm (last in DC #4, '91)
VILLAINS: Reavers: Bonebreaker, Lady Deathstrike, Donald Pierce, Murray Reese; Pierce's Wolverine andr
(becomes Albert, also in photo & pfb), Elsie-Dee (also in diagram & pfb), Molokai, Reno (prev 2 Jocko & Sal
enforcers, 1st but chr last in W #73, '93 fb), Jocko, Sally (prev 2 crooked betting parlor owners) & their employe
(some in pfb) inc Duffy (bts, attacked by Storm) & Lumpy
OTHER CHARACTERS: Travelers inc Bunny & Cyndi, betting parlor patrons inc Cloris, football players
TV), vagrants, bystanders; birds; Molokai's cousin (mentioned, frozen yogurt salesman), cigar-smoking wom
(mentioned, mistaken for Wolverine); Silver Surfer, models (prev 2 as paintings)
LOCATIONS/ITEMS: California: Stockton rest stop (bts), Los Angeles inc Jocko & Sally's betting parlors (Santa Monica Boulevard, Hollywc
Hills (prev 2 destroyed), 1 in fb, others bts), Radio Hut stores (bts), bus station, freeway & Venice Beach w/Boulevard, boardwalk & warehou
Reavers' Australian outback HQ / Elsie-Dee's bag (also in pfb), security camera (bts in pfb), employee's gun (in pfb), Jocko & Sally's mo
(some in pfb), guns, flyers, TVs, VCR, videotape (bts), transmitters (all but 1 bts), tracking device w/headphones & car w/carphone, Sal
toupee & pretzel bowl, bus station pay phone, Wolverine's bus, Reno's crowbar & machine gun, Lumpy's gun, Molokai's Mercury (pa
destroyed) & machine gun, Elsie-Dee's computer equipment (bts) inc modem & circuit boards, monitor, tools, blowtorch & Corvette w/train
blocks (bts), Pierce's monitor, Deathstrike's healing tank & replacement bionic arm, Bunny & Cyndi's surfboards, Radio Hut computer manu
Duffy's gun, Albert's sensors & infrared dampers (prev 4 bts), paintings (destroyed)
FLASHBACK: Elsie-Dee and the Wolverine android rob a betting parlor (p).
SYNOPSIS: Storm confronts LA crooks Jocko and Sally, who are offering $10,000 for Wolverine's capture, and learns that he is appare
robbing their betting parlors. At the bus station, Wolverine lets enforcers Molokai and Reno capture him. Pierce's Wolverine android robs anot
parlor; Jocko and Sally track him with a hidden transmitter as Reno and Molokai arrive. Hearing that his double is in Venice Beach, Wolver
frees himself and steals Molokai's car. In Australia, Pierce explains that the double will draw Wolverine's attention, while Elsie-Dee, made enti
of plastic explosive, will kill him — but Bonebreaker worries that he accidentally made her too intelligent. Elsie-Dee upgrades the andre
naming him Albert; he now hopes to kill Wolverine so that she won't have to blow herself up. Wolverine arrives at Venice Beach, followed
Storm, Jocko, Sally and their enforcers. Albert attacks but Wolverine disembowels him, while Storm swamps the goons with a tidal wave. Sett
a warehouse on fire, Elsie-Dee calls to Wolverine for help…
NOTE: Elsie-Dee's name is a pun; it sounds like "LCD," or liquid crystal display. Elsie-Dee names Albert after scientist Albert Einstein. Albe
claws make a "snekt" sound effect, instead of Wolverine's standard "snikt."

WOLVERINE #39 (May 1991)

"Deconstruction" (22 pages)

CREDITS: Larry Hama (writer), Marc Silvestri (pencils), Dan Green (inks), Pat Brosseau (letters), Mark Chiar
(colors), Suzanne Gaffney (asst editor), Bob Harras (editor)
FEATURE CHARACTER: Wolverine
GUEST STAR: Storm
VILLAINS: Reavers: Donald Pierce, Murray Reese (both chr next in W/Pun #1, '93), Bonebreaker (chr next v
only in W/Pun #1, '93) (all next in UXM #281, '91), Lady Deathstrike (next in W #43, '91); Albert, Elsie-Dee, Joc
Sally, Molokai, Reno
OTHER CHARACTERS: Bunny, Cyndi, reporters inc Cindy Cates (News 57 reporter), Radio Hut employ
NSA employees, FBI agents, police inc Lieutenant, bystanders; rabbit (dies), birds, swans, ducks
LOCATIONS/ITEMS: Venice Beach, California inc warehouse (partly destroyed), boardwalk, canals & Ra
Hut; Australian house, Maryland: Fort Holabird (bts, see NOTE), NSA's underground bunker / pottery, flammable waste (prev 2 destroye
Elsie-Dee's blowtorch & detonation circuit (bts) w/proximity fuse, Deathstrike's replacement bionic arm, NSA's Cray computers & printout, F
Holabird's security system (bts), Jocko & Sally's guns & car (partly destroyed), Albert's laser scanner & thumb modem, Radio Hut's compu

…nuals, computers (1 w/modem) & printers w/printouts, Cindy's microphone, reporters' cameras & police band radio, police cars & guns, NSA …nsor (bts) & guns

NOPSIS: Storm reminds Wolverine that Albert had a little girl accomplice, but Wolverine enters the burning warehouse to save her anyway. … walks through fire to reach Elsie-Dee; deeply touched that Wolverine would go through such pain for her, she concentrates and overrides … detonation circuit. In Australia, Bonebreaker tries to tell Pierce about his mistake, but reconsiders out of fear. On the boardwalk, Albert limps …ay, encountering and befriending Jocko and Sally. Elsie-Dee reveals that she's a living bomb and warns Wolverine to flee. Believing that she … …more than just a construct, Wolverine refuses, but Elsie-Dee's concentration slips and the explosion countdown begins. At a Radio Hut, Albert …ed-reads computer manuals and hacks into the NSA's computers, trying to break Elsie-Dee's countdown code. Ignoring Storm's protests, …lverine encourages Elsie-Dee not to give up. Albert cracks the code as police and FBI surround the Radio Hut. He transmits it to Elsie-Dee, …using her countdown at one second, just as they open fire, tearing Albert apart.

…TE: Page 15 is incorrectly run out of sequence between pages 11-12. Although an NSA employee here references a backup security system …Fort Holabird, that base closed in 1973.

WOLVERINE #40 (June 1991)

"Reconstruction" (22 pages)

CREDITS: Larry Hama (writer), Marc Silvestri (pencils), Dan Green (inks), Pat Brosseau (letters), Glynis Oliver (colors), Suzanne Gaffney (asst editor), Bob Harras (editor), Josef Rubinstein (c inks)
FEATURE CHARACTER: Wolverine
GUEST STARS: X-Men: Forge (mutant inventor, last in XFac #70, '91), Storm (next in Dlk #4, '91)
SUPPORTING CAST: Jubilee (Jubilation Lee, animates exploding plasmoids, last in DC #4, '91), Elsie-Dee (also in diagram)
VILLAINS: Jocko, Sally, Molokai, Reno (all next in W #74, '93), Albert
OTHER CHARACTERS: Air Force military police, fighter pilots, security guards inc Murray & their Pentagon superior (bts on phone), FBI agents, Venice police, diner patrons, cook & waitress, pool hall patrons, cabbies, reporter (on TV), bystanders

…CATIONS/ITEMS: Westchester, New York inc diner & X-Mansion underground complex; New York City: Bronx pool hall, Manhattan inc East …le Highway, East River & World Trade Center roof; California: Venice police station w/cells & property room, Palmdale's Air Force Plant 42 w/ …rthrop hangar; news studio (on TV); skies over Chicago, Illinois & Elizabeth, New Jersey / Forge's prosthetic hand & leg (prev 2 hereinafter …nsidered his standard equipment and not listed separately), scanners & car, confiscated objects (incorporated into Albert) inc Blaupunkt radio, …apons (prev 2 bts), electronics, handcuffs & Kevlar vests, Albert's satellite (bts), needle & thread, police & FBI guns, cell door (destroyed), …ie-Dee's motor oil, Wolverine's motorcycle & money, diner TV, B-2 stealth bomber (also in photo, destroyed) w/umbilicals, targeting systems, …ar & ejection seat, pool hall wiring system (bts), electrical outlet, cues, balls, soda machine & TV, taxis, 747 airplane (bts), Air Force security …mputers (bts), electrified fence (destroyed), guns, vehicles & F-16 fighters w/radios, radar (prev 2 bts), Vulcan cannons & heat-seeking missile

NOPSIS: At the X-Mansion, Forge determines that Elsie-Dee is highly explosive, and that her countdown is only paused, not stopped. In …nice, police find Albert rebuilding himself from property room objects. They flee, and Albert releases Jocko, Sally and their enforcers from …tody, then steals an Air Force stealth bomber, still planning to kill Wolverine to free Elsie-Dee from exploding. As Wolverine, Forge, Jubilee …d Elsie-Dee relax at a pool hall, Elsie-Dee receives a weak transmission from Albert, and has Wolverine take her somewhere with better …eption — the World Trade Center roof. The Pentagon scrambles jets to intercept Albert, but they cannot detect the bomber. Closing on …nhattan, Albert activates the bomber's targeting system, making him visible to radar, and slams into Wolverine as he flies past the tower. …ting his way inside, Wolverine battles Albert until Elsie-Dee explains that her detonation sequence is paused. Albert realizes that he is free …: as the jets shoot down the bomber, which crashes in the East River.

…TE: Albert seems unaware that Elsie-Dee's countdown was paused, even though he helped pause it last issue; the police assault may …ve damaged his memory. Having decided not to kill Wolverine, Elsie-Dee is no longer listed as a Villain; similarly, Albert will leave the Villain …egory next issue. Although Jubilee is an X-Man, who are normally Guest Stars, she has been Wolverine's unofficial sidekick since UXM #252, …: as such, she is listed under Supporting Cast. Air Force military police, who wear blue berets, are incorrectly colored with green berets here.

WOLVERINE #41 (Early July 1991)

"Down in the Bottoms" (18 pages)

CREDITS: Larry Hama (writer), Marc Silvestri (pencils), Dan Green (inks), Pat Brosseau (letters), Glynis Oliver (colors), Suzanne Gaffney (asst editor), Bob Harras (editor)
FEATURE CHARACTER: Wolverine (also in fb1 between W:O #5, '06 fb & W #50, '07 fb; also in fb2/implant between W #10, '89 fb & W #48, '91 fb)
GUEST STARS: Cable (Nathan Summers, X-Force's leader, last in XFac Ann #6, '91), Nick Fury (bts, called in by Forge, last in Av #333, '91, chr last in Pun/Cap #2, '92), Forge
SUPPORTING CAST: Silver Fox (seemingly dead, in fb1 between W:O #5, '06 fb & W #50, '07 fb), Albert, Elsie-Dee, Jubilee
…LAINS: Sabretooth (also in fb2/implant between W #10, '89 fb & W #48, '91 fb bts), Vole (bts in fb2/implant between W #10, '89 fb bts & W …, '91 fb bts)
…HER CHARACTERS: Masque (flesh-altering Morlock leader, last in NM #100, '91), Morlocks (sewer-dwelling mutants, some or others last …NM #100, '91), Mount Logan bar patrons (possibly disguised Weapon X agents, all but 1 bts, in fb2/implant during & also in W #10, '89 fb), …ce, bystanders; fish (1 dies), albino alligators (some dead), rats, insects
…CATIONS/ITEMS: Manhattan inc dock (bts), East River & sewer tunnels inc Grate 23 (mentioned) & South Street outlet, Morlock tunnels …Alley (large central tunnel) & Valve Room #5; Mount Logan (in fb1); Weapon X Program's Windsor warehouse (in fb2) / B-2 stealth bomber …ckage w/ejection seat, police boat & blankets, grate bars (some destroyed), Jubilee's umbrella, phone booth, Morlock pipe & grate controls, …oon stage set, props inc cake slice (prev 3 in fb2), Cable's guns, sewer debris (bts), door lock

FLASHBACKS: Wolverine carries Silver Fox's body to the saloon (1). In an implanted memory, Sabretooth taunts Wolverine and a wom implies that the two men are related (2).

SYNOPSIS: Forge and Jubilee swim down to the bomber wreckage, but find only a missing ejection seat and Albert's inert form. As a lar rainstorm breaks, Elsie-Dee drags a badly injured Wolverine into the storm drains for cover. She leaves him behind to get help, and Wolveri hallucinates about Silver Fox's death. Elsie-Dee passes an unconscious Sabretooth, who awakens; aboveground, Forge calls in a favor. T Morlock tunnels begin flooding, and Masque orders all the water vented into the storm drains. In the tunnels, Sabretooth attacks Wolveri proclaiming himself to be his father, which Wolverine refuses to believe. Elsie-Dee runs into Cable, who has entered the tunnels searching Sabretooth. Fleeing vermin interrupt Wolverine and Sabretooth's fight, followed by a rushing wall of water. Wolverine crawls into a side-tunn but finds the other exit blocked. Sabretooth follows him in just as Masque closes the grates, sealing them both in; their fight continues as water rises. In the East River, Albert awakens…

NOTE: This issue also has a 2-page "Wolverine Gallery" centerspread pin-up by Mike Mignola featuring Wolverine and Cable, a 1-pa "Wolverine Gallery" pin-up by Art Thibert featuring Wolverine and Sabretooth, and a 1-panel letters-page preview of W:RT, '91. The series beg biweekly publication again here. The Morlock Caliban broke Sabretooth's back in NM #91, '90. Next issue clarifies that Sabretooth is not actua Wolverine's father. W #50, '92 reveals that parts of this issue's flashback are memory implants, presumably including the woman's implicati Cable was revealed as a time-traveling adult version of Cyclops' son Nathan Summers in Cable #6-8, '93-94. Page 17 has a note for the colo in the margin: "underwater." This issue also has a 2nd printing with a gold cover.

WOLVERINE #42 (Late July 1991)

"Papa Was a Rolling Stone!" (20 pages)

CREDITS: Larry Hama (writer), Marc Silvestri (breakdowns), Dan Gre (finishes), Pat Brosseau (letters), Glynis Oliver (colors), Suzanne Gaffney (a editor), Bob Harras (editor)
FEATURE CHARACTER: Wolverine
GUEST STARS: Cable, Forge, Nick Fury
SUPPORTING CAST: Albert, Elsie-Dee, Jubilee
VILLAIN: Sabretooth
OTHER CHARACTERS: Masque, Morlocks, SHIELD agents (some or oth last in NF:AoS #27, '91) inc pilot (voice only) & corpsman, bystanders
LOCATIONS/ITEMS: Manhattan inc East River & sewer tunnels inc Grate (destroyed) & main causeway, Morlocks' Valve Room #5 / Cable's guns (1 destroyed), door lock (destroyed), sewer debris, Morlock pipe & gra controls, grate self-cleaning mechanism (destroyed), Elsie-Dee's auxiliary batteries (bts) & plastic-explosive body (destroyed) w/detonat circuit (bts), SHIELD emergency rescue helicopter w/infrared scanner, tetanus booster shots (prev 2 bts), computer & medical equipment needles, Sabretooth's restraints (destroyed) & Valium sedative (bts), Fury's gun & cigars, B-2 stealth bomber wreckage

SYNOPSIS: Wolverine and Sabretooth battle viciously as the tunnel floods. Cable and Elsie-Dee hear their battle through a door; Ca refuses to risk drowning by opening it, so Elsie-Dee bites his leg, steals his gun and blasts the door open. The escaping water carries all f downstream until they hit a grate blocked by debris. Elsewhere, Masque activates the grate's self-cleaning mechanism, which begins crush the debris — and the four combatants. Elsie-Dee climbs onto the mechanism, removes her head and detonates her body, destroying the gra Everyone tumbles into the East River, where a helicopter summoned by Forge's contact, Nick Fury, rescues them. Elsie-Dee's head reveals t her backup batteries are failing. Sabretooth breaks loose and attacks Wolverine again, but Elsie-Dee's head bites his neck and the two tum out of the helicopter. Blood tests reveal that Sabretooth is not really Wolverine's father, and Nick Fury implies that he knows why Sabreto believes he is. In the river, Albert drives Sabretooth off and rescues Elsie-Dee's head.

NOTE: This issue also has a 1-panel letters-page preview of W:RT, '91. W #46, '91 reveals that Sabretooth thinks he is Wolverine's father c to memory alterations. Sabretooth's costume and hair are reddish-pink on p.6, the result of a color-plate printing error. SHIELD changed meaning of its acronym to "Strategic Hazard Intervention Espionage Logistics Directorate" in NF:AoS #7, '90. This issue also has a 2nd print with a gold cover.

WOLVERINE #43 (Early August 1991)

"Under the Skin" (19 pages)

CREDITS: Larry Hama (writer), Marc Silvestri (breakdowns, c art), Dan Green (finishes), Pat Brosseau (lette Steve Buccellato (colors), Suzanne Gaffney (asst editor), Bob Harras (editor)
FEATURE CHARACTER: Wolverine
GUEST STARS: Cable (next in Q #28, '91 fb), Forge (next in Dlk #2, '91), Nick Fury (next in Av #337, '91)
SUPPORTING CAST: Albert, Elsie-Dee, Jubilee (all next in W #45, '91)
VILLAINS: Lady Deathstrike (last in W #38, '91), Sabretooth (both next in W #45, '91), Linus Dorfman (ment ill sadist, as zoo janitor, next bts in W #89, '95, next in W #90, '95 bts)
OTHER CHARACTERS: Hunter in Darkness (bts, captured by Parvenue & Tabeshaw, also on billboard & photo, in W #34, '90), Ronald Parvenue (1st bts, advertising Hunter in Darkness, also in photo), Masque (all next in W #45, '91 Morlocks (others next in W #45, '91), Harry Tabeshaw (bts, unnamed, tracked Hunter for Parvenue, next in W #48, '9 SHIELD agents (some or others next bts in Av #337, '91, next in InfG #3, '91) inc corpsman, zoo janitor (dead), prostitute, limo driver (voice only); wolve (next bts in W #89, '95), squirrel, lions, seals, tigers; Linus' therapists (mentioned), hamsters (mentioned, killed by Linus); models (on billboards)
LOCATIONS/ITEMS: Manhattan inc Times Square, Brooklyn Bridge, East River, sewer tunnels inc Grate 23 & Central Park inc Zoo; Atlan City, New Jersey's Parvenue Casino (mentioned) / Wolverine's bandages, SHIELD emergency rescue helicopter, agent's coat, Fury's gu cigar, prostitute's lighter, Parvenue's billboard, Hunter in Darkness' chains (on billboard & photo), grate wreckage, Elsie-Dee's dress scr animals' cages w/lock (destroyed), Linus' gun (destroyed), stolen uniform, trash barrel, knife & steak, Deathstrike's limousine & newspaper

SYNOPSIS: Angered that Nick Fury won't reveal Sabretooth's connection to him, Wolverine demands to be let out of the helicopter. leaps down onto a Times Square rooftop, not seeing a billboard advertising a large captive creature. As Masque and two Morlocks sur the destroyed sewer grate, Albert arrives and intimidates Masque into aiding him; he plans to build Elsie-Dee a new body. Wolverine blows

am in Central Park, but hears animals howling. Following the sounds to the Central Park Zoo, closed for the night, he discovers a bleeding Wolverine and a deranged lunatic, Linus, who had been impersonating a janitor and tormenting the animals. Linus pulls a gun, but Wolverine blocks the barrel with a claw and it explodes. Wolverine finds the real janitor's body in Linus' trash barrel, and frees the wolverine from its cage; he pursues Linus, who flees. Elsewhere, Lady Deathstrike reads a newspaper article about the captive creature and decides to investigate, while Sabretooth surfaces, planning revenge.

NOTE: This issue also has a "Wolverine Gallery" pin-up by Silvestri & Green. Linus' last name is revealed in W #89, '95. Tabeshaw's name and involvement with the Hunter's capture are revealed in W #48, '91. Wood Buffalo National Park is again incorrectly called "Buffalo Woods" here. The first two captions on p.10 panel 3 are reversed.

WOLVERINE #44 (Late August 1991)

"Babes at Sea" (23 pages)

CREDITS: Peter David (writer), Marc Silvestri (art, p.1; c pencils), Larry Stroman (pencils, pp.2-23), Al Milgrom (inks, pp.2-23), Pat Brosseau (letters), Steve Buccellato (colors), Suzanne Gaffney (asst editor, uncredited), Bob Harras (editor)
FEATURE CHARACTER: Wolverine (also in his own dream in fb; also in fb between Av #333, '91 & W #38, '91; next in InfG #2-3, SS #52, InfG #3, SS #54, InfG #4, SM #8-12, all '91, Namor #21-25, '91-92, W:BC, '91)
VILLAIN: Invisible creature (in fb, also as disembodied jaws in Wolverine's dream in fb, dies)
OTHER CHARACTERS: Cruise patrons: Brenda, Rachel (prev 2 die) & Gretchen (prev 3 pregnant friends), others (2 die); Gretchen's unborn child (bts, also as spirit, also as spirit in Wolverine's dream), Brenda & Rachel's unborn children (prev 2 bts, die), ship's crew (bts attending to Rachel's body) & security guards; women's obstetrician (mentioned) (all in fb)
LOCATIONS/ITEMS: Atlantic Ocean (also in dream), harbor (bts), Bona Venture (cruise ship, also in dream) w/Wolverine, Brenda & Gretchen's cabins, pool, engine room, hold, lower decks & elevator shafts (all in fb), Manhattan's Central Park / Brenda's spare key (bts), ship's propellers & elevators (2 destroyed) w/cables (1 set destroyed), Gretchen's mirror
FLASHBACK: Wolverine, who has been dreaming of an infant's spirit begging for help, has booked passage on the cruise ship he saw in his dream. He meets three pregnant women, Rachel, Brenda and Gretchen; Rachel goes for a swim, but something rips her throat out. Wolverine dives into the pool and battles an invisible creature, which escapes. That night, Wolverine goes prowling for the creature — but it strikes again, killing Brenda and hanging her in the elevator shaft. Wolverine attacks the creature, but it severs the elevator cables, dropping one car and killing passengers. The infant's spirit manifests to Wolverine again, who realizes that it is Gretchen's unborn child. The creature attacks Gretchen, but Wolverine intervenes; it reveals that it has been fighting this battle since the dawn of time. Wolverine tackles the creature into the ocean and pushes it into the ship's propellers, destroying it. Later, he checks on Gretchen, commenting that her baby will be very special.
SYNOPSIS: Wolverine reminisces about his cruise ship adventure.
NOTE: This was a fill-in issue; a new splash page was created to segue into the flashback story. The eternal war in which the creature and the baby are involved is never elaborated upon.

WOLVERINE: BLOODY CHOICES (June 1991)

"Bloody Choices" (59 pages)

CREDITS: Tom DeFalco (writer), John Buscema (art), Janice Chiang (letters), Gregory Wright (colors), Dawn Geiger (design), Ralph Macchio (editor), Chris DeFilippo (2nd print asst editor), Pat Garrahy (2nd print editor), Joe Jusko (c art), Michael Avon Oeming (2nd print c art)
FEATURE CHARACTER: Wolverine (also as a boy in fb between Origin #4-5, '02, see NOTE; next in X:TF #3, '99, W #45, '91)
GUEST STAR: Nick Fury (last in InfG #3, '91, next in X #1, '91)
VILLAINS: Mr. Bullfinch (child-abusing drug smuggler, dies), Shiv (Bullfinch's chief enforcer), Mr. Kapeland (Bullfinch's lawyer, dies), Dr. Corbel (corrupt doctor, dies), Bullfinch's guards (some die), Far East drug cartel (bts, in business with Bullfinch) inc Stewart (mentioned) & Kapeland's pilot (dies), child abusers (bts, supplied by Bullfinch), assassins
OTHER CHARACTERS: Bullfinch's captive boys: Palo, his brother (dies), others (bts, sensed by Wolverine); bar patrons inc Moose & Squirrel, parade performers (1 as Kamehameha the Great) & attendees, restaurant patrons & waiter, SHIELD medics & agents (some or others last in InfG #3, next bts in W #47, next in X #1, all '91) inc Sergeant, Corbel's nurse & patients, hotel clerk, bartender, Bullfinch's pilot & freighter crew, bystanders; Ellen Barkin, Julia Roberts, Tina Turner (prev 3 mentioned by crew), SHIELD agent's children (mentioned); hooded figure, horse (prev 2 as statues)
LOCATIONS/ITEMS: Hawaiian islands: Oahu inc restaurant, Corbel's clinic, Wolverine's hotel, bars, docks, SHIELD base, hospital (bts) & Bullfinch's estate w/roof helipad, Sand Island (former Japanese-American Detention Camp, 1 building destroyed) inc Bullfinch's room & SHIELD underground bunker, Bullfinch's island inc cabana w/pool; Pacific Ocean, Bullfinch's freighter w/hold, Canadian wilderness (in fb) / parade float & instruments, boy's gun, Shiv's wrist blades (destroyed) & knife, Bullfinch's laser security system (bts), window (destroyed), limousine, helicopter, records & crates (destroyed) w/coffee beans & cocaine, guards' guns, Corbel's lime aftershave, sedative, luggage & handgun, patients' bandages, Fury's note, cigar, gun, stun grenade, car & SHIELD weaponry inc steel training cable, bio-electric taser (prev 2 destroyed) & sense-dulling gas, SHIELD guns, radios, ambulance, stretcher, computers & equipment, motion sensors (bts), assassins' guns, boys' chains (in Wolverine's thoughts), barbed wire fences (1 destroyed), Kapeland's disk, helicopter (prev 2 destroyed) & speedboat (bts)
FLASHBACK: A loincloth-clad boy runs through the Canadian wilderness.
SYNOPSIS: In Hawaii, Wolverine sees a boy shoot at Bullfinch. He saves the boy from Shiv and takes him to Corbel's clinic, learning that he was abused and that Bullfinch has his brother Palo. Wolverine searches Bullfinch's freighter, discovering cocaine, but is confronted by Shiv, who resembles him. Wolverine floods the hold and swims to shore, where Nick Fury explains that SHIELD plans to arrest Bullfinch. Wolverine decides that Bullfinch should be punished personally; he sneaks onto his estate, but finds the boy dead. Shiv defeats Wolverine while Bullfinch escapes; when SHIELD arrives, Wolverine demands to join the case. Bullfinch offers to betray the cartel for immunity; Fury agrees over Wolverine's objections. Realizing that Corbel returned the boy to Bullfinch, Wolverine interrogates him. When assassins arrive to kill Corbel,

Wolverine declines to stop them. He swims to Bullfinch's island and battles Shiv, wondering if they are brothers but ultimately rejecting the ide Defeated, Shiv reveals Bullfinch's whereabouts. When Kapeland brings Palo to Bullfinch for "companionship," Fury loses his temper, but is s obligated to protect Bullfinch, attacking Wolverine when he arrives. Kapeland betrays Bullfinch, copying his testimony for the cartel. Wolveri defeats Fury, who seems relieved. He destroys Kapeland's helicopter, then finds the fleeing Bullfinch and deals out justice.

NOTE: This issue was published as a magazine-sized MGN softcover. The story is preceded by a title page, 2 credits pages, and a 1-pa introduction by Macchio; the story is followed by a logo-free reprint of the cover. Barflies "Moose" and "Squirrel" take their nicknames from 1960s *Rocky & Bullwinkle* cartoon. Shiv's similarities to Wolverine, including hairstyle and alleged healing factor, are never explained. Althou Wolverine told an ambiguous tale of a feral boy as a bedtime story in W #25, '90, this issue has him recall a similar boy in a much more concre way: it is clear that he is thinking of himself here. This marks the first true fb to Wolverine's childhood, but does not automatically validate W # '90's story, as that tale does not correspond to later revelations from the Origin, '01-02 series. This issue was reprinted in 1993 as a comic-siz bookshelf-format edition with a new cover, and new art on the inside front and back covers.

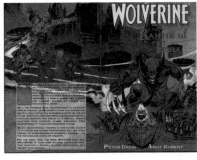

WOLVERINE: RAHNE OF TERRA (August 1991)

(Untitled, 64 pages)

CREDITS: Peter David (writer), Andy Kubert (art), Jim Novak (letters), Sherilyn Valkenburgh (colors), Suzanne Gaffney (design, asst editor), Bob Harras (editor)
FEATURE CHARACTER: Wolverine (chr last in UXM #268, '90, chr next in NM #93, '
GUEST STARS: New Mutants (Cable's students, see NOTE): Boom-Boom (Tabi Smith, explosive generator), Sunspot (Roberto Da Costa, solar-fueled strength), Wolfsba (Rahne Sinclair, lycanthrope, also as Princess Rain) (all chr last in NM Spec, '90), Ric (Julio Richter, seismic mutant, chr last in NM Ann #6, '90), Cannonball (Samuel Guth rocketlike flight), Cable (prev 2 chr last in X Ann #14, '90) (all chr next in NM #93, '
VILLAIN: Magnus (corrupt Geshem magician, also as psychic projection, dies)
OTHER CHARACTERS: Rain (Princess of Geshem, becomes Queen, also painting & mystic vision, next in W:KT, '95), Tabitha ("Tabby," Rain's serving girl), Rain's personal guard: Richard, Robert, Samuel (prev 4 also briefl their New Mutant analogs in Wolfsbane's thoughts); Mage (Cable analog, next bts in W:KT, '95) & his staff (techno-organic creature, Warlock anal dies), Rain's father (King of Geshem, see NOTE; also in painting, dies), king's archers & knights (some die, some or others next in W:KT, '95 Hubert (dies), priest, citizens of Geshem (some or others next in W:KT, '95) inc Doug (Cypher analog, chr next in W:KT, '95 fb, next bts in W:KT, '95 his mother; Pendragon (Samuel's horse), knight's horse, moat monster (dies), creatures (dead, as skeletons), lion, deer (prev 2 dead, as decoratio Rain's mother (previous Queen of Geshem, as painting), knights, religious figures, animals (prev 3 as statues & relief carvings), wolf (as pendant)
LOCATIONS/ITEMS: X-Mansion grounds & underground complex, Geshem (Earth-1991) inc Magnus' laboratory, cemetery w/kin mausoleum & city (partly destroyed) inc castle (partly destroyed) w/moat & Rain's chambers / Rain's straitjacket & bed (prev 2 destroye Wolfsbane's wolf pendant & towel, Tabby's bottles (destroyed), water jug, ropes & torch, Richard's Quake Mallet (destroyed) & alcoh Pendragon's armor, Cannonball's enchanted rifle), Samuel's seven-league boots & cape, castle bells (bts), swords & torch, knigl shields (1 destroyed), armor, spears, axes & swords, king's sword & carriage w/casket, Magnus' restraints & potions, headstone (destroye city drawbridge & well, archers' bows & arrows, door bolts, Mage's wards (bts) & crossbow
SYNOPSIS: The New Mutants worry about Wolfsbane, seemingly gone mad and claiming to be a princess. In Geshem, a bloodthirsty Wolver attacks the Mage. In the castle, Princess Rain's servant worries about the prophecy that a beast will kill her; Rain hallucinates that her guards are New Mutants. Wolverine attacks Samuel, who flees to the castle, reporting the "beast." The ailing king dies; elsewhere, Magnus reveals that he brou Wolverine to his dimension to fulfill the prophecy, and magically brainwashes her. Rain sneaks out to attend her father's funeral, encountering Do a familiar-seeming peasant. Wolverine attacks at the cemetery, but the king's knights battle him while Rain and Doug flee. Rain suddenly becom a werewolf and drives Wolverine off, then flees into the castle. Wolverine fights his way in, but Tabby lights him on fire, and his healing factor cle his mind. Magnus arrives, growing to immense size; as he tries to crush Rain, Wolverine leaps into his ear and destroys his brain. Magnus collaps and Wolverine suddenly returns home. The Mage explains that "Rain" is Wolfsbane; he switched the two and brainwashed Wolfsbane to avoid Ra prophesied death. He switches both girls back; the New Mutants disbelieve Wolfsbane's story until Wolverine arrives with her regal pendant.
NOTE: This issue occurs before Cable turned the New Mutants, Xavier's third class of students, into the paramilitary X-Force. Rictor's f name is revealed in XFor #25, '93. Doug Ramsey, aka Cypher, was a New Mutant who died in NM #60, '88; he was resurrected in XNec/2, ' Geshem is designated Earth-1991 in OHMU:AU, '05. The Mage claims that Wolverine is unique to his own dimension; this is untrue, as ma multiversal analogs of Wolverine have been seen over the years (notably in Exiles #85-86, '06), but Geshem does not have a Wolverine anal "Geshem" is a Hebrew word for rain, one of several "Rahne/Rain" puns in this issue. Richard incorrectly calls Rain "Princess Rahne" once he Ex #93, '96 revealed that Wolfsbane's father was Reverend Craig; if this is true in Geshem as well, then the unnamed King would be a Cr analog. W:KT, '95 reveals that the prophecy was a metaphor; Rain was meant to bond with the mystic energy of Geshem.

WOLVERINE #45 (Early September 1991)

"Claws Over Times Square!" (18 pages)

CREDITS: Larry Hama (writer), Marc Silvestri (breakdowns), Dan Green (finishes), Pat Brosseau (letters), St Buccellato (colors), Suzanne Gaffney (asst editor), Bob Harras (editor)
FEATURE CHARACTER: Wolverine
SUPPORTING CAST: Albert, Elsie-Dee, Jubilee
VILLAINS: Lady Deathstrike (also on TV), Sabretooth (both last in W #43, '91), Emmy Doolin (Sgt. Dool daughter, unnamed, 1st but chr last in W #46, '91 fb), mugger (dies) & his drug supplier (bts awaiting paymen
OTHER CHARACTERS: Hunter in Darkness (also on billboard, last in W #34, '90), Ronald Parvenue (cas owner, 1st on-panel app, also on TV), Masque (all last bts in W #43, '91), Morlocks (others last in W #43, ' some or others chr next (all but 1 bts) in W #54, '92, next in W #51, '92), newsreader (bts reporting on Hunt mugger's victim, Parvenue's pilot, bystanders; Queenie (victim's dog); Irina (Parvenue's ex-girlfriend, mentione

model (on billboard)

LOCATIONS/ITEMS: Manhattan inc Times Square w/rooftops & Doolin's room, Morlock tunnels, sewer tunnels; Atlantic City, New Jersey's Parvenue Casino (mentioned) / Parvenue's helicopter, camera, microphone, remote control & billboard w/bunting, spotlights, speakers & projection TV screen, Hunter's chains (on billboard) & suspended cage (destroyed) w/screen, Emmy's chair (as shooting rest) & rifle w/scope & mercury-tipped bullets, Elsie-Dee's new body (partly built), Albert's bypass circuits (bts), pliers & equipment inc particle accelerator (bts, partly built), Morlock power cables & city power lines, mugger's knife & clothes, victim's sunglasses & purse w/money, Queenie's leash, water tower (destroyed)

SYNOPSIS: Wolverine stews about the Hunter in Darkness, captured by Ronald Parvenue and about to be displayed in Times Square. Jubilee tries to raise his spirits, but nearby, a sniper takes aim. In the Morlock tunnels, Albert has partly rebuilt Elsie-Dee, but his plans to upgrade her systems require a particle accelerator and ever-growing power supplies. Elsewhere, Sabretooth stops a mugger, then mugs the victim himself, stealing clothes for a disguise. As Parvenue's show begins, his billboard transforms into a giant screen; he broadcasts from a nearby helicopter with Lady Deathstrike, who has seduced him into an alliance. Parvenue unveils the Hunter, dangling his cage from the helicopter, but the sniper shoots at it. Wolverine leaps into the cage, and Sabretooth and Deathstrike both rush to attack him. Albert severs Midtown's main power line and the city goes dark; Jubilee generates fireworks, blinding Parvenue's pilot, who crashes the cage into a water tower. Wolverine and his opponents realize that the Hunter is free…

NOTE: This issue also has a 2-page "Wolverine Gallery" pin-up by Art Thibert. Emmy's name is revealed next issue, and her ammunition is revealed as mercury-tipped "poison bullets." Wood Buffalo National Park is once again incorrectly called "Buffalo Woods."

WOLVERINE #46 (Late September 1991)

"Home Is the Hunter…" (18 pages)

CREDITS: Larry Hama (writer), Marc Silvestri (pencils), Dan Green (inks), Pat Brosseau (letters), Steve Buccellato (colors), Suzanne Gaffney (asst editor), Bob Harras (editor), Hilary Barta (c inks)
FEATURE CHARACTER: Wolverine (also in rfb2)
SUPPORTING CAST: Albert, Elsie-Dee (both next in W #51, '92), Jubilee (chr next in MColl/3, '92, next in Dlk #4, '91)
VILLAINS: Lady Deathstrike (next in UXM #281, '91), Sabretooth (chr next in Mvk Spec, '97 fb, next in MCP #98/2, '92), Emmy Doolin (named, also as Wrangler in Wolverine & Sabretooth's hallucination; also in fb1, fb2 & fb3, her chr 1st app, prior to W #45, '91; next in DW #78, '09)
OTHER CHARACTERS: Hunter in Darkness (in rfb1, next in W #51, '92), Ronald Parvenue (next in W #76, '93), Masque (next in W #51, '92), Sgt. Doolin (in rfb1 & rfb2, also in fb1 between W #34, '90 fbs; also in fb2 between W #34, '90 fb & W #34, '90; also bts in fb3, dead in coffin, following W #34, '90), Mounties (in fb3), Parvenue's chauffeur (bts driving limo); albino alligator (dies)
LOCATIONS/ITEMS: Times Square rooftop & alley, Morlock tunnels, sewer tunnels, Wood Buffalo National Park (in rfb1 & rfb2), Doolins' Canada home (in fb1, fb2 & fb3), Canadian church (in fb3), "painscape" (in hallucination, see NOTE) / Hunter's cage (destroyed), bear trap (in fb1) w/chain (destroyed), city main power line, Elsie-Dee's new body (partly built), Albert's B-2 stealth bomber (partly rebuilt, see NOTE), spare parts (incorporated into bomber), bypass circuits (prev 3 bts), screwdriver & equipment inc particle accelerator w/hyper-cryogenic electromagnet (bts), Emmy's newspaper (in fb3) & rifle (destroyed) w/scope & mercury-tipped bullets, Sgt. Doolin's rifle (in rfb2) & casket (in fb3), Wrangler's armor (in hallucination), Dumpster, Parvenue's car
FLASHBACKS: Wolverine frees the Hunter in Darkness from a bear trap; Sgt. Doolin shoots Wolverine, thinking he is the Hunter (W #34, '90 fbs). Sgt. Doolin raises Emmy (1), but becomes obsessed after his encounter with the "Hunter" (2). Sgt. Doolin is buried, and Emmy, blaming the Hunter for his decline, learns about its capture (3).
SYNOPSIS: Sabretooth and Lady Deathstrike continue attacking Wolverine, but when the Hunter recognizes Wolverine's scent, it leaps to his defense. Underground, Albert's particle accelerator creates strange matter to power Elsie-Dee's new body. The sniper, Emmy Doolin, cannot tell which combatant is the Hunter, so she shoots them all, knocking Deathstrike off the roof; the Hunter flees. Wolverine realizes who Emmy's father was, but her poisoned bullets cause both him and Sabretooth to hallucinate her as a Wrangler, an armored figure that Wolverine only partly recognizes. Sabretooth suddenly calls Wolverine his partner, believing that the two are back at "the Project" together. Jubilee tackles Emmy and Wolverine recovers; he destroys her rifle and Jubilee punches her out. Wolverine wonders about Sabretooth's ties to his past, but finds that the villain has fled. Elsewhere, Ronald Parvenue recovers Deathstrike, and the Hunter makes a new home in the sewer tunnels.
NOTE: This issue also has a 1-panel preview of X #1, '91, and a 1-page preview of W:RT, '91. Sabretooth realizes here that his memory has been altered to make him believe he is Wolverine's father. Called a "visual analog of a suffusion-chelation bath" here, the spiky landscape that Wolverine and Sabretooth hallucinate soon becomes a staple of Wolverine's altered memories, creeping around panel edges or growing into scenes. W #63, '92 reveals that Psi-Borg planted this imagery in Wolverine and his teammates' minds to help cement their memory implants; the spikes are symbolic and intentionally graphic, meant to conjure instinctive revulsion and pain. For brevity, this Index will refer to this spiky vista as a "painscape." The "surprise" Albert mentions here is revealed in W #51, '92 as a rebuilt B-2 stealth bomber. Wood Buffalo National Park is still incorrectly called "Buffalo Woods."

WOLVERINE #47 (October 1991)

"Dog Day" (20 pages)

CREDITS: Larry Hama (writer), Gerald DeCaire (pencils), Don Hudson (inks), Pat Brosseau (letters), Glynis Oliver (colors), Suzanne Gaffney (asst editor), Bob Harras (editor), Kirk Jarvinen (c pencils), Brad Vancata (c inks)
FEATURE CHARACTER: Wolverine (also in fb between XO:Sabre, '09 & W #50, '07 fb; next in MColl/3, '92; Dlk #4-5, X #1-3, MCP #85-92 & 89/4, Q #28, all '91, MCP #93, 94-96 bts, 97-99 & 100/3-4, '91-92, GR/W/Pun, '91, W #54, '92, W #48, '91)
SUPPORTING CAST: Silver Fox (in fb between XO:Sabre, '09 & W #50, '07 fb)
VILLAINS: Tracy (drug-addicted punk, dies) & his supplier (bts, meeting him later)
OTHER CHARACTERS: Police: Jim & Deidre (prev 2 "Adam-5" unit), dispatch officer (voice only on radio); Mr. Singh (store owner), Tiffany (Singh's employee) (prev 2 die), Sean & Megan (prev 2 Deidre's children), metermaid, SHIELD agents (bts contacting metermaid, some or others last in W:BC, '91, next in X #1, '91), judge (bts granting court order), Tracy's mother, ice cream vendor & patrons, bystanders; Blue (Wolverine & Silver Fox's dog, in fb, dies off-panel), Sandy (Deidre's dog), rabid dog (dies); Tracy's father (mentioned, dead)

LOCATIONS/ITEMS: Manhattan's World Trade Center, Westchester County inc Tracy's mother's house, Singh's store, highway & street, Wolverine & Silver Fox's cabin (Mount Logan, in fb) / Wolverine's rifle (in fb), registration (bts), motorcycle, chain & lock, metermaid's computer (bts) & ticket pad, SHIELD agents' ID cards (bts), Tracy's mother's court order (bts), car (destroyed), groceries, trunk, gun & belongings inc VCR & camera, police guns & car w/radio, ice cream truck, Singh's freezer windows (destroyed), cash register, mop & bucket, Tracy's stolen money & beer, cars (destroyed), traffic lights, Sean & Megan's bicycles (1 or both destroyed)

FLASHBACK: Wolverine and Silver Fox's dog comes home rabid. Silver Fox urges Wolverine to shoot him, but he hesitates.

SYNOPSIS: A metermaid confronts Wolverine as he collects his motorcycle from the World Trade Center. When he explains his recent battles, she rips up the ticket. In Westchester, a teenage thug named Tracy steals from his mother to buy drugs; when she pulls a gun, he beats her savagely. Nearby, Wolverine sees police shoot a rabid dog. Tracy robs the store where he used to work, shooting his former boss and co-worker. Driving erratically, he aims for two children crossing the street. Later, Wolverine sees Tracy's car and notices mangled bicycle handlebars in the grill. Tracy panics and runs him over, but Wolverine destroys the car. Tracy shoots Wolverine until he runs out of bullets; Wolverine keeps coming but hesitates when he reaches him. The police arrive and shoot Tracy, one officer noting that he almost ran over her children. Wolverine tells her that he once had a dog, but when it came home rabid he couldn't shoot it — so Silver Fox did.

NOTE: The series returns to monthly publication here. Wolverine left his motorcycle at the World Trade Center in W #40, '91. The DMV database lists him as "N.F.N. Logan," standing for No First Name. Tracy says that he shot Wolverine three times and Singh twice; however, he is drawn shooting Wolverine five times and Singh only once, though the colorist added a second muzzle flash. Deidre says she has to do paperwork for ten shots fired, but she is only shown firing nine. However, her partner fired once; she may have been counting both guns. Page 19 panel 4 is uncolored.

WOLVERINE #48 (November 1991)

"Dreams of Gore: Phase One" (21 pages)

CREDITS: Larry Hama (writer), Marc Silvestri (pencils), Dan Green (inks), Pat Brosseau (letters), Steve Buccellato (colors), Suzanne Gaffney (asst editor), Bob Harras (editor), Tom Orzechowski (c letters)
FEATURE CHARACTER: Wolverine (also in fb3/implant between W #41, '91 fb & W #49, '91 fb; also in rfb1/fb during MCP #73, '91 fb; also as Experiment X in rfb2/fb2 during & also in MCP #80, '91)
SUPPORTING CAST: Team X (Weapon X's espionage agents, 1st, unnamed): Kestrel (John Wraith, teleporter, 1st, unnamed, as "Carlisle," "dies," Mastodon (1st) (both in fb3/implant prior to W #49, '91 fb), Wildcat (Christoph "David North" Nord, absorbs kinetic energy, 1st, unnamed, as "Morse," "dies," in fb3/implant between Mvk #2, '97 fb & W #49, '91 fb), Silver Fox (in fb3/implant between W #63, '92 fb & W #49, '91 fb); Jubilee (last in MCP #89/4, '91, next in W #50, '92)
VILLAINS: Weapon X Program senior staff: Professor Truett "Andre Thorton" Hudson (also bts in rfb1 & as simulation in rfb & fb2; also in voiceover & as Andre in fb3/implant between W #63, '92 fb & W #49, '91 fb, "dies"), Dr. Abraham Cornelius, Carol Hine (all bts monitoring simulation in rfb/fb2 during MCP #80, '91 bts); Vole (bts in fb3/implant between W #41, '91 fb bts & W #49, '91 fb bts; also bts in rfb2/fb2 during MCP #80, '91 bts, see NOTE), Sabretooth (in fb3/implant between W #41, '91 fb & W #49, '91 fb), Weapon X agents (in rfb1/fb1 during & also in MCP #73, '91 fb)
OTHER CHARACTERS: Harry Tabeshaw (tracker, 1st on-panel app, last bts in W #43, '91, next in W #83, '94); animals (bts, took over Hunter's old lairs); Shiva (1st mention); Wranglers (Weapon X security, as simulations, in rfb/fb2 during & also in MCP #80, '91, some die, some voice only) inc engineer (voice only) & Harras, Professor's superior (as simulation, bts in rfb2)
LOCATIONS/ITEMS: Former Weapon X Program facility (Alberta, Canada) w/crawlspace, Professor's quarters (prev 2 as simulation in rfb/fb2), Zone 3 (also as simulation in rfb2/fb2) & garage, Canadian bar (in rfb1/fb1), revolutionaries' apartment (Windsor, Ontario, Canada; in fb3 soundstage and/or psychic image), Wolverine & Silver Fox's cabin (in photo) / Wolverine, Mastodon & Sabretooth's bulletproof vests (bts) guns (1 of Sabretooth's also in main story), Mastodon's radio (bts), Sabretooth's radio, revolutionaries' weapons (most bts) inc rifles (Silver Fox destroyed), Andre's fake beard, calendar (all in fb3), "painscape" spikes (in fb2 & fb3), Experiment X's wires & battery packs, Wranglers' infrared sensors, C-4 explosives (prev 2 bts), guns & armor w/radios (bts), Professor's communicator & intercom (prev 2 bts) (prev 9 as simulations rfb2/fb2), agents' stun gun (in rfb1/fb1) w/thorazine dart (bts in rfb1), Wolverine's flashlight & Lotus Seven (also in rfb1/fb1) w/rearview mirror (destroyed in fb1), Silver Fox's medicine pouch (also in fb3) w/Psi-Borg's tooth (bts in pouch, see NOTE) & Wolverine's keys, facility detector (bts) & fence w/chains (destroyed) & warning signs, Jubilee's backpack, rollerblades & flashlight, Shiva's injection-mold casing

FLASHBACKS: Weapon X agents tranquilize Wolverine, he fights back and they pistol-whip him into unconsciousness (1 / MCP #73, '91, see NOTE). In a simulation, Experiment X rampages through the Program base, using his new Adamantium claws to kill guards and menace the Professor (2 / MCP #80, '91, see NOTE). In an implanted memory, Wolverine, Sabretooth and Mastodon raid a revolutionary group's hideout, killing everyone but Silver Fox; Wolverine morphs into a spike-covered nightmare during the firefight (3, see NOTE).

SYNOPSIS: Harry Tabeshaw leads Wolverine to an abandoned facility that he discovered during his search for the Hunter in Darkness. It feels oddly familiar to Wolverine, and he begins searching it, finding his old car along with a medicine pouch attached to its key ring. Seeing claw marks and signs of a fight all around the facility, Wolverine begins flashing back to his time as a Weapon X experiment and Team X member, reliving memories both real and false. He decides to ask Professor X for help sorting through his memories, and leaves without seeing a large man-shaped mold labeled "Shiva."

NOTE: Cover-labeled "Shiva Scenario, Part 1." This issue reveals that Harry Tabeshaw helped Ronald Parvenue locate the Hunter in Darkness prior to W #43, '91. This arc is a sequel to MCP #72-84, '91, which revealed the origin of Wolverine's Adamantium skeleton: the Weapon X Program kidnapped him, implanted the metal and tried to brainwash him into a living weapon, but he ran amok and escaped. This issue's fb1 and fb2 are partly rfbs; they each retell scenes from the MCP arc but add many new details. Only the new portions of each fb are chronologized above. As MCP #84, '91 reveals, rfb2/fb2 is a simulation; Wolverine isn't attacking Wranglers or the Professor, he's just being made to think it is. The painscape spikes in fb2 and fb3 indicate that Vole, later known as Psi-Borg, telepathically ran both scenarios, placing him bts in both. Whether Team X were actively (if unknowingly) participating in fb3 as the memory was being implanted, or whether it was completely fabricated by Psi-Borg is unrevealed; everyone shown in fb3 is at least bts receiving the memory. Weapon X's operatives are named Team X in TX/T '96; OHMU:X, '04 clarifies that the Weapon X Program implanted Wolverine's Adamantium decades after Team X's dissolution. "Carlisle" and "Morse" are false names only used in memory implants. Wildcat is better known as Maverick. His, John Wraith's and Psi-Borg's seldom-used Team X codenames are revealed in W #50, '92, but they are not linked to these men until W #61-62, '92 (Maverick's through inference). Wraith's real name is revealed in W #60, '92; Maverick's longtime alias is revealed in X #6, '92, his last name in Mvk Spec, '97, and his first name in Mvk #3, '97. The Professor's longtime alias' first name is revealed here, his alias' last name in WX #23, '04, and his real name in W:O #33, '09, which also reveals that he is related to Wolverine. A Wrangler's nametag reads "Harras," after editor Bob Harras. The terrorists' apartment is 3G, named after long-running comic strip Apartment 3-G. W #64, '92 reveals that Psi-Borg's tooth is inside Wolverine's medicine pouch. Next issue reveals that Wolverine set off the facility's detection equipment here.

WOLVERINE #49 (December 1991)

"Dreams of Gore: Phase 2 (Remembrance? Of Things Past?)" (22 pages)

CREDITS: Larry Hama (writer), Marc Silvestri (pencils, c art), Dan Green & Hilary Barta (inks), Pat Brosseau (letters), Steve Buccellato (colors), Suzanne Gaffney (asst editor), Bob Harras (editor), Tom Orzechowski (c letters)

FEATURE CHARACTER: Wolverine (also in rfb1, rfb2 & as corpse in psychic image, also in W #50, '92 fb, also in fb3 between W:O #49, '10 fb & W #65, '93 fb; also in fb4/implant between W #48, '91 fb & W #62, '92 fb; also as Emilio Garra in fb2 between W #60-61, '92 fbs; also as Experiment X in fb5 between MCP #78-79, '91; also as Experiment X in fb1 during MCP #80, '91)

GUEST STARS: X-Men: Jean Grey (formerly Marvel Girl, telekinetic & telepath, also as psychic images), Professor X

SUPPORTING CAST: Team X: Kestrel (as Carlisle, "dead," bts), Wildcat (as Morse, "dead") (both in fb4/implant between W #48, '91 fb & W #63, '92 fbs), Silver Fox (in fb3 between W:O #49, '10 fb & W #65, '93 fb; also in fb4/implant between W #48, '91 fb & W #62, '92 fb; also bts as Zora de Plata in fb2 between W #60-61, '92 fbs) (all also as psychic images), Mastodon (in fb4/implant between W #48, '91 fb & W #61, '92 fb)

VILLAINS: Weapon X Program senior staff: Professor Truett Hudson (also as Andre, "dead," in fb4/implant between W #48, '91 fb & MCP #72, '91; also voice only in fb5 between MCP #78-79, '91), Carol Hines (also voice only in fb5 between MCP #78 & 84 fb, '91) (both last in MCP #84, '91, chr last in WX #23, '04), Dr. Abraham Cornelius (voice only in fb5 between MCP #78-79, '91) (all also voice only as psychic images, also bts monitoring simulation in fb1 during MCP #80, '91 fb); Vole (in fb4/implant between W #48, '91 fb bts & W #62, '92 fb bts; also bts in fb1 during MCP #80, '91), Sabretooth (in fb4/implant between W #48, '91 fb & W #62, '92 fb; also as El Tigre & Julio in fb2 between Sabre #3, '93 fb & W #61, '92 fb; also in rfb2 & as psychic image), Cuban soldiers (in fb2, some or others next in W #61, '92 fb)

OTHER CHARACTERS: Lee Harvey Oswald (Kennedy's alleged assassin, see NOTE; chr last in M:LG #4, '00, chr last bts in MK #2, '99 fb), Jack Ruby (Oswald's assassin), police inc detectives Jim Leavelle & L.C. Graves (all on TV), el Tigre's informant (bts), Cuban newsreader (voice only), bar patrons & bartender (all in fb2), US Department of Agriculture secretary (voice only on phone); Blue (in rfb1); John F. Kennedy (mentioned as assassinated in fb2), Team X "cleaners," Ottawa government (prev 2 mentioned in fb4); Fidel Castro (on poster in fb2), Wranglers (as simulations in fb1 during MCP #80, '91, some "die;" also as psychic images); bear (as simulation in fb5, "dies"), birds (as psychic images)

LOCATIONS/ITEMS: Mindscape inc recreations of X-Mansion, cantina (Palma Soriano, Cuba; in fb2), police HQ (Dallas, Texas; on TV in fb2), revolutionaries' Windsor apartment (also in fb4) & Weapon X Program facility's Zone 3 (in fb1) & nearby woods (also in fb5); "painscape," X-Mansion inc psi-lab, Salem Center gas station, Professor's office (US Department of Agriculture, Pest Control section, Washington DC); Mount Logan: Wolverine & Silver Fox's cabin (in fb3, also in rfb1 & as photo in fb4), saloon (in rfb2); Cuba: Havana, Guantanamo Bay (prev 2 mentioned in fb2) / Professor's intercom (bts), Experiment X's wires & battery packs (all in fb1 & fb5), support strut (destroyed, in fb1), Wranglers' guns & armor w/radios (bts) (also in fb1), Ruby's gun, Oswald's handcuffs (prev 2 on TV), cantina TV set, el Tigre's machine gun, soldiers' rifles (prev 6 in fb2), Mastodon's shotgun, Andre's glasses (destroyed) & gun, Wolverine, Mastodon & Sabretooth's bulletproof vests (prev 4 in fb4), Cornelius' & Hines' intercoms (bts), Experiment X's infrared goggles (prev 2 also in fb5), Wolverine's guns (1 also in fb2), Jean's notepad, Professor X's remote control, Shiva vault door, calendar (all as psychic images), painscape tree (in fb5, see NOTE) w/radiator & Silver Fox's handcuffs (prev 2 also as psychic images in fb4), mindscape doors, Professor X's Shi'ar hover-chair (hereinafter considered his standard equipment and not listed separately, also as psychic image) & needle w/stimulant, psi-lab restraints (bts, destroyed), Wolverine's brown costume (destroyed) & motorcycle, phone booth, Hines' scrambler (bts), Wolverine's shotgun (in rfb1) & father's knife (in fb3, see NOTE), Sabretooth's cake slice (in rfb2/implant)

FLASHBACKS: Wolverine takes aim at his rabid dog (W #47, '91 fb). In an implanted memory, Sabretooth scrapes frosting off a cake slice (W #10, '89 fb). In a simulation, Experiment X battles Wranglers (1). In Cuba, an undercover Wolverine and Sabretooth learn of President Kennedy's assassination and realize that they must now complete their end of a mission. Silver Fox outs them as spies, Cuban soldiers attack and Sabretooth returns fire (2). Wolverine and Silver Fox carve their names on their cabin door (3). In an implanted memory, Sabretooth interrogates the revolutionary Silver Fox (4). In a simulation, Experiment X is made to kill a bear, then fed shocking imagery to install an "activation switch" (5).

SYNOPSIS: Wolverine explores a symbolic mindscape of his own memories with Professor X and Jean Grey's help, but finds several inaccessible. Professor X warns him that his mind has been booby-trapped; prolonged exploration could revert him to an animalistic mindset. Wolverine interacts with the "revolutionary" version of Silver Fox, but sees their cabin pictured on a calendar and fears that their happiness might also be an implanted memory. Returning to the real world, a surly Wolverine leaves in search of answers. Hines, tailing him, reports his movements to the Professor.

NOTE: Cover-labeled "Shiva Scenario, Part 2." In line with decades of conspiracy theories, this issue's fb2 claims that Lee Harvey Oswald did not kill John F. Kennedy. Several other comics have offered alternate takes on JFK's assassination: in WBN #38, '76, the extradimensional Three Who Are All claimed responsibility; Stryfe, '93 claimed that the External Gideon was involved; in MK #2, '99, Candy Calder claimed that CIA mind-control was involved; and in IHulk #19, '00, Gen. John Ryker claimed that Castro hired two Corsican mercenaries to kill JFK, which Ryker covered up. It is unknown which, if any, scenarios are true on Earth-616. This issue's fb4 leads into a hallucination where Silver Fox, handcuffed to a radiator, is swallowed up by a painscape tree. A radiator chained to a tree soon becomes another common motif in Wolverine's painscape memories. "Zora de Plata" (incorrectly spelled "del Plata" here) is a slightly modified spelling of "Zorra de Plata," Spanish for Silver Fox. "Garra" is Spanish for claw. The reference to Wolverine's "father's knife" is never followed up on; given the Origin, '01-02 series' revelations about his parentage, the knife likely did not truly belong to his father.

WOLVERINE #50 (January 1992)

"Dreams of Gore: Phase 3" (36 pages)

CREDITS: Larry Hama (writer), Marc Silvestri (pencils), Dan Green (co-inks, c inks), Hilary Barta & Tom Palmer (co-inks), Pat Brosseau (letters), Steve Buccellato (colors), Suzanne Gaffney (asst editor), Bob Harras (editor), Tom Orzechowski (c letters)

FEATURE CHARACTER: Wolverine (also on monitor & in rfb, also in fb2 between W:O #26, '08 fb & WWHs:C/W #1, '10 fb; also in fb3/implant between XO:Sabre, '09 & W #63, '92 fb; also in fb1 during W #49, '91; next in X:OMO, '08; X #4-7, MCP #101-108, all '92, XMU #47, '03 fb)

GUEST STARS: X-Men: Cyclops (last in Q #28, '91), Professor X (both chr next in X:OMO, '08, next in X #4, '92), Jean Grey (chr next in X:OMO, '08), Forge (bts helping analyze data, also in fb1 between X #3, '91 & this issue's main story; next bts in X #4, '92) (prev 2 next in X #5, '92); Nick Fury (last in XFor #5, '91, next in NF:AoS #30, '91)

SUPPORTING CAST: Jubilee (next in X #4, '92)

VILLAINS: Shiva (termination program using robot bodies, 1st, also on monitor, next in W #60, '92), Professor Truett Hudson (dies, possibl[y] next as spirit in W #176, '02, see W #4, '82's NOTE), Carol Hines (next in W #62, '92), Hydra (global terror organization): Silver Fox (als[o] mentioned as Fox on target list, also in fb3/implant between XO:Sabre, '09 & W #63, '92 fb; last in W #10, '89 fb, chr last in W #-1, '97, next b[ts] in W #55, '92, next in W #56, '92), Parsons, other agents (some or others last in MCP #93/4, '92, next in SM #22, '92)

OTHER CHARACTERS: Citicorp café waiter & patrons, SHIELD agents (some or others last in XFor #1, '91, next in NF:AoS #31, '92) inc Lieutenar[t] & Security Seven, Director of Central Intelligence (bts releasing Wolverine's file), US Department of Agriculture secretary, intruders (dead), WW[II] soldiers (in fb2), Castroville prom attendees (in fb3/implant, possibly disguised Weapon X agents, see NOTE), bystanders; deer (dead, as mounte[d] head), birds (others on inner cover photo); Sabretooth (mentioned on target list, also as psychic image, on inner cover photo & rfb), Reavers: Wad[e] Cole, Angelo Macon, Murray Reese; Hand ninjas (prev 4 in rfb); Security Committee (mentioned, mandated Shiva's creation), Kestrel, Mastodon, Vole[,] Wildcat (prev 4 mentioned on Shiva's target list), Hirohito (mentioned on invitation); James & Heather Hudson, Mariko Yashida, fish (dead) (prev 4 on inner cover photos); Lady Deathstrike, Shingen Harada, Ogun, Shadowcat (prev 4 as psychic images), historical figures (on stamp & as painting[)]

LOCATIONS/ITEMS: Manhattan inc Hydra office & Citicorp Building w/café & roof, US Department of Agriculture building inc Professor's Pes[t] Control section office, skies over New York's Chautauqua Lake, Weapon X Program's Windsor warehouse w/command center & nearby rooftop "painscape", Forge's X-Mansion workshop (in fb1), WWII battlefield (in fb2), Castroville, California in photo & fb3/implant), revolutionaries' apartment, Reavers' Australian outback HQ (prev 2 in rfb) / Wolverine's guns (in rfb), motorcycle & yellow costume, Citicorp elevators, SHIELD jet fuel, fax, modem, disks (prev 4 bts), radios, armor, guns & Helicarrier w/jets, helicopters & armored window (destroyed), Forge's device & tools (prev 2 in fb1), Fury's guns, NSA computers (bts), Hydra computers w/monitoring programs (bts) & hovercraft w/telescope, Professor's computer, gun, binoculars, prosthetic hook & steel-plated door, X-Men's Blackbird jet, Cyclops' ruby quartz visor (hereinafter considered his standard equipment and not listed separately), Wolverine's NSA file w/warehouse lease, Weapon X proposal (prev 2 bts) & Shiva's target list, Jubilee's rollerblades, stage sets (some destroyed) inc Silver Fox's San Francisco apartment & Castroville prom ballroom, Mount Logan saloon, sawmill, living room, computer lab & jungle, props inc Professor's glasses (destroyed), gun, calendar & cake slice, warehouse's custom-tailored stench, surveillance cameras (prev 2 bts), monitor & intruder eliminator w/spikes, Shiva's command pad, vault door (also on monitor) & robo[t] bodies (2 destroyed, others bts) w/sound dampers & electronic triggers, Silver Fox's claws (bts), gun & medicine pouch w/Psi-Borg's tooth (bts in pouch) & Wolverine's keys, Sabretooth's pistol, ninjas' swords, soldiers' rifles w/bayonets, Reavers' guns (prev 5 in rfb)

FLASHBACKS: Wolverine is attacked by revolutionaries in an implanted memory (W #48, '91 fb), Hand ninjas (W #3, '82) and Reavers (UXM #251, '89 fb). Forge tells Wolverine where the SHIELD Helicarrier refuels (1). Wolverine serves in WWII (2). In an implanted memory, Wolverine is Silver Fox's prom date, but other students beat him up for dating a Native American, and he dumps her (3).

SYNOPSIS: Wolverine storms the docked SHIELD Helicarrier on his motorcycle, demanding that Fury release his NSA file. Nearby, Hydra's monitoring computers detect Wolverine's file being accessed. Wolverine learns that the Department of Agriculture's Pest Control section is a[t] Weapon X front, but fails to confront the Professor there. Discovering a Weapon X-owned warehouse, he has the X-Men fly him there; as they pore through his file, the Professor, Hines and a Hydra officer monitor Wolverine. In the warehouse, Wolverine discovers soundstage sets, some matching portions of his memories; he realizes that they must have been staged implants, but is relieved to not find a soundstage of his cabin[.] When Wolverine unlocks a vault door, a Shiva robot attacks; he easily destroys it, but another appears. The Hydra officer, revealed as Silver Fox, confronts the Professor, but recognizes the soundstages from her memories. As Wolverine defeats the second Shiva, the X-Men find the Professor dead, ripped apart by claws. Hines explains that Shiva has reset to its second target: Sabretooth.

NOTE: Labeled "Shiva Scenario, Part 3" on the inner cover. This issue has a die-cut cover and a second "inner cover;" it also has Wolverine pin-ups by Bill Sienkiewicz and Jim Lee. Wolverine reclaims his classic yellow costume here. Although this issue reveals that the Weapon X Program acted out false memories on soundstages, W #63, '92 reveals that they later hired Psi-Borg to implant them telepathically. Presumably memories with images that could not be feasibly acted out were Psi-Borg's work. Silver Fox's memories here match the stage sets exactly, and so were likely acted; the "prom attendees" may have been Weapon X employees. However, Wolverine's espionage memory in W #48-49, '91[)] contained graphic deaths, so though it seems to have been staged on a re-dressed "apartment" set, it was likely Psi-Borg's work — as was Wolverine's simulated rampage through the Weapon X facility in MCP #79-84, '91. This issue's "saloon" soundstage, complete with cake slice implies that Wolverine fighting Sabretooth after Silver Fox's death in W #10, '89 fb was an implant — but although Silver Fox is revealed here as alive, W:O #5, '06 clarified that the fight was real. Weapon X apparently added details to Wolverine's memory including Sabretooth taunting him with the cake, and made him think that Silver Fox died. Team X codenames Fox, Kestrel, Vole and Wildcat are revealed here. Kestrel is identified as John Wraith in W #61, '92, and the others' identities are implied in W #62, '92; W #63, '92 clarifies that Vole was not a field operative. This issue implies Silver Fox has some type of hidden claws, likely implanted by Weapon X, and clarifies that "Andre" is an alias. Despite the Professor's claim that Wolverine and Silver Fox's cabin was an implant, W #65, '93 reveals that it is real. Wood Buffalo National Park is, a[t] long last, named correctly.

WOLVERINE #51 (February 1992)

"Heartbreak Motel!" (22 pages)

CREDITS: Larry Hama (writer), Andy Kubert (pencils, c art), Dan Green (inks), Pat Brosseau (letters), Steve[n] Buccellato (colors), Suzanne Gaffney (asst editor), Bob Harras (editor), Tom Orzechowski (c letters)
FEATURE CHARACTER: Wolverine (also as virtual reality construct)
GUEST STARS: X-Men: Jean Grey (chr next in W #63, '92), Storm (prev 2 next in UXM #287, '92), Professor X (next bts in W #53, '92, chr next in W #63, '92), Forge (all last in UXM #286, '92), Cyclops (last in X #7, '92, chr next in W #65, '93) (prev 3 next in X Ann #1, '92)
SUPPORTING CAST: Albert, Elsie-Dee (both last in W #46, '91), Jubilee (last in X #7, '92)
OTHER CHARACTERS: Mystique (Raven Darkhölme, shapeshifter, also as Jean Grey, Silver Fox & blonde woman, last in XFac #70, '91), Spiral (last in X #5, '91), Hunter in Darkness (also as "Puppy"), Masque (next in XFor #6, '92) (prev 2 last in W #46 '91), Morlocks (some or others last in W #45, '91; others chr last in W #54, 1[,] or another next in XFor #6, some or others next in XFor #11, all '92), Auger Inn patrons & bartender, performers (on TV), fish; Lady Deathstrike, Shingen Harada, Ogun, Sabretooth (prev 4 as virtual reality constructs); Patsy Cline, Buddy Holly, Otis Redding, Stevie Ray Vaughan (prev 4[,] mentioned, musicians on jukebox, see NOTE), bullfighter, bull (prev 2 bts as painting)

LOCATIONS/ITEMS: X-Mansion inc Danger Room w/control booth, Salem Center's Auger Inn (bar) & Cloud 9 Motel w/Mystique's room, Morlocks' Alley[,] Manhattan's East River / Danger Room combat modules (destroyed), sensors (bts), computers & window display, virtual reality visualizer w/sensors & dummy[,] simulations of Shingen & Ogun's swords, Wolverine's motorcycle, Auger Inn cues, balls & jukebox, Mystique's money, Jubilee's rollerblades, Cloud 9 soda machine & TV, Elsie-Dee's new body (hereinafter considered her standard equipment & not listed separately) w/strange matter reactor & Body Shoppe sensors (prev 2 bts), Albert's underwater tunnel & B-2 stealth bomber (rebuilt) w/strange matter reactor (bts), Spiral's sensor probes (bts) & swords

SYNOPSIS: As Wolverine easily defeats Danger Room robots, Professor X and Forge discuss his recent personality changes: he has become surly, combative and restless, much like he was when he first joined the X-Men. Hoping to take his new measure, Professor X has Wolverine don a virtual reality headset; Wolverine battles simulations of several foes, and howls when he defeats them, worrying the X-Men. Later, as Wolverine shoots pool at a bar, a woman asks him to dance. That night, Jubilee rollerblades past a motel and spots Wolverine's motorcycle. Spying, she sees Wolverine with Jean Grey — but after Jubilee leaves, "Jean" reveals herself as Mystique. In the Morlock tunnels, Albert and the rebuilt Elsie-Dee befriend the Hunter in Darkness; all three take off in the rebuilt stealth bomber. Jubilee returns home, seeing Jean and realizing that the woman at the motel was an impostor. Mystique explains that she's worried about Spiral, her former Freedom Force teammate; detecting her name being spoken, Spiral teleports in.

NOTE: Cover-labeled "The Crunch Conundrum, 1 of Three." Sean is named in W #65, '93. The Auger Inn's name is a pun; to "auger in" is to crash a plane. Wolverine finally gets the joke in W #62, '92. All the musicians that Mystique notes on the Auger Inn jukebox died in plane or helicopter crashes.

WOLVERINE #52 (March 1992)

"Citadel at the End of Time" (22 pages)

CREDITS: Larry Hama (writer), Marc Silvestri (pencils), Dan Green (inks), Pat Brosseau (letters), Steve Buccellato (colors), Suzanne Gaffney (asst editor), Bob Harras (editor), Tom Orzechowski (c letters)
FEATURE CHARACTER: Wolverine
SUPPORTING CAST: Albert, Elsie-Dee, Jubilee
VILLAINS: Mojo (lord of TV-obsessed dimension, last in X #6, '92), Abcissa (alternate-future Jubilee, space-time teleporter, 1st), Plasma Wraiths (sentient energy fields, 1st, die)
OTHER CHARACTERS: Gateway (in image, last in UXM #281, '91), Mystique (also as Mojo), Spiral, Hunter in Darkness (as "Puppy"), Siksika (Blackfoot) natives (dead, as skeletons, some or others chr last in W #84, '94 fb), Earth-94102 Wolverine (dead, as skeleton, 1st but chr last in W #86, '94 fb), time travelers (most bts, traveling toward Crunch) inc alternate-timeline versions of Gateway & Spiral (prev 2 as images), performer (on TV), drivers; butterflies; bullfighter, bull (prev 2 as painting)
LOCATIONS/ITEMS: Cloud 9 motel w/Mystique's room (destroyed), X-Mansion, timestream, Citadel at the End of Time, Siksika burial ground (Alberta, Canada, near Weapon X Program facility) / Spiral's cloaking field (bts) & swords (others in image) w/circuits (bts), Cloud 9 painting, TV (prev 2 destroyed) & soda machine, Mojo's temporal seeker & uncertainty nullifier beams, Albert's B-2 stealth bomber w/umbilicals & antimatter implosion initiator (rebuilt cruise missile), Elsie-Dee's Body Shoppe sensors (bts), alternate-Gateway's staff (in image), Wolverine's motorcycle, Jubilee's rollerblades, truck (destroyed), Mojo's bio-technological chair (hereinafter considered his standard equipment and not listed separately), Abcissa's chains, helmet & rollerblades
SYNOPSIS: As Spiral worries that she can be traced, a Plasma Wraith appears and attacks. Wolverine and Spiral defeat it; Spiral generates a cloaking field and explains to Wolverine and Mystique that time-travelers across many realities are being drawn toward "the Crunch," the Big Bang's opposite — the end of time itself. An uncertainty nullifier beam suddenly erupts from the TV, nearly hitting them. Realizing that they are vulnerable in the past, Spiral generates a temporal vortex to the Crunch, sucking in the room's furnishings and Wolverine's motorcycle — and narrowly missing Jubilee, just arriving outside. As Jubilee investigates the empty room, Mojo suddenly appears, demanding Spiral's whereabouts. Wolverine, Mystique and Spiral arrive in the far future and defeat another Wraith; Spiral reveals that Mojo's scheme threatens all existence. At the hotel, Mojo and his teleporter Abcissa capture Jubilee. In Canada, the Hunter in Darkness leads Albert and Elsie-Dee to a native burial ground, where they discover an Adamantium skeleton with claws…

NOTE: Cover-labeled "The Crunch Conundrum, 2 of Three." Abcissa is revealed as an alternate-future Jubilee next issue. The Wolverine skeleton's native reality is designated in OHMU HC5, '08.

WOLVERINE #53 (April 1992)

"The Chimerical Mystery Tour!" (22 pages)

CREDITS: Larry Hama (writer), Marc Silvestri (pencils), Dan Green (co-inks, c inks), Hilary Barta & Klaus Janson (co-inks), Pat Brosseau (letters), Joe Rosas, Kevin Tinsley & Marie Javins (colors), Suzanne Gaffney (asst editor, uncredited), Bob Harras (editor), Tom Orzechowski (c letters)
FEATURE CHARACTER: Wolverine (next in W #55, '92)
GUEST STARS: Fantastic Four (family of super-heroic explorers): Mr. Fantastic (Dr. Reed Richards, stretchable body, last in Wlk&IW #3, '92, chr next in SH #48, '93, next bts in ASM #362, '92, next in ASM #363, '92), Thing (Ben Grimm, rocky hide & super-strength, last in FF #365, '92, next in SH #39, '92); X-Men: Professor X (bts forwarding Jubilee's call, last in W #51, '92, chr next in W #63, '92), Beast (Henry McCoy, blue fur, heightened agility & intelligence, last in X #7, '92) (prev 2 next in X Ann #1, '92), Gambit (Remy LeBeau, charges objects with explosive kinetic energy, next in W #55, '92) (prev 2 last in X #7, '92), Nick Fury (last in UXM #286, next bts in W #55, chr next in W #61, next in Dlk #10, all '92)
SUPPORTING CAST: Albert (also as image), Elsie-Dee (both chr next in W #84, '94 fb, next in W #82, '94), Jubilee (next in W #55, '92)
VILLAINS: Mojo (next in X Ann #1, '92), Abcissa (erased from time) (both also on monitor), Plasma Wraiths (some or all die, some or others next in Venom:TC #2, '96)
OTHER CHARACTERS: Gateway (in image, next in W #72, '93), Mystique (next in UXM #289, '92), Spiral (also in W #84, '94 fb, next in XFac Ann #7, '92), Hunter in Darkness (as "Puppy," chr next in W #84 fb, next bts in W #83, next in W #84, all '94), time travelers (bts, trapped in vortex) inc alternate-timeline versions of Gateway & Spiral, Siksika tribesmen (dead, as skeletons, some or others next in W #82, '94), Earth-94102 Wolverine (dead, as skeleton, also as digital reconstruction, next in TInc #9, '03, see NOTE), Roppongi police (some or others next in W #55, '92), arrestee
LOCATIONS/ITEMS: Citadel at the End of Time w/vortex crater, Siksika burial ground, Four Freedoms Plaza (Fantastic Four's Manhattan skyscraper), X-Mansion (bts), Tokyo's Roppongi District police station / Wolverine's motorcycle w/headlight, Spiral's tracer (bts) & sword, Mojo's ultra-gas plasma projection monitor (destroyed) & holovision sensor cameras, Jubilee's rollerblades, Abcissa's chains, helmet & rollerblades

(prev 4 also on monitor), Albert's B-2 stealth bomber (also in image) w/antimatter implosion initiator (also in image), scanners (bts), computer & monitor, FF's cards & chips, police handcuffs

SYNOPSIS: Wolverine, Mystique and Spiral assault Mojo's Citadel. Mojo taunts Wolverine with a captured Jubilee, and sends Plasma Wraith against them. In Canada, Albert and Elsie-Dee identify the skeleton as Wolverine's. Spiral reveals that Mojo is preventing the Crunch, which wi also retroactively prevent the Big Bang. Mojo offers to spare Wolverine if Jubilee becomes his slave. Gateway manifests, revealing that Albert's antimatter missile will kick-start the Crunch. Wolverine sends Spiral and Mystique back through time to retrieve it, as Mojo reveals that Abcissa is a future version of Jubilee. Spiral sends Albert, Elsie-Dee and the Hunter in Darkness back in time to investigate the skeleton; she then sends the missile forward, as the skeleton vanishes. As Wolverine rides the missile toward Mojo, Jubilee declines his offer and Abcissa vanishes. Jubilee and Wolverine dive through the vortex as the antimatter missile bears down on Mojo … Wolverine awakens at a super-hero card game in the present, and gets a call from Jubilee — who appeared in Tokyo.

NOTE: Cover-labeled "The Crunch Conundrum, 3 of Three." Gambit's last name is revealed in X #8, '92. Despite Mojo's implication that the Wolverine skeleton is from Abcissa's timeline, where he sent Wolverine into the past after Jubilee agreed to serve him, W #86, '94 reveals that it is from a timeline where Wolverine and Forge traveled to Earth-616's past chasing the Adversary. The skeleton has reappeared by TInc #9 '93; it seems Albert and Elsie-Dee's interference had no permanent effect on the timeline. The Tokyo police station is clarified to be in Roppong District in W #55, '92.

WOLVERINE #54 (May 1992)

"Station Identification" (22 pages)

CREDITS: Fabian Nicieza (writer), Darick Robertson (pencils), Don Hudson (inks), Pat Brosseau & Michae Heisler (letters), Kelly Corvese (colors), Suzanne Gaffney (asst editor), Bob Harras (editor), Josef Rubinstein (inks), Tom Orzechowski (c letters)
FEATURE CHARACTER: Wolverine (chr last in GR/W/Pun, '91, chr next in W #48, '91)
GUEST STARS: X-Force (former New Mutants): Shatterstar (Gaveedra-Seven, Mojoverse gladiator, chr ne in Cap #406, '92), Cannonball (chr next in XFac #77, '92) (both chr last in XFor #5, '91); Rogue (chr last in MCF #89/4, '91, chr next in X #4, '91)
VILLAINS: Vidkids (movie-themed murdering gang, some die) inc Jester (see NOTE), Cueball, K-Scope & Lin
OTHER CHARACTERS: Morlocks (1 dies, also on video; others bts, dead; some or others chr last in W #45 '91, others chr next in W #51, '92), newsreader (on TV), police (also on TV), bag lady, reporters, cameramer paramedics; Oliver Stone, John Ford (prev 2 mentioned as influences by Vidkids); Magneto, Savage Land tribesmen, dinosaurs (prev 3 a Danger Room simulations); Mickey Mouse (on shirt)
LOCATIONS/ITEMS: New York City inc church (on TV), South Bronx & lower Manhattan w/subway station & tunnels, X-Force's Adirondac Mountains base (upstate New York), news studio (in New York), X-Mansion w/Danger Room, Savage Land (in simulation) / Vidkids' cameras (some destroyed), videotapes (bts), tape box, lights & weapons inc claws (see NOTE), swords (1 destroyed), clubs, knife, wrecking ball & knuckle spikes, Link's chain, Cueball's bola, pool balls & cue, Jester's juggling balls, stretchers (1 on TV), X-Force's monitor & computer w/holographi display, Shatterstar's swords, tribesmen's bows & arrows (prev 2 as illusion), subway train (bts), bag lady's cart, police cars, ambulance handcuffs (bts), reporters' cameras & microphone
SYNOPSIS: The Vidkids chase down a Morlock and beat him to death, taping the attack. They send the video, their fourth recorded murder, to TV studio. Shatterstar, formerly an arena-warrior entertainer from Mojo's TV-obsessed dimension, sees the news report; unpleasantly reminde of himself, he decides to find the Vidkids. At the X-Mansion, Rogue and Wolverine work out in the Danger Room, and Wolverine sees the Vidkids on the news. He investigates their last attack, but encounters Shatterstar. Each believing the other to be a Vidkid, they briefly clash unt Shatterstar recognizes Wolverine, who is a revered entertainment icon on his homeworld. The Vidkids chase a bag lady into the subway tunnels but Wolverine and Shatterstar rescue her and battle the gang. Shatterstar nearly kills one, but Wolverine stops him, destroying their camera instead. The two watch as the Vidkids are arrested, but arriving reporters continue to give them the audience they crave. Uncomfortable Shatterstar ponders his place in his new world.
NOTE: This issue, a fill-in, takes place out of sequence prior to W #48, '91. Jester is not named on-panel, but the back of his jacket reads "Jester" and he wears a jester's cap. One of the Vidkids wears a makeshift Wolverine costume, complete with claws. Shatterstar's real name is revealed in XFor #39, '94. X-Force's base is formerly Larry Trask's Sentinel base, seen in X #58-60, '69. Cannonball wears a "Button Your Fly shirt, referencing a 1991 Levi's jeans commercial starring X-Force artist Rob Liefeld.

WOLVERINE #55 (June 1992)

"Thirty Slashes Over Tokyo (or 'Sayonara Yellow Brick Road')" (22 pages)

CREDITS: Larry Hama (writer), Marc Silvestri (pencils), Dan Green (inks), Pat Brosseau (letters), Steve Buccellato (colors), Suzanne Gaffney (asst editor), Bob Harras (editor), Tom Orzechowski (c letters)
FEATURE CHARACTER: Wolverine
GUEST STARS: Nick Fury (bts dispensing waiver, chr next in W #61, '92, next in Dlk #10, '92), Gambit (both las in W #53, '92), Sunfire (Shiro Yoshida, solar-blasting mutant, Mariko's cousin, last in UXM #286, '92)
SUPPORTING CAST: Mariko Yashida (last in NW #20, '91), Yukio (last in KP&W #6, '85), Jubilee
VILLAINS: Cylla Markham (former Reaver, also as Izzy, last as Skullbuster in UXM #281, '91, see NOTE), Lady Deathstrike (between UXM #281, '91 & Cap #411, '92), Silver Fox (bts monitoring SHIELD, last in W #50, '92), Matsu Tsurayaba (Hand ninjas' Jonin (leader), last in X #7, '92), Death Touch Cult Hand ninjas (use modern weaponry, 1s unnamed), Roppongi police (some or others last in W #53, '92) inc van driver & guard, punk girls, cabbie (prev working for Hand)
OTHER CHARACTERS: Reiko (last in W #33, '90), Eddie (warehouse employee), Jotaro Isuzu (customs official), Honda & Suzuki (prev Isuzu's police aides), Clan Yashida members (some or others last in NW #20, '91), airline announcer, helicopter pilot (prev 2 voice only), airpo security guards, travelers, cabbie, Matsuo's chauffeur (bts driving limo), jail matron, arrestees, bystanders; mouse, car (prev 2 as carwash sign
LOCATIONS/ITEMS: Los Angeles International Airport, Acme Storage Corp. warehouse, Deathstrike's base, Tokyo inc Narita Airport, Shingen Citadel compound & Roppongi District w/carwash & police station w/cells, evidence room & roof / Wolverine's security waiver (bts), luggage &

motorcycle, Gambit's playing cards (hereinafter considered his standard equipment and not listed separately), staff & luggage, guards' guns, metal detector & X-Ray machine, Cylla's crate (destroyed) & cybernetic implants inc maintenance program (voice only), monitoring programs, HUD displays, telecom system, voice synthesizer, targeting suite (prev 5 bts) & molybidium steel arm blades, airline computers (bts), Eddie's forklift, taxis (1 destroyed), ninjas' armor, swords, guns, van & helicopter w/radio, cabbie's gun, Matsuo's prosthetic hand (see NOTE) & limousine w/car phone, satellite (bts), Clan members' phone tracer (bts) & swords, police van, bolt-cutters, crowbar & guns, Jubilee's handcuffs, Isuzu's X-Ray machine (bts), paperwork & business card, Reiko's poisoned cane-sword, Sunfire's power-enhancing armor, confiscated objects inc gun & chainsaw

SYNOPSIS: Wolverine and Gambit try to fly to Japan to retrieve Jubilee, but security detects Wolverine's claws. He requests a security waiver from SHIELD, but the cyborg Cylla's monitoring program detects his call, activating her. In a Roppongi jail, Jubilee fends off her cellmates with fireworks; one sends a message to the Hand. In Tokyo, a cabbie secretly working for the Hand drives Wolverine and Gambit into a carwash; ninjas attack, but the mutants defeat them. Matsuo Tsurayaba pressures Mariko, seeking to purchase the criminal activities that she wishes to rid Clan Yashida of. Matsuo orders the police to move Jubilee in a van with Reiko, who he blinded as punishment for Dai-Kumo's death. Cylla ships herself to Japan, addressed to Wolverine. When police take Wolverine to the crate, she bursts out and attacks. Sunfire arrives, aiding Gambit as ninjas attack the police station. Reiko tries to poison Jubilee as Matsuo ordered, but realizes that she is Wolverine's friend and spares her. As Reiko leaves, Jubilee encounters Yukio…

NOTE: Although Sunfire and Mariko share a surname, they spell it differently ("Yoshida" vs. "Yashida"). Since both are Anglicized spellings of Japanese characters, both are equally valid. Shingen's Tokyo Citadel is not the same building as the Yashidas' ancestral manor, which is near Agarashima. This issue reveals Dai-Kumo to have been in the Hand's employ, and specifies that Jubilee arrived in Tokyo's Roppongi District (misspelled "Ropongi" throughout this arc). The Reavers were nearly destroyed by Sentinels in UXM #281, '91; Deathstrike and Cylla were the only two immediate survivors. W #77, '94 confirms that Deathstrike is Cylla's informant here. Cylla is not the original Skullbuster, bts in W #23, '90; she replaced him after he was killed in UXM #255, '89. Wolverine cut off Matsuo's hand in X #7, '92. The Death Touch Cult are named in W #108, '96; they are one of several Hand factions that Matsuo commands.

WOLVERINE #56 (Early July 1992)

"We Got Cylla, Can Mothra Be Far Behind?" (22 pages)

CREDITS: Larry Hama (writer), Marc Silvestri (pencils), Dan Green (inks), Pat Brosseau (letters), Steve Buccellato (colors), Suzanne Gaffney (asst editor), Bob Harras (editor)
FEATURE CHARACTER: Wolverine
GUEST STARS: Sunfire (also on monitor, next in W #60, '92), Gambit
SUPPORTING CAST: Jubilee, Yukio, Mariko Yashida
VILLAINS: Cylla Markham, Matsuo Tsurayaba, Death Touch Cult Hand ninjas (some also on monitors, some possibly die), Silver Fox, Hydra agents (some die, some or others last in SM #23, '92), Kojiro (mercenary, 1st), Roppongi police (working for Hand)
OTHER CHARACTERS: Silver Samurai (last in W #3, '89, chr last in W #150, '00 fb), Reiko, Matsuo's chauffeur (voice only), Tokyo police (in shadow), firemen (bts extinguishing fire), Yashida Clan members; Black Blade (last in W #3, '89); Japanese politicians (mentioned, owe Yashidas favors)

LOCATIONS/ITEMS: Tokyo inc Yukio's rented room, docks, Shingen's Citadel compound & Roppongi District police station (destroyed) w/ evidence room & nearby alley / Cylla's cybernetic implants inc targeting suite & arm blades, Sunfire's power-enhancing armor, Gambit's staff & stolen taxi, confiscated objects inc brass knuckles, guns & chainsaw, police guns & cars, ninjas' armor, swords, guns, tiger claws, crossbow, arrow & camera w/radio, Yukio's trunk of weapons inc sais, chains, axes, shuriken & ropes, Reiko's valuables & poisoned cane-sword, freighter, Kojiro's van & chained maces, Hydra's guns, fire truck, Wolverine's motorcycle, Mariko's chart, Clan member's sword, Silver Samurai's armor

SYNOPSIS: Wolverine and Cylla battle in the evidence room, while Sunfire and Gambit battle ninjas in the police station lobby, and Matsuo monitors the attacks from his limousine. Cylla explains that she's not fighting Wolverine on anyone's orders, she just loves the thrill of combat. As two allies try to sneak past Sunfire, he unleashes a plasma blast at them, severing a structural support and collapsing the building. He and Gambit then confront Cylla, who flees. Jubilee and Yukio hear police cars heading for the battle, and follow. Reiko tries to buy passage out of Japan, but is captured by Silver Fox, who requires her services. Jubilee and Yukio see Matsuo giving orders to his ninjas, and shadow him. As Mariko and Yashida businessmen discuss how to rid themselves of their criminal ties, Silver Samurai interrupts, demanding to lead the family. Wolverine and Gambit enter as well, just as ninjas surround the Yashida compound — and Matsuo arrives, seeking revenge for his severed hand.

NOTE: The series begins biweekly publication again here. A scene showing police fleeing out the station front door is incorrectly captioned "on the roof."

WOLVERINE #57 (Late July 1992)

"Death in the Family!" (22 pages)

CREDITS: Larry Hama (writer), Marc Silvestri (pencils), Dan Green (co-inks, c inks), Al Milgrom & Josef Rubinstein (co-inks), Pat Brosseau (letters), Steve Buccellato (colors), Suzanne Gaffney (asst editor), Bob Harras (editor)
FEATURE CHARACTER: Wolverine (also in photo, also in W #150, '00 fb & W:O #24, '08 fb, next in W #60, '92)
GUEST STAR: Gambit (next in W #60, '92)
SUPPORTING CAST: Jubilee, Yukio (both next in W #60, '92), Mariko Yashida (also in photo, dies, also in W #150, '00 fb & W:O #24, '08 fb, next bts in W #60, '92, possibly next as spirit in W #111, '97, see W #60, '92's NOTE)
VILLAINS: Cylla Markham (next in W #77, '94), Matsuo Tsurayaba (next in W #60, '92), Death Touch Cult Hand ninjas (some also on monitor, some die, some or others next in W #87, '94), Silver Fox (next bts in W #61, '92, next in W #62, '92), Hydra agents (some or others next in W #62, '92), Kojiro
OTHER CHARACTERS: Silver Samurai (becomes Clan Yashida Oyabun, next in Cable #2, '92), Reiko (dies), Clan Yashida members (some or others next in Cable #2, '92), Tokyo police (bts, obstructed by Matsuo), Matsuo's chauffeur (bts driving limo); Black Blade; dogs (die); Shingen Harada (mentioned, built traps), Muramasa (mentioned, crafted dagger)

LOCATIONS/ITEMS: Shingen's Citadel compound w/chapel, roof & nearby rooftop / Silver Samurai's armor, Gambit's staff, ninjas' camera (bts), armor, swords & guns, Clan Yashida's Honor Sword, Shingen's spiked trap & razor-blade maze, Matsuo's prosthetic hand & limousine w/ monitors, Reiko's bonds (bts), cane-sword & poisoned dagger, Hydra hovercraft w/machine gun, Wolverine's brown costume, Kojiro's chained mace, Silver Fox's gun, power line (destroyed), Cylla's cybernetic implants inc infrared detectors, audio direction finders, pulse-Doppler rada (prev 3 bts), targeting suite & arm blades, Clan member's sword, Yashida underworld holdings (bts), Mariko's photo, Yukio's throwing blade

SYNOPSIS: Wolverine, Gambit, the Silver Samurai and Mariko retreat into the compound; booby-traps kill several ninjas that follow. Silve Fox arrives with Reiko, offering Matsuo another way to exact revenge. Mariko apologizes for failing to fully eliminate Clan Yashida's underworld ties, but Wolverine understands. On the compound's roof, Cylla attacks Jubilee and Yukio; Wolverine comes to their aid. Reiko navigates the compound's maze and offers Mariko a deal: Matsuo will purchase and dissolve her criminal holdings if Mariko cuts off her finger. Reiko cut herself to demonstrate the blade's purity, but when Mariko begins her cut, she is racked with pain — the blade was poisoned, but Reiko wa immune. Hearing Mariko's screams, Wolverine rushes to her side; Reiko, realizing that Wolverine is Mariko's beloved, kills herself in shame Mariko bids Wolverine farewell, asking him to use his claws to spare her an agonizing death. On the roof, Jubilee and Yukio electrocute Cylla who limps away. Inside, Gambit and the Samurai hear Wolverine's claws, and see him silently holding Mariko's lifeless body.

WOLVERINE #58 (Early August 1992)

"Monkeywrenching!" (22 pages)

CREDITS: D.G. Chichester (writer), Darick Robertson (pencils), Josef Rubinstein (inks), Pat Brosseau (letters) Ariane Lenshoek (colors), Suzanne Gaffney (asst editor), Bob Harras (editor), Tom Orzechowski (c letters)
FEATURE CHARACTER: Wolverine (chr last in W #65, '93)
GUEST STARS: Professor X (chr last in W #65, '93), Terror (absorbs abilities & sensations from stolen body parts, last in TInc #5, '92)
SUPPORTING CAST: Jubilee (chr last in W #65, '93)
VILLAINS: Ecotage (Nature Defense League fringe group, unnamed): Monkeywrench (Johnny Bloodcede, also in drawings, 1st but chr last in W #59, '92 photo), Pick Axis (pickaxe-wielding trio), Lance (dies), Paul, Bunyan (prev 2 midgets)

OTHER CHARACTERS: Barton Hoff (logging magnate), Alison "Alice" Hoff (Barton's daughter, 1st bts kidnapped, also in photo), Jacob "Jake" Grenfire (Nature Defense League founder, also in drawings) (prev 2 chr last in W #59, '92 photo), ba patrons & bartender, night coroner (bts, bribed to leave), James J. Chan (dead in morgue); Night Wind (Alice's horse, in photo), birds; Luke Perry (mentioned, appearing on TV), model (on poster)

LOCATIONS/ITEMS: X-Mansion w/Danger Room (bts), Oregon bar, logging site & morgue / Alice's scrapbook w/photo & lock of hair, Professo X's wheelchair, Jubilee's napkin drawing, loggers' bulldozers (1 destroyed), Lance's grenades & monkeywrench pendant, Terror's drawing & assimilated body parts inc Lance's eye & ear, illustrator's fingers, Chan's legs & Talita's arm w/metal armor (see NOTE), Monkeywrench's mallet wrenches & explosive spikes, Pick Axis' pickaxes, Paul & Bunyan's saw

SYNOPSIS: Wolverine overhears Professor X's associate Barton Hoff ask for help finding his daughter Alice, kidnapped by a radica environmentalist group. Needing something to take his mind off Mariko's death, Wolverine decides to investigate. He and Jubilee travel to Oregon and learn that fringe group Ecotage split from the peaceful Nature Defense League. Having little success befriending the environmentalists they follow Ecotage member Lance to a logging site and witness him planting grenades in bulldozers. Lance detonates a grenade when they interrupt; Wolverine tries to question him, but Lance impales himself on a shard of wreckage. Wolverine summons Terror to the morgue; he removes Lance's eye and ear, attaching them to his body and absorbing Lance's recent experiences, including holding Alice prisoner. Ecotage leader Monkeywrench and his followers attack the morgue to reclaim Lance's body. Paul and Bunyan sever Terror's legs, but he takes new ones from a corpse. Wolverine, Jubilee and Terror defeat Ecotage, but Monkeywrench drives an explosive stake into Wolverine's chest.

NOTE: This issue and next, fill-ins, take place out of sequence following W #65, '93. Alice's full first name is given as Alison in her scrapbook. Jake Grenfire's full first name is revealed next issue. OHMU:ME #28, '93 establishes that Terror's armored left arm belonged to his lover; her name i revealed in TInc #1, '07. Ecotage's name is revealed in OHMU:Hor, '05. Wolverine's blue trunks are incorrectly colored yellow in one panel here.

WOLVERINE #59 (Late August 1992)

"Unnatural Resources" (22 pages)

CREDITS: D.G. Chichester (writer), Darick Robertson (pencils), Josef Rubinstein (inks), Pat Brosseau (letters) Ariane Lenshoek (colors), Suzanne Gaffney (asst editor), Bob Harras (editor)
FEATURE CHARACTER: Wolverine (next in X Ann #1, '92, see NOTE)
GUEST STAR: Terror (next in DD #305, '92)
SUPPORTING CAST: Jubilee (next in X Ann #1/2, '92)
VILLAINS: Ecotage: Monkeywrench (also in photo, his chr 1st app, prior to last issue), Pick Axis, Paul, Bunyan OTHER CHARACTERS: Alice Hoff, Jake Grenfire (prev 2 also in photo, their chr 1st apps, prior to last issue) NDL members, Barton Hoff & his work crews (bts, told to stop work) & aide, drunk; birds; Gaea (mentioned)
LOCATIONS/ITEMS: Oregon lake, gas station w/bathroom & forest w/logging sites & Monkeywrench's camp dam construction site (in photo) / Terror's traps & assimilated body parts inc arm wrestler & safari guide's hands

sonar operator's ear & Talita's arm w/metal armor, Monkeywrench's explosive spikes (all but 1 bts), wrenches (destroyed), torch & photo, Alice's banner (in photo), ropes (destroyed), chains & gag, Wolverine's sunglasses, NDL members' chains (1 set destroyed), keys & sand (prev 2 bts) loggers' bulldozers, Grenfire's throat protector, Pick Axis' pickaxes, Paul & Bunyan's saw

SYNOPSIS: Terror submerges Wolverine in the freezing water of an icy lake, cooling the explosive spike. Wolverine slips under the ice bu follows Jubilee's fireworks to the surface; he cuts his way free and Terror extracts the spike. At Ecotage's camp, Monkeywrench exhorts hi followers to feel nature's pain, and berates a chained Alice. Wolverine gives himself a buzz cut to infiltrate Ecotage, posing as an NDL membe When Ecotage confronts NDL, Wolverine demands more extreme action, pretends to choke Grenfire and "defects." Monkeywrench chains Alice high in a tree, planning for her father's loggers to cut it down and kill her. He then begins to initiate Wolverine into Ecotage, but Wolverine smells Alice on him; Jubilee and Terror attack and capture the other Ecotage members while Wolverine climbs up to Alice. Monkeywrench destroys the tree with explosive spikes, but Wolverine leaps clear with Alice, then pursues Monkeywrench into the woods. At the NDL protest, Barton has given in and halted logging. Wolverine returns, reuniting him with Alice — but also threatening him to be more ecologically minded.

NOTE: It is unclear if Wolverine actually kills Monkeywrench. Grenfire's full first name, Jacob, is revealed here; Bunyan's name is misspelled "Bunyon." See the Index entry for W #65, '93 for Wolverine's full chronology following this issue. Grenfire's shirt changes color twice over two pages

MARVEL COLLECTOR'S EDITION (1992)

"U Can't Touch … the Eel!" (8 pages)

CREDITS: Tony Isabella (writer), Alan Kupperberg (art, front c art), Rick Parker (letters), Janice Cohen Parker (colors), Glenn Herdling (editor)
FEATURE CHARACTER: Spider-Man (also in rfb & pfb, chr last in WoSM #72, '91, chr next in ASM #344, '91)
SUPPORTING CAST: Mary Jane Watson-Parker (Spider-Man's wife, in pfb, chr last in SpecSM #172, '91, chr next in ASM #344, '91; also in rfb)
VILLAIN: Eel (Edward Lavell, electricity-generating suit, last in AvS #29/2, '90, next in Cap #411, '93)
OTHER CHARACTERS: Police inc Sgt. Demeo, salesman (in pfb), society columnist (bts writing column), wealthy couple (bts in Bahamas), Eel's lawyer (bts demanding payment); lions (as statues)
LOCATIONS/ITEMS: New York City inc jewelry store (in pfb), New York Public Library & rich couple's penthouse, Anna Watson's home (in rfb) / Eel's electronic lock (bts), suitcase & frictionless suit w/electrical field, Atimor brooch (in pfb), Spider-Man's wallet (in pfb), handkerchief, automatic camera & spider-signal belt, rich couple's electronic security system (bts) & jewelry
FLASHBACKS: Mary Jane introduces herself to Peter (ASM #42, '66). Mary Jane admires a brooch, but tells Peter that they can't afford it (p).
SYNOPSIS: Hoping to earn money to buy Mary Jane an anniversary gift, Spider-Man searches for crime to photograph. He spots the Eel breaking into a penthouse and confronts him. Spider-Man is unable to get a grip on the frictionless villain, so he knocks him off the rooftop and into a webbing net. Explaining that the net will dissolve in an hour, Spider-Man convinces the Eel to surrender. Spider-Man snaps photos as the police collect the villain.
NOTE: This flipbook one-shot was sponsored by Charleston Chew, sent to fans who mailed in one candy wrapper and 50 cents. Each story is followed by a 1-page multiple-choice quiz about that story's plot. (This story's Quiz #1 features a Spider-Man image by John Romita.) An answer card is stapled into the book's center; submitting it with the correct answers for all four quizzes entered readers into a contest to win one of 50 prizes including a Marvel jacket, an X-Men handheld video game or a year's subscription to WoSM, SS, W or GR.

2ND STORY: "The Leader" (6 pages)
CREDITS: George Carragonne (writer), Nelson DeCastro (art), Steve Dutro (letters), George Roussos (colors), Glenn Herdling (editor)
FEATURE CHARACTER: Silver Surfer (Norrin Radd, spacefaring cosmic hero, between SS #66-67, '92)
VILLAINS: Silicon Hosts (Krell robots, destroyed, some or others also in pfb)
OTHER CHARACTERS: Light Raiders (Krell rebels): Alas Longrun, new recruits, others (in pfb, die); Longrun's steed; Krell gods (mentioned) inc Dakar & Ceeara
LOCATIONS/ITEMS: Krell (ruined planet, also in pfb) / Silver Surfer's surfboard (hereinafter considered his standard equipment and not listed separately), Silicon Hosts' blasters (some or others in pfb), master computer (bts) & hover-platforms, Light Raider's gun (in pfb), Longrun's blaster & laser sword
FLASHBACK: The Silicon Hosts wipe out most of the Light Raiders (p).
SYNOPSIS: On Krell, the Silver Surfer saves Alas Longrun from a pursuing robot. She explains that her planet's robots conquered its people, and she is the last surviving rebel. She asks the Surfer to fight with her, but he refuses, explaining that the Krell people must win their own battle for it to have meaning. Several other robots attack; the Surfer briefly aids Longrun but lets her destroy most of them. Her valiant actions inspire several bystanders to join her cause.
NOTE: This story is followed by Quiz #2 (1 page), featuring a Silver Surfer image by Ron Lim.

3RD STORY: "Gimme a Break" (8 pages)
CREDITS: Richard Howell (plot), Larry Hama (script), Sam Keith (art, back c art), Ken Lopez (letters), Joe Rosas (colors), Jim Salicrup (editor)
FEATURE CHARACTER: Wolverine (chr last in W #47, '91, chr next in Dlk #4, '91)
SUPPORTING CAST: Jubilee (chr last in W #46, '91, chr next in Dlk #4, '91)
LOCATIONS/ITEMS: X-Mansion Danger Room & infirmary / Danger Room control panel (destroyed), debris & traps inc net, piledriver & robot (destroyed) w/vise clamps, Jubilee's cast
SYNOPSIS: As Wolverine and Jubilee clean the Danger Room after an aggressive workout, a damaged control panel accidentally activates the maximum threat level program. A piledriver knocks the wind out of Wolverine, and a robot descends from a ceiling panel and threatens to crush him. Jubilee attacks the robot, but it throws her into a wall — enraging Wolverine, who destroys it. Later, the two laugh about the incident as Jubilee recuperates from a sprained ankle, suffered after tripping over a piece of debris.
NOTE: This issue is a flipbook; the 3rd & 4th stories appear on the reverse side of the comic. This story occurs before Wolverine reverted to his yellow costume in W #50, '92. The story is followed by Quiz #3 (1 page), featuring a Wolverine image by Steve Lightle. The quiz clears up a continuity error in the story: Wolverine claims to have broken some ribs, which is impossible given his Adamantium skeleton. The quiz states that he must have been exaggerating.

4TH STORY: "You've Got to Have Friends" (6 pages)
CREDITS: Howard Mackie (writer), John Hebert (pencils), Jimmy Palmiotti (inks), Rick Parker (letters), Ariane Lenshoek (colors), Glenn Herdling (editor)
FEATURE CHARACTER: Ghost Rider (Dan Ketch, Kale's mortal host, last in MCP #118/3, '92, next in GR #24, '92)
SUPPORTING CAST: Noble Kale (Spirit of Vengeance, unnamed, last in MCP #118/3, '92, next in GR #24, '92)
VILLAIN: Devil Grip (burly criminal)
OTHER CHARACTERS: Mike "Mouse" McCormick (Dan's friend) & his mother, neighborhood kids (some bts); Mike's father (mentioned, dead); Barbara Ketch (Dan's sister), Hector Collazo (prev 2 names on graves), devil (as tattoo)
LOCATIONS/ITEMS: Brooklyn, New York inc Cypress Hills Cemetery / Ghost Rider's chain & flaming motorcycle (also as regular motorcycle) & Medallion of Power (also as fuel cap) (all hereinafter considered his standard equipment and not listed separately), cemetery fence (destroyed), Barbara & Hector's gravestones

SYNOPSIS: Shy "Mouse" McCormick flees from Devil Grip, a criminal whom he had reluctantly begun working for to impress the neighborhood kids. He runs past Dan, who notices that Mouse is bleeding and transforms into Ghost Rider. Devil Grip corners Mouse and moves to crush his head, saying that he shouldn't have pried so deeply into his operations. Ghost Rider arrives and uses his penance stare on Devil Grip, then drives Mouse home — who is grateful to finally have a friend.

NOTE: This story is followed by Quiz #4 (1 page), featuring a Ghost Rider image by Javier Saltares. Kale's name is revealed in GR #77, '9 He assumes full control of Dan's physical form when he becomes Ghost Rider, hence his inclusion in the Supporting Cast. Hector Collazo is Marvel artist; he may have worked on this story in some capacity.

WOLVERINE #60 (Early September 1992)

"Counting Coup" (22 pages)

CREDITS: Larry Hama (writer), Dave Hoover (pencils), Keith Williams (inks), Pat Brosseau (letters), Kev Tinsley (colors), Suzanne Gaffney (asst editor), Bob Harras (editor), Larry Stroman (c pencils), Dan Green inks), Tom Orzechowski (c letters)

FEATURE CHARACTER: Wolverine (also as Experiment X in his own thoughts & as mannequin, also as a b in fb2/implant between W #62, '92 fb & W #49, '91 fb; also as Logan in fb1 between X #6, '92 fb & W #61, '92 f

GUEST STARS: Gambit (last in W #57, '92, next in X Ann #1, '92), Sunfire (last in W #56, '92, next in X #25, '9

SUPPORTING CAST: Team X: Mastodon (bts, aging rapidly, also bts in fb1, reassigned, between W #61, '92 & this issue's main story; last in W #49, '91 fb), Maverick (formerly Wildcat, as North in fb1 between X #6, '92 & W #61, '92 fb), John Wraith (formerly Kestrel, named, also in Sabretooth's hallucination, also fb1 between #61, '92 fbs; last in W #61, '92 fb), Silver Fox (bts as a girl in fb2/implant between W #62, '92 & W #49, '91 fb bt

Mariko Yashida (bts, dead in grave, possibly next as spirit in W #111, '97, corpse next bts in W #11, '11, see NOTE) (prev 2 also in Wolverine thoughts), Jubilee (chr last in W #57, '92), Yukio (next in UXM #311, '94)

VILLAINS: Sabretooth (also in fb2/implant between W #62-63, '92 fbs; also as Creed in fb1 between X #6, '92 fb & W #61, '92 fb; last in X # '92, chr last in UA #4, '98), Shiva (last in W #50, '92, next in W #64, '92), Psi-Borg (formerly Vole, unnamed, bts manipulating Mastodon, al bts in fb2/implant between W #62, '92 fb bts & W #63, '92 fb; last bts in MCP #84, '91, next in W #62, '92), Omega Red (bts in fb1 between #6, '92 fb & W #61, '92 fb), Matsuo Tsurayaba (last in W #57, '92, next in X #18, '93), Hand ninjas (some die, others last in X #4, '92, some others next in IM #283, '92), muggers, skinheads

OTHER CHARACTERS: Janice Hollenbeck (double agent, dead in fb1 between X #6, '92 fb & W #61, '92 fb), Major Arthur Barrington (Tea X's CIA liaison, bts arranging helicopter in fb1 between X #5-6, '92 fbs), wrestlers, audience, referee, subway conductor (voice only), Japa finest swordsmith, Mandarin's armorer (prev 2 bts crafting Matsuo's hand), Japanese government (bts asking Wolverine to leave), chauffeur (driving limo); Plasma Wraith (in Wolverine's memories)

LOCATIONS/ITEMS: Tokyo inc cemetery & Matsuo's penthouse, Manhattan inc Madison Square Garden & subway inc Penn Station tunnels, East Berlin (in fb1), Sabretooth's cabin (in fb2, psychic image), "painscape" (in Wolverine's thoughts), Mystique's Cloud 9 Mot room (in Wolverine's memories) / Mariko's memorial tablet, Jubilee's umbrella, Experiment X's wires & battery packs (prev 2 in Wolverine thoughts), wrestler's club, Shiva's robot bodies (both destroyed) w/electronic triggers (bts), subway train, Wraith's book, gun & shape charge, Matsuo's Wolverine mannequin (destroyed) & prosthetic hand (destroyed) w/piston-mounted steel finger blades, ninjas' swords (som destroyed), Sunfire's power-enhancing armor, Carbonadium Synthesizer (bts), Barrington's helicopter (mentioned), Team X's body arm Wraith's jeep & bazooka w/shell (prev 5 in fb1), Sabretooth's axe & belt, Silver Fox's medicine pouch w/Psi-Borg's tooth (bts in pouch) Wolverine's keys (prev 4 in fb2), Wolverine's limousine

FLASHBACKS: As Team X escapes with the Carbonadium Synthesizer, John Wraith stays behind to delay the pursuing Omega Red (1). In implanted memory, Sabretooth is enraged to find that his son, a young Wolverine, has been seeing a young Silver Fox (2).

SYNOPSIS: Wolverine sits at Mariko's grave, wrestling with his grief and fighting the urge to lose control. In New York, Sabretooth atten a wrestling match, but Shiva attacks him. Muggers confront John Wraith on the subway, but when skinheads confront the muggers, Wra intimidates both groups. Matsuo gloats over Mariko's death and tests his prosthetic hand's blades on a Wolverine mannequin, ignoring his ninja warnings to leave Tokyo to avoid Wolverine's vengeance. Sunfire relays the Japanese government's request that Wolverine leave the country. New York, Sabretooth decapitates a Shiva robot, but another attacks. Wraith arrives, destroys the second robot with explosives and retreats w Sabretooth. On the way to the airport, Wolverine smells Matsuo. Tracking and confronting him, Wolverine defeats Matsuo's ninjas and destroy his prosthetic hand. He slices Matsuo's face, and promises to take slow revenge, returning again and again to mutilate Matsuo more each time

NOTE: This issue occurs shortly after W #57, '92. Carbonadium (misspelled Carbonadum here) is a more malleable, less durable derivative Adamantium. Barrington's first name is revealed in Mvk #2, '97; Psi-Borg's codename is revealed in W #63, '92. Next issue explains that Wra is gathering the former Team X because Mastodon has lost his age-suppression factor. W:WXF, '09 clarifies that Psi-Borg arranged that los hence both are bts here. W #175/2, '02 reveals that Wolverine made good on his promise to Matsuo for the next several years. In W #111, '9 Ogun appears to raise Mariko's spirit from the afterlife, but as discussed in W #4, '82's NOTE, it could have simply been an illusion.

WOLVERINE #61 (Late September 1992)

"Nightmare Quest!" (22 pages)

CREDITS: Larry Hama (writer), Mark Texeira (art), Pat Brosseau (letters), Steve Buccellato (colors), Lisa Patri (asst editor), Bob Harras (editor)

FEATURE CHARACTER: Wolverine (also in his own dream & hallucination, also as Emilio Garra in fb3 himself in fb1 between W #49, '91 fb & XO:Sabre, '09 fb; also as Logan in fb2 between W #60, '92 fb & X # '92 fb)

GUEST STAR: Nick Fury (last in W #53, '92, last bts in W #55, '92, next in W #65, '93)

SUPPORTING CAST: Team X: Mastodon (also as Elefante in fb3 between W #49, '91 fb & W #60, '92 fb bt Maverick (as North in fb2 between W #60, '92 fb & X #7, '92 fb bts; also in Wolverine's hallucination), John Wra (also as himself & Carlisle in Wolverine's dream, also as Halcon in fb3 & himself in fb1 between W #63, '92 fb W #60, '92 fb; also in fb2 between W #60, '92 fb & W #60, '92); Jubilee

VILLAINS: Sabretooth (also in Wolverine's dream & hallucination, also as Emilio Garra in fb3 & himself in fb1 between W #49, '91 fb & XO:Sabre, '09 fb; also as Creed in fb2 between W #60, '92 fb & X #7, '92 fb), Silver Fox (bts, located by Wraith, also in Wolverine's dream; also bts as Zora de Plata in fb3 between W #49, '91 fb bts & W #1, '97), Omega Red (Arkady Rossovich, lethal pheromone secretion & Carbonadium arm coils, in fb2 between W #60, '92 fb & X #2, '91 bts), Cuban soldiers (in fb3, some or others last in W #49, '91 fb), young burglars

OTHER CHARACTERS: Janice Hollenbeck (dead, in fb2 between W #60, '92 fb & X #7, '92 fb), SHIELD agents (some or others last in SM #21, '92, next in W #65, '93) inc pilot (voice only), Asian woman (in fb1, dies), tentacled creature (in fb3), bystanders; "specters from Wolverine's past" (in his hallucination), Fidel Castro, John F. Kennedy, Nikita Khrushchev (prev 3 mentioned in fb3)

LOCATIONS/ITEMS: "Painscape" (in dream & hallucination), skies over California, South Central Los Angeles inc Wraith's home, Southeast Asian jungle (in fb1), East Berlin (in fb2), Cuban jungle (in fb3) / Silver Fox's medicine pouch & guns, Sabretooth & Wraith's guns, painscape tree w/handcuffed radiator (all in dream), airplane, SHIELD Helicarrier & helicopter, Wraith's flashlight, guns, TV & shaped charge, girl's bonds (bts in fb1), Team X's guns (in fb1 & fb3), Carbonadium Synthesizer (bts), Omega Red's Carbonadium coils (hereinafter considered his standard equipment and not listed separately), Team X's body armor, Wraith's jeep & bazooka (prev 5 in fb2), El Tigre's fence cutters, missile w/mobile launch platform & blind, soldiers' fence (destroyed) & rifles, Halcon's shaped charge (prev 7 in fb3), Shiva's head (destroyed) w/electronic triggers (bts), burglars' machine guns (destroyed), Mastodon's wheelchair, Sabretooth's restraints

FLASHBACKS: On a Team X mission, Wraith plans to spare a woman who had spotted them, but Sabretooth shoots her (1). In East Berlin, Omega Red attacks Wraith, who teleports away (2). In 1963, Team X tries to destroy missiles left behind in Cuba — but Silver Fox, who had defected, attacks them with a tentacled creature (3).

SYNOPSIS: Wolverine dreams about enemy and friendly versions of Silver Fox, Sabretooth and John Wraith. Jubilee wakes him when their flight from Japan is diverted to the SHIELD Helicarrier. Nick Fury explains that someone with considerable influence needs to see Wolverine immediately, and drops him and Jubilee off in what seems to be an abandoned war zone. Wraith arrives and uses the decapitated Shiva head to jog Wolverine's suppressed memories. Revealing that they are in a bad L.A. neighborhood, Wraith takes Wolverine and Jubilee to his house, where they scare off young children stealing Wraith's TV. Wraith reveals that Mastodon's artificial age-suppression factor has failed, and that he is gathering Team X to investigate before the same happens to the others. He explains that Silver Fox is still alive, startling Wolverine — then reveals that he has Sabretooth chained up in the basement.

NOTE: John Wraith is confirmed as both Carlisle and Kestrel here. Omega Red's last name is revealed as Russovich in Cable #9, '94; its correct Anglicized spelling is clarified as Rossovich in XMan #2, '95, and confirmed in GenX #11, '96.

WOLVERINE #62 (October 1992)

"Reunion!" (22 pages)

CREDITS: Larry Hama (writer), Mark Texeira (art), Pat Brosseau (letters), Marie Javins (colors), Lisa Patrick (asst editor), Bob Harras (editor), Tom Orzechowski (c letters)

FEATURE CHARACTER: Wolverine (also in rfb, also as a boy in fb/implant between W #49, '91 fb & W #60, '92 fb)

SUPPORTING CAST: Silver Fox (also seemingly dead in rfb, also as a girl in fb/implant between W #49, '91 fb & W #60, '92 fb), Maverick (last in X #6, '92), Mastodon (dies), John Wraith; Jubilee

VILLAINS: Sabretooth (also in rfb1; also in fb/implant between W #49, '91 fb & W #60, '92 fb), Psi-Borg (Aldo Ferro, "Il Topo Siciliano," telepath, 1st on-panel app, last bts in W #60, '92) & his guards, Hydra agents (some or others last in W #57, '92, chr next in SSWP #1, '92, next in NF:AoS #44, '93)

OTHER CHARACTERS: Carol Hines (last in W #50, '92), Ornette Higgenbotham (paraplegic hacker), Mrs. Higgenbotham (Ornette's mother), pizza delivery boy, vandals (bts defacing hovercraft), US government officials (bts assigning Maverick to Psi-Borg), drive-by shooters (mentioned), crippled Ornette), covert government agencies, Cuban crime families (prev 2 mentioned as Professor's allies), Wolverine spirit (mentioned in fb/implant)

LOCATIONS/ITEMS: Wraith & Higgenbothams' South Central Los Angeles homes, Psi-Borg's island fortress (off the coast of Seattle, Washington), skies over Pacific Ocean; Minneapolis, Minnesota (bts); Mount Logan inc saloon (prev 2 in rfb), Sabretooth's cabin (in fb, psychic image) / Sabretooth's restraints (destroyed), cake slice (bts in rfb), belt (in fb) & cigar, Wraith's gun, smoke bombs & shaped charge w/remote detonator (destroyed), Silver Fox's energy field disruptor (bts), blaster, handgun, armor & medicine pouch (also bts in fb) w/Psi-Borg's tooth (bts in pouch) & Wolverine's keys, Mastodon's wheelchair, Hydra VTOL hovercraft (destroyed) w/fuel cells (bts) & navigational computer, Jubilee's towels, Ornette's wheelchair & computer, NSA computers (bts), pizza, drive-by shooters' guns (mentioned), vandals' spray paint (bts), Psi-Borg's radar system, life-support armor, gold tooth (prev 3 bts), weights & surface-to-air missile, guards' smoke bombs (bts), blasters & armor w/targeting systems, image-intensifiers & infrared goggles, Hines' armor & handgun, Maverick's body armor & gun (prev 2 hereinafter considered his standard equipment and not listed separately)

FLASHBACKS: Wolverine holds Silver Fox's body; Sabretooth taunts him (W #41, '91). In an implanted memory, a young Silver Fox flirtatiously gives a young Wolverine her medicine pouch, but flees when she hears her father Sabretooth coming.

SYNOPSIS: Sabretooth breaks free and attacks Wolverine, but the two are shocked by the arrival of Silver Fox, whom both thought dead. When Wolverine rushes to greet her, she reveals that she harbors a deep grudge against him, though Wolverine does not know why. Silver Fox reveals that she and her Hydra agents have captured Carol Hines, the Weapon X Program senior staff's last survivor. Mastodon suddenly melts, his advanced age catching up to him, and a shocked Hines agrees to help. Wraith's next-door neighbor, a young hacker, breaks into the NSA computers and locates information on Team X, including the name Ferro. Hines recognizes Ferro as a Cuban mobster who aided Weapon X; the group travels to his Seattle island to confront him, but their hovercraft is shot down. They defeat Ferro's guards and storm his fortress, where they find him inexplicably young — and guarded by Maverick.

NOTE: The series returns to monthly publication here. Abraham Cornelius, the other surviving Weapon X staffer, was killed in X #7, '92. Next issue reveals that Maverick was assigned to protect Psi-Borg by the US government. W #64, '92 reveals that Psi-Borg's youth is an illusion; he is an old man in a robotic suit. Psi-Borg's real name is revealed here, his Team X codename (Vole) is correctly guessed, and Silver Fox's codename (Fox) is confirmed; Maverick's codename (Wildcat) can thus be deduced by process of elimination. Sabretooth is accidentally missing from the computer's Team X roster readout. The Hydra hovercraft was vandalized while parked in L.A.; several names spray-painted on it are comic creators, including Steve Biasi, Frank Frazetta, Larry Hama, Bob Harras, Jimmy Palmiotti and Lisa Patrick. As the hovercraft crashes, Wolverine finally gets the pun in the Auger Inn's name, from W #51, '92.

WOLVERINE #63 (November 1992)

"Bastions of Glory!" (22 pages)

CREDITS: Larry Hama (writer), Mark Texeira (art), Pat Brosseau (letters), Marie Javins (colors), Lisa Patrick (asst editor), Bob Harras (editor)
FEATURE CHARACTER: Wolverine (also as psychic image, also in fb1 between W #50, '92 fb & W #10, '89 fb)
GUEST STARS: X-Men: Professor X (chr last bts in W #53, '92), Jean Grey (both chr last in W #51, '92, next in W #65, '93)
SUPPORTING CAST: Team X: Maverick (also in fb5/implant between W #49, '91 fb & W #87, '94 fb), Silver Fox (also in fb2/implant between W #50, '92 fb & W #48, '91 fb) (both also as psychic images), John Wraith (also in fb4/implant between W #49, '91 fb bts & W #61, '92 fb); Jubilee
VILLAINS: Weapon X Program senior staff: Professor Truett Hudson (in fb1 between WX #23, '04 & MCP #72, '91), Dr. Abraham Cornelius (in fb1, his chr 1st app, prior to MCP #72, '91) (both also as psychic images); Psi-Borg (named, also as painscape tree, Professor X & Jean Grey, also in fb1 (his chr 1st app) & bts in fb2/implant prior to W #10, '89 fb bts; also in fb3/implant, bts in fb4/implant & in fb5/implant between W #60, '92 fb bts & MCP #79, '91 bts), Sabretooth (also as psychic image, also in fb2/implant between XO:Sabre, '09 & W #10, '89 fb; also in fb3/implant between W #60, '92 fb & Sabre #3, '93 fb)
OTHER CHARACTERS: Carol Hines (dies, also as psychic image; also in fb1, her chr 1st app, prior to MCP #72, '91), tentacled creature (as psychic image
LOCATIONS/ITEMS: Psi-Borg's island fortress w/computer chamber, X-Mansion, "painscape" (in Wolverine's thoughts), Weapon X Program facility (in fb1 & as psychic image), Wolverine & Silver Fox's cabin (in fb2), sawmill (in fb3), sky (in fb4), fight location (in fb5) (prev 4 psychic images) / Team X's body armor & machetes, table saw (in fb3), bomber, missile, chains (prev 3 in fb4), painscape tree's handcuffed radiator (al as psychic images), Experiment X's wires & battery packs (prev 2 in fb1 & as psychic image, see NOTE), Psi-Borg's life-support armor w/weights, gold tooth & computer mainframes (1 destroyed), Silver Fox's blaster, gun, wrist computer, armor w/radio & medicine pouch w/Psi-Borg's tooth (bts in pouch), Hines' armor & hurled brick, Cerebro (Professor X's mutant-detecting machine, bts), Wraith's shaped charges (bts) detonator & gun, Sabretooth's radio, Wolverine's biopsy sample (prev 2 bts)
FLASHBACKS: Psi-Borg demonstrates his powers on Wolverine, offering to telepathically brainwash Team X (1). In implanted memories Sabretooth savages Silver Fox (2) and battles an opponent in a sawmill (3), John Wraith is strapped to a falling cruise missile (4) and Maverick has his head stomped on (5).
SYNOPSIS: Maverick states that Ferro is under government protection. Wolverine explains that they only came to talk, but Ferro telepathically attacks the group — including Maverick. Hines names Ferro as Psi-Borg, and reveals that he worked with the Weapon X Program in exchange for an extended lifespan, but Psi-Borg telepathically kills Hines and escapes. Wolverine realizes that Silver Fox may hate him because of an implanted memory, not a real event. At the X-Mansion, Professor X briefly detects Psi-Borg with Cerebro. Team X, now fully reunited, locates and investigates an underground chamber in Psi-Borg's fortress that contains several computers. Silver Fox hacks into one, learning that they are trying to crack Wolverine's genetic code — but Psi-Borg reappears and captures her, leaving only her medicine pouch behind. Aboveground Jubilee is relieved to see Professor X and Jean Grey arrive — unaware that they are Psi-Borg's illusions.
NOTE: This issue's fb1 shows Wolverine naked and covered in wires and batteries, as he appeared when his Adamantium was implanted in MCP #79-84, '91. However, OHMU:X, '04 clarified that Team X was active, and disbanded, decades before that event. Psi-Borg is likely causing Wolverine to recall his appearance incorrectly here. Psi-Borg explains here that he deliberately created the "painscape" spikes that grow throughout many of Team X's implanted memories and hallucinations, intending them to evoke instinctive and visceral revulsion, and linked them to their pain receptors.

WOLVERINE #64 (December 1992)

"What Goes Around..." (22 pages)

CREDITS: Larry Hama (writer), Mark Pacella (pencils), Dan Panosian (inks), Scott Hanna (art assist), Pat Brosseau (letters), Marie Javins & Kevin Tinsley (colors), Lisa Patrick (asst editor), Bob Harras (editor)
FEATURE CHARACTER: Wolverine (also as Experiment X in illusion)
SUPPORTING CAST: Team X: Maverick (next in X #10/2, '92), John Wraith (both also in rfb), Silver Fox (dies); Jubilee
VILLAINS: Sabretooth (also in rfb, next in Btide #2, '93), Psi-Borg (also as painscape tree, Professor X & Jean Grey, also in rfb, next in Sabre #1, '93), Shiva (last in W #60, '92)
LOCATIONS/ITEMS: Psi-Borg's island fortress w/computer chamber, Wolverine & Silver Fox's cabin (in illusion), sawmill, sky, fight location (prev 3 in rfb, psychic images) / Psi-Borg's computer mainframes (some destroyed) armor (destroyed, also in rfb as psychic image) & gold tooth, Silver Fox's medicine pouch (destroyed) w/Psi-Borg's tooth, Wraith's gun & shaped charge, elevator (destroyed) w/cables, Experiment X's wires & battery packs, party decorations (prev 3 in illusion), table saw, bomber, missile, chains, Psi-Borg's gun (prev 5 in rfb as psychic images), Hydra hovercraft (destroyed), Shiva's robot body (rebuilt & destroyed)
FLASHBACK: In implanted memories, Psi-Borg battles Sabretooth, drops Wraith from a plane and stomps on Maverick's head (W #63, '92 fbs).
SYNOPSIS: Enraged, Wolverine begins destroying Psi-Borg's computers. The villain reveals his true form and tackles Wolverine into an elevator; Wolverine cuts the cables and they tumble into the basement. Team X follows, finding an illusion of Wolverine and Silver Fox's cabin. Psi-Borg implies that he tried to rape Silver Fox years ago, but she knocked his tooth out; he used that traumatic event to cement Wolverine's implanted memory of her death, and reveals that her medicine pouch contains his tooth. Psi-Borg explains that he has spent decades trying to decode Team X's age-suppression factor, and denies that Wolverine and Silver Fox's memories of being in love were implanted, saying that creating happy memories was a waste of time. Psi-Borg holds Wolverine immobile and telepathically forces Sabretooth to kill Silver Fox for real. Shiva, now targeting Psi-Borg, arrives and attacks — freeing Wolverine, who cradles Silver Fox's body. Badly wounded by Shiva, Psi-Borg retreats, seemingly transforming into a painscape tree and vanishing, leaving his gold tooth behind.
NOTE: Psi-Borg's gold tooth appears in all the illusory forms he takes. His Team X codename is confirmed here, and his true form as an old man in life-support armor is revealed. Psi-Borg's attempted assault on Silver Fox was apparently the basis for one of his additions to Wolverine's memory in W #10, '89 fb: Sabretooth's taunt that Silver Fox "said no." This issue also shows that Psi-Borg helped implant Sabretooth's sawmill battle memory. W #50, '92 previously implied that both memories were acted out on soundstages (although W:O #5, '06 confirmed that most of W #10, '89 fb really occurred); presumably they were initially implanted that way, and Weapon X had Psi-Borg "retouch" them later. Page 12 of this issue has visible issue and page numbers at the top of the first panel.

WOLVERINE #65 (January 1993)

"State of Grace!" (23 pages)

CREDITS: Larry Hama (writer), Mark Texeira (art), Steve Biasi (art assist), Pat Brosseau (letters), Marie Javins (colors), Lisa Patrick (asst editor, uncredited), Bob Harras (editor)

FEATURE CHARACTER: Wolverine (also as virtual reality construct & in his own thoughts & rfb, also in fb between W #49, '91 fb & XO:Sabre, '09; next in W #58-59, X Ann #1 & 1/2, X #8, GR #26, X #9, GR #27 & 29, MCP #109-116, Cap #402-407, DrS #41, all '92, W:Evil, '94; UXM Ann #16/2, X #10-11, InfW #1, FF #367, InfW #2, MK #41, WM #13, FF #368, InfW #3, NW #27, AFlt #110, Q #38, Wlk&IW #8, InfW #4, FF #369, AFlt #111, WM #14, Q #39, InfW #5, WM #15, InfW #6, FF #370, AWC #87-88, HA #1-5, all '92, MCP #117-122, '92-93; Whead #8-9, C:Gene #1-4, all '93, DHII2 #1-4, '92-93; X #12-13, Ex #57-58, all '92; DA #9-10, MTW #1-4, DA #11-12, all '93; XFac #84, X #14, XFor #16, UXM #295, XFac #85, X #15, XFor #17, all '92; UXM #296, XFac #86, X #16, XFor #18, SecDef #1-3, all '93, Btide #1-4, '92-93, FF #374, '93)

GUEST STARS: X-Men: Jean Grey (chr next in UXM #287, '92), Professor X (chr next in W #58, '92) (both last in W #63, '93), Cyclops (chr last in W #51, '92, chr next in X Ann #1, '92) (all next in XFor #18, '93); Nick Fury (last in W #61, '92, chr next in Dlk #10, '92, next in NF:AoS #43, '93)

UPPORTING CAST: Jubilee (chr next in W #58, '92, next in XFor #18, '93), Silver Fox (bts, dead in coffin, also as virtual reality construct & rfb, also in fb between W #49, '91 fb & XO:Sabre, '09; next bts, dead, in W #84, '94), John Wraith

THER CHARACTERS: Sean (Auger Inn bartender), Auger Inn patrons inc biker (next in W #92, '95), Salem Center priest, SHIELD agents all but 1 bts in hovercraft, some or others last in W #61, '92, chr next in Dlk #10, '92, next in NF:AoS #43, '93) inc pilot; birds, butterflies (both in b); Team X's superiors (mentioned, sent Wolverine on "Terry Adams" mission); Sabretooth (as virtual reality construct)

OCATIONS/ITEMS: X-Mansion Danger Room, Salem Center: Auger Inn & church, skies over Canada, Mount Logan (also in rfb) inc Wolverine & Silver Fox's cabin (also in fb & simulation) / Danger Room computers, virtual reality visualizer w/sensors, Auger Inn cues & alls, patron's money & brass knuckles, Jean's handkerchief, SHIELD paperwork & hovercraft w/drop lines & cargo loader, Wolverine's shovel another in fb) & blindfold, Silver Fox's dipper, bucket (prev 2 in fb) & coffin, navigation satellite (bts), cabin door (also in fb, becomes Silver Fox's rave marker)

LASHBACKS: Wolverine carries Silver Fox's body (W #41, '91 fb). Wolverine digs a well and shares happiness with Silver Fox.

YNOPSIS: Reeling from Mariko and Silver Fox's deaths, Wolverine wallows in misery, savagely battling a virtual Sabretooth in the Danger Room. During the session, Wolverine recalls Team X's "Terry Adams" mission, where his kill order was rescinded at the last minute. Later, Wolverine beats a roughneck at pool, then lets the sore loser hit him in the face with brass knuckles. Jean Grey arrives, asking why Wolverine s putting himself through so much torment. He explains his confusion and anger over learning that many of his memories were fake, and the ain of regaining Silver Fox but immediately losing her again. Later, John Wraith arrives and reveals that he's located Wolverine's old cabin. Wraith and Nick Fury transport Wolverine and Silver Fox's corpse to the overgrown and remote cabin, where Wolverine is overwhelmed with elief to learn that his happy memories of their time together were real after all. He buries Silver Fox there, and promises to return every spring o visit her grave.

NOTE: The window of the Auger Inn is mistakenly labeled "Augie's Bar" here. Sean is not the same bartender seen in either W #51, '91 or next ssue. Although John Wraith mentions here that he owes Wolverine for the Terry Adams mission, next issue makes clear that Wraith did not go n the mission and knew very little about it.

WOLVERINE #66 (February 1993)

"Prophecy" (22 pages)

CREDITS: Larry Hama (writer), Mark Texeira (art), Steve Biasi (art assist), Pat Brosseau (letters), Steve Buccellato (colors), Lisa Patrick (asst editor), Bob Harras (editor)

FEATURE CHARACTER: Wolverine (also as himself & hallucination in pfb1, also in pfb2 & pfb3)

GUEST STARS: X-Men: Jean Grey (next in X #19, '93), Cyclops (both last in SpecSM #199, '93), Colossus (last in XFor #17, '92), Professor X (also in pfb2, last in UXM #297, '93, last bts in NW #31, '93 fb), Storm (last in XFor #18, '93, next in X #17, '93)

SUPPORTING CAST: Jubilee (last in UXM #297, '93), John Wraith (next in Mvk Spec, '97)

VILLAINS: Ahmed, Yuri (both Kazakh border guards, 1st)

OTHER CHARACTERS: Prophecy desk clerk (also as Richard Nixon in Wolverine's hallucination) & janitor (also as Archie Bunker in Wolverine's hallucination), snow shoveler, Auger Inn bartender (in pfb1), Mounties (bts investigating cache), CIA, FBI & NSA officials (prev 3 bts informing X-Men), Kazakh bus driver (dies), goat (dies); James T. Kirk, Spock (prev 2 n stained glass window), John Lennon, Paul McCartney, George Harrison, Ringo Starr, Janis Joplin, Elvis Presley, John F. Kennedy, Jacqueline Kennedy, John Glenn, Fidel Castro, wino (also as Howdy Doody), angel (also in pfb1), Janice Hollenbeck, maggots (prev 16 in Wolverine's allucination); Reverend Mike (mentioned, previously ran Prophecy); Wranglers, tentacled creature (prev 2 as psychic images in pfb2); demonic women (also in Wolverine's hallucination), devil, demons (prev 3 on pinball game in pfb1), Four Horsemen of the Apocalypse & their horses prev 2 on stained glass window), criminal (as practice target)

OCATIONS/ITEMS: Prophecy (Christian flophouse, Ottawa, Canada) w/Wolverine's old room (formerly #23), X-Mansion (also in pfb2) w/Wolverine's room (destroyed, also in pfb3) & psi-lab (in pfb2), Auger Inn (in pfb1), "painscape" (in pfb2), Wraith's home, Kazakhstan inc rain station / Angel's harp (in pfb1), wino's bottle & crowbar (all in hallucination), janitor's mop & bucket, Auger Inn pinball machine (in pfb1), Wolverine's possessions (destroyed, most bts), clothes, hat & mission cache w/guns, Swiss Francs, Kruger Rands, US dollars, diplomatic ouch, Federal Air Marshall & UN Peacekeeping Force badges & security ID cards inc KGB, CIA, GRU, MI6 & Shin Beth, Professor X's straps ots) & psi-equipment inc electrodes & gel, Wranglers' guns (as psychic images), painscape tree w/chains & radiators (prev 8 in pfb2), Wraith's un & practice target, Kazakh train & bus, border guards' machine guns, binoculars & armored personnel carrier, goat's chain (destroyed)

LASHBACKS: At the Auger Inn, Wolverine hallucinates an angel reminding him about the Terry Adams mission (p1). Wolverine asks Professor X to try to telepathically sort out his memories; Professor X enters Wolverine's mind and tells him to remember Terry Adams (p2). Wolverine awakens in confusion, believing that he must complete his mission (p3).

SYNOPSIS: Hallucinating that it is 1967 and he is still assigned to the "Terry Adams" mission, Wolverine travels to the Prophecy flophouse. Th X-Men find Wolverine's room destroyed; Professor X realizes that his mental tampering unbalanced Wolverine. Hallucinating phantoms from h past, Wolverine recovers a hidden mission cache containing money and false Russian security ID. The X-Men ask John Wraith for details abou the Terry Adams mission, but he knows very little and refers them to Maverick. A week later, the X-Men track Wolverine's false ID and discove that he is heading for Russia. In Kazakhstan, two corrupt border guards spot Wolverine buying a bus ticket with US money. They confront hir but although Wolverine presents his security ID, they shoot him, steal his belongings and leave him for dead.

NOTE: This issue's 3 pfbs intertwine in a complex fashion. Although Wolverine believes he is in 1967, he hallucinates two people that he ha not yet met then: Janice Hollenbeck, who was killed on a later mission (X #5-7, '92 fb), and the wino from the Prophecy (mentioned in MC #72, '91), whom Wolverine encountered just before Weapon X kidnapped him and implanted his Adamantium. He also hallucinates som famous figures from after 1967: Richard Nixon became President in 1969, and Archie Bunker debuted on *All in the Family* in 1971. W #67-6 '93 establish that the angel resembles the wife of Epsilon Red, Wolverine's target on the "Terry Adams" mission.

WOLVERINE #67 (March 1993)

"Valley O' Death!" (23 pages)

CREDITS: Larry Hama (writer), Mark Texeira (pencils, co-inks, c inks), Jimmy Palmiotti (co-inks), Pat Brossea (letters), Steve Buccellato (colors), Lisa Patrick (asst editor), Bob Harras (editor), Todd Klein (c letters)
FEATURE CHARACTER: Wolverine (also in photo)
GUEST STARS: X-Men: Iceman (Robert "Bobby" Drake, creates ice, last in SpecSM #199, '93), Professor (next in X #17, '93), Psylocke (last in Btide #4, '93), Colossus, Cyclops
SUPPORTING CAST: Maverick (last in X #11/2, '92, next in XMU #3, '94), Jubilee
VILLAINS: Ahmed, Yuri (both die), Hand ninjas (bts placing bounty on Wolverine, some or others last in Noma #6, '92, next in X #18, '93), serial killer (bts killing telekinetic)
OTHER CHARACTERS: Epsilon Red (1st bts, behind door, chr last in W #68, '93 fb), Elena Ivanovna (Epsilo Red's daughter, telepath, unnamed, 1st but chr last bts in Mvk #6, '98 fb), low-level telekinetic (dead), trading po patrons, Tyuratam security guards & employees; Sasha (guard dog), vultures (some die), jackals; Uncle Sam (as doll), Israeli & Syrian soldier (prev 2 bts in tanks), angel, Vietnamese protestors, hippies, US soldiers (prev 7 in Wolverine's hallucination)

LOCATIONS/ITEMS: Kazakhstan desert (also in photo) & Tyuratam Space Center (aka Baikonur Cosmodrome, also in satellite photo) v discontinued projects bunker (unnamed) & launchpad, X-Mansion w/Wolverine's room, Manhattan penthouse, Hindu Kush trading post Kazakh bus, Wolverine's belongings (destroyed, most bts), clothes, hat & GRU ID, penthouse doors (destroyed), telekinetic's telephone w cord, protestors' sign & Uncle Sam doll, soldiers' rifles, Israeli & Syrian tanks (prev 5 in hallucination), border guards' machine guns & armore personnel carrier w/turret gun, wanted poster, Professor X's database & monitor, Maverick's satellite photos, Tyuratam mines (bts, also bts i satellite photo), shuttle w/launch assembly & tanker truck w/hose, bunker's steel door (destroyed), X-Men's Blackbird jet w/navigation compute security guards' rifles, mortar launcher & goggles, Sasha's leash

SYNOPSIS: Wolverine awakens and knocks away jackals chewing at him. Still believing that it is 1967, he hallucinates the angel again, notin that her scarred face seems familiar. The X-Men locate Maverick, who is investigating an anti-mutant serial killer. Wolverine travels acros the Kazakh desert; he kills and eats a vulture to keep his strength up. At a trading post, the border guards see Wolverine's face on a wante poster; they return to the bus to reclaim his body, but find him gone. Maverick reveals that "Terry Adams" is slang for Kazakhstan's Tyurata Space Center; the X-Men depart for Tyuratam in the Blackbird. Wolverine reaches Tyuratam, but the border guards catch up to him and attac Wolverine breaches their armored vehicle and kills them, then uses the vehicle and his false ID to bluff past Tyuratam's security. Inside, h spots a young woman who resembles the angel — who recognizes Wolverine as the man who decades ago came to kill her cosmonaut fathe Epsilon Red.

NOTE: The serial killer that Maverick tracks here is never identified or mentioned again. Elena's name and psi-powers are revealed next issu Although she claims here that her mother "told" her about Wolverine, next issue reveals that her mother was killed just as she was born, but sh telepathically absorbed her mother's final memories. Epsilon Red's bunker is named next issue. Colossus' metal face is incorrectly colored a flesh in one panel here, and Psylocke's first name is misspelled "Elisabeth," a common error.

WOLVERINE #68 (April 1993)

"Epsilon Red" (22 pages)

CREDITS: Larry Hama (writer), Mark Texeira (art), Steve Biasi (background art), Pat Brosseau (letters), Stev Buccellato (colors), Lisa Patrick (asst editor), Bob Harras (editor), Todd Klein (c letters)
FEATURE CHARACTER: Wolverine (also on monitor, in his own hallucination & as Experiment X & himself i psychic image, also in fb between Mvk #2, '97 fb & D:DW #1, '10 fb; next in X #17-19, '93, W:IF, '92)
GUEST STAR: X-Men: Colossus, Cyclops, Iceman, Psylocke (all next in X #17, '93)
SUPPORTING CAST: Jubilee (next in X #17, '93)
VILLAIN: Sabretooth (in fb between Mvk #2, '97 fb & W #11, '11 fb; also as psychic image)
OTHER CHARACTERS: Epsilon Red (genetically altered cosmonaut, 1st on-panel app, also on monitor; als in fb, his chr 1st app, prior to W #67, '93), Elena Ivanovna (named, also bts in fb, unborn, her chr 1st bts app, prio to Mvk #6, '98 fb bts; next in Mvk Spec, '97), Epsilon Red's wife (in fb prior to Mvk #6, '98 fb bts, dies) (all als in Wolverine's hallucination), Tyuratam security guards (some or others next in Cable #10, '94; others bts in fb, fighting Sabretooth, Researc Direktor Lashniev (unnamed, next in Cable #10, '94), KGB border guards (bts in fb fighting Sabretooth), Team X's superiors (bts in fb recallin Wolverine); Neil Armstrong (in photo); Silver Fox (as psychic image)

LOCATIONS/ITEMS: Tyuratam Space Center (also in fb & hallucination) w/discontinued projects bunker (named), launchpad & missio control, skies over Russia, outer space, "painscape," moon's surface (in photo) / Epsilon Red's photo, repair station w/tools & containment su (also in fb & hallucination) inc armatures w/clamp, probe (prev 2 destroyed & repaired), torch & buzzsaw, border guards' armored personne carrier, bunker's sensors, camera (prev 2 bts) & steel door (destroyed), X-Men's Blackbird jet w/electronic countermeasures, cloak, radi codebreaking computer & heat vents, Armstrong's spacesuit & lunar lander (prev 2 in photo), Tyuratam sensors, infrared detectors (prev ts), fence, mission control computers (prev 2 destroyed) & shuttle w/launch assembly, security guards' radio (bts) & guns (destroyed, others ts in fb), Direktor's radio & monitor, Wolverine & Sabretooth's body armor & machine guns (prev 2 in fb), Silver Fox's rifle, Sabretooth's belt, Experiment X's helmet (prev 3 as psychic images), painscape tree w/handcuffed radiator

FLASHBACK: Wolverine is about to kill Epsilon Red, who loathes his new form and wants to die, when Sabretooth arrives and delivers orders aborting the mission. Epsilon Red asks Sabretooth to kill him; Sabretooth instead kills Red's pregnant wife.

SYNOPSIS: Epsilon Red confronts Wolverine, who attacks, still believing that he is in the past. Wolverine hallucinates that Red's wife interferes and he accidentally scars her face. She explains that Red was altered to exist in space, and cannot survive on Earth without his containment suit. Wolverine snaps back to reality; Red explains that he was originally targeted because he was intended to be the first person to walk on the moon. He then telepathically clears out much of Wolverine's psychic clutter, unlocking several blocked memories. Tyuratam security arrives, but Wolverine disarms them. The X-Men land as a shuttle launches, and Wolverine explains that he helped Epsilon Red go into space, where he could be happy. As the X-Men depart, Elena thinks about her birth — via Caesarian as her mother died — and, revealing that she was the telepath, not Red, muses that the clues she gleaned from Wolverine's mind about Sabretooth will help her find and kill him.

NOTE: Called only "Direktor" here, Lashniev's full title and last name are revealed in Cable #10, '94, which establishes that Epsilon Red and Omega Red were created by the same program. Wolverine now believes it is early 1968, not late 1967; a period of time seems to have elapsed in his hallucinatory narrative. In Wolverine's hallucination, Epsilon Red becomes bloated when he removes his suit; however, since he was engineered to exist in airless space, Earth's atmosphere should have crushed him. It is unclear if any of Wolverine's hallucination actually occurred during the mission; much of it is broadly consistent with the actual flashback. This issue implies that the scarred angel Wolverine hallucinated in W #66-67, '93 was based on Epsilon Red's wife.

WOLVERINE: INNER FURY (November 1992)

"Inner Fury" (48 pages)

CREDITS: D.G. Chichester (writer), Bill Sienkiewicz (art), Michael Heisler (letters), Sherilyn van Valkenburgh (colors), Suzanne Gaffney (editor), Bob Harras (group editor)
FEATURE CHARACTER: Wolverine (also as Ahab in his own dream, next in TInc #9-10, AFlt #121, InfC #1-2, WoSM #104, Wlk&IW #19, WoSM #105, InfC #3, Dhawk #30, WoSM #106, Wlk&IW #20, InfC #4-5, AFlt #127 & 127/2, InfC #6, UXM #299 bts, UXM #300, X #20-21, MCP #123-131, all '93)
GUEST STAR: Nick Fury (last in Dlk #17, '92; chr last in NF:AoS #47, chr next in SSWP #17, next in XFor #20, all '93)
VILLAINS: Baron Wolfgang von Strucker (Hydra founder, bts ordering Whale guarded, last in DD #309, '92, chr last in NF:AoS #47, '93, next in SSWP #15, '93), Hydra agents (some or others last in IM #283, '92, chr last in NF:AoS #47, '93, next in NF:AoS #47, '93, next in TInc #9, '93): Big (nanotech project's diminutive co-leader, dies), George Leon dies), courier (bts, captured by SHIELD, allegedly dies, see NOTE), substation personnel (bts at base, 1 voice only) inc Lt. Maximillian Braniff unnamed, next in TInc #9, '93), mobile unit (dies) inc guards, scientists & "White Line Fever," Big's operatives (die) & cyborgs (some die, also in Wolverine's dream) inc Foster (dies), Serpentine Metalworks agents (die) inc Johnson
OTHER CHARACTERS: Whale (nanotech project's aquatic co-leader, also as shark in Big's story & as Moby Dick in Wolverine's dream), SHIELD agents (some or others last in Motor #6, '92, chr last in NF:AoS #47, '93, next in SSWP #17, '93) inc cleanup crew (bts investigating trainyard) & others (voice only inc Maintenance); Club Dogmeet patrons, employees of Small Sy's, pet store, Ed's Used Cars & movie theater, harbor master (bts, bribed by Big), customs officials (bts, bribed by Whale), bystanders; fish (1 dies; 1 bts, dies, eaten by Whale; 1 in Wolverine's dream), geese (bts in Helicarrier stabilizers, die); Hydra assassination department, SHIELD galley staff (prev 2 mentioned); Pequod crew (in Wolverine's dream, also as cyborgs), chicken (on sign in Wolverine's dream); Whale's victims (in Big's story)
LOCATIONS/ITEMS: Illinois inc Hydra Substation (Lake Michigan warehouse, bts), highway, Chicago trainyard, Club Dogmeet, Serpentine Metalworks Custom Collectibles (foundry, Hydra front), Small Sy's Clothing, pet store, Ed's Used Cars, harbor, movie theater, Big's motel room & Whale's hideout (abandoned logging site), Bering Strait (mentioned, see NOTE), ocean (in dream) / Whale's nanites (some bts), equipment some destroyed), gun, car (prev 2 bts), bucket, new pants, ejection switch, winches w/hooks, cameras (all but 1 bts) w/microphones & life-support tank (destroyed) w/mouth & earpiece, Hydra substation comm system (bts), Hydra files, mainframes, van (prev 3 destroyed), guns, knife & mobile unit (tractor-trailer truck, destroyed) w/computers, monitors & comm system, scientists' eye implants, guards' armor & guns, Leon's helicopter, Big's chainsaw (destroyed), gun w/ammo clip & hovercraft (destroyed) w/radio (bts) & armature, train (destroyed), Foster's radio (bts) & binoculars, SHIELD rifles & Helicarrier w/stabilizers, comm system (prev 2 bts) & jet, courier's communique (bts), cyborgs' swords (some destroyed) w/rejected nanites (also in dream), Wolverine's bottle (destroyed), telescope, harpoon (prev 2 in dream), Adamantium & white blood cells (prev 2 also in dream), Pequod (Ahab's ship), Whale's sign & magnifying glass (prev 3 in dream)
SYNOPSIS: The Whale, co-developer of a Hydra nanite project, doesn't want his inventions used for evil; he crashes the project's transport and escapes. Later, alerted by Nick Fury, Wolverine disrupts Hydra's planned ambush of him, but a cyborg cuts him with a nanite-laced sword. Big intervenes, killing a cyborg and explaining that families of the Whale's victims hired him. Later, a woman at a bar cuts herself on an Adamantium sliver protruding from Wolverine's hand; Big explains the Whale's nanites are stripping the Adamantium from Wolverine's skeleton. Wolverine and Big raid the Whale's former workshop; Adamantium begins protruding from Wolverine's fingers and spine as his healing factor forces the metal out. The two track down the Whale as Wolverine's condition worsens. They locate the Whale's hideout and capture him, but as Big gloats, Wolverine realizes that he smelled Big's scent at the workshop, and confronts him. Big reveals that he was the nanites' other developer, and that he had Wolverine infected. Wolverine decides to give his healing factor something more important to focus on, and stabs himself in the brain. Big tries to destroy Wolverine's body, but his chainsaw shatters on an Adamantium bone, flinging Big onto a hook and impaling him. Wolverine recovers and takes the Whale to safety.
NOTE: Braniff's rank, name and bts appearance here are revealed in TInc #9-10, '93, which also reveals the substation's location. Leon's first name is revealed in W:WXF, '09. Fury comments that his agents dropped a Hydra courier off the Helicarrier into the Bering Strait, but he may have been joking. It is never established how Wolverine expelled the nanites from his system or re-bonded the Adamantium that they had stripped; it is likely that the Whale reprogrammed them to rebuild Wolverine's skeleton shortly after the issue ended.

WOLVERINE #69 (May 1993)

"Induction in the Savage Land!" (22 pages)

CREDITS: Larry Hama (writer), Dwayne Turner (pencils), Chris Ivy (inks), Pat Brosseau (letters), Steve Buccellato (colors), Lisa Patrick (asst editor), Bob Harras (editor)
FEATURE CHARACTER: Wolverine
GUEST STARS: X-Men: Professor X (on monitor, next bts in W #71, '93, next in X #23, '93), Rogue (both last in X #21, '93), 1 other (bts piloting Blackbird, see NOTE)
SUPPORTING CAST: Jubilee (last in X #21, '93)
VILLAINS: Savage Land Mutates (natives artificially evolved by Magneto): Amphibius (froglike appearance), Barbarus (four arms), Gaza (blind, uses radar sense) (all last in UXM #274, '91), Brainchild (computer-like mind, last in UXM #275, '91), Equilibrius (affects balance, last in Av #105, '72); Sauron (Dr. Karl Lykos, pteranodon form, last in Sleep #17, '92), Magneto (bts, tampered with Brainchild's mind, last in XMU #1, '93, next in XFor #24, '93), Savage Land barbarians (some or others last in UXM #275, '91)
OTHER CHARACTERS: Forge (bts, built X-Men's gear, between UXM #300-301, '93), Fall People (Savage Land tribe, some or others last in XMU #1, '93 fb), Pteranodon Riders (Savage Land tribe, aka Sky People, unnamed) inc Gronk (unnamed); Savage Land buzzards & dinosaurs inc Tyrannosaurus rex, triceratops & Riders' telepathic pterosaurs ("soarers," some bts); Ka-Zar (mentioned, told Rogue about citadels); Bori (voice only, on Jubilee's cassette)
LOCATIONS/ITEMS: Savage Land inc Pteranodon Riders' cliffside Aerie (unnamed), Brainchild's citadel ruins & Sauron's citadel, X-Mansion (on monitor) / X-Men's Blackbird jet & supply cases: PD (perimeter & diversions: computer games, CDs & force field generator w/remote), S (shelter & environment: inflatable geodesic dome), CI (communications & instrumentation: comm unit & magnetic anomaly detectors) & FW (see NOTE), Professor X's comm system (bts), Jubilee's David Copperfield novel & Walkman w/cassette (bts) & headphones, barbarian ropes, spears, axes & knives, Barbarus & Riders' spears, Rogue's flashlight, Brainchild's chains & Genetic Transformer, Gaza & Amphibius clubs, Magneto's helmet (bts) & metal fist, Sauron's armor w/claws
SYNOPSIS: Wolverine, Rogue and Jubilee arrive in the Savage Land, sent by Professor X to investigate rumors of Magneto's return. Tyrannosaurus attacks, but Wolverine drives it off. They activate a force field and make camp, and Rogue and Wolverine search the area, leaving Jubilee behind. Wolverine finds several Savage Land Mutates and barbarians, who have captured two Fall People. Rogue's equipment detects a magnetic anomaly; she investigates a ruined citadel and finds Brainchild and Gaza, who knock her out. A Pteranodon Rider flies over the X-Men's force field and snatches Jubilee. Wolverine follows the Mutates to another citadel and interrupts their human sacrifice. The Rider deposits Jubilee in a cliffside cave; she slips and dangles from the cave mouth. Rogue awakens chained to Brainchild's Genetic Transformer. She sees a giant metal statue of a fist and begins to mention Magneto, but Brainchild panics, fighting mental blocks that prevent thinking of him. Wolverine defeats the Mutates, but is challenged by their new leader — Sauron!
NOTE: Magneto apparently died in X #3, '91. His name is never spoken in this story arc, a deliberate decision to heighten suspense about his return, which occurred in XFor #25, '93. The Blackbird's pilot is either Archangel, Bishop, Colossus, Jean Grey, Iceman or Storm; the pilot appears here roughly between X #21, '93 & W #71, '93. Gronk is named next issue, which also names the Aerie and reveals the telepathic bond between Rider and pterosaur. The tribe is named as the Pteranodon Riders in W #71, '93; OHMU HC10, '09 reveals that they are also called the Sky People. Amphibius' name is also misspelled Amphibious here; Equilibrius is misspelled Equilibrious. Jubilee is listening to U2's cover of the Beatles' "Helter Skelter," from the album Rattle and Hum. The X-Men's supply cases are each labeled with two letters; the "FW" case is unidentified and unopened, but likely stands for food & water.

WOLVERINE #70 (June 1993)

"Tooth and Nail" (22 pages)

CREDITS: Larry Hama (writer), Dwayne Turner (pencils), Richard Bennett (inks), Pat Brosseau (letters), Steve Buccellato (colors), Lisa Patrick (asst editor), Bob Harras (editor)
FEATURE CHARACTER: Wolverine
GUEST STAR: Rogue
SUPPORTING CAST: Jubilee
VILLAINS: Sauron, Savage Land Mutates: Amphibius, Barbarus, Brainchild, Equilibrius, Gaza; Savage Land barbarians inc Thunder Lizard Drovers
OTHER CHARACTERS: Fall People (1 bts), Pteranodon Riders inc Gronk (named); Riders' telepathic pterosaurs ("flyers"), Savage Land lizard (devolved) & dinosaurs inc Tyrannosaurus rexes & triceratops
LOCATIONS/ITEMS: Savage Land inc Pteranodon Riders' cliffside Aerie (named), Brainchild's citadel ruins & Sauron's citadel w/Chasm of Fire / Sauron's movable citadel floor & armor w/claws, barbarians' axes, spears & hurled boulders, Gronk's spear, Brainchild's chains (destroyed) & Genetic Transformer, Magneto's metal fist, Jubilee's Walkman w/headphones, X-Men's force field generator (bts) & inflatable geodesic dome
SYNOPSIS: As Wolverine battles Sauron, the citadel floor retracts, exposing a flaming pit. At the Riders' Aerie, Jubilee falls from the cave and lands on a pterosaur; it flies off with her on its back. At Brainchild's citadel, a lizard crawls into the Genetic Transformer's path. Rogue quickly breaks free; the beam hits the lizard, devolving it into a vicious dinosaur. Rogue defeats it, then chases down Brainchild, who still cannot speak of Magneto, but reveals that Sauron is making a bid for power. Wolverine tackles Sauron into the pit, but Sauron flies free and has the Mutates and barbarians rain boulders down on Wolverine, burying him. Jubilee knocks a pursuing Rider off his mount and panics, wishing she could save him — and her pterosaur responds, swooping down and catching him. Realizing that she has forged a mind-link with the pterosaur, the Rider welcomes her into their tribe. Wolverine digs himself free, but the barbarians herd stampeding dinosaurs into the pit…
NOTE: The telepathic link between Rider and pterosaur is revealed here. As Jubilee is able to forge a mind-link, it must be the pterosaurs that are telepathic, not the Riders. Called "soarers" last issue, the pterosaurs are called "flyers" here. Gronk's hair changes from a black ponytail last issue to a brown mohawk here.

WOLVERINE #71 (July 1993)

"Triassic Park" (22 pages)

CREDITS: Larry Hama (writer), Dwayne Turner (pencils), Richard Bennett, Hilary Barta & Josef Rubinstein (inks), Pat Brosseau (letters), Steve Buccellato (colors), Lisa Patrick (asst editor), Bob Harras (editor), Klaus Janson (c inks)
FEATURE CHARACTER: Wolverine (next in X #23, MCP #132-136, all '93)
GUEST STARS: X-Men: Bishop (Lucas Bishop, absorbs & rechannels energy, last in XMU #1, '93), Storm (last in X #21, '93) (both next in UXM Ann #17, '93), Professor X (bts, concerned about mission, last in W #69, '93), Rogue (prev 2 next in X #23, '93)
SUPPORTING CAST: Jubilee (next in X #23, '93)
VILLAINS: Sauron, Savage Land Mutates: Barbarus, Brainchild, Gaza (all next in XMU #6, '94), Amphibius (next in XX:SL #3, '02), Equilibrius; Savage Land barbarians (some or others next in TMU, '97) inc Thunder Lizard Drovers
OTHER CHARACTERS: Fall People (bts, some or others next in XMU #6, '94), Pteranodon Riders (named, bts celebrating) inc Jubilee's would-be bride; Savage Land dinosaurs (some die, others also in Sauron's thoughts) inc Tyrannosaurus rexes & triceratops; Savage Land tribesman, "civilized" humans (prev 2 in Sauron's thoughts)
LOCATIONS/ITEMS: Savage Land (also in Sauron's thoughts) inc Pteranodon Riders' cliffside Aerie (bts), Brainchild's citadel ruins & Sauron's citadel w/rafters & Chasm of Fire, civilization (in Sauron's thoughts) / Sauron's armor w/claws, falling boulders, barbarians' spears, Magneto's metal fist, Brainchild's Genetic Transformer w/restraints (destroyed), tribesman's spear (in Sauron's thoughts), X-Men's long-range monitoring system (bts) & Blackbird jet w/sensors, targeting computer, external speakers (prev 3 bts) & laser
SYNOPSIS: As dinosaurs tumble into the pit, Wolverine kills them, piles their bodies up and climbs out. Sauron attacks the arriving Rogue, and the two fight an aerial duel. A dinosaur bites Wolverine, but he claws free, grabs Sauron and threatens to throw him to the hungry reptiles. Rogue offers to help Sauron, who tells the Mutates and barbarians to stand down — but Wolverine knocks Sauron out and they take him to Brainchild's Genetic Transformer. Rogue intends to transform Sauron back to human, but Sauron argues that fighting and conquering is the Savage Land's natural order, and the X-Men should not impose their "civilized" values on him. Wolverine grudgingly agrees and frees Sauron; Brainchild and Gaza also flee. Bishop and Storm, concerned by Wolverine's radio silence, arrive with a grumpy Jubilee — whom they found being given a bride by the Riders, who has mistaken her for a boy. The X-Men head home, worried that the metal fist statue means that their greatest foe has returned…
NOTE: Bishop's first name is revealed, and his codename revealed to be his last name, in XX #1, '01. Gaza, allegedly struck mute by Magneto prior to W #69, '93, can speak again here. This issue also has a 16-page insert, "Maximum Anniversary X-Perience" (Jim Krueger & Jeffrey Lee Simons, writers; Suzanne Gaffney, designer; Dana Moreshead, colors; Bob Harras, Ralph Macchio, Nel Yomtov, Suzanne Gaffney & Terry Kavanagh, consulting editors), which previews various comics celebrating the X-Men and Avengers' 30th anniversaries including W:Kill, '93, W #75, '93, and a Wolverine limited series by Alan Grant, John Wagner & Mike Manley that never saw print.

WOLVERINE #72 (August 1993)

"Sleeping Giant" (22 pages)

CREDITS: Larry Hama (writer), Dwayne Turner (pencils), Josef Rubinstein (inks), Pat Brosseau (letters), Kevin Somers (colors), Lisa Patrick (asst editor, uncredited), Bob Harras (editor), Todd Klein (c letters)
FEATURE CHARACTER: Wolverine (also in rfb2 & rfb3)
GUEST STAR: Professor X (bts sending Wolverine to investigate base, last in UXM #303, '93 fb, next in XFor #23, '93)
SUPPORTING CAST: Jubilee (last in UXM #303, '93; also her past self bts, displaced by her present-day self, chr last in GenX #24, '97 fb, chr next in this issue's fb; also in fb between this issue's past events & UXM #244, '89)
VILLAINS: Earth-1191 future Sentinel (also in rfb3, reactivated, last in UXM #281, '91; some or others also in rfb1), Hunter Brawn (villainous businessman, unnamed, 1st bts hiring Molokai & Reno, next bts in GenX #50, '99, next in GenX #51, '99), Molokai, Reno (prev 2 chr 1st app, next in W #73, '93 fb) (prev 3 in past), cyborg Hunter-Killer dingo (dies, some or others last in UXM #252, '89)
OTHER CHARACTERS: Gateway (as image, last in W #53, '92, next in GenX #1, '94), Dr. & Mrs. Lee (prev 2 Jubilee's parents, chr next in W #73, '93 fb, found dead, following W #73, '93 fb), Estellita (Lees' maid) (prev 3 in past), the "other" Dr. & Mrs. Lee (prev 2 Jubilee's neighbors, Cynthia, Jennifer (prev 2 Jubilee's friends, 1 following GenX #24, '97 fb, see NOTE), Cynthia's mother, police (prev 4 in fb); Reavers: Lady Deathstrike (also in Wolverine's thoughts), Donald Pierce, Bonebreaker (prev 3 in rfb1 & Sentinel's thoughts), Wade Cole, Murray Reese (prev 3 noted as dead, see NOTE); Albert, Elsie-Dee (prev 2 in Wolverine & Sentinel's thoughts); historical figure, elephant (prev 2 as statues in fb)
LOCATIONS/ITEMS: Reavers' Australian outback base (also in rfb1, rfb2, rfb3 & Wolverine's thoughts); California (in fb): Los Angeles streets & Beverly Hills inc Jubilee's home (also in past) & "other" Lees' home / Wolverine & Jubilee's flashlights, Earth-1191 Sentinels (destroyed), Bonebreaker's blaster (in rfb1) & tank assembly (also in rfb1), Wolverine's cross & boots (prev 2 in rfb2), Pierce's equipment (destroyed), power line (bts) & cyber-synthesizer tanks (also in Wolverine's thoughts) w/electrolyte bath, high-voltage cables & power switch (prev 3 also in rfb3), dingo's cybernetic implants (destroyed), reactivated Sentinel's mutant sensors, magnetic flux detector, long-range microphone, sound enhancement computer, image processors (prev 5 bts), palm blasters & moly-steel optical blast irises, Gateway's space/time vortex, Lees' security gate (bts) & TV, Reno's list & shotgun, Molokai's pistol (prev 5 in past), Cynthia's mother's car, police cars, "other" Lees' tacky furnishings (prev 3 in fb)
FLASHBACKS: The future Sentinels attack the Reavers (UXM #281, '91). Wolverine has been crucified by Pierce (UXM #251, '89). Wolverine shuts off the power, awakening the Sentinel (this issue). A young Jubilee returns home to find police, who explain that her parents died when their car skidded off Mulholland Drive.
SYNOPSIS: Wolverine and Jubilee investigate the Reavers' base, finding the aftermath of the villains' losing battle against Sentinels. They find Pierce's damaged android-creation tanks leaking fluid over an inert Sentinel; Wolverine shuts the power down, inadvertently reactivating the Sentinel. As it repairs itself, Wolverine and Jubilee continue searching the complex and discover Gateway's temporal vortex active; Jubilee touches it and finds herself in the past, at her parents' house on the day they were to die in a car crash. Molokai and Reno burst in and order the Lees to get their car; Jubilee realizes that the "crash" was actually a murder as Wolverine pulls her back to the present. The Sentinel discovers

that the electrolytic fluid has given it sentience. It confronts Wolverine and Jubilee, and explains its desire to make Earth a paradise for Sentine‑ — by wiping out mankind. Wolverine attacks, but the Sentinel grabs Jubilee…

NOTE: Trevor Fitzroy's future Sentinels attacked the Reavers in UXM #281, '91. Despite being noted here as reduced to "greasy smudges the wall," Bonebreaker, Cole and Reese return in XX Ann '01 along with most of the other Reavers. Pierce presumably rebuilt them, but ho he reconstituted their organic components is unrevealed to date. The future Sentinel's native timeline is designated in OHMU:AU, '05; Fitzr‑ brought it to the present between UXM #287, '92 fb & UXM #281, '91. Brawn is named in GenX #51, '99. Despite Jubilee's theory that the "oth‑ Lees were Molokai and Reno's real target, GenX Ann '99 reveals that Brawn was laundering money through Jubilee's father's bank, and order‑ Jubilee's parents killed after her father threatened to report him. GenX #24, '97 mistakenly conflates Cynthia and Jennifer into a single perso‑ "Cynthia Jennifer." This issue also contains a bound-in "Hunt for Magneto" contest scratch-and-win game piece with trivia question, and a tradi‑ card (#2 in the Maximum Anniversary X-Perience series) featuring Trevor Fitzroy and Magneto's Acolytes, with art by Lee Weeks.

WOLVERINE #73 (September 1993)

"The Formicary Mound!" (22 pages)

CREDITS: Larry Hama (writer), Dwayne Turner (breakdowns), Josef Rubinstein (finishes), Pat Brosse‑ (letters), Paul Becton (colors), Lisa Patrick (asst editor), Bob Harras (editor)
FEATURE CHARACTER: Wolverine (also as Experiment X in his own thoughts)
SUPPORTING CAST: Jubilee (also in her own thoughts)
VILLAINS: Earth-1191 future Sentinel (becomes 3.14159), Mark II Sentinels (mutant-killing robots, some others last in MSH #7, '91): 23, 66, 86, 99 (1 bts, 1 in shadow, prev 4 last in Av #102, '72, see NOTE), Molok‑ Reno (in fb between W #72, '93 & W #38, '91, also in Jubilee's thoughts)
OTHER CHARACTERS: Dr. & Mrs. Lee (both in shadow, in fb between W #72, '93 & W #72, '93 fb bts), ding‑ Wranglers, bear (prev 2 in Wolverine's thoughts); cyborg Hunter-Killer dingos (cover only)
LOCATIONS/ITEMS: Australia: Reavers' outback base, Ant Hill (Sentinels' former Great Western Des‑ base); Los Angeles' Mulholland Drive (in fb & Jubilee's thoughts); Earth, sun, outer space (prev 3 in holographic projection), timestrea‑ "painscape" / Wranglers' armor & gun, Experiment X's wires & battery packs, painscape spikes & trees w/handcuffed radiator (all as psyc‑ images), Gateway's space/time vortex, Sentinel's sensors, palm blasters, boot jets & solar flare generator w/turret & tracking module, bould‑ (destroyed), Ant Hill's memory banks (bts), power system & holographic projector, Lees' Mercedes-Benz (in fb)
FLASHBACK: As Molokai and Reno watch, the Lees' car skids off a cliff on Mulholland Drive.
SYNOPSIS: Holding Jubilee hostage, the Sentinel steps into Gateway's vortex. Wolverine leaps after it and the trio emerges at the Ant Hill, t‑ Sentinel's former base on the other side of Australia. Wolverine cuts off the Sentinel's hand, freeing Jubilee, but the Sentinel blasts Wolveri‑ injuring him badly. Enraged, Jubilee shoots fireworks at the Sentinel, but they are more powerful than usual and she collapses from exhausti‑ The Sentinel, strangely touched by Jubilee's emotional action, enters the Ant Hill and reactivates the base's systems, renaming itself 3.141‑ Jubilee awakens and helps Wolverine toward the base; she expresses a desire to find and murder her parents' killers, but Wolverine warns ‑ against such drastic actions. A pack of hungry dingos attack, but the still-wounded Wolverine scares them off. Sentinel 3.14159 rebuilds t‑ Sentinels' solar flare generator, intending to incinerate all life on Earth. Wolverine fully recovers and attacks 3.14159, who calls in reactivat‑ Mark II Sentinels as backup.
NOTE: 3.14159 is the first six digits of the irrational number π (pi). The Ant Hill-based Sentinels battled the Avengers in Av #102-104, '72 a‑ some appeared, deactivated, in MSH #6-7, '91. Since Mark II Sentinels are largely identical, and 23, 66, 86 and 99 were never named pr‑ to this issue, it is impossible to determine which of those four appeared on-panel in which issues, and which were bts. However, Av #102, ' showed the entire group of Sentinels on-panel, making it these four's last definite on-panel app. Although Wolverine claims here that he h‑ never seen the Ant Hill, he was there in MSH #6-7, '91. Sentinel 3.14159 incorrectly claims that 23, 66, 86 and 99 destroyed Sentinel 2 in ‑ #104, '72; it was actually Sentinels 3, 5 and 10, who were themselves destroyed in MSH #7-8, '91. Although Wolverine battles Pierce's cyb‑ dingos on this issue's cover, he faces normal dingos in the story.

WOLVERINE #74 (October 1993)

"Jubilee's Revenge" (22 pages)

CREDITS: Larry Hama (writer), Jim Fern (pencils), Art Nichols (inks), Pat Brosseau (letters), Marie Javi‑ (colors), Lisa Patrick (asst editor), Bob Harras (editor)
FEATURE CHARACTER: Wolverine (next in PWZ #19, '93, W:Kill, '93)
SUPPORTING CAST: Jubilee (next in W:Kill, '93)
VILLAINS: Molokai, Reno (both also in rfb), Jocko, Sally (all last in W #40, '91), Sentinel 3.14159, Mark‑ Sentinels: 23, 86 (prev 2 destroyed), 66, 99
OTHER CHARACTERS: Molokai & Reno's victim, bystanders; Dr. & Mrs. Lee (prev 2 bts in rfb); model (‑ magazine cover)
LOCATIONS/ITEMS: Ant Hill; California inc Mulholland Drive (also in rfb), Jocko & Sally's Los Angeles offi‑ & victim's Burbank home / Sentinels' transmitters, infrared sensors & solar flare generator (destroyed) w/tu‑ & tracking module, Sentinel 66 & 99's optic blasters, Sentinel 23's faceplating, Sentinel 86's optical sensors (destroyed) & audio analys‑ suite, Sentinel 3.14159's time/stasis field projector, Lees' Mercedes-Benz (in rfb), Gateway's time/space vortex, Sally's toupee, Jocko & Sall‑ Mercedes-Benz & bootleg merchandise, Molokai's shotgun (destroyed) & Mercury, Reno's pistols (destroyed)
FLASHBACK: The Lees' car plummets off Mulholland Drive (W #73, '93 fb).
SYNOPSIS: Wolverine and Jubilee are surrounded by Sentinels, but Wolverine slices 23 in half and the two mutants flee. The damaged ‑ requests assistance, but 3.14159 coldly strips it for parts to repair itself. Jubilee tells Wolverine that her fireworks are getting more powerful, a‑ they ambush two Sentinels, decapitating 86. Sentinel 66 cradles 86's head, concerned for its ally, and the dying 86 expresses fear. Touche‑ Jubilee can't bring herself to destroy 86's head. 3.14159 arrives, confused by the emotional behavior of both its allies and foes, and as‑ Wolverine and Jubilee to explain empathy. 3.14159 decides to destroy the solar flare generator, and reconfigures the Ant Hill to comp‑

otions — a process which will take 2137 years. Jubilee has the Sentinel teleport her and Wolverine to Los Angeles, where they track down
  confront Molokai and Reno. Jubilee blasts them and considers killing them, and Wolverine lets Jubilee make the decision herself. She
  nately decides against it, and Wolverine consoles her.
 TE: The Mark II Sentinels were presumably expressing emotions as an unintended side effect of being reprogrammed by the sentient
 4159. Sentinel 99 is incorrectly labeled 23 in one panel, and Sentinel 66 mistakenly calls to itself for help.

WOLVERINE: KILLING (September 1993)

"Killing" (48 pages)

CREDITS: John Ney Rieber (writer), Kent Williams (art & design), Bill Oakley (letters), Sherilyn van Valkenburgh
(colors), Suzanne Gaffney (editor), Bob Harras (group editor), Sally Rieber, Molly Ward, Chris Brewer, Shepherd
Dobson & Hardback staff (special thanks)
FEATURE CHARACTER: Wolverine (also on monitor, in his own dream & in rfb1 & rfb2, next in X #24, '93,
W/NF:SR, '94; MCP #137-142, Sabre #2-3, W:GJ, all '93)
SUPPORTING CAST: Jubilee (last in W #74, '93, next in X #24, '93)
VILLAINS: Tane (Tribune of the Mandate, influences minds), Slith (serpentine Mandate member, possibly dies)
OTHER CHARACTERS: Mandate (hidden Tibetan society): Nirissa (Mandate's matriarch), Serra (Nirissa's
daughter, also on monitor), old man, Tane's prisoners, others; Chinese border guards (die, others bts turning
Wolverine away), squatters (bts, rioting according to headline), pilot (bts flying airplane), New York bystanders
(also in Wolverine's dream); crying tree (also in rfb2); Humphrey Bogart (bts on movie screen); slaghounds
andate animals, mentioned); Tibetan goddess & demon (prev 2 as statues)
CATIONS/ITEMS: Manhattan (also in rfb1 & dream) inc Ollopa Theater, X-Mansion, industrial factory (in dream), skies over Pacific Ocean,
et inc Chinese checkpoint (bts), campsite, temple (prev 2 also in rfb2) & Mandate's Himalayan enclave w/garden (also on monitor), Serra's
m & Tane's compound / Wolverine's note & motorcycle (also in rfb1) w/chain (destroyed), machinery (in dream), X-Men's couch (destroyed),
ards' rifles, tree branch (destroyed), old man's lotus (also in rfb2), Tibetan statue, Tane's camera (bts), monitor, torture device, missiles &
emical rig w/ tubes (destroyed)
ASHBACKS: Wolverine cuts his motorcycle chain (this issue); Wolverine sees a crying tree and bleeding lotus (this issue).
NOPSIS: Wolverine grows increasingly aggravated with mankind and technology. After an unsettling dream, he decides to take a trip to
et. However, his dream was manipulated by Tane, whose matriarch Nirissa wants to lure Wolverine to their hidden city, where she hopes
will impregnate her daughter Serra, adding his healing factor to their bloodline. Serra overhears Nirissa's plan and flees. In Tibet, Wolverine
s attacking Chinese border guards. When he casually slashes a tree branch, an old man appears and shows him the tree's pain. When the
man animates a temple statue to attack, Wolverine suppresses his violent urges; the old man asks him to ponder his casually lethal nature.
er, Wolverine finds Serra half-dead in the snow; he returns her to the Mandate's city, where Tane's enforcer Slith attacks and poisons him.
lverine awakens in the city, where he and Serra begin to fall for one another, infuriating the sadistic Tane, who secretly wanted Serra for
self. Tane tries to injure a sleeping Serra, but Wolverine confronts him. Tane attacks, using chemicals to heighten his power and broadcast
ychic pain. Wolverine destroys Tane's chemical system and moves to kill him, but recalls the old man's words and spares Tane. Leaving Serra
arewell note, Wolverine departs.
TE: The Ollopa Theater's name is a reversal of "Apollo," a famous Harlem music hall. It is unclear if Slith actually dies; Wolverine injures him
d pronounces him dead, but Slith grabs Wolverine's arm immediately afterward.

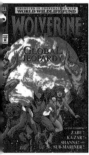

WOLVERINE IN GLOBAL JEOPARDY (December 1993)

"The Heart of Animals" (16 pages)

CREDITS: Peter David (writer), Richard Howell (pencils & colors), Bill Anderson (inks), Steve Dutro (letters),
Gerry Ellis (photography), Glenn Herdling (editor)
FEATURE CHARACTER: Wolverine (also in symbolic splash image), next in UXM #304, '93, Gam #1, '93, MCP
#150-151, '94, X #25, '93, W #75, '93)
GUEST STARS: Sub-Mariner (Namor McKenzie, Atlantean/human hybrid mutant, monarch of Atlantis, between
Namor #40-41, '93), Ka-Zar (Kevin Plunder, lord of the Savage Land), Shanna O'Hara Plunder (Ka-Zar's wife)
(prev 2 last in XMU #1, '93 fb), Zabu (Ka-Zar's sabretooth tiger, last in Cap #416, '93) (prev 3 next in TMU, '97) (all
also in symbolic splash image), Devil Dinosaur (Earth-78411 mutant dinosaur, last in FA #8, '87, chr last in MCP
#174/2, '95, next in GR #83, '97)
OTHER CHARACTERS: Conservator (extreme ecologist, also in symbolic splash image), Dr. Coral Mollison
anna's friend, monitors illegal wildlife trading, on monitor), campers inc Harry, Selma (married couple) & Dennis (their son), hunters, pilot (bts
orting island), WWF official, Conservator's audience, security guard, photographers; grizzly bear, monk seals, white rhinoceros, porpoise,
a turtle, eel, fish, bird, squirrel, crocodile, lizard, flying squirrel, shrew, platypus, turacos, frill-necked lizard, king snake, prairie dog, ibis,
ose, opossums, owl, manatee, gray kangaroos, African lions; William Harvey (quoted); bird (as Conservator's clasp design), panda (as
VF logo); grizzly bear, orangutan, harp seal, white rhinoceroses, Bengal tigers, crocodile, mountain lion, mountain gorillas, scarlet macaw,
hid, gray kangaroos, African elephant, ctenosaur lizard, giant panda, African lions, tropical rain forests (prev 16 endangered animals, plants
ecosystems, in photo section, see NOTE)
CATIONS/ITEMS: Montana campground, Mediterranean Sea, Ka-Zar's African estate, X-Mansion, Coral's research location (on monitor),
stillo (Conservator's Pacific island) w/lab, WWF auditorium / Conservator's teleportation equipment, electrical field generators (prev 2
stroyed), cages, paperwork & microphone, campers' garbage, tents, car & shotgun, polluted water, hunters' rifles, Ka-Zar's vine, speedboat
nife, X-Men's scanners & monitor, Coral's camera (bts), Shanna's transmitter (bts) & monitor, pilot's plane & radio (prev 2 bts), hurled rock,
otographers' cameras
NOPSIS: Wolverine investigates reports of vanishing animals. He intercedes when a bear spooks a camping family, but the bear disappears.
he ocean, the Sub-Mariner bemoans the polluted water and sees a family of seals vanish. Ka-Zar and Shanna stop hunters from poaching
hino, but the animal disappears. Wolverine tracks the teleport signal, and the Sub-Mariner has sea creatures lead him to their missing
ows. Shanna hears of an island crowded with endangered species; she and Ka-Zar investigate and find Wolverine already there. The Sub-

Mariner arrives, but blames Wolverine for the animal abductions; the two briefly brawl until flying debris injures Shanna. The island's owner, Conservator, breaks up the fight, explaining that he is trying to protect endangered species. He imprisons the heroes in electrical fields, but Za summons Devil Dinosaur, who was already on the island, to smash the Conservator's equipment. Shanna convinces the Conservator to h animals by fighting to improve the entire planet; he agrees and turns his island into a wildlife preserve.

NOTE: This issue, sponsored by the World Wildlife Fund, has an embossed cover with a metallic fifth ink on the image of Earth. The ind. drops the word "in" from the cover title, reading "Wolverine: Global Jeopardy." The inside front cover has an article about the WWF; the ins back cover has a list of conservation tips and a dedication to animal-loving Marvel staffer Carol Kalish (1955-1991), written by Marvel presid Terry Stewart. Kalish was penciler Richard Howell's longtime girlfriend and writer Peter David's good friend; both worked on this issue as a trib to her. P.1 and the even-numbered pages from 2-30 contain the story; the odd-numbered pages from 3-31 and p.32 have photos of endange animals and plants with short paragraphs about each. Devil Dinosaur's home reality is designated in MM:FoUB, '06.

WOLVERINE #75 (November 1993)

"Nightmares Persist" (38 pages)

CREDITS: Larry Hama (writer), Adam Kubert (pencils), Mark Farmer (co-ir c inks), Dan Green & Mark Pennington (co-inks), Pat Brosseau (letters), Ste Buccellato (colors), Lisa Patrick (asst editor), Bob Harras (editor)
FEATURE CHARACTER: Wolverine (also on monitor & in photo, also as hims & Experiment X in psychic images)
GUEST STARS: X-Men: Jean Grey, Professor X (both also on monitor), Cyclo Psylocke (all next in X Ann #2, '93), Bishop, Gambit, Rogue (prev 3 next in SM: #1, '94), Iceman, Storm (prev 2 next in Av #368, '93), Beast (next in DCut #1, '9 Quicksilver (Pietro Maximoff, mutant speedster, next in XFac #94, '93) (all last in #25, '93), Shadowcat (last in UXM #304, '93, next in Ex #71, '93)

SUPPORTING CAST: Jubilee (last in X #25, '93, next in X Ann #2, '93)
OTHER CHARACTERS: Moira MacTaggert (geneticist, also on monitor, last in X #25, '93, next in X Ann #2, '93), father & son; birds, swa geese, butterfly, flies; Lady Deathstrike, Magneto, Sabretooth, Sentinels, Wranglers, Dr. Abraham Cornelius, Carol Hines, Illyana Rasputin, fi bear, dinosaur (prev 11 as psychic images); Mariko Yashida (in photo); Mickey Mouse (as clock), Bamf, animals (prev 2 as dolls), eagle Harley Davidson logo)
LOCATIONS/ITEMS: Low Earth orbit, Wolverine's mindscape inc recreations of Avalon (Magneto's space station) & Weapon X Progr. facility, X-Mansion (also on monitor) w/Danger Room & Breakstone Lake, New Jersey home, skies above New York / Wranglers' armor & gu Experiment X's cross, helmet, battery packs & wires, Wolverine's Adamantium, Weapon X Program's Genesis Tank w/Adamantium feed tub (all as psychic images), X-Men's computer (bts) & Blackbird jet w/heat shield (bts), fly-by-wire interface, right wing, power assists, hatch d (prev 5 destroyed), main computer (bts), holographic HUDs, canopy blast shields & manual override controls, Medi-unit (also on monitor) bandages, intubation tubes & vital sign monitors, meta-morphine syringe, Professor X & Moira's headsets (also on monitors), transmitters (& monitors, Moira's medi-cart w/sutures & autoclave (prev 3 bts), Danger Room battle droids, Jubilee's popcorn, Silver Fox's medicine pou Wolverine's photo, luggage, cowboy hat, notes & motorcycle, Illyana's Bamf doll, Clan Yashida's Honor Sword
SYNOPSIS: As the X-Men struggle to pilot the Blackbird down from orbit, Professor X and Jean Grey tend to Wolverine, grievously wound after Magneto ripped the Adamantium from his skeleton. The Blackbird begins to deteriorate, and Wolverine's healing factor cannot cope w his extensive injuries. Professor X contacts Moira for medical advice, but Wolverine seems resigned to dying. Jean holds the damaged Blackt together telekinetically as Professor X telepathically restrains Wolverine from the white light that beckons him. The Blackbird's hatch breaks sucking Jean out; Wolverine hears her plight and wills himself to live, grabbing her hand and saving her. Weeks later, a still-healing Wolver tests himself in the Danger Room, but is shocked when he instinctively pops claws made of bone. Wolverine reasons that he must have alwa had bone claws, which his implanted Adamantium simply coated. His healing factor burned out and his reflexes diminished, Wolverine decic to leave the team. He says goodbye to Jubilee, leaves notes for the X-Men, and rides off on his motorcycle.
NOTE: Cover-labeled "Fatal Attractions," part of the crossover celebrating the X-Men's 30th anniversary. A trading card-sized hologram Wolverine is affixed to this issue's cover, based on art by Kubert & Farmer. This issue is continued from X #25, '93, where Magneto tore Adamantium off of Wolverine's skeleton. Wolverine's preexisting bone claws, first revealed here, were hinted at in MCP #74, '91 fb, when Weapon X Program staff noted excess Adamantium draining to Wolverine's forearms during the bonding process. Illyana Rasputin, Colos younger sister, died of the mutant-killing Legacy virus in UXM #303, '93 (although Index #7, '09 clarified that this was actually Earth-8280's Illya switched with Earth-616's Illyana in NM #73, '89). Wolverine's note to Cyclops and Jean is seen in X #30, '94. This issue also has a 16-pa insert, "Siege of Darkness" (Jeffrey Lee Simons, writer; Vito Incorvaia, art director; Cathy Colbert, production; Joel Rodgers, Jim DeSimone, M Bernardo & Wendy Geyer, colors), which previews the 17-part crossover of the same name; see Index entries for GR #44-46, '93-94.

WOLVERINE #76 (December 1993)

"Northern Dreams" (21 pages)

CREDITS: Larry Hama (writer), Tomm Coker (pencils), Al Milgrom (inks), Pat Brosseau (letters), Kevin Som (colors), Lisa Patrick (asst editor), Bob Harras (editor), Dwayne Turner (c pencils), Richard Bennett (c inks)
FEATURE CHARACTER: Wolverine (also in his own dream & as "Logan W. Logan")
GUEST STARS: Alpha Flight (Canada's premiere super hero team): Guardian (Heather Hudson, wears cybern battlesuit), Puck (both last in DM #2, '94)
VILLAINS: Lady Deathstrike (last in Cap #411, '93, last bts in Cap #414, '93), Ronald Parvenue (last in W #46, '
OTHER CHARACTERS: Sturgis (Parvenue's chauffeur, unnamed, bts driving limo), bikers inc Wiley (dies Diane; fox (dies off-panel), rabbit (dies), wild dogs; Psi-Borg (mentioned, given research grant), Carol Hines Monica Hines, see NOTE; mentioned, wrote immunology paper), Miss Gradenko (hostage) & her captor (pre mentioned in newspaper); Mariko Yashida (as skeleton), Magneto, Weapon X agents (prev 3 in Wolverine's drea
LOCATIONS/ITEMS: Ontario inc Thousand Islands (bts), Guardian's home (138A Laurier Drive, Ottawa), Route 401 & Country Bunker b Manhattan's Parvenue Towers, Canadian bar, Avalon (prev 2 in dream) / Wolverine's gun (bts) & Lotus Seven, Weapon X agents' stun gun

azine darts (all in dream), Wolverine's motorcycle, bandages, razor, luggage, passport, keys & wallet (prev 4 bts) w/Guardian's address, n Yashida's Honor Sword (bts), Parvenue's helicopter, newspaper & limousine, Guardian's cybernetic costume (hereinafter considered her dard equipment and not listed separately), window (destroyed) & computer, Wiley's motorcycle (destroyed) w/sissy bar, bikers' bungee ds (bts), motorcycles & knife, Canadian government databanks (bts), Hines' immunology paper (on monitor)

NOPSIS: As Wolverine rides his motorcycle to Ottawa, a rabbit and fox run into the road. Wolverine runs over the rabbit and crashes, ring himself and the fox. Wolverine follows the fox into the woods, hoping to help, but wild dogs attack it. Wolverine finds bikers back at his orcycle; misinterpreting their concern as a threat, he pops his bone claws, but passes out from the pain. In Manhattan, Ronald Parvenue Lady Deathstrike that he detected Wolverine crossing the Canadian border; the two head for Ontario. The bikers find Guardian's address Volverine's wallet and bring him to her house. He dreams of Magneto's attack and awakens two days later, explaining to Guardian that his ling factor is all but gone. Deathstrike tracks Wolverine, attacking and interrogating the bikers who helped him. Wolverine has Guardian hack Canada's government database looking for Weapon X information. Puck interrupts, alerting them to a suspicious limousine outside — just Deathstrike crashes in through the window.

TE: Sturgis is named next issue. Carol Hines' first name is given as Monica here; she may have written the paper under a partial alias. ther Hudson is the wife of James McDonald Hudson, Alpha Flight's original Guardian; when he returned from seeming death in AFlt #90, he took the name Vindicator and she adopted his old alias. A note on Guardian's computer monitor reads "call Lisa & Bob," referring to this e's editors. Wolverine incorrectly appears to still have Adamantium claws on this issue's cover.

WOLVERINE #77 (January 1994)

"The Lady Strikes" (21 pages)

CREDITS: Larry Hama (writer), Adam Kubert (pencils), Mark Farmer (co-inks, c inks), Mike Sellers & Mark Pennington (co-inks), Pat Brosseau (letters), Steve Buccellato (colors), Lisa Patrick (asst editor), Bob Harras (editor), Dwayne Turner (2nd print c pencils), Richard Bennett (2nd print c inks)
FEATURE CHARACTER: Wolverine (also in rfb)
GUEST STARS: Alpha Flight: Guardian (next in AFlt #128, '94), Puck (next in AFlt #129, '94)
VILLAINS: Bloodscream (last in W #17, '89), Cylla Markham (last in W #57, '92), Lady Deathstrike (next in Dom #1, '97), Ronald Parvenue (next in X #29, '94)
OTHER CHARACTERS: Sturgis (named), Guardian's neighbor, diner patron & waitress
LOCATIONS/ITEMS: Ottawa inc diner, Guardian's home (partly destroyed) & her neighbor's house / Guardian's window, computer, refrigerator, furnace & oven w/gas line (all destroyed), Parvenue's limousine & money, neighbor's telephone, Wolverine's Adamantium (in rfb), bandages, motorcycle, luggage & wallet w/money, Sturgis' fire extinguisher, Clan Yashida's Honor Sword, Cylla's cybernetic implants inc infrared scanner
FLASHBACK: Wolverine's Adamantium is pulled out through his pores (X #25, '93).
SYNOPSIS: Lady Deathstrike tackles Wolverine, smashing through Guardian's house. Guardian runs to get her battlesuit; Puck comes to Wolverine's aid but Deathstrike swats him away. The battle severs a gas line, causing an explosion that knocks the combatants into the cellar. Outside, Ronald Parvenue bribes Guardian's neighbor to stop her from calling the fire department. Wolverine pops his claws, revealing that he no longer has his Adamantium. Lady Deathstrike is staggered — her sole reason to hate Wolverine was the belief that her father's Adamantium-bonding formula was stolen and used to create Wolverine's metal skeleton; now that he no longer has it, she is unsure what to do. Deathstrike decides to leave, vowing to settle the score with Wolverine later. However, as she and Parvenue drive away, Cylla Markham and Bloodscream stop their limo, seeking Wolverine's whereabouts in order to gain vengeance of their own. Wolverine says goodbye to Puck and Guardian and continues his northward trek, as Bloodscream and Cylla dog his trail.
NOTE: This issue also has a pin-up by Tony Daniel & Jon Holdredge, featuring Wolverine and a Sentinel. The er uses the same art as p.11, with additional background details. Cylla confirms here that Deathstrike was her informant in W #55, '91. Wood alo National Park is incorrectly called "Buffalo Wood" once again. This issue was reprinted in 2006 as part of the Marvel Legends toy line, uring the cover of W #76, '93 and released with the Lady Deathstrike figure. This issue's new corner box art is from MA #131, '93's cover.

WOLVERINE #78 (February 1994)

"Deathstalk: a Test of Mettle" (20 pages)

CREDITS: Larry Hama (writer), Adam Kubert (pencils), Mark Farmer & Mike Sellers (inks), Pat Brosseau (letters), Steve Buccellato (colors), Lisa Patrick (asst editor), Bob Harras (editor)
FEATURE CHARACTER: Wolverine (also in pfb, also as Cpl. Logan in fb2 between W #34, '90 fb & W #1000/5, '11; next in WI? #60, X #30, MCP #152-155, all '94)
VILLAINS: Bloodscream (also in pfb; also in fb2, his chr 1st app, prior to W:Carni, '10), Cylla Markham (in pfb, dies, next in W #80, '94), Japanese bandit lords (in fb1, some or all die), Nazi soldier (dead, in fb2 possibly following W #34, '90 fb)
OTHER CHARACTERS: Masamune (swordsmith), Hoken Yashida (12th-century Clan Yashida Oyabun) & his troops (all in fb1), Sir Francis Drake (in fb2 following SSwConan #62/2, '81) & his pirates, Dagoo (voodoo necromancer, dies), Drake's victims (prev 3 in fb2), Cooley (Heath Junction station master, dies), Whistle Stop ress (next in W #80, '94), hunter (bts, shot wolf), trainyard employees (bts, delivered motorcycle) (prev 4 in pfb); humans & animals (dead in as skulls); wolf (dead, as pelt; also as himself & pelt in pfb, dies), birds (in pfb, 1 dies), bandit lords' horses (in fb1); Shingen Harada (quoted); iko Yashida (mentioned, told Wolverine legend of Honor Sword), demon swordsmiths (mentioned, created Unholy Blade), Légion Étrangère a French Foreign Legion, mentioned)
CATIONS/ITEMS: Alberta inc mountains, Heath Junction inc train station (all in pfb) & Logan (also in pfb) inc Whistle Stop Café (in pfb), -century Japan (in fb1) inc Caves of Kyushu (mentioned) & Masamune's forge, Atlantic Ocean, Normandy (prev 2 in fb2) / Clan Yashida's or Sword (also in pfb, also as Unholy Blade in fb1), Wolverine's bandages, wolf pelt, motorcycle w/nametag (prev 4 also in pfb), hunter's rifle,

Alberta freight train (prev 2 bts), Wolverine's rope & wolf shank, Bloodscream's ropes, Cylla's cybernetic implants inc long-range sensors & holographic display (prev 8 in pfb), bandit lords' bows (bts), arrows, swords & armor, Yashidas' swords, spear & shield, Masamune's tong hammer (prev 9 in fb1), Drake's ship, pirates' rowboats, pistols, swords & boarding ropes, victims' pistol (bts), swords & galleon, Dagoo's cha (destroyed) & potion, Bloodscream's flashlight & handgun, Wolverine's Fairbairn knife (prev 13 in fb2)

FLASHBACKS: 800 years ago, Hoken Yashida defeats bandit lords and has Masamune re-forge their Unholy Blade, made from a metec into the Honor Sword (1). 400 years ago, Dagoo makes a fatally wounded pirate undead; told that he needs an immortal's blood to replenish un-life, the pirate spends centuries searching and encounters Wolverine at the Battle of Normandy (2). Wolverine heads north through Albe killing a rabid wolf and using its meat and pelt for food and warmth. Cylla Markham and Bloodscream track Wolverine; Bloodscream kidn the Heath Junction stationmaster and consumes him slowly as they press on. Wolverine smells his pursuers, and uses the Honor Sword lodestone to navigate a blizzard. After weeks of travel, Wolverine finds the town of Logan and discovers that his motorcycle was shipped th from Heath Junction due to his name on its shipping tag. Starving, Bloodscream and Cylla catch up to Wolverine; Bloodscream drains Cy life, re-invigorating himself. Wolverine rides toward Bloodscream, sword drawn (p).

SYNOPSIS: Wolverine slices Bloodscream with the Honor Sword, seemingly killing him.

NOTE: This issue's art is printed noticeably smaller than normal; a great deal of white space is present around all four edges of most pa Bloodscream's shapeshifting power and thirst for blood are revealed here. Despite his weakness against "metal not made by man," and issue's revelation that the Honor Sword was forged from meteorite iron, W #80, '94 reveals that Bloodscream did not die here.

WOLVERINE #79 (March 1994)

"Cyber! Cyber! Burning Bright!" (21 pages)

CREDITS: Larry Hama (writer), Adam Kubert (pencils), Mark Farmer & Mike Sellers (inks), Pat Bross (letters), Steve Buccellato (colors), Lisa Patrick (asst editor), Bob Harras (editor)
FEATURE CHARACTER: Wolverine (also in photos & as skeleton in Cyber's hallucination)
VILLAIN: Cyber (Silas Burr, Adamantium-laced skin, hallucinogenic claws & psionic tracking powers, also in also as Burr in fb, possibly his chr 1st app prior to W:O #14, '07 fb, see NOTE; last in MCP #136, '93)
OTHER CHARACTERS: Zoe Culloden (LL&L expediter, 1st but chr last in Dp #-1, '97), William Burke (1 century murderer, dead, as skeleton; also possibly in fb prior to issue, see NOTE), William Hare (Bun accomplice) & their victim (bts under sheet) (prev 2 in fb, see NOTE), SAS (Special Air Service) troops inc Num One, bank teller, Edinburgh University Anatomy Department chairman, tourists, Edinburgh Castle gunners; Pe Chief Tai (mentioned, suspected that Wolverine killed Chang); Puck, Inez (both bts), Loyalist soldiers (some Ernest Hemingway, Chang (prev 5 in photos); historical figures (as busts)
LOCATIONS/ITEMS: Edinburgh, Scotland (also in fb) inc Princes Street, Edinburgh Castle, Edinburgh University's Department of Anatomy & Fiduciary Trust bank (Highmarket Street, also in pfb) w/LL&L branch office; Madripoor, Guernica (prev 2 in photos) / SAS troops' jeeps (1 destroy rifles, gas masks, handgun & tanks, Wolverine's check, bandages & luggage, Zoe's ID cards, weights, photo, computer, sports car, weapons axes, swords & shuriken, scanning headpiece & wrist computer (prev 2 hereinafter considered her standard equipment and not listed separa w/monitor & spectrographic analyzer, bank cameras (also bts in pfb) & vault door (destroyed, also in pfb), Clan Yashida's Honor Sword, Cyl Adamantium-laced skin & finger claws w/poison & hallucinogens (prev 4 hereinafter considered his standard equipment and not listed separat Burke's wheelbarrow, tarp (prev 2 in fb), skeleton & coffin, Wolverine's Adamantium skeleton (in hallucination), filing cabinet (destroyed) w/Wolve paperwork inc photos & news clippings, Bloodscream's blood (bts), railing (destroyed), gunners' watch & "One O'Clock Gun" Howitzer
FLASHBACKS: Cyber rips open the bank vault (p). In the 1820s, Burke and Hare discuss destroying a body with young Silas Burr (see NO
SYNOPSIS: SAS troops surround Wolverine at an Edinburgh bank when he tries to withdraw money from his LL&L trust. Zoe Culloden calls troops off, explaining that a man claiming to be Wolverine assaulted the bank earlier; Wolverine recognizes him as his old foe Cyber. Elsewh Cyber forces an Edinburgh professor to show him William Burke's bones, but hallucinates Wolverine's Adamantium skeleton instead, inten to claim it for himself. Zoe takes Wolverine to her office, where she attacks, accusing him of killing her mentor, LL&L's Chang. Wolverine Zoe to scan his Honor Sword for the blood of Chang's true murderer. Wolverine leaves, but Cyber tracks him down and attacks. Disappoi to find that Wolverine's skeleton is now bone, Cyber grabs Wolverine's arm and stomps on his claws, snapping them off. Zoe, who has ver Wolverine's claims, drops a filing cabinet on Cyber. As the SAS arrive, she and the injured Wolverine flee the scene, heading for Muir Islan
NOTE: This issue's title is a takeoff on the first line of William Blake's poem "The Tyger." Bloodscream (as Bloodsport) killed Chang in W #6 fb; he was cut with the Honor Sword last issue. Wolverine dropped Cyber into a vat of hallucinogens in MCP #92, '91, hence his hallucinat here. Cyber's real name is revealed here, and if his flashback is accurate, he was a young man in 1827. W:O #14, '07 established that C was alive in 1912, lending weight to the theory that he ages slowly, but Cyber is also hallucinating here, and his "flashback" may be a fant Wolverine's name on his bank account is Logan, Esq., NMI, NGN, standing for "no middle initial, no given name." While in the USA, "E generally refers to lawyers, it is a general title of respect in the UK. Landau, Luckman & Lake is also incorrectly called "Landau and Lockn here. In one panel, the office's glass door and its LL&L logo are seen from the inside; the letters are mirrored, but their order is not altered — door reads "Uadnal, Namkcul dna Ekal."

WOLVERINE #80 (April 1994)

"…In the Forest of the Night!" (23 pages)

CREDITS: Larry Hama (pencils), Ian Churchill (pencils), Al Milgrom (inks), Pat Brosseau (letters), Kevin Son (colors), Bob Harras (editor)
FEATURE CHARACTER: Wolverine (also in photos & his own dream)
VILLAINS: Bloodscream (last in W #78, '94, next in W #82, '94), Cyber (also in Wolverine's dream)
OTHER CHARACTERS: Zoe Culloden, Dr. Jaime Munoz (molecular biologist, in recording), Cylla Mark (dead, possibly next as spirit in W #176, '02, see W #4, '82's NOTE), Whistle Stop waitress (prev 2 last in W '94), Col. Mack (SAS officer, 1st), ambulance drivers inc Roddy, Edinburgh police inc Inspector McCleod (Doris, Willy (prev 2 married couple, die), SAS troops (1 dies), reporter, Alberta detective, Black Spot barter landlord (prev 2 bts) & patrons, ferry captain, bystanders; Nightcrawler (in photo); pensioner (mentioned, di two-headed calf (mentioned)

CATIONS/ITEMS: Scotland inc Firth of Forth w/dock, Black Spot pub, highway & Edinburgh's First Fiduciary Trust bank; Logan, Alberta Whistle Stop Café; "painscape" (in dream), Johns Hopkins University lecture hall (in recording), Federal storage depot (bts) / Experiment helmet, painscape spikes (both in dream), Zoe's video player (destroyed), first aid kit, sports car w/afterburner, gas can, flares & wrench weapons inc grenade, bullets, shuriken, handgun & rocket launcher, Wolverine's biopsy sample (in recording) & bandages, Clan Yashida's nor Sword, SAS troops' gas masks & rifles, reporter's microphone, ambulance (destroyed, also as psychedelic cars in hallucination) w/ etcher, sheet & oxygen tank, filing cabinet (destroyed) w/Wolverine paperwork inc photos & news clippings, waitress & detective's flashlights, odpile tarp, Cylla's cybernetic implants, Doris & Willy's tow truck, Scottish ferry

ASHBACK: In a recording, Dr. Munoz delivers a lecture on bonding Adamantium to human bone. He mentions that he studied government-stored ue samples from a subject called "Logan X," and implores the subject to come forward, explaining that he discovered a DNA instability in the samples.

NOPSIS: Wolverine awakens in Zoe's car and panics when he remembers his destroyed claws. In Edinburgh, the SAS load Cyber into an ambulance, he recovers and commandeers it, heading after Wolverine. Zoe and Wolverine stop in a pub; Wolverine drinks heavily, but without his healing factor he n gets sick. In Alberta, a weakened Bloodscream kills a couple and steals their truck. As Cyber tracks Wolverine's brainwaves, Wolverine explains his amantium loss to Zoe, who shows him a video of Dr. Munoz's lecture. Cyber catches up and attacks, trying to force Zoe's car off the road; Wolverine os into the ambulance and battles him, cracking an oxygen tank. Cyber slashes Wolverine with his hallucinogenic claws, and Wolverine uses gasoline a road flare to blow up the ambulance. He returns to Zoe's car; they drive onto the ferry and ask to be taken to Muir Island.

TE: Following from last issue's title, this issue's title paraphrases the second line of William Blake's poem "The Tyger." This issue's assistant tor is unknown; it is either Lisa Patrick or Ben Raab.

WOLVERINE #81 (May 1994)

"Storm Warning!" (21 pages)

CREDITS: Larry Hama (writer), Adam Kubert (pencils), Mike Sellers & Mark Farmer (inks), Pat Brosseau (letters), Marie Javins (colors), Ben Raab (asst editor), Bob Harras (editor)
FEATURE CHARACTER: Wolverine (next in W #175/2, '02 fb)
GUEST STARS: Excalibur (UK-based mutant team): Britanic (Brian Braddock, flight & super-strength, bts recuperating between Ex #75-76, '94) Shadowcat (last in Ex #75, '94) Nightcrawler (last in Ex #75/2, '94) (prev 2 also as themselves & Magneto in Wolverine's hallucination)
VILLAIN: Cyber (chr next in W:O #12, '07 fb, next in W #93, '95)
OTHER CHARACTERS: Moira MacTaggert (last in Ex #75, '94), Zoe Culloden (both also as themselves & Magneto in Wolverine's hallucination), Inspector McCleod, Col. Mack (prev 2 next in W #93, '95), Reg, Daphne (prev 2 pleasure boaters, die), ferry captain (bts on ferry), SAS troops; birds, pelican, bees; Jean Grey, Guardian, ilee, Silver Fox, Mariko Yashida (prev 5 in Wolverine's hallucination)

CATIONS/ITEMS: Muir Island (Moira MacTaggert's Scottish research facility & Excalibur's base) w/power plant (destroyed), dock & Moira's , Firth of Forth w/dock, Isle of Tight (mentioned), "painscape" (in hallucination) / Zoe's restraining gun, ferry, Moira's scanners & pneumatic podermic, tow truck, ambulance wreckage, SAS troops' rifles & diving gear, Reg & Daphne's speedboat, Wolverine's cross, painscape spikes ev 2 in hallucination), lab's storm shutters (bts), diagnostic equipment w/restraints & holographic display, security gurney w/restraints (some stroyed) & emergency battery (bts) w/manual override, Muir Island intruder alert system w/infrared sensors (bts), power generator (bts) & kup (prev 2 destroyed) & neutralization module ("meat locker") w/stasis field, psi-shields (prev 2 bts), hydraulic moly-steel door & handprint lock

NOPSIS: Wolverine arrives on Muir Island, hallucinating badly from Cyber's chemical attack and ranting that his friends are conspiring with gneto against him. After a struggle, Excalibur tranquilizes him. On the Scottish mainland, the SAS cannot find Cyber's body; in the water arby, Cyber commandeers a speedboat, murders its owners and heads for Muir Island. In the lab, Moira debates how to flush the toxins m Wolverine's system, as Nightcrawler notices Wolverine's face changing slightly. Moira decides to lock Wolverine in a neutralization module il they can treat him, but Wolverine nearly breaks free, hallucinating that everyone is Magneto. Cyber arrives on Muir Island and destroys power generators. Wolverine breaks loose and attacks Shadowcat, but she phases through his attack; realizing that he almost killed her, lverine snaps out of his daze. Cyber attacks Wolverine, but accidentally tackles them both into the neutralization module. Shadowcat follows d tells Zoe to lock the door; she then phases Wolverine free, leaving Cyber trapped inside.

TE: Wolverine's damaged claws have grown partway back between last issue and this issue. His brow lowers here as he begins taking a more devolved state. Cyber incorrectly calls bees "bluebottle flies" here. This issue includes a bound-in uncut sheet of three trading cards turing Spider-Man and the Lizard with art by Mark Bagley, a promo item for a Fleer card line.

WOLVERINE #82 (June 1994)

"Omnia Mutantur" (22 pages)

CREDITS: Larry Hama (writer), Adam Kubert (pencils pp.1-6 & 12-22, c pencils), Bob McLeod (pencils, pp.7-11), Mark Farmer, (inks, pp.1-16), Joe Kubert (inks, pp.17-22), Pat Brosseau (letters), Steve Buccellato (colors), Ben Raab (asst editor), Bob Harras (editor)
FEATURE CHARACTER: Wolverine (also as "Joe Culloden" & as samurai in rfb (see NOTE) & Amiko's drawing)
GUEST STARS: Excalibur: Nightcrawler (next in XMU #4, '94), Shadowcat (next in Ex #76, '94)
SUPPORTING CAST: Albert, Elsie-Dee (both last in W #53, '92, chr last in W #84, '94 fb), Yukio (last in UXM #313, '94, next in XFac #113, '95), Amiko Kobayashi (also in rfb, last in KP&W #6, '85, next in W Ann '96/2)
VILLAINS: Bloodscream (last in W #80, '94), Hand ninjas (some or others last in BAxe #2, '93, chr next in GR #74, '96 fb, next in OtEdge #8, '96), Tosh & his wife (prev 2 Amiko's foster parents)
OTHER CHARACTERS: Zoe Culloden (next in W #92, '95), Moira MacTaggert (next in Ex #78, '94), Silver murai (last in XMU #3, '93, next in W Ann '96), Nobu, Teru (prev 2 Yukio's schoolmates), Siksika tribesmen (dead, as skeletons, some or ers last in W #53, '92), Zoe's pilot (bts in helicopter), Japanese child welfare authorities (bts, bribed by Samurai), bystanders; cat, birds; nkey-Clan ninjas & their foes (prev 2 on TV)

CATIONS/ITEMS: Tokyo (also in rfb) inc temple, Yukio's rented room & Tosh's Nomi-Ya (drinking shop) w/upstairs apartment, Siksika ial ground, former Weapon X Program facility, Muir Island / Wolverine's incense, bandages & pantyhose mask, Clan Yashida's Honor Sword,

Hand ninjas' swords & chained scythes, Yukio's knife, Bloodscream's stolen clothes & tow truck w/battery & jumper cables, Albert & Elsie-De batteries, Albert's spectrographic & carbon-dating sensors (prev 3 bts), Zoe's sports car & business card, LL&L helicopter, Amiko's sch uniform (destroyed) & drawing, Tosh's slushy machine (bts), golf club, ski pole, margarita glasses (prev 3 destroyed), Mercedes-Benz, turtle wa motorcycles, electronics, big-screen TV & vibro-loungers, Monkey-Clan ninjas' swords (on TV), Silver Samurai's armor

FLASHBACK: Wolverine saves Amiko after a building collapses, killing her mother (UXM #181, '84, see NOTE).

SYNOPSIS: In Tokyo, Wolverine lights incense on the anniversary of Mariko's death. Yukio arrives, warning him of a Hand ninja ambus Wolverine battles the ninjas, but Yukio convinces them that he is an impostor, pointing out his bone claws and lack of healing factor. Wolver explains that he is balancing the scales with all his old friends, believing that he will die soon. In Alberta, Bloodscream discovers Elsie-D interred in a Siksika burial mound. He jump-starts her batteries; Elsie-Dee reveals that she has been asleep for 300 years. As she reawake Albert, Bloodscream lies, claiming to be Wolverine's friend. On Muir Island, Moira worries about Wolverine's physical regression, but Zoe h some ideas on how to address it. Posing as a social worker, Wolverine interviews Amiko's foster parents, who prove neglectful, abusive a greedy. That night he breaks in and takes Amiko away, much to her delight. Wolverine returns the Honor Sword to Silver Samurai, who convinc Japan's child welfare authorities to accept Yukio as Amiko's new guardian.

NOTE: Although this issue claims that the title translates to "everything changes," a more accurate translation is "everything gets change Veteran artist Joe Kubert inks his son Adam's pencils on pp.17-22. Wolverine's appearance continues to change; his hair is larger, his nose broader and his lower canine teeth protrude. His claws have grown back, but with a pronounced lump where they were broken. Amiko incorrec remembers Wolverine's super hero costume as samurai armor in this issue's rfb. W #175/2, '02 reveals that Hand ninjas are after Wolveri here not because he sliced Matsuo Tsurayaba's face a year ago, but because he attacked Matsuo and cut off his arm earlier that day, the f of many mutilations that he promised to inflict on Matsuo in W #60, '92.

WOLVERINE #83 (July 1994)

"Cold Comfort" (22 pages)

CREDITS: Larry Hama (writer), John Nadeau (pencils), Bud LaRosa & Keith Champagne (inks), Pat Brosseau (lette Digital Chameleon (colors), Ben Raab (asst editor), Bob Harras (editor), Adam Kubert (c pencils), Mark Farmer (c inks FEATURE CHARACTER: Wolverine
GUEST STARS: Vindicator (James MacDonald Hudson, wears cybernetic battlesuit, last in AFlt #130, '9 Guardian (last in North #4, '94)
SUPPORTING CAST: Albert, Elsie-Dee
VILLAINS: Bloodscream, grave robbers inc Epstein, "Roach-Face," "Skunk" & "Too-Tall"
OTHER CHARACTERS: Hunter in Darkness (bts, escaped from ice, also as digital reconstruction, last in #53, '92, chr last in W #84, '94 fb) & his pack (1st, all but 1 bts, some or others chr last in W #84, '94 fb), Ha Tabeshaw (last in W #48, '91), Hudsons' research team: DeLong (biologist), Simpson (geologist), Sverdr (physicist, dies), Siksika tribesmen (dead, as skeletons); Tabeshaw's father (mentioned, died of lung cancer)
LOCATIONS/ITEMS: Hudsons' Arctic research station, Siksika burial mound / Harry's sutures, clamps (prev 2 bts) & Douglas C-47 w/skis destroyed), landing strut (damaged) & research supplies, Vindicator's cybernetic costume (hereinafter considered his standard equipment a not listed separately), Sverdrup's freight-loader suit, Simpson's 3-D contour mapping scanners, seismic probes (prev 2 bts), bandages, therm cold-weather suit & tracked cargo vehicle, DeLong's rifle w/scope, station's computers, monitor & dry freezer w/door lock & frost-free moist control, ice core sample, grave robbers' shotguns & ropes, Albert & Elsie-Dee's internal modems (bts), Bloodscream's stolen tow truck
SYNOPSIS: Wolverine hitches a ride with Harry Tabeshaw, who is delivering supplies to the Hudsons' Arctic research station. Harry crac a landing strut upon arrival, delaying his departure. Guardian and Vindicator show Wolverine an ice sample they discovered with an anim shaped impression in it. Their scientists have digitally reconstructed the animal that had been frozen; Wolverine and Harry recognize it as Hunter in Darkness. In Alberta, a group of grave robbers attack Bloodscream, Albert and Elsie-Dee, but are swiftly defeated. Bloodscream as the androids' help to find Wolverine, whom he claims is deathly ill. At the research station, Wolverine asks Vindicator to be the executor of estate. A Hunter in Darkness breaks in, gravely wounding Simpson. Wolverine and the Hudsons attack it, but Wolverine realizes that it is not same Hunter he met. Sverdrup tries combating it in his freight-loading armor, but the Hunter swiftly kills him. The survivors barricade themselv in the station's freezer, but Harry hears the Hunter howling — calling to the rest of its pack.
NOTE: Ronald Parvenue's last name is misspelled "Parvenu" here and next issue. James Hudson is one of Wolverine's closest friends; Jam and Heather found Wolverine in the woods after his Adamantium implantation and helped re-integrate him into society, and as founder of Alp Flight, James convinced Wolverine to become a costumed super hero. W:O #33, '09 reveals that James Hudson and Wolverine are dista cousins. Driven by instinct and hunger, the Hunters are not technically considered Villains. Harry's plane is identified in W #85, '94.

WOLVERINE #84 (August 1994)

"Things That Go Bump in the Night!" (22 pages)

CREDITS: Larry Hama (writer), Ron Wagner (breakdowns, pp.1-9, 15-19 & 21-22), Yancey Labat (penc pp.10-14 & 20), Bill Reinhold, Tom Palmer, Al Milgrom & Younger (finishes, pp.1-9, 15-19 & 21-22, see NOT Matt Banning (inks, pp.10-14 & 20), Pat Brosseau (letters), Steve Buccellato (colors), Ben Raab (asst editor), B Harras (editor), Adam Kubert (c pencils), Mark Farmer (c inks)
FEATURE CHARACTER: Wolverine (also in rfb3)
GUEST STARS: Guardian (next bts in W #91, '95, next in W #92, '95), Vindicator (next in W #91, '95)
SUPPORTING CAST: Albert, Elsie-Dee (both also in rfb2, also in fb between W #53, '92 & W #82, '94, also in #86, '94 fb during fb; next in W #86, '94), Silver Fox (bts, dead in grave, last in W #64, '93, last bts in W #65, '9 VILLAINS: Bloodscream (also in rfb1, next in W #86, '94), Siksika rebels (in fb prior to W #86, '94 fb)
OTHER CHARACTERS: Hunter in Darkness (also in rfb2 & rfb3, also as "Puppy" in fb between W #53, '92 W #83, '94 bts, also in W #86, '94 fb during fb) & his pack (some die, some or others also in fb, their chr 1st app, prior to W #83, '94), Spiral fb during W #53, '92), Harry Tabeshaw, Hudsons' research team: Sverdrup (dead, as bones), Simpson (dies), DeLong; Siksika tribesmen (in some or others also in W #86, '94 fb during fb, chr next in W #52, '92, dead); horse (in fb), fish, butterflies; Shingen Harada (mentioned, ga fighting advice); Dagoo (in rfb1), Earth-94102 Wolverine (dead, as skeleton), Mystique (prev 2 in rfb2)

LOCATIONS/ITEMS: Canada: Hudsons' Arctic research station, Hudson Bay & Alberta inc Siksika burial mound (in rfb2), 18th-century Siksika village (in fb) & Wood Buffalo National Park (in rfb3), Atlantic Ocean (in rfb1), Wolverine & Silver Fox's cabin / Harry's handgun, flashlight & Douglas C-47 w/landing strut (bts, repaired), station's generator line (destroyed), satellite bounce transmitter, power line, flares, thermite, fire extinguishers & dry freezer w/door lock, Simpson's bandages (bts) & thermal cold-weather suit, DeLong's rifle w/scope, Sverdrup's freight-loader suit, Albert & Elsie-Dee's batteries (bts in fb), Albert's internal modem, long-range infrared, spectrographic & pheromone scanners (prev 4 bts) & B-2 stealth bomber (also in rfb2) w/homing beacon (bts), satellite (bts), Dagoo's chains (destroyed), Drake's ship (prev 2 in rfb1), Siksika's knives & shotgun (prev 2 in fb), bear trap (in rfb3) w/chain (destroyed), Vindicator's welding equipment (bts), Wolverine's bouquet, Silver Fox's grave marker

FLASHBACKS: Bloodscream chokes Dagoo (W #78, '94 fb). Albert and Elsie-Dee ask Spiral to send them back in time (W #53, '92). Wolverine frees the Hunter in Darkness from a bear trap (W #34, '90 fb). Spiral sends Albert, Elsie-Dee and the Hunter back in time, where they search unsuccessfully for Wolverine. The Hunter eventually finds and joins a pack of his own kind.

SYNOPSIS: Wolverine theorizes that the Hunters were frozen in ice until holes in the ozone melted their prison. Needing to get medical help for Simpson, Wolverine and Vindicator make a run for the station's transmitter. Hunters swarm them, but although they get the transmitter back to the freezer, Simpson dies. The pack cuts the power lines; Guardian and Vindicator distract them while Wolverine races for Sverdrup's freight-loader suit. Elsewhere, Albert scans for Wolverine but instead detects the Hunter, whom he last saw in the past. Wolverine battles the Hunters with the loader suit until the pack leader comes forward — the Hunter in Darkness that Wolverine met twice before, now hundreds of years old. Recognizing Wolverine, the Hunter calls off the attack and the pack withdraws. Later, Albert and Elsie-Dee locate their B-2 bomber, and Wolverine completes his trip to Canada by visiting Silver Fox's grave.

NOTE: Elsie-Dee claims here that she and Albert never found Wolverine in the past, but W #86, '94 fb shows that they did. Co-inker Younger's first name is unknown.

WOLVERINE #85 (September 1994)

"The Phalanx Covenant: Final Sanction, Part One — Full Shred Thrash" (37 pages)

CREDITS: Larry Hama (writer), Adam Kubert (pencils), Mark Farmer (co-inks, c inks), Josef Rubinstein (co-inks), Pat Brosseau (letters), Lovern Kindzierski & Joe Andreani (colors), Ben Raab (asst editor), Bob Harras (editor)

FEATURE CHARACTER: Wolverine (next in Cable #16, GR #57, GR/W/Pun, W #87, all '94)

GUEST STARS: Cable (also as Nathan Dayspring in rfb, also as Nathan Dayspring in fb1 & fb2 during AC&P #2, '94; last in Cable #15, '94), Phoenix (Jean Grey, also as Redd Dayspring in rfb & Cable's hallucination, also as Redd Dayspring in fb1 & fb2 during AC&P #2, '94), Cyclops (prev 2 last in UXM #316, '94), X-Men: Archangel, Iceman (prev 2 last in UXM #314, '94), Bishop (last in UXM Ann #18/2, '94), Gambit (last in DD #330, '94), Storm (last in XMU #5, '94), Beast, Rogue (prev 7 bts, detected by Cerebro), Psylocke (prev 3 last in X #34, '94) (all next in Cable #16, '94), Professor X (bts contacting Wolverine & Cable, last in XFac #106, '94 fb, next in XFac #106, '94 fb)

VILLAINS: Phalanx (humans absorbed into techno-organic alien hivemind, others last in X #36, '94, next in XFor #38, '94): Cameron Hodge (last in XFac #106, '94), Steven Lang (last in X #36, '94) (both next in Cable #16, '94), Egon, Larissa, Nkotha (prev 3 named, die; last in XFac #106, '94 fb)

OTHER CHARACTERS: Harry Tabeshaw (next bts in W #87, '94), Apocalypse's Earth-4935 dog soldiers (in fb2 during AC&P #2, '94) inc Marl; Daysprings' schmule (in fb1 during AC&P #2, '94), birds; Moira MacTaggert (mentioned, created database self-destruct failsafe)

LOCATIONS/ITEMS: Muir Island w/Moira's lab, Phalanx's citadel (Mount Everest, Tibet), Crestcoast (Earth-4935 38th-century city, in rfb, fb1 & fb2), astral plane / Cyclops & Phoenix's mini-jet (destroyed), Phalanx's techno-organic mesh (some destroyed) & psi-dampers, Harry's rope & Douglas C-47 w/ instruments (some destroyed), Wolverine's parachute, Muir Island computers, Cerebro sub-frame (prev 2 destroyed), data banks (destroyed) w/ self-destruct timer & weather station w/trunk line, Cable's teleporter (bts), hand cannon & shoulder-mounted plasma cannon w/power cells (bts)

FLASHBACKS: As Redd Dayspring, Jean teaches young Nathan how to disguise his techno-organic arm (AC&P #3, '94). Nathan talks to Redd (1). Nathan accidentally drops his disguise in front of Apocalypse's soldiers; Redd reassures him that everything will be all right (2).

SYNOPSIS: Cyclops and Phoenix find Muir Island swarming with Phalanx. Wolverine parachutes in and helps battle the creatures, explaining that Professor X summoned him. As the Phalanx attempt to absorb Moira's data on mutants, Cable joins the fight, revealing that the Phalanx have captured the X-Men. Cyclops, realizing that they must access Muir Island's Cerebro to find their teammates, devises a plan: Cable and Phoenix attack the Phalanx on the astral plane, while Cyclops and Wolverine storm the building. Cable begins remembering his adoptive mother, Redd, unaware that "Redd" was Phoenix in a different body, which distracts him during the psychic battle. As Cyclops and Wolverine locate the X-Men with Cerebro, the Phalanx prey on Cable's techno-organic infection, trying to absorb him. Wolverine rescues Cable and the mutants retreat on Harry's plane. Moira's self-destruct sequence activates, blowing up the Phalanx-riddled lab, and the X-Men head for Tibet to rescue the X-Men.

NOTE: Cover-labeled "Phalanx Covenant: Final Sanction Part 1." This crossover is split into three segments: "Generation Next" in UXM #316-317 & X #36-37, "Life Signs" in XFac #106, XFor #38 & Ex #81, and "Final Sanction" in W #85 & Cable #16, all '94, all focusing on various aspects of the Phalanx's capture of the X-Men and offensive on mutants. This story concludes in Cable #16, '94, where Cable, Cyclops, Phoenix and Wolverine rescue the X-Men and destroy the Phalanx's main base. In XFac #67-68, '91, Cyclops' infant son Nathan was infected with a techno-organic virus and sent to the far future; he grew up to become Cable, and eventually time-traveled back to the present. In AC&P #1-4, '94, Cyclops and Jean Grey's minds were pulled into the same future; they inhabited cloned bodies and spent twelve years as "Slym" and "Redd" raising young Nathan. Cyclops and Jean married in X #30, '94; Jean took the codename Phoenix in AC&P #4, '94. Earth-4935 is designated in OHMU:AU, '05. Harry's plane is identified here. This issue's newsstand cover replaces the foil stripe with a red stripe.

WOLVERINE: EVILUTION (September 1994)

"Evilution" (48 pages)

CREDITS: Ann Nocenti (writer), Mark Texeira (layouts), John Royle (pencils), Philip Moy (co-inks, c inks), Andre Pepoy (co-inks), Dave Sharpe (letters), Monica Bennett (colors), Suzanne Gaffney (editor), Bob Harras (group edito
FEATURE CHARACTER: Wolverine (also in his own dream, chr last in DrS #41, '92, chr next in UXM Ann #16/2, '9
GUEST STARS: Boom-Boom (also in Red Water Fall's dream, chr last in XFor #5, '91, chr next in XFor #6, '92
Professor X (bts researching Prescott, chr last in X:Bish #3, '09, chr next in UXM #289, '92)
VILLAINS: "Saviour" (undead entity, also as spirit & corpse), Devos (teenage anti-technology cult) inc Jimmy
Steven, Gycon president (Jimmy's father) & staff
OTHER CHARACTERS: Red Water Fall (Native American landowner), Suzy (Jimmy's sister), Jimmy's mothe
friends, classmates & teacher, Boom-Boom's friend, children (most bts, some or all die, some also in photo
Masons inc Steven's father, Daily Bugle reporter (bts writing article), pilot (bts flying plane), French farmer (b
inventing hybrid fruit), African doctors (bts inventing polio vaccine), polio patients (bts, temporarily cured), inventor (bts inventing roach kille
young woman, switchboard operator, bystanders; frogs (most die), chickens (1 dies, others dead), dogs (1 dead), cat, rabbit (prev 2 dea
birds (1 dies), Jimmy's cat; Silvio (retired coal miner, mentioned); Native American goddess (as totem, also in photos), man (head only, a
mannequin), horse (as rocking horse)
LOCATIONS/ITEMS: Prescott, New York inc nuclear plant (also in Wolverine & Red Water Fall's dreams), museum (bts), diner, wood
church, Gycon boardroom, Prescott High School, Jimmy's house, Red Water Fall's garden & nearby town's homes, outer space (in Wolverine
dream), X-Mansion, shantytown inc garbage dump & children's clubhouse, Germany Historical Museum and Archive, switchboard operato
office, French farm, Midwestern home, African hospital, inventor's forum (prev 4 bts) / Jimmy's mannequin head, stage blood, drink, show
newspaper, scalpels & war paint, nuclear warhead, Wolverine's talisman (prev 2 in Wolverine's dream) & pack, garbage inc rocking horse & tox
waste canister, Native American totem (also in photos), Silvio's (TV (mentioned), children's paintbrush (in photo), camera (bts) & TV, Saviou
coffin & wrappings, Spear of Destiny (also in Red Water Fall's dream) w/display case (destroyed), Steven's glass cutter, Red Water Fall's pho
Boom-Boom's cross (in Red Water Fall's dream) & newspaper, Jimmy's father's TV (destroyed), microphone & car w/engine (destroye
students' scalpels, teacher's diagram, Devos' ropes (also in Red Water Fall's dream), plaque (bts), candles, book, ladder, knives & telephor
cords, airplane, Gycon staff's clubs, knife & broken bottle, Jimmy's mother's cookies, nuclear plant's pipes (some destroyed), dog's leas
phone booth, telephone, switchboard (prev 4 destroyed), farmer's gene-splicing equipment, Midwestern man's fusion jar, African polio vaccin
inventor's insect-killing tin (prev 4 bts), electrical outlet, sink, toaster, woman's makeup
SYNOPSIS: Wolverine dreams of a disaster at Gycon's nuclear plant. Some children find toxic waste in a garbage dump; after playing with
several die. At a mall, Boom-Boom sees Jimmy advocating violent rejection of technology. Wolverine investigates the nuclear plant and mee
Red Water Fall, who explains that the plant had to suspend operations after he refused to sell them his land, and that he senses a malevole
presence growing. Hearing voices, Jimmy digs in the woods until he uncovers a corpse. In Germany, Jimmy's friend steals the Spear of Destir
from a museum. Jimmy and the anti-technology Devos try to reanimate the corpse through animal sacrifice. Boom-Boom investigates, but th
Devos capture her. Red Water Fall induces a vision to learn about the entity; Gycon's staff attacks while he sleeps, hoping to claim his land, b
Wolverine fights them off. Jimmy plots to use the Spear to reverse time, eliminating technology. As the Devos prepare to sacrifice Boom-Boo
to the corpse's spirit, unnatural occurrences begin happening worldwide. Wolverine arrives, scattering the Devos and rescuing Boom-Boom, bi
the spirit manifests physically, seeking to remake the world "as it should be." Wolverine stabs the spirit with the Spear, dissipating it and releasir
the Devos from its influence.
NOTE: This story is preceded by a short introductory paragraph on the inside front cover. This issue occurs well before Wolverine's Adamantiu
was removed in X #25, '93. Red Water Fall is also incorrectly called Red Fall and Red Falls here. The chicken blood leaking from Jimmy's pock
on pp.29-30 is colored light blue. The Spear of Destiny changes size several times in this issue, from less than a foot long to over five feet.

WOLVERINE & NICK FURY: SCORPIO RISING (October 1994)

"Scorpio Rising" (44 pages)

CREDITS: Howard Chaykin (writer), Shawn McManus (art), Chris Eliopoulos (letters), Gloria Vasquez (colors
Joe Kaufman (design), Mike Marts (asst editor), Nel Yomtov (group editor)
FEATURE CHARACTERS: Nick Fury (chr last in Cap #420, '93, chr next in X #25, '93), Wolverine (chr last
X #24, '93, chr next in MCP #137, '93)
SUPPORTING CAST: Scorpio (also in photo, becomes Carpasian acting President, last in W/NF:SC, '89, ne
in FoS #1, '95), la Contessa Valentina de Fontaine (chr last in NF:AoS #47, '93, chr next in SSWP #24, '94)
VILLAINS: Baltazar Pavel (descendant of Carpasian monarchy), Hydra inc Pavel's advisors, assassins (1 a
tailor, 1 as blind man) inc Niki, High Command (bts arranging coup) & agents (some or others chr last in SS
#7, '93, chr next in SSWP #26, '94, next in FoS #1, '95) inc spy (as SHIELD agent) & helicopter pilot (voice onl
Hydra LMDs (as Carpasian rebels, most or all destroyed; 1 other as Amber D'Alexis, destroyed)
OTHER CHARACTERS: Carpasian President Milovan Tankosic & his Cabinet Ministers: Dmitri Cabrinovic (Interior), Josip Potiorek (Industry
Sofia Rudavsk (Foreign Affairs) & Jasnia Schweik (Defense) (all die); SHIELD agents (some or others chr last in Cap #420, '93, chr next in A
#368, '93; 1 next in NThr #16, '94, some or others next in Nova #11, '94) inc Team Bravo (bts, sent after Scorpio), Arnett (CNN reporter, b
predicting rebel victory), UN representative (bts, had meeting scheduled with Rudavsk), Carpasian Defense Force (unnamed, some die on
panel), Carpasian citizens: Duffy (bartender), Schweik's guards (bts, dead), Tankosic's mistress (Miss Carpasia) & driver (prev 2 bts in limo, die
partiers, nun, children, bar patrons, police, reporters, ad hoc committee, bus driver (bts driving bus), bystanders; dog (dies), birds; King Djura
Pavel (Baltazar's father, unnamed, mentioned, abdicated throne to Communists), Schweik's son (mentioned, died in revolution)
LOCATIONS/ITEMS: Republic of Carpasia inc Crnilobara (capital city, unnamed) w/Schweik & Rudavsk's offices & Central Square, Hydra
LMD processing plant (as nuclear power facility), church (prev 2 destroyed), alley, tailor shop, war zone, warehouse, docks, bar, Hydra agen
room & Fury's hideout, SHIELD's artificial island w/Section Seven, Pavel's European office / Carpasian flags & bus, Tankosic's limousi
(destroyed) & microphone, Schweik's paperwork & bronzed baby shoes, Cabrinovic's liquor bottle, Potiorek's tie, Rudavsk's paperwork
window, dog's harness & dynamite, Defense Force's rifles, jeep & comm unit, SHIELD security systems (bts), holding tank (destroyed

onitors, bo staffs & blaster, Scorpio's tracer (bts), microphones & Cosmic Key, spy's wrist communicator, LMDs' military vehicle (destroyed) tank, Hydra LMD assembly equipment (destroyed), sensors (bts), blasters, guns, radio, listening device & helicopters w/radio (bts), Fury's cker (bts) & scuba gear, police handcuffs (bts)

YNOPSIS: The newly democratic country of Carpasia is plunged into civil war when its President and cabinet are assassinated. Nick Fury's arpasian-born son Scorpio wants to return and help his people, but Fury refuses to let him. Baltazar Pavel, exiled heir to the Carpasian throne, nfers with Hydra, who masterminded the assassinations. Scorpio steals the Cosmic Key and escapes the SHIELD base. Wolverine arrives Carpasia, and learns that the rebels are far better supplied than the democratic forces. Fury sneaks into Carpasia as well, and runs into both olverine and Scorpio at a bar. The three brawl, but two female Hydra agents arrive and help Scorpio escape. Wolverine and Fury compare tes as, elsewhere, Hydra produces an army of LMD "rebels." The Hydra agents seduce Scorpio — but he is rattled when his dead mother ddenly arrives. Fury and Wolverine track down Scorpio and burst in; Wolverine decapitates Scorpio's "mother," revealing her as an LMD. corpio reveals where he hid the Cosmic Key, but Hydra had bugged him, and they learn its location. Wolverine, Fury and Scorpio race Hydra the Key; after a brief skirmish, Wolverine snatches it and destroys the LMD factory, ending the war. Pavel is arrested, and Scorpio is soon pointed Carpasia's acting President.

OTE: This story is preceded by a title page, credits page with a frontispiece taken from p.31 panel 2, and introduction by Peter Sanderson. e indicia says only "Scorpio Rising." This issue occurs before Wolverine's Adamantium was removed in X #25, '93. Rudavsk's last name is so incorrectly spelled Rudasvki. Tankosic and both Pavels' first names are revealed in MAtlas #1, '08, which also names Crnilobara and the arpasian Defense Force.

WOLVERINE #86 (October 1994)

"Claws Along the Mohawk" (22 pages)

CREDITS: Larry Hama (writer), Ron Garney (pencils), Al Vey & Bud LaRosa (inks), Pat Brosseau (letters), Steve Buccellato (colors), Ben Raab (asst editor), Bob Harras (editor)

SUPPORTING CAST: Albert, Elsie-Dee (both also in fb1 during W #84, '94 fb, next in GenX #42, '98)

VILLAINS: Bloodscream (next in XMU #9, '95), Earth-94102 Adversary ("Drummer With No Sound," chaotic trickster god), Man-Killer Wolf (Adversary's Siksika vessel) (prev 2 in fb1 & fb2, also in holographic projection & as painting), Siksika rebels (in fb1 following W #84, '94 fb), alternate-future anti-mutant forces: CX288 (cyborg, destroyed), bandits (bts in ships) & command controller (voice only) (prev 3 in future, see NOTE)

OTHER CHARACTERS: Hunter in Darkness (as "Puppy," in fb1 during W #84, '94 fb), Earth-94102 Forge (also in fb1 & fb2 prior to this issue's future events), Earth-94102 Wolverine (in fb1 & fb2, his chr 1st app, prior to W #52, '92), Earth-94102 Wolverine's alternate-future self (diverged during fb2), Albert & Elsie-Dee's alternate-future lves, Siksika tribesmen (in fb1, some also as painting, some or others chr last & chr next in W #84, '94 fb) inc shaman, alternate-future rebels, an-Killer Wolf's victim (dead, in fb1 as hand & bone, also in shadow in fb2 as hand); wolf (dead, in fb1 & in shadow in fb2 as Man-Killer Wolf's eaddress), cows (dead, as skulls), bird (prev 2 in fb1); Pikuni war chief (mentioned, arrow taken from him); horse (as painting)

OCATIONS/ITEMS: Muir Island, future war zone (see NOTE), 18th-century Alberta (in fb1): Man-Killer Wolf's camp (also in holographic ojection), waterfall (also in fb2) & Siksika village / Man-Killer Wolf's bone club, Siksika's spears, axes, shotgun, clubs, torch, bow & hurled cks, Forge-94102's blaster (also in fb2), tent, painting & equipment inc holographic display w/remote scanner (bts) & remote control, Pikuni row (all in fb1), Albert's long-range pheromone scanners (bts) & B-2 stealth bomber, Phalanx psi-shields (bts) & tendril, Wolverine-94102's mor (destroyed) & box, CX288's transmitter (bts) & blasters, controller's radio (bts), Forge-94102 & Albert's armor, rebels' blasters, armor & ansports, bandits' ships (all but 1 bts), Elsie-Dee's dress (prev 11 in future)

LASHBACKS: Albert, Elsie-Dee and the Hunter in Darkness arrive in the past during a Siksika battle, and help repulse Man-Killer Wolf and s fanatics. They are greeted by Earth-94102's Forge and Wolverine, who have pursued the demonic Adversary back in time. Man-Killer Wolf tacks again, now empowered by the Adversary; Forge and Wolverine chase after him. The Siksika make Albert run a gauntlet; he survives d becomes the tribe's war chief. Albert and Elsie-Dee see a far-off explosion and realize that the Adversary blasted Wolverine and Forge out time (1). Wolverine falls out of the time vortex ten years later (2).

YNOPSIS: On Muir Island, Albert scans for Wolverine while Elsie-Dee recounts their adventure, telling Bloodscream that when their batteries n down, the Siksika buried them. Albert detects Wolverine and they fly off. Decades later, in a war-torn future, Wolverine-94102 battles a borg while carrying Elsie-Dee's head. They reunite with Forge-94102, who also arrived in this future; he explains that Albert and Elsie-Dee's e travel negated Wolverine's previous fate of landing in the past; instead, he was swept to the future. Wolverine and Elsie-Dee join Forge's bels, including Albert, and continue the fight for freedom…

OTE: Earth-616's Wolverine does not appear in this issue, although Albert detects him in Tibet, a reference to the events of Cable #16, '94. arth-94102 seemingly diverged from Earth-616 sometime after W #40, '92, as its Forge recalls that issue's events, but either before X #25, '93 after W #145, '99 fb, as its Wolverine still has his Adamantium. It is unclear if the future timeframe that this issue's Forge and Wolverine end up is their native Earth-94102, or a different alternate future. Albert, Elsie-Dee and Bloodscream's plotline is dropped after this issue; their quest locate Wolverine is never resolved, and whether the Phalanx tendril that was reaching for their jet boarded or infected it is never revealed.

WOLVERINE #87 (November 1994)

"Showdown in Lowtown!" (22 pages)

CREDITS: Larry Hama (writer), Adam Kubert (pencils), Mark Farmer, Dan Green, Tim Townsend & Josef Rubinstein (inks), Pat Brosseau (letters), Marie Javins (colors), Ben Raab (asst editor), Bob Harras (editor)

FEATURE CHARACTER: Wolverine (also as Logan in fb between XO:Sabre, '09 & Mvk #2, '97 fb)

GUEST STARS: Gambit (next in W #89, '94), Professor X (bts paying Archie, next in Bish #1, '94) (both last in X Ann #3, '94)

SUPPORTING CAST: Archie Corrigan, Tyger Tiger (both last in MCP #155, '94), O'Donnell (last in W #18, '89), Police Chief Tai (last in PWZ #22, '93) (all next in W #98, '96), Maverick (also in fb between W #63, '92 fb & Mvk #2, '97 fb; last in XMU #3, '93, next in W Ann '95/2)

VILLAINS: Sabretooth (as Creed, in fb between XO:Sabre, '09 & Mvk #2, '97 fb), Death Touch Cult Hand ninjas (die, some or others last in W #57, '92, others next in W #107, '96): Kuro Ryu, Shiro Tora; enemy troops (in fb)

OTHER CHARACTERS: Harry Tabeshaw (bts, bought Archie's plane, last in W #85, '94), Rose Wu (metamorph, also in painting, last in UX #261, '90, next in W #98, '96), Princess Bar band (bts), patrons & bartender, party guests inc prostitutes, bystanders; birds

LOCATIONS/ITEMS: Lowtown inc docks & Princess Bar w/rooftop, enemy base (in fb) / Team X's stolen information (bts), body armor guns, catwalk (destroyed), enemy blasters & body armor (all in fb), Princess Bar window, table & skylight (prev 3 destroyed), Wolverine's ca (destroyed) & telegram (bts), Rose's painting, Professor X's check, Archie's Douglas DC-3 (prev 2 bts), ninjas' plasma rifles, swords & shurike Maverick's cowl (destroyed), binoculars, smoke grenades, blasters (1 destroyed) w/laser spotter (bts) & body armor w/faceplate, wooden boa bystanders' cards

FLASHBACK: Sabretooth is wounded during a Team X mission, but refuses to let the team retreat despite heavy odds. He destroys the team exit route, forcing them to stand and fight.

SYNOPSIS: Gambit accompanies Wolverine to Madripoor, wanting to talk about Professor X's attempt to rehabilitate Sabretooth. The tw sense trouble in the Princess Bar and burst in, but find only a surprise party for Wolverine. Rose Wu reveals that she retired from LL&L a bought the Princess Bar, and Wolverine's old friends welcome him back to town. As Wolverine dances with Tyger Tiger, two Hand ninjas pl an ambush, but Maverick arrives and shoots them. Wolverine and Gambit investigate, but Maverick targets them as well. The two chase a confront Maverick, who threatens to kill Wolverine, but Wolverine calls his bluff. Maverick reveals that he has contracted the fatal Legacy viru and wanted to be killed in battle. Wolverine advises him to make the most of his last days instead of worrying about dying, but Wolverine is take aback when Maverick tells him to heed his own advice.

NOTE: Wolverine's broken claws are now fully healed. The X-Men captured Sabretooth in XMU #3, '93 and Professor X decided to try to cu his bloodlust; he has been a "guest" in the X-Mansion's cellblock since then. Stryfe arranged the airborne release of the mutant-targeting Lega virus in XFor #18, '93. Rose's metamorphing powers are revealed here. It is unclear if she only bought O'Donnell's half of the bar, or wheth Wolverine sold his half back to O'Donnell previously and Rose acquired the entire bar. With this issue, Marvel began offering two versions each X-book: a "Deluxe" edition with glossy paper that better showcased the digital coloring (and carried the word "deluxe" below the iss number block on the cover), and a "Standard" edition which was cheaper, printed on lower-grade paper, and was published two weeks later (a did not have the word "deluxe"). The two versions were published through W #99, '96.

WOLVERINE #88 (December 1994)

"It's D-D-Deadpool, Folks!" (22 pages)

CREDITS: Larry Hama (writer), Adam Kubert (pencils, pp.1-11; c pencils), Fabio Laguna (pencils, pp.12-2 Mark Farmer & Tim Townsend (inks), Pat Brosseau (letters), Marie Javins (colors), Ben Raab (asst editor), B Harras (editor)
FEATURE CHARACTER: Wolverine (next in FF #394, '94 bts, FF #395, '94)
VILLAIN: Deadpool (Wade Wilson, insane mercenary with healing factor, also as cartoon in title, last in SSW #30, '94, next in W Ann '95/2)
OTHER CHARACTERS: Grand Guignol troupe: Weapon X (Garrison Kane, cyborg), Copycat (Vaness Carlysle, metamorph, also as prop head) (both last in Dp #4, '93, next in Cable #37, '96), Milo (director), Yolan (actress), makeup artist (all also on poster), others (on poster); cabbie (also in license photo), bystanders; fli (bts, attracted by ketchup); Vindicator (mentioned, asked Wolverine to check on Weapon X)

LOCATIONS/ITEMS: San Francisco inc Grand Guignol Theater (also on poster) & Weapon X & Copycat's apartment / Weapon X & Copyca door (destroyed) & poster w/frame (destroyed), Deadpool's guns, swords & grenade, Copycat's kimono (destroyed) & prop head w/wires, Mil clipboard, Yolanda's ketchup & prop knives & axe, taxi w/master cylinder (bts), rearview mirror, door (prev 3 destroyed) & emergency brake (bt Weapon X's synthetic cyborg limbs, stage lights, Wolverine's motorcycle

SYNOPSIS: Arriving at Weapon X and Copycat's apartment, Wolverine is attacked by Deadpool, who is looking for Copycat, his ex-girlfrier The two battle fiercely until Deadpool stabs Wolverine through the chest and departs. At a nearby theater, Weapon X struggles with his new j as an actor, while Copycat encourages him to embrace the new life they are building together. Slowly recovering, Wolverine notices a poster an acting troupe that includes Weapon X and Copycat. He hails a cab and heads for the theater, realizing that his healing factor is beginning return. Deadpool arrives at the theater and attacks Weapon X, murderously jealous over Copycat's affections. The taxi's brakes die while goi down a hill; Wolverine slices off the taxi door and rides it down the street. Deadpool throws swords at both Weapon X and Copycat. Weapon blocks one sword; Wolverine bursts through the door and stops the other, and Deadpool retreats. Later, Wolverine wishes the couple good lu and departs.

NOTE: Kane and Deadpool were both empowered by the same iteration of the Weapon X Program, which succeeded the group that implante Wolverine's Adamantium. Like Wolverine, Kane was given the codename "Weapon X," which seems to be assigned to the Program's main fie operative. Deadpool's healing factor is a derivative of Wolverine's and was artificially implanted.

WOLVERINE #89 (January 1995)

"The Mask of Ogun" (22 pages)

CREDITS: Larry Hama (writer), Fabio Laguna (pencils), Josef Rubinstein (inks), Pat Brosseau (letters), Ma Javins (colors), Ben Raab (asst editor), Bob Harras (editor), Adam Kubert (c pencils)
FEATURE CHARACTER: Wolverine (also in rfb, also in fb between W #103, '96 fb bts & W #169, '01 fb; ne in X #40, '95)
GUEST STARS: Gambit (last in W #87, '94, next in XMU #7, '94), Ghost Rider (last in Morb #29, '95, next GR #58, '95)
VILLAINS: Ogun (as spirit & Wolverine, also in rfb, also in fb between W #103, '96 fb & W #169, '01 fb; next in #111, '97), Sabretooth (last in X #38, '94), Linus Dorfman (bts taking hostages, also in photo on TV, last in W #43, '9 **OTHER CHARACTERS:** Trish Tilby (reporter, on TV, last in Namor #56, '94), Dan Ketch (bts as Ghost Ride host body, last in GR/W/Pun, '94, next in GR #58, '95), tollbooth attendant, street gangs, museum guards (dead SWAT teams, hostage negotiators (prev 2 bts, dealing with Linus), Linus' victims (dead) & hostages (prev 2 bts in apartment), Japanese

ernment (bts loaning artifacts); Linus' animal victims (bts, dead in apartment) inc wolverine (last in W #43, '91); birds (others in fb), rats; adowcat (in rfb); Sun Tzu (quoted), Egyptian pharaohs (as statues)

CATIONS/ITEMS: New Jersey highway, George Washington Bridge, Manhattan inc Metropolitan Museum w/Egyptian wing, Tokyo astruction site (in rfb), bamboo grove (Kanazawa, Japan, in fb, see NOTE), news studio (on TV), Linus' apartment (bts), X-Mansion w/ oretooth's cell / Wolverine's motorcycle & money, street gangs' guns, car (destroyed), museum's doors, display case (prev 2 destroyed) & nple of Dendur recreation, Japanese armor & weapons, Ogun's mask (destroyed) & sword (prev 2 also in rfb), bamboo, Wolverine & Ogun's ken (prev 2 in fb), TV camera (bts), Sabretooth's TV & phased disruption force field (unnamed)

ASHBACKS: Wolverine kills Ogun and destroys his mask (KP&W #6, '85). An unarmed Ogun tells his pupil Wolverine to attack him, but lects all of his strikes until Wolverine loses his temper. He savagely beats Ogun, but is ashamed of his actions.

NOPSIS: Wolverine rides his motorcycle into New York, heading home to the X-Mansion at last, when Ghost Rider approaches, claiming t Ogun's spirit has returned. Wolverine follows Ghost Rider to the Metropolitan Museum, where some force has killed the guards. Wolverine hocked to see Ogun's demon mask in a Japanese exhibit. The two are distracted by a crash, and see that a suit of armor has vanished — d when they turn back, the mask is gone as well. Clad in both, Ogun attacks; he throws his sword up, daring Wolverine to attack an unarmed oonent. Ghost Rider deflects the falling sword; Wolverine catches it and splits Ogun's mask in half. The heroes see a glimpse of Wolverine's e before the empty armor falls; Wolverine explains that Ogun was attacking him with a part of himself. At the X-Mansion, Gambit taunts oretooth, saying that Wolverine is coming home…

TE: How Ogun's spirit returned is never explained. Linus Dorfman's last name is revealed here. The signs for the West Side Highway's north d south exits are accidentally reversed. Next issue specifies the type of force field restraining Sabretooth. Ogun's dojo is revealed to be in hazawa in W #113, '97 fb.

WOLVERINE #90 (February 1995)

"The Dying Game" (30 pages)

CREDITS: Larry Hama (writer), Adam Kubert (pencils, c pencils), Mark Farmer & Dan Green (inks), Pat Brosseau (letters), Marie Javins (colors), Ben Raab (asst editor, uncredited), Bob Harras (editor), Greg Hildebrandt & Tim Hildebrandt (c painting)
FEATURE CHARACTER: Wolverine (next in GR #61, X:P, UXM #322, all '95)
VILLAINS: Sabretooth (next bts in X:P, '95, next in XFor #44, '95), Linus Dorfman (nicknamed "Linus the Heinous," in pfb, also in photo on TV)
OTHER CHARACTERS: Eamon X. Reilly (police chief, 1st), Trish Tilby (both next in Venom:STA #1, '95), Dr. Sybil Survess (National Council of Personality Disorder Specialists director) (all on TV), police: Mendoza (bts, dies, killed by Linus), others (in pfb); David Letterman (last in Pun:Prize, '90, next in Cap&Falc #8, '04), Roseanne Barr xt bts in Tstrike #9, '94) (prev 2 voice only on TV), Mike (studio crew, bts running footage), newsreader (voice only), Linus' victims (dead) & stages (some die) (prev 2 bts in apartment), criminals (bts), ATF agent (prev 2 in recording); Linus' animal victims (bts, dead in apartment) inc lverine; Cyclops, Guardian, Jubilee, Phoenix, Shadowcat, Storm (prev 6 mentioned, threatened by Sabretooth) Forge (mentioned, explained ze field to Wolverine), Tom Arnold (mentioned on TV); Ben & Bob (ice cream makers, caricatures on carton, see NOTE)

CATIONS/ITEMS: X-Mansion w/Sabretooth's cell, Linus' apartment (bts) w/nearby street (in recording), news studio, compound, Late Show dio (prev 3 on monitor) / Sabretooth's phased disruption force field (named, destroyed), TV & restraints, police handcuffs (bts) & batons, ATF guns ar (prev 2 in recordings), Wolverine's weights, speed bag & bathtub, TV cameras (bts), Trish's microphone (on TV), M'kraan Crystal (bts, see NOTE)
ASHBACK: In a recording, Linus is apprehended and viciously beaten by police.

NOPSIS: At the X-Mansion, Wolverine confronts Sabretooth in his cell. Sabretooth throws himself against the force field, but it holds. bretooth dares Wolverine to kill him, but Wolverine refuses; he leaves the cellblock and spends the evening trying to take Sabretooth off his nd. Wolverine watches news footage of serial killer Linus Dorfman's brutal arrest. A psychologist points out that Linus was so difficult to subdue cause he used to beat himself, gradually desensitizing himself to pain, and Wolverine realizes that Sabretooth had been doing the same thing. the cellblock, Sabretooth throws himself at the force field again, and finally breaks through — but finds Wolverine waiting for him. The two fight a gthy and vicious battle; Sabretooth again challenges Wolverine to kill him, and begins threatening to torture and murder all of Wolverine's loved es otherwise. Enraged, Wolverine snaps and pops his claws through Sabretooth's brain — just as the entire world turns to crystal and shatters.
TE: The first and last two pages of this issue are foldouts, resulting in two 4-page spreads and two 3-page spreads. Almost all of the naining story pages are 2-page spreads. The shattered world at this issue's end is due to the events of X #41, '95, where the M'kraan Crystal efly "crystallized" all of reality after Professor X's time-traveling son Legion accidentally killed his father 20 years in the past. See WX #1, '95's TE for more details. Linus' last name is misspelled "Dorfmann" here. "Ben & Bob's real New Hampshire ice cream" is named for editors Ben ab and Bob Harras. This issue includes two bound-in trading cards, advertising the '95 Fleer Ultra X-Men card set.

WEAPON X #1 (March 1995)

"Unforgiven Trespasses" (23 pages)

CREDITS: Larry Hama (writer), Adam Kubert (breakdowns), Karl Kesel, Dan Green & Chris Warner (finishes), Pat Brosseau (letters), Mike Thomas (colors), Ben Raab (asst editor, uncredited), Bob Harras (editor), Richard Starkings & Comicraft (c letters), Todd Klein (logo)
FEATURE CHARACTER: Weapon X (James "Logan" Howlett, last in X:A, '95)
SUPPORTING CAST: Jean Grey (last in X:A, '95)
VILLAINS: Apocalypse (ruler of North America, last in XCal #1, '95, next in XMan #1, '95), Apocalypse's Horsemen: Abyss (Nils Styger, living portal, next in AmazX #1, '95), Holocaust (Apocalypse's son, next in AX #2, '95); Havok (also in holographic projection), Cyclops (prev 2 Sinister's Prelates), Beast (Sinister's chief

scientist, in holographic projection) (prev 3 next in FacX #1, '95) (prev 5 last in X:A, '95), Magma (Amara Aquilla, controls lava, dies), Infini (Apocalypse's genetically engineered soldiers, some die, rest recycled off-panel; others last in Gam&X #1, '95, next in XMan #1, '95) inc Ra Control Center Director, Central Dispatch (bts teleporting Havok), Balrog-class meta-cyborg

OTHER CHARACTERS: Human High Council: Brian Braddock, Emma Frost, Bolivar Trask, Moira Trask, Mariko Yashida (all last in X:A, '9 Sentinels (some or others last in XCal #1, '95, 1 destroyed, rest next in AmazX #1, '95), Human Defense League troops (unnamed, bts airships); Sinister (mentioned, created meta-cyborg)

LOCATIONS/ITEMS: Great Sea Wall's Mid-Atlantic Sector Five (Atlantic Ocean) w/Sensor Control Center, Central Dispatch (bts), Apocalyps citadel (Apocalypse Island, formerly Manhattan), Beast's laboratory (in holographic projection); Palace of Westminster clocktower (London, Engla United Europe) / Weapon X's Adamantium skeleton (hereinafter considered his standard equipment and not listed separately), Infinites' armor (so destroyed), Sensor Control Center's transmitter, scanners, visual sensors (prev 3 bts), security door, switching console (prev 2 destroyed), mon & transporter w/antenna, Sentinel's electronic counter-measure suite (destroyed), sensors, turbines (prev 3 bts), blasters & detachable hands, S Wall's laser & plasma cannons w/tracking systems (bts), Central Dispatch's transporter (bts), Sentinels' transport modules, Apocalypse's hologra projector, Beast's camera (bts), restraints & bone saw (prev 2 in holographic projection), Holocaust's life support armor, Human High Council's airsh gun emplacements & protective outfits

SYNOPSIS: On a mission for Europe's Human High Council, Weapon X and Jean Grey assault Apocalypse's Sea Wall sensor control center w a Sentinel. As Weapon X and Jean infiltrate the base, the Infinites request backup; Havok teleports in. Jean holds him off while Weapon X locates a destroys the main console, shutting down the entire section of sea wall. Weapon X defeats Havok and flees with Jean; the Sentinel pushes Havok into transporter. As Weapon X and Jean return to Europe on the damaged Sentinel, they witness dozens of other Sentinels rushing toward America across inactive sea wall. Elsewhere, Cyclops briefs Apocalypse that Sinister has had Weapon X deliver data to the Human High Council, while Beast operate separate Havok from the transporter-fused Sentinel hands. In Europe, Apocalypse's assassin Magma attacks the Council, but Weapon X kills her. Wea X and Jean are shocked to discover that the Council is planning a nuclear strike on America; Weapon X approves, but Jean does not.

NOTE: The Weapon X miniseries replaced Wolverine on Marvel's publishing schedule during the four-month "Age of Apocalypse" event; all oth X-titles were similarly replaced with new books. All of these new series occur in the alternate world of Earth-295, created when Legion accident killed Charles Xavier in the past in X #41, '95, ultimately allowing Apocalypse to conquer North America, oppressing humans and creating a dystop mutant-dominated society opposed only by underground rebels, including lovers Weapon X and Jean Grey. All characters that appear here are na to Earth-295; they presumably share the same real names as their Earth-616 counterparts. Weapon X's missing left hand was blasted off years bef by Cyclops. Weapon X and Jean delivered Sinister's data to the Human High Council in X:A, '95. The Sentinels' Great Airlift, rescuing humans fr America, occurred in AmazX #1-2, '95. Abyss' real name is revealed in Cable #40, '97. Bolivar's wife Moira Trask is Moira MacTaggert's Earth-2 counterpart. Emma Frost has several scars on her head; presumably her telepathic powers were surgically excised, explaining her presence on Human High Council. The Human Defense League is named in WX #3, '95. Earth-295 is designated in OHMU:X, '05. This issue's "X-Facts" featu an editorial page advertising each month's X-books, has a map of the world under Apocalypse's rule. Some of Brian Braddock's word balloons pp.22-23 are out of order. This issue also has a 2nd-print "X-Tra Edition" with a faded cover background.

WEAPON X #2 (April 1995)

"Fire in the Sky!" (22 pages)

CREDITS: Larry Hama (writer), Adam Kubert (pencils), Dan Green (inks), Pat Brosseau (letters), Joe Rosa Digital Chameleon (colors), Ben Raab (asst editor, uncredited), Bob Harras (editor)
FEATURE CHARACTER: Weapon X
SUPPORTING CAST: Jean Grey (next in FacX #3, '95)
VILLAINS: Brotherhood of Mutants (see NOTE): Box (Madison Jeffries, transmutes metal), Copycat (both c last in AmazX #2, '95); Donald Pierce (cyborg, 1st on-panel app, also on monitors) & his altered humans: Cle Slocum (prev 2 die) (prev 3 last bts in AmazX #2, '95)
OTHER CHARACTERS: Human High Council: Brian Braddock, Emma Frost, Bolivar Trask, Moira Trask, Mar Yashida; human refugees (some die), Sentinels (some or others next in XCal #2, '95) (prev 2 last in Ama #2, '95, some of each bts), Human Defense League troops (some bts, some die) inc airship captain (also monitors, dies); birds; Shingen Harada, Apocalypse's dog soldiers, breeding pen rejects (prev 3 mentioned); girl, rabbit (prev 2 as dolls)

LOCATIONS/ITEMS: England: Bristol coastline, skies above London, Cornwall airstrip / Human Defense League's body armor, plas rifles, headsets, paperwork, stretchers & mutant/weapons scanners w/alarms, humans' luggage & supplies, Sentinels' transport modu (bts), Box's poncho & morphing armor w/blasters, Copycat's poncho & satchel, children's dolls, Human High Council's airships (2 destroye analog guidance system (bts, destroyed) & protective outfits, Pierce & altered humans' cyborg implants (hereinafter considered their stand equipment and not listed separately), Jean's airplane, Weapon X's motorcycle

SYNOPSIS: Weapon X finds Jean helping the mutant refugees that the Sentinels brought back from America. He tries to convince her tha nuclear strike on Apocalypse is the best option, but she still hopes for a less deadly solution. Box and Copycat, stowaways on the airlift, reve themselves and begin shooting humans, allowing Donald Pierce and his cyborgs to slip through the sensors. Recalling her time as a priso in Apocalypse's pens, Jean snaps; she and Weapon X kill Box and Copycat. Later, Weapon X visits the Council's airship, where Mariko Yash confides in him that Brian Braddock is acting strangely. Pierce and his cyborgs assault another airship; Weapon X leaps aboard and batt them, but Pierce crashes the airship, destroying the guidance system for the Council's doomsday strike. Weapon X senses Jean leaving to wa America about the strike; at the airstrip, she tells him he will have to kill her to stop her. Unable to do it, Weapon X watches Jean fly off.

NOTE: Box and Copycat's group is called the Brotherhood of the Chaos in AmazX #1, '95 and the Brotherhood of Mutants in AmazX #2, '95 is unrevealed why the mutant/weapons scanners detected Box's armor as a weapon but not him or Copycat as mutants, but it is likely that B had generated technology to suppress their mutant nature. AoA Spec/3, '05 reveals some of Weapon X and Mariko's history together; AoA '05 reveals that she secretly bore his daughter, Kirika.

WEAPON X #3 (May 1995)

"The Common Right of Toads and Men" (22 pages)

CREDITS: Larry Hama (writer), Adam Kubert (pencils), Dan Green (co-inks, c inks), Mike Sellers (co-inks), Pat Brosseau (letters), Joe Rosas & Digital Chameleon (colors), Ben Raab (asst editor, uncredited), Bob Harras (editor), Derek Bellman (c colors)
FEATURE CHARACTER: Weapon X (also in his own memories)
VILLAINS: Apocalypse (bts, assigned Pierce to Wundagore, last in FacX #3, next bts in AX #3, next in AmazX #3, all '95), Donald Pierce (prev 2 also in Weapon X's memories) & his altered humans: Dead-Eye, Mangle, Vultura (prev 3 die); Infinites (in holographic recording, some or others chr last in Blink #1, '01, these prior to WX #4, '95 fb)
OTHER CHARACTERS: Human High Council: Bolivar Trask, Moira Trask (both next in XUniv #2, '95), Brian Braddock, Emma Frost, Mariko Yashida; Carol Danvers (Human Defense League operative, 1st), Gateway, Infinites' victims (dead in holographic recording, some or others prior to WX #4, '95 fb) inc refugee's parents [s]iblings inc Alia, Human Defense League troops (named, bts in airships), human refugee (also bts in holographic recording); Scarlet Witch [W]anda Maximoff Lehnsherr, name on gravestone); Jean Grey (in Weapon X's memories)
[LO]CATIONS/ITEMS: Transia's Wundagore Mountain inc ruins of X-Men's former base w/Gateway's tower (destroyed), Palace of Westminster [clo]cktower, culling site (in recording), skies over London, Cornwall airstrip (prev 2 in Weapon X's memories) / Dead-Eye's transmitter, sensors [wi]th bts), targeting eyepiece & kinetic energy gun (all destroyed), Mangle's facial recognition program (bts), Weapon X's parka, Scarlet Witch's [gra]vestone, Carol's blasters & grenades, refugee's holographic camera (also bts in recording), Infinites' weapons (bts) & armor (prev 2 in [re]cording), Council's airships (1 in Weapon X's memories) & protective outfits, Gateway's monitors (some destroyed), whirligig & computers w/ [ho]le, Jean's airplane (in Weapon X's memories), Vultura's transmitter (bts) & wings, Pierce's transmitter (bts), bandages & airplane w/bombs
[FL]ASHBACK: In a holographic recording, Apocalypse's Infinites massacre humans.
[SY]NOPSIS: Arriving at Wundagore Mountain, Weapon X is ambushed by two of Pierce's cyborgs, but defeats them easily. He enters the [rui]ns of the X-Men's old base and encounters Carol Danvers, who escorts him to Gateway's tower. In London, the Council listens to a refugee [de]scribe conditions in America, and note that Brian Braddock continues to be on edge. Weapon X finds Gateway watching several monitors [at o]nce, trying to absorb as much of humans' fading culture as he can. Gateway reads Weapon X's mind, learning his objective, but refuses to [hel]p guide the Council's airships to America. The damaged cyborgs attack again, and Carol destroys them — but they led Pierce to Gateway's [to]wer, which he destroys with bombs. Gateway teleports himself, Weapon X and Carol onto Pierce's airplane. Pierce battles Weapon X, but [Ca]rol tackles him out of the plane, destroying them both with a grenade. Shaken by her sacrifice, Gateway agrees to meet with the Council.
[NO]TE: This issue's title is a line from the Emily Dickinson poem, "A Toad Can Die of Light!" Although a version of the X-Men exist in this reality, they [we]re founded by Magneto. The image of Apocalypse seen in Weapon X's memories is incorrectly depicted as the Earth-616 version of Apocalypse.

WEAPON X #4 (June 1995)

"Into the Maelstrom!" (22 pages)

CREDITS: Larry Hama (writer), Adam Kubert (pencils), Dan Green (inks), Pat Brosseau (letters), Joe Rosas & Digital Chameleon (colors), Ben Raab (asst editor, uncredited), Bob Harras (editor)
FEATURE CHARACTER: Weapon X (next in X:Ω, '95; AoA Spec/4, AoA #1-6, all '05, UXFor #12-13 & 19.1, '11-12, AoA #1 & 10-13, '12-13)
GUEST STAR: Magneto (X-Men's leader, bts being tortured, last in XMan #4, '95, next in X:Ω, '95)
VILLAINS: Apocalypse (last in Gam&X #4, '95), Rex (Apocalypse's flunky, last in AX #4, '95) (both next in X:Ω, '95), Donald Pierce (dies), Infinites (some bts in ships, others last in FacX #4, '95, next in X:Ω, '95; others in holographic recording following WX #3, '95 fb, some or others chr next in X:A, '95), Apocalypse's torturers (1 voice only, other or others bts)
OTHER CHARACTERS: Human High Council: Bolivar Trask, Moira Trask (both last in XUniv #2, '95, next in [X:]Ω, '95), Brian Braddock (dies), Emma Frost, Mariko Yashida; Gateway (next bts in X:Ω, '95, next in UXFor #12, '11), Carol Danvers (dies), [Inf]inites' victims (dead in holographic recording following WX #3, '95 fb) inc Jodie Craig (dies), Human Defense League troops (some bts in [air]ships, some die) & techs (bts digitizing footage), human refugee, altered humans, Apocalypse's vat-techs (bts monitoring altered humans)
[LO]CATIONS/ITEMS: Paris, France, United Europe inc Eiffel Tower ruins, culling site (in recording), Apocalypse's citadel w/lab, skies above [No]rth Atlantic Ocean inc Great Sea Wall's North Atlantic security platforms / Infinites' armor & rifle (both in recording), Jodie's diary (as digital [pro]jection), refugee's holographic camera (also bts in recording), Council's holographic projectors (bts), protective suits & airships w/guidance [sy]stems, compasses (prev 2 bts) & nuclear bombs, altered humans' techno-organic infection (bts), vats & plasma pistol, Brian's cerebral cortex [im]plant (bts) & gun, Gateway's headset & whirligig, Weapon X's rope, Pierce's homing beacon (bts) & headset, Carol's wings (formerly Vultura's) [&] blasters, Sea Wall's radio, radar system (prev 2 bts) & Interceptor aircraft, Apocalypse's agents list (bts), Emma's headset & axe
[FL]ASHBACK: In a holographic recording, Apocalypse's Infinites kill young Jodie Craig.
[SY]NOPSIS: The Council shows Gateway footage of Apocalypse's atrocities, but he remains unmoved until Weapon X shows him a young [vic]tim's diary. Gateway agrees to guide the Council's airships, and the armada launches. Weapon X tells Emma Frost that he believes in their [att]ack, but feels terrible that it may kill Jean. Pierce alerts the Sea Wall to the approaching armada and attacks the lead airship alongside Carol [Da]nvers, whom he has rebuilt into a cyborg. Pierce demands that Brian Braddock, revealed as an unwilling double agent, aid him — but Brian [reb]els and blasts Pierce. Carol shreds Weapon X's good arm, struggling to overcome her programming, but the wounded Pierce kills her and [be]gins strangling Gateway. Weapon X pops the claws in his other arm, which were retracted in his forearm when he lost his hand, and kills [Pie]rce. The Sea Wall's aircraft attack, but Gateway generates a portal and the armada flies through, preparing to destroy Apocalypse's empire…
[NO]TE: Since Brian Braddock and Carol Danvers were both forced to betray their allies, neither is listed as a Villain here. The X-Men successfully [se]nd Bishop back in time in X:Ω, '95, where he saves Charles Xavier and restores Earth-616 — and indeed, next month Wolverine and all the [ot]her regular X-books returned to Marvel's publishing schedule — but XMan #53, '99 & AoA Spec/4, '05 reveal that Earth-295 continued on, [an]d AoA #4-5, '05 reveals that Jean channeled the Phoenix Force to prevent most of the nuclear bombs from detonating.

WOLVERINE #91 (July 1995)

"Path of Stones, Wood of Thorns" (23 pages)

CREDITS: Larry Hama (writer), Duncan Rouleau (pencils), Josef Rubinstein (inks), Pat Brosseau (letters), Ma Javins & Digital Chameleon (colors), Ben Raab (asst editor, uncredited), Bob Harras (editor), Adam Kubert (c penc
FEATURE CHARACTER: Wolverine (also in photo, holographic projection & as Experiment X in rfb, next in W Ann '
GUEST STARS: X-Men: Bishop, Psylocke (both last in X #44, '95), Beast (last in X #43, '95), Professor X next in W Ann '95), Cyclops (next in Cap #445, '95) (prev 2 last in XFor #44, '95), Phoenix (last in Cable #21, ' chr next in DCvM #1, '96, next in X Ann '95) (prev 2 also in photo), Archangel (Warren Worthington III, me winged flyer, last in UXM #322, '95, last bts in X #42, '95), Storm (last in X #42, '95, next bts in XFor #45, '95) (p 2 next in UXM #323, '95); Guardian (bts, invited to X-Mansion), Vindicator (on monitor) (prev 2 last in W #84, '
VILLAINS: Sabretooth (bts undergoing physiological changes, last bts in X #42, '95, next in XFor #44, '95), Bob Higg (abusive husband, 1st, unnamed)

OTHER CHARACTERS: Linda Higgins (Bob's abused wife), Richard & Jane Higgins (prev 2 Bob & Linda's children) (all next in W #132, ' frog (cover only), butterflies; Bill (children's uncle, mentioned); Magneto, "inner demons" (prev 2 in Wolverine's thoughts); ants (on Beast's shor
LOCATIONS/ITEMS: X-Mansion w/Bio-Chem Lab, Cyclops & Phoenix's boathouse & grounds w/Spuytin Dyvil Cove, Higgins' home nearby pond, Vindicator's lab (on monitor), Weapon X Program facility (in rfb) / Richard & Jane's wagon & flowers, X-Men's photos, Cyclo poker, X-Mansion tree (destroyed) & sensors (bts), lab's holographic projector, transmitter (prev 2 bts) & monitors, Vindicator's transmitter (bt Wolverine's biopsy sample (on monitor), Linda's sling & cordless phone, Bob's hand wrappings, Experiment X's helmet & wires, Weapon Program's Genesis Tank (prev 3 in rfb)
FLASHBACK: Adamantium is bonded to Wolverine's skeleton (MCP #73, '91).
SYNOPSIS: Increasingly feral, Wolverine has begun living in the woods outside the X-Mansion. Two neighbor children bring home flowers for th injured mother; their father feels Wolverine watching them. The X-Men discuss Wolverine's near-fatal attack on Sabretooth, worried that he is becom dangerous and unpredictable. As Wolverine howls in the night, Professor X, Beast and Storm study his medical scans and confer with Vindica who believes that Wolverine's mutation is naturally devolving him into a beast, and his Adamantium had been suppressing that transformation. At t neighbor's house, the husband catches his abused wife trying to call the police, and chases her. The X-Men check on Wolverine in the woods just the wife runs out of her house. Wolverine attacks the pursuing husband, but the X-Men hold him back, afraid he will murder the man. The wife refus the X-Men's help, saying that she knows her husband loves her deep down. The X-Men try to convince Wolverine to come inside, but he refuses.
NOTE: The Higgins' last name and Bob's first name are revealed in W #132, '98. Beast incorrectly calls Vindicator by his former codenar Guardian here. With this issue, Marvel relocates the cover's issue number to the UPC box, where it remains until W #101, '96.

WOLVERINE '95 (September 1995)

"Lair of the N'Garai" (35 pages)

CREDITS: Larry Hama (writer), J.H. Williams III (pencils), Mark McKenna (co-inks, c inks), Mick Gray & Jim Palmiotti (co-inks), Richard Starkings & Comicraft (letters), Kevin Somers & Electric Crayon (colors), Mark Powe (editor)
FEATURE CHARACTER: Wolverine (also in fb between UXM #143-144, '81)
GUEST STARS: X-Men: Sprite (Kitty Pryde), Colossus (both in fb between UXM #143-144, '81), Bishop (ne in UXM #325, '95), Psylocke (next in UXM #323, '95) (prev 2 next bts in GenX #6, '95), Beast, Professor X (ne in XFor #45, '95) (prev 4 last in W #91, '95); Nightcrawler (last in Ex #87, '95, chr next bts in DCvM #1, '96, c next in DCvM #4, '96, next in UXM #326, '95) (prev 2 also in fb between UXM #143-144, '81), Boomer (forme Boom-Boom, between XFor #44-45, '95)
VILLAINS: Kierrok ("Shatterer of Souls," descendant of N'Garai Elder Gods, last in X #96, '75, last bts in UX #143, '81, next in X #75, '98 fb), N'Garai demons (many die, some or others last in MCP #145/2, '94, next in XMU #9, '95)
OTHER CHARACTERS: Spider, mouse, ladybug; Storm (in rfb)
LOCATIONS/ITEMS: X-Mansion grounds (also in rfb & fb) & hangar bay, N'Garai dimension / N'Garai cairn (destroyed, also destroyed in rfb fb) & living corridors, Professor X's wheelchair (in fb), computers & monitors, X-Men's Blackbird jet w/hydraulic system, Nightcrawler's wren Beast's screwdriver, Nightcrawler's shotgun (hereinafter considered his standard equipment and not listed separately), rag & circuit tester, Boome instruction manual, X-Mansion cameras, sensors, motion detectors & alarm system (prev 4 bts)
FLASHBACKS: Storm destroys the N'Garai cairn (X #96, '75). Professor X has the X-Men destroy the cairn again.
SYNOPSIS: Prowling the woods, Wolverine sees that the N'Garai cairn has restored itself. Spotting a N'Garai demon heading for the X-Mansio he attacks. Inside, the visiting Nightcrawler worries about Wolverine, while Boomer seems sympathetic to Sabretooth. The X-Mansion's senso detect the N'Garai, but it flees back through the cairn and Wolverine pursues. Nightcrawler investigates; deducing where Wolverine went, follows, arriving in the N'Garai dimension. Nightcrawler sees Wolverine slaughtering several N'Garai, and is disturbed by his savage behavi Kierrok learns of the mutants' arrival and sends more N'Garai after them. As Wolverine berates Nightcrawler for judging him, the N'Garai atta and Wolverine kills several more. Kierrok battles Wolverine, wounding him grievously, but Wolverine refuses to give up. Fearing that Wolveri will kill all his demons, Kierrok sends some N'Garai to Earth; the mutants pursue and Wolverine kills them, and Kierrok closes the portal behi them. The X-Men recover Nightcrawler, but Wolverine has returned to the woods.
NOTE: From 1989-1994, Marvel published yearly squarebound prestige-format one-shots that served as Wolverine's de facto "Annua (W:Jun, '90, W:Bl, '90, W:RT, '91, W:IF, '92, W:Kill, '93 & W:Evil, '94). This issue, although it does not say "Annual" either on the cover or in t indicia, is considered Wolverine's first official Annual and the first issue of the yearly W Ann series. Although the prestige-format one-sh continue, they are no longer considered Wolverine's "Annuals" beginning with W:KT, '95, published the month before this issue.

2ND STORY: "What the Cat Dragged In" (18 pages)
CREDITS: Chris Golden (writer), Ben Herrera (pencils), Vince Russell (inks), Richard Starkings & Comicraft (letters), Ian Laughlin (color Mark Powers (editor)
FEATURE CHARACTER: Wolverine (next in XFor #46, GenX #6, UXM #323-324, W #92, all '95)
GUEST STARS: Beast (next in XFor #45, '95), George Washington "G.W." Bridge (SHIELD Commander, last in Cable #4, '93, next in Pun #7, '9

SUPPORTING CAST: Maverick (also in pfb, last in W #87, '94, next in Mvk Spec, '97)

VILLAINS: Slayback (Greg Terraerton, morphing cyborg, also in pfb, last in Dp #4, '93), Dr. Westergaard (also bts in pfb ordering attack) & her troops (some or others also bts in pfb, attacking Maverick) & scientists inc Dr. Chadwick

OTHER CHARACTERS: Deadpool (last in W #88, '94, next in XFor #46, '95), SHIELD agents (some or others last in GR #65, '95, next in Pun #104, '95), Mr. Tucci & his entourage, Maverick's sources (bts informing him); birds (bts); Moira MacTaggert (mentioned, studying Legacy virus)

LOCATIONS/ITEMS: X-Mansion w/infirmary & grounds, Westergaard's facility (on Canadian/American border, destroyed) w/waterfall, Maverick's Manhattan safehouse (in pfb) / Maverick's shuttle (destroyed), body armor w/faceplate (all also in pfb), speed lift (in pfb), gun (others in pfb) & explosive charge, Deadpool's restraints (destroyed) & cell samples, Westergaard's alarm, self-destruct system (prev 2 bts), computers, monitoring wires & robotic arm-mounted needle, troops' armor & guns (prev 2 also bts in pfb), Slayback's regenerating cyborg limbs (1 also destroyed in pfb), SHIELD guns & restraints, Beast's microscope

FLASHBACK: Slayback and Dr. Westergaard's troops attack Maverick, wanting him for their experiments. He is badly wounded, but escapes (p).

SYNOPSIS: Wolverine finds Maverick collapsed on the X-Mansion grounds. Elsewhere, Dr. Westergaard experiments on a captive Deadpool, hoping that his healing factor can cure the Legacy virus. Maverick recovers and tells Wolverine that Westergaard is kidnapping fast-healing mutants, and that Wolverine may be next. Westergaard plans to sell the cure to the highest bidder, but Slayback simply enjoys torturing Deadpool, his old enemy. Maverick convinces Wolverine to help him rescue Deadpool; the two assault Westergaard's base and free him. Westergaard and Slayback try to capture all three for their experiments, but Maverick defeats Slayback and Westergaard flees, activating the base's self-destruct sequence. Wolverine, Maverick and Deadpool escape over a waterfall, and find that SHIELD has captured Westergaard. Days later, Deadpool sends samples of his cells to the Beast, who sadly confirms that they cannot combat the Legacy virus. Maverick resolves to spend his last days hunting for a cure.

NOTE: This story is followed by three pin-ups: Omega Red by Olivier LeDroit, Bloodscream by John Van Fleet, and Team X (Logan, Victor Creed, Maverick) by Terese Nielsen. Slayback's first name is revealed in OHMU #6, '06; his last name is misspelled "Terraterton" here. This story correctly claims that Maverick has an implanted derivative of Wolverine's healing factor. He actually has an implanted age-suppression factor.

WOLVERINE #92 (August 1995)

"A Northern Exposure" (22 pages)

CREDITS: Larry Hama (writer), Adam Kubert (pencils), Dan Green (inks), Pat Brosseau (letters), Joe Rosas & Digital Chameleon (colors), Ben Raab (asst editor), Bob Harras (editor), Cam Smith (c inks), Steve Buccellato & Brian Buccellato (c colors)

FEATURE CHARACTER: Wolverine (also as holographic projection, also in fb between W #34, '90 fb & AFlt #33, '86 fb; next in W/Gam #1-4, IHulk #434, all '95, DCvM #1-4, '96, UXM #325, '95, W:KT, '95)

GUEST STARS: X-Men: Beast (last in UXM #324, '95, chr next in DCvM #1, '96, next in X Ann '95), Professor X (last in GenX #6, '95, chr next in DCvM #1, '96); Boomer (last in XFor #47, '95) (prev 2 next in UXM #326, '95), Guardian, Vindicator (prev 2 also as Heather & James Hudson in Wolverine's hallucination, also as Heather & James Hudson in fb between AFlt #34, '86 fb & AFlt #33, '86 fb; next in W #95, '95)

VILLAINS: Sabretooth (also as holographic X-ray projection, last in XFor #47, '95, next in UXM #326, '95), Bob Diggins (next in W #132, '98), poachers (in fb, some die)

OTHER CHARACTERS: Noah DuBois (telepathic LL&L operative, unnamed, last in UXM #323, '95), Zoe Culloden (last in W #81, '94), biker (last in W #65, '93) & his girlfriend, Zoe's operator & superior (prev 2 voice only); bears (dead), poachers' sled dogs (prev 2 in fb), birds

LOCATIONS/ITEMS: X-Mansion Medi-Lab, Danger Room & grounds, Wood Buffalo National Park (in fb), Graymalkin Lane (Salem Center, Westchester, New York) w/blind curve / Hudsons' packs & shotgun, poachers' rifles & dogsleds w/ropes (all in fb), lab's holographic projector (bts), computers, monitors, medical scanners & arm-mounted beds w/restraints, Wolverine's sensor array, Guardian's staff & gun, Vindicator's monitoring equipment w/headsets, Danger Room monitors, biker's motorcycle, Bob's car (destroyed) & beer, Zoe's aura-cloaking dampers, infrared shields, psi-suppressors & communicator (prev 4 bts), operator & superiors' comm units (bts)

FLASHBACK: Living ferally in the woods, Wolverine attacks poachers, who chase him. He smells James and Heather Hudson; assuming them to be poachers too, he prepares to attack.

SYNOPSIS: Professor X, Beast and the visiting Guardian and Vindicator run comparative scans on Wolverine and Sabretooth, who was seemingly lobotomized by Wolverine's attack. Wolverine, believing Sabretooth is faking, struggles to hold his temper when Boomer fawns over Sabretooth. The X-Men test Wolverine's reactions in the Danger Room, but an Arctic simulation dredges up bad memories. He flees the mansion, needing to run free, but he is still wearing his sensor array and the X-Men monitor him. Wolverine spots the X-Men's abusive neighbor driving drunk toward a blind curve, and a biker approaching from the other side. He tries to flag down the car, but the neighbor vengefully runs him over, crashing the car. The X-Men are astonished to see Wolverine's healing factor restore him in seconds; Wolverine controls his rage and cuts the neighbor from the wreck. The X-Men relax, but Zoe Culloden is also secretly monitoring Wolverine…

NOTE: This issue's fb reveals the real reason that Wolverine attacked the Hudsons in AFlt #33, '86; that issue claimed that he was merely hungry. Noah's first name is revealed in W #95, '95, and his last name in Dp #22, '98. Beast incorrectly calls Vindicator "Guardian" again here. The abusive husband's beer is branded "Bob," after editor Bob Harras. Wood Buffalo National Park is still incorrectly called "Buffalo Wood." This is the last issue of the series to use hand lettering until W #73/2 & 74, '09.

WOLVERINE: KNIGHT OF TERRA (August 1995)

(Untitled, 64 pages)

CREDITS: Ian Edginton (plot), John Ostrander (script), Jan Duursema (pencils), Rick Magyar (inks), Richard Starkings & Comicraft (letters), Tom Vincent (colors), Jaye Gardner (asst editor), Kelly Corvese (editor)

FEATURE CHARACTER: Wolverine (also in scrying glass image, next in W #93, '95)

GUEST STARS: X-Men: Bishop (last in UXM #325, '95), Professor X (last in XMan #10, '95) (both next in W #93, '95); Wolfsbane (also as Queen Rain, between Ex #90-91, '95)

VILLAINS: Beast (manifestation of Geshem's wild magic, see NOTE), rebellious Duke & his mechanical army (some bts) (prev 2 in pfb), enemy army (bts battling Mage & Doug), looters (die)

OTHER CHARACTERS: Moira MacTaggert (last in Ex #90, '95, next bts in W #93, '95, next in GenX Ann '95), Queen Rain (also as herself, her human & animal halves in her own thoughts, last in W:RT, '91), Doug (Prince Consort) (prev 2 also in painting), Mage (prev 2 bts quelling revolt), Shaman (Professor X analog) (prev 3 also in Rain's thoughts), Hector (Shaman's familiar, Beast analog) (prev 3 also in pfb), Lady Jehan Grey (Phoenix analog), Mistress Mistral (Storm analog), Lord Paladin (Bishop analog), Lord Summerisle (Cyclops analog), Lilian (Magik analog & her brother (likely Colossus analog, bts quelling revolt), Dukes of the Shires inc Duke Handfast (dies), Knights of Geshem (dead, some as bones; others bts quelling revolt; some or others also in pfb), citizens of Geshem (1 dead, as skull), palace guards (some or others of prev last in W:RT, '91), Beast's human host (Sabretooth analog, dies), Rain's unborn embryo (bts); horses (Lord Handfast's dies), birds; Magnus (in scrying glass image), Richard, Robert, Samuel (prev 3 in Rain's thoughts); wolves (as Queen's symbol, Wolfsbane's pendant & Shaman's staff), dragons (as statue & in painting)

LOCATIONS/ITEMS: Geshem inc city w/castle (also in pfb) inc Shaman's tower laboratory, Muir Island w/Moira's lab, Rain's mindscape, Knights' bows (bts), arrows, spears, axes, dagger, swords & shields, Shaman's door, window (prev 2 destroyed), wand (in pfb), staff, experiment & scrying glass, Wolfsbane's curtain, trinket box & wolf pendant, hurled crockery (destroyed) & rocks, Summerisle's armor & Basilisk Mask, Shard of Kym (Paladin's enchanted sword), Paladin's armor & knives, looters' cart, Moira's medical scanner, Dukes' swords, Rain & Doug' portrait, Doug's sword (in pfb) & metal arm (in pfb & portrait), villagers' swords (1 destroyed) & spears, Lilian's sword, Wolverine's royal pendant, Rain's stone plinths, mental door (prev 2 as psychic images) & sword, guards' telescope, axe, spears, swords, shields & cannons w/tampers

FLASHBACK: Doug helps repulse an army of transformed metal soldiers, but is mortally injured. The Shaman transforms him partly into metal to save his life (p).

SYNOPSIS: Transported to Geshem by the Shaman, Wolverine battles the Beast, who has killed hundreds of knights and now targets Queen Rain. The Beast injures Wolverine badly; elsewhere, a worried Shaman activates his backup plan. On Muir Island, Wolfsbane sees her pendant glowing; Professor X, Moira and Bishop find Rain in her room. Recovering, Wolverine heads for the castle, as Wolfsbane finds herself back in Geshem. The Shaman explains that Rain should have bonded with Geshem's wild magic; when she did not, the Beast manifested physically. The Shaman asks Wolfsbane to impersonate Rain; she agrees, and rallies Geshem's Dukes against the Beast. Elsewhere, villagers mistake Wolverine for the Beast, but he convinces the warrior Lilian of his intent, and she loans him a horse. Professor X telepathically discovers that Rain is suppressing her wild magic. The Beast reaches the castle, defeats its guardians and confronts Wolfsbane. Professor X convinces Rain to embrace her true nature, and she vanishes back to Geshem. Wolverine arrives and attacks the Beast, which is weakened by Rain's bonding with its magic. Wolverine kills the Beast's human host and its spirit dissipates. A grateful Rain knights Wolverine, and the Shaman sends the mutants back to Earth.

NOTE: The Beast, not to be confused with the X-Men's Hank McCoy (or Hector, who is Geshem's McCoy analog), is called the Great Beast on this issue's back cover. As discussed in W Ann '95's NOTE, with the launch of the W Ann series, Wolverine's squarebound prestige-format one-shots are no longer considered his de facto "Annuals."

WOLVERINE #93 (September 1995)

"A Tavern in the Town" (22 pages)

CREDITS: Larry Hama (writer), Adam Kubert (pencils), Dan Green & Matt Ryan (inks), Richard Starkings & Comicraft (letters), Joe Rosas & Digital Chameleon (colors), Ben Raab (asst editor), Bob Harras (editor), Steve Buccellato (c colors)

FEATURE CHARACTER: Wolverine (next in NiMvW #0, Rune #2/2, PR:Gen, PR:Rev, all '95)

GUEST STARS: X-Men: Cannonball (next in W #96, '95), Beast (both last in UXM #325, '95), Storm (last in Cable #23, '95), Professor X (prev 3 next in EvX #0, '95), Bishop (next in PR:Gen, '95) (prev 2 last in W:KT, '95), Boomer (last in UXM #326, '95, next in XFor #48, '95)

VILLAINS: Dark Riders (Genesis' superhuman fanatics): Harddrive (cyborg, as projection), Hurricane (generates wind), Lifeforce (siphons life energy), Spyne (reptilian mutant); Genesis (bts ordering attack) (all last in X Ann '95), Cyber (last in W #81, '94, chr last in W:O #12, '07 fb), Juggernaut (Cain Marko, unstoppable avatar of Cyttorak, last in X #42, '95, chr last in DCvM #1, '96, chr last bts in DCvM #4, '96, next in Exiles #∞, '95), Cyttorak (mystical deity of the Crimson Cosmos, bts empowering Juggernaut, last in DrS #49, '93, last bts in X #42, '95, chr last bts in DCvM #4, '96, next bts in Exiles #∞, '95, next in XMU #12, '96)

OTHER CHARACTERS: Moira MacTaggert (bts turning Cyber over to Mack, last in W:KT, '95, next in GenX Ann '95), Zoe Culloden, Noah DuBois (prev 2 next in W #95, '95), Inspector McCleod, Col. Mack (prev 2 last in W #81, '94, die), Zoe's superior (bts ordering Juggernaut removal), Auger Inn bartender & patrons; deer, squirrel, birds; African figure (as bust)

LOCATIONS/ITEMS: Edinburgh Castle dungeon, X-Mansion w/Medi-Lab & grounds, Auger Inn / Cyber's SHIELD restraints & cell door (both destroyed, see NOTE), Harddrive's teleporter (bts) & cyborg implants (in projection), Storm's plants, Wolverine's motorcycle, Juggernaut' monitoring equipment (destroyed), Auger Inn wall, door (prev 2 destroyed), beer & tap, Zoe & Noah's aura-cloaking dampers, infrared shields & psi-suppressors (prev 3 bts), Zoe's sidereal time transporter

SYNOPSIS: The Dark Riders teleport into Cyber's Scottish prison, killing McCleod and Mack and taking Cyber to meet with their master Genesis. On the X-Mansion grounds, Wolverine is stalking a deer when Cannonball flies by, accidentally interrupting the hunt. Envious of Cannonball's flight, Wolverine grabs his motorcycle and challenges him to a race. In the X-Mansion's Medi-Lab, Juggernaut awakens from his coma; still afraid of his mysterious assailant, Onslaught, he flees. At the Auger Inn, Wolverine buys the victorious Cannonball drinks, bonding with him over their shared dislike of Boomer and Sabretooth's friendship. Juggernaut smashes into the bar and begins drinking straight from the tap; the drunken Cannonball attacks him but is easily repulsed. Wolverine stares Juggernaut down; he leaves, but is confronted in the alley by Zoe and Noah, who transport him to another dimension, claiming he "knows too much." Storm arrives; the three mutants fail to locate Juggernaut, but Wolverine comments that the voice he heard in the alley was familiar.

NOTE: Juggernaut, injured by Onslaught, was rendered comatose in UXM #322, '95. He apparently recovered for his appearances in DCvM #1-4, '96, but must have relapsed prior to this issue. LL&L banish him for having clues to Onslaught's true identity, although their specific connection to Onslaught is never revealed. Marvel purchased Malibu Comics in late 1994, and was publishing several crossovers between the two companies at this time. Juggernaut is transported to the Malibu "Ultraverse" here; he went on to join the cast of the Malibu series "All-New Exiles." The Ultraverse is designated Earth-93060 in OHMU:AU, '05. Although this issue states that Moira provided the equipment keeping Cyber imprisoned, W #97, '96 states that SHIELD designed it. Likely, Moira simply provided SHIELD-designed equipment. Lifeforce's word balloons are accidentally rendered in the font and color of Spyne's balloons in one panel.

WOLVERINE #94 (October 1995)

"The Lurker in the Machine" (22 pages)

CREDITS: Larry Hama (writer), Chris Alexander (pencils), Mike Sellers & Al Milgrom (inks), Richard Starkings & Comicraft (letters), Joe Rosas & Malibu's Hues (as Violent Hues) (colors), Ben Raab (asst editor), Bob Harras (editor), Adam Kubert (c pencils), Steve Buccellato (c colors)
FEATURE CHARACTER: Wolverine (also in dfb following this issue)
GUEST STARS: Generation X (X-Men's new class of mutant students): Banshee (Sean Cassidy, sonic scream, co-headmaster), Emma Frost (telepath, co-headmaster), Chamber (Jonothon Starsmore, vessel of psionic energy), Husk (Paige Guthrie, skin-shedding biomorph), M (Claudette & Nicole St. Croix, combined as "Monet St. Croix," flight, telepathy & heightened strength, durability & intelligence), Synch (Everett Thomas, power-duplicating aura), Skin (Angelo Espinosa, extendible epidermis), Jubilee (see NOTE) (prev 2 also in dfb) (all between GenX #7-8, '95); Professor X (bts, updated Banshee on Wolverine, last in EvX #0, '95, next in XCD #1, '96)
VILLAINS: Candra (immortal External, bts loaning Jamil to Genesis, last in Rogue #4, '95, chr last in NiM/Gam #3, '96, next in X #60, '97), Jamil (Candra's servant, Karima's psychic creation, see NOTE; last in XMU #7, '94, next in W #99, '96), Genesis (bts generating gateway), Dark Riders: Harddrive (bts, busy elsewhere, next in XMan #46, '98), Hurricane, Lifeforce, Spyne; Cyber
OTHER CHARACTERS: Karima (mutant thief, bts animating Jamil, see NOTE; last in XMU #7, '94, next in W #99, '96, next in X #60, '97), Token (wraith, bts haunting Biosphere, also in dfb following this issue; next bts in GenX #35, '98, next in GenX #36, '98), Akkaba victims (dead, last in Cable #18, '94, last bts in Cable #19, '95, next in W #99, '96); vultures; soccer players (as game pieces); turtle (cover only)
LOCATIONS/ITEMS: Ruins of Akkaba, Egypt; Xavier's School for Gifted Youngsters (Snow Valley, Massachusetts, also in dfb) w/rec room & Biosphere (also in dfb) w/control booth / Dark Riders' ropes & VTOL aircraft, Jamil's knives, Generation X's perimeter sensors (bts) & tabletop soccer game, M's nail file, Biosphere computer system, Banshee's scanners, Skin's flashlight (in dfb)
FLASHBACK: Seeing Wolverine sneaking back to the Biosphere at night, Generation X wakes Jubilee. The two follow and witness Wolverine confronting a wraith-like entity, which retreats. Unsettled, Wolverine tells them it was a Token, says goodbye to Jubilee and heads back into the woods (d).
SYNOPSIS: The Dark Riders take Cyber to Egypt, where they show off their massacre at Akkaba. Wolverine visits Jubilee at Generation X's academy, revealing that he made the trip to Massachusetts on foot. Despite his growing feral nature, he wants to teach Jubilee everything he knows; Banshee and Emma Frost ask him to give a guest lecture on fighting skills. Wolverine spars with Generation X in the campus Biosphere, then challenges them to find him in the dense underbrush. They locate him, but he is listening intently — and suddenly orders them to evacuate, telling Banshee and Emma that he sensed a malevolent presence. The next day, Jubilee and Skin explain that Wolverine drove the token off during the night. Banshee, pointing out that tokens hate being around their own kind, worries for what Wolverine is becoming.
NOTE: Having joined Generation X in UXM #318, '94, Jubilee is no longer considered a member of Wolverine's Supporting Cast. "Monet" is revealed as merged twins in GenX #31, '97; their names are revealed in GenX #34, '98. GenX #39, '98 reveals that a real Monet St. Croix exists, and GenX #40, '98 reveals her to be trapped in the form of Penance, a Generation X member not seen here. Genesis and the Dark Riders murdered everyone in Akkaba in Cable #18, '94; Akkaba was Apocalypse's birthplace millennia ago. X #61, '97 reveals that Jamil is not real; he is Karima's psionic projection, subconsciously created to combat her loneliness.

WOLVERINE #95 (November 1995)

"Manhattan Rhapsody" (22 pages)

CREDITS: Larry Hama (writer), Adam Kubert (pencils), Dan Green & Matt Ryan (inks), Richard Starkings & Comicraft (letters), Joe Rosas & Malibu's Hues (colors), Ben Raab (asst editor), Bob Harras (editor), Tim Townsend (c inks), Todd Klein (c letters)
FEATURE CHARACTER: Wolverine (also as android)
GUEST STARS: Guardian (next in MFan #2, '96), Vindicator (chr next in AFlt #19, '99 fb, next in AFlt #13, '98) (both last in W #92, '95)
VILLAINS: Dark Riders: Dirt Nap (absorbs victims & takes their form, 1st, also as Wolverine, Daryll Smith, Algernon & rat, next in W #98, '96), Gauntlet (firearms expert, last in X Ann '95, next in W #99, '96), Hurricane, Lifeforce, Spyne; Genesis (Tyler Dayspring, Cable's adopted son, would-be heir of Apocalypse), Cyber (also on monitors)
OTHER CHARACTERS: Senator Robert Kelly (Chairman of Senate Sub-Committee on Mutant Affairs, last in X:P, '95, next in X #46, '95), Zoe Culloden (Noah DuBois (prev 2 last in W #93, '95), Special Agent Daryll Smith (FBI Mutant Task Force, 1st bts, unnamed, previously absorbed & used as template by Dirt Nap), Algernon (boy, 1st, unnamed, absorbed by Dirt Nap) (prev 2 next bts in W #98, '96, next in Venom:TC #3, '97), Showalter (New York Times reporter), Kelly's secretary (prev 2 voice only), police (bts in cars), coffee shop waiter, bystanders; rats (1 absorbed by Dirt Nap, next bts in W #98, '96, next in Venom:TC #3, '97), birds, cat; Graydon Creed (mentioned, running for President), Zoe's superiors (mentioned); Charles Oakley (New York Knicks basketball player), cowboys (prev 2 on billboards); eagle (as flagpole ornament)
LOCATIONS/ITEMS: Genesis' Egyptian citadel, Manhattan inc Hoppers Coffee Shop, Kelly's Washington DC office, roadway / Dark Riders' Wolverine android (destroyed), sensors (bts) & computers, Dirt Nap's headset, police cars, Kelly's glass (destroyed), speaker system (bts), newspaper & telephone bank, Zoe's sports car & cellular phone, coffee shop window (destroyed)
SYNOPSIS: In Genesis' citadel, Cyber battles and destroys a Wolverine android. The Dark Riders monitor his performance, paying special attention to his Adamantium skin. Wolverine, deciding that the X-Mansion grounds are too tame, goes walking through the "urban jungle" of Manhattan. Guardian and Vindicator watch him from a rooftop, worried that he will lose control and attack a passerby. A street hustler called Dirt Nap tries to engage Wolverine; when Wolverine brushes him off, he targets a boy instead. Wolverine confronts Dirt Nap, but Vindicator misunderstands and intervenes, and Dirt Nap flees. Elsewhere, Zoe updates Noah, telling him that Dirt Nap was sent out too early. Wolverine senses Dirt Nap again, but finds him in the form of the boy. Dirt Nap suddenly consumes Wolverine, transforming into a twisted version of him — but finds that Wolverine's healing factor makes him impossible to fully absorb. Dirt Nap expels Wolverine; quickly consuming and transforming into a rat, he escapes into the sewers, hinting that his boss has big plans for Wolverine...
NOTE: Daryll Smith is named in W #108, '96, but is not linked to Dirt Nap's initial template form until Venom:TC #3, '97, which also names Algernon. The happy face on Dirt Nap's shirt, which appears on every form he takes, changes expressions depending on his mood. Zoe's

implication that she advised someone (either LL&L or Genesis) on dispatching Dirt Nap to tempt Wolverine is never followed up on. Lifeforce's word balloon incorrectly points toward Gauntlet here. Two of the storefronts in Manhattan are "Bob 'n' Ben's Place," referring to editors Ben Raab and Bob Harras, and the Joe Kubert School, an art school run by penciler Adam Kubert's father. P.16 panel 1 is an homage to Edward Hopper's 1942 painting *Nighthawks*; the diner in the image has been renamed Hoppers Coffee Shop.

WOLVERINE #96 (December 1995)

"Campfire Tales" (24 pages)

CREDITS: Larry Hama (writer), Adam Kubert (pencils, pp.1-19; c pencils), Luciano Lima (pencils, pp.20-24), Dan Green (inks), Richard Starkings & Comicraft (letters), Joe Rosas & Malibu's Hues (colors), Ben Raab (asst editor, uncredited), Bob Harras (editor), Jesse Delperdang (c inks), Brian Buccellato (c colors)
FEATURE CHARACTER: Wolverine (also in photo, also in fb between UXM #173-174, '83; next in GR #68, '95, XCD #1-2, '96, XMU #9, '95, UXM Ann '95, X&SM #3, '09; UXM #329-330, X/Brood #1-2, X #50, all '96)
GUEST STARS: X-Men: Cannonball (last in W #93, '95), Storm (also in fb between UXM #173-174, '83; last in UXM #326, '95) (both next in XCD #1, '96), Ariel, Colossus, Rogue (prev 3 in fb between UXM #173-174, '83), Caliban (super-strong mutant tracker, between XFor #47-48, '95)
VILLAINS: Cyber (dies, possibly next as spirit in W #176, '02, see W #4, '82's NOTE; chr next as spirit in W:C #12, '07 fb, next as spirit in W:O #11, '07), Dark Riders: Spyne (next in W #100, '96), Hurricane, Lifeforce (prev 2, next in W #99, '96); Genesis
OTHER CHARACTERS: Noah DuBois (next in Dp #1, '97), Zoe Culloden; mutant deathwatch beetles (1 dies), rabbit (dies off-panel), owl, grizzly bear, eagle; Mariko Yashida (in photo); Spider-Man, Thing (prev 2 on comic book covers), cartoon character (as Caliban's hat)
LOCATIONS/ITEMS: Canadian Rockies, X-Mansion (in fb), Genesis' Citadel / X-Men's sticks, rock climbing gear w/ropes & camping supplies w/cooler, first aid kit, water bottles & portable stove, Caliban's comic books, Wolverine's beer, photo, vase (prev 3 in fb) & firewood, Cannonball's S'mores w/marshmallows, Clan Yashida's Honor Sword (in fb), Storm's plants (in fb) w/mutant flower, Zoe & Noah's aura-cloaking dampers, infrared shields & psi-suppressors (prev 3 bts), Zoe's sidereal time transporter, Noah's impulse weapon, Dark Riders' booth window (destroyed) & chamber door, Genesis' blaster & armatures, Cyber's Adamantium skin
FLASHBACK: Distraught over his cancelled wedding to Mariko, Wolverine takes to drinking. Storm shows him a hybrid flower that mutated into something new and unique. She cuts it, explaining that all beauty blooms and fades, and we must appreciate it while it is here.
SYNOPSIS: Wolverine and Storm take Cannonball and Caliban on a strenuous mountain-climbing trip. Reaching the top, they enjoy the beauty of the sunset. The mutants make camp; later that night, they bond around a fire. Cannonball and Caliban want to hear stories of the X-Men's greatest fights, but Wolverine instead impresses on them the importance of loyalty and friendship. Zoe and Noah observe, cloaked, but a bear startles Noah and he blasts it. The wounded bear charges the X-Men's camp; Storm, Cannonball and Caliban prepare to fight, but Wolverine instead distracts it with marshmallows, calming the animal. Later, Wolverine ponders his increasingly animalistic worldview. Elsewhere, the Dark Riders force Cyber into a sealed chamber and release mutant deathwatch beetles, which quickly consume all of his flesh and organs — leaving only his Adamantium behind.
NOTE: Zoe continues to imply here that LL&L has a vested interest in Wolverine's feral regression, a plot point that is never elaborated on.

LOGAN: PATH OF THE WARLORD (February 1996)

"Path of the Warlord" (49 pages)

CREDITS: Howard Mackie (writer), John Paul Leon (pencils), Shawn Martinbrough (inks), Richard Starkings & Comicraft (letters & design), Gregory Wright (colors), Mark Powers (editor)
FEATURE CHARACTER: Wolverine (chr last in RamW, '09 fb, also & chr next in W #40, '06 fb)
VILLAINS: Kimora (immortal warlord of Kageumbra), Oracle (precognitive telepath), Shadow Walker (Mahog, manipulates & travels through shadows), Shadow Dancer (Sydia, Mahog's wife, creates shadow daggers, dies), Kimora's elite guard (1 dies), tower guards & army inc monk (all Kageumbrans), Kimora's Earth-616 assassins (some die, others bts attacking Chang) & guards (die)
OTHER CHARACTERS: Dr. Michael Carling (scientist, invented dimensional portals, dies), Rose Carling (Michael's daughter, chr 1st app, chr next as Rose Wu in UXM #257, '90), Chang (chr last in W #97, '96 fb, chr next in W #5, '89), Kani (LL&L guard, bts, dead), Miyagi (Wolverine's sparring partner), Wolverine's Jasmine Falls sensei (prev 2 possibly during W #40, '06 fb), Chang's backup (bts, arriving shortly), LL&L scientists; Kageumbran dogs, bird & snakes; Jhen (Carling's dead wife, unnamed; mentioned, killed by Kimora)
LOCATIONS/ITEMS: Japan inc Jasmine Falls (mountain village, 1st), cemetery, LL&L's Tokyo branch office & Kimora's hideout, Kageumbra (Kimora's home dimension, unnamed) inc Kimora's palace w/dungeon / Wolverine's handgun, knives, katana, bokken & leaf bandage, assassins' weapons (some bts) inc swords, staffs, ropes, net & knife, Kimora's ropes, dimensional transporter (prev 2 destroyed), katana, axe & snake-whips, Miyagi's katana, LL&L's dimensional transporter w/protective suits & rocket capsule, scientists' equipment, Chang's gun & dagger, Shadow Dancer's poisoned shadow blades, Shadow Walker's dagger, Rose's rifle, knife & sword, Carling's wheeled restraint device, army's tanks, airships & weapons, guards' blasters, staff, chain, knife & rifles, elite guard's axe & quills, hurled equipment
SYNOPSIS: In the late 1940s, Logan occasionally works with LL&L. Assassins attack his meeting with Dr. Carling, kidnapping the inventor; Chang blames Kimora, their immortal, other-dimensional foe. As Kimora tortures Carling for information on his dimensional transporter, Logan arrives and attacks. Kimora defeats Logan, rattling him badly, but Carling decapitates Kimora. Five years later, Chang tracks down a retired Logan in Jasmine Falls. Logan fails to tame his rage; his disappointed sensei gives him a wooden bokken sword. Chang reveals that Kimora has returned and kidnapped Carling again, seeking to open a large portal and invade Earth. Logan agrees to help; LL&L transports the two to Kageumbra, where they meet Carling's half-Kageumbran daughter Rose. Realizing that Kimora's telepathic Oracle has duplicated Carling's transporter, the three attack his palace. Logan refuses to kill, but when Rose is endangered, he snaps and mows through Kimora's guards. Kimora kills Carling, driving Logan further into a berserker rage; he savagely but ineffectually attacks Kimora. Rose throws Logan his bokken, reminding him to control his anger. Realizing that he cannot kill Kimora, Logan throws him into the rift between dimensions and destroys the transport device. Later, back on Earth, the three mourn Carling. Rose joins LL&L, and Logan thinks about doing the same.

WOLVERINE #97 (January 1996)

"…Bump in the Night" (19 pages)

CREDITS: Larry Hama (writer), Adam Kubert (pencils), Dan Green (inks), Richard Starkings & Comicraft (letters), Joe Rosas & Malibu's Hues (colors), Ben Raab (asst editor), Bob Harras (editor)
FEATURE CHARACTER: Wolverine (also as feral extrapolation on monitor, also in fb between Logan #3, '08 fb & Blade #5, '07 fb)
GUEST STAR: Phoenix (last in UXM #331, '96)
VILLAINS: Chimera (generates psychic serpents, 1st, next bts in W #99, '96, next in Venom:TC #2, '97), Genesis (bts hiring Chimera), Chang's foes (bts in other dimension), Madripoor soldier (prev 2 in fb)
OTHER CHARACTERS: Zoe Culloden, Chang (in fb, his chr 1st app, prior to L:PW, '96), Emmet (LL&L office boy, 1st, next bts in W #99, '96, next in Venom:TC #1, '96), Mr. Ramavishnu, Miss Kierkegaard (prev 2 LL&L staff, dead), bystanders; SHIELD scientists (mentioned, designed Cyber's cell), Mr. Landau (LL&L principal, mentioned as not being human); historical figure (as statue)
LOCATIONS/ITEMS: Edinburgh inc First Fiduciary Trust bank w/LL&L branch office (destroyed) & Edinburgh castle w/dungeon, Lowtown's LL&L branch office (in fb), inter-dimensional corridor, LL&L's other-dimensional main offices / SHIELD cell door (bts), Mack's gun (both destroyed), Phoenix's hi-tech helicopter, LL&L's safe, desk (prev 2 destroyed), Warp Chamber door (another in fb), filing cabinets, paperwork, computer, monitors & security door (destroyed) w/psi-shield, soldier's machine gun, Chang's paperwork, blaster & pistol, Wolverine's money & package (prev 6 in fb), Ramavishnu & Emmet's blasters, Zoe's sidereal time transporter & parcel w/key & note (prev 2 bts)
FLASHBACK: Wolverine asks Chang to retrieve a package that LL&L is holding for him. Chang arms himself, enters a door marked "WC," and emerges mere seconds later disheveled, with two days of beard growth, and holding a different weapon.
SYNOPSIS: Wolverine investigates Edinburgh Castle's dungeon, learning that someone freed Cyber. Phoenix takes Wolverine to the local LL&L office, which has been destroyed. Wolverine finds a WC door in the rubble; explaining that it stands for Warp Chamber, he opens it, revealing a portal. Wolverine and Phoenix step through, arriving in Mr. Landau's office, where something has killed several employees. Emmet, the office boy, introduces himself and reveals that the assailant is still present in an adjoining room. As soon as Wolverine enters, the door slams; Wolverine sees Chimera reviewing a computer extrapolation of how he will soon appear if his feral regression continues. She attacks, but Wolverine stabs her through the hand; she teleports away just as Emmet and Phoenix break down the door. Zoe arrives; handing Wolverine a package and explaining that he has urgent business on Earth, she teleports him and Phoenix away…
NOTE: This issue reveals that Landau, Luckman & Lake is an interdimensional holding firm, and that Zoe now holds Chang's former title of Expediter. The contents of Zoe's parcel are revealed next issue.

WOLVERINE #98 (February 1996)

"Fade to Black" (19 pages)

CREDITS: Larry Hama (writer), Ramon Bernado (pencils), Nick Napolitano, Al Milgrom & Mark Morales (inks), Richard Starkings & Comicraft (letters), Joe Rosas & Malibu's Hues (colors), Ben Raab (asst editor), Bob Harras (editor), Adam Kubert (c pencils)
FEATURE CHARACTER: Wolverine (also in pfb)
GUEST STAR: Phoenix (in pfb, next in FAC&P #1, '96)
SUPPORTING CAST: Archie Corrigan, O'Donnell (both dead), Tyger Tiger (all last in W #87, '94)
VILLAINS: Dirt Nap (as rat, last in W #95, '95), Genesis (bts influencing Baran & Coy), Police Chief Tai (last in W #87, '94, next in W #127, '98), Prince Baran (dies, last in W #31, '90), General Coy (last in PWZ #22, '93, next in SM #73, '96), Coy & Baran's thugs (die) inc Imak & Ivan
OTHER CHARACTERS: Special Agent Daryll Smith (last bts in W #95, '95), Algernon (last in W #95, '95) (both bts inside Dirt Nap), Rose Wu (dies, also in painting, last in W #87, '94), Zoe Culloden, Madripoor police inc Sergeant, Princess Bar patrons (dead); rats (1 bts, used as Dirt Nap's template form, last in W #95, '95)
LOCATIONS/ITEMS: Lowtown inc Princess Bar & ruins of LL&L branch office, Hightown police headquarters w/maximum security cell & Tai's office, Manhattan's Rockefeller Center (in pfb), inter-dimensional corridor / Zoe's parcel (bts in pfb) w/key & note (prev 2 also in pfb), Rose's painting (destroyed), police car & guns, Wolverine's manacle, pipe (destroyed), Tyger's handgun, car & parcel w/hacksaw & Wolverine's costume, thugs' rocket grenade launcher (bts), guns, machetes, bats, chains, axe, chainsaw, knives & brass knuckles, Tai's bribe (bts), Imak & Ivan's claws, Coy's handgun, LL&L's Warp Chamber door
FLASHBACK: Wolverine and Phoenix materialize in Manhattan, and Wolverine opens Zoe's parcel (p).
SYNOPSIS: Wolverine awakens groggily and finds himself in the Princess Bar, surrounded by bodies including Archie Corrigan and O'Donnell. Realizing that they were slashed by claws, Wolverine worries that he killed them in a feral rage. Rose Wu dies in his arms but does not reveal the culprit. Tai arrives and confronts him, and Wolverine allows himself to be arrested. However, when he overhears Tai conspiring to kill him in his cell, and Dirt Nap arrives to taunt him, Wolverine begins to suspect that he is innocent. Soon, Baran and Coy arrive with several thugs, some wearing wrist-mounted claws. Wolverine realizes that they killed his friends; he slaughters the thugs and pursues Coy and Baran. Coy shoots Baran but is shot by Tyger Tiger, who also hit Tai with her car. Retrieving an address and key from Zoe's parcel, Wolverine travels to LL&L's Madripoor office, and unlocks its Warp Chamber door. He steps through, where Zoe awaits him…
NOTE: LL&L's Lowtown office address, 23 Hotei Way, is revealed here. O'Donnell's name is also incorrectly spelled "O'Donnel." Tai is now listed as a Villain, having accepted a bribe to let Wolverine be killed. Wolverine observes that someone or something seems to be making Baran and Coy more bloodthirsty than usual; given Dirt Nap's appearance in Wolverine's cell, the culprit is likely Genesis. Despite appearances, neither Coy nor Tai die this issue.

WOLVERINE #99 (March 1996)

"Of Mythic Metal Forged" (19 pages)

CREDITS: Larry Hama (writer), Val Semeiks (pencils), Dan Green, Dan Panosian & Chad Hunt (inks), Richard Starkings & Comicraft (letters), Joe Rosas & Malibu's Hues (colors), Ben Raab (asst editor), Bob Harras (editor), Adam Kubert (c pencils), John Dell (c inks), Arno (c colors, see NOTE)
FEATURE CHARACTER: Wolverine
GUEST STARS: X-Men: Cannonball (last in X #50, '96), Professor X (bts, asked Cannonball to visit Wolverine between UXM #331-332, '96)
SUPPORTING CAST: Tyger Tiger (next in W #125, '98)
VILLAINS: Dark Riders: Deadbolt (generates skeletal weapons, last in X Ann '95), Gauntlet (last in W #95, '95), Dirt Nap (as rat), Hurricane, Lifeforce (prev 2 last in W #96, '95), Chimera (bts leaving footprints, also as hologram, last in W #97, '96, next bts in Venom:TC #1, '96, next in Venom:TC #2, '97), Jamil (last in W #94, '95, next in X #60, '97), Genesis, Madripoor thugs
OTHER CHARACTERS: Special Agent Daryll Smith, Algernon (both bts inside Dirt Nap, Karima (bts animating Jamil, last in XMU #7, '94 last bts in W #94, '95, next in X #60, '97), Emmet (bts, busy elsewhere, last in W #97, '96, next in Venom:TC #1, '96), Zoe Culloden, Akkaba victims (dead, as skeletons, last in W #94, '95), Egyptian farmers; rat (bts, used as Dirt Nap's template form), vultures, cobra; Cable, Storm (prev 2 mentioned, told Wolverine about Akkaba)
LOCATIONS/ITEMS: Inter-dimensional corridor, Egypt inc ruins of Akkaba & Genesis' citadel w/bonding room, Lowtown: Princess Bar & LL&L branch office / LL&L's Warp Chamber doors, Dark Riders' ropes, pain-sticks & VTOL aircraft, Zoe's scanner, hologram projector & sidereal time transporter, Jamil's knives, Cannonball's duffel bag, thugs' machetes, gun & club, Tyger's car & submachine gun, citadel's minefield & laser enfilade, Gauntlet's guns & targeting eyepiece, Genesis' blaster & bonding tanks w/Adamantium-reshaping equipment, brain implants (prev 2 bts) & feed tubes, Cyber's Adamantium (re-fashioned into a skeleton)
SYNOPSIS: Wolverine emerges from the Warp Chamber in Akkaba, where Zoe shows him the Dark Riders' massacre. Zoe locates Chimera's footprints and leaves to track her down, telling Wolverine that they will rendezvous at Genesis' citadel. As Wolverine wonders how to get there, Jamil arrives to guide him there. Cannonball arrives in Lowtown, looking for Wolverine at Professor X's request, but discovers the trashed Princess Bar. Thugs confront him, but Tyger Tiger arrives and drives them off, then takes Cannonball to LL&L's Warp Chamber door. Jamil leads Wolverine to the citadel, where a distrustful Wolverine elects to sneak in the back; he makes his way past Genesis' defenses and sees the Dark Riders herding captured farmers inside. Cannonball arrives in Akkaba and follows Wolverine's tracks across the desert. Wolverine infiltrates the citadel; he locates and pursues Dirt Nap but encounters Genesis, who promptly blasts him unconscious. As Genesis gloats, the Dark Riders prepare to brainwash Wolverine — and bond Cyber's Adamantium onto his skeleton!
NOTE: This issue's UPC box incorrectly lists the issue number as "X99". The letters page features fan art by H.J. Davies. This is the last issue to offer both deluxe and non-deluxe versions. Cover colorist Arno's full name is unknown.

WOLVERINE #100 (April 1996)

"Furnace of His Brain, Anvil of His Heart" (36 pages)

CREDITS: Larry Hama (writer), Adam Kubert (pencils), Dan Green (inks), Richard Starkings & Comicraft (letters), Joe Rosas & Electric Crayon (colors), Ben Raab (asst editor), Bob Harras (editor), John Dell (c inks)
FEATURE CHARACTER: Wolverine (also on monitor, next in UXM #332, '96)
GUEST STARS: Elektra (Elektra Natchios, ninja mercenary, last in Elek:RE #4, '95, chr last in DCvM #4, '96), Cannonball (both next in UXM #332, '96)
VILLAINS: Dark Riders: Dirt Nap (as rat, next in Venom:TC #1, '96), Gauntlet (next in X:SFC #1, '00), Spyne (last in W #96, '95), Deadbolt, Hurricane, Lifeforce (prev 4 next bts in XNec, '09, next in XFor #21, '10); Genesis (prev 5 die), Apocalypse (possibly bts inside sarcophagus, see NOTE; also as image on sarcophagus)
OTHER CHARACTERS: Special Agent Daryll Smith, Algernon (both bts inside Dirt Nap, next bts in Venom:TC #1, '96, next in Venom:TC #3, '97), Zoe Culloden (next in UXM #332, '96), Stick (Elektra's Chaste mentor, last in DD #350, '96, next in W #105, '96), Egyptian farmers (bts in sarcophagi); rat (bts, used as Dirt Nap's template form, next bts in Venom:TC #1, '96, next in Venom:TC #3, '97); ancient Egyptians (as images on sarcophagi); people & animals (prev 2 as hieroglyphics)
LOCATIONS/ITEMS: Genesis' citadel w/bonding room & resurrection chamber, Stick's mountaintop retreat / Genesis' bonding tanks (destroyed) w/brain implants, scanners (prev 2 bts), Adamantium-reshaping equipment, computers, status board & feed tubes, Cyber's Adamantium, Gauntlet's guns & targeting eyepiece, Apocalypse's revival crèche w/sarcophagi, Zoe's research papers (bts) & sidereal time transporter, Lifeforce's fire extinguisher, Stick's bo staff

SYNOPSIS: As Wolverine endures the Adamantium bonding, Genesis celebrates, planning to make him into Apocalypse's new Horseman. Cannonball and Zoe, spying on the procedure, see the kidnapped farmers locked in sarcophagi that drain their energy into a larger unit, and Cannonball realizes that Genesis means to resurrect Apocalypse. Zoe urges Cannonball not to interfere, implying that she knows how the procedure will turn out, and teleports away. As Wolverine begins succumbing to the brain implants, a frustrated Cannonball attacks the Dark Riders, damaging the bonding equipment. The Riders quickly overpower Cannonball; seeing his teammate's plight, Wolverine begins willing the Adamantium out of his body. He expels it explosively, spraying shrapnel that kills two Riders — but the ordeal devolves him into a savage, animalistic creature. Wolverine stalks and butchers the remaining Riders, then savagely attacks and kills Genesis. Cannonball opens Apocalypse's sarcophagus, but finds it empty. Wolverine struggles to speak, then flees into the night. Elsewhere, Stick senses Wolverine's plight, and sends Elektra to help him regain his humanity.
NOTE: This issue's cover has a hologram that varies between images of Wolverine and his skeleton, depending on the angle at which it is viewed. The newsstand cover shows only the Wolverine image. Apocalypse apparently died off-panel in XFor #18, '93. This issue casts doubt over whether he was actually inside the sarcophagus; if he was, he appears bts here between Cable #19, '94, where he appears in shadow, at least partly revived, and UXM #335, '96, where he fully revives. It is possible that once Wolverine broke free, Apocalypse left the sarcophagus to finish

reviving elsewhere. Although Genesis fails to re-implant Wolverine's Adamantium and brainwash him into Apocalypse's Horseman of Death here, Apocalypse succeeds in doing exactly that in W #145, '99 fb. The blood that Gauntlet finds on p.27 is incorrectly colored luminous blue.

WOLVERINE #101 (May 1996)

"The Helix of an Age Foretold" (19 pages)

CREDITS: Larry Hama (writer), Val Semeiks (pencils), Chad Hunt (inks), Richard Starkings & Comicraft (letters), Joe Rosas & Malibu's Hues (colors), Ben Raab (asst editor), Bob Harras (editor), Adam Kubert (c pencils), Dan Green (c inks)
FEATURE CHARACTER: Wolverine (also as Ozymandias' animated statue & image carved on helix)
GUEST STARS: X-Men: Cannonball, Iceman (both next in UXM #333, '96), Cyclops, Phoenix (prev 2 next in X #51, '96); Elektra (all last in UXM #332, '96)
VILLAIN: Ozymandias (Apocalypse's living stone chronicler, last in UXM #332, '96, next in UXM #335, '96)
OTHER CHARACTERS: Gauntlet, Hurricane, Magneto (all as Ozymandias' animated statues, last in UXM #332, '96, destroyed); Professor X, Thing, many others (prev 3 images carved on helix); Spyne (as Ozymandias' animated statue, cover only)
LOCATIONS/ITEMS: Ozymandias' Moroccan temple / Ozymandias' carved helix & animated stone statues (both destroyed), rock outcropping, Professor X's wheelchair (image carved on helix), Elektra's sais, hurled rocks
SYNOPSIS: As Cyclops falls into the chasm surrounding Ozymandias' helix, the villain's animated statues attack the other X-Men. Having devolved past logical thought, the feral Wolverine dives after Cyclops, who strikes his head on a rock as he falls. Wolverine catches Cyclops and digs into the chasm wall with his claws, stopping their plunge. A groggy Cyclops notices that Professor X is carved near the bottom of the helix, and wonders how long Ozymandias has been transcribing their history in stone. Above, the X-Men battle the statues and Phoenix briefly senses someone covertly watching them. As Wolverine climbs the helix with Cyclops, two statues move to ambush the X-Men, but Elektra — whom Phoenix had sensed — stealthily knocks them into the chasm. The X-Men destroy the other statues; Ozymandias, sensing defeat, destroys the helix to preserve its secrets. Iceman rescues Wolverine and Cyclops just as the helix crumbles to dust, and Ozymandias dissolves as well. As the X-Men depart, Wolverine briefly senses Elektra watching from the shadows.
NOTE: This issue is continued from UXM #332, '96, where the X-Men track down Wolverine, who has stumbled upon Ozymandias' temple. In a minor glitch, UXM #332, '96 ends with the Magneto statue strangling Phoenix, but she is free when this issue begins. Cyclops' head injury is implied to have affected the previously damaged section of his brain that keeps him from mentally controlling his optic blasts, but the hint is never followed up on. This issue's letters page incorrectly claims that Rose Wu survived W #98, '96, but W #111, '97 shows Wolverine drinking a toast to honor her memory, confirming her death. With this issue, the issue number moves from the UPC box back to the info block on the cover's top left corner. The words "the All-New, All-Different" run above this issue's cover logo, a reference to Wolverine's feral mutation and to X #94-111, '75-78, which also carried that banner.

WOLVERINE #102 (June 1996)

"Unspoken Promises" (22 pages)

CREDITS: Larry Hama (writer), Adam Kubert (pencils), Dan Green (inks), Richard Starkings & Comicraft (letters), Joe Rosas & Malibu's Hues (colors), Ben Raab (asst editor), Bob Harras (editor)
FEATURE CHARACTER: Wolverine (also on monitors; also mentioned in Elektra's story, bts as Cpl. Logan, see NOTE)
GUEST STARS: Elektra (also mentioned as a girl & young woman in her own story), Professor X (last in UXM #332, '96, next in X #51, '96)
VILLAINS: Thug, drug dealer (both die)
OTHER CHARACTERS: Teenage boy (would-be thug), his mother & her unborn child (bts), train conductors (bts driving trains), blind beggar (dies), drug dealer's customers, young couple (die) & their baby, priest, police, bystanders; birds, cat; Hugo Natchios (Elektra's father), Christina (Elektra's mother), Niko (would-be assassin, unnamed, dies), Athos, Stavros, Theo, Natchios' cook, Nazis inc Luftwaffe Col. Schlage (bts, unnamed, ordering Stavros' family's death), Fallschirmjaegers (paratroopers), SS troops (die) & Gestapo, English army officers, Stavros' sisters & mother (prev 2 die), fish (dead) (prev 15 mentioned in Elektra's story); Mary (mother of Jesus, on medal)
LOCATIONS/ITEMS: X-Mansion (also on monitors), Salem Center train station, New York City inc alley, train station & boy's bedroom; Elektra's Greek family home inc olive grove, kitchen & garden w/shed, Stavros' family house & underground hideout (prev 6 mentioned in story) / Saplings (1 dies), Elektra's hoe, Stavros' Fairbairn knife, explosives, gun, piano wire, whetstone & knife, Nazis' nails & sign, Christina's pistol, Theo & Niko's rifles, diagram & knife (all mentioned in story), Professor X's cameras (bts) & monitors, Amtrak trains, mother's medal, coins & cart, boy's handgun, beggar's wheelchair, cup & sign, customers' car, dealer's money, gun & bulletproof vest, thug's submachine gun, baby carriage, Elektra's sais & sword, police car
FLASHBACK: Elektra recalls her childhood working with family gardener Stavros. When she accidentally killed a sapling, Stavros explained that all lives have value. Soon, Elektra overheard the servants discussing Stavros' past as a freedom fighter; how Nazis murdered his family and he became a ruthless killer. Confused, Elektra looked for Stavros, but was captured by two would-be assassins targeting her father. Stavros killed one, but Elektra begged him to spare the other, reminding him that all lives have value.
SYNOPSIS: The bestial Wolverine sneaks out of the X-Mansion and travels to the city. A teenage boy meets his thug friend; nearby, the boy's mother gives money to a beggar. The deformed Wolverine startles her, but she offers him money as well. The boy and thug rob a drug dealer, and the thug shoots a young couple who saw him. Wolverine attacks and kills the thug, then chases the boy, who shoots Wolverine several times but falls into the path of a train. Smelling the mother's scent on him, Wolverine saves the boy, then collapses from his wounds. The boy aids him, but the drug dealer returns and threatens to shoot them both. Elektra arrives and stabs him; Wolverine returns the mother's money to the boy.
NOTE: This issue is silent, aside from caption boxes narrating Elektra's story about her childhood. Larry Hama has written several other silent stories, most famously GIJoe #21, '84. Most of Elektra's story here is told on-panel in Elektra #18, '98 fb, where Niko is named. Schlage is named in W #106, '96, which also reveals that Stavros learned how to kill from Wolverine.

WOLVERINE #102.5 (1996)

"Slay-Per-View" (11 pages)

CREDITS: Dan Slott (writer), Mark Buckingham (art), Arnie Sawyer Studios (letter & trading card design), Paul Mounts & Bongotone Studio (colors), Marc Robinson (art director), Dan Buckley (trading card director), Steve Alexandrov (production), Mike Pasciullo (marketing), Marcy McKinstrie (project manager), Matthew Morra (editor), Jennifer Caudill, Matt Melnick & Christine Dattolo (special thanks), Boris Vallejo (c art)

FEATURE CHARACTER: Wolverine (also on TV; also in story & on TV in pfb, chr last in W #103, '96, chr next in UXM #333, '96)

GUEST STARS: X-Babies (juvenile Mojoverse versions of the X-Men): Cyke (Cyclops analog), Ice-Baby (Iceman analog) (prev 2 named), Shower (Storm analog), Sugah (Rogue analog) (prev 2 unnamed, see NOTE), "Archangel" (prev 3 next in XB, '98) (all also in pfb), "Bishop," "Gambit" (prev 2 also bts in pfb, next in XB:R, '00) (all last in X #47, '95); Longshot (luck-manipulating Mojoverse mutant, also in story & on TV in pfb, last in X #11 '92, chr last in MFan #5, '97, next in XFor/Yb, '96), Dazzler (last in X #47, '95, chr last in XFor/Yb, '96 fb, next in Yb/XFor, '96), Elektra (also in Wolverine's memory, chr between W #103-104, '96) (prev 2 also in pfb)

VILLAINS: Mojo II (Mojo's flawed clone, on TV, also on TV in pfb; last in X #11, '92, chr last in MFan #5, '97, next in Yb/XFor, '96), Spiral (also as Phoenix & herself in pfb; last in X #32, '94, chr last in MFan #5, '97, next in XFor #60, '96), Warwolves (Mojo's skin-wearing lupine servants, also as Deathbird (also in pfb), Sasquatch (also on TV), Magneto (on TV), Dirt Nap (as rat), Cyber, Deadpool, Lady Deathstrike, Omega Red, Razor-Fist, Sabretooth & Shiva; some or others also in pfb, those also as Cable, Vindicator (prev 2 also on TV), Weapon X (Kane), Beast, Bishop, Bloodscream, Brood, Cyclops, Gambit, Hulk, Jubilee, Maverick, Silver Samurai, Stryfe & Thing; some or others last in Ex #41, '91, next in FF #7, '98)

OTHER CHARACTERS: Gog (Mojo's enforcer, last in X #47, '95, next in XFor #59, '96), Mojoworld denizens (many bts watching TV; some or others also in pfb, many bts watching TV) inc Spineless Ones

LOCATIONS/ITEMS: Mojoverse (TV-obsessed dimension) inc Mojo II's stadium (also on TVs, also in story & on TVs in pfb) & Dazzler & Longshot's base (in pfb), wilderness (also in pfb) / Warwolves' costumes (1 also in pfb, others in pfb, some of both on TVs, some of both also on TVs, some of both destroyed), prop weapons (others in pfb) & energy lattice (in pfb), Mojo II's broadcasting equipment (bts, also bts in pfb), TV monitor & floating cameras (prev 2 also in pfb), Mojoverse denizens' TV sets (many bts; some or others also in pfb, many bts) w/remote controls, Elektra's sais & sword (prev 2 in pfb), Longshot & Dazzler's TVs, emergency broadcast system (prev 2 in pfb) & dimensional transporter (bts), Dazzler's Nielsonometer (ratings detector, also in pfb) & remote control, stadium roof (destroyed), Spiral's sword (also in pfb)

FLASHBACK: As Wolverine and Elektra meditate, the X-Men seemingly arrive for a visit. Smelling "Phoenix," Wolverine realizes that she is a disguised Spiral, and attacks. The other "X-Men," revealed as Warwolves, capture Wolverine and transport him to the Mojoverse. There, Mojo II pits Wolverine against Warwolves disguised as his greatest foes, broadcasting the battles and hoping to gain enough ratings to conquer the entire dimension. Dazzler, Longshot and the X-Babies track down Mojo II's stadium (p).

SYNOPSIS: Wolverine battles a horde of disguised Warwolves, but the Mojoverse audience slowly begins tuning out, feeling that Wolverine has no hope of winning the one-sided brawl. Dazzler, Longshot and the X-Babies arrive; Dazzler exhorts Wolverine to throw the fight. Understanding, Wolverine lets himself be overrun; the viewers become bored and tune out completely. As soon as Mojo II's power base vanishes, Dazzler, Longshot and the X-Babies attack, helping Wolverine defeat the Warwolves and shut off Mojo II's transmission. Victorious, the heroes transport Wolverine back to Earth.

NOTE: This story was originally presented on the backs of the 99 main cards in the Fleer Ultra X-Men: Wolverine '96 trading card set. Assembling the cards in 3x3 grids created the story pages. This comic-format reprint was distributed by Fleer/Skybox; its cover is taken from from card #93 of the 1996 Marvel Masterpieces trading card set. Wizard Magazine offered a variant edition with a small holographic sticker on the cover; several of these were autographed by Boris Vallejo and came with a certificate of authenticity. Despite its numbering, this issue actually occurs after W #103, '96, as Elektra is now mentoring Wolverine. Although most of the X-Babies debuted with the same names as their Earth-616 counterparts, they later adopted different, derivative names shortly before this issue. Shower's new name is revealed in XB, '98, and Sugah's in XB:R, '00. "Archangel," "Bishop" and "Gambit's" derivative names, if any, are unrevealed to date. Dazzler joined Longshot's Mojoverse rebellion in X #5, '92; they overthrew Mojo in X #11, '92 with the help of Mojo II and the X-Men.

2ND STORY: "Costume Re-Partee" (1 page)

CREDITS: Dan Slott (writer), Mike Wieringo (art), Arnie Sawyer Studios (letters & trading card design), Chuck Maiden (colors), Marc Robinson (art director), Dan Buckley (trading card director), Steve Alexandrov (production), Mike Pasciullo (marketing), Marcy McKinstrie (project manager), Matthew Morra (editor), Jennifer Caudill, Matt Melnick & Christine Dattolo (special thanks)

FEATURE CHARACTER: Wolvie (X-Babies' Wolverine analog, also as Weapon X (Earth-295), Patch, Experiment X & Wolverine, last in Ex:MM, '89, next in XB, '98)

GUEST STARS: X-Babies: Cyke, Ice-Baby (both next in XB, '98), "Jubilee" (1st, unnamed, next in XB:R, '00)

OTHER CHARACTER: Charlie X ("Prof," Professor X analog, unnamed, in painting)

LOCATIONS/ITEMS: Clubhouse for Gifted Youngsters (X-Babies' Mojoverse treehouse, unnamed) / Cyke & Wolvie's costumes & trick-or-treat bags

SYNOPSIS: Wolvie, unwilling to wear his standard costume for trick-or-treating, tries on several Wolverine-themed costumes — a samurai, Patch, Experiment X, the Age of Apocalypse's Weapon X and the feral, devolved Wolverine — but Cyke dislikes all of them. Finally, Wolvie dresses as the full-sized adult Wolverine, and Cyke approves.

NOTE: This story was originally presented on the backs of the 9 Fleer Ultra X-Men: Wolverine '96 holoflash chase cards. It is followed by a Wolverine pin-up by Julie Bell, from card #92 of the 1996 Marvel Masterpieces trading card set. Wolvie is the only X-Baby to debut with a derivative name instead of sharing his Earth-616 counterpart's codename. Charlie X is named in XB, '98, his 1st on-panel app, which also names the Clubhouse. "Jubilee's" derivative name, if any, is unrevealed to date.

WOLVERINE #103 (July 1996)

"Top of the World, Ma!" (22 pages)

CREDITS: Larry Hama (writer), Val Semeiks (pencils), Chad Hunt (inks), Richard Starkings & Comicraft (letters), Joe Rosas & Malibu's Hues (colors), Ben Raab (asst editor), Bob Harras (editor)
FEATURE CHARACTER: Wolverine (also bts in fb2 between W #126, '98 fb & W #89, '95 fb; next in W #102.5, '96, UXM #333, '96, W #175/2, '02 fb, W/Herc #1, '11 fb; Storm #1 & 4, UXM #334, X #54, Ons:XM, UXM #335, all '96)
GUEST STAR: Elektra (also in fb1 between Elektra #-1, '97 & Elek:RE #2, '95 fb; chr next in W #102.5, '96)
VILLAIN: Ogun (in fb2 between W #113, '97 fb & W #89, '95 fb)
OTHER CHARACTERS: Elektra's sparring partners (in fb1); Hugo Natchios (dies), policeman (bts), Matt Murdock (prev 3 in rfb1), Stick, Chaste members, Elektra's sensei, Hand ninjas (prev 4 in rfb2); Sun Tzu (quoted)
LOCATIONS/ITEMS: World Trade Center w/rooftop & Windows on the World restaurant w/kitchen, Manhattan rooftop; Columbia University (in rfb1), Elektra's bedroom, Chaste's mountain sanctuary, Hand's headquarters (prev 3 in rfb2), Elektra's dojo in fb1), Ogun Ryu Dojo (Kanazawa, Japan, unnamed, in fb2) / Elektra's sais, scroll, staff, paint & sword w/scabbard, Wolverine's staff, walk-in refrigerator inc door (destroyed) w/bolt, police gun (bts), Hugo's bonds (prev 2 in rfb1), Chaste & Hand ninjas' swords, sensei's sai (prev 2 in fb2), Ogun's scroll, swords & demon mask (prev 3 in fb2)
FLASHBACKS: Elektra falls for Matt Murdock; Elektra's father is killed (DD #168, '81 fb). Elektra climbs the Chaste's mountain but Stick rejects her (Elek:RE #2, '95 fb); the Hand recruit Elektra and trick her into murdering her sensei (DD #190, '83 fb). Elektra practices martial arts (1). Ogun teaches Wolverine the attributes of the samurai (2).
SYNOPSIS: Wolverine climbs the World Trade Center, completing the first task assigned to him by Elektra, who hopes to help him regain his humanity. Elektra sets up a dojo in the skyscraper's closed restaurant, displaying a Chinese scroll that Wolverine seems to recognize. Elektra then trains Wolverine exhaustively, believing that if he can reclaim his reasoning skills and mental conditioning, his humanity will follow. After a lengthy training period, Wolverine meditates calmly, and Elektra likens him to an unsheathed sword. She tricks him inside a refrigerator and locks it, explaining that she is testing him. Wolverine recalls that he last saw the scroll in the dojo where Ogun trained him. He frees himself, claims the sword that Elektra left behind and tracks her to a rooftop, where he attacks. Elektra seems to defeat him, but Wolverine lures her closer and sheathes the sword in the empty scabbard she carries — successfully completing the test.
NOTE: Wolverine regains the mental capacity to speak clearly here, the first step in his slow transformation back to normal, but his word balloons remain lettered in the "jagged" font introduced in W #100, '96. Ogun's dojo's name and location are revealed in W #113, '97 fb. This issue also contains a 6-page "Onslaught Is Coming" section, recapping the villain's previous appearances.

WOLVERINE #104 (August 1996)

"The Emperor of the Realm of Grief" (22 pages)

CREDITS: Larry Hama (writer), Val Semeiks (pencils), Chad Hunt (inks), Richard Starkings & Comicraft (letters), Joe Rosas & Malibu's Hues (colors), Ben Raab (asst editor), Bob Harras (editor)
FEATURE CHARACTER: Wolverine (also in photo & scenes from W #57, '92 & X #25, '93)
GUEST STARS: X-Men: Professor X (in scene from X #25, '93; also in past during X #25, '93), Phoenix (also in shadow in scene from X #25, '93), Cyclops (prev 2 bts asking Wolverine to consult Gateway, last in UXM #335, '96, next in Ex #100, '96), Gambit (prev 3 also in photo), Rogue; Quicksilver (prev 3 in shadow in scene from X #25, '93), Elektra (also in scene from DD #190, '83; chr last in W #102.5, '96, next in W #106, '96)
VILLAINS: Magneto (in scene from X #25, '93; also in past as himself & his dark ego's manifestation during X #25, '93), Onslaught (psionic entity, merger of Professor X & Magneto's dark urges, also in Wolverine's memory; chr 1st app in past as psionic seed planted inside Professor X, chr next in X&Doom Ann '98)

OTHER CHARACTERS: Gateway (last in X #50, '96, next in X Ann '96); Mariko Yashida, Gambit, Silver Samurai, Black Blade, Death Touch Cult Hand ninjas (prev 5 in scene from W #57, '92), Daredevil (in scene from DD #190, '83); Death, Hugo Natchios, tormented souls (some as skulls), Hand ninjas (prev 4 in Elektra's vision); Generation X: Emma Frost, Banshee, Skin, Mondo, M, Chamber, Husk; X-Factor: Forge, Polaris, Wild Child; X-Men: Archangel (also as Angel), Beast, Colossus, Iceman, Professor X, Psylocke, Storm (prev 17 in photos)
LOCATIONS/ITEMS: Xavier's School for Gifted Youngsters, Shingen's Citadel compound w/chapel, Hand's church hideout, Avalon, astral plane, underworld (in Elektra's vision) / Gateway's bull-roarer, Silver Samurai's armor, Gambit's staff, ninjas' armor, swords & gun, Reiko's poisoned dagger, Elektra's sais, Death's boat w/oar, ninjas' short swords (prev 3 in Elektra's vision), X-Men's group photos, Wolverine's Adamantium skeleton (destroyed), Professor X's exo-skeleton
FLASHBACKS: Wolverine, Gambit and the Silver Samurai battle Hand ninjas; poisoned, Mariko Yashida asks Wolverine to end her pain (W #57, '92). Daredevil's love mystically cleanses the resurrected Elektra's soul (DD #190, '83). Magneto rips out Wolverine's Adamantium, and Professor X wipes Magneto's mind (X #25, '93).
SYNOPSIS: Traveling to Generation X's academy, Wolverine asks Gateway for advice on defeating Onslaught, Professor X's "dark side," which recently manifested and is attacking New York. Gateway makes Wolverine relive Mariko's death, unnerving him badly. Elektra arrives; when she asks Gateway for help, he shows Elektra a vision of the underworld and makes her relive her resurrection by the Hand. Elektra realizes that Gateway is showing them these traumatic moments to prepare them for the truth about Onslaught. Gateway then transports them both to Avalon, where Wolverine relives Magneto tearing the Adamantium from his skeleton. Shifting to the astral plane, Wolverine and Elektra witness a horrified Professor X shut down Magneto's mind — but they also see a split-second transfer, as Magneto's psychic dark ego plants a "seed" in Professor X's mind. Returning to the present, Wolverine realizes that this was Onslaught's origin, and is guilt-ridden that his injuries indirectly caused Professor X to be infected.
NOTE: Wolverine is now rational and articulate, but his body is still mutated and animalistic. Gateway has been mainly residing at Generation X's academy since GenX #1, '94. Onslaught was revealed as a deranged, evil Professor X in X #54, '96; this issue clarifies that he is a separate entity corrupting Professor X's psyche. This issue also contains a 6-page "Onslaught and Beyond Update" section, previewing the upcoming Heroes Reborn titles.

WOLVERINE #105 (September 1996)

"Faces in the Fire" (22 pages)

CREDITS: Larry Hama (writer), Val Semeiks (pencils), Chad Hunt, Vince Russell & Harry Candelario (ink Richard Starkings & Comicraft (letters), Chris Lichtner, Joe Andreani & Malibu's Hues (colors), Ben Raab (as editor), Bob Harras (editor), Anthony Winn (c pencils), Dan Panosian (c inks)
FEATURE CHARACTER: Wolverine (next in Ons:MU fb, UXM #337, X #57, all '96)
GUEST STAR: Human Torch (Johnny Storm, generates & controls flame, last in UXM #336, '96, next in I #416, '96)
OTHER CHARACTERS: Stick (last in W #100, '96, next in Elektra #1, '96), Sean (young boy) & his mother siblings, firemen, paramedics, looters, bystanders; animals (as Sean's stuffed dolls) inc Mr. Winky (teddy bear) **LOCATIONS/ITEMS:** Manhattan apartment building (destroyed) inc lobby, rooftop, Sean's bedroom & near store / Wolverine's mask & costume shirt, firemen's net (bts), axes & trucks w/hoses & ladders, store wind (destroyed), stolen electronics, Sean's dolls, flaming debris, Stick's bo staff, paramedic's medical kit, water tower (destroyed)
SYNOPSIS: Wolverine helps firemen battle blazes caused by Onslaught's assault on New York. When a mother realizes that her young s Sean is still inside, Wolverine enters the building and locates him, earning his trust by giving the boy his mask. As the collapsing walls cut Wolverine's exit, a man appears and guides Wolverine to the fire stairs. Wolverine covers Sean with his water-soaked shirt and races throu the flaming lobby to the street. As the firemen and Sean's grateful mother look on, Wolverine's burns quickly heal and he heads back inside rescue the man. However, when the man attacks him, Wolverine realizes that he is Stick, Elektra's ghostly mentor, and he is testing Wolverir The two spar through the burning building as Stick explains that neither he nor Elektra can truly restore Wolverine's humanity — Wolverine mu do that himself. Stick points Wolverine through the fire to safety; as Wolverine emerges, the Human Torch arrives and recruits him for the fir attack against Onslaught.
NOTE: Wolverine has replaced his standard cowl with a bandana-like mask. His facial features are now slightly more human; his healing fact is slowly reversing his feral mutation. Onslaught was physically separated from Professor X in UXM #336, '96, and is defeated in Ons:MU, ' fb. This issue also contains a 6-page "Heroes Reborn Update" preview section.

WOLVERINE #106 (October 1996)

"Openings and Closures" (22 pages)

CREDITS: Larry Hama (writer), Val Semeiks (pencils), Chad Hunt & Al Milgrom (inks), Richard Starkings Comicraft's Kolja Fuchs (letters), Derek Bellman & Malibu's Hues (colors), Jason Liebig (asst editor), Ma Powers (assoc editor, see NOTE), Bob Harras (editor), Adam Kubert (c pencils)
FEATURE CHARACTER: Wolverine (also as Cpl. Logan in fb between WWHs:C/W #2, '10 fb & W #34, '90 f next in Elektra #1 & 3, '96-97, W Ann '96)
GUEST STAR: Elektra (also in rfb, last in W #104, '96, next in OtEdge #8, '96)
VILLAINS: Nazis (in fb): Luftwaffe Col. Schlage (named, bts, transferred to Russia, following Elektra #18, '98 bts) & his superiors (bts transferring him), SS troops (bts, killed Stavros' family, die; following Elektra #18, '98 fb others (bts in planes, die); Sawyer (last surviving kidnapper of Hugo, named, last in DD #168, '81 fb)
OTHER CHARACTERS: Athos (Natchios' bodyguard, last in DD #168, '81 fb), Stavros (Natchios' gardene also in fb, his chr 1st app, prior to Elektra #18, '98 fb; chr last in Elektra #18, '98 fb, chr last bts in Elektra #2, '96 fb), Theo (Stavros' adopte son) (prev 2 1st on-panel app) (prev 3 next in Elektra #18, '98), Natchios (cook (prev 2 chr last in Elektra #18, '98 fb), English army officers (bt sent Logan to Greece), Stavros' mother (bts, killed by SS, following Elektra #18, '98 fb), Greek resistance fighters (prev 3 in fb), pilot (bts flyir plane), travelers, cabbie; fish (dies), wolves, seabirds; Matt Murdock (in rfb); Silver Fox (name on gravestone); Nick Fury, John Wraith (prev mentioned, Wolverine asked them to bury him with Silver Fox), Hugo's deceased kidnappers (mentioned, died in various ways) inc Carlos Louie, mobsters, prisoner (prev 2 mentioned, each killed a kidnapper), parole board (mentioned, paroled Sawyer & another kidnapper)
LOCATIONS/ITEMS: Canadian wilderness inc Wolverine & Elektra's campsite, Wolverine & Silver Fox's cabin, skies above Atlantic Ocea Columbia University (in rfb), Greece inc Stavros' underground hideout (in fb), SS compound (destroyed) & Elektra's family home w/wir cellar / Elektra's sais, Wolverine & Elektra's luggage & camping gear inc axe & provisions, Silver Fox's grave marker, Wolverine's explosive entrenching tool (prev 2 in fb), Fairbairn knife (also in fb) & bouquet, airplane, taxi, Athos' crutch & pistol, Stavros' map (in fb) & lantern, Theo rifle, Sawyer's ropes (destroyed), Nazi airplanes (some destroyed), Greek underground's explosives (bts) & rifles (prev3 in fb), prisoner's knif heroin (prev 2 mentioned)
FLASHBACKS: Elektra and Matt Murdock fall in love (DD #168, '81 fb). Cpl. Logan teaches Stavros' underground cell how to fight Nazis. Whe they receive word that the SS murdered Stavros' mother, Logan volunteers to help Stavros exact vengeance.
SYNOPSIS: In the Canadian woods, wolves surround Wolverine and Elektra, but Wolverine quickly befriends them. The two continue the journey and arrive at Wolverine's old cabin, where he visits Silver Fox's grave. Wolverine then travels with Elektra to Greece, where they visit he childhood home and its staff — including Theo, the would-be assassin whom Elektra convinced Stavros to spare years before. Over a mea Stavros reminisces about WWII, unaware that Wolverine was the Corporal he met decades earlier. Stavros tells Elektra that the servants know the location of Sawyer, last survivor of the group that kidnapped Elektra's father years ago — but Elektra, tired of vengeance, asks them nc to confront him. Later, Stavros frees Sawyer from the cellar where the servants had secretly imprisoned him; Wolverine forcefully convince Sawyer not to go to the police, and hides Stavros' actions from Elektra.
NOTE: Elektra received a solo ongoing series the month after this issue, which was later written by Larry Hama. This issue reveals that Atho lost a leg and an eye in the events of DD #168, '81 fb. Mark Powers, who joined Wolverine's editorial team this issue, is inconsistently credite from W #106-122, '96-98; his title switches back and forth randomly between "associate editor" and "editor," often within the same issue. Thi index credits him correctly regardless of his apparent in-book title. This issue also has a 6-page feature promoting several Marvel-produced Sta Trek comic book titles.

"The Last Ronin" (40 pages)

CREDITS: Jeph Loeb (plot), Ralph Macchio (script), Ed McGuinness (pencils), Nathan Massengill & Norman Lee (inks), Richard Starkings & Comicraft (letters), Gloria Vasquez & Malibu's Hues (colors), Mark Powers (editor), Michael Golden (c pencils)
FEATURE CHARACTER: Wolverine (also on monitor)
GUEST STAR: Sunfire (also in rfb & pfb, last in X #25, '93, next in AFlt #1, '97)
SUPPORTING CAST: Yukio (last in XFac #113, '95)
VILLAINS: Bastion (merged Nimrod/Master Mold Sentinel construct, Operation: Zero Tolerance leader, last in X #57, '96, next in Ons:Ep, '97), Kingpin (in shadows, last in DCvM #4, '96, next in X #62, '97), Hand ninjas (some or others last in OtEdge #8, '96, next in Elektra #14, '98), General Hirito (government official)
OTHER CHARACTERS: Red Ronin (enormous samurai-themed robot, last in SAv #15/2, '89), Silver Samurai (also on monitor, last in W #82, '94, next bts in W #108, '96, next in Elektra #15, '98), Fujikawa Electronics engineers inc Tsu Fwon (cyberneticist, also on monitor, dies), Japanese troops (some on monitor) & government officials, Samurai & Yukio's sources (bts informing them), reporter (on TV), pilot (bts flying plane), bystanders; bird; Magneto (bts in rfb); SHIELD agents (mentioned, delivered Red Ronin to Fujikawa); Mariko Yashida (in photo)
LOCATIONS/ITEMS: Japan (also in rfb & pfb) inc Yashidas' ancestral manor, government meeting room, Fujikawa Electronics' Tokyo facility (destroyed), Hirito's base, news studio (on TV) & military compound (also on monitor) w/Sunfire's heat-resistant cell, skies over Pacific Ocean, Manhattan (in hologram) / Mariko's grave marker w/photo, Silver Samurai's armor & katana, Bastion's hologram projector w/remote control, Fujikawa's skylight & scaffolding w/elevator (prev 3 destroyed), Yukio's rope & Ultraudio 2400 listening device, compound's door (on monitor), video monitors (bts) & fence, Sunfire's inhibitor collar & cell door (prev 5 destroyed), guard's gun, ninjas' staff, shuriken, nunchuks & swords, engineer's energy lance, Tsu Fwon's comm system (bts) & remote interface system w/learning chip, Hirito's communication screen, Red Ronin's circuit boxes (all but 2 bts), detachable hand (prev 2 destroyed) & internal laser grid, bus, news camera (bts), Clan Yashida's Honor sword, airplane
FLASHBACKS: Sunfire is caught in Magneto's electromagnetic pulse (X #25, '93); his powers flare out of control (p).
SYNOPSIS: At Mariko's grave, the Silver Samurai confronts Wolverine and reveals that Sunfire has been imprisoned after his flare-up. Elsewhere, Bastion meets with Japanese officials, trying to gain support for Operation: Zero Tolerance, but Gen. Hirito stating that Japan has its own anti-mutant resource: Red Ronin. At Fujikawa, engineers debate the government's seizure of Red Ronin as Yukio spies on them. Wolverine and the Samurai break Sunfire out of his military cell; the Samurai then reveals that the Hand plans to steal Red Ronin. Wolverine investigates the Fujikawa facility and encounters Yukio. Hand ninjas burst in, but Red Ronin suddenly activates, controlled remotely by Hirito's cyberneticist Tsu Fwon. Sunfire arrives, but Ronin quickly captures him. Wolverine breaks into Ronin's head and destroys its circuit boxes, disabling it. Sunfire turns free but begins losing control again; Wolverine calms him down and later takes him to Canada, hoping the Hudsons can help him. Hirito kills Fwon on their mysterious "benefactor's" orders.
NOTE: X #63, '97 identifies Hirito's shadowed benefactor to be the Kingpin, Fujikawa's secret CEO. Bastion's true nature is revealed in MM&B Ann '98. In a story error, Wolverine acts as though he has never fought the Hand before this issue. Although not presented as such, pp.9-11 would be a three-page spread if viewed side-by-side. Fujikawa Electronics is also incorrectly spelled "Fujikama" once.

2ND STORY: "The Golden Temple" (15 pages)

CREDITS: Joe Kelly (writer), Tommy Lee Edwards (pencils), Richard Case (inks), John Workman (letters), Paul Becton (colors), Mark Powers (editor)
FEATURE CHARACTER: Wolverine (also as beggar & as the Golden Samurai in Amiko's drawings, next in UXM #338, '96, X #58, '96, MHol '96/5, Venom:TC #1-3, '96-97; UXM #339, X #59, UXM #340, DC/M:AA #2, all '96, X Ann '96, W #½, '97, W #107, '96)
SUPPORTING CAST: Amiko Kobayashi (also in photo, her own drawing & as samurai in her own imagination; also in fb, her chr 1st app, prior to UXM #181, '84; last in W #82, '94), Yukio (both next in W #107, '96)
VILLAINS: Robbers
OTHER CHARACTERS: Mr. & Mrs. Kuan (Amiko's occasional caregivers), Amiko's mother (in fb, her chr 1st app, prior to UXM #181, '84; also in photo), Shinkansen driver (bts operating train); ninjas (in Amiko's imagination & as her action figures); Buddhist gods (as statues)
LOCATIONS/ITEMS: Japan inc Golden Temple (also in fb & Amiko's imagination), train tracks & Kuans' Tokyo home / Amiko's sword & samurai armor, ninjas' swords, shuriken & dagger (all in Amiko's imagination), Amiko's school disciplinary file (mentioned), backpack, wooden sword, drawings, action figures & locket w/photo, Wolverine's coat & wrappings, Shinkansen bullet train, robbers' club, chain & switchblade
FLASHBACK: Amiko and her mother take a trip to the Golden Temple.
SYNOPSIS: Amiko imagines an exciting life as a samurai as she follows train tracks to the temple she remembers from her youth. As the frantic Kuans tell Yukio that the troubled and restless Amiko ran away, Wolverine eavesdrops outside. Later, Amiko encounters a beggar; when she mentions that she is looking for the Golden Temple, he offers to take her there. When the beggar falls in the path of an oncoming train, Amiko rushes back to pull him free. Later, they make camp, but robbers surround them. As Amiko confronts them, the "beggar" secretly pops his claws behind her, scaring them off. The two arrive at the temple, but find it abandoned and run-down. The beggar reveals himself as Wolverine, and tells Amiko that the hardest life lesson is accepting change and loss — but he has seen her courage, and knows that she can withstand the many changes her life has gone through.

LOGAN: SHADOW SOCIETY (December 1996)

"Shadow Society" (48 pages)

CREDITS: Howard Mackie (plot), Mark Jason (script), Tomm Coker (pencils), Keith Aiken & Octavio Cariello (inks), Richard Starkings & Comicraft's Emerson Miranda (letters), Christie Scheele & Malibu's Hues (colors), Richar Starkings & Comicraft's John Roshell (design), Dan Hosek (asst editor), Mark Bernardo & Mark Powers (editors)
FEATURE CHARACTER: Wolverine (chr last in W #26, '90 fb, chr next in MCP #72, '91)
GUEST STAR: Carol Danvers (CIA agent, also as "Miss Daniels," chr last in MsM #36, '09 fb, chr next in W #-1, '97
VILLAINS: Sabretooth (chr last in S&M #3, '97 fb, chr next in W #54, '07 fb), Sebastian Shaw (Hellfire Clu higher-up, absorbs kinetic energy, chr last in X:HC #4, '00 fb, chr next in X #29, '94 fb), Jacques Preen (arm dealer) & his sources (bts) & thugs inc Javert, Marius, Michel & Phillipe (prev 4 die), "Mutant Agenda" conspirator Sidney Hallorman (Defence Ministry bureaucrat, dies), Malcolm (Defence Ministry investigator, dies), CIA officia (dead); conspirators' assassins (some bts, die), Hellfire Club soldiers (some or others chr last in Cable #50, '98 fl 1 or another chr next in CX #6, '87, some or others chr next in CX #7/2, '87)
OTHER CHARACTERS: Neil Langram (Wolverine's Defence Ministry partner, secretly a mutant, dies), Patrick Hoolin ("Stranger Than Strange host, on TV), Dr. Perry Edwards (mutant-investigating author, also on TV, dies), Warren Worthington Jr. (Archangel's father), Warren Worthingto III (prev 2 chr last in XFac #47, '89 fb, chr next in X #29, '94 fb), Bob, Doug (prev 2 Dept. H guards), Hellfire Club members & doormen in Jonathan, Canadian Defence Ministry officials (bts working with CIA), technicians (bts providing computer), operator (bts on phone) & agent Carol's CIA superiors (bts sending her against Preen), pilot (bts flying plane), US intelligence group (bts gathering mutants), bar patron bystanders; Edwards' cats (bts in apartment); Senator Robert Kelly, Carol's next-door neighbor, Edwards' source (prev 3 mentioned); wome (on playing cards & in painting)
LOCATIONS/ITEMS: Canada inc Yukon, US/Canadian border w/secret installation & Ontario inc Dept. H complex (National Defence Headquarter Ottawa), Logan's apartment, Carol's hotel room, hockey stadium & Toronto bar w/Preen's showroom; "Stranger Than Strange" studio (on TV Greenwich Village (Manhattan) w/Edwards' apartment, Hellfire Club's New York branch w/nearby rooftops, Carol's safehouse / Neil's car & handgur TV cameras (bts), Carol's gas grenade (bts), rope, briefcase w/money & guns w/silencers, thugs' guns, Logan's knives, blanket, handgun, spik & sword, bar & apartment building windows (destroyed), pay phones, agents' masks, scanners & ambulance, police car, experimental comput (destroyed), Defence Ministry's computer mainframe (bts), assassins' cologne (bts), machine guns, rope lines & pistols (some bts) w/silencer (bts), Doug's gun, Bob's electronic key, Dept. H computer (destroyed), airplane (bts), "The Shadow Society" (Edwards' book), Hellfire Club windo (destroyed), limousines & computer, Jonathan's walkie-talkie, soldiers' radios (bts), rifles & armor, Sabretooth's bonds & bomb w/timer
SYNOPSIS: Sabretooth attacks and kills Logan's partner Neil Langram. Dr. Perry Edwards gives interviews, describing a secretive group calle "mutants." CIA agent Carol Danvers' cover is blown as she tries to buy weapons from an arms dealer, but Logan intervenes and saves her. Caro and Logan learn of Neil's death; knowing that Neil was investigating something, Logan tries unsuccessfully to hack into the Defence Ministry mainframe. That night, assassins attack Logan and Carol; realizing that the Ministry sent them, the two infiltrate its Dept. H subsection an discover a file labeled "Mutant Agenda" that bears Edwards' name. They travel to Manhattan and save Edwards from more assassins. Edward reveals that several mutants belong to the Hellfire Club. Logan breaks in and learns of a secret Canadian installation, as Sebastian Sha assigns Sabretooth to kill Logan. Locating the installation, Logan and Carol find all of its project heads — including several Ministry officials – dead, along with Edwards. Sabretooth attacks, explaining that organizations are competing to recruit mutants. He reveals that he killed Nei secretly a mutant, for refusing to join the Hellfire Club. Enraged, Logan savagely attacks Sabretooth, but the villain sets off a bomb, destroyin the complex. Later, Logan and Carol wonder who they can trust...
NOTE: This one-shot occurs just before Wolverine is kidnapped by his old employers, the Weapon X Program, who bond Adamantium to hi skeleton. Despite this issue's implication, Shaw is not yet a member of the Inner Circle; he later becomes Black Bishop, Black King and finall Lord Imperial. Carol becomes the super heroine Ms. Marvel; Warren Worthington III becomes Wolverine's X-Men teammate Archangel. Th Defence Ministry department that Wolverine works for here is clarified as Dept. K in OHMU:X, '04 — not to be confused with Dept. H, which thi issue reveals existed before James Hudson was assigned to run it. Bob and Doug are named for Bob and Doug McKenzie, fictional hosts c SCTV's "Great White North" sketch. Some of Carol's dialogue on p.29 is incorrectly attributed to Edwards.

WOLVERINE #107 (November 1996)

"Once Upon a Time in Little Tokyo" (22 pages)

CREDITS: Larry Hama (writer), Anthony Winn (pencils), Dan Green (inks), Richard Starkings & Comicraft' Kolja Fuchs (letters), Gloria Vasquez (colors), Jason Liebig (asst editor), Mark Powers (assoc editor), Bob Harra (editor), Adam Kubert (c pencils)
FEATURE CHARACTER: Wolverine (also in photo, rfb1 & rfb2)
SUPPORTING CAST: Amiko Kobayashi (also in rfb2), Yukio (both also in photo, last in W Ann '96/2)
VILLAINS: Pale Flower (Shirohana, Double Jade Clan Oyabun, 1st; also in fb, her chr 1st app, prior to issue Akatora (filmmaker, Death Touch Cult's new jonin, 1st; also as Kojiro, 1st), Emi, Sumi (prev 2 Akatora's brainwasher 1st, unnamed), Miho (Akatora's enforcer), Death Touch Cult Hand ninjas (some die, 1 voice only on phone, som or others last in W #87, '94) inc Akatora's spies (bts following Wolverine) & stage crew, Akatora's superior (bt ordering Amiko's kidnapping, see NOTE), Double Jade Clan Yakuza gangsters (some die)
OTHER CHARACTERS: Dai-Kumo & his Yakuza gangsters (both dead in fb following W #33, '90), Japanese special tactical forces, Yukio's neighbors, gambling parlor patrons & servants, singer (on TV), Akatora's victims (dead, as bones), bystander rats, flies; Silver Samurai (in rfb1), Amiko's mother, green dragon (prev 2 in rfb2); dragons (as tattoo & decoration), Japanese demon (as tattoo) Hello Kitty, koala bear (prev 2 as Amiko's dolls), horses (as Amiko's carousel)
LOCATIONS/ITEMS: Tokyo (also in rfb2 & as stage set) inc Yukio's rented room (in rfb1), Double Jade Clan's Shinjuku district gamblin hall, Yukio & neighbor's apartments w/nearby rooftop & Akatora's Tokyo Bay island w/soundstage, dungeon & Amiko's playroom, Dai-Kumo' mansion (in fb) / Wolverine's image inducer (bts) & presents inc bicycle, noodle vendor's cart & cellphone, ninjas' phone (bts), swords, guns & wrist radio, Yukio's chains & photo w/frame (destroyed), special forces' bullhorn, tank, spotlight, armored vehicle & rifles w/infrared scope, Silve Samurai's armor, Clan Yashida's Honor Sword (prev 2 in rfb1), apartments' windows & wall (prev 2 destroyed), neighbor's motorcycle, Akatora'

nines (all but 1 bts), cellphone, Kojiro costume & blast door w/security system (bts), prop tanks & jets, crew's camera, fan, fire extinguisher & negaphone, Yakuza swords & guns, Shirohana's sword & blowfish, Miho's submachine gun, Amiko's carousel, balloons & ice cream, Reiko's lower & umbrella sword (prev 2 in fb)

FLASHBACKS: Wolverine gives Silver Samurai the Honor Sword (W #82, '94). Wolverine cradles Amiko and her dying mother (UXM #181, 84). Pale Flower stands over the bodies of her father Dai-Kumo and his henchmen.

SYNOPSIS: Wolverine finds Hand ninjas ransacking Yukio and Amiko's apartment. He kills the ninjas, but Japanese soldiers surround the building, demanding his surrender. Wolverine smashes into the neighbors' apartment, borrows their motorcycle and flees. Elsewhere, ninja jonin Akatora takes a break from filming a monster movie to get a progress report from his informant, a noodle vendor. Wolverine asks for sanctuary at a Yakuza gambling hall, citing his ties to Clan Yashida. Pale Flower, Oyabun of the Double Jade Clan, agrees to his request. Akatora taunts the captive Yukio, but his servants pamper Amiko. Akatora orders Amiko's subliminal brainwashing and has the noodle vendor alert the soldiers of Wolverine's location. Pale Flower feeds Wolverine a meal, but reveals that she is Dai-Kumo's daughter, and that she has just poisoned Wolverine for his part in Dai-Kumo's death. Wolverine shrugs off the poison's effects — just as the soldiers burst in…

NOTE: Wolverine uses an image inducer to appear human in W #107-109 & 111-114, '96-97; his healing factor slowly restores his body to normal in the meantime. Akatora's name is a play on the word "actor." His character Kojiro's name is intentionally similar to Gojira, Godzilla's original Japanese name. W #109, '97 reveals that most of his stage crew are also ninjas, and that he is acting on orders from an unnamed Hand master. Akatora's title of jonin is revealed in OHMU HC5, '08; it remains unrevealed how or when he took control of the Death Touch Cult from Matsuo Tsurayaba, or if Matsuo ever took it back. Emi and Sumi are named next issue. This issue also includes a 6-page feature promoting Marvel Vision's "Time Slip" feature.

WOLVERINE #108 (December 1996)

"East Is East…" (22 pages)

CREDITS: Larry Hama (writer), Anthony Winn (pencils), Dan Green & Vince Russell (inks), Richard Starkings & Comicraft's Kolja Fuchs (letters), Joe Rosas (colors), Jason Liebig (asst editor), Mark Powers (assoc editor), Bob Harras (editor), Adam Kubert (c pencils)
FEATURE CHARACTER: Wolverine
SUPPORTING CAST: Yukio, Amiko Kobayashi
VILLAINS: Iron Monk (nearly indestructible Hand master, dies), Yohei (Hand spy, infiltrated Clan Yashida, 1st, see NOTE), Akatora, Emi, Sumi, Death Touch Cult Hand ninjas (named) inc Cyber-Ninjas (1st), Blue Monkey Gang (dockland street gang)
OTHER CHARACTERS: Silver Samurai (bts sending Yohei, last in W Ann '96, next in Elektra #15, '98), Pale Flower, noodle vendor, Tokyo police, Akatora's victims (dead, as bones), paramedics (bts at police station); rat, lies, seagulls; Dai-Kumo (mentioned, sent Pale Flower to Swiss boarding school), Special Agent Daryll Smith (named), FBI Mutant Task Force (prev 2 mentioned, hired noodle vendor), vendor's other clients (mentioned); Hello Kitty, Bart Simpson, Raggedy Ann, animals (prev 4 as Amiko's dolls), horses (as Yukio's carousel)
LOCATIONS/ITEMS: Tokyo inc waterfront, Akatora's island w/dungeon & Amiko's playroom & Shinjuku District inc police station holding cells w/underground passageway, Pale Flower's Swiss boarding school (mentioned) / Wolverine's image inducer (bts), police machine guns, Iron Monk's gong & rosary beads, cell doors (destroyed) w/bars, cinderblock (destroyed), Silver Samurai's note, Clan Yashida's Honor Sword, Amiko's dolls, sweets & carousel, Yukio's chains, Sumi's whip, Akatora's cellphone & blast door w/security system (bts), ninja's gun, noodle vendor's cart & cellphone, ambulances (bts), Blue Monkey Gang's club, chain & knives, Emi & Sumi's knives & bandages, Yohei's lighter, dock crane w/chains & crate, Cyber-Ninjas' swords, guns & cybernetic parts
SYNOPSIS: As Wolverine and Pale Flower sit in jail, the Iron Monk attacks, revealing that he cannot be harmed by mortal weapons. As the Monk batters Wolverine, Yohei arrives and delivers the Honor Sword, a gift from the Silver Samurai. Wolverine impales the Monk with the Honor Sword; forged from meteorite iron, it kills him. Elsewhere, Emi and Sumi continue grooming Amiko with candy and gifts, while the noodle vendor informs Akatora of the Monk's failure. At the docks, Yohei easily defeats a gang of thugs. Pale Flower reveals that Yohei is Clan Yashida's secret weapon; he rebuts by revealing that Pale Flower is a mutant. Learning that the noodle vendor has been selling secrets to the FBI, Akatora sends Emi and Sumi to kill him, but they fail. Wolverine explains that he must rescue Yukio and Amiko. Yohei volunteers to aid him — as does Pale Flower, who now sees Wolverine's nobility. Akatora decides to send his cybernetic ninjas against both the noodle vendor and Wolverine.
NOTE: Having joined Wolverine's rescue mission, Pale Flower will no longer be listed as a Villain; however, Yohei is revealed as a Hand spy next issue. Pale Flower's mutant powers are never revealed, but are implied to be a limited form of telepathy. Venom:TC #3, '97 reveals that Daryll Smith, first mentioned here, vanished because Dirt Nap absorbed him. The digital lettering on several pages is off-register, most notably on p.10, where balloons cover Wolverine's face and point to empty spaces instead of characters. This issue also includes a 2-page feature promoting the '97 CoH series.

WOLVERINE #109 (January 1997)

(Untitled, 22 pages)

CREDITS: Larry Hama (writer, uncredited), Anthony Winn (pencils, uncredited), Dan Green (inks, uncredited), Richard Starkings & Comicraft (letters, uncredited), Jason Liebig (asst editor), Mark Powers (assoc editor), Bob Harras (editor, uncredited), Adam Kubert (c pencils)
FEATURE CHARACTER: Wolverine (also in Amiko's hallucination)
SUPPORTING CAST: Amiko Kobayashi (also in her own hallucination), Yukio (both next in Elektra #15, '98)
VILLAINS: Akatora (also as Kojiro & bear), Yohei (dies), Emi, Sumi, Death Touch Cult Hand ninjas (some die, some or others next bts in Elektra #15, '98) inc Cyber-Ninjas (die) & Akatora's stage crew & actors (also as Monsters from Beyond the Pacific Rim, die) inc Toshi
OTHER CHARACTERS: Pale Flower, noodle vendor; flies, rat, starfish; green dragon (also as Wolverine), Amiko's mother (prev 2 in Amiko's hallucination); horses (as Amiko's carousel), bear (as Amiko's doll)
LOCATIONS/ITEMS: Tokyo (also in hallucination & as stage set) inc dockside alleyway & Tokyo Bay inc Akatora's island w/dungeon (bts) & Amiko's playroom / Wolverine's image inducer (bts), Cyber-Ninjas' cybernetic parts (some destroyed), swords, guns, mace & axe, noodle

vendor's knife, cleaver, machine gun & cart w/pan, bowl & chopsticks, Yohei's handguns & poisoned dagger, Pale Flower's sword, guns & knives, Akatora's bicycle, gun, sword, Kojiro costume, bear costume w/hypnotic hat & bear doll w/disguised poison dagger, Amiko's calliope & carousel, Emi & Sumi's bandages, ferry w/life raft & oars, actors' guns & costumes (destroyed) w/morphing guns & steel tentacles, crew's lights, set & slate & cameras w/headsets, Clan Yashida's Honor Sword, ninjas' swords, Yukio's chains (bts)

SYNOPSIS: As Cyber-Ninjas menace the noodle vendor, Wolverine interrupts but refuses to help. The vendor defeats the ninjas, but others arrive; Wolverine agrees to help battle them, but demands to know Yukio and Amiko's location. Elsewhere, Emi, Sumi and Akatora hypnotize Amiko, convincing her that the dragon that killed her mother was Wolverine in disguise. Amiko wants revenge; Akatora gives her a poisoned dagger hidden inside a doll. Wolverine, Yohei, Pale Flower and a reluctant noodle vendor pilot a ferry to Akatora's island, where Akatora films a monster movie on the beach. Wolverine crashes the set, but the cast attacks him, impaling themselves on his claws and weighing him down. While Wolverine's allies assault the island and rescue Amiko and Yukio, Wolverine defeats Akatora. The villain taunts Wolverine, claiming that one of his allies is a Hand sleeper agent. Wolverine smells blowfish toxin on Yohei's blade and quickly kills him; Akatora escapes. Wolverine and his allies depart the island, unaware that Amiko has been brainwashed.

NOTE: This issue has no interior title or creator credits. Most creators can be deduced from their styles, but the colorist is unknown. This issue reveals that most of Akatora's crew are ninjas, and that Akatora was carrying out an unnamed Hand master's orders. Amiko reports to the Hand in Elektra #15, '98, but her brainwashing plotline is dropped after that; presumably Emi and Sumi's work wore off. Some of Akatora's dialogue on p.20 is incorrectly attributed to Wolverine. This issue also includes a 2-page feature promoting Marvel's online CyberComics.

WOLVERINE #110 (February 1997)

"Lesser Beasts" (22 pages)

CREDITS: Tom DeFalco (writer), Joe Bennett (pencils), Joe Pimentel (inks), Richard Starkings & Comicraft's Emerson Miranda (letters), Joe Andreani, Paul Becton & Graphic Colorworks (colors), Jason Liebig (asst editor), Mark Powers (assoc editor), Bob Harras (editor), Adam Kubert (c pencils), Tim Townsend (c inks)
FEATURE CHARACTER: Wolverine (next in M:S&L, '97, MFan #2, '96; X #61, IHulk #454-455, all '97, X Ann '97)
GUEST STAR: Shaman (Dr. Michael Twoyoungmen, Sarcee mystic, last in OtEdge #2, '95, next in AFlt #3, '97)
VILLAINS: Great Beast (other-dimensional mystical creature, as spirit & possessing bear, also as cave painting, others last in AFlt #64, '88, next in XMan #39, '98), William "Jocko" Jacquomo, Peter "Petey" Hale (prev 2 robbers)
OTHER CHARACTERS: Bob & Catherine Totebind (vacationing married couple), Alan Totebind (their son), convenience store employees & patrons, Mounties; bears (1 also possessed by Great Beast, another in cave painting) animal (as bones), birds; Elektra, Stick, Professor X (prev 3 in Wolverine's thoughts); Catherine's father (army Major), Shaman's grandfather, Sarcee children (prev 3 mentioned), raven spirit (bts, spoke to Shaman in dream); cavemen, buffalo (prev 2 in cave painting)
LOCATIONS/ITEMS: Canadian convenience store & wilderness preserve w/cave / Great Beast's clay pot, Jocko's bandage, shotgun, backpack & stolen money & beer, Petey's handgun, backpack & stolen car, Mounties' guns & barricades, Shaman's medicine pouch (hereinafter considered his standard equipment and not listed separately) w/animal bones, Totebinds' Jeep (destroyed) & camping equipment inc hammer & tent w/spikes & pole, Alan's video game, Stick's bo staff (in Wolverine's thoughts)
SYNOPSIS: When a bear opens a clay pot in a cave, a spirit emerges and possesses it. Elsewhere, Jocko and Petey rob a convenience store. Mounties learn that they are hiding in a wilderness preserve, and Shaman asks Wolverine to help track them down, warning that he has mystically sensed a Great Beast's revival. Mounties stop the Totebinds from entering the preserve; Catherine berates the meek Bob into sneaking in, but the family soon encounters Jocko and Petey. Wolverine tracks down the robbers and orders them away from the Totebinds, but the possessed bear suddenly attacks. Catherine, Alan and the robbers flee, leaving Bob behind. As Wolverine savagely battles the bear, Bob tries to help but is knocked aside. Struggling to control his animal urge to kill, Wolverine sheathes his claws and knocks the bear out; Shaman arrives and exorcises the Beast. Elsewhere, the robbers decide to shoot Catherine and Alan, but Wolverine arrives and stops Petey — and Bob, finding his courage, knocks out Jocko.
NOTE: It is unclear which Great Beast appears here. Aside from this issue, only seven Great Beasts have ever appeared on-panel — but Snowbird transforms into a previously unknown eighth Beast in Herc #119, '08, so others may exist, and this may be another Beast. However it vaguely resembles Ranaq the Great Devourer; if this is Ranaq, he appears here following AFlt #18, '85. This issue also includes a 2-page feature promoting the MVision magazine.

WOLVERINE #111 (March 1997)

"Restoration" (22 pages)

CREDITS: Larry Hama (writer), Anthony Winn (pencils), Dan Green (inks), Richard Starkings & Comicraft (letters), Dana Moreshead & Graphic Colorworks (colors), Jason Liebig (asst editor), Mark Powers (editor), Adam Kubert (c pencils)
FEATURE CHARACTER: Wolverine
GUEST STARS: X-Men: Phoenix (also as Marvel Girl in photo), Cannonball (next in NM:TD #1, '97), Storm (next in W #113, '97) (all last in UXM Ann '97), Bishop (last in Cable #41, '97), Gambit, Beast (prev 2 last in XMU #14, '97) (prev 3 next in UXM #341, '97), Cyclops (last in Cable #44, '97, next in UXM #342, '97); Iceman (last in X Ann '97, next in XMU #15, '97) (prev 3 also in photo)
SUPPORTING CAST: Mariko Yashida (as spirit, also in Wolverine's memory, last in W #57, '92, last bts in W #60, '92, possibly next as spirit in Herc #129, '09, see NOTE; corpse next bts in W #11, '11)
VILLAIN: Ogun (as spirit, last in W #89, '95)
OTHER CHARACTERS: Zoe Culloden (in hologram, last in UXM #332, '96, last bts in Venom:TC #1, '96, next in Dp #1, '97), Stick (last in Elektra #2, '96, next in Elektra #7, '97 fb), cabbie (voice only), FedEx driver (bts delivering package), Harry's Hideaway staff (bts serving X-Men), Auger Inn bartender, motorcycle salesman; Madeline Drake, William Drake (prev 2 Iceman's parents), Professor X (also mentioned in government custody), Angel (prev 4 in photos), O'Donnell (bts), Archie Corrigan, Silver Fox, Rose Wu (prev 4 in Wolverine's memory); Big Bopper, Patsy Cline, Buddy Holly, Glenn Miller, Ricky Nelson, Otis Redding, Lynyrd Skynyrd, Ritchie Valens, Stevie Ray Vaughan (prev mentioned, musicians on jukebox)
LOCATIONS/ITEMS: X-Mansion w/Danger Room, Salem Center inc Harry's Hideaway (X-Men's favorite eatery), Auger Inn & motorcycle

hop / Wolverine's image inducer (bts), luggage, motorcycle & new motorcycle w/keys, Clan Yashida's Honor Sword, taxi, X-Men's table, car & olographic projectors, Iceman's photos & belongings, FedEx truck (bts) & package, Zoe's holographic projector, wooden box w/artifact (bts), Storm's pruning shears & plants w/mutant flower, Auger Inn jukebox, Danger Room remote control, Ogun's energy sword, Stick's bo staff
SYNOPSIS: Wolverine returns to the X-Mansion, checking in with Cannonball, who has been caring for his motorcycle, and learning that Iceman is leaving to care for his injured father. Zoe Culloden delivers a mysterious artifact, asking Wolverine to keep it safe. Storm gives Iceman one of her mutant flowers as a going-away present, and comments that it is unable to survive in a standard environment — seemingly like many of the X-Men. The team visits Harry's Hideaway, but Wolverine goes to the Auger Inn, drinking toasts to his dead friends. Depressed, Wolverine enters the Danger Room, but a spirit appears and raises Mariko Yashida's soul, offering to bring her back to life. Wolverine rejects the offer and drives the spirit off. Stick appears, putting Mariko back at rest and warning Wolverine that he and Elektra were preparing him for this foe all along. Wolverine buys Cannonball a new motorcycle and rides off on his old one, determined to prove that he can survive in the real world.
NOTE: Wolverine's posture is extremely hunched here. Though he continues to use an image inducer in his own series, his appearances without it in other books show that he still looks partly animalistic. Wolverine returns to wearing his standard cowl this issue, although he still occasionally appears in other titles with his bandana mask. Iceman's father heckled anti-mutant Presidential candidate Graydon Creed in X #58, '96, and was badly beaten by Creed's thugs prior to UXM #340, '97. Iceman's photo of the X-Men was first seen in UXM #289, '92. The artifact that Zoe entrusts to Wolverine is never revealed. This issue's letters page has a LOC from future Marvel Handbook writer David Wiltfong. This issue also includes a 3-page feature promoting the '97-98 KZ series. In Herc #129, '09, many deceased characters' spirits appear in the afterlife, including Mariko's; however, as discussed in W #4, '82's NOTE, it is uncertain if anything that living characters witness there is real.

WOLVERINE #112 (April 1997)

"The Light at the End of the Day" (22 pages)

CREDITS: Larry Hama (writer), Anthony Winn (pencils), Dan Green (inks), Richard Starkings & Comicraft's Emerson Miranda (letters), Joe Rosas & Graphic Colorworks (colors), Jason Liebig (asst editor), Mark Powers (editor), Adam Kubert (c pencils)
FEATURE CHARACTER: Wolverine (also in W #113, '97)
GUEST STAR: Phoenix
VILLAINS: Ogun (as spirit & possessing mime), Sturm, Drang (prev 2 street thugs)
OTHER CHARACTERS: Helen Bach (construction site foreman, 1st but chr last in W #114, '97 fb), Clive (Kirsten's paraplegic boyfriend), Kirsten (apartment superintendent) (prev 2 last in Venom:STA #5, '95), juggling mime (also possessed by Ogun), Wolverine's landlord (bts talking to Kirsten about Wolverine), crazies, cook (voice only), winos, garbage truck & ambulance drivers (prev 3 bts, heard outside), café patrons, volunteer construction workers, charitable foundation officers (bts funding construction project), hot dog vendor (in shadow), bystanders inc Elmore & his mother; birds; Uma Thurman, Jackie Estacado, model, girl (prev 4 on posters); John Donne (quoted)
LOCATIONS/ITEMS: Manhattan's East Village inc basement, park, diner, Wolverine's new apartment, Third Eye Café & Augean construction site / Kirsten's guitar & order pad, Clive's wheelchair & laptop, mime's mask, unicycle & Indian clubs, Wolverine's image inducer (bts), luggage, pull-up bar & motorcycle (destroyed) w/chain, Clan Yashida's Honor Sword, Ogun's chain, knives & cleaver, pay phone, garbage truck, ambulance (prev 2 bts), Helen's hammer, screwdriver & lunchbox, workers' tools (some bts), boards & hard hats, hot dog vendor's cart, Sturm's handgun
SYNOPSIS: Wolverine arrives in the East Village, and stops two thugs from hassling Kirsten and Clive. Kirsten offers to get Wolverine an apartment in her building; nearby, a spirit leaves a street mime into a basement. Wolverine calls Phoenix and explains that he's testing himself, seeing if he can live in the normal world. Over the next few days he explores the East Village, but can't stop blaming himself for Professor X's transformation into Onslaught. Late one night, Wolverine sees the mime ride past, looking much more sinister than before. Wolverine decides to get a job; Kirsten recommends a construction site where volunteers are rebuilding an apartment complex destroyed during Onslaught's attack. Wolverine joins the crew and befriends the foreman, Helen Bach, who makes it clear that she abhors violence. Heading home, Wolverine and Helen discover the thugs destroying Wolverine's motorcycle; when one grabs Helen she snaps and beats him badly. Wolverine disarms the other, but Helen refuses to explain herself. Wolverine enters his apartment, where the mime awaits…
NOTE: Sturm and Drang's names reference "Sturm und Drang," a German artistic movement dating from the 1760s that emphasized extremes of violent emotion. This issue's final panel occurs after the first panel of next issue. Anthony Winn, a Top Cow Studio alumnus, included several Top Cow references in this issue's background: a poster advertises Top Cow's "the Darkness," and graffiti includes several Top Cow artists' names, including Marlo Alquiza, Eric Basaldua, Joe Benitez and Joe Weems. This issue's letters page seems to have been meant for next issue; it refers to Storm appearing here (she appears next issue) and teases Lady Deathstrike's appearance "next issue" (she appears in W #114, '97). This issue also includes a 3-page feature promoting IHulk #454, '97.

WOLVERINE #113 (May 1997)

"The Wind from the East" (22 pages)

CREDITS: Larry Hama (writer), Leinil Francis Yu (pencils), Edgar Tadeo (inks) (see NOTE), Richard Starkings & Comicraft's Emerson Miranda (letters), Joe Rosas (colors), Jason Liebig (asst editor), Mark Powers (editor), Adam Kubert (c pencils), Matt Banning (c inks), Liquid! (c colors)
FEATURE CHARACTER: Wolverine (also in W #112, '97, also in fb between W:O #17, '07 fb & W #62, '08 fb)
GUEST STARS: Daimon Hellstrom ("Hellstorm," lord of Hell, last in NiM #2/2, '95); X-Men: Storm (last in W #111, '97), Phoenix
VILLAINS: Ogun (as spirit & possessing Phoenix, Helen & mime; also as Japanese Army Captain in fb, his chr 1st app, prior to W #103, '96 fb), Japanese Army Sergeant (in fb, dies)
OTHER CHARACTERS: Ancient One (powerful mage, as Sorcerer Supreme in fb between MW:SW, '06 & DrS #75, '86 fb), Stick (in fb, his chr 1st app, prior to Elek:RE #2, '95 fb), Helen Bach, juggling mime (prev 2 also possessed by Ogun), Clive, Kirsten, Japanese soldier, Shanghai bystanders (prev 2 in fb), New York bystanders; historical figure (as painting), singers (on poster), Jollibee (fast food mascot, on bystander's shirt), dragons (as crystal stand)
LOCATIONS/ITEMS: East Village inc Wolverine's apartment, Hellstrom's Necromanteion (Fire Lake, Massachusetts); Shanghai, China seaport (in fb) / Wolverine's image inducer (bts) & motorcycle, mime's unicycle & mask, Ogun's sword, gun (prev 2 in fb), knives & cleaver,

wooden box (also in crystal & in fb) w/artifact (bts), Stick's bo staff, soldier & Sergeant's rifles w/bayonets (prev 3 in fb), Phoenix's note, Kirsten guitar, Clive's wheelchair, Hellstrom's cane & scrying crystal

FLASHBACK: In Shanghai, young Stick and the Ancient One keep the box away from Japanese troops. The Sergeant beats the Ancient One until Wolverine intervenes. Ogun kills the Sergeant for dishonorable conduct, but Wolverine makes him spare the other soldier. Impressed, Ogun offers to tutor Wolverine, but he declines.

SYNOPSIS: The mime taunts Wolverine, juggling knives and the artifact box. Sensing something familiar about him, Wolverine grabs the mime — who breaks his own wrist escaping Wolverine's grasp, but continues fighting. Wolverine realizes that the mime is possessed. Helen decides to return to Wolverine's apartment and explain her outburst, but is discouraged when she sees the gorgeous Phoenix and Storm entering the building. The two mutants interrupt Wolverine's battle and disable the mime. Phoenix tries to exorcise the spirit, but it possesses her body and throws one of the mime's knives at Storm. Wolverine leaps in front of it; stunned by his selflessness, the spirit is distracted and Phoenix expels it. Outside, the spirit possesses Helen; elsewhere, Daimon Hellstrom senses the artifact…

NOTE: Artists Leinil Yu and Edgar Tadeo are collectively sub-credited as "Starfire Visuals" in W #113-118, '97; referring to Whilce Portacio's art studio, which they both work for. This issue's first panel occurs before the final panel of last issue. Ogun's dojo's name and location are revealed here. Wolverine's word balloon on p.4 panel 1 incorrectly points off-panel. Hellstrom uses the last name "Hellstorm" here, a common alias. Names on the buzzer of Wolverine's apartment building include BMX bikers Dennis McCoy and Mat Hoffman, rock musician James Iha and Filipina actress Amanda Page. This issue's letters page once again seems to have been meant for next issue; it teases the X-Men's battle with Bastion "next issue" (it occurs in W #115, '97). This issue also includes a 3-page feature promoting IHulk #454, '97.

WOLVERINE #114 (June 1997)

"For the Snark Was a Boojum, You See!" (22 pages)

CREDITS: Larry Hama (writer), Leinil Francis Yu (pencils), Edgar Tadeo (inks), Richard Starkings & Comicraft's Emerson Miranda (letters), Joe Rosas (colors), Jason Liebig (asst editor), Mark Powers (editor), Adam Kubert (c pencils), Liquic (c colors)

FEATURE CHARACTER: Wolverine (next in CDawn #1, UXM #342, X #62-66, all '97, W #58, '07 fb)

GUEST STARS: X-Men: Phoenix, Storm (both next in UXM #342, '97); Daimon Hellstrom (next in Pun #1, '98)

VILLAINS: Lady Deathstrike (last in Dom #3, '97, next in Cap #1, '98), Ogun (a spirit, shadow, & possessing Deathstrike & Helen, next in Ex #111, '97), Iraqi elite guard unit (in fb)

OTHER CHARACTERS: Helen Bach (also in photo; also in fb, her chr 1st app, prior to W #112, '97), Clive, Kirsten, Helen's army co-pilot (in fb), bystanders inc Marvin & Sabine; Helen's dog; Donald Pierce (mentioned, gave Deathstrike a self-repair program), Helen's superior (mentioned, discharged her; 1 or another also in photo in fb); Weezer: Brian Bell, Rivers Cuomo, Matt Sharp, Patrick Wilson (prev 4 on poster), Helen's loved ones (in photos); Garfield (as doll), cat (as canister), eagle (as Helen's patch)

LOCATIONS/ITEMS: East Village w/alley, Helen's apartment (also in fb), Marvin & Sabine's apartment (destroyed) & Wolverine's apartment, astral plane, Iraq (in fb) inc Baghdad prison (mentioned in fb) / Wolverine's image inducer (bts) & window (destroyed), Clive's wheelchair, Kirsten guitar, Deathstrike's cybernetic healing circuits w/metamorphic plastic skin, wooden box w/artifact (bts), Helen's guns, knives, grenades, ammo belt (prev 4 also in fb) & Blackhawk helicopter (in fb, destroyed), water tower (destroyed), Ogun's psychic chains (destroyed) & energy sword, Iraqi guards' helicopter & guns (prev 2 in fb)

FLASHBACK: Iraqi soldiers capture and abuse Helen during the Gulf War. After her release, she makes a bunker in her apartment, determined not to be hurt again.

SYNOPSIS: Wolverine tracks the possessed Helen, but encounters Daimon Hellstrom, who warns him to keep the artifact safe. Lady Deathstrike attacks Wolverine, revealing that the box belongs to her family and demanding its return. At Wolverine's apartment, Phoenix and Storm look in the box and realize the danger of its contents falling into the wrong hands. As Wolverine and Lady Deathstrike battle, the possessed Helen reaches "her" apartment and discovers a weapons cache. Wolverine agrees that the box belongs to Deathstrike, but asks her to let him discuss its contents with Zoe Culloden before returning it. Deathstrike, curious to learn more, agrees to a truce. Helen bursts into Wolverine's apartment, shooting at Phoenix and Storm, but Phoenix telepathically exorcises the spirit possessing her. As Wolverine and Deathstrike arrive, the spirit returns and possesses Deathstrike, reshaping her synthetic face and revealing its identity — Ogun — before fleeing into the night.

NOTE: This issue's title is the final line from Lewis Carroll's 1874 nonsense poem, "the Hunting of the Snark." Phoenix notes here that Wolverine's feral regression has more or less halted itself; his posture has improved noticeably here, and the special font used for his word balloons has become less jagged. Some of Helen's dialogue on p.19 is incorrectly attributed to Phoenix. The artifact plotline is dropped after this issue, and never resolved. Although previous issues have had reprints or newsstand editions with different or altered covers, this is the first issue of the series to have a true variant cover. This issue also has a 3-page feature promoting the '97-99 AFlt series.

WOLVERINE #-1 (July 1997)

"A Whiff of Sartre's Madeleine!" (22 pages)

CREDITS: Larry Hama (writer), Leinil Francis Yu (pencils, p.1 background), Cary Nord (pencils, c pencils), Edgar Tadeo (inks, p.1 background), Scott Hanna (inks), Richard Starkings & Comicraft's Emerson Miranda (letters), Joe Rosas (colors), Jason Liebig (asst editor), Mark Powers & Bob Harras (editors), Tim Townsend (c inks)

FEATURE CHARACTER: Wolverine (also in rfb & photo, on monitor & bts & as hologram in scene from W #115, '97; chr last in AFlt #3/2, '83, chr next in UXM #147, '81 fb)

GUEST STARS: Black Widow (Natalia "Natasha" Romanova, Russian spy, chr last in BW:DO #2, '10 fb), Carol Danvers (chr last in L:SS, '96), Nick Fury (chr last in W/NF:SC, '89 fb) (all chr next in BFF:Ben #1, '00), Ben Grimm (chr last in Thing #10, '84 fb, chr next in MFan #46/2, '89), James Hudson (chr last in AFlt #3/2, '83 fb), Heather Hudson (chr last in AFlt #-1, '97 fb) (prev 2 also in rfb, chr next in UXM #147, '81 fb), Stan Lee (Marvel Comics founding father, as chef, see NOTE)

VILLAINS: Sabretooth (also in photo, chr last in W #54, '07 fb, chr next bts in W #126, '98 fb, chr next in W:O Ann, '07 fb), Silver Fox (also on monitor, chr last in W #61, '92 fb, chr next in W #50, '92), Hydra agents (some or others chr last in Tb #-1, '97, chr next in XMF #4, '01 fb) inc covert team (some or all die)

OTHER CHARACTERS: Dr. Myron MacLain (inventor of Adamantium, chr last in Av Ann '01/2, chr next in Av #66, '69), CIA Special Agent Lawson (as bum), diner patron, James' government connections (bts arranging Wolverine's flight), cabbie (in shadow), MacLain's secretary, travelers; Maverick (in photo), Captain America & his assailant (bts), Lord Dark Wind & his subject (prev 4 in MacLain's thoughts); X-Men: Cannonball, Cyclops, Phoenix, Storm; OZT troops (prev 5 bts & as holograms), Prime Sentinels (some bts, all also as holograms), Bastion, Jubilee (prev 8 in scene from W #115, '97)

LOCATIONS/ITEMS: OZT's base (in story & as hologram in scene from W #115, '97), Ottawa airport w/snack bar, Wood Buffalo National Park (in rfb) w/Hudsons' cabin, Washington DC (also on monitor) inc Hydra base & Department of Agriculture's Annex B w/alley & MacLain's lab, battlefield, Dark Wind's lab (prev 2 in MacLain's thoughts) / OZT transport jet (also as hologram), troops' armor, blasters & hover-platforms, X-Men's power-dampening restraints, Storm's polymer prison (prev 5 as holograms), Bastion's holographic projector (bts), Jubilee's restraints & memory-reading helmet (all in scene from W #115, '97), Hudsons' rifle (in rfb), Stan's spatula, Ben's experimental jet w/ejection seats, taxi, Lawson's walkie-talkie, Hydra's surveillance cameras (1 in car), infrared scanners, comm system, seeker missile (prev 4 bts), computers, monitor & photos, secretary's intercom (bts), Hudson's letter (mentioned), MacLain's X-ray machine, assailant's gun (bts), Captain America's shield, Dark Wind's sword (prev 3 in MacLain's thoughts), Sabretooth's handgun & cowboy hat, covert team's masks, guns & cars (destroyed) w/comm unit, Fury's car (destroyed), handguns, cigars & lighter, Carol's gun, Black Widow's bazooka, Wolverine's luggage

FLASHBACK: Wolverine attacks the Hudsons, who shoot him; later, he discovers his metal claws (AFlt #33, '86 fb).

SYNOPSIS: Stan Lee interrupts the regularly scheduled issue to present a tale of Wolverine's past. James Hudson sends the amnesiac Wolverine, who seeks answers about his metal skeleton and claws, to Adamantium inventor Dr. Myron MacLain; test pilot Ben Grimm flies Wolverine to Washington DC. As the CIA and Hydra spy on him, Wolverine meets with MacLain, who is astonished that Adamantium could be bonded to bone. CIA agent Sabretooth interrupts; pleased that Wolverine does not recognize him, Sabretooth pulls a gun — but a Hydra team attacks, trying to capture Wolverine. Nick Fury and Carol Danvers crash the brawl and rescue Wolverine; Hydra pursues them, but the Black Widow arrives and destroys their vehicle, telling Wolverine not to ally with any of their organizations. Sabretooth catches up, intent on finishing his assignment, but Wolverine defeats him and departs, confused. Hydra aims a missile at Wolverine from afar, but their leader Silver Fox orders him spared — for now.

NOTE: Most Marvel titles dated July '97 were "Flashback" issues, numbered #-1, which told stories set in the past and had 1960s-style panel layouts, lettering and letters pages. Stan Lee introduced each issue, interrupting any ongoing storylines; p.1 features Lee standing on the art from W #115, '97 p.1, the issue that would have otherwise have been published this month. Though Lee also poses as the airport chef when introducing the story, he is not an actual in-universe character and thus has no chronology. Nick Fury incorrectly remarks here that Wolverine and Carol Danvers don't know one another. They have worked together on several prior occasions, including L:SS, '96, but Fury may not be aware of their history. This issue's letters page is temporarily re-titled "Letters to Logan!"

WOLVERINE #115 (August 1997)

"In the Face of It" (22 pages)

CREDITS: Larry Hama (writer), Leinil Francis Yu (pencils), Edgar Tadeo (inks), Richard Starkings & Comicraft's Emerson Miranda (letters), Joe Rosas (colors), Jason Liebig (asst editor), Mark Powers (editor)

FEATURE CHARACTER: Wolverine (also as Daria, as hologram, on monitor & in rfb)

GUEST STARS: X-Men: Cannonball, Cyclops, Storm (all also as Prime Sentinels), Phoenix (also as Bastion) (all also as holograms & on monitor, last in X #66, '97); Professor X (between X #66-67, '97), Jubilee (also bts in rfb, between GenX #29-30, '97)

VILLAINS: Bastion (last in X #66, '97, next in Cable #45, '97), Prime Sentinels (cyborgs with Sentinel hardware & programming, some also as holograms & on monitor, some die; some or others of this unit last in X #65, '97), Operation: Zero Tolerance troops (some also as holograms & on monitor, some die; some or others of this unit last in Ons:Ep, 1 last in X #66, some or others next in W #117, all '97)

OTHER CHARACTERS: Daria (Bastion's nanotech-enhanced aide, between GenX #29-30, '97); Reavers: Wade Cole, Angelo Macon; Lady Deathstrike, Sentinel, Hand ninjas (prev 5 in rfb)

LOCATIONS/ITEMS: Operation: Zero Tolerance base (former Hulkbuster base, New Mexico desert; also as holograms & on monitors) w/Hole & ultra-containment block), incineration chamber & Professor X's cell; Reavers' Australian outback HQ, Lowtown, Ant Hill, Times Square (prev 4 in rfb) / OZT transport jet, hover-platforms, X-Men's power-dampening restraints, Storm's polymer prison, furnace (all also as holograms), Prime Sentinels' cybernetic implants (some bts, some destroyed, hereinafter considered their standard equipment and not listed separately), troops' armor (some also on monitors, some destroyed) & blasters (some of prev 3 also as holograms), Bastion's interactive monitors & holographic projectors (bts) w/remote control, Jubilee's power-dampening restraints & memory-reading helmet, Cyclops' implanted nanotech bomb (bts, see NOTE), base security cameras (destroyed, all but 1 bts), elevators, comm system & blast door, cells' psi-shields, blast dampers, hidden cameras (prev 3 bts) & master switch, memory scanner, Hand ninjas' swords & sais (prev 2 in rfb), OZT aircraft, vehicles (prev 2 also on monitor, destroyed) & hovercraft

FLASHBACK: Jubilee remembers Wolverine battling Reavers (UXM #251, '89 fb), Hand ninjas (UXM #268, '90), a Sentinel (W #74, '93) and Lady Deathstrike (W #46, '91).

SYNOPSIS: Bastion taunts the captive Jubilee and Professor X as his troops unload the unconscious X-Men, captured after OZT shot down their plane, and take them to specially crafted cells. As Wolverine appears to have died in the crash, the troops throw his body into a furnace. Wolverine revives and bursts out, killing the troops and stealing their armor. He then enters the cellblock, overpowers the guards and frees the X-Men. Security begins patrolling the base; Phoenix telepathically disguises herself as Bastion and gives each guard unit a different password. When the units meet and their passwords do not match, each group suspects the other of being disguised X-Men, and attacks. The X-Men near the exit, but Bastion seals the blast doors and sends waves of Prime Sentinel cyborgs against them. The X-Men battle bravely, but are overwhelmed — until Jubilee lunges past Bastion, hitting the door controls and letting the X-Men escape into the desert.

NOTE: Cover-labeled "Operation: Zero Tolerance", part of an event where Bastion and his Prime Sentinels launched a coordinated assault on the various X-teams. After "Flashback Month," all Marvel titles were revamped with a retro cover layout and a gatefold front cover that featured a 2-page recap section inside. The image of Wolverine in the cover's corner box is based on the cover of W #½, '97. Professor X was taken into

government custody in X #57, '96 for his unwitting part in Onslaught's destructive rampage. Bastion captured Jubilee in GenX #25, '97. W #1
'97 reveals that OZT implanted a nanotech bomb in Cyclops' chest during or just before this issue. Wolverine now looks completely hum
again; apparently his healing factor finished reverting his feral mutation while it healed his massive injuries from X #65, '97's plane crash
however, his word balloons remain lettered in the "slightly jagged" font introduced in W #114, '97. P.1 has several differences from the prelimina
version seen in W #-1, '97, including an expanded first panel, added narration and some dialogue changes.

WOLVERINE #116 (September 1997)

"What the Blind Man Saw" (22 pages)

CREDITS: Larry Hama (writer), Leinil Francis Yu (pencils), Edgar Tadeo (inks), Richard Starkings & Comicra
Emerson Miranda (letters), Joe Rosas (colors), Jason Liebig (asst editor), Mark Powers (editor)
FEATURE CHARACTER: Wolverine (also in dfb)
GUEST STARS: X-Men: Cannonball, Cyclops, Phoenix, Storm
VILLAINS: Bastion (last in Cable #47, '97, chr last in XFor #82, '98 fb, next in GenX #31, '97), Harper (shap
shifting Prime Sentinel developer, also mentioned as "Dr. Prospero," last in UXM #343, '97), Prime Sentin
(others as psychic images, some or others of this unit next in GenX #31, '97)
OTHER CHARACTERS: Senator Kelly (last in UXM #344, '97), Henry Peter Gyrich (Commission
Superhuman Activities official, last in Cable #45, '97 fb) (both next in X #68, '97), Mustang (blind ex-pilot, 1
also in fb prior to issue), clinic patients (some bts on bus) inc Arvell, Debra, Felipe, Helmut & Morgan (pre
unnamed), air show pilots & audience (prev 2 in fb), clinic truck driver (bts in dfb), Kelly's chauffeur (bts driving limo); coyotes (1 in dfb; others b
scared off by X-Men); federal authorities, smugglers (prev 2 mentioned); Sharon Kelly (Senator Kelly's dead wife, name on gravestone); ang
(as statues); OZT trooper (recap page only)
LOCATIONS/ITEMS: New Mexico desert inc Prospero Clinic (in dfb) & trailer park (former smuggling camp) w/underground bunker, lo
airfield (in fb), Washington DC's Arlington National Cemetery / Cyclops' implanted nanotech bomb (bts), Mustang's dialysis shunt (b
bandages & leg braces, OZT's radar, infrared sensors & telekinetic scanners (prev 3 mentioned), airplanes (in fb) inc Sally (Mustang's P-
Mustang, destroyed), Prime Sentinel cybernetic implants (in dfb, others bts in Mustang & clinic patients inc mutant sensors & Mustang's eye
clinic's electric fence, tractor-trailer truck (prev 2 in dfb), OZT hovercraft (bts) & jet w/sensors (bts), clinic bus, Harper's activation modu
Sharon's headstone, Kelly's limo
FLASHBACKS: Wolverine investigates a shipment heading for the Prospero Clinic, and learns that it is full of cybernetic Prime Sentinel pa
(d). Mustang's plane engine gives out during an air show; he steers the plane away from the audience but is badly wounded in the crash.
SYNOPSIS: The X-Men discover a trailer park in the desert. The blind Mustang befriends them, explaining that Prospero Clinic patients l
there. Wolverine smells Mustang's prosthetics and Storm obscures the X-Men's footprints with a wind gust; Mustang realizes that they a
mutants, but is sympathetic. That night, Wolverine sneaks away to investigate the clinic. The next morning he reveals that Mustang and 1
others are unknowingly being transformed into Prime Sentinel sleeper units. When Cannonball hears an OZT jet approaching, Mustang hic
the X-Men in an underground bunker. Other clinic patients arrive; Mustang tries to explain what Wolverine discovered, but they don't believe h
so Mustang reveals the X-Men's presence — as, on the jet, Harper activates three of the sleeper Sentinels. In Washington DC, Senator K
decides that OZT's war on mutants is wrong, and decides to speak to the President about stopping it.
NOTE: Cover-labeled "Operation: Zero Tolerance." Next issue reveals the clinic patients' names, and that "Dr. Prospero" is OZT's Harper.

WOLVERINE #117 (October 1997)

"A Divine Image" (23 pages)

CREDITS: Larry Hama (writer), Leinil Francis Yu (pencils), Edgar Tadeo (inks), Richard Starkings & Comicra
Emerson Miranda (letters) & Jason Medley (recap design), Joe Rosas & Chris Sotomayor (colors), Jason Liel
(asst editor), Mark Powers (editor)
FEATURE CHARACTER: Wolverine
GUEST STARS: Jubilee (also on Sentinel's scanner, last in GenX #31, '97), X-Men: Cannonball, Cyclo
Phoenix, Storm
VILLAINS: Bastion (last in X #68, '97, next in XMan #30, '97), Harper, Prime Sentinels (some or others of t
unit last in GenX #31, '97) inc Arvell, Felipe & Helmut (prev 3 named, also as clinic patients), OZT troops (1
monitor, some or others of this unit last in W #115, '97)
OTHER CHARACTERS: Mustang (also as hologram & Prime Sentinel), clinic patients (many as silhouet
in tubes) inc Debra & Morgan (prev 2 named), Master Mold (Sentinel-creating robot, head only); coyotes, chameleon; Sabra, Daria (pre
mentioned); William Blake (quoted); man (as painting); Senator Kelly (recap page only)
LOCATIONS/ITEMS: New Mexico desert (also on scanner) inc Prospero Clinic & trailer park w/underground bunker / Cyclops' implant
nanotech bomb (bts), Mustang's bandages, Prime Sentinel cybernetic implants (some in Mustang & clinic patients, some bts, so
destroyed) inc mutant sensors (bts), nanotech metamorphic tissue, paralysis ray & Mustang's eyes, OZT jet w/computers, monitors, con
unit & holographic projector, Harper's files, Sentinel creation tubes (prev 2 destroyed), telephone & escape hatch, Jubilee's power-dampen
restraints (destroyed), cactus, Prime Sentinel's mutant & infrared sensors, power cell, communications suite, targeting system (prev 5 bts
visual receptors (prev 3 destroyed), clinic bus, Bastion's activation module (bts)
SYNOPSIS: As Mustang reveals the X-Men to the clinic patients, three suddenly morph into Prime Sentinels and attack. The X-Men fight ba
careful to disable the Sentinels without killing them. A patient tries to interfere but a Sentinel blasts him, revealing his cybernetic parts; the oth
realize that Mustang's claims are true. The X-Men defeat the Sentinels and decide to shut down the Prospero Clinic. Nearby, Bastion ale
Harper that the President is about to order SHIELD to shut them down. Elsewhere, Jubilee flees across the desert; Wolverine smells her fr
afar as the X-Men prepare to assault the base, and races to her rescue. A Prime Sentinel locates Jubilee, but Wolverine arrives and destro
it. The two return to the clinic, but find that the enraged patients stormed it while Wolverine was gone. The X-Men find the Sentinel-creat
equipment trashed; "Prospero" has fled. Elsewhere, Bastion learns that one sleeper Prime Sentinel is left, and activates it. At the clinic, Musta
convulses and transforms...

OTE: Cover-labeled "Operation: Zero Tolerance." Dr. Prospero is revealed as Harper here; his alias is also misspelled "Propero." The Master old head, which Harper is presumably using to help transform the clinic patients, is a duplicate; the original was destroyed in X #16, '66 and e Mark II Master Mold is actually part of Bastion, as MM&B Ann '98 reveals. Daria freed Jubilee in GenX #31, '97. Although the X-Men make point of subduing the Prime Sentinels without lethal force, p.7's art seems to depict Wolverine decapitating Helmut and Cyclops destroying his ad — however, Helmut is seen intact on p.8. Also, although Helmut claims to only use his "temporary paralysis" ray on Debra, he does enough mage to expose many of her cybernetic parts.

WOLVERINE #118 (November 1997)

"Out of Darkness Into Light" (23 pages)

CREDITS: Larry Hama (writer), Leinil Francis Yu (pencils), Edgar Tadeo (inks), Richard Starkings & Comicraft's Emerson Miranda (letters), Jason Wright (colors), Jason Liebig (asst editor), Mark Powers (editor)
FEATURE CHARACTER: Wolverine (also on Mustang's scanner, also as Experiment X in rfb, also in fb1 between W:Hunger, '09 & W #34, '90 fb; also in fb2 between X:L #218, '09 fb & X #94, '75; next in UXM #350, X #70, GR #88, all '97; X #71, UXM #351-352, all '98; Elektra #10, ASM #429, XMU #17, all '97, KP:AoS #1-3, '97-98, W Ann '97)
GUEST STARS: X-Men: Professor X (in fb2 between X:L #218, '09 fb & X #94, '75), Cannonball (also on Mustang's scanner), Cyclops (also on Mustang & Sentinel's scanners), Phoenix, Storm; Jubilee (prev 5 next in UXM #350, '97), G.W. Bridge (last in Cable #47, '97, next in Tb #6, '97)
VILLAINS: Prime Sentinels (some destroyed, some or others next in X Ann '00), OZT troops

THER CHARACTERS: Mustang (also as Prime Sentinel), clinic patients (1 also on Mustang's scanner), SHIELD agents (some bts on ships, hers last & next in X #69, '97) inc medics; deer (in rfb); President William Clinton (mentioned, authorized OZT's shutdown)
OCATIONS/ITEMS: Prospero Clinic (also on scanner), skies above New Mexico desert, Weapon X Program facility (in rfb), Wood Buffalo ational Park (in fb1), X-Mansion (in fb2) / Weapon X Program's Genesis Tank w/Adamantium feed tubes, Experiment X's helmet (all in rfb), yclops' implanted nanotech bomb (bts, also on scanner), clinic window (destroyed), OZT jets, troops' armor, SHIELD air fighters & command ip, Bridge's handgun, agents' guns & mutant sensors, medics' scanners & wrist monitor, Harper's computer disks
LASHBACKS: Adamantium is bonded to Wolverine's skeleton (MCP #73, '91). A feral Wolverine hunts deer in the woods (1). Wolverine uggles to repress his rage (2).
YNOPSIS: Transformed into a Prime Sentinel, Mustang takes aim at the X-Men. Wolverine tries to reason with him, but although Mustang uggles against his programming, he ultimately snaps and attacks. The X-Men evacuate the clinic patients as Wolverine battles Mustang, couraging him to assert his humanity. Jubilee blasts Mustang in the face with fireworks, disabling his Sentinel eyes; the trauma of being nded again shocks him back to his senses. Outside, the X-Men see SHIELD fighter jets chasing an armada of OZT troops and Prime entinels. A passing Sentinel blasts Cyclops; SHIELD medics land and attend to him. They detect a nanotech device inside his chest, and noenix realizes that it was implanted during their OZT captivity. Wolverine encourages Mustang to stay with SHIELD, certain that they can verse his transformation. The X-Men steal an OZT jet and head for the X-Mansion seeking medical help, but Cyclops feels the device reading — and realizes that it is a bomb.
OTE: Cover-labeled "Operation: Zero Tolerance Epilogue." SHIELD was mobilized against OZT in X #69, '97. Bridge incorrectly states here at Bastion is "on the run"; Bastion was captured during SHIELD's initial strike. The X-Men extract Cyclops' nanotech bomb in X #70, '97.

WOLVERINE '97 (1997)

"Heart of the Beast" (38 pages)

CREDITS: John Ostrander & Joe Edkin (writers), Leonardo Manco (art), Richard Starkings & Comicraft's Kolja Fuchs (letters) & Jason Medley (recap design), Shannon Blanchard (colors), Kelly Corvese (editor), Mark McNabb (c colors)
FEATURE CHARACTER: Wolverine (also on monitor & in rfb1 & rfb2, also in fb1 between XO:Sabre, '09 & UToS #-1, '97; next in X #71-72, '98, SM/King, '97, Elektra #14, '98, W #119, '97)
VILLAINS: Volk (Ilya Dubromovitch Skorzorki, wolflike Russian agent, also in fb1 & fb2 prior to issue), Bowser (OZT "hound-master," in shadow, last in XFac #137, '97), Russian soldiers (in fb1, some or all die) inc Yuri, Volk's employer (bts in fb2, hiring him)

THER CHARACTERS: Dimitri Suhkarov (Soviet nuclear arms designer, in fb1, dies), Viktoria Suhkarov (Dimitri's daughter, Canadian cret Service agent, also in fb1 prior to issue), Bull Hosek (bartender, dies), Volk's victims (die), KGB scientists (bts mutating Volk) (prev in fb2), Hot Bar patrons, hotel maid, FedEx driver, pilot (bts flying plane), bystanders; wolves (another as Wolverine's belt buckle), birds; abretooth (in rfb1), Weapon X Program employees (in rfb2), Frasier Crane, Eddie (Martin Crane's dog) (prev 2 on billboard), models (on pin-up billboard); X-Men: Cannonball, Cyclops, Phoenix; Jubilee (prev 4 recap page only)
OCATIONS/ITEMS: Russia (also in fb2) inc KGB lab (in fb2), Ul'yanovsk Airport & Ural mountains (also in fb1) w/Jensei River bridge, John raith's home (in rfb1), Weapon X Program facility (in rfb2), Bowser's OZT headquarters, Manhattan inc Washington Square Park, Times Square, ot Bar & Viktoria's Biltmore Hotel suite / Wolverine's KGB file, getaway airplane (prev 2 bts) & knife, soldiers' machine guns, Dimitri's handgun (all fb1), Volk's handgun (another in fb1) & Canadian Secret Service file (also bts in fb1), employees' monitors, Weapon X Program's Genesis tank w/ damantium feeder tubes (prev 3 in rfb2), KGB's DNA-alteration equipment (in fb2), Bowser's monitors, Statue of Liberty, Hosek's shotgun, hurled air (destroyed) & table, bar window (destroyed), Viktoria's keycard, handgun & lamp, pay phone, airplane, Wolverine's rented Jeep
LASHBACKS: Wolverine battles Sabretooth (W #62, '92). Adamantium is bonded to Wolverine's skeleton (MCP #73, '91). Wolverine tries help Dimitri and Viktoria Suhkarov defect from Soviet Russia, but Volk and his soldiers pursue them. Volk defeats Wolverine and kills Dimitri t, impressed by Wolverine, lets him leave with Viktoria (1). The KGB infuses Volk with wolf DNA, giving him lycanthropic powers; he soon comes a mercenary (2).
YNOPSIS: Bowser hires Volk to kill Wolverine. Learning this, Viktoria alerts Wolverine, but he knows that she longs to avenge her father. olverine lets Volk track him down at a friend's bar. Wolverine attacks, but as the fight progresses, Volk becomes more wolflike. He kills

Wolverine's friend, exhorting him to fight harder, but Wolverine calms himself instead. Displeased, Volk flees. Wolverine realizes too late th Volk is targeting Viktoria; Volk kidnaps her, taking her to Russia and challenging Wolverine to final battle. Wolverine travels there and locat Volk, who attacks viciously — but during the savage battle he finally transforms fully into a wolf. Wolverine knew that Volk wanted this all alon and lets him run off into the woods — but Viktoria, still seeking vengeance, pursues him.
NOTE: Viktoria's name is also incorrectly spelled "Victoria Sukharov." On several pages, this issue's coloring incorrectly shows Wolverine claws shining as if they were still metal.

WOLVERINE: DOOMBRINGER (November 1997)

"Doombringer" (48 pages)

CREDITS: Doug Moench (writer), Michal Dutkiewicz (pencils), Jimmy Palmie (inks), Richard Starkings & Comicraft's Emerson Miranda (letters) & John Rosh (design), Mark McNabb, Dennis Calero & Atomic Paintbrush (colors), Dan Hos (asst editor), Mark Bernardo (editor)
FEATURE CHARACTER: Wolverine (also as "Patch," also in rfb2, chr last in #3, '89, chr next in MA Ann #4, '88)
SUPPORTING CAST: Archie Corrigan (his chr 1st app, chr next in W #4, '8 Mariko Yashida (also in dfb1 prior to issue; chr last in KP&W #6, '85, chr next in #150, '00 fb)
VILLAINS: Doombringers ("Walkers Between Worlds," other-dimension creatures, 1 dies, 1 arm only), 10th-century Clan Yashida sages (die, also in fb1 prior to issue) & samurai (die, some also in rfb1, 1 also in fl prior to issue) inc archer (also in dfb2 & dfb1), other-dimensional beings (in fb1), traitorous Clan Yashida members (die), arm wrestler
OTHER CHARACTERS: Silver Samurai (also in rfb2, also in fb2 between UXM #174, '83 & SecWars2 #7, '86; chr last in W #3, '89, chr ne in W #150, '00 fb), Clan Yashida members (some or others chr last in UXM #174, '83, chr next in XFac #63, '91) inc Mariko's bodyguards (som or others also in dfb1 prior to issue), 10th-century sages (die, some also in rfb1, some also in fb1 prior to issue) & army (die, some also rfb1), Princess Bar patrons, waitress & bartender, doctors (bts treating Samurai), Japanese bystanders (in dfb2), Madripoor bystanders; bir Bodhisattvas (1 also in fb1), Buddhist demons, victims (dead, as skulls), dogs, hydras, fish (prev 6 as statues)
LOCATIONS/ITEMS: Thailand (also in fb1) inc sage's workshop (in fb1) & rainforest inc Tangkor Marat temple (also in fb1 & rfb1) w/northe temple (also in rfb1) & southern temple, Princess Bar, Yashidas' ancestral manor (also in fb2 & dfb1), Japanese city (in dfb2), hospital (b another in rfb2) & airstrip / Sages' scroll (bts, also in fb1), horns (all but 1 bts), crystal (destroyed), drums, torches, vapors, gong & malle samurai & army's swords (1 destroyed), armor (1 of prev 2 also in fb1), spears, arrows (prev 4 also in rfb1) & bows (also bts in rfb1), seism detectors (bts), arm wrestler's gun (destroyed) w/bullet, archer's armor, sword (prev 2 also in dfb1 & dfb2), bow (also in dfb2), arrows & ma sage's herbs (in fb1), Silver Samurai's armor, katana (prev 2 also in rfb2) & bandages, Clan Yashida's Honor Sword (also in fb2), Clan membe swords (some destroyed), dagger (destroyed), guns & sonic equipment, Archie's knife & Douglas DC-3 w/parachutes, chrysanthemum
FLASHBACKS: The sages stop time (this issue). Wolverine battles the Silver Samurai (UXM #173, '83). A thousand years ago, two grou of sages disagree on how to handle a prophesied apocalypse — one advocates halting time, the other seeks to hasten the destruction — other-dimensional visitors manipulate them (1). The Silver Samurai meditates with the Honor Sword (2). The thousand-year-old archer petitio Mariko to finish what Clan Yashida began a millennium ago (d1). The modern world bewilders the archer (d2).
SYNOPSIS: A millennium ago, sages summon an other-dimensional "doombringer," while an opposing group casts a spell to stop time. As bo groups' armies clash and the doombringer's arm emerges through a portal, time halts in the temple. A thousand years later, an earthquake "awakens time-frozen archer. Mariko asks Wolverine to investigate, unsure which side the ancient Clan Yashida was on. The Silver Samurai tells Wolverine that th archer recruited twenty Yashida clansmen; the two travel to Thailand and find the temple. Inside, the clansmen break the spell and restart time. The arch welcomes the doombringer, but it kills him; the sages and soldiers quickly age and crumble to dust. As a second doombringer emerges, Wolverine an the Samurai close the portal, then defeat the traitorous clansmen. The first doombringer attacks and badly injures Wolverine, but the Samurai interven and Wolverine kills it. Later, Wolverine reassures Mariko that the ancient Yashidas opposed the doombringer, but Mariko knows he is lying.
NOTE: This issue also has a Dynamic Forces silver foil variant cover; 1500 of these were autographed by inker Jimmy Palmiotti. This iss occurs during Wolverine's time as "Patch" in Madripoor. In a departure from his standard behavior at this time, Wolverine brandishes his claw and displays his healing factor openly while dressed as Patch. The Silver Samurai's given name is misspelled "Keniuchio" here.

WOLVERINE #½ (1997)

"Resolutions" (12 pages)

CREDITS: Ben Raab (writer), Joe Phillips (pencils), Mark Lipka (inks), J Babcock (letters), Don Skinner (colors), Steve Blackwell (art director), Darr Sanchez (production director), John Dokes (Marvel promotions), Ben Plavin Mike Marts (Wizard promotions), Dan Hosek (editor), Leinil Francis Yu (c pencil Edgar Tadeo (c inks)
FEATURE CHARACTER: Wolverine (also in rfb1 & symbolic image, chr last in Ann '96, chr next in W #107, '96)
GUEST STAR: Cable (also in rfb2, also as Nathan Dayspring in fb between Cab #25, '95 & XFor #1, '91 fb, also in XFor #2, '04 fb & Cable #5, '93 fb during fb; c last in X Ann '96, chr next in Yb/XFor, '96)
OTHER CHARACTERS: Tyler Dayspring (in fb, his chr 1st app, prior to XFor #1, '91 fb; also as Genesis in rfb1 & bts in rfb2), Jenskot (Aliy Cable's wife, in fb between Cable #25, '95 & Cable #1, '93 fb; also in rfb2 & as psychic projection in fb), Larry (diner proprietor), Larry's patron Tyler's friends (in fb); butterflies (in fb), birds; Egyptian farmers (bts), Cannonball, Dark Riders: Deadbolt, Dirt Nap, Gauntlet, Hurricane, Spy (prev 7 in rfb1), Stryfe & his Canaanite troops (prev 2 bts), Clan Chosen: Boak, Dawnsilk, Silo, Tetherblood, 1 other (prev 7 in rfb2); Apocalyp (on busts & sarcophagus in rfb1), ancient Egyptians (as images on sarcophagi in rfb1); Blaquesmith (as psychic projection in fb); frog (on be sign), cartoon duck (on billboard); techno-organic creatures (cover only)

LOCATIONS/ITEMS: Larry's (New York diner, see NOTE), Genesis' citadel (in rfb1) w/bonding room & resurrection chamber, Earth-4935's 38-th centuries: Clan Chosen camp (in fb), Grand Canyon (in rfb2) / Genesis' bonding tank w/Adamantium-reshaping equipment, brain implants (rev 2 bts), computers & feed tubes, Cyber's Adamantium, Apocalypse's revival crèche w/sarcophagi (all in rfb1), Cable & Tyler's energy staffs (rev 2 in fb), Clan Chosen's armor & blasters, Stryfe's thermite explosive (bts), Canaanite's blaster (prev 4 in rfb2), Tyler's football, patrons' car keys, Larry's metal plate (prev 3 bts), Cable & Wolverine's drinks

FLASHBACKS: Genesis tries to re-bond Adamantium to Wolverine's skeleton, but Wolverine breaks free and kills him (W #100, '96). As the Clan Chosen battles Stryfe's forces, an explosion kills Jenskot (Cable #1, '93). Tyler grows up, playing with friends, honing his powers and learning the art of battle.

SYNOPSIS: Cable and Wolverine sit grimly at Larry's, drinking and telepathically discussing Wolverine's recent killing of the villainous Genesis, Cable's adopted son. Wolverine explains that Genesis' experiments had accidentally devolved him to a feral state, and that he had lashed out at his tormentor like a savage beast. Cable reminisces about Tyler's childhood in their future timeline, and explains that the villainous Stryfe had kidnapped and brainwashed him into becoming evil. Larry tries to interrupt so he can close the diner for the night, but soon gives up and tells the two to lock up when they leave. Cable and Wolverine both regret what became of Tyler. Wolverine apologizes, and the two men shake hands.

NOTE: This sendaway one-shot, part of Wizard Magazine's #½ line, was available through a special offer in Wizard #75, '97 and came with a certificate of authenticity. Wizard also produced a variant special edition with blue foil on Wolverine's costume. This issue also has a 4-page sketchbook section with script and pencil excerpts, which reveal that the diner was originally intended to be Harry's Hideaway, and Larry was originally its operator Harry Morrel. Although p.1's caption states that the diner is in Westchester's Salem Center, p.12 shows it in New York City; the city backdrop may have been the reason for the diner's name change. As the sketchbook section confirms, this story is set in the past, shortly after Wolverine killed Genesis.

WOLVERINE #119 (December 1997)

"Not Dead Yet, 1 of 4" (22 pages)

CREDITS: Warren Ellis (writer), Leinil Francis Yu (pencils), Edgar Tadeo (inks), Richard Starkings & Comicraft's Emerson Miranda (letters) & Jason Medley (recap design), Jason Wright (colors), Jason Liebig (asst editor), Mark Powers (editor), Todd Klein (c letters)
FEATURE CHARACTER: Wolverine (also in fb2 between W #13, '11 fb & W #120, '98 fb; also in fb1 between W #121, '98 fbs)
VILLAINS: Roddy McLeish ("White Ghost," "Gweilo", assassin, 1st, bts hiring killers; also in fb2, his chr 1st app, prior to W #120, '98 fb; also in fb1 between W #121, '98 fb & this issue) & his hired killer (bts), Triad members (Chinese mobsters, 1 dies, rest bts pressuring Wong) & their police mole (bts reporting Wong's death), McLeish's driver (dies) (prev 3 in fb1)
OTHER CHARACTERS: Ai-Chia Wong (Wolverine's girlfriend, 1st, also in photo, prior to W #121, '98 fb), Tak-ah Wong (Ai-Chia's father, movie producer, dead, also in photo) & his movie star (bts, sought by Triads), Mandarin filmmakers (bts making movie), bar patrons & waiter, Hong Kong bystanders (all in fb1), restaurant waiter (in fb2), homeless veteran (dead), New York bystanders; chickens (dead, in fb2); Maud (hired McLeish) & her husband (killed by McLeish), McLeish's other victims (prev 3 mentioned in fb1), Triad enforcer (killed by Wolverine), Japanese killer & soldier (prev 3 mentioned in fb2); Bruce Lee (named on marquee); models inc Miss Chun Li (on posters in fb1), Tak-Wah's wife (in photo in fb1), man (on poster in fb2); animals (as statues in fb1); Mustang, Prime Sentinels (prev 2 recap page only)
LOCATIONS/ITEMS: Hong Kong: movie theatre (bts), Wongs' home (also in photo), bar, streets, docks (all in fb1) & restaurant (in fb2), Japanese fields (mentioned in fb2), East Village inc Wolverine's apartment (destroyed) / McLeish's tree saw (mentioned), camera (bts) & limousine, Wolverine's motorcycle, Triad's boat, handgun & suitcase w/money (prev 5 destroyed) (all in fb1), McLeish's knife (also in fb1 & fb2), beach (in fb2) & photograph, plastic explosive w/arming switch, Adamantium shards, pay phones
FLASHBACKS: Wolverine and his friend McLeish drink in a Hong Kong bar; McLeish brags about his contract killings. Wolverine takes his girlfriend Ai-Chia to a movie, but they leave early — and return home to find Ai-Chia's father dead and McLeish fleeing. Wolverine chases McLeish's car on his motorcycle, but McLeish sideswipes him and escapes. Later, McLeish accepts payment from the Triad member who hired him — but Wolverine throws his motorcycle at McLeish from above, breaking his back. The Triad shoots at Wolverine, but sparks ignite the motorcycle's gas tank, which explodes (1). Months earlier, McLeish tells Wolverine that he recently saw his healing factor and claws in action. McLeish points out ways to kill Wolverine despite his powers (2).
SYNOPSIS: Wolverine finds a homeless veteran dead in his apartment, a photo of Ai-Chia's father's corpse taped to his forehead. Wolverine discovers McLeish's knife and a plastic explosive bomb with Adamantium shards protruding from it; he dives out the window as the bomb explodes, realizing that McLeish is alive. As an entire bank of pay phones begins ringing, Wolverine runs…
NOTE: Cover-labeled "Not Dead Yet, Part 1 of 4." McLeish's first name is revealed in W:WXF, '09. This issue's cover incorrectly credits Larry Hama as writer. A model on a poster is named Chun Li, a reference to the character from the "Street Fighter" video game franchise.

WOLVERINE #120 (January 1998)

"Not Dead Yet, 2 of 4" (22 pages)

CREDITS: Warren Ellis (writer), Leinil Francis Yu (pencils), Edgar Tadeo (inks), Richard Starkings & Comicraft's Emerson Miranda (letters) & Jason Medley (recap design), Jason Wright (colors), Jason Liebig (asst editor), Mark Powers (editor), Todd Klein (c letters)
FEATURE CHARACTER: Wolverine (also in fb1 & fb2 between W #119, '97 fb & W #121, '98 fb)
VILLAINS: Roddy McLeish (also in fb1 & fb2 between W #119, '97 fb & W #121, '98 fb) & his hired killers (1 dies, 1 voice only on phone), assassins (in fb1)
OTHER CHARACTERS: New York bystanders; Hong Kong police (mentioned in fb2, fought Wolverine); Miss Chun Li (on poster in fb2), angel (as painting in fb1); Ai-Chia Wong, Hong Kong bystanders (prev 2 recap page only)

LOCATIONS/ITEMS: Hong Kong: bar (in fb2) & McLeish's suite (in fb1), Manhattan inc Sam's Bike Shop, upstate New York road & town McLeish's house / Killers' cars (destroyed), cellphone (bts) & handguns, garage door (destroyed), Wolverine's motorcycle, McLeish's cellpho

FLASHBACKS: McLeish throws a party for the world's premier assassins, but Wolverine feels uncomfortable and leaves (1). Wolverine te McLeish about his temper, explaining that when he gets angry enough he stops thinking. McLeish listens attentively, grinning (2).

SYNOPSIS: Wolverine races through the Manhattan streets, wondering how McLeish could still be alive and trying to plan his next mo Two cars suddenly smash into Wolverine from opposite directions, pinning him between them. One of the drivers gets out, passes along greeting from McLeish and shoots at Wolverine, but he fires lazily and misses. Wolverine hooks the gun with his claws and threatens the kil demanding to know McLeish's location, but the killer passes out. Wolverine frees himself; when his legs heal he heads to the bike shop hous his motorcycle. He finds another killer waiting there for him, but quickly disarms him and rides out of the city, needing to get far away from anyo that McLeish might hurt to get at him. In a small upstate town, McLeish receives a report that Wolverine is heading his way…

NOTE: Cover-labeled "Not Dead Yet, Part 2 of 4." The recap page, with a large amount of space to fill, features sarcastic profiles of the assass who attack Wolverine (calling them "Nameless Assassin #1 & 2") and the cars that they slammed into him. For some reason, a bystander wearing a Starfleet uniform from *Star Trek: the Next Generation.* This issue's letters page apologizes for crediting Larry Hama on last issue's cov

WOLVERINE #121 (February 1998)

"Not Dead Yet, 3 of 4" (22 pages)

CREDITS: Warren Ellis (writer), Leinil Francis Yu (pencils), Edgar Tadeo & Gerry Alanguilan (inks), Rich Starkings & Comicraft's Kolja Fuchs (letters) & John Marasigan (recap design), Jason Wright (colors), Jas Liebig (asst editor), Mark Powers (editor)

FEATURE CHARACTER: Wolverine (also in fb1 between W #120, '98 fb & W #119, '97 fb; also in fb2 betwe W #119, '97 fb & W #126, '98 fb)

VILLAINS: Roddy McLeish (bts killing Ai-Chia, also as voice in recording, also in fb1 between W #120, '98 f W #119, '97 fb) & his hired killers

OTHER CHARACTERS: Ai-Chia Wong (dead, also in fb2 between W #119, '97 fb & this issue), villagers (dead in town), plane ground crew (in fb2); McLeish's victims (mentioned in fb1)

LOCATIONS/ITEMS: Hong Kong bar (in fb1) & airport (in fb2), upstate New York town (mentioned, ro & woods / Wolverine's luggage (in fb2) & motorcycle (destroyed), airplane (in fb2), killers' radio & guns w/Adamantium bullets, McLeis preservatives (bts), cassette player (destroyed) w/motion sensor & board w/ropes & release mechanism

FLASHBACKS: A drunken McLeish brags to Wolverine about his decades of killing (1). After Ai-Chia's father's murder, Wolverine deci to leave Hong Kong. A grief-stricken Ai-Chia asks why Wolverine used to associate with McLeish, and says that she can't bear the though being with him anymore (2).

SYNOPSIS: Wolverine rides upstate, seeking a remote town in which to lie low and wondering how McLeish could be alive. Killers ambush I at a fork in the road, but Wolverine charges them on his motorcycle. After defeating the killers, Wolverine realizes that some of their bullets w Adamantium, and wonders where McLeish is getting so much of the rare metal. Briefly confused about which road to follow, Wolverine resolv to let McLeish stop manipulating him, and follows his instincts. However, Wolverine soon finds Ai-Chia's body strung up in the woods, along w a cassette player broadcasting a message from McLeish, who promises more like her in a nearby town. Wolverine snaps and races up the ro promising to find and kill McLeish all over again.

NOTE: Cover-labeled "Not Dead Yet, Part 3 of 4."

WOLVERINE #122 (March 1998)

"Not Dead Yet, 4 of 4" (22 pages)

CREDITS: Warren Ellis (writer), Leinil Francis Yu (pencils), Edgar Tadeo (inks), Richard Starkings & Comicra Emerson Miranda (letters) & John Marasigan (recap design), Jason Wright (colors), Jason Liebig (asst edit Mark Powers (editor), Dusty Abell (c pencils), Drew Geraci (c inks)

FEATURE CHARACTER: Wolverine (next in Mvk #4, '97; UXM #353, 354 fb & 353-354, AFlt #9, UXM #3 X #73-75, all '98, W #175/2, '02 fb)

VILLAINS: Roddy McLeish (dies, possibly next as spirit in W #2, '10, see NOTE) & his hired killers, Tr members inc dead Triad's son (dies)

OTHER CHARACTERS: Villagers (dead); mouse; Triad's father's men (mentioned, told son of father's dea assassins (mentioned, found McLeish), McLeish's son (mentioned, lives in British Columbia); dragons (as tatto

LOCATIONS/ITEMS: Upstate New York road & town w/McLeish's house (destroyed) / Killers' rifles, McLeis floodlights, speakers, boards, ropes, gasoline bomb & handgun w/poisoned Adamantium bullets, Triads' microphone (destroyed), machine g & handgun w/Adamantium bullets, gasoline tanks (destroyed)

SYNOPSIS: Wolverine runs through the small town, defeating McLeish's killers without breaking stride. Floodlights activate, revealing town's residents killed and strung up along the road. A small bomb explodes beneath Wolverine as McLeish taunts him over a loudspeak explaining how he survived the Hong Kong explosion. Wolverine enters McLeish's house but finds a young Triad at the microphone, who clai that he has been impersonating McLeish to avenge the death of his father — the Triad who hired McLeish years before. Wolverine kills Triad and smells the real McLeish in the next room, now old and infirm — but McLeish shoots Wolverine with a poisoned bullet, overwhelm his healing factor. Thinking fast, Wolverine claims to have found and killed McLeish's son; McLeish lunges angrily at Wolverine, who catc his head between his two outer claws and threatens to pop the center claw. McLeish dies of fear and ill health; Wolverine burns his body a ponders the fitting irony of killing McLeish with lies.

NOTE: Cover-labeled "Not Dead Yet, Part 4 of 4." This issue contains a LOC from future comic artist Lee Ferguson. McLeish's spirit, along w those of several other deceased characters, appears in W #2, '10 when Wolverine is taken to Hell. However, as discussed in W #4, '82's NOT it is uncertain if anything Wolverine witnesses in the afterlife is real.

WOLVERINE #123 (April 1998)

"Better Than Best!" (22 pages)

CREDITS: Tom DeFalco (writer), Denys Cowan (pencils), Bill Sienkiewicz (inks), Richard Starkings & Comicraft (letters) w/ John Marasigan (recap design), Jason Wright (colors), Jason Liebig (asst editor), Mark Powers (editor), Mat Broome (c pencils)
FEATURE CHARACTER: Wolverine (also in pfb & his own thoughts)
VILLAINS: Bloodscream (last in XMU #9, '95), Roughouse (also in pfb, last in W #23, '90) (both next in ASM #435, '98), Black Tarantula (Carlos LaMuerto, superhuman crimelord, bts employing Bloodscream & Roughouse, last in ASM #432, last bts in ASM #433, next in ASM #434, all '98), extortionists (1 in pfb)
OTHER CHARACTERS: Deli employee, bystanders (both in pfb), police; model (on poster in pfb); Marrow (mentioned, nearly killed Wolverine), Storm (mentioned, taught Wolverine to pick locks); Roddy McLeish, Miss Chun Li (prev 2 recap page only)
LOCATIONS/ITEMS: East Village inc deli, subway, Wolverine's apartment ruins (all in pfb) & warehouse (also in pfb) w/basement, X-Mansion (mentioned in pfb) / Wolverine's belongings (in pfb, destroyed), manacles, lockpicks, bandages & boot w/hidden heel compartment, deli's money (also bts in pfb), extortionists' guns (1 in pfb) & ladder, warehouse's coffee & spices (prev 2 in pfb), light bulbs (1 destroyed), forklift, support beams (destroyed), debris, police car
FLASHBACK: Wolverine examines his ruined apartment, then stumbles across a deli robbery and follows the thief back to his warehouse hideout. Roughouse suddenly attacks, and Wolverine realizes that he was set up (p).
SYNOPSIS: Wolverine awakens in manacles, thinking about his recent New Year's resolution to once again become "the best there is at what he does." Roughouse and Bloodscream torture Wolverine, then leave to let him recuperate. Wolverine breaks his own arm to escape from the manacles, then uses hidden lockpicks to free his other arm. Roughouse convinces Bloodscream to stop torturing Wolverine and just kill him — but when he returns, Wolverine runs him over with a forklift. The two battle savagely as Wolverine tries to put his resolution into action. Bloodscream attacks, but Wolverine stabs him through the chest, then tricks Roughouse into destroying support beams, collapsing the roof on him. Wolverine holds his claws to the weakened Roughouse's neck and convinces him to surrender. Police arrive and Wolverine departs, pondering how best to reach his goal.
NOTE: Black Tarantula's real name is revealed in ASM #436, '98. Wolverine made his New Year's resolution in X #73, '98. Though Roughouse reformed in W #21-23, '90, he is back to his villainous ways here with no explanation. Although W #4 & 6, '89 implied that Roughouse is Asgardian, Wolverine first explicitly speculates it here. Footnotes incorrectly refer to Wolverine and Bloodscream's last battle as W #81, '94; their last battle in this series was W #78, '94, and they clashed again in XMU #9, '95.

WOLVERINE #124 (May 1998)

"Invisible Destroyers!" (22 pages)

CREDITS: Tom DeFalco (writer), Denys Cowan (pencils), Bill Sienkiewicz (inks), Richard Starkings & Comicraft's Emerson Miranda (letters), Jason Wright (colors), Jason Liebig (asst editor), Mark Powers (editor), Mat Broome (c pencils), Sean Parsons (c inks)
FEATURE CHARACTER: Wolverine (also in his own thoughts)
GUEST STAR: Captain America (Steve Rogers, patriotic super-soldier, also on poster, between Cap #4-5, '98)
VILLAINS: Rascal (wears invisibility suit), Rodents (Rascal's hired thugs, 1 as truck driver)
OTHER CHARACTERS: Mabel (martial arts instructor) & her students, show employees, security guard, stuntmen, audience, bystanders; Spice Girls (mentioned); Storm, Bloodscream, Roughouse (prev 3 recap page only), people (dead as skulls), worm (prev 2 cover only)
LOCATIONS/ITEMS: New York City inc Madison Square Garden & Mabel's dojo / Wolverine's bokken, blindfold & luggage, students' bokken, Mabel's staff, Captain America's poster & triangular shield replica (see NOTE), Rascal's truck & invisibility suit w/sound dampers (bts), goggles & explosive device, Rodents' blasters & invisibility suits w/sound dampers (bts) & goggles, police baton
SYNOPSIS: Wolverine trains at Mabel's dojo, hoping to get his edge back. Later, as Wolverine stews about his recent defeats, he sees a poster advertising Captain America's charity appearance at Madison Square Garden. Wolverine suddenly smells a dozen men behind the Garden, but sees and hears nothing. Perplexed, Wolverine breaks into the backstage area and begins fighting what seems like empty air, wondering if his senses have gone haywire. Captain America arrives; Wolverine finally scores a hit, disabling his opponent's invisibility suit. Wolverine dons the man's helmet, letting him see several others surrounding him. Rascal introduces himself and his Rodents, who attack, hoping to assassinate Captain America live on stage. Wolverine tosses Captain America a second helmet and he joins the fight. Wolverine asks if Captain America has ever lost his edge, and is heartened by Cap's affirmative answer. The Rodents are quickly defeated, and Rascal readies an explosive device on his costume — but Wolverine deduces that he is bluffing, and has Captain America knock Rascal out.
NOTE: Page 14 panel 1 has several lettering errors: two of Wolverine's word balloons are reversed, and two caption boxes repeat the same words. Captain America circular shield was lost at sea in Cap #2, '98; he began using a replica of his original WWII triangular shield in Cap #3, '98.

WOLVERINE #125 (June 1998)

"Logan's Run!" (40 pages)

CREDITS: Chris Claremont (writer), Leinil Francis Yu (pencils), Edgar Tadeo (co-inks, c inks), Gerry Alanguilan (co-inks), Richard Starkings & Comicraft's Emerson Miranda (letters), Jason Wright (colors), Jason Liebig (asst editor), Mark Powers (editor), Jae Lee (variant c art), Chris Sotomayor (c colors)
FEATURE CHARACTER: Wolverine (also in Jubilee's & his own dreams)
GUEST STARS: X-Men: Phoenix (last in UXM #355, '98), Psylocke (last in X #73, '98), Rogue (last in X #75, '98) (all also in symbolic splash image & as serpents in Wolverine's dream); Jubilee (last in GenX #41, '98), Shadowcat (last in Ex #121, '98) (all also in Jubilee's dream), Black Widow (last in JIM #519, '98)

SUPPORTING CAST: Jessica Drew (last in SenSM Ann '96/2), Tyger Tiger (last in W #99, '96), Yukio (last Elektra #15, '98) (all also in symbolic splash image, Jubilee's dream & as serpents in Wolverine's dream)

VILLAIN: Viper (Ophelia Sarkissian, terrorist, also bts in Jubilee's dream, also as herself & Jubilee in Wolverine's dream, last in Beast #3, '97, last bts in S&L #3/3, '98)

OTHER CHARACTERS: Gateway (also in Jubilee's dream, last in GenX #25, '97, next in W #141, '99), Lockhe (Flock alien, Shadowcat's pet dragon, last in Ex #120, '98); Hellfire Club soldiers (bts in car in Jubilee's dream Silver Fox, Mariko Yashida, Sabretooth, Mount Logan bystanders (prev 4 in Wolverine's dream); historical figure painting); Bloodscream, Roughouse, Captain America, Rodents, people (dead, as skulls) (prev 5 recap page or

LOCATIONS/ITEMS: Chicago alley (in Jubilee's dream), Reavers' Australian outback HQ (also in Jubile dream), Berkshire Mountains inc Xavier's School for Gifted Youngsters, Mount Logan (named, also in Wolverin dream) inc saloon (destroyed), Yashidas' ancestral manor (also in Wolverine's dream), Princess Bar catacom & owner's suite / Kitty Pryde's clothes, soldiers' car (destroyed), Wolverine's cross & bonds, Tyger's short swc (all in Jubilee's dream), Psylocke's sword, Yukio's throwing blades (prev 2 also in Jubilee's dream), Viper's victi green costumes, lipstick & hair dye (some of prev 3 also in Jubilee's dream), Viper's poisons (bts, also bts Wolverine's dream), teleport ring (bts), handguns & dagger, Shadowcat's backpack, Gateway's bull-roarer, Jubilee's clothes, mirror & bon mining equipment, Wolverine's whiskey, cigar & bo staff (prev 3 destroyed), Tyger's fixative gun, blowfish toxin (bts), Clan Yashida's Ho Sword, Viper's helicopter (bts) w/rope ladder (prev 4 in Wolverine's dream), Black Widow's "Widow's Bite" bracelets

SYNOPSIS: Jubilee finds herself in Chicago, where Phoenix destroys a pursuing car — then suddenly in Australia, reliving her first meet with Wolverine. She realizes that she is dreaming as Phoenix, Psylocke, Rogue, Jessica Drew, Tyger Tiger and Yukio, all clad in green, stalk and Wolverine. Shadowcat awakens Jubilee, explaining that Viper has enthralled Wolverine's closest female friends and tried to do the same them. Phoenix and Rogue attack; Jubilee has Gateway teleport them away, and they decide to find Wolverine. They check Mount Logan, but enthralled women attack again. Gateway teleports the girls to Japan, where they find Wolverine, but Psylocke arrives and telepathically captu him. Wolverine awakens in the Princess Bar, as Viper has Phoenix try to alter his mind. Black Widow arrives and frees Jubilee and Shadowc the three cause a distraction and Wolverine attacks Viper, but she reminds him of his oath. Phoenix telepathically clears the others' minds, they find Wolverine standing by Viper's side — announcing that she is his wife.

NOTE: Mount Logan, the town where Wolverine and Silver Fox lived, is named here. Viper's real name is revealed in IM:DoS Ann, '08. Thou this issue states that she enthralled Wolverine's friends via poisons, Jubilee is attacked telepathically. Presumably after poisoning one or b of the telepaths, Phoenix or Psylocke, Viper had them telepathically attack some or all of the others. This issue opens with Jubilee reliv Shadowcat's memories from X #131, '80 pp.1-2, likely a result of Phoenix or Psylocke inadvertently linking their minds. Jubilee then relives own memories of meeting Wolverine, from UXM #251, '89 p.22. Although Wolverine claims here that Viper is his wife, they are not yet marri he is announcing his intent to marry her.

WOLVERINE #126 (July 1998)

"Blood Wedding" (22 pages)

CREDITS: Chris Claremont (writer), Leinil Francis Yu (pencils), Edgar Tadeo & Gerry Alanguilan (inks), Rich Starkings & Comicraft's Emerson Miranda (letters) & John Marasigan (recap design), Jason Wright (colors), Jas Liebig (asst editor), Mark Powers (editor), J.H. Williams III (c pencils), Mick Gray (c inks), Chris Sotomayor (c colo

FEATURE CHARACTER: Wolverine (also in fb2 between X:TF #3, '99 & W #103, '96 fb bts; also in fb1 betwe W #121, '98 fb & SM/W #2, '03 fb; also in fb3 between X Ann #4, '80 & X #139, '80)

GUEST STARS: X-Men: Phoenix, Rogue (both next in UXM #356, '98), Psylocke (next in X #77, '98); Bl Widow (chr next in IM #6, '98 fb, next in IM #5, '98), Jubilee (next in XMU #20, '98), Shadowcat (also as Sprit fb3 between X Ann #4, '80 & X #139, '80)

SUPPORTING CAST: Jessica Drew, Tyger Tiger (both next in W #128, '98), Yukio (next in W #150, '00)

VILLAINS: Sabretooth (also bts in fb1 between W #-1, '97 & W:O Ann, '07 fb; last in XFac #142, '98), Viper (a in fb1 during Cap #113, '69 fb), Matsuo Tsurayaba (bts allied with Hydra, last in X #32, '94, chr last in W #175/2, '02 fb), Hand ninjas (some others last in Elektra #19, '98), Hydra agents (some or others last in Cap #6, '98), Wolverine & Viper's foes (in fb1)

OTHER CHARACTERS: Lockheed (next in Ex #124, '98), Seraph (diminutive bar proprietor, in fb2 between W:O Ann, '07 fb & W:O #9, '0 bts; also in fb1 between W:O #19, '08 fb & W:O Ann '07 fb), Seraph's patrons (in fb2), priest (dies); birds; historical figure (as painting), and (as statues)

LOCATIONS/ITEMS: Lowtown: Jessica's apartment & Princess Bar (also as Seraph's in fb1 & fb2) w/catacombs (also in fb1), Baran's form palace, Tyger's Hightown suite, airstrip (in fb1), X-Mansion Danger Room (in fb3) / Viper's victims' green costumes, lipstick and hair dye, Bl Widow's "Widow's Bite" bracelets (bts), Shadowcat's backpack, airplane (another in fb1), Viper & foes' handguns, Seraph's tomb (prev 2 in fb Wolverine's whiskey & cigar (another of prev 2 in fb1), Hydra rifle w/scope, Hand ninjas' sword, bow & arrow, Matsuo's prosthetic hand, a ear & nose (prev 4 bts, see NOTE), Sabretooth's Adamantium skeleton (bts, hereinafter considered his standard equipment and not lis separately) w/finger claws

FLASHBACKS: Seraph, Viper and Wolverine adventure together; when Sabretooth mortally injures Seraph, Viper saves Wolverine, w swears an oath to her on Seraph's tomb (1). Seraph kisses Wolverine (2). During a Danger Room session, Sprite phases through Wolverine claws, but her super-dense structure still makes her ill (3).

SYNOPSIS: Wolverine's friends berate him angrily, but Wolverine is resolute: he will marry Viper. Shadowcat stays behind as the others dep Wolverine explains that the dying Seraph made him swear to grant Viper one request, whatever it may be — and this was it. Nearby, H ninjas and Hydra agents plan to assassinate Wolverine, but Sabretooth kills them, wanting Wolverine for himself. Shadowcat attends Wolverine seaside wedding ceremony — but as soon as the priest pronounces Wolverine and Viper married, Sabretooth attacks. Shadowcat phases V to safety; Wolverine battles Sabretooth, noting that his healing factor is greatly enhanced. Sabretooth grabs and shatters Wolverine's bone cl — revealing that he now possesses an Adamantium skeleton and retractable finger-claws. Shadowcat phases Wolverine out of Sabretoo grasp; he falls into the ocean, but Sabretooth wounds Shadowcat...

NOTE: It has never been revealed who gave Sabretooth his Adamantium skeleton and upgraded his healing factor, but W #162, '01 implies that the revived Weapon X Program was responsible. As W #175/2, '02 fb reveals, Wolverine has attacked Matsuo as revenge for Mariko's death three times at this point, cutting off his left arm, right ear and nose. All are therefore prosthetics here, as is his previously lost right hand.

WOLVERINE #127 (August 1998)

"I'm King of the World!" (21 pages)

CREDITS: Chris Claremont (writer), Leinil Francis Yu (pencils, pp.1-6, 15-16 & 20-21; c pencils), Cary Nord (pencils, pp.7-8), Mike S. Miller (pencils, p.9-10 & 17-19; co-inks), Jeff Matsuda (pencils, pp.11-12), Mel Rubi (pencils, pp.13-14), Carlos Pacheco (pencils, pp.17-19), Edgar Tadeo (co-inks, c inks), Jon Holdredge & Marlo Alquiza (co-inks), Richard Starkings & Comicraft's Emerson Miranda (letters) & John Marasigan (recap design), Jason Wright & Tom Smith (colors), Jason Liebig (asst editor), Mark Powers (editor), Chris Sotomayor (c colors)
FEATURE CHARACTER: Wolverine (also as Beast, Captain America, Hulk, Human Torch & Thing)
GUEST STAR: Shadowcat
SUPPORTING CAST: Police Chief Tai (last in W #98, '96, next in W:O Ann, '07)
VILLAINS: Viper (bts, captured), Sabretooth, Matsuo Tsurayaba, Bao Tien (Madripoor ganglord) & his goons (bts capturing Viper) & bodyguards, Hand ninjas (some die), Hydra agents (some die) inc Cadre Leader & Cadre Commander
OTHER CHARACTERS: Madripoor's Directorate (bts, planning to name successor to throne), dockworkers, Tien's party guests; bird, cat, rat; Gen. Thaddeus "Thunderbolt" Ross (mentioned, pursuing Hulk), Madripoor's Free Militia (mentioned); Hulk (as himself & "Joe Fixit" in holographic projection); historical figure (as painting), frog (on sign), dragons (as statues)
LOCATIONS/ITEMS: Baran's former palace, Lowtown inc Princess Bar & waterfront, Hightown inc Tien's skyscraper, Madripoor harbor w/ docks & Hydra's floating base (oil tanker) / Hand ninjas' swords, bow, arrow, shuriken & poisoned knife, Hydra bio-tags (some destroyed), remote sensors (prev 2 bts), tank (destroyed), bio-tagged guns w/scopes & hovercraft w/computer (bts), base's cameras, power inhibitors (prev 2 bts), computers, monitors, hologram projector & trap door, Matsuo's prosthetic hand, arm, ear & nose, Wolverine's fire suit, pressor rifle (prev 2 bts), whiskey, cigar, flamethrower, binoculars, parasail, garbage can lid, computer w/modem, mortar (bts) w/remote detonator & fans w/generator (bts), Madripoor immigration registry computers (bts), bodyguards' guns, Tien's handgun, fire hydrant
SYNOPSIS: Sabretooth gloats over Wolverine's easy defeat, and ponders what to do with Shadowcat. Later, Hand ninjas and Hydra agents enter Lowtown, having allied to seize control of the island. A shield-bearing figure attacks and defeats them; they take him to be Captain America, but he proves to be Wolverine wielding a garbage can lid. Elsewhere, Matsuo Tsurayaba and a Hydra commander are informed that the Hulk has arrived in Madripoor; a false lead created by Wolverine. Using props and impersonating several other heroes, Wolverine attacks several Hydra and Hand groups, making them think that they face an army. Meanwhile, Sabretooth and Shadowcat have allied, having realized Hydra and the Hand's goal, and learn that the Hand has captured Viper. Tai tells Wolverine that the invaders seek to have Matsuo appointed as the new prince, and that they need a strong alternative candidate; Tai suggests Viper. Wolverine locates Hydra's base and finds Shadowcat and Sabretooth waiting there — but Matsuo springs a trap, capturing all three.
NOTE: Wolverine wears his brown costume this issue and next. P.16's art seems to show Sabretooth and Shadowcat being caught in an explosion, but the explosion is heavily obscured by narrative captions and not referenced later in the issue. Writer Chris Claremont originally planned this story arc to be six issues; the explosion may have been a story element that was cut, but not redrawn, when he compressed the arc to four issues.

WOLVERINE #128 (September 1998)

"Green for Death" (22 pages)

CREDITS: Chris Claremont (writer), Stephen Platt (pencils, pp.1-10 & 20-22), Angel Unzueta (pencils, pp.11-19), Matt Banning, Jaime Mendoza, Harry Candelario, Rob Hunter & Jason Martin (inks), Richard Starkings & Comicraft's Emerson Miranda (letters) & John Marasigan (recap design), Wayne Robinson (colors), Jason Liebig (asst editor), Mark Powers (editor), Leinil Francis Yu (c pencils), Edgar Tadeo (c inks), Liquid! (c colors)
FEATURE CHARACTER: Wolverine (also in Shadowcat's illusion & on poster)
GUEST STAR: Shadowcat (also on poster, next in Ex #122, '98)
SUPPORTING CAST: Jessica Drew (next in HFH #18, '98), Tyger Tiger (next in IM:DoS Ann, '08) (both also on TV)
VILLAINS: Sabretooth (also in Shadowcat's illusion, chr next in Mvk #6, '98, next in Gam #8, '99), Viper (becomes Madripoor's ruling Prince, also on TV, chr next in W #131, '98 fb in W #131, '98), Matsuo Tsurayaba (chr next in W #175/2, '02 fb, next in W #175/2, '02), Hand ninjas (some or others next in W Ann '99/2) & sorcerers (die, others next in W Ann '99/2) inc Magus, Hydra agents (some or others next in W #131, '98) inc Cadre Commander
OTHER CHARACTERS: Madripoor's Directorate (bts crowning Viper); X-Men: Phoenix (also as Marvel Girl), Angel, Banshee, Beast, Colossus, Cyclops, Iceman, Nightcrawler, Professor X, Storm; cabbie (prev 11 in Wolverine's illusion); fish (dead, in Shadowcat's illusion)
LOCATIONS/ITEMS: Madripoor harbor w/Hydra's floating base, mountains (in Shadowcat's illusion), X-Mansion (in Wolverine's illusion), Princess Bar / Matsuo's prosthetic hand, arm, ear & nose, Shadowcat's Adamantium claws (in her illusion), base's internal sensors (bts), computers & sensory deprivation tanks, Hand ninjas' swords, Hydra agents' guns (1 destroyed), taxi, Wolverine's luggage, hurled sand (prev 3 in Wolverine's illusion), Viper's poisons (bts), poisoned knife & wanted posters, Princess Bar TV, Wolverine's whiskey & cigar
SYNOPSIS: Matsuo Tsurayaba plans to enslave the unconscious Wolverine, Sabretooth and Shadowcat. Hand sorcerers cast the three into illusory worlds, mystically swapping their personality attributes and placing them in situations that tempt them to betray their ideals, which would make them into Hand slaves. Shadowcat receives Sabretooth's savagery, but phases free of the illusory world. Wolverine receives Shadowcat's innocence, and savage illusory X-Men attack him — but Sabretooth awakens and kills the sorcerers, ending the illusions. Hydra attempts to brainwash recent captives Viper, Tyger Tiger and Jessica Drew, but Shadowcat phases the women free. Hydra agents attack, but Viper knocks out the savage Shadowcat before she can kill anyone, which would have doomed her. Sabretooth, who received Wolverine's sense of honor, teams with Wolverine; they defeat the Hand and Hydra. Viper tries to kill Sabretooth, but Shadowcat recovers and phases him through her blade. Days later, the mutants' personalities have returned to normal — but Viper has been appointed Madripoor's new Prince, which was her true goal all along.

NOTE: Wolverine drinks a shot of whiskey and smokes a cigar in every issue of this arc, toasting his dead lovers. In W #125, '98 he toasts Silver Fox; in W #126-128, '98 he toasts Seraph. On p.10, Colossus is miscolored in two different ways in two consecutive panels. On p.12, Iceman and Beast are miscolored as each other, and Nightcrawler is given pink skin and orange hair. Viper's green hair is miscolored blue on p.21.

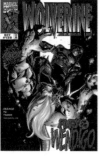

WOLVERINE #129 (October 1998)

"Survival of the Fittest, Part One: Whatever It Takes…" (23 pages)

CREDITS: Todd Dezago (writer), Leinil Francis Yu (pencils), Edgar Tadeo (inks), Richard Starkings & Comicraft's Emerson Miranda (letters) & John Marasigan (recap design), Jason Wright (colors), Jason Liebig (asst editor), Mark Powers (editor), Dean & Monica Kubina (c colors)
FEATURE CHARACTER: Wolverine (also as Experiment X in rfb1 & rfb2, also in rfb3)
VILLAINS: Wendigo (Andre Mornet, cursed cannibal, also in Wolverine's thoughts, 1st but chr last in W #130, '98 fb), Wendigo spirit (bonded to Canadian cannibals by ancient curse, also bts in rfb3, bts empowering Mornet, last in Blaze #12, '95, last bts in MFan #3, '96)
OTHER CHARACTERS: Dept. H employees (some or others last in AFlt #14, '98, next in AFlt #15, '98), mugging victim; zebra (dies), leopard; Psi-Borg (bts), Wrangler (dead), Professor Truett Hudson (prev 3 in rfb1), Wendigo (Paul Cartier), Wendigo (also as Georges Baptiste), Alpha Flight: Shaman, Snowbird; Hulk, Nightcrawler (prev in rfb3); X-Men: Phoenix, Psylocke, Rogue, Sabretooth, Viper (prev 5 in Wolverine's thoughts); Shadowcat (recap page only)
LOCATIONS/ITEMS: African veldt, city streets, Canada: Dept. H headquarters (Ottawa, Ontario), North Woods (Quebec), Hudson Bay (prev 2 in rfb3) & Alberta inc former Weapon X Program facility (also in rfb1 & rfb2) / ATM machine, victim's ATM card & money (prev 2 bts), mugger's steel pipe, Psylocke's sword (in Wolverine's thoughts), facility's bio-scanners (bts), Humvee (destroyed), Canadian flag (also as Wolverine's bandages) & motion detectors w/lasers, Wolverine's lockpick, Wrangler's armor (in rfb1), Experiment X's helmet (in rfb2), Weapon X Program Genesis Tank (also in rfb2) w/Adamantium feed tubes (in rfb2), Dept. H computers & monitors
FLASHBACKS: In an implanted memory, Experiment X rampages through the Weapon X facility and attacks the Professor (MCP #81, '91). Adamantium is bonded to Wolverine's skeleton (MCP #73, '91). Hulk and Wolverine battle Paul Cartier as the Wendigo, and Georges Baptiste takes on the curse (IHulk #181, '74), but Wolverine and Alpha Flight later cure him (X #140, '80).
SYNOPSIS: In Africa, a leopard kills a zebra; in the city, a mugger robs a man: creatures do what they must to survive. In the Canadian woods, Wolverine thinks about recent events; his broken claws have not yet grown back. Wolverine breaks into the abandoned Weapon X Program facility, and wonders if he still has his edge. Suddenly, Wendigo bursts in, having smelled his old foe; without his claws Wolverine is at a disadvantage and Wendigo nearly eviscerates him. Wolverine bandages his wounds and finds a Humvee; he tries to run Wendigo down, but the creature destroys the vehicle and begins crushing Wolverine. Desperate and realizing that he has gone from hunter to prey, Wolverine slashes Wendigo's face with his half-grown claw nubs. Wendigo flees in pain, as the badly injured Wolverine passes out…
NOTE: Andre's first name is revealed in CM #3, '00, and his last name in W:WXF, '09. This issue's digital lettering has several typos.

WOLVERINE #130 (Early November 1998)

"Survival of the Fittest, Part Two: …To Survive!" (22 pages)

CREDITS: Todd Dezago (writer), Leinil Francis Yu (pencils), Edgar Tadeo (inks), Richard Starkings & Comicraft's Emerson Miranda (letters) & John Marasigan (recap design), Jason Wright (colors), Jason Liebig (asst editor), Mark Powers (editor), Dexter Vines (c inks), Chris Dickey (c colors), Mike Wieringo (special thanks)
FEATURE CHARACTER: Wolverine (also in Wendigo's thoughts, next in X #76, UXM #356, X #77-78, UXM #359, all '98, W #900/3, '10; UXM&FF Ann, UXM #360, X #80, ½ & 81, all '98)
VILLAINS: Wendigo (also in Wolverine's thoughts, also as Andre Mornet in fb, his chr 1st app prior to W #129, '98; next in CM #2, '00), Wendigo spirit (next bts in CM #2, '00, next in CM #3, '00)
OTHER CHARACTERS: Tommy Jarman (farmer's son); Jake (Tommy's dog, dies), animals (bts, healed by Wolverine) inc cows; Jim Jarman (mentioned, Tommy's father), Tommy's mother & older brothers (prev mentioned), Mornet's brother (mentioned in fb); X-Men: Beast, Colossus, Cyclops, Nightcrawler, Rogue, Storm (prev 6 in Tommy's thoughts); Viper (recap page only)
LOCATIONS/ITEMS: Saskatchewan, Canada inc Jarmans' North Battleford farm w/barn (destroyed); Wisconsin woods (in fb) w/underground cavern / Canadian flag (as Wolverine's bandages), Jarmans' tractor (bts) & axe, Tommy's food, water, tray, pole, heater, first aid kit & kerosene w/tank (destroyed), Mornet's axe & bandages, fallen tree (prev 3 in fb), Wolverine's note, shed door (destroyed), Jake's collar
FLASHBACK: As Andre Mornet chops wood, the ground collapses; a tree pins him down and his axe severs two of his fingers. Days pass, and a desperate and starving Mornet decides to eat his own severed fingers.
SYNOPSIS: Young Tommy Jarman and his dog Jake discover the badly injured Wolverine in his family's barn. Elsewhere, Wendigo dimly recalls how he came to be cursed. As days pass, Tommy bonds with the recovering Wolverine, who explains his injuries by saying that creatures do what they must to survive. Wolverine knows that Wendigo will track him down, and sneaks away one night — but soon realizes that his scent is all over the Jarmans' shed, and races back. Wendigo smashes into the barn; Tommy and Jake hide, but Jake growls and barks, refusing to be silent. As Wendigo approaches the noise, a tearful Tommy is forced to break Jake's neck. Wolverine returns and attacks, splashing kerosene on Wendigo's facial wounds and striking a spark. The barn explodes in flames; Wendigo flees as Wolverine carries Tommy to safety.
NOTE: Though Wolverine battled Wendigo in Alberta last issue, the Jarmans' farm is in neighboring province Saskatchewan. It is not clear how Wolverine made it so far with his injuries; perhaps he drove several miles in the Humvee last issue before Wendigo destroyed it. The recap page shrinks from 2 pages to 1 page here. Viper is profiled on the recap page despite not appearing in the issue. This issue's digital lettering has several noticeable typos.

WOLVERINE #131 (Late November 1998)

"It Fell to Earth" (22 pages)

CREDITS: Todd Dezago (plot), Brian K. Vaughan (script), Cary Nord (pencils), Scott Hanna & Rob Hunter (inks), Richard Starkings & Comicraft's Emerson Miranda (letters) & John Marasigan (recap design), Kevin Tinsley (colors), Jason Liebig (asst editor), Mark Powers (editor)

FEATURE CHARACTER: Wolverine (also in rfb & pfb, next in HFH #18-19, '98-99, W:BR, '98)

VILLAINS: Viper (also in rfb & pfb, also in fb1 & fb3 between W #128, '98 & this issue's pfb; last in W #128, '98, next in W #139, '99), Hydra agents (some or others last in W #128, '98, next in Tb #0, '99) inc Akihiko & hazmat team (1 dead (also bts in pfb), 1 dies; 1 mentioned, died (prev 2 also in pfb) (prev 3 also in fb2 (some or all possibly bts) & fb3 prior to pfb; all but 1 other bts, died on mountain (also in fb2 (some bts) & fb3 (some or all bts) prior to issue)); spider-like alien (dies)

OTHER CHARACTERS: Khan (Viper's servant, also in fb1), alien's victims (dead), monk (prev 2 in fb3), pilot
ts flying helicopter); X-Men: Phoenix, Psylocke, Rogue; Shadowcat, Tyger Tiger, Sabretooth, Hand ninja (prev 7 in rfb); person, crane (also in
3), deer (prev 3 as statues), bird, dragon (prev 2 as paintings); Wendigo (recap page only); George Leigh-Mallory (quoted)

)CATIONS/ITEMS: Namjagbarwa Feng (Himalayan mountain, also in fb2 & fb3) w/base camp (bts) & creature's cave (also in fb3), Viper's
ghtown palace (also in fb1, fb3 & pfb) w/bio-lab (also in pfb), Princess Bar catacombs & owner's suite, Baran's palace, Madripoor harbor (bts) w/
vdra's floating base (prev 5 in rfb) / Wolverine's radio (bts), vial (destroyed), ropes, harness, backpack, bomb & shoe spikes, Hydra radio, tracking
it (prev 2 bts), helicopter & level four protective suits, Viper's poisons (bts), Viper's victims' green costumes, lipstick & hair dye (prev 4 in rfb),
er's disease & tracking device (prev 2 bts), bio-lab access panel, containment pods & acid pit, hazmat team's tent, binoculars (prev 2 in fb2),
ar (destroyed) & cold-weather suits (1 of each of prev 2 in main story, more in fb2 & fb3), alien's victim's steamer trunk (destroyed) & rifle (in rfb3)

ASHBACKS: Khan kneels before Viper (1). A Hydra hazmat team searches for what they think is a virus in the Himalayas (2). A monk tells
er of the alien, but the team she sends fails to find it; several die of exposure but three return (3). Viper shows Wolverine the three agents,
w infected, and asks him to find the virus so she can create an antidote (p).

'NOPSIS: Wolverine struggles to climb a Tibetan mountain. In Madripoor, Viper monitors the dead and dying Hydra agents, and demands
dates on Wolverine's search. Wolverine locates a cave with a survivor from the hazmat team, who is terrified of a creature. The agent
plains that they never found the virus; Wolverine realizes that Viper infected the men herself to convince him to help. Suddenly, a spider-like
en creature attacks, stinging Wolverine with potent venom. Wolverine's healing factor nearly succumbs, but he wills himself to fight back and
anages to kill the creature. Wolverine burns its body and returns to Madripoor with a sample — but destroys it before Viper's eyes.

)TE: Wolverine's claws have now grown back fully. This issue's original printing had a typo in p.5's digital lettering that resulted in an accidental
inic slur. Marvel recalled the comic and issued a corrected printing.

WOLVERINE: BLACK RIO (November 1998)

"Black Rio" (48 pages)

CREDITS: Joe Casey (writer), Oscar Jimenez (pencils), Eduardo Alpuente (inks), Richard Starkings & Comicraft's Emerson Miranda (letters) & John Marasigan (design), Gina Going (colors), Zena Tsarfin (asst editor), Ruben Diaz (editor)

FEATURE CHARACTER: Wolverine (also in fb between UToS #-1, '97 & WWHs:C/W #1, '10 fb; next in X:Lib #1-4, '98-99, XMU #22, '99, Av #10, '98, W #132, '98)

VILLAINS: Ezra Asher (Antonio's former wife, vampire), Saint Cyrus Leviticus (long-lived madman) & his alien symbiote (prev 2 die), bate-bola boys (costumed muggers, die, resurrected, destroyed)

OTHER CHARACTERS: Antonio Vargas (detective, dies, also in fb prior to issue),
nar (Vargas' acquaintance), Devil's Grill patrons & staff (prev 2 in fb), Cyrus & Asher's victims (dead, some resurrected & destroyed), diner
ok, travelers, police, Carnaval performers & attendees, hotel bartender & patrons, priest, funeral attendees, crane operator, sanitation
rkers, bystanders; shark, moth (prev 2 die), birds, spider; Jesus Christ (as statues), models (on posters), cartoon duck (as wall graffiti)

)CATIONS/ITEMS: Rio de Janeiro, Brazil inc Cañita Bravo's (diner), Devil's Grill (Vargas' tavern, in fb), Centro (downtown Rio) inc rooftops &
enida Rio Branco, Vargas' apartment & Central Police Precinct office, São Conrado cove, Hotel Dix bar, bate-bola boys' hangout, airport, bars,
metery & favelas (slums) w/church / Wolverine's bottle (in fb), chains (destroyed), luggage & liquor, airplane, Vargas' paperwork, handgun, key,
ffin, gravestone & rubber gloves, patron's knife, hurled chair (prev 2 in fb), Asher's mirror (destroyed), performers' costumes & instruments,
endees' costumes, police handgun, bate-bola boys' costumes, motorcycles, bats, bolas, pumpkin & nerve toxin, cemetery crane, sanitation
rkers' hose, brooms & street sweeper, church pew (destroyed), Leviticus' cloak

ASHBACK: Working as Vargas' bouncer, Wolverine brawls with patrons at the Devil's Grill.

'NOPSIS: Wolverine travels to Rio for Carnaval. He visits his old friend Antonio Vargas, now a detective, and helps him investigate vampiric
ngs. A shark attacks them at a cove where more bodies have been found, but Wolverine kills it. Elsewhere, vampire Ezra Asher plots with
Cyrus Leviticus. Wolverine parties hard, and defeats a gang of thugs who try to mug him; later, Ezra attacks and kills the thugs. Wolverine
d Vargas drink and reminisce, but Cyrus and Ezra ambush them at Vargas' home. Wolverine is knocked out, and Vargas recognizes Ezra
his long-missing wife — just before she kills him. Later, as a furious Wolverine searches for the villains, he encounters the muggers again
now undead creatures. Wolverine lets himself be captured; he awakens to Ezra feeding on him. Cyrus reveals that he hosts a parasitic alien
mbiote, and that Ezra's undead servants will kill everyone at Carnaval; the symbiote will harvest their death energy, making Cyrus immortal.
rus leaves; Wolverine breaks free and battles Ezra, who flees. Wolverine then locates and destroys the undead muggers, then battles Cyrus
the Carnaval attendees watch, killing him and his symbiote. Later, Wolverine visits Vargas' grave, as Ezra watches from the shadows.

)TE: All the blood shown in this issue is colored purple. Carnaval is spelled "Carnival" on the back cover.

WOLVERINE #132 (December 1998)

"A Rage in the Cage" (22 pages)

CREDITS: Fabian Nicieza (writer), Leinil Francis Yu (pencils), Edgar Tadeo, Scott Koblish, Scott Elmer & Har[...] Candelario (inks), Richard Starkings & Comicraft's Emerson Miranda (letters) & John Marasigan (recap desig[...] Jason Wright (colors), Jason Liebig (asst editor), Mark Powers (editor), Brandon Peterson (c pencils)

FEATURE CHARACTER: Wolverine (also in rfb, next in UXM #362-363, '98-99; X #83 fb, UXM #364, X #8[...] XMU #25/2, all '99)

VILLAIN: Bob Higgins (named, also in rfb & pfb, last in W #92, '95)

OTHER CHARACTERS: Linda Higgins (dead, also in photos; also in pfb, dies), Richard & Jane Higgins (prev 2 al[...] in pfb) (all also in rfb, last in W #91, '95), Dr. Kellan (Jane's doctor), Michelle Kole (Linda's sister, see NOTE), John K[...] (Michelle's husband), Mike (forensics expert), police inc Cowaher, Dunleavy, Farley & Jackson, trauma resident, nurs[...] hotel maid, travelers, airport security guards; X-Men: Beast, Professor X, Storm (prev 3 in rfb); person, animal (prev[...] as paintings), Tyrannosaurus rex (as statue), bear, rabbit (prev 2 as Jane's dolls); Sabretooth, Wendigo (prev 2 recap page only)

LOCATIONS/ITEMS: Salem Center inc Higgins' home (also in rfb & pfb), X-Mansion grounds (in rfb), Graymalkin Lane (also in rfb), bar (bts), Mik[...] house, police station & hospital w/morgue, highways inc Rte. 87, hotels (all but 1 bts) inc Hideaway Hotel w/Higgins' room, Albany Airport / Linda's t[...] tag, police fingerprinting equipment (bts), computer, crime scene tape, camera w/Polaroid pictures & cars w/radios, Wolverine's sensor array (in rfb)[...] motorcycle, Bob's hand wrappings (in rfb), receipt (bts), handgun (in pfb), beer cans (also in pfb) & car (also in rfb & pfb) w/oil, Higgins' shovel (also pfb), Richard's crayons & paper, hotel TV (bts) w/remote control, maid's cart & duster, Jane's bandages & dolls, guards' guns

FLASHBACKS: Seeing Bob beating Linda, Wolverine attacks but the X-Men restrain him (W #91, '95). Bob runs Wolverine down with his car (W #[...] '95). Bob beats Linda, but she threatens him with a gun. A panicked Richard hits Linda with a shovel; she falls, landing on Jane, and breaks her neck (p[...]

SYNOPSIS: As Police examine Linda Higgins' body, a doctor lists Jane in critical condition. Wolverine eavesdrops, assuming that Bob is [...] blame and feeling guilty for not stopping him months before. Outside the Higgins' home, Wolverine finds empty beer cans and a trail of oil fro[...] Bob's leaking car. As Wolverine follows the trail, Bob and Richard spend the night at a hotel. The police determine that a blunt object hit Lind[...] and recover a shovel. Wolverine finds the hotel; Bob and Richard are gone, but Richard left behind a scrawled message naming an airpo[...] As Jane recovers, police discover Richard's fingerprints on the shovel. At the airport, Wolverine confronts Bob, but Richard confesses to th[...] accidental killing. Wolverine points out that Bob created the hostile situation to begin with, and airport security arrests Bob.

NOTE: The Higgins family's last name is revealed here. Michelle Kole also calls herself "Aunt Laura" here; "Laura" may be a family nickname [...] her middle name. Bob's car must not have been as badly damaged as W #92, '95's crash made it appear; he is still driving the same car her[...]

WOLVERINE #133 (January 1999)

"Losing Control" (22 pages)

CREDITS: Erik Larsen (writer, variant c pencils), Jeff Matsuda (pencils), Jonath[...] Sibal (inks), Richard Starkings & Comicraft's Emerson Miranda (letters) & Jo[...] Marasigan (recap design), Jason Wright (colors), Jason Liebig (asst editor), Ma[...] Powers (editor), Chris Dickey (c colors)

FEATURE CHARACTER: Wolverine (also in symbolic image, also possessed by Aria[...]

GUEST STAR: Warbird (Carol Danvers, also in symbolic image, also as M[...] Marvel & Binary in her own thoughts, also as Danvers in rfb, last in IM #12, '99[...]

VILLAIN: Powerhouse (energy draining & projecting mutant, also on TV, last in S[...] #15, '91, next in SMU #4, '04)

OTHER CHARACTERS: Collector (Taneleer Tivan, collection-obsessed Elder of t[...] Universe, bts running Prison World, last in FF #389, '94), Trish Tilby (on TV, last in SMU #22, '98, next in Av Ann '99), Aria (body-possessing Zenna[...] 1st, unnamed, spirit also possessing Wolverine, Jh'az, pilot & witness), Prison World guards (some or others next in W #135, '99) inc Jh'az (Sau[...] alien, also possessed by Aria), Prison World staff: pilots (1 possessed by Aria, some bts in ships; some or others next bts in W #135, '99, 1 or anoth[...] next in W #137, '99) & Central Command officer (voice only, next in W #135, '99); Prison World captives (bts, imprisoned), police (some or others a[...] on TV) inc Sgt. Pierce (unnamed), Hardcase's patrons & waitress, newsreader (on TV), cameraman (bts on TV, filming Trish), crash witnesses (1 a[...] possessed by Aria), bystanders; butterfly; Captain Marvel (in rfb); X-Men: Colossus, Marrow, Nightcrawler, Rogue, Shadowcat, Storm; Cerebro (p[...] 7 recap page only)

LOCATIONS/ITEMS: Prison World (Collector's artificial planetoid, 1st, unnamed) w/hangar bay, Manhattan inc United Nations building (also on T[...] & Hardcase's bar w/alley, news studio (on TV), New York road (near Congers) w/nearby woods, Kree Earth outpost (in rfb), outer space (in Warbir[...] thoughts) / Prison World ships, Jh'az's blaster & comm unit, Central Command's comm system (bts), crew's equipment, guards' blasters, Hardcase's T[...] & pool table, balls & cues, Carol's drinks, Kree Psyche-Magnitron (bts in rfb, destroyed), news cameras (bts), police cars (destroyed, 1 on TV) & riot ge[...] (some or others on TV), Trish's microphone (on TV), Wolverine's motorcycle, debris, witness' car, tanker truck, mailbox (prev 3 destroyed)

FLASHBACK: Carol Danvers gains superpowers when a Kree Psyche-Magnitron explodes (CM #18, '69).

SYNOPSIS: On an artificial planet, Aria's spirit leaves her body and possesses a guard. Other guards try to intercept her, but Aria switches into a pilot's bo[...] and escapes in his spaceship. In New York, Wolverine and Warbird play pool and reminisce. But Warbird is bitter about her recent split from the Avenge[...] she drinks heavily, making Wolverine uncomfortable. The two see a news report that the human-hating Powerhouse is attacking the UN, and Wolver[...] decides to intervene. Warbird insists on helping, denying that she is impaired, but when they confront Powerhouse, Warbird's drunken attacks endan[...] bystanders. Nearby, two friends discover Aria's crashed spaceship; one investigates the cockpit just as the pilot awakens. Powerhouse easily defe[...] Warbird, but Wolverine gets fed up and knocks Powerhouse out. A car suddenly barrels into the fight scene and crashes; Wolverine checks on the dri[...] who is possessed by Aria. Warbird awakens seconds later to find that Aria has now possessed Wolverine!

NOTE: This issue's cover is labeled "The Great Escape, Part 1 of 6," but the rest of the arc does not carry this label on either the covers [...] story titles. This issue also has a variant cover. Next issue names Sgt. Pierce and Prison World, and reveals the Collector's involvement and [...] captives' existence. Aria is named in W #135, '99. Hardcase's bar is owned by the Harriers' leader Hardcase, as revealed in W #139, '99. Bet[...] known as Ms. Marvel, Carol took the codename Warbird in Av #4, '98, but quit the Avengers in Av #7, '98 when they court-martialed her o[...] her growing alcoholism.

WOLVERINE #134 (Early February 1999)

"Choice in the Matter" (22 pages)

CREDITS: Erik Larsen (writer), Jeff Matsuda (pencils), Jonathan Sibal (inks), Richard Starkings & Comicraft's Emerson Miranda (letters) & John Marasigan (recap design), Jason Wright (colors), Jason Liebig (asst editor, uncredited), Mark Powers (editor)

FEATURE CHARACTER: Wolverine (also in his own thoughts, also possessed by Aria)

GUEST STARS: Avengers (Earth's premier super hero team): Firestar (Angelica Jones, generates microwaves), Justice (Vance Astrovik, telekinetic), Vision (synthozoid) (all last in Av #12, '99, next in Av Ann '99); New Warriors (teenage superteam): Rage (Elvin Haliday, super-strength & durability), Speedball (Robbie Baldwin, generates kinetic field) (prev 2 last in Hawk, '98, next in Av #13, '99); Black Cat (Felicia Hardy, tech-enhanced adventurer, last in SenSM #30, '98, next in PPSM #5, '99), Black Widow (last in XFor/Ch Ann, '98, chr last in DD #9, '99, chr next in DD #14, '01, next in BW #1, '99), Darkhawk (Chris Powell, bonded to alien armor, next in NW #1, '99), Falcon (Sam Wilson, wears glider suit, next in BP #16, '00) (prev 2 last in Av #4, '98), Human Torch (last in FF #12, '98, chr last in DD #8, '99, next in SM #4, '99), Moon Knight (Marc Spector, avatar of Khonshu, last in MK #4, '98, next in MK #1, '99), USAgent (John Walker, strength-enhanced patriot, last in Cap #10, '98, last bts in Cap #11, '98, next in Tb #23, '99), Warbird (next in W #138, '99)

OTHER CHARACTERS: Cardiac (Dr. Elias Wirtham, cyborg vigilante, last in SMU #14, '96), Solo (James Bourne, anti-terror vigilante, last in Solo #4, '94) (both next in W #140, '99), Starjammers (interstellar freebooters): Ch'od (Saurid alien), Corsair (Christopher Summers, Cyclops & Havok's father), Mam'selle Hepzibah (Mephitisoid alien), Raza Longknife (alien cyborg) (prev 4 last in Starj #4, '96); Aria (body bts in holding cell, also as chess piece; spirit possessing Wolverine, also as vision & symbolic image), Collector, Prison World staff: Space Parasite (Randau, energy-absorbing Xeronian alien, last in IHulk #103, '68, next in W #136, '99), Torgo (robotic Mekkan alien, last in IHulk #270, '82), Uroc (Asgardian Uru rock troll, last in Thor #450, '92, next in W #137, '99), Collector's aide (Solon alien); Prison World guards & captives (prev 2 on monitors), police (some bts in cars) inc Sgt. Pierce (named), witness, paramedic, driver, Collector's alien trophies (dead, in tubes), Xem alien (unnamed, dead, as rug); X-Men: Colossus, Cyclops, Nightcrawler, Phoenix, Storm (prev 5 in Wolverine's thoughts); Powerhouse, Jh'az, Prison World pilot (prev 3 recap page only)

LOCATIONS/ITEMS: Manhattan inc rooftop & United Nations building, Prison World (named, see NOTE): cells (on monitors, 1 bts) & Collector's control room / Pierce's handgun, witness & driver's cars, parked van (prev 3 destroyed), Firestar's power-regulating costume, news van w/camera, police cars, Falcon's glider suit, USAgent's motorcycle & shield, Black Widow's "Widow's Bite" bracelets, Solo's weaponry inc guns w/laser sight, Cardiac's armor (destroyed), beta particle reactor (bts) & staff, rubble, Darkhawk's amulet, Black Cat's agility & balance-boosting devices (bts) & strength-enhancing costume w/claws, water tower (destroyed), aide's tracking computer (bts), Collector's chess pieces (destroyed), trophy cases & monitors, Aria's body's holding cell (bts), Uroc's Uru metal body, Starjammers' floating cage

SYNOPSIS: Aria forces the possessed Wolverine to attack Warbird and the police, as Wolverine realizes to his horror that his body is no longer under his control. The Avengers arrive; Wolverine defeats Firestar and Vision, then breaks free from Justice's telekinetic bubble and flees. Wolverine tries to fight Aria's control, begging her not to use lethal force. Several other heroes attempt to subdue Wolverine, but the possessed hero easily defeats Moon Knight, USAgent and Falcon. Black Widow tries to calm Wolverine, but he uses her as a human shield. Wolverine defeats Solo and Cardiac, makes short work of Darkhawk, Rage and Speedball, then badly injures the Black Cat and douses the Human Torch with a water tower. Aria is pleased by her "test" of Wolverine's abilities, and explains that she chose him based on his fearsome reputation to help her rescue thousands of captive aliens from a prison planet. Wolverine is furious at her methods, but grudgingly agrees. On Prison World, the Collector and his staff plan for Aria's return...

NOTE: Each X-book shipped biweekly for one month during the winter of '98-99; Wolverine shipped twice this month. The recap section expands back to 2 pages, but is eliminated next issue. Although W #136, '99 clarifies that Prison World does not have an official name, Aria first uses its longstanding nickname here. The Xem race is named in OHMU:U #1, '10. One of the Collector's trophies is the head of a xenomorph from the *Alien* film series. Aria says "Help me, Wolverine – you're my only hope!", unknowingly paraphrasing an iconic line from *Star Wars Episode IV: A New Hope*.

WOLVERINE #135 (Late February 1999)

"From Bad to Worse" (22 pages)

CREDITS: Erik Larsen (writer), Jeff Matsuda (pencils), Jonathan Sibal (inks), Richard Starkings & Comicraft's Emerson Miranda (letters), Jason Wright (colors), Jason Liebig (asst editor), Mark Powers (editor), Liquid! (c colors)

FEATURE CHARACTER: Wolverine (also possessed by Aria)

OTHER CHARACTERS: Starjammers: Ch'od, Corsair, Hepzibah, Raza; Aria (named, spirit possessing Wolverine & guard, also as vision), Collector, Prison World staff: Torgo, Central Command officer (Elan alien, last voice only in W #133, '99), pilots (bts in ships, some or others last in W #133, '99, 1 next in W #137, '99) & Collector's aide; Prison World guards (some or others last in W #133, '99) inc Xxan Xxar (Xixix alien, last in FF #262, '84), Marik (squad leader), Chameleoid alien (unnamed, also possessed by Aria), Lem alien & Tribbitite alien, Prison World captives (all but 1 bts, imprisoned), Sidrian Hunters (Sidri aliens); Collector's alien trophies (dead, as skulls)

LOCATIONS/ITEMS: Outer space, Prison World w/Central Command office, hangar bay & Collector's control room / Aria's stolen spaceship (destroyed), Prison World's scanners, shields, trapping field (prev 3 bts) & air ducts, pilots' ships, Starjammers' floating cage, Central Command computer & comm system (prev 2 bts), guards' blasters, Marik's comm unit (bts) & lock disabling device, Chameleoid guard's blaster & restraints, Sidrian Hunter's leash

SYNOPSIS: As Aria's spaceship traverses deep space, Wolverine reprimands Aria, whose spirit still possesses him, for her earlier actions. The ship arrives at Prison World, and Wolverine is awed by its sheer size. A tractor beam pulls the ship into the docking bay and guards board it. Wolverine battles them, but realizes that Aria is no longer possessing him. A stray shot causes the ship to explode, and Wolverine uses the opportunity to slip away. The Collector orders the mechanical Torgo to find Wolverine, and taunts his other captives, the Starjammers. Elsewhere

in Prison World, Wolverine crawls out of an air duct, wondering where Aria went and how he is supposed to free the artificial planet's ent population by himself. A squadron of guards detects Wolverine, but he ambushes and defeats them. Another guard soon confronts Wolverin but turns out to be possessed by Aria. She tells Wolverine to pose as her prisoner — but Torgo suddenly confronts the two, with a pair of dea Sidri aliens by his side…
NOTE: The Chameleoid race is named in FF #51, '02. Wolverine comments "I've got a bad feeling about this," quoting another iconic line fr Star Wars Episode IV: A New Hope.

WOLVERINE #136 (March 1999)

"Trust" (22 pages)

CREDITS: Erik Larsen (plot, co-script), Eric Stephenson (co-script), Jeff Matsuda (pencils), Jonathan Sib (inks), Richard Starkings & Comicraft (letters), Jason Wright (colors), Mark Powers (editor), Sean Chen (c penci
FEATURE CHARACTER: Wolverine
VILLAIN: Galactus (Galan, devourer of worlds, bts, detected by Blip, last in FF #8, '98)
OTHER CHARACTERS: Starjammers: Ch'od, Corsair, Hepzibah, Raza; Aria (spirit also possessing guard, al as vision), Collector, Prison World staff: Space Parasite (last in W #134, '99, next in Anni:HoG #1, '07), Torgo (al in rfb; also in fb between FF #174, '76 fb & FF #91, '69), Collector's aide (next in W #138, '99), Central Comma officer, Blip alien & Ovoid alien; Prison World captives inc Vuk (D'bari alien, last in SH #46, '92), Bzztl (Vuk's sc 1st), Vaag alien (prev 3 unnamed), Badoon alien, Judan alien, Korbinite alien, Kree alien, Krogarrian alien, Xant alien, Zen-Whoberian alien & Zn^rx alien, Prison World guards inc Chameleoid alien (possessed by Aria), Sidri Hunters, Torgo's alien opponent (in fb); Kral IV Skrulls (1 also in symbolic image in fb), Fantastic Four: Human Torch, Mr. Fantastic, Thing (pr 4 in rfb)
LOCATIONS/ITEMS: Prison World w/Central Command office, holding cells & Collector's control room, Skrulls' Kral IV arena (in fb & rfb Starjammers' floating cell, guards' testing equipment (bts) & handheld teleporter, Aria's stolen spaceship (destroyed) & power-inhibiting colla Sidrian Hunter's leash (bts), Chameleoid guard's restraints (bts) & blaster, Prison World's scanners (bts) & shields, Ovoid's body-switchi equipment
FLASHBACKS: Impressed with the Thing's nobility, Torgo helps the Fantastic Four defeat their Skrull captors (FF #93, '69). Torgo batt opponents in the Skrulls' arena.
SYNOPSIS: The Collector's guards return Raza to the Starjammers' cell; Raza reports that something seems amiss in Prison World. Elsewhe Torgo has the Sidri incapacitate the guard that Aria possesses, but convinces Wolverine to hear him out, explaining that the Collector has th best interests of all the aliens held there at heart. Meanwhile, a Blip returns to Prison World and delivers bad news to the Collector's aide. Tor takes Wolverine to a holding area, and tells him to mingle with the aliens to learn more about Prison World — but as soon as Torgo leaves, th aliens viciously attack, assuming that Wolverine is allied with the Collector. Elsewhere, Prison World staff force Aria's spirit back into her bo and affix a collar that prevents her from possessing anyone else. Wolverine's battle ends when a D'bari captive recognizes him as an X-Ma Wolverine begins rallying the prisoners for a mass escape. Elsewhere, the Starjammers hear the aide's bad news, and realize that they mu aid the Collector against Wolverine.
NOTE: Writer Erik Larsen's first name is misspelled "Eric" here, a common error. Dark Phoenix destroyed the D'bari homeworld in X #135, ' Vuk and Bzztl are named in OHMU #3, '06, which also confirms that Vuk is the same D'bari seen in Av #4, '64, SH #43-46, '92-93 & UXM #38 '00. The Vaag race is named in MM:WMD/3, '05. The Krogarrian tells Wolverine "He doesn't like you. Neither do I," unknowingly paraphrasi another iconic line from Star Wars Episode IV: A New Hope. The assistant editor of this issue and next is unknown; it is either Jason Liebig Pete Franco.

WOLVERINE #137 (April 1999)

"Countdown to Destruction" (22 pages)

CREDITS: Erik Larsen (writer), Jeff Matsuda (pencils), Jonathan Sibal (inks), Richard Starkings & Comicraf Oscar Gongora (letters), Mark Bernardo (colors), Mark Powers (editor)
FEATURE CHARACTER: Wolverine
VILLAIN: Galactus
OTHER CHARACTERS: Starjammers: Ch'od, Corsair, Hepzibah, Raza; Aria, Collector (bts freei Starjammers), Prison World staff inc Uroc (last in W #134, '99), Torgo, Blip alien, Ovoid alien & pilot (som or others last in W #133, '99, some or others last bts in W #135, '99), Prison World captives inc Vuk (next Starhammer in UXM #387, '00), Bzztl & Courga alien, Prison World guards inc Millie
LOCATIONS/ITEMS: Prison World w/holding cells, main power grid & hangar bay / Guards' blasters truncheon, captives' possessions, Aria's power-inhibiting collar, Prison World's ships (1 destroyed), shields (b & air ducts, Millie & Torgo's comm units, cell door's locking mechanism (destroyed), power grid's bridge (destroyed), engine & breakers, Uro Uru body, Corsair's blaster, rubble, Taa II (Galactus' worldship, bts)
SYNOPSIS: Torgo and the Starjammers lead the guards in a thorough search of the cells, looking for Wolverine. Elsewhere, Wolverine snea into Aria's cell and defeats the guards; the two then infiltrate Prison World's main power grid, planning to shut it down and open the ce Wolverine disables the grid, but Uroc attacks him. Wolverine's claws break on Uroc's Uru body, but Uroc accidentally shatters a bridge str dropping him into the engine core. With the power shut down, prisoners flood the halls; guards try to stop them and a riot breaks out. Tor vainly tries to secure the hangar bay as prisoners steal ships and attempt to flee. The Starjammers confront Wolverine, revealing that most the prisoners are the last of their kinds, and that the Collector wasn't imprisoning them — he was protecting their races from extinction. Cors further explains that the world-devouring Galactus was approaching, and with Prison World's power down, so are the shields that kept it hidde As Prison World begins to quake, Galactus arrives.
NOTE: Wolverine's first thought balloon on p.12 incorrectly points to Uroc.

WOLVERINE #138 (May 1999)

"Doomsday!" (22 pages)

CREDITS: Erik Larsen (writer), Jeff Matsuda (pencils, pp.1-15), Steve Scott (pencils, pp.16-19), Yancey Labat (pencils, p.20-22), Jonathan Sibal, Scott Elmer & Scott Koblish (inks), Richard Starkings & Comicraft's Oscar Gongora (letters), Mark Bernardo (colors), Pete Franco (asst editor), Mark Powers (editor), Leinil Francis Yu (c pencils)

FEATURE CHARACTER: Wolverine

GUEST STAR: Warbird (last in W #134, next bts in IM #15, next in Av #16, all '99)

VILLAIN: Galactus (also in symbolic image, also possessed by Aria, next in Sup/FF, '99)

OTHER CHARACTERS: Starjammers: Sikorsky (Chr'ylite physician, last in IHulk #415, '94), Ch'od, Corsair, Hepzibah, Raza (all next in Galact #5, '00); Aria (spirit also possessing Galactus, dies), Collector (next in SH:CC, '09), Prison World staff (many bts, many die) inc Torgo (possibly dies), Collector's aide (last in W #136, '99), pilots e, all but 1 bts in ships) & Ovoid alien, Prison World guards (many bts, many die) inc Kerivak, Chameleoid alien & Tribbitite alien, Prison World otives (many bts, many die) inc Bzztl & Zn^rx alien, restaurant patron

)CATIONS/ITEMS: Prison World (destroyed) w/hangar bay, outer space, Seattle restaurant / Taa II, rubble, Prison World ships (many stroyed) w/comm systems (all but 1 bts), Starjammer (Starjammers' spaceship) w/teleporter & medi-lab (prev 2 bts), Ch'od's repair equipment s), Collector's vessel, Aria's power-inhibiting collar (destroyed) w/Ovoid's remote control, Galactus' Elemental Converter, pilot's robot body, ia & Wolverine's parachutes

✔NOPSIS: As Galactus manifests, Prison World's inhabitants panic and Wolverine realizes that he made a terrible mistake. Pilots begin acking Galactus, hoping to delay his feeding so others can escape. Wolverine finds Bzztl in the crowd, crying because he cannot find his her. Wolverine delivers Bzztl to the Starjammers, who are packing their ship with prisoners, then decides to try to stop Galactus. The Collector oukes Aria for destroying his refuge and condemning thousands to death, then flees. Torgo tells Wolverine that they must destroy Galactus' emental Converter. Aria manages to briefly possess Galactus, but he quickly expels her; Wolverine's claws shatter against the Converter, but continues desperately pounding against it. Torgo delivers the fatally injured Aria to the Starjammers, who convince Wolverine that he must e. Torgo continues trying to destroy the Converter — but as Wolverine watches from the departing ship, angrily blaming himself, Galactus nsumes Prison World and Sikorsky reports Aria's death. Days later, back on Earth, a saddened Wolverine explains the adventure to Warbird.

)TE: Wolverine's claws seem to have grown back fully in the short span of time between last issue and this one. Oddly, when he breaks them ain here, they do not grow back by next issue, a longer period of time. Most or all the Prison World staff, guards and captives seen on-panel identified in previous issues are likely bts here — though it is impossible to say with any certainty, as several unidentified people fled Prison orld in ships last issue. This issue's letters page has a B&W preview of the cover and 2 pages from next issue.

WOLVERINE #139 (June 1999)

"The Freaks Come Out At Night" (22 pages)

CREDITS: Erik Larsen (writer), Leinil Francis Yu (pencils), Dexter Vines (inks), Richard Starkings & Comicraft (letters), Joe Rosas (colors), Pete Franco (asst editor), Mark Powers (editor)

FEATURE CHARACTER: Wolverine (next in UXM #365, Gam #1, X #85, X:MW, UXM #366, X #86, UXM #367, X #87, PPSM #4, Dp #27, UXM #368, X #88, UXM #369, X #89, UXM #370, X #90, W #145 fb, Hulk #8, UXM #372 bts, AX #1-3, X #95, W #145, all '99)

GUEST STARS: X-Men: Nightcrawler (bts, listened to Wolverine), Storm (bts, told Cable about Wolverine) (both between X #84, '99 & UXM #365, '99); Cable (last in XMan #47, '99, next in Cable #64, '99)

VILLAINS: Viper (last in W #131, '98, next in GenX #54, '99), Arnim Zola (fanatical geneticist, last in Tb #24, '99 fb, next in Cap #50/6, '02), Primus (Zola's android, last in NW #73, '96, next in Tb #103, '06), Doughboy (Zola's malleable creation, last in Cap #396, '92, next in Tb:II, '08), Zola's creatures inc Monkeyboy

THER CHARACTERS: Hardcase, Harriers: Blindside (Bobbi Chase), Longbow (Amelia Greer) (all last in UXM #261, '90); Stacey Kramer able's waitress friend, between Cable #63-64, '99), Hardcase's patrons & waitress, Babel's patrons, Harriers' benefactor (bts hiring them), la's creatures' victims (bts, dead), police (bts in cars); Harriers: Lifeline, Warhawk (prev 2 mentioned, got married), Timebomb (mentioned, got trouble); Spider Jerusalem (on magazine cover), cartoon dog (on poster)

)CATIONS/ITEMS: Manhattan inc rooftops, docks, Hardcase's bar & Babel's diner / Cable's Psimitar, bar window (destroyed), Monkeyboy's licopter (destroyed) w/machine gun, Longbow's handgun, Hardcase's broom, dock (destroyed), Zola's control device & artificial body w/ESP x

✔NOPSIS: Wolverine catches up with Hardcase, who has semi-retired from the mercenary business. Cable arrives, checking in on Wolverine er hearing about his experience on Prison World. Suddenly, the brutally beaten Longbow is thrown through the bar window. Wolverine and able chase down her attacker, but are shocked to discover that it is a lobster-like creature. A helicopter rescues the monster and flies away, t Cable damages it with a psionic blast. Back at Hardcase's, Longbow explains that she and Blindside were hired in Madripoor to investigate aths and disappearances linked to similar monsters. Wolverine and Cable locate the helicopter's crash site, but are attacked by monkey- and ant-like creatures and captured by the living ship Doughboy, as Arnim Zola reveals himself to be the creatures' master. Cable grabs Zola's ntrol device and wards the creatures off, but Zola ejects the two from Doughboy in midair. Cable lowers them telekinetically, and as the two onder what Zola's agenda was, Zola gloats over his captive — Wolverine's wife, Viper.

)TE: The Viper subplot is never continued; in her next appearance she is free without explanation, and the "acquaintance" that Zola plans to ke her to is never identified.

WOLVERINE #140 (July 1999)

"Vengeance" (22 pages)

CREDITS: Erik Larsen (writer), Leinil Francis Yu (pencils), Dexter Vines (inks), Richard Starkings & Comicra[ft?]
Albert Deschesne (letters), Joe Rosas (colors), Pete Franco (asst editor), Mark Powers (editor)
GUEST STARS: X-Men: Colossus (last in GenX #52, '99), Nightcrawler (last in X Ann '99) (both next in UX
#372, '99), Marrow (Sarah, removable bone outgrowths) (prev 2 chr last in CM #6, '00 fb), Professor X (prev 2 la
in X #91, '99, next in Gam Ann '99)
VILLAINS: "Wolverine" (Skrull imposter, see NOTE, 1st but chr last in CM #6, '00 fb, next in XMU #24, '9
Reanimator (robot-controlling mutant, 1st, unnamed, next in Nova #3, '99) & his refurbished robots (destroye[d])
Spider-Slayers (Spencer Smythe's Spider-Man-hunting robots): Mark II (last in ASM #58, '68), Mark VI (last
ASM #191, '79) (another of prev 2 next in ASM #20, '00), Mark III (last in ASM #105, '72); Thing robot (prev 2 ne
in W #149, '00), Magneto robot
OTHER CHARACTERS: Cardiac (next in MTU #5, '05), Solo (next in Cable&Dp #7, '04) (both last in W #134, '99), witnesses (bts reporti[ng]
Magneto sightings), police (bts in cars), diner staff & patrons, bystanders; woman (as mannequin), singer, historical figures (prev 2 as painting[s])
LOCATIONS/ITEMS: New York inc diner & West Side junkyard, X-Mansion / Reanimator's other robots (destroyed) w/blaster & energy swo[rd?]
Spider-Slayers' clawed tendrils, crushed cars (destroyed), debris, police cars (all but 1 bts), Nightcrawler's image inducer, Solo & Cardia[c's]
police band radios (prev 2 bts), Solo's weaponry inc knives & guns, hurled chair & dumpster, Cardiac's beta particle reactor (bts), staff & arm[or?]
Professor X's wheelchair
SYNOPSIS: Wolverine and Nightcrawler investigate reports that Magneto was sighted in a junkyard. They are attacked by robots, one
which resembles Magneto — but although the two destroy their opponents, they fail to notice the nearby shadowy figure controlling the robo[ts.]
Wolverine and Nightcrawler then eat at a diner, where they discuss the X-Men's adventure on the Skrull homeworld, and Professor X's rece[nt]
attitude change and harsh training regimens. Wolverine bumps into a belligerent patron, spilling his drink, and a brawl breaks out — whi[ch]
escalates when Solo attacks, seeking revenge for Wolverine's recent rampage through Manhattan. Cardiac arrives and attacks Wolveri[ne]
as well, but Nightcrawler interrupts, explaining that Wolverine had been possessed by Aria at the time. The two vigilantes grudgingly belie[ve]
Nightcrawler and leave, and Nightcrawler lectures Wolverine for jumping straight into a fight instead of trying to explain. Back at the X-Mansi[on,]
Marrow objects to Professor X's haranguing. When Wolverine tries to convince Professor X to relax, he is sharply rebuked as well.
NOTE: Although readers were unaware of it at the time, the true Wolverine does not appear in W #140-143, '99. UXM #375, '99 and W #14[?]
'99 reveal that Skrulls working for Apocalypse kidnapped Wolverine just after X #90, '99, and replaced him with a Skrull imposter implante[d]
with Wolverine's memories. Apocalypse brainwashed Wolverine into becoming the Horseman Death, while the imposter spied on the X-Me[n.]
Professor X acts curt here because he has subconsciously sensed that something is amiss, and is subjecting the X-Men to stress in hop[es]
of flushing out a traitor. Marrow's last name is unrevealed to date. Reanimator is named in Nova #7, '99; his junkyard hideout is specified
on Manhattan's West Side in W #149, '00. Two of his robots resemble the Transformers' Optimus Prime and *Lost In Space*'s Robot B-9. T[he]
Spider-Slayers seen here may be replicas, not refurbished originals. The X-Men's adventure on the Skrull homeworld occurred in X #89-90[,]
UXM #370, all '99.

WOLVERINE #141 (August 1999)

"Broken Dreams" (22 pages)

CREDITS: Erik Larsen & Eric Stephenson (writers), Leinil Francis Yu (pencils), Dexter Vines (inks), Richa[rd]
Starkings & Comicraft (letters), Marie Javins (colors), Pete Franco (asst editor, uncredited), Mark Powers (edito[r)]
Liquid! (c colors), Jay Faerber (special thanks)
GUEST STARS: Generation X: Banshee (last in XFor #91, '99), M (Monet St. Croix, flight, telepathy
heightened strength, durability & intelligence, see NOTE), Chamber, Emma Frost, Husk, M, Synch (all also
symbolic images), Jubilee, Skin (prev 7 last in GenX #56, '99) (all next in GenX #57, '99); Professor X (bts sendi[ng]
"Wolverine" to Academy, see NOTE; last in Gam Ann '99, next in UXM #372, '99)
VILLAINS: "Wolverine" (Skrull, last in W/Pun #4, '99), Donald Pierce (also in pfb, last in Cable #53, '98, next
GenX #69, '00 fb)
OTHER CHARACTERS: Gateway (last in W #125, '98, next in XX #4, '01), Khyber (vengeful cyborg) & [his?]
troops, Hank, Jean, Scott (prev 3 last in XFor #8, '92, chr last in MTU #19, '06), Bobby (last in Cable #1, '92), Warren (prev 5 Cable's robo[t]
assistants, destroyed), Massachusetts Academy students (some or others last in GenX #53, '99, next in GenX #57, '99), Pierce's robo[t]
henchmen (destroyed); Cable's Russian friend (in photo)
LOCATIONS/ITEMS: Massachusetts Academy (formerly Xavier's School for Gifted Youngsters, see NOTE), Swiss Alps (in pfb) inc Cabl[e's]
chalet (destroyed, also in pfb) w/Pierce's workshop, Khyber's storage cache (bts) / Wolverine's cowboy hat, Jubilee's cellphone, Generati[on]
X's computers w/security files (bts) & disks, Gateway's bull-roarer, Cable's sky cycle (in pfb), photo, chair & computers (also in pfb) w/fil[es]
(bts), Pierce's cables (others also in pfb) & new cyborg body w/morphing arms (1 destroyed) & stolen Adamantium, henchmen's tools & f[ire?]
extinguishers, Khyber's teleporter (bts), hover-bike & cybernetic implants, troops' armor, blasters & hover-bikes w/guns
FLASHBACK: The injured Pierce finds and breaks into Cable's Alps chalet (p).
SYNOPSIS: At the Massachusetts Academy, Wolverine runs tests on Generation X's security files, waving off Banshee's protests a[nd]
explaining that he's just following Professor X's request. Wolverine then leaves with Jubilee to catch up, but the other Generation X membe[rs]
stage a mock attack on him, hoping to test themselves against a real X-Man — a fight quickly broken up by Emma Frost. Suddenly, Gatew[ay]
appears and teleports Wolverine and Jubilee to Cable's Swiss Alps chalet. Cable's robot assistants attack, and Donald Pierce reveals that [he]
has taken over the house. Pierce explains that Cable's files led him to a hidden Adamantium cache, which he upgraded his cyborg body wi[th]
Wolverine battles Pierce, but Khyber interrupts the fight, claiming that the Adamantium belongs to him and viciously attacking Pierce. Wolveri[ne]
rescues Jubilee just in time as Khyber's men destroy the chalet. Khyber defeats Pierce and teleports away, leaving Wolverine and Jubilee [to]
wonder what Gateway's purpose was in sending them there.
NOTE: Given that the Wolverine Skrull is a spy, his claim that Professor X sent him to check Generation X's security files may be false, a[nd]
Professor X may not actually be bts here. Synch fails when trying to copy Wolverine's mutant powers, a clue that "Wolverine" is an imposte[r.]

onet St. Croix was freed from the Penance form in GenX #40, '98 and adopted the codename M — formerly used by her sisters Claudette and Nicole, who merged into a single being and were posing as Monet while she was trapped. Xavier's School admitted non-mutant students and reverted to its former name, the Massachusetts Academy, between GenX #49-50, '99. Cable's robotic assistants are named after the five original X-Men. This issue includes three bound-in trading cards featuring the Hulk, Captain America and She-Hulk, promo items for a "Got Milk?" campaign, with art by Andy Kubert and colors by Paul Mounts.

WOLVERINE #142 (September 1999)

"Reunion!" (22 pages)

CREDITS: Erik Larsen & Eric Stephenson (writers), Leinil Francis Yu (pencils), Dexter Vines & Scott Koblish (inks), Richard Starkings & Comicraft (letters), Glynis Oliver (colors), Pete Franco (asst editor), Mark Powers (editor)
GUEST STARS: Alpha Flight: Aurora (Jeanne-Marie Beaubier), Northstar (Jean-Paul Beaubier) (prev 2 twin siblings & mutant speedsters), Sasquatch (Dr. Walter Langkowski, transforms into animalistic powerhouse), Guardian (James Hudson), Shaman (also in pfb), Puck; Beta Flight (Dept. H's trainee team): Murmur (Arlette Truffaut, controls minds via touch), Flex (Adrian Corbo, transforms limbs into blades) (prev 2 next bts in HoM #8, '05), Radius (Jared Corbo, generates force field, next in UXM #401, '02), Ghost Girl (Lilli Stephens, becomes intangible) (prev 4 in pfb) (all last in AFlt #20, '99), Vindicator (James Hudson's synthoid clone, last as Guardian in AFlt #20, '99, also in pfb); Heather Hudson (Alpha Flight/Dept. H liaison, last as Vindicator in AFlt #20, '99)
VILLAINS: "Wolverine" (Skrull, also on monitor), Weapon X (Kane, last in Cable #39, '97), AIM (Advanced Idea Mechanics, scientific arms dealers & developers): MODOK (George Tarleton, Mental Organism Designed Only for Killing, AIM leader, last in IM/Cap Ann '98), agents (some or others last in Av #13, '99)
OTHER CHARACTER: Dept. H official (in pfb, see NOTE)
LOCATIONS/ITEMS: Canadian AIM base (also on monitor) w/lab, Dept. H headquarters (in pfb) / Heather's gun, AIM armor (some destroyed), guns, winch, restraints, rappelling cables, comm unit & android w/blasters & remote control, Alpha Flight's comm units (bts) & training robot (in pfb) w/missiles, base's cameras (bts), monitors, computers, gas & retractable walls, MODOK's comm unit (bts) & anti-grav chair, lab's medical equipment & steel partitions, Weapon X's synthetic cyborg limbs
FLASHBACK: Dept. H assigns the less-experienced Alphans to Beta Flight, and the new team trains with Alpha Flight (p).
SYNOPSIS: Wolverine and Alpha Flight assault a secret Canadian AIM base. A large android attacks them, but the heroes grab its control device and turn it against the AIM agents. Wolverine and the Alphans enter the base and begin searching for Guardian and his synthoid double Vindicator, who were kidnapped by AIM, as MODOK observes them from afar with a shadowy ally. Wolverine and Heather talk about all the changes that Alpha Flight has gone through over the years, when the heroes are suddenly separated by sliding steel partitions and gassed. AIM agents restrain the unconscious Alpha Flight, but find Wolverine missing. Nearby, Wolverine accesses a computer and finds Guardian's location; he battles his way into the lab, finds Guardian and Vindicator attached to sinister-looking medical equipment, and bullies an AIM agent into sealing the lab. Nearby, MODOK gloats over the captive Alpha Flight, and orders his ally — Weapon X — to eliminate Wolverine.
NOTE: James Hudson has returned to his original codename of Guardian; Heather briefly retook the codename Vindicator before retiring from Alpha Flight shortly before this issue. AFlt #1-20, '97-99 featured a seemingly de-aged James Hudson as Guardian, while another Guardian claiming to be the true James Hudson returned in AFlt #13, '98. AFlt #20, '99 revealed that one of them was a synthoid clone, but did not clarify which one; this issue reveals that the younger James is the clone, and that he took the codename Vindicator after Heather retired. Ghost Girl's first name is revealed in OHMU HC1, '08. Despite appearances, the Dept. H official demoting the newer Alphans to Beta Flight is not General Jeremy Clarke, who died in AFlt #12, '98. He may be Agent Skimmer, who is 1st bts in AFlt #1, '04 fb and 1st in AFlt #8, '04.

WOLVERINE #143 (October 1999)

"Rebirth" (18 pages)

CREDITS: Erik Larsen & Eric Stephenson (writers), Leinil Francis Yu (pencils), Dexter Vines (inks), Richard Starkings & Comicraft's Jason Levine (letters), Marie Javins (colors), Pete Franco (asst editor), Mark Powers (editor), Gerry Alanguilan (c inks), Mike Rockwitz (c colors)
GUEST STARS: Alpha Flight: Aurora, Northstar (both next in UXM #379, '00), Puck (next in GenX #58, '99), Shaman (next in W #171, '02), Guardian, Sasquatch; Snowbird (Narya, Inuit demi-goddess, last as spirit in AFlt #68, '89), Heather Hudson (next in W #173, '02), Vindicator (dies)
VILLAINS: "Wolverine" (Skrull), Weapon X (chr next as Garrison Kane in WXD:AZ, '02, next as Garrison Kane in Dp #57, '01), MODOK (next in X51 #11, '00), AIM agents
LOCATIONS/ITEMS: Canadian AIM base w/labs / Lab's medical equipment, AIM armor (some destroyed), guns, restraints, aircraft & android battle suit (destroyed), Snowbird's tube (destroyed) & feed cables, base's equipment & computer w/database (bts), MODOK's anti-grav chair
SYNOPSIS: Guardian and Vindicator awaken, and Wolverine deduces that AIM was stealing information straight from their minds. They escape through a hole that Wolverine tore in the wall, but are stunned to find Snowbird — Alpha Flight's long-dead teammate — unconscious in the next lab. Weapon X attacks and battles Wolverine, but Vindicator knocks him out with an electrical blast. Elsewhere, AIM agents discuss the source of Shaman's powers, and Heather realizes that this AIM faction is studying the supernatural. MODOK gloats to Heather, but Wolverine interrupts; as AIM agents swarm Wolverine, Sasquatch transforms back to human form, slips out of his restraints and frees the other Alphans. Vindicator joins the fray, piloting a giant AIM battle suit, but MODOK damages it with a power blast and flees with the AIM agents. Guardian flies to get to Vindicator, but the battle suit explodes, killing the synthoid. Alpha Flight escapes the base, happy to have regained Snowbird but shaken by Vindicator's death.
NOTE: Starting this month, Marvel removes the cover date from all of its titles, leaving only the issue number. As Guardian and Vindicator's powers come solely from their cybernetic costumes, which they do not have here, Vindicator should not have been able to blast Weapon X; however, his synthoid nature may have granted him additional, previously unrevealed powers.

2ND STORY: "Loose Ends" (4 pages)
CREDITS: Eric Stephenson (writer), Rob Jensen (pencils), Bob Wiacek (inks), Richard Starkings & Comicraft (letters), Gina Going (colors Pete Franco (asst editor), Mark Powers (editor)
GUEST STARS: Alpha Flight: Guardian, Sasquatch; Snowbird (all next in GenX #58, '99), Dum Dum Dugan (bts investigating AIM lab, last i Cap #20, '99)
VILLAINS: "Wolverine" (Skrull), AIM agents (some or others next in Cap #27, '00)
OTHER CHARACTERS: SHIELD agents (bts investigating AIM lab, some or others last in X Ann '99) inc Millie (unnamed), Dept. H official (bts reacting to Vindicator's death) & employees (some or others last in AFlt #20, '99), AIM's newborn creations
LOCATIONS/ITEMS: Dept. H lab, AIM base / Guardian's testing equipment (bts), microscope & clipboard, SHIELD aircraft (bts) w/comm system, Dept. H comm unit (bts), Snowbird's diagnostic bed, AIM aircraft, armor, guns & maturation chambers
SYNOPSIS: Guardian puzzles over Snowbird's resurrection, and confides in Wolverine that Dept. H's top officials have been acting oddly latel Sasquatch theorizes that because of Snowbird's half-god heritage, her body regenerated after death and eventually returned to life. Guardia realizes that AIM was trying to create other beings like Snowbird — as, elsewhere, AIM agents monitor two infants.
NOTE: Sasquatch's explanation of Snowbird's recovery overlooks the fact that he himself is inhabiting Snowbird's original body. Afte Snowbird's death in AFlt #44, '87, the evil Pestilence reanimated and possessed her corpse. Sasquatch, whose own body had been destroyed in AFlt #24, '85 and whose spirit was bodiless, entered Snowbird's body in AFlt #45, '87 to force Pestilence out. Sasquatch's spirit remained there permanently, and in AFlt #68, '89, Snowbird's spirit manifested and transformed her old body to resemble his. Therefore, Sasquatch explanation here that Snowbird's body regenerated while in its grave cannot be accurate. W #172, '02 reveals that the Inua (the gods of th North) had a hand in resurrecting Snowbird, but the exact mechanics of her return are unexplained. SHIELD agent Millie is named in Hulk #8 '99. The hints dropped here and next issue that something is wrong with Department H are never followed up on.

WOLVERINE/CABLE (October 1999)

"Guts 'n' Glory" (48 pages)

CREDITS: Joe Casey (writer), Stephen Platt (pencils), Matt Banning (as "Batt," co-inks, c inks), Lary Stucker, Bo Wiacek, Mark Pennington, Johnny Greene, Scott Koblish & Rodney Ramos (co-inks), Michael Heisler (letters Colorgraphix (colors), Pete Franco (asst editor), Mark Powers (editor), Chris Dickey (c colors)
FEATURE CHARACTERS: Nathan Dayspring Askani'Son (aka Nathan Summers, also on Kray's scanner & as boy & himself in his own thoughts, also in fb between Cable #-1, '97 fb & Cable #-1, '97; chr last in Cable #-1, '97, chr next a Traveler in XFor #1, '04 fb, see NOTE), Wolverine (chr last in SM/W #2, '03 fb, chr next in Fury, '94)
GUEST STAR: James Hudson (also on monitor, chr last in W:FCBD, '09, chr next in AFlt #52, '87 fb)
VILLAINS: Vulture (Adrian Toomes, wears winged suit, chr last in ASM #241, '83 fb, chr next in ASM #2, '63 D'von Kray (Canaanite warrior, dies, also on monitors, also in fb prior to issue) & his squad (in fb, die, all but 1 bts
OTHER CHARACTERS: Security guards inc Franklin H. Rhodes (dies, also on Kray's scanner, also as Shadow Company agent in pfb, see NOTE), NYC police inc Sal, Rhodes' friends inc Chuck, "You Name the Price" hosts (on TV) inc Bob, Dept. H agent (some bts in aircraft & cell bay; others bts, die; some or others chr last in X #140, '80 fb, chr next in AFlt #10/2, '84), reporters (1 on TV, 1 voic only on radio), cameraman (bts filming reporter), news vendor, Wolverine's lover, Moose Jaw Mounties (bts responding to Kray's rampage eyewitnesses (bts reporting Kray) & police, librarian, hostages, paramedics (bts in ambulances), Rhodes' barber (bts cutting Nathan's hair) & customer, Shadow Company agents (in pfb), bartender, Federal agents (bts taking Kray's body), bystanders; birds; Charles Xavier (mentioned lectured on mutation, also in photo), Tribune Haight (mentioned, placed bounty on Nathan), rebel forces (mentioned, trained by Shadow Company), Chuck's superior officer (mentioned); model (on billboard), man in newspaper photo), people on magazine covers; Cyclops (a Slym), Apocalypse, Adolf Hitler, Nazis, astronauts (bts in capsule), US soldiers, Clan Chosen members (prev 7 in Nathan's thoughts)
LOCATIONS/ITEMS: Manhattan inc Times Square, New York Public Library & Jewelry Exchange, Queens inc bar w/bathroom & Rhodes gun shop w/apartment (bts) & spare bedroom, Wolverine's northern Canada cabin, Dept. H headquarters (also on monitors) w/cell bay (bts & lab, Saskatchewan's Moose Jaw, Salem Center cemetery, broadcast location, "You Name the Price" set (prev 2 on TV), Earth-4935's 39t century battlefield (in fb & Nathan's thoughts) & lab (in fb), farmhouse (destroyed), sewer (prev 2 in pfb), Germany, Vietnam, Earth orbit (pre 3 in Nathan's thoughts) / Reporters' microphone (on TV) & broadcast equipment (bts), news camera (bts), vendor's newsstand (destroyed newspapers & magazines, Hudson's comm system (bts) & paperwork, Wolverine's comm system, shortwave radio & helicopter w/headset sensor scope, library's microfilm & viewer, police cars, barricades & guns, Jewelry Exchange's alarm (bts), vault door (destroyed) & jewel Vulture's backpack, winged suit & bomb w/timer, Rhodes' window (destroyed), flashlight, firearms, TV & gravestone, Kray's time machine (in fb memory banks, radar jammer, homing tracer (prev 3 bts), guns, medical tubes, VTOL rockets & internal tracking devices, electrical wires, Dep H security system (bts), hovercrafts, computers & medical monitors, ambulances, customer's rifle w/scope, host's microphone, car (prev 2 o TV), Shadow Company's armor, guns & flamethrower, doll (prev 4 in pfb), Nathan's weaponry (in fb & Nathan's thoughts), books (destroyed Nazis' guns, nuclear bombs, NASA re-entry capsule, Nathan's psimitar, Clan Chosen blasters (prev 5 in Nathan's thoughts)
FLASHBACKS: Rhodes serves with the Shadow Company, but becomes uncomfortable with their work (p). After Nathan kills Kray's Canaanit squad, Kray genetically re-engineers himself and follows Nathan back in time, but the journey drives him insane.
SYNOPSIS: Freshly arrived from the 39th century, Nathan Dayspring learns about present-day society. In Canada, James Hudson alert Wolverine to a rampaging creature. Nathan researches Charles Xavier, but the Vulture's nearby jewelry heist interrupts him. Nathan intervenes but is caught in an explosion when the Vulture blasts the vault door open. Security guard Franklin Rhodes rescues Nathan; sensing an ex-militar kindred spirit in him, Rhodes offers Nathan the spare bedroom behind the gun shop that he runs. Wolverine defeats the mindlessly rampagin D'von Kray. Dept. H experiments on Kray, hoping to make him into a Canadian agent over Wolverine's objections. Kray suddenly reactivates tracking Nathan, he heads for New York. Nathan and Rhodes bond over shared wartime experiences, but when Kray suddenly attacks the arm themselves in Rhodes' shop. Wolverine arrives; the two mutants battle Kray, but when Rhodes tries to aid them he is fatally shot. Enrage Wolverine and Nathan behead Kray. Later, the two mutants part ways, and Nathan visits Rhodes' grave, pondering his mission in this era.
NOTE: This issue's cover subtitle, "Guts and Glory," is not in the indicia. This one-shot occurs in the early Silver Age, before the Vulture's publi debut. Rhodes' claim of having been a SHIELD agent for eight years cannot be true, as SHIELD was still being created at this time; it is likely tha Rhodes actually served under Nick Fury in the CIA. Nathan Dayspring has not yet adopted the codename Cable. His first meeting with Charle Xavier, shortly after this issue, is described and quoted in Cable #45, '97, but not shown on-panel.

WOLVERINE #144 (November 1999)

"First Cut!" (22 pages)

CREDITS: Erik Larsen & Eric Stephenson (writers), Mike S. Miller (pencils), Vince Russell (inks), Richard Starkings & Comicraft's Saida Temofonte (letters), Marie Javins & Joe Rosas (colors), Pete Franco (asst editor), Mark Powers (editor), Steve Buccellato (c colors)
FEATURE CHARACTER: Wolverine (in fb between AFlt #9/2, '84 & W:FCBD, '09; also in rfb)
GUEST STARS: Hercules (Heracles, Greek demigod, in fb between Thor #228, '74 & MTU #28, '74), James Hudson (in fb between AFlt #127/2, '93 fb & W:FCBD, '09), Heather Hudson (in fb between AFlt #8/2, '84 & AFlt #17, '84 fb), Dum Dum Dugan (also bts in scene from Hulk #7, '99, next in Hulk #8, '99)
VILLAINS: "Wolverine" (Skrull, next & also in scene from Hulk #7, '99), Leader (Samuel Sterns, evil gamma-spawned genius, in fb between MFeat #11, '73 & IHulk #224, '78 fb) & his Humanoids (robotic servants, in fb, some or others chr last in IHulk #147, '72, chr next in IHulk #224, '78 fb)

OTHER CHARACTERS: Karkas (Deviant gladiator, in fb, his chr 1st app, prior to Et #8, '77), Dept. H officials (bts meeting with "Wolverine," some or others in fb) inc Major Chasin (in fb between AFlt #117, '93 fb & GSX #1, '75), SHIELD agents (bts flying plane, also in scene from Hulk #7, '99, all but 1 next bts in Hulk #8, '99, some or others next in Dlk #5, '00) inc Millie (next in Hulk #8, '99), actors (as terrorists), Dept. H employees (some or others chr last in AFlt #10/2, '84, chr next in IHulk #181, '74) (prev 2 in fb); Canadian Minister of Defence's daughter mentioned as target by "terrorists" in fb), Hulk (on monitor & mentioned in fb; also in rfb, also in scene from Hulk #7, '99), Wendigo (Baptiste), Wendigo spirit (bts) (prev 2 in rfb); birds (in scene from Hulk #7, '99)

LOCATIONS/ITEMS: Canada: Dept. H headquarters, abandoned Ontario warehouse (prev 2 in fb) & Quebec's North Woods (in rfb); Leader's underground lair (New Mexico desert, in fb, destroyed), Florida woods (also in scene from Hulk #7, '99) / Chasin's file, terrorists' chair (destroyed), bomb & guns, Dept. H's hidden cameras (bts) & van w/monitors, receivers & headphones, Leader's teleporter, bio-signature tracer (prev 2 bts), Omnichair, monitor, robot, gamma-nullifying plasma bath (destroyed) & flying saucer, Wolverine's steel bar w/restraints, Hercules & Karkas' chains, lair's pylon & security tendrils (prev 3 destroyed) (all in fb), SHIELD aircraft, Wolverine's drop suit (prev 2 also in scene from Hulk #7, '99), SHIELD agents' flight helmets (in scene from Hulk #7, '99)

FLASHBACKS: Wolverine attacks the Hulk and Wendigo (IHulk #181, '74). As Wolverine discusses super hero costumes with the Hudsons, Dept. H's Major Chasin orders him to take out a small terrorist cell — a phony assignment, designed to make Wolverine look good to Dept. H's top brass. Wolverine battles the "terrorists" while James monitors him, but is suddenly teleported away — and finds himself a captive of the Leader, along with Hercules and Karkas. The Leader explains that he plans to submerge the Hulk in plasma that will transform him into Bruce Banner permanently, but he needs his captives' aid capturing the Hulk. Wolverine slips out of his bonds and frees Hercules and Karkas, and the three battle the Leader's Humanoids. Wolverine chases the fleeing Leader, who activates a large robot — but it accidentally smashes the plasma bath, soaking the Leader. Wolverine returns to Dept. H, having proven himself beyond a doubt.

SYNOPSIS: Wolverine finishes telling Dugan his story as their aircraft nears the Hulk's location. Doing SHIELD a favor, Wolverine dons a parachute and bails out, preparing to confront the behemoth.

NOTE: This issue continues into Hulk #8, '99, where the Hulk fights "Wolverine," celebrating the 25th anniversary of Wolverine's debut in IHulk #180, '74. Although the Skrull imposter's story to Dugan is mostly a factual account from Wolverine's past, details about receiving his "first costume" and being assigned his "first Dept. H mission" are inaccurate; W/Cable, '99 established that Wolverine has been a costumed Dept. H operative since before ASM #2, '63. Presumably the Skrull's implanted memories of Wolverine's past are slightly faulty. Major Chasin's last name is misspelled "Chasen" here, a common error; his first name is unrevealed to date. This issue's p.22 repeats and expands upon a scene from Hulk #7, '99 pp.21-22. The Dept. H van's license plate is THX1138, referencing George Lucas' film of the same name. This issue also contains "Fast Lane, Part 1 of 4," an 8-page anti-drug story starring Spider-Man which was bound into many Marvel comics published this month. It is indexed as Av #22/2, '99 in Index #14, '11.

WOLVERINE #145 (December 1999)

"On the Edge of Darkness" (38 pages)

CREDITS: Erik Larsen (writer), Leinil Francis Yu (pencils), Dexter Vines (inks), Richard Starkings & Comicraft (letters), Marie Javins (colors), Pete Franco (asst editor), Mark Powers (editor), Bill Sienkiewicz (variant c pencils), Liquid! (c colors)
FEATURE CHARACTER: Wolverine (as Death, also in rfb1 & rfb3, also as Death in rfb2; also in fb1 & fb2 between X #90, '99 & Hulk #8, '99; next as Death in Cable #75, '00, X #96, '00)
GUEST STARS: X-Men: Colossus, Gambit (both also bts in rfb1), Nightcrawler, Storm (all also in fb1 between X #90, '99 & UXM #371, '99), Shadowcat (prev 3 also in rfb1), Marrow (also bts in rfb1), Professor X (also in shadow in rfb1) (prev 3 also bts in fb1 between X #90, '99 & UXM #371, '99), Rogue, Cyclops, Phoenix (all last in XMU #25, '99, next in UXM #376, '00), Hulk (also as hologram, also as himself & Joe Fixit in rfb3; last in Galact #2, '99, next in Hulk #9, '99) (all also in rfb2)
VILLAINS: Apocalypse (also in fb2 between X #90 bts & Cable #66; last in UXM #374, last bts in X #95, next in Cable #74, all '99), Sabretooth (in fb2

between Mvk #7, '98 & Gam #8, '99), "Wolverine" (Skrull, as himself & Wolverine in fb1, his chr 1st on-panel app, between X #90, '99 bts & UXM #371, '99; also bts in rfb1, also in rfb2 & rfb3), Apocalypse's Skrull henchmen (bts in rfb1; also in fb1 & fb2 following X #90, '99 bts, also bts i UXM #371, '99 fb during fb; some or others chr next in X #92, '99)

OTHER CHARACTERS: Mary Purcell (energy being, also bts in rfb1 & rfb2, bts inside Gambit in fb between X #90, '99 bts & UXM #37 '99 bts); birds; Generation X: Banshee, Jubilee; Alpha Flight: Guardian, Northstar, Heather Hudson (prev 5 in rfb2); Tyrannosaurus rex (in rfb3 Anubis (as statue in fb2)

LOCATIONS/ITEMS: X-Mansion (also in rfb2) w/Danger Room (in rfb2), Apocalypse's Egyptian base (also in fb2), wooded valley, Earth orbit (i rfb1, rfb2 & fb1), Muir Island, Massachusetts Academy, Canadian AIM lab, New Mexico carnival, Skrulls' headquarters (prev 5 in rfb2), Florid woods (in rfb2 & rfb3), Quebec's North Woods; Dallas, Texas; Savage Land (prev 3 in rfb3) / X-Men's Skrull spaceship (in rfb1, also in fb1 & fb1 Skrull blaster (in fb1) & shuttle (in fb1 & bts in rfb1) w/weaponry (bts in rfb1), Generation X's computers (in rfb2) w/security files (bts), Death sword (also in rfb2) & robotic steed, Marrow's bone knife, trees (destroyed), Apocalypse's holographic projector (bts), hovership w/tractor bear & Adamantium reshaping & bonding equipment (in fb2) w/restraints & feed tubes, Sabretooth's Adamantium skeleton (in fb2, destroyed; also a Wolverine's new Adamantium skeleton, hereinafter considered his standard equipment and not listed separately)

FLASHBACKS: The X-Men's spaceship is attacked (X #90, '99). The Wolverine Skrull begins discrediting Professor X (UXM #371, '99 visits Generation X and Alpha Flight (W #141 & 143, '99), and battles the Hulk (Hulk #8, '99), showing only minor indications that he was a imposter (UXM #372, '99) — but after a suspicious Professor X temporarily disbands the X-Men (X #92, '99), "Wolverine" is attacked and kille by Death (AX #3, '99), who is unmasked as the true Wolverine (X #95, '99). The Hulk battles Wolverine (IHulk #181, '74 & #340, '88 & #454 '97) and the Wolverine Skrull (Hulk #8, '99). Skrulls board the unconscious X-Men's spaceship, abduct Wolverine and leave a Skrull operativ in his place (1). Wolverine awakens to find himself a captive of Apocalypse. Sabretooth attacks Wolverine, revealing that they are fighting t become Apocalypse's Horseman of Death. Horrified by the thought of Sabretooth in that role, Wolverine savagely defeats him and claims th title, gambling that he can someday break free. Apocalypse strips out Sabretooth's Adamantium and re-bonds it to Wolverine's skeleton (2).

SYNOPSIS: As the X-Men reel from the revelation that Wolverine has been brainwashed, Apocalypse orders Wolverine to kill the Hulk Wolverine tracks down and attacks the Hulk with his newly restored Adamantium claws. Wolverine gains the advantage after a brutal battle, bu hesitates, unable to deliver the killing blow. The Hulk recovers, savagely pounds Wolverine into the ground and departs; Apocalypse reclaims hi fallen Horseman, telling him that there are many more battles ahead.

NOTE: This issue also has four variant covers: a Dynamic Forces chrome variant using p.32's art that came with a certificate of authenticity, wraparound sendaway variant sponsored by Nabisco, a newsstand edition without foil on Wolverine's claws, and a 2nd printing that uses gol foil. This issue celebrates the 25th anniversary of Wolverine's debut in IHulk #180, '74. The X-Men traveled from the Skrull homeworld back t Earth in X #90, '99. "Wolverine" was revealed as a Skrull post-mortem in UXM #375, '99; this issue reveals how and when the switch was made Guardian is incorrectly drawn in rfb2 as wearing his cybernetic costume; he did not have it in W #142-143, '99.

WOLVERINE #146 (January 2000)

"Through a Dark Tunnel" (22 pages)

CREDITS: Fabian Nicieza & Erik Larsen (writers), Mike S. Miller (pencils), Armando Durruthy, Nathan Massengi & Mike Christian (inks), Richard Starkings & Comicraft's Wes Abbott (letters), Marie Javins (colors), Pete Franc (asst editor), Mark Powers (editor), Chris Dickey (c colors)

FEATURE CHARACTER: Wolverine (also as Death, also as Death in rfb1, also in rfb2, rfb3, rfb4, rfb8, rfb9 rfb10 & rfb11, also bts in rfb5)

GUEST STARS: X-Men: Archangel (also in his own thoughts, also in rfb1, also as Angel in rfb6, rfb7 & rfb8 Nightcrawler (also in rfb1 & rfb12, also voice only in rfb5), Psylocke (also bts in rfb2), Shadowcat (also in rfb1, als as Ariel in rfb4, also bts as Sprite in rfb5); Jubilee (also in rfb9 & rfb10) (all last in X #96, '00)

OTHER CHARACTERS: Moira MacTaggert (last in X #96, '00, also bts in rfb7); Shadow King (mentioned, trapped b Psylocke's telepathy); "Wolverine" (Skrull, also dead as himself), X-Men: Colossus, Cyclops, Gambit, Rogue; Cable Sabretooth (prev 7 in rfb1), Apocalypse (as symbolic image in rfb1, also in rfb3), Morlocks (some dead in rfb2, others in rfb4), Caliban, Leech, Masque Sunder (prev 4 in rfb4), Callisto (in rfb4 & rfb6), Storm (in rfb4 & bts in rfb7), Professor X (bts in rfb7), Molokai, Reno (prev 2 in rfb9), butterfly (in rfb1C

LOCATIONS/ITEMS: X-Mansion (also in rfb1, rfb7 & bts in rfb5) w/grounds (in rfb10 & rfb11) & Med Lab (in rfb1), Morlock tunnels (also in rfb2 w/Alley (large central tunnel, also in rfb4 & rfb6), astral plane, New Mexico carnival, Skrulls' headquarters (prev 2 in rfb1), Apocalypse's Egyptia base (in rfb1 & rfb3), Manhattan (in rfb8), Mulholland Drive (in rfb9) / Cerebro w/monitors, Archangel's backpack w/club & bola, Shadowcat' backpack w/swords (1 destroyed), Death's sword (also in rfb1), rock, support beam (destroyed), rubble; Cable's psimitar, X-Men's medica equipment, Gambit's staff (prev 3 in rfb1), Apocalypse's Adamantium reshaping & bonding equipment (in rfb3) w/restraints & feed tubes Callisto's Morlock law book, Ariel's wedding dress (prev 2 in rfb4), Angel's restraints (in rfb6)

FLASHBACKS: Death battles the X-Men (AX #2, '99) and kills "Wolverine" (AX #3, '99), who is revealed as a Skrull (UXM #375, '99); Deat is unmasked as the real Wolverine (X #95, '99), having fought Sabretooth for the title (W #145, '99 fb), and the X-Men battle him once more (X #96, '00). Wolverine looks for survivors after the Morlock Massacre (UXM #212, '86). Apocalypse re-bonds Adamantium to Wolverine's skeleto (W #145, '99 fb). The X-Men intervene when the Morlocks try to forcibly marry Ariel and Caliban (UXM #179, '84). Nightcrawler teases Wolverin (UXM #153, '82, see NOTE). Callisto taunts the captive Angel (UXM #169, '83). Angel quits the X-Men over his dislike of Wolverine (UXM #148 '81). Angel and Wolverine square off (UXM #242, '89). Jubilee attacks Molokai and Reno (W #74, '93). Jubilee talks with Wolverine after hi Adamantium was removed (W #75, '93). Wolverine and Nightcrawler spar (UXM #148, '81).

SYNOPSIS: Psylocke uses Cerebro to monitor the X-Men as they search for Wolverine in the Morlock tunnels, hoping to return him to his righ mind. Psylocke stimulates Wolverine's memories while the X-Men disorient him with a physical assault, but Psylocke senses something wron in Archangel's mind. Shadowcat fights a duel with Wolverine, but he nearly kills her until Archangel intervenes. Jubilee and Nightcrawler implor Wolverine to come back to them, as Psylocke makes a final telepathic push. Struggling, Wolverine overcomes Apocalypse's brainwashing — but Archangel suddenly begins transforming…

NOTE: Cover-labeled "Apocalypse: the Twelve," part of a sprawling X-book crossover. This issue continues from X #96, '00, where the X-Me drove Death into the Morlock tunnels. This issue's cover carries a "60 Years of Super Heroes" slug, celebrating MC #1, '39. This issue's rfb5 is a "audio only" flashback; it is a single word balloon with no visual component. Psylocke is dressed as Lady Mandarin when she helps Wolverine' true personality break free on the astral plane, a reference to UXM #258, '90, where Wolverine helped Psylocke overcome similar brainwashing b the Hand. This issue also contains the bound-in Spider-Man story "Fast Lane, Part 2 of 4"; that story is indexed as ASM #13/2, '00 in Index #11, '1C

WOLVERINE #147 (February 2000)

"Into the Light" (22 pages)

CREDITS: Fabian Nicieza (plot), Erik Larsen (script), Roger Cruz (pencils), Derek Fridolfs & Andy Owens (inks), Richard Starkings & Comicraft's Oscar Gongora & Wes Abbott (letters), Wilson Ramos (colors), Pete Franco (asst editor), Mark Powers (editor), Michael Ryan (c pencils)

FEATURE CHARACTER: Wolverine (also as Death in rfb1, rfb5 & rfb6, also in pfb, next in UXM #377, X51 #7 & 8 fb, all '00, UXM Ann '99, X #98, '00, W Ann '99)

GUEST STARS: X-Men: Archangel (also in rfb1 & rfb4, also as Death in rfb3 & rfb7, also as Death in fb during XFac #23, '87; also in pfb), Psylocke (also in rfb2), Nightcrawler, Shadowcat; Jubilee (prev 3 on monitor) (all next in UXM #377, '00)

VILLAIN: Shadow King (evil psychic entity, also bts in rfb2, last in X #78, '98, next in XX Ann, '01)

OTHER CHARACTERS: Moira MacTaggert (also on monitor, next in UXM #377, '00), Abraham Kieros, paralyzed former Horseman, also as War in rfb3, also as War in fb during XFac #23, '87; last as War in UXM #295, '92), Ship (Apocalypse's sentient Celestial ship, in fb during XFac #23, '87; also in rfb3 & rfb7), patients inc Candy, doctors, nurses, hospital visitors & receptionist; Horsemen of Apocalypse: Pestilence, Famine (prev 2 in rfb3); Apocalypse (in rfb3, rfb5 & rfb7), Ozymandias (in rfb4)

LOCATIONS/ITEMS: New York City (also in rfb3, rfb7 & fb) inc rooftops & hospitals inc Candy & Kieros' rooms, X-Mansion, Morlock tunnels (also on monitor, also in rfb1 & pfb), astral plane (in rfb2), loft apartment (in rfb4), Apocalypse's Egyptian base (in rfb5 & rfb6) / Archangel's techno-organic wings (also in rfb1, rfb3, rfb4, rfb7, pfb & fb, see NOTE), Cerebro w/monitors, X-Men's comm system, doctor's stethoscope, patients' stretcher, IV & bandages, Candy's IV & medical chart, Kieros' IV; Apocalypse's regeneration equipment, Horsemen's robotic steeds (prev 2 in rfb3), Apocalypse's Adamantium reshaping & bonding equipment (in rfb5) w/restraints & feed tubes, Death's sword (in rfb6)

FLASHBACKS: Archangel battles Wolverine (last issue). Psylocke imprisons the Shadow King (X #78, '98). Apocalypse transforms Angel into Death (XFac #19, '87), who leads the Horsemen (XFac #24, '88). Archangel's metal wings molt, revealing feathered wings underneath (UXM #338, '96). Apocalypse re-bonds Adamantium to Wolverine's skeleton (W #145, '99 fb). Wolverine stands proudly as Death (W #145, '99). Angel stands proudly as Death (XFac #24, '88). Archangel flees the Morlock tunnels (p). War and Angel talk about their transformations.

SYNOPSIS: His wings now made of energy, a strangely driven Archangel lands near a hospital. Wolverine follows as Psylocke monitors them through Cerebro; Moira worries that Psylocke's continued use of telepathy will let the Shadow King escape his psychic prison. His perceptions changed, Archangel feels the emotions of a hospital's patients and staff, and uses his energy to help a terminally ill girl make peace with her fate. Wolverine realizes that Archangel is looking for paralyzed former Horseman Abraham Kieros. Wolverine ambushes Archangel in Kieros' room, but Archangel asks for Wolverine's trust, explaining that when Apocalypse transformed him, he challenged Archangel to embrace hope — which he has finally done. Just before the Shadow King can break free, Archangel convinces Psylocke to disengage from Cerebro. He then pours his energy into Kieros, healing him and transforming Archangel back to normal.

NOTE: Cover-labeled "Apocalypse: the Twelve." This issue continues into UXM #377, '00, where a large group of X-Men attack Apocalypse's base. XFor #4, '08 reveals that Archangel's Apocalypse-given wings are made of techno-organic material, explaining how they seemingly "molted" from metal to feathers in UXM #338, '96, and how they transformed into energy here. This issue also contains the bound-in Spider-Man story "Fast Lane, Part 3 of 4"; that story is indexed as ASM #15/2, '00 in Index #11, '10.

WOLVERINE #148 (March 2000)

"Same As It Never Was" (23 pages)

CREDITS: Erik Larsen (writer, c pencils), Roger Cruz (pencils), Andy Owens & Scott Koblish (inks), Richard Starkings & Comicraft's Saida Temofonte & Oscar Gongora (letters), Wilson Ramos (colors), Pete Franco (asst editor), Mark Powers (editor)

GUEST STAR: Cyclops (bts, merged with Apocalypse, last in Cable #77, '00, next bts in XMU #26, '00, next in X #98, '00)

VILLAIN: Apocalypse (bts creating altered reality, also mentioned in altered reality as defeated by High Lord; last in Cable #77, '00, next bts in XMU #26, '00, next in X #98, '00)

OTHER CHARACTERS: New Fantastic Four: Hulk (also as Joe Fixit & Bruce Banner), Ghost Rider, Spider-Man, Wolverine; May Parker (Spider-Man & Mary Jane's young daughter), Noble Kale (bts inside Ghost Rider), President Robert Kelly (bts, assassinated), Doombots (most or all destroyed), Lurch (reprogrammed Sentinel), Dr. Doom clone, Arnim Zola (prev 2 die), Annihilus, Blastaar, Harpy, Mary Jane Watson-Parker, Stacey Kramer, Graydon Creed & his bodyguards & supporters, diner patrons; X-Man (mentioned, became High Lord), Fantastic Four: Human Torch, Invisible Woman, Mr. Fantastic, Thing; Avengers, X-Men (prev 2 exact members unspecified), Dr. Doom (prev 7 mentioned, killed in final battle with High Lord), Magneto (mentioned, annexed Latveria) (all Apocalypse's creations, see NOTE)

LOCATIONS/ITEMS: New York City inc Four Freedoms Plaza & Babel's Diner, Washington DC inc White House (destroyed) & Washington Monument (all Apocalypse's creations) / Fantastic Four's Fantasti-Car (destroyed), Fantasti-Flare & Negative Zone portal w/steel iris (destroyed) & control computer, Annihilus' Cosmic Control Rod, Hulk's gamma gun, Ghost Rider's sky-cycle (destroyed), Doombots' weaponry (bts) w/scope, Ghost Rider's bonds, Zola's bomb w/timer & artificial body w/viewscreen & ESP box, clone's armor w/self-destruct program (bts), supporters' signs (all Apocalypse's creations)

SYNOPSIS: In an altered reality, Ghost Rider, the Hulk, Spider-Man and Wolverine have become the new Fantastic Four. As they open the Negative Zone portal, planning to throw the Harpy in, Annihilus and Blastaar burst through and attack. The heroes quickly rally; Spider-Man hurls the Harpy at Annihilus, knocking the villains through the portal, which the heroes seal. Ghost Rider leaves on a personal mission, lamenting how bad the world became during the High Lord's reign, but is attacked. Wolverine visits his girlfriend Stacey, but is soon summoned back to the FF's headquarters. Banner announces that Dr. Doom has assassinated President Kelly — and Doombots suddenly burst in. After defeating them, Wolverine, Hulk and Spider-Man race to Washington DC, where they find Ghost Rider a prisoner. Wolverine reveals "Dr. Doom" to be a flawed clone, and Arnim Zola appears, claiming responsibility. The clone self-destructs explosively; the FF escape, but Zola is apparently killed. Outside, the team sees the anti-mutant Graydon Creed being sworn in as President.

NOTE: Cover-labeled "Ages of Apocalypse," part of an altered-reality X-book crossover. This issue continues from Cable #77, '00 and into XM# #26, '00 (though p.23 incorrectly directs readers to X #98, '00). Apocalypse merged with and possessed Cyclops in X #97, '00; he then began manipulating space and time, creating alternate worlds including the one seen this issue, which is designated Earth-2841 in OHMU HC2, '0 However, he only altered reality within a very small sphere, and the only people he had to "work with" were those present at the end of X #97, ' — none of whom appear here. Therefore, all characters seen on-panel in this issue are creations of Apocalypse. The X-Men escape Apocalypse altered reality in X #98, '00. This issue's p.1, an introductory text page repeated from UXM #377, '00, is badly blurred. The New Fantastic Fo previously appeared in FF #347-349, '90-91. Like last issue, this issue also contains the bound-in Spider-Man story "Fast Lane, Part 3 of 4."

WOLVERINE '99 (1999)

"Crying Wolf!" (25 pages)

CREDITS: Marc Andreyko (writer), Walter McDaniel (pencils), Walden Wong & Scott Koblish (inks), Micha Heisler & Revenge Graphics (letters), Gina Going (colors), Mark Powers (editor), Tyson McAdod (c inks), Chr Sotomayor (c colors)
FEATURE CHARACTER: Wolverine
GUEST STAR: Deadpool (between Dp #37-38, '00)
VILLAIN: Lycus (werewolf, also as "Hunter-Wolf" in Vess' story)
OTHER CHARACTERS: Duncan Vess (werewolf turned author, also in his own story), Council (mystic werewolf elders), Vess' fans inc Tim Fairholm; birds; Shadowcat (mentioned, likes Vess' work); Spider-Man, Ma Powers (prev 2 in newspaper photos), snake (in story), lions (as Vess' decorations)
LOCATIONS/ITEMS: New York City bookstore, Vess' brownstone w/rooftop & wine cellar, New York woods & cliffsic (prev 2 in story) / Vess' ponytail (destroyed), knife (both in story), pen & candelabra, copies of "Blood Moon" (Vess' newest novel), Deadpool's pac swords, dagger & glass cutter, brownstone's skylight, door, floor (prev 3 destroyed), table & alarm system, Wolverine's metal pipe
SYNOPSIS: Wolverine attends author Duncan Vess' book signing, hoping to get Shadowcat an autographed copy of Vess' newest werewo novel. However, when both men catch the other's scent, Vess becomes agitated and leaves; Wolverine realizes that Vess is more than huma Outside, Wolverine notices Deadpool stalking Vess from the rooftops. Vess arrives home, but finds the werewolf Lycus waiting to kill hir Wolverine attacks Deadpool and they crash through Vess' skylight, but their battle is interrupted when Lycus blindsides them both. The tw retreat, coming across Vess, who reveals that he is a werewolf who wishes to live in the human world. Lycus attacks Wolverine again, whi Deadpool decides to do what he was hired for — and kill Vess. Suddenly, the mystical werewolf Council manifests. Tired of Vess' novels exposir their community, they hired Deadpool to make Vess' death look normal, but Lycus' savage attack risks exposing them further. The Counc punishes Lycus, but the breaking dawn weakens them and they depart, threatening to deal with Vess later.
NOTE: The Wolverine series did not publish an Annual in 1998. Like W #146, '99, the cover carries a "60 Years of Super Heroes" slug. A footnot incorrectly states that this issue occurs prior to X #90, '99. Lycus implies here that "Duncan Vess" is an alias.

2ND STORY: "Beer Run" (12 pages)
CREDITS: Marc Andreyko (writer), Massimiliano Frezzato (colors, uncredited; art), Michael Heisler & Revenge Graphics (letters), Mark Power (editor)
FEATURE CHARACTER: Wolverine (next in XMU #26/2, '00 & 35/2, '02, UXM #379, '00, W #149, '00)
GUEST STARS: She-Hulk (Jennifer Walters, gamma-powered super-strong attorney), Nick Fury (both last in Hulk #11, '00, next in FF #2 '00), Captain America (last in Hulk #11, '00 fb, next in FF #26, '00), Thing (last in Hulk #9, '99, next in FF #24, '99)
VILLAINS: Hand ninjas (some die, some or others last in W #128, '98) & sorcerers (others last in W #128, '98) (some or others of both next i NW #5, '00), thieves (all but 1 in shadow), dragon (dies)
OTHER CHARACTERS: Convenience store clerk (bts selling Wolverine beer), announcer (voice only on TV); fly
LOCATIONS/ITEMS: New York City inc convenience store, alley, Fury's apartment & Hand's sewer hideout / Fury's playing cards (som destroyed), keys, TV w/remote control & SHIELD hover-car (partly destroyed) w/electrified tendrils (destroyed) & alarm, Wolverine's bee manhole cover, sorcerers' summoning brazier w/gemstone (destroyed), Hand ninjas' swords (1 destroyed), nunchuks & sai, thieves' siphon a lug wrench
SYNOPSIS: Wolverine and his fellow heroes play cards, but when they run out of beer, Nick Fury loans Wolverine his flying SHIELD car t get more. After buying a case of beer, Wolverine drops the car key. As he picks it up, a thief steals his beer — and when Wolverine reacts, hi claws scratch the car, activating its defensive tendrils. Wolverine claws his way free and chases down the thief, but suddenly a burst of energ sucks him down a manhole and into a Hand lair, where ninjas swarm him and sorcerers summon a dragon that tries to eat him. Wolverine kill the dragon, sucking the ninjas into its closing dimensional portal. Wolverine reclaims his beer, but finds Fury's car stripped and defaced. By th time he gets back, all of his poker buddies are asleep. Wolverine settles down to watch TV, but when he opens a beer it explodes with foam.

WOLVERINE #149 (April 2000)

"Resurrection" (22 pages)

CREDITS: Erik Larsen (writer), Graham Nolan (pencils), Jimmy Palmiotti (inks), Richard Starkings & Comicraf (letters), Marie Javins (colors), Pete Franco (asst editor), Mark Powers (editor), Sean Chen (c pencils)
FEATURE CHARACTER: Wolverine (also on Marvel Burger poster, next in X #99, UXM #380, BlSun:X #3-5 all '00, W/Herc #1, '11 fb)
GUEST STARS: New Warriors: Aegis (Trey Rollins, wears enchanted breastplate), Turbo (Michiko Musashi wears Torpedo suit), Speedball (all last in NW #7, '00, last bts in Av #25, '00), Bolt (Chris Bradley, electric mutant last in NW #7, '00), Namorita (Namorita Prentiss, Atlantean-human hybrid, last in FF #29, '00), Nova (Richar Rider, wields Xandarian Nova Force, last in Av #25, '00) (all next in NW #8, '00)
VILLAINS: Reanimator (last in Nova #7, '99) & his refurbished robots (destroyed): Spider-Slayers: Mark I (replica see NOTE), Mark III (last in W #140, '99) (another of prev 2 next in ASM #20, '00), Mark V (last in ASM #169, '77'
Android Man (Mad Thinker's android, last in FF #79, '68, chr last in FF:WGCM #1, '01), Fourth Sleeper (Red Skull's robot, last in Cap #410, '92'
Impact 739 (SHIELD training robot, last in Cap #226, '78), Quintronic Man (Stark International robot, last in Nova #3, '99, next in LastDef #3, '08)

a Sentinel (some or others last in X51 #8, '00 fb, next in NX #114, '01), Tomazooma (Russian robot, last in MYiR '92/13), Walking Stiletto (AIM robot, last in Cap #114, '69), Hulk robot (last in Nova #3, '99), Thing robot (last in W #140, '99), Captain America robot, Iron Man robot, Thor robot

OTHER CHARACTERS: Bernie Dillon (Nova's friend, last in Nova #7, '99, next in NW #9, '00 fb), Marvel Burger patrons & employees, Speedball's friend (bts on phone), police; Nightcrawler (mentioned, told Wolverine about junkyard), Spider-Man (on Marvel Burger poster & as action figure), Daredevil, Thing (prev 2 on Marvel Burger poster)

LOCATIONS/ITEMS: New York City inc Marvel Burger (Nova & Bernie's workplace), New Warriors' Brooklyn firehouse headquarters & West Side junkyard (identified, also on monitors) w/Reanimator's warehouse / High Evolutionary's broadcasting satellite array (bts), Wolverine's bandages, junkyard's cameras (bts) & barbed wire fence, warehouse door (destroyed), Reanimator's sensors (bts), computers & other robots (destroyed) w/Big Wheel's wheel, Captain America robot's shield, Thor robot's hammer, Impact 739's staff & Spider-Slayer's tendrils, Nova's comm badge (bts, destroyed), Speedball's cordless phone, Turbo's Torpedo suit, Aegis' enchanted breastplate, police car, Bernie's mop

SYNOPSIS: With his healing factor gone after the High Evolutionary erased all mutants' powers, Wolverine's newly regained Adamantium skeleton is slowly killing him. When he buys coffee at Marvel Burger, where Nova works in his secret identity, Nova recognizes him. Wolverine continues on to the junkyard, where his Skrull imposter once fought robots; he climbs the fence but falls, not used to being without his enhanced senses. Inside, Wolverine discovers a warehouse full of patched-together robots — and confronts the Reanimator, who orders the robots to attack. Nova suddenly bursts in, having followed Wolverine, and begins wrecking the robots. Wolverine painfully pops his claws and follows suit. Nova summons the rest of the New Warriors, who capture the Reanimator; the villain explains that he cannot turn the robots off, as he too has lost his mutant powers. Wolverine and the New Warriors destroy the remaining robots and turn the Reanimator over to the police. Later, a bandaged Wolverine thanks Nova, gives him some crimefighting advice and departs.

NOTE: The High Evolutionary stripped the world's mutants of their powers in UXM #379, '00; the X-Men reversed the effect in UXM #380, '00. Some or all of the robots seen here may be replicas; the Mark I Spider-Slayer was confirmed as a replica in OHMU HC11, '09. Marvel Burger is a restaurant chain with super hero-themed food; menu items in this issue include Fantastic Fries, the Galactus Burger, Hunk o' Hulk, Power Punch and the Silver Slushie. This issue has a LOC from future Index head writer Daron Jensen.

WOLVERINE #150 (May 2000)

"Blood Debt" (30 pages)

CREDITS: Steve Skroce (writer, pencils), Lary Stucker (inks), Richard Starkings & Comicraft's Troy Peteri (letters), Steve Buccellato (colors), Pete Franco (asst editor), Mark Powers (editor), Adam Pollina (variant c pencils), Rob Stull (c inks), Tim Smith III (sketchbook design), Larry Wachowski & Wendi Higenbottam (special thanks)

FEATURE CHARACTER: Wolverine (also on monitor & in rfb1, also as Death in rfb2, also in fb2 during W #57, '92; also in fb4 during UXM #181, '84)

SUPPORTING CAST: Yukio (last in W #126, '98), Amiko Kobayashi (also as baby in fb4 during UXM #181, '84; last in Elektra #15, '98) (both on monitor), Mariko Yashida (in fb2 during W #57, '92; also in fb3 between W:Doom, '97 & XFac #63, '91; also in photo & rfb1)

VILLAINS: Clan Kaishek (Mongolian crime family, 1st): Yolyn Kaishek (Clan Kaishek patriarch, also in photo, also in fb1 between W #153, '00 fb & this issue, also in W #153, '00 fb during fb1), Haan Kaishek (Clan Kaishek heir apparent), Gom Kaishek (Haan's scheming brother), Kia Kaishek (Haan & Gom's sister), Otou (Haan's aide) (all 1st), Gom's men (2 on monitor, 3 die off-panel), Haan's men (some die), punk

OTHER CHARACTERS: Silver Samurai (also in pfb, also in fb3 between W:Doom, '97 & W #56, '92; last in XMU #24, '99), Amiko's friends inc Sukie, Yolyn's father (former Clan Kaishek patriarch, dies, in fb1 between W #153, '00 fb & this issue, also bts in W #153, '00 fb during fb1; also in photo), Amiko's mother (dead in fb4 during UXM #181, '84), tea house proprietor & patrons, Japanese industrialist (bts refusing Haan) & his son (in pfb), Gom's doctors, bystanders; Shingen Harada (mentioned, resisted Yolyn), Amiko's previous assailant (mentioned, arm broken);

Yolyn's two brothers (in photo); Apocalypse (in rfb2); Eddie (doll, destroyed); Buddha (as statues), Kaisheks' honored dead & conquered enemies (prev 2 as wall decorations, also in fb1), historical figure (on wall scroll), cartoon characters (on billboards) inc dog & fish, birds (on sword hilt, also in fb1), lion (as statue)

LOCATIONS/ITEMS: Clan Kaishek's Outer Mongolian fortress (also in photo & fb1), Yashidas' ancestral manor (also in fb3), Tokyo (also in fb4) inc Shingen's Citadel compound chapel (in rfb1 & fb2), teahouse & Yukio's new apartment w/nearby rooftop, Apocalypse's Egyptian base (in rfb2), industrialist's son's bedroom (in pfb), Gom's Japanese safehouse (also on monitors) / Yolyn's sword (also in fb1) & memento box w/ photo, Mariko's grave marker w/photo, blowfish toxin (bts in rfb1 & fb2), Silver Samurai's armor (also in fb3), swords (1 also in fb3 & fb4), IV, Gom's men's knife (on monitor) & guns (some on monitor) w/scope, Wolverine's luggage, Amiko's Eddie doll (destroyed) & book, Death's sword (in rfb2), tea house window (destroyed), punk's knife & gold teeth, Otou's dagger & rifle, Yukio's window (destroyed), hurled table & first aid kit w/ needle & surgical thread, Haan's men's guns & knife, Haan's pistols, Gom's cameras (1 bts), limo, monitors, dagger & handgun, Kia's cloth, Yukio & Amiko's bonds

FLASHBACKS: Wolverine holds the poisoned Mariko Yashida in his arms (W #57, '92). Wolverine serves as Death (W #145, '99). Yolyn Kaishek murders his father, gaining control of Clan Kaishek (1). Mariko begs Wolverine to end her pain (2). Silver Samurai fails to force Mariko to give him control of Clan Yashida (3). Wolverine carries the infant Amiko away from her dead mother (4). Silver Samurai cannot bring himself to kill a boy on Haan's orders (p).

SYNOPSIS: A depressed Yolyn Kaishek thinks about his patricide. Wolverine visits Mariko's grave and encounters an upset Silver Samurai, who implies that Clan Yashida is in trouble. Later, Wolverine and Yukio find Amiko brawling in a teahouse. Wolverine talks with Amiko, apologizing for his frequent absences. That night, an injured Samurai arrives at Yukio's apartment, explaining that Haan Kaishek had usurped control of Clan Yashida. Haan's men burst in; Wolverine defeats many of them, but Haan stabs the Samurai. Gom and Kia, Haan's siblings, arrive and help Wolverine and the Samurai escape — but later, Gom reveals that he has captured Yukio and Amiko. Threatening their lives, Gom order Wolverine to assassinate Haan, so Gom can inherit control of Clan Kaishek.

NOTE: Cover-labeled "Revolution," referring to a line-wide revamp of the X-books that jumped six months ahead. This issue also has three variant covers: a variant by Bill Sienkiewicz, a Dynamic Forces limited edition that came with a certificate of authenticity, and a chrome editio of the standard cover with several logo elements removed. This issue also has an 8-page sketchbook section featuring artist Steve Skroce character designs and penciled pages from this issue and next. Gom and Kia's family name is never explicitly stated to be Kaishek, but the name can be safely assumed; Yolyn's family name is confirmed in W #153, '00. Clan Kaishek's fortress' location is revealed in W #152, '00. The Yashida ancestral manor in Agarashima is incorrectly called the Yashida compound, which is a completely different building in Tokyo. This issue also contains the bound-in Spider-Man story "Fast Lane, Part 4 of 4"; that story is indexed as ASM Ann '00/2 in Index #11, '10.

WOLVERINE #151 (June 2000)

"Blood Debt, Part 2" (22 pages)

CREDITS: Steve Skroce (writer, pencils), Lary Stucker (inks), Richard Starkings & Comicraft's Saida Temofonte (letters), Steve Buccellato (colors), Pete Franco (asst editor), Mark Powers (editor), Larry Wachowski & Wendi Higenbottam (special thanks)
FEATURE CHARACTER: Wolverine
SUPPORTING CAST: Yukio, Amiko Kobayashi
VILLAINS: Clan Kaishek: Yolyn Kaishek (also in fb, his chr 1st app, prior to W #152, '00 fb), Gom Kaishek (dies), Haan Kaishek, Kia Kaishek, Tupa (Kia's aide, 1st), Otou, Yolyn's men (in fb, some or others chr next in W #152 '00 fb), Gom's men (some die), Haan's men (many die)
OTHER CHARACTERS: Silver Samurai, Yolyn's brother (dies) & his men (most dead) (prev 2 in fb), Gom's doctor (bts telling Samurai to recuperate), commuter; birds (on sword hilt in fb), cartoon characters (on billboards) inc devil & fish
LOCATIONS/ITEMS: Clan Kaishek's Outer Mongolian fortress, Yolyn's brother's home (in fb), Tokyo inc Gom's safehouse & Haan's Shinjuku District penthouse w/garage / Yolyn & his brother's men's guns, Yolyn's sword (both in fb), Yukio & Amiko's bonds, Gom's van, gate, door (prev 3 destroyed), handgun & car, Haan's windows (destroyed), limo, cellphone & pistol, Haan's men's explosives (bts), guns, swords, spears, axe & cellphone, bus shelter (destroyed), Silver Samurai's bandages, Gom's men's guns, Amiko's chopstick, Kia's handgun, van & gun w/tranquilizer darts
FLASHBACK: After a battle between their forces, Yolyn kills his brother, his first step towards seizing control of Clan Kaishek.
SYNOPSIS: A remorseful Yolyn remembers murdering his brother. At Gom's safehouse, Kia is kind to the captive Yukio and Amiko, but Gom plans to kill them regardless of Wolverine's success. Wolverine breaks into Haan's penthouse, but discovers that Haan knew of his attack; two hundred troops swarm Wolverine while Haan escapes. Driven into a berserker rage, Wolverine tears through the attackers and escapes. Gom gloats to the recovering Silver Samurai that once Wolverine kills Haan, he will inherit all Kaishek dominions, including Clan Yashida. Wolverine returns to Gom's safehouse, furious that Haan was ready for him — but Haan secretly follows Wolverine, and his troops attack the safehouse. Kia knocks out Yukio, Amiko and the Samurai, delivering them to her aide, while Haan corners and kills Gom. Kia tells Wolverine that his loved ones are now her prisoners, and orders him to protect her — as she fears that she will be Haan's next target.
NOTE: Next issue reveals that Kia alerted Haan to Wolverine's imminent attack.

WOLVERINE #152 (July 2000)

"Blood Debt, Part 3" (22 pages)

CREDITS: Steve Skroce (writer, pencils), Lary Stucker (inks), Richard Starkings & Comicraft's Saida Temofonte (letters), Steve Buccellato (colors), Pete Franco (asst editor), Mark Powers (editor), Larry Wachowski & Wendi Higenbottam (special thanks)
FEATURE CHARACTER: Wolverine
SUPPORTING CAST: Yukio, Amiko Kobayashi
VILLAINS: Clan Kaishek: Yolyn Kaishek (also in fb between W #151, '00 fb & W #153, '00 fb), Haan Kaishek (dies, also in rfb), Kia Kaishek, Otou, Tupa, Yolyn's men (in fb, some or others chr last in W #151, '00 fb, others next in W #153, '00), Haan's men (some die)
OTHER CHARACTERS: Silver Samurai, Yolyn's other brother (in fb, dies); Gom Kaishek (in rfb, dies); woman (on billboard), man (as sculpture); birds (on sword hilt in fb)
LOCATIONS/ITEMS: Clan Kaishek's Outer Mongolian fortress (also in fb), Tokyo: Gom's safehouse (in rfb), Shingen's Citadel compound (bts), Kia's safehouse, Haan's Shinjuku District penthouse & Yukio's apartment / Yolyn's sword (in fb), Tupa's handgun, cellphone & serving tray, Yukio's window (destroyed), bonds & bandages, Amiko's bonds, Silver Samurai's bonds, bandages, armor & swords, safehouse pipes (1 destroyed), Haan's pistol (also in rfb) & security system (bts), Haan's men's guns, Kia's cellphone & handgun, Otou's rifle, Wolverine's luggage
FLASHBACKS: Haan shoots Gom (last issue). Yolyn's other brother begs for peace, but Yolyn kills him anyway, continuing to seize control of Clan Kaishek.
SYNOPSIS: A despairing Yolyn remembers murdering his other brother. The captive Yukio gives Amiko a pep talk, readying her to fight. As Haan ponders his fratricide, Wolverine and Kia burst in; Kia asks to talk about peace. Tupa brings food to her prisoners, but Amiko breaks free and knocks her down; Amiko and the bound Yukio struggle to overpower Tupa. Kia asks Haan why the Kaisheks have always eliminated their loved ones to gain power. Her cellphone rings; it is Yukio, shouting to Wolverine that they are free. Wolverine attacks Kia, but she dodges him and suddenly shoots Haan, then tosses Wolverine her gun. When Haan's guards burst in, Kia blames Wolverine, and escapes while he battles and defeats the guards. The dying Haan realizes that Kia has been manipulating everyone, and warns Wolverine that their father Yolyn is her next target. Wolverine reunites with Amiko and the Samurai, but Yukio has taken off after Kia — and Wolverine follows.

WOLVERINE #153 (August 2000)

"Blood Debt, Conclusion!" (22 pages)

CREDITS: Steve Skroce (writer, pencils), Lary Stucker (inks), Richard Starkings & Comicraft's Saida Temofonte (letters), Colorgraphix (uncredited) & Steve Buccellato (colors), Pete Franco (asst editor), Mark Powers (editor), Larry Wachowski & Wendi Higenbottam (special thanks)
FEATURE CHARACTER: Wolverine (next in IF/W #1-4, '00-01; X #102-103, UXM #384, X #104, UXM #385, all '00, X Ann '00; X #105-106, Av #35, X #107, XMU #29, all '00, MaxS #3, '01, S #4, '00)
SUPPORTING CAST: Yukio (next bts in W #158, '01, next in W #173, '02), Amiko Kobayashi (next in W #158, '01)
VILLAINS: Clan Kaishek: Yolyn Kaishek (dies, also in rfb, also in fb between W #152, '00 fb & W #150, '00 fb, also in W #150, '00 fb during fb), Kia Kaishek (dies), Yolyn's men (some or all die, others last in W #152, '00 fb)
OTHER CHARACTERS: Silver Samurai (next in Elektra #3, '01), Yolyn's father (in fb, his chr 1st app, prior to & also in W #150, '00 fb; also in rfb); Kublai Khan (mentioned, Kaisheks' ancestors served him); Kaisheks' honored dead & conquered enemies (prev 2 as wall decorations, also in rfb & bts in fb); birds (on sword hilt, also in rfb & fb)
LOCATIONS/ITEMS: Outer Mongolia inc Clan Kaishek's fortress (destroyed, also in fb & rfb) / Yolyn's window, door (both destroyed) & sword (also in fb & rfb), Kia's guns, Amiko's poncho, canteen, supplies & sling w/stones, Silver Samurai's poncho, binoculars, armor & swords, Yukio's rope (also in rfb), Yolyn's men's guns, gas pipes (destroyed)
FLASHBACKS: Yolyn watches his father die (W #150, '00 fb). Yolyn stabs his father, claiming control of Clan Kaishek by right of birth.
SYNOPSIS: As Yolyn regrets murdering his family, Kia enters and confronts him. Outside Clan Kaishek's fortress, Wolverine tells Amiko and the Silver Samurai to stay put, and enters looking for Yukio. Kia shoots Yolyn, claiming full control of Clan Kaishek — but Yukio bursts in and attacks her. The two women duel through the fortress until they encounter Wolverine battling Yolyn's guards. Kia flees, then ambushes and shoots the pursuing Yukio. Amiko interrupts, having disobeyed Wolverine and snuck inside, but Kia takes Amiko hostage and flees deeper into the fortress. Wolverine follows, attacks Kia and frees Amiko; the Silver Samurai helps Amiko and Yukio escape the fortress. Wolverine and Kia fight a brutal battle that ruptures several gas lines. Fatally injured, Kia strikes her sword on Wolverine's claws, creating a spark; the gas ignites and the fortress explodes. Amiko rushes to the badly burned Wolverine's side, but he reassures her that he will be fine.
NOTE: Yolyn Kaishek's family name is confirmed here. Colorgraphix's credit is given in the "Wolverine: Blood Debt" TPB. This issue has another LOC from Daron Jensen.

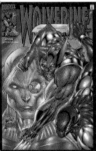

WOLVERINE #154 (September 2000)

"All Along the Watchtower" (22 pages)

CREDITS: Rob Liefeld (plot, pencils), Eric Stephenson (script), Norm Rapmund (inks), Richard Starkings & Comicraft's Troy Peteri (letters), Digital Broome (colors), Pete Franco (asst editor), Mark Powers (editor)
FEATURE CHARACTER: Wolverine (also in pfb, also on monitors in pfb)
GUEST STAR: Siryn (Theresa Rourke Cassidy, sonic scream, last in XFor #100, '00)
VILLAINS: Scourge (mercenary group): Mini Max, Pigskin, Reckless Eric, Vance Rebus (prev 4 also in pfb), Deadeye Dick, Mega Max, 1 other; Deadpool (also in pfb, last in Gam #18, '00), Administrator (Watchtower's cyborg leader, 1st, also as hologram, also bts in pfb ordering Wolverine's capture), Levon (as bartender, also as Leon), Janine (also as waitress) (prev 2 mercenaries, in pfb), Watchtower guards (bts responding to break-in)
OTHER CHARACTERS: Geronimo Crowe (former SHIELD agent, Administrator's son, see NOTE), Cargo (teleporter), Hardwire (reprogrammed Sentinel), Shooter (cyborg, unnamed) (all 1st), Deadpool's surveillance assistant (in pfb); Neil Young (mentioned in pfb)
LOCATIONS/ITEMS: Swags (bar, destroyed, in pfb, also on monitors in pfb) w/nearby woods (also in pfb), Watchtower facility / Pigskin's gun, Deadeye Dick's cyborg implants, Mega Max's shoulder cannon, Deadpool's knives, swords, guns w/tranquilizer darts & van (in pfb) w/hidden cameras (bts, destroyed) & monitors, assistant's earpiece, Janine's guns (prev 2 in pfb), Administrator's hard-light hologram projector (bts, see NOTE) & eyepiece (also as hologram), Siryn's healing tube w/chemical bath & breathing tube, Wolverine's bonds, Crowe & Hardwire's comm units (bts), Shooter's cyborg limbs w/gun-arm
FLASHBACK: Deadpool secretly monitors Wolverine as he drinks at a bar. The waitress hits on Wolverine, but when she calls the bartender by a different name than he used, Wolverine surmises that it is a trap. The "waitress" begins shooting at Wolverine; Deadpool realizes that other mercenaries have targeted Wolverine, and Vance Rebus destroy the bar (p).
SYNOPSIS: Deadpool and the Scourge confront Wolverine; Deadpool explains that someone has offered an enormous bounty for Wolverine's capture. Deadpool and Wolverine fight, and Deadpool knocks Wolverine out with tranquilizer darts. Wolverine awakens in the Watchtower's facility; he easily defeats the Scourge, but the Administrator knocks him out with one slap. Elsewhere, Deadpool checks on former X-Force member Siryn, whom he has feelings for, and worries about whether the Watchtower can heal her throat. Wolverine discovers that the Watchtower has drained much of his blood; the Administrator explains that they study mutants to find ways to heal humans. Suddenly, Geronimo Crowe and his team burst in, free Wolverine and confront the Administrator — whom Crowe calls father…
NOTE: Crowe is named on this issue's letters page, but his last name is misspelled "Crow." Shooter is named next issue. Crowe's team is initially shown as four human-sized silhouettes; either the massive Hardwire was drawn incorrectly, or the team has a fifth member who does not fully appear on-panel. Siryn's throat was cut in XFor #90, '99. Next issue reveals that the Administrator appears in holographic form in this issue's final scene.

WOLVERINE #155 (October 2000)

"All Along the Watchtower, Part 2" (22 pages)

CREDITS: Rob Liefeld (plot, pencils), Eric Stephenson (script), Norm Rapmund (inks), Richard Starkings & Comicraft's Troy Peteri (letters), Digital Broome (colors), Pete Franco (asst editor), Mark Powers (editor), Kev Senft (as "Blond," c colors)
FEATURE CHARACTER: Wolverine
GUEST STAR: Siryn (chr next in Dom #3, '03, next in Dp #56, '01)
VILLAINS: Deadpool (next in Dp #46, '00), Administrator (as hologram), Watchtower guards (prev 2 next in XFor #4, '0
OTHER CHARACTERS: Shooter (named), Geronimo Crowe, Hardwire
LOCATIONS/ITEMS: Watchtower facility (destroyed) & safehouse w/nearby woods / Shooter's cyborg limbs w/gu arm, Administrator's eyepiece (as hologram) & hard-light hologram projector (bts), guards' guns, Hardwire's muta scanners (bts), Siryn's healing tube (destroyed) w/chemical bath & breathing tube, Deadpool's knives & swords

SYNOPSIS: As Geronimo Crowe's team battles the Watchtower guards, Wolverine attacks the Administrator, but discovers that he is just holographic projection, which fades away. Crowe tells a confused Wolverine that there are many more facets to the human/mutant conflict tha the X-Men are aware of, and has Hardwire scan the facility for other captive mutants. Hardwire detects Siryn and smashes his way to her locatio where Deadpool stands vigil over her healing tube. Wolverine and Shooter attack Deadpool, knocking him into Siryn's tube, which shatters — a Siryn emerges, her voice and powers fully restored. Siryn explains that Deadpool captured him for the Watchtower's twisted medical researd in exchange for their healing her, but although Siryn is disappointed in Deadpool, she is still grateful; they leave together. Wolverine agrees to he Crowe's team track down the Administrator. Wolverine infiltrates a Watchtower safehouse, but finds another hologram of the Administrator, whic taunts him before disappearing. Wolverine swears to expose the Watchtower and end their experimentation on mutants.
NOTE: Crowe's last name is spelled correctly here. Cargo does not appear in this issue; presumably after teleporting Crowe and Shooter in the facility last issue, he teleported away. Wolverine finally locates and deals with the Administrator in XFor #4, '05. This issue's cover is a homage to that of IHulk #340, '88.

WOLVERINE #156 (November 2000)

"Going Underground" (22 pages)

CREDITS: Rob Liefeld (plot), Eric Stephenson (script), Ian Churchill (pencils), Norm Rapmund (inks), Richa Starkings & Comicraft (letters), Digital Broome (colors), Pete Franco (asst editor), Mark Powers (editor)
FEATURE CHARACTER: Wolverine
GUEST STAR: Spider-Man (last in S/Void, '01)
VILLAINS: Mole Man (Harvey Rupert Elder, underground monarch, last in Wlk #4, '99) & his creatures (1 dies Morlock offshoot group (bts warring with Mole Man) inc Fugue (bts killing people) & Carver
OTHER CHARACTERS: Moloid subterraneans (underground race, Mole Man's subjects, some or others last Wlk #4, '99), Joanna Chen (ANN reporter), police inc Lt. Tara Curson & her SWAT team (die) inc Giordano, victim (dead, all but 1 bts), cameraman, paramedics
LOCATIONS/ITEMS: Abandoned subway station (Manhattan's Lower East Side) & tunnels / Cameraman earpiece & camera, Joanna's microphone & cigarette, paramedics' stretcher & sheet, police flashlights & floodlights, scrap of victim's dres SWAT team's spotlights (bts), guns, armor & goggles, Spider-Man's camera, Mole Man's electrical staff

SYNOPSIS: Joanna Chen reports on a murder in an abandoned subway station, the sixth similar killing in as many weeks. Wolverir investigates the murders, his hyper-senses leading him deep into abandoned subway tunnels. He encounters a SWAT team, who initial believe him to be the killer, but their commander Lt. Curson recognizes Wolverine as an X-Man. Suddenly, large rocky creatures smash into th tunnel; Wolverine battles them, but finds their hides very difficult to damage. The creatures kill the entire team except Curson; Wolverine pursue them down the tunnels and discovers one creature battling Spider-Man, who had ventured into the tunnels to try to take news photos for th Daily Bugle. After a prolonged battle, the two heroes manage to defeat the creature; Lt. Curson catches up, shaken but insistent on helping. Th heroes debate where the creatures came from, but as they round a corner, they discover the answer — as the rest of the creatures await, alon with the Mole Man and his Moloid army…
NOTE: Next issue reveals that the creatures were bred to combat the attacking Morlock offshoot group and that Fugue killed the victims, an specifies that Curson's squad is a SWAT team. This issue includes a 2-page preview of UltSM #1, '00.

WOLVERINE #157 (December 2000)

"Right Underneath It" (23 pages)

CREDITS: Rob Liefeld (plot), Eric Stephenson (script), Ian Churchill (pencils), Norm Rapmund (inks), Richar Starkings & Comicraft's Troy Peteri & Oscar Gongora (letters), Peter Pantazis (colors), Pete Franco (asst editor Mark Powers (editor), Tanya Horie & Richard Horie (c colors)
FEATURE CHARACTER: Wolverine (next in W #166, '01 fb, W Ann '00)
GUEST STAR: Spider-Man (chr next in ASM #36, '01, next in SM:Mys #1, '01)
VILLAINS: Mole Man (next in AFlt #4, '04) & his creatures, Morlock offshoot group inc Carver (impenetrable ski & retractable arm blades) & Fugue (feral creature) (prev 2 die)
OTHER CHARACTERS: Lt. Tara Curson, Moloid subterraneans (some or others next in AFlt #4, '04)
LOCATIONS/ITEMS: Abandoned subway tunnels, Morlock offshoots' underground caverns inc makeshift aren w/chasm / Curson's armor & guns, Mole Man's electrical staff & makeshift litter, Morlock offshoots' advance

weaponry (mentioned)
SYNOPSIS: Wolverine attacks the Mole Man as the Moloids swarm over Spider-Man and Lt. Curson, but when one of the rocky creature grabs Curson, the Mole Man comes to her defense, zapping the creature with his staff. Wolverine explains that the creatures killed severa policemen, and the Mole Man grows concerned, claiming that they should not act without his orders; they were bred solely to combat a

marauding Morlock offshoot group. Suspecting that the marauders are the killers he seeks, Wolverine has the Mole Man lead them to their caverns. The three are soon captured, and Carver explains that the mindless Fugue is the murderer. Wolverine challenges Carver to combat under Morlock law. The two battle by a chasm, but an earth tremor suddenly knocks Fugue in. Spider-Man catches him on a web, but it breaks; Carver grabs it, but the two fall into the chasm. The heroes suspect that the Mole Man engineered the quake, but he waves off their questions and leads them back to the surface.

NOTE: This issue's letters page has a 1-page B&W preview of W #159, '01.

WOLVERINE 2000 (2000)

"Family" (40 pages)

CREDITS: Frank Tieri (writer), Jorge Santamaria (pencils), Rodney Ramos (uncredited) & Nathan Massengill (inks), Richard Starkings & Comicraft's Saida Temofonte (letters), Hi-Fi Design (colors), Pete Franco (asst editor), Mark Powers (editor), Jorge Lucas (c pencils), Nestor Pereyra (c inks)
FEATURE CHARACTER: Wolverine (also in rfb, also as himself & hologram in pfb, next in UXM #388, Bish #16, X #108, UXM #389 fb, W #158, all '01)
GUEST STAR: Beast (last in UXM #387, next bts in Hcat #2, next in Hcat #3, all '00)
VILLAINS: Brood (parasitic insectoid aliens; some also in fb, also bts on monitor in fb; some or others last in CoC2 #5, '99, others next in X4 #1, '05) inc "Ulara," "Zet," "Jexia" (prev 3 also in fb, see NOTE), Hotel Ripley "guests," "staff" & "security," Queen (another in rfb) & her bodyguards (1 also in fb), Tyrus' embryo (also in fb), Wolverine's embryo (another bts in rfb), others (in fb only) (all die); Malcolm Colcord (1st bts, controlling Wolverine, see NOTE; chr last in W #166, '01 fb, chr next bts in W #166, '01 fb, next in 1st on-panel app in W #160, '01)
OTHER CHARACTERS: Tyrus Krill (alien bounty hunter, also in pfb, also in fb prior to pfb), Ulara (Tyrus' wife), Zet (Tyrus' son), Jexia (Tyrus' daughter) (prev 3 also in fb prior to issue, see NOTE) (all transformed into Brood & back, die), fast food staff (bts in pfb) & patrons (in pfb) inc Greg & John, Hotel Ripley guests, staff (all but 1 of prev 2 transformed into Brood, die) & security (transformed into Brood, die), Tyrus' alien trophies (dead, heads in cases) inc D'bari (see NOTE) & Skrull; an Acanti (alien space whales used as Brood's living starships, in fb, also on monitor in fb; another in rfb; some or others last in UXM #166, '83, next in X4 #4, '05), M'zara blood flies (alien parasites); Brood: Ship-Master & his crew (prev 2 bts) inc Weaponeer, Cyclops' Queen embryo, Hannah's Queen embryo (bts), Ghost Rider's embryo, "Fang," "Harry Palmer," "Fred," "Nancy"; Apocalypse, Cyclops, Ghost Rider, Psylocke, Rogue, Temptress, Hannah Conover, Acanti Prophet-Singer (prev 17 in rfb)
LOCATIONS/ITEMS: New York's Ripley Hotel w/lobby & pool, fast food restaurant (in pfb), Apocalypse's safehouses (mentioned in pfb), outer space (in rfb & fb); Denver, Colorado; New Orleans, Louisiana; Sedonia, Arizona; "Sleazeworld" (prev 3 in rfb) / Guests' car & luggage, hotel baggage cart, employee's walkie-talkie, security's walkie-talkies (bts), John's car, restaurant window (prev 2 in pfb, destroyed), Krill's trophy cases, holographic projector (prev 2 in pfb), scent masking device (bts), Brood sensor (prev 2 also bts in pfb), scientific equipment, hypo-spray w/depressant compound (prev 3 in fb), weaponry inc blaster (in fb), knife (in pfb), staff (also in pfb), gun & sonic device, personal spaceship (also in pfb) w/autopilot & family spaceship (in fb) w/sensors, hyperdrive (prev 2 bts), monitors, security alarm & escape pods, Wolverine's Weapon X brain implants (bts in pfb, see NOTE) & sheets, Brood eggs (see NOTE)
FLASHBACKS: The Brood pursue the Acanti Prophet-Singer as Cyclops transforms (UXM #166, '83), "Harry Palmer" commands the Brood-controlled Rogue and Psylocke (UXM #233, '88), Wolverine threatens "Fang" (UXM #162, '82), Ghost Rider transforms (GR #26, '92), two of Hannah Conover's followers transform (X/Brood #1, '96). Tyrus arrives on Earth and locates Wolverine, who has been having vivid dreams of killing. Tyrus informs him of a Brood infestation (p). The Brood attack Tyrus' family's spaceship and infect him. He suppresses the transformation medically, but discovers that his family has been transformed as well, and flees in horror.
SYNOPSIS: Wolverine enters the Ripley Hotel and begins killing everyone he sees, but detects and spares one uninfected employee. Tyrus infiltrates the hotel, but convulses as his Brood embryo tries to transform him. Wolverine finds a massive Brood infestation; he is swarmed and overwhelmed until Tyrus arrives, unleashing specialized weapons that kill most of the Brood. The Queen battles Tyrus; her bodyguards infect Wolverine, but his healing factor defeats the embryo. Wolverine kills the Queen, but Tyrus suddenly transforms into a Brood and attacks him. Wolverine fatally stabs Tyrus, who reverts and explains that these Brood were his family. His family reverts as well and they die together. Later, Beast reprograms Tyrus' spaceship and Wolverine sends their bodies back to their homeworld.
NOTE: This Index treats Brood hatchlings as separate entities from their hosts; thus Krill's family and the Broods they became are listed separately. Although generally only Queens can implant embryos in host bodies, the Queen's bodyguards seem to have this ability here as well. Wolverine's healing factor has destroyed implanted Brood embryos twice before, in UXM #162, '82 & 234, '88. Krill's D'bari trophy may be K'hari, lifemate of G'aspix. MHeroes #33, '11 claims that Krill killed K'hari, and although that story was set on Earth-9411, it seems to have been a deliberate reference to this issue. W #166, '01 reveals that the new Weapon X Program's director has begun controlling Wolverine remotely via leftover Weapon X brain implants; Wolverine's vivid dreams, first mentioned here, are his mind's way of coping. This issue includes homages to the *Alien* film series, the inspiration for the Brood: the Ripley Hotel is named after lead character Ellen Ripley, and Brood eggs are shown that resemble xenomorph eggs. (Only the Brood Empress, who does not appear here, lays eggs; these may have been stored on the Brood ship.) Also, a sign advertises *Invasion of the Body Snatchers*, a film about aliens secretly replacing humans.

WOLVERINE #158 (January 2001)

"Manhunt" (22 pages)

CREDITS: Joe Pruett (writer), Sunny Lee (pencils), Harry Candelario (inks), Richard Starkings & Comicraft (letters), Hi-Fi Design (colors), Pete Franco (asst editor), Mark Powers (editor), Jorge Lucas (c pencils), Nestor Pereyra (c inks)
FEATURE CHARACTER: Wolverine (next in UXM #389, '01, W #166, '01 fb)
SUPPORTING CAST: Yukio (bts informing Wolverine of kidnapping), Amiko Kobayashi (both last in W #153, '00, next in W #173, '02)
VILLAINS: Zaran (Maximillian Zaran, "Weapons Master," assassin, last in Gam #19, '00, next in W #167, '01), Shinji Kizaki (Yakuza boss) & his ninjas (die)
OTHER CHARACTERS: Helicopter pilot; Velociraptor (dies), lion, deer (prev 2 dead, heads as trophies); Amazon tribe (mentioned, developed pheromone-masking elixir); dragons (as decoration)

LOCATIONS/ITEMS: Zaran's private island (South China Sea) inc helipad & home w/cellblock, Yukio's apartment (bts) / Wolverine's helicopter parachute & binoculars, Zaran's ransom note, hidden cameras (prev 2 bts), bow (destroyed), arrows, pike, knives, shotgun & blowgun w/ poisoned dart, cell door lock, Kizaki's closed-circuit television (prev 2 bts), ninjas' swords, bows & arrows, twig (destroyed), poison antidote

SYNOPSIS: Wolverine parachutes onto Zaran's private island, complying with the ransom note that Zaran left behind after he kidnapped Amiko. A Velociraptor suddenly attacks him; assuming that Zaran imported it from the Savage Land, Wolverine kills the creature. He locates Amiko, but Zaran poisons him with a blowdart. Zaran explains that he wishes to regain his reputation, and plans to hunt and kill Wolverine to impress Yakuza boss Shinji Kizaki. Zaran gives Wolverine a head start, then attacks him from the woods, but Wolverine soon tracks Zaran down and defeats him. Kizaki frees Amiko and offers Wolverine the antidote to Zaran's poison, but Wolverine's healing factor has already neutralized it. Kizaki, realizing that Wolverine could become a powerful enemy, decides to kill him now. He orders his ninjas to attack, but Wolverine gets Amiko to safety and ambushes the ninjas in the woods, killing them. As his helicopter arrives, Wolverine makes Kizaki swear to leave him and his family alone, but as soon as Wolverine departs, Kizaki begins plotting revenge.

NOTE: This issue was polybagged with a Marvel Online CD-Rom. Kizaki has not exacted his revenge to date.

WOLVERINE #159 (February 2001)

"The Best There Is" (22 pages)

CREDITS: Frank Tieri (writer), Sean Chen (pencils), Norm Rapmund (inks), Richard Starkings & Comicraft' Saida Temofonte (letters), Hi-Fi Design (colors), Pete Franco (asst editor), Mark Powers (editor), Danny Miki (c inks), Steve Buccellato (c colors)

FEATURE CHARACTER: Wolverine (also on scope & in his own dream)

GUEST STARS: X-Men: Nightcrawler (last in Cable #88, '01, next in W #161, '01), Rogue (last in UXM #389, '01, next in XMU #31, '01) (prev 2 also in Wolverine's dream), Colossus (last in UXM #389, '01 fb, next in X #109, '01)

VILLAINS: Mr. X (telepathic serial killer, see NOTE) & his Murder Avant-Garde (group unnamed): Blok (Mr. X's enforcer, also possessed by Ogun) (both chr last in W #169, '01 fb), Major & his men (die) inc Johnson, Peters Riley & Rogers, Lady Killers (group unnamed): T, A (all 1st); Ogun (bts possessing Blok, last in KP:AoS #3, '98 chr last in W #169, '01 fb), Viper (bts informing Mr. X about Wolverine, last in GenX #54, '99, next in X #109, '01) Weapon X agents (1st bts, planting car bomb, some or others chr last in W #166, '01 fb)

OTHER CHARACTERS: John Merchant (former Weapon X employee, dies, last in MCP #79, '91) & his wife (both also as stick figures in drawing), Nanci Merchant & her sister (prev 2 John's daughters) (all chr last bts in W #166, '01 fb), Miss Pennyfeather (Mr. X's secretary, voice only on intercom), Tony (nightclub doorman), police (1 also on scope), bartender (bts serving Wolverine), restaurant staff & patrons (prev a dead), nightclub patrons, bystanders (1 dies, also on scope; some or others also on scope); dog (on scope); Mr. Spencer, conference ca participants (prev 2 mentioned by Pennyfeather), litigants (mentioned, suing Hub); Cable, Phoenix (prev 2 in Wolverine's dream)

LOCATIONS/ITEMS: New York (also on scopes) inc restaurant, rooftop, Diesel bar, Hub nightclub & Mr. X's office, X-Mansion (also in dream) Merchants' home / Miss Pennyfeather's intercom (bts), Mr. X's intercom, binoculars, rifle, cellphone & limousine, police car (on scope), bonds & gag, Major's radio (bts), binoculars, cellphone, handguns & knife, computer monitor (destroyed), apple, violin bow (prev 3 used as weapons) Major's men's flamethrower (destroyed), guns, goggles, rappelling lines & headsets w/radios (bts), car (destroyed), T & A's cellphone, car, whip sword & dagger, John's car (destroyed) & briefcase, Weapon X car bomb (bts)

SYNOPSIS: From his skyscraper office, Mr. X shoots and kills a jogger on the street. Wolverine awakens from a nightmare that he has killed the X-Men, but he snaps at his teammates when they check on him, unwilling to admit that the dreams have gone on for months. Fearing that they are an aftereffect of his time as Death, Wolverine heads into New York City to drink, but notices a small squad observing him from a rooftop. Thei leader, the Major, reports in to Mr. X, who is eating at a restaurant after having murdered everyone inside. The Major orders his men to attack but Wolverine ambushes them and battles savagely, killing the entire squad. Nearby, T and A are barred from a nightclub, so they viciously beat the doorman until the Major calls, asking for their aid. Elsewhere, John Merchant gets in his car, which suddenly explodes. Wolverine attacks the Major, interrogating him about who ordered the assault — but T, A and Blok arrive and attack Wolverine...

NOTE: Though the name "Mr. X" is given in last issue's teaser box, it is not used in-story until Wolverine nicknames his foe as such in W #161 '01. The character is technically unnamed; neither his real name nor a self-chosen codename have been revealed to date. Mr. X's telepathic powers are revealed in W #168, '01. T and A's names are a play on the phrase "T&A." Their sub-group the Lady Killers is named next issue; Mr X's larger group the Murder Avant-Garde is named in W #161, '01. The Merchants' last name is revealed in OHMU HC13, '10. Wolverine's dream here is a reaction to Weapon X's Director making him stalk the Merchants prior to this issue, as W #166, '01 fb reveals.

WOLVERINE #160 (March 2001)

"The Best There Is, Part Two of Three" (22 pages)

CREDITS: Frank Tieri (writer), Sean Chen (pencils), Norm Rapmund (inks), Richard Starkings & Comicraft's Saida Temofonte (letters), Hi-Fi Design (colors), Mike Raicht (asst editor), Mike Marts (editor), J.H. Williams III (c pencils), Mick Gray (c inks), José Villarrubia (c colors)

FEATURE CHARACTER: Wolverine (also in W #166, '01 fb)

VILLAINS: Malcolm Colcord (Weapon X Program director, unnamed, 1st on-panel app, chr last & next bts in W #166, '01 fbs), Sabretooth (last in Bish #16, '01) (both next in W #162, '01), Mr. X, Murder Avant-Garde: Blok (also possessed by Ogun), Major, Lady Killers (group named): T, A; Ogun (bts possessing Blok), Weapon X agents (1st on-panel app, some in shadow, some or others next in W #162, '01), street gang (die)

OTHER CHARACTERS: Peter Craigo (unnamed), Michael Herana (both former Weapon X employees, die, see NOTE), Miss Pennyfeather (bts on phone), Campbell, Hampton, Johnson, Sanderson, Turnbull (prev 5 Mr. X's sparring partners, die) & their wives (mentioned by Mr. X, receiving condolence packages), bystanders; other former Weapon X employees (mentioned, killed); model (on poster), people (dead, as skulls, cover only)

LOCATIONS/ITEMS: Manhattan's West 108th Street inc 1313 (Weapon X front), New York rooftop, Mr. X's gymnasium, city street & warehouse / Sabretooth's note, gang's guns, Blok's spear & tie, T & A's whip, sais (some destroyed), daggers, guns & bandages, Major's handguns (destroyed), bandages (bts) & cellphone, Weapon X's machine guns (in shadow), knockout gas & car, Mr. X's cellphone & invitation

arring partners' padding & truncheons, Miss Pennyfeather's phone (bts), Michael's newspaper, Wolverine's Weapon X brain implants (bts)

YNOPSIS: In Manhattan, Sabretooth kills a street gang, then meets with a potential new client. Sabretooth is shocked by the man's face, d as knockout gas pumps into the room, the man states that Sabretooth will work exclusively for him now. Meanwhile, T, A and Blok press eir attack on Wolverine. A embeds a dagger in Wolverine's throat as the Major attacks from behind. Wolverine defeats the Major, but T and A gin swinging him into Blok's punches; Wolverine ducks and Blok knocks out A. The major reports to Mr. X, who kills all of his sparring partners. olverine flings T away and begins choking Blok with his own tie, but the Major intervenes, giving Wolverine an invitation for a one-on-one battle h Mr. X. Later, two nervous men meet to discuss John Merchant's fate, but are both killed in a drive-by shooting. That night, Wolverine arrives Mr. X's warehouse; the two fight viciously, but Mr. X easily sidesteps all of Wolverine's attacks and quickly defeats him.

DTE: Malcolm Colcord's first name is revealed in WX #1, '02, and his last name in WX #6, '03. Called just "Mike" here, Michael Herana's full st name is revealed next issue, as is Peter's first name. Their last names are revealed in OHMU HC13, '10. Although they were employees the original Weapon X Program, it is not revealed what their jobs were, where and when they served, or if they were ever seen on-panel; erefore this Index cannot determine either man's last app, if any. W #166, '01 fb reveals that Weapon X's Director made Wolverine track down e two men between pages of this issue. Sabretooth claims here to have been involved with killing Senator Robert Kelly, but Kelly was shot by anti-mutant protestor in X #108, '01. Although the Major states that Blok is mute, Block cries out in pain earlier in this issue.

WOLVERINE #161 (April 2001)

"The Best There Is, Part Three of Three" (22 pages)

CREDITS: Frank Tieri (writer), Sean Chen (pencils), Norm Rapmund (inks), Richard Starkings & Comicraft's Saida Temofonte (letters), Avalon's Raymund Lee (colors), Mike Raicht (asst editor), Mike Marts (editor), J.H. Williams III (c pencils), Mick Gray (c inks), José Villarrubia (c colors)

FEATURE CHARACTER: Wolverine (next in X #109, '01, XMU #37, '02, X:Dec, '00, UXM #390, '01, W #176, '02 fb; ASM #36, XMU #30/4, W:SC, all '01)

GUEST STAR: Nightcrawler (last in W #159, '01, next in X #109, '01)

VILLAINS: Mr. X ("named"; also as himself, boy & symbolic image in fb, his chr 1st app, prior to W #169, '01 fb, also in W:MrX, '10 during fb; next voice only in W #163, '01, next in W #167, '01), Murder Avant-Garde (named): Blok (also possessed by Ogun, next in W #168, '01), Major, Lady Killers: T, A; Ogun (possessing Blok, also in Wolverine's imagination, next in W #168, '01)

THER CHARACTERS: Drexel Walsh (US Senator, former Weapon X employee, 1st but see NOTE), Postlewaite (Mr. X's lawyer), Bryars Walsh's aide), Mr. X's parents, accident victim, martial arts masters, fighters, vagrant (prev 5 die), Mr. X's old girlfriend, powerful man (prev 2 ead) (others of prev 3 mentioned, killed by Mr. X), driver (bts in car), Mr. X's parents' maid (bts cooking soufflé), Mr. X's date & psychiatrist, diences, referee, bystanders (prev 14 in fb), Mr. X's victim trophies (dead, some as heads & skulls); Sparky (Mr. X's puppy, in fb), mouse (prev die), cobra, birds; John Dillinger (mentioned, Mr. X owns his tommy gun), Saddam Hussein (mentioned, gave Mr. X a flamethrower), African ieftain (mentioned, killed by Mr. X), doctors (mentioned in fb, treating Mr. X); Peter Craigo, Michael Herana, John Merchant, police (prev 4 in otos); Grim Reaper (as statue), bear, mouse, horse (prev 3 as Mr. X's toys in fb), cartoon dog (on bottle in fb), dragon (as tattoo)

OCATIONS/ITEMS: Mr. X's private island w/dining room & trophy room, Walsh's Washington DC office, ocean, city street (others in photo fb); Mr. X's childhood home, restaurant, vacation spot, psychiatrist's office, ex-girlfriend's bedroom, martial arts dojos, fighting arenas (prev 7 fb), Merchants' home (in photo) / Wolverine's restraint chair (destroyed), raft, note, eggs benedict & ball gag, Major's bandages, T's sling, A's andage, brace & handgun, Postlewaite's briefcase & documents, Mr. X's records (destroyed), car, oven, rope, knives, rifle, childhood toys (prev in fb), trophy cases (1 destroyed), sword (destroyed, another in fb), spears, axe, limo & semi-automatic flamethrower, driver & powerful man's rs, psychiatrist's notebook, master's sword (prev 3 in fb), cobra's cage, Walsh's newspaper, trophy room door lock, John Dillinger's tommy n, Blok's bandages, X-Men's Blackbird jet

LASHBACK: As a boy, Mr. X witnesses a woman die and is transfixed. Depressed for years afterward, he kills his puppy on a whim, and ddenly realizes that death is the thrill he craves. He practices killing, then studies with martial arts masters, perfecting their styles and then urdering them. He soon considers his killings to be an art form.

YNOPSIS: Wolverine finds himself strapped down, positioned so he cannot pop his claws without gutting himself. A removes his ball-gag, t Wolverine bites her. Mr. X serves Wolverine with papers officially claiming the title "the best there is." He asks Wolverine to join his staff of urderers, but Wolverine becomes enraged, pops his claws and tears free despite the pain, attacking Mr. X. Meanwhile, Senator Walsh realizes at the recent deaths are connected — and that he may be next. Wolverine battles Mr. X, but as he gains the upper hand, Blok intervenes d knocks him out. Wolverine awakens on a raft in the ocean, with a note apologizing for Blok's interference. Wolverine later returns to Mr. X's nd, but finds no trace of him.

DTE: Peter Craigo's first name and Michael Herana's full first name are revealed here. Like them, Senator Walsh's Weapon X position or ior on-panel appearances have never been specified, therefore this Index cannot determine his last app, if any. Mr. X's trophies include Han olo trapped in Carbonite. This issue's letters page runs responses from an online survey asking what readers wanted to see in future issues.

WOLVERINE: SON OF CANADA (April 2001)

"Son of Canada" (14 pages)

CREDITS: Howard Mackie (writer), Ron Lim (pencils), Walden Wong (inks), Dave Sharpe (letters), Sotocolor (colors), Ralph Macchio (editor)

FEATURE CHARACTER: Wolverine (next in W #166, '01 fb, W #162, '01)

GUEST STARS: Hulk (last in IHulk #26, '01), Silver Surfer (last in MaxS #3, '01) (both next in Def #1, '01), Spider-Man (during ASM #25, '01), Captain America (last in Cap #39, '01, chr last in Cap #1, '02 fb, chr next in X #111, '01 fb), Thor (Thor Odinson, Norse god of thunder, last in IHulk Ann '01) (prev 2 next in Av #38, '01), Storm (last in XMU #30/2, '01, chr next in XX #2, '01 fb, next in G&B #1, '01 fb), Thing (between FF #39-40, '01) (prev 3 chr last in ASM #36, '01)

VILLAINS: Blastaar (self-declared Negative Zone monarch, last in Web:TS #14, '00, next in CM #24, '01), Darkforcers (black energy creatures) inc Darkforce (see NOTE)

THER CHARACTERS: Bystanders; Green Goblin, Puck (prev 2 mentioned, see NOTE)

LOCATIONS/ITEMS: Canada: Calgary, Alberta inc Banff Springs Hotel; Signal Hill, Newfoundland inc Cabot Tower; Vancouver's Gre█ Unlimited, Toronto's CN Tower, Ottawa's Parliament Building, Quebec, Nova Scotia; distortion field (space between Negative Zone & Earth-61█ / Doritos truck, hurled chunk of snow, Blastaar's energy transmitters (destroyed), Mjolnir (Thor's enchanted Uru hammer), Captain America█ Vibranium shield (prev 2 hereinafter considered his standard equipment and not listed separately)

SYNOPSIS: Spider-Man, the Hulk and Wolverine find themselves teleported to Vancouver. Wolverine notices a portal above them, and Hu█ grabs his companions and leaps through; Spider-Man cautiously fires a webline back to Earth. The three find themselves in the distortion fie█ between Earth and the Negative Zone, and see several other captive heroes. Spider-Man yanks on his webline, but the three are pulled ba█ to Alberta instead. Hulk grabs a Darkforce creature from the portal, who brags about Blastaar's plan to capture all of Earth's heroes and invac█ Leaping through the portal again, the three arrive in Toronto, where they find an energy transmitter powering the portals. Reasoning that the█ need help, the three return to the distortion field and free the others. The heroes split up, following the portals across Canada and destroyi█ the auxiliary transmitters. They regroup in Newfoundland at the main transmitter just as Blastaar begins to invade — but the heroes smash th█ device just in time, closing the final portal and thwarting the villain.

NOTE: This giveaway one-shot was sponsored by Doritos and distributed exclusively in Canada. It was limited to 65,000 copies, ea█ individually numbered on the front cover's UPC box. Many Canadian businesses are namechecked on signs in the background. Given the█ names, Darkforce and his Darkforcers are likely empowered by the energies of the Darkforce Dimension. Spider-Man comments here th█ he was hot on the trail of his foe the Green Goblin before he was teleported away; more accurately, he was chasing reports of Green Gob█ sightings all across New York.

WOLVERINE #162 (May 2001)

"The Hunted, Part One" (22 pages)

CREDITS: Frank Tieri (writer), Sean Chen (pencils), Norm Rapmund (inks), Richard Starkings & Comicraf█ Saida Temofonte (letters), Avalon's Raymund Lee (colors), Mike Raicht (asst editor), Mike Marts (editor), Hi█ Design (c colors)

FEATURE CHARACTER: Wolverine (also in video, also in W #166, '01 fb)

GUEST STAR: Beast (also as Humphrey Bogart, last in X #111, '01 fb)

VILLAINS: Sabretooth (also on monitor, next in W #164, '01), Malcolm Colcord (in shadow, last in W #160, '0█ chr last in W #166, '01 fb), Dr. Rich Duncan, Dr. Zanna Zira (prev 2 Weapon X doctors, unnamed, 1st but chr la█ in W #166, '01 fb, next in W #166, '01), Weapon X agents (some in shadow, others bts killing former employe█ some or others last in W #160, '01, next in W #164, '01)

OTHER CHARACTERS: Trish Tilby (on TV, last in FF #40, '01, next in X #111, '01), Senator Drexel Walsh (die█ also in photo & video; chr next in W #166, '01 fb), Ben Urich (Daily Bugle reporter, bts on phone, last in ASM #24, chr next in SM/DD, '02, ne█ in DD #27, '02), Walsh's guards (on monitors, others also on monitors, all die; some also in W #166, '01 fb) inc Smithers, former Weapon █ employee (bts, killed, also on photo on TV; others as photos), police (bts investigating former employee's murder), FBI (bts investigating Walsh█ murder), Daily Bugle operator (bts on phone), Weapon X doctors, diner patron & waiter, newsreader (voice only on TV), Walsh's wife & childre█ (prev 2 mentioned); bystanders (in photo); elephant (on diner logo)

LOCATIONS/ITEMS: News studio (on TV), US Senate (in photo), Walsh's summer home (upstate New York, also on monitors & video█ X-Mansion, Gunga Diner w/nearby roadway, Weapon X program facility / TV cameras (bts), elevator shaft (mentioned), Walsh's TV, diske█ (prev 2 destroyed), guns, files, monitors & watch, guards' guns w/scopes, summer home's security cameras, phone line (prev 2 bts), titaniu█ reinforced doors (prev 2 destroyed), laser perimeter detectors & bulletproof windows w/bars, Wolverine's car (destroyed) & Weapon X bra█ implants (bts, destroyed), Weapon X's hidden camera (bts, see NOTE), Weapon X doctors' helmets, scalpels, vital sign monitors & Adamantiu█ reshaping & bonding equipment, Sabretooth's new Adamantium skeleton (hereinafter considered his standard equipment and not liste█ separately), Beast's image inducer (bts)

SYNOPSIS: Senator Walsh watches a news report of another mysterious death, knowing that it is connected to the others and fearing th█ he is next despite his guards' reassurances that he is well protected. Walsh decides to call the newspapers and reveal the truth, but sudden█ Wolverine bursts into his home, tears through the guards and murders him in cold blood. Wolverine awakens from a nightmare, shaken by th█ vivid images of killing Walsh. Still worried that Apocalypse is behind the dreams, Wolverine goes for a drive to clear his head, but Beast ta█ along. Wolverine refuses to explain what is wrong, so Beast threatens to beat the information out of him. The two begin to spar, but Wolveri█ loses his temper and cuts Beast badly before regaining his composure. Humbled, he tells Beast about his dreams. Elsewhere, the Weapon █ program re-bonds Adamantium to Sabretooth's skeleton. At a diner, Wolverine is shocked to see a news report about Walsh's death — comple█ with surveillance footage that shows Wolverine committing the murder.

NOTE: Dr. Duncan and Dr. Zira's last names are revealed in W #166, '01, and their first names in OHMU HC13, '10. Like W #95, '95 p.1█ this issue's p.22 panel 1 is an homage to the painting *Nighthawks*. This issue implies that the Weapon X Program gave Sabretooth his fi█ Adamantium skeleton prior to W #126, '98. W #166, '01 fb reveals that Colcord was spying on Wolverine with a hidden camera at the end█ this issue.

WOLVERINE #163 (June 2001)

"The Hunted, Part Two" (22 pages)

CREDITS: Frank Tieri (writer), Mark Texeira (pencils), Norm Rapmund (inks), Richard Starkings & Comicraf█ Saida Temofonte (letters), Avalon's Raymund Lee (colors), Mike Raicht (asst editor), Mike Marts (editor), Se█ Chen (c pencils)

FEATURE CHARACTER: Wolverine (also in photo & symbolic image, also as himself & Death in rfb)

GUEST STARS: SHIELD: Sharon Carter (SHIELD's new Executive Director), Dum Dum Dugan (next█ USAgent #1, '01) (both last in Cap #39, '01), Nick Fury (also as LMD, last in Cap #37, '01, chr last in Cap #1, '0█ fb); Beast (also as Harrison Ford & O.J. Simpson)

SUPPORTING CAST: Maverick (last in Mvk #12, '98)

VILLAINS: Brent Jackson (Weapon X mole within SHIELD, 1st but chr last in WX #23, '04), Malcolm Colcord (b█ giving Jackson orders), Mr. X (voice only on phone, as "a friend," last in W #159, '01)

OTHER CHARACTERS: Shiver Man (Caleb Jackson, intangible bounty hunter, 1st, also in symbolic image, next in W #165, '01), Senator Drexel Walsh (dead, bts, buried, also in rfb, chr last in W #166, '01 fb), President George W. Bush (1st bts, speaking at Walsh's funeral & assigning Jackson to manhunt, next in 1st on-panel app in Cap Ann '01), SHIELD agents (some or others last in Cap #38, '01, next in Cap #40, '01), truck stop waitresses inc Flo & patrons inc Red, newsreader (voice only, on radio), Mini-Mart clerk, FBI (bts, searching for Wolverine), security guard (bts patrolling office), motel owner, Mr. X's government contacts (bts informing Mr. X of Weapon X, see NOTE); politicians mentioned, grooming Walsh for Presidential bid)

LOCATIONS/ITEMS: Southern US inc truck stop & motel w/Wolverine & Beast's room (destroyed) & nearby Mini-Mart & gas station, Walsh's summer home (also in rfb), Apocalypse's Egyptian base (in rfb), secret SHIELD base (disguised as deli), government office / Clerk's radio & newspaper, Beast's image inducer (bts), Wolverine's Weapon X brain implants (bts in rfb) & newspaper, Death's sword (in rfb), Shiver Man's photo & guns w/flaming bullets, waitresses' pad & tray, Maverick's comm device (bts) & body armor w/faceplate, government computer, pay phone (destroyed), Jackson's forged letter w/fake scent, Nick Fury LMD (destroyed), SHIELD agents' guns

FLASHBACK: Wolverine kills Walsh (last issue) and serves as Death (W #145, '99).

SYNOPSIS: The subject of a nationwide manhunt, Wolverine has gone into hiding with Beast. Haunted by the surveillance footage and his vivid dream, Wolverine suspects that he may be guilty, but Beast believes in his innocence. Elsewhere, Nick Fury learns that he will not be handling the Wolverine manhunt; the President fears a conflict of interest and requested that new agent Brent Jackson take over. Fury worries that Jackson is out to kill Wolverine, and hires a bounty hunter to find Wolverine first: the supernatural Shiver Man. Maverick digs into Walsh's background and discovers a lengthy period of his past that is classified. Wolverine receives a mysterious call from "a friend," telling him to look to his own past for answers. The Shiver Man locates Wolverine and attacks, but Wolverine and Beast manage to drive him off. They receive a note from Fury telling them to meet him clandestinely, but when they arrive, Wolverine realizes that "Fury" is an LMD — just as SHIELD agents surround the two mutants.

NOTE: Shiver Man's real name is revealed in AT:Shiv, '09. Jackson's status as a Weapon X mole, and Colcord's bts presence here giving him orders, are revealed in W #166, '01. Wolverine's "friend" is revealed as Mr. X in W #167, '01; W #168, '01 reveals that his government contacts had alerted him that the Weapon X Program was manipulating Wolverine. Sharon Carter became SHIELD's Executive Director in Cap #31, '00.

WOLVERINE #164 (July 2001)

"The Hunted, Part Three" (22 pages)

CREDITS: Frank Tieri (writer), Sean Chen (pencils), Norm Rapmund (inks), Richard Starkings & Comicraft's Saida Temofonte (letters), Avalon's Raymund Lee (colors), Mike Raicht (asst editor), Mike Marts (editor), Tom Chu (c colors)
FEATURE CHARACTER: Wolverine (also in rfb)
GUEST STARS: SHIELD: Sharon Carter (next in X #111, '01 fb), Nick Fury; Beast
SUPPORTING CAST: Maverick (bts sending note, next in W #166, '01)
VILLAINS: Mr. X (bts as "a friend," sending note), Sabretooth (also on monitor, last in W #162, '01), Brent Jackson, Malcolm Colcord, Weapon X agents (some or others last in W #162, '01) (prev 2 in shadow), Mauvais (1st bts), Montgomery Battle ("Constant Battle," Cage warden), Cage guards inc Caleb "Reb" Tillis (Warden's right-hand man) & Axel (unnamed), Cage inmates (1 dies) inc Absorbing Man (Carl "Crusher" Creel, absorbs objects' properties, last in Dp #43, '00, next in Cap #50, '02), Batroc the Leaper (Georges Batroc, master of savate, last in Gam #19, '00, next in Cap #41, '01), General (Russian mob boss, 1st, next bts in W #170, '02), Kangaroo (Brian Hibbs, leaping athlete, last in SpecSM #246, '97, next in TWoS #16, '02), Red Ghost (Ivan Kragoff, intangible Russian scientist, last in Dp #39, '00) & his Super Apes: Igor (shape-shifting baboon), Miklho (super-strong gorilla), Peator (magnetic orangutan) (prev 3 last in FF #3, '98, next in NW #2, '05), Wrecking Crew (Asgardian-powered villains): Thunderball (Dr. Eliot Franklin, magically-enhanced strength, next in Thing #1, '02), Wrecker (Dirk Garthwaite, wields enchanted crowbar, next in Tb:LS, '01) (prev 2 last in Thor #29, '00), Brothers (Cage's black faction) inc Mo Money (corrupt rap mogul, Brothers' leader) & Axe (axe-wielding gladiator, last in NM #29, '85); Skulls (Red Skull-worshipping Neo-Nazis) inc Aryan (Skulls' leader, 1st); Maggia (organized crime cartel): Silvermane (Silvio Manfredi, senior mobster, last in Av #31, '00) (prev 2 next in U #1, '06), Hammerhead (steel-skulled mobster, last in Tb #53, '01, next in PPSM #50, '03); Cruisers (prison rapists, 1st, some or others next in TWoS #17, '02)

OTHER CHARACTERS: Peepers (Peter Quinn, enhanced vision, last as Occult in NW #6, '00), helicopter pilot (bts flying helicopter), prison officials (bts making inquiries); Battle's fellow soldiers (mentioned, killed in Vietnam), Mo Money's hip-hop rival (mentioned, murdered); Shiver Man, Senator Drexel Walsh (prev 2 in rfb); Red Skull (as banner)

LOCATIONS/ITEMS: Cage (superhuman prison built into remote island) w/courtyard, cellblock, cafeteria, Hole, Battle's office & remains of le Prison de la Morte (18th-century French prison, bts, unnamed), Walsh's summer home (in rfb), SHIELD headquarters, Weapon X program facility / Cage's power-dampening field (bts), force field & retractable helipad, Wolverine's Weapon X brain implants (bts in rfb), medical shots (bts), bonds, claw restraints & lunch tray, Wrecker's oversized shiv, guards' helmets, shields & electrified truncheons, supply helicopter, Mo Money's weights, Skulls' banner & tattoo needle, Red Ghost's chess set, inmate's soap-on-a-rope, Silvermane's wheelchair & newspaper, Maverick & Mr. X's notes, cafeteria chair, inmates & Axe's shivs, Weapon X doctors' vital sign monitors, Tillis's keys, Axel's flashlight

FLASHBACK: Wolverine kills Walsh (W #162, '01).

SYNOPSIS: Wolverine and Beast have been sent to superhuman prison the Cage, where the inmates' powers are suppressed. Surrounded by angry super villains, the two have been involved in fights every day since their arrival. Wolverine steps in as the Absorbing Man pummels Beast; the warden and guards intervene, but are clearly prejudiced against the two X-Men. Later, Wolverine finds a smuggled-in note from Maverick, which reveals that Walsh's death was one of many, all connected somehow. Fellow mutant Peepers befriends Wolverine and Beast, but when the Skulls harass the three, tempers flare. Another brawl breaks out, and the guards step in and mercilessly electrocute Wolverine and Beast. Elsewhere, a recovering Sabretooth tries to attack his benefactors, but discovers that he is mentally inhibited from harming them. Head guard Caleb Tillis plans to have Wolverine killed, and shows another guard a secret section of the prison. Wolverine is thrown in solitary confinement in the Hole; without him around, the other prisoners grow bold — and stab Beast in the chest.

NOTE: Axel is named next issue, as is le Prison de la Morte, the abandoned facility that the Cage was built on top of.

WOLVERINE #165 (August 2001)

"The Hunted, Part Four" (22 pages)

CREDITS: Frank Tieri (writer), Sean Chen (pencils), Norm Rapmund (inks), Richard Starkings & Comicraft's Saida Temofonte (letters), Avalon's Raymund Lee (colors), Mike Raicht (asst editor), Mike Marts (editor)
FEATURE CHARACTER: Wolverine (also as himself & Death in rfb)
GUEST STARS: Dr. Strange (Dr. Stephen Strange, Earth's Sorcerer Supreme, last in SM:L #3, '01, next in De #1, '01), Beast (also in rfb), Nick Fury
VILLAINS: Mauvais (Jean-Pierre Beaubier, 18th-century cannibal sorcerer, 1st on-panel app, next in W Ann '01), M X (bts as "a friend," sending note, next in W #167, '01), Warden Montgomery Battle (bts ordering Beast's treatmen delayed, next in DR:LL #1, '09), Cage guards (some die, some or others in rfb, some or others next in DR:LL #1, '09 inc Caleb "Reb" Tillis (next in DR:LL #1, '09), Axel (named) & Mike, Cage inmates: Dmitri (Super-Ape, 1st), Red Gho (prev 2 next in Dline #2, '02), a Skull (some or others next in U #1, '06); Sabretooth (joins Weapon X Program), Malcol Colcord (voice only, on headsets), Brent Jackson (bts obtaining Cage access codes), Weapon X agents
OTHER CHARACTERS: Wong (Dr. Strange's manservant, last in FF Ann '99, next in Def #1, '01), Peepers (next in WX #26, '04), Shiver Man (als in rfb, last in W #163, '01), Cage doctors (bts leaving Beast overnight), bystanders; Bill Carruthers (mentioned, showed Mauvais to Tillis), Ancient On (mentioned, imprisoned Mauvais); Brent Jackson (in photo); Apocalypse, Senator Drexel Walsh (prev 2 in rfb), mystical being (as statue)
LOCATIONS/ITEMS: Dr. Strange's Sanctum Sanctorum (Greenwich Village, Manhattan), Cage w/courtyard (in rfb), hole, cellblock, medica ward, nearby ocean & remains of le Prison de la Morte (named), Walsh's summer home, Southern US, Apocalypse's Egyptian base (prev in rfb), alley / Cage's power-dampening field (bts), force field, false rock & retractable helipad, Tillis' flashlight & pump w/hose & drugged liquic Wolverine's Weapon X brain implants (bts in rfb), bonds (destroyed) & claw restraints, guards' helmets & shields, Death's sword (prev 3 in rfb Peepers' hover tray, Beast's bandages, Skull's shiv & medical cart, Fury's photo, Mr. X's note, Weapon X agents' hovercraft, guns, headset handheld computer & rappelling lines, Malcolm's transmitter (bts), guards' electrified truncheon (some or others also in rfb) & guns
FLASHBACK: Wolverine kills Walsh; the Shiver Man confronts him; guards beat Wolverine and Beast (W #162-164, '01); Wolverine serve as Death (W #145, '99).
SYNOPSIS: Tillis reveals Mauvais, a motionless, rotten body hidden below the prison — which suddenly awakens when the guard touches Peepers visits Wolverine in the Hole, and tells him that the Beast was stabbed; Wolverine warns Peepers that the inmates may try to finish th job. Tillis tells Mauvais that they awakened him to kill Wolverine. Elsewhere, Nick Fury asks the Shiver Man to follow Brent Jackson. Wolverine "friend" has a note smuggled in that reveals the connection between the recent deaths, worrying him greatly. Tillis drugs Wolverine and bring him to Mauvais — but to his shock, Mauvais begins eating chunks of Wolverine's flesh. Peepers saves the groggy Beast from a Skull, stabbin his foe viciously, but Weapon X agents suddenly burst in and capture Beast. Mauvais tears out Wolverine's eye and eats it; having regained h strength, he teleports away. Tillis decides to shoot Wolverine himself, but he is stopped — by Sabretooth.
NOTE: Mauvais' real name is revealed in OHMU HC7, '09. Next issue reveals that Jackson gave Weapon X the Cage access codes. This is th last issue to feature the Comics Code Authority logo, as Marvel was in the process of switching to an in-house rating system.

WOLVERINE #166 (September 2001)

"The Hunted, Conclusion" (40 pages)

CREDITS: Frank Tieri (writer), Sean Chen (pencils, pp.1-4 & 10-40), Barry Windsor-Smith (art, pp.5-9), Norr Rapmund (inks, pp.1-4 & 10-40), Richard Starkings & Comicraft's Saida Temofonte (letters), Avalon's Raymun Lee (colors), Mike Raicht (asst editor), Mike Marts (editor), J.H. Williams III (c pencils), Mick Gray (c inks), Jos Villarrubia (c colors)
FEATURE CHARACTER: Wolverine (also on monitors & on monitor in fb6, also as James Howlett in symboli image, also in rfb1, also as Experiment X in fb1 between X23 #1, '05 & MCP #84, '91, also in W #175, '02 t during fb1; also in fb3 between W #157, '00 & W Ann '00; also in fb4 between UXM #389, '01 & W #159, '01; als in fb5 between W:SC, '01 & W #162, '01, also in W #162, '01 during fb)
GUEST STARS: Beast (also on monitor in fb6), Nick Fury (also on monitor)
SUPPORTING CAST: Maverick (next in WXD:AZ, '02), John Wraith (next in W #1, '10)
VILLAINS: Weapon X Program (government program using mutants as weapons, 1st on-panel app as group): Malcolm Colcord (also bts rfb1, also in fb1 & fb2 during WX #23, '04, also in W #175, '02 fb during fb1, also in WX #23, '04 during fb2; also in fb3 between W #23, '04 W Ann '00 bts; also bts controlling Wolverine in fb4 between W Ann '00 & W #160, '01; also bts controlling Wolverine in fb5 & in fb6 between W #160, '01 & W #162, '01), Sabretooth (also in Colcord's thoughts), Dr. Rich Duncan (also in fb3 & fb6, his chr 1st app, prior to W #162, '01), D Zanna Zira (also in fb3, her chr 1st app, prior to W #162, '01) (prev 2 last in W #162, '01), Brent Jackson (all chr next in WXD:AZ, '02, next in D #57, '01), agents (some die, some or others also in rfb1, some or others also in fb3, their chr 1st app, prior to W #159, '01 bts; some or othe chr next in WXD:AZ, '02, next in Dp #58, '01) inc Shaun Criden (dies) & control room personnel (voice only)
OTHER CHARACTERS: Shiver Man (next in AT:Shiv, '09), Senator Drexel Walsh (dead in fb5 between W #162, '01 & W #163, '01 bts; als in rfb1), John Merchant (bts inside house in fb4 between MCP #79, '91 & W #159, '01; also bts in rfb2), Nanci Merchant & her mother & siste (prev 3 bts inside house in fb4, their chr 1st bts app, prior to W #159, '01), original Weapon X Program guards (many die, some or others chr la in X23 #1, '05) inc Andrew Potts (unnamed), Colcord's commanding officer (prev 2 in fb1), doctors, military men (prev 2 in fb2), Walsh's guard (dead, in fb5 during W #162, '01), FBI (bts, misled by Fury), bar patron (also on monitor); Kathleen Colcord (Malcolm's ex-wife), Suzie & Jimm Colcord (prev 2 Malcolm's children) (prev 3 unnamed, mentioned, left Malcolm after his disfigurement); Peter Craigo, Michael Herana (prev in rfb1); Apocalypse, Chamber, Deadpool, Magneto, Marrow, Mystique, Nightcrawler, Rogue, Toad (prev 9 in Colcord's thoughts); Dog Loga Rose O'Hara (prev 2 in symbolic image, unnamed); historical figures (in portraits in fb2); eagle (as Presidential seal in rfb1)
LOCATIONS/ITEMS: Weapon X Program facilities (1 destroyed, also in fb3 & fb6) w/control room (bts), New York City's Millennium Hotel w rooftop & Wraith's room, bar; commanding officer's office (in fb1), former Weapon X program facility (in fb1 & fb3), hospital, Colcord's office government briefing room (prev 3 in fb2), Merchants' home (in fb4 & rfb2), city street, Walsh's office (prev 2 in rfb1), Walsh's summer hom (in fb5), roadway (on monitor in fb6), Howlett estate (Alberta, in symbolic image, see NOTE) / Wolverine's Weapon X brain implants (bts i fb3, fb4 & fb5), restraints & eyepatch, Weapon X's sensors (some or others also in fb3), computers, Experiment X helmet, monitoring devic

re-implantation equipment, control room's comm unit & teleporter (prev 2 bts) (all destroyed), former facility's alarms (bts), guards' rifles (1 destroyed) & flamethrower (prev 3 in fb1), medical equipment, X-rays, Colcord's computers (prev 3 in fb2), facility's computers, Duncan & Zira's laptops, Malcolm's microphone (prev 3 in fb3), John's car (in fb4, also destroyed in rfb2), Weapon X's car, machine guns (prev 2 in rfb1), car bomb (bts in rfb2), hidden cameras (1 bts, another bts in fb6) & monitors (another in fb6, all but 1 destroyed), Maverick's grenade, armor w/ faceplate & gun (destroyed) w/titanium bullets, agents' guns, Shiver Man's guns w/flaming bullets, hotel window (destroyed), Dog's scythe (in symbolic image), Malcolm & Criden's walkie-talkies, Sabretooth's headset, facility's self-destruct system (bts)

FLASHBACKS: Weapon X agents kill Peter and Michael after Wolverine tracks them down; Senator Walsh realizes the pattern (W #160-161, '01). John's car explodes (W #159, '01). Malcolm is assigned to the Weapon X facility, but days later Experiment X escapes, attacking him and mutilating his face (1). Malcolm refuses to have his face fixed, and rises through the ranks despite his disfigurement, eventually convincing the military to restart Weapon X (2). Discovering information about Wolverine's mental implants, Malcolm finds that he can control Wolverine remotely (3). Malcolm has Wolverine stalk John Merchant (4). Malcolm has Wolverine kill Walsh, but the shock of committing murder shorts out the implants (5). Malcolm learns that the implants no longer work (6).

SYNOPSIS: Wolverine awakens a captive of the reborn Weapon X Program, whose director bears a grudge against Wolverine for ravaging his face. Elsewhere, John Wraith and Sabretooth tell Maverick that Weapon X is re-recruiting or killing all its old agents. Malcolm reveals that he made Wolverine kill Walsh, a former employee. He explains that Weapon X will reward the mutants that join, but when Wolverine rejects the offer, Malcolm orders him brainwashed. Maverick refuses to rejoin; Sabretooth fatally injures him, then attacks Wraith for good measure. Shiver Man, having learned Wolverine's innocence, bursts in and frees him. As Wolverine slaughters Weapon X guards, Malcolm activates the base's self-destruct and teleports Sabretooth back; Wolverine battles Sabretooth viciously until Shiver Man convinces him to get Beast to safety. Shiver Man tackles Sabretooth as the base explodes. Later, Wolverine discusses the new Weapon X with Nick Fury, while the Program plans their next move…

NOTE: Shaun Criden's first name is revealed in OHMU HC13, '10. Andrew Potts is named in WX #1, '02. Malcolm's family's first names are revealed in WX #6, '03; their last name is never given, but can be safely assumed to be Colcord. This issue's rfb2 reveals that Wolverine was bts during the drive-by shooting in W #160, '01. Brent Jackson is revealed as a Weapon X mole here. Barry Windsor-Smith, who wrote and drew the "Weapon X" serial in MCP #72-84, '91, draws this issue's 5-page flashback to that story. At this time, the Origin miniseries had been solicited but not yet published; this issue's symbolic image is based on preview art for the series. Origin #1, '01 names Dog and reveals Rose's first name; Rose's last name is revealed in W #11, '11. The Howlett estate is specified as being in Alberta in Origin #3, '02.

WOLVERINE #167 (October 2001)

"Blood Sport, 1 of 3" (22 pages)

CREDITS: Frank Tieri (writer), Dan Fraga (pencils), Norm Rapmund (inks), Richard Starkings & Comicraft's Saida Temofonte (letters), Avalon's Raymund Lee (colors), Mike Raicht (asst editor), Mike Marts (editor), Barry Windsor-Smith (c pencils), Tom Chu (c colors)

FEATURE CHARACTER: Wolverine (as "Patch," also as himself in pfb)

GUEST STARS: Beast (bts in pfb awaiting magazine, chr next in XX #3, '01 fb, next in NX #117, '01), Nick Fury (bts arranging Wolverine's exoneration, next in Cap #41, '01)

VILLAINS: Mr. X (as Bloodsport's Champion, also bts as "a friend" in pfb, sending letter; last in W #161, '01, last bts in W #165, '01), Anaconda (Blanche Sitznski, extendable arms, last in Cap #437, '95, next in Cap #30, '04), Cat (Shen Kuei, martial arts master, last in HFH #19, '99, next in Cable&Dp #7, '04), Eel (last in SM:L #3, '01, next in SecWar #3, '04), Forearm (Michael McCain, four-armed mutant, last in XFor #68, '97, next in XFor #4, '05), Gamecock (Carlos Cabrera, wears taloned costume, dies, last in Cap #371, '90, last bts in Cap #394, '91), Headhunter (sword-wielding swordsman, dies), Oddball (Elton Healey, wields weaponized juggling balls, dies, last in Hawk, '98), Puma (Thomas Fireheart, mystical feral transformation, last in SMU #15, '97), Razor-Fist (Douglas Scott, blades for hands, last in SM #81, '97, next in Dline #2, '02), Speed Demon (James Sanders, super-speed, last in Tb #36, '00, next in MKSM #6, '04), Taskmaster (Tony Masters, photographic reflexes, last in Av #38, '01, chr last in Dp #68, '02 fb), Toad (Mortimer Toynbee, mutant leaper w/extendable tongue, last in Tb #53, '01, next in NX #132, '02), Zaran (last in W #158, '01, next in GLA #2, '05 fb), Viper (last in X #109, '01) & her men

OTHER CHARACTERS: Jae Lo (Wolverine's Bloodsport assistant, 1st), Bloodsport staff & audience inc Chris & Justin, pilot (bts flying plane), flight attendant, mailman (bts delivering X-Men's mail), airport ground crew, travelers, bystanders; strippers (mentioned, working in Foxy Den, also on sign), Tony Hawk, Steven Hawking (prev 2 mentioned in magazine); skateboarder (on magazine cover); Senator Drexel Walsh (in photo), Ogun (in Wolverine's imagination); Bodhisattva (as statue), cat (as tattoo)

LOCATIONS/ITEMS: Skies over Pacific Ocean, X-Mansion (in pfb), Madripoor airport, Lowtown inc Foxy Den (strip club, formerly Princess Bar) & Bloodsport arena / Airplane, Wolverine's eyepatch (also in pfb), cigar (another in pfb), newspaper & luggage, attendant's ashtray, Beast's "Science and Skateboarding" magazine, skater's skateboard (on magazine cover), Mr. X's letter (prev 3 in pfb), Lo's Humvee, Viper's men's guns, Bloodsport bell (bts), cylinder, water tank & cage w/curtain, Headhunter's sword, Oddball's weaponized juggling balls, Cat's nunchuks, Taskmaster's shield, bow, arrows & billy club, Razor-Fist's prosthetic razor attachments, Zaran's sais & staff, Anaconda & Forearm's strap, Eel's frictionless suit w/electrical field, Speed Demon's throwing blades

FLASHBACK: Wolverine receives a letter from his "friend," inviting him to Madripoor's Bloodsport competition and revealing that he is the reigning champion (p).

SYNOPSIS: On the flight to Madripoor, Wolverine reads a newspaper "revealing" that the Senator Walsh murder video was a hoax, and mentally thanks Nick Fury. He briefly spies a demonic face in the clouds, unnerving him. Jae Lo picks Wolverine up at the airport, introducing himself as Wolverine's Bloodsport assistant. At the arena, Wolverine encounters Viper; he briefly believes her to be his mysterious "friend," but he doesn't know what he means. The Bloodsport's first round proceeds quickly, with Headhunter, Puma, Taskmaster, Zaran, Anaconda and Toad victorious. Wolverine defeats Speed Demon and moves forward to the second round, where Taskmaster and Puma prevail. Wolverine battles the Toad, and although initially unprepared for Toad's new powers, Wolverine ultimately wins. Headhunter then steps into a curtain-draped cage to battle the previous year's champion, but is beheaded almost instantly. The curtain rises, revealing that the champion — and Wolverine's "friend" — is Mr. X.

NOTE: Cover-labeled "Bloodsport, Part 1 of 3." Wolverine quits smoking this issue, due to Editor in Chief Joe Quesada's decision that heroic characters should not be depicted smoking. Wolverine's eye has not yet grown back; luckily, he is traveling to the one place on Earth where he is known for wearing an eyepatch. Razor-Fist's real name is revealed in NAvF, '06. Taskmaster's real name is revealed in Task #3, '11. Toad received a power upgrade in XMF #6, '01 that brought him in line with his depiction in the X-Men feature film. Viper's trademark green hair is miscolored blue this issue. Several characters appear to die here, only to reappear in later books without explanation; presumably they we merely badly injured and recovered. Some panels of this issue are noticeably repeated from previous panels; it seems that some of this issu gorier moments were concealed prior to publication.

WOLVERINE #168 (November 2001)

"Blood Sport, 2 of 3" (22 pages)

CREDITS: Frank Tieri (writer), Dan Fraga (pencils), Norm Rapmund (inks), Richard Starkings & Comicra Saida Temofonte (letters), Avalon's Raymund Lee (colors), Mike Raicht (asst editor), Mike Marts (editor), J Williams III (c pencils), José Villarrubia (c colors)

FEATURE CHARACTER: Wolverine (also as "Patch," also as himself & Experiment X in rfb)

VILLAINS: Mr. X (also as Bloodsport's Champion, also as himself & boy in rfb, next in W:MrX, '10), Blok (also posses by Ogun, last in W #161, '01, next in DpTU #891, '10 fb), Ogun (as spirit, also possessing Blok & Viper's man, las W #161, '01), Puma (next in SenSM #26, '06), Taskmaster (also in rfb, next in Cap #44, '01), Viper & her men (1 a possessed by Ogun)

OTHER CHARACTERS: Jae Lo, Bloodsport staff (1 dies), announcer & audience inc Chris & Justin; Cap America, Daredevil (prev 2 mentioned, fighting styles copied by Taskmaster); Jean Grey, Annie Richardson, Mar Yashida, accident victim (prev 4 in rfb); Mr. T (on shirt); people (dead, as skulls, cover only)

LOCATIONS/ITEMS: Bloodsport arena (also in rfb), w/backstage & lower level, Wolverine's Madripoor hotel room; city street, Gre Annandale-on-Hudson, New York home, former Weapon X Program facility, Shingen's Citadel compound (prev 4 in rfb) / Wolverine's eyepa & luggage, Bloodsport cage (floor destroyed, also in rfb), electrical cables (bts), bell & boxes w/nunchuks, sais, mace & championship belt, L drugged water, announcer's microphone, Taskmaster's shield (also in rfb), billy club, bow & arrows (some destroyed) inc flame arrow, Weap X Program's Genesis Tank (in rfb) w/Adamantium feed tubes

FLASHBACKS: Mr. X sees a woman die (W #161, '01 fb); Jean Grey's friend dies in her arms (BA #27, '81 fb); Mr. X fights Wolverine and Taskmaster (this issue); Adamantium is bonded to Wolverine's skeleton (MCP #73, '91); Wolverine holds the dead Mariko Yashida (W #57, '!

SYNOPSIS: Wolverine demands to know why Mr. X helped him; Mr. X retorts that he didn't want Wolverine getting "credit" for Walsh's de Energy passes from Blok into one of Viper's men. Jae Lo gives Wolverine a drugged drink before his match with Puma. Wolverine ba defeats his foe; Lo blames Viper. After Mr. X defeats and humiliates Taskmaster, Wolverine and Mr. X face off as the final two contenders — Taskmaster interrupts their battle with a surprise attack. Wolverine notices that Mr. X anticipated the attack, and realizes that he is telepat reading his opponents' minds to determine their strategies. Wolverine slips into a mindless berserker rage and soon gains the upper hand — Mr. X wins the Bloodsport by default when Wolverine knocks him within reach of the championship belt, and Mr. X and Blok escape. Later, Wolverine packs for home, a startled Viper announces that Ogun has returned.

NOTE: Cover-labeled "Bloodsport, Part 2 of 3." This issue reveals that Mr. X's government contacts informed him that the Weapon X Program targeted Wolverine, and implies that Viper was the unnamed "friend from Madripoor" who alerted Mr. X to Wolverine's existence prior to W #159, '(

WOLVERINE #169 (December 2001)

"Blood Sport, 3 of 3" (22 pages)

CREDITS: Frank Tieri (writer), Dan Fraga (pencils), Norm Rapmund (inks), Richard Starkings & Comicra Oscar Gongora (letters), Avalon's Raymund Lee (colors), Mike Raicht (asst editor), Mike Marts (editor), Williams III (c pencils), José Villarrubia (c colors)

FEATURE CHARACTER: Wolverine (also possessed by Ogun, also in rfb, also in fb1 between W #89, '95 f W:O #9, '07 fb; next in UXM #392, X #112, UXM #393, X #113, all '01, WX #21, '04 fb, W Ann '01)

VILLAINS: Ogun (as spirit & possessing Wolverine, Viper, Viper's man, fish vendor & bystanders; also Wolverine's imagination; also as spirit & possessing Helen Bach, Blok & Viper's man in rfb; also in fb1 betwee #89, '95 fb & KP&W #1, '84; also as spirit & possessing Blok & hosts inc Mr. X's opponent in fb2 between KP:A #3, '98 & W #159, '01; possibly next as spirit in W #2, '10, see W #122, '98's NOTE), Mr. X (in fb2 between W #1 '01 fb & W #159, '01), Blok (in fb2, his chr 1st app, prior to W #159, '01, also possessed by Ogun; also posses by Ogun in rfb), Viper (also possessed by Ogun, next in XX #10, '02) & her men (1 possessed by Ogun, 1 other possessed by Ogun in rfb), L Ugama Hana (crimelord) & his ninjas (prev 2 in fb1, die)

OTHER CHARACTERS: Ogun's hosts (possessed by Ogun) inc Mr. X's opponent, audience (all in fb2), fish vendor (also possessed Ogun), bystanders (some possessed by Ogun); Helen Bach (possessed by Ogun in rfb); people (dead, as skulls, cover only)

LOCATIONS/ITEMS: Lowtown inc Foxy Den, marketplace & docks, Ogun Ryu Dojo (in fb1), fighting arena (in fb2), East Village, New rooftop, Bloodsport arena backstage (prev 3 in rfb) / Ogun's swords & incense, Wolverine's sword, ninjas' nunchuks, spears, swords, s chains, tiger claws, bows, arrows, knives, shuriken & throwing blades, Hana's Honor Sword (all in fb1), Wolverine's eyepatch, Viper's laser pis Viper's men's knife, club & hurled bottles, fish vendor's knives, bystanders' broom & hurled fruit

FLASHBACKS: Ogun possesses Helen Bach (W #114, '97), Blok (W #160, '01) and Viper's man (last issue). As Ogun tutors Wolver Ugama Hana confronts Ogun over a grievance. Ogun dares Hana to murder him, and Hana runs Ogun through — but Ogun laughs, pulls the sword and beheads Hana. Ogun then explains to an astonished Wolverine that death is a state of mind (1). Ogun discovers Mr. X w searching for an ideal host, but Mr. X's telepathy repulses Ogun's possession attempt, so he possesses Blok instead (2).

SYNOPSIS: Wolverine and Viper track Ogun's host, but he flees into a nearby marketplace. Ogun suddenly begins body-hopping, forc bystanders to attack Wolverine and Viper in quick succession. Viper shoots into the crowd, but Wolverine stops her. Ogun flees, challeng Wolverine to meet him that night for a reckoning. Wolverine does so, but finds Ogun possessing Viper. Ogun reveals that he wants Wolve as his final host, and tries to possess him — but he cannot cope with Wolverine's bestial mind, and flees back inside Viper. Wolverine sudde stabs Viper, gravely injuring her. With no suitable hosts, Ogun's spirit disperses; Wolverine promises to get Viper a doctor if she grants hi divorce, and Viper grudgingly agrees.

NOTE: Cover-labeled "Bloodsport, Part 3 of 3." Viper's costume this issue resembles that of Lara Croft, Tomb Raider. Ogun incorrectly sta here that he possessed Helen Bach after his last encounter with Wolverine in W #114, '97; he actually possessed Helen during the encou then fled in the body of Lady Deathstrike afterward.

WOLVERINE 2001 (2001)

"The Watch" (27 pages)

CREDITS: Frank Tieri (writer), Matthew Marsilia (pencils), Victor Llamas, Rich Perrotta & Scott Elmer (inks), Richard Starkings & Comicraft's Oscar Gongora (letters), Avalon's Raymund Lee (colors), Mike Raicht (asst editor), Mike Marts (editor), J.H. Williams III (c pencils), José Villarrubia (c colors)

FEATURE CHARACTER: Wolverine (next in Tb #57 & 58 bts, '01-02, Cap #50/6, '02, XMU #47, '03 (voice only), Cyclops #1 & 4, '01-02, UXM #394, '01; Dp #60-61, SM:SC bts, all '02)

VILLAINS: Bloodscream (last in ASM #435, '98), Mauvais (last in W #165, '01), Vermin (Edward Whelan, transforms into ratlike creature, last in MKn #15, '01) (all next in W #170, '02)

OTHER CHARACTERS: Ravencroft security guards (die) inc Lou, homeless people (some die, some also as pseudo-zombies) inc "Squeegie Man" (dies), cabbie, commuter, commuter's friend (bts on phone), shelter employee, Squeegie Man's son, bystanders; rats (some die), pigeons, dog

LOCATIONS/ITEMS: New York City inc sewer, homeless shelter & Mauvais' hideout, Ravencroft Institute (mental institution) w/Vermin's cell, Squeegie Man's son's apartment / Hobos' fire barrel, commuter's car (destroyed) & cellphone, Squeegie Man's watch, squeegee, towel & spray bottle, employee's board, Bloodscream's swords, guards' guns & security monitors, Vermin's straitjacket (destroyed), Mauvais' hacksaws, chains & meat hooks

SYNOPSIS: As three homeless men discuss recent hobo disappearances, they are attacked. Later, a hobo tries to wash a commuter's windshield, but enraged commuter beats him. Wolverine intercedes and befriends the hobo, nicknamed "Squeegie Man," who shows Wolverine his watch — an heirloom that he hopes his estranged son will one day take. Wolverine visits Squeegie Man's shelter later but finds the hobo gone; he discovers the watch left behind and suspects foul play. That night, Bloodscream sneaks into the shelter, but Wolverine ambushes him. Bloodscream flees and reports his new master Mauvais, who has Bloodscream enthrall and recruit Vermin. As Wolverine searches the street for Squeegie Man, Bloodscream attacks. Wolverine pursues Bloodscream into the sewers, where Vermin commands rats to swarm him. Wolverine duels Bloodscream and cuts off his hands, but the villains are suddenly teleported away. Wolverine, assuming that Squeegie Man is dead, delivers the watch to his son. Elsewhere, Mauvais prepares to feast on the dead hobos, including Squeegie Man, that Bloodscream has brought him.

NOTE: This is the final issue of this volume of Wolverine Annual; the series is relaunched in 2007. Wolverine's eye has grown back after Mauvais consumed it in W #165, '01.

2ND STORY: "Red Snow" (13 pages)

CREDITS: Matt Nixon (writer), Kilian Plunkett (art), Richard Starkings & Comicraft's Oscar Gongora (letters), Avalon's Raymund Lee (colors), Mike Raicht (asst editor), Mike Marts (editor)

FEATURE CHARACTER: Wolverine (next in W #170, '02)

VILLAIN: Thomas Grant (Holly's former sheriff, dies)

OTHER CHARACTERS: Father Thomas Braun (Catholic priest, agent of Office of Inquisition, 1st, next in W #177, '02), Michael Standish (Holly's new sheriff, dies, see NOTE) & his wife (Thomas' daughter, dead), Peter Standish (Michael's son, deputy), Gus (motel proprietor, bts in hotel in fb, dies), Gert (Gus' sister, bts on phone), Holly townspeople (dead; others bts, die; some also in fb prior to story), Plodex eggs (alien eggs that adapt by absorbing others' DNA, chr last in AFlt #3, '04 fb; some bts on ship, chr next & also in scene from AFlt #4, '83 fb; some bts on ship, next (most bts) in AFlt #3, '04 fb, next in AFlt #5, '04; 1 also as bear-hybrid, also in scene from AFlt #4, '83 fb, dies) inc eggs that will become bear (unnamed; next (possibly bts) in AFlt #3, '04 fb; next in AFlt #5, '04), Marrina (Marrina Smallwood, Alpha Flight member) & her mate (prev bar next & also in scene from AFlt #4, '83 fb) (prev 3 bts on ship), bear (dies), Catholic saint (as statue)

LOCATIONS/ITEMS: Arctic Circle (also in scene from AFlt #4, '83), outer space; Holly, Alberta, Canada inc hospital (bts), church, police station, movie theater, gas station, Gus' lodge (ruins, also destroyed in fb) & Grant's manor house (destroyed); Gert's Vancouver home (bts) / Plodex Devourer Ship (unnamed) w/drive unit (destroyed) & egg-ejecting equipment (bts) (prev 3 also in scene from AFlt #4, '83 fb), Thomas & Michael's guns w/scopes, Wolverine's motorcycle, townspeople's guns (bts), torches (prev 2 in fb), car (destroyed) & bullet casings, Peter & Michael's Jeeps, Braun's sword w/case, Plodex's shackles (bts), police car, Thomas' candle, pay phone

FLASHBACK: Angry townspeople burn down Gus' lodge (p).

SYNOPSIS: 40,000 years ago, a Plodex ship crashes on Earth and ejects thousands of alien eggs. 40 years ago, Sheriff Grant discovers an egg while hunting a bear. In the present, Wolverine arrives in a small Canadian town to check on his friend Gus, whose sister Gert is worried about him. Wolverine discovers Gus' ruined lodge, but when he asks the deputy, Grant's grandson, what happened, the agitated deputy orders Wolverine to leave. Wolverine investigates a foul odor from a church and meets Father Braun, who reveals that Grant has made the townspeople worship a captive demon for decades. Braun explains that he tried to intervene, but they killed Gus while trying to get at him; Braun then released the demon, which killed most of the townspeople. Wolverine tracks down the odor, finding Grant and the deputy battling the "demon" — an alien Plodex that had partially absorbed a bear's DNA. The creature kills Grant, but Wolverine manages to destroy it. Later, Wolverine regretfully informs Gert of Gus' death.

NOTE: Braun's position with the Office of Inquisition is revealed in W #177, '02, and his first name is revealed in W:WXF, '09. Devourer Ships are named in AFlt #3, '04; Mar is named in AFlt #10, '05. The back of Michael's police Jeep reads "J. Standish"; it is possible that "Michael" is a middle name or a nickname.

WOLVERINE #170 (January 2002)

"Stay Alive! Part 1 of 3" (22 pages)

CREDITS: Frank Tieri (writer), Sean Chen (pencils), Norm Rapmund (inks), Richard Starkings & Comicraft's Saida Temofonte (letters), Avalon's Raymund Lee (colors), Mike Raicht (asst editor), Mike Marts (editor), Mike McKone (c art), José Villarrubia (c colors)

FEATURE CHARACTER: Wolverine (also in Mauvais' vision)

VILLAINS: Mauvais (also as doctor & Grotts, also as himself & Grotts on TV), Bloodscream (next in MKSM #6, '04), Vermin (next bts in Alias #26, '03, next in SH #5, '04) (prev 2 also as paramedics) (all last in W Ann '01), Radioactive Man (Dr. Chen Lu, emits & controls radiation, last in IM #40, '01, next in TWoS #13, '02), Omega Red (last in UXM #380, '00, next in W #173, '02), General (bts hiring Omega Red, last in W #164, '01), Sabretooth (last in Dp #61, '02), Wendigo spirit (bts empowering Wendigo), Wendigo (prev 2 last in CM #3, '00), Tiberius Stone (corrupt TV mogul, last in IM Ann '01/2, next bts in IM #56, '02, next in IM #57, '02), Nikolai Vernoff (drug dealer, dies) & his bodyguards (die)

OTHER CHARACTERS: Inua (bts summoning Wolverine, also in Mauvais' thoughts): Hodiak, Nelvanna, Turoq (all last in AFlt #45, '87, next in #172, '02); Grotts (Stay Alive host, dies), Bartlet (Stay Alive producer, dies off-panel), Stay Alive contestants (die, also in recording, all but 1 also on (some bts) & as bones, some also as bones on TV) inc Casey & Terri, Stay Alive announcer (voice only) & actor (prev 2 in recording), entertainment reporter (on TV), helicopter pilot (in shadow, dies), Jake's Diner waiter, nightclub patrons, Omega Red's toady, airplane pilot, Stone's control room personnel (bts on phone); wolf (in recording), seal (bts biting contestant), polar bears (die, others in recording); Milo Stevens (Stone's former employer, mentioned, suggested shooting in Arctic, see NOTE); waiter's wife (mentioned, watches Stay Alive); tribal spirit animal (as totem pole in recording)

LOCATIONS/ITEMS: Canada: Arctic Circle (also in recording, on TV & in Mauvais' vision), hospital & Jake's Diner, news studio (on TV), Stone broadcast control room (bts) & office, Brooklyn's Pyramid Nightclub / Actor's horn, contestants' equipment, binoculars, walking sticks, cold-weather gear (all in recording) & torches (also on TV), Stone's monitors, newspaper & cellphone, Stay Alive's helicopter (destroyed), remote-controlled cameras (bts) w/controllers, Grotts' microphone, stretcher w/restraints, diner TV, Terri's card (on TV), Wolverine's black leather costume (see NOTE), parachute (destroyed), backpack, goggles & snowmobile, Vernoff's drugs (bts) & champagne, bodyguards' guns, Omega Red's death spores (hereinafter considered part of his "standard equipment" and not listed separately), Weapon X Program's teleporters, Sabretooth override transmitter (prev 2 bts), pilot's airplane & headset

SYNOPSIS: Tiberius Stone rages about the dismal ratings of his reality show "Stay Alive," broadcast live from the Arctic. An injured contestant airlifted out; as the helicopter arrives at the hospital, Mauvais ambushes and kills the show's host, assuming his likeness. He departs for the Arctic as Bloodscream and Vermin consume the injured contestant. Later, Wolverine idly watches "Stay Alive" and is shocked when the host transforms into Mauvais and attacks the contestants. Elsewhere, Omega Red kills a drug dealer as Sabretooth secretly observes. Wolverine charters a plane and parachutes into the Arctic on a snowmobile. Stone is ecstatic over the potential ratings boost of Mauvais' massacre; when his assistant balks, Stone orders him killed. Mauvais arranges the contestants' half-eaten bodies and casts a spell, seeking revenge against the Gods of the North who imprisoned him centuries ago. He senses Wolverine's approach and commands polar bears to attack, but Wolverine defeats them. Mauvais reveals that his cannibalism was meant to attract the Wendigo — and on cue, the creature arrives.

NOTE: This issue's cover is labeled "Stay Alive, Part 1 of 3," but the next two issues' covers do not carry this label. This issue debuts a 9/11 memorial slug on the cover, which runs until W #180, '02. The new corner box art that debuts here is taken from last issue's cover. Wolverine's black leather X-jacket and costume, which debuted in UXM #394, '01 as part of the X-titles' 2001 revamp, belatedly begins appearing in this series starting here, but Wolverine wears a variant version without the large "X" across the body through W #176, '02. This issue reveals that Tiberius Stone orchestrated Milo Stevens' death in IM #38, '01 fb. W #174, '02 reveals that Sabretooth has gone rogue and overridden the Weapon X program's teleporters. Bloodscream's hands are intact here without explanation; Mauvais may have magically reattached them.

WOLVERINE #171 (February 2002)

"Stay Alive, Part 2 of 3" (22 pages)

CREDITS: Frank Tieri (writer), Sean Chen (pencils, letters), Norm Rapmund (inks), Avalon's Raymund Lee (colors), Mike Raicht (asst editor), Mike Marts (editor), José Villarrubia (c colors)

FEATURE CHARACTER: Wolverine

GUEST STARS: Alpha Flight: Guardian, Puck, Sasquatch, Snowbird (all last in GenX #58, '99), Aurora (last in UXM #379, '00), Shaman (last in W #143, '99)

VILLAINS: Lady Deathstrike (last in X Ann '00), Sabretooth (both next in W #173, '02), Mauvais (becomes Wendigo), Wendigo (dies), Wendigo spirit (bts empowering Wendigo & Mauvais), Japanese mobsters (die)

OTHER CHARACTER: Buddha (as statue)

LOCATIONS/ITEMS: Canadian Arctic, Japanese temple / Stay Alive's remote-controlled cameras (bts) w/controller, hurled tree (destroyed), mobsters' sword (destroyed) & guns, Weapon X Program's teleporters (bts), Sabretooth override transmitter (bts) & binoculars, snow column (created & destroyed), Wendigo's heart (destroyed)

SYNOPSIS: Wolverine and Wendigo attack Mauvais simultaneously. Mauvais tries to fight them off, but is staggered until the raging Wendigo suddenly turns on Wolverine. Mauvais bites Wendigo; the creature responds by smashing him with an enormous tree, but Mauvais animates the tree's limbs to attack his foes. In Japan, mobsters confront Lady Deathstrike, but she quickly kills them all as Sabretooth secretly observes. Wolverine and Wendigo hammer Mauvais' mystic shields until they shatter, but Wendigo suddenly turns on Wolverine again, hurling him away from the fight. Mauvais raises a column of snow under Wolverine, lifting him high in the air, then dissipates it, dropping him. Mauvais then generates an energy sword, slicing deep into Wendigo's chest; he leaps on Wendigo, pulls out his heart and consumes it. As Wolverine watches in horror, Mauvais gains the Wendigo power and appearance. Wolverine attacks, but the newly empowered Mauvais easily defeats him, hammering Wolverine brutally until he is nearly unconscious. A sudden energy blast hits Mauvais, who turns and sees Alpha Flight...

NOTE: Cover-labeled "'Nuff Said," part of a month-long line-wide stunt where most of Marvel's books had no dialogue of any kind. This issue also has a 6-page feature presenting writer Frank Tieri's plot.

WOLVERINE #172 (March 2002)

"Stay Alive! Conclusion!" (22 pages)

CREDITS: Frank Tieri (writer), Sean Chen (pencils), Norm Rapmund (inks), Richard Starkings & Comicraft's Saida Temofonte (letters), Mike Raicht (asst editor), Mike Marts (editor), José Villarrubia (c colors)

FEATURE CHARACTER: Wolverine

GUEST STARS: Alpha Flight: Aurora (also as Jeanne-Marie), Snowbird (also as Wendigo & snow leopard), Puck (next in W #173/2, '02), Guardian, Sasquatch, Shaman

VILLAINS: Great Beasts: Kariooq (the Corrupter), Tolomaq (the Fire Beast) (both last in AFlt #24, '85), Somon (the Great Artificer), Tundra (the Land Beast) (prev 2 last in XMan #39, '98) (all next in ChW:AFlt, '11); Mauvais (becomes Wendigo), Wendigo spirit (bts empowering Mauvais, next bts in Sabre #1, '04), Wendigo (dead, briefly reanimated)

OTHER CHARACTERS: Inua: Hodiak (Sky-Father, chr next in Herc #117, '08 fb, next in Herc #116, '08), Nelvanna (Hodiak's daughter), Turoq (the Shaper) (prev 2 next in ChW:AFlt, '11) (all last in AFlt #45, '87, last bts in W #170, '02), mythological Canadian creatures (dead, reanimated & destroyed)

LOCATIONS/ITEMS: Canadian Arctic, Great Beasts' otherdimensional realm / Stay Alive's remote-controlled cameras (bts) w/controllers, Shaman's magical vine (destroyed) & staff, hurled tree, Somon's staff

SYNOPSIS: Alpha Flight attacks the Wendigo-powered Mauvais. Shaman tells Wolverine that they were alerted when Snowbird lost contact with the Inua; Mauvais' spell has created a mystical energy column blocking them from manifesting on Earth. Mauvais attacks Aurora's mind, unlocking her split personality Jeanne-Marie. Shaman tries to disrupt Mauvais' column with a magically growing vine, but Mauvais destroys it and resurrects Wendigo — along with several other creatures from Canadian mythology — to attack the heroes. Alpha Flight splits their focus, half blasting the column while the others battle the creatures; Puck talks Jeanne-Marie into accessing Aurora's powers and rejoining the fight. Mauvais' power fades and the creatures crumble; Wolverine uses his claws to destroy the weakened column. The Inua manifest and hurl Mauvais through a portal into the dimension of their ancient enemies, the Great Beasts. Mauvais has a prophetic vision as the portal closes; he taunts Wolverine that dark events will soon befall him. The Inua thank the heroes and depart, but Mauvais' parting words have unsettled Wolverine.

NOTE: This issue's colorist is uncredited, but is likely Avalon's Raymund Lee. Mauvais' first name is revealed this issue. Shaman states here that the Inua orchestrated Snowbird's resurrection prior to W #143, '99, but does not elaborate how or why.

WOLVERINE #173 (April 2002)

"The Logan Files, 1 of 3" (17 pages)

CREDITS: Frank Tieri (writer), Sean Chen (pencils), Norm Rapmund (inks), Richard Starkings & Comicraft's Saida Temofonte (letters), Avalon's Raymund Lee (colors), Mike Raicht (asst editor), Mike Marts (editor), David Finch (c pencils), José Villarrubia (c colors)

FEATURE CHARACTER: Wolverine

GUEST STARS: X-Men: Beast (bts caring for Nightcrawler, chr next in NX #114, '01, next in NX #124, '02), Cyclops (next in XFac #2, '02) (both chr last in W #174, '02 fb), Nightcrawler (also in photo, last in Cap #50/6, '02, also in W #174, '02 fb, chr next in UXM #395, '01, next in UXM #404, '02); Alpha Flight: Sasquatch (bts near crash site), Shaman (also bts in W #173/2, '02, next in BP #43, '02), Guardian; Heather Hudson (last in W #143, '99) (prev 2 also on monitor & in photo)

SUPPORTING CAST: Yukio (last in W #153, '00, last bts in W #158, '01), Amiko Kobayashi (last in W #158, '01) (both also in photo)

VILLAINS: Sabretooth (leaves Weapon X Program), Lady Deathstrike (both last in W #171, '02), Omega Red (last in W #170, '02), Weapon X Program: Malcolm Colcord (all also in mystic vision), Brent Jackson (prev 2 last in Dp #61, '02, chr last in W #173/2, '02), Mr. Sinister (Nathaniel Essex, machiavellian geneticist, 1st as Dr. Robert Windsor, last in XMU #30/2, '01, next as Windsor in W #175, '02), Weapon X agents (some or others last in Dp #60, '02, chr last in W #173/2, '02)

OTHER CHARACTERS: Leech (cancels mutants' powers, last in GenX #68, '00, last bts in GenX #69, '00, next in W #175, '02), Claire McNeil Hudson (Guardian & Heather's unborn daughter, unidentified, 1st bts app as embryo), Amiko's friends, bystanders (others in photo); Jubilee, Shadowcat, Warbird (prev 3 mentioned, possible targets of Sabretooth), Father Hildago (mentioned, taking confession); Wendigo spirit (bts), Bloodscream, Mauvais, Mr. X, Ogun, Vermin, Wendigo (prev 7 in mystic vision), cartoon pig, octopus & dog (prev 3 on signs)

LOCATIONS/ITEMS: Bronx, New York inc St. Ann's Church & East River, Alpha Flight Compound (Vancouver, unnamed, also on monitor), Alberta (also on monitor), Tokyo (also in photo) inc pachinko parlor, X-Mansion (also on monitor) w/Infirmary (bts), Weapon X Compound (Program's mountain base), Earth orbit, Bellagio Hotel (Las Vegas, Nevada) w/Sabretooth's suite / Lady Deathstrike's filtration mask, car (destroyed), Alpha Flight's comm system, Guardian's jet (destroyed) w/comm unit (bts), Heather's headset (also on monitor), parlor window (destroyed), Yukio's throwing blade, X-Men's life support equipment (bts) & comm system, Weapon X Program's teleporters (bts), satellite & Mutant Power Cannon w/computers & remote control, Sabretooth's override transmitter (bts), photographs & disks (all but 1 bts) w/Weapon X files (bts, unidentified, see NOTE) inc Logan files

SYNOPSIS: As Nightcrawler prays at a Brooklyn church, Omega Red and Lady Deathstrike attack him, injuring him badly and dumping him into the river. In Canada, Shaman is unable to give Wolverine any mystical insight into Mauvais' prophecy. Guardian and Heather call Alpha Flight's base from their jet, and Heather reveals that she is pregnant. Deathstrike and Omega Red secretly sabotage the jet, which crashes, and Shaman realizes that the prophecy may have referred to Wolverine's loved ones. In Japan, Deathstrike and Omega Red kidnap Amiko and savagely injure Yukio. Cyclops tells Wolverine about Nightcrawler's attack, and Wolverine realizes that Shaman's hunch was right. At the Weapon X Program compound, Colcord shows new employee Dr. Windsor their Mutant Power Cannon, which projects captive mutants' powers at targets anywhere in the world — when the cannon, currently imprisoning the power-dampening Leech, suddenly fires. Jackson notes that the culprit used Colcord's security codes; Wolverine realizes that his powers have vanished. In Las Vegas, Sabretooth laughs at the misery he is causing his old foe…

NOTE: "Dr. Windsor" is revealed as a disguised Mr. Sinister in WX #13, '03; his alias' first name is revealed in WX #26, '04. Heather Hudson gives birth in XMU #45, '03; her daughter's name is revealed in AFlt #2, '11. The Alpha Flight Compound, the team's new base, is named and its location is given in W #179, '02. Next issue reveals that Sabretooth's disk contains stolen Weapon X files including "the Logan Files," which W #175, '02 reveals contain information about Wolverine's past. WX #½, '02 reveals that Sabretooth stole more than one disk. This issue's letters page has 1-page B&W previews of WXD:S, '02 & next issue.

2ND STORY: "Laying the Groundwork" (5 pages)

CREDITS: Matt Nixon (writer), David Finch (pencils), Norm Rapmund (inks), Richard Starkings & Comicraft (letters), Avalon's Raymund Lee (colors), Mike Raicht (asst editor), Mike Marts (editor)

FEATURE CHARACTERS: Alpha Flight: Aurora (as Jeanne-Marie, next in WXD:WC, '02), Snowbird (next in BP #44, '02 fb), Puck (all last in W #172, '02), Sasquatch (prev 2 next in BP #43, '02), Shaman (bts on phone, during W #173, '02)

VILLAINS: Weapon X Program: Malcolm Colcord, Brent Jackson (both chr last in Dp #61, '02, chr next in W #173, '02), Weapon X agents (some or others chr last in Dp #60, '02, chr next in W #173, '02)

OTHER CHARACTERS: Ambulance driver (dies); Wild Child (mentioned, will be assigned to Aurora)

LOCATIONS/ITEMS: Alberta inc roadway & medical clinic, Shaman's suggested mental hospital (mentioned), Alpha Flight Compound (bts), Weapon X Compound, Manitoba Psychiatric Hospital for Women (Ontario, unnamed, bts) / Ambulance w/window (destroyed), Aurora's stretcher w/restraints, Sasquatch's cellphone, Alpha Flight's comm system (bts), Weapon X agents' gun (bts), motorcycles & truncheon

SYNOPSIS: Alpha Flight reluctantly decide to send Aurora, her fragile psyche damaged by Mauvais, to a mental hospital. Sasquatch rides in the ambulance with her, but when Shaman calls to alert him of Guardian's jet crash, he races to their aid. Soon after, Weapon X agents attack the ambulance and kidnap Aurora. At the Weapon X compound, Colcord tells Jackson that she will be taken to an unrelated mental hospital, then be "rescued" by Weapon X agent Wild Child.

NOTE: This story occurs between pp.7 & 12 of this issue's first story. The Weapon X Program appears here first, then there. Wild Child retrieves and recruits Aurora in WXD:WC, '02, where the Manitoba Psychiatric Hospital is named. Aurora's last name is misspelled "Baubier" here.

WOLVERINE #174 (May 2002)

"The Logan Files, 2 of 3" (22 pages)

CREDITS: Frank Tieri (writer), Sean Chen (pencils), Norm Rapmund (inks), Richard Starkings & Comicraft's Sa
Temofonte (letters), Avalon's Raymund Lee (colors), Mike Raicht (asst editor), Mike Marts (editor), David Finch
pencils), Joe Weems (c inks), José Villarrubia (c colors)
FEATURE CHARACTER: Wolverine
GUEST STARS: X-Men: Beast (in fb between UXM #394, '01 bts & W #173, '02), Cyclops (in fb between U
#394, '01 & W #173, '02), Nightcrawler (in fb during W #173, '02), Phoenix (bts in fb, trying to read Nightcrawler's mi
between UXM #394, '01 & XFac #1, '02); Guardian, Heather Hudson (prev 2 in fb between W #173, '02 & BP #42, '
SUPPORTING CAST: Yukio (next in XX #36, '04), Amiko Kobayashi (also in Wolverine's thoughts)
VILLAINS: Lady Deathstrike, Omega Red (both also on monitors), Sabretooth; Weapon X Program: Brent Jacks
(next in WX #½, '02), Malcolm Colcord (prev 2 chr last in W #173, '02), Garrison Kane (last in Dp #59, '01), Weapon
agents (some or others chr last in W #173, '02)
OTHER CHARACTERS: Claire McNeil Hudson (bts in fb, unborn, between W #173, '02 bts & BP #42, '02 bts), Bellagio patrons, security guards
staff inc doorman, Cirque du Soleil performers & audience, bystanders; Mariko Yashida (in photo); tiger (in painting)
LOCATIONS/ITEMS: Yashidas' ancestral manor, Tokyo hospital, Weapon X Compound, skies over Pacific Ocean, Bellagio Hotel w/Cirque du So
stage & Sabretooth's suite, East River, X-Mansion, Alberta (prev 3 in fb) / Mariko's grave marker w/photo, Wolverine's rose & borrowed Alpha Flu
jet & cybernetic Guardian costume, Guardian's jet (destroyed), X-Men's winch & medical sensors (prev 3 in fb), Yukio's support bed, breathing tu
& IV drips, Kane's cybernetic implants w/computer interface cables, Weapon X Program's files (mentioned) inc Logan Files (named) & computers
monitor, Bellagio windows, slot machines (prev 2 destroyed), fountain & trash can, Lady Deathstrike's filtration mask, hurled pillar, guard's handg
Director's chair, Jackson's control chip (bts), Weapon X agent's gun, performer's flaming top hat, Cirque du Soleil curtain (destroyed), Amiko's rope
FLASHBACK: The X-Men recover the injured Nightcrawler; Guardian escapes with Heather before their jet crashes.
SYNOPSIS: Wolverine visits Mariko's grave and apologizes for having to neglect his obligation; although it is the anniversary of her death, he urge
needs to rescue Amiko. Visiting Yukio in the hospital, Wolverine learns that Lady Deathstrike carved the villains' Las Vegas location onto Yuki
back. With severe spine damage, Yukio asks Wolverine to kill her if she does not recover, unsettling Wolverine deeply. At the Weapon X compou
Kane discovers that Sabretooth has escaped with sensitive data including something called the Logan Files. Wolverine arrives in Las Vegas, whe
Deathstrike and Omega Red promptly ambush him. His powers gone, Wolverine has borrowed one of Guardian's suits to protect him, but the villa
still injure him badly. Elsewhere, Jackson taunts Colcord about Sabretooth's escape; Colcord snaps, beats Jackson and orders him suspend
Wolverine flees, but Deathstrike and Omega Red catch up and knock him unconscious. Wolverine awakens to find a gloating Sabretooth hold
Amiko captive.
NOTE: Mariko's surname is misspelled "Yoshida" on her grave marker here. However, as discussed in W #55, '92's NOTE, both "Yashida" a
"Yoshida" are valid Anglicized spellings of the Japanese characters in her name, and Mariko's cousin Sunfire uses the latter spelling. Wolverine's yea
obligation to Mariko is revealed in W #175/2, '02. Yukio fully recovers by XX #36, '04.

WOLVERINE #175 (June 2002)

"The Logan Files, Conclusion!" (23 pages)

CREDITS: Frank Tieri (writer), Sean Chen (pencils), Norm Rapmund (inks), Richard Starkings & Comicraft's Sa
Temofonte (letters), Avalon's Raymund Lee (colors), Mike Raicht (asst editor), Mike Marts (editor), J.H. Williams III
pencils), José Villarrubia (c colors)
FEATURE CHARACTER: Wolverine (dies, also bts in rfb1 & as James Howlett in rfb2, also as Experiment X in
during W #166, '01 fb)
SUPPORTING CAST: Amiko Kobayashi
VILLAINS: Lady Deathstrike (next in W #183/2, '03), Omega Red (next in WX #3, '03), Sabretooth (next in Sabre #
'02), Weapon X Program: Malcolm Colcord (also in fb during W #166, '01 fb), Mesmero (Vincent, mutant hypnotis
Wild Child (Kyle Gibney, feral mutant) (prev 2 last in Dp #61, '02), Garrison Kane (prev 3 next in WX #½, '02),
Sinister (as Dr. Robert Windsor, last as Windsor in W #173, '02, next as Windsor in WX #½, '02), Weapon X agents
OTHER CHARACTERS: Leech (last in W #173, '02, next in WX #5, '03); original Weapon X Program senior staff: Professor Truett Hudson (bts
rfb1), Dr. Abraham Cornelius; original Weapon X Program employee (prev 2 voice only in rfb1), John Howlett, Thomas Logan (prev 2 dead in rfb2)
LOCATIONS/ITEMS: Sabretooth's Bellagio Hotel suite, former Weapon X Program facility (also in fb & bts in rfb1) w/exhaust pit & nearby woo
Weapon X Compound (also in Sabretooth's thoughts), Howlett estate (in rfb2) / Wolverine's bandages, sharpened stakes & borrowed cyberne
Guardian costume (destroyed), Omega Red & Sabretooth's champagne bottles (Omega's destroyed), Amiko's ropes (some destroyed), Sabretooth
override transmitter & disks (all but 1 bts) w/Weapon X files inc Logan Files, Weapon X Program's teleporters (bts), airships, Mutant Power Canni
& computers w/monitor, suite window (destroyed), Logan Files disk container (also in Sabretooth's thoughts), Kane's cybernetic implants inc senso
former Weapon X Program's observation window, gas tanks & equipment (prev 3 destroyed) inc scalpel, tubing & medical bed, Weapon X age
guns & headset, Colcord's rifle (in fb) & comm device, Thomas Logan's shotgun (in rfb2)
FLASHBACKS: Dr. Cornelius and a Weapon X employee react to Experiment X (MCP #73-75, '91, see NOTE). James Howlett stares at the bod
of John Howlett and Thomas Logan (Origin #2, '01). Experiment X mauls Colcord.
SYNOPSIS: Sabretooth, Omega Red and Lady Deathstrike toast Wolverine's defeat — but when Sabretooth's allies demand their promis
rewards, Sabretooth teleports away with Wolverine and Amiko. Wolverine finds himself in a forest; Sabretooth reveals that he stole Weapon X's Log
Files, containing information on Wolverine's past. Powerless, Wolverine flees to find Amiko; Kane tracks Sabretooth's teleport and Colcord orders
massive Weapon X attack. Sabretooth stalks Wolverine, who realizes that they are near the original Weapon X facility. He finds an injured Amiko insid

Sabretooth savagely attacks, claiming that the Logan Files are empty; the real reason Wolverine cannot recall his past is because his brain "heals" ... r traumatic memories. Colcord fires the Mutant Power Cannon at Sabretooth as his agents storm the facility. Sabretooth fatally injures Wolverine, realizes that his powers are gone when Wolverine stabs him back. As Colcord arrives, Sabretooth teleports away and Wolverine falls, dead.

...TE: Mesmero's first name is revealed in WX #8, '03; his last name is unrevealed to date. This issue's rfb1 is an "audio only" flashback; word ...oons with no visual component. Given Colcord's distress over their theft last issue, Sabretooth's claim that the Logan Files are empty is likely false.

...D STORY: "The Vow" (8 pages)
...EDITS: Frank Tieri (writer), Georges Jeanty (pencils), Ray Snyder (inks), Richard Starkings & Comicraft's Oscar Gongora (letters), Avalon's ...ymund Lee (colors), Mike Raicht (asst editor), Mike Marts (editor)
...ATURE CHARACTER: Wolverine (dead, also in rfb, also in fb1 between W #81-82, '94; also in fb2 between UXM #333, '96 & W/Herc #1, '11 ...also in fb3 between X #75, '98 & W #123, '98)
...LAINS: Matsuo Tsurayaba (also in fb1 & fb2 between X #32, '94 & W/Herc #1, '11 fb; also in fb3 between W/Herc #1, '11 fb & W #126, '98; also ...04 between W #128, '98 & W/Herc #1, '11 fb; last in W #128, '98, chr last in W/Herc #1, '11 fb; chr next in Psy #3 fb, next bts in Psy #1, next in Psy ...all '10) & his employees (in fb1, some or all die) & bodyguards (1 in fb2, dies off-panel; others in fb3, some on monitors), Hand ninjas (in fb2, die, ...ne or others chr last in GR #74, '96 fb, others chr next in OtEdge #8, '96), Weapon X agent
...HER CHARACTERS: Matsuo's scientists & martial arts trainers (both in fb4); Mariko Yashida (in rfb), dragon (as mural), dog (as statue in fb1)
...CATIONS/ITEMS: Matsuo's Japanese estate (in fb1, fb2, fb3 & fb4, also on monitors in fb3), Shingen's Citadel compound chapel (in rfb), ...ner Weapon X program facility / Matsuo's clock (also in fb1 & fb3), laptop, paperwork, sword (prev 3 in fb1), cameras, lasers, motion detectors (prev ...ts), monitors (prev 4 in fb3), energy swords, laser pistols (prev 2 bts), battle armor, cybernetic arm (prev 4 in fb4), paper, daisho (seppuku swords) ...ase & prosthetic hand (also in fb1, fb2, fb3 & fb4), arm (in fb3), ear (in fb3 & fb4) & nose (also in fb4), blowfish toxin (bts in rfb), employees' guns (in ...), ninjas' swords (in fb2), bodyguards' guns (1 in fb2; others in fb3, some on monitors), Weapon X Program bodybag
...ASHBACKS: Wolverine holds the poisoned Mariko Yashida (W #57, '92). On the first anniversary of Mariko's death, Wolverine attacks and cuts off ...tsuo's arm (1). On the second anniversary, Wolverine battles through Hand ninjas and cuts off Matsuo's ear (2). On the third anniversary, Wolverine ...aks in and cuts off Matsuo's nose (3). Matsuo gets cybernetic implants and martial arts training to prepare for the fourth anniversary (4).
...NOPSIS: On the fifth anniversary of Mariko's death, a scarred and dispirited Matsuo Tsurayaba awaits Wolverine's yearly attack. He plans to ...Wolverine to allow him an honorable suicide, but Wolverine never arrives. The astonished Matsuo wonders why his persistent foe failed to attack; ...ewhere, a Weapon X agent packs Wolverine's corpse into a bodybag.
...DTE: Wolverine is incorrectly depicted with metal claws in the first three flashbacks; he had bone claws at those times. We do not see Wolverine's ...rth attack, where he destroys Matsuo's gall bladder, on-panel; this event is later shown in W/Herc #1, '11 fb.

...D STORY: "A Good Man" (8 pages)
...EDITS: Jason Aaron (writer), Udon Studios (art, colors), Richard Starkings & Comicraft (letters), Mike Raicht (asst editor), Mike Marts (editor)
...ATURE CHARACTER: Wolverine (also as himself & Experiment X in rfb, chr last in W #176, '02, chr next in Av #51, '02 fb)
...LAINS: Hunters (die)
...HER CHARACTERS: Churchgoing woman; hunters' dogs (all die); Paul (woman's husband), woman's mother (prev 2 mentioned, dead); Mariko ...shida (in photo in rfb)
...CATIONS/ITEMS: Alabama woods, road & church (mentioned) w/graveyard, former Weapon X Program facility, Moon's Blue Area, Yashidas' ...cestral manor (prev 3 in rfb) / Experiment X's helmet, wires & battery packs, Mariko's grave marker w/photo, Wolverine's rose (all in rfb), woman's ...le & car w/tire (destroyed), hubcap, jack, lug wrench & spare tire, hunters' shotguns, dogs' collars
...ASHBACK: Experiment X rages (MCP #79, '91); Wolverine thinks of Phoenix (X #137, '80); Wolverine visits Mariko's grave (last issue).
...NOPSIS: Wolverine runs through Alabama, pursued by dogs and hunters. He encounters a woman with a flat tire; anxious to get her out of ...rm's way, he quickly changes the tire. The woman calls Wolverine a good man, but he disagrees. The dogs catch up and attack; Wolverine quickly ...patches them, but the hunters arrive and shoot wildly — killing the woman. Wolverine slaughters the hunters; he buries the dogs and the woman, ...t leaves the hunters' bodies in the road.
...DTE: This story occurs after Wolverine's recovery next issue. Writer Jason Aaron was the winner of Marvel's 2001 Wolverine talent competition; ...ting this story was his prize. Aaron went on to write various Wolverine arcs, one-shots and miniseries, and became the series' regular writer with ...#1, '10.

WOLVERINE #176 (July 2002)

"The Logan Files, Epilogue" (22 pages)

CREDITS: Frank Tieri (writer), Sean Chen (pencils), Norm Rapmund (inks), Richard Starkings & Comicraft's Saida Temofonte (letters), Avalon's Raymund Lee (colors), Mike Raicht (asst editor), Mike Marts (editor), José Villarrubia (c colors)

FEATURE CHARACTER: Wolverine (dead, revives, also possibly as spirit, see NOTE; also as himself, Cpl. Logan & "Patch" in rfb1; also in rfb2; also as himself, Experiment X & Death in rfb3; also in fb1 between X #109, '78 & CX #28/2, '88; also in fb2 between UXM #390, '01 & ASM #36, '01; next in W #175/3, '02, Av #51, '02 fb; XFor #116, NX #114-116, UXM #395-398, all '01, XMU #6, '05 fb, NX Ann '01, NX #139, '03 fb, XFor #120, '01, NX #117-122, '01-02; Pun #16-17, NX #123-126, all '02, W:Saud, '06; Order #5-6, BP #41-43 & 44 fb, UXM #400, Dp #69, all '02)

GUEST STARS: X-Men: Colossus (possibly as spirit, see NOTE; also in rfb1; also in fb1 between X #109, '78 & CX #28/2, '88; also dead in fb2 between UXM #390, '01 & this issue; last in UXM #390, '01, chr next in AX #5, '04 fb, next ...AX #4, '04), Nightcrawler (in fb2 between XMU #37, '02 & XMU #30/2, '01), Cyclops (in fb2 between XMU #37, '02 & ASM #36, '01) (prev 2 also in ...l between X #109, '78 & CX #28/2, '88), Storm (prev 2 also in rfb2) (prev 3 also in rfb1), Banshee (prev 2 in fb1 between X #109-110, '78), Gambit ...fb2 between UXM #390, '01 & XMU #30/2, '01), Phoenix (Jean Grey, in fb2 between XMU #37, '02 & Cable #92, '01); also as Marvel Girl in rfb1 & ...an Grey in rfb2), Professor X (in fb2 between UXM #390, '01 & X #110, '01; also in painting in fb1), Rogue (in fb2 between X #109, '01 & XX #3, '01 ...; Archangel (in fb2 between IM #37, '01 & Tb #57, '01; also as Angel in rfb1), Phoenix (Phoenix Force, cosmic entity, as Jean Grey in fb1 between ...#109, '78 & CX #28/2, '88)

...UPPORTING CAST: Amiko Kobayashi (also in rfb1, next in W:Xisle #1, '03)

VILLAINS: Stonewall (Louis Hamilton, cannot be knocked down, last in UXM #255, '89), Super Sabre (Martin Fletcher, speedster, last in NM A[#7/2], '91) (both next in shadow in XNec, '09, next in XFor #21, '10), Cyber (last in W #96, '95, chr next as spirit in W #11, '07), Geist (last in W #23, '90), Mastermind (Jason Wyngarde, mutant illusionist, last in UXM Ann #17, '93), Pyro (St. John Allerdyce, cont. flame, last in Cable #87, '01, next in IHulk #83, '05), Stryfe (Cable's evil clone, last in G&B #6, '01, next in shadow in Cable #10, '09, next in XFor/C:M '09), Shingen Harada (last in W #4, '82, next in W #60, '08), Cameron Hodge (last in Cable #16, '94, next in XFor #3, '08), Professor Truett Huds. (last in W #50, '92), Cylla Markham (last in W #80, '94), Roche (Madripoor's former crimelord, last in MCP #10, '89) (all possibly as spirits, see NOT. Weapon X Program: Malcolm Colcord (bts returning Amiko, chr next in WXD:AZ, '02, next in WX #½, '02), Weapon X agents (die, some or others rfb1; others next in WX #½, '02)

OTHER CHARACTERS: Rose O'Hara (Wolverine's childhood friend & first crush, possibly as spirit, see NOTE; last in Origin #6, '02), people fr. Wolverine's past (bts, heard dimly, see NOTE); Sabretooth (as himself & Creed in rfb1, also in rfb3), Guardian (also as James Hudson), Wend. (Cartier), Wendigo spirit, Claire McNeil Hudson, Nazi soldiers (prev 3 bts), Heather Hudson, Malcolm Colcord, Hulk, Lady Deathstrike, Maveri. Ogun, Omega Red, Yukio, X-Men: Beast, Iceman, Thunderbird (prev 16 in rfb1), Havok, priest (prev 2 in rfb2), Magneto, Mariko Yashida (prev 2 in rft. Magik, Nikolai Rasputin, Alexandra Rasputina (prev 3 mentioned, in afterlife)

LOCATIONS/ITEMS: Afterlife (also as Howlett estate grounds), former Weapon X Program facility (also in rfb1 & rfb3) w/exhaust pit & nearby woc (prev 2 in rfb1), skies above Canada, X-Mansion (also in fb1 & fb2) w/grounds (in rfb2), Bellagio Hotel w/Sabretooth's suite, East River, Alberta, Tok. Normandy, Princess Bar, Kanazawa, East Berlin, Wood Buffalo National Park, North Woods, South Pacific Ocean (prev 12 in rfb1), Shingen's Cita. compound chapel, Avalon, Apocalypse's Egyptian base (prev 3 in rfb3) / Bellagio fountain, Amiko's ropes (some bts), Wolverine's Fairbairn knife borrowed cybernetic Guardian suit, Weapon X agents' guns, Guardian's jet, Heather's headset, Team X's guns & body armor, Hudsons' packs in rfb1), Cyclops & Jean's ribbon, priest's Bible (prev 2 in rfb2), blowfish toxin (bts), Experiment X's wires & battery packs, Wolverine's Adamantiu. Death's sword, Logan Files disk container (prev 6 in rfb3), X-Men's playing cards (in fb1), Colossus' casket, Professor X's wheelchair (prev 2 in fb2), Cylla's cybernetic implants, Geist's exoskeleton w/razor attachment, Shingen & Roche's swords, Professor's handgun, Stryfe's armor, Hodg. cybernetic body, Pyro's flamethrowers, Rose's rose (prev 9 possibly afterlife manifestations), Weapon X Program's bodybag (destroyed), airship. medical equipment inc sensors & breathing tube, Wolverine's bandages, Amiko's poncho, Colcord's note (destroyed)

FLASHBACKS: Omega Red defeats Wolverine and brings him to Sabretooth; Sabretooth battles Wolverine; Weapon X agents interrupt; Nightcraw. lands in the East River; Guardian's jet crashes; Deathstrike stabs Yukio; Amiko is gravely injured (W #173-175, '02); Cpl. Logan attacks Nazis (W #. '90 fb); Patch visits the Princess Bar (W #15, '89); Wolverine trains with Ogun (W #89, '95 fb); Team X performs espionage (X #5, '92 fb); Wolver. attacks the Hudsons (AFlt #33, '86 fb); Wolverine attacks Hulk and Wendigo (IHulk #181, '74); the X-Men charge into action (GSX #1, '75). As Cyclc. marries Jean (X #30, '94), Wolverine skulks in the woods (WI? #60, '94). Wolverine holds the poisoned Mariko Yashida (W #57, '92); Experimen. suffers (MCP #78, '91); Magneto rips out Wolverine's Adamantium (X #25, '93); Wolverine serves as Death (W #145, '99); Sabretooth holds the em. disk container (last issue). The X-Men play cards (1). Wolverine skulks outside during Colossus' memorial service (2).

SYNOPSIS: Wolverine awakens in the afterlife, where a familiar redheaded woman explains that he must comes to terms with his feelings. She as. about Wolverine's longstanding love for Jean Grey, points out that Wolverine hasn't had a meaningful relationship since Mariko's death, and confir. that Wolverine's mind "heals" over emotional trauma. She urges Wolverine to accept that it's all right to fail and to hurt, and offers him a chance to lea. about his past. Suddenly, the spirits of several of Wolverine's former foes attack; Wolverine is overwhelmed until the spirit of the recently deceas. Colossus arrives and helps defeat them. Wolverine suddenly fades out, "resurrected" by his returning healing factor. Wolverine kills the Weapon. agents and returns to the X-Mansion; Colcord soon returns a healed Amiko, apologizing for Sabretooth's unsanctioned attack.

NOTE: Colossus committed suicide in UXM #390, '01, but AX #5-6, '04 reveal that the alien Ord stole his body shortly afterward and resuscitat. him. Depending on when Colossus was revived, he may not have actually been dead at this time — which casts doubt on whether any of the oth. spirits seen here are real. They could have been illusions, as demons like Mephisto often manipulate living people who visit the afterlife — or Wolveri. may have simply hallucinated the entire experience while healing from his grave wounds. The chronologies given here assume that all the spirits a. real. It is unclear who the voices that Wolverine dimly hears belong to, although they are implied to be characters from the Origin, '01-02 miniserie. is also unclear if they are spirits or simply Wolverine's memories. This issue also has a 4-page preview of CallD:B #1/2, '02. This issue's letters pa. is the series' last until W #43, '06.

WOLVERINE #177 (August 2002)

"The Shadow Pulpit, Book 1 of 2" (22 pages)

CREDITS: Matt Nixon (writer), Dan Fraga (pencils), Lary Stucker (inks), Richard Starkings & Comicraft's Sai. Temofonte (letters), Avalon's Raymund Lee (colors), Mike Raicht (asst editor), Mike Marts (editor), Sean Chen. pencils), Norm Rapmund (c inks), José Villarrubia (c colors)

FEATURE CHARACTER: Wolverine

VILLAINS: Cardinal Panzer ("Shadow Pope," head of corrupt Office of Inquisition faction), Dogma ("Bishop. Assassins," energy form in malleable containment suit), Cardinal Parente (Panzer's ally), Sister Inquisitor (Panzer. torturer, unnamed) (all 1st), Panzer's foot soldiers

OTHER CHARACTERS: Father Braun (last in W Ann '01/2), Father Davidson (Catholic priest, dies), Lois (Iri. Ayes bartender), Irish Ayes patrons, police (bts in cars); Pope John Paul II (mentioned, Panzer's likely target); pig (. oven mitt)

LOCATIONS/ITEMS: New York City: St. Ann's Church (see NOTE), Brooklyn Bridge, East River, Greenwich Village inc Irish Ayes pub; Vatican City. dungeon & Panzer's office; Rome, Italy / Davidson's Bible & confession booth screen (destroyed), Dogma's swords, bolas & malleable containment s. (see NOTE), Braun's sword & chains, police cars (bts), Lois' oven mitt & water bucket, Panzer's Extra-Low Frequency Vibration Emanations (ELVE. device (destroyed), foot soldiers' knives, van, guns, electrified net & helicopter w/rappelling lines, Sister Inquisitor's crop, Wolverine's chains (bts)

SYNOPSIS: While taking confession, Father Davidson is strangled. Later, Father Braun meets with Wolverine, whose enhanced senses are bei. painfully affected by an external source. Braun reveals that a corrupt Vatican faction led by his former mentor, Cardinal Panzer, plans to overthrc. the Pope. He explains that Davidson discovered the plot and was murdered, and that Panzer is using an extra-low frequency device to subtly conve. all New Yorkers to Panzer's worldview. Wolverine, realizing that the device is dampening his senses, barely senses the arrival of Dogma, Panze. assassin. Dogma easily overpowers Wolverine, burying his sword in the mutant's back, but flees when Wolverine damages his suit. Braun hel. Wolverine extract the sword and the two track Panzer's device to the Brooklyn Bridge. Braun destroys the device, restoring Wolverine's enhanc. senses, but Panzer's foot soldiers capture him; Dogma attacks again, knocking Wolverine into the river. Later, in Vatican City, Panzer confers with h. ally Cardinal Parente, while Braun is tortured for information and Panzer's soldiers guard an unconscious Wolverine.

OTE: W #177-178, '02 were published biweekly. Braun's position with the Office of Inquisition is revealed here. Sister Inquisitor's title and Dogma's
ture as an energy being in a containment suit are revealed next issue. St. Ann's Church, located in the Bronx, is incorrectly stated to be in Lower
anhattan here.

WOLVERINE #178 (August 2002)

"The Shadow Pulpit, Book 2 of 2" (23 pages)

CREDITS: Matt Nixon (writer), Dan Fraga (pencils), Lary Stucker (inks), Richard Starkings & Comicraft's Jason Levine (letters), Avalon's Raymund Lee (colors), Mike Raicht (asst editor), Mike Marts (editor), Sean Chen (c pencils), Norm Rapmund (c inks), José Villarrubia (c colors)
FEATURE CHARACTER: Wolverine
VILLAINS: Sister Inquisitor (named), Cardinal Panzer, Cardinal Parente, Dogma & his assassins, Panzer's foot soldiers
OTHER CHARACTERS: Father Braun (dies), Parente's guards, restaurant staff & patrons, pilot (bts flying plane), bystanders; College of Cardinals (mentioned as "the Council," Parente claims they will judge Panzer); historic & mythological figures (as statues)
LOCATIONS/ITEMS: Vatican City inc dungeon, sewer tunnels & Panzer's office, Roman airport / Foot soldiers' van & guns, Wolverine's chains (destroyed), Braun's chains, Sister Inquisitor's crop, assassins' sword, nunchuks & staff, arente's scrolls, Dogma's sword & containment suit (destroyed), Panzer's gun, airplane (in shadow)
YNOPSIS: Wolverine awakens, finding himself chained in a van by Panzer's foot soldiers. He breaks free and attacks; one soldier flees into a sewer nnel, and Wolverine notes its location. In the dungeon, the Sister Inquisitor demands to know what Braun told Wolverine, but Braun refuses to break. olverine investigates the sewers and avoids guard patrols; he picks up Braun's scent but several assassins suddenly assault him, forcing him back to street level, where Dogma attacks again. The two battle furiously, but Wolverine punctures and shreds Dogma's costume, which deflates — and olverine realizes that Dogma was an energy being. Retracing his steps down to the dungeon, Wolverine arrives to find Panzer beating Braun. ealizing that without Braun, Wolverine can prove nothing, Panzer shoots Braun dead. Wolverine attacks, but Parente intervenes, arresting Panzer d claiming that he will face justice. Unsure whether to trust Parente, Wolverine threatens him and leaves. Later, Parente lectures the freed Panzer, orried that Wolverine may have become a more dangerous enemy than Braun.
OTE: Sister Inquisitor's title is revealed here. Wolverine's standard X-jacket, with the large "X" across the body, makes its first appearance in olverine's title this issue. Although Wolverine does not seem to have his costume when he is captured and brought to Rome, he wears it after his scape. His X-jacket may be reversible, and might have been the coat he was wearing when he was captured.

WOLVERINE #179 (September 2002)

"Of Lesser Demons…" (23 pages)

CREDITS: Matt Nixon (writer), Ethan Van Sciver (pencils), Lary Stucker (inks), Richard Starkings & Comicraft's Saida Temofonte (letters), Avalon Studios (colors), Mike Raicht (asst editor), Mike Marts (editor), Sean Chen (c pencils), Norm Rapmund (c inks), José Villarrubia (c colors)
FEATURE CHARACTER: Wolverine
GUEST STARS: Alpha Flight: Puck, Sasquatch (both also possessed by demonic shaman, last in BP #44, '02 fb), Snowbird (also as monstrous insect, last in CitV #3, '02) (all next in UXM #421, '03), Shaman (last in BP #43, '02)
VILLAINS: Demonic shaman (undead spirit, also as skeleton & monstrous insect, dies), demonic spider, scorpion & crab (prev 3 die), evil force (bts, sensed by Shaman)
OTHER CHARACTERS: Charles "Chuck" Moss (Shaman's protégé, 1st); flies (some die), birds, gecko, grubs
LOCATIONS/ITEMS: Vancouver inc Alpha Flight Compound (named), X-Mansion grounds, astral plane / Shaman's mputer (bts), pouch, staff & mystical bowl, Moss' computer (bts), Humvee & luggage, gecko's mouth stitches (destroyed), hurled rock, demon's ganic growths (some destroyed), Wolverine's belt compartment
YNOPSIS: After a mystical swarm of flies invades the Alpha Flight Compound, Shaman uses an enchanted gecko to contact Wolverine for help. olverine travels to the compound, now enveloped by demonic growths; Shaman explains that a demon has overtaken the building and captured uck, Sasquatch and Snowbird. Flies envelop the two as they enter the transformed compound, but Shaman sucks them into his medicine pouch, en gives Wolverine grubs that will break the demon's hold on his teammates. A possessed Sasquatch attacks, but Wolverine attaches a grub to m, freeing his mind. The two begin chasing the similarly possessed Puck, but encounter the demon and the captive Snowbird, both in the form monstrous insects. As Wolverine attacks the demon, Shaman confronts it on the astral plane — releasing the captured flies, which swarm and onsume the villain's spirit. The compound reverts to normal and Puck and Snowbird are freed, but Shaman senses a larger evil force at work — one at wants to corrupt his arriving protégé, Chuck Moss.
OTE: The Alpha Flight Compound is revealed to be located in Vancouver this issue. Chuck's full first name is confirmed next issue.

WOLVERINE #180 (October 2002)

"Everything's Zen" (23 pages)

CREDITS: Matt Nixon (writer), Jorge Lucas (art), Richard Starkings & Comicraft's Saida Temofonte (letters), Avalon Studios (colors), Mike Raicht (asst editor), Mike Marts (editor), Andy Kubert (c pencils)
FEATURE CHARACTER: Wolverine (next in Venom #6-10, '03-04, UXM Ann '01, UXM #401, '02)
GUEST STAR: Shaman (next bts in AFlt #1, '04, next in AFlt #2, '04)
VILLAIN: Evil force (in shadow, as wind & bears)
OTHER CHARACTERS: Chuck Moss (next as Earthmover in UXM #421, '03); elk, birds, worm; Chuck's father (mentioned, nominated Chuck for training)
LOCATIONS/ITEMS: British Columbia woods inc cave & Shaman's Prince George cabin / Shaman's tent, Moss' Humvee & necklace, twig (destroyed), Wolverine's bokken & blindfold, dead tree

MARVEL WOLVERINE
NIXON FG LUCAS

SYNOPSIS: As Chuck begins his mystical training, Shaman has Wolverine teach him how to be at peace with the world. The two journey into th woods, where Wolverine explains the Bushido mindset. Wolverine demonstrates his oneness with nature by sneaking up to touch an elk — but Chu steps on a twig and the startled elk violently kicks Wolverine away. Chuck is horrified, but Wolverine quickly heals. The two practice swordfightir Chuck tires and asks to stop, but Wolverine continues battering him, explaining that real combat has no time-outs. He then has Chuck cross a fall tree above a gorge. Chuck nearly falls, but Wolverine has him do it again while blindfolded; Chuck trusts his instincts and succeeds. That nigl Wolverine has Chuck remain in a cave to discover his animal totem. Chuck has visions of looming evil spirits, but the next morning awakens to discov a worm in his hand — his new totem. In the woods, Wolverine is astonished to see Chuck calmly walk up and touch the elk.

NOTE: Chuck's full first name, Charles, is confirmed here. After he receives the worm totem, Wolverine calls him an "earthmover"; UXM #422, ' reveals that Chuck takes this as his codename prior to UXM #421, '03. This issue's "Cutting Edge" page contains no letters; it is a farewell from th departing editorial team, and the last "Cutting Edge" page until W:RTH, '10.

WOLVERINE #181 (November 2002)

"Chasers" (22 pages)

CREDITS: Frank Tieri (writer), Sean Chen (pencils), Tom Palmer (inks), Richard Starkings & Comicraft's Saic Temofonte (letters), Avalon Studios' Edgar Tadeo (colors), John Miesegaes (asst editor), Axel Alonso (editor), Esa Ribic (c art)

FEATURE CHARACTER: Wolverine (also in pfb)

VILLAINS: Nicky Dell'adera, Joey Fucillo, "Mad Dog" Mike Perretta (all mobsters, bts in pfb, questioned by Wolverine Pazzo family mobsters (group unnamed), bartender (prev 2 dead; also in pfb, die off-panel)

OTHER CHARACTERS: Westchester bar owner (bts in pfb, borrowed money from mob) & his daughter (also bts i basement in pfb) (both next in W #184, '03); actors (on TV in pfb); Ricky Bertel (gambler, killed), John Cerilli (Mad Dog victim), Billy Perretta (Mad Dog's brother), Loretta (Mad Dog's girlfriend) & her boss, Nicky's victim (killed), Wolverine'; victim (prev 7 mentioned in pfb); Spider-Man (mentioned, daughter thinks Wolverine is him); boxers (bts on posters also on posters in pfb); snake (as tattoo, also as tattoo in pfb)

LOCATIONS/ITEMS: Chez Bippy's (mob-affiliated bar, also in pfb) w/basement, Eighteenth Avenue, Mott Street, Nicky's victim's business, Loretta'; brokerage firm, Westchester bar (prev 5 mentioned in pfb) / Mobster's gun (also in pfb) & hand, bartender's shotgun (also in pfb), Wolverine's drink (in pfb) & bag, daughter's ropes; Nicky's pickle barrel, Bertel & bar owner's borrowed money, Joey's ropes & Cadillac, Mad Dog's hammer, bos; wheelchair (prev 6 mentioned in pfb)

FLASHBACK: Wolverine orders a drink at a bar. At a nearby table, three Mafia members swap stories of their fellow mobsters' misdeeds: Nick Dell'adera killed a man and stuffed him in a pickle barrel, Joey Fucillo dragged a gambler to death with his car over a hundred dollar debt, and Mike "Mad Dog" Perretta assaulted his girlfriend's wheelchair-bound boss. The mobsters notice Wolverine eavesdropping and confront him; Wolverine buys them drinks and tells a story of his own. When a bar owner's daughter became ill, he borrowed money from the mob to pay for her medical care, bu he couldn't repay them, so the mobsters kidnapped his daughter. Wolverine explains how he visited Dell'adera, Fucillo and Perretta, and convinced them to reveal the guilty parties: the mobsters he's drinking with right now. The crew's leader and the bartender go for their guns, but Wolverine pops his claws (p).

SYNOPSIS: Wolverine rescues the girl from the basement, telling her not to look as he carries her past the carnage in the bar.

NOTE: Beginning this month, Wolverine and most other Marvel titles switched to a lower-case lettering font. Next issue reveals that the three mobsters belong to the Pazzo crime family. W #183, '03 reveals that the bar owner's debt is $20,000.

WOLVERINE #182 (December 2002)

"Three Funerals and a Wedding" (23 pages)

CREDITS: Frank Tieri (writer), Sean Chen (pencils), Tom Palmer (inks), Richard Starkings & Comicraft (letters), Avalon Studios' Edgar Tadeo (colors), John Miesegaes (asst editor), Axel Alonso (editor), Esad Ribic (c art)

FEATURE CHARACTER: Wolverine (next in Bhood #8, W/Hulk #1-4, XX #18, XMU #35/3, UXM #408-409, WXD:AZ, all '02)

VILLAINS: Pazzo family (mobsters, 1st on-panel app as group, named): Freddo Pazzo (Godfather, also in portrait, also as himself & boy in photos), Salvatore "Sal" Pazzo (former Don, in pfb; also in photos), Johnny Delacavva (underboss, also in photo, also in pfb), Freddo's soldiers inc Tony Ditello (all 1st), Sal's bodyguard (in pfb), mobster (dead, as hand); Roman (1st bts, warring against Pazzos) & his men (bts attacking wedding)

OTHER CHARACTERS: Joseph "Joe Bats" Cavellia (Pazzo family capo) & his men (prev 2 bts, killed at wedding, also dead in photo); Bats' niece & her husband (prev 2 mentioned, wedding attacked), Freddo's mother (mentioned in pfb, Sal promised her he'd make something of Freddo), Tony's victim (mentioned, killed); Al Capone & his men, John Dillinger & his gang, Dutch Schultz & his bodyguard, Benjamin "Bugsy" Siegel (prev 7 in photos); Jim Malone, Eliot Ness, George Stone, Oscar Wallace (prev 4 characters in movie still), Michael Corleone, Frank Pentangeli (prev 2 characters in movie); Freddo's dog (in portrait), snake (on tattoo)

LOCATIONS/ITEMS: Pazzo home (also in photo & pfb) w/Freddo's office; Brooklyn's Bay Ridge reception hall, New York streets, Las Vegas' Flamingo Hotel & Casino, Freddo's childhood home (prev 4 in photos), restaurant (in movie still), Corleone's study (in movie) / Bats' gun, Dillinger's car & machine gun, Schultz's car, bodyguard's gun, Freddo's guns, toy pistols & cowboy costume (all in photos), Johnny's Daily Bugle (destroyed), Sal's IV, breathing tube & vital sign monitor (prev 3 in pfb), photos, pipe (in portrait), TV, notepad, ring, laptop, Daily Bugle & DVD player w/remote control, Wolverine's box w/mobster's hand, soldiers' guns (destroyed)

FLASHBACK: The dying Don Sal Pazzo names his callow son Freddo the new Godfather, hoping responsibility will mature him, and makes Johnny promise to support Freddo (p).

SYNOPSIS: Pazzo underboss Johnny Delacavva worries about rival Mafioso the Roman, successfully waging a mob war against his family. Tony Ditello urges Johnny to simply kill Freddo, their spoiled and selfish Godfather, and take over — but despite his unhappiness with Freddo's recent decisions, including kidnapping the Westchester bar owner's daughter, Johnny believes in the Mafia code of honor and loyalty. As Freddo and Johnny discuss the Chez Bippy's massacre, Tony interrupts to say that someone has arrived with proof of the killer's identity. Wolverine enters, bearing a box containing one of the dead mobsters' hands. He reveals that he is the killer and destroys Freddo's soldiers' guns with a quick swipe of his claws.

olverine demands that Freddo waive the bar owner's debt; in exchange, he volunteers his own services, offering to wipe out the Roman and his ldiers. Johnny has misgivings, but Freddo quickly agrees.

)TE: Despite the Pazzo family members' varying motivations and morals in this arc, they are all mobsters and killers, and are thus all listed as lains. Freddo and Sal's last names are confirmed as Pazzo next issue, which also reveals Johnny and Tony's last names and Freddo's title of dfather. Sal's full first name is revealed in W #185, '03. Freddo watches *The Godfather, Part II* here.

WOLVERINE #183 (January 2003)

"…And Got Yourself a Gun" (21 pages)

CREDITS: Frank Tieri (writer), Sean Chen (pencils), Tom Palmer (inks), Richard Starkings & Comicraft's Saida Temofonte (letters), Avalon Studios' Edgar Tadeo (colors), Warren Simons & John Miesegaes (asst editors), Axel Alonso (editor), Esad Ribic (c art)
FEATURE CHARACTER: Wolverine
GUEST STAR: Punisher (Frank Castle, criminal-killing vigilante, between Pun #26-27, '03)
VILLAINS: Kingpin (last in DD #30, '02, next in DD #42, '03) & his henchman, Sweeper (freelance assassin, 1st), Pazzo family: Freddo Pazzo (also in photo), Johnny Delacavva, soldiers (some or others also on recap page) inc Tony Ditello; Roman (rival mobster, 1st on-panel app), Vincente (Roman's aide), Bruno (Roman's soldier, dies off-panel), Roman's crew (all but 1 die) inc Tony (dies), Roman's other crews (bts, killed by Wolverine), diamond smugglers (die off-panel, also bts in bucket as ashes)
HER CHARACTERS: Police (1 bts in car), FBI agents, fruit stand proprietor (on monitor), hot dog stand proprietor, lions' victims (dead, as bones), standers (1 on monitor); Cleopatra (Roman's cat), lions inc Nero (another as statue); Federal witness (mentioned, will testify against Freddo), Jason ambi, Lou Gehrig (prev 2 mentioned, baseball skills compared); historical figures (as statues); eagle (as chair design); Sal Pazzo, mobster (dead, as nd), snake (bts as tattoo) (prev 3 on recap page)
)CATIONS/ITEMS: New York City inc Sons of Italy (private club), smugglers' Chinatown hideout, Kingpin's office, Pazzo home & Roman's home lion pit / Punisher's weapons (bts) & newspaper, Tony's newspaper, crew's cards & guns, club window (destroyed), police car, Johnny's binoculars car, FBI agents' car & video camera w/monitor, fruit stand w/merchandise (some also on monitor, some destroyed), Roman's costume (also on onitor), wooden sword, pit trapdoor & lion statue w/trapdoor button, hot dog stand w/merchandise, smugglers' diamonds, Sweeper's gasoline tank, h bucket, gun w/case & diamond box w/note, Freddo's Daily Bugle (destroyed) & ring, Wolverine's toothpick
NOPSIS: Wolverine massacres one of the Roman's crews, unintentionally aggravating the Punisher, who had targeted the same crew. Johnny atches from a nearby car, wondering what will happen if Wolverine ever turns on them. Nearby, the ranting Roman assaults a fruit stand, dressed tattered rags and wielding a wooden sword. The FBI agents tailing him suspect that he fakes madness to avoid prosecution; sure enough, when e Roman returns home he discards his costume and takes on a regal air. His soldier Bruno bursts in to report Wolverine's most recent attack, but e Roman admonishes him for talking business while the FBI might be listening in, and feeds Bruno to his lions. The Roman decides to hire help of own: an assassin named the Sweeper, currently killing jewel smugglers for the Kingpin. Freddo congratulates Wolverine on turning the mob war's e, and asks him for another favor: to murder a witness who will soon testify against the family. Wolverine refuses and leaves, secretly stalked by the veeper…
)TE: Beginning this month, Marvel re-introduced recap pages to most of their books, this time placed on p.1. However, as they generally have no w art, this Index will not count them as story pages. Freddo's title and Johnny Delacavva and Tony Ditello's last names are revealed on this issue's cap page, and Freddo and Sal's last names are confirmed as Pazzo. The crew that Wolverine kills here resembles the cast of HBO's *The Sopranos*; is issue's title is a reference to that show's theme song.

ID STORY: "Restraining Order" (20 pages)
REDITS: Matt Nixon (writer), Ryan Bodenheim (pencils), Mark Morales (inks), Richard Starkings & Comicraft (letters), Avalon Studios (colors), Mike aicht & Nova Ren Suma (asst editors), Mike Marts (editor)
EATURE CHARACTER: Wolverine (chr last in XXX #1, '03, chr next in W:Net #1, '02)
ILLAINS: Lady Deathstrike (last in W #175, '02, next in XX #25, '03), Nicopetti (Oyabun of Kobe) & his henchmen (prev 2 possibly die, see NOTE), ker gang
THER CHARACTERS: USA Cantina doormen & would-be patrons, Nicopetti's former enemies (dead, as trophies), golfers; women (on sign & llboard)
)CATIONS/ITEMS: Kobe, Japan inc highway, golf driving range & USA Cantina (nightclub) w/Nicopetti's office / Wolverine's motorcycle (destroyed) katanas, gang's motorcycles (destroyed) & lead pipe, Deathstrike's money & fake passport, Nicopetti's window (destroyed), handkerchief & trophy ases w/preservatives, doormen's cordons, golfers' clubs, tees & balls, Lady Deathstrike's finger talons (destroyed, see NOTE), henchmen's car & ns
YNOPSIS: Wolverine pursues a biker gang through the streets of Kobe, destroying their motorcycles and demanding to know where Lady eathstrike is hiding. Nearby, underworld leader Nicopetti thanks Deathstrike for the many assassinations she has performed for him, but refuses help in her war against Wolverine, pointing out how irrational her hatred is. Wolverine arrives just as Deathstrike throws Nicopetti out the window. eathstrike flees, and Wolverine pursues her on his motorcycle as Nicopetti orders his men to follow. Seeking revenge for her recent attack on miko and Yukio, Wolverine catches up to Deathstrike and demands to settle their ongoing conflict with a duel of honor. The two fight with swords but eathstrike soon gains the upper hand, running Wolverine through. Wolverine tells Deathstrike to kill him, but taunts her with the thought that once he dead, her life will no longer have a purpose. Enraged, Deathstrike realizes that Wolverine is right and admits defeat. Wolverine leaves as Nicopetti d his men arrive; they surround Deathstrike and attack.
OTE: This story occurs soon after the mob storyline concludes in W #185, '03. Penciler Ryan Bodenheim was the winner of Marvel's 2001 Wolverine lent competition; penciling this story was his prize. Nicopetti and his men's final fates are unrevealed, but it is likely that Deathstrike kills them all. eathstrike's finger talons seem to no longer be made of Adamantium, as Wolverine is able to sever them with a sword. This story is Wolverine's last ostumed appearance in his own title for nearly two years; he wears street clothes in this series until W #20, '04.

WOLVERINE #184 (February 2003)

"When In Rome…" (22 pages)

CREDITS: Frank Tieri (writer), Sean Chen (pencils), Tom Palmer (inks), Richard Starkings & Comicraft (letters), Aval
Studios' Edgar Tadeo (colors), Warren Simons & John Miesegaes (asst editors), Axel Alonso (editor), Esad Ribic (c a
FEATURE CHARACTER: Wolverine
VILLAINS: Sweeper (dies, also dead as ashes), Pazzo family: Freddo Pazzo (also in photo), Johnny Delacavv
soldiers inc Tony Ditello, Johnny's hitmen (die); Roman & his soldiers (prev 2 die)
OTHER CHARACTERS: Westchester bar owner (1st on-panel app, last bts in W #181, '02) & his daughter (last in
#181, '02), Clyde's staff & patrons, Federal witness (bts, located by Tony), lions' victims (dead, as bones), bystande
Cleopatra, lions (another as statue); Attila the Hun (as bust), historical figure (as statue), women (on posters); eagle (
chair design); Roman's crew (recap page only)
LOCATIONS/ITEMS: New York City inc Clyde's (diner), Rub You Longtime Massage Parlor, Plaza 5 hotel, Freddo
office & Roman's home w/lion pit / Wolverine's newspaper & note, pay phone, Sweeper's cigarettes, ash bucket & gun w/case, Roman's papi
(destroyed), bust, globe, pit trapdoor & lion statue w/trapdoor button, hitmen's car, cellphone & machine guns, Johnny's car (destroyed), cellphone, gun
ropes, Freddo's ring (bts), cellphone, laptop & Daily Bugle, Tony's cellphone, Roman's soldiers' guns & van, Freddo's soldier's gun, bar owner's handcur
SYNOPSIS: The Sweeper follows Wolverine into a diner and lights a cigarette. Wolverine confronts him, subtly threatening the assassin wh
lecturing about the dangers of cigarette smoking. His hands hidden by the table, the Sweeper assembles his gun, but Wolverine kills him and delive
his ashes to the Roman in a bucket. Johnny, increasingly nervous that Wolverine will turn on the Pazzos, arranges a hit against him. Wolverine defea
the hitmen and confronts Johnny, but the Roman's soldiers interrupt, claiming that their boss wants to see Wolverine. Elsewhere, Tony discovers whe
the FBI is hiding their witness. The Roman tries to bribe Wolverine to switch sides; when Wolverine refuses, the Roman throws Johnny into the lii
pit. Wolverine follows and stares down the lions, then grabs the Roman's foot and pulls him in. As the lions devour the Roman, Wolverine and John
call Freddo, reporting that the debt is repaid — but Freddo reveals that he has kidnapped the bar owner and his daughter, and orders Wolverine
kill the witness.

WOLVERINE #185 (March 2003)

"Sleeping With the Fishes" (21 pages)

CREDITS: Frank Tieri (writer), Sean Chen (pencils), Tom Palmer (inks), Richard Starkings & Comicraft's Jimn
Betancourt (letters), Avalon Studios' Edgar Tadeo (colors), Warren Simons & John Miesegaes (asst editors), Ax
Alonso (editor), Esad Ribic (c art)
FEATURE CHARACTER: Wolverine (also in Freddo's imagination)
VILLAINS: Pazzo family: Freddo Pazzo (dies off-panel, also in photo), Johnny Delacavva, Tony Ditello, other soldie
(bts in safehouse)
OTHER CHARACTERS: Westchester bar owner & his daughter (prev 2 bts in safehouse, also in photo), Fede
witness (also in Freddo's imagination), Federal agents (also dead in Freddo's imagination), courtroom bailiff
audience, judge (in shadow), jury (bts in jury box), Freddo's lawyers, reporters, bystanders; woman (on TV); Poli
Chief Vincent Aiello, Lucy Aiello, David "Noodles" Aaronson, Max Bercovicz, Patrick "Patsy" Goldberg, nurse, infant g
(prev 7 characters in movie); Lady Justice (as courthouse statue)
LOCATIONS/ITEMS: Hospital, brothel (both in movie), New York City inc safehouse (in photo), Plaza 5 hotel (also in Freddo's imaginatioi
courthouse & Pazzo home (also in photo) w/Freddo's office, Holland Tunnel, New Jersey highway & Pine Hollow woods / Hospital & brothel telephon
(in movie), Freddo's cellphone (bts), TV, gun, ring, Daily Bugle, DVD player (bts) w/remote control, box w/photo & daughter's pigtail & limousine w/gi
& bullets, soldiers' cellphone, knife & camera (prev 3 bts), agents' guns (some also in Freddo's imagination), hotel doors (destroyed
Freddo's imagination), daughter's Daily Bugle (in photo), Johnny's gun, flashlight & shovel, lawyers' paperwork, bailiff's gun & Bible, Tony's cellphon
gun, car, shovel & pickaxe, reporters' cameras (bts), van & microphones, courthouse cordons
SYNOPSIS: Freddo repeats his order to kill the FBI's witness, and gives Wolverine a box containing the captive girl's severed pigtail. As Wolverii
stalks out, Johnny confronts Freddo, feeling that the young Godfather has crossed the line — but remembers his promise to Freddo's father and stan
down. Freddo gloats in court the next day, but is enraged when the witness arrives. He signals Tony to order the captives' death, but Johnny stops To
outside. Later, an infuriated Freddo gets in his limo, but the driver reveals himself to be Wolverine. He locks Freddo in and drives to the New Jers
woods, where Johnny and Tony await. They tell Freddo that despite Johnny's vow of loyalty, they would never be party to killing a child. Wolveri
reveals that he doesn't know the bar owner; he simply overheard his story and decided to investigate to amuse himself. Johnny and Tony march Fred
into the woods, where they have dug a shallow hole. As Wolverine drives off, he hears gunshots ring out.
NOTE: Salvatore Pazzo's full first name is revealed here. Freddo watches Once Upon a Time in America.

WOLVERINE #186 (April 2003)

"See Ya Around, Frankie" (21 pages)

CREDITS: Frank Tieri (writer), Terry Dodson (pencils), Rachel Dodson (inks), Richard Starkings & Comicraft's Jimn
Betancourt & Wes Abbott (letters), Avalon Studios' Edgar Tadeo (colors), Warren Simons & John Miesegaes (as
editors), Axel Alonso (editor), Esad Ribic (c art)
FEATURE CHARACTER: Wolverine (next in UXM #409, XX #19, XFac #3 & 4 fb, all '02, XMU #39/2, '03, NX #12
& 133, '02, XXX #1, '03, W #183/2, '02, W:Net #1-4, '02-03, UXM #410-413, '02; XXX #2, XMU #44, UXM #417-42
XMU #45, all '03, Pun #33-37, '03-04)
GUEST STAR: Punisher (last in Pun #27, '03, next in AgentX #2, '02)
OTHER CHARACTERS: Restaurant cooks & patrons, mall staff & patrons, bystanders; fish (some or all c
off-panel); Spider-Man, others (prev 2 as action figures), models (as mannequins & on posters), bodybuilders (
magazine photos); ape, bears (prev 2 as dolls); Pazzo family: Freddo Pazzo, Johnny Delacavva, Tony Ditello (prev
recap page only)

LOCATIONS/ITEMS: Mall inc Toys R Fun (toy store), Yuki's (Japanese restaurant), Elizabeth's Mystery (lingerie store) & motorcycle store / Punisher's satchel, guns, knife, grenades, rope, baseball bat, bicycle chain, stolen motorcycle & magazines inc Guns+Ammo & Men's Body, Toys R Fun window & wall (prev 2 destroyed), toys inc ball pit (destroyed), keyboard & gorilla's hammer, Yuki's wall, spear, fish tank (prev 3 destroyed), grills, knife, shuriken & gong, motorcycle store window (destroyed), Elizabeth's Mystery mannequins & windows (prev 2 destroyed)

SYNOPSIS: When the Punisher attacks Wolverine in a mall, Wolverine hurls his foe through a toy store window, angry at the shabby treatment that he endured the last time the two met. The Punisher knocks Wolverine into the store's ball pit, tossing grenades after him; the blast blows the two through the wall into a restaurant. Explaining that he's displeased that Wolverine spared the Pazzo family, Punisher shatters an aquarium, drenching Wolverine as he retreats. Wolverine follows; Punisher ensnares his neck with rope and drags him through the mall with a motorcycle until Wolverine frees himself. Punisher calls Wolverine a mass murderer, but Wolverine reminds Punisher that they both are. Their fight spills into a lingerie shop; Punisher tries to strangle Wolverine, but Wolverine knocks him out a window and explains that wiping out the Pazzos would have changed nothing; organized crime will always exist. When the Punisher's satchel spills open, Wolverine mocks his foe for carrying men's bodybuilding magazines, then departs as the Punisher struggles to remain conscious.

NOTE: This issue is the series' response to Pun #16-17, '02, which mocked and humiliated Wolverine. This issue's title has a double meaning as a farewell to departing writer Frank Tieri.

WOLVERINE #187 (May 2003)

"Down the Road" (22 pages)

CREDITS: Daniel Way (writer), John McCrea (art), Richard Starkings & Comicraft's Jimmy Betancourt (letters), Avalon Studios (colors), Warren Simons & John Miesegaes (asst editors), Axel Alonso (editor), Esad Ribic (c art)
FEATURE CHARACTER: Wolverine
VILLAIN: Murderous hillbilly (dies, also bts in pfb)
OTHER CHARACTERS: Red Onion bartender & patrons, hillbilly's victims (2 dead, in shadow; 1 also in pfb, dies; others mentioned), truck driver (bts in truck), person (on TV); bear (dead, as head on wall), armadillo (dead), flies; James Beam (mentioned, Wolverine met him), woman (mentioned by hillbilly); Native American (as statue); pig (as car decoration); gecko (cover only)
LOCATIONS/ITEMS: Southern USA (also in pfb) inc Sunny's Grocer/Gas/Liquor, Red Onion Saloon w/bathroom & roadways w/bridge / Wolverine's motorcycle, hillbilly's truck (destroyed), tarp & moonshine, Red Onion pool table, balls & cues, tractor-trailer truck, victim's truck (in pfb), bridge sign

FLASHBACK: The hillbilly shoots a victim in the back (p).

SYNOPSIS: Wolverine smells a familiar scent in a saloon parking lot. Inside, he finds a hillbilly departing to continue his cross-country trip. Wolverine asks if he can hitch a ride with him, and the hillbilly agrees. The two set off in his truck and begin drinking moonshine and swapping stories. Wolverine asks why dead bodies are hidden in the back of the truck; the hillbilly comments that the men wronged him, but does not elaborate. When the drunken hillbilly nearly gets into an accident, Wolverine takes over driving for a while. Later, the hillbilly confesses that the men were unarmed strangers whom he shot simply for sport, and that he has been killing for years. Relieved to have finally been caught, the hillbilly decides to drive his truck off a bridge but when he cannot bring himself to do so, Wolverine offers to drive again. The hillbilly gratefully agrees, and Wolverine sends the truck plummeting to the gorge below.
NOTE: W #187-188, '03 were published biweekly.

WOLVERINE #188 (May 2003)

"Good Cop / Bad Cop, Part One" (22 pages)

CREDITS: Daniel Way (writer), Staz Johnson (pencils), Danny Miki (inks), Richard Starkings & Comicraft (letters), Avalon Studios (colors), Warren Simons & John Miesegaes (asst editors), Axel Alonso (editor), Esad Ribic (c art)
FEATURE CHARACTER: Wolverine
VILLAINS: Detective Scott McLawry (corrupt narcotics officer, 1st); street gang inc Lo-Lo
OTHER CHARACTERS: Detective Lester Brown (Internal Affairs officer, 1st), Michael Bloomberg (New York Mayor, 1st bts app ending investigation of Snow shooting, next bts in MK4 #1, '04, next in Nc #5, '05), Juwan Barnes (possible witness), Tawanda Barnes (Juwan's mother) (prev 2 die off-panel), police inc Murphy (McLawry's partner), Snow's neighbor, Bernie's Liquor clerk (bts selling Brown liquor), Brown's Internal Affairs superior, Sullivan's patrons & waitress, bystanders; Elijah "No-Show" Snow (drug dealer, mentioned, killed by McLawry)
LOCATIONS/ITEMS: New York City: Barnes' apartment building w/stairwell & Snow & Tawanda's apartments, Bernie's Liquor, police station w/superior's office, Sullivan's (bar, unnamed) / Brown's flask, badge, cellphone, car, business card, liquor bottle & gun holster, police outline chalk (bts), guns, nightsticks, computers, files & log-in sheet, neighbor's door chain, Juwan's key & groceries, Snow's drugs (mentioned), McLawry's drink

SYNOPSIS: Beaten-down detective Lester Brown drinks on duty, then unsuccessfully canvasses the neighbors of a dead drug dealer. Young Juwan Barnes spots Brown and runs; Brown pursues him but trips, knocking Juwan down a stairwell. Juwan's mother Tawanda berates Brown, ignoring his explanation that he suspects Scott McLawry, the officer who shot the dealer, of being corrupt. Juwan's superiors calls, telling him to halt his investigation; frustrated Brown drinks heavily. Later, Tawanda enters the police station, loudly accuses Brown of brutality toward her son and stalks out; Brown's boss lectures and reassigns him. McLawry's partner comments that McLawry left the station suddenly; Brown realizes that he may have surmised that Juwan witnessed the shooting. Brown races back to the Barnes' apartment but finds them missing. He asks a street gang what they witnessed, they steal his gun and beat him until Wolverine intervenes. Brown awakens later and goes to a bar; McLawry gloatingly buys him a drink. Brown threatens to expose McLawry and storms out. Wolverine finishes Brown's drink.
NOTE: Cover-labeled "Good Cop Bad Cop, Part 1 of 2." Juwan and Tawanda's deaths are confirmed next issue, which also names Sullivan's bar.

WOLVERINE #189 (June 2003)

"Good Cop / Bad Cop, Part Two" (22 pages)

CREDITS: Daniel Way (writer), Staz Johnson (pencils), Danny Miki & Crime Lab Studios (inks), Richard Starki█ & Comicraft (letters), Avalon Studios (colors), Warren Simons & John Miesegaes (asst editors), Axel Alonso (edit█ Esad Ribic (c art)
FEATURE CHARACTER: Wolverine (next in XMU #46, 46/2 & 48, '03)
VILLAIN: Detective Scott McLawry
OTHER CHARACTERS: Detective Lester Brown, Juwan Barnes (also on recap page), Tawanda Barnes (p█ 2 bts, dead, buried by McLawry), police inc Murphy, Brown's Internal Affairs superiors, Tawanda's co-worker (█ reported her missing), Brown's neighbor (bts, buzzed Brown in), bartender (bts serving Murphy), bar patron█ waitress, bystanders (bts in cars); Elijah "No-Show" Snow (mentioned); angel (as statue, cover only)
LOCATIONS/ITEMS: Police station w/superior's office, Tawanda's workplace & apartment (prev 2 mentioned), ba█ w/bathroom & nearby alley, Lincoln Tunnel, New Jersey woods (also on map) & highway / Brown's bandage & gun, police guns (all but 1 bts)█ computers, McLawry's car, shovel & gun, Wolverine's ropes, drink & envelope w/map
SYNOPSIS: Brown's superiors question him about the Barnes' disappearance, suspicious that Tawanda accused him of police brutality, th█ vanished. Brown explains his suspicions that Juwan witnessed McLawry murder Snow, and that when McLawry heard that Juwan had met Bro█ he realized that Juwan might implicate him, so he killed both Barnes. The superiors, believing McLawry's claim that he shot Snow because the dea█ was reaching for a weapon, suspend Brown. McLawry celebrates being cleared at a bar, but Wolverine confronts him, implying that he has proof t█ McLawry deliberately murdered Snow and the Barnes. McLawry knocks Wolverine out and stuffs him into his car trunk, then drives out to the woo█ He admits killing Juwan and Tawanda and burying them nearby, rants about protecting the city at any cost, and shoots Wolverine in the head. A█ McLawry drives off, Wolverine revives. Later, at a bar, Brown receives an envelope containing his gun and a map to the Barnes' bodies. As he rac█ out to prove McLawry guilty, Wolverine finishes Brown's drink.
NOTE: Cover-labeled "Good Cop Bad Cop, Part 2 of 2." Sullivan's, the bar where Brown confronted McLawry last issue, is named here. This is █ final issue of this volume of Wolverine; the series is immediately relaunched with a new #1.

WOLVERINE #1 [#190] (June 2003)

(Untitled, 22 pages)

CREDITS: Greg Rucka (writer), Darick Robertson (art), Chris Eliopoulos (letters), Studio F (colors), Warren Simo█ & John Miesegaes (asst editors), Axel Alonso (editor), Esad Ribic (c art)
FEATURE CHARACTER: Wolverine (also as "Mean Man")
VILLAINS: Cry (1st bts app sending Brothers against Lucy, next in 1st on-panel app in W #4, '03), Brothers of █ New World (doomsday cult, 1st, unnamed, some or others next in W #3, '03, these next in W #5, '03), Wolverin█ assailant (bts stabbing Wolverine)
OTHER CHARACTERS: Lucy Braddock (Doggie Diner waitress, dies), Louise (Lucy's co-worker), Doggie Di█ cook (bts cooking food) & patrons, police, coroner, bystanders; man (on poster); dog (as diner statue & logo)
LOCATIONS/ITEMS: Portland, Oregon: Doggie Diner, apartment building w/Wolverine & Lucy's apartment█ Wolverine's books (1 destroyed) & tip, Lucy's journal, coffee pot, door chain, X-acto knife & bookshelf w/books, patro█ money, assailant's knife, Brothers' machine guns, apartment doors (destroyed), police tape (destroyed) & guns, coroner's van
SYNOPSIS: Lucy Braddock works in a Portland diner, where every morning Wolverine quietly reads a different book. Lonely, Lucy nicknames t█ stoic Wolverine "Mean Man," but when he leaves an enormous tip, she suspects that he cares about her. That night, Lucy writes in her journal, worri█ about "brothers" who will soon come for her. Hearing noise in the hallway, she sees a stabbed Wolverine stagger to his apartment, across from he█ The next day, Lucy sees Wolverine in the diner without a scratch, and knows that he can protect her. When Wolverine leaves a book behind, Lu█ ventures into his apartment to return it. The two talk briefly; Lucy senses Wolverine's noble spirit and hints that she is in danger. She borrows a boo█ cuts the pages out and hides her journal inside. That night, two men enter the building, shoot through her and Wolverine's doors with machine gu█ and flee. Wolverine finds Lucy dead, discovers her journal and its plea for his help, and decides to avenge her.
NOTE: The bracketed secondary issue number above is retroactive, stemming from the series' return to the previous volume's numbering w█ W #300, '12. Neither this volume nor subsequent ones actually feature dual numbering on the covers. W #3, '03 reveals that this issue occ█ in Portland, although why Wolverine has rented a Portland apartment is never revealed. Lucy calls the shooters her "brothers" here; next iss█ reveals that she was referring to their group's name, which is fully revealed in W #3, '03. Though the shooters are definitively next seen in W #█ '03, they may be present among the Brothers seen in W #3-4, '03. Lucy wears a shirt with a three-eyed smiley face, a reference to the DC/Verti█ series Transmetropolitan, also illustrated by artist Darick Robertson. Wolverine reads *Smoker, Walden, Cat's Cradle, Fight Club, Catcher in the R█ Confederacy of Dunces, Complete Stories and Poems of Edgar Allan Poe, Catch-22* and *Manufacturing Consent.*

WOLVERINE #2 [#191] (August 2003)

(Untitled, 21 pages)

CREDITS: Greg Rucka (writer), Darick Robertson (pencils), Tom Palmer (inks), Chris Eliopoulos (letters), Studi█ (colors), Warren Simons & John Miesegaes (asst editors), Axel Alonso (editor), Esad Ribic (c art)
FEATURE CHARACTER: Wolverine (also in photo)
VILLAIN: Thomas Leeds (Leeds Arms owner, 1st)
OTHER CHARACTERS: Sycamore Blaine (My Cold Dead Hand owner, 1st, also in photo, next in W #7, '0█ Cassandra "Cassie" Lathrop (ATF agent, 1st, undercover as Leeds' assistant) & her ATF contact (bts on walkie-talki█ Blaine's customer, gun show vendors & attendees, Suds bartender & patrons, bystanders; deer (dead, as stuff█ heads, next in W #7, '04); Dennis Terril (mentioned, bought guns for Brothers), Brothers of Christ, Brothers of Freedo█ Brothers of Revolution, Brothers of White Pride (prev 4 mentioned by Blaine), shooters, victim, commentators (prev█

ntioned by customer); model, girl (prev 2 on posters), soldiers, dogs (prev 2 in photos & on poster), eagles (on jacket, poster & shirt), cat (on shirt)
)CATIONS/ITEMS: Portland: Wolverine's apartment, My Cold Dead Hand (Blaine's gun shop) w/back room; Klamath County, Oregon: Suds (bar), ibit hall, Smitty's Motel w/Cassie & Leeds' rooms; Laos (in photo); Leeds Arms (mentioned) / Wolverine's bullet, books & motorcycle, Lucy's journal, ns (on posters), Blaine's photo, Wolverine & Blaine's machine guns, soldiers' helicopter (prev 2 in photos), Cassie's rucksack, gun, cellphone, letproof vest & walkie-talkie, vendors' booths & guns, attendees' driver's licenses, Leeds' guns (1 destroyed), keycard & business card, McNally's lkie-talkie (bts), M-16s w/ammunition, Brothers' machine guns & conversion kits (prev 4 mentioned)
✓NOPSIS: Wolverine cuts a bullet out of his body, and visits his old army buddy Blaine's nearby gun shop. He asks about groups called "Brothers"; ine examines the bullet and reminds Wolverine that there are scores of militias and survivalist groups in the area. Determining that the group's apons are modified Mac-10s, Wolverine tries to track the guns back to the Brothers; Blaine suspects that shady gun dealer Tom Leeds may have ld the weapons. Wolverine attends a local gun show, buying a handgun from Tom and his assistant Cassie Lathrop. He hints that he wants to rchase illegal weapons and modification kits; Tom suggests they meet later. That night, the two negotiate for M-16s; Wolverine subtly asks about ac-10s, but Tom mentions that he sold his entire supply recently. Later, Wolverine ambushes Leeds in his motel room, demanding to know who ught the Mac-10s. After extracting the name Dennis Terril, Wolverine rides off. Cassie watches him, reporting to her unseen superiors that they may ve a problem.
)TE: Although last issue's cover was not labeled, this issue is cover-labeled "Brotherhood, Part II." However, W #4, '03's recap page names this story : "The Brothers." Thomas Leeds' full first name is confirmed next issue, and Cassie's in W #4, '03. Chris McNally's first name is revealed next issue, d his last name in W #8, '04. Blaine's first name is revealed in W #7, '04, which also clarifies that Wolverine and Blaine are two of the soldiers in the 71 Laos photo seen here. Lathrop's undercover status is revealed next issue. This issue partially reveals the Brothers' group name. Wolverine drinks ein brand beer here, a reference to Wolverine creator Len Wein. The motel has a Poti cola vending machine, another Transmetropolitan reference.

WOLVERINE #3 [#192] (September 2003)

(Untitled, 22 pages)

CREDITS: Greg Rucka (writer), Darick Robertson (pencils), Tom Palmer (inks), Chris Eliopoulos (letters), Studio F (colors), Warren Simons & John Miesegaes (asst editors), Axel Alonso (editor), Esad Ribic (c art)
FEATURE CHARACTER: Wolverine
VILLAINS: Brothers of the New World (group named; some or others mentioned, took Joe's eye; some or others last in W #1, '03), Dennis Terril (corrupt Westfall sheriff, 1st), Thomas Leeds (also on monitor)
OTHER CHARACTERS: Joe Braddock (Lucy's father, 1st, also in photo) & his friends inc Jeremiah "Jerry" Lowe (unnamed), ATF agents inc Cassie Lathrop (also bts on monitor), Chris McNally (Cassie's ATF superior) & Rucka, reporter, RR Café waitress & patrons, guard, bystanders; dog, birds; Cry (named, mentioned, bought desert property), Topeka resident (mentioned, dead, Wolverine's motorcycle registered in his name), Lucy's classmates (mentioned, arrested for drinking), Oregon State Police (mentioned, never contacted by Terril); Lucy Braddock, fish (dead) (prev 2 photo); bear (as Leeds' doll)
)CATIONS/ITEMS: Medford, Oregon inc police station interrogation room (also on monitor) & Leeds Arms (Leeds' gun shop) w/bedroom; estfall, Oregon inc jail (mentioned), RR Café & Joe's home; lake (in photo), Brothers' Oregon desert land (mentioned) / ATF computers (bts), vans, rs, guns, handcuffs & bulletproof vests, Leeds' guns (bts) & teddy bear, Cassie's report (bts), gun, car, map & Jeep w/radio, reporter's microphone, olverine's motorcycle & loganberry pie (see NOTE), pay phone w/phone book, Lucy's fishing pole (in photo) & journal, interrogation room camera s) & monitor, guard's gun, Chris' radio (bts), Joe's phone, Brothers' truck & machine guns, Terril's patrol car w/loudspeaker
✓NOPSIS: ATF agents arrest Leeds for weapons trafficking; Cassie reveals that she is an undercover agent and worries about the short man who nted M-16s. Wolverine arrives in Westfall and orders pie at a diner, but when he drops Dennis Terril's name, a one-eyed man named Joe confronts n. When Wolverine mentions Lucy Braddock, Joe and his friends attack; Wolverine subdues them and learns that Joe is Lucy's father. Cassie ughly "interrogates" Leeds until he reveals that Wolverine wanted Terril's name; she heads for Westfall to learn why. Later, Joe explains to Wolverine at the Brothers of the New World recently settled nearby; their leader, Cry, has an unsavory taste for younger women. A year ago, Sheriff Dennis ril called Joe, claiming to have arrested and released Lucy, but Lucy never came home. When Joe tried to find his daughter, the Brothers gouged t his eye. Wolverine explains Lucy's fate; Joe is saddened, but relieved that she eventually escaped Cry. Suddenly, Terril and the Brothers arrive and gin firing into Joe's house…
)TE: Cover-labeled "Brotherhood, Part III." Thomas Leeds' full first name is confirmed here. Jerry Lowe's name is revealed next issue; Chris Nally's last name is revealed in W #8, '04. ATF agent Rucka is named for writer Greg Rucka. Wolverine is interrupted while eating a piece of pie re; Rucka intended to introduce a running gag where Wolverine can never finish a slice of pie in peace, but the joke only occurred once more, in W 3, '04. Another Poti cola vending machine is seen here.

WOLVERINE #4 [#193] (October 2003)

"The Brothers, Part IV" (22 pages)

CREDITS: Greg Rucka (writer), Darick Robertson (pencils), Tom Palmer (inks), Chris Eliopoulos (letters), Studio F (colors), Warren Simons & John Miesegaes (asst editors), Axel Alonso (editor), Esad Ribic (c art)
FEATURE CHARACTER: Wolverine
VILLAINS: Cry (Brothers' leader, 1st on-panel app, last bts in W #1, '03), Sheriff Dennis Terril (dies), Brothers of the New World
OTHER CHARACTERS: Agent Cassie Lathrop, Joe Braddock, Cry's captive "wives" inc Kim & Lynn, bystanders; Healey (mentioned, Joe's friend); Lucy Braddock (in photo), criminals (on wanted posters)
LOCATIONS/ITEMS: Westfall inc Lowe & Healey's homes (mentioned), riverbed, Terril's office & Joe's house, Brothers' compound (abandoned Oregon desert mine) w/wives' cell, lake (in photo), Rte. 84 (mentioned) / Cassie's Jeep, badge & gun, Brothers' trucks (others mentioned) & machine guns, Terril's gun, mace, lamp & patrol car, Joe's or, windows & photo (prev 3 destroyed), Kim's washcloth, compound gate
✓NOPSIS: When Cassie asks about Terril in Westfall, the locals turn cold, but reveal that he is the sheriff. Terril and the Brothers cease fire and estigate Joe's house, but Wolverine and Joe have escaped into the woods. Wolverine tells Joe to go to Blaine's gun shop for safety, then turns back. issie sees men enter Terril's empty office; when she investigates, one of them introduces himself as Cry. He suddenly blinds Cassie with a lamp and

maces her; his followers beat her unconscious. Terril orders the Brothers to find Wolverine, then drives off — but Wolverine, hidden in the back se
ambushes Terril and painfully extracts the location of Cry's compound. When Terril insults Lucy, an enraged Wolverine kills him. Investigating Ter
office, Wolverine notices Cassie's scent and wonders why she is involved. At the compound, the Brothers throw Cassie into a cell with several ot
captive women. Most have been deeply conditioned to love their captors, but one, Kim, still rebels. Outside, Wolverine arrives and plans his attack
NOTE: Although this issue is cover-labeled "Brotherhood, Part IV," the recap page names the story arc "the Brothers." Jeremiah Lowe is named he
and Cassie's full first name is confirmed. The Brothers call one of Cry's captives "sister"; they might be called the Sisters of the New World. Lucy's nan
is scratched into the cell wall along with the typical hash marks that prisoners use to count days. Marvel restructures their internal rating system t
month; the Wolverine series goes from PG to PSR: "Parental Supervision Recommended."

WOLVERINE #5 [#194] (November 2003)

"The Brothers, Part V" (22 pages)

CREDITS: Greg Rucka (writer), Darick Robertson (art), Chris Eliopoulos (letters), Studio F (colors), Warren Sime
& John Miesegaes (asst editors), Axel Alonso (editor), Esad Ribic (c art)
FEATURE CHARACTER: Wolverine
VILLAINS: Cry (dies), Brothers of the New World (most die; some last in W #1, '03, die) inc Carl & Len
OTHER CHARACTERS: ATF agents inc Cassie Lathrop, Cry's captive "wives" inc Kim & Lynn, Leonard Bradfc
(contestant), Phil & his partner (prev 2 announcers) (prev 3 voice only, on TV, see NOTE), singers (on TV, see NOT
birds, flies; Will (Leonard's son, mentioned on TV); performers, models, eagle, horse (prev 4 on posters)
LOCATIONS/ITEMS: Brothers' compound w/kitchen (mentioned), main room, storage room, wives' cell & Cr
bedroom, show venue (on TV, see NOTE) / Brothers' truck, TV, machine guns, boxes w/wives' belongings, food cart
milk & pool table w/balls & cue, compound generator (bts), windows (prev 2 destroyed) & gate, wives' lipstick & mir
(destroyed) w/glass shard, Cassie's sock, ATF helicopter & cars, singer's microphone (on TV, see NOTE)
SYNOPSIS: As Wolverine gauges the compound's forces, Cassie shatters a captive's mirror, making a crude knife from the glass. At suns
Wolverine leaps over the compound wall and sneaks inside. He grabs a guard, ordering the Brother to lead him to the generator, but when they pa
a storeroom, Wolverine catches Lucy's scent and investigates. Finding boxes full of clothes, Wolverine realizes that the Brothers have kidnapped a
abused many other young women. Guards surround Wolverine, but he becomes enraged and attacks viciously. When a Brother delivers the captiv
dinner, Cassie ambushes and stabs him, then grabs his gun and flees. Kim helps her navigate the compound, but the lights suddenly go out; Wolveri
has destroyed the generator and is rampaging through the compound, killing the Brothers. Smelling the two Brothers that shot Lucy, Wolverine k
them, then tracks down and corners Cry. Cassie hears screams; she arrives to see Wolverine standing over Cry's body, but he quickly departs. Lat
as ATF agents arrive, Cassie resolves to track down Wolverine.
NOTE: Cover-labeled "Brotherhood, Part V," although the recap page still gives the conflicting title "the Brothers" for this arc. The audio from a TV
the Brothers' compound indicates that a game show is playing, but the screen shows a band in concert. Although the recap page states that Cry h
six captive wives, at least seven are seen on-panel.

WOLVERINE #6 [#195] (December 2003)

"So, This Priest Walks Into a Bar" (22 pages)

CREDITS: Greg Rucka (writer), Darick Robertson (pencils), Tom Palmer (inks), Virtual Calligraphy's Rus Woo
(letters), Studio F (colors), Warren Simons (editor, see NOTE), Axel Alonso (supervising editor, see NOTE), Es
Ribic (c art)
FEATURE CHARACTER: Wolverine (also as sketches (all but 1 bts), on poster & in Cassie's dream, next in SM
#4 fb, 1 fb, 2 fb, 3 fb, 2 fb, 3 fb, 4 fb & 1-4, XX #20-22, all '03, W/Cap #1-4, '04, DD #53-55, '03-04; W/Doop #1-2, XS
#11, UXM #423, all '03, X23 #6, '07 fb; Exiles #28-30, W:Xisle #1, 5 fb, 1 fb & 1-5, XMU #50, W:Snikt #1 fb, 2-4,
4-5, NX #135 & 137-138, all '03, UXM #429-434, '03-04, NX #138-139, '03, X23 #6, '07 fb; NX #140, XX #25-30, N
#5, H/W:6 #1-4, all '03, UXM #438-441, '04, NX #142-146 & 148-150, '03-04; WX #18 fb, UXM #442-443, NX #1
WX #15, SecWar #2 fb, all '04, SecWar:FNF, '05 bts, SecWar #3 fb & 5 fb, '04-05, WX #16-18, '04)
GUEST STAR: Nightcrawler (also as priest, between UXM #422-423, '03)
OTHER CHARACTERS: ATF agents inc Cassie Lathrop (also in her own dream), Jo (mutant Box bartender, 1st, next in W #19, '04), Brady (muti
Box employee), Box's mutant patrons inc Mike, sketch artist; X-Men: Beast, Bishop, Psylocke, Rogue, Sage, Storm, Thunderbird; Deadpool, oth
(prev 9 on posters), criminal (on wanted poster)
LOCATIONS/ITEMS: Portland: Cassie's house (also in dream), ATF office; the Box (mutant-centric bar, New York City) / Artist's pencil, satche
sketch pad, agents' computers & cellphone, Nightcrawler's image inducer (bts), Wolverine's motorcycle & money, Lucy's symbolic drink, Cassie's g
(in dream) & Jeep
SYNOPSIS: Cassie works with a sketch artist to create a picture of Wolverine, but rejects each sketch, complaining that they don't reflect
personality. Nightcrawler, disguised as a priest, meets a dejected Wolverine at a New York bar. Wolverine snaps at Nightcrawler for his disgui
pointing out that the bar's employees and clientele are all mutants. Wolverine pours three glasses of beer; he and Nightcrawler drink two, and c
glass stands alone. Nightcrawler toasts Colossus' memory and tries to make small talk, but Wolverine is surly and unpleasant. Meanwhile, Cas
has a sensual and disturbing dream about Wolverine. Nightcrawler eventually asks Wolverine who he failed to save, and Wolverine explains Luc
fate, confessing that he killed twenty-seven evil men. Nightcrawler points out that evil begets evil, but when Wolverine wonders if he is evil hims
Nightcrawler reminds him that wolves cull sick animals from herds. As the bar closes and the two mean leave, Wolverine stands in the rain, tryin
convince himself that he is not an animal.
NOTE: Wolverine drinks Wein beer again here. The colorist has given Nightcrawler barely visible facial tattoos on p.6, a possible reference to
look in the 2003 X-Men feature film X2. They were removed when this issue was reprinted in the "Wolverine: the Brotherhood" TPB, '04. Nightcraw
mentions seeing Shadowcat recently, a reference to XMU #38, '02, also by writer Greg Rucka and penciler Darick Robertson. The posters on the B
walls are heavily blurred covers and pages from various Marvel comics, including the cover of W Ann '99 and the variant cover of XX #2, '01. Edit
Warren Simons and Axel Alonso's new titles are first given in W #12, '04.

WOLVERINE #7 [#196] (January 2004)

"Coyote Crossing, Part One" (21 pages)

CREDITS: Greg Rucka (writer), Leandro Fernández (art), Virtual Calligraphy's Rus Wooton (letters), Studio F (colors), Warren Simons (editor), Axel Alonso (supervising editor)
FEATURE CHARACTER: Wolverine (also as sketch & in photo)
VILLAINS: Angelica Rojas (1st bts app smuggling heroin inside immigrants, next in 1st on-panel app in W #9, '04), Ian Ritter (1st bts app smuggling immigrants into Texas), Merrick (dies), Lake (also on TV) (prev 2 Ritter's employees)
OTHER CHARACTERS: Sycamore Blaine (also in photo, last in W #2, '03), Néstor Garcia (Cerveza Fria owner), Ángel (bartender, next in W #9, '04) (prev 2 1st), Agent Cassie Lathrop, Marcia Zandi (reporter), police, Border Patrol agents (prev 3 on TV, 1 or another bts on phone), service station employee, illegal immigrants (prev 2 dead), pizza restaurant employee (bts on phone), cameraman (bts taping Zandi), Cerveza Fria patrons, bystanders; deer (dead, as stuffed heads, last in W #2, '03), cow (dead, as skull), vultures, flies; Oscar (Néstor's son, mentioned, found by Wolverine); model (on poster), soldiers (on poster & in photos), men (in photos), snake (on poster), scorpion (as tattoo)
LOCATIONS/ITEMS: El Paso, Texas: Border Patrol headquarters (on TV), Cerveza Fria (Néstor's bar) w/Néstor's office; Texas service station w/ garage & nearby land, My Cold Dead Hand w/back room, Cassie's house, Portland pizza restaurant (bts), Laos (in photo) / Wolverine's motorcycle, Merrick's gun & tractor-trailer truck w/chain & padlock, attendant's truck w/keys (bts), garage window (destroyed), Cassie's Jeep, badge, sketch & cordless phone, Blaine's guns (1 bts), newspaper, medals, photos & coffee pot, Wolverine & Blaine's machine guns (in photo), immigrants' heroin-filled balloons (bts, see NOTE), pay phone, Néstor's paperwork, Border Patrol's handcuffs (bts) & nightsticks, Zandi's microphone (prev 3 on TV)
SYNOPSIS: Wolverine arrives at a Texas service station; finding it abandoned, he investigates and finds two criminals, Merrick and Lake, and a dead employee. Wolverine kills Merrick and forces Lake to explain their actions; Lake shamefacedly leads Wolverine to a tractor-trailer truck full of dead illegal immigrants, explaining that they suffocated while he and Merrick smuggled them into Texas. Wolverine forces Lake to reveal his boss' name, then locks him in the trailer. In Portland, Cassie tracks down Blaine and asks him about Wolverine, reassuring him that she's searching for Wolverine for personal reasons, not legal ones. Blaine eventually reveals Wolverine's real name, but refuses to help Cassie find him. In El Paso, Wolverine reports the truck to the authorities, then visits his old friend Néstor Garcia at his bar, asking him to help track down the human traffickers. In Portland, Cassie has just given up her search for Wolverine when she sees a news report about the truckful of immigrants, and hears Lake shouting about a man with claws…
NOTE: Cover-labeled "Coyote Crossing, Part 1." W #7-8, '04 were published biweekly. The series' rating rises from PSR to PSR+ here. Ritter's first name is revealed next issue, and Rojas' in W #11, '04. W #10, '04 reveals that the immigrants were smuggling heroin for Rojas.

WOLVERINE #8 [#197] (January 2004)

"Coyote Crossing, Part Two" (22 pages)

CREDITS: Greg Rucka (writer), Leandro Fernández (art), Virtual Calligraphy's Rus Wooton (letters), Studio F (colors), Warren Simons (editor), Axel Alonso (supervising editor)
FEATURE CHARACTER: Wolverine (also as sketch)
VILLAINS: Ian Ritter (human trafficker, dies), Mendes (Rojas' employee), Lake
OTHER CHARACTERS: Agent Cassie Lathrop, Néstor Garcia, Border Patrol agents inc Len & Special Agent Aguinaga, food truck employee, firemen (bts, called to Ritter's), bystanders; birds; dog; father & daughter (prev 2 characters on TV); Kelly Dean (El Paso ATF head, mentioned), Chris McNally (mentioned, met Aguinaga), Angelica Rojas (mentioned, targets desperate immigrants), immigrants (mentioned, hired by Rojas), would-be immigrants (mentioned, caught by Border Patrol); Jesus Christ (in painting)
LOCATIONS/ITEMS: El Paso inc Paisano Drive (mentioned), Cerveza Fria, Border Patrol headquarters w/ interrogation room & Ritter's garage (destroyed) w/office; Rio Grande (Ciudad Juárez, Chihuahua, Mexico) / Aguinaga's notepad & binoculars, border patrol vehicles, food truck, would-be immigrants' gas cans (mentioned), Cassie's badge, sketch & gun, Wolverine's motorcycle, Mendes' truck (destroyed), tools, gun, matches & gas cans, Ritter's TV (destroyed), paperwork & fax machine, fire truck (bts)
SYNOPSIS: Cassie observes as Border Patrol agent Aguinaga questions Lake, getting him to name Ian Ritter as the smuggling operation's US head. As the Border Patrol agents procure a warrant, Cassie shows Aguinaga a sketch of Wolverine, suggesting that he is the clawed man that Lake mentioned. Meanwhile, Wolverine arrives at Ritter's garage and beats him viciously, ordering him to divulge the name of his Mexican counterpart. Ritter's employee Mendes suddenly enters and shoots both combatants, then pours gasoline throughout the garage and lights it on fire. Wolverine tackles Mendes as Border Patrol agents arrive. Cassie sees Wolverine's motorcycle and leaps into the spreading fire to find him, but Wolverine is soon forced to rescue her. He relates Mendes' confession that he secretly worked for Ritter's counterpart, Rojas, and tells Cassie to stop following him. Later, Néstor tells Wolverine about Rojas' drug smuggling operation, and Wolverine decides to pay the crimelord a visit. As Cassie watches through binoculars, Wolverine climbs over the border fence and swims across the Rio Grande into Mexico.
NOTE: Cover-labeled "Coyote Crossing, Part 2." Chris McNally's last name and Ian Ritter's first name are revealed here.

WOLVERINE #9 [#198] (February 2004)

"Coyote Crossing, Part Three" (21 pages)

CREDITS: Greg Rucka (writer), Leandro Fernández (art), Virtual Calligraphy's Rus Wooton (letters), Studio F (colors), Warren Simons (editor), Axel Alonso (supervising editor)
FEATURE CHARACTER: Wolverine (also bts on monitors)
VILLAINS: Angelica Rojas (drug trafficker, 1st on-panel app, last bts in W #7, '04), Hector (dies, also bts on monitors), Ruben, Sandro (prev 3 Rojas' recruiters), Rojas' guards (some or all die) inc Felix, heroin den doorman
OTHER CHARACTERS: Cassie Lathrop, Special Agent Aguinaga, Néstor Garcia, Ángel (last in W #7, '04), Angelica Murillo (Rojas' unborn daughter, 1st bts app, unidentified, see NOTE), heroin addicts, Cerveza Fria patrons, bystander; goat; Ismael Araoz, Pedro de Mendoza, Juan Carlos Moxica, Peter Roberts, others (prev 5 names on Cassie's suspect list); Biblical figures (in painting), men (in photos), spirits (as figurines)

LOCATIONS/ITEMS: Ciudad Juárez inc Rio Grande, heroin den & Rojas' estate w/guard post, Border Patrol's El Paso headquarters, Cerveza Fr w/Néstor's office / Bystander's satchel & laundry, recruiters' cards, heroin den door (destroyed), doorman's knife, addicts' needles, spoon, tie, lighter knife, Border Patrol's files, Aguinaga's cellphone, Cassie's notepad, men's guns (in photos), Ruben's pistol & cellphone, Felix's cordless phone, guard cameras (bts), monitors, guns & spotlights, Hector's truck (destroyed)
SYNOPSIS: Wolverine's arrival in Mexico catches the attention of three small-time criminals. Wolverine enters a heroin den and assaults the doorma he tries to interrogate the addicts about Rojas' whereabouts, but they are too high to respond. Wolverine notices one of the criminals following hi and questions the man, learning that the three recruit drug mules for Rojas. In El Paso, Cassie pores through Border Patrol files and deduces th Néstor knows Wolverine; she travels to his bar, but Néstor asks why she is so determined to find Wolverine, telling her that she's not the first woma to become entranced by his odd machismo. In Mexico, the criminals shoot Wolverine, but he subdues all three and forces one to drive him to Roja estate. Another calls ahead and warns Rojas' guards; when the criminal's truck arrives, they spray it with bullets. Wolverine survives and battles his wa through Rojas' guards and to the estate's front door — where he discovers that Rojas the crimelord is a heavily pregnant woman.
NOTE: Cover-labeled "Coyote Crossing, Part 3." Rojas' daughter is born next issue and given a first name in W #11, '04; her last name is neve specified, but to differentiate her from her mother, this Index presumes that the infant was given her adoptive parents' last name.

WOLVERINE #10 [#199] (March 2004)

"Coyote Crossing, Part Four" (21 pages)

CREDITS: Greg Rucka (writer), Leandro Fernández (art), Virtual Calligraphy's Rus Wooton (letters), Studio F (colors Warren Simons (editor), Axel Alonso (supervising editor)
FEATURE CHARACTER: Wolverine (also in W #11, '04 fb)
VILLAIN: Angelica Rojas
OTHER CHARACTERS: Angelica Murillo (1st on-panel app, also in W #11, '04 fb), Agent Cassie Lathrop, Néstc Garcia, Cerveza Fria patrons & bartenders inc Ángel, Rey (Rojas' aide, bts, fled from Wolverine), Rojas' guards (dead Border Patrol (mentioned, thought Rojas was male); Biblical figures (in painting), fertility goddess (as statue), men (i photos)
LOCATIONS/ITEMS: Cerveza Fria w/bedroom & Néstor's office, Rojas' estate / Cassie & Néstor's drinks, men guns (in photos), Rojas' statue (destroyed), telephone & drugs (mentioned) inc heroin, Wolverine's blanket
SYNOPSIS: Ángel closes the bar for the night, but Cassie refuses to leave. Néstor reminds her that Wolverine is not here; Cassie points out that h will return eventually, and the two toast Wolverine. In Mexico, Rojas freely admits her crimes, stating that life is cheap in the shantytowns surroundin her estate. She challenges Wolverine to kill her, but he cannot bring himself to harm her unborn baby. Rojas taunts Wolverine, suggesting that he is onl using the dead immigrants as a justification to fuel his love of murder. Wolverine snaps and attacks Rojas, but misses her at the last instant. Verging o a berserker rage, Wolverine struggles to regain control of himself; he eventually sheathes his claws and departs, but Rojas suddenly goes into labc Wolverine returns to Néstor's bar, tells Cassie about Rojas and grudgingly lets her sleep on the couch. The next day, Cassie finds Wolverine gone. Sh fears that he has reconsidered and left to kill Rojas, but Wolverine suddenly returns — holding a newborn baby.
NOTE: Cover-labeled "Coyote Crossing, Part 4." This issue reveals that W #7, '04's dead immigrants were smuggling heroin for Rojas.

WOLVERINE #11 [#200] (April 2004)

"Coyote Crossing, Part Five" (21 pages)

CREDITS: Greg Rucka (writer), Leandro Fernández (art), Virtual Calligraphy's Rus Wooton (letters), Studio F (colors Warren Simons (editor), Axel Alonso (supervising editor)
FEATURE CHARACTER: Wolverine (also in fb during W #10, '04)
VILLAIN: Angelica Rojas (in fb, dies; also in photo)
OTHER CHARACTERS: Angelica Murillo (named; also in fb, her chr 1st on-panel app, during W #10, '04), Ager Cassie Lathrop, Néstor Garcia, Ángel, Maria Murillo (Rojas' sister), Mr. Murillo (Maria's husband), their children (prev also in photos), paperboy (bts delivering Maria's paper), looters; birds; Rojas & Maria's father (in photo); Néstor's wife children (prev 2 mentioned); Jesus Christ, Biblical figure (prev 2 in paintings), spirits (as figurines)
LOCATIONS/ITEMS: Cerveza Fria w/bedroom, Rojas' estate (also in fb), Murillos' home (4388 W. Oak, Evanstor Illinois; also in photos), church, reunion location (prev 2 in photos), Cassie's house / Wolverine's blanket (also in fb) & motorcycle, Rojas' water pan (in fb), photo w/frame (destroyed) & belongings inc rug, painting, speakers, clock, furniture, TV & toilet, Angelica's diapers bottles, baby formula & baby clothes, looters' knife (destroyed), truck & crowbar, Maria's cashier's checks (bts), letter, newspaper & coffee pot, Murillo SUV, computer & diplomas, Ángel's bag, Cassie's Jeep
FLASHBACK: Wolverine returns to Rojas' estate, finding her in labor. He helps her give birth and she dies.
SYNOPSIS: Néstor sends Ángel to buy baby supplies, and urges Cassie to talk to Wolverine. The brooding Wolverine asks why Cassie keep following him; she admits that she honestly isn't sure. Wolverine blames himself for Rojas' death, explaining that he killed or scared away everyone who could have helped her, but Cassie points out that he saved an innocent life. Wolverine and Néstor discuss what to do with the baby. Wolverin returns to Rojas' estate, finding looters picking it clean; one looter attacks but Wolverine easily disarms him. He finds a letter and learns that Rojas ha a sister, Maria. Wolverine travels to Maria's Illinois home, learning that she has a happy and stable family. He tells Maria of Rojas' death and explain that the baby needs a loving home. Maria and her family soon adopt the newborn, naming her Angelica. Later, Wolverine arrives at Cassie's Portlan house, where she happily lets him in.
NOTE: Cover-labeled "Coyote Crossing, Part 5."

WOLVERINE #12 [#201] (May 2004)

"Dreams" (24 pages)

CREDITS: Greg Rucka (writer), Darick Robertson (pencils; inks, pp.1-8 & 10-24), Tom Palmer (inks, p.9), Virtual Calligraphy's Rus Wooton (letters), Studio F (colors), Warren Simons (editor), Axel Alonso (supervising editor)
FEATURE CHARACTER: Wolverine (also as himself & his animal side in his own dream)
OTHER CHARACTERS: Agent Cassie Lathrop (also in Wolverine's dream); X-Men: Nightcrawler, Phoenix, Rogue; Mariko Yashida, Yukio, Professor Truett Hudson, Wolverine's victims (dead) inc Wranglers, intelligence agents (1 dies), mutants inc bartender, fish-people; deer (dead), bird, cat (prev 15 in Wolverine's dream); Heather Hudson, Rose O'Hara, Herodotus, mythological phoenixes (prev 4 mentioned in Wolverine's dream); Captain America (in photo)
LOCATIONS/ITEMS: Cassie's home; Wolverine's British Columbia cabin (see NOTE), woods, lake, bedroom, bar, the Box, cage (prev 7 in dream) / Wolverine's sack (destroyed), boat, hat, costumes, tuxedo, fishing pole & water dish, victim's sword, Wranglers' armor, Mariko & Yukio's chili, cabin's door (destroyed) & tools, agents' guns, earpieces, atchbook & sack, bartender's birdseed (all in dream), Cassie's coffee pot & newspaper
SYNOPSIS: Asleep next to Cassie, Wolverine dreams. He hears a woman asking to be killed, and sees a field full of corpses. Wolverine follows a d bird, then fishes using Nightcrawler as bait, scaring away half-human fish. In Wolverine's cabin, Mariko makes dinner for the Professor. Wolverine's imal side swipes at him; Yukio asks to be killed, but Wolverine cannot move and the Professor looms above him. Wolverine gnaws at a deer carcass d plays with a cat, but the bird returns, now with human eyes. At a bar, Rogue serves Wolverine while intelligence agents harass mutants. Wolverine es Rogue's bruised face and punches an agent, who shatters. At the Box, a mutant feeds the bird. Wolverine's animal side abducts Mariko and stabs olverine, but he feels nothing. Wolverine follows the bird to a field, where Phoenix lies naked in the snow. They kiss passionately while discussing gine mechanics, but agents abduct and cage Wolverine like an animal. In the morning, Wolverine tells Cassie that he did not dream.
OTE: Phoenix was killed by Kuan-Yin Xorn in NX #150, '04. In his dream, Wolverine says he smuggled liquor during Prohibition. WSaga, '09 clarifies at he actually did, and that this was how he met James Beam, an encounter mentioned in W #187, '03. W #15, '04 reveals that Wolverine used to live but cannot remember, the cabin he dreams about here. A newspaper headline reads "Capt. America Captures Osama," but this is a background ke, not a reference to a canonical event. Editors Warren Simons and Axel Alonso's new roles, begun in W #6, '03, are named here.

WOLVERINE #13 [#202] (June 2004)

"Return of the Native, Part I" (22 pages)

CREDITS: Greg Rucka (writer), Darick Robertson (art), Virtual Calligraphy's Rus Wooton (letters), Studio F (colors), Warren Simons (editor), Axel Alonso (supervising editor)
FEATURE CHARACTER: Wolverine
VILLAINS: Sabretooth (last in NX #142, '03), Workshop (Weapon X Program offshoot group, 1st, unnamed): Murray (unnamed), Willoughby (prev 2 Workshop heads, 1st), Bowen, Peary (prev 2 die, see NOTE)
OTHER CHARACTERS: Native (feral Weapon X Program escapee, also in photos & on scope, 1st but chr last bts in W #14, '04 fb), Agent Cassie Lathrop (next in W #19, '12), Jenkie's Diner waitress & patrons inc Don; fish (die, 1 also on scope), eagle, bears, birds, deer; Bigfoot hoax perpetrator (mentioned, confessed)
LOCATIONS/ITEMS: British Columbia mountains (also in photos & on scope), Cassie's house, Oregon/Montana highway, Workshop's office (Seattle, Washington), Jenkie's Diner (Montana) / Sabretooth's backpack & money, abretooth & Bowen's infrared binoculars, Bowen & Peary's backpacks, restraints & tranquilizer guns w/darts, Wolverine's cigar (see NOTE), torcycle (prev 2 destroyed) & apple pie, Cassie's Jeep, tree, hoax perpetrator's Bigfoot photos (mentioned), Workshop's Native files & photos
SYNOPSIS: Sabretooth and two hunters stalk the Native, a ragged, animalistic woman who lives ferally in British Columbia's mountains. The hunters oot her with tranquilizers, but she recovers and kills them both, then viciously claws Sabretooth and flees. In Portland, Wolverine sneaks out of the eeping Cassie's house and rides off, but loses control when he swerves to avoid a deer and crashes his motorcycle. As Wolverine resigns himself to alking, it begins to rain. In Seattle, Sabretooth reports to the Workshop, furious that they didn't tell him the truth about Native before hiring him to find er. Murray apologizes and points out that it will be harder to find Native a second time, but Sabretooth has decided to let someone else do the work r him. Wolverine orders a slice of pie at a Montana diner, but Sabretooth arrives and interrupts, needling Wolverine by consuming the pie himself. abretooth then gives Wolverine a file on Native, revealing that she is an escaped Weapon X experiment, just like Wolverine.
OTE: Cover-labeled "Return of the Native, Part 1." W #13-14, '04 were published biweekly. Starting with this issue, the series is published under the arvel Knights banner until W #39, '06. Murray is named next issue. The Workshop's lab is named "the Workshop" in W #17, '04; OHMU HC13, '10 arifies that it is the group's name as well. Sabretooth calls Bowen and Peary "Company" types, implying that the Workshop has CIA ties. Wolverine's sappointment when a cigar is ruined in his crash is incongruous, as he gave up smoking in W #167, '01. This issue features the second and final stance of Wolverine being unable to eat a slice of pie without interruption. Native's healing factor, implied here, is confirmed in W #17, '04.

WOLVERINE #14 [#203] (June 2004)

"Return of the Native, Part 2" (22 pages)

CREDITS: Greg Rucka (writer), Darick Robertson (art), Virtual Calligraphy's Rus Wooton (letters), Studio F (colors), Warren Simons (editor), Axel Alonso (supervising editor)
FEATURE CHARACTER: Wolverine (also in Native's drawing, also in fb between MCP #84, '91 & X23 #1, '05)
VILLAINS: Workshop: Murray (named), Willoughby; Sabretooth
OTHER CHARACTERS: Native (also in her own drawing, also bts in fb, her chr 1st bts app, prior to W #13, '04), Nancy (Willoughby's secretary); animals (dead, as bones), eagle; Native's parents, Wranglers (dead), Weapon X captive (see NOTE) & agents (prev 4 in Native's drawing); soldiers (mentioned, came after Native previously)
LOCATIONS/ITEMS: British Columbia mountains inc Native's cave, Workshop's Seattle office, Weapon X Program facility (in fb, also in Native's drawing) / Wolverine's stick, backpack, flashlight, coffee pot, frying pan, canned food & dog tags, Experiment X's wires (in fb), Weapon X Program's tubes (1 destroyed) & equipment, Wrangler's gun (prev 3 in ative's drawing), Native's cigar box w/knickknacks inc lighter, scope, knife, pocketknife, compass & dog tags

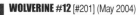

FLASHBACK: Wolverine screams at the Native while escaping the Weapon X facility.

SYNOPSIS: Smelling smoke from a far-off campfire, Native knows that someone is in her territory. Sabretooth tells the Workshop that he has manipulat[ed] Wolverine into tracking and befriending Native, and he will just follow Wolverine's scent. In the mountains, Wolverine realizes that Native is watching h[im]. He waits patiently; eventually she approaches the fire and curiously investigates Wolverine's belongings. Wolverine talks calmly, but Native has a sudd[en] flash of memory from the Weapon X Program and attacks, popping bone claws similar to Wolverine's. When Wolverine does not fight back, Native fle[es]. Wolverine soon finds her cave and discovers a crude drawing depicting Native's abduction and experimentation, and her escape during Wolverin[e's] Weapon X rampage. Disturbed that he doesn't recall her, Wolverine then finds Native's box of knickknacks, including dog tags nearly identical to his ow[n]. Native returns to her cave, but spots Wolverine and flees. Wolverine pursues her; the two briefly fight and circle each other warily, then begin to kiss.

NOTE: Cover-labeled "Return of the Native, Part 2." The story title's chapter notation switches from Roman numerals to numbers here. It is unknow[n] whether Native's bone claws, healing factor and animal senses were derived from Wolverine and implanted by the Weapon X Program, or if s[he] coincidentally has the same mutation as Wolverine, but her drawing seems to show her with claws while being abducted. This issue reveals th[at] the Weapon X Program had other captives at the time they implanted Wolverine's Adamantium; Native's drawing shows a third captive besid[e] herself and Wolverine, but their identity is unrevealed. Wolverine's dog tags end in X001-1 and Native's end in X001-6; this could indicate at least s[ix] captives. Native's dog tags read "Feral;" they were changed to "Native" when this issue was reprinted in the "Wolverine: Return of the Native" TPB, '0[6?]. Presumably the character's original name was Feral, and was likely changed to avoid confusion with the X-Force character of the same name. W[ith] this issue, the recap page begins showcasing previous issues' covers. This Index will not list characters that appear only on those covers.

WOLVERINE #15 [#204] (July 2004)

"Return of the Native, Part 3" (21 pages)

CREDITS: Greg Rucka (writer), Darick Robertson (pencils), Jimmy Palmiotti & Tom Palmer (inks), Virtual Calligraph[y's] Rus Wooton (letters), Studio F (colors), Warren Simons (editor), Axel Alonso (supervising editor)
FEATURE CHARACTER: Wolverine
VILLAINS: Workshop: Murray (bts canceling Sabretooth's contract), Willoughby (voice only on radio); Sabretooth
OTHER CHARACTERS: Native (also in her own drawing); eagle; Native's parents, Wranglers (dead, all but 1 bt[s]), Weapon X agents (some bts) & captive (prev 4 in Native's drawing)
LOCATIONS/ITEMS: British Columbia mountains inc Native's cave & Wolverine's former cabin, Workshop's Seat[tle] office (bts), Weapon X Program facility (in Native's drawing) / Sabretooth's Humvee (bts, see NOTE), backpack, rad[io] (destroyed) w/tracker (bts, see NOTE) & rifle w/scope, Workshop's bomb (bts, see NOTE) w/timer & transmitt[er], Willoughby's radio (bts), Weapon X Program's tubes (1 destroyed) & equipment, Wrangler's gun (prev 3 in Nativ[e's]

drawing), cabin's tools & books

SYNOPSIS: Sabretooth tracks Wolverine through the mountains, noticing several signs of his fight with Native. Willoughby contacts Sabretooth f[or] an update, but the villain blows him off. Nearby, Wolverine and Native awaken in her cave; Wolverine tries to explain that Sabretooth and his employe[rs] want to capture her. Native points to her crude drawing of Wolverine, but he still does not remember her. As the two exit the cave, Sabretooth shoo[ts] them, incapacitating Wolverine — but Native stabs Sabretooth in the groin and the eyes and he retreats. Wolverine recovers, wanting to purs[ue] and attack the injured Sabretooth, but Native leads him elsewhere. Nearby, Willoughby contacts Sabretooth again, telling him that the Worksho[p is] canceling his contract, and Sabretooth spitefully decides to kill the Native to keep them from capturing her. Elsewhere, Native leads Wolverine to a[n] abandoned cabin that seems naggingly familiar. Recognizing the scents and noticing the books strewn around, Wolverine realizes that he used to li[ve] there — as Native utters her first word to him, "home."

NOTE: The cover label for this story arc disappears here; it returns on W #17, '04's cover. This issue implies that Wolverine and Native lived togeth[er] in a British Columbia cabin after their escape from the Weapon X Program facility. The books, tools and mattress shown, plus next issue's revelati[on] that Native knows Wolverine's real name, imply that they lived and communicated somewhat like humans. However, all other flashbacks to Wolverine['s] post-escape period show him living ferally in Alberta's Wood Buffalo National Park — and Wolverine doesn't recall the cabin, despite his esca[pe] occurring after Weapon X altered his memories. Wolverine may have mentally degenerated and fled after a period of time in the cabin, or it is possib[le] that he and Native knew one another and lived there prior to their abduction. Next issue reveals that the Workshop planted a tracker in Sabretooth['s] radio; W #17, '04 reveals that they planted a bomb on his Humvee.

WOLVERINE #16 [#205] (August 2004)

"Return of the Native, Part IV" (21 pages)

CREDITS: Greg Rucka (writer), Darick Robertson (pencils), Jimmy Palmiotti (inks), Virtual Calligraphy's Rus Wooto[n] (letters), Studio F (colors), Warren Simons (editor), Axel Alonso (supervising editor)
FEATURE CHARACTER: Wolverine (also in photo)
VILLAINS: Workshop: Dr. Vapor (1st bts, contacted to prep lab), Murray, Willoughby, agents (some die) inc Rams[ey] (dies); Sabretooth, Workshop's CIA contacts (bts arranging surveillance)
OTHER CHARACTER: Native (also in photo)
LOCATIONS/ITEMS: McChord Air Force Base (Tacoma, Washington), CIA contacts' office (bts), British Columb[ia] woods (also in photo) inc Wolverine's former cabin (destroyed) & Native's cave / Workshop's tracker (destroye[d]), computers, GPS satellite (all bts) & helicopters (2 destroyed) w/loudspeaker, missiles, gun & rappelling lines, CIA s[py] satellite (bts), Murray's radio (bts) & private jet, Willoughby's satellite photo, Sabretooth's backpack, cabin's table, too[ls] & books (prev 3 destroyed), agents' gas masks (2 destroyed), radios (bts), armor, guns, taser & gas grenades, Ramsey's headset (destroyed)

SYNOPSIS: Having tracked Sabretooth via GPS, the Workshop's spy satellite locates Wolverine and the Native in the mountains. Murray mobilize[s] his agents, ordering Wolverine killed and Native captured alive. As Sabretooth hunts Native, planning to murder her, he sees several Worksho[p] helicopters fly overhead and realizes that his plans must change. Native explains in stuttered, broken English that Wolverine used to live in th[e] cabin. Frustrated at not remembering, Wolverine lashes out, but suddenly senses Workshop agents outside. The agents throw in gas grenades, b[ut] Wolverine tosses them out again; they explode and Wolverine uses the smoky cloud for cover and attacks. He and Native quickly defeat the agent[s], but a helicopter's missile destroys the cabin. Wolverine leaps onto the helicopter and crashes it, then disables a second — but several agents captu[re] Native while he is distracted. Wolverine tries to free Native, but the agents taser him into unconsciousness and depart. Hours later, Sabretooth find[s] the still-recovering Wolverine, and offers to team up to destroy the Workshop.

WOLVERINE #17 [#206] (September 2004)

"Return of the Native, Part V" (21 pages)

CREDITS: Greg Rucka (writer), Darick Robertson (pencils), Nelson DeCastro (inks), Virtual Calligraphy's Rus Wooton (letters), Studio F (colors), Warren Simons (editor), Axel Alonso (supervising editor)
FEATURE CHARACTER: Wolverine
VILLAINS: Workshop: Dr. Vapor (sadistic biologist, 1st), Murray, Willoughby, agents (some dead), doctors; Sabretooth, potential buyers (bts, interested in Native's ovaries)
OTHER CHARACTERS: Native, Wolverine & Native's unborn child (1st bts app as embryo, see NOTE); cow (dead, as skull), horses; Mick Jagger (quoted)
LOCATIONS/ITEMS: Workshop's Montana lab (also called "Workshop," disguised as ranch) w/decontamination chamber & front gate, British Columbia woods, Montana roadway / Workshop helicopters (2 destroyed), computers (bts), gate alarm (destroyed) & bomb w/timer & transmitter (prev 2 destroyed), agents' armor, guns & map, Native's ovaries (bts, removed), shackles, knockout gas mask & stretcher w/restraints, doctors' prod & medical equipment, decontamination chamber's comm system (bts), computers & gas, Sabretooth's Humvee, Vapor's tranquilizer, scalpel, tongs, microscope, vital sign monitors, radiation suit, biohazard container, head-mounted camera, medical bed w/clamps & radioactive pellet w/tube
SYNOPSIS: Native arrives at the Workshop's Montana lab, where Dr. Vapor looks forward to operating on her. An agent orders her to work quickly, as several interested buyers have already contacted the Workshop. In the mountains, Sabretooth explains why he and Wolverine should work together — Wolverine wants Native back and Sabretooth wants to make the Workshop pay — but Wolverine remains silent. He finds and disarms a Workshop bomb hidden on Sabretooth's Humvee, infuriating Sabretooth further, and the two drive off together. Vapor decontaminates Native and prepares her for surgery, inserting a radioactive pellet into Native's side to distract and weaken her healing factor. While running a blood test, Vapor discovers that Native is pregnant. On the road, Sabretooth tries to make conversation, but Wolverine remains silent. They arrive at the Workshop; Sabretooth gets out, destroys the alarm and opens the gate — but Wolverine suddenly runs him over, pinning Sabretooth with the Humvee and swearing that he will never be partners. Meanwhile, Vapor extracts Native's ovaries.
NOTE: The story arc's cover label returns here, listing this issue as "Return of the Native, Part 5." Native's healing factor is confirmed here. Wolverine slept with Native between W #14-15, '04, but there is no way to tell when her pregnancy took hold. Although she could have become or been pregnant in W #15-16, '04, this Index considers this issue to be the embryo's first official bts appearance. Wolverine seems to stab Sabretooth in the head here, which is impossible given Sabretooth's Adamantium skeleton. Wolverine must have retracted his claws and punched Sabretooth in the head.

WOLVERINE #18 [#207] (October 2004)

"Return of the Native, Part VI" (21 pages)

CREDITS: Greg Rucka (writer), Darick Robertson (pencils; inks, p.1), Tom Palmer (finishes, pp.2-12), Jimmy Palmiotti (finishes, pp.13-21), Virtual Calligraphy's Rus Wooton (letters), Studio F (colors), Warren Simons (editor), Axel Alonso (supervising editor)
FEATURE CHARACTER: Wolverine (also as Tex, also on monitor)
VILLAINS: Workshop: Murray, Willoughby, Dr. Vapor (all die), agents (most die, 1 also in photo, others bts transporting ovaries) inc Tex; Sabretooth
OTHER CHARACTERS: Native, Wolverine & Native's unborn child (bts as embryo); cow (bts, dead as skull), deer (dead, as stuffed heads); religious figures (in painting)
LOCATIONS/ITEMS: Workshop's secure facility (bts) & Montana lab (also on monitor) w/front gate / Agents' radio (bts), vehicles (1 bts), ID & guns w/flashlights, gate alarm (mentioned), Sabretooth's Humvee, Tex's radio, gun, hat & shirt, Workshop cameras, comm system (prev 2 bts), monitors & electronic door locks (1 destroyed), Native's ovaries (bts), IV & knockout gas mask, Vapor's scalpel & radioactive pellet
SYNOPSIS: Workshop agents respond to the destroyed gate alarm, and find a furious Sabretooth pinned under his own Humvee. Elsewhere, Wolverine ambushes other agents, steals their clothes and ID, and infiltrates the lab. Murray and Willoughby notice Wolverine on a security monitor and order a silent response, not wanting to disturb Vapor's operation. Several agents begin stalking Wolverine, but he ambushes them, killing nearly everyone, and orders the lone survivor to lead him to Native. Elsewhere, Sabretooth is brought to see Murray and Willoughby. He confronts them about the bomb they planted; they apologize and offer him five million dollars to stop Wolverine from derailing their plans. Sabretooth rejects the offer, murders Murray and Willoughby, then turns on the Workshop's remaining agents. Wolverine finds a recovering Native and cuts the radioactive pellet out of her. Vapor mentions that Native is pregnant, but when she reveals that the Workshop sold Native's ovaries, an outraged Wolverine kills Vapor. Sabretooth watches the couple flee, and decides to returns to his original plan: kill Native.
NOTE: Cover-labeled "Return of the Native, Part 6."

WOLVERINE #19 [#208] (November 2004)

"Last Rites" (21 pages)

CREDITS: Greg Rucka (writer), Darick Robertson (pencils), Tom Palmer (inks), Virtual Calligraphy's Rus Wooton (letters), Studio F (colors), Warren Simons (editor), Axel Alonso (supervising editor)
FEATURE CHARACTER: Wolverine (also on poster in pfb1, also in pfb2 & bts in pfb1 contacting Nightcrawler, next in W/Pun #1-5, '04, RamW/3, '09, W:ONO, '09; AX #1, UXM #444, WX #20-21 & 23-25, Nc #3, X #157-160, all '04, Nc #3 & 4 fb, '05; UXM #444-449, XStat #26 fb, XMU #4 & 4/2, DX #4, UXM #450-451, all '04, WM #5, '07 fb, XMU #9/2, '05 fb, X #161-164, '04-05, XMU #5 & 5/2, '04; UXM #452-454, Mys #23, all '05, MKSM #6, '04, Nc #5 & 6 fb, X #165, Herc #1 fb, XMU #10, MTU #1 fb, 1-2 & 5, Jubilee #3 & 5-6, all '05, MHol '04/2, Cable&Dp #7-10, '04-05, X4 #1-5, '05, W:Debt, '11, UXM #455 & 456 fb, '05, AX #1-6, '04)
GUEST STAR: Nightcrawler (also as himself & priest in pfb1, last in NX #156, '04, next in XMU #7, '05)

VILLAIN: Sabretooth (in pfb2, next in IDisc #1, '04)

OTHER CHARACTERS: Native (dead; also in pfb2, dies), Wolverine & Native's unborn child (bts as embryo, dead; also bts as embryo in pfb dies), Jo (also in pfb1, last in W #6, '03), Box patron & employee (prev 2 in pfb1); fish (dies), raccoon, flies, birds (prev 4 in pfb2); X-Men: Beast, Bishc Psylocke, Rogue, Sage, Storm, Thunderbird; others (prev 8 on posters), Deadpool, others (prev 2 on posters in pfb1)

LOCATIONS/ITEMS: The Box (also in pfb1), Montana woods inc restricted area, British Columbia mountains inc ruins of Wolverine's former cab (prev 4 in pfb2) / Nightcrawler's image inducer (bts, also bts in pfb1), warning sign, barbed wire, Workshop's helicopter (prev 3 in pfb2, destroyed Wolverine's shirt (in pfb2) & sheet, Jo's washcloth

FLASHBACKS: Nightcrawler arrives at the Box, telling Jo that Wolverine will meet him there shortly (p1). Sabretooth stalks Wolverine and Native they move north through the Montana woods. Farther ahead, the two rest for a short time, and Native confirms that she is pregnant. She tells Wolverin to go home, but he refuses to abandon her; he asks Native to come back with him, but she knows she will not fit into human society. Later, as Wolveri runs through the woods, he belatedly realizes that Native has stopped following. He doubles back to look for her, but Sabretooth attacks, claiming th Native is neither human nor animal and is better off dead. Sabretooth savagely tears into Wolverine, incapacitating him, and departs. Native return the ruins of Wolverine's cabin and waits; Sabretooth eventually catches up. Telling Native that people will never give up trying to exploit her, he attac Wolverine arrives a few hours later, and is horrified to find Native dead (p2).

SYNOPSIS: Wolverine arrives with Native's body, and asks Nightcrawler for last rites.

NOTE: Cover-labeled "Return of the Native, Part 7." The X-Men reverted to traditional super hero costumes in the X-titles' 2004 revamp. Nightcrawle new costume appears on this issue's cover, but this story arc occurs before the revamp; Nightcrawler wears street clothes in the story itself.

WOLVERINE #20 [#209] (December 2004)

"Enemy of the State, Part 1" (24 pages)

CREDITS: Mark Millar (writer), John Romita Jr. (pencils Klaus Janson (inks), Virtual Calligraphy's Rus Wootc (letters), Paul Mounts (colors), Jennifer Lee (editor), Ax Alonso (exec editor), Richard Isanove (variant c colors Eric J. Moreels (special thanks)

FEATURE CHARACTER: Wolverine (die resurrected, also in W #59, '08 fb & W #22, '05 fb)

GUEST STARS: Elektra (last in Elektra #35, '04 Nick Fury (last in AX #6, '04, chr last in Cap #12, '0 Shadowcat (last in AX #6, '04, chr next in UXM #459, '0

VILLAINS: Gorgon (Tomi Shishido, telepathic mutant prodigy, transforms people stone, also as hologram, 1st but chr last in W #26, '05 fb, also in W #59, '08 fb & W #22, '05 fb), "Baron Strucker" (1st bts app facilitating Hydra's alliance with Gorgon, als in W #22, '05 fb), Elsbeth von Strucker (1st bts app conspiring with Gorgon, next 1st on-panel app in W #23, '05), undead Hand ninjas (1st, many destroyed, othe bts murdering churchgoers, some chr next in W #59, '08 fb, some or others chr las in W #26, '05 fb, next in W #23, '05), Hydra agents (bts discussing alliance & outfittin Wolverine, some or others last in Mys #19, '04), Dawn of the White Light (1st bts ap allied with Hand & Hydra, next in 1st on-panel app in W #27, '05), kidnappers (die)

OTHER CHARACTERS: Ichiro (Mariko Yashida's cousin, chauffeur, named, la in UXM #173, '83), Fukuko (Ichiro's wife, 1st, unnamed) (both also in photo, next i W #27, '05), Rikuto (Ichiro's son, unnamed, dies off-panel, also in photos, next b in W #31, '05), SHIELD agents (others bts decoding Hydra transmissions & locatin Wolverine; some or others last in AX #6, '04, chr last in Cap #9, '05) & doctor (dies, last bts in W/NF:SC, '89, chr last & next bts in W #14, '11 fb), Ichiro employer & his son, children, umpire, baseball audience, police, reporters (bts covering kidnapping), priests, nuns, fanatics (prev 3 dead), bystander pigs (bts, ate Rikuto), unborn birds (bts, dead inside eggs); Captain America, Mr. Fantastic (prev 2 also on cover), Iron Man, Professor X, others (pre 5 mentioned, Hand targets), Adam Sandler (mentioned, in airline film), Wolverine's seatmate (mentioned), Jenny Lee (as coffee logo), saints (a statues); Fantastic Four: Human Torch, Invisible Woman, Thing; X-Men: Beast, Cyclops, Emma Frost (prev 6 cover only)

LOCATIONS/ITEMS: Nagasaki, Japan: employer & Ichiro's homes, Glover Park, police station, graveyard; Minneapolis, Minnesota churc Argentina (bts), South Atlantic Ocean / Ichiro's employer's limousine & cookie basket, baseball bats, ball (prev 2 bts), padding & gloves, umpire mask, kidnappers' car & guns, police paperwork & computer, Wolverine's bandages, new costume, sacks w/note & laundry & Hydra implants (bts) in targeting array, ninjas' swords, sais, shuriken & spear, airplane, seatmate's Tetris game (prev 2 mentioned), Gorgon's sword, Rikuto's bird eggs, Ichiro photos, SHIELD comm unit (bts), cars, cameras, flashlights, guns, earpieces, medical equipment & aircraft carrier w/cameras, security alarm (pre 2 bts), monitors & generator (destroyed) w/backup (bts), Hand's files, Fury's holographic projector, doctor's paperwork & water bottle, Elektra's sais

SYNOPSIS: Ichiro's son Rikuto plays baseball with Ichiro's rich employer's son, but kidnappers suddenly pull Rikuto into a car, apparently havin confused the two boys. They demand an exorbitant ransom, and a desperate Ichiro calls Wolverine. Traveling to Japan, Wolverine meets th kidnappers, but scores of undead Hand ninjas ambush him and he realizes he has been set up. Gorgon suddenly impales Wolverine with a swor reveals that Rikuto is dead, and kills Wolverine. Days later, Shadowcat unsuccessfully investigates Wolverine's disappearance. A month later, Nick Fur asks Elektra to help investigate a Hand plot, explaining that SHIELD has discovered that Hydra, the Hand, and Gorgon's cult the Dawn of the Whit Light have allied and are targeting super heroes. Fury learns that Wolverine has been discovered in Argentina, barely alive; SHIELD transports him t their aircraft carrier. Wolverine awakens, his morality gone and a Hydra mission pounding insistently in his head. He murders his doctor and destroy the ship's generator; as SHIELD agents mobilize in the darkness, Wolverine confronts Elektra…

NOTE: Cover-labeled "Enemy of the State, Part 1 of 6." W #20-21, '04 were published biweekly. This issue has a variant cover, a WizardWorld Texa sketch variant, and a Marvel's Greatest Comics edition, published in July 2011 with a lower price, ads mainly for other Marvel books, and an altere cover label: "Enemy of the State, Part 1." W #22, '05 reveals that the Hand resurrected Wolverine, and that Hydra implanted cybernetic devices inside him. Gorgon's real name is revealed in W #26, '05. Fukuko and Rikuto are named in W #27, '05; their surname is unrevealed to date. Fury believe that Kyoto gangs murdered Gorgon and the Hand resurrected him; W #26, '05 fb reveals that Gorgon killed himself. Wolverine returned to a traditiona super hero costume in AX #1, '04. The series reverts to all-caps lettering with this issue. Jenny Lee coffee is named for editor Jennifer Lee.

WOLVERINE #21 [#210] (December 2004)

"Enemy of the State, Part 2 of 6" (23 pages)

CREDITS: Mark Millar (writer), John Romita Jr. (pencils), Klaus Janson (inks), Virtual Calligraphy's Rus Wooton (letters), Paul Mounts (colors), Jennifer Lee (editor), Axel Alonso (exec editor), Cory Sedlmeier (special thanks)
FEATURE CHARACTER: Wolverine (also in NTb #4, '05)
GUEST STARS: Fantastic Four: Human Torch, Mr. Fantastic (both bts inside Baxter Building), Invisible Woman (Susan Storm Richards, turns objects invisible & creates force fields), Thing (all last in X4 #5, '05); X-Men: Storm (last in Cable&Dp #10, '05, next in W #25, '05), Shadowcat (prev 2 chr last in UXM #460, '05), Emma Frost (bts detecting Wolverine, last in AX #6, '04, chr between UXM #459-460, '05); Elektra, Nick Fury (prev 4 next in W #23, '05)
VILLAINS: Gorgon (also bts in NTb #4, '05), "Baron Strucker," Hydra agents (prev 3 bts monitoring Wolverine, see NOTE)
OTHER CHARACTERS: Franklin Richards (last in MK4 #13, '05, last bts in MK4 #14, '05), Valeria Richards (last in MK4 #13, '05) (prev 2 Mr. Fantastic & Invisible Woman's children, bts inside Baxter Building), President George W. Bush (last in Cable&Dp #9, '05, next in W #25, '05) & his pilots (prev 2 bts on Air Force One), Xavier Institute students (some or others last in AX #6, '04, chr last in UXM #459, '05, next in W #23, '05) inc Updraft (Johan Schumann, flight) & Bartholomew Grice, Baxter Building employees inc Avril (receptionist, bts explaining evacuation), SHIELD agents (many die, others bts discovering breach & breaking Hydra's codes, some or others next in W #23, '05) inc Captain, non-essential Pentagon personnel (bts, evacuated), bystanders; sharks (1 dies); Hand's targets (on monitor); Colossus (mentioned, returned from seeming death; also in photo)
LOCATIONS/ITEMS: South Atlantic Ocean, skies above Manhattan, X-Mansion, Baxter Building (Fantastic Four's Manhattan office & home) SHIELD comm units, mainframe (both bts), guns (1 destroyed), flashlight, paperwork, helicopters w/winches, Helicarrier w/monitor & aircraft carrier (destroyed) w/piping, lifeboats, radiation suit & explosives (bts) w/timer, Elektra's sais (destroyed), Wolverine's SHIELD psych file (bts) & Hydra implants, defense codes, Pentagon files, White House security details (prev 4 bts), Fury's guns & earpiece, Hand's files, Air Force One, students' bedpans (bts) & blankets, X-Mansion trip beams, Storm's luggage, Shadowcat's photo & candles, employees' paperwork, Mr. Fantastic's think-tank (bts), Fantastic Four's voice-controlled computer & force field generator
SYNOPSIS: As Wolverine murders the SHIELD agents without remorse, Elektra realizes that he has been brainwashed by Hydra. She attacks Wolverine, but an explosive that he had set suddenly tears a hole in the aircraft carrier, and rushing water interrupts their battle. As SHIELD agents drown, Wolverine swims away, struggling vainly against the evil thoughts that fill his head. A shark attacks him, attracted by the dead agents, but he swiftly guts it. Later, as rescue crews arrive, Elektra realizes that Wolverine hacked the SHIELD mainframe and stole several sensitive files. The next day, Nick Fury holds a security meeting detailing Wolverine's resurrection and conversion by Hydra and the Hand, and explains that they plan to do the same to other heroes. As Fury orders nationwide security measures taken, the President arrives to take refuge in the Helicarrier. At the X-Mansion, Shadowcat explains the heightened security and reassures the frightened students. The Fantastic Four erect a force field around their headquarters — unaware that Wolverine is already inside the building.
NOTE: Cover-labeled "Enemy of the State, Part 2 of 6." Updraft's codename, last name and powers are revealed in OHMU HC13, '10. Next issue reveals that Gorgon, "Strucker" and several Hydra technicians are monitoring and directing Wolverine from a hidden base. The Xavier Institute went public as a school for young mutants prior to NX #114, '01; the X-Men are now teachers to a large class of new students. The alien Ord revived Colossus prior to AX #5, '04 fb.

WOLVERINE #22 [#211] (January 2005)

"Enemy of the State, Part 3 of 6" (22 pages)

CREDITS: Mark Millar (writer), John Romita Jr. (pencils), Klaus Janson (inks), Chris Eliopoulos (letters), Paul Mounts (colors), Jennifer Lee (editor), Axel Alonso (exec editor), Cory Sedlmeier (special thanks)
FEATURE CHARACTER: Wolverine (also in fb between W #59, '08 fb & W #20, '04; next in W #23, '05 fb, Loners #2, '07 fb, Inv #6, '05)
GUEST STARS: Iron Man (Anthony Stark, armored inventor, last in MK4 #13, '05, last bts in Cap #4, '05, chr last in Cap #13, '06), Yellowjacket (Dr. Henry Pym, size-changing scientist, last in AvFin, '05, next in MAv #15, '08) (both also as monitor images), Fantastic Four: Mr. Fantastic (all also as VR projections), Human Torch, Thing (prev 2 also on monitor), Invisible Woman (prev 4 next in Inv #9, '05)
VILLAINS: "Baron Strucker" (imperfect clone of Hydra head Wolfgang von Strucker, 1st on-panel app, see NOTE; chr next bts in W #23, '05 fb, next in Inv #6, '05), Gorgon (chr next bts in W #23, '05 fb, next bts in Inv #6, '05) (both also in fb during W #20, '04), Elsbeth von Strucker (bts, arriving shortly), Hand sorcerers (in fb following W #59, '08 fb, 1 or another next in W #24, '05, some or others next in NAv #27, '07), Hydra agents (some or others chr next in W #23, '05 fb, next in Inv #6, '05)
OTHER CHARACTERS: Franklin Richards (next in MK4 #15, '05), Valeria Richards (next bts in MK4 #15, '05, next in MK4 #18, '05) (both on monitor), Diana, Sabrina (prev 2 paramedic's cousins, Human Torch's dates, bts on phone), United Nations officials (bts, cautiously optimistic about terraformer), paramedics (die, 1 also on monitor), firemen, hospital burn unit (bts standing by) & dispatch operator (voice only on radio), bystanders (bts, killed in explosion); fetal monsters (bts on monitor); AIM, Hand (prev 2 mentioned, to be contacted by Hydra), super heroes mentioned, killed & resurrected by Hydra, see NOTE); X-Men: Cyclops, Shadowcat, Storm; Captain America, Falcon (prev 5 monitor images)
LOCATIONS/ITEMS: Baxter Building (also on monitors) w/nursery (on monitor), Micro-verse (see NOTE) & data room, Hydra base (also in fb), non-space (virtual reality), Iron Man & Yellowjacket's log-in locations, Manhattan (also on monitor) inc Beth Israel hospital (bts) & gas station, monsters' nursery (bts), parallel worlds, Earth's core (prev 3 on monitors) / Human Torch's tools, earpiece & 1957 Thunderbird (destroyed) & Thing's steroid cream, Wolverine's bandages, IVs & Hydra implants (bts) inc ocular cameras & comm system, Hydra teleporter, comm unit (prev 2 bts), monitors, eyepieces, guns, hover-sled & control equipment, Baxter Building blueprints (bts), Fantastic Four's alarm system, voice-activated computer, time machine (prev 3 bts), cables (destroyed), security robots (some destroyed), intercom, monitors & fire suppression system, Hand's spikes & altar (prev 2 in fb), Mr. Fantastic's terraformer (as VR projection), synthetic personality chip (bts), think-tank, VR interface helmet & hard drive, Iron Man & Yellowjacket's VR interface suits, Invisible Woman's comm unit, gas pumps (destroyed), fire truck, ambulance (also on monitor), fireman's radio, operator's radio (bts)

FLASHBACK: Gorgon telepathically brainwashes the newly resurrected Wolverine.

SYNOPSIS: Wolverine spies on the Fantastic Four as Gorgon and Baron Strucker monitor him from a Hydra base. In virtual reality, M Fantastic shows Iron Man and Yellowjacket designs for a terraformer designed to remake harsh landscapes, but detects Wolverine hacking int his systems. Thing and Human Torch attack, but Wolverine uses the building's fire suppression system to defeat the Torch, and stabs throug Thing's rocky hide. Mr. Fantastic envelops Wolverine, but Hydra teleports him free. The Invisible Woman immobilizes Wolverine with her forc field, but he calls for an extraction — and a Hydra hover-sled smashes through the building. Wolverine gives the pilot a hard drive stolen fro Mr. Fantastic, then tackles the pursuing Human Torch. The two crash into a gas station, which explodes. Paramedics recover a burn victir they believe he is the Torch until the "victim" suddenly pops his claws and kills them. Strucker has the hard drive sent to AIM, ordering them t weaponize Mr. Fantastic's inventions.

NOTE: Cover-labeled "Enemy of the State, Part 3 of 6." Although Strucker seems to be in charge of Wolverine's missions here, Wolverine wa sent to attack Strucker in NTb #4, '05. NTb #17, '06 reconciles this inconsistency by revealing that the "Baron Strucker" seen in W #22-25, 'C is a genetically engineered clone, created to give the illusion that Strucker was in charge of this Hydra faction. OHMU HC1, '08 clarifies tha Gorgon and Elsbeth conspired to have the clone created, and thus control this Hydra faction by proxy. Although this issue and next mentio that Hydra has killed and resurrected other heroes besides Wolverine, they are never identified. The Baxter Building's "Micro-verse" area has n known connection to the Microverse dimension.

WOLVERINE #23 [#212] (February 2005)

"Enemy of the State, Part 4 of 6" (22 pages)

CREDITS: Mark Millar (writer), John Romita Jr. (pencils), Klaus Janson (inks), Chris Eliopoulos (letters), Pa Mounts (colors), Jennifer Lee (editor), Axel Alonso (exec editor)

FEATURE CHARACTER: Wolverine (also in dfb, also in fb between W #22, '05 & Inv #6, '05, also in Loner #2, '07 fb during fb)

GUEST STARS: X-Men: Colossus (bts, told Shadowcat that Emma met Gorgon, last in AX #6, '04, chr last i UXM #460, '05), Emma Frost (last in AX #6, '04, last bts in W #21, '05, chr last in UXM #460, '05), Shadowca (last in W #21, '04); Captain America (last in Inv #9, '05), Falcon (last in AvFin, '05, chr last in Cap #14, '06), Iro Man (bts in Helsinki), Nick Fury (all next in W #25, '05), Elektra (prev 2 last in W #21, '04), Daredevil (last in MK #14, '05)

VILLAINS: Elsbeth von Strucker (Wolfgang von Strucker's 3rd wife, elderly Satanist, 1st on-panel app, also o monitor), Gorgon (also bts monitoring Wolverine in fb between W #22, '05 & Inv #6, '05 bts; last bts in Inv #6, '05), "Baron Strucker" (also bt monitoring Wolverine in fb between W #22, '05 & Inv #6, '05; last in Inv #6, '05) (prev 2 also bts in Loners #2, '07 fb during fb), Hydra agent (others bts monitoring Wolverine; some or others also in fb between W #20, '05 bts & Inv #6, '05, some bts monitoring Wolverine, those also bt in Loners #2, '07 fb during fb; some or others last in Inv #6, '05 fb), undead Hand ninjas (some destroyed, some or others last in W #20, '04' would-be rapists (in dfb, die)

OTHER CHARACTERS: Stepford Cuckoos (three-in-one telepathic gestalt): Mindee (originally Irma, see NOTE), Celeste, Phoebe (all last i AX #5, '04, next in XPx #1, '05); Hornet (Eddie McDonough, wears cybernetic flight pack, dead; also bts in fb, fatally injured & dies off-pane between NW #1, '99 & this issue, also in Loners #2, '07 fb during fb; last in NW #1, '99), SHIELD agents (others bts profiling Wolverine's attacks some or others last in W #21, '05, also in AntM #1, '07 fb), Xavier Institute students (1 last in MKSM #6, '04, some or others last in W #21, '05 next in W #25, '05), Vatican (bts hiring Elektra, see NOTE), Stark International security guards (in fb, die), eyewitnesses (bts reporting attack t SHIELD, also bts witnessing attack in fb prior to issue), paramedics (all but 1 bts treating Hornet), hotel employee, cathedral explosion victim (bts, injured), reporters (bts reporting explosion), "Strucker's" child victim (bts, sacrificed) & servants, party attendees (bts having orgy), babie (bts, dead, as drum skins), policeman (others bts, killed by Wolverine, also on cover), Navy soldiers (bts, bombed by Wolverine), assault victir (in dfb), bystanders; dog (in fb), birds; Black Widow (mentioned, described Daredevil's senses), Dawn of the White Light (mentioned, laughed a Magneto), Helena Blavatsky (mentioned, rumored as Elsbeth's old friend), kings, presidents (prev 2 mentioned, rumored as Elsbeth's lovers' corporate heads (mentioned, rumored as Satanists), worldwide security services (mentioned, on high alert), Emma's friend (mentioned involved with Gorgon years ago); historical figure (as bust), model, cowboys (prev 2 on billboards)

LOCATIONS/ITEMS: Stark International (Iron Man's Long Island corporate office, also in fb), New York City (also in dfb) inc IRS complex, powe stations (prev 2 bts), Girl Scout hall (Hydra front), rooftops, Elektra's hotel & Daredevil's Hell's Kitchen brownstone, X-Mansion, "Strucker's" hom (Georgetown, Washington DC); Helsinki, Finland; cathedral, banks, credit union (prev 3 destroyed), ocean (prev 5 bts); Kyoto, Japan; Europ (prev 2 mentioned) / Stark International defense programs (destroyed) & files (both bts), guards' guns & earpieces, Hydra flight backpacks (a in fb) & blasters (others in fb), SHIELD satellite (bts), helicopters, crane, guns, jetpacks, hover-platform, handheld computer & Helicarrier w monitors & situation map, paramedic's tarp & medical kit, Hornet's cybernetic flight pack (also bts in fb), Elektra's sword, weights, earpiece map w/pins & guns w/case, room service trolley, ninjas' bows, arrows, sais (prev 3 bts), swords, mace, spears & scythes, hurled ice, roofto pipe, Fury's earpiece & guns, Wolverine's explosives, transmitter, gas bomb & EMP generator (prev 4 bts), X-Men's hover-platforms, Cerebr (X-Men's upgraded Cerebro), "Strucker's" knife (bts) & piano, Elsbeth's handmade bowl (bts) & walking stick, servants' brooms, cloth & spra bottle, attendees' baby-skin drums (bts), Captain America's earpiece, Falcon's earpiece & glider suit, ATM security camera (bts in dfb), powe generators (bts, destroyed)

FLASHBACKS: Wolverine stops an attempted rape (d). Wolverine attacks Stark International with Hydra agents, kills Hornet, then pats a dog

SYNOPSIS: SHIELD investigates the aftermath of Wolverine's assault on Stark Industries. Elektra decapitates Hornet's body, explaining tha it is the only way to prevent the Hand from reanimating and corrupting him. Later, Elektra reflects on the wave of terror attacks that Hydra i making Wolverine perform. Undead Hand ninjas attack her, but she defeats them and brainstorms a way to capture Wolverine. Later, at Elektra' suggestion, Emma uses Cerebra to amplify all the precognitive and psychic students and try to predict Wolverine's next targets. Elsewhere Hydra's bankroller Elsbeth von Strucker humiliates her husband the Baron, deriding his plans and bedding the Gorgon. Various heroes pitc in to help SHIELD shut down all the Hydra cells they can find, but Wolverine continues spearheading assaults on America's financial center. and destroys Manhattan's power grid. That night, Wolverine and several ninjas infiltrate Daredevil's home; the sleeping hero awakens to fin Wolverine ready to impale him.

NOTE: Cover-labeled "Enemy of the State, Part 4 of 6." UXM #514, '09 reveals that Mindee Cuckoo's first name was originally Irma. W #31, '0! reveals that the Vatican hired Elektra to assassinate the Gorgon once his nihilist plans were made public. Eyewitnesses and a SHIELD ager istake Hornet for Spider-Man, which may be an inside joke: Spider-Man initially created the Hornet costume as an alternate identity in SenSM #27, '98; Eddie McDonough adopted the identity prior to Sling #0, '98. Though Iron Man is said to be at a Bilderberg Group meeting in Helsinki, Finland, the group only met in Helsinki in 1994. Their 2005 meeting was in Rottach-Egern, Germany.

WOLVERINE #24 [#213] (March 2005)

"Enemy of the State, Part 5 of 6" (22 pages)

CREDITS: Mark Millar (writer), John Romita Jr. (pencils), Klaus Janson (inks), Virtual Calligraphy's Randy Gentile (letters), Paul Mounts (colors), Jennifer Lee (editor), Axel Alonso (exec editor), Richard Isanove (c colors)
FEATURE CHARACTER: Wolverine
GUEST STARS: Daredevil (next in SecWar #3, '04), Elektra (dies, resurrected off-panel, next in W #26, '05)
VILLAINS: Gorgon, "Baron Strucker," Elsbeth von Strucker, undead Hand ninjas (some destroyed), Hand sorcerer (some or others last in W #22, '05 fb, this one or another chr next in W #13, '11 fb, some or others next in NAv #27, '07), Hydra agents
OTHER CHARACTERS: SHIELD agents (die, others bts guarding other heroes) inc McGurk, café waitress, bystanders; Nick Fury (mentioned, McGurk told to contact him), President George W. Bush (mentioned, Hydra's next target), drug kingpin (mentioned, killed by Elektra); Hugo Natchios (bts in Elektra's memories); people (as busts)

LOCATIONS/ITEMS: Daredevil's brownstone w/nearby rooftop, Hydra base, Washington DC café, Washington Monument; Budapest, Hungary (mentioned) / Ninjas' spears, scythes (all but 1 of prev 2 bts), swords, sais, bows & arrows, Elektra's gun (destroyed) & sniper rifle destroyed, another mentioned) w/scope, agents' comm unit (bts) & guns, Daredevil's window, punching bag (prev 2 destroyed), SHIELD beeper (bts), couch, screwdrivers, weights & billy clubs, Gorgon's swords (1 destroyed) & earpiece (bts), Elsbeth's comm unit (bts), Hydra cameras (bts), earpieces & teleporter, Elsbeth & "Strucker's" laptops, Wolverine's Hydra implants (bts), sorcerer's spears, Hand altar
SYNOPSIS: As Wolverine threatens Daredevil, Elektra aims her rifle from a nearby rooftop, having predicted Wolverine's attack. Her shot misses; Daredevil uses the ensuing confusion to hurl Wolverine away, but the ninjas attack him. Elektra sees that the Gorgon spoiled her shot. He slaughters the SHIELD agents backing her up, transforming some to stone with his gaze, then challenges Elektra. Inside, Daredevil destroys the ninjas, but Wolverine rejoins the fight. The two battle all through Daredevil's house until Wolverine is knocked off-balance and falls, impaling his chest on a ninja's sword. Nearby, Elektra and Gorgon duel, but Gorgon soon gains the upper hand. Gloating that Elsbeth has promised him Hydra if Strucker's plans fail, he mercilessly beats Elektra to death. Wolverine's injury clears his mind; he warns Daredevil that Hydra plan to have him assassinate the President the following night, but Strucker and Elsbeth teleport him back to their base. Daredevil realizes that Elektra was the villains' true target that night — as elsewhere, the Hand prepares to resurrect her…
NOTE: The cover label disappears for this issue. The credits incorrectly attribute this issue's cover pencils to Greg Land.

WOLVERINE #25 [#214] (April 2005)

"Enemy of the State, Part 6 of 6" (23 pages)

CREDITS: Mark Millar (writer), John Romita Jr. (pencils), Klaus Janson (inks), Virtual Calligraphy's Randy Gentile (letters), Paul Mounts (colors), Jennifer Lee (editor), Axel Alonso (exec editor), Richard Isanove (c colors)
FEATURE CHARACTER: Wolverine (also in AntM #1, '06 fb)
GUEST STARS: X-Men: Marvel Girl (Rachel Grey, Cyclops & Jean Grey's telepathic & telekinetic daughter from Earth-811, next in W #30, '05), Cyclops (both last in UXM #460, '05), Shadowcat (also in NX #13, '05), Emma Frost (prev 2 last in W #23, '05), Beast (last in NX #13, '05), Colossus (last in UXM #460, '05, last bts in W #23, '05), Gambit (last in X4 #5, '05), Storm (last in W #21, '04), Iceman (prev 8 next in NX #13, '05), Havok (prev 2 last in UXM #459, '05), Rogue (bts hunting Wolverine, last in Cable&Dp #10, '05) (prev 2 next in XPx:E #5, '05), Northstar (dies, last in X #164, also in NX #13 & W #30 fb, next dead in NX #13, all '05, see NOTE); Mr. Fantastic (bts, mind read by Marvel Girl, last in MK4 #18, '05, last bts in W #23, '05), Falcon (prev 2 next in NX #13, '05), Captain America (also bts on TV, also in NX #13, '05, next in YAv #1, '05), Nick Fury (prev 3 last in W #23, '05), Dum Dum Dugan (bts aboard Helicarrier, last in Cable&Dp #10, '05, chr last in AntM #1, '06 fb)
VILLAINS: "Baron Strucker" (dies off-panel), Gorgon, Elsbeth von Strucker, undead Hand ninjas (bts killing teenage mutant), Hydra agents
OTHER CHARACTERS: Danielle "Dani" Moonstar (New Mutants squad advisor, casts illusions, in silhouette, between NX #12-13, '05), Xavier Institute students (some or others last in W #23, '05, next in NX #13, '05) inc New Mutants (Dani's squad): Elixir (Josh Foley, healer), Prodigy (David Alleyne, absorbs skills & knowledge), Surge (Noriko Ashida, manipulates electricity), Wind Dancer (Sofia Mantega, manipulates wind); Paragons (Wolfsbane's squad): Trance (Hope Abbott, projects astral form, unnamed), Wolf Cub (Nicholas Gleason, wolflike form, see NOTE) (prev 6 in silhouette, during NX #13, '05); President George W. Bush (last in Cable&Dp #9, last bts in W #21, next voice only in SecWar #5/3, all '05, next in W:O #1, '06), SHIELD agents (some die, some or others also & chr next in AntM #1, '06 fb) inc Mitch Carson, Veronica King, Chris McCarthy, Eric O'Grady (prev 4 1st bts app, aboard Helicarrier, during AntM #1, '06 fb) & doctors, super heroes (bts guarding Washington DC), teenage mutant (bts, killed by Hand); people (on TV); agent's girlfriend & baby (mentioned, detected by Marvel Girl)
LOCATIONS/ITEMS: X-Mansion inc hangar & grounds, Washington DC inc White House's Oval Office, Iowa (bts), Hydra base, skies above USA / SHIELD helicopters, broadcast equipment (both bts), guns, paperwork, jets, Helicarrier & medical equipment w/restraints, Wolverine's terraformer (destroyed), cloaking device & Hydra implants (bts) inc ocular cameras, Cerebra, Fury's guns, Iron Man's armor (hereinafter considered his standard equipment and not listed separately), Falcon's glider suit, Hydra teleporter & monitors, X-Men's Blackbird jet, trees (destroyed) w/branch, Gambit's aftershave (bts) & staff, Rogue's breath mints (bts), doctor's medical kits, "Strucker's" ring, Gorgon's sword
SYNOPSIS: Wolverine infiltrates the X-Mansion with a Hydra cloaking device and grabs Marvel Girl. Threatening to activate a terraformer, obliterating the mansion and all its students, he orders her to use Cerebra to telepathically kill the President. As SHIELD and various heroes guard the White House, Nick Fury learns that the Hand are killing small-time superhumans. Marvel Girl uses Cerebra to read Mr. Fantastic's mind, letting her telekinetically disassemble the terraformer, then attacks Wolverine and alerts the X-Men. Wolverine commandeers the Blackbird, blasting it through the mansion and into the woods, but the X-Men, SHIELD troops, and other arriving heroes pursue and attack him. Wolverine lunges at Shadowcat, who phases; Wolverine passes through her and impales Northstar, killing him. Assaulted on all sides, Wolverine is staggered; Captain America delivers a crashing blow with his shield, knocking Wolverine out. In Hydra's base, Elsbeth and the Gorgon execute

Strucker for his failure. Later, aboard the Helicarrier, Fury worries about a fanatical Gorgon-led Hydra and wonders what to do with Wolverine.
NOTE: Cover-labeled "Enemy of the State, Part 6 of 6." Northstar joined an ad hoc X-Men team in UXM #392, '01, and later joined the X-Men
teaching staff in UXM #414, '02. NX #13, '05 clarifies the identities of several students seen only in silhouette here. Dani's squad names
themselves after her old team, the original New Mutants, in NX #2, '04. NX:Ybook, '05 reveals Wolf Cub's codename, and names Trance and
reveals her powers. AntM #1, '06 fb reveals that Dugan, Carson, King, McCarthy and O'Grady are aboard the Helicarrier during this issue.
Carson's last name is revealed in AntM #2, '07, and King's in AntM #5, '07. Although this issue mentions that SHIELD has recruited many super
heroes to guard Washington DC, most are never seen or identified.

WOLVERINE #26 [#215] (May 2005)

"Agent of S.H.I.E.L.D. Part 1 of 6" (24 pages)

CREDITS: Mark Millar (writer), John Romita Jr. (pencils), Klaus Janson (inks),
Virtual Calligraphy's Randy Gentile (letters), Paul Mounts (colors), Jennifer Lee
(editor), Axel Alonso (exec editor), Greg Land (c pencils), Marc Silvestri (variant c
pencils), Eric Basaldua (variant c inks), Richard Isanove (c colors), Steve Firchow
(variant c colors)
FEATURE CHARACTER: Wolverine (also as himself & on monitor in simulation)
GUEST STARS: X-Men: Polaris (Lorna Dane, controls magnetism, last in X #16,
also in NX #13, next in XPx:E #5, all '05), Iceman (during & also in NX #13, '05),
Elektra (also on monitor, last in W #24, '05), Nick Fury (also "dies" in
simulation), Dum Dum Dugan (bts on Helicarrier)
VILLAINS: Gorgon (also in fb between SecWs #11, '10 fb & W #20, '04), Elsbeth von Strucker, Northstar (dead, last dead in NX #13, '05),
Slyde (Matthew Beacher, wears stepbrother's frictionless suit, see NOTE; dies, last as Matt in SMU #6/2, '94) (prev 2 resurrected off-panel),
Knickknack (Nick Grossman, juggles dangerous weapons, last in Tb #53, '01), Leap-Frog (Buford Lange, wears leaping suit, last in DD #1,
'01 fb), Poison (Cecilia Cardinale, empowered by extradimensional warrior, last in SM #64, '96), SHOC (Todd "Neil Aiken" Fields, bonded
w/Darkforce-wielding armor, last in SM #90, '98), Spot (Dr. Johnathon Ohnn, controls portals to "Spotworld" dimension, last in TWoS #17, '02),
Vibro (Prof. Alton Vibereaux, generates vibratory energy, last in IM #267, '91), many other heroes & villains (prev 8 die & resurrected off-panel,
see NOTE) (prev 10 also on monitor), Sickly Ones (ancient Hand founders, 1st bts app, supporting Gorgon; 1 also in fb, his 1st on-panel app
prior to issue; all next in 1st on-panel app in W #29, '05), undead Hand ninjas (some or others in fb, their chr 1st app, prior to W #20, '04, some
destroyed; some or others next in W #29, '05), Hydra agents (bts hacking SHIELD mainframe)
OTHER CHARACTERS: Dani Moonstar (during & also in NX #13, '05), "Baron Strucker" (bts, dead, buried on beach), Dr. Weinberg (SHIELD
psychotherapist, last as Rabble Rouser in ST #119, '64, also "dies" in simulation), SHIELD agents (1 dies; some or others also in simulation,
most "die"; some or others chr last & also in AntM #1, '06 fb, chr next in AntM #2, '07 fb) inc Chris McCarthy (chr last in AntM #2, '07 fb),
Mitch Carson, Veronica King, Eric O'Grady (prev 3 chr last in AntM #1, '06 fb, chr next in AntM #2, '07 fb) (prev 4 bts aboard Helicarrier),
Artie, Carmine, Melcher, Mills, Nico (prev 5 aboard Helicarrier, possibly bts, see NOTE) & Dubrowsky (in simulation, see NOTE), doctor (also
in photo, dies); Dawn of the White Light (mentioned, terrorized Japan), Gorgon's parents, siblings & only friend (prev 3 mentioned, killed by
Gorgon), Spot's wife (mentioned, ran up several bills), TV personalities (mentioned in fb, nicknamed Gorgon), Japanese citizens (mentioned in
fb, terrorized by Gorgon); SHIELD agent's unborn baby (bts in simulation, detected by Wolverine)
LOCATIONS/ITEMS: Hand's secret city (Akamatu, Japan, in fb) w/forgotten forest, Hydra safehouse (Fussen, Germany), New York City inc
St. Mary's Church & NYU Medical Center, skies above Arkansas (also in simulation), Japan (mentioned in fb) inc TV stations, "Strucker's" burial
site (beach, mentioned) / Gorgon's paintings, opera, formula (all mentioned), sword & blindfold, hurled log, Sickly Ones' tesseract house, ninja
scythes, spear, mace, candles (all in fb), swords, nunchuks (others of prev 2 also in fb), daggers & sai, Elektra's jet-boots, swords (prev 2 also
on monitor), sais & throwing daggers, Slyde's frictionless suit (also on monitor), doctor's bonesaw, SHIELD guns, earpieces, protective suits
(prev 3 also in simulation), satellite (bts), paperwork & Blackhawk Helicarrier (also in simulation) w/shields, cameras (prev 2 bts), computers &
monitors, Northstar's will (bts) & explosives (also on monitor), Hydra teleporter & computer (prev 2 bts), Weinberg's protective suit, handheld
computer & deprogramming equipment w/monitor, Fury's gun (prev 5 also in simulation) & earpiece, Wolverine's anesthetic (bts), villains' staff
guns, earpiece (prev 3 bts, also bts on monitor), armor, explosives & jet-boots, SHOC's Darkforce armor, Leap-Frog's leaping suit (prev 5 also
on monitor)
FLASHBACK: Gorgon seeks out the Hand, slaughtering his way to an audience with a Sickly One. He pledges loyalty to their nihilist ideals,
then impales himself with his sword and asks the Hand to resurrect him.
SYNOPSIS: Gorgon and Elsbeth discuss the villains that the Hand has recently killed and resurrected. Spot teleports to a meeting with Slyde,
but arrives to find the Hand murdering him. Elsewhere, the X-Men steel themselves to decapitate Northstar's corpse, but Elektra and the Hand
suddenly teleport in and steal the body. As SHIELD tracks the mounting reports of murdered villains, Dr. Weinberg reports to Nick Fury on his
progress deprogramming Wolverine. Suddenly, Wolverine awakens and breaks free, rampaging through the Helicarrier. He kills Fury, but pauses
when he realizes that a SHIELD agent is pregnant. Weinberg appears and congratulates him; the rampage has been a simulation, one of many
they have recently put Wolverine through, and his moment of mercy was a breakthrough. SHIELD suddenly detects a swarm of resurrected
villains flying directly at the Helicarrier — led by Elektra and Northstar.
NOTE: Cover-labeled "Agent of ... S.H.I.E.L.D. 1 of 6." This issue has a variant cover. W #29, '05 reveals that Elektra is working undercover in W
#26-29, '05, and as such she is not listed as a villain. Next issue names agents Artie, Carmine, Melcher and Nico; AntM #2, '07 fb names Mills.
Though they are aboard the Helicarrier here, it is unclear if they appear on-panel or not. It is unrevealed whether Dubrowsky and the pregnant
SHIELD agent also exist in reality, or are just characters in the simulation. MEnc #5, '05 gave Rabble Rouser's real name as Vitold Niyazov;
however, after this issue revealed his last name as Weinberg, OHMU HC9, '09 clarified that Niyazov was an alias. Weinberg's true first name
is unrevealed to date. Contrary to the SHIELD agents' gossip, Rabble Rouser never broke the Human Torch's jaw. Leap-Frog's first name is
revealed in OHMU #4, '06; OHMU HC4, '08 clarifies which of the various Leap-Frogs was killed and resurrected by the Hand. Slyde, who is
black, is depicted here as white; SM:BiBH, '07 fixes this error by clarifying that the Slyde seen here is the original Slyde's stepbrother. The Spot's
real name is a reference to the phrase "Johnny on the spot." The vast majority of the resurrected heroes and villains seen in this issue and next
are never identified. The Helicarrier's location over Arkansas is revealed next issue.

WOLVERINE #27 [#216] (June 2005)

"Agent of S.H.I.E.L.D. Part 2 of 6" (23 pages)

CREDITS: Mark Millar (writer), John Romita Jr. (pencils), Klaus Janson (inks), Virtual Calligraphy's Randy Gentile (letters), Paul Mounts (colors), Jennifer Lee (editor), Axel Alonso (exec editor), Greg Land (c pencils), Joe Quesada (variant c pencils), Danny Miki (variant c inks), Richard Isanove (c colors), Morry Hollowell (variant c colors)

FEATURE CHARACTER: Wolverine (also in AntM #3, '07 fb, next in Cable&Dp #13, '05)

GUEST STARS: Elektra (next in W #29, '05), Dum Dum Dugan (bts aboard Helicarrier, chr next in AntM #2, '07 fb), Nick Fury (also in AntM #2-3, '07 fbs)

VILLAINS: Knickknack (next bts in UJack #1, '06), Spot (next in CW:WarC, '07), Leap-Frog, Poison, SHOC, Slyde, Vibro (prev 5 die), Northstar, Gorgon, Elsbeth von Strucker, Dawn of the White Light (Gorgon's mutant terrorist cult, Brotherhood splinter group, 1st on-panel app, group last bts in W #20, '04), Hydra agents (some or others next bts in W #30, '05, next in W #31, '05), AIM agents (some or others last in Cap 3, '05, next in W #30, '05), many other resurrected heroes & villains (many or all die, some also in AntM #2, '07 fb)

OTHER CHARACTERS: Ichiro, Fukuko (both last in W #20, '04, next in W #31, '04), Dr. Weinberg (also in AntM #3, '07 fb), SHIELD agents (many die, some or others chr last & also in AntM #2, '07 fb, also in AntM #3, '07 fb; others bts preparing escape pod & manning other stations inc England & Germany, many presumably die) inc Mitch Carson (chr last in AntM #2 fb, chr next in AntM #3 fb, next in AntM #2, all '07), Veronica (chr last & also bts in AntM #2, '07 fb, next in AntM #3, '07 fb), Chris McCarthy (next in AntM #2, '07 fb), Eric O'Grady (during & also in AntM #2, '07 fb, next as Ant-Man in AntM #1, '06), Mills (also in AntM #2, '07 fb) (prev 5 bts aboard Helicarrier), Artie, Carmine, Melcher & Nico, rescue crews (some or others chr last in AntM #3, '07 fb), Hydra servant; Libertas (as Statue of Liberty, cover only)

LOCATIONS/ITEMS: Arkansas, Hydra safehouse, Ichiro's home, Wakanda (mentioned) / Villains' earpiece (bts), explosives, armor, staff, guns & jet-boots, SHOC's Darkforce armor w/flashlight, Slyde's frictionless suit, Leap-Frog's leaping suit, Fury's guns, Weinberg's protective suit & deprogramming equipment w/monitor (bts), SHIELD armor, earpiece (all possibly destroyed), guns (others possibly destroyed) & Blackhawk Helicarrier (destroyed) w/computer, Elektra's jet-boots (bts) & swords, Hydra weapons, comm system (prev 2 bts), doomsday devices (all but 1 bts) & construction equipment, Wakandan materials (mentioned), rescue crews' temporary shelters & medical equipment inc IVs, metal pole (bts), Wolverine's cellphone, SHIELD & Weinberg's bandages

SYNOPSIS: The villains assault the Helicarrier, blasting their way in and causing massive damage. Northstar attacks Nick Fury and beats him severely. As villains begin breaking into Weinberg's lab, the desperate doctor releases Wolverine, still unsure if he is fully deprogrammed. The villains burst in, but Wolverine slaughters them all one by one — then proceeds through the Helicarrier, killing every other villain he finds and working his way to the command center, where he finds Elektra and Northstar holding a nearly dead Fury. Explosions suddenly rip through the damaged Helicarrier and the massive ship crashes, killing hundreds. Elsewhere, Gorgon and Elsbeth observe Hydra and AIM's construction of doomsday weapons from Mr. Fantastic's hard drive, and gloat about SHIELD's destruction. Later, as rescue crews feverishly aid the crash survivors, Wolverine calls Ichiro and Fukuko. He belatedly explains that Rikuto is dead, and Fukuko asks Wolverine to make those responsible pay dearly. Weinberg finds Wolverine suiting up, preparing to kill every last member of Hand, Hydra and Dawn of the White Light.

NOTE: Cover-labeled "Agent of … S.H.I.E.L.D. Part 2 of 6." This issue's cover is an homage to NF:AoS #4, '68. This issue also has a variant cover. Fukuko and Rikuto are named here. SHOC's codename is incorrectly given as Shock; Slyde's last name is incorrectly spelled "Beecher." Despite their seeming deaths here, Knickknack and Spot have gone on to appear elsewhere; any or all of the other resurrected heroes and villains may have also survived. The Helicarrier's location over Arkansas is specified here.

WOLVERINE #28 [#217] (July 2005)

"Agent of S.H.I.E.L.D. Part 3 of 6" (23 pages)

CREDITS: Mark Millar (writer), John Romita Jr. (pencils), Klaus Janson (inks), Virtual Calligraphy's Randy Gentile (letters), Paul Mounts (colors), James Taveras (production), Jennifer Lee (editor), Axel Alonso (exec editor), Greg Land (c pencils), Richard Isanove (c colors), Walter N. Cosby Jr. (special thanks)

FEATURE CHARACTER: Wolverine (also on scanner, next in W #13, '11 fb)

GUEST STARS: Nick Fury (bts recovering from injuries), Dum Dum Dugan (bts as acting SHIELD commander, chr last in AntM #2, '07 fb, next in W #30, '05)

VILLAINS: Northstar (next in W #30, '05), Dawn of the White Light (die) inc Gas, Quake, Rockslide, Space-Bomb, Sparks & Thermos (all also on scanner)

OTHER CHARACTERS: Sentinels (see NOTE, others last in WX #22, '04, chr last in SS1 #1, '06): Three (unnamed, destroyed), One, Two; Dr. Weinberg (next in W #30, '05), SHIELD agents (others mentioned, seized Sentinels), Northstar's victims (dead) inc bar patrons, police, truck driver (bts dumping bodies), bartender, bystanders; birds; Russian mob, Iraqis (prev 2 mentioned, tried to sell & buy Sentinels)

LOCATIONS/ITEMS: US towns, garbage dump, bar, SHIELD remote base (bts) & emergency outpost, Alaskan oil refinery (Dawn of the White Light's hideout, possibly on Kenai Peninsula, destroyed) / Police flashlights, camera, tarps & cars, ambulance, dump truck, Northstar's pills (mentioned), jukebox w/CDs, Dawn of the White Light's restraints (destroyed), truncheon & shotgun (prev 2 possibly destroyed), SHIELD trucks, guns, paperwork & comm system, Wolverine's earpiece & mutant gene-cloaking device, Sentinels' mutant scanners (prev 3 bts)

SYNOPSIS: Given command of the Dawn of the White Light mutant cult, Northstar begins a cross-country spree, killing bigots and homophobes. Wolverine tracks Northstar and the Dawn to a bar; feeling responsible for having killed Northstar to begin with, Wolverine gives him a chance to repent — but Northstar angrily declines, and has the Dawn beat Wolverine into unconsciousness. Elsewhere, Dr. Weinberg vouches that Wolverine is deprogrammed, and points out that with SHIELD in shambles, Wolverine's vendetta may be exactly what the heroes need. Wolverine awakens imprisoned at the Dawn's secret base, but the villains discover technology in his neck that cloaks his mutant gene. Suddenly, Sentinels burst in and begin wiping out the cult members en masse — Wolverine had obtained the robots from SHIELD storage before tracking down Northstar. Wolverine interrogates Northstar about the location of Gorgon's base, but Northstar refuses to answer. Wolverine knocks him out and alerts SHIELD of the battle, then climbs aboard a Sentinel's shoulder and heads to his next target — the Hand.

NOTE: Cover-labeled "Agent of … S.H.I.E.L.D. Part 3 of 6." The Marvel Knights logo disappears from the cover for two issues starting here, b the series is still published under that imprint. Wolverine references the "New Avengers" this issue, even though this arc occurs before that tea forms. He also mentions that he heard that these Sentinels were recovered after a battle with the Avengers, but it is unclear if this is a referen to a previously published story, a heretofore-unknown event, or pure hearsay. Their numeric designations were likely assigned by SHIELD a are not traditional Sentinel numbers; Three's designation is not given, but can be easily deduced.

WOLVERINE #29 [#218] (August 2005)

"Agent of S.H.I.E.L.D. Part 4 of 6" (23 pages)

CREDITS: Mark Millar (writer), John Romita Jr. (pencils), Klaus Janson (inks), Virtual Calligraphy's Randy Gent (letters), Paul Mounts (colors), James Taveras (production), Jennifer Lee (editor), Axel Alonso (exec editor), Jo Quesada (c pencils), Danny Miki (c inks), Morry Hollowell (c colors), Walter N. Cosby Jr. (special thanks)
FEATURE CHARACTER: Wolverine
GUEST STARS: Elektra (last in W #27, '05), Nick Fury
VILLAINS: Sickly Ones (1st on-panel app for group, die; 1 last in W #26, '05 fb, group last bts in W #26, '05 undead Hand ninjas (destroyed)
OTHER CHARACTERS: Sentinel Two (destroyed, other Sentinels next in WX:DoFN #1, '05), SHIELD agen (others mentioned, modified Sentinels), Wolverine's victims (bts, killed for information); Fukuko, Rikuto (prev mentioned, in Wolverine's thoughts)

LOCATIONS/ITEMS: Hand's secret city w/forgotten forest, SHIELD top secret hospital (Manhattan, see NOTE) / Ninjas' swords, spear scythes, bows, arrows, shuriken, nunchuks, maces, daggers & tiger claws (of some or all destroyed), Rikuto's books, toys, Pocky & bi eggs (prev 4 mentioned), Sickly One's tesseract house w/trapdoor, Wolverine's SHIELD technology (bts, see NOTE) & earpiece (bts), Elektra swords, SHIELD guns & helicopter, Fury's bandages & IVs
SYNOPSIS: Wolverine learns the location of the Hand's secret city. The ninjas inside prepare for an attack, but are surprised when a Sentin bursts through their outer wall. The robot fries scores of ninjas as Wolverine guides it towards the main house, but other ninjas leap onto th Sentinel and hack at it, eventually causing it to crash. Wolverine continues on foot, letting anguished thoughts of Rikuto fuel his rage. The Sick Ones welcome Wolverine and reveal that Elektra is the Hand's new queen. They order her to kill Wolverine, but Elektra silently signals a pla to him, and the two suddenly turn on the Sickly Ones and murder them. Elektra reveals that since she has been resurrected before, the Hand brainwashing did not take: she has merely been undercover, and now knows all of Hydra's secret locations. The two gleefully slaughter eve ninja in the city and report back to SHIELD. Nick Fury smiles from his hospital bed, knowing that SHIELD can finally shut down Hydra for goo
NOTE: Cover-labeled "Agent of … S.H.I.E.L.D. Part 4 of 6." This issue's recap page shows this issue's cover, instead of the standard image the previous issue's cover. The SHIELD hospital's secret location is revealed as Manhattan next issue. Although the Sickly Ones reference th SHIELD technology hidden in Wolverine's belt, and although a belt is traditionally part of his costume, Wolverine is not wearing a belt this issu

WOLVERINE #30 [#219] (September 2005)

"Agent of S.H.I.E.L.D. Part 5 of 6" (23 pages)

CREDITS: Mark Millar (writer), John Romita Jr. (pencils), Klaus Janson (inks), Virtual Calligraphy's Randy Genti (letters), Paul Mounts (colors), Tom Valente (production), Jennifer Lee (editor), Axel Alonso (exec editor), Richa Isanove (c colors), Walter N. Cosby Jr. (special thanks)
FEATURE CHARACTER: Wolverine (also in rfb)
GUEST STARS: X-Men: Beast, Emma Frost (both next in SecWar #5, '05 fb), Shadowcat (also in rfb), Icema (all last in NX #13, '05), Marvel Girl (last in W #25, '05) (prev 2 next in XPx:E #5, '05); Dum Dum Dugan (last W #28, '05), Elektra, Nick Fury
VILLAINS: Constrictor (Frank "Schlicting" Payne, wields Vibranium arm coils, last in Cable&Dp #12, '05, chr ne in SecWar #3, '04, next in SecWar #5, '05 fb), Man-Bull (William Taurens, super-strong & durable horned mutate last in Gravity #1, '05, next in U #3, '06), Rhino (Aleksei Sytsevich, super-strong, wears durable hide, on monitc last in MKSM #10, next bts in MTU #7, next in MTU #11, all '05), Tombstone (Lonnie Lincoln, super-strong & durable albino, last in MKSM #1 '05, next in MKSM #18, '05), Warhawk (Mitchell Tanner, metallic skin, last in X #11/2, '92), Northstar (as hologram, also in rfb, also in fb during V #25, '05; last in W #28, '05), Gorgon (on monitor), Elsbeth von Strucker (dies), AIM agents (many die, some or others last in W #2 '05, next in GLA #2, '05), Hydra agents (bts in European bases, many die, some or others last in W #27, '05), undead Hand ninjas (destroyed)
OTHER CHARACTERS: Dr. Weinberg (also in photo, last in W #28, '05), SHIELD agents (some die, some or others as holograms) & doctors hotel guests; Special Forces soldiers & officers (prev 2 mentioned, train with rabbits), rabbits (mentioned, killed & eaten by soldiers); Rikut (dead in Wolverine's thoughts), Northstar's victims (dead in Northstar's thoughts, on monitor as holograms); birds (psychic illusions); gargoyl (as statue, cover only)
LOCATIONS/ITEMS: X-Mansion grounds (in rfb/fb), astral plane, SHIELD emergency outpost (also as hologram) & top secret hospita Manhattan hotel inc Gorgon's penthouse (destroyed), Hydra's European factories (some bts) inc St. Petersburg, Russia (on monito Amsterdam, Netherlands & Brussels, Belgium / Frost's floating pillows (psychic illusions), SHIELD protective suits (as hologram), teleporte (bts), trucks, guns, armor, monitors, earpieces, jet-boots, energy lances & helicopters w/cloaking devices, cameras (prev 2 bts) & missiles Weinberg's hologram projector & deprogramming equipment (as hologram) w/monitors, Dugan's handheld computer, Wolverine & Elektra' guns & smart-suits (unnamed) w/psi-blockers (destroyed), teleporters & intangibility switches (prev 2 bts), Wolverine's earpiece (bts) & jetpac Elektra's swords, throwing daggers & nunchuks, Null (Mr. Fantastic's anti-Galactus robot, half-built), Hydra's construction equipment, AIM blasters & handheld computers, Constrictor's Vibranium coils, ninjas' swords, wooden beam, Fury's bandages
FLASHBACK: As Wolverine impales him (W #25, '05), Northstar screams.
SYNOPSIS: In Emma Frost's psychic therapy group, Shadowcat blames herself for Northstar's death, but the other X-Men reassure her she is not to blame. At SHIELD's emergency outpost, Dr. Weinberg tells Wolverine that his deprogramming technique isn't working on Northsta for some reason. Wolverine mentally prepares for SHIELD's assault on Hydra, focusing on thoughts of Rikuto. Dum Dum Dugan explains tha the agents will be hitting seven worldwide Hydra facilities simultaneously; Wolverine and Elektra load up with technological gadgets, and SHIELL

ffers reduced jail sentences to several incarcerated super villains in exchange for participating in the assault. As troops and criminals swarm ydra's bases, cloaked SHIELD helicopters fire missiles into Gorgon's Manhattan penthouse, killing Elsbeth. Wolverine and Elektra teleport in nd grievously injure Gorgon, but he manages to fight back, murdering the accompanying SHIELD team and pinning Wolverine to a wall with sword. Gorgon reads Elektra's mind, learns Nick Fury's location, and teleports to SHIELD's hospital, intent on killing the convalescing Fury... OTE: Cover-labeled "Agent of … S.H.I.E.L.D. Part 5 of 6." The Marvel Knights logo returns to the cover this issue. The SHIELD hospital's cation is revealed here. Wolverine and Elektra's smart-suits are named next issue.

WOLVERINE #31 [#220] (October 2005)

"Agent of S.H.I.E.L.D. Part 6 of 6" (23 pages)

CREDITS: Mark Millar (writer), John Romita Jr. (pencils), Klaus Janson (inks), Virtual Calligraphy's Randy Gentile (letters), Paul Mounts (colors), James Taveras (production), Jennifer Lee (editor), Axel Alonso (exec editor), Richard Isanove (c colors)

FEATURE CHARACTER: Wolverine (next in W #14, '11 fb, W #59, '08 fb; XFor #4-6, SecWar #4 & 5 fb, Pulse #9, 6 & 9, GLA #2 fb, XPx:E #1-5, all '05, XMU #12, '06; X #166 bts & 167-170, W:Soul #1-5, AX #7-9, 10 fb & 11-12, XMU #9, NAv #4-6 & 8 fb, all '05, NAv #42, '08; MTU #10, 10/2 & 11-13, Rogue #7 voice only & 11-12, all '05, Gam #2, '04 fb; Gam #4-5 & 6 fbs, X #171 & 174, NX #14, NAv #7-10, all '05, GSAv/5, '08, Herc #4-5, '05, YAv #11-12, '06, IM:K&K/2, '10, GSAv/4, '08; ASM #519-522, MKSM #13-14 & 18, all '05, NAvF, '06 voice only, X:KPSF #1, '05 bts, Nc #8-12, '05-06; X #175, BP #8, X #176, BP #9, X:Col #1, all '05, XMU #12/2 & 14/2, '06, HoM #1, '05, NAv #42, '08 bts; HoM #1 & 3 fb bts, W #33 fb, all '05)

UEST STARS: Nick Fury (chr next in W #14, '11 fb), Dum Dum Dugan (both next in NFHC #1, '05), Elektra (next in MAv #16, '08), Shadowcat ext in SecWar #5, '05 fb), Spider-Man (last in SMU #10, '05, next in SecWar #3, '05)

ILLAINS: Gorgon (dies, next in SecWs #2, '09), Northstar (next in NX #16, '05), Hydra agents (1 or another chr next in MAv #16, '08, some others next in ASM #519, '05), criminals (dead)

THER CHARACTERS: Ichiro, Fukuko (both last in W #27, '05), Rikuto (bts, dead, buried in field, last in W #20, '04), Elsbeth von Strucker dead), SHIELD doctors (some dead) & agents (some dead, some die; some or others next in NFHC #1, '05) inc Captain (dies), police (bts forming SHIELD of Wolverine's actions), homeless people

OCATIONS/ITEMS: Manhattan inc warehouse, SHIELD top secret hospital & ruins of Gorgon's hotel penthouse, SHIELD emergency utpost & temporary HQ, Hydra base, New Jersey alley, docks, bar, X-Mansion, Japanese field / Elektra's swords, nunchuks & throwing aggers, SHIELD armor, guns, monitor, helicopters & energy lances, Wolverine's earpiece (bts), bandages & smart-suit (named) w/jetpack & eleporter (bts) inc GPS (destroyed), Fury's replacement teeth & lungs (prev 2 bts), bandages, sling & computer w/voice recognition software ts), microphone & monitors, hospital window, warehouse skylight (prev 2 destroyed), doctors' handheld computer, Weinberg's deprogramming quipment, Shadowcat's laptop

YNOPSIS: Wolverine tries to teleport to the hospital, but his equipment is damaged. Gorgon kills Nick Fury's guards and prepares to ecapitate him — but Wolverine uses his jetpack and bursts through the wall, tackling Gorgon out the window. The two brawl savagely, and Gorgon telepathically dredges up all the horrible acts that Hydra made Wolverine commit. Gorgon prepares to turn Wolverine to stone, but Wolverine uses his claws to reflect Gorgon's gaze back into his own eyes. Gorgon transforms into stone, and Wolverine shatters him. Weeks ter, Fury e-mails Shadowcat, explaining that Elektra has vanished and is rumored to be restarting the Hand, and Hydra is likely reforming sewhere. Fury lies, claiming that Northstar's body was never found, while Northstar screams in a SHIELD deprogramming unit. Fury tells hadowcat that Wolverine hasn't been seen since the final battle, but hundreds of criminals have been found dead. In Japan, Wolverine finally arns where Rikuto was buried; he summons Ichiro and Fukuko to a barren field, where all three grieve.

OTE: Cover-labeled "Agent of … S.H.I.E.L.D. Part 6 of 6." This issue reveals that the Vatican secretly hired Elektra to assassinate Gorgon. ick Fury misspells Northstar's last name "Baurbier" in his e-mail to Shadowcat, but he also apologizes for his spelling errors, blaming his voice-ecognition software. Northstar is eventually deprogrammed in X Ann '07. Wolverine joins the New Avengers shortly after this issue. NAv #31, 7 reveals that Elektra is replaced by a Skrull sometime after this issue; MAv #16, '08 clarifies that it is actually the Skrull who rebuilt the Hand.

WOLVERINE #32 [#221] (November 2005)

"Prisoner Number Zero" (23 pages)

CREDITS: Mark Millar (writer), Kaare Andrews (art), Virtual Calligraphy's Randy Gentile (letters), José Villarrubia (colors), Cory Sedlmeier (asst editor), Axel Alonso (editor), Andrew Devenney & Andrew Wickliffe (special thanks)

FEATURE CHARACTER: Wolverine (also as symbolic image, chr last in W:O #20, '08 fb, chr next in I♥M:MMH, '06 fb)

VILLAINS: Nazis: Major Bauman (Sobibor's Commandant, dies), General Reinhard Heydrich (Bauman's mentor, dies off-panel), Muller, Schenker (prev 2 Bauman's aides), Sobibor's previous two Commandants (bts, committed suicide) & later Commandant, General Kurt Daluege (Heydrich's successor, see NOTE; bts appointing later Commandant), soldiers

THER CHARACTERS: Sobibor prisoners (some die off-panel, some dead) inc Jews, Communists & homosexuals, Czech assassins (bts illing Heydrich); Gustav Reifsnyder (Nazi, mentioned, reported mutant sighting), mutant boy (possibly Max Eisenhardt, see NOTE; mentioned, estroyed armored car), Bauman's allies (mentioned, cited his potential), Bauman's father (mentioned, Bauman promised to pass his wine to is own children), Satan (as skull on wine label)

OCATIONS/ITEMS: Sobibor death camp (Lublin, Poland) w/Commandant's house (destroyed), crematorium & gas chamber / Sobibor's urnace (bts), train, coal bunkers & barbed wire fences, Bauman's wine bottles, books, bookshelf, lantern (prev 4 destroyed), car, gun & reakfast tray, soldiers' gas masks & guns w/bayonets, prisoners' wheelbarrow, Völkischer Beobachter (Nazi newspaper), Heydrich's car (prev mentioned), Wolverine's bonds, later Commandant's car

YNOPSIS: After the previous two Commandants' suicides, Major Bauman is assigned to run Sobibor death camp. During an inspection, Bauman ees a short, hairy prisoner staring at him, and has him shot. That night, Bauman hears an eerie whistling and is startled to discover the same prisoner, inexplicably alive. Bauman has the prisoner shot again, but continues hearing whistling at night. Days later, Bauman spots the same prisoner again; he shoots him and begins to doubt his senses. Bauman has the soldiers search Sobibor every week; they keep finding the same man and killing him over and over. Bauman soon begins drinking heavily. When the soldiers report that the prisoner has survived the gas chamber, Bauman ties him to a cha and demands to know why the prisoner is tormenting him. The prisoner merely grins; Bauman snaps and assaults him, knocking over wine bottles an a lantern. The wine ignites, killing Bauman. Later, Sobibor's new Commandant arrives, and sees a short, hairy prisoner staring at him from the crowd…

NOTE: This issue occurs in 1942. W #32-35, '05 were published biweekly. This issue also has a 4-page preview of NFHC #1, '05, and a 1-pag afterword by Mark Millar lauding industry legend Will Eisner, who died in January 2005. Millar describes Eisner's contributions to this issue' plot, including the suggestion to keep Wolverine almost completely silent. Wolverine only utters one on-panel sound this issue — "nnf" — afte being struck. It is unexplained why Wolverine allowed himself to be imprisoned for so long; he may have been on a covert mission. Althougl Bauman lists beheadings as one of the unsuccessful methods of killing Wolverine, this must be an exaggeration, as Wolverine could not survive a beheading. Bauman mentions that a mutant boy was seen destroying an armored car; this may be a reference to Max Eisenhardt, later know as Magneto, whose powers manifested in mid-1942 according to X:MT #3, '09. In real life, Sobibor became operational in April 1942 and ha only two Commandants, Lt. Franz Stangl and Lt. Franz Reichleitner, before closing in October 1943 after a mass escape. Heydrich was a real-lif individual, as were the assassins who killed him. Daluege is referred to only as "Heydrich's successor" in this issue; his identity is surmised from real-world records. This issue also has a black & white edition with different (and fewer) ad pages, advertising other Marvel books.

WOLVERINE #33 [#222] (November 2005)

"Chasing Ghosts, Part One of Three" (24 pages)

CREDITS: Daniel Way (writer), Javier Saltares (breakdowns), Mark Texeira (finishes), Virtual Calligraphy's Jo Caramagna (letters), Paul Mounts (colors), James Taveras (production), Cory Sedlmeier (asst editor), Jennife Lee (editor), Axel Alonso (exec editor), Joe Quesada (c pencils), Danny Miki (c inks), Richard Isanove (c colors)

FEATURE CHARACTER: Wolverine (SHIELD Red Guard commander, in fb2 between HoM #3, '05 fb bts W #34, '05 fb bts; also in rfb)

VILLAINS: Human guerrilla fighters (in fb2, die; others as embassy staff in fb2, die; others bts stealing Sentine in fb2 prior to W #35, '05 fb)

OTHER CHARACTERS: Mystique (SHIELD Red Guard agent, also in rfb, also as herself, Price & a vine in fb between X #174, '05 & W #34, '05 fb bts; also in fb1 during HoM #3 '05; last in HoM #3, '05), Col. Sebastian Shav (Director of SHIELD, last in UXM #454, '05, chr last in IM:K&K/2, '10, last bts in Pulse:HoM, '05), Magneto (rule of the House of Magnus, bts donating Sentinel in fb2 between HoM #1, '05 bts & SM:HoM #4, '05 bts; also in portraits), Paula D'Onofrio (Hous of Magnus' assistant press secretary, 4-armed mutant) & her family (bts in fb2, vacationing), Devin Price (House of Magnus' foreign relation minister), mutant SHIELD agents (some bts flying jets; others bts reporting to Coleridge, those also bts witnessing Mystique in fb1 prior to issue some or others last bts in HoM #3, '05) inc Agent Coleridge (voice only), Sentinels (some or others last in HoM #3, '05, next in IM:HoM #1, '05 another in fb2 prior to W #35, '05 fb, some or others chr last in NEx #9, '06 fb, 1 or another chr last in SM:HoM #4, '05), Mexican & America diplomats (some die), Marines, bartender, photographer (prev 4 in fb2); Earth-58163 Nick Fury, Red Guard trainees (as "Fury's Hellions") in Earth-58163 Wolverine (prev 3 in photo); Libertas (as Statue of Liberty)

LOCATIONS/ITEMS: Earth-58163: skies above Manhattan (also in rfb & fb1), Mexico (in fb2): Chiapas' Sierra Madre de Chiapas mountains Mexico City's Four Seasons Hotel & American Embassy; Hellions' base (in photo) / Guerrilla fighters' machetes, pole, knives, cleaver, machin guns & weaponized acid, D'Onofrio's ropes (destroyed), Mystique's comm unit (bts) & knife, Wolverine's gun & pills, Marines' guns, SHIEL helicopters w/searchlights, photographer's camera (all in fb2), SHIELD jets & Helicarrier (also in rfb & fb1) w/security cameras (bts in rfb & fb1 Wolverine & Mystique's reports, Mystique's gun (also in fb2), Shaw's laptop & photo, Wolverine's knife, Fury & trainees' guns (prev 2 in photo)

FLASHBACKS: Wolverine leaps off the Helicarrier (HoM #3, '05). Mystique screams (1). In Mexico, Wolverine and Mystique rescue Paul D'Onofrio from human guerrilla fighters. Later, a surly Wolverine abuses pills and alcohol as the two prepare to attend a party at the America Embassy, held to celebrate the House of Magnus donating a Sentinel to Mexico. At the party, Wolverine drinks heavily — but more guerrilla disguised as waitstaff suddenly attack, dousing Wolverine in acid and attacking the diplomats. Mystique poses as the foreign relations ministe and kills a guerrilla, while Wolverine and the arriving Marines slaughter the rest — however, they soon discover that the attack was a distraction and the Sentinel has been stolen (2).

SYNOPSIS: Col. Shaw interrogates Mystique about the Sentinel theft, suspecting that it may have been an inside job. Mystique explains tha ever since the House of Magnus won the war against humankind, Wolverine has been restless and angry, still wanting enemies to fight. Sha shows Mystique an old photo of Wolverine with Nick Fury, and Mystique identifies Fury as the guerrillas' leader.

NOTE: Cover-labeled "House of M," part of a line-wide altered-reality event. In HoM #1, '05, the mentally unstable Scarlet Witch transforme Reality-616 into an alternate dimension (Reality-58163, see next issue's NOTE), where her father Magneto rules and mutants are the majorit lording over the second-class "Sapien" minority. Wolverine leaped off the Helicarrier in HoM #3, '05 after regaining his Earth-616 memories an realizing what the Scarlet Witch had done. SM:HoM #1-5, '05 indicate that a period of several days or more elapses between the reality war and Wolverine's realization; it is in that period of time that this issue's fb2 occurs. Reality-58163 is designated in OHMU #6, '06. This issue als has a 4-page preview of NFHC #1, '05.

WOLVERINE #34 [#223] (December 2005)

"Chasing Ghosts, Part Two of Three" (23 pages)

CREDITS: Daniel Way (writer), Javier Saltares (breakdowns), Mark Texeira (finishes), Virtual Calligraphy' Randy Gentile (letters), Paul Mounts (colors), Tom Valente (production), Cory Sedlmeier (asst editor), Jennife Lee (editor), Axel Alonso (exec editor), Kaare Andrews (c art)

FEATURE CHARACTER: Wolverine (bts leaving infirmary in fb2 between W #33, '05 fb & W #35, '05 fb)

OTHER CHARACTERS: Mystique (also bts discovering Wolverine's absence in fb2 between W #33, '05 W #35, '05 fb), Col. Sebastian Shaw, mutant SHIELD agents (bts flying jets), Earth-58163 residents (see NOTE Red Guard trainees (also in fb3 during fb, some bts off-panel) inc Wolverine (prior to W #35, '05 fb, also in fb during fb) & Earshot (Travis Spangler, long-range voice caster), human SHIELD officers (all but 2 bts, kille inc Nick Fury (dies, also in fb3 during fb) & General, Jacob (Fury's son), General's family (prev 2 bts, captive

SHIELD command (bts kidnapping officers' families) & agents (prev 10 in fb1); Earth-58163 historical figures (in painting in fb1); Earth-58163 human-built Sentinels (cover only)

LOCATIONS/ITEMS: Earth-58163: skies above Manhattan, SHIELD training facility (in fb1 & fb3) w/motor pool (in fb1, destroyed), Mexican SHIELD infirmary (in fb2) / SHIELD tanks (some destroyed), airplane, guns & vehicles, Fury's knife (bts, also in fb3), Jeep (destroyed), handcuffs & paperwork, assassin's cigar, gasoline drums (prev 2 destroyed), note & bomb w/timer (all in fb1), Wolverine's oxygen mask (in fb2), SHIELD jets & Helicarrier, Shaw's laptop & records book, Mystique's gun

FLASHBACKS: Twenty years ago, mutants gain control of SHIELD. They kidnap Nick Fury's son and force Fury to create an elite mutant unit, Red Squad. Fury humiliates cocky young trainee Earshot, and decides to teach another trainee, Wolverine, responsibility by making him squad leader. Wolverine soon challenges Fury and the two begin to fight. Fury tries to turn the battle into a lesson for the other trainees, but Wolverine becomes enraged and pops his claws… That night, Earshot gets a note telling him to lure Fury to the motor pool. He does so, and when Fury arrives, a bomb explodes, apparently killing him (1). After the guerrillas' attack, Mystique finds Wolverine's hospital room empty (2). Fury stabs Wolverine in the ear, ending their fight, and swears to someday wipe out all mutants (3).

SYNOPSIS: Mystique refuses to believe that Wolverine could have colluded with Fury. Shaw reveals that Fury has been presumed dead for twenty years, but that his body was never found. Mystique realizes that Fury could have faked his death if he had an accomplice.

NOTE: Cover-labeled "House of M." Although the HoM, '05 series suggested that the Scarlet Witch transformed Reality-616 and gave everyone else memories, several events indicate that Reality-58163 is a separate, pre-existing alternate dimension. (Notably, Proteus-58163 leaves the "House of M" reality in Exiles #71, '05, traveling across the multiverse, and still exists after the Scarlet Witch restores Earth-616, as shown in Exiles #72-82, '06 & NExiles Ann., '09. However, X:L #231, '10 shows that Proteus-616 also exists on Earth-616; thus Proteus-58163 cannot be an altered Proteus-616, and must have always been a separate individual.) The Scarlet Witch likely detected Reality-58163 subconsciously in HoM #1, '05 and temporarily "overlaid" it atop Reality-616, merging the two and giving the 616 residents their 58163 counterparts' memories. Thus, any flashbacks to points before the "House of M" reality warp began actually take place on the true Earth-58163, not the altered Earth-616, and feature that dimension's inhabitants. This issue's fb1 & fb3 occur on Earth-58163; this issue's fb2 occurs on the altered Earth-616. Nick Fury is depicted on this issue's cover as a skull with an eyepatch, but Fury-58163 does not wear an eyepatch. It is unrevealed who prompted Earshot to set up Fury, but Wolverine seems to be the likeliest suspect.

WOLVERINE #35 [#224] (December 2005)

"Chasing Ghosts, Conclusion" (25 pages)

CREDITS: Daniel Way (writer), Javier Saltares (breakdowns), Mark Texeira (finishes), Virtual Calligraphy's Randy Gentile (letters), Paul Mounts (colors), Tom Valente (production), Cory Sedlmeier & Michael O'Connor (asst editors), Jennifer Lee (editor), Axel Alonso (exec editor), Kaare Andrews (c art)

FEATURE CHARACTER: Wolverine (in fb3 between W #34, '05 fb & HoM #2, '05; also voice only in rfb & as symbolic image; next in HoM #2-5, Cap #10, HoM #5-8, all '05; NX #20, '06, HoM #8, '05; GenM #1 fb, NX #20, HoM:Day, X #177-179, NX #21, UXM #466, Run #10 fb, 10 bts & 11-12, NAv #14-15, all '06, MAv #14, '08, NAv #15, '06, AF #13, '05 fb, MTU #14, '06, CW:Choos/6, '06, S #1-2, '05, AX #13, GenM #5, NX #24, DocS #1-2, all '06, W/Herc #1-4, '11, I♥M:MMH, '06)

VILLAINS: Veranke (Skrull Queen, as Red Guard agent Jessica Drew, see NOTE; in fb1 between HoM #1, '05 & NAv #45, '08), human guerrilla fighters (in fb3 following W #33, '05 fb bts, die)

OTHER CHARACTERS: Mystique (also in rfb & as Earth-58163 Nick Fury, also in fb1 between W #34, '05 fb bts & this issue's fb3; also as Earth-58163 Fury in hologram & as herself in fb3 between fb1 & Pulse:HoM, '05 bts; next in NX #16, '05), Col. Sebastian Shaw (next in Pulse #10, '05), Earth-58163 Wolverine (in fb2 & fb4 following W #34, '05 fb), Earth-58163 Mystique (in fb2 & fb4), Sentinel (destroyed, in fb1 following W #33, '05 fb, others chr next in NAv #45, '08), mutant SHIELD agents (chr 1st on-panel app, some or others next in NX #16, '05) & scientist, pilot

LOCATIONS/ITEMS: Earth-58163: skies above Manhattan (also in fb2 & fb4), Mexico: SHIELD infirmary (in fb1), abandoned Unified Steel Corp mill (in rfb & fb3, destroyed) / Mystique's holographic projector (bts), detonator (in hologram), satchel (also in rfb), map, binoculars, explosives & stolen airplane, door chain (also in rfb), Sentinel's data core (bts), guerrilla fighters' masks & guns, hurled gears, metal I-beam (prev 6 destroyed) (all in fb3), Wolverine's oxygen mask, Veranke's gun (prev 2 in fb1), Mystique's gun (also in fb1, fb3 & bts in rfb), Shaw's desk (destroyed), laptop & records book, SHIELD guns & Helicarrier w/computer, forensic equipment, comm system, palm scanner & cell door w/lock, evidence scraps, Fury's personnel file (bts) w/access log, Wolverine-58163's pills (in fb2 & bts in fb4)

FLASHBACKS: Wolverine shouts Fury's name (this issue). Despite Wolverine's scrawled message not to follow him, Mystique does (1). Mystique begs Wolverine to stop drinking, asking him to accept that the war is over, and he begins to tell her about the one foe he respected (2). Mystique tracks down the stolen Sentinel to a steel mill, and arrives to see Wolverine battling more guerrillas. Wolverine then finds a holographic projection of Nick Fury, who gloats that his forces now know how to defeat the Sentinels, and threatens to topple the House of Magnus. Wolverine swears to track him down, but Fury detonates explosives; Wolverine rescues Mystique from the burning mill (3). Wolverine tells Mystique about Fury (4).

SYNOPSIS: Shaw throws Mystique in the brig for disobeying Wolverine's order not to follow him. Later, SHIELD's forensics lab points out that Mystique accessed Fury's personnel file recently. Shaw realizes that Mystique organized the theft of the Sentinel, posing as the deceased Fury, to give Wolverine back his purpose in life. Releasing Mystique, he orders her to find Wolverine and bring him back.

NOTE: Cover-labeled "House of M." This issue's fb2 & fb4 occur on the true Earth-58163; this issue's fb1 & fb3 occur on the altered Earth-616. Mystique tracks down Wolverine in HoM #3, '05; the Scarlet Witch restores Earth-616 in HoM #7, '05. NAv #42, '08 reveals that Skrulls abducted the real Jessica Drew prior to this issue, replacing her with Queen Veranke. The series begins running a "next issue" page here, showcasing the following issue's cover. As with recap pages that showcase previous issues' covers, this Index will not list characters that appear only on those upcoming covers.

WOLVERINE #36 [#225] (January 2006)

"Origins & Endings, Chapter One" (22 pages)

CREDITS: Daniel Way (writer), Javier Saltares (breakdowns), Mark Texeir (finishes), Virtual Calligraphy's Randy Gentile (letters), J.D. Smith (colors), Debora Weinstein (production), Michael O'Connor (asst editor), Axel Alonso (editor), Jo Quesada (c pencils, variant c pencils), Danny Miki (variant c inks), Richard Isanov (c colors)

FEATURE CHARACTER: Wolverine

GUEST STARS: Avengers: Luke Cage (super-strength & steel-hard skin), Captai America, Spider-Man (all last in S #2, '05), Iron Man (last in GenM #2, '06); Emm Frost (last in NX #24, chr next in W:O #4, next bts in SM/BCat #5, next in X #183, a '06), Dum Dum Dugan (last in Cap #10, '05) (prev 2 also on monitors)

VILLAIN: Veranke (as Spider-Woman, last in S #2, '05)

OTHER CHARACTERS: Silver Samurai (last in X:KPSF #5, '05, last bts in HoM #3, '05), Japanese Prime Minister Junichiro Koizumi & hi driver & security cadre, SHIELD agents (some as jogger & would-be patron, some or others last in DocS #2, '06), bar staff & bouncers, woulc be bar patrons, subway train conductor (bts driving train), hotel staff & patrons, American, Canadian, Russian & British military officials (1 dies bystanders; rats

LOCATIONS/ITEMS: Tokyo inc tunnel (also on monitor), Shinjuku bar, subway tunnel, parking garage, hotel & rooftop, SHIELD headquarters X-Mansion (on monitor), American & Russian military bases, Canadian Secret Service base, British Royal Air Force base / Wolverine's parce public telephones, SHIELD earpieces (some bts), van, guns, palm scanner, rifles w/scopes & comm system w/monitors, subway train, cables Prime Minister's limousine, convoy's cars, tunnel camera (bts), security's guns (some destroyed), Silver Samurai's armor & katanas, X-Mansio comm unit, military computers, Weapon X paperwork (some of prev 2 destroyed), officials' incendiary (bts), sledgehammers, furnace & handgun, Royal Air Force helicopter

SYNOPSIS: In Tokyo, Wolverine waits by a public phone until Emma Frost calls him, but Emma has been unable to locate Wolverine's targe Wolverine realizes that he's being tailed by SHIELD, and forces his way into the back room of a nearby bar, bullying the bouncers into closing th bar behind him. Wolverine cuts a hole in the floor and enters Tokyo's underground tunnels, making his way to a subway line and jumping atop train. Wolverine arrives beneath a manhole cover just as the Japanese Prime Minister's limo passes overhead; he pops his claws up through th chassis, causing the limo to crash. SHIELD mobilizes, wondering if Wolverine has gone bad again, but Wolverine's true target is the Minister' new security chief — the Silver Samurai. As Wolverine and the Samurai begin to fight, Dum Dum Dugan and Wolverine's Avengers teammate contact Emma Frost, who reveals that Wolverine has regained all of his real memories. Military officials worldwide, monitoring the call, panic an begin destroying Weapon X-related evidence…

NOTE: Cover-labeled "Decimation," part of the fallout from the House of M event, and "Origins & Endings, Part I of V." This issue also has variant cover. Wolverine regained his full, unaltered memories in HoM #2, '05 thanks to the Scarlet Witch's reality alterations. This issue's cove is an homage to Origin #1, '01; the series' logo changes for this arc, adopting the same font used for the Origin, '01-02 series' logo. The serie returns to monthly publication here.

WOLVERINE #37 [#226] (February 2006)

"Origins & Endings, Chapter Two" (22 pages)

CREDITS: Daniel Way (writer), Javier Saltares (breakdowns), Mark Texeira (finishes), Virtual Calligraphy Randy Gentile (letters), J.D. Smith (colors), James Taveras (production), Michael O'Connor (asst editor), Axe Alonso (exec editor), Kaare Andrews (c art)

FEATURE CHARACTER: Wolverine (also in his own dream)

GUEST STARS: Avengers: Luke Cage (next in Cable&Dp #20, '05), Spider-Man (chr next in SM/BCat #1, '02 next in SM/BCat #4, '06), Captain America, Iron Man; Dum Dum Dugan (next in W #39, '06)

VILLAIN: Veranke (as Spider-Woman, next in Pulse #12, '06)

OTHER CHARACTERS: Silver Samurai (next in W:O #2, '06), General Annato (Japanese military official Canadian, Russian, British & other military officials (prev 5 on monitor), SHIELD agents (1 or another next in V #39, '06, some or others next in W:O #1, '06), police, freighter crew (bts piloting freighter), Dept. K officer (voic only on radio) & soldiers, bystanders; Itsu, Janet, Rose O'Hara, Silver Fox, conspirators (in shadow) (prev 5 in Wolverine's dream); actor (o billboard); samurai (as painting, cover only)

LOCATIONS/ITEMS: Canadian, Russian, Japanese, British & other military bases (all on monitor), SHIELD headquarters, Tokyo inc tunnel & harbor, Pacific Ocean, British Columbia harbor, former Weapon X Program facility (now Department K facility) / SHIELD comm system w monitors, military bases' comm units (bts), police cars, motorcycle, gun, barricades & helicopters w/searchlights, Silver Samurai's armor katanas, convoy's cars, tunnel wall (destroyed) w/Wolverine's painted mark, freighter w/anchor, conspirators' kill light (bts), Itsu's umbrella (pre 2 in dream), fallen tree, Dept. K fence (destroyed), radios (1 bts), Jeeps & guns

SYNOPSIS: As Dugan discusses Wolverine's returned memories with panicked military officials, Wolverine and the Silver Samurai continu their duel. Wolverine asks the Samurai several questions, but the answers he receives distract him enough for the Samurai to impale him injuring Wolverine badly. Wolverine is forced to cut off the Samurai's hand to escape; he limps away, cutting a hole in a large water pipe an letting himself be washed into the harbor. There, he climbs aboard a Canada-bound freighter, stows away and collapses. Wolverine drifts in an out of consciousness on the lengthy journey, and is eventually forced to eat his own regenerating flesh to survive. He dreams of the women h has loved and watched die — including a mysterious Japanese woman, whose face Wolverine cannot quite see before shadowy conspirator surround and capture him. Wolverine awakens, fully recovered, and dives into the Canadian harbor; he makes his way to the former Weapon : facility, now taken over by Department K. Despite his instinctive revulsion, Wolverine sneaks inside…

NOTE: Cover-labeled "Decimation" & "Origins & Endings, Part II of V"; the recap page titles this story "Origins and Endings, Part II of V." Thoug it is not made explicit this issue, the Silver Samurai tells Wolverine that his escape from the Weapon X Program facility years ago was not a accident; someone secretly helped him. Wolverine's other questions and the Samurai's answers are unrevealed.

WOLVERINE #38 [#227] (March 2006)

"Origins & Endings, Chapter Three" (22 pages)

CREDITS: Daniel Way (writer), Javier Saltares (breakdowns), Mark Texeira (finishes), Virtual Calligraphy (production) w/Randy Gentile (letters), J.D. Smith (colors), Michael O'Connor (asst editor), Axel Alonso (exec editor), Kaare Andrews (c art)

FEATURE CHARACTER: Wolverine (also in photo, also as symbolic image on monitor & Experiment X in rfb; also in fb between W:O #35, '09 fb & W:O #3, '06 fb, also in W #40, '06 fb during fb)

GUEST STARS: Winter Soldier (James "Bucky" Barnes, Captain America's WWII partner & former brainwashed Soviet assassin, see NOTE; also in fb between W #40, '06 fb & Cap #11, '05 fb; last in Cap #14, '06), Avengers: Captain America (next in W:O #3, '06), Iron Man (chr next in IM:T/3, '10, next in Pulse #12, '06)

VILLAINS: Muramasa (villainous swordsmith, 1st in fb between W:O #35, '09 fb & W #40, '06) & his henchmen (die, in fb following W:O #35, '09 fb, also in W #40, '06 fb during fb)

OTHER CHARACTERS: Weapon X Program employees (dead, as skeletons, last (some or all possibly bts) in X23 #1, '05 fb; some or others rfb, 1 dies, 1 voice only, others bts); Weapon X Program senior staff: Professor Truett Hudson, Carol Hines (prev 2 bts in rfb), Dr. Abraham Cornelius (voice only in rfb)

LOCATIONS/ITEMS: Department K facility (also as Weapon X Program facility in rfb), Muramasa's mountain (near Jasmine Falls, in fb), Avengers Tower (Avengers' Manhattan skyscraper), Winter Soldier's hideout / Weapon X Program's shielded door (destroyed) & Genesis Tank w/Adamantium feed tubes (all in rfb), Dept. K's shelving, brick wall (prev 2 destroyed), concrete & paint, Weapon X Program's computers w/diagnostic bed (also in rfb) w/needles, cables & monitor (prev 3 in rfb), Wolverine's ropes (destroyed), Muramasa's cauldron, henchmen's swords, dagger & armor w/helmets (1 destroyed) (prev 6 in fb), Winter Soldier's bionic arm (also in fb, hereinafter considered his standard equipment and not listed separately), gun (another bts in fb) & computer w/monitor, Iron Man's jet, mask, welding torch & military telephone

FLASHBACKS: Experiment X screams (MCP #76, '91), kills a Weapon X employee (MCP #74, '91), attacks the senior staff (MCP #84, '91), suffers through experiments (MCP #76, '91) and is implanted with Adamantium (MCP #73, '91). Muramasa tells his men to dispose of a semiconscious Wolverine, saying that he has served his purpose and will someday return if he is worthy. The men carry Wolverine into the woods, but are attacked and killed by a shadowy foe. Wolverine awakens and tries to fight, but his "liberator" incapacitates him expertly.

SYNOPSIS: Wolverine enters the Dept. K facility, finding new walls and floors erected in a hasty attempt to disguise and seal off the original base. Wolverine slashes them until he finds a hidden door; he enters the base's catacombs and finds skeletal bodies strewn everywhere, left over from his rampage years before. Wolverine discovers bullet holes in some bodies' skulls and realizes that the Samurai told him the truth: someone helped him escape. Realizing that the same man freed him from Muramasa's men years before, Wolverine calls Captain America — and asks the whereabouts of his former partner, Bucky.

NOTE: Cover-labeled "Decimation" & "Origins & Endings, Part III of V"; the recap page titles this story "Origins and Endings, Part III of V." Cap #11, '05 fb revealed that Bucky was recovered by the Soviets after the fateful WWII explosion in Av #4, '64 fb; they revived and brainwashed him into an assassin called the Winter Soldier. This issue implies, and next issue's recap page confirms, that Winter Soldier was bts making sure Wolverine escaped the Weapon X Program in MCP #84, '91; he appeared there between Cap #11, '05 fb & Cap #1, '05 fb. Although normally a Soviet agent, W:O #5, '06 fb reveals that in this issue's fb, Winter Soldier was taking orders from a shadowy manipulator, named as Romulus in W #53, '07 and revealed to be the mastermind behind a decades-long conspiracy manipulating Wolverine in W:O Ann., '07. Romulus was therefore also behind Winter Soldier's involvement in Wolverine's escape in MCP #84, '91; he appears bts in that issue between W #54, '07 fb & W:O #28, '08 fb bts.

WOLVERINE #39 [#228] (April 2006)

"Origins & Endings, Part Four" (22 pages)

CREDITS: Daniel Way (writer), Javier Saltares (breakdowns), Mark Texeira (finishes), Virtual Calligraphy's Randy Gentile (letters), J.D. Smith (colors), Kate Levin (production), Michael O'Connor (asst editor), Axel Alonso (exec editor), Kaare Andrews (c art)

FEATURE CHARACTER: Wolverine

GUEST STARS: Dum Dum Dugan (also on monitor, last in W #37, '06, next in W:O #1, '06), Winter Soldier

OTHER CHARACTERS: SHIELD agent (some or others last in W #37, '06, next in W:O #1, '06), Pentagon officials (also on monitor), Montreal smugglers (bts transporting Wolverine to Europe), Winter Soldier's sniper, bystanders; Akihiro (1st mention, thought dead), Itsu (mentioned, killed by Winter Soldier)

LOCATIONS/ITEMS: SHIELD field office, United States Disciplinary Barracks (Fort Leavenworth, Kansas) (both also on monitor); Department K facility (destroyed); Montreal, Quebec, Canada; Yugoslavia (prev 3 mentioned); Belgrade, Serbia inc hotel (mentioned), rooftop & printing facility / SHIELD gun & comm system w/monitor, Pentagon officials' belts, shoes (prev bts) & comm unit w/monitors, Dugan's gun, Wolverine's rucksack, smugglers' vehicle (bts), sniper's rifle w/scope, padlock (destroyed), printing press w/ink, Winter Soldier's handcuffs (destroyed), ATM card (bts) & knife

SYNOPSIS: Dum Dum Dugan confers with frightened Pentagon officials who have taken refuge inside Fort Leavenworth. They panic when they hear that Wolverine torched the former Weapon X Program facility; Dugan reassures them that they are secure, but begins to worry about his own safety. Wolverine travels to Belgrade, having made sure that his travel plans were leaked in hopes of drawing out the Winter Soldier. He is shot by a sniper outside a printing press; Wolverine races into the massive building, but Winter Soldier has covered himself in ink to hide his scent and easily ambushes Wolverine, stabbing him and cuffing his hands. Winter Soldier tries to calm Wolverine down, but Wolverine slips into berserker rage and attacks. The two fight brutally; Wolverine breaks the cuffs, pops his claws and lunges at Winter Soldier — but the sniper intervenes, shooting Wolverine. Winter Soldier pays the sniper and tells her to flee for her own safety, explaining that Wolverine has every right to be furious: he killed Wolverine's wife and unborn child.

NOTE: Cover-labeled "Decimation" & "Origins & Endings, Part IV of V"; the recap page titles this story "Origins and Endings, Part IV of V." This is the last issue to be published under the Marvel Knights banner.

WOLVERINE #40 [#229] (May 2006)

"Origins & Endings, Part Five" (24 pages)

CREDITS: Daniel Way (writer), Javier Saltares (breakdowns), Mark Texeira (finishes), Virtual Calligraphy'
Randy Gentile (letters), J.D. Smith (colors), Kate Levin (production), Michael O'Connor (asst editor), Axel Alon
(exec editor), Kaare Andrews (c art)

FEATURE CHARACTER: Wolverine (also in fb between L:PW, '96 & W #38, '06 fb, also in L:PW, '96, W
#27, '08 fb, W:O #35, '09 fb & W #38, '06 fb during fb; also in W:O #25, '08 fb; next in W:O #1-15, '06-07, Pul
#12-13, '06, MHol '05/2, ASM #525, '05; MKSM #20-21, ASM #527, FNSM #4, MKSM #22, UXM #470-471, E
#14, all '06)

GUEST STAR: Winter Soldier (also in fb between Cap #11, '05 fb & W #38, '06 fb; also in W:O #25, '08 fb, ne
in Cap #16, '06 fb)

VILLAINS: Romulus (bts giving Winter Soldier orders in fb, between W:O #33, '09 fb bts & W:O #5, '06 fb
Muramasa (also in fb, his chr 1st app, prior to W:O #35, '09 fb) & his henchmen (some in fb prior to W #38, '06 fb, also in W:O #35, '09 fb &
#38, '06 fb during fb; others in fb during W #38, '06 fb)

OTHER CHARACTERS: Itsu (Wolverine's wife, dies off-panel in fb, also in W:O #27, '08 fb & W:O #5, '06 fb during fb), Akihiro (Wolverine
Itsu's unborn son, unidentified, 1st bts app as fetus in fb prior to his chr 1st app as infant in W:O #5, '06 fb), Suboro Bando (Jasmine Falls founde
see NOTE), Jasmine Falls villagers (some former ninjas, some or others also in L:PW, '96), Winter Soldier's espionage unit (bts in fb, operatir
in China), Wolverine's extractors (bts recovering Wolverine in fb) & acquaintances (bts creating false IDs), train conductor, passengers & tick
agents, bystanders; Ogun (mentioned, told Wolverine to seek out Suboro); Avengers: Captain America, Iron Man, Spider-Man (prev 3 cover onl

LOCATIONS/ITEMS: Belgrade sewers, Jasmine Falls (in fb) inc Wolverine's home (built), Muramasa's mountain (also in fb), Chinese tra
station; Madripoor (mentioned) / Wolverine's bamboo, rocks, rope (all become his home), eyepatch & rucksack, Itsu's fan, Muramasa's swor
henchmen's dagger (bts), armor & swords (all in fb), Winter Soldier's gun (another in fb) & knife, Chinese passenger train, Wolverine's forge
passport & visa (prev 2 bts), walking stick & rucksack w/brown costume, Muramasa Sword (healing factor-neutralizing blade, mystically forge
from Wolverine's rage, 1st)

FLASHBACK: Soon after WWII, a world-weary Wolverine settles in Jasmine Falls, where former ninjas live peacefully. After four years Wolverir
marries Itsu; she soon becomes pregnant. The villagers celebrate with a carefully choreographed dance symbolizing their self-control, but a
explosion on a nearby mountain distracts Wolverine, who pops his claws and injures a villager, shaming himself deeply. Wolverine decides
leave, but when he returns home to bid Itsu farewell, he finds her dead. Wolverine snaps and charges up the mountain, finding swordsmi
Muramasa and demanding the means to extract vengeance. Later, Winter Soldier sees Muramasa's men carrying Wolverine away and intervene

SYNOPSIS: Winter Soldier apologizes for killing Itsu; he was brainwashed and following orders at the time. Wolverine explains that he wa
tracking Winter Soldier to ask about his involvement in the Weapon X escape, and had no idea that he was involved in Itsu's death. After gettir
more details about Winter Soldier's mission, Wolverine departs for Japan. He returns to Muramasa's mountain and claims the Muramas
Sword, swearing vengeance on those who manipulated him for decades.

NOTE: Cover-labeled "Decimation" & "Origins & Endings, Part V of V"; the recap page titles this story "Origins and Endings, Part V of "
The series drops the Marvel Knights logo from the cover with this issue. This storyline spins off into the ongoing W:O, '06-10 series, where
Wolverine's regained memories help him discover and unravel a massive conspiracy that had secretly manipulated him for nearly a centur
Wolverine learns in W:O #5, '06 that his unborn son was ripped from Itsu's womb and survived. The infant's real name, given to him by adoptiv
parents that Romulus placed him with, is revealed in W:O #26, '08. His codename as an adult, Daken, is revealed in W:O #12, '07. Daken fir
appears on-panel (in shadow on the astral plane) in W:O #4, '06. Suboro Bando's name is extremely similar to that of Wolverine's friend Sabu
Bando, seen in W #26, '90; Suboro may be Saburo's grandfather or another relative. It is unrevealed why Wolverine is wearing an eyepatch
this issue's fb. Despite their mutual creator, MyA:Book, '07 clarifies that the Muramasa Sword is different from the sentient Black Blade seen
W #1-3, '88-89. The sword's healing factor-neutralizing properties are revealed in W:O #6, '06; its origin is revealed in W:O #35, '09 fb. Wolverine
re-obtains his brown costume for W:O #1-27, '06-08, but does not wear it in this series.

WOLVERINE #41 [#230] (June 2006)

"The Package" (34 pages)

CREDITS: Stuart Moore (writer), C.P. Smith (art, colors), Virtual Calligraphy's Randy Gentile (letters), Micha
O'Connor (asst editor), Axel Alonso (exec editor)

FEATURE CHARACTER: Wolverine (next in FNSM #6, BP #16, X #186, XRun, MTU #21 & 22 bts, X:DG #1-
NAv #17-20, NAv Ann #1, MTU #23, 23/2 & 24-25, Thing #8, IM #8 & 10-12, X #189/2, all '06, MHol '07, Claw
#1-3, '06, Claws2 #1-3, '11)

GUEST STAR: Black Panther (T'Challa, warrior king of Wakanda, during BP #15, '06)

VILLAINS: General Lago (would-be Zwartheid ruler, dies) & his rebel troops (some die) inc assassin (bts killir
Mayamba) & child soldiers

OTHER CHARACTERS: Zwartheid President Mayamba (dead) & his soldiers & infant daughter, daughter
caretaker (see NOTE), villagers (some conscripted by Lago, die); elephant (dead), mosquitoes (all but 1 bts
python, ants; UN officials (mentioned, rank Zwartheid last in Quality of Life), tribes, warlords, diamond merchants (prev 3 mentioned, discusse
peace with Mayamba), coup masterminds (mentioned, ousted Mayamba), women (mentioned, infected with HIV), Western corporation head
(mentioned, exploited Zwartheid citizens); Spider-Man (on comic book cover)

LOCATIONS/ITEMS: Free Republic of Zwartheid (war-torn African nation) inc Samaya River (bts), villages, jungle & Central Governmer
Building / Lago's helicopter, Lago's troops' trucks, Jeeps (1 of prev 2 destroyed), tanks, guns, bows, arrows & rocket launcher, Black Panther
airplane & headset, Wolverine's parachute, cigarettes & carrying harness, villagers' guns, truck, car & paperwork, assassin's poison (bts
Zwartheid's diamonds (mentioned), Mayamba's soldiers' tank & machine guns, conscripted villagers' bandages, crutch, axe, knife, guns
machete, child soldiers' camera & machine guns

SYNOPSIS: In Zwartheid, Wolverine and Black Panther watch from an airplane as Lago's troops advance on the capital. Black Panther ask
Wolverine to get a package safely out of the country; Wolverine parachutes out. He arrives at the capital to find that President Mayamba ha

en murdered, and is given the "package" — Mayamba's infant daughter. Wolverine heads for the border, but soldiers stop him; unsure of their yalties, he offers them cigarettes and they let him pass. He hacks his way through tall grass, but Lago's troops attack; Wolverine steals a Jeep d flees into the jungle, but the vehicle soon crashes and Wolverine continues on foot. He encounters a village of maimed, conscripted soldiers, ho attack; Wolverine struggles to suppress his berserker rage, focusing on keeping the baby safe. Lago's troops riddle Wolverine with arrows d child soldiers surround him. Lago demands the baby, but when he approaches, Wolverine kills him. Wolverine points out that the children e free now, and they let him safely cross the border.

OTE: Wolverine tells Mayamba's soldiers that he's taking the baby to her mother; if true, this implies that the woman who gave him the baby is ot the child's mother. The maimed villagers, forced to fight by threats and torture, are not considered Villains. This issue's production coordinator unknown. This issue's cover says "tortoise fill with triangles" in small type below artist C.P. Smith's signature, possibly a digital coloring note at was accidentally left in.

WOLVERINE #42 [#231] (July 2006)

"Vendetta" (22 pages)

CREDITS: Marc Guggenheim (writer), Humberto Ramos (pencils), Carlos Cuevas (inks), Virtual Calligraphy's Randy Gentile (letters), Edgar Delgado (colors), Michael O'Connor (asst editor), Axel Alonso (exec editor)

FEATURE CHARACTER: Wolverine (dies, revives, also in scenes from CW #1, '06, also in W #48, '07 fb & CW #1, '06, next in BP #17, '06)

GUEST STARS: Avengers: Iron Man (also in scenes from CW #1, '06; during CW #1, '06), Luke Cage (also in scene from CW #1, '06; last in CW #1, '06, next in DD #83, '06); X-Men: Emma Frost (last in Claws #1, '06, last voice only in Claws #3, '06), Cyclops (last in Claws #1, also in CW #1, next bts in XFac #8, all '06) (prev 2 next in CW #2, '06), Marvel Girl (prev 2 also in scenes from CW #1, '06), Colossus Iso in scene from CW #1, '06) (prev 2 last in Thing #8, '06, next in CW #1, '06); Sub-Mariner (in shadow, last in NAv:I, '06, next in BP #17, '06)

ILLAINS: Crusader (Arthur Blackwood, faith-based powers, last in NAv #3, '05 fb, last bts in NAv #7, '05, next in NAv #35, '07) & his followers ie), Nitro (bts on the run, also in recording & symbolic image, last in CW #1, '06), Veranke (in scene from CW #1, '06; during CW #1, '06), lantean Royal Guard (unidentified): Amir, Politus (prev 2 sleeper agents, 1st, unnamed, also as suburban couple); restaurant kitchen staff

THER CHARACTERS: Sentinel Squad O*N*E (Alexander Lexington, Rajani Dhama, Jake Slayton & Tracy Skylark, Sentinel pilots, 3 also scene from CW #1, '06, see NOTE; full group last in BP #16, 3 inc Lexington last in CW #1, 1 next in CW #2, full group next in NX #26, all 6), Paul & Amir's children inc Lily, Carol (Amir's friend, bts on phone), Ishiguro (restaurant owner), SHIELD agents (bts claiming to search for tro, more or others last in IM #12, '06, next in CW #1, '06), 198 (mutant refugees living on X-Mansion grounds, as silhouettes, see NOTE; oup last in X #184, next bts in NX #27, next in CW:X #1, all '06), FAA employee (bts discovering Wolverine's "body"), waitress, reporters (bts oadcasting Stamford footage), Sub-Mariner's aide (in shadow), firemen, helicopter pilot (bts flying helicopter), truck driver (bts, Nitro hid in his uck), restaurant staff & patrons; cats; Cloak, Dagger, Young Avengers: Vision (Jonas), Wiccan (prev 4 in scene from CW #1, '06 bts), Hawkeye ate Bishop), Hulkling, Patriot, Stature; Avengers: Captain America, Iron Man, Spider-Man; Fantastic Four: Invisible Woman, Mr. Fantastic, ning; Iron Fist (as Daredevil), Criti Noll (as Yellowjacket), Black Cat, Dr. Strange, Falcon, Hercules, Nighthawk, She-Hulk, Valkyrie, Wasp, amford victim (prev 21 in scene from CW #1, '06); New Warriors: Namorita, Night Thrasher; Coldheart, Nitro (prev 4 in recording); Lily's soccer oach & teammates, piano teacher & math tutor (prev 4 mentioned by Amir), recovery workers & bureaucrats (prev 2 mentioned, smelled by olverine); Donald Duck (on TV); baseball player (in photo)

OCATIONS/ITEMS: Lindsborth, Kansas (unnamed) inc cornfield & bar; Stamford, Connecticut (also on TVs & in scene from CW #1, '06); oomstadt (capital of Latveria); Amir & Politus' Port Washington, New York home; New York City: Baxter Building (also in scene from CW #1, 6), Japanese restaurant w/alley; Raft (superhuman prison, bts), X-Mansion / Crusader's sword, armor, stolen money (some destroyed) & acked C-130 airplane (destroyed), followers' spears & wrench, FAA jacket, Wolverine's Avengers & X-Men pagers, bar TV, helicopter (bts) 'camera, aide's recording (bts) & TV w/remote control, New Warriors' camera, Coldheart's sword (prev 2 bts), Night Thrasher's batons (1 estroyed), school bus (prev 4 on TV), rescue helicopter, rubble, Sentinel Squad O*N*E's manned Sentinel units (prev 2 also in scene from CW , '06), children's ball, Amir's cordless phone, kitchen staff's knives, nunchuks & cleaver, 198's tent city, Emma's laptop, SHIELD containment ld, pickup truck (prev 2 bts)

YNOPSIS: Wolverine battles the Crusader and his followers aboard a hijacked airplane. Desperate, Crusader crashes the plane, but Wolverine urvives. He recovers at a nearby bar, but the X-Men and Avengers both page him suddenly, and Wolverine sees the Stamford disaster reported TV. In Latveria, two men watch the footage, seeing the explosive Nitro detonate while battling Namorita, killing hundreds. The X-Men and vengers volunteer at the disaster site, clearing rubble and rescuing survivors. Elsewhere, a suburban couple receive a mysterious assignment. the days that follow the disaster, Congress debates making superhumans register themselves, and anti-hero sentiment grows. Wolverine asked to leave a restaurant, and the kitchen staff briefly try to fight him. Later, a gathering of heroes debate the Registration Act; Wolverine minds Luke Cage that government Sentinels now watch the X-Men's every move, and wonders why nobody is looking for Nitro. Cyclops and nma tell him not to get involved, but Wolverine ignores them. In Stamford, he locates Nitro's scent, and begins hunting…

OTE: Cover-labeled "Civil War," part of a sprawling line-wide event where, after Nitro exploded in Stamford, killing 600 people, the US overnment passed a law requiring superhumans to register their identities, causing an ideological schism within the super hero community. his issue also has a 2nd printing cover, featuring interior art from p.21 and cover-labeled "Civil War: Vendetta." Politus (called only "Paul" here) d Amir are named in W #45, '06; they are revealed as undercover members of the Atlantean Royal Guard in W #44, '06. The cornfield and r's locations are revealed in W #48, '07. Every issue of this arc begins with the words "People call me Wolverine. I'm the best there is at what I ." When the Scarlet Witch restored Earth-616, she wiped out the powers of nearly all the world's mutants, as seen in HoM #8, '05 & HoM:Day, 5. The X-Men were largely unscathed, but most of the students were depowered. Worldwide, mutants found themselves hunted; several took fuge at the X-Mansion, forming a tent city and naming themselves "the 198" (referencing an early estimate of the world's remaining mutants). he government dispatched Sentinel Squad O*N*E to guard the X-Mansion in HoM:Day, '06, ostensibly protecting the mutants but also strictly upervising their comings and goings. As the Sentinels are identical, and as the 198 are often depicted as faceless crowds, it is largely impossible track individual character chronologies; this Index will instead chronologize them as groups. This issue's production coordinator is unknown.

WOLVERINE #43 [#232] (August 2006)

"Revenge" (22 pages)

CREDITS: Marc Guggenheim (writer), Humberto Ramos (pencils), Carlos Cueva (inks), Virtual Calligraphy (production) w/Randy Gentile (letters), Edgar Delga (colors), Michael O'Connor (asst editor), Axel Alonso (exec editor)
FEATURE CHARACTER: Wolverine (dies, revives, also in W #48, '07 fb)
GUEST STAR: Iron Man (last in CW:FL #2, '06, next in W #45, '06)
VILLAINS: Nitro (Robert Hunter, detonates & reconstitutes body, also in pho also in W #48, '07 fb), Walter Declun (corrupt Damage Control CEO, unnamed, 1 on-panel app, last bts in CW #1, '06), Atlantean Royal Guard: Janus (sleeper age 1st, also as surfer), Amir, Politus
OTHER CHARACTERS: SHIELD pilot (bts flying plane) & Superhuman Restra Unit ("Cape-Killer Squad," die, some or others last in CW:FL #2, '06) inc Abrams (unit leader), truck driver (dies), bar patrons, Wolverine's victim (bts, beaten for information), emergency room personnel (bts treating victims), surfers; Captain Marvel, New Warriors (prev 2 mentioned, kill by Nitro); man (in photo); shark (on surfer's shirt)
LOCATIONS/ITEMS: California: Stockton biker bar, Big Sur inc Nitro's cabin (destroyed); Florida's Daytona Beach, Washington DC inc Capi Building / Bar window (destroyed), patrons' motorcycles, pickup truck, Nitro's cash (mentioned), MGH (Mutant Growth Hormone), newspap cellphone & Range Rover, Wolverine's motorcycle & whetstone, Janus & surfer's surfboards, SHIELD airplane, guns, armor & helmets cameras (prev 5 destroyed), Declun's car & cellphone
SYNOPSIS: Wolverine tracks down the truck driver who smuggled Nitro out of Stamford, and forcefully extracts Nitro's location: Big S California. Iron Man arrives and asks Wolverine to stop his hunt, reminding him that in the current political climate, Wolverine's vigilante actio could damage all heroes. Iron Man explains that a special anti-superhuman SHIELD team is preparing to arrest Nitro — and asks if Wolverin truly seeks justice, or if he just wants an excuse to kill. In Florida, the suburban couple track down a surfer named Janus. Wolverine grudgin accompanies the SHIELD strike team, but when they assault Nitro's cabin, the villain explodes violently, killing the entire team — and burni Wolverine down to his Adamantium skeleton. Nitro recovers, pops pills and calls his secretive backer, but the backer severs their ties, claimi that Nitro is too unpredictable and high profile for his needs. Elsewhere, Janus and the couple learn Nitro's location from the truck driver, th kill him. Nitro prepares to flee the scene, but a half-healed Wolverine awakens and attacks...
NOTE: Cover-labeled "Civil War." This issue also has a 2nd printing cover, featuring interior art from pp.15-16 and cover-labeled "Civil Wa Vendetta," which apparently was the original name for this story arc. Declun is named in W #45, '06. The Superhuman Registration Act becan law in CW #2, '06; Wolverine's activities are now considered unsanctioned vigilantism. Wolverine sharpens his claws on a whetstone here; sin that would have no effect on his Adamantium, he is presumably trying to intimidate the SHIELD agents. Although no longer called "Cutti Edge," this issue features the series' first letters page since W #176, '02.

WOLVERINE #44 [#233] (September 2006)

"Justice" (22 pages)

CREDITS: Marc Guggenheim (writer), Humberto Ramos (pencils), Carlos Cuevas (inks), Virtual Calligraphy Randy Gentile (letters), Edgar Delgado (colors), Brad Johansen (production), Michael O'Connor (asst edito Axel Alonso (exec editor)
FEATURE CHARACTER: Wolverine (also on scope & bts in rfb1)
GUEST STAR: Sub-Mariner (last in BP #17, '06)
VILLAINS: Nitro (also in rfb1, bts in rfb2 & on scope), Walter Declun (also bts in rfb1, next in W #46, '0€ Atlantean Royal Guard (named): Amir, Janus, Politus
OTHER CHARACTERS: Henry Ackerdson (Damage Control public relations manager, last in DC #4, '91, ne in W #46, '06), Damage Control (superhuman battle damage repair corporation) employees (some or others la in Thing #6, '06, next in W #46, '06), SHIELD Superhuman Restraint Unit (dead, as skeletons); Anne Marie Hoa (mentioned, aggravated Henry); Namorita (in rfb2, dies); Charles Dudley Warner, Sir Francis Bacon (prev 2 quoted)
LOCATIONS/ITEMS: Big Sur (also in rfb1 & on scope), Sub-Mariner's location, Damage Control's Manhattan office (Flatiron Buildin Stamford (in rfb2) / Nitro's cellphone (in rfb1) & MGH, Amir & Sub-Mariner's comm units, Janus' injector & water-breathing mask, Janus & Ami multi-bladed weapons, Politus' binoculars & stun gun, Henry's cellphone (mentioned)
FLASHBACKS: Nitro calls his backer (last issue). Nitro's explosion kills Namorita (CW #1, '06).
SYNOPSIS: Wolverine attacks Nitro, staying close after surmising that Nitro has a protective aura surrounding him, in which objects are sa from his explosive power. Janus and the couple observe from the woods as Wolverine beats Nitro brutally, and report to their king. Desperat Nitro reveals that his powers were enhanced by Mutant Growth Hormone when he exploded at Stamford, and implies that his supplier is pa of a larger conspiracy. Wolverine grudgingly promises Nitro's safety in exchange for more information — but Janus attacks Wolverine befo Nitro can explain, and the couple move to capture the villain. Realizing that Nitro is telling the truth, Wolverine resigns himself to defending hi In Manhattan, Nitro's former backer returns to his company, encouraging an employee to remain loyal through this crisis. In Big Sur, the fi superhumans brawl through the woods. The attackers reveal themselves as Atlantean sleeper agents, activated to capture and punish Nitro f killing Namorita — just as their king, the Sub-Mariner, arrives.
NOTE: Cover-labeled "Civil War." His clothes incinerated by Nitro's blast last issue, Wolverine is naked for this entire issue. In the past, Nitr explosive power worked differently: he literally detonated and re-formed his physical body. Wolverine notes here that Nitro now has an aura th generates explosive force outward and protects anything inside it; OHMU:U #4, '07 clarifies that Nitro's MGH abuse altered how his powe operate.

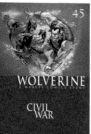

WOLVERINE #45 [#234] (October 2006)

"Vengeance" (23 pages)

CREDITS: Marc Guggenheim (writer), Humberto Ramos (pencils), Carlos Cuevas (inks), Virtual Calligraphy's Randy Gentile (letters), Edgar Delgado (colors), Kate Levin (production), Michael O'Connor (asst editor), Axel Alonso (exec editor)

FEATURE CHARACTER: Wolverine (also as Iron Man, also in CW #2, '06 & ASM #533, '06)

GUEST STARS: Iron Man (last in W #43, '06, next in MsM #5, '06), Sub-Mariner (also in ASM #533, '06, next in BP #18, '06) (both also in rfb)

VILLAINS: Nitro (next in Sub #1, '07 fb), Atlantean Royal Guard: Politus (dies), Amir (prev 2 named), Janus

OTHER CHARACTERS: SHIELD Superhuman Restraint Unit member (dead, as skeleton; others next in CW #2, '06), Atlanteans, bar patrons; fish; X-Men: Cyclops, Emma Frost (prev 2 in rfb); Michel Foucault (quoted)

LOCATIONS/ITEMS: Big Sur, Pacific Ocean inc New Pangea (Atlantean province, also in rfb), Stockton, Mansion (prev 2 in rfb), bar / Skeleton's clothes, Janus' injector & water-breathing mask, Amir's sword & multi-bladed weapon, Wolverine's llphone (bts), Iron Man's aquatic armor (model 35), New Pangea oxygen barrier, Politus' torture devices, Emma's laptop (in rfb)

LASHBACK: Sub-Mariner questions Wolverine's honor (this issue); Iron Man questions Wolverine's motivations (W #43, '06); Emma tells olverine not to get involved (W #42, '06).

YNOPSIS: Wolverine dresses himself with a dead SHIELD agent's clothes, then attacks Sub-Mariner and his agents, determined to keep Nitro fe. Sub-Mariner loses his patience and knocks Wolverine out; Wolverine awakens to find Nitro gone, and summons Iron Man for a favor. Later, ad in Iron Man's aquatic armor, Wolverine descends to the undersea city of New Pangea and confronts Sub-Mariner, explaining that he gave s word to Nitro and needs information from him. Sub-Mariner derides Wolverine's need to treat a mass murderer honorably, and Amir mentions at Politus is interrogating Nitro. They take Wolverine to the cellblock, but are shocked to find that Nitro has freed himself and mortally wounded litus. Wolverine slices off Nitro's hand; realizing that his vow to the villain isn't worth keeping, Wolverine leaves him with the Atlanteans. Later, lb-Mariner tells Wolverine that Politus learned Nitro's supplier's name and told Amir as he died: Walter Declun, CEO of Damage Control.

DTE: Cover-labeled "Civil War." Walter Declun is named here. Iron Man's aquatic armor designation is revealed in IManual, '08.

WOLVERINE #46 [#235] (November 2006)

"Payback" (22 pages)

CREDITS: Marc Guggenheim (writer), Humberto Ramos (pencils), Carlos Cuevas (inks), Virtual Calligraphy's Randy Gentile (letters), Edgar Delgado (colors), Brad Johansen (production), Michael O'Connor (asst editor), Axel Alonso (exec editor)

FEATURE CHARACTER: Wolverine (also in rfb, also in pfb, also in dfb during pfb)

GUEST STARS: X-Men: Cyclops (last in ASM #533, next bts in CW #3, next in XFac #9, all '06), Emma Frost (between CW #2-3, '06); Forge (mutant inventor, last in BP #16, '06, next in NX #25, '06) (all in pfb)

VILLAINS: Mandroids (armored guards, also in pfb, some or others last in YAv #10, '06) inc Eddie (unnamed), Walter Declun (last in W #44, '06)

OTHER CHARACTERS: Atlantean Royal Guard: Amir, Janus (both bts following Wolverine); Anne Marie Hoag (Damage Control president, last in DC2 #4, '90), Henry Ackerdson (last in W #44, '06), Damage Control nployees (some or others last in W #44, '06, next in AntM #10, '07): Anne (receptionist, last in DC #2, '89, next in AntM #8, '07), Amy (public ations), Larry (acquisitions) (prev 2 bts helping Declun buy Roxxon office), 1 other (voice only); Damage Control clients & security guards, cationers, bank customers, manager & security guard, focus groups (bts disliking bulldog logo), reporter (voice only) (all in pfb), Joel Begleiter Jesthaven fund manager), Westhaven security guards (prev 2 in dfb); birds, dog (prev 2 in pfb); Declun's secretary (mentioned by Anne) & estors (mentioned, helped Declun buy Damage Control), 911 operator, SHIELD agents (prev 2 mentioned, called by Declun); Professor (mentioned, installed Wolverine's psi-shields), Iron Man (mentioned, used to sleep with Emma), Rogue (mentioned, absorbed Emma's emories), Whirlwind (mentioned, Mandroids repurposed his technology) (prev 7 in pfb); Veranke (as Spider-Woman), Blackout, Brothers imm, Captain America, Crusader, Dagger, Goliath, Iron Man, Ms. Marvel, Nitro, Speedball, Speedfreek, Spider-Man, Thor clone (prev 14 in); model (on magazine cover); eagle (as Eagle Plaza statue), bulldog (as Damage Control's logo) (prev 3 in pfb); Billy Joel (quoted)

OCATIONS/ITEMS: Damage Control's new Long Island headquarters (former Roxxon office, also in pfb), Flatiron Building office & Pier 46 arehouse, Eagle Plaza (Forge's Dallas, Texas skyscraper), Royal Bank Financial Group (Grand Cayman Island bank), X-Mansion (prev 5 in), Geffen-Meyer chemical plant, skies over Lindsborth, Stamford, Raft (prev 4 in rfb), Westhaven Mutual Fund office (in dfb) / Anne's headset, tro's MGH, Forge's computers, monitors & data-miner, office's air ducts, Damage Control's construction equipment, guard's gun (destroyed), nk vault, Ackerdson's proposed new logo, reporter's broadcast equipment (bts) (all in pfb), Mandroids' armor (also in pfb, 1 destroyed) w/ hirlwind's buzzsaw, Thor clone's hammer, Spider-Man's "Iron Spider" armor (prev 2 in rfb), Damage Control's stock (bts), Begleiter's computer rev 2 in dfb)

LASHBACKS: Registered heroes battle underground heroes (CW #3-4, '06, see NOTE); Wolverine fights the Crusader (W #42, '06); peedball faces Raft escapees (CW #1, '06); Spider-Woman tries to contain the Raft breakout (NAv #2 & 3 fb, '05, see NOTE). Wolverine rives at Damage Control's office demanding a meeting. He alleges to Anne Marie Hoag that Walter Declun sold Nitro MGH to cause more werful explosions. As Anne Marie, disturbed, explains how Declun came to own controlling shares in the company, Declun arrives and orders olverine off his property. Wolverine leaves a data-miner behind, then later breaks in and retrieves it; Forge decodes its data and confirms that eclun is instigating superhuman fights so Damage Control can make money cleaning them up. Despite Cyclops' protests, Wolverine begins ining Damage Control financially, looting their bank accounts and forcing their stockholders to liquidate their shares. Declun counters by buying new office building, showing confidence to the public — but when Wolverine investigates the building, armored Mandroids attack him (p). olverine breaks into a stockholder's office and intimidates him into liquidating all his Damage Control stock (d).

YNOPSIS: The Mandroids subdue Wolverine and begin cutting off his head.

OTE: Cover-labeled "Civil War." As Forge realizes that Declun is manufacturing superhuman battles, we see a montage of fight scenes, veral of which are from CW #3-4, '06. However, although this issue was published after CW #3-4, '06, it occurs beforehand. The montage correctly shows Blackout attacking Dagger, but they have never met on-panel. Their "battle" here is likely an art error; Blackout was present in

NAv #2 & 3 fb, '05, and Dagger was present in CW #3-4, '06. Next issue reveals that, per Wolverine's request, Amir and Janus are shadowi
him here; they therefore transition from Villains to Other Characters. Eddie is named next issue.

WOLVERINE #47 [#236] (December 2006)

"Retribution" (22 pages, see NOTE)

CREDITS: Marc Guggenheim (writer), Humberto Ramos (pencils), Carlos Cuevas (inks), Virtual Calligraph
Randy Gentile (letters), Edgar Delgado (colors), Kate Levin (production), Michael O'Connor (asst editor), A:
Alonso (exec editor)
FEATURE CHARACTER: Wolverine (dies, revives, also in dfb, also in W #59, '08 fb & W #48, '07 fb; next in XF
#9, NX #26 & 29, BP #18, NX #31 bts, X:DG #6, all '06, NX #32, '07, X #189-191 & 193, '06-07, GSW #1, '06)
GUEST STARS: Sentry (Robert Reynolds, schizophrenic hero, last in CW:Ret/2, '07, next in BP #18, '06), Ir
Man (bts giving Sentry Wolverine's file, last in NAv #23, '06, next in CW #3, '06)
VILLAINS: Walter Declun (in dfb, next in ASM Ann '08), Mandroids (some or others next in MCP #5/2, '08) i
Eddie
OTHER CHARACTERS: Maria Hill (Director of SHIELD, last in CW:YAv&Run #4, chr last bts in Cap #22 fb, ne
in CW #3, all '06), Miriam Sharpe (mother of Stamford victim, last in CW #2, '06, next in CW #4, '06), Damage Control: Lenny Ballinger (forema
last in FF:Foes #3, '05), John Porter (account executive, last in DC #4, '91) (prev 2 next in FF #542, '06), Albert Cleary (comptroller, last in S
#6, '04), Henry Ackerson (prev 2 next in WWHulk:DC #1, '08), Anne Marie Hoag (next in AntM #8, '07) (prev 5 in dfb), Atlantean Royal Guar
Amir, Janus; SHIELD agents (some or others last in NAv #23, '06, next in CW #3, '06) inc Herrick Goldman, SHIELD Superhuman Restra
Unit (some or others last in NAv #23, chr last in Cap #22 fb, next in CW #3, all '06), unregistered superhuman, cabbie, bystanders (prev 2 in df
President George W. Bush (mentioned, Declun's friend), New York Times reporters, state & Federal investigators (prev 2 mentioned, looking in
Damage Control's finances); bulldog (as Damage Control logo in dfb); Louis Brandeis (quoted)
LOCATIONS/ITEMS: Damage Control's new Long Island headquarters, skies above USA, Manhattan (in dfb) inc Damage Control's Flatir
Building office, Stamford / Mandroids' armor (2 destroyed) w/Whirlwind's buzzsaw (destroyed), headquarters' skylight (destroyed), SHIEL
shackles, level 10 power-nullifying collars (1 each of prev 2 destroyed), guns, armor, monitors, rappelling lines, helmets w/cameras & Helicarr
w/window (destroyed), Hill's earpiece & handgun, office window (destroyed), Declun's MGH (prev 2 in dfb)
FLASHBACK: As Damage Control's senior staff berate Walter Declun for his conduct and threaten to retake the company from him, Wolveri
arrives, having recovered from his plunge off the Helicarrier. Declun takes MGH, goes berserk and tackles Wolverine out a window; the two bra
through the city streets until Wolverine savagely stabs Declun through both eyes (d).
SYNOPSIS: The Mandroid's buzzsaw breaks against Wolverine's Adamantium vertebrae, stopping the villains from decapitating him. Amir a
Janus burst in and attack the Mandroids; Wolverine recovers, but the Sentry suddenly arrives with a SHIELD squad, declaring Wolverine und
arrest for violating the Superhuman Registration Act. Wolverine tries to fight, but the Sentry easily knocks him unconscious. Wolverine awake
shackled on the Helicarrier, where new SHIELD Director Maria Hill tells him to stop pursuing Declun, who has friends in high places. Wolveri
breaks free of his restraints and leaps off the Helicarrier, frantically slicing off his power-nullifying collar as he falls toward the city. Later, aft
Declun's defeat, Wolverine commiserates with Miriam Sharpe, whose son died in Stamford.
NOTE: Cover-labeled "Civil War." This issue's title is incorrectly given as "Payback," which was last issue's title. The correct title is reinstat
when this issue is reprinted in the "Civil War: Wolverine" TPB, '07; this Index has chosen to correct the typo and present the issue's intended ti
This issue reveals that Amir and Janus were following Wolverine last issue. Despite appearances, Declun does not die here. Maria Hill becan
Director of SHIELD in SecWar #5/3, '05. This issue also has a 2-page preview of Anita:GP #1, '06.

WOLVERINE: SAUDADE (2006)

"Saudade" (46 pages)

CREDITS: Jean-David Morvan (writer), Philippe Bouchet (art), RAM (letter
Walter Pezzali (colors), Chiara Benassi (design), DRZ (graphic designer), Mai
Corticelli (art director), Laurent Frémont (supervision), Matteo Losso & An
Rodella (editorial coordinators), Olivier Jalabert (editor), Marco Lupoi (editor
director), Sébastian Dallain (deputy director), Alain Guerrini (director); Alexand
Hain-Cole (UK translation), Paul Gravett (UK biography text); Larry Hama (L
adaptation), Dave Sharpe (US letters), John Denning (US asst editor), Cory Levi
(US editor), Mark Beazley & Jennifer Grünwald (US special projects editors), J

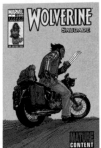

Youngquist (US senior editor)
FEATURE CHARACTER: Wolverine (also in his own imagination, also in fb between XFac #70, '91 & DC #
'91; chr last in NX #126, '02, chr next in Order #5, '02)
GUEST STARS: X-Men: Phoenix (chr last in XX #9, '02, chr next in Order #5, '02), Professor X (in fb betwe
XFac #70-71, '91, also in picture), others (bts in fb, preparing to search for Wolverine, exact members unspecifie
team chr last in XFac #70, '91, chr next in W #40, '91)
VILLAINS: Kuhrra Daïzonest (mutant phaser, healer & telepath, dies) & his death squad inc Jorge (see NOT
(all in fb)
OTHER CHARACTERS: Andre Mexer (casts disorienting illusions, also in Wolverine's imagination, also in pictur
prior to issue), Xavier Institute students (some or others chr last in NX #126, chr next bts in XFac #4, chr next in V
#131, all '02), Kuhrra's penitents & aides inc Pedrao, Mexer's friends (die), mermaid (also as partier, on banne
& as pendant & statue), partiers, bus driver & passengers, penitents' neighbor (bts driving them to Kuhrra), squa
member's children, miners, guards, bystanders; fish (some also on banner & as earrings, another as statu
rats, seagulls (prev 16 in fb); Mexer's mother (mentioned in fb, died giving birth at age 12), garbage collectors (mentioned in fb, found newbo
Mexer), Portuguese Colonials' descendants (mentioned in fb, control Brazil's wealth); cartoon cats (on Wolverine's clothes & child's shi
historical & mythological figures (prev 2 as statues), spirits (as skeleton pendants), model (as truck decoration), girl (as child's doll) (prev 6 in f
Magneto (bts), Omega Red, Sabretooth, waitress, bar patron (prev 5 in Wolverine's imagination)

LOCATIONS/ITEMS: Brazil: Fortaleza, Ceará w/train station (mentioned), docks & beach; Sergipe inc Kuhrra's Sergipe Heights home & Jarambu w/beach & Mexer's shanty, Sertão (Brazilian outback, mentioned), Pará's Serra Pelada gold mine; Atlantic Ocean (all in fb); X-Mansion (also in fb) w/hangar & grounds, battlefields, bar (prev 2 in Wolverine's imagination) / Death squad's guns (some destroyed), ropes (1 destroyed), truncheon, Jeep, knife, sack, tape & trucks (1 destroyed) w/tires (some destroyed) & CB radios (bts), Wolverine's truck, Jeep, X-phone w/GPS (bts) & motorcycle w/oil (bts) & keys, cargo ship, dock crane, forklift, Cerebro (bts), Mexer's friend's switchblade, penitents & dancers' offerings, mermaid's pendant, bus, dumpster (mentioned), Kuhrra's car (bts), gate (destroyed) & operating curtain, banner wrap, pay phone, Professor X's earpiece & wheelchair w/monitor, squad member's car (destroyed), clothes, bandages, guns & trophy case w/ stolen cellphones, aide & guards' guns, miner's packs, Mexer's pickaxe (all in fb), X-Plane (X-Men's jet), Mexer's sponge & bucket

FLASHBACK: Professor X contacts Wolverine, vacationing in Brazil, to report that Cerebro detected a mutant near him. Mexer suddenly attacks Wolverine with disorienting illusions; he and his friends steal Wolverine's motorcycle and flee from a pursuing death squad. Elsewhere, healer Kuhrra Daïzonest is stricken by a wave of pain caused by Mexer's power usage. Wolverine rescues the boys from the squad; they take him to a beach party where an exotic woman gives Wolverine a mermaid pendant. Wolverine tells Mexer about the X-Men, but Professor X reveals that Mexer is not the mutant Cerebro detected. The death squad attacks again, capturing Mexer. They riddle Wolverine with bullets and dump him in the ocean; Wolverine's pendant begins glowing, attracting a mermaid. Wolverine later awakens on the beach, fully healed. The squad brings Mexer to Kuhrra, who telepathically lobotomizes the boy. Wolverine forces a squad member to reveal Kuhrra's location, and assaults Kuhrra's home. The healer attacks, phasing inside Wolverine's body and pulling out his muscles — but Wolverine's Adamantium stops Kuhrra from extracting Wolverine's heart. Wolverine kills Kuhrra, and later finds the lobotomized Mexer laboring in a gold mine.

SYNOPSIS: Wolverine tells the students of his time in Brazil. Mexer works as the Institute's janitor, and Wolverine sadly wonders how the boy could have turned out.

NOTE: This French-language graphic novel was originally created and published in Europe as an oversized hardcover by Panini Comics, Marvel's foreign licenser. Panini also published a special edition, limited to 2000 copies, that includes an 8-page interview/sketchbook section and an original soundtrack CD by Brazilian musician DJ Dolores. This issue was translated into English and printed in the UK as part of Panini's "Marvel Europa" TPB, '07, along with new biographical blurbs about the creators. It was then re-dialogued and reprinted in the US by Marvel, in standard comic book format, in 2008. The US edition, which carries a Mature Content warning, uses the original back cover as the front cover, includes the original front cover and limited edition back cover as pin-ups, includes the UK TPB's biographies on the inside back cover, and uses the limited edition front cover as the back cover. The cover of both French editions credits the writer and artist by their last names, but credits the colorist by his first name. This story takes place before "M-Day," where the Scarlet Witch depowered most of the world's mutants. Mexer's first name is revealed in OHMU HC13, '10. Jorge is named in the US edition. Kuhrra's telepathy, implied in the original edition, is made explicit in the US edition. It is unrevealed why Mexer's power usages cause Kuhrra pain. Wolverine's ringtone is "Kirbyleebyrne," referencing X-Men writer Stan Lee and artists Jack Kirby and John Byrne. In real life, the Serra Pelada gold mine closed in 1986.

GIANT-SIZE WOLVERINE (December 2006)

"House of Blood and Sorrow" (34 pages)

CREDITS: David Lapham (writer), David Aja (art), Virtual Calligraphy's Joe Caramagna (letters), José Villarrubia (colors), Warren Simons (editor)
FEATURE CHARACTER: Wolverine (also in pfb, next in W #48, '07)
VILLAINS: Hydra agents (some or all die, also bts in pfb, some or others last in NAv #23, '06, 1 or another last in SH #10, '06, some or others next in WS:WK, '07)
OTHER CHARACTERS: Horace Buchman (Waverly farmer, dies), Leelee Buchman (Horace's daughter, also in fb prior to issue), Waverly Sheriff & residents (others mentioned, died) inc Mose (bts on phone, reported crash) & Sweeney (dies), Benny's Tavern patrons inc Mike & Sam, Leelee's mother (dead, also in fb prior to issue) & her living tumor (another in fb), doctors, Leelee's deformed siblings (prev 2 in fb); horse, deformed goat & chicken (prev 3 possibly die), birds; State Troopers (mentioned, Sheriff plans to call them), patron's daughter (mentioned, punished for going near Buchmans), Horace's family (mentioned, owned farm); game show contestants (bts) & host (prev 2 on TV)

LOCATIONS/ITEMS: Waverly, North Dakota (also in pfb & fb) inc river (bts), Horace's house & barn (prev 2 destroyed), Sheriff's office, Benny's Tavern & former cemetery; game show set (on TV), hospital (in fb) / Horace's truck (bts), tractor (destroyed), TV, shotgun & liquor bottles, Hydra radios (all but 1 bts), car, ring, blasters, guns, robot (destroyed, also in pfb) w/machine guns & hovercraft w/rappelling lines, Sweeney's shotguns (destroyed) & truck, Leelee's rag & water bowl, Sheriff's truck & gun, patrons' cars & guns, doctors' scalpels, scissors, knives & bowls (prev 4 in fb), Wolverine's shovel, water main (bts)

FLASHBACKS: Wolverine battles a flying Hydra robot (p). Doctors remove an enormous tumor from Leelee's newborn mother; years later, all her babies except Leelee are similarly deformed.

SYNOPSIS: Leelee Buchman sees a robot crash-land near her farm. Sweeney discovers the wreckage and assumes that it is an alien craft; he alerts the town sheriff, who distrusts the Buchmans. Leelee discovers and shelters the badly burned Wolverine. The robot soon reactivates and attacks, but Wolverine destroys it. As the sheriff recruits locals to help deal with the Buchmans, undercover Hydra agents overhear. Leelee tells Wolverine that her deformed siblings were drowned at birth, but although she was normal, the doctor tried to drown her anyway; when her mother lashed out to save Leelee, the sheriff shot her. Wolverine sees a tentacle protruding from Leelee's father Horace's back, and traces it to the basement, where an enormous tumor-like creature has grown out of the mother's corpse. The sheriff and his mob arrive, and the Hydra agents spot Wolverine and attack. A brawl breaks out; Sweeney shoots Horace and the tumor reacts violently, demolishing the house and killing Sweeney and the agents. Leelee demands that the tumor stop, and it calms down and slithers away. Later, Wolverine and Leelee bury her mother's body.

NOTE: Strangely, this issue has a house ad for itself.

2ND STORY: (Untitled, 21 pages)
NOTE: Reprinted from X #6, '92, with the original story title ("Farther Still") removed.

3RD STORY: (Untitled, 23 pages)
NOTE: Reprinted from X #7, '92, with the original story title ("Inside … Out!") and all footnote boxes removed.

WOLVERINE #48 [#237] (January 2007)

"Vendetta — Epilogue: Knocking On Heaven's Door" (21 pages)

CREDITS: Marc Guggenheim (writer), Humberto Ramos (pencils), Carlos Cuevas (inks), Virtual Calligraph
Randy Gentile (letters), Edgar Delgado (colors), Michael O'Connor (asst editor), Axel Alonso (exec editor)
FEATURE CHARACTER: Wolverine (also as himself, James Howlett & Experiment X in Purgatory visions
fb1, also as himself, Experiment X & "Patch" in Purgatory visions in fb2, also in rfb1 & rfb2, also as himself & Ir
Man in rfb3; also as spirit in fb1 during W #42, '06; also as spirit & revives in fb2 during W #43, '06; also as sp
in fb3 between W #59, '08 fb & W #47, '06)
VILLAINS: Lazaer (Azrael, angel of death, also as Phoenix, Silver Fox, Mariko Yashida & Wolverine in Wolverine
afterlife visions, also as WWI soldier in Wolverine's thoughts; 1st as Lazaer in fb1, fb2 & fb3 between W #58, '
fbs), Nitro (in fb2 during W #43, '06; also in rfb2 & rfb3)
OTHER CHARACTERS: Amir (also in rfb3, next in W #57, '07); Crusader, his followers (all but 1 bts); FAA employ
(bts) (prev 3 in rfb1), SHIELD Superhuman Restraint Unit inc Abrams, Walter Declun (bts) (prev 3 in rfb2), Atlantean Royal Guard: Janus, Politus; Su
Mariner, Forge, Mandroids, Sentry, Maria Hill (bts) (prev 7 in rfb3); Phoenix (also as Marvel Girl, in Purgatory visions in fb1 & fb2), Silver Fox, Mar
Yashida (prev 2 in Purgatory visions in fb1), Phaedra, WWI troops (prev 2 in Wolverine's thoughts); angel (on Lazaer's sword)
LOCATIONS/ITEMS: Amir's bedroom, Purgatory (in fb1, fb2 & fb3), Lindsborth (named, in rfb1), Big Sur (in rfb2, rfb3 & fb2) inc Nitro's cal
(in rfb2), New Pangea, Eagle Plaza, Damage Control's Long Island headquarters, skies over USA (prev 4 in rfb3), Shingen's Citadel compoun
Howlett family estate, Weapon X Program facility, Avalon (prev 4 in Wolverine's afterlife visions); Ypres, Belgium (unnamed); Hydra base (prev
in Wolverine's thoughts) / Crusader's armor, sword, stolen money (prev 2 bts) & hijacked C-130 airplane (destroyed), FAA jacket (bts) (all in rfb
SHIELD airplane, guns, armor & helmets w/cameras (prev 5 destroyed), Nitro's cellphone (prev 6 in rfb2), Janus' water-breathing mask, Ir
Man's aquatic armor, Mandroids' armor w/Whirlwind's buzzsaw, Hill's handgun, SHIELD power-nullifying collar (destroyed) & Helicarrier (b
w/window (destroyed) (prev 8 in rfb3), Weapon X Program's Genesis Tank w/Adamantium feed tubes, Wolverine's Adamantium, Experime
X's helmet (prev 4 in Purgatory visions), Wolverine's staff & rifle w/bayonet (prev 3 in Wolverine's thoughts), Lazaer's sword, Amir's injector
water-breathing mask
FLASHBACKS: Crusader crashes his stolen airplane; Wolverine later awakens in the rubble (W #42, '06). SHIELD assaults Nitro, wl
explodes; the blast burns Wolverine down to a skeleton, but he eventually recovers and attacks Nitro (W #43, '06). The Atlantean Royal Gua
interrupt Wolverine beating Nitro; Wolverine confronts Sub-Mariner and Nitro, consults with Forge, fights Mandroids and the Sentry and lea
off the Helicarrier (W #44-47, '06). Wolverine dies in the plane crash and his soul arrives in Purgatory, where he sees a cloaked figure await
him (1). Wolverine dies in Nitro's explosion and his soul meets Phoenix in Purgatory. He soon revives, seeing Nitro passed out from the eff
of exploding; Wolverine's nervous system and muscles slowly regrow (2). Wolverine dies from the Helicarrier fall; his soul arrives in Purgato
where Lazaer attacks. The two duel and Wolverine wins, gaining the right to return to his body (3).
SYNOPSIS: After sleeping with Amir, Wolverine tells her about Lazaer, noting that he has begun battling Wolverine's soul more and more oft
Amir asks why Lazaer attacks; Wolverine refuses to explain, but thinks back to WWI.
NOTE: Cover-labeled "Casualties of War," part of the fallout from the Civil War event. The "Vendetta Epilogue" in this story's title confirms W #
'06's implication that "Vendetta" was meant to be the name of this story arc. Lazaer is revealed as Azrael, the Angel of Death in W #58, '07. I
is incorrectly depicted wearing a WWI uniform in Wolverine's thoughts. Lindsborth, Kansas is named here; Ypres, Belgium is named in W #
'07. This issue clarifies that Wolverine and Nitro took a lengthy amount of time to recover from W #43, '06's explosion. In W #64, '08, Wolver
mentions that he has tried Atlantean water therapy to manage pain; he may have learned it here. W #48-55, '07's production coordinato
unknown. This issue contains the series' final letters page until W #3, '11.

WOLVERINE #49 [#238] (February 2007)

"Better to Give..." (34 pages)

CREDITS: Rob Williams (writer), Laurence Campbell (pencils), Kris Justice (inks), Virtual Calligraphy's Ran
Gentile (letters), Paul Mounts (colors), Michael O'Connor (asst editor), Axel Alonso (exec editor)
FEATURE CHARACTER: Wolverine (next in Blade #5, '07, CW #6, '06 bts, FF #543, '07 fb, XPx:W #1-5, '06-0
GUEST STAR: Kitty Pryde (bts asking Wolverine to shop for her, last in X #190, '06, next in NX #35, '07)
VILLAINS: "Black Christmass" (kidnappers posing as death cult, also as elves, some die) inc Cave, Justin (p
2 die) & Barry, corrupt Lacy's employee (as Santa Claus)
OTHER CHARACTERS: Toulouse Lexington (wealthy businessman's daughter), Toulouse's bodyguar
Pinter (former policeman), others (die); Lacy's manager (bts closing Santa's Grotto), shoppers, employee
security guard, Toulouse's father (bts paying for Toulouse's shopping trip), police, helicopter pilot (voice on
bystanders; Croatian veterans (mentioned, met Cave); Santa Claus, models (prev 2 on posters), soldiers, bea
deer, penguins (prev 4 as decorations), angels (as statues); Jesus Christ (quoted)
LOCATIONS/ITEMS: Manhattan inc Rockefeller Plaza & Lacy's department store w/Santa's Grotto / Wolverine's pack, Lacy's Christm
decorations & speaker system (bts) w/microphone, "Sex Panther" perfume, Toulouse's glasses, Pinter's gun, Santa's Grotto's "temporar
closed" barriers (bts) & exit chute, employee's Santa costume, kidnappers' walkie-talkies (some bts), guns (1 destroyed), toy sack, elf & Sa
costumes, shopping cart w/plastic explosives & bombs (destroyed) w/timers, Cave's gun, elf & Santa costumes & plastic explosive harne
(destroyed) w/remote control, police cars, guns, barricades & megaphone, news helicopter, Rockefeller Plaza's Christmas decorations
SYNOPSIS: At Lacy's, Wolverine grudgingly runs errands for Kitty Pryde. He bumps into heiress Toulouse Lexington, who accidentally spra
perfume on herself. Toulouse later visits the store Santa Claus, but he suddenly seizes her — and the "elves" pull out guns, shooting all
Toulouse's bodyguards except Pinter, who flees. The elves' leader, Cave, straps an explosive harness onto Toulouse. Pinter discovers Wolver
standing over a pile of dead elves; the two find Cave's men planting bombs, but discover that the explosives are just for show. Cave lou
announces that he plans to destroy Lacy's as a strike against consumerism, but admits privately that the attack is a distraction; he really wants
kidnap and ransom Toulouse. Wolverine and Pinter battle through Cave's men, but the bombs detonate and the panicked crowd flees outside
along with Cave and the captive Toulouse. Wolverine tracks the perfume's scent and locates Toulouse; Cave panics and activates her explos
harness, but Wolverine cuts her free and absorbs the blast himself, while Pinter shoots Cave.

WOLVERINE #50 [#239] (March 2007)

"Evolution, Chapter One: First Blood" (22 pages)

CREDITS: Jeph Loeb (writer), Simone Bianchi (pencils), Simone Bianchi & Andrea Silvestri (inks & washed halftones), Richard Starkings & Comicraft (letters), Paul Mounts (colors), Michael O'Connor (asst editor), Axel Alonso (editor), Morry Hollowell (c colors)

FEATURE CHARACTER: Wolverine (also in rfb, also in fb between W #47, '91 fb & W #10, '89 fb, also in W:O #5, '06 fb, W #41, '91 fb, W #10, '89 fb & XO:Sabre, '09 during fb)

GUEST STAR: Rogue (last in MsM #10, '07, next in X #194, '07)

SUPPORTING CAST: Silver Fox (alive & seemingly dead in fb between W #47, '91 fb & W #10, '89 fb, also in W:O #5, '06 fbs, W #55, '07 fb & W #41, '91 fb during fb)

VILLAINS: Romulus (millennia-old manipulator, bts influencing Wolverine's dreams; also in shadow in Wolverine's dream; chr last in W:O #31, '09 fb, last voice only in W:O #2, '06, chr last bts in W:O #15, '07), Sabretooth (also in rfb, also in fb between XO:Sabre, '09 & W #10, '89 fb, also in W:O #5, '06 fb, W #55, '07 fb, W #10, '89 fb & XO:Sabre, '09 during fb; last in X #193, '07)

OTHER CHARACTERS: Horses (in fb); models (on TV); Lupine (fictitious race allegedly evolved from prehistoric wolves, some dead) inc "Blondie" (blond-haired pack leader, dies) & "Pup" (black-haired pack leader); saber-tooth tiger (dies) (prev 4 in Wolverine's dream)

LOCATIONS/ITEMS: X-Mansion w/grounds, Mount Logan (in fb) inc saloon (in rfb) & Wolverine & Silver Fox's cabin, beach (on TV), prehistoric valley (in dream) / X-Mansion window (destroyed) & TV, Wolverine's firewood, coat & boots, Silver Fox's snowball, woodpile (prev 5 in fb), saloon window (in rfb, destroyed), saber-tooth tiger's fang (in dream)

FLASHBACKS: Wolverine and Sabretooth crash through the saloon window (W #10, '89 fb). Wolverine and Silver Fox flirt and kiss as Sabretooth secretly observes; Wolverine later returns home to find Silver Fox dead and a birthday greeting scrawled on the wall in blood. He finds Sabretooth in town and attacks, but Sabretooth defeats him and says "Quod sum eris."

SYNOPSIS: Wolverine has a recurring dream of a prehistoric battle where Lupine kill a saber-tooth tiger. The dark-haired pack leader then murders the blond leader as a shadowy figure watches. Disconcerted by the dreams, Wolverine returns to the X-Mansion unhappy that Sabretooth recently joined the X-Men. He challenges Sabretooth and tackles him out a window; the two begin to brawl viciously across the mansion grounds. Wolverine recalls their earlier battle and asks what "quod sum eris" meant; Sabretooth translates it as "I am what you will be" and implies that as Wolverine ages, he will become as savage and bloodthirsty as Sabretooth is. As Sabretooth buries his claws in Wolverine's heart, Wolverine pops his claws through Sabretooth's throat...

NOTE: This issue also has an ad-free black & white edition that features a 1-page Simone Bianchi sketchbook; the B&W edition also has a New York Comic Con variant cover. Sabretooth asked the X-Men for asylum from the powerful Children of the Vault in X #188, '06; he joined Rogue's X-Men strike team to battle the Children in X #192, '06. The Lupine are surmised to be evolved from prehistoric wolves in W #53, '07, but revealed as fictitious creations of Romulus in W #312, '12. W #55, '07 reveals that Romulus is manipulating Wolverine's dreams in this story arc.

2ND STORY: "Puny Little Man" (12 pages)

CREDITS: Jeph Loeb (writer), Ed McGuinness (pencils), Dexter Vines (inks), Richard Starkings & Comicraft (letters, uncredited), Dave McCaig (colors), Michael O'Connor (asst editor), Axel Alonso (editor), Len Wein, Herb Trimpe, John Romita, Damon Lindelof & Leinil Francis Yu (special thanks)

FEATURE CHARACTER: Wolverine (also in his own dream, chr last in W #55, '07, chr next in W:O Ann, '07)

OTHER CHARACTERS: Hulk, Earth-1610 Hulk, Earth-1610 Wolverine (all in Wolverine's dream, see NOTE); Heather Hudson (mentioned in Wolverine's dream, added whisker design to his cowl)

LOCATIONS/ITEMS: Canada inc North Woods (in dream), Earth-1610 Tibet (in dream) / Boulder (destroyed)

SYNOPSIS: Wolverine dreams about his first battle with the Hulk. He wonders why the Canadian government decided to make a clawed psychopath into a super hero, and notes bitterly that no matter who he works for, they always want to mold him in their image. Wolverine's dream suddenly takes a strange turn, as the Hulk grabs him and — as Wolverine's costume switches to a different look — Hulk savagely rips his legs off his torso. Wolverine awakens in Canada, unsettled by his nightmare.

NOTE: This story occurs after the conclusion of the story arc begun in this issue's first story. Initially, Wolverine's dream roughly follows the events of IHulk #181, '74, then segues into the events of UltWHulk #1, '06 fb. The latter issue occurred on Earth-1610, aka the "Ultimate universe." Though Earth-616's Wolverine should not have been aware of those events, various Marvel characters have occasionally tapped into alternate realities via dreaming or imagination. Notably, Nc #3, '86 established that Kitty Pryde once subconsciously connected with Earth-5311 when telling Illyana Rasputin a bedtime story in UXM #153, '82; a similar connection could have occurred during Wolverine's dream. Although Wolverine notes that his counterpart's costume is unfamiliar, he wore the same costume in UXM #423-424 & Exiles #28-20, all '03.

WOLVERINE #51 [#240] (April 2007)

"Evolution, Chapter Two: Déjà Vu" (22 pages)

CREDITS: Jeph Loeb (writer), Simone Bianchi (pencils), Simone Bianchi Andrea Silvestri (inks & washed halftones), Richard Starkings & Comicraft (letter Paul Mounts (colors), Michael O'Connor (asst editor), Axel Alonso (editor), Mor Hollowell (c colors)

FEATURE CHARACTER: Wolverine (also in his own thoughts, next in FallSon:W FallSon:Av, FallSon:SM, FallSon:IM, X #200-204, NX #38-39, 40 bts & 41, all 'C MCP #8/3, '08; X:ES, NX #42, X #201/2 fb, SH #16, NAv #28 fb, 29 fb, 30 fb & 2 31, all '07, Pun #3, '09 fb, W #31, '07, DD #112, '08 fb, NAv #31-34 & 36 fb, '07-C MAv #8, '08, NAv #36, 35 bts & 37, '07-08; Cable&Dp #43-44, NW #2-3, all '07, Ann #1, '12, WWHulk:X #1-3, '07, WWHulk:DC #1 bts & 2-3, '08)

GUEST STAR: Storm (last in FF #543, '07, chr last in BP #34, '08, next in FallSon:IM, '07)

VILLAINS: Romulus (bts influencing Wolverine's dream, also in shadow in Wolverine's dream), Sabretooth (also in Wolverine's thoughts, ne in X #195, '07 fb)

OTHER CHARACTERS: Neanderthals (dead), "Pup" (both in Wolverine's dream); Psylocke, Boomer (prev 2 in Wolverine's thoughts); deer "dead"), rabbits, unicorns (prev 3 as holograms in Wolverine's thoughts)

LOCATIONS/ITEMS: Sky, desert, prehistoric valley (in dream) w/lake, field (in holographic illusion), Danger Room w/control booth (prev in thoughts) / X-Men's Blackbird jet w/trajectory sensors (bts) & cockpit canopy, Wolverine's chains (all destroyed), saber-tooth tiger's fan Neanderthals' fire (prev 2 in dream), Danger Room security cameras (bts), control booth window (destroyed) & computers, Sabretooth restraints (prev 4 in thoughts)

SYNOPSIS: Wolverine has another unsettling dream, in which the black-haired Lupine pack leader that he has nicknamed "Pup" howls over th bodies of Neanderthals he has just killed. However, when "Pup" accidentally steps into their fire, he is set ablaze. A shadowy figure grabs hi and dunks him in a lake, saving his life. Wolverine awakens and finds himself chained to the X-Men's Blackbird jet, which a recovered Sabretoo is piloting. Wolverine breaks free and smashes into the cockpit, attacking Sabretooth. Wolverine realizes that Sabretooth was deliberately takin him somewhere, but with neither mutant focusing on flying, the Blackbird crashes. The two combatants are badly injured, but continue fightin savagely in the wreckage. As they battle, Wolverine recalls a time when the X-Men were caring for Sabretooth after Wolverine lobotomized hi with his claws — but Sabretooth recovered, broke free and brutally injured Psylocke. Wolverine blames himself for not being there to save he Suddenly, Wolverine and Sabretooth's brawl is interrupted by a lightning bolt, wielded by Storm...

NOTE: This issue also has an ad-free black & white edition that features a 1-page Simone Bianchi sketchbook. Wolverine popped a cla through Sabretooth's brain in W #90, '95. Wolverine thinks about Sabretooth's attack on Psylocke in UXM #328, '96 here, but as he notes, was not present for the incident; his recollection is based on second-hand information and is not entirely accurate. Storm married the Bla Panther in BP #18, '06, becoming Queen of Wakanda; her married name is now Ororo Iqadi T'Challa, as revealed in AX #25, '08. Despi appearances, there is a lengthy gap between this issue and next, wherein Wolverine and Sabretooth are calmed down and return to the X-Me Sabretooth soon betrays Rogue's X-Men strike team and is thrown into the ocean in X #198-199, '07; from there he is captured and brought Wakanda, where Storm and the Panther summon Wolverine next issue.

WOLVERINE #52 [#241] (May 2007)

"Evolution, Chapter Three: Blood on the Wind" (22 pages, see NOTE)

CREDITS: Jeph Loeb (writer), Simone Bianchi (pencils), Simone Bianchi Andrea Silvestri (inks & washed halftones), Richard Starkings & Comicraft (letters Simone Peruzzi (colors), Michael O'Connor (asst editor), Axel Alonso (edito Morry Hollowell (c colors)

FEATURE CHARACTER: Wolverine (also in fb between MCP #98, '92 fb & #53, '07 fb)

GUEST STARS: Black Panther, Storm (both last in FF #550, '07)

VILLAINS: Romulus (bts influencing Wolverine's dream, also in Wolverine dream; also in fb, his chr 1st app, prior to W #53, '07 fb), Sabretooth (also as Vict Creed in fb between XO:Sabre, '09 & W #53, '07 fb; last in Cable&Dp #41, '0 Hand ninjas (in fb, others chr last in Elek:Hand #5, '05 fb, another chr next in W:O Ann, '07 fb, others chr next in UXM #268, '90 fb)

OTHER CHARACTERS: Wakandan archaeologists (bts discovering Lupine graveyard) & guards (die), Japanese prostitutes (in fb, some bt killed by Sabretooth); elephants (dead as skeletons; others also die in Wolverine's dream); Janice Hollenbeck (see NOTE), Psylocke, Silv Fox (prev 3 mentioned, attacked by Sabretooth); guards' wives & children (prev 2 mentioned by Black Panther); Lupine: black-haired leade blond-haired leader, others; ancient warriors (prev 4 in Wolverine's dream); Bast (Panther God, as statue)

LOCATIONS/ITEMS: Wakanda, Africa (Black Panther's kingdom) inc archaeological dig site (also as battlefield in dream) & palace; Tokyo (fb) / Sabretooth's chains (destroyed), Romulus' fake Lupine skeletons (see NOTE) & scent-masking oils (bts), Wolverine's bonds (destroye off-panel), ninja's sword (prev 3 in fb), Romulus' sword, Lupines' armor, swords & shields, leaders' wrist-mounted blades, warriors' swords spears, elephants' armor (prev 8 in dream)

FLASHBACK: Over a century ago, the Hand capture a young Wolverine in Tokyo, and a shadowy figure orders him to stop a man who is killin prostitutes. Wolverine confronts the man, Victor Creed — but when he cuts off Victor's hand, Victor simply reattaches it and heals.

SYNOPSIS: Wolverine daydreams about a Lupine battle against warriors in ancient Africa. Romulus promises a reward for the most kills, b at the battle's end, both leaders' counts are equal — so the black-haired leader quickly decapitates the blond leader. In Wakanda, Wolverin emerges from his daydream to learn that Storm and the Black Panther have Sabretooth captive. Storm tries to tell Wolverine about a rece archeological discovery, but Sabretooth breaks free, murders two guards and flees. Black Panther chases and attacks him, but Sabretoot quickly begins choking him. Wolverine frees Black Panther by cutting off Sabretooth's hand. Storm points out that they are fighting in the archeologists' discovery — a boneyard littered with Lupine skeletons, and looking just like the battlefield from Wolverine's dream…

NOTE: This issue also has an ad-free black & white edition that features a 1-page Simone Bianchi sketchbook. A lettering error drops out the word "Evolution" in this issue's title; this Index has chosen to correct the typo and present the issue's intended title. Although this issue implies that the battle in Wolverine's dream occurred in Wakanda, the human warriors seen there appear European, not African. W #312, '12 reveals that Romulus falsified and planted the "Lupine skeletons" discovered here. Sabretooth incorrectly refers to Janice Hollenbeck as "Jenny" in this issue.

WOLVERINE #53 [#242] (June 2007)

"Evolution, Chapter Four: Insomnia" (22 pages)

CREDITS: Jeph Loeb (writer), Simone Bianchi (pencils), Simone Bianchi & Andrea Silvestri (inks & washed halftones), Richard Starkings & Comicraft (letters), Morry Hollowell (colors), Michael O'Connor & Daniel Ketchum (asst editors), Axel Alonso (editor)

FEATURE CHARACTER: Wolverine (also in fb between W #52, '07 fb & W:O #49, '10 fb)

GUEST STARS: Sasquatch (last in CW:In, '07, chr last in MCP #12/4, '08), Wolfsbane (last in WWHulk:X #3, '07) (both also on monitor), Storm (next in FNSM #24, '07), Black Panther

VILLAINS: Romulus (named, bts influencing Wolverine's dream & giving Wild Child orders, also in Wolverine's dream, also in fb between W #52, '07 fb & W:O #14, '07 fb bts), Sabretooth (also as Victor Creed in fb between W #52, '07 fb & XO:Sabre, '09, chr next in W #310, '12, next in W&X #3, '12), Wild Child (last in W:O #15, '07)

OTHER CHARACTERS: Feral (Maria Callasantos), Thornn (Lucia Callasantos) (prev 2 sisters, depowered catlike mutants, see NOTE; also on monitor, last in HoM:Day, '06), Wakandan archaeologists (bts studying Lupine remains), guards (die), citizens (dead, as skulls) & nurse; Magneto (mentioned, allegedly coined term "Homo superior"); Lupine: blond-haired leader (dies), black-haired leader (prev 2 see NOTE); spectators, white tigers (die), historical figures (as statues) (prev 5 in Wolverine's dream); prehistoric fish, shark, tortoise, crocodile, gila monster, wolf, gorilla, Neanderthal, man, various stages of evolving Lupine (prev 10 on monitor); mythological figures (as masks), giraffes as pattern on fabric)

LOCATIONS/ITEMS: Black Panther's Wakandan palace w/underground tunnels, Sabretooth's cell & Wolverine's room, Tokyo (in fb1), Flavian Amphitheater (aka the Colosseum; Rome, Italy; in dream) / Fake Lupine skull, Black Panther's computers w/monitor, guards' shields & pikes, Sabretooth's cell door & shackles w/shock collar, Wild Child's poison & transportation (prev 2 bts), Wolverine's sword (in fb2), nurse's cloth & water bowl, tiger's chain (destroyed), leaders' armor, swords, shields & axe (prev 5 in dream)

FLASHBACK: In Tokyo, a young Wolverine defeats Victor Creed — but when he tries to kill him, a shadowy figure knocks him out.

SYNOPSIS: Wolverine dreams that two Lupine gladiators perform in ancient Rome, battling tigers and one another. The dark-haired gladiator wins, and when Romulus gives him a thumbs-down, he beheads his blond opponent. Black Panther studies the bones and theorizes that the Lupine are a separate species, evolved from wolves into something similar to humans. Wolverine visits the imprisoned Sabretooth and demands to know more about Romulus, the figure from his dreams, but Sabretooth is afraid to answer. Wolverine returns later, but finds the guards dead and Sabretooth gone. Wolverine tracks Sabretooth to the palace's underground tunnels, but is suddenly ambushed by former Alpha Flight member Wild Child, who is stronger and faster than ever before. Wolverine succumbs to Wild Child's poisoned claws, and awakens days later — to find Sasquatch, Wolfsbane, Feral and Thornn gathered in Wakanda, asking him to accompany them to the old Weapon X Program facility…

NOTE: This issue also has an ad-free black & white edition that features a 1-page Simone Bianchi sketchbook. The Lupine leaders seen in this issue's dream are not the same as the two from previous dreams. W #312, '12 implies that Romulus was trying to create a new species, and invented the "Lupine" to trick Wolverine and the Wakandan scientists into studying feral mutations in greater detail, effectively furthering Romulus' research for him. Black Panther claims that Feral and Thornn have mutations with a Lupine component, but both are catlike, not wolflike. Black Panther also shows a picture of Sasquatch when listing Lupine-like mutations, but Sasquatch's powers are magical and derive from the Great Beast Tanaraq. Feral and Thornn were depowered on "M-Day" along with most of the world's mutants. Next issue implies that Romulus restored them, but W #55, '07 reveals that only their physical appearances were restored, not their powers.

WOLVERINE #54 [#243] (July 2007)

"Evolution, Chapter Five: Wake the Dead" (22 pages)

CREDITS: Jeph Loeb (writer), Simone Bianchi (pencils), Simone Bianchi & Andrea Silvestri (inks & washed halftones), Richard Starkings & Comicraft (letters), Simone Peruzzi (co-colors), Morry Hollowell (co-colors, c colors), Aubrey Sitterson & Daniel Ketchum (asst editors), Axel Alonso (editor)

FEATURE CHARACTER: Wolverine (also in his own dream, also in fb between MCP #74, '91 fb & MCP #74, '91)

GUEST STARS: Black Panther (bts loaning Wolverine his jet, next in FNSM #24, '07), Sasquatch, Wolfsbane

VILLAINS: Romulus (bts influencing Wolverine's dream, also in shadow in Wolverine's dream, also in shadow in fb between W:O #27, '08 fb & MCP #84, '91 bts), Sabretooth (in fb between L:SS, '96 & W #-1, '97), Sabretooth clone (1st, see NOTE), Professor Truett Hudson (in fb between MCP #74, '91 fb & MCP #74, '91), Wild Child (also in Wolverine's dream)

OTHER CHARACTERS: Feral (dies), Thornn, Canadian Air Force (bts, escorts diverted); Mr. Sinister, Professor X (prev 2 mentioned in fb, studying genetics); Captain America, Wild Child, Nazis (some die) (prev 3 in Wolverine's dream)

LOCATIONS/ITEMS: Skies above British Columbia & Alberta, Department K facility (also as Weapon X Program facility in fb), Italian Alps (in dream) / Black Panther's private jet, Weapon X Program's computer (in fb), sensors, battery packs & Genesis Tank (destroyed, also in fb), Adamantium feed tubes (in fb), Professor's paperwork (in fb), Nazis' guns & tank, Wolverine's sword, Wild Child's grenade (prev 4 in dream)

FLASHBACK: As "Experiment X," Wolverine floats in a tank after his Adamantium bonding. Sabretooth and Romulus arrive to check on his progress, and Romulus orders the Professor to wipe Wolverine's memory.

SYNOPSIS: In Wolverine's dream, he and Captain America fight Nazis in 1942. Wolverine unmasks the Nazi leader — Wild Child — but knocked away and lands at Romulus' feet. Wolverine awakens just as his group's jet lands at the former Weapon X facility. Sasquatch notes that their planned military escort was missing, and worries that something is wrong. Wolverine orders the others to stay in the jet, but Feral, Thornn and Wolfsbane decide to follow anyway — and Wild Child suddenly ambushes Sasquatch. Wolverine finds Sabretooth floating in a tank, but he bursts free and attacks savagely; Wolverine notes that Sabretooth's rational mind appears to be completely gone. Sabretooth gouges out Wolverine's eyes; by the time Wolverine recovers and follows, he finds Sasquatch badly wounded, Wolfsbane and Thornn in shock — and Sabretooth crouched over Feral's corpse.

NOTE: This issue also has an ad-free black & white edition that features a 1-page Simone Bianchi sketchbook. This issue implies that Romulus restored Feral and Thornn's mutated appearances. XFac #142, '98 fb showed Wild Child's teenage years, establishing that he is not old enough to have been alive in WWII; this may have been the first clue that Romulus' dreams were false scenarios. Wolverine notes here that Sabretooth's scent smells different; W #311, '12 reveals that Romulus switched Sabretooth with a wild, more feral clone between this issue and last, so that the real Sabretooth could go underground for a time.

WOLVERINE #55 [#244] (September 2007)

"Evolution, Chapter Six: Quod Sum Eris" (23 pages)

CREDITS: Jeph Loeb (writer), Simone Bianchi (pencils), Simone Bianchi & Andrea Silvestri (inks & washed halftones), Richard Starkings & Comicraft (letters), Simone Peruzzi & Frank D'Armata (colors), Aubrey Sitterson (asst editor), Axel Alonso (editor), Greg Land (variant c pencils), Jay Leisten (variant c inks), Morry Hollowell (c colors), Justin Ponsor (variant c colors)

FEATURE CHARACTER: Wolverine (also as himself & Experiment X in rfb3, also in rfb2 & pfb, next in W #50/2, '07, W:O Ann, '07, W:O #16-20, '07-08; Sub # fb & 3 fb, NX #43, W Ann #1, all '07)

GUEST STARS: X-Men: Cyclops, Emma Frost (both last in WWHulk:X #3, '07, next in NX #43, '07); Sasquatch (bts directing Wolverine to hospital in pfb, next in MAv #21, '09), Wolfsbane (in pfb, next in XFac #25, '08)

SUPPORTING CAST: Silver Fox (seemingly dead in fb between W:O #5, '06 fb & W #50, '07 fb; also alive & seemingly dead in rfb2)

VILLAINS: Sabretooth (in fb between W:O #5, '06 fb & W #10, '89 fb; also in rfb1, rfb3 & symbolic image), Sabretooth clone (dies, also in rfb1 & pfb; possibly seen as spirit in W:RTH, '10, see NOTE; next in W #310, '12), Romulus (in shadow, also in rfb3 & in shadow in pfb), Wild Child (also in pfb)

OTHER CHARACTERS: Feral (dead in pfb, also dead in rfb1, next in shadow in XNec, '09, next in NM #8, '10), Thornn (in pfb), Psylocke, prostitute (prev 2 in rfb1), Black Panther, Captain America, Storm, "Blondie" (dies), "Pup," elephant (prev 6 in rfb3)

LOCATIONS/ITEMS: X-Mansion (also in rfb3) w/Danger Room (in rfb1), Department K facility (in pfb & rfb1, also as Weapon X Program facility in rfb3), Tokyo (in rfb1), Wolverine & Silver Fox's cabin (ruins, also in fb & rfb2), Alberta hospital (bts), Italian Alps, prehistoric valley, Wakanda inc battlefield, skies, Flavian Amphitheater (prev 6 in rfb3) / Muramasa Sword, Weapon X Program sensors (in pfb, rfb1 & symbolic image), battery packs (in pfb) & Genesis Tank (in rfb3) w/Adamantium feed tubes, Romulus' scent-masking oils (bts, also bts in pfb), Black Panther's private jet, Wolfsbane's blanket, facility gas cans (prev 3 in pfb), Silver Fox's snowball, Wolverine's coat & boots (prev 3 in rfb2), saber-tooth tiger's fang, X-Men's Blackbird jet, Experiment X's helmet (prev 3 in rfb3)

FLASHBACKS: Sabretooth attacks prostitutes (W #52, '07 fb), Feral (W #54, '07) and Psylocke (UXM #328, '96). Silver Fox lies dead; Wolverine and Silver Fox flirt (W #50, '07 fb). Captain America fights (W #54, '07); "Pup" kills "Blondie," Romulus charges into battle and gives a thumbs-down (W #50 & 52-53, '07); Sabretooth flies the Blackbird, Storm and Black Panther study the Lupine (W #51 & 53, '07); Experiment X pops his claws (MCP #74, '91) and floats in the Genesis Tank (MCP #73, '91); Wolverine lobotomizes Sabretooth (W #90, '95). Sabretooth flees, frightened by an unseen presence; Wolfsbane reveals that Wild Child gathered their group, tricking them into bringing Wolverine there (p). Sabretooth savages Silver Fox.

SYNOPSIS: Wolverine reclaims the Muramasa Sword from Cyclops and travels to Silver Fox's cabin, now a ruin. Sabretooth soon attacks, but Wolverine lops his arm off with the sword and makes a final entreaty to Sabretooth's buried rational side. Sabretooth haltingly agrees that he needs to be stopped — and Wolverine decapitates him. Wild Child appears, congratulating Wolverine and stating that Romulus affected Wolverine's dreams to illustrate that black-haired and blond leaders always emerge from the Lupine ranks and fight to the death. Wolverine briefly smells Romulus nearby, and swears to hunt him down.

NOTE: This issue also has a variant cover that is an homage to EC Comics' Crime SuspenStories #22, '54, and an ad-free black & white edition that features a 1-page Simone Bianchi sketchbook. Wolverine entrusted Cyclops with the Muramasa Sword in W:O #5, '06. This issue's implication that Wolverine, Sabretooth and Wild Child may be Lupine descendants is made moot by W #312, '12's revelation that the Lupine never actually existed. In W:RTH, '10 & W #2-5, '10-11, Sabretooth's spirit appears when Wolverine is sent to Hell, but since W #311, '12 reveals that Sabretooth was not dead at that time, this may have been the clone's spirit. However, as discussed in W #4, '82's NOTE, it is uncertain if anything Wolverine witnesses in the afterlife is real. Wolverine finally comes face-to-face with Romulus in W:O #39, '09 and defeats him in W:O #48, '10.

WOLVERINE ANNUAL #1 (December 2007)

"The Death Song of J. Patrick Smitty" (36 pages)

CREDITS: Gregg Hurwitz (writer), Marcelo Frusin (art, colors), Todd Klein (letters), Aubrey Sitterson (asst editor), Axel Alonso (editor)

FEATURE CHARACTER: Wolverine (also in pfb & rfb1, next in W #56, '07)

VILLAINS: Scarred crimelord (dies, also in pfb), criminals (1 also on monitor in pfb): Tarell (dies, also in pfb, also as security guard in Smitty's imagination), others (some die off-panel, also die in rfb1, also in pfb; some dead, also die off-panel in pfb; 1 dead off-panel, also dies in pfb; 1 dies, also in pfb; 1 dies in pfb); hubcap thief

OTHER CHARACTERS: J. Patrick Smitty (reluctant criminal, dies, also on monitor, also bts in rfb1, also as boy & himself in pfb), Glenda (Smitty's mother), Smitty's father & friend, priest, churchgoers, record store clerk & patrons, homeless man, crimelord's bodyguards, couple, police (prev 11 in pfb), convenience store clerk, mugging victim (prev 2 in pfb, also in Smitty's thoughts), old woman (dies in pfb, also in Wolverine & Smitty's thoughts & as angel statue in Smitty's imagination), bank employees (1 or more die in pfb; also in Smitty's thoughts, some bts), customers (die in pfb, some off-panel; some in Smitty's thoughts, some bts) & security guard (dies off-panel in pfb, also dies in rfb2, also as Tarell & drug addicts in Smitty's imagination), drug addicts (as security guard in Smitty's imagination), crimelord's wife, bystanders (others in pfb); birds, dog (prev 2 in fb), crabs (also in pfb), worms; friend's father (mentioned in pfb, friend threatens to make him sue); Led Zeppelin: John Bonham (bts off-panel), John Paul Jones, Jimmy Page, Robert Plant; Richard Cole, Peter Grant, Glynis Johns, Jim Morrison, Sandy Olsen, Danny Zuko, Jagdstaffel (WWI German pilots, 1 bts off-panel), others (prev 12 on posters in pfb), Jesus Christ (as statue in pfb), Hulk (on poster in pfb), dragon (as tattoo), angel (as statue, as old woman in Smitty's imagination), chimpanzees (as graffiti)

LOCATIONS/ITEMS: New York City (also in pfb) inc criminals' hideout (5122 Silent Sea Lane, Apt. #22, also in pfb & rfb1), Global Trust Bank (in rfb2 & on monitor in pfb), Smitty's parents' apartment, convenience stores, record store, burgled home, bar, criminal's garage (prev 7 in pfb), church (also in pfb) w/confession booth (in pfb), crimelord's home, Smitty's apartment, factory (prev 3 also in pfb) & rooftops, Smitty's mother's crack pipe, priest's rosary, clerk's mop & bucket, Smitty's gun, money, stocking mask & stolen beer, cassette & electronic equipment, victim's purse, criminals' van, guns, bags, note, stocking masks, spray paint & stolen money, bystander's car, old woman's flowers (also in Smitty's thoughts), crimelord's stocking mask (destroyed) & shotgun, bank window (destroyed) & security cameras (bts), security guard's handgun, police cars & tape (all in pfb), broken bottle (bts, also in rfb1), crimelord's fish tank, molten metal tanks (prev 2 also in pfb), Smitty's door (destroyed) & corkscrew, angel statue, addicts' works & crack pipe, crimelord's handgun, Tarell's welding mask & equipment, factory's waste chain & crane w/remote control, bystander's spray paint, flower

FLASHBACKS: Wolverine kills criminals (this issue). Smitty shoots the security guard (this issue). Young Patrick Smitty grows up enjoying church, but falls into a life of crime and joins a crimelord's crew. An old woman gives Wolverine a flower — but the crimelord's crew rush past, knocking her over, and she dies. They rob a bank, but when the criminal's mask rips he shoots all witnesses, and Smitty kills the security guard. Wolverine tracks the criminals down (p).

SYNOPSIS: Wolverine kills everyone except Smitty, ordering him to deliver a threat to the crimelord. Smitty sinks into depression, but suddenly notices how precious life is. The crimelord soon orders Smitty to shoot Tarell, whom he fears will go to the police, but Smitty hesitates. Wolverine suddenly attacks, killing Tarell; the crimelord knocks him into a vat of molten metal and flees, but Smitty sees Wolverine crawl out. Wolverine soon kills the crimelord in his home; he then attacks Smitty, who flees across rooftops to a church — then embraces his fate, leaping onto Wolverine's claws. Later, Wolverine recalls the old woman's kindness.

NOTE: The Wolverine Annual series relaunches here after six years. Unlike the previous volume, which numbered using years of publication, this volume uses issue numbers. This issue's title is a reference to T.S. Eliot's poem "The Love Song of J. Alfred Prufrock"; some of Smitty's narration references lines from the poem. The crimelord's scar accidentally switches sides when he views his reflection this issue.

WOLVERINE #56 [#245] (October 2007)

"The Man In the Pit" (36 pages)

CREDITS: Jason Aaron (writer), Howard Chaykin (art), Virtual Calligraphy's Cory Petit (letters), Edgar Delgado (colors), Rich Ginter (production), Aubrey Sitterson (asst editor), Axel Alonso (editor)

FEATURE CHARACTER: Wolverine (also in photos, next in BICMW #1/6, '10)

VILLAINS: Romulus (voice only, off-panel, next voice only in W:O #35, '09, next in W:O #36, '09), Wild Child (next in W:O #38, '09), gunners (some possibly die off-panel, see NOTE) inc Wendell Rayfield (conflicted ex-policeman, also in fb2 & fb1 prior to issue), guards (some die, others likely die off-panel) inc Karl

OTHER CHARACTERS: Cindy (Wendell's ex-wife), Doris (photographer), security guard (prev 2 possibly die off-panel, see NOTE), collection agency employees (voices only, in recording), Wendell's victim (in fb1) & father (also in fb2 prior to issue), couriers (bts delivering photographs to Romulus, die off-panel); comedian (mentioned, coming to town), nightclub employee (mentioned, knows Wendell), Wendell's mother (mentioned, died in childbirth); cowboy, horse (prev 2 in portrait), cartoon characters, football players (prev 2 on TV in fb2), joker (on wine bottle in fb2), dragon (as tattoo), devil (on food can)

LOCATIONS/ITEMS: Wendell's home, office building w/pit (also in photos) & parking lot, Cindy's motel, city street (in fb1), Wendell's childhood home (in fb2), Krouton Assisted Living rest home, Romulus' headquarters, cartoon courtroom, football stadium (prev 2 on TV in fb2), nightclub, bank (prev 2 mentioned) / Wendell's coffee, scotch (both bts), nightstick (in fb1), sling (in fb2), iron, lunchbox, car, keycard, money, trash, gun, alarm clock, answering machine & whiskey flask, security guard's cameras (bts) & monitors, office's hand scanner, countdown clock & machine gun assembly, guards' armor, guns, flamethrowers & X-ray scanner, gunner & Wendell's earphones, Doris' Polaroid camera w/photos, stress balls, Newton's cradles, show tickets (prev 3 mentioned), Cindy's perfume (bts), Wendell's father's wine bottle (destroyed), belt, plunger (prev 3 in fb2) & wheelchair, Wild Child's envelope & pushpins

FLASHBACKS: As a policeman, Wendell beats a man (1). Wendell's father beats him, blaming him for everything (2).

SYNOPSIS: Wendell Rayfield reports to his job, one of many gunners who take shifts constantly firing a machine gun at Wolverine, who has been trapped in a pit for weeks. Later, Wendell awkwardly flirts with co-worker Doris; Wolverine taunts him, aware that Wendell's wife recently left him. That night, Wendell delivers his ex-wife's alimony, comes home to collection agency voicemails, and returns to work miserable. Wolverine

continues talking as days pass, and Wendell soon opens up to Wolverine even as he continues shooting him. Just as the two bond, Wolver
tells Wendell that his abusive father was right, then stops talking altogether, leaving Wendell shaken. His life continues to spiral into mise
Wendell soon decides to die. He begs his elderly father to shoot him, but the old man does not. Wendell finally frees Wolverine, hoping to
killed, but Wolverine spares him and leaves. Elsewhere, Wild Child decorates Romulus' wall with photos of the bullet-riddled Wolverine.
NOTE: Although Romulus and Wild Child are obviously responsible, the exact circumstances of Wolverine's capture are unrevealed. After be
freed, Wolverine promises to kill everyone in the building on his way out. He likely kills all the armed guards and any other gunners still prese
but it is unknown if he also kills Doris and the security guard, who are relative innocents.

WOLVERINE #57 [#246] (November 2007)

(Untitled, 22 pages)

CREDITS: Marc Guggenheim (writer), Howard Chaykin (art), Virtual Calligraphy's Cory Petit (letters), Edg
Delgado (colors), Anthony Dial (production), Aubrey Sitterson (asst editor), John Barber (editor), Axel Alon
(exec editor), Arthur Suydam (c art)
FEATURE CHARACTER: Wolverine (dies, also as spirit in W #58, '07 fb, also in fb between W:O #12, '07 fb
W #58, '07 fb)
GUEST STARS: Iron Man (also as monitor image, last in IM:DoS Ann, '08), Avengers (team last in WWHulk:D
#3, '08, chr last in BICMW #1/6, '10, next in NAv Ann #2, '08), X-Men (team last in NX #43, '07, chr next in X&S
#4, '09, next in AX #23, '08) (prev 2 bts, too busy to help Wolverine, exact members unspecified)
VILLAINS: Shogun (fragment of Wolverine's soul given physical form, unnamed, 1st but chr last in W #58, '07 f
next in W #60, '08), Scimitar (terrorist group, 1st) agents (die, 1 as Iron Man, others next in W #61, '08), Germa
soldiers (in fb, some die, others (some bts in planes) prior to W #58, '07 fb)
OTHER CHARACTERS: Amir (dies, last in W #48, '07), Maria Hill (last in IM:DoS Ann, '08, next in NAv Ann #2, '08), SHIELD agents (son
or others last in IM:DoS Ann, '08), Canadian, British & French soldiers (in fb, die, some prior to W #58, '07 fb; others bts in planes in fb prior
W #58, '07 fb; others bts in tanks in fb, see NOTE), Atlantean intelligence operatives (bts intercepting transmissions); people (dead, as skulls
vultures (prev 2 cover only)
LOCATIONS/ITEMS: Ypres, Belgium (in fb); Fadhil, Iraq inc Scimitar hideout; skies over USA, waterfront, Afghanistan, Darfur (prev
mentioned) / Allied tanks (see NOTE), airplanes, pistol & rifles w/bayonets (some destroyed), German airplanes, chlorine gas, gas masks
rifles w/bayonets, Wolverine's wrist wrappings (all in fb), Scimitar Helicarrier (destroyed, also as SHIELD Helicarrier in holographic illusion
on monitor), image inducers (bts), guns, files, missile launcher & computer w/monitor, Atlantean espionage equipment (bts), Amir's gun, mu
bladed weapon & water-breathing mask, X-Jet (X-Men's supersonic aircraft), Wolverine & Amir's earpieces, Shogun's gun, throwing sta
Adamantium armor & bomb w/remote detonator, SHIELD helicopters, earpieces, paperwork & stretcher
FLASHBACK: In World War I, Wolverine fights in Belgium. The Germans release poison gas, killing all the Allied soldiers except Wolverine –
who finds two bayonets, mounts them on his wrists and attacks the gas-masked German troops.
SYNOPSIS: Wolverine helps Amir investigate Scimitar, a new terrorist group that the Atlanteans are concerned about. The two fight the
way inside a Scimitar base and uncover a plot to assassinate Tony Stark, now director of SHIELD. Wolverine and Amir race to the Helicarrie
Wolverine intercepts the assassin, but notices him wearing Adamantium armor and realizes that this was a trap. The "Helicarrier's" imag
inducer deactivates, revealing it as a massive Scimitar ship. Wolverine battles the assassin, noting that his foe is just as agile and ruthless a
himself. When the assassin kills Amir, Wolverine snaps and attacks in a berserker rage — but the assassin suddenly shoves a small bon
down Wolverine's throat and detonates it. Later, SHIELD agents investigate the Scimitar ship's crash site and find Wolverine — perfectly heale
physically, but brain-dead.
NOTE: This issue is titled "Logan Dies" when it is reprinted in the "Wolverine: the Death of Wolverine" TPB, '08. However, that is a retroactiv
title designed to match W #59-61, '08, and does not indicate an omission here. Shogun is named in W #58, '07 and revealed as a fragment
Wolverine's soul in W #61, '08. Iron Man became director of SHIELD in CW #7, '07. Though W:O #17, '07 establishes that Wolverine fought wi
the Devil's Brigade in WWII, they are not the Canadian unit seen here. In the real world, tanks were not used in WWI until September 1916. Th
X-Men's X-Jet is a different craft than both the Blackbird and the X-Plane.

WOLVERINE #58 [#247] (December 2007)

"Curaetar" (22 pages)

CREDITS: Marc Guggenheim (writer), Howard Chaykin (art), Virtual Calligraphy
Cory Petit (letters), Edgar Delgado (colors), Brad Johansen (production), Aubr
Sitterson (asst editor), John Barber (editor), Axel Alonso (exec editor), Arth
Suydam (c art), Clint Langley (variant c art)
FEATURE CHARACTER: Wolverine (dead & as spirit, also in rfb, also in fb1
fb8 between W #57, '07 fb & W #59, '08 fb; also as spirit in fb2 during W:O An
'07; also as spirit in fb3 between NX #130, '02 fb & MCP #78, '91; also as spirit
fb4 during CX #10/2, '87; also as spirit in fb5 during MCP #5, '88; also as spirit
fb6 between X #66, '97 & W #115, '97; also as spirit in fb7 during W #57, '07 fb)
GUEST STARS: Dr. Strange (last in WWHulk:DC #2, '08), Iron Man (next i

Penance #2, '07)
VILLAINS: Lazaer (in fb1 & fb8, his chr 1st app, prior to W #59, '08 fb; also in fb2 between W #60, '08 fb & Venus #14, '51; also in fb3,
fb5 & fb6 between Venus #14, '51 & W #48, '07 fb, see NOTE; also in fb7 between W #48, '07 fb & W #61, '08; also as Azrael in Wolverine
thoughts), German soldiers (die in fb1 & dead in fb8 between W #57, '07 fb & W #59, '08 fb; others bts in planes in fb1 following W #57, '07 ft
OTHER CHARACTERS: Wong (last in WWHulk #3, '07, next in NAv Ann #2, '08), SHIELD agents (some bts flying planes, some or othe
next in Penance #2, '07) & doctor, Canadian soldiers (others next in W #59, '08 fb), British soldiers, French soldiers (some of prev 3 dead
fb1 & fb8, others bts in planes in fb1, all following W #57, '07 fb); bartender (as Purgatory illusion); Amir (dead in rfb); people (dead, as skulls
Death (prev 2 in Wolverine's thoughts)

CATIONS/ITEMS: Ypres (in fb1 & fb8), skies over USA, Dr. Strange's Sanctum Sanctorum, Purgatory (as bar, also in fb2, fb3, fb4, fb5, fb6
b7), Scimitar's Iraq hideout (in rfb) / German gas masks (1 destroyed), airplanes & rifles w/bayonets, Allied airplanes (all in fb1), Wolverine's
yonets & wrist wrappings (prev 2 in fb1 & destroyed in fb8), German chlorine gas (in fb1 & fb8), Lazaer's sword (in fb1, fb2, fb3, fb4, fb5, fb6,
", fb8 & Wolverine's thoughts), SHIELD Helicarrier & jets, Wolverine's oxygen mask, Experiment X's helmet, wires & battery packs (prev 3 in
), Amir's water-breathing mask, Shogun's throwing star (prev 2 in rfb), Azrael's spear & scythe (prev 2 in Wolverine's thoughts)

ASHBACKS: Amir dies in Wolverine's arms (last issue). Wolverine kills German troops in WWI until he notices a cloaked figure doing the
me. Wolverine instinctively recognizes him as a foe, and the two square off and begin to duel (1). Wolverine battles Lazaer as "Patch" (2)
d Experiment X (3), and in his yellow costume (4), his brown costume (5) and his bandana mask (6). Shaken by Amir's death, Wolverine's
solve weakens and Lazaer defeats him (7). In WWI, Lazaer impales Wolverine on his sword — but Wolverine removes the blade and kills
zaer with it (8).

NOPSIS: Dr. Strange boards the SHIELD Helicarrier and discusses the brain-dead Wolverine with Iron Man. Strange explains that Wolverine's
ul is missing, and takes his body back to his Sanctum. Later, Strange travels to Purgatory, discovering Wolverine drinking endlessly at a bar.
range reminds Wolverine that, ever since he defeated Lazaer in WWI, his soul has dueled Lazaer again every time he died — with victory
aning a return to life. This time, however, Lazaer won. Strange then reveals that "Lazaer" is actually Azrael, the angel of death.

OTE: This issue's indicia is incorrectly dated "November 2007." This issue also has a zombie-themed variant cover. This issue is subtitled
gan Dies, Part 2 of 5" when it is reprinted in the "Wolverine: the Death of Wolverine" TPB, '08. However, that is a retroactive title designed to
atch W #59-61, '08, and does not indicate an omission here. Shogun is named here. Lazaer may also be the same character as Darkangel
Angel of Death; if so, he would appear in HA #1, '92 following this issue's fb5, and in DA #14, '93 prior to this issue's fb6. Wolverine's memory
his claws must be suppressed at this point, as he enjoys fighting with bayonets on his arms, but does not know why. The German soldiers in
s issue's fb1 are incorrectly called Nazis.

WOLVERINE #59 [#248] (January 2008)

"Logan Dies (Part 3 of 5): Odyssey" (22 pages, see NOTE)

CREDITS: Marc Guggenheim (writer), Howard Chaykin (art), Virtual Calligraphy's Cory Petit (letters), Edgar
Delgado (colors), Anthony Dial (production), Aubrey Sitterson (asst editor), John Barber (editor), Axel Alonso
(exec editor), Arthur Suydam (c art)

FEATURE CHARACTER: Wolverine (revives, also as spirit; also as himself & in his own thoughts in rfb; also
as himself, James Howlett & Experiment X in Purgatory visions; also in fb1 between W #58, '07 fb & W #60, '08
fb; also dead in fb2 & resurrected in fb5 between W #20, '04 & W #22, '05 fb; also in fb3 between W #14, '11 fb &
XFor #4, '05; also in fb4 between W #47, '06 & W #48, '07 fb)

GUEST STAR: Dr. Strange

VILLAINS: Lazaer (in fb1 between W #58, '07 fb & W #60, '08 fb; also in rfb), Gorgon (in fb2 between W #20,
'04 & W #22, '05 fb; also as Purgatory vision), Phaedra (traitorous Hand high priestess, unnamed, 1st in fb2 & fb5
or to W #60, '08; also in Wolverine's thoughts in rfb), Shogun (in fb2 & fb5, his chr 1st app, prior to W #57, '07; also bts in rfb), German soldiers
fb1, 1 dies; others dead in fb1, some bts off-panel, following W #58, '07 fb), undead Hand ninjas (in fb2 following W #20, '04, some or others
r next in W #23, '05), Hand sorcerers (in fb2, some or others chr last in NW #5, '00, these prior to W #22, '05 fb)

THER CHARACTERS: Canadian soldiers (in fb1, 1 bts in plane, others last in W #58, '07 fb, some or others next in W #60, '08 fb); SHIELD
ents (die), Nitro (bts), Amir (prev 3 in rfb); X-Men: Cyclops, Emma Frost, Gambit, Storm; Magma, Acanti Prophet-Singer (dead), kidnapper
es) (prev 7 as Purgatory visions); historical figures (in photos in fb1 & Purgatory); man (in silhouette on poster in fb1), cowboy, horse (prev 2
portrait in Purgatory); Elizabeth Howlett, Shingen Harada (prev 2 quoted in Purgatory)

OCATIONS/ITEMS: Ypres (also in Wolverine's thoughts in rfb), Allied army base (also in rfb), bars, battlefields (all in fb1), Purgatory (as bar,
owlett estate, Ypres, Weapon X Program facility, Canada, "Sleazeworld," Yashidas' ancestral manor, Avalon, X-Mansion grounds & Nagasaki
aveyard, also in rfb), Nagasaki graveyard (in fb2), Hydra base (in fb2 & fb5), South Atlantic Ocean, Amir's bedroom, Scimitar's Iraq hideout,
g Sur (prev 4 in rfb), city streets (in fb3, others in fb4), Dr. Strange's Sanctum Sanctorum / Lazaer's sword (also in rfb), Allied trucks, tank &
ane, Allied & German rifles w/bayonets, Wolverine's pistol (all in fb1) & rifle w/bayonet (in fb1 & in his own thoughts in rfb), German chlorine
s (in fb1 & Purgatory vision), Experiment X's wires & battery packs (prev 2 in rfb & Purgatory vision), Wolverine's Adamantium, bayonets &
ist wrappings, Shingen's bokken, X-Men's baseball equipment (prev 5 in Purgatory visions), Gorgon's sword (in fb2 & Purgatory vision), Hand
appings & altar, Shogun's Adamantium armor (prev 3 in fb2 & fb5), SHIELD gun & aircraft carrier, Amir's water-breathing mask, Shogun's
mb (bts) w/remote detonator, Experiment X's helmet (prev 6 in rfb), Dr. Strange's orb

LASHBACKS: The brainwashed Wolverine slaughters SHIELD troops (W #21, '04); Wolverine thinks about WWI (W #48, '07); Wolverine is
pressed (this issue's fb1); Shogun kills Wolverine (W #57, '07); Nitro kills Wolverine (W #43, '06); Wolverine's soul battles Lazaer (last issue's
). Wolverine stands over Lazaer's body, but Lazaer reappears, congratulating him and warning that they will meet again. A powerful depression
on grips Wolverine; he begins drinking excessively and making sloppy mistakes in battle. Eventually Wolverine realizes that he should be
ad, and points a gun at his head (1). Phaedra and the Hand prepare to resurrect Wolverine (2). Wolverine wanders aimlessly (3). Wolverine
s dead after falling from the Helicarrier (4). With Shogun by her side, Phaedra resurrects Wolverine (5).

YNOPSIS: Dr. Strange tells Wolverine that he must fight his own way out of Purgatory. Wolverine leaves the "bar" and battles his way through
rsions of himself from different points in his life, who remind him that he hasn't been the same since the Hand killed and resurrected him.
olverine realizes that Phaedra did something to him when she resurrected him; he returns to his physical body, and prepares to track her
wn.

OTE: This issue's subtitle, "Odyssey," is mistakenly omitted from the issue; it is reinstated when the issue is reprinted in the "Wolverine: the
eath of Wolverine" TPB, '08. This Index has chosen to correct the typo and present the issue's intended title. Phaedra is named and revealed
a former Hand high priestess next issue. This issue also has several short features: Fury's Files (facts & trivia, 1 page), Portfolio Review (Tom
ummett's character sketches for Exiles #1, '08, 2 pages), Look Who's Talking! (Matt Fraction interview, 1 page) and Questions That Need
swers! (creator poll, 1 page). Some of the Wolverine silhouettes on this issue's cover erroneously have four claws instead of three.

WOLVERINE #60 [#249] (February 2008)

"Logan Dies (Part 4 of 5): Wake the Dead" (23 pages)

CREDITS: Marc Guggenheim (writer), Howard Chaykin (art), Virtual Calligraphy's Cory Petit (letters), Edg Delgado (colors), Irene Lee (production), Aubrey Sitterson (asst editor), John Barber (editor), Axel Alonso (ex editor), Arthur Suydam (c art)
FEATURE CHARACTER: Wolverine (also as toys, also in rfb, also in fb between W #59, '08 fb & W:O #' '07 fb)
GUEST STAR: Dr. Strange (bts giving Treskara to Wolverine, next in NAv Ann #2, '08)
VILLAINS: Lazaer (in fb between W #59, '08 fb & W #58, '07 fb), Phaedra (named, also in rfb & Wolverin memory projection, last in W #59, '08), Shogun (also in rfb, last in W #57, '07), Shingen Harada (resurrected c panel, last in W #4, '82, possibly last as spirit in W #176, '02, see W #4, '82's NOTE), Hand ninjas (die, 1 off-par some or others last in NAv #31, '07, next in PWJ #20, '08)
OTHER CHARACTERS: Naicho (Japanese intelligence) agents: Shiori Masakuma (formerly Asano Kimura's lover), others (bts tracki Scimitar); Canadian soldiers (in fb, some or others chr last in W #59, '08 fb), toy store employees (all but 1 bts fleeing from fight) & custome (bts fleeing from fight); Nightcrawler (mentioned, owns 5 image inducers); Amir, Scimitar agents (die), Hand sorcerer (prev 3 in rfb); bears (son also on TV), Elmo, Teletubbies, dragons, rabbits, dogs, ladybug, gorilla, monkeys, cats, blobs (prev 11 as toys), crab (as Yashida family sea dragon (as wall scroll), cartoon characters (on TV & poster)
LOCATIONS/ITEMS: Allied army base (in fb), Tokyo inc Harajuku toy store (Hand front), Shiori's apartment & Scimitar's Mt. Fuji headquarte Fadhil inc Scimitar hideout, skies over USA, Hydra base (prev 4 in rfb), Akihabara toy store (mentioned) / Wolverine's pistol, Lazaer's sword (bo in fb), store's toys & dolls, ninjas' swords, Dr. Strange's Treskara (memory projector), Amir's water-breathing mask, Scimitar Helicarrier (al as SHIELD Helicarrier), guns & computer (bts) w/monitor, Hand altar (bts) & wrappings (prev 7 in rfb), Scimitar image inducers (others in rf Shogun's Adamantium armor (partly destroyed, also in rfb), Naicho espionage equipment (bts), Wolverine's bomb w/timer, Yashida family se
FLASHBACKS: Wolverine learns of the "attack" on Iron Man; the Scimitar ship decloaks (W #57, '07). Phaedra prepares to resurrect Wolveri (last issue's fb). Wolverine kills Scimitar agents (W #57, '07). As Wolverine considers shooting himself, Lazaer reappears, explaining th Wolverine's depression is punishment for defying the natural order. He threatens to rematch with Wolverine someday, then vanishes.
SYNOPSIS: Wolverine enters a Tokyo toy store, revealing that he knows that it is a Hand front. Ninjas reveal themselves and attack, b Wolverine defeats them all; he asks the lone survivor where to find Phaedra, and the ninja reveals that she defected to Scimitar. Wolveri wonders why Scimitar went to so much trouble to trap and kill him. He consults with a Japanese intelligence agent and deduces the locati of Scimitar's main base: underneath Mt. Fuji. Wolverine infiltrates the base, locates Shogun and attacks, turning the tables on the villain attaching a bomb to his chest and detonating it. Wolverine then finds and confronts Phaedra, who reveals that she has resurrected one Wolverine's most vengeful foes — Shingen Harada.
NOTE: This issue names Phaedra and reveals that she was a Hand high priestess. Shiori's lover Asano Kimura died in W #3, '82. It is uncle how Wolverine's bomb blows a hole in Shogun's Adamantium armor; it may have been Adamantium mail held together with lesser metal. Th issue also has several short features: Questions That Need Answers! (creator polls, 2 pages), Fury's Files (facts & trivia, 1 page) and Lo Who's Talking! (Brian Reed interview, 1 page).

WOLVERINE #61 [#250] (March 2008)

"Logan Dies (Part 5 of 5): Soul Survivor" (22 pages)

CREDITS: Marc Guggenheim (writer), Howard Chaykin (art), Virtual Calligraphy's Cory Petit (letters), Edg Delgado (colors), Brad Johansen (production), Aubrey Sitterson (asst editor), John Barber (editor), Axel Alon (exec editor), Arthur Suydam (c art)
FEATURE CHARACTER: Wolverine (also dead, on monitor & as himself & spirit in rfb, next in Penance #3 5, NAv Ann #2, W:Fb, all '08)
VILLAINS: Lazaer (also in rfb, last in W #58, '07 fb), Phaedra (dies, also in rfb), Shogun (destroyed, also in rf Shingen Harada (dies, revives, also dies off-panel in rfb, possibly next as spirit in W #2, '10, see NOTE), Scimit agents (others last in W #57, '07)
OTHER CHARACTERS: Mariko Yashida (mentioned, Phaedra offers to resurrect her); Amir (dead), Gorgc Cassandra Nova, Dr. Weinberg, German soldiers (1 dies, some bts in planes), SHIELD agents (some di kidnapper (dies), Hand sorcerer (prev 8 in rfb), Bruce Springsteen (quoted)
LOCATIONS/ITEMS: Yashidas' ancestral manor, Ypres, Purgatory, Lindsborth, X-Mansion, Scimitar's Iraq hideout, Nagasaki graveyard, Sou Atlantic Ocean, skies above Arkansas, Hydra base (all in rfb), Scimitar's Mt. Fuji headquarters / German planes, chlorine gas & rifles bayonets, Wolverine's bayonets & wrist wrappings, Experiment X's helmet, wires & battery packs, Amir's water-breathing mask, Shogun throwing star, Gorgon's sword, SHIELD gun, aircraft carrier & protective suits, Weinberg's handheld computer & deprogramming equipment monitor, Hand altar (bts) & wrappings (all in rfb), Shingen's sword (another in rfb), Shogun's Adamantium armor (destroyed) & helmet, Lazae sword (prev 3 also in rfb), Scimitar intruder alarm (bts) & guns
FLASHBACK: Wolverine kills Shingen (W #4, '82); kills Germans (W #58, '07 fb); kills Lazaer (W #59, '08 fb) and duels him in Purgatory (#58, '07 fb); returns to life (W #42, '06); battles Cassandra Nova (NX #116, '01); battles Lazaer again (W #48, '07 fb); and is defeated by Laza (W #58, '07 fb); Amir dies in Wolverine's arms (W #57, '07); Gorgon kills Wolverine (W #20, '04); a brainwashed Wolverine battles SHIELD troo (W #21, '04); and is deprogrammed (W #26, '05); Phaedra prepares to resurrect Wolverine (W #59, '08 fb).
SYNOPSIS: Wolverine duels Shingen fiercely, eventually killing him once again. Phaedra's resurrections have drawn Lazaer's attention; attacks, claiming that Wolverine has killed more than his share of people. Lazaer reveals that Phaedra kept a piece of Wolverine's soul when s resurrected him — which she transformed into Shogun. Wolverine snatches Lazaer's sword and chops Shogun up, then deduces that Phaedra resurrections are more of an affront to Lazaer than his own killings. Wolverine offers to kill Phaedra if Lazaer restores his soul. Lazaer agree but nullifies their previous arrangement; Wolverine's next death will be permanent. Phaedra desperately offers to resurrect Mariko Yashida, b Wolverine kills her. As Wolverine charges into battle against Scimitar agents, his soul restored and his depression gone, Shingen revives…

OTE: Shingen's spirit appears in W #2, '10 when Wolverine is taken to Hell, implying that he died again after this issue; however, as discussed W #4, '82's NOTE, it is uncertain if anything Wolverine witnesses in the afterlife is real. Shingen's last name is given as "Yashida" here. This sue also has a Look Who's Talking! feature (Mike Benson interview, 1 page).

WOLVERINE: FIREBREAK (February 2008)

"Firebreak" (22 pages)

CREDITS: Mike Carey (writer), Scott Kolins (pencils), Troy Peteri (letters), Moose Bauman (colors), Aubrey Sitterson (editor)
FEATURE CHARACTER: Wolverine
VILLAINS: Hydra agents (some or all die, some or others last in Av:In Ann/3, '08, chr next bts in SecWs #2, '09 fb, next in Av:In Spec, '09) inc Seven, Hydra's Eastern European client (bts commissioning incendiary)
OTHER CHARACTERS: Peter, Sue (prev 2 estranged couple), Ginny (Peter & Sue's daughter); bear (dies), fish; rangers (mentioned, Sue wants to warn them about fire), local law enforcement officials (mentioned, Wolverine will report to them), woman (mentioned, Peter apologizes for sleeping with her); Mister Beak (Ginny's parrot doll)
LOCATIONS/ITEMS: Woodlands (destroyed) inc ranger station (mentioned), Hydra base (bts), river & Peter & Sue's cabin / Peter's blanket, car & wallet, Sue's cellphone (mentioned), Hydra experimental incendiary (bts), ansport, blasters, gas masks, thermal detonator w/timer & containers (1 destroyed) w/viruses, toxins & explosives inc iron thermite ingredients
YNOPSIS: Peter and Sue's marriage has become strained. When Peter notices that the nearby woods are ablaze, the two flee their cabin w eir daughter, but are confronted by an angry bear. Wolverine leaps from the fire and kills the bear, but reveals that toxins in the flames have endered him blind. The group flees, Peter and Sue describing the terrain to Wolverine, who helps them leap over a river that blocks their path. he group stumbles across Hydra agents evacuating an underground base; Wolverine kills two agents and forces another to explain that their cendiary experiments started the blaze. Wolverine has Peter and Sue find ingredients for explosive thermite in the Hydra transport, intending create an explosion that sucks the oxygen from the air. Wolverine and Peter set up the thermite, but other Hydra agents ambush them; they ve into the river as the bomb explodes, extinguishing the blaze. Wolverine's sight returns; Peter reunites with Sue, admitting that he cheated n her and hoping to work through it.
OTE: This story's inker is uncredited.

ND STORY: "Little White Lies" (10 pages)
REDITS: Macon Blair (writer), Vasilis Lolos (art), Troy Peteri (letters), Nestor Pereyra (colors), Aubrey Sitterson (editor)
EATURE CHARACTER: Wolverine (also in pfb, next in NAv #38-39, '08, X&SM #4, '09, AX #14-22, 23 fb & 22-24, '06-08, GSAX #1, '08, :MC, '07; UXM #492, XFac #25, NX #44, X #205, UXM #493, XFac #26, NX #45, X #206, UXM #494, XFac #27, NX #46, X:L #208 fb, NX 46, X #207, X:L #208 fb, X #207, W #62, all '08)
ILLAINS: Carmelo de lo Santo Silva ("Carmelo S.S.", international drug lord), Dr. Yow (sadistic doctor, dies), Carmelo's associates & guards some die) inc Felix, clowns (die)
THER CHARACTERS: Chief William Lacey (Director, White House Office of National Drug Control Policy, also in pfb, also in fb prior to pfb), amuel (Lacey's son, dies, also in fb prior to issue), pilot (bts flying jet), helicopter pilot (bts waiting to extract Wolverine), Wolverine's sources ots reporting Carmelo's location); wild boar (dead); angels, saints (prev 2 as statues)
OCATIONS/ITEMS: Carmelo's compound, city street (in pfb), Lacey's home (in fb) & office (Washington DC), Madripoor (mentioned) / Volverine's parachute, jet, branch, guards' guns & uniform, Carmelo's roasting spit, clowns' stilts (destroyed), torch & throwing blades, Orange ater formula (bts), alarm system (bts) w/tripwire, Lacey & Carmelo's helicopters (bts)
LASHBACKS: Lacey hires Wolverine to rescue his estranged son Samuel (p). Lacey disowns Samuel.
YNOPSIS: Parachuting into Carmelo's compound, Wolverine sees the drug lord throwing a party complete with clowns. Carmelo announces that, hurt Lacey, he has kidnapped Samuel and Dr. Yow has infected him with the lethal Orange Eater formula. Wolverine steals a guard's uniform, ocates Samuel and tries to sneak out, but triggers a tripwire. Wolverine defeats the guards, but the clowns suddenly attack. They throw knives at Volverine and set him ablaze, but Wolverine kills them. Dr. Yow reveals that Carmelo has fled, and that Orange Eater is incurable; Wolverine kills ow, then euthanizes the suffering Samuel. Later, Wolverine lies to Lacey, saying that Samuel was shot during their escape attempt.

WOLVERINE #62 [#251] (April 2008)

"Get Mystique! Part 1 of 4" (23 pages)

CREDITS: Jason Aaron (writer), Ron Garney (art), Virtual Calligraphy's Joe Caramagna (letters), Jason Keith (colors), Aubrey Sitterson (asst editor), Axel Alonso (editor)
FEATURE CHARACTER: Wolverine (also in pfb, also in fb1 & fb2 between W #113, '97 fb & W #63, '08 fb)
GUEST STAR: Cyclops (in pfb, last in X #207, chr next in Cable #6 fb, next in UXM #495 fb, all '08)
VILLAIN: Mystique (also as Wolverine, also in fb1 & fb2, her chr 1st apps, prior to W #63, '08 fb; also as herself & worshipper in pfb; last in X #207, '08)
OTHER CHARACTERS: Firing squad (in fb1, possibly die), villagers (1 dies, vorshippers (die), bystanders (prev 2 in pfb); seagulls (in pfb), birds (in pfb, others in fb1), cow (dead, as skull, in fb1); Big Pearl, Honeypot May, One-Eyed Ande, Pete the Pygmy, Six-Fingered Soapy (prev 5 mentioned in fb2, unnamed, Mystique's friends in Kansas City); horse (mentioned a fb1, stolen by Wolverine); people (on billboard in pfb)
OCATIONS/ITEMS: Mexico's Sonoran Desert (in fb1 & fb2) w/Nogales bar (mentioned) & prison; Tehran, Iran mosque (destroyed); Muir sland (prev 2 in pfb), Afghanistan's Safed Koh Mountains / Wolverine's shackles, squad's rifles (some also in fb2), handgun, sword & poles, Volverine & Mystique's ropes & blindfolds (all in fb1), villagers' sticks, machine guns & ammo belts, Mystique's bomb (bts in pfb) w/remote etonator, squad member's knife (in fb2)

FLASHBACKS: Wolverine, about to be executed for horse thievery in 1921 Mexico, meets fellow condemned prisoner Mystique as the firing squad takes aim (1). Wolverine breaks free and kills the firing squad. Mystique suggests that the two of them, both obviously superhuman, should work together (2). After the X-Men's disastrous battle against the Marauders, Cyclops asks Wolverine to find and kill Mystique for betraying the team. Wolverine tracks Mystique to Iran, but she blows up a mosque to distract him while she escapes (p).

SYNOPSIS: "Wolverine" stalks through the Afghanistan mountains searching for Mystique; he roughly interrogates local children, angering the villagers. "Wolverine" smells Mystique's scent and brutally stabs a woman — but his victim proves to not have been Mystique. "Wolverine" demands that the villagers give Mystique to him, or more blood will flow. Later, Wolverine enters the Afghanistan mountains and sees a dead woman with three claw holes. Realizing that Mystique has posed as him and framed him for murder, Wolverine turns to find several gun-wielding villagers, while Mystique gloats from an alley…

NOTE: Cover-labeled "Divided We Stand," part of the fallout from the "Messiah CompleX" crossover, where the X-Mansion was demolished by Sentinel attack and Mystique, who joined the X-Men in X #181, '06, betrayed the team to the Marauders. This issue also has a 2nd printing cover featuring interior art from p.6. This issue's credits page incorrectly lists Edgar Delgado and Cory Petit as the colorist and letterer respectively; the recap page provides the correct credits. The production coordinator of W #62-64, '08 is unknown. This issue also has two short features: Portfolio Review (Yanick Paquette's pencils for YX #1, '08, 2 pages) and Look Who's Talking! (Mark Millar interview, 1 page).

WOLVERINE #63 [#252] (May 2008)

"Get Mystique!" (23 pages)

CREDITS: Jason Aaron (writer), Ron Garney (art), Virtual Calligraphy's Cory Petit (letters), Jason Keith (colors), Aubrey Sitterson (asst editor), Axel Alonso (editor)
FEATURE CHARACTER: Wolverine (also in pfb, also in fb between W #62, '08 fb & W #64, '08 fb)
VILLAINS: Mystique (also as Sister Betty (nun) & Mistress Zahira (prostitute), also as herself & woman in fb between W #62, '08 fb & W #64, '08 fb), card players (in fb) inc Jeb
OTHER CHARACTERS: Big Pearl, Honeypot May, One-Eyed Ande, Pete the Pygmy, Six-Fingered Soapy (all Mystique's grifters, 1st in fb prior to W #64, '08 fb), Miles Brickman (US Senator, dies, last in X51 #4, '99), Mordad (bts in cave) & his guards inc Salah, villagers (some also in pfb; others in pfb), US soldiers & Marines, Green Zone bartender, orphans, Brickman's coordinators (bts scheduling him for meetings), trolley operator (bts driving trolley), bystanders (prev 2 in fb); birds, lizard; Punisher, Wendell Rayfield, Bushwhacker, Sentinels, SHIELD agents, aliens (prev 6 mentioned, shot Wolverine), police, judges (prev 2 mentioned in fb, on the take), May's clients (mentioned in fb, robbed), Jason "the Monster" Gorlewski (on wanted poster), ancient Egyptians, jackal (prev 2 as stone carvings)
LOCATIONS/ITEMS: Kansas City, Missouri (in fb) w/North End (mentioned), downtown, West Bottoms & grifters' apartment; Afghanistan's Safed Koh Mountains (also in pfb); Iraq inc Green Zone Café (Baghdad), brothel (Iraq/Syria border) & Mordad's caves (Al Anbar) / Kansas City trolley, Pearl's chocolates & dress w/flap, bystander's money clip, Soapy's cards, Jeb's knife & gun, Mystique's bank blueprints (all in fb), clients' wallets & tenpins w/diamonds (prev 3 mentioned in fb), villagers' shotgun, ammo belts (prev 2 in pfb) & machine guns (also in pfb) w/bullets; Punisher, Rayfield, Bushwhacker, aliens & SHIELD agents' guns (prev 5 mentioned), Wolverine & Mystique's drinks, Green Zone window (destroyed), army truck w/window (destroyed), Marines' guns & Humvees, guards' machine guns
FLASHBACKS: The villagers shoot Wolverine (p). Mystique introduces Wolverine to her group of grifters, who busily fleece Kansas City's residents. Angry card players discover Six-Fingered Soapy's extra digit; they try to cut it off, but Wolverine intervenes. Mystique asks Wolverine to join her group, explaining that she has a big score planned.
SYNOPSIS: The villagers throw Wolverine off a cliff. He slowly recovers and continues tracking down Mystique, eventually finding her at a bar for US soldiers, disguised as a nun and surrounded by orphans. She quietly asks why Wolverine is taking her betrayal so personally, then loudly accuses him of being lewd and flees. As a soldier confronts Wolverine, Mystique steals a van and escapes. Later, Senator Brickman visits a prostitute while in Iraq — but she strangles him, reveals herself as Mystique and takes his place. Wolverine catches up, finds Brickman's body and realizes that Mystique is now protected by US Marines. Deciding to seek out help, he calls in a favor from a man named Mordad…
NOTE: Cover-labeled "Divided We Stand." Unlike this arc's other three parts, this issue's story title does not contain a chapter number. XFac #139, '97 established that one of Mystique's many cover-identities was "Mallory Brickman," Senator Brickman's wife — meaning that she kills and impersonates her own husband this issue.

WOLVERINE #64 [#253] (June 2008)

"Get Mystique! Part 3" (22 pages)

CREDITS: Jason Aaron (writer), Ron Garney (art), Virtual Calligraphy's Cory Petit (letters), Jason Keith (colors), Aubrey Sitterson (asst editor), Axel Alonso (editor)
FEATURE CHARACTER: Wolverine (also in pfb & his own thoughts, also in fb between W #63, '08 fb & W #65, '08 fb)
VILLAIN: Mystique (also as Senator Miles Brickman & Miss December; also dies in Wolverine's thoughts; also as herself, flapper & Mr. Butterworth (bank president) in fb between W #63, '08 fb & W #65, '08 fb)
OTHER CHARACTERS: Big Pearl, Honeypot May, One-Eyed Ande, Pete the Pygmy, Six-Fingered Soapy (all in fb between W #63, '08 fb & W #65, '08 fb), Mordad (Iraqi freedom fighter, also as policeman, also in pfb) & his guards (some or others also as police, some or others also in pfb) inc Jassim, US soldiers, police (some or all in fb prior to W #65, '08 fb), bank employees & customers (prev 2 in fb prior to W #65, '08 fb); vulture, birds; Russian soldiers (mentioned, tried to kill Wolverine), US officials (mentioned, praised & condemned Mordad), Iraqi police (mentioned, IDs stolen by Mordad), ninjas (mentioned, Wolverine learned their tricks); Miss December (Playpen playmate, in photo); angel as statue in fb)
LOCATIONS/ITEMS: Kansas City's Federal Reserve Bank (in fb), Iraq inc US Army headquarters (Baghdad) & Al Anbar w/Mordad's caves (in pfb); Afghanistan mountains (mentioned) / police guns & nightsticks, grifters' guns & getaway car, Soapy's drill, saw, stethoscope & toolbox, employees' wallets & watches (prev 2 bts), Mystique's sack (all in fb), Mordad's car, body bag (prev 2 destroyed), C-4 with detonator (destroyed) & stolen police IDs (bts) & Jeep, guards' machine guns (some or others also in pfb), alien painkillers (mentioned), soldiers' truck, machine guns & Playpen magazine, "Brickman's" chair (destroyed), Mystique's guns, grenades, missile launchers & ammo belt

FLASHBACKS: Wolverine asks his old friend Mordad to help him fake his own death (p). Mystique asks Wolverine to help her rob the Federal Reserve Bank. Despite serious reservations about their plan, Wolverine eventually agrees. Later, Mystique and her grifters burst into the bank with guns; Soapy begins breaking into the vault while Wolverine and Ande wait outside. When they hear a strange noise, Mystique flees and Ande fears that she has sold them out. Soapy opens the vault, to find police awaiting him inside…

SYNOPSIS: Wolverine blows himself up with a car bomb. Posing as police, Mordad and his men deliver Wolverine's burned body to Baghdad's U.S. Army base, and the soldiers bring the "suicide bomber" inside for identification. Wolverine recovers and tracks down Mystique, still posing as Brickman. The two brawl furiously, but "Brickman" soon summons security guards to distract Wolverine and flees. Posing as a supermodel, she steals a truck full of weapons and escapes the base. As Wolverine follows her into the desert, Mystique prepares for her final stand…

NOTE: Cover-labeled "Divided We Stand." This issue reveals that Wolverine tried Atlantean water therapy to deal with pain; he may have learned about the therapy from Amir in or around W #48, '07.

WOLVERINE #65 [#254] (July 2008)

"Get Mystique! Conclusion" (23 pages)

CREDITS: Jason Aaron (writer), Ron Garney (art), Virtual Calligraphy's Cory Petit (letters), Jason Keith (colors), Anthony Dial (production), Aubrey Sitterson (asst editor), Axel Alonso (editor)

FEATURE CHARACTER: Wolverine (also on Mystique's scope, also in fb between W #64, '08 fb & W #10, '11 fb; next in W:Amaz/2, '08)

VILLAIN: Mystique (also in fb between W #64, '08 fb & XX #1, '01 fb; next in X:MD #1, '08)

OTHER CHARACTERS: Big Pearl, Honeypot May, One-Eyed Ande, Pete the Pygmy (all die off-panel), Six-Fingered Soapy (dies), bank employees & customers (some or all of each bts off-panel), police (all in fb following W #64, '08 fb); birds (others in fb); eagle (as decoration)

LOCATIONS/ITEMS: Kansas City's Federal Reserve Bank, railroad tracks (both in fb), Iraq's Syrian desert (also on scope) / Soapy's drill, saw, stethoscope & toolbox (all bts), police guns & nightsticks, grifters' guns & getaway car, Pearl's dress w/flap, Wolverine's pack & reward money, train w/boxcar (all in fb), soldiers' truck, Mystique's paint (bts), knife, guns, grenade, Claymore mine, missile launcher & sniper rifle (destroyed) w/scope, pay phone (mentioned)

FLASHBACK: The police shoot Soapy and the other grifters — then thank Wolverine for tipping them off and give him a reward. Later, a conflicted Wolverine boards a train car, but discovers Mystique hiding on it as well. She claims that she understands why he betrayed her; Wolverine counters that she would have betrayed the group for her own gain eventually as well. Mystique offers to let bygones be bygones, but suddenly kicks Wolverine out of the boxcar.

SYNOPSIS: Mystique and Wolverine battle savagely. Mystique taunts Wolverine, claiming that he too will one day betray the X-Men. Enraged, Wolverine lunges at Mystique; she pulls a gun and shoots him in the face just as he stabs her through the chest. The two collapse simultaneously. Wolverine soon recovers and finds the badly wounded Mystique crawling away. He tells her that he's worked hard to atone for his mistakes — and that she should examine her own choices, and where they've led her. Wolverine drops a gun at her feet and walks away as Mystique curses him.

NOTE: Cover-labeled "Divided We Stand." Having transformed fully back to her natural state, Mystique is naked for this issue's entire present-day portion. This issue also has a Look Who's Talking! feature (Aron Coleite interview, 1 page) and a 5-page preview of Et #1, '08.

WOLVERINE: THE AMAZING IMMORTAL MAN AND OTHER BLOODY TALES (July 2008)

"The Amazing Immortal Man!" (11 pages)

CREDITS: David Lapham (writer), Johnny Timmons (art), Artmonkeys Studios (letters), José Villarrubia (colors), Alejandro Arbona (asst editor), Warren Simons (editor), Simone Bianchi (c art)

FEATURE CHARACTER: Wolverine (also as Amazing Immortal Man, also in pfb & on wanted poster, also in dfb1, also in dfb2 following main story; chr last in W #10, '11 fb, chr next in W:O Ann, '07)

VILLAINS: Maximillian "Max" Ernesto Seville (circus owner & bank robber, also in dfb1 prior to story) & his circus employees (some also in dfb1 prior to story) inc Raúl (fire-eater, also on poster in pfb), Arabian Knights (circus swordsmen), lion tamer (in pfb) & Armand

OTHER CHARACTERS: Olga (lion tamer's assistant & lover, dies off-panel, also in pfb; also in dfb1 between pfb & story; also bts, dead in grave, in dfb2 following story), "Teddy Fingers" (Max's safecracker, also in dfb1 prior to story), Lydia (gypsy midwife), Kansas Governor Harry Woodring (bts, called about manhunt), Olga's son (unborn, in pfb; also bts, unborn, in dfb1 between pfb & story), circus barker (also in pfb), audience (others also in dfb1 prior to story), police officers mentioned, crowd control at shows), bystanders (others in pfb); horses (1 also in pfb), lions, elephants; Tennessee police (mentioned in pfb, arrested Wolverine for stealing chickens), sideshow geek (mentioned in pfb, shot by Armand); Man-Frog (on poster in pfb)

LOCATIONS/ITEMS: Greenland, Kansas fairgrounds; Missouri fairgrounds (in pfb); Wellington, Kansas inc bank (bts, also in dfb1) & fairgrounds (also in dfb1) w/Max's trailer (in dfb1), Chicago, woods (in dfb2), Tennessee (mentioned) / Max's bed of nails (bts), trailers, gun, car, lock w/money, cage (destroyed) w/lock & circus tent (destroyed, also in pfb & dfb1) w/posters (in pfb), Wolverine's chains (destroyed, others mentioned), spikes (also in dfb1) & cage, lion tamer's gun (prev 2 in dfb1), Olga's gravestone (in dfb2), Raúl's torch, fire guns, Knights' swords (1 destroyed, 1 also in dfb2), wanted poster, Teddy's hat

FLASHBACKS: Olga befriends Wolverine, captured and displayed in Max's sideshow as a "wild man" — but when Olga's jealous lover shoots him, Wolverine's rapid healing leads to a new position (p). Max's men rob the towns that their circus visits, but Wolverine refuses to perform unless they stop, so Olga can safely give birth in the town hospital. Max reassures Wolverine, then plots a robbery anyway (d1). Wolverine leaves Olga's grave (d2).

SYNOPSIS: As the "Immortal Man," Wolverine survives injuries to amuse the audience. Max locks Wolverine in a lion cage, leaves Olga with a midwife, and robs the town bank. Wolverine breaks free and defeats the attacking sideshow performers, but discovers that Olga died in childbirth and howls — startling Max so much that he flees, never to return.

NOTE: This story occurs in the 1930s. This issue has a Look Who's Talking! feature (Aron Coleite interview, 1 page) between the first and second stories. Governor Woodring is unnamed here; his identity is surmised from real-world records.

2ND STORY: "The Animal Man" (11 pages)

CREDITS: David Lapham (writer, pencils), Stefano Gaudiano (inks), Artmonkeys Studios (letters), Avalon Studios' Matt Milla (colors), Alejan Arbona (asst editor), Warren Simons (editor)

FEATURE CHARACTER: Wolverine (in pfb, also as animal man in Animal's thoughts, next in MChan #3 fb, ASM #555, X:DWS #2, all '08

VILLAINS: Street gang (in pfb, some possibly die), would-be rapists

OTHER CHARACTERS: Animal (disturbed bus driver, also becomes Animal in pfb), Claire (Animal's daughter, in pfb), passengers (a as demons in Animal's thoughts, others in pfb), Animal's boss (bts making him promise to call Claire), police (bts in car), bystanders (in p scorpion (as tattoo in pfb)

LOCATIONS/ITEMS: New York City (also in pfb) inc hospital & Animal's Bronx apartment (prev 2 in pfb) & passenger's Bronx apartm building / Gang's switchblades, abandoned wheelchair, hospital IV & breathing tube, Animal's weights, drugs, journal & razor blade (all in p Animal's wrist-mounted knives (destroyed) & bus (prev 2 also in fb), witch's broom (in Animal's thoughts), rapist's knife, police car (bts)

FLASHBACK: A New York bus driver stands up to a street gang who try to assault a woman on his bus, but they stab him. Wolverine interve and attacks the gang, impressing the driver. As he recuperates, the driver becomes obsessed with Wolverine — exercising, taking drugs to h faster, and building wrist-mounted knives to emulate his new hero (p.)

SYNOPSIS: Returning to work with a "Wolverine" hairstyle, the disturbed driver views everyone that boards his bus as evil. He sees two n get off; they follow and confront a young woman. The driver intervenes, proclaiming himself "Animal" — but as he waves his arms, his w mounted knives fall apart. The men stab the driver and flee; the young woman comforts the wounded "Animal" as police approach.

3RD STORY: "Coney Island Baby" (11 pages)

CREDITS: David Lapham (writer), Kelly Goodine (pencils), Paul Neary (inks), Avalon Studios' Ian Hannin (colors), Alejandro Arbona (a editor), Warren Simons (editor)

FEATURE CHARACTER: Wolverine (next in FF #556-557 & 562, '08-09; XFor #1-2, XFor:Aint/2, XFor #3-6, W:DG/2, all '08)

OTHER CHARACTERS: Sideshow freaks (some also on posters) inc Rosalyn (parasitic infant), geek, pinhead, snake charmer & Rosaly mother, gangsters, gunman (prev 2 dead), shooter's victims (bts, some dead, others critical), Coney Island barker & patrons (1 or more di inc bodybuilder (dies off-panel), police, ticket agent; parasitic creature (mentioned, Wolverine encountered one decades ago); Rat-Faced E python (prev 2 on posters)

LOCATIONS/ITEMS: Gangsters' hideout, Coney Island (Brooklyn, New York) boardwalk w/Sideshows by the Seashore building / Hide windows (destroyed), perfume, kielbasa, hot dogs, suntan oil (prev 4 bts), barker's cane, gunman's guns, Coney Island roller coaster, frea bat, torch, mallet & knives

SYNOPSIS: Wolverine tracks a gunman who murdered several gangsters, but also shot several bystanders. The trail leads to Coney Isla but Wolverine finds the gunman dead with a bizarre stomach wound. Hearing more gunshots, he finds a bodybuilder childishly running an with a handgun. The bodybuilder accidentally shoots his own hand, but feels no pain. Wolverine chases the man across the park, but sees t he has the same stomach wound as the gunman. Wolverine tracks the man to the Coney Island sideshow, where the circus freaks protect culprit — a parasitic infant who burrows inside hosts. They explain that the gangsters had kidnapped the infant, who just wanted to get ba home to them. Wolverine relents, but suspects that he may have to return one day to kill it.

NOTE: This story's letterer is uncredited, but is likely Artmonkeys Studios, Dave Lanphear's production company. This issue also has a 5-pa preview of Et #1, '08.

WOLVERINE: DANGEROUS GAMES (August 2008)

"Tally Ho!" (22 pages)

CREDITS: Simon Spurrier (writer), Ben Oliver (art), Blambot's Nate Piekos (letters), Nestor Pereyra (colo Aubrey Sitterson (editor), Boo Cook (c pencils)

FEATURE CHARACTER: Wolverine (also as himself & fox creature in pfb, chr last in W:KMS/2, '08, chr n in W Ann #2, '08)

VILLAINS: Sir Damien Spencer (hunter of men, possibly dies off-panel), Ben (hippie hired by Spencer, dies c panel) (both also in pfb), Spencer's thugs (in pfb)

OTHER CHARACTERS: Hippies inc Moonbeam & Pixiedust, hunters inc Gregory & Julian, police (bts, arrivi at bar), diner patrons & waitress (all in pfb); Spencer's hunting dogs (die off-panel, also in pfb), birds, toads (pre bts, making noise), foxes (some die off-panel, also in pfb), dogs (others of prev 2 mentioned in pfb, videotaped, pre 3 in pfb), Gaea (mentioned, praised by hippies), Spencer's agents (mentioned, researched Wolverine), Brit lawmakers (mentioned, outlawed fox hunting), chickens (mentioned, allegedly threatened by foxes) (prev 4 in pfb); 5th Dimension: Billy Da Jr., Florence LaRue, Marilyn McCoo, Lamonte McLemore, Ron Towson (prev 5 voice only in recording in pfb)

LOCATIONS/ITEMS: Louisiana: New Orleans bar, diner, hunters' camp w/nearby woods (all in pfb), hippies' tent city (also in pfb), swa / Wolverine's pack, clothesline, ropes, tape, fox costume & spring-loaded trap, hippies' knife & snacks w/laxatives (bts), hunters' bugle (b saddle straps (some destroyed), gun (destroyed), rope, riding crops & cars w/trailers, Spencer's truck (all in pfb), hippies' tents, Spence pheromone marker cocktail, guns w/tranquilizer darts & combat suit w/IR tracker & satellite-linked HUD (prev 7 also in pfb), satellite, also i in pfb), Ben's car (also in pfb) w/radio (in pfb), Wolverine's brandy bottle (also as Molotov cocktail, also in pfb), Spencer's hover-steed (destroye w/weapons cache (bts)

FLASHBACK: After Wolverine gets into a bar fight, a hippie named Ben offers to hide him from the police. They travel to Ben's commu where the other hippies ask Wolverine to help sabotage a local foxhunt. The snooty hunters annoy Wolverine; he agrees, and helps the hipp ambush hunters and spring traps. Soon the hunters flee, and Ben offers Wolverine a celebratory drink. Later, Damien Spencer approac Wolverine in a diner, explaining his perverse love of hunting animal activists. He reveals that Ben dosed Wolverine with a trackable pheromo cocktail, and challenges him, knowing that he loves a good fight. Wolverine grudgingly agrees, taking some brandy for the road (p).

SYNOPSIS: In the swamp, Wolverine evades Spencer's specially bred hunting dogs, but Spencer shoots Wolverine with a nauseati tranquilizer. Stumbling across the hippie commune, Wolverine finds Ben's tent and vomits on him. The hunting dogs, smelling the pheromon swarm on Ben — and Wolverine ignites the brandy and uses it to kill the dogs. When Spencer catches up, Wolverine ambushes him fr above...

NOTE: This story takes place some time after this issue's second story, during a time when Wolverine is globetrotting. Spencer's final fate is unrevealed, but Wolverine likely kills him.

2ND STORY: "Purity" (10 pages)
CREDITS: Rick Remender (writer), Jerome Opeña (art), Blambot's Nate Piekos (letters), Michelle Madsen (colors), Aubrey Sitterson (editor)
FEATURE CHARACTER: Wolverine (next in Logan #1-3, UXM #495-499, X:P&D, all '08, W:MD #1-2, 4 fb & 3-4, '08-09; XFor:Aint, YX #6, W:KMS, all '08)
VILLAINS: Dao (drug syndicate head) & her enforcers (both die), pimps (others mentioned, preyed on Dao), Dao's syndicate members (prev bts, intimidated by Dao)
OTHER CHARACTERS: Buddhist monks: Klahan (Wolverine's old friend, dies), others (dead); worshippers, bystanders; women (on signs), dancers, government figures (prev 2 in pictures), Buddha, crane (prev 2 as statues), doves (as tattoos), bear (on belt buckle)
LOCATIONS/ITEMS: Bangkok, Thailand inc noodle house (mentioned), temple & Dao's apartment / Dao's window (destroyed), gun, cellphone – home-cooked meal, enforcers' gun & machetes
SYNOPSIS: Wolverine meditates at a Bangkok temple. His friend Klahan congratulates his recent efforts to intimidate local crime syndicates, lauding him for not resorting to physical violence. A woman named Dao overhears, and offers to cook Wolverine a meal to thank him. That night, the two begin to kiss and undress; Wolverine notices the woman's dove tattoo but leaves before sleeping with her, citing his desire to earn control over his animal urges. Wolverine returns to the temple, but finds the monks slaughtered by gangland enforcers. Over the dying Klahan's calls to refrain from violence, Wolverine loses control and kills the enforcers, noticing that one has a dove tattoo. Realizing that Dao is the crimelord, Wolverine apologizes to Klahan's memory, then returns to Dao's apartment and kills her.
NOTE: This issue also has a 6-page preview of UltO #1, '08.

WOLVERINE: KILLING MADE SIMPLE (October 2008)

"Killing Wolverine Made Simple" (22 pages)

CREDITS: Christopher Yost (writer), Koi Turnbull (pencils), Sal Regla (inks), Virtual Calligraphy's Cory Petit (letters), Beth Sotelo (colors), Michael Horwitz (asst editor), John Barber (editor), Stephen Segovia (c art), John Rauch (c colors)
FEATURE CHARACTER: Wolverine (also in pfb, also dies in his own thoughts)
VILLAINS: Nanny (armored scientist obsessed with mutant children, also voice only in pfb), Orphan-Maker (Peter, childlike mutant in armored suit, also in pfb) (both last in Sling #9, '99)
OTHER CHARACTERS: Trance (also in pfb, also in photo & on scope in pfb, last in NX #46, '08, next in X:MD #2/3, '08), Blindfold (Ruth Aldine, precognitive mutant, bts in pfb foreseeing Orphan-Maker's attack, last in YX #6, '08, next in X:MD #3/3, '09), Trance's father (also in photo & on scope in pfb) & mother (prev 2 in pfb); X-Men: Archangel, Beast, Emma Frost, Nightcrawler, Rogue (prev 5 dead), Cyclops; Nimrod, Proteus, Stryfe, Elizabeth Howlett (dies) (prev 10 in Wolverine's thoughts)
LOCATIONS/ITEMS: Michigan (also in pfb) inc lake & Abbotts' Bloomfield house (destroyed, in pfb & on scope in pfb), mountains, X-Mansion, Central Park, sun, Muir Island, Howlett estate (prev 6 in Wolverine's thoughts), ocean (mentioned) / Hope's bonds, Wolverine's chains (destroyed), Nanny's armor, blaster & bug-ship (prev 3 also bts in pfb) w/comm system, self-destruct device (destroyed) & escape pod, Abbotts' hot water tank (destroyed) & car (prev 2 in pfb), Orphan-Maker's gun & armor (destroyed) (prev 2 also in pfb) w/comm unit (bts in pfb), Wolverine's Adamantium skeleton, Muramasa Sword, Asteroid M, Stryfe's armor (prev 4 in Wolverine's thoughts), magnet (mentioned)
FLASHBACK: Wolverine watches former Xavier Institute student Trance's house after the precognitive Blindfold predicted danger. Orphan-Maker suddenly attacks, trying to kill Trance's parents. Wolverine battles him, but Orphan-Maker stuns Wolverine and Trance; Nanny orders him to leave the parents and capture Wolverine. Later, a frightened Trance waits for Wolverine to save the day, but Wolverine explains that he's all too mortal (p).
SYNOPSIS: Wolverine describes several ways he can be killed, including Adamantium poisoning, beheading, drowning, being burned to the bone, thrown into the sun, destroyed by a reality warper, or time travelers killing his mother before he was born. Wolverine also points out that if Nanny de-ages him, his metal skeleton won't change size with his body. As Nanny enters, preparing to do just that, Trance panics and projects her astral self, zapping Wolverine's chains. He breaks free and savagely attacks Orphan-Maker, tearing his armor apart. Nanny and Orphan-Maker flee, activating the ship's self-destruct device — but Trance disables it with her astral form, gaining the courage to fight for herself.
NOTE: The Xavier Institute was closed, and all students sent home, after Sentinels demolished the X-Mansion in UXM #493, '08. Although Wolverine did survive being burned to a skeleton in W #43, '06, he did so by dueling Lazaer for another chance at life, as W #58, '07 revealed. With that arrangement nullified as of W #61, '08, Wolverine likely would not survive another such injury.

2ND STORY: "Disturbing Consequences" (11 pages)
CREDITS: Todd Dezago (writer), Steve Kurth (pencils), Serge LaPointe (inks), Virtual Calligraphy's Cory Petit (letters), Joel Seguin (colors), Michael Horwitz (asst editor), John Barber (editor)
FEATURE CHARACTER: Wolverine (next in W:DG, '08, W Ann #2, '08)
OTHER CHARACTERS: Officials (bts sending Wolverine to investigate base), researchers (1 dies, others dead), virus-like organism (dies)
LOCATIONS/ITEMS: Antarctica inc secret research facility / core sample pit / Wolverine's cold-weather gear & snowmobile w/GPS, HUD & heated seat, researchers' ice core sample (destroyed), pickaxe, ice cutting tools & core sample drilling equipment w/drill bit, facility's kerosene & blast door
SYNOPSIS: Wolverine is asked to investigate an Antarctic research facility that recently broke off radio contact. Wolverine deduces that the researchers were studying ice core samples, but is suddenly attacked by a crazed man covered in oozing sores. Wolverine locks the man in a lab and investigates the rest of the facility, finding the other researchers dead. He examines the enormous ice drilling shaft outside, but the infected man frees himself and tackles Wolverine. They fall in, but a drill bit impales the man and his symptoms vanish, manifesting on Wolverine's body. Wolverine realizes that he was sent here so that his healing factor could kill a mobile virus that the researchers found in the ice. Wolverine eventually overcomes the virus, frees himself and torches the facility.
NOTE: This issue also has an 8-page preview of W:FC #5, '08.

WOLVERINE ANNUAL #2 (November 2008)

"Roar" (35 pages)

CREDITS: Duane Swierczynski (writer), Mike Deodato Jr. (art), Virtual Calligraphy/ Cory Petit (letters), Val Staples (colors), Daniel Ketchum & Sebastian Girner (assistant editors), Axel Alonso (editor)
FEATURE CHARACTER: Wolverine (next in Av/Inv #2-12, '08-09, X:MD #5, '0 bts, AX #25-30, '08-09, X:MD #2/3 & 5/2, '08-09; UXM #500, MCP #12/2, W:t #21-28, X:OS, X:L #217, W:O #29, all '08; X:L #218, W:O #30-31, 32 fb & 31-3 HulkTU, all '09, UXM #501-503, '08, Cable #6 fb, 7 & 9-10, '08-09, XFor Ann, '1 SecInv #1-2 & 4-7, Tb #125, all '08, SecInv #7-8, '08-09, NAv #48, '09, XFor #7-1 '08-09; X:Worlds #4, X:MD #3/3, UXM #506, W:Chop, all '09)
VILLAINS: Nanabozho (Coyote, Native American trickster god, bts & as symbol vision in fb3 during DrS #25, '91), coyote creature (Navajo boy inside monstrous body with deafening roar, dies, boy also as spirit, also bts a creature in rfb, also as boy & creature in fb3 & as creature in fb2 & in shadow as creature in fb1 prior to issue)
OTHER CHARACTERS: Dina Wolkow (dowser, also in fb2 & fb1 prior to issue), diggers (in fb2 & fb1, die off-panel, also in rfb) inc Victc Doolittle, Roamer town officials (bts hiring geologist in fb2), sheriff & residents (some dead) inc Netos' Store employee, workers (die), geologis (prev 2 in fb2), Navajo tribesmen (die), cowboys (prev 2 in fb3), rescue crews, paramedics; Jerusalem crickets (others in fb3), horses (in fb3); ki (mentioned, Googled Roamer for Wolverine), doctor (mentioned in fb1, tended to diggers); Bob Barker (quoted)
LOCATIONS/ITEMS: Roamer, New Mexico (Chavez County, also in fb1, fb2 & as Navajo land in fb3) inc Netos' Store, Sheriff's office & Dina house; Roswell, New Mexico (mentioned) / Diggers' shovels (in fb1 & fb2), Dina's applewood dowsing rod (in fb1 & destroyed in fb2) & shotgu (also bts in fb2), Wolverine's pack, kid's portable computer (mentioned), resident's car, trailer home (destroyed), sheriff's guns, paper, marker blood, hydraulic digging equipment (destroyed in fb2), building windows (destroyed), creature's blood, Navajo teepees, knife, axe, shield, spea bow & arrows, cowboys' guns (prev 8 in fb3), rescue crew's van, paramedics' ambulance, stretcher & medical equipment
FLASHBACKS: Diggers stare at what they uncover (this issue). Diggers uncover something that bursts their eardrums (1). Dowsing fc water, young Dina detects a powerful source, but diggers uncover a buried coyote creature, whose roar deafens them. They re-bury it, b decades later others dig there. Ignoring Dina's warnings, the workers accidentally free the creature, which deafens and slaughters them (2). Afte cowboys massacre a group of Navajo, the lone survivor prays for revenge; he is given a creature's body and made to slumber underground (3
SYNOPSIS: Wolverine finds Roamer's residents in a state of shock. An enormous coyote creature attacks, his roar bursting Wolverine eardrums. Wolverine drives the creature away; realizing that the entire town is now deaf, Wolverine has a written conversation with the sheri who refuses to help. Wolverine meets Dina, who has learned to lip-read; but the creature attacks again. Wolverine cuts it open, revealing a youn Navajo boy inside. The boy begins to roar, but Wolverine slices his voice box, explains that the people who killed his family are long dead, an euthanizes the boy.
NOTE: This issue also has a 2nd-printing cover. Contrary to Dina's claims, Jerusalem crickets do not make sounds like crying children. Thi issue's fb1 occurs during fb2.

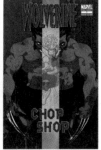

WOLVERINE: CHOP SHOP (January 2009)

"Chop Shop" (22 pages)

CREDITS: Mike Benson (writer), Roland Boschi (art), Jeff Eckleberry (letters), Dan Brown (colors), Joe Sabin (production), Daniel Ketchum (editor), Axel Alonso (exec editor), Tomer Hanuka (c pencils)
FEATURE CHARACTER: Wolverine (also in pfb, next in W:Sb, '09)
VILLAINS: Organ-smuggling ring: Annabel (model turned seductress), Sebastian (ringleader), Dr. Phillip (vivisectionist), Jeffrey (Phillips' assistant) (prev 3 die), enforcers (die) inc Ludwig & Yuri; criminals (in pfb, all bu 1 dead)
OTHER CHARACTERS: Wolverine's source (bts in pfb, alerting him about organ smugglers), hotel patron & bartender, smugglers' victims (die), St. Vincent's Hospital receptionist & doctors, cabbie (bts driving taxi), ba patron & bartender; José Javier (drug lord, mentioned, uses smugglers' services), Koratev Brothers (mentioned smugglers' rivals), Annabel's father (mentioned, alcoholic) & mother (mentioned, threatened by smugglers) enforcer's grandfather (mentioned, believed in avenging spirits); mythological figure (as tribal mask)
LOCATIONS/ITEMS: Hotel w/bar & Annabel's room, criminal's home (in pfb), smugglers' hideout w/nearby river, Annabel's apartment Sebastian's penthouse, Manhattan inc bar & St. Vincent's Hospital / Annabel's perfume, soap, shampoo (all bts), door chain (destroyed), drink & case w/syringe & paralyzing drugs, smugglers' van, stretcher, tarps, organ containers & cleaning supplies, criminals' guns (in pfb), Phillips' ca spotlights, scalpels & medical equipment, enforcers' guns, receptionist's computer, taxi
FLASHBACK: Wolverine tracks down leads on an organ smuggling ring (p).
SYNOPSIS: Annabel buys Wolverine a drink at a hotel bar. The two flirt, and soon go back to Annabel's room and sleep together. Afte Wolverine is asleep, Annabel injects him with paralyzing drugs and summons enforcers, who deliver his body to organ smugglers — just a Wolverine had intended. Dr. Phillips removes many of Wolverine's organs and the enforcers throw his body in the river, but Wolverine eventuall recovers and returns to the smugglers' hideout, swearing revenge. He kills Phillips, luring the enforcers outside; as the men slowly becom panicked, Wolverine picks them off one by one, and Phillips' terrified assistant dies of a heart attack. Wolverine then tracks down Annabel an forces her to reveal the ringleader's identity. He makes her visit the ringleader under false pretenses and drug him; Wolverine then cuts out th ringleader's organs and forces Annabel to deliver them to a hospital. The next night, a woman offers to buy Wolverine a drink, but he declines.
NOTE: This issue showcases artist Tomer Hanuka's alternate cover concepts on the credits page, which runs after the story.

WOLVERINE: FLIES TO A SPIDER (February 2009)

"Swallowed the Spider" (34 pages)

CREDITS: Gregg Hurwitz (writer), Jerome Opeña (pencils, co-inks), John Lucas (co-inks), Virtual Calligraphy's Joe Caramagna (letters), Michelle Madsen (colors), Sebastian Girner (asst editor), Axel Alonso (editor), Tim Bradstreet (c art), Enrica Jang (special thanks)
FEATURE CHARACTER: Wolverine (chr last in XFor #12, '09, chr next in W #74/2, '09)
VILLAINS: Road Dawgs (biker gang, some also in pfb) inc enforcer, drug-running mobster (also in portrait, also bts in pfb) & his thugs, corrupt sheriff & deputies (all die)
OTHER CHARACTERS: Clancy Jordan (trucker, also in pfb), Ruthie Jordan (Clancy's niece, 2nd grader, dies in pfb, also in photo), Los Diablos (rival biker gang, die in pfb), Daily Bugle reporter (bts writing about Ruthie's death), Rat Trap bartender & patrons inc bikers, mobster's women; animal (dead, as stuffed head), Road Dawg member's dog; Mr. Jordan (Clancy's brother) & his wife (prev 2 mentioned, unnamed, Ruthie's parents), Road Dawg member's victim (mentioned, killed as initiation rite), town citizens (mentioned, scared of Road Dawgs); Santa Claus, reindeer (prev 2 as Rat Trap decorations), devil (as graffiti, also in pfb as Los Diablos logo), model (on poster), biker (in silhouette on bathroom door), woman, snake (prev 2 as tattoo), rat (in silhouette on Rat Trap sign), dog (dead as skull in Road Dawgs logo & tattoos), bears (on hat, pin, lighter, graffiti & belt buckle)
LOCATIONS/ITEMS: Rat Trap (biker bar, destroyed), Road Dawgs' hideout, Sheriff & mobster's offices, highway, Los Diablos' warehouse, gas station (prev 2 in pfb) / Road Dawgs' motorcycles (destroyed), guns (1 destroyed) (some or others of prev 2 also in pfb), banners, drinks, lighter, cellphones, wrench, razor blade & satchels (another also in pfb, destroyed) w/cocaine (bts, some also in pfb), bikers' motorcycles, Santa's motorcycle & sleigh (prev 2 as decorations, destroyed), pool cues (1 destroyed), tables & balls, Rat Trap decorations, windows (prev destroyed) & banner, Los Diablos' guns & motorcycles, Clancy's truck, lollipops (prev 4 in pfb), mobster's money & cordless phone, sheriff's truck (destroyed) & rifle, deputies' rifles & badges, Wolverine's ropes, gag, motorcycle, Daily Bugle, plastic explosives & lighter w/detonator, bodyguards' trucks & guns (prev 2 destroyed)
FLASHBACK: When the Road Dawgs ambush rival biker gang Los Diablos, stray bullets kill Clancy's young niece Ruthie (p).
SYNOPSIS: The Road Dawgs party in their bar and harass embittered trucker Clancy. When Wolverine, elsewhere in the bar, blocks one biker's pool shot, two men attack — but Wolverine snaps the biker's cue and stabs them. Other bikers attack, but Wolverine quickly kills them. As the last biker hides and telephones the Dawgs' leader for backup, Clancy befriends Wolverine. More bikers arrive, including the group enforcer, but Wolverine makes short work of them. The Dawgs' leader contacts their drug lord backer, who orders the town's corrupt sheriff to intervene. The last biker attacks Wolverine; the deputies arrive to find the biker tied up. Wolverine ambushes them, then kills the sheriff. Furious, the drug lord travels to the bar with his men — but Wolverine detonates plastic explosives that he had planted in the parking lot, killing them all. Wolverine shows the dying drug lord a newspaper headline about Ruthie's death, then nods to Clancy and departs.
NOTE: This issue occurs out of publication sequence, shortly after MDigHol, '08, due to its New Year's Eve references. Clancy and his brother's last names are not given, but can be inferred from their relationships to Ruthie.

WOLVERINE: SWITCHBACK (March 2009)

"Switchback" (23 pages)

CREDITS: Joseph Clark (writer), Das Pastoras (art, colors), Dave Lanphear (letters), Sebastian Girner (asst editor), Axel Alonso (editor)
FEATURE CHARACTER: Wolverine (also in pfb)
VILLAINS: Sheriff MacReedy (corrupt Pottsville lawman, also in pfb, dies), Brett (diner brawler, in pfb)
OTHER CHARACTERS: MacReedy's victims (dead, some also alive & dead in photos in main story & pfb, some also in Wolverine's imagination), gas station attendant, diner waitress & patrons, bystanders (prev 4 in pfb); deer (in pfb, others dead as stuffed head in pfb & dead in photo), birds (in pfb), fish (stuffed), bobcat (as stuffed head), animals inc wolverine (as skulls) (prev 4 dead in pfb), Bazooka Joe (gum mascot, on wrapper in main story & pfb); deer (as logo on hat in pfb), eagle (on uniform patch)
LOCATIONS/ITEMS: Pottsville (Northwestern US town, also in pfb) inc switchback curve (also in pfb, also in photos in main story & pfb), gas station, diner (prev 2 in pfb) / MacReedy's barn & office (in pfb) w/cell / MacReedy's bubble gum (some also in pfb), patrol car (also in pfb), coffee maker (in pfb), gun, stinger, stick, ropes, beer, Polaroid camera & photo album w/photos (others in pfb), victims' cars & clothes (prev 2 destroyed, some or others destroyed in photos in main story & pfb), Wolverine's car (destroyed, also in pfb), wallet & passport (prev 2 in pfb)
FLASHBACK: Driving through a switchback curve in the mountains, Wolverine smells death. He pulls over and detects that several car accidents have recently happened at the exact same spot — and that the same man's scent appears at each one, smelling of bubble gum. In the nearby town, locals confirms that tourists often crash at the curve, but mention that Sheriff MacReedy plans to post a warning sign. When a waitress hits on Wolverine, a burly patron grows jealous; Wolverine picks a fight and winds up in jail, where he smells MacReedy's bubble gum. When Wolverine casually mentions the dangerous road, the sheriff threatens him and orders him to leave town. Wolverine obliges, and drives toward the curve (p).
SYNOPSIS: MacReedy looks through photos of wrecks, then lays a tire-destroying stinger across the road at the curve. Wolverine, speeding, deliberately hits the stinger and crashes. Wolverine awakens hanging upside down in a barn full of corpses and car parts. MacReedy taunts Wolverine and reveals that he hates tourists; Wolverine asks MacReedy for a last beer, then kills him.
NOTE: Although Wolverine smells 12 victims at the crash site, MacReedy has at least 20 corpses in his barn; some may have been too old for Wolverine to detect.

2ND STORY: "Punching Bag" (8 pages)
CREDITS: Gregg Hurwitz (writer), Juan Doe (art, colors), Dave Lanphear (letters), Sebastian Girner (asst editor), Axel Alonso (editor)
FEATURE CHARACTER: Wolverine (also in pfb, next in NAv #48-50, W:O #32-36, Av:FCBD, MAv #21 & 23, AoAtlas #4-5, W:O #36-40, YX #10 bts & 11-12, XInf #2-4, W #73, RamW, all '09)

VILLAINS: Kidnappers (die, also in pfb), carjacker
OTHER CHARACTERS: Kidnappers' victim (also in pfb; others dead as skulls in main story & pfb, 1 also on poster in pfb), bar patrons, bartender, carjacker's victim; muggers, burglars, bank robbers (prev 3 mentioned in pfb, thwarted by Wolverine), kidnapper's parents & do█, strip club patrons, horse (as shirt logo) (prev 4 mentioned as taunts)
LOCATIONS/ITEMS: Bar (in pfb) w/nearby cave (also in pfb) & street, bank (mentioned), strip club (mentioned as taunt) / Kidnapper's truc█ (in pfb) & bat (also in pfb) w/nails, missing persons posters, Wolverine's pack & drink (prev 3 in pfb), kidnapper's car, steak, rope & mother█ shirt (prev 4 mentioned as taunts), carjacker's gun, victim's car
FLASHBACK: Wolverine, run ragged by several adventures in a row, enters a bar hoping to relax with a drink. Before he can take a sip, h█ sees a woman outside being kidnapped. Wolverine tracks the kidnappers to a cave littered with skulls of several previous victims. He attack█ but is knocked into the ceiling, where his claws lodge in the rock (p).
SYNOPSIS: Wolverine taunts the kidnappers. They beat him, loosening his claws; Wolverine frees himself and kills the villains. Wolverin█ leaves hoping to finish his drink, but spots a carjacking…
NOTE: This issue also has a 6-page preview of AoAtlas #1, '09.

WOLVERINE #66 (August 2008)

"Old Man Logan, Part 1" (24 pages)

CREDITS: Mark Millar (writer), Steve McNive█ (pencils), Dexter Vines (inks), Virtual Calligraphy█ Cory Petit (letters), Morry Hollowell (colors), Iren█ Lee (production), Michael Horwitz & Aubrey Sitterso█ (asst editors), John Barber (editor), Axel Alonso (grou█ editor), Michael Turner (variant c pencils), Herb Trimp█ (DF variant c pencils), Mark Roslan (variant c inks█ Peter Steigerwald (variant c colors)
FEATURE CHARACTER: Logan (downtrodde█ pacifist farmer, 1st, also in his own imagination, als█ as Wolverine in fb between W #70, '09 fb & W #68, '0█ fb, also in W #70, '09 fb during fb; chr last as Wolverin█ in W #70, '09 fb)
GUEST STAR: Hawkeye (Clint Barton, blind archer █ former Avenger, 1st)
SUPPORTING CAST: Maureen (Logan's wife█ Scotty, Jade (prev 2 Logan & Maureen's children)
VILLAINS: Hulk Gang (Hulk's inbred descendants█ some or others next bts in W #72, '09): Charlie Banne█ Otis Banner (1 of prev 2 also in Logan's imaginatio█ (prev 2 next, possibly bts, in W:OML, '09), Bobbi-J█ Banner (next in W:OML, '09); undercover SHIEL█ agents (bts as rebels, hiring Hawkeye to deliver seru█ next in 1st on-panel app in W #71, '09) inc Tobias
OTHER CHARACTERS: Robert Bruce Banne█ Jr. (Hulk's infant son, unnamed, chr next in W:OML█ '09, next as adult in FF #560, '08), Abe Donovan (bt█ declining pigs, next in 1st on-panel app in W #72, '09█ Jolene (market employee, bts offering to buy X-Box█ Becky's mother (bts telling Jade about Logan's past█ train operator (bts driving train in fb between W #7█ '09 fb bts & W #68, '08 fb bts), Hawkeye's West Coas█ contacts (bts arranging Hawkeye's delivery, see NOTE█ Logan's pigs (others mentioned, lost by Abe) & hors█ Becky (Jade's friend, mentioned), Logan's neighbo█ (mentioned, punished for not paying rent), Hawkeye'█ ex-wife (mentioned, helped customize Spider-Mobil█ see NOTE); Red Skull (as President), Dr. Doom, Hulk, Kingpin of Crime (prev 4 liste█ on map, rule sections of Amerika), Abomination, Magneto (prev 2 listed on map, formerl█ ruled sections of Amerika); women (as Jade's dolls); Captain America (dead, as skeleton█ Venom symbiote, Tyrannosaurus rex (prev 2 cover only)
LOCATIONS/ITEMS: Earth-807128: Westchester (in fb) w/train tracks, Logan'█ family farm (Sacramento, California, Hulkland, Amerika, see NOTE, also in Logan'█ imagination) w/nearby marketplace & neighbor's home (prev 2 mentioned), Ab█ Donovan's farm (bts) / Freight train (in fb), Logan's bandages & tractor w/engin█ (destroyed), Scotty & Jade's X-Box (mentioned) w/long-life battery, Jade's Gamebo█ & dolls, Scotty's shotgun, Hulk Gang's Fantasticar, Hawkeye's customized Spider█ Mobile (Spider-Man's former buggy) w/satnav GPS system & briefcase (bts) w/Super█ Soldier serum (see NOTE), navigation satellite (bts)
FLASHBACK: A bloody Wolverine staggers through the woods and kneels in fron█ of train tracks.

YNOPSIS: Logan crosses the wastelands of California and returns to his family's farm. He tells his wife Maureen that their neighbor declined to buy eir pigs; Maureen suggests selling the children's toys, but Logan refuses to stoop that low for money. When their daughter Jade mentions that she erheard that Logan was a super hero decades ago, before the villains conquered the nation, Logan changes the subject. Days later, the Hulk Gang rives and demands their rent money, which Logan's family does not have. Logan fantasizes about killing the Hulks, but instead meekly accepts a cious beating. The Hulks orders Logan to pay double next month. Later, an aged and blind Hawkeye visits, offering to pay Logan for help navigating ross the ravaged nation to deliver a package. Needing money, Logan accepts, but reminds Hawkeye that he's not Wolverine anymore, and he uses to hurt anyone ever again. The two depart for the East Coast in Hawkeye's refurbished Spider-Mobile.

OTE: Cover-labeled "Old Man Logan." This issue also has seven variants: regular and sketch versions of Michael Turner's variant cover, a ynamic Forces variant limited to 1,999 copies, a 2nd printing featuring interior art from p.14, a 3rd printing featuring a sketch version of the andard cover, a 4th printing that interlocks with reprint covers of W #67-70, '08-09, and a Marvel's Greatest Comics edition, published in May 10, with a lower price and ads only for other Marvel books. The "Old Man Logan" arc occurs in an alternate future, designated as Earth-807128 OHMU HC5, '08, where super villains conquered the USA and divided it up into sections. All characters that appear in this arc are native to arth-807128. Although this Index normally refers to Wolverine by his standard codename even during times when he is not actively using it, in s timeline he has deliberately rejected the Wolverine identity. Robert Bruce Banner Jr.'s last name is confirmed in FF #558, '08; his first name, iddle name and suffix are revealed in FF #560, '08. Bobbi-Jo's first name is revealed in W:OML, '09. The President of Amerika is revealed the Red Skull in W #69, '09. Hawkeye's clients are revealed as undercover SHIELD agents, his West Coast contacts are established, and s cargo is revealed as Super-Soldier Serum in W #71, '09. The ex-wife who helped Hawkeye customize the Spider-Mobile is likely Tonya, roduced next issue. A map of Earth-807128's altered USA, named as "Amerika" next issue, is shown here; locations shown on the map but t visited in this arc are Kree Haven, the Negative Zone opening, Clyde's Pit, the Lair of the Creel Gang and the Lizard King's domain. Writer ark Millar has stated that Clyde's Pit is the holding facility for Earth-1219 mutant Clyde Wyncham, who was brought to Earth-616 in 1985 #6, 3. Clyde is freed in FF #568, '09 fb; OHMU:U #2, '10 incorrectly designates that fb as "Earth-21923," but Millar has confirmed that Clyde is eed on Earth-807128 during the villainous uprising. Earth-1219 is designated in OHMU HC12, '09.

WOLVERINE #67 [#256] (September 2008)

"Old Man Logan, Part 2" (22 pages)

CREDITS: Mark Millar (writer), Steve McNiven (pencils), Dexter Vines (inks), Virtual Calligraphy's Cory Petit (letters), Morry Hollowell (co-colors, c colors), Christina Strain (co-colors), Paul Acerios (production), Jody LeHeup (asst editor), John Barber (editor), Axel Alonso (group editor)

FEATURE CHARACTER: Logan (also as Wolverine in fb during W #70, '09 fb)

GUEST STARS: X-Men (exact members unknown, as Apocalypse, Omega Red, Sabretooth & Mr. Sinister in Mysterio's illusion in fb, team during W #70, '09 fb), Hawkeye

VILLAINS: Ghost Riders (biker gang, die), Mysterio (bts casting illusions in fb during W #70, '09 fb), Kingpin of Crime (bts planning to execute Ashley's group) & his thugs (bts capturing Ashley's group), Ashley (Hawkeye & Tonya's daughter, 1st, see NOTE), Moloid subterraneans

OTHER CHARACTERS: Ultron 8 (benevolent Ultron descendant), Tonya (Spider-Man's daughter & Hawkeye's ex-wife), Daredevil, Punisher (prev 2 bts captured by Kingpin's men), Ghost Riders' contact (bts informing them of Hawkeye's shipment), memorabilia vendors, worshippers, bystanders; dog, cat; Iron Man, Spider-Man, Thor (prev 3 as memorabilia), Captain America (mentioned, killed) (prev 2 also dead on cover), Red Skull (as President, mentioned, tolerates hero memorabilia), Absorbing Man, Magneto (prev 2 mentioned, killed Thor), super villains (mentioned, ignored Hawkeye), San Francisco citizens (mentioned, killed by Moloids); Cyclops, Daredevil, Ms. Marvel, Spider-Man, Thing (prev 5 dead, cover only)

LOCATIONS/ITEMS: Earth-807128: Northern California inc San Francisco estroyed), X-Mansion (in fb), Kingdom of the Kingpin: Hammer Falls (formerly Las Vegas, Nevada) inc Tonya's garage, Kingpin's cellblock isk Lake City, formerly Salt Lake City, Utah); Europe, Asia (prev 2 mentioned) / Hawkeye's bow, arrows, briefcase w/Super-Soldier serum ts) & Spider-Mobile w/satnav GPS system, bystanders' cars, carts & scooters, navigation satellite (bts), Logan's light-stick, Ghost Riders' otorcycles, spear, hooked chains & spiked club, vendors' super hero memorabilia, Thor's hammer, Tonya's car, rag & file, cell's energy bars

LASHBACK: Wolverine viciously battles several villains.

YNOPSIS: As they drive, Logan explains to a skeptical Hawkeye that he has given up being Wolverine and become an avowed pacifist. awkeye sheepishly admits that he is ferrying drugs. The two arrive in San Francisco, but find its buildings sunk into the ground. Logan spots nneling Moloids; Hawkeye explains that they have been attacking cities, and that they may be the planet's immune response to humans. hecking for survivors, the two are attacked by the Ghost Riders biker gang. Logan lets a biker beat him savagely, but Hawkeye, guided by their nouts, kills the bikers with his arrows. Hawkeye lectures Logan for not helping, but Logan repeats that he takes his pacifism very seriously. The o drive to Hammer Falls, where citizens worship Thor's hammer and pray for heroes to return. Ultron 8 greets Hawkeye, telling the two old en to visit Hawkeye's ex-wife Tonya, Spider-Man's daughter. Tonya tells Hawkeye that their daughter Ashley tried to depose the Kingpin, but as captured — and faces execution.

OTE: Cover-labeled "Old Man Logan." This issue also has three variant covers: a sketch variant, a 2nd printing featuring interior art from p.19, nd a 3rd printing that interlocks with reprint covers of W #66 & 68-70, '08-09. Last issue's map is used on the recap page of W #67-72, '08-09, ith an inset showing Logan and Hawkeye's current location. This issue is dedicated to the memory of artist Michael Turner, who died in June 008. Next issue reveals Ashley's plan to usurp the Kingpin's throne, hence her inclusion as a Villain here. One of the cars seen here resembles erbie, the Volkswagen Beetle from Disney's *Love Bug* movies.

WOLVERINE #68 [#257] (October 2008)

"Old Man Logan, Part 3" (23 pages)

CREDITS: Mark Millar (writer), Steve McNiven (pencils), Dexter Vines (ink Virtual Calligraphy's Cory Petit (letters), Morry Hollowell (co-colors, c colors), Jus Ponsor & Jason Keith (co-colors), Joe Sabino (production), Jody LeHeup (as editor), John Barber (editor), Axel Alonso (group editor)

FEATURE CHARACTER: Logan (also as Wolverine in fb between W #66, ' fb & W #70, '09 fb)

GUEST STAR: Hawkeye

VILLAINS: Kingpin of Crime (ruler of section of Amerika, see NOTE; 1st on-par app, dies) & his thugs (some die, all but 2 also on scope), Moloid subterranea (bts destroying Cedar City), Ashley

OTHER CHARACTERS: Daredevil, Punisher (prev 2 Ashley's friends, die, see NOTE), Ultron 8, Tonya, tra operator (bts driving train in fb between W #66, '08 fb bts & W #70, '09 fb bts), Cedar City victims (bts, killed ■ Moloids) & survivor, spectators, bystanders; Velociraptors; Magneto (mentioned, killed by Kingpin); dragons (i tattoos)

LOCATIONS/ITEMS: Earth-807128: Tonya's garage, Westchester train tracks (in fb), Cedar City of Champio■ (destroyed, formerly Cedar City, Utah), Fisk Lake City inc Rice-Eccles Stadium w/nearby rooftop & Kingpir headquarters (former Walmart) w/cellblock / Tonya's car, tools & equipment, Hawkeye's bow, arrows, sword Spider-Mobile, Ultron 8's X-Men keychain, freight train (in fb), Kingpin's loudspeaker (bts) & cane, Daredevil Punisher's chains & post, stadium floodlights, thugs' guns, Logan's binoculars w/heat sensor, cell's energy ba w/control panel (destroyed), cellblock wall & door (prev 2 destroyed)

FLASHBACK: A train speeds toward Wolverine.

SYNOPSIS: Hawkeye, proud of Ashley for trying to become a super hero, promises to rescue her from th Kingpin. Logan refuses to get involved, but relents when Hawkeye promises that Logan only has to read th roadmap. Ultron 8 gives Logan an X-Men keychain for luck, but it only stirs up painful memories. The two drive through Cedar City, findin that it too has been sunk into the ground by Moloids. In Fisk Lake City, the Kingpin publicly executes Ashley's captured friends, dressed a Daredevil and the Punisher, by releasing dinosaurs that devour the would-be heroes. Logan spies on the Kingpin and locates Ashley, dresse as her grandfather Spider-Man. Hawkeye has Logan drive the Spider-Mobile up a building and crash through the prison wall; Hawkeye attacl Kingpin's thugs and frees Ashley. The Kingpin bursts in, but Ashley swiftly decapitates him. She then attacks Hawkeye, revealing that sh overthrew the Kingpin because she intends to claim his throne. In the Spider-Mobile, Logan grudgingly realizes that he must take action…

NOTE: Cover-labeled "Old Man Logan." This issue also has two variant covers: a 2nd printing featuring interior art from p.23, and a 3rd printir that interlocks with reprint covers of W #66-67 & 69-70, '08-09. Daredevil, Punisher and the Kingpin are not Matt Murdock, Frank Castle Wilson Fisk, but are new, unrelated characters. Hammer Falls and Fisk Lake City are referred to as Las Vegas and Salt Lake City here.

WOLVERINE #69 [#258] (January 2009)

"Old Man Logan, Part 4" (23 pages)

CREDITS: Mark Millar (writer), Steve McNiven (pencils), Dexter Vines (inks Virtual Calligraphy's Cory Petit (letters), Morry Hollowell (colors), Joe Sabir (production), Jody LeHeup (asst editor), John Barber (editor), Axel Alonso (grou editor)

FEATURE CHARACTER: Logan (also as Wolverine in fb during W #70, '09 fb)

GUEST STARS: X-Men (exact members unknown, dead in fb as Lac Deathstrike, Mr. Sinister & Omega Red in Mysterio's illusion, team during W #7l '09 fb), Hawkeye

VILLAINS: Mysterio (bts casting illusions in fb during W #70, '09 fb), Ashle Moloid subterraneans, Venom symbiote, Kingpin's thugs (most or all die)

OTHER CHARACTERS: Loki (dead, as skeleton), Millar's bartender (bts serving drinks) & patrons, security guard, bystanders; dinosau (possibly die); Human Torch, Thing (prev 2 mentioned, killed); Invisible Woman, Mr. Fantastic (prev 2 mentioned, missing, see NOTE), Kai (mentioned, allegedly defeated Invisible Woman & Mr. Fantastic), Shocker, gossiper (prev 2 mentioned, heard about Kang's victory); Thoma Jefferson, Abraham Lincoln, Theodore Roosevelt, George Washington, Red Skull (prev 5 as Mount Rushmore statues)

LOCATIONS/ITEMS: Earth-807128: Fisk Lake City inc underground caverns & Kingpin's cellblock, Wyoming: Paste Pot Creek & Electrovill■ South Dakota inc Mount Rushmore (prev 4 unclaimed territory), Millar's bar (Des Moines, Iowa, Doom's Lair), X-Mansion (in fb) / Thugs' car vans, trucks (all destroyed) & guns, Hawkeye's dinosaur repellant spray (bts), bow, arrows & Spider-Mobile w/fender, cellblock wall & windo (prev 2 destroyed), guard's handgun, building windows (destroyed), Logan's light-stick, Baxter Building (destroyed)

FLASHBACK: Wolverine stands over several villains' bodies.

SYNOPSIS: As Ashley attacks Hawkeye, Logan grabs him and smashes the Spider-Mobile out through a window, landing roughly on th ground below. They soon spot a convoy of Kingpin's men chasing them through the desert, but a chasm suddenly opens beneath the car Logan awakens underground and sees Moloids consuming the Kingpin's men. Logan locates Hawkeye, pinned under the Spider-Mobile an hidden from the Moloids. Logan chases the Moloids off and the two drive up the chasm wall to safety. Continuing east, they encounter herc of roaming dinosaurs, drive past Loki's giant corpse, and are unknowingly stalked by a hostless Venom symbiote. They discuss the heroes' fa decades ago, and drive past Mount Rushmore, which has the Red Skull's face carved into it. They stop at a bar; Hawkeye wonders why Ashle turned out so badly. Teased by a drunk, Logan nearly attacks the man, but quickly exits the bar. Hawkeye asks what happened to hurt Logan s deeply, and Logan decides to finally discuss it…

NOTE: Cover-labeled "Old Man Logan." This issue also has a 2nd printing variant cover that interlocks with reprint covers of W #66-68 & 7('08-09. This issue reveals that the Red Skull is President of Amerika. FF #560-561, '08-09 reveal that Mr. Fantastic and the Invisible Woma

entioned here as missing, did survive the villainous uprising. Hawkeye explains here that the packs of dinosaurs roaming the Midwest are from ⁞e Savage Land; they were imported by the wealthy years ago as a fad, but were ultimately abandoned.

WOLVERINE #70 [#259] (February 2009)

"Old Man Logan, Part 5" (22 pages)

CREDITS: Mark Millar (writer), Steve McNiven (pencils), Dexter Vines (inks, pp.1-14 & 17-22; c inks), Mark Morales (inks, pp.15-16), Virtual Calligraphy's Cory Petit (letters), Morry Hollowell (colors, pp.1-14 & 17-22; c colors), Justin Ponsor (colors, pp.15-16), Joe Sabino & Damien Lucchese (production), Jody LeHeup (asst editor), John Barber (editor), Axel Alonso (group editor)
FEATURE CHARACTER: Logan (also as Wolverine in fb, his chr 1st app, prior to W #66, '08, also in W #67, 69, 66 & 68, '08-09 fbs during fb)
GUEST STARS: X-Men: Beast, Nightcrawler (both prior to W #72, '09), Cannonball, Colossus, Cyclops, Forge, Gambit, Havok, Iceman, Longshot, Polaris, Kitty Pryde, Psylocke, Storm, others (all also as Absorbing Man, Apocalypse, Blob, Dr. Octopus, Green Goblin, Klaw, Lady Deathstrike, Mr. Hyde, Mr. Sinister, Omega Red, Sabretooth, Scorpion, Shocker, Silver Samurai, Stryfe, Trapster, Ultron & others in Mysterio's illusion), Jubilee (also as herself & Bullseye in Mysterio's illusion) (all die in fb, some also in W #67, '08 fb during fb, some also in W #69, '09 fb during fb); Hawkeye
VILLAINS: Mysterio (Quentin Beck, illusionist, in fb, also bts in W #67 & 69, '08-09 fbs during fb), Red Skull (bts employing Mysterio in fb prior to W #72, '09 fb), Venom symbiote (merged with Tyrannosaurus rex)
OTHER CHARACTERS: Dwight (young boy with Ant-Man's helmet), Fantastic Four: Invisible Woman (prior to FF #557, '08), Thing (prior to W #72, '09), Human Torch, Mr. Fantastic (prev 4 bts in fb, sending distress call); Avengers (exact members unknown), SHIELD agents, Wakandan agents (prev 3 bts in fb, sending distress calls), Xavier Institute students (in fb), train operator (bts driving train in ⁞, also bts in W #66 & 68, '08 fbs during fb), Dwight's victims (dead, as skeletons); dinosaurs inc Tyrannosaurus rex (merged with Venom ⁞mbiote), ants (bts, controlled by Dwight), sheep (in fb)
⁞OCATIONS/ITEMS: Earth-807128: Westchester inc train tracks & X-Mansion w/evacuation tunnels (all in fb), Avengers' headquarters, ⁞HIELD headquarters, Fantastic Four's headquarters, Wakanda (prev 4 bts in fb), Las Vegas (mentioned in fb), Iowa: Des Moines & Dwight's ⁞oll; Doom's Head, Illinois: Doom's Lair / X-Mansion walls, Dr. Octopus' mechanical arms, Klaw's sonic prosthesis (all destroyed), Bullseye's ⁞nives (all but 1 bts), Stryfe's armor, Shocker's gauntlets, Absorbing Man's ball & chain, Scorpion's stinging tail, Silver Samurai's armor & sword, ⁞reen Goblin's glider & pumpkin bomb, Trapster's armor, rubble (all in Mysterio's illusion), Avengers, SHIELD, FF & Wakanda's distress systems ⁞rev 4 bts), X-Men's comm system w/monitors, Forge's prosthetic leg (destroyed) & hand (bts), freight train (all in fb), Hawkeye's Spider-Mobile, ⁞wight's Ant-Man helmet, victims' cars (destroyed)
⁞LASHBACK: As Wolverine and Jubilee monitor sudden distress signals from heroes worldwide, the mansion wall explodes. Several villains ⁞our in and attack Wolverine, gloating that they have finally organized and risen up to eliminate the super heroes. Kitty Pryde evacuates the ⁞stitute students, wondering where the other X-Men are, as Wolverine savagely murders dozens of opponents. He battles Bullseye at length ⁞nd finally kills him, but "Bullseye's" corpse transforms into Jubilee. Mysterio appears and reveals that the "villains" were illusions that he cast ⁞ and Wolverine is horrified to see all the X-Men lying slaughtered at his feet. Mad with grief, Wolverine staggers into the woods and jams his ⁞ead under a speeding train's wheels, hoping to die.
⁞YNOPSIS: Logan tells Hawkeye how the X-Men died fifty years prior, and how he swore off the violent life of Wolverine. Driving on, they pay a ⁞mall toll to Dwight, a young boy with Ant-Man's helmet who threatens them with his swarm of ants. As they continue east, the Venom symbiote ⁞ossesses a roaming Tyrannosaurus rex and attacks…
⁞OTE: Cover-labeled "Old Man Logan." This issue also has three variant covers: a 2nd printing featuring interior art from pp.4 & 19, a 3rd ⁞rinting sketch variant, and a 4th printing that interlocks with reprint covers of W #66-69, '08-09.

WOLVERINE #71 [#260] (May 2009)

"Old Man Logan, Part 6" (23 pages)

CREDITS: Mark Millar (writer), Steve McNiven (pencils), Dexter Vines (inks), Virtual Calligraphy's Cory Petit (letters), Morry Hollowell (co-colors, c colors), Paul Mounts (co-colors), Irene Lee (production), Jody LeHeup (asst editor), John Barber (editor), Axel Alonso (group editor)
FEATURE CHARACTER: Logan (also on monitor)
GUEST STARS: Hawkeye (also on monitor, dies), Black Bolt (Blackagar Boltagon, elderly Inhuman with destructive voice), Emma Frost
VILLAINS: Venom symbiote (also merged with Tyrannosaurus rex, dies, also on monitor), Dr. Doom (ruler of section of Amerika), undercover SHIELD agents (also as rebels, 1st on-panel app, last bts in W #66, '08) inc Tobias, Red Skull's troops

⁞THER CHARACTERS: Giant-Man (dead, as skeleton), mutants, bystanders; Tyrannosaurus rex (also merged with Venom symbiote, also ⁞n monitor); Dormammu (mentioned, allied with other villains), Mandarin, Hawkeye's plant (prev 2 mentioned, played cards with Hawkeye ⁞ears ago), Emma Frost's husband (mentioned, married as a pact to spare mutants, see NOTE), Hawkeye's West Coast contacts (mentioned, ⁞iding rebels); Red Skull (as President, also as statue), Absorbing Man, Bullseye, Mr. Sinister, Sabretooth, Scorpion, Silver Samurai (prev 7 on ⁞illboards), heroes inc Captain America & Thor (prev 3 as statue)
⁞OCATIONS/ITEMS: Earth-807128: Illinois: Doom's Head (also on monitor) & Forbidden Quarter (mutant sanctuary, near Chicago); Osborn

County (Ohio, unclaimed territory, see NOTE); President's Quarter: Pym Falls (West Virginia, see NOTE) & New Babylon (formerly Washingto DC) inc "rebel hideout" / Hawkeye's earpiece (mentioned), Spider-Mobile w/Gatling gun & briefcase w/Super-Soldier serum, Forbidden Quarter cameras, teleporter, auto repair tools (prev 3 bts), computers & monitors, Black Bolt's walking stick, troops' guns & armor, Captain America shield, Thor's hammer (prev 2 as statue), SHIELD agents' guns & prosthetic arm

SYNOPSIS: Logan and Hawkeye flee the Venom-possessed dinosaur as their predicament is monitored from nearby. Suddenly, an aged Blac Bolt appears and uses his sonic powers to blast the symbiote off of the dinosaur. Logan and Hawkeye are teleported to the Forbidden Quarte where Emma Frost greets them. She explains that there are only 20 mutants remaining in the world, and most of them have taken shelter at he refuge. Hawkeye upbraids Emma for her traitorous marriage, but she defends her actions as necessary to save mutant lives. The two depa nearing the East Coast and driving underneath Giant-Man's enormous skeleton, and soon arrive at their destination: New Babylon. Hawkey reveals that his cargo was Super-Soldier serum, and takes Logan to meet underground rebels who plan to create new super heroes and retak the world. Hawkeye asks for a place on the proposed team, but the rebels suddenly gun down Logan, reveal themselves as undercover SHIEL agents, loyal to the Red Skull — and shoot Hawkeye in the head.

NOTE: Cover-labeled "Old Man Logan." This issue also has a 2nd printing variant cover featuring interior art from pp.1-2. Doom's Head is adde to the recap page map this issue. Two locations are named in-story differently than on the map: Osborn City is called Osborn County (though th two may be separate, the city existing within the county), and Pym Cross (incorrectly stated here as being in Connecticut) is called Pym Fall The man Emma married to spare mutant lives is not identified, but may be Dr. Doom.

WOLVERINE #72 [#261] (June 2009)

"Old Man Logan, Part 7" (27 pages)

CREDITS: Mark Millar (writer), Steve McNiven (pencils), Dexter Vines (co-ink c inks), Jay Leisten (co-inks), Virtual Calligraphy's Cory Petit (letters), Morr Hollowell (co-colors, c colors), Nathan Fairbairn & Paul Mounts (co-colors), Jaco Chabot (production), Jody LeHeup (asst editor), John Barber (editor), Axel Alons (group editor)

FEATURE CHARACTER: Logan (becomes Wolverine, next in W:OML, '09)
GUEST STAR: Captain America (James "Bucky" Barnes, dies off-panel in fb)
SUPPORTING CAST: Maureen, Scotty, Jade (all dead, last in W #66, '08; ne bts, dead, in W:OML, '09)
VILLAINS: Red Skull (President of Amerika, dies, also as statue, also in fb betwee W #70, '09 fb bts & this issue's main story), Hulk Gang (bts killing Logan's family, some or others last in W #66, '08; all next, some bts, in W:OML '09) inc Elrod Banner, Rufus Banner & Woody Banner (prev 3 unnamed), Heinz (Red Skull's aide), SHIELD agents (some die) inc Tobias

OTHER CHARACTERS: Beast, Nightcrawler (both last in W #70, '09 fb), Thing (last bts in W #70, '09 fb), Archangel, Vision (all dead, a body parts in trophy cases), Hawkeye (dead), Abe Donovan (Logan's neighbor, 1st on-panel app, last bts in W #66, '08, next in W:OML, '09 bystanders inc Silas; Redwing (Falcon's falcon, dead, stuffed); Abomination, Dr. Doom, Magneto (prev 3 mentioned in fb, plan to divide up USA Red Skull's wife (mentioned, thinks he is morbid); eagle (as Nazi logo)

LOCATIONS/ITEMS: Earth-807128: Capitol Building (destroyed in fb), New Babylon's White House w/trophy room, skies over Amerik California inc Logan's family farm / Silver Surfer's surfboard, Dr. Strange's Eye of Agomotto & Cloak of Levitation, Thor's helmet, Spider-Man mask & web-shooters, Daredevil's costume & billy club, Iron Man's armor sections, Captain America's costume & shields, Cyclops' ruby quar visor, Captain Marvel's costume & Nega-Bands, Nova's helmet & gauntlet, Ghost Rider's chain & leather jacket, Punisher's costume & gun Hulk's pants, Darkhold, Storm's tiara, Spider-Woman, Iron Fist & Black Panther's masks, Elektra's sais, Black Knight's Ebony Blade, Moo Knight's costume & throwing crescents, Sentry & Falcon's costumes, Fantastic Four's logo, Cloak's cloak, other heroes' objects (some part destroyed, all as Red Skull's trophies), Red Skull's sidearm (in fb) & trophy cases (destroyed), SHIELD agents' explosives, radios (prev bts), tarps, guns & armor, Hawkeye's briefcase w/Super-Soldier serum, Tobias' briefcase w/money, chair (destroyed), trophy room blast door (destroyed) w/automatic locks, Silas' cart, Logan's tractor

FLASHBACK: As Washington DC burns, a gloating Red Skull kills Captain America.

SYNOPSIS: As the Red Skull muses in his trophy room full of vanquished heroes' equipment, SHIELD agents deliver Hawkeye and Logan bodies. Red Skull tells the agents to keep the cash they lured Hawkeye with, but Logan suddenly awakens — breaking his pacifistic code an assaulting the Red Skull, who knocks him into a trophy case. Red Skull retrieves the Black Knight's sword, but Logan blocks his attack wi Captain America's shield — then angrily uses it to decapitate the villain. Logan grabs the cash and dons Iron Man's armor, then takes off an heads for California. The armor's power eventually dies 500 miles from home; Logan runs the rest of the way and finally arrives, bearing enoug money to save his family. However, he discovers that the Hulk Gang got bored, came back early — and slaughtered his wife and children. Starin at his family's bodies, Logan pops his claws for the first time in fifty years, and reclaims the name Wolverine.

NOTE: Cover-labeled "Old Man Logan." This issue also has a 2nd printing variant cover featuring interior art from p.11. Due to delays, this issu was published out of sequence, two weeks after W #73, '09. The "Old Man Logan" story arc concludes in W:OML, '09, where Elrod, Rufu and Woody Banner are named; other Hulk Gang members may have participated in this issue's attack, but they are not specifically identified.

RAMPAGING WOLVERINE (June 2009)

"Sense Memory" (22 pages)

CREDITS: Joshua Hale Fialkov (writer), Paco Diaz Luque (art), Dave Sharpe (letters), Michael Horwitz (ass editor), John Barber (editor), Nelson DeCastro (c art)

FEATURE CHARACTER: Wolverine (also in fb1 between Blade #5, '07 fb & L:PW, '96; next in W #73, '0 RamW/2, '09)

VILLAINS: Duck-Hwan (Chin-Mae's hired hand, dies, also in fb1 & fb2 prior to story), Chul-Moo (corrupt hote magnate, dies off-panel in fb1, also in fb2 during fb1) & his enforcers (in fb1, 1 dies), pirates (in fb1, some or a possibly die off-panel)

OTHER CHARACTERS: Chin-Mae Ho (Korean fisherman), Byung-Soon Ho (Chin-Mae's wife) (prev 2 die i fb1, also in fb2 during fb1), bartender, bar patrons inc soldiers (prev 3 in fb2); fish (some die, others dead), Chir

Mae's water buffalo, birds, monkeys (prev 4 in fb1); Dong-Sun Ho (Chin-Mae & Byung-Soon's son, mentioned in fb1, drowned), Madripoor's citizens (mentioned, benefited from Duck-Hwan's improvements); Buddha (as statue in fb1)

LOCATIONS/ITEMS: Madripoor inc beach (also in fb1), bar (in fb2) & Chin-Mae's house (destroyed in fb1 & fb2) w/nearby jungle (in fb1), South China Sea (in fb1), Duck-Hwan's university (mentioned in fb1) / Chul-Moo's sling (also in fb2), satchel & gun, pirates' swords, prosthetic hand, machine gun, abandoned Japanese war boat & rifles w/bayonets, buffalo's packs & leash, Byung-Soon's cloth, Chin-Mae's fishing net, enforcer's knife (all in fb1), Duck-Hwan's knife (in fb1) & ropes, Wolverine's shovel

FLASHBACKS: Shortly after WWII, Wolverine battles pirates near Madripoor. Shot, Wolverine falls into the ocean and washes ashore, where Korean fisherman Chin-Mae finds him. Wolverine heals and befriends Chin-Mae and his wife Byung-Soon; he helps Chin-Mae and his assistant Duck-Hwan fish, and finds great pleasure in the simple activity. When "land baron" Chul-Moo tries to intimidate Chin-Mae into selling his land, Wolverine attacks Chul-Moo — but the violence disturbs Chin-Mae, so Wolverine distances himself from his new friends. Later, he smells smoke, and rushes back to find Chin-Mae dead, and Chul-Moo's enforcers killing Byung-Soon. Wolverine kills Chul-Moo and mourns his friends. The pirates locate Wolverine and attack again, but are defeated (1). Duck-Hwan offers to lure Wolverine away so that Chul-Moo can talk to Chin-Mae, but instead Chul-Moo burns Chin-Mae's house down (2).

SYNOPSIS: Having regained his memories, Wolverine finds that Madripoor now reminds him of Chin-Mae and Byung-Soon's deaths. Seeking justice, Wolverine buries the now-elderly Duck-Hwan up to his neck at the beach, and waits for the tide to come in.

NOTE: This 48-page B&W one-shot mimics the style of Marvel's 1970s B&W magazines (and in particular, its title parodies "Rampaging Hulk"). It was followed by several similar one-shots: MKF, '09, IndIM, '09, MysDrS, '10 & SavAxe, '10. All four stories in this issue feature Wolverine on an island; the first three occur during W #73, '09. Wolverine regained his memories in HoM #8, '05. The monkeys seen in this story's fb may be Madripoorian spider-monkeys, wiped out in W #31-32, '90.

2ND STORY: "Unconfirmed Kill" (11 pages)

CREDITS: Chris Yost (writer), Mateus Santolouco (art), Troy Peteri (letters), Jody LeHeup (asst editor), John Barber (editor)

FEATURE CHARACTER: Wolverine

VILLAINS: Hydra agents (bts on island, some or others last in W #73, '09, next in SecWs #3, '09) & sniper (dies)

OTHER CHARACTERS: Espionage officials (bts asking Wolverine to investigate island, see NOTE); fishermen, spies, tourist, terrorists, seals, others (all mentioned, sniper's victims, die)

LOCATIONS/ITEMS: Hydra's Indian Ocean island (also on scope) w/secret base / Sniper's headset, handgun & rifle w/scope, X-Men's Blackbird jet (destroyed) w/fuel line (see NOTE), Wolverine's camera (bts, see NOTE), Hydra comm system (bts), sniper's knives, guns, explosives & hammer (prev 4 mentioned)

SYNOPSIS: A sniper guards the beach of Hydra's island base, following orders to shoot anything that approaches. He fires on a low-flying Blackbird jet, crashing it. The pilot staggers out of the wreckage, but the sniper shoots him. The sniper sees a man running up the beach; he shoots him as well, but when he sees a third man he realizes that, impossibly, they are all the same person. The sniper shoots the approaching man over and over, beginning to wonder if he is going crazy. Suddenly, the sniper hears something behind him — and turns to see Wolverine lunging at him, claws extended. Later, Wolverine salutes his slain foe's marksmanship.

NOTE: This issue's next story clarifies several points in this one: it explains that Wolverine was asked to investigate the Hydra base, reveals the island's Indian Ocean location, and specifies the presence of Wolverine's camera and the destruction of the Blackbird's fuel line. The project that Hydra is pursuing on the island is never revealed.

TEXT STORY: "Kiss, Kiss" (4 pages)

CREDITS: Robin Furth (writer), Nelson DeCastro (illustrations), John Barber (editor)

FEATURE CHARACTER: Wolverine (also in his own hallucination, next in W #73, '09, W:Anniv, '09)

VILLAIN: Bio-engineered mutant black widow spider (dies, also as Jean Grey in Wolverine's hallucination; others mentioned, destroyed decades ago)

OTHER CHARACTERS: SHIELD, AIM, Hydra & other agents (all dead), scientists, doctors; Hydra scientists (mentioned, created spiders decades ago), First Canadian Parachute Battalion officers (mentioned, gave mission briefings), espionage officials (mentioned, asked Wolverine to investigate island, see NOTE); bats, wildcats (prev 2 mentioned, left droppings in cave)

LOCATIONS/ITEMS: Hydra's Indian Ocean island w/cave, espionage base, Canadian army briefing room (mentioned), X-Mansion (in hallucination) / animal droppings, spider's webs, scientists' analysis equipment (bts), X-Men's Blackbird jet w/fuel line (destroyed) & cloaking device, Wolverine's camera, sniper's rifle, Hydra's biological engineering equipment (prev 6 mentioned)

SYNOPSIS: Wolverine, needing to heal after the sniper's attacks, sleeps in a cave. He seems to awaken in the X-Mansion, where Jean Grey gives him sharp, painful kisses. Wolverine shakes off a strange lethargy and realizes that he is actually suspended in webs, being stung with hallucinogenic venom by an enormous intelligent spider. Wolverine kills the creature and brings it back to his superiors, who confirm that it was the last survivor of a decades-old Hydra experiment.

NOTE: The espionage organization asking Wolverine to investigate the Hydra island is never named, but may be SHIELD. It is never specified whether or not Wolverine shut down the Hydra project alluded to in the previous story.

3RD STORY: "Modern Primitive" (11 pages)

CREDITS: Ted McKeever (writer, art, letters), Jody LeHeup (asst editor), John Barber (editor)

FEATURE CHARACTER: Wolverine (chr last in W/Pun #5, '04, chr next in W:ONO, '09)

GUEST STAR: Nightcrawler (chr last in XMU #7, '04, chr next in UXM #444, '04)

VILLAIN: Sauron (bts battling Wolverine in midair, chr last in WX #18, '04, chr next bts in NAv #1, '05, chr next in NAv #2, '05)

OTHER CHARACTERS: Wild boar (dead), monkeys (1 dies)

LOCATIONS/ITEMS: Island w/cave / X-Men's Blackbird jet

SYNOPSIS: After shredding Sauron's wing during an aerial battle, Wolverine plummets from the sky onto a small island. After several days of surviving on his own, killing a boar for food, Wolverine spots a group of curious monkeys staring at him from afar. Days later, the monkeys return, but the largest of the group challenges and attacks Wolverine. The monkey bites a large chunk off of Wolverine's arm, but Wolverine soon slices the animal to pieces, and the other monkeys consider Wolverine their new leader. Nightcrawler finally shows up in a jet to rescue Wolverine, who debates bringing the monkeys home with him.

NOTE: This story occurs shortly prior to the X-Men's 2004 revamp, as Wolverine is still wearing his leather X-jacket here.

WOLVERINE: THE ANNIVERSARY (June 2009)

"The Anniversary" (23 pages)

CREDITS: William Harms (writer), Jefte Palo (art), Virtual Calligraphy's Joe Caramagna (letters, uncredited), Lee Loughridge (colors), Sebastian Girner (asst editor), Axel Alonso (editor), Simone Bianchi (c pencils), Andrea Silvestri (c inks), Simone Peruzzi (c colors)
FEATURE CHARACTER: Wolverine (also in his own dream, also in W #73, '09)
VILLAINS: Holy War Brigade (Japanese terrorist group, some or others also bts attacking power plant, train & resort): Masaru (Brigade leader, dies) & his bodyguards (some or all die) inc Isamu, hijackers (also as flight attendants, die) inc Cosby & Shin
OTHER CHARACTERS: Judy (flight attendant, dies), delivery man, airplane pilots, air marshal (prev 2 die) & passengers, air traffic control employees (bts on radio); Masaru's crested ibis; Mexican tourist (dead), New York commuters (prev 2 in photos); others mentioned, killed by terrorists, Chinese conservationists (mentioned, care for ibises), Shin's family (mentioned, ordered killed by Masaru); Guantanamo Bay prisoners (mentioned, release demanded by Masaru); Mariko Yashida (as herself & corpse in Wolverine's dream); Japanese demon (as statue)
LOCATIONS/ITEMS: Masaru's home (outside Tokyo), skies above Pacific Ocean, air traffic control center (bts), power plant (destroyed), New York commuter train route, Mexican resort (prev 3 mentioned), Japanese field (in dream); Honolulu, Hawaii; Guantanamo Bay Naval Base, Cuba (prev 2 mentioned) / Delivery truck, bodyguards' guns, Masaru's cellphone, newspapers & swords, ibis' cage, blowfish toxin (bts in dream), Flight 319 (Pac-Air jumbo jet) w/cargo (some destroyed), windshield, bathroom floor (prev 2 destroyed), weight sensors, support beams (prev 2 bts), speaker system & oxygen masks, Shin's headset, knife, cellular phone, emergency insulin box & bomb w/timer & heart monitor, hijackers' headsets, guns & knives, pilot's headset, air traffic control comm system (bts)
SYNOPSIS: Affluent terrorist leader Masaru enjoys his recent purchase of a rare crested ibis. On an airplane to Japan, Wolverine dreams of Mariko. Shin and his fellow hijackers rise up, kill the pilots and overtake the plane. Shin takes over flying the plane and activates a bomb that is attuned to his heartbeat. Via telephone, Masaru demands that the US release all Guantanamo Bay prisoners. Wolverine challenges a hijacker and is shot; he is dumped in the back hallway, where he slices a hole into the cargo bay and cuts several crates loose, destabilizing the plane's flight. Wolverine then climbs around the plane's exterior to the cockpit, smashes through the window, grabs Shin and throws him out; the bomb explodes harmlessly in midair. Wolverine kills the other hijackers, then picks up Shin's phone and listens to Masaru. Days later, Wolverine attacks Masaru at his home. He explains that he heard the ibis squawk over the phone and simply tracked down the endangered bird's owner, then kills Masaru.
NOTE: Both stories in this issue occur during Wolverine's trip to Japan in W #73, '09. This issue's subtitle is misspelled "Anniversay" in the indicia. Despite the subtitle's implication, this issue does not occur on the anniversary of Mariko's death, which occurred in W #57, '92. It may occur on another significant date, such as the anniversary of Wolverine and Mariko's first meeting, first date or planned wedding. Letterer Joe Caramagna, uncredited here, receives credit when this story is reprinted in the "Wolverine: Flies to a Spider" TPB, '09.

2ND STORY: "Ghosts" (8 pages)
CREDITS: Jonathan Maberry (writer), Tomm Coker (art), Virtual Calligraphy's Joe Caramagna (letters), Daniel Freedman (colors), Sebastian Girner (asst editor), Axel Alonso (editor)
FEATURE CHARACTER: Wolverine (also in his own dream, next in W #73, '09)
VILLAINS: Ninjas (die)
OTHER CHARACTERS: Mariko Yashida (dies in Wolverine's dream); cartoon animal (on billboard)
LOCATIONS/ITEMS: Wolverine's Japanese room w/nearby rooftop, Japanese field (in dream) / Blowfish toxin (bts in dream), ninjas' swords (1 destroyed), scythe & throwing stars, room window (destroyed)
SYNOPSIS: Wolverine once again dreams of killing Mariko, but this time she warns him to wake up. Wolverine does so, and finds himself menaced by ninjas. Unsure how Mariko could have warned him, Wolverine wonders if his attackers are ghosts as well, possibly men he has killed, seeking revenge. He battles the ninjas, thinking about simply giving up, letting himself be killed and finally rejoining Mariko — but ultimately he decides to fight on, and defeats his attackers.

FREE COMIC BOOK DAY: WOLVERINE — ORIGIN OF AN X-MAN (May 2009)

"Kingdom of No" (22 pages)

CREDITS: Fred Van Lente (writer), Gurihiru (art, colors), Dave Sharpe (letters), Anthony Dial (production), Ralph Macchio (consulting), Nathan Cosby (editor), Ed McGuinness (c pencils), Mark Farmer (c inks), Justin Ponsor (c colors)
FEATURE CHARACTER: Wolverine (also in photos & on scope, also in rfb, chr last in AFlt #-1, '97, also in W #9, '89 fb bts, BFF:Ben #1-3, '00, W #13, '11 fb, W #119-121, 119, 121 & 126, '97-98 fbs, SM/W #2, '03 fb, W/Cable, '99, Fury, '94, AFlt #52, '87 fb, X #14, '11 fb, AFlt Spec, '92, MCP #51, '90 fb, AFlt #127/2, '94 fb, W #9, '89 fb, W/NF:SC, '89 fb, UXM #228, '88 fb, AFlt #9/2, '84 & W #144, '99 fb, chr next in W:O #28, '08 fb)
GUEST STAR: James Hudson (during AFlt #3/2, '83, also in W/Cable, '99, AFlt #52, '87 fbs, AFlt #8/2, '84, AFlt Spec, '92, AFlt #127/2, '93 fb & W #144, '99 fb)
OTHER CHARACTERS: Madison Jeffries (chr last in AFlt #30, '86 fb, chr next bts in AFlt #1, '83, chr next in AFlt #16, '84), Dept. H doctor & officials (1 or another also voice only on loudspeaker) inc Admiral, Defence Ministry commandos (also in photos & as knights) & pilot, Harbordale residents; squirrel (prev 2 as living dioramas), Madison's seahorse (destroyed) & scarab robots; Wolverine's sparring partner (in photo); bomber squadron (mentioned, suggested as alternative attack), Dept. H psychiatrists (mentioned, unable to jog Wolverine's memory), Royal Air Force paratroopers (mentioned, trained Wolverine); Hulk, Wendigo (prev 2 in rfb)
LOCATIONS/ITEMS: Canada inc Dept. H headquarters (also in photos), North Woods (in rfb) & Harbordale, New Brunswick w/Madison's auto body shop / James' paperwork, photos, parachute & slide projector, iron bars (destroyed), guns (prev 2 in photos), Defence Ministry bombers (mentioned) & troop transport plane, Wolverine's book on brain functions, pilot's headset, car (destroyed), Madison's assimilated metallic plating, Convergence Zone vat & construction robots w/sensors & restraint cables, lovers' car, hockey players' sticks, knights' armor, sword, spear & axe (prev 6 as metallic plating), doctor's stethoscope, Dept. H speaker system (bts) w/microphone

FLASHBACK: Wolverine attacks the Hulk and Wendigo (IHulk #181, '74).

SYNOPSIS: James Hudson pitches Dept. H's new superhuman agent, Wolverine, to the program's military backers, who just lost three commandos to a crisis. Later, as Wolverine reads a book about the brain in hopes of understanding his amnesia, James briefs him on the crisis: Harbordale is being slowly coated with metal. Wolverine arrives; robotic scarabs sense his Adamantium and summon a large trucklike robot, which captures Wolverine. The robot carries Wolverine past metallic dioramas of boyhood memories and begins dipping him into a tank of metal coating, but Wolverine breaks free. He discovers and destroys a robotic seahorse, then follows a thin energy trail to semi-conscious mutant Madison Jeffries. Defeating three "knights," actually the metal-coated commandos, Wolverine awakens Madison, halting the robots. Later, Wolverine explains that the brain book taught him that the seahorse represented memory centers. James theorizes that Madison lost control of his power after wartime stress, and subconsciously recreated childhood memories out of metal. Years later, Dept. H summons Wolverine to battle the Hulk…

NOTE: This one-shot, published at slightly reduced dimensions, was produced for Free Comic Book Day, a yearly industry event where publishers create special issues that comic stores give away for free. Although the bulk of this issue takes place soon after FF #1, '61 and details Wolverine's first official Dept. H mission, the final page takes place years later, just before IHulk #180, '74. Unlike most Marvel comics, whose publication dates are two months ahead of their on-sale dates, this issue's publication date and on-sale date match: the issue was released in May 2009, along with other Marvel books dated July 2009.

WOLVERINE

WOLVERINE #73 [#262] (July 2009)

"A Mile In My Moccasins, Part One" (11 pages)

CREDITS: Jason Aaron (writer), Adam Kubert (pencils), Mark Farmer (inks), Virtual Calligraphy's Cory Petit (letters), Justin Ponsor (colors), Jody LeHeup (asst editor), John Barber (editor, uncredited), Axel Alonso (group editor, uncredited), Marko Djurdjevic (variant c art)

FEATURE CHARACTER: Wolverine (also in RamW/1-2 & /text, '09, W:Anniv/1-2, '09; next in AT:WPun #1-6, '08-09, UXM #508, '09, MDigHol, '08; XFor #12, W:Flies, W #74/2, all '09)

GUEST STARS: Avengers: Luke Cage (next in Time #1, '09), Captain America (James "Bucky" Barnes, next in W #74/2, '09), Ronin (Clint Barton, archer & martial artist, next in DR:NN/5, '09), Spider-Man (chr last in MsM #34, '09 fb, next in ASMFam #3/4, '09) (all last in AoAtlas #5, '09), Spider-Woman (Jessica Drew, last in Av:FCBD, '09), X-Force (Cyclops' black ops strike team): Archangel (last in YX #7, '08, last bts in XInf #1, '09), Domino (Neena Thurman, manipulates probability, last in XFor #11, '09) (prev 2 next in UXM #508, '09), Warpath (James Proudstar, enhanced strength & senses, last in UXM #506, '09, next in MDigHol, '08); X-Men: Cyclops (last in XInf #4, '09, next in MDigHol, '08), Iceman (last in X:MD #3/3, '09, next in UXM #508, '09), Deadpool (last in Dp #7, '09, next in MsM #40, '09), Gambit (last in X:L #214, '08, next in X:L #220, '09), Ghost Rider (John Blaze, Spirit of Vengeance's mortal host, last in XFor #10, '09, chr next in GR #26, '08, next in GR #35, '09), Punisher (last in PWJ #25, '09, chr next in AT:WPun #1, '08, next in GR #32, '09), Thing (last in MAv #21, '09, next in FF #564, '09), She-Hulk (last in IHulk #600, '09, next in Thor #11, '08, next in Thor #602, '09) (prev 2 last in MAv #23, '09)

SUPPORTING CAST: Yukio (last in W:Soul #5, '05, next in Psy #2, '10)

VILLAINS: Serpent Society (cabal of snake-themed villains): Black Mamba (Tanya Sealy, Darkforce control & telepathy, next in Av:In #26, '09), Anaconda (prev 2 last in Nova #19, '09), Bushmaster (Quincy McIver, prosthetic arms & snakelike lower torso, last in PWJ #15, '08) (prev 2 next in X:TS&P #2, '11), Cottonmouth (Burchell Clemens, extendible jaw & neck, last in AmE:Just, '08, next in BScars #3, '12), others (exact members unknown, bts in ships, team last in Nova #19, '09, next in X:TS&P #2, '11); Absorbing Man (last in SH #23, '08, next in DR:LL #1, '09 fb), Black Talon (Samuel Barone, controls zombies, last in U #5, '06, last in MZ4 #1, '09), Cyber (last in W:O #32, '09, possibly next as spirit in W #2, '10, see W #122, '98's NOTE), Cyttorak (bts empowering Juggernaut, last in CB&MI13 #3, '08, last bts in X:L #219, '09, next bts in IHulk #602, '09, next in UXM #542, '11), Juggernaut (last in X:L #219, '09, next in IHulk #602, '09), Mystique (last in X:MD #5, '09, next in DXM #3/2, '09), Purifiers (anti-mutant religious zealots, some or all die, some or others last in XFor:Aint, '08, next bts in X:SC #1, '10, next in UXM #523, '10), Red Hulk (Thaddeus "Thunderbolt" Ross, gamma-fueled powerhouse, last in Hulk #12, '09, next in IHulk #600, '09), clones of MODOK (some or others next in FoH:RH #1, '10), Hydra agents (some or others last in Av:In #24, '09, next in RamW/2, '09), Hellfire Club soldier (dies, some or others last in X:L #217, '08, others in XNec, '09), Asgardian giant, bank robbers, Wolverine's assailants inc demon-masked villains (dead) & pyrokinetic

OTHER CHARACTERS: Zarathos (Spirit of Vengeance, last in XFor #10, '09, chr next in GR #26, '08, next in GR #35, '09), zombies (some or all destroyed), policeman, Golden Grasshopper & Golden Grizzly patrons, bank employees & patrons, card-playing hero, reporter (voice only on TV), bar patrons, Bangkok & Tokyo bystanders; "Dark" Avengers (on TV, 1 bts): "Captain Marvel" (Marvel Boy), "Hawkeye" (Bullseye), Iron Patriot (Green Goblin), "Ms. Marvel" (Moonstone), "Spider-Man" (Venom), "Wolverine" (Daken), Ares, Sentry; Happy Samurais, cartoon characters inc octopus (prev 3 on billboards), grasshopper, bear (prev 2 on bar signs), snakes (as Black Mamba's costume decorations)

LOCATIONS/ITEMS: San Francisco, Golden Grasshopper (Bangkok, Thailand bar), Golden Grizzly (northern Siberia bar), deserts, bank, gas station, bar, jungle, torturer's hideout, Japan inc Zen garden, temple & Yukio's Tokyo apartment (Shinjuku District), various battle locations, poker game location / Police nightstick & gun, Wolverine's glass (destroyed), newspaper, motorcycle & X-Force costume, San Francisco trolley, Spider-Woman's web-shooters (see NOTE), Ronin, Black Talon, Deadpool & assailant's swords, Captain America's shield, Ghost Rider's chain & flaming motorcycle (prev 3 hereinafter considered their standard equipment and not listed separately), Bushmaster's cybernetic limbs & lower body, Serpent Society's ships, Punisher, Domino, Hydra, Deadpool & assailants' guns, Warpath's Vibranium knives, cars, truck (prev 2 destroyed), Mystique's flamethrower, robbers' shotguns (1 destroyed), Cyber's Carbonadium pacemaker (bts), MODOK clones' anti-grav chairs, heroes' cards & chips, bar TVs, pool tables, balls & cues, assailants' bomb & masks, Absorbing Man's ball & chain, torturer's battery (bts), cables & bonds, torn cloth, Yukio's sword

SYNOPSIS: Wolverine lives a breakneck life, fighting a new battle nearly every day. He fights Juggernaut, the Serpent Society with the Avengers, Black Talon with Ghost Rider and Punisher, Purifiers with X-Force, Mystique with Cyclops and Hydra with Spider-Man, then relaxes in a Bangkok bar. The next week, Wolverine stops bank robbers with Iceman, battles Cyber, fights MODOK clones with Deadpool, then relaxes in a Siberia bar.

The next week, Wolverine fights a giant with Thor, battles Red Hulk, plays cards with other heroes, sees reports of Daken posing as him, stab a Hellfire Club soldier, then meditates in Japan. The next week, Wolverine is shot, stabbed, blown up, attacked by the Absorbing Man, set on fire and electrocuted. Wolverine sleeps after a fight; she tries to talk about his constant battles, but he leaves to continue adventuring.
NOTE: This issue also has a 70th anniversary variant cover and a 2nd printing featuring interior art from pp.2-3 & 6-7. Part 2 of this arc appear in W #74/2, '09, though that story does not occur directly after this one. Wolverine's appearances in RamW/1-2 & /text, '09 & W:Anniv/1-2, '0 weave in and out of this story's globetrotting events. Cottonmouth's real name is revealed in OHMU HC10, '09. Red Hulk's identity is reveale in Hulk #22, '10. In addition to being an X-Man and Avenger, Wolverine has been the leader of the new X-Force, a secret team that proactivel eliminates threats to mutantkind, since UXM #493, '08. James Barnes, formerly Bucky and the Winter Soldier, became Captain America in Ca #34, '08 after Steve Rogers' seeming assassination in Cap #25, '07. The "live report" unveiling Norman Osborn's Avengers, including Dake posing as Wolverine, must be a recording; Wolverine already saw the report in W:O #33, '09. Spider-Woman uses web-shooters here; she may have borrowed them from Avengers teammate Spider-Man.

2ND STORY: "One-Percenter, Part One" (11 pages)
CREDITS: Daniel Way (writer), Tommy Lee Edwards (art, colors), John Workman (letters), Jody LeHeup (asst editor), John Barber (editor) Axel Alonso (group editor, uncredited)
FEATURE CHARACTER: Wolverine (also as "Mr. Claremont," chr last in DR:Elek #5, '09, also in dfb following this story)
VILLAIN: Ram (Burning Sons' co-leader)
OTHER CHARACTERS: Burning Sons (biker gang) inc Horrorshow (Henry McLaury, also bts in dfb following this story), Warhorse (prev co-leaders), Hotbox & Level (prev 2 bts, killed), Dennis (policeman), Shelly (Horrorshow's ex-wife, dies), New Saints (rival biker gang): Henry McLaury Jr. ("Junior," Horrorshow's younger son), heroin cooker (dead) (prev 3 in pfb); Level's girlfriend (dies), strip club dancers, patrons & bartender; birds; Daken (mentioned, Wolverine couldn't see him), Eric McLaury (Horrorshow's older son, mentioned, died), Level's girlfriend' mother (mentioned, girlfriend staying with her), state troopers (mentioned, beaten by Horrorshow), soldier (in silhouette on flag), people (in photos); woman (as neon decoration)
LOCATIONS/ITEMS: Desert highway, Horrorshow's home & strip club, cooker's home (in pfb), Level's girlfriend's mother's house w/nearby street, San Francisco, New York (prev 2 mentioned) / Wolverine's motorcycle & fake ID, police car, Burning Sons' motorcycles, cooker's heroin shotgun & drug processing equipment (prev 3 in pfb), Ram's gun, motorcycle & New Saints jacket
FLASHBACKS: Shelly overdoses and dies, and her lover, the New Saints' "cooker," kills himself out of grief (p). Wolverine asks Horrorshow fo Henry Jr.'s location (d, see NOTE).
SYNOPSIS: Riding through the desert on his motorcycle, Wolverine runs into the Burning Sons, led by his old friend Horrorshow. The two catch up; Horrorshow explains that he made the Sons give up drugs, but his wife left him and took their son, Henry Jr., who now rides with rival gang the New Saints. Ram bursts in, announcing that Henry Jr. just killed two Sons, but Horrorshow refuses to retaliate until he investigates. Ram challenges Horrorshow, but ultimately backs down. Wolverine promises to look into the situation, and visits one of the dead Sons' girlfriends; she asks if Ram sent him — but is suddenly shot by a biker wearing the New Saints logo.
NOTE: Next issue completes both stories begun in this issue, but reverses their order: part 2 of this arc appears in W #74, '09's first story. "One percenters" are biker gang members. Wolverine's alias here is likely a nod to longtime X-Men writer Chris Claremont. This issue's dfb is an "audi only" flashback; it is three word balloons with no visual component. This is the first story in the series since W #92, '95 to use hand lettering.

WOLVERINE #74 [#263] (August 2009)

"One-Percenter, Part Two" (11 pages)

CREDITS: Daniel Way (writer), Tommy Lee Edwards (art, colors), John Workman (letters), Jody LeHeup (ass editor), John Barber (editor), Axel Alonso (group editor, uncredited)
FEATURE CHARACTER: Wolverine (also in pfb, chr next in UXM #509, '09)
VILLAIN: Ram (dies)
OTHER CHARACTERS: Burning Sons inc Horrorshow & Warhorse, Henry McLaury Jr. (in pfb), Level's girlfriend (dead), police, paramedic; police dogs; Daken (mentioned in pfb, refused Wolverine's help), Leve (mentioned in pfb, hooked on drugs)
LOCATIONS/ITEMS: Level's girlfriend's mother's house, Horrorshow's strip club, underpass (in pfb), woods gas station w/bathroom / Police car, gun, nightstick & caution tape, Horrorshow's gun, Junior's ropes (destroyed in pfb), Ram's heroin (mentioned in pfb), Wolverine's motorcycle

FLASHBACK: Wolverine captures Henry Jr., who denies the murders, but reveals that he supplies Ram with drugs. Wolverine realizes tha Ram wants to return the Burning Sons to drug-running — so he framed Henry, hoping that Horrorshow would balk at waging war on his son and be deposed. Wolverine orders Henry to leave town, and decides to fake his death (p).
SYNOPSIS: Ram tells Horrorshow that Henry Jr. killed Level's girlfriend, pressing him to declare war on the New Saints — but Wolverine claims that there is no need, as Henry is dead. Assuming that Wolverine killed his son, Horrorshow becomes enraged and shoots him Wolverine awakens later in the woods and hears police approaching. Wolverine deduces that Ram wanted the authorities to find a corpse with Horrorshow's bullets in it, to frame him for murder. Wolverine tracks down Ram and kills him.
NOTE: The New Saints are incorrectly called the "New Sons" here. This is the last story in the series to use hand lettering.

2ND STORY: "A Mile In My Moccasins, Part Two" (11 pages)
CREDITS: Jason Aaron (writer), Adam Kubert (pencils, inks pp.4-5), Mark Farmer (inks pp.1-3 & 6-11), Virtual Calligraphy's Cory Petit (letters) Edgar Delgado, Morry Hollowell & Paul Mounts (colors), Jody LeHeup (asst editor), John Barber (editor), Axel Alonso (group editor)
FEATURE CHARACTER: Wolverine (next in ASME #2/2, '09, PlSkaar, Time #1-2, Time:X, Time #3-4, all '09, WWHs:C/W #1, '10 fb; MsM #40-43 Cap #50, DR:Elek #4-5, W #73/2 & 74, UXM #509-511, Et #7-8 & 9 fb, Run #10, all '09, W:MrX, '10, W:Rev, '09)
GUEST STARS: Avengers: Captain America (last in W #73, '09, chr next in Cap #43, '08, next in MsM #41, '09), Spider-Man (last in Bahia, '09 next in ASME #2/2, '09); Cyclops (bts on phone, last in XFor #12, '09, next in UXM #509, '09)
VILLAINS: Wrecking Crew: Piledriver (Brian Calusky, magically enhanced strength), Thunderball, Wrecker (all last in NAv #50, '09, next i DR:Hood #1, '09); Cyclops & Wolverine's foes (bts, described by reporter), anti-mutant gang (bts, killed by Wolverine), would-be robbers
OTHER CHARACTERS: Earl (Ronson's bartender), reporters (1 voice only on TV), cameraman, police (bts investigating gang's death)

onson's Bar patrons, bystanders; fly, pigeons; Firelord, Hulk, Juggernaut (prev 3 mentioned, fought Spider-Man), Beyonder (mentioned, made oor fashion choices); Happy Samurais (on poster), people (in photo); "Dark" Avengers: Ares, Iron Patriot, "Ms. Marvel," Sentry, "Spider-Man," "Wolverine" (prev 6 next issue page only, see NOTE)

OCATIONS/ITEMS: Rooftop, Spider-Man's apartment, gang's hideout, Ronson's Bar w/nearby street / Wrecker's crowbar, Thunderball's ball chain, Captain America's gun, Spider-Man's camera, reporter's microphone & camera, patrons' motorcycles, pool table, balls & cues, bar nenu, Wolverine's costumes (mentioned), robbers' shotguns (destroyed)

YNOPSIS: Wolverine, Spider-Man and Captain America fight the Wrecking Crew. Over the next week, Spider-Man hears reports of Wolverine's near-constant heroics, and becomes concerned. Spider-Man finds Wolverine in a bar and tries to talk to him, pointing out that his onstop fighting is unhealthy, runs him ragged and may get him killed. Wolverine loses his temper and tries to throw Spider-Man out of the bar. lobbers suddenly burst in, but panic when they see an angry Spider-Man and Wolverine staring them down and are quickly defeated. Wolverine idmits that Spider-Man is right: ever since he regained his memories, he has been tormented by all the horrible things he has done, and the nly way to make up for them and avoid dwelling on them is to play hero every waking minute. Wolverine thanks Spider-Man and trudges off to the night.

IOTE: The recap page gives this story's title as "A Mile In My Moccasins, Part 2 of 2." This is the last issue of this series in its current form; the eries changes its title to "Dark Wolverine" with #75, '09, and switches focus to Wolverine's son Daken, who joined Norman Osborn's villainous vengers team in DAv #1, '09, publicly adopting Wolverine's codename and brown costume to annoy his father. The DW series continues until 90, '10; as this Index will not be covering the revamped series, the characters shown on the "next issue" page are listed here. Wolverine's solo dventures continue in his ongoing stream of one-shots and the spinoffs W:O, '06-10 and W:WX, '09-10.

WOLVERINE: REVOLVER (August 2009)

"Revolver" (22 pages)

CREDITS: Victor Gischler (writer), Das Pastoras (art, colors), Virtual Calligraphy's Joe Caramagna (letters), Sebastian Girner (asst editor), Axel Alonso (editor)
FEATURE CHARACTER: Wolverine (next in DR:Elek #5, FF #569, IHulk #601-603, ASM #595, NAv #51-54, ASM #600 & 601/2, all '09, SW #7, '10, AX #31-35, '09-10, AX:Xeno #1-5, '10-11, W:WX #1, '09)
VILLAINS: Russian mobsters (die), shapeshifting demon (also as human)
OTHER CHARACTERS: Russian Roulette competitor (dies) & audience (some or all die); shady characters (mentioned, interrogated by Wolverine), Native American medicine man (chief's brother, mentioned, told Wolverine about demon), tribal chief & members (prev 2 mentioned, killed by demon)
LOCATIONS/ITEMS: Underground betting parlor (Las Vegas), southwestern US inc canyons & cave, Oklahoma, Native American reservation (prev 2 mentioned) / Russian Roulette revolver w/bullets, audience's noney, mobsters' guns, Wolverine's sacks, shovel & Jeep

YNOPSIS: Wolverine attends a mob-run Russian Roulette tournament. The champion is extremely calm; the challenger shoots himself in ne head to the audience's delight. The mobster calls for the next participant; Wolverine stands up, but asks that the gun be loaded with two ullets, not just one. The champion agrees and the game begins; Wolverine shoots himself, but staggers to his feet and demands that the game ontinue. As the shocked audience watches, the champion shoots himself in the head — but he does not die either. The champion transforms ito a demon; the mobsters attack but are all killed. Wolverine explains that he tracked the demon down after it recently killed a tribal chief. he two fight; Wolverine severs the demon's arm, but it reattaches the limb easily. Wolverine cuts the demon into several different pieces and eparates them. He then takes a cross-country drive, tossing the demon's body parts into various canyons. The demon's head begs for mercy, ut Wolverine leaves it in a cave, facing the wall.

IOTE: This issue's story is preceded by a title/credits page.

WOLVERINE: WEAPON X #1 [#264] (June 2009)

"The Adamantium Men, Part 1 of 5" (22 pages)

CREDITS: Jason Aaron (writer), Ron Garney (art), Virtual Calligraphy's Cory Petit (letters), Jason Keith (colors), Jody LeHeup (asst editor), John Barber (editor), Axel Alonso (group editor), Adam Kubert (variant c art A), Olivier Coipel (variant c art B), Alan Davis (variant c pencils C), Mark Farmer (variant c inks C), Justin Ponsor (variant c colors A & B), Rob Schwager (variant c colors C)
FEATURE CHARACTER: Wolverine (also in photo & rfb1, also as Experiment X in rfb2)
SUPPORTING CAST: Maverick (also in rfb1, last in W:O #8, '07, next in W:WX #3, '09), Melita Garner (San Francisco Post reporter, 1st)
VILLAINS: Strikeforce X (Blackguard's enhanced black ops squad, 1st, unnamed, some bts off-panel) inc Binderup, Comfort, Klein, Overfield, Pierce, Pottratz & Sever (prev 7 unnamed), muggers
OTHER CHARACTERS: Colombian protesters (die) & villagers (some die, some dead) inc Alvaro (dies off-panel), Roxxon miners (bts mining coal), subway conductor (bts driving train), commuters; scorpion (dies), dogs (dead), parrots, ants, birds;

Grecian (mentioned, unnamed, sold Blackguard plans), Blackguard's Chief Executive (mentioned unnamed, bought Weapon X files) & scientis (mentioned, created Strikeforce X), Maverick's moth (mentioned as taunt); bushmasters, anacondas, frog killer bees, parasitic catfish (prev 5 mentioned, li in jungle), fish (mentioned, dead, studied by Melit wolves (in rfb2, some die); X-Men: Beast, Colossu Cyclops, Emma Frost, Storm (prev 5 in phot mythological figures (as statues), angel (on playi card), person (in advertisement)

LOCATIONS/ITEMS: Colombia jungle inc villa (near Magdalena River), Roxxon's Cerrejón co mine (mentioned) & protesters' temple hideout, S Francisco docks & subway system inc Civic Center station, Blackguard's research facility (Washington, along US/Canadian border), East Ber (in rfb1), Weapon X Program facility (in rfb2) / Villager's stick, Alvaro's branch, bananas & machete, Strikeforce X's Adamantium skeletor healing nanites (prev 2 bts), laser claws (prev 3 hereinafter considered their standard equipment and not listed separately), guns, grena & playing card, protesters' guns, knife & newspaper clippings, bystander's newspaper, BART subway train, Melita's purse & phone, mugge guns, Maverick's Blackguard paperwork, Weapon X Program's files (mentioned) & Genesis tank (in rfb2) w/Adamantium feed tubes, Wolveri & Maverick's guns & body armor (in rfb1), Blackguard's Genesis Tanks

FLASHBACKS: Wolverine and Maverick perform espionage (X #5, '92 fb). Experiment X kills wolves (MCP #77, '91) and has Adamantiu bonded to his bones (MCP #73, '91).

SYNOPSIS: In Colombia, a villager returns home to find his friends and neighbors slaughtered, and is ambushed by a soldier. Near protesters plan violent strikes against Roxxon's Colombian coal mine. The villager staggers in and coughs up a grenade, which explode Several protesters flee, but soldiers shoots them; the sole survivor is impaled by green glowing laser claws similar to Wolverine's. In S Francisco, muggers confront reporter Melita Garner on the subway; she gives them her purse but refuses to relinquish her phone. Wolveri asleep on a nearby seat, awakens and quickly defeats the muggers. Melita introduces herself, but Wolverine is disinterested. He later mee with Maverick, who reveals that military contractor Blackguard, a Roxxon subsidiary, has somehow obtained the old Weapon X Program's Determined to keep anyone from restarting the program, Wolverine tracks down Blackguard's research facility. It is abandoned — but Wolveri discovers a dozen empty Adamantium bonding tanks.

NOTE: Although the W:WX, '09-10 series, launched between W #71-72, '09, was originally a spinoff, it became the de facto "main" Wolveri title when the regular series became DW with #75, '09. The bracketed secondary numbering continues on this title; its 16 issues were includ when Marvel renumbered the regular series with W #300, '12. This issue also has seven variant covers: regular and sketch editions of "varia A" by Adam Kubert, "variant B" by Olivier Coipel, "variant C" by Alan Davis, a Hero Initiative blank variant, a Dynamic Forces "virgin variant" w the trade dress removed (but run on the back cover over an identical image), and a 2nd printing featuring interior art from W:WX #2, '09 p.10 Dynamic Forces "negative virgin variant," featuring an inverted color scheme and signed by artist Ron Garney, was solicited but never release W:WX #1-15, '09-10 & DRL:W, '09's recap pages use background art featuring Experiment X and Wranglers, taken from MCP #81, '91 p drawn by Barry Windsor-Smith and recolored by Richard Isanove for the cover of W:WX HC, '07. This issue also reprints two Official Handbo profiles: OHMU HC6, '09's Maverick (Nord) entry (2 pages), and OHMU:W, '04's Weapon X Program entry (3 pages). This issue also has 6-page preview of GRs #1, '09. Strikeforce X's Adamantium skeletons are confirmed, and their healing nanites revealed, next issue. W:WX # '09 names Strikeforce X, Binderup, Comfort, Klein, Overfield and Pottratz, and reveals the Chief Executive's title. Pierce and Sever are nam in W&X #16, '12. Grecian's name and involvement in selling Weapon X's files are revealed in W:WX #5, '09. Maverick, depowered on M-D mentions here that he has also lost the acid-generating power that the new Weapon X Program gave him in WXD:AZ, '02. Wolverine wears X-Force costume in this story arc.

WOLVERINE: WEAPON X #2 [#265] (July 2009)

"The Adamantium Men, Part 2 of 5" (22 pages)

CREDITS: Jason Aaron (writer), Ron Garney (art), Virtual Calligraphy's Cory Pe (letters), Jason Keith (colors), Jody LeHeup (asst editor), John Barber (editor), A Alonso (group editor), Marko Djurdjevic (variant c art)
FEATURE CHARACTER: Wolverine (also in photos)
GUEST STARS: Sons of the Tiger: Abe Brown (next in DW #90, '10), B Diamond (next bts in DW #90, '10, next in W #5.1, '11), Lin Sun (next in W:WX #1 '10) (all bts, interviewed about dropping crime rates, last in W:MD #4, '09)
SUPPORTING CAST: Melita Garner
VILLAINS: Iron Patriot (bts making speech to American Legion, last in DAv #6, 'C next in DR:GL, '09), Simon Trask (anti-mutant activist, bts calling for Proposition vote, last in UXM #509, '09, next in Utopia, '09), Strikeforce X (group's 1st full app) inc Binderup, Comfort, Klein, Overfield, Pierce, Pottratz & Sev
OTHER CHARACTERS: San Francisco Post editor & reporters inc Pete, American Legion members (bts attending Osborn's speec Canadian military secretary (bts on phone), airplane pilot (bts flying plane), passengers (all but 1 bts on plane) & flight attendant, El Barc bartender & patrons, Colombian locals (bts telling Wolverine about Strikeforce X); Melita's cat, birds, spider; Black Panther (Shuri, mentione profiled by Post), Ghost Rider (mentioned, allegedly told woman to set fires), X-Men (mentioned, send press releases to Post), wom (mentioned, burned down gift shops), photographers (mentioned, photographed Angel); falcon, ant (prev 2 mentioned, trackable by Wolverine Louis L'Amour (author), Archangel (bts), Punisher, criminal (prev 4 in photos), flapper (on poster), cowboys (on book cover)
LOCATIONS/ITEMS: San Francisco Post offices, Melita's apartment, Canadian woods (in photo), skies over Pacific Ocean, Colombia i jungle, El Barcito bar & Casa Suelta hotel, American Legion hall, San Francisco: Balboa Park gift shops (destroyed), Chinatown, Laurel Heigh Hunter's Point (prev 5 mentioned) / Reporter & editor's photos, Melita's notes, photos, research books & cordless phone, airplane, Wolverine pack, drinks & money, Strikeforce X's guns (some destroyed), binoculars & sniper rifle w/scope & cancer-causing bullets, trees (destroyed)

YNOPSIS: Melita Garner suggests that the Post do an exposé on Wolverine, but her editor declines the idea. She decides to investigate 'olverine herself, but has little luck — until she receives a mysterious phone call from someone who hints that she will find all the answers by vestigating Blackguard. Meanwhile, Wolverine journeys to Colombia in search of Blackguard's Adamantium-enhanced strike force. Deciding let his foes come to him, Wolverine visits a local bar and treats the patrons to a round of drinks. Much later, a seemingly drunk Wolverine aggers back to his hotel, observed by two Strikeforce X members hiding in the trees. They plan their attack, but suddenly lose track of their rget. Wolverine ambushes them and the three fight a lengthy battle; Wolverine learns that both men match his powers, including techno-rganic healing factors and laser claws. Their brawl ends in a stalemate, but when the other ten Strikeforce members arrive, Wolverine realizes at he is outmatched. He flees into the jungle, and Strikeforce X pursues…

OTE: This issue also has a variant cover. Strikeforce X's Adamantium skeletons are confirmed, and their healing nanites revealed, here; 'olverine theorizes that they may also have bionic implants and drug-heightened senses. Melita's research books include *Animal Life of the 'anadian Wilderness*, *Properties of Adamantium*, *A Secret History of Department H*, *The Yakuza*, and *Yeti and Wendigo* (misspelled "Wenidgo").

WOLVERINE: WEAPON X #3 [#266] (August 2009)

"The Adamantium Men, Part 3 of 5" (22 pages)

CREDITS: Jason Aaron (writer), Ron Garney (art), Virtual Calligraphy's Cory Petit (letters), Jason Keith (colors), Jody LeHeup (asst editor), John Barber (editor), Axel Alonso (group editor), Salvador Larroca (variant c art), Morry Hollowell (c colors), Frank D'Armata (variant c colors)
FEATURE CHARACTER: Wolverine
SUPPORTING CAST: Melita Garner (next in W:WX #5, '09), Maverick
VILLAINS: Strikeforce X (named, some bts off-panel) inc Klein (also on monitor), Binderup, Comfort, Overfield, Pottratz (prev 5 named), Pierce & Sever, Blackguard's Chief Executive (1st, also on monitor) & Human Resources Department (Chief Executive's enforcers, die), corrupt US Senators

THER CHARACTERS: Mr. Bender (Blackguard vice president), Roxxon miners (bts in trucks), Blackguard doctors & lawyers, US Senators, earing attendees; Melita's cat (next in W #17, '11), snake; Blackguard shareholders (mentioned, promised Wolverine's head), Strikeforce X's ctims (mentioned, raped, tortured or killed) & military superiors (mentioned, discharged them), Christopher Columbus (as statue), historical ures (in paintings), cartoon character (on shirt); lion (on ring)

OCATIONS/ITEMS: Colombian jungle w/cave, Roxxon coal mines w/Blackguard Security Station Zebra, Chief Executive's office (prev 2 also n monitor), San Francisco: Coit Tower & Melita's apartment, US Senate Chambers (Capitol Building) / Strikeforce X's earpieces, knife & guns /cancer-causing bullets, Wolverine's punji sticks (bts) & tracking device w/transponder, Station Zebra's comm system & medical equipment, oxxon bulldozer, backhoe, dump trucks & mining equipment, Chief Executive's laptop, Bender's personnel files, Human Resources' van, guns, arpiece & knife, Maverick's guns & sniper rifle w/scope, Senate's microphones & cameras, Melita's door (destroyed), handgun & MP3 player 'headphones, San Francisco Post

YNOPSIS: Strikeforce X hunts Wolverine through the jungle, but Wolverine uses guerrilla tactics and booby traps to wear them down, apturing squad member Pottratz and shooting another member with the team's own cancer-causing bullets. Klein reports failure to an angry hief Executive, who has bribed several Senators to award Blackguard a massive defense contract, and cannot have Strikeforce X's actions in olombia revealed. Melita meets with Bender, a disgruntled Blackguard vice president, who gives her files on Strikeforce X — all dishonorably scharged soldiers. Blackguard's "Human Resources Department" later confronts Bender, but a concealed Maverick shoots them all. In olombia, Wolverine tortures Pottratz for information. Pottratz escapes, but Wolverine secretly planted a tracking device behind the soldier's ye. A Blackguard assassin attacks Melita in her home, but Maverick bursts in and kills him. Later, in a Congressional meeting, Senators grill the hief Executive about Melita's newspaper article alleging Strikeforce X's crimes in Colombia. Wolverine follows the tracker, but finds that Pottratz as gouged out his own eye to avoid pursuit…
OTE: This issue also has a variant cover.

WOLVERINE: WEAPON X #4 [#267] (October 2009)

"The Adamantium Men, Part 4 of 5" (22 pages)

CREDITS: Jason Aaron (writer), Ron Garney (art), Virtual Calligraphy's Cory Petit (letters), Jason Keith (colors), Jody LeHeup (asst editor), John Barber & Jeanine Schaefer (editors), Axel Alonso (group editor), Adi Granov (variant c art), David Finch (70th variant c art), Jim Cheung (70th variant c frame art), Morry Hollowell (c colors, 70th variant c colors)
FEATURE CHARACTER: Wolverine
SUPPORTING CAST: Maverick
VILLAINS: Chief Executive (also on monitor),

uman Resources Department, Strikeforce X: Klein (dies), 1 other
THER CHARACTERS: Bob (Blackguard's Chief Financial Officer, dies off-panel), HAMMER agents (Norman Osborn's peacekeeping oops, some or others last in Herc #127, '09) inc Gertrude Jacks (Maverick's ex-lover), Blackguard executives (1 dies off-panel, others dead), hief Executive's chauffeur, subway conductor (bts driving train), bus driver (bts driving bus), schoolchildren, bystanders; rat; Norman Osborn nentioned, wants Blackguard to succeed), US Senators (mentioned, excited about Strikeforce X), Spetsnaz regiment (mentioned, killed by 'olverine), Rolling Stones (mentioned, still performing), Boon Hogganbeck, Old Ben (prev 2 mentioned, characters in book); Spider-Man (on utton), man (as ice sculpture)
OCATIONS/ITEMS: New York City inc highway, subway tracks, gas station & Chief Executive's condo (also on monitor) w/parking garage, ob's San Francisco office w/nearby street, Caribbean resort, Pentagon, Syria's Golan Heights, Afghanistan (prev 3 mentioned) / Chief

Executive's comm system (bts), limousine (destroyed), money & files, Bob's laptop, Human Resources' gun, blindfold & cigarette, HAMME
guns, camera, flashlight & investigative tools, Jacks' cellphone, Maverick's earpiece (bts), cellphone, gun & sniper rifle w/scope, champag
bowl, Klein's book, Wolverine's motorcycle (destroyed) & earpiece, subway train & tracks, school bus, gas pump (destroyed), Boon's kn
(mentioned)
SYNOPSIS: The Chief Executive, panicking after Melita's exposé, has his Human Resources Department murder any potential informan
As HAMMER investigates the murder of Blackguard's chief financial officer, Maverick contacts Agent Gertrude Jacks, his ex-lover, who fee
him information on Blackguard. Maverick reports to Wolverine that Blackguard's executives are hiding at a Caribbean resort — but Wolverine
already at the resort and has killed them all, determined to send a message to anyone else who tries to restart the Weapon X Program. Realizi
that Wolverine will target him next, the Chief Executive demands that Klein move him to a safer location. However, Wolverine attacks the Ch
Executive's limousine en route, crashing it. Klein assaults Wolverine; the two fight a vicious battle across New York City, only pausing when th
notice horrified schoolchildren staring at them. Maverick attacks the Chief Executive, but another squad member fires his laser claws into Maveric
chest. Exhausted, Klein and Wolverine continue battling. Wolverine finally kills Klein but collapses; HAMMER agents arrive and arrest him.
NOTE: This issue also has two variant covers, including a frame variant celebrating Marvel's 70th anniversary. Melita Garner's first name
incorrectly given as "Alita" on this issue's recap page. Norman Osborn and HAMMER replaced Tony Stark and SHIELD in SecInv #8, '09.

WOLVERINE: WEAPON X #5 [#268] (November 2009)

"The Adamantium Men, Part 5 of 5" (22 pages)

CREDITS: Jason Aaron (writer), Ron Garney (art), Virtual Calligraphy's Cory Pe
(letters), Jason Keith (colors), Jody LeHeup (asst editor), John Barber & Jeani
Schaefer (editors), Axel Alonso (group editor), Carlos Pacheco (variant c pencils
Danny Miki (variant c inks), Justin Ponsor (variant c colors)
FEATURE CHARACTER: Wolverine (next in NAv #55, Utopia, UXM #514, D/
#8, Exodus, UXM #515-516, X:L Ann, all '09, X:L #228-229, '09-10, Dp #16-18, '0
10, Hulk #14-17, '09-10; WoSM #9, Psy #1 fb & 2-4, NatX #1, NatX:XF, XFor:S&
#1-3, all '10; XFor #12-13, XFor/C:MW, Cable #13, XFor #14, Cable #14, XFor #1
Cable #15, XFor #16-20, XNec, all '09; XFor #21-25, NatX #3/3, all '10, DRL:X, '0
DW #80, '09, W:O #41-43, 48 fb & 43-45, '09-10, DRL:W, '09)
SUPPORTING CAST: Maverick (next in W #3, '11), Melita Garner (chr next in W:WX #8, '10 fb, next in W:WX #8, '10)
VILLAINS: Iron Patriot (Norman Osborn, corrupt HAMMER director, last in DR:GL, '09, next in X:L #225, '09), Grecian (Blackguard contracte
dies), Chief Executive (next in W #304, '12), Strikeforce X (some bts off-panel; some die, possibly next as spirits in W #2, '10, see W #122, '98
NOTE; Pierce, Sever & 1 other next in W #304, '12) inc Klein (dead), Pottratz (dies), Binderup, Comfort, Overfield, Pierce & Sever
OTHER CHARACTERS: HAMMER doctor & agents (some or others next in X:L #225, '09) inc Gertrude Jacks, reporter (on monitors), L
Senators (bts vetoing Blackguard's contract), Wall Street traders (bts reacting to Senate vote), San Francisco Post employees; shark (die
birds, starfish, crab; Professor X (mentioned, psychoanalyzed Wolverine), Blackguard's supporters (mentioned, angry at Wolverine); Melit
cat (in photo)
LOCATIONS/ITEMS: HAMMER morgue & interrogation facility w/nearby street, Pacific Ocean w/island, news studio (on monitors), L
Senate chambers (bts), Manhattan's Wall Street (mentioned), Blackguard offices, parking garage, Grecian's office w/nearby alley / Jacks' hoo
& Vibranium restraints, HAMMER guns, Maverick's car & gun, oil rig (destroyed) w/alarm system, Strikeforce X's guns, Pottratz's eyepatc
Chief Executive's bandages, knife & handheld TV, news camera (bts), Wolverine's helicopter (destroyed) w/missiles & machine gun, Post's TV
Blackguard's computer w/Strikeforce X files (bts, destroyed), Grecian's files & money
SYNOPSIS: Wolverine awakens in a HAMMER facility, confronted by Agent Jacks. He plays on Jacks' conflicted loyalties, promising to destr
the corrupt Blackguard; Jacks reluctantly lets him leave. Maverick tells Wolverine that Strikeforce X and the Chief Executive are hiding
a Pacific Ocean oil rig, awaiting the Senate's vote. Maverick reminds Wolverine that battling Strikeforce X hand-to-hand would be suicid
Wolverine instead attacks the rig with a helicopter, blowing it up. Pottratz leaps onto Wolverine's helicopter and destroys it; Wolverine lat
washes up on a small island with the Chief Executive and the surviving squad members. He drowns Pottratz and maroons the others on th
island; later, the Senate votes to deny Blackguard's defense contract. Jacks erases Blackguard's Weapon X files, but is later arrested by Norma
Osborn. Wolverine tells Melita that he was the one who tricked her into investigating Blackguard. Elsewhere, Maverick kills Grecian, who so
the Weapon X files to Blackguard — but Maverick is troubled, as he sold them to Grecian to begin with.
NOTE: This issue also has a variant cover.

WOLVERINE: OLD MAN LOGAN GIANT-SI
(November 2009)

"Old Man Logan, Conclusion" (32 pages)

CREDITS: Mark Millar (writer), Steve McNiv
(pencils), Dexter Vines (co-inks, c inks), Ma
Morales (co-inks), Virtual Calligraphy's Cory Pe
(letters), Morry Hollowell (colors), Jody LeHeu
(asst editor), Jeanine Schaefer & John Barb
(editors), Axel Alonso (group editor), Ed McGuinne
(variant c pencils), Paolo Rivera (variant c art), Ch
Sotomayor (variant c colors)
FEATURE CHARACTER: Wolverine (chr last in
#72, '09, chr next as Hooded Man in FF #560, '08 fb, FF #558-562, '08-09, FanFor #1-4, '09)
SUPPORTING CAST: Maureen, Scotty, Jade (all bts, dead in graves, also in photos; last in W #72, '09)
VILLAINS: Hulk Gang: Hulk (ruler of section of Amerika), Charlie Banner, Otis Banner (prev 2 possibly bts), Beau Banner, Bobbi-Jo Banne
Elrod Banner, Eustace Banner, Luke Banner, Rufus Banner, Woody Banner, others (all die), Billy-Bob Banner (possibly dies, see NOTE)

OTHER CHARACTERS: Robert Bruce Banner Jr. (chr last in W #66, '08, chr next as adult in FF #560, '08 fb), Abe Donovan (last in W #72, '09), Hulk Gang's victims (dead, as body parts), Stark's Bar bartender, Heff's Mansion madam & prostitutes, Billy-Bob's friend (bts loaning movies), Logan's neighbors; cow (dies), horse; She-Hulk (mentioned, slept with Hulk & spawned Hulk Gang), Jim Belushi (mentioned, Hulk Gang plan to watch his movies), Jerry Lee (dog, mentioned, character in a Jim Belushi movie); Raggedy Ann (as doll)

LOCATIONS/ITEMS: Earth-807128: Hulk Gang's trailer park w/cave & watering hole, Sonny Stark's Bar, Heff's Mansion (whorehouse), Logan's family farm / Hulk Gang's TV, Billy-Bob's movies (both bts), Jade's Gameboy & doll, bar window, car, Hulk Gang's trailers, Fantasticar (rev 4 destroyed) & flashlight, Wolverine's chains (destroyed), bedroll, supplies & plastic explosive w/timer, hurled debris, Scotty's baseball & cards, Maureen's Bible, family's grave markers, Bruce's baby carrier

SYNOPSIS: Two Hulk Gang members wash their bloodstained clothes in a river and discuss murdering Wolverine's family — but Wolverine suddenly ambushes and kills them both. Three other Hulks celebrate in a bar, but Wolverine slaughters all three. Other Hulks exit a whorehouse, but find Wolverine waiting for them. At the Hulks' trailer park, Bobbi-Jo cares for the infant Bruce Jr. with an elderly Bruce Banner. The Hulks' Fantasticar suddenly smashes into the park and explodes, killing several Hulks; Wolverine slaughters the last survivors, but the elderly Bruce surprises Wolverine with super-strength. As the two battle savagely, Bruce reveals that he killed Wolverine's family to provoke him; Bruce misses the villainous lifestyle. Bruce transforms into a gigantic Hulk and consumes Wolverine — but Wolverine bursts out of the Hulk's stomach, killing him. Later, Wolverine stands over his family's graves, deciding that he has hidden as Logan long enough. Vowing to bring order to the lawless nation, Wolverine straps Bruce Jr. to his back and rides off into the sunset.

NOTE: This one-shot concludes the "Old Man Logan" arc from W #66-72, '08-09. It also has two variant covers. This issue also has a sketch and cover gallery featuring the preliminary and final pencils for W #66, '08 pp.2-4, penciler Steve McNiven's concept sketches, the standard covers for W #66-72, '08-09, pencils and inks for W #71, '09's cover, Wizard Magazine promotional art by McNiven, Vines & Hollowell, W #66, '08's Crimpe and Turner variant covers, both of this issue's variant covers, and an unused cover for W #66, '08 by McNiven & Hollowell. All characters appearing here are native to Earth-807128. Bobbi-Jo's first name is revealed here. Luke Banner is almost identical to one of the two Hulk Gang members seen in W #66, '08 (named as Charlie and Otis, though that issue did not specify who was who); the two may be twins. Billy-Bob's fate is unrevealed, though Wolverine likely killed him. One of the movies that the Hulk Gang plans to watch is from Jim Belushi's K-9 series.

DARK REIGN: THE LIST — WOLVERINE (December 2009)

"All We Want Is the World and Everything In It" (22 pages)

CREDITS: Jason Aaron (writer), Esad Ribic (pencils, c art), Tom Palmer (inks), Jared Fletcher (letters), Matthew Wilson (colors), Anthony Dial (production), Jody LeHeup (asst editor), Jeanine Schaefer & John Barber (editors), Frank Cho (variant c art), Michael Choi (2nd print c art), Sonia Oback (2nd print c colors)

FEATURE CHARACTER: Wolverine (also as monitor images, next in XvAtlas #1-2, '09-10, UXM #516-517, '09-10; NatX #1/3, UXM #520-522, NatX #1/2, 2/4 & 4/3-4, W:WX #8 fb, all '10, W:WX #6, '09)

GUEST STAR: Marvel Boy (Noh-Varr, genetically-altered Reality-200080 Kree, last in DAv #5, '09, next in SWORD #2, '10)

VILLAINS: Iron Patriot (last in DRL:Hulk, '09, next in DRL:ASM, '10), Project: Deathlok (cybernetically animated corpses, destroyed, some also on monitor) inc Agent D-18

OTHER CHARACTERS: Fantomex (Charlie-Cluster 7, "Jean-Phillipe," Weapon XIII, artificially evolved mercenary, also as monitor image, last in Mys #24, '05, next in UXM #519, '10), EVA (Fantomex's sentient nervous system, last in Mys #21, '05, last bts in Mys #23, '05, next in UXM #520, '10), World (newly sentient Super-Sentinel factory, also on monitors, last in XPx:W #5, '07, next in UXFor #5, '11) & its superhuman creations (some or others last in NX #143, '03, next in UXFor #5, '11) inc Allgod (Weapon XVI, gaseous living religion); Dr. David Heimerdinger (HAMMER scientist, 1st, unnamed, next in W:WX #13, '10), truck driver; Daken (mentioned, served on "Dark" Avengers with Marvel Boy), Dr. Doom (mentioned, Fantomex stole his shrinking ray); Captain America, Huntsman (bts), Ultimaton (prev 3 as monitor images)

LOCATIONS/ITEMS: London, England inc World's location (also on monitors) & nearby church; HAMMER base, San Francisco sushi bar, alternate dimensions (mentioned) / HAMMER monitors, X-Men's Blackbird jet w/ keys, Allgod's containment canister, World superhumans' nanotech (bts) & cybernetic limbs, corpses' cybernetic implants (some bts), Fantomex's nanites, stolen shrinking ray (prev 2 bts), guns & flashlight, Heimerdinger's Project: Deathlok schematics & computers w/transmitter, Kree anti-deity equation (mentioned), World's brain (partly destroyed), Marvel Boy's transforming gauntlet & energy nunchuks, truck

SYNOPSIS: Norman Osborn decides to claim the superhuman-generating World facility. Marvel Boy, who recently defected from Osborn's Avengers, warns Wolverine, but when the two arrive at the World, a gas takes over Wolverine's mind. Wolverine and the World's superhumans chase Marvel Boy; he flees but encounters Osborn's cybernetically animated corpse troops. Fantomex arrives and the two evade the troops; Fantomex explains that the gaseous Allgod is a living religion, co-opting anyone with faith, and that the World has become sentient and is protecting itself. The two fight their way to the World's giant brain; Fantomex has Marvel Boy kiss it, reassuring it that they are no threat. Wolverine and the superhumans come out of their religious daze; all three heroes destroy the corpse troops. One corpse rips off a chunk of the brain; Wolverine severs its hand, but the hand crawls away. Later, Fantomex shrinks the World and departs with it. As an introspective Wolverine catches a ride to a nearby church, the truck unknowingly runs over the crawling hand.

NOTE: This issue, part of the "Dark Reign: the List" series of one-shots that detail Osborn's various schemes, also has a variant cover and a 2nd print cover. This issue also has a gallery with the script, pencils and inks for p.15, and reprints two Official Handbook profiles: OHMU HC4, '08's Fantomex entry (2 pages), and OHMU HC7, '09's Marvel Boy (Noh-Varr) entry (2 pages). Dr. Heimerdinger's last name is revealed in W:WX #13, '10, and his first name in W:WX #14, '10, which reveals that his Project: Deathlok experiments become the basis for Earth-10511's future Deathlok program. Given that the World is in London, it is unclear how Wolverine plans to hitchhike home. Also, the truck that picks him up is incorrectly depicted as driving on the right, with the driver on the left.

2ND STORY: "A Good Man" (8 pages)
NOTE: Reprinted from W #175/3, '02.

WOLVERINE: WEAPON X #6 [#269] (December 2009)

"Insane in the Brain, Part 1 of 5" (22 pages)

CREDITS: Jason Aaron (writer), Yanick Paquette (pencils), Michel LaComb▮ (inks), Virtual Calligraphy's Cory Petit (letters), Nathan Fairbairn (colors), Jo▮ LeHeup (asst editor), John Barber & Jeanine Schaefer (editors), Axel Alons▮ (group editor), Adam Kubert (c pencils), Joe Kubert (variant c pencils), Jus▮ Ponsor (c colors), Laura Martin (variant c colors)

FEATURE CHARACTER: Wolverine (as Patient X, also on monitors as Patie▮ X, also as "Spider-Man")

VILLAINS: Dr. Rot (Algernon J. Rottwell, originally Bentley Newton, insa▮ sanatorium head, also as woman, 1st but chr last in W:WX #8, '10 fb), Nurse Fest▮ (Rot's diseased assistant, unnamed, 1st in silhouette), sanatorium guards (some ▮ others chr last in W:WX #8, '10 fb)

OTHER CHARACTERS: Sanatorium orderly (1 or another next in W:WX #8, '10) & inmates (some also as chef, clown, cowboy, mime, Nativ▮ American, pharaoh, soldier, tribal figure, anime characters, devil, goblin, ape, bird, frog, fox, pig, rabbit, rooster & others) inc Dwarves (next ▮ W:WX #9, '10), Biter, Charlie Chainsaws, Wendell & Widow, Rot's victims (dead as brains, bts in basement, some or others chr last dead ▮ W:WX #8, '10 fb), Wendell's victims (dead as brains, most bts in sack); ravens; Thomas Logan (see NOTE), wolves (others on variant cove▮ Silver Fox, X-Men (prev 4 mentioned, remembered by Wolverine); Spongebob Squarepants, people (prev 2 on TV), men (as paper cutouts▮ Maverick, Grecian (prev 2 recap page only, see NOTE)

LOCATIONS/ITEMS: Dunwich Sanatorium (Dr. Rot's asylum, 1st, also on monitor) w/Patient X's cell (also on monitor) & incurable war▮ Howlett family estate, Wolverine & Silver Fox's cabin, moon, Charlie's cabin (prev 4 mentioned) / Dr. Rot's surgical equipment (bts), camera▮ (all but 1 bts), monitor, papers, costume, mask, microphone w/speaker & God Brain Machine (bts, unnamed) w/controls, Patient X's blood▮ straitjacket, orderly's rag & bucket, guards' armor & truncheons, Charlie's chainsaws (mentioned) & checkers, Biter's helmet, Widow's scissor▮ veil & chains, sanatorium key, TV & medicine bell, Fester's bandages & "medicine" inc button, candy, jelly bean & pencil eraser, patients' sutur▮ & masks, Wolverine's Spider-Man mask, Wendell's costume, suitcase & sack

SYNOPSIS: Bound in a straitjacket, Wolverine recounts his life to Dr. Rot, who points out that the events sound crazy. Unable to think straigh▮ Wolverine believes himself insane and wants to be cured; Rot makes him sleep using a strange machine. Later, Wolverine wanders the dayroo▮ with the other inmates. The guards warn him harshly away from the incurable ward's basement entrance; an inmate claims that Rot is buildi▮ a giant machine out of brains. Nurse Fester hands out medicine, but Wolverine dimly realizes that the "pills" are assorted random object▮ The inmate invites Wolverine on an escape attempt, but the addled mutant declines. The next day, Wolverine sees the inmate slumped in th▮ dayroom with a massive lobotomy scar. Later, Dr. Rot throws a costume party for Wendell, who is being discharged. Wolverine tells Rot that h▮ recalls killing people, piquing the doctor's interest. Hours later Wendell returns in a panic, carrying a sack of freshly harvested human brain▮ Pleased, Rot brings him to the basement, where Wendell screams…

NOTE: This issue also has a variant cover by Joe Kubert, father of regular cover artist Adam Kubert. This issue and next issue's story title▮ incorrectly label this as a five-part arc. W #306, '12 reveals Dr. Rot's birth name, explains that he legally changed it and clarifies that "Rottwe▮ is his mother's family name. Nurse Fester is named next issue. Dr. Rot's God Brain Machine, made from his victims' brains and responsibl▮ for muddling the inmates' thinking, is partially revealed next issue, and named and fully revealed in W:WX #8, '10. Patient X's room change▮ from a padded cell to a standard hospital room between panels. Wolverine dimly recalls "killing his father" here; Wolverine killed groundskeepe▮ Thomas Logan in Origin #2, '01 after Thomas slew Wolverine's presumed father John Howlett. W #4, '11 confirms Origin #1-2, '01's implicatio▮ that Thomas was Wolverine's biological father, and reveals that Wolverine learned this years ago. Beginning with W:WX #2, '09, the series' reca▮ page returned to showing panels from previous issues instead of covers; as such, this Index will resume listing the characters appearing therei▮

WOLVERINE: WEAPON X #7 [#270] (January 2010)

"Insane in the Brain, Part 2 of 5" (22 pages)

CREDITS: Jason Aaron (writer), Yanick Paquette (pencils), Michel LaCombe (inks), Virtual Calligraphy's Co▮ Petit (letters), Nathan Fairbairn (colors), Jody LeHeup (asst editor), Jeanine Schaefer (editor), Axel Alonso (grou▮ editor), Adam Kubert (c pencils), Justin Ponsor (c colors)

FEATURE CHARACTER: Wolverine (as Patient X, also as Patient X on monitor, also as Experiment X in hi▮ own dream)

VILLAINS: Dr. Rot (also as woman), Nurse Fester (named, voice only), mobsters: Paulie (bts on phone▮ Frankie, 1 other (prev 2 die); sanatorium guards (some also on monitor, die)

OTHER CHARACTERS: Sanatorium inmates (1 dies; others mentioned, made into assassins) inc Biter (ne▮ in W:WX #10, '10) & Charlie Chainsaws, State Attorney General (bts, targeted for assassination), Rot's victim▮ (dead as brains, some bts in basement); Dr. Marshall Swinson (mentioned, formerly ran sanatorium), mobster▮ uncle Tony (mentioned, obtained assassins at sanatorium); Wolverine's victims (dead in his dream); Charles Manson (quoted)

LOCATIONS/ITEMS: Dunwich Sanatorium w/Patient X's cell (also on monitor) & incurable ward, Weapon X Program facility (in dream) / D▮ Rot's camera (bts), monitor, cleavers, mask, knife, IVs, restraints, syringe, mirror, tongs, surgical equipment, electroshock machine, God Bra▮ Machine w/controls, microphone w/speaker & "weapons" inc saw, drill, knives, awl & chain, guards' armor, gun, truncheons, pressure suits, fi▮ hose, cattle prods & laughing gas tank w/mask, Charlie's muffin, Fester's bandages (prev 2 mentioned), Experiment X's wires & battery pack▮ (prev 2 in dream), Frankie's car & cellphone, mobster's gun & restraints, Charlie's chainsaws & activation switch, inmate's casts & makesh▮ noose, Patient X's cage w/sign, Biter's helmet

SYNOPSIS: During "therapy," sadistic guards torment Wolverine as Dr. Rot exhorts him to unleash his rage, but the addled Wolverine is to▮ afraid. Later, Wolverine sees Charlie Chainsaws break an inmate's arm; he vaguely feels that someone should intervene, but cannot reca▮ what to do. That night, Wolverine sees a screaming Charlie, whose hands have been cut off, chased by a cleaver-wielding Rot. Mobsters arriv▮ hoping that the sanatorium can provide them with a lunatic to perform a seemingly random assassination, as it has in the past. Rot shows th▮ mobsters Charlie, his hands now replaced with actual chainsaws. When the mobsters panic, Rot has Charlie kill one, and captures the othe▮ –

owing him a giant machine made of floating brains in tanks before extracting the mobster's own brain. The next day, Wolverine sees guards ...eak the inmate's other arm, and nearly pops his claws. Rot electrocutes and humiliates Wolverine during further "treatment"; when the guards ...at him again, Wolverine snaps, pops his claws and attacks them savagely, pleasing Rot.

...OTE: Dr. Swinson's first name is revealed next issue.

WOLVERINE: WEAPON X #8 [#271] (February 2010)

"Insane in the Brain, Part 3 of 4" (22 pages)

CREDITS: Jason Aaron (writer), Yanick Paquette (pencils), Michel LaCombe (inks), Virtual Calligraphy's Cory Petit (letters), Nathan Fairbairn (colors), Jody LeHeup (asst editor), Jeanine Schaefer (editor), Axel Alonso (group editor), Adam Kubert (c pencils), Todd Doney (c colors)
FEATURE CHARACTER: Wolverine (also as Patient X, also as Patient X on monitors & in illusion, also in fb1 between NatX #4/4, '10 & W:WX #6, '09)
SUPPORTING CAST: Melita Garner (also in fb1 between W:WX #5, '09 & this issue)
VILLAINS: Dr. Rot (also in fb2 & fb1, his chr 1st app, prior to W:WX #6, '09), Nurse Fester, mobsters inc Paulie, sanatorium guards (1 or another dies in illusion, also dead on monitor; some or others also in fb2 & fb1, their chr 1st app, some or others chr next in W:WX #6, '09), serial killer (former sanatorium inmate, dies in fb1, also in photo in fb1)

...THER CHARACTERS: Charlie Chainsaws, former sanatorium staff (some also in fb2; others in fb2, dead or die) inc Dr. Marshall Swinson ...rmer sanatorium head), sanatorium inmates (in fb2; others mentioned, made into assassins) & orderly (dies, 1 or another last in W:WX #6, ...9), Rot's victims (dead as brains; some or others dead as brains in fb1, some or others chr next bts, dead, in W:WX #6, '09), killer's victims ...ead as body parts), homeless people (prev 2 in fb1), Rot's neighbor's cat & childhood victims (prev 2 mentioned, attacked by young Rot), ...overnment agents, mobsters, businessmen (prev 3 mentioned), obtained assassins at sanatorium), serial killers (in photos in fb1), nurse (in ...sion, also in photo in illusion & on monitor), Wolverine's victims (dead), slaughter victims (in photos) (prev 2 in illusion), victims, chimp (prev 2 ...entioned in newspaper in illusion); politician (on poster)

...OCATIONS/ITEMS: Dunwich Sanatorium (also on monitors, in illusion & in fb2) w/incurable ward, San Francisco: 8th Street Rescue Mission, ...rking garage, killer's apartment (prev 3 in fb1), Melita's apartment, Rot's childhood neighborhood, mountain shack w/nearby town (prev 3 ...entioned) / Nurse's Chardonnay (mentioned) & medicine, guard's newspaper, sanatorium window & electrical junction box (prev 2 destroyed) ...ll in illusion), guards' armor (some also in fb1, another on monitor) & truncheons (others of prev 2 in fb2, another of prev 2 in illusion), Dr. ...ot's bone saws (destroyed), camera (bts), drill, acid, 2x4 (prev 3 mentioned), monitors, dolly, scalpel, tongs & God Brain Machine w/controls, ...ectrodes, printout & portable unit (in fb1), Wolverine's restraints (some destroyed) & IVs (some of prev 2 also on monitor), killer's jars, Melita's ...otos & car, guards' vans & snare poles (prev 5 in fb1), Charlie's chainsaws, staff's cages, Swinson's wheeled board, inmate's knife (in fb2), ...ot's father's lawnmower (mentioned) w/gasoline, Fester's bandages, orderly's armor & truncheon, mobsters' car & guns

...LASHBACKS: Wolverine deals with a deranged serial killer. He meets with Melita, who observes that several recent killers stayed at the same ...elter. As Wolverine stakes out the shelter, Dr. Rot arrives and activates his brain-dampening machine; his guards easily capture Wolverine (1). ...ottwell sparks a riot and takes over the sanatorium (2).

...YNOPSIS: Dr. Rot makes Wolverine think he is running amok in the sanatorium, but Wolverine refuses to kill a nurse and breaks free from the ...usion. Rot brings a chained Wolverine to the incurable ward, where the sanatorium's mutilated staff are imprisoned. The facility's former director, ...w a quadruple amputee, explains that the sanatorium used to manufacture lunatic assassins until Rot took over and began his own bizarre ...ojects. Unable to saw through Wolverine's Adamantium skull, Rot inserts electrodes into Wolverine's scalp; needing more power, Rot kills an ...derly and adds the man's brain to his machine. Elsewhere, Melita awakens with a sudden psychic awareness of Wolverine's predicament. As ...obsters arrive looking for their missing friends, Rot is delighted by the previous brainwashing he detects in Wolverine's mind...

...OTE: This issue's story title now correctly labels the arc as a four-part story. It is never explained how Melita psychically detected Wolverine's ...cation, but Wolverine may have been able to amplify and broadcast his thoughts through the God Brain Machine.

WOLVERINE: WEAPON X #9 [#272] (March 2010)

"Insane in the Brain, Conclusion" (22 pages)

CREDITS: Jason Aaron (writer), Yanick Paquette (pencils), Michel LaCombe (inks), Virtual Calligraphy's Cory Petit (letters), Nathan Fairbairn (colors), Jody LeHeup (asst editor), Jeanine Schaefer (editor), Axel Alonso (group editor), Adam Kubert (c pencils), Morry Hollowell (c colors)
FEATURE CHARACTER: Wolverine (also in his own imagination, also in pfb, next in W:Worst, '10, W:Bwalk, '10)
GUEST STARS: X-Men: Nightcrawler (also on monitor in pfb), Psylocke (both in pfb, last in X:Pixie #4, '10, next in Doomw #1, '10)
SUPPORTING CAST: Melita Garner (also in pfb)
VILLAINS: Dr. Rot (next in W #304, '12), Nurse Fester (next in W #305, '12) (both also in pfb), mobsters (die in pfb, some also on monitor in pfb)

...THER CHARACTERS: Charlie Chainsaws (also in pfb, also on monitor in pfb, next in W #306, '12), sanatorium inmates (in pfb, 1 or more ...es, some also on monitor in pfb) inc Biter (last in W:WX #7, '10) & Dwarves (last in W:WX #6, '09), Rot's victims (dead; others dead as skin in ...b, next in W #305, '12; others dead as brains in pfb, others next in W #305, '12), Wolverine's victim (dead), Artemis Nicodemus Rottwell (Dr. ...ot's great-great-grandfather, mentioned, came to America, see NOTE); politician (on poster), man in silhouette on fire extinguisher)

...OCATIONS/ITEMS: Melita's apartment (also in pfb) w/nearby alley, Dunwich Sanatorium (in pfb, also on monitors in pfb), dirt road / Dr. Rot's ...meras (bts), monitors, microphone, syringes, hooks, cleavers, surgical tape, oversized nutcracker, makeshift psychic bomb & God Brain ...achine (destroyed) w/controls, Nightcrawler's metal pipe, mobsters' guns (1 also on monitor), inmates' knives (some also on monitor), sutures ...n monitor), stick & cleaver, Fester's fire extinguisher (destroyed) & syringe, battery, paper clip, cheese grater, hummingbird heart, Chrysler ...haust fan (prev 5 mentioned) (all in pfb), victims' phone book (bts) & camper van, Dr. Rot's knife, Fester's bandages (also in pfb), needle & ...read, Charlie's chainsaws (bts, also in pfb), Melita's cordless phone

FLASHBACK: Melita summons Nightcrawler and Psylocke, explaining Wolverine's predicament. The two X-Men investigate the sanatoriu. basement and discover the God Brain Machine. Psylocke begins disabling it; upstairs, the inmates battle the mobsters as Rot gleefully watch. Wolverine stands amid the carnage, unsure what to do, but as soon as Psylocke deactivates the machine, Wolverine regains his mind. He quic. guts Rot, but to his surprise, the doctor does not fall; Fester attacks Wolverine while Rot creates a makeshift psychic bomb from an inmate's bra. The bomb drives everyone present briefly mad; when the X-Men regain their minds, they find that Rot and Fester have escaped (p).

SYNOPSIS: Wolverine staggers to Melita's apartment and collapses in her arms. The next morning, as Dr. Rot is stitched up by Nurse Fest. he calls Melita's apartment, having learned her name from scanning Wolverine's mind. When Wolverine answers, Rot whispers something a. Wolverine enters a trance. Melita awakens later to find Wolverine dazed and covered in blood; outside, a man lies dead in an alley with his bra. missing…

NOTE: It is not made explicit, but Rot quickly brainwashed Wolverine and set him free between last issue and this issue's pfb. Wolverine overcomes this brainwashing in W #308, '12. Artemis Rottwell, called only Dr. Rot's "ancestor" here, 1st appears in W #306, '12, which reveal his exact relation to Dr. Rot.

WOLVERINE: UNDER THE BOARDWALK (February 2010)

"Under the Boardwalk" (32 pages)

CREDITS: Stuart Moore (writer), Tomm Coker (art), Jeff Eckleberry (letters), Daniel Freedman (colors), Dami. Lucchese (production), Sebastian Girner (asst editor), Axel Alonso (editor)
FEATURE CHARACTER: Wolverine (also in rfb & his own thoughts & imagination, also in fb3 & fb1 between '. Ann #1, '12 fb & CX #26/2, '88 fb; next in W:Wend, '10)
VILLAINS: Phil DeBlasio (mobster, also in rfb, also in fb1 prior to issue) & his enforcers (in fb1; also in rfb, 1 bts. Amber DeBlasio (Phil's daughter) & her thugs, criminal
OTHER CHARACTERS: Katrina McCann (waitress, also in rfb & photo, also in fb3 & fb1 prior to issue), Phi. victim (dead as skeleton, also in rfb, also dead in fb1 prior to issue), Wolverine's FBI contact (bts providing info. Phil), airline announcers (voice only on loudspeaker), travelers, casino employees & patrons, strip club patro. dancer (others of prev 2 in fb3), bartender, police (also in Wolverine's imagination, others bts in police cars), pil.

(bts flying plane), bystanders (others in fb2); seagulls; Beast, Iron Man, Mr. Fantastic (prev 3 mentioned, could trace text message), Mr. Corvas. (Katrina's boss, mentioned, ordered Amber away), mobsters (mentioned, prevalent in Atlantic City); X-Men: Colossus, Cyclops, Emma Fro. Nightcrawler (prev 4 in Wolverine's thoughts); Katrina's husband (in photo); hamburger mascot (as statue)
LOCATIONS/ITEMS: San Francisco International Airport; Coney Island inc boardwalk (also in fb1 & rfb), strip club, Katrina's bedroom (pre. 2 in fb3) & amusement park; Atlantic City, New Jersey inc beach (also in fb2), boardwalk (also in Wolverine's imagination), bar, jail, C. Hall, Amber's hotel room, Katrina's apartment & Casino Alexandria w/café; JFK International Airport (bts), skies over USA; battleground. Wolverine's thoughts); Nome, Alaska; Atlantic Ocean (prev 2 mentioned) / Wolverine's luggage, cellphone & ticket, Air Alaska airplanes (1 bts. Amber's bail money, cellphone (prev 2 bts) & gun, enforcer's gun (in fb1 & rfb), satellite (bts), casino chips & betting table, FBI files, Australi. bound ship, DeBlasio's bank accounts (prev 3 mentioned), boardwalk lampposts (1 also in fb1 & rfb) & slats (destroyed, some also destroyed. fb1 & bts in rfb), police guns (also in Wolverine's imagination) & cars (bts), Katrina's photo & knives, thugs' guns, roller coaster
FLASHBACKS: DeBlasio buries the body (this issue's fb1). Wolverine watches as mobster Phil DeBlasio buries a body under a boardwalk (1. Tourists walk in Atlantic City (2). Wolverine sleeps with DeBlasio's girlfriend Katrina (3).
SYNOPSIS: Wolverine receives a text message summoning him to Atlantic City and mentioning DeBlasio; Wolverine recalls seeing him bu. the body. In Atlantic City, Wolverine meets a young woman named Amber and encounters Katrina again; he assumes that she summoned hi. Wolverine investigates, learning that DeBlasio vanished decades ago. He sees a familiar lamppost, recalls that the body is buried below it a. digs up the boardwalk, but finds nothing. Later, Wolverine confronts Katrina; she denies sending the text and reminds him that the body wa. buried on Coney Island, not Atlantic City. Wolverine travels there and finds the body, but Amber suddenly arrives, revealing herself as DeBlasio. daughter; she was simply trying to manipulate Wolverine into finding her absent father, and didn't know about the body. Wolverine defeats h. thugs and stalks off; later, he encounters an elderly man who resembles DeBlasio, but no longer trusts his memory.
NOTE: This issue's story is preceded by a title/credits page. This issue also has a 2-page feature with photos from the MarvelFest NYC 200 outdoor festival.

WOLVERINE: WENDIGO! (March 2010)

"Wendigo!" (22 pages)

CREDITS: Frank Tieri (writer), Paul Gulacy (art), Jeff Eckleberry (letters), Thomas Mason (colors), Jacob Chab. (production), Sebastian Girner (asst editor), Axel Alonso (editor), Ben Oliver (c pencils)
FEATURE CHARACTER: Wolverine (also in recording in dfb prior to this issue, next in W:WX #10, '10)
VILLAINS: Wendigo (Luc LeMay, cursed cannibal, 1st, in recording, also voice only in pfb, also in dfb followi. this issue), Wendigo spirit (bts empowering LeMay in pfb, also bts empowering LeMay in pfb & in d. following this issue, also as bobblehead; last in CM #3, '00, last bts in Hulk #9, '09, next bts in IHulks #630, '11). **OTHER CHARACTERS:** "Monsters, Myths and Marvels" cast & crew: Gordon Allsworth (host, also in recordin. in pfb & dfb, last in MChan #3, '08), Jimmy (cameraman, also voice only in recording, also bts holding camera. recording in pfb & dfb, last in MChan #1, '08, last bts in MChan #3, '08) (both also in pfb & dfb), Diane (actres. also dies in recording), Mike (actor, also as Wendigo, also as himself & Wendigo in dfb & recording in pfb), cre.

member (bts on set); Andre Simard (cryptozoologist, in pfb, also in recording in pfb) (prev 3 die off-panel) (prev 4 also dead in photo), Jean G. (investigator), Sonja (Guy's deputy), Mounties, police, Canadian government agents, bystander; birds, fish; Georges Baptiste, Paul Carti. Francois Lartigue (prev 3 mentioned, recent Wendigo hosts), Real Besson (mentioned, truck was stolen), Diane's agent & lawyer (prev. mentioned), Lac Saint Jean residents (mentioned, trustworthy), Roberval residents (mentioned, hold Wendigo festival), thief (mentioned, sto. Besson's truck), moose (mentioned, hunted by residents), Bigfoot, Loch Ness Monster (prev 2 mentioned, local legends); Alpha Flight: Auror. Guardian, Northstar, Puck, Shaman, Snowbird (prev 6 in ad), Man-Thing, Silver Surfer, Sub-Mariner, woman, fish (prev 5 in show intro)
LOCATIONS/ITEMS: Lac-Saint-Jean-Est, Quebec inc woods (also in recording, photo, pfb & dfb, also in recording in pfb & dfb), Lac Sai. Jean (lake), Le Bonet (pastry shop, mentioned), police station & gas station; Roberval, Quebec (mentioned); Florida swamp, Atlantis, out.

pace (prev 3 in show intro) / Mike's Wendigo costume (also in photo, dfb & recording in dfb), Gordon's microphone (bts in pfb, also in recording in pfb), clipboard & map, Jimmy's camera (also in pfb & bts in dfb, also bts in recording & recording in pfb & dfb), floodlights (1 also in photo) & ar, Diane's cellphone (also in recording), Mounties' camera (bts), TV, photo, duffel bag & DVD player w/remote control, crew's tents (in photo, or another also in dfb & recording in dfb), Guy's boat, beer, paperwork & fishing rod w/hook, police cars & fingerprint analysis computer ots), snowmobile, hockey equipment, Besson's truck (prev 3 mentioned), Wendigo spoor (in recording in pfb) & bobblehead, agent's laptop, Wolverine's motorcycle

LASHBACKS: As Jimmy films, Andre Simard hears a Wendigo howl and runs toward it (p). As Gordon and Jimmy cower in their tent, Mike es to hide with them, but the Wendigo drags Mike away. It returns for Gordon and Jimmy, but Wolverine suddenly cuts its arm off (d).

YNOPSIS: As a tabloid crew films a Wendigo reenactment in the Quebec woods, a real Wendigo suddenly beheads the actress. Later, vestigator Jean Guy interviews Gordon and Jimmy about the massacre of their crew. Jimmy explains that a Wendigo attacked; Guy is keptical, but Jimmy points to the evidence in the recordings. He explains that he and Gordon fled after a clawed man saved them by cutting off e Wendigo's arm, but Mounties reveal a severed human arm recovered at the scene. Government agents instruct Guy to claim that a serial iller committed the slaughter; Guy agrees, but reveals that the arm belonged to Luc LeMay, recently suspected of succumbing to the Wendigo urse. Later, Gordon and Jimmy pass Wolverine at a gas station.

NOTE: This issue's story is preceded by a title/credits page. Wolverine appears in only five panels of this story, and speaks only one line.

ND STORY: "Wolverine vs. Thor, Part One" (7 pages)
NOTE: Reprinted from WvThor #1, '09.

RD STORY: "Wolverine vs. Thor, Part Two" (7 pages)
NOTE: Reprinted from WvThor #2, '09.

TH STORY: "Wolverine vs. Thor, Part Three" (7 pages)
NOTE: Reprinted from WvThor #3, '10.

WOLVERINE: WEAPON X #10 [#273] (April 2010)

"Love and the Wolverine" (22 pages)

CREDITS: Jason Aaron (writer), C.P. Smith (art, colors), Virtual Calligraphy's Cory Petit (letters), Jody LeHeup (asst editor), Jeanine Schaefer (editor), Axel Alonso (group editor), Adam Kubert (c pencils), Morry Hollowell (c colors)

FEATURE CHARACTER: Wolverine (also in fb between AstSMW #4, '11 & MCP #93, '91 fb; next in W:Sav, '10)
GUEST STARS: X-Men: Emma Frost (last in X:Pixie #4, '10), Storm (on monitor, last in NatX #4/4, '10, chr next in BP #9, '09) (both next in Doomw #1, '10), Rogue (last in X:L #234, '10, next in S:FallSun, '10); Black Widow (last in InvIM #22, '10, next in IHulk #607, '10), Luke Cage (next in AvAtlas #1, '10), Jessica Jones (Cage's wife, super-powered former private detective, chr next in NAv #63, '10 fb, next in NAv #62, '10) (prev 2 last in NAv Ann #3, '10), Lin Sun (martial arts instructor, last in W:MD #4, '09, last bts in W:WX #2, '09, next in DW #90, '10)
SUPPORTING CAST: Yukio (last in Psy #4, '10, next in W #2, '10), Melita Garner (chr next in W #1, '10 fb, next in DW #90, '10)

VILLAINS: Mystique (also as homeless woman, last in DXM #5, '10, chr next in W #5/2, '11, next in D:DW #1, '10), ninjas (die)
OTHER CHARACTERS: Jubilee (last in NatX #2, '10, next in Girl #3/2, '10), Danielle Cage (Luke & Jessica's infant daughter, last in NAv Ann #3, chr next in NAv #63 fb, next in NAv #62, all '10), migrant worker (in fb), martial arts students, bystanders; Seraph, Silver Fox, Viper prev 3 mentioned, involved with Wolverine), Lady Deathstrike (also on cover), Sabretooth (prev 2 mentioned, might hypothetically attack Melita), Spider-Man, Tom Cruise, John Wayne (prev 3 mentioned, Melita dislikes them), Morrissey, Robert Smith (prev 2 mentioned, Melita likes hem), Brotherhood of Evil Mutants (mentioned, fought Wolverine), Bobby Hornberger, Navy soldier (prev 2 mentioned, Melita's ex-boyfriends), worker's father (mentioned in fb, attacked Wolverine) & family (mentioned in fb, moved on), aliens, Wolverine's lover (prev 2 mentioned, slept with Wolverine), Melita's parents (mentioned, mixed-race couple); Freddie Foxxx (rapper, music on Wolverine's computer); Mariko Yashida (in photo); man (in silhouette as target), women (as mannequins), dragon (as tattoo), tiger (as dojo sign & medallion); Domino, Phoenix (prev 2 cover only)
LOCATIONS/ITEMS: California sugar beet fields (mentioned) & orange grove (in fb), Melita's apartment, Japan, Wakanda (on monitor), pool all, shooting range, mall, Luke & Jessica's hotel room, Sons of the Tiger dojo w/nearby alley, Yashidas' ancestral manor, Utopia (X-Men's sland nation), San Francisco Post offices w/nearby alley, Sonora, Mexico; supermarket meat locker, fight location (prev 3 mentioned) / Worker's ather's hoe, Wolverine's tent, Bobby Hornberger's car, burning car, signal device, GPS tag (all mentioned), ninjas' shurikens (bts) & swords, Yukio's sword, Wolverine's chess set & laptop w/camera, Storm's comm unit (bts), pool table, cues & balls, Black Widow's target (destroyed) & machine guns, Jubilee's purchases, Luke's luggage w/Danielle's pacifier (bts), Sun's medallion, X-Men's Blackbird jet (bts), Mariko's grave narker w/photo

FLASHBACK: A beautiful migrant worker seduces a young Wolverine.
SYNOPSIS: Wolverine and Melita snuggle and trade stories about their dating histories, but Wolverine grows uncomfortable. Later, Wolverine attles ninjas in Japan, but when Yukio propositions him, he strangely turns her down. Wolverine and Storm discuss his rejection of Yukio during a chess game, and Storm surmises that Wolverine has a girlfriend. Playing pool with Rogue, Wolverine denies having feelings for Melita, but ventually admits that he does. Wolverine visits Black Widow and Jubilee, who give him dating advice; Wolverine also visits Luke Cage and essica Jones, and manages to calm their screaming baby. Melita studies self-defense at a dojo; when Wolverine surprises her outside she kicks him in the face, impressing him. Wolverine takes Melita to Mariko's grave, explaining that all his past loves have died. Melita understands he danger, but wants to give a relationship a try anyway. They spend the night together on Utopia, then Wolverine drops Melita off at work. Nearby, disguised as a vagrant, Mystique spies on Melita...

NOTE: This issue also has a 6-page preview of UltNUlts #1, '10. Wolverine's comment that he has "not really" ever been married references his ham marriage to Viper in W #126-169, '98-02, but overlooks his marriage to Itsu in W #40, '06 fb. The X-Men founded Utopia, an artificial island or mutants off San Francisco's coast, in Exodus, '09. Wolverine wears all three of his standard costumes here. Jubilee's name is misspelled as "Jubillee" on her customized earrings. Wolverine's computer desktop contains folders labeled "vacation," "ninja vacation," "Omega Red" and Wolverine Weapon X #10," as well as a thumbnail image of WXNoir, '10's cover and a folder containing the rap album *Freddie Foxxx Is Here*.

WOLVERINE: SAVAGE (April 2010)

"Sushi" (22 pages)

CREDITS: Ryan Dunlavey (writer), Richard Elson (art), Dave Sharpe (letters), Veronica Gandini (colors), Anthony Dial (production), Michael Horwitz (asst editor), Nathan Cosby (editor), J. Scott Campbell (c pencils), Ed McGuinness (variant pencils), Mark Farmer (variant c inks), Christina Strain (c colors), Chris Sotomayor (variant c colors & design)
FEATURE CHARACTER: Wolverine (next in Doomw #1, 3 fb, 1-2 & 3 fb, ANOlym, Herc #138-149, 141 & 141/2, Herc:Fall #1 fb, AvAtlas #1 & 4, IHulk #607-608, FoH:SSH #2, WWHs:C/W #1-2, FoH:SSH #3, Hulk #22, all '10, WvThor #1-3, '09-10; Siege #3, NAvFin, Siege #4, Av:In #35, NAv #1, Av #1-6, all '10, ASM #648, '11; W:O #46, DW #85, W:O #47, DW #86, W:O #48-50, FC #19, DW #89, FC #20,
X23 #2 fb, OMtL #3-5, W:WX #11, all '10)
VILLAIN: Lizard (Dr. Curt Connors, regenerative reptilian alter ego, last in WoSM #6/3, '10, next in ASM #630, '10)
OTHER CHARACTERS: "Pops" (master chef), sushi chef (Pops' daughter) (both also in pfb & photo), their family (in pfb), restaurant patron (others in pfb, another bts placing large order), waiter (in pfb, others mentioned), boat owner, bystanders; sea monster, monster's victims (dead as bones), fish (others dead as sushi, others dead as sushi in pfb, another on restaurant sign), jellyfish (dead as chili), seagulls, shark, octopus, food critics (mentioned, reviewed restaurant), sea lion (mentioned, dissolved in stomach acid); Deadpool (as Wolverine, variant cover only)
LOCATIONS/ITEMS: Pier inc sushi bar (also in pfb & photo) w/kitchen, Pacific Ocean w/island, Las Vegas (mentioned) / Bystanders' cameras, sushi bar window (destroyed & repaired), dishes, tables (some of prev 2 destroyed), pots, pans, vegetables & cutting block, chef's knives (destroyed), Lizard & monsters' tails (destroyed), Pops' ladle, knives, chef jacket, jellyfish chili & indigestion concoction, Wolverine's money, apron & sushi platters, monster's eggs (others bts in ramen in pfb), magazines (mentioned), "Boggins" (Wolverine's boat) w/rope & net
FLASHBACK: Business booms at the sushi bar thanks to Pops' secret ingredient (p).
SYNOPSIS: Wolverine battles and defeats the Lizard, but their fight wrecks a sushi bar. Yelling that Wolverine ruined a large and important order, the chef stabs Wolverine with her knives, but this merely breaks them. She grows despondent; Wolverine offers to help and slices up sushi with his claws. The chef explains that business became bad when her father disappeared while searching for more of his secret ingredient. Wolverine volunteers to find him; he buys a small boat and tracks Pops' scent across the ocean to an island. There Wolverine finds a giant sea monster's eggs, but the monster attacks and swallows him. He discovers Pops living inside the monster's cavernous stomach; Pops gives the monster indigestion using a foul recipe he created, and it vomits up Pops and Wolverine. Pops gathers several eggs, his secret ingredient, while Wolverine defeats the monster. Pops reunites with his daughter and the sushi bar soon regains its popularity, but Wolverine is relegated to dishwashing.
NOTE: This issue also has a Deadpool-themed variant cover, which uses a retouched and recolored version of W:FCBD, '09's cover and Wolverine wears his brown costume here.

WOLVERINE: MR. X (May 2010)

"Unfinished Business" (32 pages)

CREDITS: Frank Tieri (writer), Paco Diaz & Guillermo Ortego (art), Jared K. Fletcher (letters), Ulises Arreola (colors), Damien Lucchese (production), Jody LeHeup (asst editor), Jeanine Schaefer (editor), Francesco Mattina (c art)
FEATURE CHARACTER: Wolverine (also in rfb2, photo & Mr. X's imagination, chr last in Run #10, '09, chr next in W:Rev, '09)
VILLAINS: Mr. X (also in rfb1 & rfb2, also in fb during W #161, '01 fb, chr last in W #168, '01, chr next in Th #132, '09), Iron Patriot (chr last in DR:LL #3, chr next bts in Tb #132, chr next in Tb #133, all '09), bank robbers
OTHER CHARACTERS: Knights of Wundagore (High Evolutionary's artificially evolved animal warriors): Sir Ossilot (in fb between IM #111, '78 & MAv #22, '09 fb), Count Tagar (in fb between Thor #484, '95 & MAv #22, '09 fb), Lord Gator; Bova Ayrshire (evolved cow-woman, in shadow) (prev 2 in fb between HFH #17, '98 & MAv #22, '09 fb), Mr. X's sparring partners (1 dies, others dead, see NOTE) & kindergarten teacher (dead as head) & her students (prev 3 as "Wolverine"), bank employee & patrons, delivery boy, bystanders; wolverines (die), dinosaurs (dead as skeletons); driver (bts in car), accident victim, fighter (prev 2 die), audience, bystanders (prev 5 in rfb1); warriors (as mannequins) & their victims (as prop skulls), historical figures, horse (prev 2 as statues), Humpty Dumpty, frog, owl, fish (prev 4 as mobile), bear, bees (prev 2 on posters), dragon (on sword), lions (as kneepads)
LOCATIONS/ITEMS: City street, dojo, fighting arena (all in rfb1), Wundagore Mountain (High Evolutionary's Transia lab, in fb), Bloodsport arena (in rfb2), New York City inc Mr. X's warehouse hideout (another in rfb2), bank, classroom & Museum of Natural History w/Hall of Warriors, Iron Patriot's office, Graymalkin Industries (X-Men's Marin Headlands, San Francisco base, mentioned) / Car (in rfb1), Bloodsport cage (in rfb2, floor destroyed), Mr. X's swords (another in fb), arrow (destroyed), bow, gasoline, match, axe, cellphone, metal pipes, cage w/remote control & parcel w/note (destroyed), sparring partners' robotic suit (destroyed) & Wolverine costumes, Wolverine's eyepatch (in rfb2), motorcycle, bandage & Avengers ID card, robbers' guns (destroyed), knife & bulletproof vests, delivery boy's hat (destroyed), students' bonds, tape & masks, mannequins' prop weapons inc hook, Iron Patriot's armor, cellphone & monitors
FLASHBACKS: A woman's death triggers Mr. X's telepathy; he grows to love killing (W #161, '01 fb). Mr. X defeats Wolverine once (W #160, '01), but loses to his berserker rage (W #168, '01). Mr. X battles the Knights of Wundagore.
SYNOPSIS: Mr. X kills several sparring partners dressed as Wolverine. He then kills actual wolverines, having trained to fight creatures whose minds he cannot read. Later, as Wolverine thwarts a bank robbery, a delivery boy brings him a package; inside is a schoolteacher's head wearing a Wolverine mask. Wolverine races to the school to find Mr. X holding the children hostage. Obsessed with defeating Wolverine, Mr. X challenges him to a fight at the Museum of History. Wolverine grudgingly accepts; that night, Wolverine arrives and Mr. X attacks. Wolverine suddenly realizes that Mr. X craves this battle, and stops fighting. Enraged, Mr. X slashes at Wolverine and threatens to kill the X-Men's students, but Wolverine calmly swears that if Mr. X harms anyone, Wolverine will never fight him again. Without a worthy foe, Mr. X sinks into depression — until Norman Osborn invites him to join his Thunderbolts…

This issue occurs immediately before Mr. X joins the Thunderbolts. Mr. X's deceased sparring partners include a large fanged creature d what appears to be a Brood killed in mid-transformation.

WOLVERINE: WEAPON X #11 [#274] (May 2010)

"Tomorrow Dies Today, Part 1" (22 pages)

CREDITS: Jason Aaron (writer), Ron Garney (pencils, see NOTE), Virtual Calligraphy's Cory Petit (letters), Jason Keith (colors), Jody LeHeup (asst editor), Jeanine Schaefer (editor), Axel Alonso (group editor)
FEATURE CHARACTER: Wolverine
GUEST STARS: Steve Rogers (also as Captain America on recap page, last in EHAge/3, '10, next in W:WX #13, '10), X-Men: Cyclops (bts on comm system, last in S:FallSun, '10, next in W:Dust, '10), Nightcrawler (last in Girl #1, '10, next in W #900/2, '10)
VILLAINS: Earth-10511 future Deathloks (cybernetically enhanced murderers, 1st but chr last in W:WX #15, '10) inc Unit L17 (unnamed)
OTHER CHARACTERS: Miranda L. Bayer (waitress, 1st, unnamed), Jeffrey K. Winstone (volcanic rock body), Winston Rowe (latent telepath), Wendell Bryant (drunken romantic), Amy (Wendell's date) (prev 4 die), newborns s in maternity ward) inc Bradberry twins (die), bar patrons & bartender, hospital security guards (some or all die), nurses, Earth-10511 future sidents: Emma Frost (dead as brain sample), Kang (dead as head), General (1st bts app), rebel (prev 4 bts sending Miranda psychic messages); '; football players (on TV); Captain America (mentioned, Deathloks' next target), Iron Man (mentioned, talked to Captain America about Wolverine), or (mentioned, took Wolverine to Viking bar), Buzzsaw (Todd Bryant, Earth-10511 super hero, mentioned, Wendell & Amy's son), Melita Garner entioned by Wolverine), Himalayan murder monks (mentioned, trained Jeffrey), Viking bar owners (mentioned, make mead from Frost Giant blood), rchaser (mentioned, bought Dulohery's Pub), bank officials (mentioned, foreclosed on Richie's Bar); Hank Williams (music played on jukebox); ative American chief (as belt buckle), tribal figure (as mask), girl (as doll), gargoyle (as statue)
OCATIONS/ITEMS: New York City inc rooftop, alley, Central Park, Julio's Bar & Grill & hospital w/maternity ward, bars (bts), Drifter's Reef olynesian bar), Himalayan monastery, Oar House, Market Street Tavern, Dulohery's Pub, Richie's Bar, yuppie bar, coffee shop, Bryants' Tahiti sort, Icelandic Viking bar (prev 9 mentioned) / Deathloks' cybernetic implants (some bts), artificial intelligence units (bts) (both hereinafter nsidered their standard equipment and not listed separately), blasters & laser claws, X-Men's Blackbird jet w/comm unit, Steve & Wolverine's nks & empty glasses, Frost Giant blood mead, Steve's Super-Soldier serum (prev 2 mentioned), bar door (destroyed) & jukebox, Cyclops' mm system (bts), security guards' guns, hospital fire axe w/glass case (destroyed), rebels' temporal relay machine (bts)
YNOPSIS: Would-be vigilante Jeffrey Winstone begins his first night of crimefighting, but a Deathlok unit suddenly confronts and murders m. Nearby, Wolverine welcomes Steve Rogers, formerly Captain America, back to the land of the living by taking him on a pub crawl with ghtcrawler as designated driver. Elsewhere, a Deathlok interrupts Wendell and Amy's awkward first date; it informs them that their son will e day be a super hero, then kills them. In a Polynesian bar, Steve thanks Wolverine for staying with the Avengers while he was thought dead. olverine grudgingly admits that with Steve back and Melita in his life, he is happy; when a local criticizes his musical taste, Wolverine promptly :ks a bar fight. In New York, a Deathlok murders newborns in a maternity ward. As a battered Steve and Wolverine return home, a woman med Miranda confronts Wolverine, warning that Deathloks have arrived from the future. Nearby, the Deathloks murder their final secondary rget, and prepare for their main mission: to kill Captain America.
OTE: This issue also has a 6-page preview of ElecAnt #1, '10. Miranda Bayer is named next issue. Unit L17 is designated in W:WX #14, '10, nich also reveals how Miranda receives messages from the future. Earth-10511 is designated in OHMU TPB3, '12. Jeffrey Winstone takes e codename Slag in Earth-10511's future. The Deathloks' laser claws are derived from those of Strikeforce X. Steve Rogers returned from eming death in Cap:Re #6, '10, although James Barnes is still acting as Captain America. This arc does not have an inker; it is colored directly om Ron Garney's finished pencils.

WOLVERINE: WEAPON X #12 [#275] (June 2010)

"Tomorrow Dies Today, Part 2" (22 pages)

CREDITS: Jason Aaron (writer), Ron Garney (pencils), Virtual Calligraphy's Cory Petit (letters), Jason Keith (colors), Jody LeHeup (asst editor), Jeanine Schaefer (editor), Axel Alonso (group editor), Morry Hollowell (c colors)
FEATURE CHARACTER: Wolverine
GUEST STAR: Captain America (last in OMtL #5, '10)
VILLAINS: Earth-10511 future Deathloks (also some's past selves, some of those also on monitor, some or others chr last in W:WX #13, '10) inc Unit L17 (also his past self, chr last in W:WX #15, '10)
OTHER CHARACTERS: Miranda Bayer (named) & her Earth-10511 future self (1st, rebel squad commander), Evan Wakowski (child, 1st) & his Earth-10511 future self (1st, rebel squad member), Café Kiev employee, commuters, bystanders, Earth-10511 future residents: General (Deathlok Unit L17's alternate-future self, rebellion's hidden leader, 1st, next in W:WX #14, '10), Wolverine's Earth-10511 future self (dies), Emma Frost ead as brain sample), Kang (dead as head) (prev 2 bts sending Miranda psychic messages, next in W:WX #14, '10), rebels inc squad embers (some also on monitor), Roxxon scientists (some or others chr last in W:WX #15, '10) & sentries (all but 1 bts guarding facility), standers, Roxxon's cyborg guard dogs (bts guarding facility); Earth-10511 heroes: Spider-Man (see NOTE), Captain America, Ghost Rider, n Fist, Mr. Fantastic, Punisher, Thing (prev 7 listed as slain), Iron Man (listed as apprehended), Hulk (status unknown), Daredevil (at large), ners (prev 11 in photos); Vladimir Lenin (in portrait), Native American chief (as belt buckle), people, cat (prev 2 in posters)
OCATIONS/ITEMS: New York City inc Central Park, Café Kiev (Russian restaurant, destroyed) & subway station, future Earth-10511 (1st) inc unisher's hideout (mentioned), Howlett's bookstore w/rebel base & Roxxon facility w/lab (also on monitor) / Roxxon's security cameras (all but 1 s) & time machine, bookstore's buzzer & hidden door, rebels' temporal relay machine (bts), guns, grenades, photo wall & computers w/energy anners (bts), squad's grenades (bts), guns (some also on monitor), armor, blowtorch, binoculars & rocket launcher, Wolverine's exoskeleton & ok-hand, sentries' guns, mines & rocket launchers (prev 3 bts), Deathloks' acid, General's cybernetic implants (bts) (all Earth-10511), Deathloks' asters (some also on Earth-10511, some of those also on monitor) & scanners (bts), subway ceiling (destroyed), Captain America's gun

SYNOPSIS: 25 years from now in a Roxxon-dominated world, an older Miranda Bayer delivers bad news to her underground rebels: Roxxon Deathloks have killed the Punisher, one of the few heroes left. The rebels detect Roxxon's time machine in use and dispatch a squad to destroy it; an older Wolverine, missing both his hands, joins them. In the present, Miranda explains that she has been receiving messages from the future, and knows that Deathloks have traveled here to kill anyone suspected of being the General, the rebels' secretive leader. Nearby, the Deathloks attack Captain America; Miranda leads Wolverine to the fight and he swiftly joins in. Deathlok unit L17 targets Miranda, but experiences a paralyzing and oddly emotional system glitch. A young boy pulls Miranda to safety; she recognizes him as her future squadmate Wakowski. In the future, the rebels infiltrate Roxxon's lab and Wolverine assaults the time machine, but Deathloks douse him with acid, killing him. As the squad attacks the Deathloks, the General monitors the battle from afar.

NOTE: Earth-10511's Spider-Man's status is not visible on the photo seen here, but next issue clarifies that he has been killed. Evan Wakowski's first name is revealed in W:WX #14, '10. The General is revealed as Unit L17's future self in W:WX #15, '10.

WOLVERINE: WEAPON X #13 [#276] (July 2010)

"Tomorrow Dies Today, Part 3" (22 pages)

CREDITS: Jason Aaron (writer), Ron Garney (pencils), Virtual Calligraphy's Cory Petit (letters), Jason Keith (colors), Jody LeHeup (asst editor), Jeanine Schaefer (editor), Axel Alonso (group editor), Morry Hollowell (c colors)

FEATURE CHARACTER: Wolverine

GUEST STARS: Avengers: Spider-Man (last in OMtL #5, '10), Spider-Woman (Jessica Drew, last in NAv #1, '10, chr last in ASM #648, '11), Captain America; New Avengers (Cage's Avengers team): Iron Fist (Daniel Rand, martial arts master), Luke Cage (prev 2 last in Av #1, '10), Thing (last in OMtL #3, '10); Steve Rogers (last in W:WX #11, '10)

VILLAINS: Earth-10511 future Deathloks (also some or others' past selves, 1 dies, chr last in W:WX #14, '10, some or others chr next in W:WX #12, '10; also some's past selves, some bts fighting rebels) inc Unit L17 (also his past self, possibly bts fighting rebels)

OTHER CHARACTERS: Miranda Bayer & her Earth-10511 future self, Evan Wakowski & his Earth-10511 future self, Dr. David Heimerdinger (last in DRL:W, '09, dies), subway conductor (bts driving subway train), Deathloks' other targets (bts, guarded by Avengers), commuters, target's neighbor, bystanders, Earth-10511 future residents: Spider-Man's Earth-10511 future self (dies), Roxxon control (voice only on radio) & security guards, rioters (some die), rebel squad (some bts fighting Deathloks), "Spider-Friends" (Spider-Man arachnid robots); Heimerdinger's cybernetically enhanced animals; Iron Patriot (mentioned, exiled Heimerdinger), Melita Garner (mentioned, Spider-Woman), Luther Manning, Michael Collins (prev 2 mentioned, previous Deathloks), Heimerdinger's possums (mentioned, need cages & cybernetically animated corpses (mentioned, former soldiers), corpses' victims (mentioned, illegal immigrants); Sentinel (on poster), Native American chief (as belt buckle)

LOCATIONS/ITEMS: Subway station, targets' locations (all but 1 bts), Roadside Carcass Removal Dept. w/parking lot, future Earth-10511 Roxxon facility w/lab & nearby building (destroyed), Baxter Building, US-Mexico border (prev 2 mentioned) / Protesters' signs, bat & hurled bricks, guards' guns & armor w/radio (bts), control's comm system (bts), Deathloks' recorder (bts) & bazooka, Spider-Man's truncheons & web shooting gun w/scope, Roxxon's Most Wanted list (mentioned) & time machine (bts), squad's guns (bts) & bomb (all Earth-10511), Deathlok blasters (some or others also on Earth-10511, some bts), teleporters (bts, some or others also bts on Earth-10511) & transmitters (bts), L17 scanners, web-shooter (prev 2 bts), repulsor ray & laser claws, Captain America's gun, subway train w/window (destroyed), Avengers Quinjet w/GPS system & comm unit, Steve's wrist communicator (destroyed), animals' cages & cybernetic implants, Captain America's makeshift bandages & wrist communicator

SYNOPSIS: 22 years from now, Roxxon unleashes Deathloks against a crowd of protesters. An older Spider-Man tries to stop the massacre but the Deathloks kill him. In the present, Wolverine and Captain America continue battling the Deathloks. Unit L17 corners Miranda again, but although his human half desperately wants to kill her, his computerized brain continues glitching. Wolverine intervenes and decapitates L17; Steve Rogers and the Avengers arrive and the remaining Deathloks retreat. Miranda tells Steve about the Deathloks' remaining targets and reveals that scientist Dr. Heimerdinger will invent the Deathloks. Wolverine and Captain America bring the inert L17 to Heimerdinger, who currently experiments on cybernetically enhancing animals. Wolverine suggests killing him, but Miranda warns that his death may not prevent the future, merely alter it. L17 suddenly revives, lashes out and kills Heimerdinger, and flees with his own severed head. Elsewhere, the other Deathloks find Steve and the Avengers guarding their targets; deducing that Miranda is an intelligence leak, they target her for death. Brandishing several new powers, L17 attacks Miranda...

NOTE: This issue also has a 1-page "Celebrating the Women of Marvel" interview with writer Kelly Sue DeConnick. Dr. Heimerdinger's title and last name are revealed here. Although it is not made explicit until next issue's recap page, L17's new powers, including versions of Iron Man's repulsor rays and Spider-Man's web-shooters, manifested as a result of Heimerdinger's premature death retroactively changing the circumstances of the Deathloks' creation. One subway commuter reads Jason Aaron's DC comic "Scalped" this issue.

WOLVERINE: WEAPON X #14 [#277] (August 2010)

"Tomorrow Dies Today, Part 4" (22 pages)

CREDITS: Jason Aaron (writer), Ron Garney (pencils), Virtual Calligraphy's Cory Petit (letters) & Clayton Cowles (production), Jason Keith & Matt Milla (colors), Jody LeHeup (asst editor), Jeanine Schaefer (editor), Axel Alonso (group editor), Morry Hollowell (c colors)

FEATURE CHARACTER: Wolverine

GUEST STARS: Avengers: Spider-Man (also on shirt), Captain America, Spider-Woman; New Avengers: Luke Cage, Iron Fist, Thing; Steve Rogers

VILLAINS: Earth-10511 future Deathloks (also some's past selves, their chr 1st app, some or others chr last bts in W:WX #15, '10, also in W:WX #13, '10, these also in rfb, also in W:WX #12-13, '10) inc Unit L17 (also his past self, his chr 1st app, also as murderer, dies & revived as Unit L17, also in W:WX #15, 12 & 13, '10) & others (some or others chr last bts in W:WX #15, '10, chr next in W:WX #13, '10), Earth-10511 future Roxxon executives (some or others also bts in W:WX #15, '10) & Deathlok prototypes (in fb)

THER CHARACTERS: Miranda Bayer & her Earth-10511 future self, Evan Wakowski (dies) & his Earth-10511 future self (erased from
ne), Unit L17's childhood self (orphan), cook, security guard, bystanders; Earth-10511 future residents: Emma Frost (dead as brain sample),
ang (dead as head) (prev 2 1st on-panel app), General (prev 3 last in W:WX #12, '10), Mathew K. Edwards (Roxxon detractor, dies) & his wife
children, Roxxon scientists (die in fb, others chr next in W:WX #15, '10), prison guards, rebels inc squad members; madmen (mentioned, in
urderer's earliest memories), murderer's victims (mentioned, killed), police, judges, juries (prev 3 mentioned, caught & convicted murderer),
/ilians, government officials, super heroes (prev 3 mentioned, targeted by Roxxon), marketing department (mentioned, named "Peaceloks");
Jolverine's Earth-10511 future self (dies in rfb), Earth-10511 heroes: Captain America, Daredevil, Hulk, Spider-Man, Sub-Mariner, others (prev
in photos), Native American chief (bts as belt buckle), model (on poster); worms (in painting)
OCATIONS/ITEMS: New York City inc parking lot & Youth Development Center w/kitchen, future Earth-10511: Roxxon labs (1 also in rfb,
nother also in fb), jail, Edwards' house, rebel base; Dunwich Sanatorium (mentioned) / Executive's limousine & gun, Roxxon's logo, crematoriums,
rthing stations (prev 3 mentioned), security cameras (bts) & time machine, L17's intravenous caffeine system, endorphin regulator, reverse
uscle thrusters (prev 3 bts) & blaster, Deathloks' acid (in rfb) & bio-beds, prototypes' cybernetic implants (some bts), scientists' computers
rev 2 in fb), squad's bomb (destroyed), guns & armor, rebels' computers, photo wall & temporal relay machine, General's cybernetic implants
ts) (all Earth-10511), L17's laser claws (also on Earth-10511) & repulsor ray, Deathloks' blasters (some also on Earth-10511), transmitters &
leporters (prev 2 bts), Steve & Captain America's wrist communicators, kitchen knives
LASHBACKS: Deathloks kill the older Wolverine (W:WX #12, '10). Deathlok prototypes run amok and attack their creators.
YNOPSIS: 20 years from now, a Roxxon executive releases a remorseless murderer from prison, then shoots him. The murderer awakens
ansformed into Unit L17, one of Roxxon's new Deathlok enforcers, as executives toast their recent corporate takeover of the planet. L17 enjoys
utally enforcing Roxxon's rule, but resents his computerized brain forbidding him to kill randomly. In the present, L17 overrides his glitching
omputer and assaults Miranda, but Wolverine and Captain America tackle him while Miranda and Wakowski flee. In the future, the older
Jakowski assaults the time machine — but when Deathloks kill the young Wakowski in the present, his elder counterpart vanishes. Realizing
at time was altered, the General sends a psychic message to the younger Miranda; she immediately races into a nearby orphanage, pursued
y L17, as the other heroes arrive and attack the Deathloks. In the future, L17 confronts the older Miranda. In the present, L17 finds Miranda
olding a knife to his childhood self's throat…
IOTE: This issue's cover is an homage to that of W:WX #1, '09. Evan Wakowski and Dr. David Heimerdinger's first names are revealed here.
Jolverine appears in only seven panels of this issue, and speaks only two lines.

WOLVERINE: WEAPON X #15 [#278] (September 2010)

"Tomorrow Dies Today, Conclusion" (22 pages)

CREDITS: Jason Aaron (writer), Ron Garney (pencils), Virtual Calligraphy's Cory Petit (letters), Jason Keith
& Matt Milla (colors), Jody LeHeup (asst editor), Jeanine Schaefer (editor), Axel Alonso (group editor), Chris
Sotomayor (c colors)
FEATURE CHARACTER: Wolverine (next in W #900, '10)
GUEST STARS: Avengers: Captain America, Spider-Woman (both next in X:L #236, '10); Spider-Man (also on
shirt, next in MK #9, '10); New Avengers: Luke Cage, Iron Fist (prev 2 next in ChW #1, '10), Thing (next in UXM
#525, '10); Steve Rogers (next in UXM:HA, '10)
VILLAINS: Earth-10511 future Deathloks (die, also their past selves, chr next in W:WX #11, '10; some or others'
past selves also bts being operated on, their chr 1st bts app, chr next in W:WX #14, '10) inc Unit L17 (next in
UXFor #5, '11; also his past self, also on monitor, also in W:WX #14 & 12-14, '10, chr next in W:WX #11, '10),
arth-10511 future Roxxon executives (bts, arriving to view experiments, some or others chr next in W:WX #14, '10)
THER CHARACTERS: Miranda Bayer & her Earth-10511 future self (also on monitor, dies), Unit L17's childhood self, orphans, Earth-10511
ture residents: Roxxon scientists (others mentioned, others last in W:WX #14, '10 fb, some or others chr next in W:WX #12, '10) inc Abraham
ornson (particle physicist, bts sleeping with scientist) & Martin, General, Unit L17's victims (some die, others dead), rebels inc squad (dies);
Jinston Rowe, Jeffrey Winstone (prev 2 mentioned, Deathlok's targets), Unit
17's childhood self's tormentors (mentioned, will beat & neglect him); Native American chief (bts as belt buckle), musician (on poster)
OCATIONS/ITEMS: New York City inc Youth Development Center, future Earth-10511: Roxxon labs (1 also on monitor), victims' flophouse,
bel base; Danmar Orphanage (Wayland, Massachusetts, mentioned) / L17's laser claws (also on monitor) & cybernetic brain implants,
rmaldehyde jar, scientists' computers & surgical equipment, Miranda's gun (destroyed) & electrified truncheon (also on monitor), squad's
rmor, Roxxon's security cameras (bts) & time machine, rebels' temporal relay machine (mentioned) & computer, General's cybernetic implants
ome bts) (all Earth-10511), L17's emotional subfolder (bts, also bts in Earth-10511), blaster, lucky rabbit's foot (prev 2 also on Earth-10511),
leporter, antivirus software, personality dampening program, nanorobotic molecular propellers (prev 4 bts) & repulsor ray, Miranda's kitchen
nife, Deathloks' hearts (destroyed), blaster (some also on Earth-10511), laser claws, web-shooter & repulsor rays, Steve & Thing's wrist
ommunicators, orphanage wall (destroyed)
YNOPSIS: 20 years from now, scientists upgrade Unit L17's brain. When the scientists' romance goes sour, the computerized brain becomes
urious about emotion, but its human half suppresses those thoughts. In the present, Miranda threatens L17's childhood self until Wolverine
efuses the standoff. 25 years from now, the older Miranda recognizes L17 from her past; suddenly realizing what must occur, she lets L17 kill
er. In the present, L17's computer glitch returns. Recognizing Miranda as the woman he killed, his computerized brain suddenly re-opens its
motion files and suppresses its human half. Thanking Miranda for teaching him about compassion, L17 switches sides and helps defeat the
ther Deathloks. In the future, the older Miranda tells L17 that she loves him and dies. L17 briefly feels emotion, then enters the time machine
ith the other Deathloks, beginning their mission in the past to kill anyone who might be the General. In the present, L17 decides to explore
umanity; in the future, the General is revealed as an aged and compassionate L17.
IOTE: This issue also has a 2-page interview with paleontologist Dr. Michael J. Ryan, who classified a dinosaur "Medusaceratops lokii" after
hor's evil stepbrother Loki. This issue's future segment detailing L17's brain surgery is incorrectly labeled "25 years from now"; it is actually 20.

WOLVERINE #900 (July 2010)

(Untitled, 11 pages)

CREDITS: C.B. Cebulski (co-plot), David Finch (co-plot, pencils), James Asmus (script), Danny Miki (inks), Dave Sharpe (letters), Guru eFX (colors), John Barber (editor, uncredited), Aspen's Peter Steigerwald (c colors)
FEATURE CHARACTER: Wolverine
VILLAINS: Crimelord (possibly dies, see NOTE) & his ninjas (die)
OTHER CHARACTERS: Crimelord's bodyguards, masseuse, bystanders; Weapon X Program senior sta (mentioned, found by Wolverine); people (on poster & billboard, others dead as skulls on cover); dragons (as tattoos)
LOCATIONS/ITEMS: San Francisco's Chinatown w/rooftops & massage parlor / Ninjas' swords, shurikens, tiger claws, parlor window & door (prev 2 destroyed), crimelord's sword
SYNOPSIS: Wolverine tracks a scent across Chinatown, thinking about how easy it is for him to slip into a animalistic, instinctive hunting mode. Although the Weapon X Program gave him his Adamantium, he has alway been a killer, always been full of feral rage — which bothers him, because in many ways he is far too similar to the criminals and murderers that h fights on a daily basis. Wolverine finds his prey, a Chinatown crimelord, at a massage parlor. When the crimelord's ninjas attack, badly woundir Wolverine, he gives in to a mindless berserker rage and lashes out savagely. Later, a recovered Wolverine ponders his tenuous grip on humanit
NOTE: This one-shot's numbering, poking fun at the vast number of Wolverine one-shots, miniseries and spin-offs over the years, is take from the similarly numbered Dp #900, '09. The crimelord's fate is unrevealed, but Wolverine presumably killed him. Wolverine wears his brow costume in this story.

2ND STORY: "The Curse of the Yellow Claw" (22 pages)
CREDITS: Dean Motter (writer), Greg Scott (art), Dave Sharpe (letters), Val Staples (colors), Michael Horwitz & John Barber (editors)
FEATURE CHARACTER: Wolverine (also as Black Dragon, next in W:DevHell, W:Dust, X:SC #1, UXM #523, NM #12, X:L #235, all '10, X #260, '12 fb; X:L #235, XFor #26, UXM #524, SC:Prepare, NM #13, X:L #236, XFor #27, UXM #525, NM #14, X:L #237, XFor #28, UXM:H fb, X:SC #2, all '10, NM #20-21, '11, W:WX #16, '10)
GUEST STAR: Nightcrawler (last in W:WX #11, '10, next in X:SC #1, '10)
VILLAINS: Yellow Claw (Plan Chu, Communist villain, also in Wolverine's thoughts, last in AoAtlas #6, '07, possibly last as spirit in Atlas #5, '1 see NOTE), Ibis Consortium (land developers, bts buying buildings) & their horticulturalists & hired thugs inc Red Lotus Tong (Chinatown gang corrupt City Hall officials (bts ignoring Ibis' plans)
OTHER CHARACTERS: Mai Ling (building owner) & her partners (bts refurbishing buildings), Nari Ling (Mai's sister, bts, threatened b Ibis), Run Run (street hustler, last in W:MD #3, '09), ship captain (bts piloting ferry), Xyno addicts (in fb), street gang & their victim, cabbie (silhouette), bystanders; animals (dead; others bts, dead on Mai's doorstep), seagulls; Lin Fong (previous Black Dragon, mentioned, overthrow by Wolverine), Mai's grandfather (mentioned, died), Chinatown locals (mentioned, asked Black Dragon for help), criminals (mentioned, oppose Triads), charities (mentioned, aided by criminals) & authorities (mentioned, disliked criminals), Triads (mentioned, opposed by criminals Chinese authorities (mentioned, wiped out Xyno); Nick Fury, Jimmy Woo, Suwan (prev 3 in Wolverine's thoughts); woman (as mannequin Chinese demons (as masks)
LOCATIONS/ITEMS: San Francisco Bay w/Utopia & Alcatraz Island, San Francisco: City Hall (mentioned), Mai Ling's Alamo Squar apartment, Chinatown inc Yellow Claw's hideout, Mai Ling's Spofford Alley buildings (mentioned) & Stockton Street fireworks shop (destroyed w/basement & alley & nearby Ibis-owned buildings (mentioned), China (in fb & painting) inc opium den (in fb) / Ferry, Ibis' paint (mentioned letter, trucks, high-pressure manifolds & refrigeration, filter & air conditioning units, Run Run's smartphone, Prada handbag & powdered toa venom (prev 3 mentioned), Wolverine's bribe, laptop, cellphone & wall projection screen, Nick Fury & Jimmy Woo's guns, Suwan's sword (prev 3 in Wolverine's thoughts), yellow claw flowers (others also in fb), Xyno, addicts' drug paraphernalia (prev 2 in fb), X-Men's xenobotanic database, gang member's knife, thugs' metal pipes (1 destroyed) & environmental gear, taxi, Mai Ling's keys, fireworks shop chains, firework & hidden door (destroyed) w/bars, horticulturists' yellow claw growing equipment & control booth w/window, alarm (prev 4 destroyed) & sel destruct system, Red Lotus swords, axe, hammer, spear & clubs
FLASHBACK: Addicts smoke Xyno, a drug made from yellow claw poppies.
SYNOPSIS: Mai Ling asks for Wolverine's help as the Black Dragon to intervene against a corporation that is pressuring her to sell he fireworks shop. Wolverine visits his Chinatown contact Run Run, who explains that the block's expansive basement level used to be an opiun den, and reveals that "yellow claw" is involved — not the super villain, but the highly narcotic flower. Wolverine investigates the shop, but whe thugs attack him and flee, Wolverine realizes that they will know that Mai Ling sent him. He races to her apartment, finding her badly beate she mentions a secret passage beneath the shop and Wolverine calls Nightcrawler for help. Later, Wolverine infiltrates the basement, findin a massive yellow claw growing operation. He attacks, distracting the guards while Nightcrawler teleports into the control room and activate the operation's self-destruct system. Wolverine, Nightcrawler and Mai Ling watch the shop collapse, destroying the poppies — as nearby, th villainous Yellow Claw watches as well.
NOTE: Wolverine was crowned the Black Dragon, ruler of San Francisco's Chinatown underworld, in W:MD #4, '09. The Yellow Claw died i AoAtlas #6, '07. His appearance here may signify an as-yet-unexplained return to life, or may be an imposter or robot double.

3RD STORY: "Desperate Measures" (11 pages)
CREDITS: Todd Dezago (writer), Jason Craig (art), Dave Sharpe (letters), Thomas Mason (colors), Chris Allo, John Barber & Michael Horwit (editors)
FEATURE CHARACTER: Wolverine (also in pfb, chr last in UXM #359, '98, chr next in UXM&FF Ann '98)
GUEST STARS: X-Men: Marrow (also bts fighting Sentinels in pfb, between X #78-79, '98), Beast (also in pfb, chr next in UXM&FF Ann '98 Archangel (chr next in Ex #125, '98) (prev 2 chr last in UXM #358, '98), Cyclops (chr last in UXM #359, '98, chr next in UXM #368, '99) (pre 2 in pfb)
VILLAINS: Sentinels (bts attacking Morlocks, also in pfb, some or others chr last in UXM #337, '96, 1 chr last in Ugirl #3, '97, some or other chr next in X51 #6, '00)
OTHER CHARACTERS: Morlocks (tunnel-dwelling mutants): Ape (shapeshifter, chr last in XFac #15, '87, chr next in WX #5, '03), Matchstic Girl (pyrokinetic) (prev 2 also bts fleeing from Sentinels in pfb), Carapace (Cara, generates protective shell), Poser (duplicates powers) (prev also in pfb & on Sentinel's scanner in pfb); rats; Leech (mentioned, Poser duplicates his power), Morlock children (mentioned, nicknamed Poser

LOCATIONS/ITEMS: Morlock tunnels (beneath New York City) w/nearby entrance (in pfb) / Shrapnel (also in pfb), debris, shopping cart, crates, Matchstick Girl's gloves, Marrow's bone knives, Sentinel's mutant sensors (bts in pfb), makeshift bandages (bts)

FLASHBACK: The X-Men intervene when Sentinels attack the Morlock tunnels, but flying shrapnel injures Carapace (p).

SYNOPSIS: Beast, Marrow, Wolverine and some Morlocks flee into the tunnels with the injured Carapace, but an explosion traps them in a small chamber. Beast asks everyone to work together, but Marrow lashes out, claiming that she and Wolverine are nothing but weapons. Beast quickly formulates a plan: Poser imitates Leech's powers, canceling Carapace's protective shell. Matchstick Girl generates flame, Ape mimics mirror to amplify the light, and Beast guides Wolverine's hands, using his claws to remove Carapace's shrapnel as Marrow hacks through the debris trapping them. The operation is successful and the mutants escape; Wolverine quietly refutes Marrow's accusation.

NOTE: This story occurs during Marrow's brief tenure as an X-Man. Wolverine is incorrectly depicted with metal claws here; he had bone claws this time. Neither Archangel nor Cyclops were active X-Men at this time; they may have been visiting the team. Though Wolverine says that three Sentinels attacked, four are seen in the pfb; presumably Cyclops and Archangel defeated them during this story.

TH STORY: "One Night Only" (11 pages)
NOTE: Reprinted from W:ONO, '09.

TH STORY: "Worst There Is" (11 pages)
NOTE: Reprinted from W:Worst, '10.

TH STORY: "Birthday Boy" (18 pages)
NOTE: Reprinted from ASME #2/2, '09.

TH STORY: "Puny Little Man" (12 pages)
NOTE: Reprinted from W #50/2, '07.

TH STORY: "Hunger" (8 pages)
NOTE: Reprinted from W:Hunger, '09.

WOLVERINE: WEAPON X #16 [#279] (September 2010)

"The End of the Beginning" (22 pages)

CREDITS: Jason Aaron (writer), Davide Gianfelice (art), Virtual Calligraphy's Cory Petit (letters), Dave McCaig (colors), Jody LeHeup (asst editor), Jeanine Schaefer (editor), Axel Alonso (group editor), Ron Garney (c pencils), Morry Hollowell (c colors)

FEATURE CHARACTER: Wolverine (also in rfb2, also in fb1 between CX #2, '86 & X #94, '75; also in fb2 between X #138, '80 & X Ann #4, '80; also in fb3 between UXM #148, '81 & BMC HC, '87; also in fb4 between HFHX, '85 & SecWars2 #7, '86; next in UXM:HA, '10, W #309, '12 fb; Girl #3/2, UXM #526-527, all '10; GenHope #1-4, UXM #530-534, all '11, Doomw #6, '10, GenHope #5, '11, IAmAv #5/2, '11, Herc:Fall #1, '10, ChW #1, '10, ChW:ChK, '11, ChW #1-2, '10; ChW:DeAv #1, 2 bts & 3, ChW #5 bts, all '11, IAmAv #2/3-4, '10, NAv #1-6, '10-11, IAmAv #4, '11, NAv #7, '11; IAmAv #1, BW #1-2 & 5, W #1 fb, all '10, AstSMW #1-6, '10-11, Sland #4-5, '10-11; DW #90, X #1-2, XCurse:SG, XCurse:XV #1/4, XCurse:SB fb, all '10, X #5 fb & 3-6, '10-11; W&Jub #1-4, W #5/2, all '11, W:RTH, '10)

GUEST STARS: X-Men: Nightcrawler (also dead in rfb1, also in rfb2, also in fb2 between X #138, '80 & X Ann #4, '80; also in fb3 between UXM #148-149, '81; also in fb4 between HFHX, '85 & SecWars2 #7, '86), Colossus, Cyclops, Storm (all in fb1 between CX #2, '86 & X #94, '85), Angel (last in X:SC #2, '10, chr last in NM #21, '11, next in UXM:HA, '10, see NOTE), others (bts reading will, exact members unspecified, am last in X:SC #2, '10, chr last in NM #21, '11, next in UXM:HA, '10)

OTHER CHARACTERS: African natives, relief workers (both in fb4), priest, parishioners; monkeys (bts, stole Wolverine's supplies), bugs (bts, eaten by Wolverine), mosquitoes (1 dies); Bastion (as arm in rfb1); Phoenix (mentioned in fb2, dead), Sabuko (mentioned in fb3, Wolverine plans to kill him)

LOCATIONS/ITEMS: Utopia (also in rfb1), Venezuela mountain w/river & Church of the Holy Ascension, X-Mansion (in fb3) w/Danger Room (in fb1 & rfb2), Bard College Cemetery (in fb2), African plains (in fb4), seminary (mentioned) / Nightcrawler's will (bts), concert grand piano, mountain roads (mentioned, washed out), X-Men's hover-mounts (destroyed) & Blackbird jet, Wolverine's ropes, tarp, beans & makeshift tent, Danger Room robots (destroyed in fb1) w/head module section (also in fb1 & rfb2), Phoenix's gravestone (in fb2), relief workers' tents & truck, food, medical supplies (prev 2 in fb4)

FLASHBACKS: Nightcrawler lies dead (UXM #524, '10). Wolverine berates Nightcrawler (this issue's fb1). During an early Danger Room session, Wolverine mocks Nightcrawler's religious faith. Slicing apart a robot's head, he says that someday, when Nightcrawler is dying on the battlefield, Wolverine will watch for God to claim him (1). At Phoenix's grave, Wolverine wonders how Nightcrawler can have faith (2). As a furious Wolverine plans to kill a villain, Nightcrawler expresses worry about Wolverine's soul (3). Wolverine and Nightcrawler donate supplies to an African relief mission (4).

SYNOPSIS: Wolverine mourns Nightcrawler, recently killed in battle. As Wolverine ponders Nightcrawler's religious faith, he learns that Nightcrawler's will asked him to donate a grand piano to a mountaintop church. Knowing that Nightcrawler wanted to impart a final lesson, Wolverine accepts, but his anti-gravity generators quickly break. After days of hefting the piano by hand and remembering Nightcrawler's many lessons, Wolverine arrives, only to discover that the small church has no piano players. The priest gives Wolverine a parcel that Nightcrawler had left. Inside is the robotic head; Wolverine thinks about his promise from that day to watch for God.

NOTE: This is the final issue of the W:WX series. The main Wolverine title is relaunched with a new #1 two months after this issue; the Index's bracketed secondary numbering continues there. Nightcrawler was killed by Bastion in XFor #26, '10. In XFor #4-6, '08, Archangel gained the ability to transform back and forth from his current feathered wings to his former blue-skinned, metal-winged look. In keeping with the comics, the Index will refer to him as Angel when in feather-winged form and as Archangel when in metal-winged form. Wolverine's evolving religious beliefs are a running theme of writer Jason Aaron's run; although Wolverine expresses atheism in this issue's flashbacks, he was susceptible to Allgod in DRL:W, '09, meaning he has faith in something. In this issue he reflects on Nightcrawler's faith, and in W #1, '10 fb he expresses jealousy of people with unshakeable faith, and begins attending John Wraith's church.

WOLVERINE: ROAD TO HELL (November 2010)

"Falling" (7 pages)

CREDITS: Jason Aaron (writer), Renato Guedes (pencils), José Wilson Magalhaes (inks), Virtual Calligraphy's Clayton Cowles (letters, production), Matthew Wilson (colors), Jody LeHeup (asst editor), Jeanine Schaefer (editor), Axel Alonso (group editor), Mico Suayan (c pencils), Jason Keith (c colors)
FEATURE CHARACTER: Wolverine (soul, also as himself, James Howlett, Cpl. Logan & Experiment X in rfb, soul next in W #1, '10; body next in X23 #1-3, '10-11; D:DW #2-3, W #1, all '10)
VILLAIN: Sabretooth clone (soul as severed head, last in W #55, '07, next in W #2, '10, see NOTE)
OTHER CHARACTERS: John Howlett Jr. (Wolverine's older brother, soul), damned souls (others in their thoughts, some or others next in W #1, '10); Mystique, Red Right Hand members (prev 2 mentioned, seen by Wolverine); Thomas Logan (dead), Elizabeth Howlett (voice only), Shingen Harada, Kuan-Yin Xorn, Mariko Yashida, Nazi, Purifiers (prev 5 die), Hellfire Club soldiers, Wranglers (some of prev 2 die), X-23, Strikeforce members (prev 11 in rfb); Devil (in damned souls' thoughts)
LOCATIONS/ITEMS: Hell (also in damned souls' thoughts), Howlett family estate, Shingen's Citadel compound chapel, Hellfire Club's New York branch, Normandy, Yashidas' ancestral manor, Weapon X Program facility, Purifiers' base, Colombian jungle, Manhattan (prev 9 in rfb) / Blowfish toxin (bts), Hellfire Club soldiers' weaponry, Cpl. Logan's rifle w/bayonet, Experiment X's wires & battery packs, Wranglers' armor, Purifiers' gun, Xorn's helmet (all in rfb)
FLASHBACK: James Howlett stands over Thomas Logan's body (Origin #3, '02); Wolverine kills Mariko (W #57, '92), Hellfire Club soldiers (W #133, '80), a Nazi (W #34, '90) and Shingen Harada (W #4, '82); Experiment X kills Wranglers (MCP #84, '91); X-Force kills Purifiers (XForce '08 fb); Wolverine battles Strikeforce X (W:WX #2, '09) and kills Kuan-Yin Xorn (NX #150, '04).
SYNOPSIS: Wolverine finds himself falling through an endless black abyss. Unable to think straight, he sees flashes of people that he has killed in his mind's eye as voices torment him from the darkness. Wolverine catches a rock ledge, breaking his fall, but finds a young boy sitting on it — his older brother John Jr., whom he never knew. John brandishes Sabretooth's severed head, which bites Wolverine; he loses his grip and continues falling.
NOTE: This one-shot's three stories set up the simultaneous relaunches of W, '10-12 & X23, '10-12 and debuts of D:DW, '10-12 & UXFor, '10-13. This story is preceded by a credits/contents page listing all three stories, and followed by a 3-page Renato Guedes sketchbook. Having been separated from his physical body and its Adamantium skeleton, Wolverine's claws are bone again. W #311, '12 reveals that Sabretooth was not actually dead at this time. The spirit seen in this story arc is assumed to be the clone that died in his place, though see W #2, '10's NOT for more. John Howlett Jr. died in 1897; his grave was seen in Origin #1, '01. W:End #4, '04 fb revealed his backstory and claimed that his death was faked, but W:WXF, '09 clarified that those events occurred on Earth-4011.

2ND STORY: "Brace For Impact" (8 pages)
CREDITS: Daniel Way & Marjorie Liu (writer), Giuseppe Camuncoli (pencils, pp.1 & 5-8, see NOTE), Onofrio Catacchio (inks, pp.1 & 5-8, see NOTE), Will Conrad (art, pp.1-4, 6 & 8, see NOTE), Virtual Calligraphy's Clayton Cowles (letters, production), Marte Gracia & John Rauch (colors), Jody LeHeup (asst editor), Jeanine Schaefer (editor), Axel Alonso (group editor)
FEATURE CHARACTERS: Daken (Akihiro, Wolverine's villainous son, last in DW #90, '10, next in D:DW #1, '10), X-23 (Laura Kinney, Wolverine's female clone, also as waitress, last in X #2, '10, next in X23 #1, '10)
VILLAINS: Dr. Detlef Metzger (former Weapon X scientist, 1st, also in pfb), Malcolm Colcord (last in WX:DoFN #1, '05) (both next in D:DW #7, '11) & his soldiers
OTHER CHARACTERS: Restaurant patrons, kitchen staff & waiters inc Tammy, Metzger's dinner companions, weapons contractors (bts awarding Metzger money); Wolverine (mentioned, Metzger found his blood), Dr. Zander Rice (mentioned, Metzger found his journals)
LOCATIONS/ITEMS: Restaurant w/kitchen, rooftop & nearby rooftop, Metzger's office (in pfb) / Waitress' bonds, tape & clothes, champagne bottle (destroyed), briefcase w/Rice's journals & vial of Wolverine's blood (prev 3 in pfb), soldiers' guns & Hummers
FLASHBACK: Dr. Metzger discovers Zander Rice's journals and a vial of Wolverine's blood (p).
SYNOPSIS: Daken eats in a restaurant, observing Dr. Metzger and planning to befriend him. X-23 poses as a waitress, determined to stop Metzger; both are aware that he was just awarded billions of dollars to restart the Weapon X Program. Soldiers suddenly burst into the restaurant. Daken and X-23 slip away as Malcolm Colcord arrives and insists that Metzger come with him. Daken and X-23 race to adjacent rooftops; they watch as Colcord's soldiers drive off with Metzger, then get a brief glimpse of one another…
NOTE: Giuseppe Camuncoli drew the panels telling Daken's half of this story, and Will Conrad drew the panels telling X-23's half. This story is later continued in D:DW #7, '11 & X23 #8, '11; it is followed by a 1-page Camuncoli sketchbook.

3RD STORY: "The First Day of the Rest of Your Life" (7 pages)
CREDITS: Rick Remender (writer), Leonardo Manco (art), Virtual Calligraphy's Clayton Cowles (letters, production), Chris Sotomayor (colors), Jody LeHeup (asst editor), Axel Alonso (editor)
FEATURE CHARACTERS: X-Force (Wolverine's secret black ops strike team): Angel (also as Archangel on cover, last in X #1, '10, chr last in W #4, '11), Deadpool (last in DpTU #888, '10, chr last in Dp #31, '11), Fantomex (last in UXM #529, '10), Wolverine (prev 2 chr last in W #5, '11), Psylocke (last in X #4, '10) (all next in UXFor #1, '10)
SUPPORTING CAST: EVA (last in UXM #529, '10, chr last in W #9, '11, next in UXFor #1, '10)
VILLAINS: Egyptian priestess (dies) & her enforcers (as Horus, some or all die, others next in UXFor #1, '10)
OTHER CHARACTERS: Brood (dead as statue), homeless lunatic (bts giving Deadpool directions); Weapon Plus scientists (mentioned, programmed Fantomex to escape), Deadpool's mother (mentioned, warned him about disease), super villains (mentioned, possibly in cave), man (in photo); falcons (on enforcers' armor)
LOCATIONS/ITEMS: Northern Arizona inc Cavern-X (X-Force's secret desert base, 1st), Egypt inc alley (mentioned) & hideout's secret entrance / Wolverine's newspaper, Fantomex's bloodborne nanites (mentioned), Sentinel head (destroyed), costume tubes, Angel's sandwiche, Deadpool's swords & map, enforcers' spears & masks, priestess' energy scepter
SYNOPSIS: As Fantomex and Wolverine fly EVA to Cavern-X, Fantomex asks why Wolverine wanted him to join the new X-Force; Wolverine replies that like him, Fantomex struggles to suppress an urge to kill — and that X-Force is about channeling those urges against those who truly deserve them. The two arrive; Fantomex unsuccessfully hits on Psylocke as Angel tells Wolverine that he sent Deadpool on a mission to keep him busy. In Egypt, as Deadpool searches for a villains' hideout, a priestess and her enforcers suddenly attack. Deadpool defeats them; grasping

priestess' scepter, he is suddenly able to see an opening in the rocks…

NOTE: This story is continued in UXFor #1, '10. This issue also has an 8-page preview of Namor #1, '10 and a 6-page B&W preview of nHope #1, '11. The "Cutting Edge" page, last seen in W #180, '02, returns here. Revamped as an editorial forum instead of a letters page, it is regularly in the relaunched W, '10-12 series.

WOLVERINE #1 [#280] (November 2010)

"Wolverine Goes To Hell, Part 1" (22 pages)

CREDITS: Jason Aaron (writer), Renato Guedes (pencils), José Wilson Magalhaes (inks), Virtual Calligraphy's Cory Petit (letters), Matthew Wilson (colors), Jody LeHeup (asst editor), Jeanine Schaefer (editor), Axel Alonso (group editor), Jae Lee (c art), Steve McNiven (variant c pencils A), Arthur Adams (variant c pencils B), Marko Djurdjevic (combining variant c art), J. Scott Campbell (Deadpool variant c pencils), Dexter Vines (variant c inks A), June Chung (c colors), Justin Ponsor (variant c colors A), Christina Strain (Deadpool variant c colors)

FEATURE CHARACTER: Wolverine (possessed by demons, also soul; also in photo, also as Deadpool on variant cover; also in fb1 & fb2 between BW #5, '10 & AstSMW #1, '10)

SUPPORTING CAST: Melita Garner (also in fb2 between W:WX #10, '10 & DW #90, '10, last in DW #90, '10), John Wraith (dies off-panel, also in fb1 between W #166, '01 & this issue, last in W #166, '01, next in W #3, '11) (both also in photos)

VILLAINS: Mongrels (Wolverine's illegitimate children, 1st, unnamed) inc Cannonfoot (hurls rocks with feet), Fire Knives (wields flaming knives), Saw Fist (arm-mounted chainsaws), Shadow Stalker (S&M-themed villain) (all unnamed), Gunhawk (William Downing, sharpshooter) (all 1st, chr last in W #13, '11 fb, chr last bts in W #14, '11 fb, next in W #3, '11); Red Right Hand (Wolverine-hating organization, unnamed, 1st but some or others chr last in W #5/2, '11, next in W #3/2, '11) inc Roger (unnamed), boy, ninja, widow (prev 4 1st but chr last in W #14, '11 fb) & leader (1st on-panel app, last bts in DW #90, '10, chr last in D:DW #2, '10) (prev 5 next in W #3/2, '11); Devil (ruler of Hell, chr last bts in W #12, '11 fb, see NOTE), demons (another last in D:DW #2, '10; others bts possessing Wolverine, their 1st bts app, chr last bts in D:DW #3, '11)

OTHER CHARACTERS: Mystique (last in D:DW #3, '11), churchgoers (die, some or others also in fb1 prior to Judy's death) inc Judy (dead), San Francisco Post security guards (1 dies, 1 dead), editor & reporters, damned souls (some or others last in W:RTH, '10); insects, worms, snakes; Dr. Strange (mentioned, lost to Wolverine at cards), Sabretooth (also on variant cover), Maverick, others (prev 3 mentioned, Wraith assumed they'd attack), Weapon X Program senior staff (mentioned in fb1 by Wolverine & Wraith), super heroes (mentioned in fb1, optimistic about future); Sons of the Tiger: Abe Brown, Bob Diamond, Lin Sun; X-Men: Cyclops, Rogue; Maverick (as Agent Zero), Jubilee (also on variant cover), Daken, Silver Samurai, Tyger Tiger, Yukio, X-23, Amiko Kobayashi (prev 13 in photos); X-Men: Colossus, Nightcrawler, Professor X, Kitty Pryde; Beast, Fantomex, Havok (prev 7 variant cover only), Asta (in silhouette), Nick & Nora Charles (prev 3 on billboard, variant cover only)

LOCATIONS/ITEMS: First Kestrel Baptist Church (Wraith's church, destroyed, also in fb1) w/shed, nearby woods & Judy's nearby house (bts); San Francisco inc Melita's apartment (in fb2) & San Francisco Post offices, Red Right Hand's Mexican estate (1st), Hell / Wraith's Bible (destroyed), guns (bts), guns & security computer, Melita's Kree laser baton, military pepper spray, interstellar cellphone, mystical device, Vibranium brass knuckles (prev 5 in fb2), Skrull sonic disruptor (also in fb2), laptop, photo & purse, Cannonfoot's rocks & curved boots, Fire Knives' knives, Gunhawk's bladed handguns, Saw Fist's wrist-mounted chainsaws, Shadow Stalker's hair bolas & spiked costume (prev 7 hereinafter considered their standard equipment and not listed separately), Mystique's motorcycle & helmet, Gunhawk's wrist communicator, Red Right Hand's dossiers & monitoring station w/comm unit

FLASHBACKS: Wolverine and John Wraith talk about their pasts as killers, and Wraith explains that he found peace by becoming a pastor. Wolverine ponders faith, and comments that he's used to carrying darkness, but isn't comfortable with happiness (1). Afraid that his enemies will attack her, Wolverine gives Melita several advanced weapons (2).

SYNOPSIS: As Wraith delivers a sermon, he notes that Wolverine is conspicuously absent. Suddenly a churchgoer races in, reporting an attack by a clawed creature. Wraith arms himself and races into the woods, but a demonic-looking Wolverine attacks, covering Wraith in swarming insects. "Wolverine" sets Wraith's church on fire and stabs him in the chest; Wraith sees Hell in his attacker's eyes as he dies. Later, the Mongrels attack Melita's office, killing two security guards and demanding her location. Melita startles them with her advanced weaponry, but they begin chasing her until Mystique bursts in on a motorcycle and rescues her. As the women flee, Gunhawk reports failure to the Red Right Hand. Meanwhile, the Devil welcomes Wolverine's soul to Hell…

NOTE: In late 2010, Marvel ended all of its Wolverine-related ongoing series (DW, W:O & W:WX), then revamped and relaunched a "Wolverine family" line of titles, including this relaunched series. The line also included D:DW, '10-12 & X23, '10-12, and later W:Best, '11-12. UXFor, '10-13, is also considered a satellite "family" title, as Wolverine leads that team. This issue has seven variants: "variant A" by Steve McNiven, "variant B" by Arthur Adams, a variant that interlocks with variants of UXFor #1, X #3, GenHope #3, X23 #1 & D:DW #1, all '10, to form a larger image, a sketch variant, a Deadpool variant, a blank variant, and a 2nd printing featuring interior art from p.11. Many demons have posed as or claimed to be the Biblical Satan; it is unknown if the "Devil" seen in this arc is a new claimant, a pre-existing Hell-lord such as Asmodeus, Marduk Kurios,

Lucifer, Mephisto, Satannish or Thog, or even a gestalt of some or all of these demons. The Mongrels are named in W #3/2, '11 and revealed Wolverine's illegitimate children in W #14, '11. Cannonfoot, Fire Knives, Saw Fist and Shadow Stalker are named in W #4/2, '11; Gunhawk's re name is revealed in W #15, '11. The Red Right Hand is named in this issue's next story; their estate's location is revealed in W #9, '11. Roger named in W #12, '11; all other members' names are unrevealed to date. "Kestrel" was one of John Wraith's Weapon X codenames.

2ND STORY: "Scorched Earth, Chapter One: Last Stand of the Silver Samurai" (6 pages)
CREDITS: Jason Aaron (writer), Jason Latour (art), Virtual Calligraphy's Cory Petit (letters), Rico Renzi (colors), Jody LeHeup (asst edito Jeanine Schaefer (editor)
VILLAINS: Black Samurai (Red Right Hand's enforcers, 1st, some or all die, some or others next in W #3, '11)
OTHER CHARACTERS: Silver Samurai (dies; last in SecWs #11, '10, next in W #3, '11); Viper, Hand ninjas (both mentioned, guessed assailants), Shingen "Shin" Harada (Silver Samurai's son, 1st mention, unnamed); Mariko Yashida (in photo)
LOCATIONS/ITEMS: Yashidas' ancestral manor (destroyed) / Silver Samurai's armor & katanas, Black Samurais' armor, swords, bows arrows, Red Right Hand's hidden camera (bts), Mariko's grave marker w/photo
SYNOPSIS: The Red Right Hand's Black Samurai attack the Yashidas' manor, setting it on fire and grievously wounding the Silver Samurai. Noting that t villains' armor and fighting styles are eerily similar to his own, Silver Samurai marshals his strength, ignores his injuries and fights back. As the manor bur around him, Silver Samurai kills his attackers, staggers to Mariko's grave and dies; his final thought is of his son.
NOTE: This issue also has a 2-page Renato Guedes sketchbook. The Red Right Hand is named here. Silver Samurai's son first appears in W #300, '

WOLVERINE #2 [#281] (December 2010)

"Wolverine Goes To Hell, Part 2 of 4" (22 pages)

CREDITS: Jason Aaron (writer), Renato Guedes (pencils), José Wilson Magalha (inks), Virtual Calligraphy's Cory Petit (letters), Matthew Wilson (colors), Jared K. Fletch (design), Jody LeHeup (asst editor), Jeanine Schaefer (editor), Jae Lee (c art), Art Adams (variant c pencils), Mike Mayhew (vampire variant c art), June Chung (c colors
FEATURE CHARACTER: Wolverine (possessed by demons, also soul)
GUEST STARS: Ghost Rider (John Blaze, last in Sland #5, '11), Ghost Rid (Dan Ketch, last in Strange #4, '10), Daimon Hellstrom (last in NAv #6, '11), Pu (soul, last in NAv #16, '06, possibly last as spirit in Herc #129, '09, see W #11 '97's NOTE)
SUPPORTING CAST: Yukio (last in W:WX #10, '10), Mariko Yashida (soul, la in W #57, '92, corpse last bts in W #60, '92, possibly last as spirit in Herc #129, 'C see W #111, '97's NOTE; next in W #5, '11), Melita Garner
VILLAINS: Cyber (last in W #73, '09), Shingen Harada (last in W #61, '08), Rod McLeish (last in W #122, '98), Ogun (last in W #169, '01), Omega Red (last in W #39, '09), Sabretooth clone (last in W:RTH, '10), Shredder (oversized right har last in H/W:6 #4, '03), Ethan Warren (wraith-like skeleton form, last in Logan #3, '0 Kuan-Yin Xorn (tiny star in brain, last in NX #150, '04, last voice only in NAv #20, '0 Strikeforce X members (last in W:WX #5, '09, others next in W #304, '12), Hand ninj (some or others last in ASM #651, '11, others next in Task #3, '11), Hydra agents (son or others last in HA:Prince #1, '10, others next in Task #1, '10), Purifiers (some or othe last in X:Hell #1, '10, others next in FearIt:UXFor #1, '11), Hellfire Club soldiers (some others last in XNec, '09, others next in X:Schism #2, '11), Yakuza gangster, Nazi, bik Wolverine's other victims (all as souls), demons (some bts possessing Wolverine), De
OTHER CHARACTERS: Thomas Logan (Wolverine's biological father, soul, last in Origin #3, '02, next in W #4, '11), Zarathos (last in Sla #5, '11), Ketch's Spirit of Vengeance (unidentified spirit empowering Ketch, last in Strange #4, '10), Mystique, damned souls (others mentione broken by Devil); X-Men (mentioned, Melita plans to call them); cartoon characters (on billboard); tiger (on robe); Gorgon (cover only, s NOTE)
LOCATIONS/ITEMS: Hell, San Francisco gas station, Yukio's Tokyo apartment / Ninjas' bows (bts), arrows, swords & shuriken, Nazi's rif Ogun's mask & sword, Xorn's helmet, McLeish's guns, Shingen & Yukio's swords, Sabretooth's chain, Mystique's motorcycle, Melita & Yukic cellphones, Mariko's spiked flail
SYNOPSIS: In Hell, Wolverine battles an enormous army of ninjas as the Devil laughs, reminding him that many other dead villains want the turn at revenge. The Devil asks Wolverine to scream in agony for his pleasure; Wolverine instead demands more foes. The Devil happily obligε and scores of super villains swarm Wolverine. The Devil reveals a domesticated and obedient Sabretooth chained to his throne, and promis to break Wolverine as well. Meanwhile, Melita confronts Mystique, deducing that she is involved with Wolverine's predicament. Melita calls Yuk for assistance, but the demonically possessed Wolverine attacks Yukio as she answers the phone, stabbing her through the spine. A shock Melita hangs up just as Mystique's allies arrive: Daimon Hellstrom and the two Ghost Riders. In Hell, an exhausted Wolverine demands mo foes, but the Devil instead brings out Mariko Yashida, and orders her to whip Wolverine. After several minutes, Wolverine howls in agony — scream heard by his former Alpha Flight ally Puck, who plots with a shadowed man...
NOTE: This issue also has a variant cover, a vampire variant, and a 2nd printing using interior art from p.2. This issue's story title incorrectly labe this as a four-part arc. Gorgon appears with Wolverine's other victims on the cover; however, he does not appear in the issue and is not dead this time, having been resurrected in SecWs #2, '09. Cyber and Shingen Harada's presence in Hell here indicates that they died sometime aft their last appearance. However, there is some doubt about whether the spirits seen here are real; any or all of them could be illusions, as demo often manipulate living people who visit the various Hell-realms. The chronologies given here assume that all the spirits are real.

2ND STORY: "Scorched Earth, Chapter Two: Amiko's Story" (6 pages)
CREDITS: Jason Aaron (writer), Steven Sanders (art), Virtual Calligraphy's Cory Petit (letters), Ronda Pattison (colors), Jody LeHeup (as editor, uncredited), Jeanine Schaefer (editor, uncredited)
FEATURE CHARACTER: Wolverine (possessed by demons)

UPPORTING CAST: Amiko Kobayashi (last in W:Soul #5, '05), Yukio

ILLAINS: Demons (bts possessing Wolverine)

THER CHARACTERS: Train conductors (bts driving trains), commuters, bystanders; Silver Samurai, Mariko Yashida (prev 2 mentioned, in ell); woman, cartoon character (prev 2 on billboards)

OCATIONS/ITEMS: Tokyo inc subway & Yukio's apartment w/nearby train tracks / Amiko's sword (destroyed), cellphone & satchel, commuter ains, Yukio's sword, apartment window (destroyed)

YNOPSIS: Amiko returns home to see the possessed Wolverine standing over a badly injured Yukio. Disgusted that Wolverine is under outside ontrol yet again, Amiko grabs a sword and attacks. Wolverine destroys her sword, but Yukio manages to stab Wolverine through the heart, stracting him. The two women then jump out the window, landing on a passing train; as it speeds them away, Amiko implores Yukio to wake up…

OTE: Writer Jason Aaron's last name is misspelled "Arron" in this story's credits. W #300, '12 reveals that Yukio becomes a paraplegic as a esult of Wolverine's attack.

WOLVERINE #3 [#282] (January 2011)

"Wolverine Goes To Hell, Part 3 of 5" (22 pages)

CREDITS: Jason Aaron (writer), Renato Guedes (pencils), José Wilson Magalhaes & Oclair Albert (inks), Virtual Calligraphy's Cory Petit (letters), Matthew Wilson (colors), Jared K. Fletcher (design), Jody LeHeup (asst editor), Jeanine Schaefer (editor), Jae Lee (c art), June Chung (c colors)

FEATURE CHARACTER: Wolverine (possessed by demons, also soul)

GUEST STARS: Sons of the Tiger: Lin Sun, Abe Brown (both last in DW #90, '10), Bob Diamond (last in W:MD #4, '09, last bts in DW #90, '10) (all bts, attacked by Black Samurai) (prev 2 next in W #5.1, '11); X-Men: Colossus (last in X #6, '11), Kitty Pryde (last in GenHope #5, '11), Rogue (last in X #4, '10, next in W #6, '11); Spider-Man (last in SM&FF #4, '10, next in W #5.1, '11), Daimon Hellstrom, Ghost Rider (Ketch) (prev 2 next in W #5, '11), Ghost Rider (Blaze), Puck (soul)

SUPPORTING CAST: Yukio, Amiko Kobayashi (both next in W #300, '12), Maverick (last in W:WX #5, '09, next W #9, '11), Melita Garner (next in W #5, '11), John Wraith (dead, next in W:Best #3, '11)

ILLAINS: Mongrels: Cannonfoot, Fire Knives, Gunhawk, Saw Fist, Shadow Stalker (all last in W #1, '10, next in W #4/2, '11); Black Samurai ome or others last in W #1/2, '10), Sabretooth clone (soul), demons (some bts possessing Wolverine), Devil

THER CHARACTERS: Hope Summers (duplicates & amplifies mutant powers, last in GenHope #5, '11, next in UXM Ann #3, '11), Silver amurai (dead, also soul, last in W #1/2, '10, corpse next bts in W #300, '12), Ketch's Spirit of Vengeance (next in W #5, '11), Zarathos, Mystique, ain conductor (bts driving train), reporter, cameraman (bts filming reporter), police, damned souls inc flesh trench denizens (bts tormenting amurai); X-23, firefighters (prev 2 in rfb1), Daken, Red Right Hand's ninjas (prev 2 in rfb2); Howard the Duck (mentioned as taunt), Red Right and (mentioned, sent Wolverine to Hell); San Francisco Post security guards (mentioned, killed by Mongrels); Thomas Logan (recap page only)

OCATIONS/ITEMS: Hell inc flesh trenches (bts), San Francisco inc ex-mutant shelter (destroyed, in rfb1), docks, San Francisco Post offices, ons of the Tiger dojo & Grace Cathedral; Milan (in rfb2), Tokyo, Yashidas' ancestral manor, First Kestrel Baptist Church (prev 2 destroyed), adripoor airport, Maverick's hideout, Avengers Mansion, Utopia / Silver Samurai's armor, Black Samurais' arrows & armor, Devil's Soulcutter word, commuter train, reporter's microphone, news camera (bts), airplane, Maverick's gun, ninjas' swords, Spider-Man's cordless phone, elita's cellphone, Ghost Riders' hooked chains, Red Right Hand's truck (mentioned), demons' crosses, nails & spiked flail, Wolverine's elongings, Kitty's phasing suit, Red Right Hand's hidden cameras (bts)

LASHBACKS: X-23 recovers from a demonic attack at an ex-mutant shelter (X23 #2, '10). Daken battles the Red Right Hand's ninjas (D:DW 1, '10).

YNOPSIS: Sabretooth viciously tears into Wolverine, but when the Devil calls, Sabretooth sits obediently. The Devil threatens to train Jolverine to follow suit, but the mutant remains defiant. Deciding to teach Wolverine a lesson, the Devil chops the Silver Samurai's soul into eces with his sword. Wolverine spits in the Devil's face; the Devil slices Wolverine's ear off and orders him nailed to a wall. On Earth, the Red ight Hand's minions attack Wolverine's friends and family, including X-23, Daken, Maverick and the Sons of the Tiger. Melita tries calling vengers Mansion, but Spider-Man believes she is a prank caller. Mystique admits that she helped the Red Right Hand, but had a change of eart; Daimon Hellstrom prepares for an exorcism. In Hell, Puck tells Wolverine that every time he challenges the Devil, the demons inch closer open revolt; he exhorts Wolverine to stay defiant. Wolverine tears himself free and attacks the Devil directly — as his demon-possessed body rives on Utopia, and assaults Kitty Pryde and Colossus…

OTE: This issue's story title now correctly labels the arc as a five-part story.

ND STORY: "Scorched Earth, Chapter Three: Old Wounds" (6 pages)

REDITS: Jason Aaron (writer), Michael Gaydos (art, colors), Virtual Calligraphy's Cory Petit (letters), Jody LeHeup (asst editor, uncredited), eanine Schaefer (editor, uncredited)

UEST STAR: Lin Sun (on monitor, next in W #5.1, '11)

ILLAINS: Red Right Hand (some or others last in W #1, '10, next in W #9, '11) inc Roger, ninja, widow (prev 3 next in W #9, '11), boy (next W #10, '11) & leader (next in W #5, '11) (prev 5 last in W #1, '10); a Black Samurai (on monitor, others as monitor images)

THER CHARACTERS: Reporter, police (both on monitor), cameraman (bts filming reporter); San Francisco Post security guards (mentioned, lled by Mongrels), leader's father (in photo); X-Men: Wolverine (possessed by demons, also as statues), Colossus, Kitty Pryde; Ghost Rider laze), Ghost Rider (Ketch), Mystique, Yukio, Daimon Hellstrom, Amiko Kobayashi, demons (bts possessing Wolverine), train conductor (bts riving train) (prev 11 as monitor images)

OCATIONS/ITEMS: Yashidas' ancestral manor, Tokyo, Utopia, San Francisco inc Post offices & Sons of the Tiger Dojo (all on monitors), Red ight Hand's Mexican estate / Black Samurais' armor & swords, Daken's sword, commuter train, Kitty's phasing suit, reporter's microphone, ws camera (bts) (all on monitors), Red Right Hand's hidden cameras (bts) & monitoring station, news camera (bts), leader's gun, pocketwatch & statue garden

YNOPSIS: The Red Right Hand monitors their attacks on Wolverine's loved ones, but are upset by the security guards' deaths. Killing nocents was not their plan; some wonder if they have gone too far, but their leader reminds them that vengeance on Wolverine is all that atters, and threatens to kill anyone who breaks ranks. Storming out, the leader relaxes in a garden filled with statues of Wolverine being rmented.

OTE: The Mongrels' team name is revealed here. This issue's "Cutting Edge" page runs two fan letters, the first letters printed in this series nce W #48, '07. This issue also has a 6-page preview of BP #513, '11.

WOLVERINE #4 [#283] (February 2011)

"Wolverine Goes To Hell, Part 4 of 5" (22 pages)

CREDITS: Jason Aaron (writer), Renato Guedes (pencils), José Wilson Magalhaes & Oclair Albe**r** (inks), Virtual Calligraphy's Cory Petit (letters**r** Matthew Wilson (colors), Jared K. Fletcher (design**r** Jody LeHeup (asst editor), Jeanine Schaefe**r** (editor), Jae Lee (c art), Marko Djurdjevic (variant art), Brandon Peterson (Tron variant c pencils), Jun**e** Chung (c colors)

FEATURE CHARACTER: Wolverine (possesse**d** by demons, also soul, also as James Howlett in rfb)**r**

GUEST STARS: X-Men: Cyclops (last in X23 #3, '11), Colossus (both chr next in W #6, '11 fb), Kitty Pryde (prev 2 next in W #6, '11), Angel (ch**r** next in W:RTH/3, '10, next in UXFor #1, '10), Iceman (next in W #5.1, '11) (prev 2 last in X #5, '11); Ghost Rider (Blaze), Puck (soul)

VILLAINS: Sabretooth clone (soul), Devil, demons (some bts possessing Wolverine)

OTHER CHARACTERS: X-Club (X-Men's science squad): Madison Jeffries (last in X #5, '11, next in UXM Ann #3, '11), Kavita Rao (geneticis**t** last in W&Jub #1, '11); Cecilia Reyes (force field-projecting doctor, last in UXM #530, '11) (prev 2 next in W #6, '11 fb), Thomas Logan (sou**l** also dead in rfb, last in W #2, '10), Mystique, Zarathos, damned souls; seagulls; Magik (mentioned as taunt); John Howlett (dead in rfb); X-Me**n**: Beast, Emma Frost, Phoenix; Hulk, Silver Samurai, Tron opponent (prev 6 variant covers only)

LOCATIONS/ITEMS: Hell, Howlett family estate (in rfb), Utopia, San Francisco Bay / Devil's Soulcutter sword, Kitty Pryde's phasing suit, Re**d** Right Hand's hidden camera (bts), Wolverine's bone claws, Ghost Rider's hooked chain, Cecilia's fire blanket, souls' hurled rocks & makeshift club**s**

FLASHBACK: A young James Howlett stares at John Howlett and Thomas Logan's bodies (Origin #3, '02).

SYNOPSIS: Wolverine battles the Devil as demons and damned souls alike look on with glee. The Devil wounds Wolverine grievously, bu**t** Wolverine brandishes his blood-soaked claws, showing the rebellious demons that the Devil can be made to bleed. As Wolverine attacks th**e** astonished Devil with renewed vigor, Puck and his shadowy ally plan an uprising. On Utopia, the possessed Wolverine battles Colossus, slashin**g** through his organic steel skin. Other X-Men join the fight, but Wolverine attacks them with demonic powers. In Hell, the Devil snaps off Wolverine'**s** bone claws — but the demons suddenly revolt, swarming their former master. Wolverine lunges at the distracted Devil and uses his broken claw**s** to nail him to the wall. On Utopia, Mystique and Ghost Rider burst in, grab Wolverine and drag him off. In Hell, demons fight over the Devil's swor**d** but Puck charges with an army of damned souls. As war breaks out across Hell, Puck's ally reveals himself as Wolverine's father.

NOTE: This issue has a variant cover that interlocks with variants of W:Best #1-2, D:DW #4, X23 #4 & UXFor #3, all '11, to form a larger image as well as a Tron variant. Colossus is incorrectly depicted as bleeding when Wolverine cuts his metal skin this issue; he does not have liqui**d** blood when in his organic steel form. This issue also contains a house ad with a QR code linking to an "Age of X Historical Log" feature.

2ND STORY: "Scorched Earth, Chapter Four: Last Call" (6 pages)

CREDITS: Jason Aaron (writer), Jamie McKelvie (art), Virtual Calligraphy's Cory Petit (letters), John Rauch (colors), Jody LeHeup (asst edito**r** uncredited), Jeanine Schaefer (editor, uncredited)

SUPPORTING CAST: Tyger Tiger (last in DpTU #891, '10, next in D:DW #5, '11)

VILLAINS: Mongrels: Saw Fist (next in W #12, '11), Shadow Stalker (next in W #10, '11), Cannonfoot, Fire Knives (all named, see NOTE)**,** Gunhawk (all last in W #3, '11)

OTHER CHARACTERS: Princess Bar bouncers (some or all die); bear (dead, stuffed); Madripoor judges (mentioned, offers criminals ja**il** time or bouncer job), criminals (mentioned, most choose jail), Princess Bar patrons (mentioned, lowlifes), inmates, rats (prev 2 mentioned, i**n** prisons); Native American (as statue), Wolverine, bartender, others (prev 3 in photos)

LOCATIONS/ITEMS: Madripoor inc jails, Lowtown factories (both mentioned) & Princess Bar w/back room (destroyed), bar (in photo)**,** Princess Bar window (destroyed), bouncer's brass knuckles, patrons' knives (mentioned), Gunhawk's Molotov cocktail, Tyger's gun, Wolverine'**s** knickknacks & photos (prev 2 destroyed)

SYNOPSIS: The Princess Bar's bouncers have a reputation as Madripoor's most frightening psychopaths, but even they are no match for th**e** Mongrels, who assault the bar and quickly overwhelm the staff. Gunhawk makes his way to the back room; Tyger Tiger guards it, but Gunhaw**k** easily pushes past her into a storeroom full of Wolverine's mementos and personal items. Intent on ruining Wolverine's life, Gunhawk sets th**e** room ablaze.

NOTE: Tyger Tiger became Madripoor's ruling Princess in IM:DoS Ann, '08. Shadow Stalker and Saw Fist's codenames are given here as one wor**d** each; they are clarified as being two words each in W #11-12, '11 respectively.

WOLVERINE #5 [#284] (March 2011)

"Wolverine Goes To Hell, Part 5 of 5" (22 pages)

CREDITS: Jason Aaron (writer), Renato Guedes (pencils), José Wilson Magalhaes (inks), Virtual Calligraphy'**s** Cory Petit (letters), Matthew Wilson (colors), Jared K. Fletcher (design), Jody LeHeup (asst editor), Jeanin**e** Schaefer (editor), Jae Lee (c art), June Chung (c colors)

FEATURE CHARACTER: Wolverine (also possessed by demons, also soul)

GUEST STARS: X-Men: Emma Frost (last in X23 #3, '11), Cyclops (both chr last in W #6, '11 fb), Magneto (las**t** in XCurse:XV #1/4, '10), Sub-Mariner (last in Namor #5, '11); Ghost Rider (Blaze), Ghost Rider (Ketch), Daimo**n** Hellstrom (prev 2 last in W #3, '11), Puck (soul, next in AFlt #2, '11)

SUPPORTING CAST: Mariko Yashida (soul, corpse next bts in W #11, '11), Melita Garner

VILLAINS: Mongrels: Fire Knives, Gunhawk (both next in W #12, '11), Cannonfoot (next in W #10, '11); Dev**il** (possibly next in JIM #627, '11, see NOTE; next bts in W #12, '11), Sabretooth clone (soul, corpse next in W #310**,** '12), Red Right Hand's leader (last in W #3/2, '11, next in W #9, '11), demons (some bts possessing Wolverine)

OTHER CHARACTERS: Thomas Logan (soul, next in W #304, '12), Ketch's Spirit of Vengeance (last in W #3, '11), Zarathos, Mystiqu**e**

damned souls (some or others next in W #304, '12), bystanders; Omega Red (also on cover), Ogun, Shingen Harada, Roddy McLeish (prev 4 mentioned, torment Wolverine), Galactus, Kang (prev 2 mentioned, threats to Earth), John Howlett (mentioned, killed by Thomas), Wolverine's victims (mentioned, sent to Hell), Ghost Riders' mothers (mentioned as taunt), Thomas' ancestors, fly keepers, scream choirs, skin sculptors, bus babies, lepers, sad girl, men, women, children, flies, rats, maggots, rabid dogs (prev 14 mentioned, in Hell), damned souls' loved ones mentioned, souls taunted with them); Gorgon (see NOTE), Cyber, Hellfire Club soldier, Hydra agent (prev 4 on cover)

LOCATIONS/ITEMS: Hell inc river, caves, meat gardens, fields of submission, gore bogs, child kennels & viscera forests (prev 7 mentioned), San Francisco inc Grace Cathedral, Red Right Hand's Mexican estate / Ogun & Shingen's swords, McLeish's guns, lepers' face-sacks, sad girl's pliers & fingernail basket (all mentioned), souls' makeshift clubs, Ghost Riders' hooked chains, Mystique's holy water spray can, Hellstrom's mystic tome, Devil's Soulcutter sword, Wolverine's bone claws (bts) & spiked flail, Red Right Hand's hidden camera (bts) & monitoring station

SYNOPSIS: Wolverine is stunned to see his biological father, Thomas Logan, who warmly tells Wolverine that he is proud of him. In San Francisco, the possessed Wolverine fights his captors, stabbing Mystique and beheading a Ghost Rider, but the other Ghost Rider hurls him into the chapel, where Hellstrom begins an exorcism. In Hell, Sabretooth claims the Devil's sword; Wolverine attacks him and the two fight viciously until Wolverine grabs the sword and slices Sabretooth's soul into pieces. The demons begin bowing, and Thomas encourages Wolverine to rule Hell with him, but Wolverine throws the sword to the demons and rejects his father. Wolverine and Puck begin climbing to freedom; Wolverine tries to free Mariko, but she refuses to come with him. Puck is grabbed and hurled back into Hell, but soon manages to claim the Devil's sword for himself. Wolverine continues climbing; as the exorcism concludes on Earth, his soul returns to his physical body. Wolverine races out of the chapel and collapses in front of the arriving X-Men.

NOTE: Gorgon again appears with Wolverine's victims on the cover, despite not being dead at this time. In JIM #627, '11, Marduk Kurios resembles this story's Devil. It is unclear if Kurios was the Devil seen here, was part of a gestalt making up this Devil, or is simply impersonating him.

2ND STORY: "Scorched Earth, Conclusion: How It Started" (6 pages)

CREDITS: Jason Aaron (writer), Jason Latour (art), Virtual Calligraphy's Cory Petit (letters), Rico Renzi (colors), Jody LeHeup (asst editor), Jeanine Schaefer (editor)

FEATURE CHARACTER: Wolverine (also possessed by demons, chr last in W&Jub #4, '11, soul chr next in W:RTH, '10, body chr next in X23 #1, '10)

VILLAINS: Mystique (also as Melita Garner, chr last in W:WX #10, '10, chr next in D:DW #1, '10), Red Right Hand (some or others chr last in W #14, '11 fb, chr next in W #1, '10) inc leader (chr last in W #14, '11 fb, chr last bts in DW #90, '10, chr next in D:DW #1, '10), demons (bts possessing Wolverine, chr next bts in X23 #1, '10, chr next in W #6, '11; some or others chr last in W #12, '11 fb)

OTHER CHARACTERS: Sacrificial victims (dead), bystanders; woman, cat (prev 2 on signs), goat (as pentagram design)

LOCATIONS/ITEMS: San Francisco / Red Right Hand's chains, meat hooks & tractor-trailer truck, leader's mystic tome

SYNOPSIS: As Melita greets Wolverine, two men suddenly grab her and drag her into a truck's trailer. Wolverine chases them in, but finds a pentagram on the floor; the Red Right Hand's leader begins casting a spell, and "Melita" reveals herself as Mystique. In a flash of light, Wolverine's soul is forced out and demons possess his body. As they depart to attack Wolverine's loved ones, the leader gloats.

NOTE: This story occurs just before W:RTH, '10. A typo in this story causes the demons to refer to themselves as "T" in one panel. This issue also has a 6-page feature on Marvel's 2011 revival of Crossgen's Ruse and Sigil titles, interviewing writers Mark Waid and Mike Carey and Sales Director David Gabriel.

WOLVERINE #5.1 (April 2011)

"Happy" (22 pages)

CREDITS: Jason Aaron (writer), Jefte Palo (art), Virtual Calligraphy's Cory Petit (letters), Nathan Fairbairn (colors), Jared K. Fletcher (design), Jody LeHeup (asst editor), Jeanine Schaefer (editor), Paolo Rivera (c art)

FEATURE CHARACTER: Wolverine (chr last in UXFor #5.1, '11, chr next in Tstrike #2, '11)

GUEST STARS: New Avengers: Luke Cage (next in Tb #154, '11), Iron Fist (both last in Sland #5, '11), Spider-Man (last in W #3, '11) (prev 2 next in FF #584, '10), Ms. Marvel (Carol Danvers, next in FF #588, '11), Thing (next in SG #1, '11) (prev 2 last in ASM #654, '11); Secret Avengers (Rogers' black ops super hero team): Beast (last in Sland:MK #3, '11, chr next in AX #43, '11, next in FF #588, '11), Black Widow (last in BW #8, '11, next in Task #4, '11), Steve Rogers (last in AvAc #5, '10 fb, next in Tstrike #1, '11), Sons of the Tiger (martial artists): Bob Diamond (former actor, last in W:MD #4, '09), Abe Brown (ghetto-raised street fighter, last in DW #90, '10) (prev 2 last bts in W #3, '11), Lin Sun (last in W #3/2, '11) (prev 3 next bts in W #17, '11); X-Men: Colossus (last in X:TS&P #3/3, '11), Iceman (last in W #4, '11), Angel (bts watching for Wolverine) (prev 3 next in X:TS&P #2, '11), Cyclops (prev 2 last in UXFor #5.1, '11), Emma Frost (last in Namor #8, '11) (prev 2 bts declining invitation), Storm (last in X23 #3, '11) (prev 3 next in FF #588, '11), Rogue (last in W #3, '11, next in X:L #244, '11) (prev 2 chr last in W #8, '11), Deadpool (last in UXFor #5.1, '11, next in DpTU #885, '11), Gambit (last in X #6, '11, next in X23 #4, '11), Invisible Woman (last in SM&FF #4, '10, next in SG #1, '11), Jessica Jones (last in AvAc #6, '11, next in FF #588, '11), Spider-Woman (last in IAmAv #1, '10, next in Tstrike #2, '11), Squirrel Girl (Doreen Green, squirrel-like mutant, bts babysitting Danielle, last in ASM #653, '11, next in NAv #15, '11 fb), X-23 (between X23 #3-4, '11)

SUPPORTING CAST: Melita Garner (chr last in W #8, '11, chr next in FearIt:W #1, '11)

VILLAINS: Buzzard Brothers (cannibal siblings): Boyd, Bufford (both 1st, next in W #20, '12); Azuma Góda (1st bts app, directing ninjas, see NOTE; chr last bts in W #9, '11; next bts in W #19, next voice only in W #20, next in 1st on-panel app in W #300, all '12); Hand ninjas (Tokyo branch, some or others last in Sland:GR, '10, chr last in W #9, '11, next in W #300, '12)

OTHER CHARACTERS: Jubilee (chr last in W #8, '11, chr next in X23 #10, '11), Danielle Cage (bts, babysat by Squirrel Girl, last in ASM #653, '11, next in NAv #15, '11 fb), Terrence (trucker), police (1 dead, others bts in station), Buzzard Brothers' victims: Boy Scouts, people, animals (prev 3 dead as bones); Terrence's dog (bts, dead, eaten); vegan victim (mentioned, tasted like squirrel), American victims (mentioned, tasted like cigarettes), Boyd's lawyer, maggots (prev 2 mentioned); Rolling Stones (music on jukebox); Devil, demons (prev 2 recap page only)

LOCATIONS/ITEMS: Canadian wilderness inc police station, Melita's rented cabin & Buzzard Brothers' cabin, Avengers Mansion (New Avengers' headquarters) / Terrence's truck, Wolverine's bouquet, snow, beef jerky & birth certificate, guests' alcoholic gifts & aircraft inc Avengers Quinjet & X-Men's Blackbird jet, Melita's banners, steaks, beer, mop & birthday cake, cabin jukebox, speakers (prev 2 bts) & microphone, Deadpool's cheese dip w/bullets, Buzzard Brothers' ropes, organ jars, knives, axes, sharpener, cooking pot, bone pistols w/tooth bullets & bathtub w/fire & cooking grease, police cars, canned beans, Hand ninjas' shuriken & swords

SYNOPSIS: On his way to meet Melita, Wolverine finds an abandoned truck. Realizing that the driver has been abducted, Wolverine begins tracking him. Elsewhere, Melita has arranged a surprise party for Wolverine, inviting many of his fellow heroes, but Luke Cage bets that Wolverine won't show. Elsewhere, the trucker awakens to find himself a captive of the cannibalistic Buzzard Brothers, who drag in a bullet-riddled Wolverine and prepare to deep-fry him. As the party wears on, Melita wonders what's keeping Wolverine; guests begin to apologize and leave. Elsewhere, Wolverine recovers and cuts off Bufford's hand; Boyd immediately begins eating it, enraging Bufford, and the two brothers fight. Wolverine decides not to kill them, and instead calls the police. Later, Wolverine and the trucker arrive at Melita's rented cabin, to find her cleaning up. She explains the attempted surprise, and reveals that she located Wolverine's birth certificate — and that his birthday is a different day than he always thought. As the two embrace, Hand ninjas break the Buzzards out of jail.

NOTE: This one-shot, part of Marvel's "Point One" line designed as accessible jumping-on points for new readers, occurs after Wolverine regains his body from the demons possessing it. Beast quit the X-Men in UXM #519, '10. The Kingpin gained control of the Hand's New York branch in Sland #5, '11. W #20 & 300, '12 reveal that Azuma Góda and his Tokyo branch are recruiting outside agents, including the Buzzard Brothers, as part of a power grab.

WOLVERINE #6 [#285] (April 2011)

"Wolverine vs. the X-Men, Part 1 of 3" (22 pages)

CREDITS: Jason Aaron (writer), Daniel Acuña (art, colors), Virtual Calligraphy's Cory Petit (letters), Jared K Fletcher (design), Jody LeHeup (asst editor), Jeanine Schaefer (editor), Nick Lowe (group editor), Jae Lee (c art), June Chung (c colors)
FEATURE CHARACTER: Wolverine (also possessed by demons, also bts on TV, also as Danger Room construct & monitor images in fb1)
GUEST STARS: X-Men: Colossus (also in fb2 between W #4, '11 & this issue; next in W #8, '11), Kitty Pryde (both last in W #4, '11), Emma Frost (also in fb2 between X23 #3, '11 & W #5, '11), Rogue (last in W #3, '11) Storm (last in X23 #3, '11), Cyclops (also in fb1 between X #6, '11 & W&Jub #1, '11; also in fb2 between W #4-5 '11), Magneto, Sub-Mariner (prev 3 also as Danger Room constructs & monitor images in fb1); Daimon Hellstrom (next in Tb #155, '11), Ghost Rider (Blaze, next in X:TS&P #2/4, '11), Ghost Rider (Ketch) (prev 7 also bts on TV)
SUPPORTING CAST: Melita Garner
VILLAINS: Demons (1st on-panel app, possessing Wolverine)
OTHER CHARACTERS: Mystique (next in W #9, '11), Jubilee (last in W&Jub #4, '11), Kavita Rao (in fb2 between W #4, '11 & UXM Ann #3 '11), Cecilia Reyes (in fb2 between W #4, '11 & X23 #13, '11), Zarathos (next in next in X:TS&P #2/4, '11), Ketch's Spirit of Vengeance, reporter (on TV), cameraman (bts filming battle), police (all but 1 bts urging evacuation), bystanders; birds
LOCATIONS/ITEMS: Utopia (also in fb1) w/Danger Room (in fb1) & infirmary (also in fb2), Grace Cathedral (also bts on TV), news studio (on TV), Wolverine's mindscape, city street (as Danger Room construct in fb1) / Wolverine's Adamantium (bts, also as Danger Room construct in fb1), Danger Room computers (in fb1) w/monitors, X-Men's medical computers, oxygen mask (prev 2 in fb2) & TV monitors, Ghost Riders' hooked chains, Hellstrom's trident, cameraman's broadcast equipment & camera, Magneto & Cyclops' comm units (prev 4 bts), Jubilee's blood pack, Colossus' bandages, Kitty's phasing suit, traffic light post, mailbox, car (prev 3 destroyed)
FLASHBACKS: Concerned that Wolverine might someday be brainwashed or turn evil again, Cyclops uses the Danger Room to develop methods of killing him (1). Cyclops visits the injured Colossus in the infirmary, and assembles a team to pursue the demon-possessed Wolverine (2)
SYNOPSIS: Wolverine's soul has re-entered his body, but the demons still possess it. Wolverine fights for control, urging Melita to run, but the demons force him to lash out wildly at her. Cyclops' team confronts Hellstrom and the Ghost Riders, who explain that they have done all they can — the rest is up to Wolverine himself. As Wolverine battles the demons in his own psychic mindscape, Melita begs the heroes to give him time to triumph. As Mystique slips away, the demons force Wolverine to attack the assembled heroes. On Utopia, several other X-Men see the battle on the news, and rush to help. The possessed Wolverine defeats Hellstrom and the Ghost Riders, and begins to run amok, menacing civilians. Cyclops reluctantly orders the X-Men to follow his plan — and kill Wolverine.
NOTE: Cyclops' word balloon on page 5 incorrectly points to the Danger Room's holographic version of Cyclops.

WOLVERINE #7 [#286] (May 2011)

"Wolverine vs. the X-Men, Part 2 of 3" (22 pages)

CREDITS: Jason Aaron (writer), Daniel Acuña (art, colors), Virtual Calligraphy's Cory Petit (letters), Jared K. Fletcher (design), Jody LeHeup (asst editor), Jeanine Schaefer (editor), Nick Lowe (group editor), Jae Lee (c art), Dave Johnson (variant c pencils), June Chung (c colors)
FEATURE CHARACTER: Wolverine (also possessed by demons, also as his own mental aspects: Phoenix (Jean Grey, bts), Nightcrawler, gunslinger commando, samurai (prev 5 see NOTE), berserker (unnamed), James Howlett Logan, Experiment X, Weapon X, "Patch", Death, wild man & feral regression)
GUEST STARS: X-Men: Magneto (also as boy in his own thoughts, next in UXFor #5.1, '11), Sub-Mariner (next in Namor #6, '11), Cyclops, Emma Frost Kitty Pryde, Rogue, Storm; Fantomex (last in UXM #533, '11)
SUPPORTING CAST: Melita Garner
VILLAINS: Demons (possessing Wolverine, also as Nazi in Magneto's thoughts)
OTHER CHARACTERS: Dr. Nemesis (Dr. James Bradley, mutant super-scientist, last in X #6, '11), EVA (last in UXM #534, '11), Jubilee bystanders; bird; concentration camp prisoners (in Magneto's thoughts); Shingen Harada (see NOTE), Ogun, Sabretooth, Silver Samurai, Thomas Logan, Mariko Yashida (prev 6 names on mindscape gravestones), Adolf Hitler (mentioned, demons claim to be his master); biker (on road sign); X-Men: Archangel, Colossus (prev 2 cover only); Captain America (variant cover only)
LOCATIONS/ITEMS: Wolverine's mindscape inc forest, graveyard & fortress w/cells, San Francisco inc Bay, Golden Gate Bridge & Angel Island, Auschwitz (in Magneto's thoughts) / Wolverine's padlocks (destroyed), samurai armor & swords, gunslingers' pistols, Experiment X's helmet & battery

acks, commando's machine gun & pistol, Logan's guns, Death's sword, X-Men's swords, Melita's staff (all psychic manifestations), Wolverine's adamantium, manhole cover (destroyed, also as shrapnel), Magneto's anti-psychic helmet, Nazi's crop & knife (prev 2 in Magneto's thoughts), cars destroyed), bystanders' boats, Dr. Nemesis' hypodermic weaponry, Melita's gun, Kitty's phasing suit, Fantomex's advanced weaponry

SYNOPSIS: In Wolverine's mindscape, he takes refuge in a psychic fortress, dons samurai armor, and releases all of his various mental aspects: hero, soldier, spy, berserker and more. The pursuing demons burst in, and are attacked by a dozen different Wolverines. In the real world, Magneto begins pulling the Adamantium from Wolverine's possessed body, but the demons break his hold and force him to flash back to his childhood in Auschwitz. Sub-Mariner tackles Wolverine into the bay, but is quickly defeated when the demons set him ablaze. As Cyclops pursues Wolverine, he summons Fantomex and Dr. Nemesis as reinforcements — but the other X-Men arrive with Melita and demand one more chance to save their friend. As Storm's winds hold Wolverine immobile, Emma enters his mind with Rogue, Jubilee, Kitty Pryde and Melita. They join the psychic battle, but despite their best efforts the demons continue to slowly overtake Wolverine's mind. Elsewhere in the mindscape, Nightcrawler pursues a last-ditch attempt at victory, and opens a door marked with the Phoenix logo…

NOTE: This issue also has a variant cover celebrating Captain America's 70th anniversary. Shingen's psychic gravestone reads "Shingen Yashida." Wolverine's mental aspects wear costumes representing different periods in his life; the gunslinger and commando looks have never been seen before. The "real" Wolverine is represented by the samurai aspect. The berserker aspect is named next issue. "Phoenix" is revealed next issue as yet another aspect; despite "Nightcrawler's" claim next issue that he is the true Nightcrawler's soul, W #9, '11's recap page clarifies that he is also an aspect. This issue also has a 2-page article advertising the FearIt, '11 miniseries and its tie-ins.

WOLVERINE #8 [#287] (June 2011)

"Wolverine vs. the X-Men, Part 3 of 3" (22 pages)

CREDITS: Jason Aaron (writer), Daniel Acuña (art, colors), Virtual Calligraphy's Cory Petit (letters), Jared K. Fletcher (design), Jody LeHeup (asst editor), Jeanine Schaefer (editor), Nick Lowe (group editor), Jae Lee (c art), Dale Keown (variant c pencils), June Chung (c colors), Peter Steigerwald (variant c colors)

FEATURE CHARACTER: Wolverine (also possessed by demons, also voice only as hope & bts as memory in his own mind, also as his own mental aspects including berserker (named), James Howlett, Logan, "Patch," Death, Nightcrawler, Phoenix, samurai, gunslinger, commando, wild man & feral regression)

GUEST STARS: X-Men: Colossus (last in W #6, '11), Kitty Pryde (both next in X:TS&P #3/3, '11), Cyclops (next in Namor #8, '11), Emma Frost (also as fantasy in Wolverine's mind, next in Namor #6, '11), Rogue (next in X:L #244, '11), Storm (also bts as memory in Wolverine's mind, see NOTE; next in FF #588, '11) (prev 2 chr next in W #5.1, '11); Fantomex (chr next in W:RTH/3, '10, next in UXFor #5.1, '11)

SUPPORTING CAST: Melita Garner (chr next in W #5.1, '11, next in FearIt:W #1, '11)

VILLAINS: Demons (also possessing Wolverine, some or all possibly die)

OTHER CHARACTERS: Dr. Nemesis (next in Namor #6, '11), EVA (chr next in W:RTH/3, '10, next in UXFor #5.1, '11), Jubilee (chr next in W #5.1, '11, next in X23 #10, '11); Jewel, Mystique, Spiral, Squirrel Girl (prev 4 as fantasies in Wolverine's mind), Jean Grey (voice only as hope in Wolverine's mind), Dr. Rot (mentioned in Wolverine's mind); Thor, boxing coaches & fans (prev 3 variant cover only)

LOCATIONS/ITEMS: Angel Island, Wolverine's mindscape inc fortress w/cells, Danger Room (bts as psychic manifestation), Utopia inc infirmary / Wolverine's samurai armor & swords, Melita's staff, X-Men's swords, fantasies' crops, restraints & paddle, Nightcrawler's cutlass (all psychic manifestations), Dr. Nemesis' hypodermic weaponry inc plague, cancer & bacteria-loaded bullets, Fantomex's advanced weaponry, Kitty's phasing suit, Cyclops' borrowed boat, Colossus' bandages

SYNOPSIS: Fantomex and Dr. Nemesis begin shooting Wolverine with advanced weapons, but Storm orders them to stop, explaining that several X-Men are telepathically inside Wolverine's head. In the mindscape, the demons' attack separates the other X-Men from Wolverine and his mental aspects. As the X-Men explore various recesses of Wolverine's mind, disturbed by what they find, Nightcrawler and Phoenix suddenly appear and offer help. Emma notes with relief that "Phoenix" is another of Wolverine's mental aspects; still, her power is tremendous, and she forces the X-Men back to their physical bodies. With their teammates clear, Fantomex and Dr. Nemesis renew their assault, overloading Wolverine's healing factor — but when Wolverine mutters Jean's name, Cyclops suddenly halts the attack. In the mindscape, the Phoenix Force flares, destroying the demons; Wolverine awakens, himself again. The X-Men celebrate, but Wolverine refuses to answer Cyclops' questions about Jean and leaves to deal with a private matter. In the mindscape, Wolverine's mental aspects rebuild his psychic fortress…but the berserker demands revenge.

NOTE: This issue also has a "Thor Goes Hollywood" variant cover, an homage to the *Rocky IV* movie poster. The doors in Wolverine's mind are labeled Secrets, Faith, Self-Loathing, Mercy, Compassion, Football, Favorite Lines of Poetry, Best Dirty Jokes, Sexual Fantasies, Hopes and Dreams, Reasons to Hate Myself, Secrets of Weapon X, X-Men I've Had Sex With, How I Cheat at Cards, and People I Have To Kill Before I Die. Graffiti scrawled on the wall reads "Dr. Rot was here," a reference to the brainwashing he implanted between W:WX #8-9, '10. Jubilee sees an off-panel memory of Wolverine having sex in the Danger Room; W&X #24, '13 establishes that it was with Storm.

WOLVERINE #9 [#288] (July 2011)

"Get Mystique: Final Repose" (22 pages)

CREDITS: Jason Aaron (writer), Daniel Acuña (art, colors), Virtual Calligraphy's Cory Petit (letters), Jared K. Fletcher (design), Jody LeHeup (asst editor), Jeanine Schaefer (editor), Nick Lowe (group editor), Jae Lee (c art), Michael Ryan (variant c pencils), June Chung (c colors), Frank Martin (variant c colors)

FEATURE CHARACTER: Wolverine (also as his berserker aspect on recap page, next in W:RTH/3, '10, UXFor #1-4 & 5.1, '10-11; W #5.1, Tstrike #2 & 4-5, X:TS&P #1 fb, all '11, FF #584 & 588, '10-11; SM:BT #9, NAv #8, Av #7-12 & 12.1, all '11, Klaws #2, '10, W #1000/2, '11)

SUPPORTING CAST: Maverick (last in W #3, '11, next in W #304, '12)

VILLAINS: Red Right Hand (some or others last in W #3/2, '11) inc Roger, widow, ninja (all last in W #3/2, '11) & leader (last in W #5, '11); Lord Deathstrike (Lady Deathstrike's brother, gadget-using assassin, 1st, next in X #26, '12) & his employers, Azuma Góda (chr 1st bts app, directing ninjas; chr next bts in W #5.1, '11; next bts in W #19, next voice only in W #20, next in 1st on-panel app in W #300, all '12), Hand ninjas (Tokyo branch, some or others last in Sland:GR, '10, chr next in W #5.1, '11, next in W #300, '12)

OTHER CHARACTERS: Mystique (also as policeman, also on monitor, dies, last in W #6, '11, next in W #300, '12), Deathstrike's target (dies) his guards, bikers (die), underground doctor & his patient, garbagemen, gun store employee, underworld auctioneer & bidders, bystanders; horse (others on poster), seals (bts, dead as brains), birds; Nightcrawler (mentioned, Mystique honored his memory by helping Wolverine); soldier (as display dummy); cow (as skull on belt buckle); Beast, Professor X (prev 2 in shadow), Cable, Hope Summers (prev 4 variant cover only)

LOCATIONS/ITEMS: San Francisco inc rooftops, sewers, gun store & underground doctor's office, Red Right Hand's Mexican estate, Argentinean field, target's Chinese complex, Maverick's hideout, underworld auction house / bikers' chain, shotgun & bat, Red Right Hand's camera (bts) & computers w/monitors, Lord Deathstrike's private jet, scanner, smartphone, handguns, x-ray mask, wall-climbing shoes, phasing device & high-powered rifle w/scope, tripod, case & exploding bullet, guards' submachine guns, doctor's surgical equipment, Mystique's motorcycle (destroyed), cellphone & coffin, duct tape, Wolverine's car (destroyed) & belt-buckle communicator, Maverick's computer (bts) headset, FBI, CIA & Interpol files (prev 3 bts), mailbox, telephone pole (prev 2 destroyed), garbage truck, gun store's machine gun, grenade handgun, stolen SHIELD technology (mentioned), Hand ninjas' bow (bts), arrows, swords & axe

SYNOPSIS: The Red Right Hand watch from afar as Wolverine stalks through San Francisco looking for Mystique. In Argentina, Lord Deathstrike assassinates a well-protected target in China by literally shooting through the planet with a high-powered gun. The Red Right Hand's leader hires him to kill Mystique, fearing that she will tell Wolverine their plan. Wolverine fights his way into an underground medical clinic, but Mystique has already left. Mystique calls Wolverine, trying to warn him about the Red Right Hand, but Wolverine threatens her and refuses to listen. Lord Deathstrike suddenly attacks Mystique; she flees, but Wolverine locates and pursues her. As Mystique impersonates a policeman and confiscates a gun store's weapons to fight back, Maverick contacts Wolverine, having located the group's base. Wolverine drives Lord Deathstrike off and confronts Mystique. She tries once more to warn him of the Red Right Hand's plan, but the enraged Wolverine refuses to listen and kills her. Later, Mystique's body is sold at an underworld auction — and purchased by the Hand.

NOTE: This issue also has an "X-Men Evolutions" variant cover showcasing various stages in the life of Hope Summers. W #304, '12 confirms that Lord Deathstrike is Lady Deathstrike's brother. This issue's title references the "Get Mystique" arc from W #62-65, '08. Mystique learned the full scope of the Red Right Hand's plan, and decided she could not be a part of it, in D:DW #1, '10; this explains why she helped them send Wolverine to Hell in W #5/2, '11 but later saved Melita from the Mongrels in W #1, '10.

WOLVERINE #1000 (April 2011)

"Last Ride of the Devil's Brigade" (22 pages)

CREDITS: Rick Spears (writer), Timothy Green (art), Tom Orzechowski (letters), Veronica Gandini (colors), Michael Horwitz (editor), Stephen Segovia (c pencils), Rafa Garres (variant c pencils), Crime Lab Studios (c inks), Sonia Oback (c colors)
FEATURE CHARACTER: Wolverine (as Cpl. Logan, also as Nazi, chr last in W #1000/5, '11, chr next in Logan #1, '08 fb)
GUEST STAR: Nick Fury (chr last in Twelve #1, '08, chr next in NF:AoS #38, '92 fb)
VILLAINS: Nazis (some or all die; 1 also as werewolf, dies), Nazi pilots (1 dies, others bts in planes, 1 dies), Nazi mad scientist & his acolytes (die)
OTHER CHARACTERS: Devil's Brigade (Wolverine's Canadian special forces unit, some or others last in W:O #17, '07 fb): Lt. Jake Bugsby (pilot), Frank Marshall (communications specialist), Sgt. Ryan "Rags" Ragatello (demolitions expert), Cpl. Hank Stiggins (medic) (all die) & their commanders (bts activating backup plan); Allied pilots (bts in planes) & soldiers (others mentioned, advancing on Berlin), Soviet soldiers (bts operating tank), fetal creature (dead in jar); wolf (dead as headdress); Captain America (Rogers), Bucky (prev 2 mentioned, presumed dead), Baron Heinrich Zemo (mentioned, battled Captain America), Dr. Abraham Erskine (mentioned, killed), Adolf Hitler (mentioned, hiding in bunker), Weapon Plus Program (mentioned, developing anti-Communist weapons), Sara Stiggins (Hank's wife) & her unborn child (prev 2 mentioned), Ragatello's twin brother (mentioned, lives in Brooklyn), Saint Walpurga (patron saint of those with rabies, mentioned), Nazi scientists (mentioned, creating Wunderwaffen), Allied recon unit (mentioned, gave Devil's Brigade intel), devils, ghouls, goblins, witches (prev 4 mentioned, appear on Walpurgis Night), Nazi's family (mentioned); eagle (as statue), eagle (as statue)
LOCATIONS/ITEMS: Germany: Harz mountain range inc Elbe River (bts) & Brocken (peak) w/Nazi outpost (destroyed) inc science lab, Berlin (mentioned) inc Hitler's bunker / Devil's Brigade's airplane (destroyed) w/machine guns, Nazi Focke-Wulf fighter planes (2 destroyed) w/machine guns, Wolverine's parachute, pilot's handgun, Soviet tank (bts), Nazis' motorcycle, rifles, uniform & knife, outpost's machine guns, sirens (prev 2 bts), antenna (destroyed), barbed wire, tank & searchlights, Allied airplanes w/bombs, scientist's shackles, experiment jars & syringe w/ lycanthrope serum, lab's skylight, werewolf's War Merit Cross, soldiers' bonds (bts); Hitler's cyanide & Luger handgun, Nazi Wunderwaffen ("wonder weapons"): giant tanks, cruise missiles, night vision equipment, light-powered sun-gun, powerful bomb; Super-Soldier Serum (prev 8 mentioned)

SYNOPSIS: In 1945, as the Devil's Brigade flies through German airspace, Nazi fighter planes attack. The Brigade is killed, but Logan leaps onto one of the fighters, kills the pilot and commandeers the plane. After landing near his target, Logan continues the mission: to stop a Nazi lab from developing a counterpart to Captain America's Super-Soldier Serum. As Logan sneaks into the lab, the Allies suddenly begin bombing it. Fleeing explosions, Logan runs into a Nazi tank, which shoots him. Logan awakens later to find the base in ruins; he locates an underground lab and witnesses a crazed scientist inject a Nazi, transforming him into a werewolf. Logan battles the creature and kills it with its own silver valor medal. Nick Fury arrives and stops Logan from murdering the scientist, explaining that Captain America has been killed and the USA needs to gather new technology to win future wars. They conscript the scientist into the nascent Weapon Plus program, as Wolverine wonders if his fighting days will ever end.

NOTE: This issue also has a variant cover. Like W #900, '10, this one-shot's numbering pokes fun at the vast number of Wolverine comics published over the years; its numbering is taken from the similarly hyperbolic Dp #1000, '10. Though the Devil's Brigade have appeared and been mentioned several times before, this is the first story to name any individual members. W:O #17, '07 fb revealed that they were trained by Silas Burr, later Wolverine's nemesis Cyber. The circumstances of Captain America and Bucky's seeming deaths in WWII were detailed in Av #4, '64 fb. Weapon Plus was the parent program behind the Weapon X Program, which grafted Adamantium to Wolverine's bones.

2ND STORY: "The Legend of Crimson Falls" (22 pages)
CREDITS: Jimmy Palmiotti (writer), Rafa Garres (art, colors), Virtual Calligraphy's Joe Sabino (letters), Sebastian Girner (asst editor), Axel Alonso (exec editor)
FEATURE CHARACTER: Wolverine
VILLAINS: Evolved lycanthropes inc Alika (Lionsgate Hotel manager, also in wolf form in symbolic image) & Thomas (all also in wolf form, die; also in wolf form in photo)
OTHER CHARACTERS: Ava (nonviolent lycanthrope) & her unborn child (bts as embryo), Ryan Taylor (Ava's boyfriend), Betty (local teenager) & her boyfriend, diner patrons & staff inc Mike, construction workers (dead, 1 also in photo), townspeople (others mentioned, witnessed victim), development company (bts buying land), bar patrons & bartender, police, paramedics, firefighters; dog (another mentioned, humps Thomas' leg); Ava's parents (mentioned, killed) & friend (mentioned, lives in Brookville), FBI, state police (prev 2 mentioned, unable to find werewolf evidence), forensics (mentioned, arriving soon), Alika's parents (mentioned, knew Wolverine); trout, skunk (prev 2 mentioned)
LOCATIONS/ITEMS: Crimson Falls, New York (small Adirondack mountain town) inc lake, waterfall, Floods (diner), Tony's Pizza & Brew (mentioned), Motor Bar & Lionsgate Hotel (destroyed) w/nearby woods & housing development; Brookville (nearby town), Mike's house w/guest room, hospital, Austria (prev 6 mentioned) / Boyfriend's rowboat, flashlight & beer, construction workers' beer (mentioned), tools & truck, Wolverine's backpack, newspaper & X-Men business card, Alika's car, groceries & boxes, Thomas' whittling knife, Ava's smartphone & perfume, hotel's roof, deck & water heater (prev 3 mentioned), surveillance camera (bts) & photo, townsperson's truck, police cars, files, crime scene tape & body bags, bar pool tables, cues & balls, ambulance, stretcher, werewolf's shotgun, fire truck w/hose
SYNOPSIS: In a small Adirondack town, two teenagers discover a lake full of corpses. Wolverine soon arrives for a vacation, and is immediately attracted to hotel manager Alika. Teenage hotel resident Ava gossips that werewolves killed the recent victims, piquing Wolverine's curiosity. Later, he and Alika walk in the woods, and soon sleep together. The next day, a local asks for Wolverine's help in finding the werewolf. The police tell Wolverine that the victims were all construction workers from a nearby housing development. That night, Wolverine sees Ava sneak into town; when he follows, he interrupts a werewolf attack on Ava's boyfriend — and a lycanthropic Alika flees. Wolverine returns to the hotel, where Alika explains that all the hotel residents are werewolves, and that they killed the workers to protect their territory. They attack Wolverine, who kills them all. Later, Wolverine finds Ava in the woods, who reveals that she is also a werewolf but wants no part of the killings. Wolverine gives her the X-Men's phone number.
NOTE: This story is titled "Legend of the Crimson Falls" on the credits page. Wolverine incorrectly claims that he is single here; he has been dating Melita Garner since W:WX #10, '10.

3RD STORY: "The Adamantium Diaries" (11 pages)
CREDITS: Sarah Cross (writer), João Lemos (art), Jeff Eckleberry (letters), Chris Chuckry (colors), Sana Amanat (editor)
FEATURE CHARACTER: Wolverine (also in photos, on posters & as dolls, also as "Patch" in photo, also in rfb; next in UXFor #5-8, 10 fb & 8-9, X:L #244-246, NM #24, X:L #248, NM #25, Namor #11, W/Dp:Decoy, D:DW #9.1, Skaar:KSL #5, NAv #9-13 & 14 fb, AX #36-37, 39 & 41, AvAc #11 & 12 bts, GenHope #6, UXM #534.1, 535 & 537-538, all '11, UXM #526/2, '10; IHulks Ann, X23 #10-12, all '11, Av:Child #2-8, '10-12, MNowPO/5, '12 fb, Av:Child #9, '12; UXM #539, NAv #15 fb, NAv Ann #1, all '11, Av Ann #1, '12; Av #13 fb, FearI:1-2, AFlt #4, NAv #15 fb & 14 fb, FearI:W #1-3, Av #17 fb, FearI:6, FearI:UXFor #1-3, FearI:6, InvIM #509, all '11, FearI:7 & 7.2 fb, '11-12, AFlt #6, '12, AvAc #20, '11, AFlt #7-8, '12; FearI:7, Dp #37 fb, Av #13-15, NAv #16, Av #17-18, AvSolo #11, '11; FearI:7 #6-7 & 10-12, '12; ASM #665 fb, X #7-10, ASM #666, SI:C&D #1, ASM #667-668, SI:DF, SI:DHKF #1, ASM #668, SI:Av, Herc #7-8, all '11, ASM #670 & 672-673, '11-12, X #11, '11, W:Best #1, 11 fb, 1-4, 11 fb & 4-12, '11-12; XGS, X #12-15, GenHope #9, X #16-19, all '11, MK #6 & 12, '11-12, Annis:EF #1-4, '11-12, W #10, '11)
VILLAINS: Muggers
OTHER CHARACTERS: Teenage Wolverine fan & her teacher (bts in classroom) & classmates, diner patrons & waitress, bystanders; Sabretooth (mentioned, fights Wolverine), Edward Cullen (mentioned, fan's classmates obsessed with him), Jay Gatsby (mentioned in book report); X-Men: Colossus, Storm; Kierrok (prev 3 in rfb); X-Men (exact members unspecified), Matt Murdock (as boy), "Battling" Jack Murdock, Wolverine's foe, protestors, boxers, referee (prev 7 in photos); creature, wolf (prev 2 on posters), birds (on Latveria poster & vodka bottle)
LOCATIONS/ITEMS: Wolverine fan's bedroom & school inc classroom & library, Salem Center inc diner & Auger Inn, X-Mansion (in rfb) / Wolverine fan's pencils, pen, straws (prev 3 as "claws"), diary, books, shoulder bag, steel-toed boots & Wolverine memorabilia inc dolls, posters & clippings from magazines & newspapers inc Daily Bugle, DB! & Madripoor Herald, library computer, knife (on poster), "Wolverine Daily" fan website, Wolverine's Wikipedia entry (mentioned), diner's boxing photos & newspaper clipping, boxers' gloves (in photos), muggers' vodka bottle, Wolverine's motorcycle
FLASHBACK: Wolverine battles Kierrok the Damned (X #96, '75).
SYNOPSIS: A shy teenage girl, bullied at school, is an enormous Wolverine fan, and wishes she had his courage and attitude. One evening, she spots a man who resembles Wolverine. The man denies being the mutant hero, but invites her to join him at a nearby diner. They talk about Wolverine for hours; she expresses her admiration of the hero, and the man explains that she doesn't need claws to stand up to bullies, just confidence. As they leave the diner, muggers accost them. Fed up, the girl attacks them with her shoulder bag. The muggers flee, and she thanks her newfound friend for his advice. He smiles, pops his Adamantium claws, and rides off on his motorcycle.
NOTE: This story is titled "Adamantium Claws" on the credits page. The diner walls have framed photos of boxer "Battling Jack" Murdock, and a newspaper article featuring Jack with his son Matt, who grew up to be the super hero Daredevil. In addition to her schoolbooks, the fan is reading a book on Canadian mammals.

4TH STORY: "Development Hell" (8 pages)
NOTE: Reprinted from W:DevHell, '10. This story is not listed on the credits page.

5TH STORY: "Last Men Standing" (8 pages)
CREDITS: Vince Hernandez (writer), Luke Ross (art), Tom Orzechowski (letters), Guru eFX (colors), Michael Horwitz (editor)
FEATURE CHARACTER: Wolverine (as Cpl. Logan, chr last in W #78, '94 fb, chr next in W #1000, '11)
VILLAINS: Nazis (some die)
OTHER CHARACTERS: US soldiers (some dead) & officers inc Lieutenant
LOCATIONS/ITEMS: Belgium's Ardennes forest inc soldiers' trenches / Soldiers' binoculars, rifles, grenades, packs, shovels & coffee, Nazis' tanks & rifles
SYNOPSIS: In 1944, a small unit of US troops worries about how to hold the Ardennes forest against a heavily armed approaching Nazi force. They have suffered many casualties and are demoralized — and none of them trust Cpl. Logan, the squad's new addition, who recommends a dangerous plan to flank their foes. Suddenly, the Nazis begin shelling the troops' encampment. Logan attacks alone, drawing the Nazi tanks'

fire and giving the US troops a chance to get into position. The soldiers attack from both sides, catching the Nazis in a crossfire. Later, relieved to have finally won a battle, the soldiers welcome Logan to their ranks as he reminds himself that trust must be earned.
NOTE: Although this story only lists its timeframe as "1944," it occurs during the December 1944 Ardennes Counteroffensive, better known as the Battle of the Bulge.

WOLVERINE #10 [#289] (August 2011)

"Wolverine's Revenge! Part 1" (22 pages)

CREDITS: Jason Aaron (writer), Renato Guedes (pencils), José Wilson Magalhaes (inks), Virtual Calligraphy's Cory Petit (letters), Matthew Wilson (colors), Jared K. Fletcher (design), Jody LeHeup (asst editor), Jeanine Schaefer (editor), Nick Lowe (group editor), Jae Lee (c art), June Chung (c colors)
FEATURE CHARACTER: Wolverine (also on monitor, also on poster in fb2; also in fb1 between W #65, '08 fb & W:Amaz, '08; also in fb2 between W:O #3, '06 fb & W #11, '11 fb; also in W #14, '11 fb)
VILLAINS: Mongrels: Cannonfoot (also bts on monitor, dies, last in W #5, '11, also in W #14, '11 fb, next in W #14, '11), Shadow Stalker (last in W #4/2, '11, also on monitor); Red Right Hand (some bts off-panel; some also in fb2, the group's chr 1st app, prior to W #11, '11 fb) inc leader (also as boy in fb1 & as boy & man in fb2, his chr 1st app prior to W #11, '11 fb; also in D:DW #1, '10 fb during fb2), widow (also as woman in fb2 during W #11, '11 fb), boy (last in W #3/2, '11), Roger & ninja; Hudson Bay Company employees (in fb2, all but 1 bts giving leader information)
OTHER CHARACTERS: Leader's father (coal mine owner, dies, also in photo in fb2, possibly next as spirit in W #14, '11, see NOTE) & his miners (some die), strikebreakers inc Pinkertons, union organizers (some die) inc old woman (dies) (all in fb1), leader's father's rivals (bts bankrupting his family), leader's mother & sisters, mourners (prev 4 in fb2), widow's husband (bts, dead in casket, in fb2 following W #11, '11 fb, possibly next as spirit in W #14, '11, see NOTE); Mongrels: Fire Knives, Gunhawk, Saw Fist (prev 3 mentioned, drew straws to fight Wolverine); armed men, coyotes, copperhead snakes (prev 3 mentioned in fb1, defeated by leader's father), leader's relatives (mentioned in fb2, took in his mother & sisters), peer (mentioned in fb2, fighting WWII) & sources (mentioned in fb2, helping locate Wolverine); historical figures (as statues), man (in photo in fb2); Mystique (dead, recap page only)
LOCATIONS/ITEMS: Kentucky: miners' shantytown, father's office (both in fb1) & coal mines (destroyed, all but 1 bts), funeral home; leader's relatives' home, Texas oil wells, ammunition factory, Japan (prev 4 mentioned); Canada: Yukon Territory, Hudson Bay Company's Canadian training facility, bar, hospital, graveyard, Wolverine's various locations (prev 12 in fb2), Red Right Hand's Mexican estate (also on monitor, also in fb2) / Strikebreakers' torches, bats & pitchfork, miners' signs, hammer & sickle, Pinkertons' guns, father's liquor bottle (destroyed), Wolverine's knife (all in fb1), father & husband's coffins, leader's hammer, book, handgun, pocketwatch, grenade, mortar & rifle w/scope, train, Hudson Bay files, Wolverine's liquor bottle (destroyed), Red Right Hand's candles (prev 13 in fb2), Red Right Hand's security cameras & computer w/monitors, Mongrels' straws (mentioned), Cannonfoot's rocks (1 destroyed), leader's cane, statue (destroyed)
FLASHBACKS: Eighty years ago, a coal mine owner hires violent strikebreakers to deal with protesting employees. The strikers hire an elderly union organizer, and a "negotiator" named Logan who beats the strikebreakers badly and forces the owner to the bargaining table. The owner gets drunk and lashes out, killing the elderly organizer, and Logan stabs him to death in front of his son (1). The owner's son grows up consumed with a need for revenge. Obtaining information from the Hudson Bay Company, he tracks down Wolverine and shoots him, but Wolverine survives. The man keeps trying, but rifles, grenades and missiles are ineffective. Eventually he changes tactics, and recruits others who have lost loved ones to Wolverine. They found the Red Right Hand, dedicated to making Wolverine pay (2).
SYNOPSIS: Wolverine bursts into the Red Right Hand's estate, intent on revenge. The halls appear empty, but Cannonfoot emerges and attacks, as the Red Right Hand watch the battle on monitors from a secure room. Wolverine kills Cannonfoot, but is immediately attacked by Shadow Stalker, as the Red Right Hand gloat that their plan is unfolding perfectly.
NOTE: This issue also has a 5-page preview of Cap #1, '11. The Hudson Bay Company facility, which trained Wolverine as a soldier in the 1910s, was secretly run by Romulus and overseen by Wolverine's uncles Frederick and Elias Hudson, as revealed in W:O #33, '09. In the real world, "Hudson's Bay Company" is a Canadian business that specialized in fur trading for many years. In W #14, '11, the leader's father and widow's husband's spirits appear when the Red Right Hand arrives in Hell, as do most other members' loved ones; however, as discussed in W #4, '82's NOTE, it is uncertain if anything seen there is real. With this issue, the series switched to an accelerated "semi-monthly" schedule, often publishing two issues a month.

WOLVERINE #11 [#290] (August 2011)

"Wolverine's Revenge! Part 2" (22 pages)

CREDITS: Jason Aaron (writer), Renato Guedes (pencils), José Wilson Magalhaes (inks), Virtual Calligraphy's Cory Petit (letters), Matthew Wilson (colors), Jared K. Fletcher (design), Jody LeHeup (asst editor), Jeanine Schaefer (editor), Nick Lowe (group editor), Jae Lee (c art), June Chung (c colors)
FEATURE CHARACTER: Wolverine (also on monitor, also on posters in rfb & fb2; also in fb1 between W #10, '11 fb & W:AoAtlas #1, '08; also as Logan in fb2 between D:DW #1, '10 fb & W:O #6, '06 fb; also in W #14, '11 fb)
SUPPORTING CAST: Mariko Yashida (bts, dead in coffin, last in W #57, '92, last bts in W #60, '92, possibly last as spirit in W #5, '11, see W #2, '10's NOTE; corpse next bts in W #300, '12)
VILLAINS: Red Right Hand (some bts off-panel, some also in rfb; some also in fb2, some or others chr last in W #10, '11 fb, chr next in W #12, '11 fb) inc widow (also as woman in rfb; also as girl in fb1 & as woman in fb2, her chr 1st app, prior to W #14, '11 fb; also in W #10, '11 fb during fb2), leader (also as man in rfb; also as man in fb2 between W #10, '11 fb & D:DW #2, '10 fb), Roger, boy (prev 2 bts off-panel) & ninja; Shadow Stalker (also on monitor, dies, also in W #14, '11 fb, next in W #14, '11), Sabretooth (as Creed in fb2 between W #68, '93 fb & X #5, '92 fb), Daken (in fb2 between D:DW #1-2, '10 fbs)
OTHER CHARACTERS: Sabretooth clone (dead as head, see NOTE), Victoria Creed (Sabretooth's mother, named, dies, in fb2 following XO:Sabre, '09), widow's father (high-ranking OSS member, in fb1, dies) & husband (NSA agent, in fb2 prior to W #10, '11 fb bts, dies; also bts in rfb, dead in coffin); Landau, Luckman & Lake; Hand, Hudson Bay Company, John Sublime, Weapon II, Winter Soldier (prev 6 mentioned in fb1, in widow's father's notes), CIA, Nick Fury, Gorilla Man, Lady Deathstrike, Lord Dark Wind, Omega Red (prev 6 mentioned in fb2, in widow's husband's notes), John & Elizabeth Howlett, Itsu, Thomas Logan, Rose O'Hara, Silver Fox (prev 6 mentioned in fb2, in Red Right Hand's

notes), Dog Logan, Mystique, Seraph (prev 3 mentioned in fb1 & fb2, in father's & Red Right Hand's notes), Romulus (mentioned in fb1 & fb2, in father's & husband's notes), Senator Joseph McCarthy (mentioned in fb2, widow met husband at his rally), Zebediah Creed (mentioned in fb2, killed by Sabretooth), Communists, Asians, mutants (prev 3 mentioned in fb2, considered threats by husband), nursing home employees (mentioned in fb2, cater to Victoria), widow's boyfriends (mentioned in fb2), widow's mother (mentioned in fb1, dead); mourners (in rfb); Millie Collins, photographer (prev 2 on comic book cover); bear (as doll)

LOCATIONS/ITEMS: Red Right Hand's Mexican estate (also on monitors, also in rfb) inc greenhouse, pool & trophy room, widow's childhood home (destroyed, in fb1) & married home, pro-McCarthy rally location (mentioned), Golden Oaks Retirement Home inc Victoria's room (prev 4 in fb2), graveyard (in rfb) / Red Right Hand's security cameras (bts), computer w/monitors & display cases (some destroyed) w/Wolverine's swords & costumes & Mariko's coffin, estate's windows & walls (some of prev 2 destroyed), father's notes (destroyed) & gun, widow's comic book & doll, Wolverine's lighter (prev 5 in fb1), husband's notes, Logan's gun, Red Right Hand's knives & notes, leader's car & hammer (prev 7 in fb2), husband's coffin, Red Right Hand's candles (in rfb)

FLASHBACKS: The Red Right Hand's leader recruits the widow (last issue's fb). Following WWII, a young girl's father becomes a paranoid conspiracy theorist, obsessed with unraveling the secrets of Romulus, Weapon Plus and more. One night the girl is horrified to discover that Wolverine has assassinated her father (1). Years later, the girl has grown up and married another conspiracy theorist. She awakens to find him dead, with Sabretooth and Wolverine looming over her. Wolverine stops Sabretooth from assaulting her, but she recognizes Wolverine as her father's killer. The widow joins the Red Right Hand. One night, the leader takes her to a nursing home, where Sabretooth's mother sleeps, and she beats the old woman to death with a hammer. Later, Daken attends a Red Right Hand meeting and offers a sadistic idea for hurting Wolverine (2).

SYNOPSIS: Wolverine and Shadow Stalker battle through the Red Right Hand's estate. Wolverine is thrown into a trophy room, and is astonished to see it full of memorabilia from his own past. The battle continues; Wolverine eventually kills Shadow Stalker while the Red Right Hand watch from afar.

NOTE: This issue also has a 5-page preview of X:Schism #1, '11, and a 1-page Marvel Architects feature spotlighting several artists. Wolverine's first love Rose O'Hara's last name is revealed this issue, and Shadow Stalker's codename is clarified as being two words. The young widow reads Millie #27, '51 in this issue's fb1. The Red Right Hand have Sabretooth's severed head in their trophy room, but W #310, '12 reveals that Sabretooth is not dead at this time, and the head of the clone that died in his place is still buried at Silver Fox's cabin. This may be the head of a second Sabretooth clone, as W #310, '12 reveals that dozens had been made. The trophy room also contains Mariko Yashida's coffin; the Black Samurai likely stole it after assaulting the Yashidas' ancestral manor in W #1/2, '10.

WOLVERINE #12 [#291] (September 2011)

"Wolverine's Revenge! Part 3" (22 pages)

CREDITS: Jason Aaron (writer), Renato Guedes (pencils), José Wilson Magalhaes (inks), Virtual Calligraphy's Cory Petit (letters), Matthew Wilson (colors), Jared K. Fletcher (design), Jody LeHeup (asst editor), Jeanine Schaefer (editor), Nick Lowe (group editor), Jae Lee (c art), Joe Quesada (variant c pencils), Danny Miki (variant c inks), June Chung (c colors), Richard Isanove (variant c colors)

FEATURE CHARACTER: Wolverine (also on monitor & on poster, also in rfb; also in fb during IHulk #340, '88)

GUEST STAR: Hulk (in fb during IHulk #340, '88)

VILLAINS: Mongrels: Saw Fist (last in W #4/2, '11), Fire Knives (also bts on monitor) (both die, next in W #14, '11), Gunhawk (prev 2 last in W #5, '11); Red Right Hand (some bts off-panel; some also in fb, some or others chr last in W #11, '11 fb, chr next in W #14, '11 fb) inc Roger (named, dies; also in fb, his chr 1st app, prior to W #14, '11 fb; also bts off-panel in dfb during fb), leader (also in fb between W #13, '11 fbs), ninja, boy (prev 2 bts off-panel) & widow; Devil (bts possessing flies & anaconda; also bts possessing anaconda in fb, his chr 1st app, prior to W #1, '10; last in W #5, '11, possibly last in JIM #627, '11, see W #5, '11's NOTE), demons (possessing boy & dog in fb & dfb, their chr 1st app, some or others chr next bts in W #5/2, '11, chr next in X23 #2, '10)

OTHER CHARACTERS: Carol (Roger's wife) & her unborn daughter (bts as fetus) (both die, also in pictures in fb2), paramedics inc Bobby, commuters, reporter (voice only on radio), authorities (bts crediting Wolverine), bartender, bar patron, hobo (dies), boy, dog (prev 2 possessed by demons, also possessed by demons in dfb following fb) (all in fb), Red Right Hand's sacrificial victims (some dead, also die in fb2 prior to issue; others dead in fb2); flies (also possessed by Devil, next in W #14, '11), goat (dead), anaconda (possessed by Devil, also as itself & possessed by Devil in fb2 prior to issue); Mongrels: Cannonfoot, Shadow Stalker (prev 2 in fb); firefighter (variant cover only)

LOCATIONS/ITEMS: Texas: radio newsroom (bts) & Highway 18; X-Mansion, bar & nearby streets (also in dfb) & alley (all in fb), Red Right Hand's Mexican estate (also on monitor, also in rfb, dfb & fb) inc sacrificial altar (also bts on monitor, also in dfb & fb) / Roger's tow truck (destroyed), pictures & Wolverine costume, cars (some destroyed) w/radio, paramedics' medical kit, sacrificial restraints (all in fb), Roger's bat, Red Right Hand's hooked chains (prev 2 also in fb), security cameras (all but 1 bts) & computers w/monitors, Saw Fist's wrist-mounted chainsaws, Fire Knives' knives (1 each of prev 2 destroyed)

FLASHBACKS: Wolverine battles Cannonfoot (W #10, '11) and Shadow Stalker (last issue). The demon-possessed boy explains the terms of his offer (this issue's fb). Years ago, Roger's pregnant wife begins having labor complications. They head for the hospital, but a Wolverine/Hulk fight blocks the highway. Roger's truck accidentally hits Wolverine, destroying the vehicle. He runs for the hospital carrying his wife, but she dies. Years later, the Red Right Hand's leader approaches Roger in a bar, offering membership. Roger declines, stalks off and performs a gruesome ritual: he finds a hobo, forces him to dress as Wolverine, and beats him to death. A demon-possessed boy and dog approach, offering Roger a plan for true revenge. Roger agrees, returns to the bar and joins the Red Right Hand. Later, the group summons the Devil.

SYNOPSIS: Fire Knives and Saw Fist attack Wolverine; he quickly defeats them and they defiantly kill one another in front of him. Roger becomes agitated, yelling that Wolverine isn't suffering enough and needs to know what the Red Right Hand is doing to him. He tries to leave the secure chamber, but Gunhawk shoots him dead.

NOTE: This issue also has an "I Am Captain America" variant cover. Saw Fist's codename is clarified as being two words here. This issue's "Cutting Edge" LOC is recycled in W #13-14 & #16-19, '11-12.

WOLVERINE #13 [#292] (October 2011)

"Wolverine's Revenge! Part 4" (22 pages)

CREDITS: Jason Aaron (writer), Renato Guedes (pencils), José Wilson Magalhaes (inks), Virtual Calligraphy's Cory Petit (letters), Matthew Wilson (colors), Jared K. Fletcher (design), Jody LeHeup (asst editor), Jeanine Schaefer (editor), Nick Lowe (group editor), Jae Lee (c art), June Chung (c colors)

FEATURE CHARACTER: Wolverine (also on monitor, also in photo in fb4; also in fb2 between BFF:Ben #3, '0? & W #119, '97 fb; also in fb3 between W #28-29, '05)

VILLAINS: Mongrels: Cannonfoot, Fire Knives, Saw Fist, Shadow Stalker (all in fb4, their chr 1st app, during W #14, '11 fb bts); Gunhawk (also on monitor, dies; also in fb4, his chr 1st app, during W #14, '11 fb bts); Red Right Hand (some bts off-panel) inc ninja (also as girl in fb1 & fb4, & dies & resurrected in fb3, her chr 1st apps, prior to W #14, '11 fb), leader (also in fb4 between D:DW #2, '10 fb & W #12, '11 fb; also in fb3 between W #12, '11 fb & W #14, '11 fb), boy (bts off-panel) & widow; Hand ninjas (in fb2, die; others in fb2 & fb1, die in fb1; others in fb1 some or others chr last in Elek:Ass #1, '86 fb, chr next in fb4) inc ninja's father (in fb2 & fb1, dies in fb1), others (in fb4, some or others chr last in fb1, chr next in Elek:Ass #8, '87), others (in fb3, many die, some or others chr last in Elektra #22, '03, chr next in MAv #16, '08 fb) inc Takeo (ninja's brother, dies) & his brothers (bts, dead) inc Kaemon (1 dead ninja possibly next as spirit next issue, see NOTE); Hand sorcerer (in fb3, 1 or another chr last in W #24, '05, some or others chr next in NAv #27, '07)

OTHER CHARACTERS: Hand pupils (1 dies) & elder (both in fb1), Hand women inc ninja's mother, women's unborn children (bts as fetuses) (prev 3 in fb3)

LOCATIONS/ITEMS: Japan: house (in fb2) & Hand ninjas' cave lair (in fb1, fb3 & fb4); Red Right Hand's Mexican estate (also on monitors, also in fb3) / Hand ninjas' swords (others in fb2, fb3 & fb4) & daggers, ninja's whip & rocks (prev 2 mentioned) (prev 4 in fb1), Hand ninjas' bows (bts), arrows & shuriken, Wolverine's swords (prev 4 in fb2), ninja's rice (bts) & swords, sorcerer's altar & candle (prev 4 in fb3), Wolverine's motorcycle (in photo), leader's photo (prev 2 in fb4), Red Right Hand's security cameras (bts) & computers w/monitors

FLASHBACKS: A young girl, born into the Hand clan, trains to be a ninja. Her father and several other ninjas, defeated by Wolverine, return to the Hand's lair and commit suicide in shame (1). Wolverine defeats several ninjas, including the girl's father (2). Years later, Wolverine bursts into the lair and begins slaughtering every ninja in sight. The woman attacks, but Wolverine kills her. She awakens later, resurrected by the Hand… but only because Wolverine decimated the clan, and they need her and the other women to bear children to replenish their ranks. Disgusted, the ninja defects; she seeks out the Red Right Hand's leader, who asks her to train his newly gathered Mongrels (3). Years before, the Red Right Hand's leader tries to hire the Hand to kill Wolverine, but they decline (4).

SYNOPSIS: As Wolverine approaches the Red Right Hand's secure room, Gunhawk emerges and begins shooting at him. Wolverine fatally stabs Gunhawk, and the Red Right Hand prepare for Wolverine's arrival. Dying, Gunhawk explains that they don't want to kill Wolverine, just to hurt him. Undaunted, Wolverine charges into the chamber…

NOTE: This issue also has a 6-page preview of Ults #1, '11. This issue's pp.21-22 occur after pp.1-4 of next issue. Being generic Hand ninjas, the Red Right Hand member, her brothers and/or her father may have appeared elsewhere prior to this issue's flashbacks, but this is the chronologically earliest appearance where they are depicted as individuals. The Red Right Hand's ninja is reunited with a loved one in Hell next issue, but their identity is not revealed; see also W #10 & 14, '11's NOTE sections.

WOLVERINE #14 [#293] (October 2011)

"Wolverine's Revenge! Conclusion" (22 pages)

CREDITS: Jason Aaron (writer), Renato Guedes (pencils), José Wilson Magalhaes (inks), Virtual Calligraphy's Cory Petit (letters), Matthew Wilson (colors), Jared K. Fletcher (design), Jody LeHeup (asst editor), Jeanine Schaefer (editor), Nick Lowe (group editor), Jae Lee (c art), June Chung (c colors)

FEATURE CHARACTER: Wolverine (also in rfb1, rfb3, rfb4 & bts on monitor in rfb2; also in fb1 between W #31, '05 & W #59, '08 fb; also in fb3 during W #10, '11; also in fb4 during W #11, '11)

GUEST STAR: Nick Fury (in fb1 between W #31, '05 & NFHC #1, '05)

VILLAINS: Mongrels: Fire Knives, Saw Fist (both also in rfb3, last in W #12, '11), Cannonfoot (also in fb3 during W #10, '11; last in W #10, '11), Gunhawk (also in photo & rfb4), Shadow Stalker (also in fb4 during W #11, '11; last in W #11, '11) (all dead, also in photos in fb1; also bts in fb1, their chr 1st bts app, gathered by Daken, also in W #13, '11 fb during fb); Red Right Hand: Roger (in fb1 & fb2 between W #12, '11 fb & W #1, '10; also bts in rfb2), ninja (in fb1 & fb2 between W #13, '11 fb & W #1, '10) (prev 2 also in W #13, '11 fb during fb1), boy (also in fb1, his chr 1st app, prior to W #1, '10) (prev 3 also in rfb1, '10) (prev 3 die, also as souls), widow (also bts in rfb2; also in fb1 & fb2 between W #11, '11 fb & W #1, '10) (prev 4 die, also as souls), others (die, also as souls; some bts off-panel), also in rfb2 (some bts); some also in fb1 & fb2, some or others chr last in W #12, '11 fb, chr next in W #5/2, '11); Daken (in fb1 between W:O #15 & 24, '07-08)

OTHER CHARACTERS: SHIELD doctor (boy's mother, alive & dead in fb1 following W/NF:SC, '89, also in W #20, '04 during fb; also in rfb1 & bts in photo), teachers, mourners, orphanage worker (prev 3 in fb1), Red Right Hand members' dead loved ones (as spirits; also in photos, most bts) inc leader's father (last in W #10, '11 fb), ninja's relative (last in W #13, '11 fb) (prev 2 also bts in photos) & widow's husband (also in photo, last in W #11, '11 fb, last bts in W #10, '11 fb); flies; boy's father (mentioned in fb1, abandoned mother & boy), six foster families (mentioned in fb1, rejected boy), Hand sorcerers (mentioned in fb1, brainwashed Wolverine); Carol, widow's father, Dolores Downing (Gunhawk's mother, unnamed), other Mongrels' mothers, Red Right Hand's other loved ones (prev 2 bts) (prev 5 in photos); woman (in painting); Wolverine's victims (dead as skulls, cover only)

LOCATIONS/ITEMS: Red Right Hand's Mexican estate (also in rfb2, rfb3, rfb4, fb1, fb2, fb3 & fb4), nursing school, foster homes (prev 2 mentioned), boy's school, SHIELD base, graveyard, orphanage (prev 6 in fb1), South Atlantic Ocean (in rfb1), Hell / Red Right Hand's poisoned wine, computers w/monitors (also in rfb2), photo album & Mongrels' files, mother's coffin, boy's file, Red Right Hand's photos (prev 3 in fb1), video camera (bts in fb2) & security cameras (bts in rfb2, fb3 & fb4), SHIELD aircraft carrier & medical equipment, Wolverine's bandages (prev 3 in rfb1)

FLASHBACKS: Wolverine kills the SHIELD doctor (W #20, '04). The Red Right Hand watch Wolverine battle Cannonfoot (W #10, '11). Fire Knives and Saw Fist kill each other (W #12, '11). Gunhawk lies dead (last issue). After a brainwashed Wolverine kills a SHIELD doctor, the Red Right Hand's leader adopts him as his son. Later, the group discusses whether to use Daken's revenge plan, or to send Wolverine to Hell as the emons suggested. The boy advocates both (1). The Red Right Hand records a message for Wolverine explaining their revenge plan's true ature (2). Wolverine cripples Cannonfoot (3). Wolverine stabs Shadow Stalker (4).

YNOPSIS: The Red Right Hand members drink poison, to rob Wolverine of the pleasure of killing them. Wolverine bursts in to find everyone ead, and a recording begins: the Red Right Hand explains that Wolverine killed members of each of their families, and direct Wolverine to a lder containing pictures of familiar women and their children. The leader explains with glee that the Mongrels were Wolverine's illegitimate hildren — and that Wolverine has now murdered his own family as well. As the group arrive in Hell and reunite with their loved ones, Wolverine horrified by his actions.

OTE: This issue also has a 7-page preview of UltX #1, '11. This issue's pp.1-4 occur between and during pp.20-21 of last issue. Elizabeth owning is named next issue. As discussed in W #4, '82's NOTE, there is some doubt about whether the spirits seen here are real; any or all f them could be illusions, as demons often manipulate living people who visit the various Hell-realms. The chronologies given here assume hat all the spirits are real.

WOLVERINE #15 [#294] (November 2011)

"Wolverine: No More" (22 pages)

CREDITS: Jason Aaron (writer), Goran Sudzuka (art), Virtual Calligraphy's Cory Petit (letters), Matthew Wilson (colors), Jared K. Fletcher (design), Jody LeHeup (asst editor), Jeanine Schaefer (editor), Nick Lowe (group editor), Jae Lee (c art), June Chung (c colors)
FEATURE CHARACTER: Wolverine (also in pfb)
GUEST STARS: X-Men (bts in pfb, looking for Wolverine): Cyclops (last in X #15.1, '11, next in X:L #250/2, '11), others (exact members unspecified, team last in X #19, '11, next in X:L #250, '11)
SUPPORTING CAST: Melita Garner (in pfb, last in FearIt:W #3, '11)
OTHER CHARACTERS: Mongrels: Cannonfoot, Fire Knives, Saw Fist, Shadow Stalker (all bts, dead, buried by Wolverine), Gunhawk (dead) (all possibly next as spirits in W #304, '12, see W #2, '10's NOTE); townspeople, bartender, bar patrons (all in pfb); wild dogs; Dolores Downing (mentioned in pfb, died 30 years ago), other Mongrels' mothers (mentioned in pfb, Wolverine buried their children next to them); Sabretooth (as head), Daken, Dog Logan, Thomas Logan prev 4 as hallucination in pfb)

OCATIONS/ITEMS: Dolores' hometown inc graveyard, bar & gas station, other Mongrels' mothers' hometowns (mentioned) inc graveyards, Melita's apartment (all in pfb), Yukon mountain / Gunhawk's coffin, other Mongrels' coffins (mentioned), Wolverine's ropes, shovel & whiskey ottle, Thomas' staff (in hallucination), patron's knife, pay phone (all in pfb), Wolverine's costume (destroyed)

LASHBACKS: Wolverine drags a coffin to a small town, looking for Dolores Downing. Informed that Dolores died decades ago, Wolverine akes the coffin to the cemetery and begins burying it next to her grave. A townsperson asks who's inside; Wolverine reveals Gunhawk's body, nd admits that he killed him. Later, Wolverine wallows in self-pity at a bar. Staggering into the street, he hallucinates Sabretooth, Daken, his alf-brother Dog and his father mocking him. Three men try to mug him; incoherent and sobbing, he lashes out with his claws. The men slice Volverine's throat and flee. Later, Wolverine calls Melita; she asks where he's been and says that the X-Men are worried, but Wolverine asks er to just forget him.

YNOPSIS: Somewhere in the Yukon, Wolverine climbs a tall mountain. As soon as he reaches the peak, he jumps off. When he lands, there's brief moment of blackness where he has no pain, thinks no thoughts, and feels no shame. But his healing factor revives him, he remembers hy he's there, and he begins to climb again.

OTE: This issue's recap page titles this story "Wolverine No More." Gunhawk's mother's name is revealed here. Gunhawk's first name is also evealed; his last name can be inferred from his mother's.

ND STORY: "Periphery" (8 pages)
OTE: Reprinted from Moment/4, '02, to commemorate the 10th anniversary of the September 11, 2001 terror attacks.

WOLVERINE #16 [#295] (November 2011)

"Wolverine Forever" (20 pages)

CREDITS: Jason Aaron (writer), Goran Sudzuka (art), Virtual Calligraphy's Cory Petit (letters), Matthew Wilson (colors), Jared K. Fletcher (design), Jody LeHeup (asst editor), Jeanine Schaefer (editor), Nick Lowe (group editor), Jae Lee (c art), June Chung (c colors)
FEATURE CHARACTER: Wolverine (also in dfb between X:Prelude #4, '11 & this issue; also in X:Prelude #4 & 1-3, '11; next in X:Schism #1-3, GenHope #10, X:Schism #3-5, X:Regen, GenHope #12, X:Schism #5, all '11, W&X #2, '12 fb)
GUEST STARS: Avengers: Captain America (Rogers, next in X:Schism #2, '11), Iron Man (next bts in X:Schism #2, '11) (both also in dfb following issue, last in Annis:EF #4, '12), Hawkeye (Clint Barton, sureshot archer, last in ASM #673, '12) (prev 2 next in PointOne, '12 fb), Spider-Woman (last in ASM #671, '11, next in AvSM #1, '12); New Avengers: Luke Cage (last in MK #6, '11, next in AvAc #21, '12) (prev 2 chr last in MK #12, '12), Dr. Strange next bts in GR #7, '12, next in Venom #13.1, '12), Iron Fist (prev 2 last in ASM #673, '12), Thing (last in Annis:EF #4, chr next in ASM #692/3, ext bts in X23 #17, all '12) (prev 2 next in NAv #16.1, '11); Secret Avengers: Beast (last in W:Best #12, '12, chr last in SecAv #20, '12 fb, next in X:Regen, '11), Black Widow (last in MK #6, '11, chr last in MK #12, '12, next in X23 #20, '12); X-Force: Deadpool (last in BScars #4, '12, chr next n X #25, '12, next in UXFor #10, '11), Fantomex (last in FearIt:UXFor #3, next bts in X:Schism #2, next in UXFor #10, all '11); X-Men: Storm (last n X #15.1, chr next in X:Prelude #4, next bts in X:Prelude #1, next in X:Prelude #2, all '11), Colossus (last in X #15, '11, chr next in X:Prelude #4, 11), Magneto (last in X #258, '12) (prev 3 also in dfb between X:Prelude #4, '11 & X:Schism #1, '11), Cyclops (also in dfb between X:Prelude 3 & X:Schism #1; last in X:L #250 fb, all '11) (prev 2 chr next in X:Prelude #2, '11), Emma Frost (last in X #19, '11), Professor X (last in X:L 253, '11), Kitty Pryde (last in XGS, '11), Sub-Mariner (last in X #16, '11) (prev 4 chr next bts in X:Prelude #4, '11), Rogue (chr next bts in X:Prelude 4, '11) (prev 8 next in X:Prelude #1, '11), Gambit (next bts in X:Schism #2, '11, next in X:Schism #5, '11) (prev 2 last in X:L #258, '12), Iceman last in X #15, '11), Psylocke (last in X #14, '11) (prev 2 next in X:Schism #1, '11); Black Panther (last in BP #529, '12), Daimon Hellstrom (last

in Veng #6, '12) (prev 2 next in VFH #0.1, '12), Elektra (last in Herc #10, '12, next in Tb #1, '13), Nick Fury (last in Cap #5, '12, next in Dp #5 '12), Hulk (last in IHulk #1, chr last in IHulk #7.1, '12, next in IHulk #8, '12), Puck (last in AFlt #8, '12, next in AX #51, '12, see NOTE), Th (last in FearIt #7.2, chr last in MK #12, next in AvSM #1, all '12)

SUPPORTING CAST: Melita Garner

VILLAINS: Cyttorak (bts empowering Colossus, see NOTE; last in JIM #627, last bts in X #15, chr next bts in X:Prelude #4, next bts X:Prelude #1, all '11, next in UXM #15, '12), unidentified foe (bts menacing Utopia in dfb, last bts in X:Prelude #4, '11, see NOTE), assailan (bts attacking Wolverine with arrows), kidnappers (die)

OTHER CHARACTERS: Jubilee (between X #19-20, '11-12), Hope Summers (last in UXM #543, '11, next in X:Schism #1, '11), kidnappe children & their families; elk (dies), wolves (some die, others dead as bones); Devil (mentioned, shook hands with Dr. Strange), Kitty's boyfriend (mentioned, compared to Wolverine); wild dogs (recap page only)

LOCATIONS/ITEMS: Utopia (also in dfb) inc Professor X's office, Yukon inc families' homes & kidnappers' cabins & arena w/cages, intervie locations / Deadpool's sword, kidnappers' snowmobiles, night vision goggles, handguns, tranquilizer guns, cage truck & video cameras, Melita notepad, wolves' spiked collars, cage padlock (destroyed), heroes' aircraft (bts), Black Widow's "Widow's Bite" bracelets, assailants' bows (bts arrows & shuriken

FLASHBACK: Wolverine charges into battle alongside both the Avengers and the X-Men. (d).

SYNOPSIS: Melita interviews dozens of superhumans, asking their opinion about Wolverine. Each views him differently, but all admire hi greatly. In the Yukon, Wolverine has gone feral, living with a wolf pack. Men suddenly attack, capturing the healthy wolves and killing the wea They shoot Wolverine in the head, but he soon recovers and begins tracking them. At their cabin, the men prepare to unleash the capture wolves into an arena and film the battle, when Wolverine arrives. He slaughters the men, releases the wolves and prepares to return to th wild, when he smells the men's intended victims: kidnapped children. Wolverine returns them to their nearby town; watching the families' happ reunions, he thinks about how, if he hadn't been tricked into killing his own children, he wouldn't have been here to save these children. Melit suddenly arrives, flanked by several heroes who all want Wolverine to return home. Heartened, he agrees. Later, Melita asks Wolverine h opinion of himself; he replies that he is a work in progress.

NOTE: To commemorate the 10th anniversary of the September 11, 2001 terror attacks, this issue reprints the cover of Moment, '02 and pin-up from pp.1, 22, 3, 33-33, 57, 47 & 21 of Heroes, '01. Steve Rogers retook the mantle of Captain America in FearIt #4, '11, following Bucky Barne seeming death in FearIt #3, '11. In a bid to depower the rampaging Juggernaut, the X-Men convinced Cyttorak to remove Juggernaut's powe and transfer it to Colossus in UXM #542, '11. Puck's return to life remains unexplained, but presumably as ruler of Hell, he could simply leave a his leisure. In X:Prelude #1-4, '11, the X-Men prepare to face an imminent and unspecified threat. That battle is never seen on-panel; this Inde presumes that this issue's dfb, showing X-Men and Avengers charging toward an unspecified threat, is a scene from that battle.

WOLVERINE: DEBT OF DEATH (November 2011)

"Debt of Death" (34 pages)

CREDITS: David Lapham (writer), David Aja (art), Dave Lanphear (letters), Bettie Breitweiser (colors), Laure Sankovitch (assoc editor), Warren Simons & Alejandro Arbona (editors), Tom Brevoort (exec editor)

FEATURE CHARACTER: Wolverine (chr last in X4 #5, '05, chr next in UXM #455, '05)

GUEST STAR: Nick Fury (also on monitor, chr last in NAv #14, '06 fb, chr next in AX #3, '04)

VILLAINS: Kanaye Nakadai (Kenichi's drug-addicted son), Hiroshi Murata (Yakuza Oyabun), Takashi (Murata aide) (all die), Yakuza gangsters (some dead, others bts smuggling robots), ninja assassins

OTHER CHARACTERS: Superintendent General Kenichi Nakadai (high-ranking Japanese police official) his wife (both die, also in photos), Kiku Nakadai (Kenichi's daughter), Inspector Mori (Japanese police official SHIELD agents (some die; some bts piloting jets, pods & Red Eyes; 2 voice only; some or others chr last i Cable&Dp #10, '04, chr next in AX #3, '04) inc Brainiac, Deacon, Eggs, Hays, Kronks (prev 5 bts piloting pod also on monitors, die), Giovanni & Taggart; Ryu (Wolverine's informant), Masao (Wolverine's former sensei) & his wife, US Air Force soldier (some or all die), Japanese police, WWII Japanese scientists (bts with alibis; others mentioned, dead; all also in photos), Japanese intelligenc (bts informing SHIELD about robots), Murata's guards (some bts in house), airport announcer (voice only) & employee, reporters (bts reportin robot attack), commuters, diner employee & patrons, bystanders; birds (another in painting); Kyodai, Imura Shatei (prev 2 Yakuza, mentione planning party), witnesses (mentioned, killed), WWII US soldiers (mentioned, shot Kenichi down), Murata's female employee (mentione Kanaye likes her), Tokyo gangsters (mentioned, owed money by Kanaye)

LOCATIONS/ITEMS: Japan: US Air Force bases inc Ginowan (Okinawa), Narita International Airport (Tokyo), Nakadais' house w/crawlspace Kenichi's R&D facility (bts, also in photos), Murata's home (destroyed), Masao's apartment, diner, bar bathroom, harbor w/docks (bts), garden beach (prev 2 mentioned); atomic bomb explosion site (in photo) / Shinpu Okubetsu Kogeki Tai robots (WWII Japanese kamikaze robots, som also on monitors; some destroyed, rest bts) w/gyroscopic systems, tracking systems, facial recognition software, modern microchips (pre 4 bts), Gatling guns, bombs & self-destruct devices, Air Force jets, jeeps & machine guns (some or all of prev 3 destroyed), ninjas' sword & hooked chain, police car, Kenichi's airplane, journals (prev 2 mentioned) & handgun, SHIELD Helicarrier, jets, Red Eye spy cameras (a but 1 bts), walkie-talkies, machine guns, helicopters w/winch & hover-pods (some destroyed, some also on monitors) w/stabilizers, comn systems, machine guns, internal cameras & onboard computers (prev 2 bts) w/monitors, Brainiac's Gameboy, Murata's limo & cocaine (pre 3 mentioned), Masao's birdcage, phone booth, satellites, Chinese freighter (prev 2 bts), guards' guns, Fury's bazooka, Kanaye's handcuff (destroyed), Takashi's gun

SYNOPSIS: Japanese robots attack a U.S. Air Force base in Okinawa, then explode. Elsewhere, ninjas kill police superintendent Kenich Nakadai. Wolverine arrives in Tokyo, invited by Kenichi to help find an intelligence leak. Inspector Mori informs Wolverine of Kenichi's death; h suspects Yakuza boss Murata. Elsewhere, the robots assault another US base, destroying the SHIELD hover-pods that defend it. Nick Fun learns that the robots, developed during WWII but mothballed, were recently stolen — and that Kenichi had overseen their development. A informant tells Wolverine that Murata wants Kenichi's son Kanaye dead. Wolverine intercepts the fleeing Kanaye at the airport; SHIELD agent arrive and escort both of them to the Helicarrier. Fury meets with Wolverine, but when the robots suddenly attack the Helicarrier, Wolverin realizes that they are targeting Kanaye. He leaps from the Helicarrier with Kanaye, landing in the harbor; Murata later returns home to fin Wolverine and Kanaye waiting. Murata explains that Kanaye sold Kenichi's secrets to him, including the robots' existence, then had Murata k his father. Murata stole the robots, but when some ran amok, believing it was still WWII, he targeted Kanaye to erase evidence of his involvemen Still tracking Kanaye, the remaining robots suddenly assault the house and explode; Wolverine is the only survivor.

OTE: This story occurs before Nick Fury split from SHIELD in SecWar #5, '05.

ND STORY: "Sick Day" (12 pages)
OTE: Reprinted from Moment/3, '02, to commemorate the 10th anniversary of the September 11, 2001 terror attacks.

WOLVERINE #17 [#296] (December 2011)

"Goodbye Chinatown, Part 1" (20 pages)

CREDITS: Jason Aaron (writer), Ron Garney (pencils, see NOTE), Virtual Calligraphy's Cory Petit (letters), Jason Keith (colors), Jared K. Fletcher (design), Jody LeHeup (asst editor), Jeanine Schaefer (editor), Nick Lowe (group editor)
FEATURE CHARACTER: Wolverine (also as Black Dragon)
GUEST STARS: Sons of the Tiger: Abe Brown, Bob Diamond, Lin Sun (all bts in hospital, last in W #5.1, '11); Gorilla-Man (Ken Hale, cursed with gorilla body, last in FearIt:HF #4/2, '11)
SUPPORTING CAST: Melita Garner (next in W #19, '12)
VILLAINS: Rock of the Buddha (stony super-strong fighter), Soulstriker (physically assaults foes' souls) (both last in W:MD #4, '09), Darkstrider (mysterious six-armed fighter, last in MKF #37, '76), Razor-Fist (last in DpTU #891, '10), Jade Claw (bts running drug ring, last in AoAtlas #11, '09) & her henchmen (some die, some or others
st in AoAtlas #11, '09), red dragons
THER CHARACTERS: Master Po (Wolverine's sensei), Yuen Yee (young street hustler) (both last in W:MD #4, '09), Drunken Mantis artender (bts, killed by Jade Claw's henchmen, last in W:MD #1, '08), drug dealer (dead), police, reporters, prospective employers (bts fering Melita jobs), bystanders; Melita's cat (last in W:WX #3, '09), rat; X-Men: Angel, Dazzler, Northstar, Pixie, Storm; Collective Man (prev mentioned, fought in San Francisco), M-11 (Human Robot, mentioned, friend of Gorilla-Man), Avengers (mentioned, to be contacted for ackup), Lo Shang Cho, Lin Fong (prev 2 former Black Dragons, mentioned, dead), Black Dragon Tong, Praying Mantis Tong, Red Lotus Tong rev 3 mentioned, scattered or dead), Chinatown drug dealers (mentioned, killed); Native American chief (bts as belt buckle), dragons (on vest, atue & bar decorations), praying mantis (on bar sign), fish (on bar decorations), Native Americans, settler (prev 2 on sign); fox (as backpack go); crows (prev 4 cover only)
OCATIONS/ITEMS: San Francisco inc Hunan Garden (restaurant), hospital (prev 2 mentioned), Melita's apartment & Chinatown inc runken Mantis bar, Jade Claw's dockside warehouse & dragons' underground tunnels, X-Mansion grounds (mentioned) / Ambulance, police rs & crime scene tape, reporters' cameras & microphones, dragons' teeth (1 bts) & cart w/chains, Melita's job offers, Yuen Yee's earrings, itchblade (prev 2 bts) & wristwatches, Drunken Mantis safe (destroyed), Wolverine's money (mentioned) & Chinese food, henchmen's armor, uns, smartphone & electric prods, Jade Claw's crates (some destroyed) w/heroin, warehouse's hidden staircase w/disguised entrance button, azor-Fist's prosthetic razor attachments
YNOPSIS: In Chinatown, police investigate drug-related killings; the most recent victim was stabbed with a dragon's tooth. At Melita's partment, Wolverine explains that he has decided to return to New York and rebuild the X-Men's school. She reveals that she has received b offers from all across the country; their relationship faces an uncertain future. Yuen Yee interrupts, asking for Wolverine's aid. In Chinatown, olverine finds Master Po's bar wrecked by a drug-related attack. He apologizes for failing as Black Dragon, and offers to step down. Po tells m to resolve their current crisis first, and reveals that the attackers stole Wolverine's stash of money, which would have been used to rebuild e school. Wolverine, Po and Yuen Yee track the attackers to a warehouse; they burst in, defeat several high-tech henchmen and discover vast ipments of heroin. Gorilla-Man arrives, revealing that the Jade Claw is behind the drug smuggling. The group discovers a vast underground nnel network; there they see red dragons pulling drug-filled carts. Suddenly, several villains attack…
OTE: Cover-labeled "Regenesis," referring to a restructuring of the X-books after the X:Schism miniseries that positioned Wolverine and yclops as the heads of two ideologically different mutant factions. Wolverine decided to leave Utopia and reopen the X-Men's school in Schism #5, '11. Like W:WX #11-15, '10, Ron Garney's art on W #17-19, 300 & 304, '11-12 does not have an inker; it is colored directly from arney's finished pencils. This issue's cover gives San Francisco's population as 775,306; however, the 2010 census lists the city's population 805,235. This was the first issue of the series to be sold as both a physical comic and a digital download.

WOLVERINE #18 [#297] (January 2012)

"Goodbye, Chinatown Part 2" (20 pages)

CREDITS: Jason Aaron (writer), Ron Garney (pencils), Virtual Calligraphy's Cory Petit (letters), Jason Keith (colors), Jared K. Fletcher (design), Jody LeHeup (asst editor), Jeanine Schaefer (editor), Nick Lowe (group editor), Khoi Pham (variant c art), Edgar Delgado (variant c colors)
FEATURE CHARACTER: Wolverine (also as Black Dragon)
GUEST STARS: Fat Cobra (martial arts champion of Peng Lai Island, last in ASM #672, '11), Gorilla-Man
VILLAINS: Jade Claw (Suwan, Yellow Claw's grand-niece) & her henchmen, Darkstrider, Razor-Fist, Rock of the Buddha, Soulstriker, red dragons (another mentioned, dead, eaten by Fat Cobra)

THER CHARACTERS: Master Po, Yuen Yee, Peng Lai oracles (bts warning Fat Cobra of trouble), Jade Claw's servants & slaves, vain oman (dead; others mentioned, killed), person (dead, as skeleton), Jade Claw's enemies, hummingbirds, butterflies, bull elephant, bald eagle, rannosaurus rex, baby seal, tiger (prev 8 bts, dead, used to make Claw's dinner); worm; Soulstriker's family (mentioned, dishonored), Jade law's concubines (mentioned, Yuen Yee wants to become one), addicts (mentioned, targeted by Jade Claw); gods, wenches, chickens, turkey w 4 mentioned, fantasized about by Fat Cobra), doves (mentioned, used to make Jade Claw's pillows); Native American chief (bts as belt uckle), dragons (on vest); attackers (cover only)
OCATIONS/ITEMS: Dragons' underground tunnels inc bottomless pit & Jade Claw's greenhouses, meth caves (prev 2 mentioned), compound poppy field, Savage Land (mentioned) / Razor-Fist's prosthetic razor attachments, henchmen's armor, guns & oxygen helmets, Yuen Yee's

handgun, villains' ropes, dragons' cart (bts) & collars w/chains, Jade Claw's pillows, bra (prev 2 mentioned), carriage & elaborate dinner, slave chains, oxygen masks & poppy baskets, wine, food, cave moss & water, Wolverine's money & beef jerky (prev 6 mentioned), apples (bts)

SYNOPSIS: Wolverine and his allies battle Darkstrider, Razor-Fist, Rock of the Buddha, Soulstriker, Jade Claw's henchmen and the dragons a wild free-for-all. When the dragons capture Po and Yuen Yee, Wolverine and Gorilla-Man give up. Soulstriker ties them between two dragon who begin pulling; he then pushes Po into a pit and departs with the captive Yuen Yee to finish transporting the latest heroin shipment. As soo as the villains depart, Gorilla-Man unties the ropes; as he and Wolverine battle the dragons, Fat Cobra arrives and aids them. Elsewhere, Jac Claw's servants pamper her as she shows Yuen Yee her vast underground poppy field. She describes her ambition to become the world greatest drug lord, then enslaves him to tend the field. After defeating the dragons, Fat Cobra explains that he was sent into the tunnels k oracles that sensed trouble, but quickly became lost. None of them know how to reach Jade Claw's compound, so they decide to hitch a rid they allow the dragons to swallow them...

NOTE: Cover-labeled "Regenesis." This issue also has a "Marvel 50th Anniversary" variant cover, an homage to the cover of SM #1, '90. Th issue also has a 6-page preview of Av:XSanc #1, '12.

WOLVERINE #19 [#298] (January 2012)

"Goodbye Chinatown, Part 3" (20 pages)

CREDITS: Jason Aaron (writer), Ron Garney (pencils), Virtual Calligraphy's Cory Petit (letters), Jason Kei (colors), Jared K. Fletcher (design), Jody LeHeup (asst editor), Jeanine Schaefer (editor), Nick Lowe (grou editor)

FEATURE CHARACTER: Wolverine (also as Black Dragon; also in photo, also in pfb; next in XFac #230, W& #3 fb & 17 fb, all '12, W&X #1-3, '11-12; W&X:A&O #1-5, W #302 fb & 310-313, PointOne fb, AvSM #1, AvAc #2 bts, X23 #17 & 20, all '12, NAv #16.1, '11; AvSM #5, Av:XSanc #1, 4 fb & 3-4, Av #19, all '12, NAv #17 & 19-2 '11-12, Av #24, '12, F.F. #11, '11, FF #600, '12)

GUEST STARS: Fat Cobra (next in W #304, '12), Gorilla-Man (next in W&X #19, '12) (both also in pfb), Spide Man (in pfb, last in Annis:EF #4, '12, next in PointOne, '12 fb)

SUPPORTING CAST: Melita Garner (also in pfb)

VILLAINS: Jade Claw (also in pfb), Soulstriker, Razor-Fist, Rock of the Buddha (all next in W #304, '12), Darkstrider (prev 4 in pfb), Azun Góda (bts targeting Takenaka, last bts in W #9, '11, chr last bts in W #5.1, '11); Takenaka (bts, unnamed, traveling to America); Jade Claw henchmen (in pfb, some die), red dragons (in pfb; 1 also in main story)

OTHER CHARACTERS: Seraph Investigations (Seraph's detective agency, 1st app, unnamed): Seraph (last in W:O Ann, '07 fb), Cass Lathrop (last in W #13, '04), Lynx (feral woman, last in MCP #130, '93) (all in shadow); Harry Morrel (Harry's Hideaway proprietor, last in X #7 '98, next in W&X #24, '13), Joe "Robbie" Robertson (Daily Bugle editor-in-chief, in pfb, last in ASM #673, '12, next in ASM #679, '12), Mast Po, Yuen Yee (prev 2 also in pfb), Daily Bugle staff, Jade Claw's slaves (some also in main story) & servants, red dragon's victim (dead a skeleton) (prev 4 in pfb), Japanese government officials (bts hiring Seraph); Harry's Hideaway staff; black dragons (in pfb; some also in ma story); Mongrels: Cannonfoot, Fire Knives, Gunhawk, Saw Fist, Shadow Stalker; X-Men: Cyclops, Nightcrawler; Blackguard, Jean Grey Scho students, General George Patton, Jade Claw's concubines, wenches, demons (prev 13 mentioned in pfb); Sabretooth (bts), Silver Samur Amiko Kobayashi, Kingpin, Yakuza gangster, Hand ninjas, others (bts) (prev 7 in photos), Bugle staffer's loved ones (in photos in pfb); Kerr the Frog (on mug in pfb), Native American chief (as belt buckle, also bts as belt buckle in pfb), detective, dog (prev 2 in posters in pfb), drago (bts on vest, also bts on vest in pfb, also as tattoos in photo)

LOCATIONS/ITEMS: Harry's Hideaway (Salem Center eatery), dragons' underground tunnels (also in pfb) inc Jade Claw's compound poppy field (prev 2 destroyed), Earth's core (bts) w/dragon nest, Daily Bugle (prev 5 in pfb), Seraph Investigations' office / Slaves' oxyge masks, makeshift club & poppy baskets & bags, henchmen's armor, guns & oxygen helmets, food (mentioned), Melita's résumé, Bugle staff computers & newspapers, Razor-Fist's prosthetic razor attachments, Master Po's ropes (all in pfb), Harry's hammer, sign & beer, Wolverine money, Seraph's photos, guns & darts, Yakuza's submachine gun, Hand ninjas' swords, Silver Samurai's armor (prev 3 in photos)

FLASHBACK: The red dragons arrive at Jade Claw's compound and vomit up their "passengers." Jade Claw's henchmen attack the heroe Yuen Yee takes advantage of the confusion to seize a gun, shoot the guards and mobilize a slave revolt. Meanwhile, after a successful jc interview, the Daily Bugle hires Melita. Soulstriker tries to punch Wolverine's soul, but the traumas Wolverine has endured recently have mad him immune. Po suddenly shows up, riding black dragons that he discovered living deep within the earth. The two groups of dragons beg fighting; the black dragons ignite the poppy field and Jade Claw flees into the tunnels.

SYNOPSIS: Harry Morrel regretfully closes his restaurant, business having dried up since the X-Men moved away. Suddenly, Wolverine burs out of the underground tunnels with his allies, scores of freed slaves, and a sack of money. Harry joyfully reopens. Melita soon joins the par happy that both she and Wolverine will now be in New York. Elsewhere, shadowed figures discuss their next assignment, worried about havir to deal with Wolverine.

NOTE: Cover-labeled "Regenesis." Next issue identifies the shadowed Seraph Investigations members, reveals their group name ar Takenaka's name, and explains that the Japanese government hired them to protect Takenaka. W #300, '12 reveals that Góda targete Takenaka for death. Seraph, generally depicted as having dwarfism, is incorrectly drawn at normal height here.

WOLVERINE #20 [#299] (February 2012)

"And Then There Was War, Part 1" (20 pages)

CREDITS: Jason Aaron (writer), Renato Guedes (pencils, c art), José Wilson Magalhaes (inks), Virtu Calligraphy's Cory Petit (letters), Matthew Wilson (colors), Jared K. Fletcher (design), Jody LeHeup & Sebasti Girner (asst editors), Jeanine Schaefer (editor), Nick Lowe (group editor)

FEATURE CHARACTER: Wolverine

SUPPORTING CAST: Melita Garner (next in W #303, '12)

VILLAINS: Buzzard Brothers: Boyd, Bufford (both last in W #5.1, '11); Kingpin (last in BP #529, '12, next in " #302, '12), Sabretooth (last in W&X #3, '12), Takenaka (Yamaguchi-Gumi Yakuza Oyabun, dies), Azuma Gó (1st voice only app, unnamed), Hand ninjas (New York branch, some or others last in BP #529, '12, next in D #50, '12)

THER CHARACTERS: Seraph Investigations (1st full app, named): Cassie Lathrop, Lynx, Seraph (all next in W #304, '12); Kingpin's dyguards (some die), Takenaka's bodyguards (some die) & pilots, Japanese government official (Seraph's employer, bts on phone); abretooth's pilot (bts flying plane), hot dog vendor, Buzzard Brothers' victims (dead, as bones), bystanders; Silver Samurai (mentioned, dead); storical figure (as statue); dragons (as tattoos)

OCATIONS/ITEMS: New York City inc subway, Soho, Bronx (prev 3 mentioned), airport, warehouse & Central Park, skies over USA / ngpin's limousines & cane, Seraph Investigations' Bluetooth headsets, walkie-talkies, van & chains, hot dog vendor's cart, Buzzard Brothers' one knives & pistol w/tooth bullets, Cassie's handgun & cellphone, Seraph's business card (mentioned) & sniper rifle w/scope & experimental ASA "asteroid buster" bullets, Takenaka's private jet w/window (destroyed), Hand ninjas' swords, Sabretooth's plane (bts) & earpiece

YNOPSIS: Wolverine spots Yakuza boss Takenaka in Central Park. Takenaka meets with Kingpin, who now runs the Hand, to discuss a owing conflict in the Japanese underworld. The two make peace, but the Buzzard Brothers suddenly attack Takenaka's bodyguards, and he spects Kingpin of treachery. Cassie Lathrop intervenes, forcing the two crimelords to retreat with her, while a sniper shoots at the Buzzards om afar. Wolverine follows the crimelords to a van, but finds it driven by Lathrop and Lynx, two women he was formerly involved with — and shocked when Seraph, long thought dead, reveals herself as the sniper. Seraph explains that she now runs a detective agency, and the apanese government recently hired them to protect Takenaka. Lynx interrogates the Buzzards; they claim to work for ninjas, but Kingpin enies any involvement. Takenaka departs for Japan, while Seraph muses that a third party seems to be trying to start a war. Later, Sabretooth ursts into Takenaka's jet and throws him out the window in mid-flight.

OTE: Despite this issue's title, next issue is not "part 2"; it re-titles the story arc and begins again with a new part 1. How Seraph survived abretooth's attack in W #126, '98 fb remains unrevealed; presumably her corpse seen in W:O Ann '07 was a fake. The fact that Takenaka aveled to New York to make peace, even though he is feuding with the Tokyo-based Hand, indicates that the Kingpin has expanded his fluence and taken over the Hand's Tokyo branch since Sland #5, '11. Takenaka's Yakuza family is named in W #300, '12. Bufford is incorrectly awn with both hands in one panel this issue. This is technically the final issue of this volume of Wolverine; the series is renumbered the lowing month, effectively resurrecting the 1988-2003 volume.

WOLVERINE #300 (March 2012)

"Back In Japan, Part One — Chapter One: Welcome Back, Gaijin" (5 pages)
"Chapter Two: Secret of the Silver Samurai" (4 pages)
"Chapter Three: Young Ronin in Love" (3 pages)
"Chapter Four: Same Old Snikt" (2 pages)
"Chapter Five: Cookin' With Sabretooth" (3 pages)
"Chapter Six: Last Day on the Farm" (3 pages)
"Chapter Seven: Welcome to the Temple of the Fist" (10 pages)

CREDITS: Jason Aaron (writer), Ron Garney (pencils, pp.6-9, 15-17 & 30), Adam Kubert (art, pp.1-5, 13-14 & 21-29; c art), Steve Sanders (art, pp.10-12 & 18-20), Virtual Calligraphy's Cory Petit (letters), Paul Mounts (colors, pp.1-5, 13-14 & 21-29), Jason Keith (colors, pp.6-9, 15-17 & 30), Sotocolors (colors, pp.10-12 & 18-20), Jared K. Fletcher (design), Jody LeHeup & Sebastian Girner (asst editors), Jeanine Schaefer (editor), Nick Lowe (group editor), Geof Darrow (wraparound variant c art), Jim Cheung (variant c art), Laura Martin (c colors), Justin Ponsor (variant c colors)
FEATURE CHARACTER: Wolverine (also in photo)
GUEST STAR: Kitty Pryde (last in F.F. #11, '11, next in UXFor #19, '12)
SUPPORTING CAST: Amiko Kobayashi (also in photo), Yukio (both last in W #3, '11), Mariko Yashida (bts, dead in grave, last in W #57, '92, possibly last as spirit in W #5, '11, corpse last bts in W #11, '11)

VILLAINS: Azuma Góda (director of Hand's Tokyo branch, 1st on-panel app, named), Mystique (also as Sabretooth, last in W #9, '11), Sabretooth, Hand ninjas (Tokyo branch, some die; others also as passengers & flight attendant, die; some or others last in W #9, '11, chr last in W #5.1, '11), invisible four-armed techno-organic wall ninjas (Hand guards), Yakuza gangsters, lowlifes, sumo wrestlers, pirates (some of prev 4 die), Sky Yakuza (parachuting criminals, 1 bts flying plane), Yakuza leaders & their US agents

OTHER CHARACTERS: Quentin Quire (troublemaking telepathic student, last in W&X:A&O #5, '12, next in W&X #4, '12), Silver Samurai (Shingen "Shin" Harada, Kenuichio's son, 1st), Silver Samurai (Kenuichio Harada, bts, dead in grave, last in W #3, '11), Shirato (deep-cover Hand ninja) & his wife & son (prev 3 die), Momma (madam) & her prostitutes & patron, pilot (bts flying plane), travelers; cow (dead), birds; Kingpin (mentioned, unaware of Góda's treachery), Takenaka (mentioned, Góda ordered his death), Yamaguchi-Gumi (mentioned, Takenaka's Yakuza family) Silver Samurai, Red Right Hand, Hand's victims (prev 3 mentioned, dead), Shirato's village's residents & visitors (prev 2 mentioned, surveilled); Jean Grey, Buddha, horse (prev 3 as statues), storical figure (as painting), demon (as mask), dragons, demon (prev 2 as tattoos), snakes (as tattoo & statuette); cats (variant cover only), ople, cartoon characters (prev 2 on billboards, variant cover only)

OCATIONS/ITEMS: Jean Grey School for Higher Learning (Wolverine's new school, built on former X-Mansion grounds), skies over Pacific cean, Japan inc Narita International Airport, ruins of Yashidas' ancestral manor, Hand's Tokyo corporate lab, pool hall, biker bar, wrestling g, harbor, alley, Momma's brothel & Iwate Prefecture inc Shirato's farm & Temple of the Fist, Los Angeles International Airport / Airplane

w/windows (destroyed) & serving cart, ninjas' swords (some destroyed), shuriken (mentioned), sai, gas masks & knockout gas, Wolverine
Avengers ID (mentioned) & motorcycle (destroyed), Silver Samurai's will (mentioned), gravestone & sword, Mariko's gravestone (see NOT
Yukio's handgun & wheelchair w/armrest swords, Yashida vault w/armor, weapons, artwork & gold, Yakuza cars (1 destroyed), guns, bazool
cellphones & suitcase w/money, Shin's computer (mentioned), van, suction cups, nuclear-powered nunchuks, laser swords & armor (prev
hereinafter considered his standard equipment and not listed separately) w/blasters & boot jets, Amiko's chains (bts), ropes & goggles,
security systems, full-body liquefier, light-bending incubators (prev 3 mentioned), windows (destroyed), computers, laser grid, scanning wal
experimental power source, pool table, balls & cues, lowlifes' weapons inc shotgun & broken bottle, bikers' motorcycles, pirates' knives, hook
boat, Sabretooth's comm unit (bts), jetpack (destroyed), knife & wire lines, brothel Jacuzzi, Shirato's maps, files (prev 3 mentioned), scythes
sword, Góda's limousine, van & Bluetooth headset, Sky Yakuzas' parachutes, submachine guns & airplane w/comm system (bts), Mystiqu
airplane (bts) & cellphone

SYNOPSIS: At the Yashidas' ruined manor, Wolverine and Yukio visit Mariko and the Silver Samurai's graves. Yukio explains that Takenak
death kicked off a Hand/Yakuza war, and reveals that the Samurai had a son, Shin — who is now dating Amiko. Elsewhere, Amiko and S
break into a Hand lab to steal a power source for his armor, but Amiko is captured. Wolverine interrogates criminals and learns that Yaku
leaders will soon meet at a temple. The Yakuza offer Sabretooth a million dollars to leave the country; elsewhere, Azuma Góda, leader of 1
Tokyo Hand branch, activates a sleeper agent who reveals tunnels leading to the temple. Sabretooth arrives in Los Angeles and accepts t
Yakuza's money; the gangsters inform their bosses, who are relieved. However, as Wolverine approaches the temple, Sabretooth attacks h
Góda arrives at the temple and challenges the Yakuza leaders, revealing that he employs Sabretooth, that he had Takenaka killed, and that
plans to usurp Hand control from the Kingpin. His ninjas attack the Yakuza; Wolverine and Sabretooth crash into the temple and join the grow
battle. Shin arrives as well, clad in his new armor and hoping to free Amiko — while the "Sabretooth" in Los Angeles reveals herself as Mystiq

NOTE: With this issue, Marvel renumbered the series to #300, the issue number that it would have reached had the title not been reboot
in 2003 and 2010. The renumbering ignores the issues following the series' retitling as D:WX with #75, '09, but counts W:WX #1-16, '09-10
their place. This issue also has a variant cover, a wraparound variant, a blank wraparound variant and a 2nd printing using the standard cove
B&W art. This issue also has a 6-page preview of W #310, '12, the issue that explains Sabretooth's return prior to this storyline; a 4-page gall
showcasing the covers of W #1-189, '88-03, W #1-74, '03-09, W:WX #1-16, '09-10 & W #1-20 & 300, '10-12, including many variants; 1 pa
of Sabretooth costume sketches by Adam Kubert; and 2 pages of Silver Samurai costume sketches by Steve Sanders, with notes by Sand
and Sebastian Girner. The recap page titles this story "Back In Japan, Part 1." Called "Shin" here, the new Silver Samurai's full real name
revealed next issue. On page 12, Shin is incorrectly drawn escaping the Hand lab with Amiko, but she is shown as a captive two panels la
Mariko's grave, formerly a large stone monument with her photograph, is now a simple gravestone; presumably the Black Samurai desecrat
the original monument when they stole her corpse, and Wolverine had her re-buried after W #16, '12. When Yukio's back was injured in
#173-174, '02, she begged Wolverine to kill her if she ended up paralyzed. Here, however, she has adapted well to life as a paraplegic. W #3
'12 confirms that the Hand resurrected Mystique after her death in W #9, '11. Wolverine reads *The Sailor Who Fell From Grace With the Sea*

WOLVERINE #301 (April 2012)

"Back In Japan, Part 2 — Chapter Eight: Just Another Day in Japan" (6 pages)
"Chapter Nine: Ladies and Gentlemen…the All-New Silver Samurai!" (4 pages)
"Chapter Ten: Ninjas = 1. Yakuza = 0" (3 pages)
"Chapter Eleven: Ninja in a Coma" (4 pages)
"Chapter Twelve: In the Clutches of the Hand" (3 pages)

CREDITS: Jason Aaron (writer), Billy Tan (art, pp.1-6 & 14-20), Steve Sanders (art, pp.7-13), Virtual Calligraph
Cory Petit (letters), Jason Keith (colors, pp.1-6 & 14-20), Sotocolors (colors, pp.7-13), Jared K. Fletcher (desig
Jody LeHeup & Sebastian Girner (asst editors), Jeanine Schaefer (editor), Nick Lowe (group editor), Oliv
Coipel (c art), Justin Ponsor (c colors)
FEATURE CHARACTER: Wolverine
SUPPORTING CAST: Yukio, Amiko Kobayashi

VILLAINS: Mystique, Sabretooth, Azuma Góda, Hand ninjas, Yakuza gangsters, Sky Yakuza (some of prev 3 die), Mind ninjas (u
hallucinogenic toxins), Yakuza leaders

OTHER CHARACTERS: Silver Samurai (Shin), Mamoru Tsuruoka (undercover ninja), hospital staff; flesh-eating beetle; Silver Samu
(Kenuichio, mentioned, absent father to Shin), Shin's mother (mentioned, died of cancer), orphans (mentioned, tormented Shin), hospital ki
(mentioned, killed patients), coma patients (mentioned, murdered) & their families (mentioned, hired Tsuruoka); dragons (as tattoos); samu
(cover only)

LOCATIONS/ITEMS: Temple of the Fist w/window (destroyed), courtyard & nearby roadway, hospital inc roof, Yoshimi Hyakuana tor
(Hand's cave lair), orphanage, Amiko's bedroom (prev 2 mentioned) / Hand ninjas' swords, shuriken, dust & torches, Yakuza motorcycles
destroyed), guns, cellphones & chainsaws, Silver Samurai's bonds & first battlesuit (mentioned) w/microwave, bicycle chains & nails, Amik
gas mask (bts), chains, ropes & laser sword, hurled tree trunk, Góda's teleporter (bts), tweezers & scalpel, Yukio's wheelchair, knockout g
(bts) & swords, Tsuruoka's sword, medical chart & life-support equipment w/breathing tube (destroyed), crash cart (mentioned), Wolverin
sword, Mind ninjas' swords, knives & tiger claws

SYNOPSIS: Wolverine brawls with Sabretooth as the Hand and Yakuza battle throughout the temple. Amiko tries to strangle Góda,
Sabretooth stops her. Shin, now calling himself the Silver Samurai, moves to free Amiko, but Wolverine misunderstands and tackles him aw
Wolverine and the Samurai begin to duel in the courtyard; Wolverine warns him not to get involved with the underworld turf war, but the co
Samurai refuses to listen. Góda, Sabretooth and the Hand interrupt, capture the Samurai and teleport away, leaving Amiko behind. La
Wolverine locates his friend Mamoru Tsuruoka, a deep-cover ninja who has been in a self-induced coma for years, investigating homicides
a hospital. Wolverine awakens him; despite Tsuruoka's anger at having his cover blown, he provides Wolverine with the Hand's location. In
Hand's lair, Góda tortures the Silver Samurai, seeking control of Clan Yashida. Wolverine and Yukio prepare to assault the cave, unaware t
Amiko has followed them. Inside the cave, Sabretooth, Mystique and the mysterious Mind ninjas await their foes…

NOTE: Shin's full name is revealed here; he is named for his grandfather, Lord Shingen Harada. The Mind ninjas are presumably a sub-gro
of the Hand; their use of toxins is revealed next issue.

WOLVERINE #302 (May 2012)

"Back In Japan, Part 3 — Chapter Thirteen: Still in Hell" (3 pages)
"Chapter Fourteen: Into the Cave of the Mind Ninjas" (6 pages)
"Chapter Fifteen: Out Comes the Berserker" (7 pages)
"Chapter Sixteen: the Turning of the Worm" (4 pages)

CREDITS: Jason Aaron (writer), Billy Tan (art, pp.1-3, 8-12 & 16-20), Steve Sanders (art, pp.4-8 & 13-15), Virtual Calligraphy's Clayton Cowles (letters), Jason Keith (colors, pp.1-3, 8-12 & 16-20), Sotocolors (colors, pp.4-8 & 13-15), Jared K. Fletcher (design), Sebastian Girner (asst editor), Jeanine Schaefer (editor), Nick Lowe (group editor), Arthur Adams (c art), Peter Steigerwald (c colors)
FEATURE CHARACTER: Wolverine (also as himself & his berserker mental aspect in his own hallucination, also in photo; also in fb between W&X:A&O #5, '12 & W #310, '12)
GUEST STAR: Rachel Grey (in fb between W&X:A&O #5, '12 & W&X #4, '12)
SUPPORTING CAST: Amiko Kobayashi (also on monitor), Yukio
VILLAINS: Kingpin (last in W #20, '12, next in D:DW #21, '12), Lord Deathstrike (last in X #27, '12), Mystique (also as Yukio, also as Yukio photo), Sabretooth, Azuma Góda (also in photo), Mind ninjas (die), Hand ninjas (some die, some also as dragon in Amiko's hallucination)
OTHER CHARACTERS: Silver Samurai, Kingpin's aide, travelers; butterflies (in fb), horse (another as statue); Mongrels: Cannonfoot, Fire Knives, Gunhawk, Saw Fist, Shadow Stalker; Devil, demons, damned souls (prev 8 in Wolverine's hallucination); Amiko's mother (mentioned, died), wickedest minds in Japan (mentioned, invented Mind ninjas' toxin), Weapon X Program, Dr. Rot (prev 2 mentioned in fb, altered Wolverine's mind)
LOCATIONS/ITEMS: Yoshimi Hyakuana tombs (also on monitor & in photo), ruins of Yashidas' ancestral manor, Kingpin's New York office, Japanese airport, Hell (in hallucination) inc Sea of Atrophy, Jean Grey School for Higher Learning grounds (in fb) / Devil's floating throne, damned souls' chains (both in hallucination), Mind ninjas' swords, knives, shuriken, hooked chain, tiger claws & hallucinogenic toxins, Yukio's swords & wheelchair (destroyed) w/smoke bomb & self-destruct device, Sabretooth's gas mask & jetpack, Mystique's gas mask, camera & submachine gun, Amiko's rock, laser sword & holographic monitor, Góda's security cameras (bts), monitors & jetpack, Silver Samurai's bonds, Hulk gun, ammonia jug, fish scaler (prev 3 mentioned), Hand ninjas' swords (some destroyed), spear & dragon costume, Yashida vault w/ weapons (bts), armor, artwork & gold, Kingpin's photo, Lord Deathstrike's airplane (bts) & suitcase, Wolverine's torch
FLASHBACK: Rachel Grey teaches Wolverine psychic self-defense tactics.
SYNOPSIS: Wolverine finds himself back in Hell. The Devil gloats that Wolverine's escape was an illusion, and summons the Mongrels to attack him. In the real world, Yukio battles the Mind ninjas, whose hallucinogenic toxins have incapacitated Wolverine. Deeper in the cave, Góda watches Amiko sneak in, and threatens to kill her unless the Silver Samurai joins him. Amiko, beginning to hallucinate, sees the dragon that killed her mother. Wolverine suspects that he is hallucinating and unleashes his "berserker" mental aspect; he revives and savagely kills the Mind ninjas. The Silver Samurai arrives, grabs Amiko and flees. Sabretooth and Góda betray the Hand, leaving them to be destroyed. His berserker aspect still in control, Wolverine slaughters the ninjas and then has sex with Yukio. Afterward, "Yukio" slips away; transforming back to Mystique, she checks her camera, which recorded the event. The Samurai reveals that he has joined Góda; Amiko angrily rejects him. In New York, Kingpin learns of Góda's treachery and hires Lord Deathstrike to kill him.
NOTE: This issue also has a 6-page preview of AvX #0, '12. This issue confirms that the Hand resurrected Mystique between W #9, '11 & W #300, '12, and reveals that they heightened her shapeshifting powers in the process.

WOLVERINE #303 (May 2012)

"Back In Japan, Finale — Chapter Seventeen: No More Ninjas" (3 pages)
"Chapter Eighteen: Forgive Me, Father" (3 pages)
"Chapter Nineteen: the Day I Became Invisible" (10 pages)
"Chapter Twenty: 日本を愛してます!" (4 pages, see NOTE)

CREDITS: Jason Aaron (writer), Billy Tan (art, pp.1-3 & 17-20), Steve Sanders (art, pp.4-6, 11 & 15), Paco Diaz (art, pp.7-10 & 12-16), Virtual Calligraphy's Chris Eliopoulos (letters), Matt Milla, Sotocolors, Jim Charalampidis & Rachelle Rosenberg (colors), Jared K. Fletcher (design, uncredited), Jeanine Schaefer (editor), Nick Lowe (group editor), Brandon Peterson (c art)
FEATURE CHARACTER: Wolverine (also on monitors & in photos, also as Hand ninja, next in D:DW #21-23, W&X #4, all '12, UXFor #10-19, '11-12; W&X #4, UXFor #19-23, W&X #4, all '12)
SUPPORTING CAST: Melita Garner (last in W #20, '12), Yukio, Amiko Kobayashi
VILLAINS: Mystique (also as Azuma Góda & bodyguard, also as Yukio in photos), Lord Deathstrike (both also on monitors), Sabretooth, Silver Samurai, Azuma Góda, Hand ninjas (Tokyo branch, others next in Av #4, '13 fb), Yakuza leaders, East Asian criminal leaders (prev 4 die), burglars (bts robbing bank)
OTHER CHARACTERS: Hand ninjas' children (bts, liberated by Wolverine), Tokyo police (bts, received ninjas' children), criminal leaders' bodyguards (dead), Goda's female companions; fish (some or all die), Silver Samurai (Kenuichio, mentioned, warned Shin about Mystique), Dr. Rot, Lord Deathstrike, Kingpin (prev 3 mentioned, deadly threats), deep-cover Hand ninjas (mentioned, stationed across Japan) inc disease-maker & woman w/deadly flesh; Mind ninja (dead in photos); girls, cartoon characters (prev 2 on billboards), Maneki-neko ("beckoning cat," as statuette), Galactus, Kingpin (prev 3 mentioned, deadly threats), deep-cover Hand ninja (dead in photos); girls, cartoon characters (prev 2 on billboards), Maneki-neko ("beckoning cat," as statuette), other (as wall decoration)
LOCATIONS/ITEMS: Tokyo inc Yukio's apartment & Shibuya bank (bts) w/nearby rooftop, Góda's penthouse (also on monitors) w/rooftop garden, Yakuza boardroom w/nearby highway, ruins of Yashidas' ancestral manor, Melita's apartment, criminal leaders' meeting place; Hand temples (destroyed), Osaka inc Higashiosaka, Jean Grey School for Higher Learning (prev 4 mentioned), Yoshimi Hyakuana tombs (in photos), Hand ninjas' swords, Mystique's motorcycle & photos & handguns, Silver Samurai's motorcycle & costume-activation wrist-unit, office wall & fishtank, penthouse door & balcony (prev 4 destroyed), Góda's handgun (destroyed), security cameras (bts), monitors, sword & deep-cover list, Lord Deathstrike's scanner, submachine guns, wall-climbing shoes & handgun w/laser scope, Amiko's police radio (bts) & laser sword, Sabretooth's jetpack, Yukio's wheelchair & helicopter w/machine gun, Wolverine & Melita's cellphones
SYNOPSIS: Over several days, Wolverine kills every single Hand ninja in Tokyo. However, this fits with Góda's plan: with them gone, the Kingpin has nothing to control, and Góda can build a new organization using the sleeper agents seeded across Japan. Elsewhere, Silver Samurai kills

the Yakuza leaders, bringing their organization under Góda's control as well. As the final step in becoming the secret king of the Japane underworld, Góda arranges for his own public "assassination." Mystique poses as Góda when Lord Deathstrike attacks…but instead of allowi herself to be shot, she fights back. Sabretooth reveals that he and Mystique are betraying Góda and hijacking his newly built organization; th recruit Deathstrike and depart as Wolverine arrives and kills Góda. Later, Wolverine tries calling Melita, but she refuses to answer — Mystiqu mailed her the photos of her tryst with Wolverine. Elsewhere, Sabretooth and his allies kill the heads of many other Asian crime famili solidifying their power. Unaware of his foe's grand plans, Wolverine relaxes with Yukio and Amiko.

NOTE: This issue's recap page titles the story "Back In Japan, Part 4." The final chapter's title translates to "I love Japan!" This issue's assista editor is unknown; it is either Sebastian Girner or Jake Thomas.

WOLVERINE #304 (June 2012)

"One More Round" (20 pages)

CREDITS: Jason Aaron (writer), Ron Garney (pencils, pp.3-4), Paul Pellet (pencils, p.7), Steve Dillon (art, pp.1-2, 5-6, 10, 13 & 17-20), Mike Perkins (art, pp 9), Jefte Palo (art, pp.11-12), Daniel Acuña (art, p.14), Steve Sanders (art, p.1! Renato Guedes (art, p.16), Dave Meikis (inks, p.7), Virtual Calligraphy's Cory Pe (letters), Matthew Wilson, Matt Milla, Rain Beredo, Andy Troy & Chris Sotoma (colors), Jared K. Fletcher (design, uncredited), Jake Thomas (asst editor), Jeani Schaefer (editor), Nick Lowe (group editor), Dale Keown (c art), Guruhiru Studi (variant c art), Jason Keith (c colors)

FEATURE CHARACTER: Wolverine (also in photos, next in Dp #50-54, '1 UXFor #24-29, 31-33, 31 & 34-35, '12-13; X:L #261-263 & 265, UXM #9-10, XCI #1, CarnUSA #1-5, all '12, MHol '11/2, W&X #17 fb, 5-8 & 12 fb, '12, AX #52 fb & 48-56, '12-13, AX Ann, '13; IHulk #12, Av:Child #9, W&X # fb, W #305-308, AvX #0, AvAssem #1 & 6, W #309 voice only, AvX #1, W&X #9, NAv #24 fb, Av #28 fb, W&X #9, NAv #24, AvX #1-2, NAv #2 AvX #2, Av #25, AvX #2, W&X #10 fb, AvX #2, UXM #11, AvX #2-3, AvAc #29, W&X #10, AvX #3-4, W&X #11, AvXVs #1, AvX #4, UXM #1 AvX #5-7, Av #29, W&X #12, AvX #7-10 & 12 fb, W&X #15 & 17, AvX #11, UXM #18, AvX #11, W&X #18, UXM #19, AvX #11, X:L #273, W #18, UXM #19, AvX #12, all '12, W&X #18-19 & 21-23, '12-13, DD #13 fb, XFac #238, NM #50, AvAc #38, all '12, W #31-33, '12-13, AvX # '12, AvXCon #1, '12, Av #34, '13, NAv #31, '12, Av #2, '13 fb, A+X #1/2, '12; X:L #2-6, Hawk #6, AX #57-58, all '13, Winter #10 & 12-14, '12-1 AvAssem #9 & 11, A+X #4/2 fb, Av #1-5, all '13, UncAv #1-4, '13, AvXCon #1-5, '12-13, W #314-317, '12-13)

GUEST STAR: Fat Cobra (also as Black Dragon, last in W #19, '12, next in W&X #19, '12)

SUPPORTING CAST: Maverick (last in W #9, '11), Melita Garner (joins Seraph Investigations, next in W #306, '12), Yukio, Amiko Kobayas (prev 2 next in AX Ann, '13)

VILLAINS: Hellfire Club's new Inner Circle (rich anti-mutant children): Black King (Kade Kilgore, young arms dealer), White Queen (Wilhelmi Kensington, sadistic heiress) (both last in W&X #3, '12, next in W&X #8, '12); Strikeforce X: Pierce, Sever (prev 2 next in W&X #16, '12), 1 oth (dies off-panel) (prev 3 last in W:WX #5, '10), Blob (Earth-295's Fred J. Dukes, obese immovable mutant, last in UXFor #18, '12), Mystiqu Sabretooth (prev 3 next in UXFor #27, '12), Bloodscream (last in AvAc #4, '10), Blackguard's Chief Executive (dies, last in W:WX #5, '10), Dak (last in D:DW #23, '12, see NOTE), Kingpin (bts sending cobras, last in D:DW #21, '12) (prev 2 next in Dp #50, '12), Dr. Rot (last in W:WX # '10, next in W #305, '12), Dog Logan (Wolverine's time-displaced half-brother, last in AstSMW #6, '11, next in W&X #25, '13), Jade Claw, Raz Fist, Rock of the Buddha, Soulstriker (prev 4 last in W #19, '12), Lady Deathstrike (last in UXFor #5.1, '11, next in ASM:Ends, '12), Madc (rapid-healing lunatic, last in W:Best #12, '12, next in Cap&BW #638, '12), Roughouse (last in Av:In #24, '09), Sauron (last in NM #10, '10), Lo Deathstrike, Silver Samurai (prev 3 next in W&X #20, '13), Spiral (last in W:DevHell, '10, chr next in UXFor #3, '13 fb, next in UXFor #1, '1 Tiger Shark (last in VFH #4, '12, next in SecAv #29, '12), Wild Child (last in W:O #39, '09, see NOTE), "Dr. Doom" (bts declining invitation, eith Kristoff Vernard or a Doombot; see NOTE), security guards

OTHER CHARACTERS: Mongrels: Cannonfoot, Fire Knives, Saw Fist, Shadow Stalker (all last in W #14, '11, last bts in W #15, '11), Gunha (last in W #15, '11) (all as spirits); Seraph Investigations: Seraph, Lynx, Cassie Lathrop (prev 3 last in W #20, '12, next in W #316, '12); Bes (Kilgore's chauffeur, last in X:Schism #2, '11, last bts in W&X #3, '12, next bts in W&X #21, '13), Thomas Logan (as spirit, last in W #5, '1 damned souls (some or others last in W #5, '11), driver (dies), party victims (bts, to be beaten & killed), Tokyo police (bts reporting brawl), furri (bts, brawling), football players (on TV), server, Chinatown residents, Madripoor criminals, bar patrons, bartender & bystander; cobras (b delivered to Sabretooth), penguin, wolverine (prev 2 dead), birds; Norman Osborn (mentioned, imprisoned Jacks), HAMMER agent Gertru Jacks (mentioned, freed from prison), Jacks' boyfriend (mentioned, living with Jacks), wenches (mentioned by Fat Cobra); Jean Grey Scho students (in photo, specific members unknown); angel (as statue); girls, cartoon characters (prev 2 on billboards, recap page only); Avenge Black Widow, Captain America, Hawkeye, Hulk, Iron Man, Thor (prev 6 as children, variant cover only)

LOCATIONS/ITEMS: Madripoor's Lowtown inc Sabretooth's party location & nearby bar, New York City parking garage & rooftop w/wa tower, Pacific Ocean island, Dog's Canadian shack, Yukio's Tokyo apartment, Kabukicho furry bar (bts), Hell's Black Cavern, tunnels bene San Francisco's Chinatown; Norman Osborn's prison, Tangier (prev 2 mentioned), Jean Grey School for Higher Learning (in photo), football fie (on TV) / Deathstrikes' limousine (destroyed), Lord Deathstrike's grenade & gun, Maverick's handgun & cellphone, Wolverine's motorcycle & be phone booth, party food & drinks, Tiger Shark's water circulation suit, Kingpin's box of cobras, Dr. Rot's God Brain Machine (prev 2 mentione Soulstriker's bandages, guards' guest list, Kilgore's handgun & flying limousine, Sabretooth's door, Silver Samurai's sword (prev 2 destroye Dog's spit, laser knife, newspaper clippings & futuristic weapons & technology, Seraph's van, Lynx's knife, Cassie's handguns, Amiko's poll radio (bts), goggles & laser sword, Yukio's spears, swords & wheelchair, football cameras, pool balls (prev 2 bts), cues & table, bar TV

SYNOPSIS: Sabretooth, now the secret crimelord of Asia, throws himself a birthday party. Lord and Lady Deathstrike arrive to find the event full swing; they mingle with an unlikely assortment of villainous guests, but Dr. Rot is turned away at the door. Maverick helps Wolverine find t party's location; he crashes the event and attacks the guests. Meanwhile: on a remote island, Kade Kilgore locates Strikeforce X's survivors a recruits them to be his bodyguards. In Canada, Dog Logan kills and eats a wolverine, and reads about the Jean Grey School. Melita Garn having broken up with Wolverine, joins Seraph Investigations. In Tokyo, Amiko practices crimefighting. In Hell, Thomas Logan spends time w his grandchildren, the Mongrels. In Chinatown, Fat Cobra is crowned the new Black Dragon. At the party, Wolverine defeats all of the gues then eviscerates Sabretooth. He mentions Sabretooth's old habit of attacking every year on Wolverine's birthday, and promises to see him ne year. Wolverine finds a nearby bar, orders a beer and watches football, content.

OTE: This issue also has an "Avengers Art Appreciation" variant cover. This is writer Jason Aaron's final issue, although he continues to write e Wolverine-centric series W&X, '11-present. This issue confirms that Lord and Lady Deathstrike are siblings. Kilgore and his pre-teen allies ok over the Hellfire Club's Inner Circle in X:Schism #5, '11. Seraph calls her group "Seraph's Angels" here; this is a nickname, not the group's 'icial name. The Blob appearing here is from the "Age of Apocalypse" dimension, Earth-295; he crossed into the Marvel Universe between XFor #13-15, '11. Mystique states that Dr. Doom declined their party invitation, but Dr. Doom was trapped in another dimension at this time. ystique may have unknowingly contacted Kristoff Vernard, who ruled Latveria in Doom's absence, or one of several robotic Doombots, which affed Doom's American castle. If Kristoff, he is last in FF #604, '12, chr next in Veng #1, '11 and next in Veng #6, '12. Some or other Doombots pear last in Av:Child #3, '11 and next in IHulk #13, '12. Though Daken appeared to die in an explosion in D:DW #23, '12, Wolverine was not oled; he shows no surprise here to discover his son still alive. Wild Child was apparently killed in W:O #39, '09, but presumably his healing ctor saved him. Though it is impossible to trust anything seen in the afterlife, the chronologies given here assume that the spirits of Thomas ogan and the Mongrels are real. Sabretooth's tradition of attacking Wolverine every year on his birthday has been seen in CX #10/2, '87, W 0, '89 and XO:Sabre, '09.

WOLVERINE ART APPRECIATION (2009)

(Untitled, 31 pages)

CREDITS: John Rhett Thomas (co-writer & editor), Brian O'Dell, Eric O'Dell & Dugan Trodglen (co-writers), Blammo! Content & Design & Michael Kronenberg (design), John Denning & Alex Starbuck (asst editors), Mark Beazley & Jennifer Grünwald (special projects editors), Jeff Youngquist (senior editor), Joe Quesada (c pencils), Danny Miki (c inks), Richard Isanove (c colors), C.B. Cebulski (special thanks)

NOTE: Seventeen Marvel books dated June 2009 had variant covers with a linked theme, dubbed "Wolverine Art Appreciation Month": images of Wolverine, done in homage to a variety of artists and styles from throughout history. These covers were collected and reprinted in this one-shot, along with descriptions of the styles and artists being imitated, commentary by the writers and each cover's artist about their creative process, and biographical material and photos of each cover's artist. This issue's cover, printed on canvas stock, recycles the art from W:O #5, '06's cover, an homage to the work of artist Alphonse Mucha featuring Wolverine and Emma Frost. The issue preceded by an introduction page. Each cover feature is generally presented across two pages, with commentary on the left-hand page and e cover presented full-size without its trade dress on the right. This issue's back cover is a gallery with thumbnail images of all 17 covers, but es not include W:O #5, '06's art.

ST FEATURE: Reprints AoAtlas #9, '09's variant cover, by Gerald Parel. Done in symbolist/expressionist style in homage to the work of tist Edvard Munch.

ND FEATURE: Reprints ASM #590, '09's variant cover, by Paolo Rivera. Done in "flea market chic" style in homage to artist C.M. Coolidge's 1906 ogs playing poker" painting *Waterloo*, this cover features multiple Wolverines, each in different outfits: his 1970s yellow costume, 1980s brown ostume, "Experiment X" helmet, original "whiskered" costume from IHulk #180-182, '74, and street clothes; an empty leather X-jacket is also visible. **OTE:** This feature is presented on one page, with the art running half-size. It does not feature a photo of Rivera, but one is presented in this sue's 11th feature.

RD FEATURE: Reprints ASM #592, '09's variant cover, by Paolo Rivera. Done in surrealist style in homage to the work of artist Salvador Dali. **OTE:** This feature is presented on one page, with the art running half-size; it does not feature a photo of Rivera.

TH FEATURE: Reprints CB&MI13 #12, '09's variant cover, by Skottie Young. Done in illustration/cartoon art style in homage to the work of tist Edward Gorey, this cover features Wolverine and a little girl.

TH FEATURE: Reprints DD #118, '09's variant cover, by Russ Heath (background art) & Juan Doe (foreground art). Done in Pop Art style in mage to the work of artist Roy Lichtenstein, this cover features Wolverine, Hellfire Club soldiers, and a lovestruck woman. **OTE:** This feature does not have a photo of Heath. It also does not have biographical information on Doe, but some is provided in this issue's th feature.

TH FEATURE: Reprints Exiles #1, '09's variant cover, by Jason Chan. Done in surrealist style in homage to the work of artist René Magritte. **TH FEATURE:** Reprints GR #34, '09's variant cover, by Alina Urusov. Done in homage to the Japanese woodblock printmaking style. **TH FEATURE:** Reprints Hulk #11, '09's variant cover, by Ed McGuinness. Done in homage to the Mayan cave paintings of Naj Tunich, uatemala, this cover features Wolverine and a saber-tooth tiger.

TH FEATURE: Reprints Herc #128, '09's variant cover, by David Williams. Done in "retro" comic book style in homage to the work of artist ck Kirby, this cover features Wolverine and several unidentified henchmen.

0TH FEATURE: Reprints MK #29, '09's variant cover, by Juan Doe. Done in cubist-inspired style in homage to the work of artist Pablo casso.

1TH FEATURE: Reprints MsM #38, '09's variant cover, by Paolo Rivera. Done in illustrative style in homage to the work of artist N.C. Wyeth, is cover features Wolverine, Cyclops and Sentinels.

2TH FEATURE: Reprints Run #9, '09's variant cover, by David Lafuente. Done in art nouveau style in homage to artist Alphonse Mucha's 896 advertising poster *Job*.

3TH FEATURE: Reprints SecWs #3, '09's variant cover, by Gerald Parel. Done in symbolist style in homage to the work of artist Gustav imt, this cover features Wolverine and ninjas.

4TH FEATURE: Reprints UXM #508, '09's variant cover, by Laura Martin. Done in Post-Impressionist style in homage to the work of artist ncent van Gogh.

5TH FEATURE: Reprints WarM #5, '09's variant cover, by Fiona Staples. Done in realist-inspired style in homage to the work of artist John nger Sargent.

6TH FEATURE: Reprints W:FC #14, '09's variant cover, by Chris Eliopoulos. Done in homage to the cartoon art style of newspapers' Sunday omics, specifically *Peanuts*, *Garfield* and *Calvin & Hobbes*, this cover features Wolverine (as Charlie Brown, Jon and Calvin) and Kitty Pryde s Lucy van Pelt, Garfield and Susie Derkins).

OTE: A snippet of Eliopoulos' webcomic *Misery Loves Sherman* is visible at the very bottom of the cover.

7TH FEATURE: Reprints X:L #223, '09's variant cover, by Morry Hollowell. Done in Pop Art style in homage to the work of artist Andy Warhol. **OTE:** This cover recycles Frank Miller's art from the cover of W #1, '82. It is presented on one page, with the art running half-size, and does ot feature a photo of Hollowell.

Below are the abbreviations used in this Index. A comprehensive list can be found at http://www.marvel.com/universe/index.

1st – in chronologies this usually refers to the first appearance. When it means another first, such as the first time a character is mentioned, a clarification (1st mention) is included.
Ann – Annual
app – appearance
bts – a behind the scenes appearance, where a character was not seen, but nonetheless impacted on the story in some way.
chr – chronologically. Differentiates between the real last and next appearances, and revised last and next appearances created by flashbacks and other continuity inserts.
dfb – during flashback. A flashback set within the issue it is presented in.
fb – flashback. An appearance set in a time frame earlier than the rest of a given issue's story.
HC – hardcover
inc – including
LOC – letter of comment
pfb – prior flashback. A flashback set just before the events in the main story.
prev – previous

rfb – reminder flashback. A flashback that reshows past events with no new content.
Spec – Special
TPB – trade paperback

AC&P – Adventures of Cyclops and Phoenix
AF – Amazing Fantasy
AFlt – Alpha Flight
AgentX – Agent X
AmazX – Amazing X-Men
AmE:Just – American Eagle: Just a Little Old-Fashioned Justice (digital comic)
Anita:GP – Anita Blake, Vampire Hunter: Guilty Pleasures
Anni:HoG – Annihilation: Heralds of Galactus
Annis:EF – Annihilators: Earthfall
ANOlym – Assault on New Olympus
AntM – Irredeemable Ant-Man
AoA – Age of Apocalypse
AoAtlas – Agents of Atlas
ASM – Amazing Spider-Man
ASM:Ends – Amazing Spider-Man: Ends of the Earth
ASME – Amazing Spider-Man Extra
ASMFam – Amazing Spider-Man Family
AstSMW – Astonishing Spider-Man & Wolverine
AT:Shiv – Astonishing Tales: Shiver Man (digital comic)
AT:WPun – Astonishing Tales: Wolverine/Punisher (digital comic)
Av – Avengers

Av/Inv – Avengers/Invaders
Av:Child – Avengers: Children's Crusade
Av:FCBD – Free Comic Book Day: Avengers
Av:In – Avengers: the Initiative
Av:XSanc – Avengers: X-Sanction
Av1959 – Avengers 1959
AvAc – Avengers Academy
AvAssem – Avengers Assembl
AvAtlas – Avengers vs. Atlas
AvFin – Avengers Finale
AvS – Avengers Spotlight
AvSM – Avenging Spider-Man
AvSolo – Avengers: Solo
AvX – Avengers vs. X-Men
AvXCon – AvX: Consequences
AvXVs – AvX: Vs.
AWC – Avengers West Coast
AX – Astonishing X-Men
AX:Xeno – Astonishing X-Men: Xenogenesis
BA – Bizarre Adventures
Bahia – Spider-Man & the Human Torch: Bahia de los Muertos!
BAxe – Black Axe
BFF:Ben – Before the Fantastic 4: Ben Grimm and Logan
Bhood – Brotherhood
BICMW – Breaking Into Comics the Marvel Way
Bish – Bishop
BlSun:X – Black Sun: X-Men
BMC – Best of Marvel Comics
BP – Black Panther
BScars – Battle Scars
Btide – Battletide
BW – Black Widow
BW:DO – Black Widow: Deadly Origin

Gene – Codename: Genetix

ble&Dp – Cable & Deadpool

ble&NM – Cable and the New Mutants

IID:B – Call of Duty: the Brotherhood

p – Captain America

p&BW – Captain America & Black Widow

p&Falc – Captain America and the Falcon

p:ME – Captain America: the Medusa Effect

p:Re – Captain America: Reborn

rnUSA – Carnage USA

&MI13 – Captain Britain and MI13

Dawn – Psylocke & Archangel: Crimson Dawn

W – Chaos War

W:AFlt – Chaos War: Alpha Flight

W:ChK – Chaos War: Chaos King

W:DeAv – Chaos War: Dead Avengers

tV – Citizen V and the V Battalion

aws2 – Wolverine & the Black Cat: Claws II

M – Captain Marvel

C – Marvel Super Hero Contest of Champions

C2 – Contest of Champions II

H – Code of Honor

V – Civil War

V:Choos – Civil War: Choosing Sides

V:FL – Civil War: Front Line

V:In – Civil War: the Initiative

V:Ret – Civil War: the Return

CW:WarC – Civil War: War Crimes

CW:X – Civil War: X-Men

CW:YAv&Run – Civil War: Young Avengers & Runaways

CX – Classic X-Men

D:DW – Daken: Dark Wolverine

DA – Dark Angel

DAv – Dark Avengers

Daz – Dazzler

DC – Damage Control

DC/M:AA – DC/Marvel: All Access

DC2 – Damage Control vol. 2

DCut – Die-Cut

DCvM – DC versus Marvel

DD – Daredevil

DDs – Daredevils

Def – Defenders

DF:Av – Domination Factor: Avengers

Dhawk – Darkhawk

DHII2 – Death's Head II vol. 2

Dline – Deadline

Dlk – Deathlok

DM – Death Metal

DocS – Doc Samson

Dom – Domino

Doomw – Doomwar

Dp – Deadpool

DpTU – Deadpool Team-Up

DR:Elek – Dark Reign: Elektra

DR:GL – Dark Reign: the Goblin Legacy

DR:Hood – Dark Reign: the Hood

DR:LL – Dark Reign: Lethal Legion

DR:NN – Dark Reign: New Nation

DRL:ASM – Dark Reign: the List - Amazing Spider-Man

DRL:Hulk – Dark Reign: the List - Hulk

DRL:W – Dark Reign: the List - Wolverine

DRL:X – Dark Reign: the List - X-Men

DrS – Doctor Strange

DW – Dark Wolverine

DX – District X

DXM – Dark X-Men

EHAge – Enter the Heroic Age

ElecAnt – Electric Ant

Elek:Ass – Elektra: Assassin

Elek:Hand – Elektra: the Hand

Elek:RE – Elektra: Root of Evil

Et – Eternals

EvX – All-New Exiles vs. X-Men

Ex – Excalibur

Ex:MM – Excalibur: Mojo Mayhem

Exodus – Dark Avengers/ Uncanny X-Men: Exodus

F.F. – FF

FA – Fallen Angels

FAC&P – Further Adventures of Cyclops and Phoenix

FacX – Factor X

FallSon:Av – Fallen Son: the Death of Captain America - Avengers

FallSon:IM – Fallen Son: the Death of Captain America - Iron Man

FallSon:SM – Fallen Son: the Death of Captain America - Spider-Man

FallSon:W – Fallen Son: the Death of Captain America - Wolverine

FanFor – Fantastic Force

FC – Franken-Castle

FearIt – Fear Itself

Fearlt:F – Fear Itself: the Fearless

Fearlt:HF – Fear Itself: the Home Front

Fearlt:UXFor – Fear Itself: Uncanny X-Force

Fearlt:W – Fear Itself: Wolverine

FF – Fantastic Four

FF:Foes – Fantastic Four: Foes

FF:WGCM – Fantastic Four: the World's Greatest Comics Magazine

FFvX – Fantastic Four vs. the X-Men

FNSM – Friendly Neighborhood Spider-Man

FoH:RH – Fall of the Hulks: Red Hulk

FoH:SSH – Fall of the Hulks: Savage She-Hulks

FoS – Fury of SHIELD

Fs – Firestar

FX – First X-Men

G&B – Gambit & Bishop

Galact – Galactus the Devourer

Gam – Gambit

Gam&X – Gambit and the X-Ternals

GenHope – Generation Hope

GenM – Generation M

GenX – Generation X

GIJoe – G.I. Joe

Girl – Girl Comics

GR – Ghost Rider

GR/W/Pun – Ghost Rider/ Wolverine/Punisher

GRs – Ghost Riders

GSAv – Giant-Size Avengers

GSAX – Giant-Size Astonishing X-Men

GSW – Giant-Size Wolverine

GSX – Giant-Size X-Men

H/W:6 – Hulk/Wolverine: Six Hours

HA – Hell's Angel

HA:Prince – Heroic Age: Prince of Power

Hawk – Hawkeye

Hcat – Hellcat

Herc – Hercules

Herc:Fall – Hercules: Fall of an Avenger

HFH – Heroes For Hire

HFHX – Heroes For Hope Starring the X-Men

HoM – House of M

HoM:Day – House of M: the Day After

HulkTU – Hulk Team-Up

HW:Melt – Havok & Wolverine: Meltdown

I ♥ M:MMH – I ♥ Marvel: My Mutant Heart

IAmAv – I Am an Avenger

IDisc – Identity Disc

IF – Iron Fist

IF/W – Iron Fist/Wolverine

IHulk – Incredible Hulk

IHulks – Incredible Hulks

IM – Iron Man

IM/Cap – Iron Man/Captain America

IM:DoS – Iron Man: Director of SHIELD

IM:HoM – Iron Man: House of M

IM:K&K – Iron Man: Kiss and Kill

IM:T – Iron Man: Titanium

IManual – Iron Manual

Index – Official Index to the Marvel Universe

IndIM – Indomitable Iron Man

InfC – Infinity Crusade

InfG – Infinity Gauntlet

InfW – Infinity War

Inv – Invaders

InvIM – Invincible Iron Man

JIM – Journey Into Mystery

Klaws – Klaws of the Panther

KP&W – Kitty Pryde and Wolverine

KP:AoS – Kitty Pryde: Agent of SHIELD

KZ – Ka-Zar

L:PW – Logan: Path of the Warlord

L:SS – Logan: Shadow Society

LastDef – Last Defenders

Ls – Longshot

M:LG – Marvel: the Lost Generation

M:S&L – Marvel: Shadows and Light

MA – Marvel Age

MAtlas – Marvel Atlas

MAv – Mighty Avengers

MaxS – Maximum Security

MC – Marvel Comics

MChan – Marvels Channel: Monsters, Myths & Marvels (digital comic)

MColl – Marvel Collector's Edition

MCP – Marvel Comics Present

MDigHol – Marvel Digital Holiday Special (digital comic)

MEnc – Marvel Encyclopedia

MFan – Marvel Fanfare

MFeat – Marvel Feature

MGN – Marvel Graphic Novel

MHeroes – Marvel Heroes (Panini UK)

MHol – Marvel Holiday Special

Micro – Micronauts

Millie – Millie the Model

MK – Moon Knight

MK4 – Marvel Knights 4

KF – Master of Kung Fu
Kn – Marvel Knights
KSM – Marvel Knights Spider-
Man
M&B – Machine Man &
astion
M:FoUB – Marvel Monsters:
rom the Files of Ulysses
loodstone and the Monster
unters
M:WMD – Marvel Monsters:
Where Monsters Dwell
NowPO – Marvel Now Point
ne
Moment – Moment of Silence
Morb – Morbius, the Living
ampire
SH – Marvel Super-Heroes
sM – Ms. Marvel
T – Marvel Tales
TE – Marvel Treasury Edition
TIO – Marvel Two-In-One
TU – Marvel Team-Up
TW – Mys-Tech Wars
Vision – Marvel Vision
vk – Maverick
Vs – Mephisto vs. …
W:SW – Marvel Westerns:
trange Westerns
yA:Book – Mystic Arcana: the
ook of Marvel Magic
YiR – Marvel Year in Review
ys – Mystique
ysDrS – Mystic Hands of
octor Strange
Z4 – Marvel Zombies 4
atX – Nation X
atX:XF – Nation X: X-Factor
Av – New Avengers
Av:I – New Avengers: Illuminati
AvF – New Avengers: Most
Wanted Files

NAvFin – New Avengers Finale
Nc – Nightcrawler
NEx – New Excalibur
NExiles – New Exiles
NF:AoS – Nick Fury: Agent of
SHIELD
NFHC – Nick Fury's Howling
Commandos
NFVS – Nick Fury vs. SHIELD
NiM – Night Man
NiM/Gam – Night Man/Gambit
NiMvW – Night Man vs.
Wolverine
NM – New Mutants
NM:TD – New Mutants: Truth or
Death
North – Northstar
NTb – New Thunderbolts
NThr – Night Thrasher
NW – New Warriors
NX – New X-Men
NX:Ybook – New X-Men:
Academy X Yearbook Special
OHMU – Official Handbook of
the Marvel Universe
OHMU:AU – Official Handbook
of the Marvel Universe: Alternate
Universes
OHMU:Hor – Official Handbook
of the Marvel Universe: Horror
OHMU:ME – Official Handbook
of the Marvel Universe: Master
Edition
OHMU:U – Official Handbook of
the Marvel Universe: Update
OHMU:W – Official Handbook of
the Marvel Universe: Wolverine
OHMU:X – Official Handbook of
the Marvel Universe: X-Men
OMIX – Official Marvel Index to
the X-Men
OMtL – One Month to Live

Ons:Ep – Onslaught: Epilogue
Ons:MU – Onslaught: Marvel
Universe
Ons:XM – Onslaught: X-Men
OtEdge – Over the Edge
Penance – Penance: Relentless
PlSkaar – Planet Skaar
Prologue
PointOne – Point One
PP – Power Pack
PPSM – Peter Parker: Spider-
Man
PPSSM – Peter Parker, the
Spectacular Spider-Man
PR:Gen – Phoenix Resurrection:
Genesis
PR:Rev – Phoenix Resurrection:
Revelations
Psy – Psylocke
Pulse:HoM – Pulse: House of M
Special
Pun – Punisher
Pun/Cap – Punisher/Captain
America: Blood & Glory
Pun:Prize – Punisher: the Prize
PWJ – Punisher War Journal
PWZ – Punisher War Zone
Q – Quasar
RamW – Rampaging Wolverine
Rom – Rom: Spaceknight
Run – Runaways
S – Sentry
S&L – Shadows & Light
S&M – Sabretooth and Mystique
S/Void – Sentry vs. the Void
S:FallSun – Sentry: Fallen Sun
Sabre – Sabretooth
SAv – Solo Avengers
SavAxe – Savage Axe of Ares
SC:Prepare – Second Coming:
Prepare
SecAv – Secret Avengers

SecDef – Secret Defenders
SecInv – Secret Invasion
SecWar – Secret War
SecWar:FNF – Secret War: From the Files of Nick Fury
SecWars – Marvel Super Heroes Secret Wars
SecWars2 – Secret Wars II
SecWs – Secret Warriors
SenSM – Sensational Spider-Man
SG – Spider-Girl
SH – She-Hulk
SH:CC – She-Hulk: Cosmic Collision
SI:Av – Spider-Island: Avengers
SI:C&D – Spider-Island: Cloak & Dagger
SI:DF – Spider-Island: Deadly Foes
SI:DHKF – Spider-Island: Deadly Hands of Kung Fu
Skaar:KSL – Skaar: King of the Savage Land
Sland – Shadowland
Sland:GR – Shadowland: Ghost Rider
Sland:MK – Shadowland: Moon Knight
Sleep – Sleepwalker
Sling – Slingers
SM – Spider-Man
SM&FF – Spider-Man and the Fantastic Four
SM/BCat – Spider-Man/Black Cat
SM/DD – Spider-Man/Daredevil
SM/King – Spider-Man/Kingpin: to the Death
SM/W – Spider-Man/Wolverine
SM:BiBH – Spider-Man: Back in Black Handbook

SM:BT – Spider-Man: Big Time (digital comic)
SM:HL – Spider-Man: Hobgoblin Lives
SM:HoM – Spider-Man: House of M
SM:L – Spider-Man: Lifeline
SM:MA – Spider-Man: the Mutant Agenda
SM:Mys – Spider-Man: the Mysterio Manifesto
SM:SC – Spider-Man: Sweet Charity
SMU – Spider-Man Unlimited
SMvW – Spider-Man vs. Wolverine
SpecSM – Spectacular Spider-Man
SpEdX – Special Edition X-Men
SS – Silver Surfer
SS1 – Sentinel Squad O*N*E
SSol – Super Soldiers
SSwConan – Savage Sword of Conan
SSWP – Silver Sable & the Wild Pack
ST – Strange Tales
Starj – Starjammers
Stryfe – Stryfe's Strike File
Sub – Sub-Mariner
Sup/FF – Superman/Fantastic Four
SW – Spider-Woman
Task – Taskmaster
Tb – Thunderbolts
Tb:II – Thunderbolts: International Incident
Tb:LS – Thunderbolts: Life Sentences
Time – Timestorm: 2009/2099
Time:X – Timestorm: 2009/2099 - X-Men

TInc – Terror Inc.
TMU – Tales of the Marvel Universe
Tstrike – Thunderstrike
TWoS – Tangled Web of Spider-Man
TX/T7 – Team X/Team 7
U – Underworld
UA – Unlimited Access
Ugirl – Ultragirl
UJack – Union Jack
UltNUlts – Ultimate New Ultimates
UltO – Ultimate Origins
Ults – Ultimates
UltSM – Ultimate Spider-Man
UltWHulk – Ultimate Wolverine vs. Hulk
UltX – Ultimate X-Men
UncAv – Uncanny Avengers
UO – Uncanny Origins
Utopia – Dark Avengers/Uncanny X-Men: Utopia
UToS – Untold Tales of Spider-Man
UXFor – Uncanny X-Force
UXM – Uncanny X-Men
UXM&FF – Uncanny X-Men & Fantastic Four
UXM:HA – Uncanny X-Men: the Heroic Age
Veng – Vengeance
Venom:STA – Venom: Sinner Takes All
Venom:TC – Venom: Tooth and Claw
VFH – Villains For Hire
W – Wolverine
W&Jub – Wolverine and Jubilee
W&X – Wolverine and the X-Men
W&X:A&O – Wolverine and the X-Men: Alpha & Omega

W/**Cable** – Wolverine/Cable
W/**Cap** – Wolverine/Captain America
W/**Doop** – Wolverine/Doop
W/**Dp:Decoy** – Wolverine/Deadpool: the Decoy (digital comic)
W/**Gam** – Wolverine/Gambit: Victims
W/**Herc** – Wolverine/Hercules: Myths, Monsters & Mutants
W/**Hulk** – Wolverine/Hulk
W/**NF:SC** – Wolverine/Nick Fury: the Scorpio Connection
W/**NF:SR** – Wolverine & Nick Fury: Scorpio Rising
W/**Pun** – Wolverine/Punisher
W:**Amaz** – Wolverine: the Amazing Immortal Man and Other Bloody Tales
W:**Anniv** – Wolverine: the Anniversary
W:**AoAtlas** – Wolverine: Agent of Atlas (digital comic)
W:**BC** – Wolverine: Bloody Choices
W:**Best** – Wolverine: the Best There Is
W:**Bl** – Wolverine: Bloodlust
W:**BR** – Wolverine: Black Rio
W:**Bwalk** – Wolverine: Under the Boardwalk
W:**Carni** – Wolverine: Carni-Crawl (digital comic)
W:**Chop** – Wolverine: Chop Shop
W:**Debt** – Wolverine: Debt of Death
W:**DevHell** – Wolverine: Development Hell (digital comic)
W:**DG** – Wolverine: Dangerous Games

W:**Doom** – Wolverine: Doombringer
W:**Dust** – Wolverine: the Dust From Above (digital comic)
W:**End** – Wolverine: the End
W:**Evil** – Wolverine: Evilution
W:**Fb** – Wolverine: Firebreak
W:**FC** – Wolverine: First Class
W:**FCBD** – Free Comic Book Day: Wolverine - Origin of an X-Man
W:**Flies** – Wolverine: Flies to a Spider
W:**GJ** – Wolverine in Global Jeopardy
W:**Hunger** – Wolverine: Hunger (digital comic)
W:**IF** – Wolverine: Inner Fury
W:**Jun** – Wolverine: the Jungle Adventure
W:**Kill** – Wolverine: Killing
W:**KMS** – Wolverine: Killing Made Simple
W:**KT** – Wolverine: Knight of Terra
W:**MD** – Wolverine: Manifest Destiny
W:**MrX** – Wolverine: Mr. X
W:**Net** – Wolverine: Netsuke
W:**O** – Wolverine: Origins
W:**OML** – Wolverine: Old Man Logan Giant-Size
W:**ONO** – Wolverine: One Night Only (digital comic)
W:**Rev** – Wolverine: Revolver
W:**RT** – Wolverine: Rahne of Terra
W:**RTH** – Wolverine: Road to Hell
W:**Saud** – Wolverine: Saudade
W:**Sav** – Wolverine: Savage
W:**Sb** – Wolverine: Switchback

W:**SC** – Wolverine: Son of Canada
W:**Snikt** – Wolverine: Snikt
W:**Soul** – Wolverine: Soultaker
W:**Wend** – Wolverine: Wendigo!
W:**Worst** – Wolverine: Worst There Is (digital comic)
W:**WX** – Wolverine: Weapon X
W:**WXF** – Wolverine: Weapon X Files
W:**Xisle** – Wolverine: Xisle
War**M** – War Machine
WBN – Werewolf By Night
WCA – West Coast Avengers
Web:**TS** – Webspinners: Tales of Spider-Man
Whead – Warheads
WI? – What If?
Winter – Winter Soldier
Wlk – Warlock
Wlk&IW – Warlock and the Infinity Watch
WM – Wonder Man
WoSM – Web of Spider-Man
WS:WK – Winter Soldier: Winter Kills
WSaga – Wolverine Saga
WvThor – Wolverine vs. Thor (digital comic)
WWHs:C/W – World War Hulks: Captain America vs. Wolverine
WWHulk – World War Hulk
WWHulk:DC – World War Hulk: Aftersmash - Damage Control
WWHulk:X – World War Hulk: X-Men
WX – Weapon X
WX:DoFN – Weapon X: Days of Future Now
WXD:AZ – Weapon X: the Draft - Agent Zero
WXD:S – Weapon X: the Draft - Sauron

WXD:WC – Weapon X: the Draft - Wild Child

WXNoir – Weapon X Noir

X – X-Men

X&Doom – X-Men and Dr. Doom

X&M – X-Men and the Micronauts

X&SM – X-Men and Spider-Man

X/AFlt – X-Men/Alpha Flight

X/Brood – X-Men/Brood

X:A – X-Men: Alpha

X:Bish – X-Men: the Times and Life of Lucas Bishop

X:Col – X-Men: Colossus - Bloodline

X:Dec – X-Men: Declassified

X:DG – X-Men: Deadly Genesis

X:DWS – X-Men: Divided We Stand

X:ES – X-Men: Endangered Species

X:HC – X-Men: the Hellfire Club

X:Hell – X-Men: Hellbound

X:KPSF – X-Men: Kitty Pryde - Shadow & Flame

X:L – X-Men: Legacy

X:Lib – X-Men: Liberators

X:MC – X-Men: Messiah CompleX

X:MD – X-Men: Manifest Destiny

X:MT – X-Men: Magneto - Testament

X:MW – X-Men: the Magneto War

X:OMO – X-Men: Odd Men Out

X:OS – X-Men: Original Sin

X:P – X-Men: Prime

X:P&D – X-Men: Pixies and Demons (Free Comic Book Day)

X:Pixie – X-Men: Pixie Strikes Back!

X:Prelude – X-Men: Prelude to Schism

X:Regen – X-Men: Regenesis

X:SC – X-Men: Second Coming

X:Schism – X-Men: Schism

X:SFC – X-Men: the Search for Cyclops

X:TF – X-Men: True Friends

X:TS&P – X-Men: To Serve and Protect

X:WA – X-Men: the Wedding Album

X:Worlds – X-Men: Worlds Apart

X:Ω – X-Men: Omega

X23 – X-23

X4 – X-Men/Fantastic Four

X51 – X-51

XB – X-Babies

XB:R – X-Babies Reborn

XCal – X-Calibre

XCD – X-Men & ClanDestine

XClub – X-Club

XCurse:SB – X-Men: Curse of the Mutants - Smoke and Blood

XCurse:SG – X-Men: Curse of the Mutants - Storm & Gambit

XCurse:XV – X-Men: Curse of the Mutants - X-Men vs. Vampires

XFac – X-Factor

XFor – X-Force

XFor/C:MW – X-Force/Cable: Messiah War

XFor/Ch – X-Force/Champions

XFor/Yb – X-Force/Youngblood

XFor:Aint – X-Force: Ain't No Dog

XFor:S&V – X-Force: Sex & Violence

XGS – X-Men Giant-Size

XInf – X-Infernus

XMan – X-Man

XMF – X-Men Forever

XMU – X-Men Unlimited

XNec – X-Necrosha

XO:C – X-Men Origins: Colossus

XO:Sabre – X-Men Origins: Sabretooth

XO:W – X-Men Origins: Wolverine

XPx:E – X-Men: Phoenix - Endsong

XPx:W – X-Men: Phoenix - Warsong

XRun – X-Men/Runaways (Free Comic Book Day)

XStat – X-Statix

XUniv – X-Universe

XvA – X-Men vs. the Avengers

XvAtlas – X-Men vs. Agents of Atlas

XvHulk – X-Men vs. Hulk

XX – X-Treme X-Men

XX:SL – X-Treme X-Men: Savage Land

XXX – X-Treme X-Men X-Posé

YAv – Young Avengers

Yb/XFor – Youngblood/X-Force

YX – Young X-Men